# The Marshall Court
# and Cultural Change
# 1815–35

# The Marshall Court
# and Cultural Change
# 1815-1835
## Abridged Edition

## G. Edward White

With the aid of Gerald Gunther

New York • Oxford
*Oxford University Press*
1991

## Oxford University Press

Oxford   New York   Toronto
Delhi   Bombay   Calcutta   Madras   Karachi
Petaling Jaya   Singapore   Hong Kong   Tokyo
Nairobi   Dar es Salaam   Cape Town
Melbourne   Auckland

and associated companies in
Berlin   Ibadan

First published in 1988 by Macmillan Publishing Company, Inc., New York

First published in an abridged cloth and paperback edition
in 1991 by Oxford University Press, Inc.,
200 Madison Avenue, New York, New York 10016

Oxford is a registered trademark of Oxford University Press

Library of Congress Cataloging-in-Publication Data
White, G. Edward.
The Marshall Court and cultural change, 1815–1835 /
G. Edward White with the aid of Gerald Gunther.
p. cm.   Reprint. Originally published: New York : Macmillan Pub. Co., 1988.
Includes bibliographical references and index.
ISBN 0-19-507058-5   ISBN 0-19-507059-3 (pbk.)
1. United States. Supreme Court—History.
2. Marshall, John, 1755–1835.   3. United States—History—1815–1861.
I. Gunther, Gerald, 1927–    .   II. Title.
KF8742.W45   1991   347.73′26′09034—dc20
[347.30735009034]   90-25516

9 8 7 6 5 4 3 2 1

Printed in the United States of America
on acid free paper

*For*
*John F. Davis*

# Contents

# *Illustrations*

ix

# Preface to the Abridged Edition

THIS WORK'S initial appearance was as a volume in the *Oliver Wendell Holmes Devise History of the Supreme Court of the United States*, a series of encyclopedic reference works covering the history of the Supreme Court in predetermined phases, generally tracking the tenures of the Court's successive Chief Justices. In some instances, however, the tenure of a Chief Justice was considered sufficiently important to require more than one volume. I thus began my work on the Marshall Court under the assumption that my coverage would principally be restricted to the last twenty years of Chief Justice Marshall's tenure. Given those constraints of coverage, and methodological constraints imposed by the Holmes Devise project itself, I was faced with the prospect of writing a volume whose essential purpose would be that of a reference guide for specialists.

To an extent I rebelled against that prospect, and sought to produce a volume on the Marshall Court that was unabashedly interpretive, even revisionist, while retaining something of the format of other Holmes Devise volumes. In particular, I sought to place the Marshall Court's decisions firmly in a cultural context, taking culture to include not only features of the political, sociological, and economic landscape in which the Marshall Court functioned but also the sets of ideological belief systems that framed the Court's jurisprudential universe and informed the discourse of its decisions. My emphasis on the culture of the Marshall Court resulted in attention to some topics, such as the state of early nineteenth-century transportation facilities or the writings of James Fenimore Cooper, that might at first blush seem quite remote from cases decided by the Supreme Court of the United States.

Another way to characterize my orientation in the volume, and to distinguish that orientation from some of the other volumes in the Holmes Devise series, was that I self-consciously sought to communicate with generalist readers, those who shared my interest in late eighteenth- and early nineteenth-century American culture, as well as specialist readers who had a particular concern with the factual and doctrinal dimensions of the Marshall Court's cases. My aim, in short, was to treat the Supreme Court between 1815 and 1835 as a cultural artifact and to invite others to react to my interpretations of it in that capacity. My interpretations in this volume are, of course, informed by the fact that the Court was a legal institution whose justices employed the discourse of legal professionals, but they are also informed by my view of other institutions and discourses in the culture at large.

Happily, a sufficient number of specialist readers and reviewers discerned the generalist orientation of my Holmes Devise volume and encouraged me to prepare an edition that would be more accessible to a generalist audience. This abridged edition is the result.

The principal abridgement I have made in this edition is to eliminate chapters discussing the Marshall Court's nonconstitutional cases. While those cases represented most of the Court's docket in the years between its 1815 and 1835 Terms, the bulk of them came to the Court simply because they involved disputes between citizens of different states in which the amount in dispute exceeded $2000. Such cases qualified for litigation in the federal district courts created by Article III of the Constitution and the Judiciary Act of 1789, and could be appealed from those courts directly to the Supreme Court of the United States. The Supreme Court had no discretionary power to decline to hear such cases, as it currently does. Moreover, there was no obligation in the Court or lower federal courts to follow decisions handed down by state courts or substantive points of law, as there now is after *Erie R.R. v. Tompkins.*[1]

Many of the nonconstitutional cases on the Marshall Court's docket thus involved relatively minor disputes. But the cases can nonetheless be seen as having potentially significant implications for contemporaries. A dispute over the wording of a contract or the title to a tract of land, for example, might appear to have little interest except to the litigants, even though the case had been decided by the Supreme Court of the United States. But more was at stake in such cases than might first appear, since the Supreme Court, being a federal court, was theoretically free to decide the case on the basis of a substantive rule of law different from that promulgated by a state court on the same subject. The possibility of different substantive rules of law coexisting in the federal courts and the state courts of any given state had obvious implications for the allocation of state and federal power in the American legal system, and those implications were noted by contemporary observers, who treated the allocation of sovereign powers between the newly created federal government and the states as the most central and potentially divisive political question of their time.

Despite the potential significance of the Court's nonconstitutional cases, my conclusions about the Marshall Court's treatment of them suggest that the cases have only a limited interest to nonspecialists. The nonconstitutional cases can be subdivided into three convenient groupings. The first grouping included cases with a market component, that is, cases

---

[1] 304 U.S. 64 (1938).

raising legal issues with discernible economic implications, such as real property cases, cases involving contracts and negotiable instruments, and cases affecting corporations. The second grouping included cases in which the Court exercised explicit and implicit supervisory powers granted to it by the Constitution and the Judiciary Act of 1789, such as the power to fashion the technical limits of its own jurisdiction, the power to create federal rules for choosing between conflicting laws of different jurisdictions, and the power to define the meaning of federal criminal statutes or to declare, in a very limited context, the federal common law of crimes. The third grouping included maritime cases not raising constitutional issues, such as international law cases, prize cases, and marine insurance cases.

In the first group of cases I concluded that the Court's decisions were comparatively insignificant when compared with activity in the state courts and also with the Court's activity in constitutional cases. On the whole, I found this group of cases "more interesting in the aggregate than in the individual; more interesting as trends over time than as jurisprudential breakthroughs; more significant, on occasion, for what the Court did not do than what it did." While I found that the Court's decisions in areas related to a market economy confirmed that "in a society such as early nineteenth-century America in which economic relationships are being transformed . . . legal doctrines will both facilitate and respond to that transformation," I did not regard that finding as remarkable, and indeed suggested that "the cases confirm a view of the relationship between law and the co-economy which has in past years become entrenched."[2]

With respect to the second group of cases, I found that while "the impression is of a Court whose power to fashion nonconstitutional rules of jurisdiction and procedure for itself and the lower federal courts was taken for granted," the Court was nonetheless disinclined to invoke its appellate review powers under Section 25 of the Judiciary Act of 1789 to usurp the prerogatives of state courts where a procedural rule had substantive implications, or to "use the expanded federal criminal jurisdiction of the District of Columbia circuit court as a device to get itself into the business of reviewing substantive criminal decisions." In short, I concluded, "this batch of nonconstitutional cases revealed the Court's posture as comparable to that which it adopted in the more publicized constitutional decisions."[3] The Justices took pains to avoid the appearance of being partisan, invading state prerogatives, or making substantive criminal law decisions, while at the same time vigorously preserving the jurisdiction and discretion of the federal courts. None of these stances can be said to be counterintuitive.

---

[2] G. Edward White, *The Marshall Court and Cultural Change, 1815–1835* 834–835 (1988 ed.)

[3] Id. at 751, 883.

The maritime nonconstitutional cases, involving international law, prize disputes, and marine insurance, were arguably more significant. But their significance, I concluded, was not principally based on the results the Court reached in those cases but in the relationship between the Court's increased involvement with maritime cases and its efforts to expand its jurisdiction over domestic sovereignty disputes in the years after 1819. As I put it, "One of the decisive episodes in the history of the Supreme Court of the United States was the interval from 1812 to 1819 during which the Court, because of its established jurisdiction over a number of maritime cases, suddenly became, with the War of 1812 and the Latin American revolutions, a major forum for the adjudication of high sea disputes."[4] Out of that period came the Court's intervention in prize and piracy cases, its announcement of a positivistic interpretation of the "law of nations" in international law cases, and even its conceptualization of commercial law, to which it was first introduced in a maritime setting, as a general and uniform subject. The interventionist stance of the Court in its early maritime cases, I argued, prepared it "to emerge as a force in domestic sovereignty disputes."[5] The principal interest of the cases, then, was not in their results or even in the doctrines the Court promulgated, but in the Court's activist but cautious involvement with delicate issues of sovereignty and politics.

On the whole, then, in an edition directed toward the generalist reader, it seems appropriate to refer those who desire a detailed treatment of the nonconstitutional cases decided by the Marshall Court between 1815 and 1835 to the original edition of this work.

My decision to abridge the work to eliminate some of its specialized material should not be taken to represent a shift in the methodological focus of this edition of the volume. This book remains one whose primary emphasis is on what might be called cultural details: on an amassing of the multidimensional texture of the Marshall Court's cultural universe. I have tried to re-create that universe through the extraction of apparently discrete features in late eighteenth- and early nineteenth-century American culture and through efforts to draw connections between those discrete features. Ultimately the features and their connections are presented as a cultural matrix in which the Marshall Court's decisions are seen as not merely set but in a sense imprisoned, so that the Court and its Justices come to be characterized as distinctively time- and place-bound.

And while the volume, even in its abridged form, remains a detailed portrait of one institution, in a comparatively short time frame, it is nonetheless an interpretive portrait. It might be useful to those readers primarily interested in the work's interpretive structure to be exposed, in prefatory form, to the sorts of cultural details that have been given primary interpretive significance. I have singled out three clusters of details for

---

[4] Id. at 925.     [5] Id. at 925–926.

particular emphasis: details pertaining to tangible physical changes in the early nineteenth-century American environment; details pertaining to predominant belief systems in the discourse of early nineteenth-century American elite culture; and details pertaining to the internal practices, deliberations, and decisions of the Marshall Court, an institution whose decisions were rendered collegially.

I will reserve further discussion of those clusters of details, and their relationship, for the work as a whole. At this point it seems appropriate to note the original intuitions that led me to conclude that those clusters deserved particular emphasis. One intuition followed from my observation that not only were there objectively dramatic quantitative and qualitative changes in the American environment in the first forty years of the nineteenth century—changes in demographics, political and economic practices and institutions, the geographic boundaries of the American nation itself—but contemporaries overwhelmingly perceived their environment as one of rapid change, and increasingly began to contrast their "past" with their "present" and their projected "future." I thus intuited that the nature and meaning of cultural change would be particularly pressing issues for contemporaries of the Marshall Court.

Another intuition stemmed from my investigation of primary and secondary literature on the ideologies of republicanism and liberalism, ideologies that have been identified by historians of the early Republican period as pervasive and potentially contradictory belief systems structuring American elite thought in the late eighteenth and early nineteenth centuries. I noted that at least during the time period covered in my volume neither of those belief systems, to the extent they could be fruitfully distinguished from one another, had generated a coherent theory of cultural change which could be described as a progressive evolution in which the future represented an "advance" or an "improvement" on the past. On the contrary, to the extent either system had advanced a theory of cultural change, it was a "cyclical" rather than a "progressive" theory, one in which nations, like individuals, passed through inevitable stages of youth, maturity, and decay.

A third intuition was related to the perhaps prosaic observation that in almost no respects did the Marshall Court, in its internal practices and deliberative procedures, resemble modern Supreme Courts. While one might not have found it startling to observe that the Marshall Court's justices met in Washington for only six or seven weeks a year, or that they spent a good portion of their time riding from one federal circuit court to another on horseback or in horsedrawn vehicles, I concluded that most modern observers of the Court would be taken aback to discover some other features of its internal practices. These included the justices' exercising discretionary power to place cases or issues on the Court's docket that they as individuals wanted heard and decided, and on which they had previously announced views; justices drafting petitions for one set of liti-

gants in a case, even though they subsequently declined to decide that
case on conflict of interest grounds; justices occupying the same boardinghouse in Washington as the lawyers that argued cases before them, and
discussing and even voting on cases in that boardinghouse; opinions of the
Court not revealing the votes of individual justices; some justices "silently
acquiescing" in a given decision even though they had not supported it in
internal deliberations; justices not circulating their draft opinions after they
had delivered them orally in court, but simply sending them to the Court's
Reporter for subsequent publication; the Reporter editing and in some
instances substantially rewriting opinions, even ones in which he had been
one of the lawyers arguing the case before the Court. I concluded that
these practices were sufficiently alien to modern conceptions of judicial
accountability that they were themselves products of a distinctive culture,
one whose assumptions about the nature of judging were as premodern as
its assumptions about cultural change.

The interpretive structure ultimately derived from those intuitions
treats the significant constitutional cases of the later Marshall Court as
having a multifaceted character. At a straightforward level, those cases
were exercises in the interpretation of a Constitution that had received
only the sparest prior interpretation. At other levels, they were reflections
of changing economic arrangements and attitudes, manifestations of
evolving definitions of political sovereignty, illustrations of the inherent
ambiguity of such culturally resonant concepts as "Union," "property,"
or "commerce." And at the level most directly related to the intuitions
out of which the volume's interpretative emphasis emerged, they were
efforts on the part of a group of Supreme Court Justices to recast the
meaning of a document from their recent past—the text of the Constitution, together with the ideological assumptions they ascribed to that text—
so that it could speak to their rapidly changing present and offer some sort
of permanent guidance to their uncertain future. Those efforts took place
within a jurisprudential universe in which issues of judicial power and
judicial accountability were subsumed in a particularistic conception of
judicial "discretion," a conception that has no precise modern equivalent.

I want to express my appreciation to four colleagues whose familiarity with the original edition of this work encouraged me to think it might
have some continued appeal to a wider spectrum of readers. Thanks to
William W. Fisher III, Alfred S. Konefsky, Sanford Levinson, and H.
Jefferson Powell. I, of course, remain responsible for any decision not to
abridge portions of the original edition that arguably should not have seen
their way into print in the first place.

G.E.W.

*Charlottesville, VA*
*October 1990*

# Preface

THIS WORK has had a long and not always tranquil history. As its authorship has changed, so necessarily has its emphasis. Constant in the life of the volume has been the prodigious amount of archival research engaged in by Gerald Gunther in the years in which he was connected with the project, research that, while it has been supplemented, could not have been duplicated in the several years I have been working on the volume, and has thus been an indispensable help in allowing me to prepare a manuscript in a manageable time. Constant as well has been the difficulty of writing about the Supreme Court of the United States in what was surely one of its most famous but one of its least accessible periods.

I began work on the project in earnest in 1982; before that Professor Gunther had shipped me his research files, which contained duplicates of many of the letters, notebooks, and manuscripts from archival collections cited in the notes. On occasion I have had to reverify some sources, but for the most part I have been able to rely on the files. Despite the great saving in time and effort that has resulted, I share the conviction of another author in this series that "the vicarious enlightenment to be derived from another's research is spotty and faint."[1] Research material is only as useful as the interpretations in which it is framed, and those interpretations rarely survive the passage from one scholar to another. Consequently there was a great deal of data collected by Professor Gunther that I did not use, and perhaps even more that I used in a fashion different from that which he would have employed. Moreover, there was a sizable amount of data that I collected myself. It goes without saying, however, that my debt to Professor Gunther has been considerable.

I bear sole responsibility, however, for the manuscript of this volume. In keeping with its substantial gestation period, the life of the manuscript has not been short, and there have been some false starts and adjustments along the way. I came into the Holmes Devise series with

---

[1] Benno Schmidt in A. Bickel and B. Schmidt, *The Judiciary and Responsi-* *ble Government, 1910–21* (1984), 723.

the firm intention of writing an "interpretive" history, with a de-emphasis on the massive detail that has been characteristic of other volumes in the series. I found that the subject and the approach did not mix well, and thus this work resembles its predecessors in the series in length and to some extent in detail, although it may differ radically from some volumes in not being a "lawyer's history" but in consistently seeking to locate the Marshall Court in the larger culture of which it was a part.

This was not a book I had anticipated writing. I had not previously concentrated on late-eighteenth- and early-nineteenth-century legal history; I had no intention of writing a volume in a series; and I had no particular interest in institutional history. Through an odd combination of circumstances Professor Stanley Katz and I began discussions about the Holmes Devise series, and in some mysterious fashion those discussions evolved into a commitment on my part to take on the work of this volume. Looking back, I can only attribute the outcome to Professor Katz's unique version of sleight-of-hand. Having reluctantly and almost unconsciously taken on the volume, I should confess I have enjoyed writing it. No one, especially the authors, would remotely describe the production of a Holmes Devise history as fun, but for me it has been a stimulating experience in acculturation: working with early-nineteenth-century sources requires exposure to a great many "foreign" phenomena, from eighteenth-century calligraphy and etymology to the belief structure of republicanism. I have emerged from the project with a much keener sense for what it may have been like to live in the early days of the American nation; that sense is the closest thing to "fun" I can associate with my labors.[2]

An author invariably accumulates debts in a scholarly enterprise, and in this case the length of the project and my relatively neophyte status as a historian of the early Republic have made the list longer than usual. The persons to whom I am indebted can be subdivided into categories: those who gave me advice and critical reactions rather early, on issues that may have seemed to them elementary and tedious; those who became aware of my involvement with the project at an early stage and were somehow unable to disentangle themselves as my work progressed; and those whose counsel was requested in the later stages on specialized issues. Included in the first category are Professors Gordon Wood, Charles Hobson, and Hendrik Hartog; in the second category Kent Newmyer, Charles McCurdy, and Alfred Konefsky; and in the third William McLoughlin, Eric Freyfogle, Craig Joyce, and William Fisher. I also want to acknowledge the uncategorizable contributions of Gerald Gunther,

---

[2] I have tried to capture some of the sense of living and working as a Marshall Court Justice in "Imagining the Marshall Court," Supreme Court Historical Society *Yearbook* 77 (1986).

Stanley Katz, and John F. Davis, each of whom read the entire manuscript, sometimes at more than one stage. Messrs. McCurdy and Konefsky should be singled out a second time because they convinced me to make some substantial changes in the manuscript when I hoped it was nearly done. The result is that this volume has appeared in print later than it otherwise would have: the discriminating reader will know where to lay blame for that delay.

A group of research assistants has worked on this study, some of them rarely having the sense that they were engaged in a project that would ever come to fruition. Some may, on becoming aware of the mention of their names in connection with this project, require some effort to remember what it was, but in the time zone of academic life years are foreshortened, and I remember vividly the contribution of each. Thanks to Wendy Wysong, Joanne Schehl, Suanne Rudley, Diane Borkowski, Ann Hammersmith, Montsi Cangialose, and Wendy Rogovin. Thanks as well to Diane Moss, Madeline Branch, and the typing staff at the University of Virginia School of Law for their help with several drafts of the manuscript.

In addition, several people have been helpful during the process of evolution from completed manuscript to book. Marsha Rogers, the Archivist of the University of Virginia School of Law, and James Hutson and his staff at the Manuscript Division of the Library of Congress assisted in the selection of illustrations. Kent Olson, Head of Reference of the University of Virginia Law Library, assisted in the checking of sources. Charles E. Smith, Elly Dickason, and Nancy Brooks of Macmillan Publishing Company facilitated the volume's production. Stanley N. Katz was available when the world demonstrated its habitual indifference to an author's interests.

Despite the delays occasioned by Professors McCurdy and Konefsky, the manuscript would have been completed sooner had not two Siamese cats, Madeleine and Annabelle, regularly trod on its contents and sometimes scattered them on the floor, and had two small dogs, Lady and Nessie, been better housetrained and more reliable about their wanderings. Whatever increase in domestic tension may have occurred from the actions of those animals was offset by the pleasure they gave a household already enhanced by the presence of Susan Davis White, Alexandra V. White, and Elisabeth McC. D. White. Alexandra began high school when this work was in its first stages, and will be a sophomore in college when it is published. Elisabeth will have progressed from first to sixth grade. Susan will not have gotten any older, only better.

In looking at other prefaces written by authors of volumes in this series, I have noticed that it is customary to pay some respects to Oliver Wendell Holmes, Jr., whose bequest to the United States made the series possible, and to Felix Frankfurter, who first conceived the use of

Holmes's legacy to commission a history of the Supreme Court of the United States. I have written about Holmes on several occasions and shall write more about him; he needs no encomiums from me, and I am quite confident that if he had noted the size and detail of this study, he would no more have read it than he read the industrial commission reports Justice Louis Brandeis shipped him one summer. As for Frankfurter, I am not among the generation of authors—Julius Goebel, Carl Swisher, Charles Fairman, George Haskins, Alexander Bickel, Paul Freund—who were solicited directly by Frankfurter and "made" to undertake volumes in the series. I am not even sure Frankfurter would have approved of my entry, and had he discovered that this volume raises some questions about John Marshall's professional ethics and suggests that Justice Henry Baldwin may well have been at least temporarily insane, he might have disapproved of the result. But had it not been for Frankfurter, Holmes's legacy to the United States might still be sitting in some nameless government account, not even earning interest, and there would be no Holmes Devise volumes. I leave it to the reader to decide whether Frankfurter should have left well enough alone.

G.E.W.

Charlottesville
September 1986

# The Marshall Court
# and Cultural Change
# 1815–35

# Introduction

THE MARSHALL COURT has repeatedly been characterized, but it has rarely been studied. This work, which appears more than 150 years after Marshall's death, represents the first attempt at a detailed description of the Court's internal deliberations, the first effort to survey the Court's nonconstitutional cases between 1815 and 1835, and the first detailed investigation of the intellectual legal culture in which the Court's decisions were grounded. Often the Court has merely been noted in passing, by historians surveying early American culture, or by political scientists studying American governmental institutions, or by lawyers analyzing the evolution of constitutional doctrines.

The result of this tendency to consider analysis of the Marshall Court as an exercise tangential to other, more central scholarly pursuits has been the emergence and persistence of certain talismanic labels that in the aggregate have produced a historiographical image for the Court. The Court has been regularly labeled "nationalist," "Federalist," "property-conscious," and "Chief Justice–dominated." I have, in another place, discussed the origins and shifting emphasis of those labels.[1] A review of that discussion seems unnecessary here, but some summary comments are in order, by way of placing the emphasis of this study in context.

In brief, each of the labels advances a particular characterization of the Marshall Court. The label "nationalist" identifies the Court with a political ideology that promoted the growth and spread of the powers of the federal government and, concomitantly, sought to restrict and compress the powers of the states. The label "Federalist" identifies the Court

---

[1] G. White, "The Art of Revising History: Revisiting the Marshall Court," *Suffolk U.L. Rev.*, 16:659 (1982). Among the sources discussed in that article are A. Beveridge, *The Life of John Marshall* (4 vols., 1916–19); C. Warren, *The Supreme Court in United States History* (3 vols., 1922); C. Haines, *The Role of the Supreme Court in American Government and Politics* (2 vols., 1944); H. Laski, *The State in Theory and Practice* (1935); M. Jones, ed., *Chief Justice John Mar-* *shall: A Reappraisal* (1956); R. Faulkner, *The Jurisprudence of John Marshall* (1968); and G. White, *The American Judicial Tradition* (1976). A cogent review of Marshall Court historiography can be found in R. Clinton, "The Populist–Progressive Interpretation of American Constitutional History" (Ph.D. diss., University of Texas at Austin, 1984), 1–37. My thanks to Professor Clinton for letting me see his work in advance of its publication.

with the political party that came into being in the latter years of the Washington administration and had as its central goal the maintenance of the identity and influence of the newly created federal government. The label "property-conscious" identifies the Court with the belief that the ownership and use of property was a prerequisite to civic virtue and human happiness, and that one of the first objects of government should be the preservation of property rights. The label "Chief Justice–dominated" identifies the Court with its Chief Justice, suggesting that John Marshall was the most important and influential member of the Court, and that to a large extent the Court's views on legal issues were the equivalent of Marshall's views.

When I began this study I had a sense that these labels amounted to oversimplifications, and that a revision of the Court's image was probably necessary. I also believed that the starting point for the revision lay in the considerable amount of recent scholarship that has explored the importance of the ideology of republicanism as a central belief structure for late-eighteenth- and early-nineteenth-century American culture.[2] I suspected that the Marshall Court, like other institutions in that period, had been affected by republicanism, and that by considering the relationship between the Court's decisions and the central issues and paradoxes of republican thought a new perspective on the Court might be gained.

I have pursued that effort in this study; one might say I have explored the possibilities of attaching another label—"republican"—to the Marshall Court. I will subsequently give a brief outline of my efforts and the historiographical consequences, but at this point a caveat is in order. Entrenched historical labels do not survive merely out of inertia; they survive because they contain a modicum of truth. The difficulty with the entrenched labels for the Marshall Court is not that they mischaracterize but that they oversimplify: they conceal complexities and in the process blunt rather than sharpen understanding.

The Court's "nationalism," for example, was an eighteenth-century, anachronistic variety, oriented primarily toward preserving the federal government against centrifugal encroachments, and only secondarily toward expanding national power. Its "Federalism" was not so much a conventional partisan ideology as a collective attitude toward the proper locus of sovereignty in the American republic, an attitude that was complex and not always consistent. Labeling the Court "property-conscious" conceals the most important feature of its decisions affecting property rights, the fact that the decisions represented accommodations between two quite different conceptions of property, one of which was inimical

---

[2] I have listed the sources that have influenced my understanding of republicanism and liberalism in early America in Chapter I.

to the idea of property as a commodity to be exchanged in a market economy. A characterization of the Court as dominated by its Chief Justice fails to take into account the significance of other Justices, such as Story and Johnson, who regularly contributed to the Court's opinions, and fails to emphasize the importance of the Court's internal deliberative process, which placed a high value on the contributions of "silent" Justices, whose votes or opinions were not revealed in the Court's formal decisions.

I have therefore not employed entrenched labels in this study, except where I have deliberately sought to complicate their meaning. As part of that process I have asked whether the meaning of the labels might be deepened or enhanced by considering the Court as an institution functioning in a culture composed of the entrenched belief structure of republicanism and the emerging oppositionist belief structure of liberalism. In the process of exploring that question I have discerned that the label "republican," when applied to the institution of the Supreme Court of the United States, itself conceals significant complexities. An initial complexity is the simultaneous uniqueness and diversity of the ideology of republicanism itself. From a modern vantage point, republicanism can be made to appear wholly distant from modern thought in certain of its metaphysical assumptions, such as its theory of cultural change or its attitudes toward social stratification. The gap between such assumptions and those of moderns helps convey the time-boundedness of republicanism and emphasizes the degree to which dominant ideologies establish tacit boundaries on thought and discourse. But while a recognition of ideology as a cultural system is important, that recognition tends to obscure the diversity of viewpoints that can be held within the boundaries of an ideological universe, the extent to which ideology continually confronts, reshapes, and is reshaped by cultural experience, and the presence of potentially competitive ideologies in the same time frame. I have responded to this initial complexity by suggesting that the ideological ethos of the early nineteenth century can most accurately be described as an amalgamation of republican and liberal ideologies, with other ingredients, such as the belief that America was an exceptional and unique culture, being added to the mix.

A more basic complexity was raised by the difficulty of making meaningful correlations between ideological positions and the judgments rendered by courts. Courts are, first of all, not static entities: their personnel and the composition of their dockets change, sometimes drastically, over time. In America appellate courts, such as the Supreme Court of the United States, typically render collective judgments which deemphasize individual beliefs and emphasize "authoritative" legal sources that are taken to be neutral, apolitical, and nonideological. How does one assess the ideological posture of a court whose members try to conceal

3

their belief structures and to suggest that their judgments have nothing to do with ideology?

I have sought to respond to these complexities in several ways. First, I have made an effort to reconstruct, as far as possible, internal evidence about the Marshall Court's deliberative processes, and I have attempted to show that the working life of the Court—the manner in which cases came to it, the setting of its deliberations, its deliberative practices themselves—can be seen as having an ideological character. The working life of the Court reveals that a particular jurisprudential issue—the problem of judicial "discretion" and the related problem of distinguishing the judicial declaration of legal principles from partisan political activity—was foremost in the minds of Marshall and his contemporaries. A surprising amount of internal evidence relevant to this issue has survived, and I have employed it to reconstruct those dimensions of cases and formulations of doctrine that revealed the Justices' concern with "discretion."

Second, I have sought to penetrate the legal doctrines of the Court through certain reading techniques. One of these has been to identify words that occupied places of significance in the language of early-nineteenth-century republicanism and liberalism—words such as "property," "Union," and "commerce"—and to compare the use of such words in Marshall Court decisions with their use in the culture at large. These sorts of words may be considered as cultural signifiers, words intended to convey a bundle of associations and thereby to invoke an appeal to values perceived to be of great importance in the culture.

Another technique has been to identify, in cases raising legal disputes, the propositions opponents regarded as beyond dispute—that is, the common starting premises from which advocates of differing points of view developed their arguments. An example can be seen in the Court's decisions comprising the meaning of the Contract Clause of the Constitution, in which the question of the degree of protection for "vested" rights of property was raised. While those decisions provoked severe disagreement within the Court on how much legislative interference with property should be tolerated, and what sorts of property could be restricted, no one challenged the proposition that private property rights in a republic were entitled to autonomy and protection.

A third reading technique I have employed is to ascertain which jurisprudential issues the Marshall Court regarded as significant and controversial, and which it tacitly dismissed as settled or trivial. The Marshall Court, because of its place in history and its own deliberative practices, had a significant amount of freedom to facilitate the placement of certain cases on its docket. Many of the Court's significant constitutional cases, we shall see, were cases that the Justices arranged to hear, through use of their discretionary power to shepherd lower court cases up to the Court.

4

## Introduction

The disproportionate number of certain kinds of cases on the Court's docket (sovereignty cases, especially those testing the scope of the Court's own power to review the judgments of state courts, admiralty jurisdiction cases, piracy cases, real property cases) and the virtual or total absence of other kinds of cases (slavery cases, free speech cases, gender discrimination cases) furnish another index of those issues whose resolution the Justices regarded as pressing and significant and those issues that the Justices tacitly concluded were beyond dispute, insignificant, or too complex or diverse to merit resolution. Those sets of judgments can, of course, be seen as having ideological ramifications.

Finally, I have assumed that the formulation of legal doctrine can itself be read as an ideological exercise. The ideological dimension of Marshall Court opinions was accentuated by the place of the Court in history. The Court came into existence at a time when very few authoritative sources of legal doctrine existed in America. In 1815 there were comparatively few reported decisions of courts, relatively few interpretations of the Constitution by the Court itself, and almost no legal treatises written by American authors. By 1836 all three of those sources had significantly increased, and in many instances Marshall Court Justices had themselves been responsible for that increase. Marshall Court Justices, we will see, played an important role in the growth of reported decisions, published their own circuit opinions, wrote treatises, and added to the decisions interpreting the Constitution. In the process one can often see their starting presuppositions laid bare.

My assessment of the Court's internal deliberations and my readings of its doctrinal pronouncements have led me to advance a characterization of the role the Court occupied in early-nineteenth-century American culture. Evidence supporting the characterization will be presented throughout the study; at this juncture I offer it in stark outline.

The cultural context in which the Court did its work was composed, I believe, of three central features. One was the conception of American culture that prevailed in the early nineteenth century: that of America as a new and a republican society, freed from the feudal institutions and practices of Europe, committed to a novel form of government in which sovereignty rested in the people, who were endowed with a virgin continent and abundant resources. In the exceptional setting of the American continent, contemporaries reasoned, a republic might be created that would break the cycle of institutional decay and become permanently fixed in time, just as the burgeoning economic opportunities in America had broken European patterns of status and deference. Americans might be truly free: free from the determinism of history, free from the hierarchies of class, free from the corruption of courtiers, free to buy and sell goods and commodities in a market that was unaffected by status or influence.

5

The event that early-nineteenth-century observers most commonly associated with this sense of American exceptionalism and promise was the Revolution. In that gesture of independence, symbolic as well as real, Americans had severed themselves from the tyranny, corruption, and feudalism of the Old World. But in reflecting on the Revolution, contemporaries of the Marshall Court encountered the second pervasive feature of their time: the sense that the Revolutionary generation had passed. Fifty years spanned the Declaration of Independence and the John Quincy Adams administration; one by one the war heroes, the patriots, the Founding Fathers had died or were dying. It was apparent that the America from which the movement for independence had arisen was not the America of the 1820s: the landscape, the population, the modes of transportation and communication, even the territorial expanse of the nation had undergone massive changes. The seminal, identifying years of American culture were passing into history.

The simultaneous perception that American culture was new, free, and exceptional, but that the period most symbolic of its unique qualities was being relegated to a memory, evoked a sense of uneasiness among contemporaries of the Marshall Court. That unease was accentuated by the third central feature of early-nineteenth-century American culture: the absence of a historicist theory of cultural change. Early-nineteenth-century Americans did not embrace the idea that change was a given in social organization and that the history of cultures was, therefore, the progression of qualitative change. The absence of a historicist sensibility among Marshall's contemporaries meant that they tended to characterize evidence of change as part of a cyclical pattern of events, in which cultures were born, matured, decayed, and were dissolved. They also tended to ascribe to certain institutions or cultures a potential for being "outside time," that is, for resisting, because of their inherent soundness or their exceptional character, the inexorable process of decay.

The perception of American exceptionalism, the sense of distance from the Revolutionary experience, and the lack of a historicist sensibility fused in early-nineteenth-century Americans to create a distinctive attitude toward the relationship between the past and the future. The attitude emphasized the ability of exceptional ideas or institutions to perfect themselves over time and thereby to resist the cycle of decay. In the case of America, the cycle could be broken if successive generations would recast the insights of the Revolutionary generation as lessons to be derived from the past and applied to the future. Recasting first principles was thus a way of avoiding the full implications of permanent qualitative change.

The idea that the past could be preserved and the exceptionalism of America made permanent seemed particularly applicable to American jurisprudence. Two of the major sources of American law were the Constitution, a document written in and embodying the assumptions of the

Revolutionary period, and the common law, typically characterized by Marshall's contemporaries as a repository of principles whose authoritativeness was reaffirmed by their application to new situations. The process of legal interpretation in America, then, appeared to be simply a version of the idea of recasting itself: the derivation of first principles and their restatement as lessons for the future.

The purpose of recasting first principles was, of course, to ensure their permanence in a changing cultural environment, and here the idea of interpretation, especially judicial interpretation, appeared to raise problems for contemporaries of the Marshall Court. Judges, by virtue of the decision in *Marbury* v. *Madison*[3] and by virtue of their gradual displacement of juries as finders and declarers of legal principles, had by the close of the War of 1812 solidly established themselves as the principal expounders of common law and constitutional principles. But was their interpretation of those principles faithful to the principles themselves?

The principles embedded in the Constitution served as a case in point. Republican theorists could point to the Constitution as the source of three permanent principles: the "anticorruption" principle, embodied in the separation of legislative, executive, and judicial powers; the "antityranny" principle, embodied in the idea of a written Constitution; and the "federalism" principle, embodied in the creation of two sovereign entities, the states and the federal government, each of whose powers was limited by the other. Corruption, tyranny, and the concentration of power in one sovereign had all been evils republican government was designed to prevent. The separation of powers was intended to ensure that one group in a government could not corrupt others through its influence; the promulgation of written laws to ensure that republican citizens knew their rights and obligations, and would not be susceptible to the fiats of tyrants; and the creation of divided sovereignties to ensure that American governments could neither ignore nor become dominated by local attitudes and interests.

It is arguable, however, that the interpretation and declaration of legal principles by federal judges, so far from ensuring the permanence of these constitutional principles, violated each of them. Federal judges owed their appointments to the executive; they tended to be members of the same political party as those who appointed them. Might their decisions not merely reflect the partisan views of their patrons and thus violate the anticorruption principle? Moreover, federal judges, in fashioning their decisions, might, even in local matters, ignore the findings of state courts or legislatures, thus violating the federalism principle. Finally, federal judges, in an age in which not all judicial decisions were reported, might produce a body of unwritten common law, thus failing to give republican

---

[3] I Cranch 137 (1803).

citizens notice of their legal rights and responsibilities and violating the antityranny principle.

In the period of the Marshall Court one can see this concern about the dangers of interpretation by federal judges crystallized in two code words: "discretion" and "consolidation." "Discretion" referred to the opportunities for federal judges to make partisan decisions or to make unwritten decisions without having to account for their actions. "Consolidation" referred to the opportunities for federal judges to usurp the prerogatives of state courts or state legislatures and thereby "consolidate" the power of the Union. We will notice throughout this work the strategies developed by Marshall Court Justices to deal with criticism that their decisions were unduly "discretionary" and "consolidationist." In a nutshell, those strategies amounted to an argument that any "discretion" the federal courts possessed was a "mere legal discretion," that is, a discretion to find and declare the appropriate legal authorities, and nothing more; and an argument that the purported "consolidationist" decisions of the Court were merely applications of the language and spirit of the Constitution.

The problems for federal judges were not, however, limited to disabusing their critics about their discretion and their tendency to embrace consolidation. Their problems were basically those of all early-nineteenth-century Americans who perceived a need to preserve the special character of American culture in light of an increased distance between the Revolutionary experience and the present. Their concern, notwithstanding its legal emphasis, was the same concern exhibited by other interpreters of their time: how to invest the past with meaning for the present and future, and thereby preserve the exceptional version of American republicanism against decay, while modifying it to accommodate social and economic change.

I will be suggesting in the course of this work that the Marshall Court adopted a three-pronged response to the cultural problem outlined above. The first prong of the response was to recast the language of the Constitution, so that extracted principles could be made applicable to an altered cultural environment. The principal technique for this recasting was a linguistic analysis of the Constitution's text, developed by Chief Justice Marshall and employed by other Justices as well. By means of this analysis certain critical words in the Constitution, such as "contract" and "commerce," were given a universalistic meaning and thus converted into permanent principles. The words replaced nontextual sources of principles and were packed with nontextual meanings, such as those derived from natural law. In each of the great constitutional cases that came before the Marshall Court a critical word or group of words in the Constitution's text was recast through this technique, converted into a principle, and made applicable to a situation not explicitly contemplated by the Framers.

8

*Introduction*

The second prong of the Court's response was to recast doctrine in nonconstitutional cases as it recast textual language in constitutional cases. Rather than words being packed with meaning, universalized, and converted into principles, prior common law decisions were converted to authorities and at the same time Americanized. Thus the process of recasting doctrine often meant its modification to conform to new conditions, but the recast doctrines were treated as if they were enduring principles that had been extracted from the authorities of the past. Just as the Court did not treat its recasting of the Constitution as making new law, it did not treat its recasting of common law doctrines as lawmaking. In both areas modifications of language or doctrine were presented as the promulgation and clarification of settled principles.

The third prong of the Court's response was the creation of mechanisms to promote selective, collegial, and confidential decisionmaking, so that the discretionary features of judging would not be exposed to public scrutiny. Those mechanisms, developed during the early years of Marshall's tenure and perfected in the so-called "Golden Age" of the Court, from 1812 to 1823, when the number and identity of Justices remained constant, affected the manner in which cases came to the Court, the process by which they were decided, and the techniques for their delivery, publication, and dissemination. The primary purpose of the mechanisms was to preserve the appearance of unanimity and continuity in the Court's decisions so as to emphasize the nondiscretionary nature of the principles and authorities the Court was extracting.

It is possible to see these responses of the Marshall Court as emblematic of a broader set of responses early-nineteenth-century Americans were seeking to make to the contradictions they perceived in their cultural environment. Early-nineteenth-century Americans were anxious to preserve the institutions and principles of the Revolutionary experience in the face of an altered cultural landscape. They were anxious to maintain the uniqueness and exceptionalism of the American republic against the inevitability of decay and the prospect of change. Unwilling fully to embrace qualitative change yet aware of the distance between themselves and the generation of the Declaration and the Constitution, they sought devices to establish that change could be a perfecting process, by which first principles of republican government were periodically restated so as to ensure their permanence. The Court's treatment of constitutional language and legal doctrines, and the Court's refinement of its internal deliberative practices, can be seen as examples of such devices. In this vein, the Court can be seen as an institution whose central self-defined function was that of preserving, perfecting, and modifying the exceptional American version of republicanism in the face of cultural change.

This book thus argues that a new characterization of the Marshall Court can be made. The point of the characterization is not to label the

Court as "republican" in its ideology—the various strands of republican theory extant in early-nineteenth-century America suggest that such a label would obfuscate rather than clarify the Court's stance—but to emphasize that the Court was an institution responding to contradictions in the culture of its time. The boundaries of ideology and cultural experience meant that there were certain issues that the Marshall Court could have decided only in one fashion; certain issues that it did not think worth deciding; certain issues that so revealed the internal contradictions of the Court's belief structure as to make it unable to decide. The characterization invites us to see the Marshall Court as an important reflection of the distinctive cultural attitudes of early-nineteenth-century literate America, no less a cultural artifact because of its character as a legal institution. The Marshall Court was a phase in the history of the Supreme Court of the United States, but it was, more significantly, a Court of its age.

# CHAPTER I

*The Origins
of Marshall Court Jurisprudence* I:
*Cultural Change and
Republicanism*

HE EXTENDED ARGUMENT OF THIS STUDY is that the decisions of the
Marshall Court cannot be separated from the distinctive cultural
ethos in which they originated. As such the argument presupposes that
the distinctiveness of early-nineteenth-century American culture can be
grasped; this chapter initiates that exploration. The chapter examines the
relationship between early-nineteenth-century American culture and the
ideology of republicanism, a constellation of interconnected ideas that
arguably set the boundaries of thought and discourse during the period
covered by this work. A succeeding chapter discusses the response of
elite members of the legal profession to the central intellectual problem
facing literate Americans in the early nineteenth century, that of accommodating republican theory to dramatic and pervasive cultural change.
Taken together, the chapters suggest that the origins of Marshall Court
jurisprudence may be found in the interaction of rapid and puzzling social
change with an entrenched ideological paradigm, and a distinctive professional response to that interaction.

This chapter is divided into three sections. The first discusses observable and arguably distinctive features of the cultural landscape of
early-nineteenth-century America, and contrasts those features with the
immediate past.

The second section assesses the responses of one literate observer,
James Fenimore Cooper, to those features in the landscape. Cooper, who
wrote both novels and social commentary, was a faithful if opinionated
recorder of contemporary events as well as the best-known American
novelist writing in our period, and he was highly ambivalent about the

features of American culture he discussed. I will be examining Cooper's social commentary as well as his fiction. The choice of both literary genres is intended as an exercise in exploring the multiple levels on which contemporaries of the Marshall Court communicated their perceptions of the world they were experiencing. I am especially interested in the juxtaposition of two of those levels, the surface, "rational" reconciliation of perceived tensions in the culture, and the imaginative dramatization of those tensions, in which they appear much less easily reconcilable.

The ideological framework from which Cooper viewed the cultural landscape around him, and the issues he identified as particularly pressing ones for his contemporaries, serve as a transition to the third section of the chapter, which discusses the ideology of republicanism, the paradigmatic theoretical framework within which early-nineteenth-century Americans discussed and debated social, political, economic, and legal issues. The section discusses the intellectual sources of American republicanism, the central presuppositions of its belief structure, and the accommodation of republican theory to cultural change in early-nineteenth-century America.

In 1828 James Fenimore Cooper, already a well-known novelist, published a book of social commentary thinly disguised as a "traveller's report." The book, entitled *Notions of the Americans: Picked up by a Travelling Bachelor,*[1] was a conscious effort on Cooper's part to respond to travel accounts of America by European visitors. Two such accounts in the 1820s, Cooper felt, had presented American culture in a misleading or disparaging fashion.[2] *Notions of the Americans* was an effort to supply a correction, in the form of a "hasty and general sketch of [t]he principles of the [American] government and the state of [American] society."[3] In two concluding chapters Cooper sought to summarize the state of American society in the 1820s.

Cooper's anonymous "travelling bachelor" identified five distinctive features of early-nineteenth-century American culture. These features have been so regularly commented upon by historians of the period, and were remarked upon so often by contemporaries at the time, as to lend credence to Cooper's choices. It is the purpose of this section to suggest

---

[1] J. Cooper, *Notions of the Americans: Picked up by a Travelling Bachelor* (2 vols., 1828). I have used the American Classics edition (1963), which is a facsimile of the original with the same pagination.

[2] The travelers' accounts in question were Adam Hodgson, *Letters from North America* (2 vols., 1824) and Frederick Fitzgerald DeRoos, *Personal Narrative of Travels in the United States and Canada* (1827). See Robert Spiller's introduction to the American Classics edition of *Notions of the Americans,* v–vi.

[3] Cooper, *Notions,* I, xv.

that each of the features identified by Cooper can be seen as a symptom of rapid cultural change, but that the changes taking place occurred in a manner that obscured or qualified their radical nature. The relevant time span for this examination of cultural change is the years between 1800 and 1840, years which framed the tenure of the Marshall Court.

First on Cooper's list of features in the cultural landscape was the rapid growth and diffusion of American population. The population of the nation in 1815 had doubled that of 1790; between 1810 and 1840 the population increased at a rate of better than 32 percent each decade.[4] In 1800 the total population of the United States was estimated at 5.3 million inhabitants, the great percentage of whom lived between the eastern seaboard and the Appalachian mountains; by 1840 the population had increased to 17.1 million, more than a third of whom lived west of the Appalachians.[5] As more Americans were born, and more territory was added to the nation, contemporaries experienced a sense of "violent motion" and "fabulous growth and change."[6]

But the rapid growth and diffusion of the population, which can be traced in part to a large birth rate,[7] did not ensure that the increased number of Americans would lead longer or healthier lives. One of the paradoxes of massive population growth in early-nineteenth-century America was the continued precariousness of an individual life. From a modern perspective, the living conditions of the period appear markedly solicitous to disease.[8] Sanitation facilities were rudimentary: cities had neither systems for sewage disposal nor adequate drainage, with the result that streets became depositories for garbage and waste. Indoor plumbing was largely nonexistent, and window screens did not exist at all; as a result insect carriers of infectious diseases, such as flies and mosquitoes, had easy access both to offal in the streets and to the living quarters of

---

[4] G. Taylor, *The Transportation Revolution* (1951), 4; see the Government Printing Office monograph, *A Century of Population Growth in the United States 1790–1900* (1909).

[5] *Century of Population Growth,* 55.

[6] M. Meyers, *The Jacksonian Persuasion* (1960 ed.), 122. Meyers's observation is intended as a summary of the reactions of contemporaries. See ibid., 121–41.

[7] Taylor, *Transportation Revolution,* 4.

[8] The observations on health and medicine made in the next few paragraphs are based on R. Shryock, *Medicine and Society in America, 1660–1860* (1960), 17–49; R. Shryock, *Medicine in America: Historical Essays* (1966), 13–25, 237–50; W. Rothstein, *American Physicians in the Nineteenth Century* (1972), 41–61; C. Rosenberg, "The Therapeutic Revolution: Medicine, Meaning, and Social Change in Nineteenth-Century America," in M. Vogel and C. Rosenberg, *The Therapeutic Revolution* (1979), 3–21; and C. Warner, "The 'Nature-Trusting Heresy': American Physicians and the Concept of the Healing Power of Nature in the 1850s and 1860s," *Perspectives in Am. Hist.*, 11:291 (1978). For a contemporary account of living conditions in one section of the population, see J. Griscom, *Sanitary Condition of the Labouring Population of New York* (1845).

13

houses. Epidemics of yellow fever and influenza were common, and residents of seaport towns, such as Norfolk, Philadelphia, and New York, often relocated during the summers to avoid yellow fever. The dietary habits of nineteenth-century Americans also seem, from a modern perspective, not conducive to health. The absence of refrigeration meant that meat not eaten shortly after the animal was killed quickly became infested with bacteria. Because of the absence of extensive sewage facilities, fresh water was hard to obtain in urban areas. The selection of food and drink was, by modern standards, only moderately healthful. Current dietary theories would applaud the nineteenth-century table's emphasis on grains and unprocessed food, but would be less enthusiastic about the great amount of animal fat and the large quantities of alcoholic beverages consumed. If one equates health with safeguards against disease and a modern nutritional dietary regimen, the environment of nineteenth-century America was a comparatively unhealthy one.

While one might surmise that the precariousness of life in early-nineteenth-century America would have engendered significant developments in medicine, one of the striking features of the age was the comparative powerlessness of the medical community to reduce the average American's vulnerability to illness and death. With some exceptions—notably smallpox—illnesses were not attributed to the presence of infectious agents but to a disturbance in the body's equilibrium. The prevalent theory of pathology held that the human body was composed of various substances (the medieval humors) which needed to remain in balance to ensure health. When illness developed, medical practice responded by various techniques designed to strip the body of its "imbalance"; bleeding and the use of emetics, laxatives, and diuretics were common treatments. In the early years of the century this theory was implemented through so-called "heroic" practices, in which physicians bled patients copiously, induced them to perspire, gave them regurgitory and emissive agents, and generally attempted to produce violent "eruptions" that were believed to restore needed balance. By the 1820s and 1830s, the negligible effects of heroic practices resulted in their falling out of fashion, and some physicians became attracted to homeopathic medicine, which consisted of injecting the patient with small doses of agents that were thought to be likely to cause the disease in a healthy person. By the 1840s and 1850s, a number of physicians had concluded that the best therapeutic practice was to avoid being "heroic" at all costs, which often meant "letting nature take its course."

The significant developments in population growth and diffusion that marked the first forty years of the nineteenth century, then, had their disturbing side. Crowded conditions increased the risk of contagious diseases and made hygienic and sanitary efforts more difficult. Medical theory and practice continued to be based on intuitive, medieval beliefs about the composition of the human body. The fact that Americans were more numerous and more mobile did not mean that they could expect to be healthier than their ancestors. On the contrary, they confronted a rapidly changing human environment without the benefit of altered theories about why some people remained healthy and others suddenly took sick and died. At a more abstract level, they confronted the sudden growth of population without a clear sense of how their existing culture could accommodate that growth. Cooper, writing in 1828, projected that "in 1850, the population will probably be 24,000,000; in 1880, 48,000,00; and in 1920, near or quite 100,000,000." He then commented that "the first impression that strikes the mind is the impossibility that 100,000,000 people should consent to live quietly under the same government."[9]

The diffusion of the population had been made possible, Cooper felt, by extraordinary developments in transportation.[10] Here again historians of the period support his observation. One influential study has described the period between 1815 and 1860 as a "transportation revolution,"[11] and a comparison of the state of transportation facilities in the nation in 1800 with those in 1840 suggests that the phrase may not be excessive. In the first years of the century the principal means of long-distance transportation available were stagecoaches, horses and horse-carts, and sailing ships. Roads were simply paths cleared across land, unpaved and filled with stumps, often impassable in wet weather. Ferries or fords were usually necessary whenever water intervened. Passage on a sailing ship was dependent on the wind. Joseph Story described an 1807 trip from Boston to New York on a packet:

> I think you were last with me in a dead calm, and were kindly told that the said calm was about to please me for a day or two, in which time neither heaven nor earth afforded one beauty to the eye or ear. Luckily, I was a bad prophet. In about two hours a breeze sprang up and increased with the tide until by noon it blew with great violence. . . . We carried sail nobly and rejoiced in the expectation of reaching our haven in a few hours. . . . We arrived just before night at Hell-Gate, and were beating against the wind with a full tide, a heavy breeze, and high sea running, when suddenly our ship mis-staged and plumped ashore on Blackwell's Island. . . .
>
> As some evil spirit would have it, we were seized with mania of getting to New York that night. A fishing smack was passing by, and in an instant, with one accord, we jumped into our boat, rowed to her and, baggage and all, found ourselves crowded into one of the most miserable, filthy, vile skiffs that ever disgraced the water . . . the weather soon thickened and became rainy, and for two hours we were

---

[9] Cooper, *Notions*, II, 340–41.
[10] Ibid., 321–22.

[11] Taylor, *Transportation Revolution*, 1.

pleasantly contemplating that our crazy skiff would land in the coast and give us the additional comfort of sleeping with a wet jacket in the open air. . . .

Thanks to our stars we landed at the City about 8 o'clock, and soon found ourselves in a public coffeehouse. The residue of my time has been devoted to Morpheus, who has received from me a most religious reverence.[12]

The rudimentary state of transportation facilities markedly affected the development of national institutions. Congress and the Supreme Court remained transient bodies of government until the 1830s; the national capital was relatively inaccessible; letters, the only form of long-distance communication, were dependent upon transportation conditions; gatherings of persons from diverse localities and regions were necessarily infrequent and logistically inefficient.[13]

By 1840 this state of affairs had been, observers felt, marvelously altered. Between 1815 and 1830 a series of turnpikes, many with stone foundations and gravel dressings, were built, along with bridges and drainage ditches. The coming of the turnpike, which greatly improved short-distance overland transportation (principally provided by horse-drawn stagecoaches) was symbolized by the National Road, which began at Cumberland, Maryland. By 1818 the road stretched to Wheeling, in western Virginia, and by 1833 it had reached Columbus, Ohio. The National Road featured stone bridges, taverns, and stone and gravel roadbeds, and was financed and built, notwithstanding political and constitutional debates, by the federal government.[14]

The boom in turnpike construction was paralleled by a comparable growth in the construction of canals. With the completion and financial success of the Erie Canal, built in sections from 1817 to 1825, a network of canals was launched in the eastern and midwestern states. Between 1816 and 1840 over 3,000 miles of canals were built, at a total cost of nearly $125,000,000.[15] All of the major seacoast ports except Charleston were connected to interior waterways by canals; canals lined upcountry and tidewater areas in all states from Maine to Virginia. In addition, a series of canals connected mid-Atlantic states to states in the Ohio River Valley, and another series joined the Ohio and Mississippi rivers to the

---

[12] J. Story to Samuel P. P. Fay, May 15, 1807, quoted in W. Story, *The Life and Letters of Joseph Story* (2 vols., 1851), I, 143.
[13] G. Dangerfield, *The Awakening of American Nationalism* (1965), 195–97; J. Young, *The Washington Community 1800–1828* (1966), 41–48, 65–83. For a description of early roads in America, see C. Colles, *A Survey of the Roads of the United States of America, 1789* (W. Ristow, ed., 1961).
[14] Taylor, *Transportation Revolution*, 22.
[15] Ibid., 52

Great Lakes. Although the canal building boom had ended by 1840, it had opened up the interior of the American continent: cities such as Cincinnati, Pittsburgh, and Cleveland had become business and population centers.

While canals meant that traffic was no longer limited to the natural courses of navigable rivers in passing from the coast to the interior, they did not themselves improve the speed of the boats that used those routes. The vicissitudes of water travel evident in Story's description of his 1807 journey remained. One historian has characterized early-nineteenth-century navigation as follows:

> Transportation up the rivers [or canals] proved extremely time consuming and costly. . . . Flatboats from western Pennsylvania floated down to New Orleans in a month or six weeks. A few keelboats and barges made the return trip upriver. . . . On wide expanses of water they used sails and when the river bottom was solid, they poled. At times they rowed . . . [T]hey might [also] resort to ''bushwacking,'' pulling the boat up the river by grasping bushes or branches of trees overhanging the bank.[16]

The nineteenth-century innovation in American transportation that most directly responded to such problems was the steamboat. First launched by Robert Fulton and the Livingston family in New York in 1807, by 1820 steamboats were in service on the Hudson, Delaware, Connecticut, Ohio, Missouri and Mississippi rivers, as well as the waters around New York City and the Great Lakes.[17] According to the leading history of early-nineteenth-century transportation, during the next twenty years the steamboat ''dominated American river transportation'' and ''proved the most important factor'' in the industrial development of the Mississippi Valley region.[18] By 1840 the steamboat had eclipsed other forms of river transportation, except for particularly bulky freight, which was still carried by sailboats or flatboats. The effect on passenger transportation was particularly dramatic. Instead of a lengthy, cumbersome, uncomfortable passage in a horsedrawn vehicle over unpaved roads, or an exposed journey on a sailing ship, a passenger could ride in the relative comfort of a vessel that could provide shelter from the weather and ensure that the duration and nature of the trip would be comparatively predictable. Steamboat travel was not without its risks: boilers periodically burst, and snaggings, fires, and collisions occurred with some frequency.[19] But

---

[16] Ibid., 57.
[17] See ibid., 57–64; L. Hunter, *Steamboats on the Western Rivers* (1949), 6–24.

[18] Taylor, *Transportation Revolution*, 58, 63.
[19] Hunter, *Steamboats*, 271–303.

the presence of the steamboat revolutionized long-distance travel across America in the two decades after 1820.

An even more significant development in the history of American transportation, the railroad, lies largely outside the period covered by this study. The earliest railroads in America were built after 1826, although interest in steam travel on rails had surfaced as early as 1816. Small stretches of track were in operation near Baltimore and Charleston by 1831 and around Boston by 1835. A survey of mileage on railroads and canals in 1830 showed only 73 miles of railroad in the nation as opposed to 1,277 miles of canals.[20] In the next ten years railroad mileage grew significantly, surpassing that of canals by 1840, but most of the growth took place after 1835. Nonetheless, the possibility that steam power could be put to use on land, and the vast implications of that development, were part of the consciousness of many Americans in the 1820s and 1830s.

While these technological changes in transportation were striking in themselves, they may have had their greatest impact outside the area of technology proper. Two factors greatly altered American attitudes toward the idea of travel itself. As transportation became technologically revolutionized between 1800 and 1840, it became markedly less expensive and less time consuming.[21] The result was that personal travel shifted from a pursuit of the wealthy and leisured to a pursuit in which more persons, for more diverse reasons, could engage.[22] Meanwhile business enterprises began to employ different, and potentially competitive, modes of transportation, and began to place a premium on speed as well as on quality and price. Easier and cheaper interchange with the world that lay beyond an individual's immediate surroundings thus could alter that individual's sense of time, space, mobility, and place in society.

This last observation reminds us that the transportation revolution of the early nineteenth century took place in a culture that was deeply localized and stratified, and remained so while dramatic technological changes were taking place. One cannot assume that the persons who witnessed the dramatic changes in transportation taking place reflexively altered their thinking about themselves and their place in society because of those changes. A fairer assumption, and one that receives support in contemporary accounts, is that those early-nineteenth-century Americans who sensed the changes that new modes of transportation could make in their lives retained, at the same time, a vivid sense of the pre-"revolu-

---

[20] Taylor, *Transportation Revolution*, 76–79.

[21] See ibid., 142–52; Hunter, *Steamboats*, 417–18.

[22] Hunter, *Steamboats*, 441, describes the division of steamboat travel into "cabin passage" and "deck passage" and the large numbers of lower-income passengers that adopted the latter class of transportation, often at one-fourth the rates of cabin passage.

tionized'' world. And the reminders of that world were not merely nostalgic: locality and class were as significant a part of early-nineteenth-century America as was the promise of mobility.

In recalling that casual travel outside one's locality was a pursuit essentially limited to the wealthy in the early 1800s, one is reminding oneself not only of the state of technology at the time but also of the state of physical and social relationships. As the War of 1812 opened, America was a nation of relatively vast size, relatively small population, formidable geographic barriers, and, like other colonies of Western European nations, an established heritage of social stratification. The development of a mass culture, such as that of modern America, was precluded in the early nineteenth century by geography, communication, and attitudes toward class.

In succeeding chapters we will note the role geography played in shaping the composition of the Marshall Court and the nature of its business. We will see that the office of Supreme Court Justice was conceived from its origins as having a regional dimension: though the Court met in the nation's capital, its members allegedly represented the nation's various regions. When a Justice from one region left the Court, he was regularly replaced by another from the same region, and the duration of the Court's Term in Washington was compressed so that the Justices could return to their regions as circuit judges. The Justices' dual functions combined with the formidable physical barriers to travel in early-nineteenth-century America to make the office an itinerant one, and the Justices transients in the Washington community. We will also see the appearance of a specialized Supreme Court bar, heavily staffed by members of Congress and practitioners from Maryland and the District of Columbia; the practice of the Justices' living together in a boardinghouse while holding court; the speed with which the Justices decided cases; and the frequent injuries that the Justices suffered on their travels. Each of these phenomena can be associated with the geography of early-nineteenth-century America.

But geography was a shaping force in a more basic sense. In an age in which traveling from Boston to New York, even as late as 1833, meant a two-day journey by stagecoach or an even longer trip over water;[23] in which many roads remained merely dirt paths; in which hills or rivers could serve as barriers; and in which many passengers continued to be exposed to the elements, moving from one's local surroundings remained a formidable undertaking. As a result, provincial habits and experiences formed part of most Americans' lives, and few opportunities existed for exchange among different sections of the nation. A study of early-nineteenth-century Washington, for example, has shown that as late as

---

[23] Taylor, *Transportation Revolution*, 142.

1829 members of Congress associated with, lived with, and overwhelmingly voted with members from their own locality.[24]

Provinciality was furthered by the relative absence of any unifying means of communication. Newspapers existed in abundance, but these were primarily of local circulation. Letters, the principal means of communication between persons living in different localities, depended upon a postal service which, although it grew rapidly in scope between 1815 and 1830, continued to use horseback riders to deliver half its mail in 1825 and, until 1845, charged between six and twenty-five cents for each single sheet of paper mailed.[25] The insularity fostered by geography, when coupled with the rudimentary communication system of the age, suggests that local attitudes, conventions, and practices were a substantial force in early-nineteenth-century American culture.

An individual in early-nineteenth-century America was identified not only with a particular region or locality but also with a particular social status. Social stratification can be seen in every feature of early-nineteenth-century American life, from dress to voting requirements. Education, choice of occupation, leisure pursuits, patterns of social interchange, marriage, birth, and death were linked to a class structure that was somewhat fluid in theory but comparatively fixed in practice. Conceptual distinctions were made that separated squires from artisans, free persons from slaves, and propertyholders from those without property; those distinctions were manifested in social practices. Squires, for example, were shown deference on the street, influenced the voting patterns of others, served as creditors, educated their offspring formally, engaged in ritualistic leisure activities such as hunting and dancing, and were closely associated with the political and legal offices of their localities and regions. Artisans (sometimes called "yeomen") rarely engaged in any of these functions. Their opportunities for education, influence, leisured pursuits, and power in a community were significantly fewer.[26]

Deeply entrenched practices and institutions, then, did not suddenly change because Americans had easier access to distant places and to one another. Transportation was undeniably a loosening force, helping to break down geographic barriers that fostered provinciality and stratification. But the breakdown of those barriers took place in a culture whose practices and institutions were products of a localized and stratified environment. Geographic diversity, inaccessibility, provincialism, and

---

[24] Young, *Washington Community*, 87–153.
[25] Taylor, *Transportation Revolution*, 149–50.
[26] For contemporary sources supporting these observations, see T. Dwight, *Travels in New England* (4 vols., 1821); B. Hall, *Travels in North America* (2 vols., 1829), as well as the sources cited infra, note 63. See also R. Bushman, " 'This New Man': Dependence and Independence," in R. Bushman, ed., *Uprooted Americans* (1979).

stratification coexisted in early-nineteenth-century America with the turnpike, the canal, the steamboat, and the infant railroad.

In addition to population and transportation, Cooper noted a third
distinctive feature of America in the 1820s, the changing state of "commerce."[27] Few words were more widely and ambiguously used in the
first forty years of the nineteenth century than the word "commerce."
We shall have occasion to explore its several meanings, including its
constitutional meaning. Here the term is used in its early-nineteenth-
century lay sense, as a word incorporating many of the distributional
aspects of economic activity, and equated with "traffic," "intercourse,"
and "enterprise," while being distinguished from "manufacturing" and
"agriculture."[28] The most striking fact about American commerce in the
early nineteenth century, Cooper felt, was its increasingly "internal"
character. As new modes of transportation were opening up the interior
of the country, traffic in goods was beginning to flow westward to the
inland cities as well as eastward across the Atlantic and north and south
along the Atlantic seacoast. At the same time "immense progress" had
been made "in manufactures" since independence, and Cooper believed
that "nothing can have a greater tendency to increase the trade between
different sections of a country . . . than increasing its objects."[29] American commerce was thus more "internal" both in the sense of being more
dispersed throughout the continent and in the sense of being less directed
toward foreign trade.[30]

Cooper's perception was based on tangible evidence. In a message
to Congress in the seventh year of his presidency, James Madison had
called for a tariff to protect "the enterprising citizens whose interests are
now at stake."[31] Congress responded with the Tariff of 1816, the first
national effort to protect domestic trade against foreign competition. The
same message encouraged internal improvements; Madison at that time
assumed that such improvements could constitutionally be subsidized by
the federal government.[32] The internal expansion of the American economy was also fostered by other protectionist tariffs, new modes of trans-

---

[27] Cooper, *Notions*, II, at 326.
[28] For a discussion of the role of
"commerce" in late-eighteenth- and
early-nineteenth-century American
thought, see D. McCoy, *The Elusive
Republic: Political Economy in Jeffersonian America* (1980), 76–104,
237–44.
[29] Cooper, *Notions*, II, 326–27.
[30] Ibid., 329–31.
[31] Quoted in J. Richardson, ed.,
*Messages and Papers of the Presidents,
1789–1807* (1898), I, 567.

[32] Madison alluded to "the great importance of establishing throughout our
country the roads and canals which can
best be executed under national authority." Ibid. He was subsequently to reverse this position, vetoing an 1817
congressional bill that sought to finance
internal improvements through the use
of earmarked federal funds. See ibid.,
584.

portation, the massive influx of population into the Ohio and Mississippi valleys, the availability of interior land through public land sales, the systematic dispersal of Indian tribes, and the success of the cotton gin. Such developments, which all took place between 1800 and 1840, redirected the nation's commercial energies.

Transportation, population, migration, commerce, and national policy were interdependent forces in the period. Better communications between the Atlantic seacoast and the interior meant that more people could move westward and live comfortably away from the seacoast. Congress encouraged people to do so through public land and tariff policies, and was responsive to their interests once they did. As more people moved inland, they created larger markets, justifying greater expenditures for steamboats, canals, and the like. As those markets became profitable sources of income they formed the base for experiments in manufacturing. The industrial steam engine, the power loom, and the blast furnace, all products of the forty years after 1800, were both responses to and altering forces in the new markets for internal commerce. Thus by the 1820s, when factories had become more numerous, American commerce not only had a new geographic orientation, it included goods that had been produced by novel economic processes.[33]

But the increasingly domestic orientation of traffic in goods and the increased presence of industrializing sectors in the nation's economy did not mean that the character of American commerce was completely transformed in the forty years after 1800. The new modes of commerce and production coexisted with older, established modes, which were based on oceangoing trade, the primacy of foreign markets, coastal shipping centers, the individual household as the central unit of production as well as consumption, and the overwhelmingly rural and agrarian character of American life. In 1815 about 6 percent of the American population lived in cities; in 1830 only 9 percent. Nearly 80 percent of the population was engaged in agriculture in 1815. Approximately 75 percent of white adult males were self-employed as late as 1825. Few Americans performed specialized economic functions: an individual household combined, in its adult members, manufacturing, farming, the providing of services, and commercial exchange.[34] Those evocative symbols of urbanizing America, the factory worker and the captain of industry, were uncommon features of the landscape.

---

[33] Three general discussions of commerce in the early nineteenth century can be found in P. Gates, *The Farmer's Age: Agriculture, 1815–1860* (1960), 1–50, 398–420; C. Nettels, *The Emergence of a National Economy, 1775–1815* (1962), 205–340; and Taylor, *Transportation Revolution,* 153–206.

[34] Taylor, *Transportation Revolution,* 6; P. Conkin, *Prophets of Prosperity: America's First Political Economists* (1980), 6, 7–9.

Moreover, one section of the country, the tidewater South, continued to rely primarily on foreign commerce and exportation, and resisted industrialization; and its patterns of exchange were transplanted to settlements in the interior. New developments in technology and transportation did not alter the mode of southern commerce, they merely made cotton an important item in that commerce. Most of the South's cotton was produced in the western regions, Alabama, Mississippi, Louisiana, and Texas; most of it was prepared for market by slaves working on plantations; and most was exported to Europe. In the coastal South a similar means of production and a similar market orientation existed for rice, tobacco, and sugar. While manufacturing existed in the tidewater and interior South between 1800 and 1840, it was centered around households or plantations, not factories. "Commerce" for the South in that period meant traffic between households or plantations and coastal ports, with foreign markets as the ultimate destination. Nor was the use of slave labor in the southern economy new: the Constitution had tacitly recognized slavery, although mandating the abolition of the slave trade. The novel feature of the southern economy in the forty years after 1800 was the dramatic interaction of slave labor with technological developments in extractive agriculture, exemplified by the cotton gin. Although that interaction was a new development, both slavery and an externally oriented traffic in agricultural commodities had been fixtures in the eighteenth century.[35]

Early-nineteenth-century alterations in the character and content of American commerce, then, were superimposed on an older model of commerce as maritime, coastal, external, and mercantile; they did not displace that model. As in the case of population and transportation, the potentially radical effect of the changes was tempered by continuities; the meaning of the changes for contemporaries was ambiguous. In the realm of commerce, for example, it was by no means clear that American commercial policy should facilitate internal traffic and domestic manufacturing at the expense of external traffic and foreign trade; nor was it clear whether the interests of shippers from the interior, coastal merchants, manufacturers, and plantation owners were interdependent, complementary, or competitive. The ramifications of the rapidly changing content and direction of commercial development appeared uncertain to early-nineteenth-century Americans.

In identifying his final two distinctive features of the early-nineteenth-century American environment, Cooper turned from concrete phenomena to the more abstract realm of ideas and institutions.[36] One

---

[35] On southern commerce in the early nineteenth century see Conkin, *Prophets of Prosperity*, 9–12; D. Boorstin, *The Americans: The National Experience* (1965), 171–76.

[36] Cooper, *Notions*, II, 354.

abstract phenomenon he identified as uniquely American was the existence of a political theory that "leaves every man . . . on grounds of
perfect equality." Equality, however, was an ideal rather than an enforced
practice: "an equality of rights only." If Cooper's feature is restated as
a tension between homage to the ideal of equality in theory and circumscription of that ideal in practice, historians have largely agreed with his
assessment. Cooper acknowledged that "talents, money, and enterprise"
were "left to their natural influences," and "produce[d] their natural
effects," which were not equalizing. Moreover, "the slaves in the Southern States" were excepted even from abstract equality: they necessarily
did not possess equal rights.

But the idea of equality itself, Cooper felt, was not only entrenched
but growing: "here we have a government in which the people are the
sources of power . . . the tendency is to natural rights, at the expense of
artificial institutions."[37] The principle of abstract equality has been regularly identified by scholars as an idea that gained considerable momentum
in the forty years after 1800. Two areas of American life often singled
out as illustrating the growing deference paid to the equality principle in
those years are suffrage and education.

The early nineteenth century was one of the major periods of suffrage reform in American history, although the beneficiaries of the reform
were exclusively white males. Between 1816 and 1821 six new states
entered the Union and provided in their constitutions for universal white
male suffrage, thereby departing from the pattern of all but one of the
original states, which had limited voting to freeholders or taxpayers.[38]
And between 1820 and 1829 three influential states, Massachusetts, New
York, and Virginia, held constitutional conventions in which they reviewed suffrage conditions. Massachusetts continued to restrict suffrage
to taxpayers, but the requirement was sufficiently modest (any tax paid
to the state or a county) as to amount to universal male suffrage.[39] New
York abolished its freehold qualifications for white males and retained a
minor taxpaying requirement. It also retained freehold qualifications for
black males, which had the effect of disenfranchising nearly all eligible
black voters.[40] Virginia's situation was nearly unique. In 1829, when
Virginia held its convention, it was, along with North Carolina, the last
of the states retaining a freehold qualification for suffrage. In the convention of that year opponents of the freehold qualification pointed out
that it disenfranchised numerous farm tenants, tradesmen, and artisans.
Defenders took a more abstract philosophical stance, one asserting that

---

[37] Ibid., 333, 335, 339.
[38] Maryland was the only original
state with universal male suffrage. See
M. Peterson, *Democracy, Liberty, and*

*Property: The State Constitutional
Conventions of the 1820s* (1960), xiv.
[39] Ibid., 11.
[40] Ibid., 137

# Chapter I: *The Origins of Marshall Court Jurisprudence* I

"amongst the arguments relied upon by the advocates of a very extended suffrage, one of the most fallacious, is that which attempts to found the right upon principles of natural equality." Suffrage, the delegate continued, was not a natural right, and even if it were "the Bill of Rights . . . admits the modification which natural rights may receive by entering into society."[41] Eventually a compromise was adopted in which housekeepers and leaseholders were enfranchised, but all other nonfreeholders were excluded. The result of the compromise, one scholar has suggested, was that "over 30,000 adult white males remained outside the circle of political competence."[42]

Virginia's response was unusual for the time: one historian has suggested that "something approximating white manhood suffrage had been achieved in most states prior to 1824."[43] The extension of suffrage, as the Virginia convention illustrated, had been premised on the equality principle: the old freehold and taxpayer qualifications had suggested that one sort of person's participation in civic affairs was more desirable than another's. Suffrage reform was also notable for the presence of visible members of the judiciary—Joseph Story in Massachusetts, James Kent in New York, John Marshall in Virginia—aligned on the side of resistance to reform.[44]

Educational reform came slightly later than suffrage reform, the major growth of free public education in America taking place between 1830 and 1850.[45] But the connection between equality, the diffusion of knowledge, and free access to educational institutions had been made by the 1820s, and some tangible evidence of educational reform had occurred. In 1826 Story, in a discourse on the "Characteristics of the Age," noted that "this is emphatically the age of reading. In other times this was the privilege of the few; in ours, it is the possession of the many." The "progress" of "learning," Story felt, was "once gradually downwards from the higher to the middle classes of society"; it "now radiates in all directions, [being] aided . . . by the system of free schools."[46] The lyceum circuit, on which public lectures were given by scholars to adult audiences, was first established in 1826, and "mechanics institutes," billed as opportunities for self-improvement, were common in the early

---

[41] Philip N. Nicholas, speech before the Virginia Constitutional Convention of 1829, quoted in ibid., 387–88.

[42] Ibid., 284.

[43] E. Pessen, *Jacksonian America: Society, Personality, and Politics* (1969), 158.

[44] For samples of Story's, Kent's, and Marshall's positions, see Peterson, *Democracy, Liberty, and Property*, 78–91, 182–84, 360–64.

[45] See R. Nye, *Society and Culture in America 1830–1860* (1974), 378–99; A. Ekirch, *The Idea of Progress in America 1815–1860* (1944), 195–224.

[46] J. Story, "Characteristics of the Age," (1826) in W. Story, ed., *The Miscellaneous Writings of Joseph Story* (1852), 344–45.

1830s. The "universality of a state of high mental cultivation" was linked by advocates of free public education to a "great reorganization of society."[47]

If one observes the inexorable triumph of extended suffrage and the rapid growth of public education between 1800 and 1840, one might be tempted to identify the equality principle as the dominant impulse of that period. There were, of course, stark contradictions, such as slavery, the disenfranchisement of free blacks, the exclusion of women from the suffrage and from many educational institutions, and the dispossession of Indian tribes, and contemporaries noted these exceptions to the apparent triumph of the equality principle. But an even more striking feature of the period was the continued persistence of practices and institutions whose thrust was to confine and circumscribe equality in the very areas of American culture in which enthusiasm for the equality principle seemed most marked. Voting practices and educational patterns furnish examples.

A recent study of voting practices in Massachusetts from the 1790s to the 1840s has shown that eighteenth-century conceptions of deference and influence coexisted with the emergence of political parties, the written ticket, and the secret ballot. The patterns of change, moreover, were irregular: sometimes localities that had become highly partisanized subsequently became dominated by individuals of "standing," wealth, or power; sometimes open, oral voting was reinstituted after efforts to use secret, written ballots.[48] Oral, or viva voce, voting complemented deference politics and a qualified franchise: it assumed that persons of influence in a community could control the votes of others. Oral voting had been the dominant eighteenth-century practice, resulting in ritualistic scenes in which men of "standing" walked to the polls, declared their votes openly, and then vouched for others, who noted that they agreed with their patrons.[49] The secret ballot, by contrast, freed "dependent" sectors of the population from having to reveal their votes. A Boston newspaper, in arguing for ward voting in 1823, claimed that under the procedures extant at the time "an overbearing aristocracy" practiced a "system of dictating and browbeating," by "tak[ing] their stand and overaw[ing] those who may have more mind, more honesty, and more patriotism, but LESS MONEY."[50]

Voting practices similar to those in Massachusetts were present in many states. Like the freehold qualification, open oral voting declined between 1800 and 1840, but the decline was gradual and irregular, and

---

[47] "The Progress of Popular Intelligence," *Free Enquirer*, 4:89 (Jan. 14, 1832).

[48] R. Formisano, *The Transformation of Political Culture: Massachusetts Parties, 1790s–1840s* (1983), 128–48.

[49] For detail on such practices in late-eighteenth-century Virginia, see C. Sydnor, *Gentlemen Freeholders: Political Practices in Washington's Virginia* (1952).

[50] Boston *Statesman*, Feb. 27, 1823.

many states retained viva voce voting or an open form of written ballot through the 1830s.[51] Deference politics, with its de-emphasis on partisanship, mass appeals, and extensive suffrage, likewise remained an important part of American culture through the early 1830s.[52]

Similarly, the drive for free and universal public education was accompanied by a self-conscious effort in institutions of higher learning to preserve elitist values. Higher education, in eighteenth-century America, had principally served to provide young men of "standing" with a "liberal" exposure to the kind of knowledge a cultivated gentleman should possess. Higher education was neither a professional training ground nor, in most cases, a vehicle of upward mobility.[53] As public education came to be associated with democratizing and leveling influences, several spokesmen for private colleges responded by identifying themselves as guardians of "liberal" education, which they associated not only with "progress" but with the preservation of traditional intellectual and moral standards.[54]

The equality principle, then, appears as both an energizing and a threatening force in early-nineteenth-century America; one can catalogue affirmations of it, implicit and explicit exceptions to it, and reactions against it. Cooper's sense of a juxtaposition of equality as an abstract ideal and equality as a set of practices thus seems a perceptive observation. Appeals to the equality principle held considerable theoretical stature in the forty years after 1800—Jacksonian Democrats and self-styled reformers of all kinds consistently made such appeals—but the appeals tended to conceal the ambiguities of practice and the mixed responses that the ideal of equality generated.

In his summary of early-nineteenth-century American culture in *Notions of the Americans* Cooper finally came to the feature "of infinitely the most interest." This was the presence, and "the durability," of a "confederated government."[55] The existence of a federal republic, and the conflicting pressures engendered by the existence of that form of government in a rapidly growing and diversifying culture, dwarfed all other issues in significance during the forty years after 1800. Each of the cultural features previously discussed affected the status and potential

---

[51] See P. Bourke and D. DeBats, "Identifiable Voting in Nineteenth Century America," *Perspectives in Am. Hist.*, 9:259, 269–75 (1977).

[52] See R. McCormick, *The Second American Party System: Party Formation in the Jacksonian Era* (1967), 104–23; K. Hall, *The Politics of Justice: Lower Federal Judicial Selection and the Second Party System, 1829–61* (1979), 170–75.

[53] See L. Cremin, *American Education: The National Experience* (1950), 107–33; Ekirch, *Idea of Progress*, 212–23. Virtually all American colleges were private in the period under discussion.

[54] Ekirch, *Idea of Progress*, 212–16.

[55] Cooper, *Notions*, II, 340, 341.

future of federated republican government in America; each can also be seen as subordinate to the great question of that government's durability. No period in American history has arguably contained so many dramatic, and perplexing, changes in the composition of the nation that was being governed by a federal republic. And the idea of a federal republic itself presupposed a fragile, perhaps temporary, existence for the form of government established in 1787. As we shall see, many early-nineteenth-century social theorists perceived republics as temporary stages in the course of a nation from primitive to "corrupt" and "tyrannical" states. The perceived fragility of republican forms of government interacted with the massive cultural changes of the early nineteenth century to make acute the question whether federated republicanism, the form of government established by the Constitution, could endure in America, especially in light of the rapidly altering American cultural environment.

Federated republicanism, as established by the Constitution, was based on two late-eighteenth-century ideas, the idea that sovereignty would be distributed between the entities forming a republican government and the idea that power would be balanced among the branches of the government being formed. The form of government established by the Constitution was thus first a republic, that is to say a representative government in which power, theoretically vested in the people, was implemented by representatives; second, a federated republic, in which, as Alexander Hamilton put it in 1788, "a partial union or consolidation" had been constructed, in which "the state governments would . . . retain all the rights of sovereignty which . . . were not, by [the Constitution], exclusively delegated to the [federal government]";[56] and, third, a federated republic with a tripartite structure of powers, one branch balanced against another.

The federated republic created in 1787 can be seen as posing three large issues of political theory, none of which was resolved by the formation process. One issue was the rights of the people against the government itself, "government" being taken as encompassing both the federal union and the states. Another was the nature and scope of the powers of each of the tripartite branches of the federal government in relation to one another. A third was the nature and scope of the powers of the federal government's branches in relation to the states. All of those issues were unsettled at the time of the Constitution's framing. But the last issue was to be significantly affected by the cultural changes of the years between 1800 and 1840.

We have seen that trends in population, transportation, and commerce had both diversifying and unifying effects in the early nineteenth

---

[56] Publius [Alexander Hamilton], *The Federalist* No. 32, in New York *Daily Advertiser*, Jan. 3, 1788.

century. By the 1830s far greater numbers of Americans lived more varied lives, were separated by greater distances, were more conscious of sectional "interests," voted along more conspicuously regional lines, and participated more extensively in domestic regional markets than they had in the 1800s. Americans had greater access to one another, could more easily change their location, were more likely to engage in interstate trade and commerce, and were more aware of, and responsive to, symbols of nationhood and "Union" as the nineteenth century progressed. More states entered the Union, with the result that the national government controlled more territory and commanded more wealth and resources, but also with the result that more sovereign state governments existed.

Most of the changes in early-nineteenth-century American culture thus bore upon Cooper's "question of infinitely the most interest": how far the sovereignty of the federal government, as embodied by any of its three branches, could infringe upon the sovereignty of the states. The question may have originally been thought of as an abstract inquiry in experimental political theory, just as a tripartite federated republic had been thought of as an experimental form for a nation.[57] But since the major cultural changes of the period between 1800 and 1840 had both centripetal and centrifugal ramifications, that question radiated through much of American life as the nineteenth century matured. By the period covered by this study the question had become a practical one of constitutional law, and one that was multifaceted, complex, controversial, and increasingly urgent.

But the previous pages have suggested that while massive cultural changes did in fact occur in early-nineteenth-century America, the meaning, and sometimes even the existence, of these changes was obscured by other features of American culture that represented continuity with the eighteenth-century past. This made interpretation of cultural change a confusing and perilous process, and elevated to great importance the question of the role of the past as a source of meaning for the present. As questions of sovereignty become acute in the early nineteenth century, the Constitution, an authoritative guide from the past, was increasingly looked to as a source of answers to those questions. But the Constitution had been framed in a culture that nineteenth-century Americans now sensed as distinguishable from their own, at least in many of its tangible features. Was the document to remain a source of guidance notwithstanding the increasing remoteness of the context of its framing? More generally, how did one interpret the revolutionary past—the time in which the American experiment in federated republicanism was created—in light of the cultural landscape of the present? Were the theories of sovereignty, and the theory of republicanism itself, still relevant to early-nineteenth-

---

[57] See P. Nagel, *One Nation Indivisible* (1964), 13–31.

century America? In this fashion legal issues—such as whether the Constitution permitted or prohibited states from regranting lands they had previously granted, taxing national banks, passing insolvency legislation, or creating steamboat monopolies on interstate waterways—became exercises in the interpretation of cultural change.

How did contemporary Americans react to the massive changes taking place in their culture? I have previously suggested that the changes were less observable to contemporaries than to subsequent generations because they were concealed and deflected by practices and institutions that fostered continuity with the past. But there was little doubt that early-nineteenth-century Americans were aware that the world of their children would not resemble that of their parents; how did they view this prospect? One way to get a sense of the reaction of contemporaries is to trace in some detail the responses of an early-nineteenth-century literary artist who saw himself as a social commentator.

James Fenimore Cooper was the dominant American novelist of the period of the late Marshall Court, in sales as well as in reputation.[58] But the source of Cooper's interest in cultural change was not merely the resonance of a literary artist. He had been born in affluent circumstances in upstate New York in 1789, the son of Judge William Cooper of Cooperstown, a landowner who on his death in 1809 was one of the wealthiest men in New York state.[59] Between his father's death and the 1820s, however, a depression in land values, mismanagement of the Cooper landholdings by Cooper's brothers, and the effective use of debt collection processes by land speculators resulted in Cooper's losing most of his original family holdings.[60] At the same time Cooper began to emerge as a successful historical novelist, publishing *The Spy* in 1821, *The Pioneers* in 1823, *The Pilot* in 1824, *The Last of the Mohicans* in 1826, and *The Prairie* in 1827, most of which were well received and all of which were self-conscious efforts to write on native American themes. Cooper was thus by the 1820s both a dispossessed member of the early-nineteenth-century landowner classes and an artist with an investment in American society.

The most revealing of Cooper's volumes of social commentary, *Notions of the Americans,* appeared, we have seen, as a response to the writings of British and Continental Europeans about their travels to America between 1825 and 1840. The timing of the foreign travelers' visits was itself significant. It testified to the advancing state of transportation in America; it was also a signal of the emergence of America as a "new"

---

[58] See J. Cooper, *The Pioneers* (J. Beard, ed., 1980), xx, xlii–xlvi.

[59] Beard, in Cooper, ibid., xxx.

[60] Ibid., xx–xxxii.

culture and a distinctive nation. The best known of the traveler's reports, Alexis de Tocqueville's *Democracy in America*,[61] based on trips taken in 1831 and 1832, emphasized both these themes. The two most striking features of America for Tocqueville were the mobility of the citizenry, which he found facilitated by vast distances, abundant land, and rapidly developing modes of transportation, and the presence of democracy, the political principle that he felt distinguished America from Europe.[62] Most of the early-nineteenth-century European visitors that were motivated to travel around America at approximately the same time as Tocqueville commented on those two features. Their responses revealed that as travelers they had found American culture accessible; as observers, alien.[63]

The accounts of European visitors between 1825 and 1840 produced a composite portrait of Americans and American culture. Differences between America and Europe stood out in stark relief for the travelers, and they thus grasped essences that natives might have ignored. On the other hand the perception of Europeans that America was radically different from Europe encouraged visitors to focus on the differences; subtleties and complexities were often missed in the vividness of the contrast. To restore some balance in the accounts, the composite portrait created by European travelers is contrasted with the self-consciously corrective portrait supplied by the mythical travelers invented by Cooper in *Notions of the Americans*.

Although European travelers were more inclined to record their immediate observations, they sometimes discussed abstract characteristics of American culture. There are many more references to transportation

---

[61] A. de Tocqueville, *Democracy in America* (2 vols., 1835, 1840).

[62] See G. Pierson, *Tocqueville and Beaumont in America* (1938), 50–153.

[63] The generalizations about travelers' reactions made in the next several paragraphs, listed alphabetically: Edward S. Abdy, *Journal of a Residence and Tour in the United States* (3 vols., 1835); Bernhard, Duke of Saxe-Weimar-Eisenach, *Travels Through North America, 1825 and 1826* (2 vols., 1828); James Boardman, *America and the Americans* (1833); Michel Chevalier, *Society, Manners and Politics in the United States* (1839); Stephen Davis, *Notes of a Town in America 1832–1833* (1833); DeRoos, *Personal Narrative*; John Eyre, *The European Stranger in America* (1839); Simon A. Ferrell, *A Ramble of Six Thousand Miles Through the United States*

(1832); Asa Greene, *Travels in America* (1833); Francis Grund, *Aristocracy in America* (1839); Basil Hall, *Travels in North America in the Years 1827 and 1828* (1829); Thomas Hamilton, *Men and Manners in America* (1833); Fanny Kemble, *Journal of a Residence in America* (2 vols., 1835); Frances Lieber, *The Stranger in America* (2 vols., 1835); Frederick Marryat, *A Diary in America* (1839); Harriet Martineau, *Society in America* (2 vols., 1837); Peter Neilson, *Recollections of a Six Years' Residence in the United States* (1830); Tyron Power, *Impressions of America, 1833, 1834, 1835* (2 vols., 1836); Patrick Shireff, *A Tour Through North America* (1835); James Stuart, *Three Years in North America* (2 vols., 1833); Tocqueville, *Democracy in America;* Frances Trollope, *Domestic Manners of the Americans* (1832); and Godfrey T. Vigne, *Six Months in America* (1833).

facilities, crowds, and the haste with which Americans ate gargantuan meals than to equality, liberty, or sovereignty. Nonetheless visitors perceived that Americans were simultaneously egalitarian and snobbish, and that they were simultaneously chauvinistic in their patriotism and susceptible to bitter sectional animosities. Numerous accounts stress the endless bragging of Americans about their rivers, their climate, their food and drink, their language, their political institutions, their transportation, and their prosperity, "as if," Tocqueville suggested, Americans "doubt[ed] their own merit, [and] wished to have it constantly exhibited before their own eyes."[64] At the same time observers noted the sharp criticism residents of one section of the nation reserved for residents of another. Regional stereotypes were perpetuated. Southerners were characterized by others as lawless, hot-tempered, and irreligious; northerners as acquisitive, prudish, and cunning; westerners as ill-mannered, uneducated, and violent. There was a tendency, travelers noted, on the part of representatives of one section to attribute the nation's problems to the excessive influence of the other sections. Americans appeared to be both aggressively nationalistic and internally divided.

In the travel accounts Tocqueville and other foreign observers frequently noted the distinctive features of the nineteenth-century American cultural landscape. In reading the accounts one often has to draw inferences, but those inferences lie close to the surface of the commentary. European travelers frequently commented about crowded conditions in transit, the mingling of diverse classes of society, the apparent impatience, restlessness, and rootlessness of Americans, the apparent indifference of the population to steamboat accidents, and the great significance American society placed upon commerce, business, and the acquisition of money. From such comments one becomes aware that population growth and mobility, developing modes of transportation, and active commercial enterprise were dominant features of the American landscape. Similarly, the constant stream of observations by travelers about the openness, foolishness, informality, vulgarity, aggressiveness, materialism, and braggadocio of Americans suggest that European visitors, most of them members of the upper classes with a well-developed sense of social distinctions and niceties, were confronting a culture in which the equality principle was disconcertingly present and in which the pursuit of wealth and upward mobility were linked. Many visitors also noted the contradictions between the equality principle and entrenched practices, such as slavery, the treatment of Indians, social climbing, and subtle class distinctions.

Travelers' accounts, in short, confirmed the presence of the features of early-nineteenth-century American culture previously described, and

---

[64] Tocqueville, *Democracy in America,* II, 238.

found that those features made America less than entirely hospitable. Population growth, in most of the accounts, was disconcerting and oppressive; the transportation revolution seemed to have precipitated a chronic restlessness and impatience in the population; the great attention paid to internal commerce seemed to make Americans boring, materialistic, and unattractively shrewd; equality was noxious in its breaking down of social niceties and in its fostering of hypocrisy and cant; the American political experiment in juxtaposing a Union and sovereign states appeared to have precipitated both chauvinism and sectional discord. Not all the travelers drew negative conclusions from their experiences in America, and many marveled at the abundance, physical beauty, inexpensiveness, and accessibility of the nation, or were impressed with the cordiality, generosity, and unpretentiousness of the population. But the composite portrait was sufficiently troubling to provoke Cooper to attempt a corrective in *Notions of the Americans*.

The technique Cooper used in *Notions of the Americans* was to create a "travelling bachelor," a member of a club of persons of "inveterate peregrinating habits," who encountered, "on the road between Moscow and Warsaw," one John Cadwallader, an American.[65] The two then resolved to travel to America, Cadwallader as a returning native and the bachelor as a visitor. As preparation for the trip the bachelor, while he and Cadwallader were detained in London, read a good many English accounts of travels to America, of which Cadwallader took no apparent notice. Eventually the bachelor asked Cadwallader why he had not commented on any of the accounts, and Cadwallader responded that the writers "have been journeying in America, to ridicule, to caricature, and to misrepresent."[66] The result was that Europeans had a distorted image of American culture, demonstrated, Cadwallader thought, by the fact that the only "sufficiently correct history of the war of the revolution" was that written by the American John Marshall, Chief Justice of the United States, originally as part of his biography of George Washington.[67] Cadwallader resolved to accompany the bachelor through his travels in America; the obvious purpose of the two men's excursion was to correct that distorted image.

*Notions of the Americans* consisted of a long series of correctives. A particularly striking one was Cooper's analysis of the state of American commerce. After remarking on the beauty and efficiency of American

---

[65] Cooper, *Notions*, I, 1.
[66] Ibid., 331.
[67] Ibid., 332. Marshall's biography, *The Life of George Washington,* had originally been published in five volumes between 1805 and 1807. In 1824 the first volume was reprinted as *A History of the Colonies Planted by the English on the continent of North America, from their settlement, to the commencement of that war which terminated in their independence.* Cooper undoubtedly referred to that work.

ships and the overwhelming "maritime" orientation of the American population, Cooper noted that "real or pretended sceptics" had questioned whether the maritime emphasis of American commerce would persist, citing the internal development of the continent. He had the bachelor ask Cadwallader

> What effect will manufactures be likely to produce on the maritime character of your people? How far will the cheapness of land have a tendency to divert your population from the ocean, and what will be the probable influence of the inland States in opposing the commercial, or navigating interest of the maritime?[68]

That question was a singular compound of associations. It associated inexpensive land, population growth, the interior development of the nation, and "manufactures." It equated "commercial" and "navigating" interests. It linked sectional animosity, and potential sovereignty disputes, with economic interests, whether "inland" or "maritime." And it associated commerce with "character": America was in danger of losing her "maritime" nature.

Cadwallader's answer was equally revealing:

> [N]o parallel can be drawn between America and any other country, since no other country possesses such varied and cheap means of intelligence and communication, nor a population sufficiently active and intelligent to profit by them . . . [M]en would come from the forest to the sea to meet a demand, just as men will go from the sea to the interior, when that demand has more than met with its supply. So long as the merchant can afford to pay for labour, he will never want seamen in America, since it is commerce that makes mariners, and not mariners commerce. . . .
> As respects the supposed difference between the interests of what you call the maritime, and of the interior States, it has no real existence, and can, therefore, never produce any important results. It is difficult to imagine a state of society where there is so little competition . . . between its members, as is to be found in the United States. The unfortunate and lamentable grievance of slavery ceases to be an evil in this respect. . . . [I]n America, the southern planter has need of the shipping and manufacturers of [the north]. The converse of the proposition exhibits the principle which bonds the northern to the southern man. On all the great and leading questions of policy, their interests are identified. . . .

---

[68] Cooper, *Notions,* I, 336.

If the states of Ohio, Tennessee, and Kentucky, had the exclusive power to legislate on the commerce of the Union, they might encumber it from ignorance of its practices, though they would not be slow to perceive how useful it is, even to themselves. But commerce is regulated in the grand council of the nation, where men are assembled who know how to compare their respective wants, and where small sectional interests are completely silenced by the ones of the majority. . . .

As to manufactures, they are clearly a means of ordering commerce, when they exist in communities that can profit by both. It will be adding one more to the other numerous nautical resources of the country, let them thrive with us today . . . since . . . they will clearly increase the objects of intercommunication.[69]

One is struck by the combination of surface sanguinity and underlying uncertainty in this response. An enterprising population, "varied and cheap" transportation and communication, and the tendency of men to pursue their economic interests will result in prospective mariners coming "from the forest of the sea." The same logic, however, would result in members of a labor force going from the sea to the interior and thereby undermining maritime commerce. The differing interests of "the maritime" and "the interior" states had "no real existence," yet "the unfortunate and lamentable" presence of slavery was a signal of the differing interests of North and South. Manufacturers and commerce could "thrive" together, but manufacturers were somehow regarded as a "nautical" resource.

A particularly interesting passage in this quotation is that in which Cooper addressed the subject of interstate commerce. He was apprehensive that inland states such as Ohio, Tennessee, and Kentucky might "encumber" commerce, being "ignoran[t] of its practices." But fortunately commerce was "regulated in the grand council of the nation," by which Cooper meant Congress, "where small sectional interests are completely silenced by the voice of the majority." As we shall see, this was an astonishing characterization, both of Congress's regulatory power and of its nature. Four years before Cooper published *Notions of the Americans* the Marshall Court had held, in *Gibbons* v. *Ogden*,[70] that Congress had plenary power to regulate commerce, but Congress had not exercised that power at all. Moreover, the 1824 presidential election, in which four sectional candidates ran for the presidency and none obtained a clear popular majority, had demonstrated that Congress was composed of a set of sectional interests rather than a nationally minded majority. The passage, and the entire tenor of Cadwallader's response, appears to be a forced effort to alleviate Cooper's misgivings about potentially disruptive

---

[69] Ibid., 338–39.

[70] 9 Wheat. 1 (1824).

trends that had surfaced in nineteenth-century America. The artificiality of Cadwallader's "solutions" to the questions put by his bachelor companion only heightened the searching quality of the questions.

As the narrative of *Notions of the Americans* progressed Cooper increasingly advanced generalizations about the character of the American population, moving from travel commentary to an analysis of natural characteristics and institutions. He touched upon suffrage, public education, Congress, the presidency, the military, universities and colleges, the "learned professions" (law, medicine, and the clergy), literature, painting, architecture, language, the Supreme Court, the "system of jurisprudence" in America, religion, crime, dueling, slavery, relations between whites and blacks and whites and Indians, and the "influence of money" in American culture. The effect was to produce a catalogue of most of the customs or institutions that seemed important to an observer of early-nineteenth-century America. But the significance of *Notions of the Americans* is not only as a record of early-nineteenth-century America but also as an often unconscious revelation of the tensions elicited by Cooper's observations. Those tensions have previously been mentioned; at this point they can be recast into two broad categories. One category consisted of tensions emanating from the equality principle: Cooper's ambivalent attitudes toward democracy, freedom, social class, and order embody that set of tensions. Another category was composed of tensions emanating from the principle of dual sovereignty, exemplified by Cooper's ambivalence toward the interaction of sectional and national pressures in American culture.

Every abstract topic discussed by Cooper in *Notions of the Americans* elicited one or another of these sets of tensions. Two examples will suffice. In their visit to Congress the bachelor and Cadwallader came upon two congressmen, one "a grave looking, middle-aged man, of a slightly rustic air," the other "a gentleman-like man of sixty." The first was later revealed to be "a farmer of moderate means and good character"; the second "a man of immense hereditary landed estate." The two symbolized "the two extremes of the representation in this country—a yeoman, and a great proprietor." Congressmen, Cooper pointed out, "represent no particular interests, for all interests unite to send them here." The fact that one of the pair was "a yeoman, and the other a species of lord of the manor, produces no effect whatever." The two "meet in Congress on terms of perfect equality."[71] The message of the encounter, then, appeared to be that the equality principle triumphed over the artificialities of wealth and class.

But immediately after the encounter with the two congressmen the bachelor and Cadwallader came upon "two more members of Congress,"

---

[71] Cooper, *Notions*, I, 34–35.

who walked with them for some distance. One "was a man of a fashion-able air, and of exceedingly good manners," who spoke French, and was "agreeable and intelligent." The other had an "air which was not that of a man of the world," and "language sufficiently provincial to be remarked." The bachelor was "a little perplexed by the provincialisms of this individual," but "not less surprised at his shrewdness and intelligence." When the second pair left, the bachelor "again expressed surprise at the manifest difference in manners that existed between the two members." Cooper then employed Cadwallader to give a response Cooper especially wanted to convey:

> You will begin to know us in time. . . . These men are both lawyers. He whose air and language are so unexceptionable, is a member of a family long known in this country for its importance. You see he has not lost, nor will he be likely to let his posterity lose, the manners of the world. He is far from being rich, nor is he remarkable for talent, though rather clever. You find he has a seat in Congress. The other is the child of an affluent tradesman, who has given his son an education for the bar, but who could not give him what he has not himself—a polished exterior. But he is gleaning, and before he does, he will be in the way of imparting a better air to his descendants. In this manner is the whole of our community slowly rising in the scale of mere manners. As to talent, this provincial lawyer, for he is provincial in practice as well as by birth, has, as you must have observed, enough of it. . . . He has got the intelligence, and no small part of the feelings, of a gentleman; he may never get the air, for he began too late for that, and, like most men, he probably affects to despise an unattainable advantage. . . . Perhaps one of these parties loses a little by the intimate association which is a necessary consequence of their common situation; but the gradual approximation is, on the whole, produced by the improvement of the other. In the great essentials of soundness of feeling, minds, and common sense, they are quite on an equality.[72]

On the surface, the second encounter might be taken to convey the same message as the first: the gentleman and the provincial meet "quite on an equality" in the halls of Congress. But in the second example Cooper's language contains more than the surface appeal to equality. There are passages suggesting that the gentry life is far more attractive than that of the tradesman. The "air" and "language" of the gentleman-lawyer is "unexceptionable" to a European aristocrat: the provincial, by contrast, lacks polish. Wealth through trade cannot itself result in the development of tone and refinement. The provincial, in fact, recognizes this, and while he may "affect to despise" the "air" of a gentleman,

---

[72] Ibid., 36–37.

"he will be in the way of imparting a better air to his descendants." The status ascription that this effort represents is described by Cooper as creating a "slowly rising . . . scale" of manners. Throwing a gentleman and a provincial together in Congress results in "one of these parties los[ing] a little by the intimate association," and there is no question that it is the gentleman who is the "loser"; but "the improvement" of the provincial offsets this disadvantage. While the last sentence suggests that air, tone, breeding, manners, and polish may not be "essentials," the thrust of the passage is to contrast provincialism unfavorably with cosmopolitanism, and implicitly to suggest that equality has its drawbacks. This message, immediately following Cooper's comment about the "perfect equality" of Congress, invests that comment with an undercurrent of disquietude, and gives it the same quality of surface sanguinity that we have noted earlier. The example thus raises once more the theme of the awkward interplay between equality as an ideal and equality in practice.

A second illustrative example can be found in Cooper's discussion of the relationship between demographic and commercial changes and American maritime power. He began the discussion by claiming that "the natural order of things will accumulate the power of the republic quite fast enough"; creation of a large naval establishment was not necessary. He then described the forces composing the "natural order of things":

> [T]he Americans have been tracing the outline of their great national picture. . . . In fifty years it is physically certain that these states will contain fifty millions of souls. This number, supposing that the present marine should increase only in a numerical proportion, would give [America] a navy of rather more than two hundred sail. . . . [The American] population is getting compact; and as manufactures increase, and the usual divisions of employments follow, they will become such in a geometrical progression. Should there be a necessity for [a naval] force, there is far more probability that [the United States navy] will contain one thousand than two hundred sail in the year 1875.[73]

The above passage offers an example of Cooper's formulaic treatment of the growth and diffusion of population, trends in the American economy, and the size of national institutions. All of the factors in the formula, he believed, were interdependent and increasing in "a geometrical progression," allowing prodigious estimates of the future strength and vitality of the nation.

But this passage was again followed by a chilling afterthought:

---

Nor do I find a single plausible reason for disbelieving this result. Should a separation of the states occur, an event quite as improbable as any other act of suicide, and just as possible as all suicides, the commercial and manufacturing states would still keep together.[74]

The great trends in population and commerce Cooper had previously catalogued were revealed by these sentences to bear no necessary connection with national harmony. The trends had made possible the identification of certain states as "commercial and manufacturing." These states apparently shared economic interests, and as such were distinguishable from other states with other interests. Dissolution of the Union, like suicide, was "improbable," but "possible"; and if it occurred identity of economic interest could be expected to determine political affiliation. The afterthought suggests, then, that the changes in America Cooper had observed were placing pressure on the dual sovereignty principle as much as they were cementing the Union. Again Cooper's prognosis of a stronger and more unified nation emerging as part of "the natural order of things" appeared to be a surface reconciliation of his anxieties.

Cooper's effort in *Notions of the Americans,* then, had been to chart features of the early-nineteenth-century American landscape and to link the presence of their features to two overriding themes: the necessary interaction between a series of progressive economic forces and national power and prosperity; and the inevitable triumph in America, notwithstanding practical complications and qualifications, of the equality principle. He had not been completely successful in this effort: tensions had appeared beneath his surface optimism. But he had resolutely sought to convey the messages.

At the time that Cooper wrote *Notions of the Americans* he was full of enthusiasm for American culture and not inclined to penetrate too deeply into its contradictions and tensions. Nonetheless, he was genuinely ambivalent about the transformations in American society, and that ambivalence can be perceived beneath the surface sanguinity of his prose. *Notions of the Americans* can thus be seen as a portrait of early-nineteenth-century American culture that was conceived as a corrective but ended up being more searching and troubled than the author may have intended. Cooper saw, as had the travelers he sought to correct, a rapidly growing, economically active, increasingly diversified nation, imbued both with an egalitarian spirit and elitist habits and practices, increasingly interdependent and at the same time divided, filled with a sense of its cultural uniqueness and at the same time deeply uncertain about the institutions, practices, and ideals that it could claim as unique and permanent.

---

[74] Ibid.

✳

Neither the travelers' accounts nor Cooper's imaginary travelogue had delved deeply into the role of law in early-nineteenth-century American culture. Cooper had made a passing reference to the Supreme Court, briefly discussed the organization of the federal and state courts, showed some awareness of a few of the Marshall Court's decisions,[75] and realized that "there are not probably two [states] in the whole confederation whose forms of jurisprudence are precisely the same," and that "numberless questions of jurisdiction between the courts of the confederation and those of the States, still remained to be decided."[76] But his brief account of American jurisprudence was sketchy and not always accurate,[77] and he did not discuss the legal implications of the changes in early-nineteenth-century American culture that he described. Law was, however, a common subject of Cooper's fiction, and a significant presence in his life. His father had been a lay judge; he was a persistent litigator in the New York courts;[78] he had been deprived of much of his inheritance in legal disputes. One of Cooper's "Leather-stocking" novels, *The Pioneers,* represents his fullest account of the relationship between law and the distinctive features of American culture that he had identified in *Notions of the Americans.*

*The Pioneers,* first published in the United States in 1823, was immediately characterized as causing "a sensation" because of its descriptions of American "scenery, history, and character."[79] The favorable reception of *The Pioneers,* one reviewer suggested, was proof "that National Feeling is not dead, but sleepeth."[80] The publisher distributed 3,500 copies a few hours after publication, an unprecedented event in American book publishing at the time.[81] Reviews were generally favorable, and although by 1844 Cooper called the book's sales "only moderately successful,"[82] it established his literary reputation and made it

---

[75] Notably Gibbons v. Ogden, supra, note 70, which Cooper discussed (erroneously) in *Notions,* II, 160–61.

[76] Ibid., 154, 161.

[77] In addition to Cooper's misunderstanding of *Gibbons,* he claimed that the number of Supreme Court Justices had "recently been raised to nine." Ibid., 160. This comment was made in 1828; the number of Justices remained at seven until 1837. See C. Swisher, *The Taney Period, 1836–64* (1974), 58–63.

[78] See, e.g., Cooper v. Greeley, 1 Denio 347 (1845). That case arose out of a comment made by Horace Greeley, the editor of the New York *Tribune,* about a lawsuit that Cooper had filed

against him. Greeley wrote in the *Tribune:* "Mr. Cooper will have to bring his action to trial somewhere. He will not like to bring it in New York, for we are known here, nor in Otsego [County, the locality of Cooperstown], for he is known there." On reading Greeley's comments Cooper sued for libel. He lost.

[79] Washington *National Intelligencer,* Feb. 21, 1823.

[80] Ibid.

[81] New York *Commercial Advertiser,* Feb. 1, 1823; see Beard, in *Pioneers,* xlii.

[82] Cooper in *The Letters and Journals of James Fenimore Cooper* (J. Beard, ed., 4 vols., 1960–68) IV, 342.

possible for him to recoup some of the financial losses he had suffered in the forced sale of portions of his father's estates.

Of all of Cooper's novels, *The Pioneers* has received the greatest amount of critical attention; it is arguably his most complex, penetrating, and evocative novel. The depth and complexity of *The Pioneers* can be traced to the importance the novel assumed in Cooper's personal life. It was written at a time when Cooper had been stripped of much of his inheritance; it dealt directly with themes from Cooper's youth; it was set in the area in which Cooper grew up and peopled with characters modeled on Cooper's family, friends, and acquaintances. *The Pioneers* was also written at a period in Cooper's life in which the memories of his childhood seemed particularly vivid and in which the themes that Cooper associated with the last years of the eighteenth century, in which *The Pioneers* was set, seemed especially meaningful to contemporary Americans. All of these factors combined to make *The Pioneers* a novel of considerable richness.

The plot of *The Pioneers* is simple to the point of melodrama, but the novel's thematic organization is considerably more complex. The plot is composed of two narrative stories. One is the story of Judge Marmaduke Temple's efforts to impose some restraints on the use of his vast landholdings near Templeton in upstate New York, particularly as regards deer hunting. The other story involves the attempts of Oliver Effingham, the grandson of the original owner of the lands, to restore his claim to the lands and to keep Judge Temple from being aware of his real identity and of the concealed presence of Major Effingham, his grandfather, who is secreted in a hut in woods owned by Temple. Natty Bumppo, an aging hunter and former servant of Major Effingham, figures prominently in both stories. Bumppo continues to hunt game in the face of Temple's restrictions, and he assists Oliver Effingham in concealing Major Effingham, who is lodged in Bumppo's hut.

The connection between Bumppo and the Effingham family, the identity of Oliver Effingham (known to the Temple family as "Oliver Edwards," a hunter), and the concealed existence of Major Effingham are not revealed until the novel's conclusion. At the end of the novel the two stories are connected in a highly contrived manner. Oliver Effingham marries Judge Temple's daughter; Major Effingham, after having his existence acknowledged, subsequently dies; Judge Temple is revealed to have held the lands in trust for the Effinghams and to have offered to relinquish them, only to be rebuffed by Oliver Effingham's father (who conveniently dies in a shipwreck). On hearing the news of Oliver's father's death, Judge Temple voluntarily grants his lands to trustees, to be held for the benefit of his daughter and the Effingham family. Natty Bumppo, who had been arrested for killing a deer out of season and refusing to allow his hut to be searched, is pardoned, through Temple's good offices, by the governor of New York; he leaves Templeton to find a new area in which to hunt.

So stated, the novel appears to be a combination of late-eighteenth-century drawing-room farce and nineteenth-century romance. There are echoes of both those genres in the concealed identities, the love affair of Oliver Effingham and Elizabeth Temple, and several dramatic scenes. But the artificiality of Cooper's plot and the contrived connections between the principal characters are the least significant features of *The Pioneers*. Cooper managed those aspects of the novel so clumsily, in fact, that one has the sense that he intended them as perfunctory bows to the reading public, giving the bulk of his attention to thematic interplay. The major emphasis of *The Pioneers* was on the interaction of civilization, law, and the environment of late-eighteenth-century America; and Cooper's portrait of those forces in combination was a complex and absorbing one, all the more absorbing because it was retrospective. Cooper, writing in the 1820s, conveyed scenes from what he clearly intended to be an age that, at least in upstate New York, had nearly passed. When one compares the portrait of Templeton in the 1790s with the contemporary social history Cooper produced in *Notions of the Americans,* one senses that Cooper's readers knew that many of the conflicts presented in *The Pioneers* between the native American environment and the march of civilization had been resolved. But while Cooper identified those conflicts as related to a particular time, he presented them as recurring, and perhaps universal, features of life in America. Thus *The Pioneers,* read with those conflicts in mind, serves as both a historical portrait and a warning about the future.

The thematic structure of *The Pioneers* was designed to reveal the ambiguous nature of village culture in America, as exemplified by the village culture of Templeton, which is organized in the English fashion of a squirearchy. Judge Temple, the great landowner, is the pinnacle of that society: everyone else owes his or her place to the Judge. The village culture is a hierarchical culture, with gradations of social status signified by language, authority, and patterns of influence and deference. Judge Temple's influence is characterized as "too powerful to be opposed" in matters of religion. The "poorer and less polished part of the population" defers in church and elsewhere to "the principal personages of the village." When "Edwards" temporarily joins Judge Temple's household, the Judge, one of his employees, and his daughter Elizabeth debate at what table he is to sit at meals. The employee suggests that Edwards be placed with the housekeeper and all-purpose manservant, but Judge Temple concludes that he "is to fill the station of a gentleman," and should dine with the Temple family. In general, the Judge is afforded respect because of his position in the hierarchy.[83] His landholdings, wealth, and consequent influence give him power and compel deference. When he is vindicated at the end of the novel by being revealed as an honest and just man, the vindication is a testament to the virtue that such a culture engenders in its elite members.

Superimposed on the status gradations of village culture is the ideal of equality. The relationships among characters, while they take place within the status hierarchy, periodically demonstrate that status gradations are not fully respected. The housekeeper in Judge Temple's household complains that Elizabeth "wouldn't so much as hold discourse with me," but that she "*will* call [Elizabeth] Betsy as much as I please; it's a free country, and no one can stop me." Judge Temple feels that in America "all are equal who know how to conduct themselves with propriety," a sentiment that blends the equality principle with status conventions. The "freedom of manners that prevailed in the new settlements," Cooper says at one point, "commonly leveled all difference in rank, and with it, frequently, all considerations of education and intelligence."[84] The statement is ambiguous: one is not sure whether the leveling process is to be taken as a gain or a loss.

This sense of ambiguity pervades the treatment of village culture in *The Pioneers*. The civilizing impulse is sometimes applauded, as when the amenities of the Temple household are described or Judge Temple is identified with a careful husbanding of natural resources (he protests against the profligate cutting or burning of trees) or a moderate approach toward the hunting of wild life. Such scenes convey the message that those at the upper levels of the social hierarchy become progressively more refined, considerate, moderate, and virtuous individuals. One might compare Cooper's portrait of an uneducated woodchopper, Billy Kirby, who symbolizes the lower levels of village culture:

He was a noisy, boisterous, reckless lad, whose good-natured eye contradicted the bluntness and bullying tenor of his speech. For weeks he would lounge around the taverns of the county, in a state of perfect idleness, or doing small jobs for his liquor and his meals, and cavilling with applicants about the prices of his labour; frequently preferring idleness to an abatement of a tittle of his independence, or a cent in his wages. . . .[85]

Kirby is "boisterous and reckless": he lounges, cavils, bullies, and brags, reminiscent of the stereotypical Americans of the foreign travelers' ac-

---

[83] Cooper, *Pioneers*, 117, 122, 205, 439. Page references are to James Franklin Beard's 1980 edition.

[84] Ibid., 396.
[85] Ibid., 190–91.

counts. He also fiercely preserves his independence, taking pride in his work, refusing to be sold short, and refusing to defer. But his work is largely destructive: he chops down and burns the forest, leaving wasted, charred stumps. He lacks Temple's refinement, moderation, and virtue. But at the same time he resists, through his physical strength and independence, full deference to the status hierarchy of Templeton.

As *The Pioneers* unfolds, the equivocal nature of village culture is played out. The denizens of that culture who occupy its middle levels— Hiram Doolittle, the petty, cunning magistrate; Richard Jones, the pompous, foolish sheriff; Jotham Riddel, the voracious land grabber—are either the butts of humor or the objects of contempt. In contrast, those characters who resist the culture altogether (Bumppo and the Mohegan chief Chingachgook), or those who occupy its upper levels are honest, just, considerate, and respected. Advancing civilization in America thus appears as both a positive and a negative development. Bumppo is unrefined and illiterate, Chingachgook sometimes drunken and pitiable; but they avoid the voraciousness, cruelty, and hypocrisy of the middle-level settlers. Judge Temple, Oliver Effingham, and Elizabeth Temple suggest in their conduct that exposure to the highest levels of civilization reduces human selfishness, brutality, and profligacy. Effingham lives off the land, as Bumppo's companion, before revealing his true identity; Elizabeth refuses to make a show of her wealth or attractiveness, willingly exposes herself to dangers, and is loyal both to her father and to Effingham; Judge Temple, as previously noted, is the personification of farsightedness, moderation, and philanthropy.

This portrait of village culture in the 1790s combines with the historical setting of *The Pioneers* to produce an unsettling message. The best features of that culture, the values of gentility and virtue that surfaced in its upper echelons and the inherent nobility and humanity of the characters who operate on its fringes, are apparently passing away. There are more Kirbys and Joneses and Doolittles in America in the 1820s, just as there are better roads, more commerce, a greater dispersion of people and wealth, and a growing spirit of equality. Natty Bumppo and Chingachgook are dispossessed by the "march of the nation across the continent." Bumppo's ideal of a "great day when the whites shall meet the red-skins in judgment, and justice shall be the law, and not power"[86] seems further away at the novel's end than at its beginning.

In the last quoted sentence Bumppo articulates an image of law and its relationship to society that recurs throughout *The Pioneers*. Law is juxtaposed against both power and justice. It simultaneously functions as a device by which those in power reinforce their status and as a means

---

[86] Ibid., 456, 455.

of civilizing and humanizing social relationships in the village culture, making them more inherently just. Marmaduke Temple is the principal figure through which Cooper conveys this image of law. Temple has been designated a judge, and given the authority to resolve disputes, simply because he is the wealthiest and most powerful citizen of Templeton. He has acquired his wealth and power through legal maneuverings made possible by his friendship with Oliver Effingham's father, who made him his agent and business partner. When the senior Effingham was forced to leave America after the Revolutionary War broke out, Temple, who was a native of Pennsylvania, remained. And when British estates were confiscated after the Revolution, Temple "appeared in New York, and became the purchaser of extensive possessions at comparatively low prices."[87] One such tract of land was that surrounding Templeton.

In myriad ways Judge Temple uses law to facilitate his personal desires and to preserve his power. He secures passage in the New York legislature of a deer-season law that prevents hunting on his lands in the summer months. Bumppo violates that law and is arrested by a sheriff and magistrate that Temple commissioned and sentenced by Temple himself to pay a fine. The source of Temple's wealth is his trust agreement with Oliver Effingham's father, which enables him to have the use of necessary capital to purchase lands. At the close of the novel, however, Temple's virtue is revealed, and he demonstrates it by executing two legal documents, one a memorandum in which he itemizes his obligations to the Effinghams, the other a will in which he leaves his fortune in trust to his daughter and Oliver Effingham and their heirs. When Bumppo is arrested and imprisoned for resisting the efforts of Temple's appointed legal officers to search a hut on Temple's land, it is Temple who uses his influence to obtain for Bumppo a legal pardon from the governor.

With the exception of Judge Temple, the characters in *The Pioneers* identified with the law are depicted as disingenuous, litigious, and crafty. One is described as having an expression composed of "winks and shrewd looks"; another is characterized as having "a parenthetical style that frequently left to his auditors a long search after his meaning";[88] most of the actions of another are "grounded in cunning."[89] Lawyers aid Temple in arresting Bumppo, concealing Temple's relationship with Effingham's father, building the village of Templeton, and preparing a marriage settlement on Temple's daughter. Temple's influence does not prevent one lawyer from encouraging Effingham to sue the Judge when Temple inadvertently wounds Effingham with a shotgun in the novel's first scene.

---

[87] Ibid., 36.
[88] Ibid., 281.

[89] Ibid., 341.

The image of law in the village culture—"twisty," incomprehensible, practiced by untrustworthy people or used as the instrument of wealth and power—is pitted against the "natural law" of Natty Bumppo's environment. According to Bumppo's natural law, "doing what's right"[90] constitutes the basic principle of behavior. Bumppo continually contrasts "the troubles and divilities of the law" with his "right to shoot on these hills." Temple himself concedes that Bumppo has "a kind of natural right to gain a livelihood in these mountains." But when Natty defies the law, he is described as "an example of rebellion to the laws, and . . . a kind of out-law." Elizabeth Temple protests against the arrest of Bumppo: "those laws that condemn a man like the Leather-stocking to so severe a punishment . . . cannot be perfect in themselves." But Judge Temple counters that "society cannot exist without wholesome restraints," and "the laws alone remove us from the condition of the savages."[91]

In the implicit battle between Temple's law and Bumppo's natural rights, the sympathy of *The Pioneers* is manifestly with Bumppo. His legal offenses—killing a deer out of season and resisting the entrance of legal officials into his hut—are treated as justifiable in the circumstances. He is put in the stocks for a day and humiliated by the magistrate, Doolittle, but he gets his revenge by pointedly ignoring Doolittle's lame efforts at conversation and subsequently shooting him in the backside. He is imprisoned, but successfully escapes. He twice saves Elizabeth Temple from death. He even reveals himself in the novel's conclusion as faithful to the values of the upper levels of the village culture, since he has been a loyal servant of his former master, Effingham's grandfather. When he leaves Templeton, going "far towards the setting sun," he marches not only westward as "the foremost in [a] band of Pioneers," but toward "the great day when . . . justice shall be the law."[92]

The principal tension of *The Pioneers* comes from the fact that at the end of the novel the most sympathetic figure in the narrative, Bumppo, has abandoned the village culture. His protest against civilization has essentially been a protest against the fraudulent or oppressive use of law. He believes, for most of the narrative, that Temple has unfairly deprived the Effingham family of their lands: his "natural right" to hunt on Temple's property, he feels, derives in part from the legal rights of his master. He also appeals to "higher laws" in killing the deer and resisting entry, the laws of human self-sufficiency and loyalty. He is, then, a personification of the ideals of the American village culture, in which self-sufficiency and resourcefulness eventually can breed gentility, and in which

---

[90] Ibid., 362.
[91] Ibid., 358, 25, 112, 314, 355, 382, 383.

[92] Ibid., 455.

gentility teaches virtues such as loyalty to one's betters. Yet it is the march of the village culture, personified by Judge Temple in his effort to "tame the wilderness" so that "society [can] be tolerable" and its "ministers of justice" given respect,[93] that drives Bumppo west.

These levels of tension and ambiguity in *The Pioneers* are the source of its endurance in American letters and its place as a peculiarly representative early-nineteenth-century American novel. Not only does *The Pioneers* contain familiar features of the cultural landscape, from muddy roads and taverns to boisterous yeomen to squires and lay judges, it portrays the major sources of cultural change with a resonant and genuinely divided sensibility. One is not sure, at the close of *The Pioneers,* whether the virtues of a hierarchical society outweigh the arbitrary inequalities on which it rests; whether independence and equality will result in the loss of education, refinement, and moderation; whether the progressive march of American civilization is a liberating or a brutalizing phenomenon; whether mankind's most admirable qualities are facilitated or repressed by social organization. Nor is one sure whether law is preferable to its absence; whether law is simply the handmaiden of the powerful and influential classes in society, or a restraint on those classes as well as on the others; and, finally, whether law embodies justice or exists in contradiction to it. In *The Pioneers* one can see not only several of the central issues of Cooper's age but the inextricable connection between those issues and the image of law.

Cooper's perceptions of early-nineteenth-century America were, of course, his own, and one cannot claim too much for the portraits in *Notions of the Americans* and *The Pioneers*. But the works serve to identify three themes that are important to an understanding of the context in which the Marshall Court functioned: first, the widespread conviction among contemporaries that early-nineteenth-century America was a culture in rapid transition, with older forms of social organization and economic life giving way to newer forms; second, the disquieting and ambivalent reactions this perception of cultural change engendered, especially among literate persons who had been prominent in the hierarchies of eighteenth-century village culture; third, the close connection between law and both aspects—the liberating and the disquieting sides—of cultural change. Cooper's works are also important to an understanding of the context of the Marshall Court in that they simultaneously convey hope that the tensions engendered by rapid change can be reconciled, smoothed over, or allowed to dissipate with time and the further growth and expansion of the nation, and fear that the tensions are somehow basic, irreconcilable, and destructive of the Republic. Law is associated with both the hope and the fear: it offers a mechanism for the orderly and

---

[93] Ibid., 344.

temperate resolution of social discord, but it also has a way of reinforcing acquisitiveness, undermining virtue, and encouraging human beings to think of social relationships in terms of power rather than justice. Cooper thus suggests that the fundamental dilemmas of early-nineteenth-century American culture emanate from the process of interpreting cultural change, and that law is significantly bound up in that process.

At one point in *The Pioneers*, after Judge Temple says that "all are equal who know how to conduct themselves with propriety," Richard Jones, his gentleman associate, responds, "I call this democracy, not republicanism," and then adds, "let [Oliver Effingham] keep the law, or I shall show him that the freedom of even this country is under wholesome restraint."[94] The use of the term "republicanism" and the association of that term with the subordination of "freedom" to "wholesome restraint" under law brings us to another central source of Marshall Court jurisprudence. Republicanism was the dominant ideology of late-eighteenth-century American culture, and the accommodation of republicanism to the cultural changes of the early nineteenth century the foremost problem in social theory during the years of the Marshall Court.[95]

---

[94] Ibid., 205. For additional treatments of *The Pioneers* from a perspective that is not inconsistent with the above discussion, see J. McWilliams, *Political Justice in America* (1972); R. Ferguson, *Law and Letters in American Culture* (1984), 297–304.

[95] On the emergence of republicanism as a historiographical construct, see R. Shalhope, "Toward a Republican Synthesis: The Emergence of an Understanding of Republicanism in American Historiography," *Wm. & Mary Q.*, 29:49 (1972); D. Ross, "The Liberal Tradition Revisited and the Republican Tradition Addressed," in J. Higham and P. Conkin, eds., *New Directions in American Intellectual History* (1979), 116; R. Shalhope, "Republicanism and Early American Historiography," *Wm. & Mary Q.*, 39:334 (1982). For examples of works emphasizing the central importance of republican thought in late-eighteenth- and early-nineteenth-century America, see B. Bailyn, *The Ideological Origins of the American Revolution* (1967) and *The Origins of American Politics* (1968); G. Wood, *The Creation of the*

*American Republic* (1969); G. Stourzh, *Alexander Hamilton and the Idea of Republican Government* (1970); J. G. A. Pocock, *The Machiavellian Moment* (1975); L. Banning, *The Jeffersonian Persuasion* (1978); and McCoy, *Elusive Republic*.

Considerable criticism has been leveled at the use of republicanism as an ideological paradigm for early-nineteenth-century America, particularly by scholars who have emphasized the discontinuity between republican theories of political economy and the "market," "capitalist," or "liberal" emphasis of early-nineteenth-century American economic thought and practice. The leading critic has been Joyce Appleby. See Appleby, "Liberalism and the American Revolution," *New England Q.*, 49:3 (1976); Appleby, "The Social Origins of American Revolutionary Ideology," *J. Am. Hist.*, 64:935 (1978): Appleby, "Commercial Farming and the 'Agrarian Myth' in the Early Republic," *J. Am. Hist.*, 68:833 (1982); Appleby, "What Is Still American in the Political Philosophy of Thomas Jefferson?," *Wm. & Mary Q.*,

# Chapter I: *The Origins of Marshall Court Jurisprudence* I

Marshall Court jurisprudence can be seen as heavily influenced by a special version of republicanism, a version that represented a fusion of classical republicanism and other trans-Atlantic ideologies. This section first describes the sources of that version of republicanism and then considers the accommodation of republican theory to cultural change. The accommodation process is conveyed by tracing the modification of three propositions of American republican theory: the proposition that political activity should be nonpartisan and reflective of hierarchical social relationships, the proposition that economic activity should simultaneously protect property rights and be responsive to commerce, and the proposition that republican institutions were expected to decay with time.

Five sources contributed to the emergence of the version of republicanism that set the boundaries of discourse for Marshall and his contemporaries.[96] The first source was classical republicanism itself, an ideology that has been shown to have had roots in sixteenth-century European thought and perhaps even in ancient Greece and Rome. Classical republicanism in its eighteenth-century English formulation, however, was radical in its consequences, calling for the dismantling of corrupt governmental institutions that fostered luxury and retarded virtue. The basic premise of classical republicanism was that in the ideal form of government, a republic, individual liberty and self-fulfillment would be achieved through civic virtue, the active participation by citizens in political life. The purpose of a representative government was to ensure this citizen participation and to eradicate unrepresentative centers of power, such as institutions modeled on monarchical courts, that spawned corruption. Classical republicanism also advocated the wider distribution of property

---

39:287 (1982). For a concession that "even within the minds of Jefferson and Madison may be found tensions between liberal and republican . . . values, which set in motion a number of continuing debates within American culture," see Pocock, "The Machiavellian Moment Revisited," *J. Mod. Hist.*, 53:49 (1981).

[96] The generalizations advanced in this and succeeding paragraphs represent a distillation of insights in the sources cited in note 95 and the following additional studies: J. Appleby, *Economic Thought and Ideology in Seventeenth-Century England* (1978); D. Adair, *Fame and the Founding Fathers* (1974); J. Banner, *To the Hartford Convention* (1970); R. Buel, *Securing the Revolution* (1972); J. Crowley, *"This Sheba, Self": The Conceptuali-* *zation of Economic Life in Eighteenth-Century America* (1974); A. Hirschman, *The Passions and the Interests* (1977); D. Howe, *The Political Culture of the American Whigs* (1979); R. Isaac, *The Transformation of Virginia. 1740–1790* (1982); L. Kerber, *Federalists in Dissent* (rev. ed., 1980); J. Rakove, *The Beginnings of National Politics* (1979); R. Tuck, *Natural Rights Theories* (1979); M. Wilson, *Space, Time, and Freedom* (1974); R. Berthoff, "Independence and Attachment, Virtue and Interest: From Republican Citizen to Free Enterpriser, 1787–1837," in Bushman, *Uprooted Americans,* 97; Bushman, " 'This New Man' "; J. Murrin, "The Great Inversion," in J. Pocock, ed., *Three British Revolutions* (1980), 368.

among citizens so as to forestall the kind of dependence that led to demagoguery and mass unrest. But both civic participation and the distribution of wealth were to be limited by the imperatives of social class: the virtuous citizens that managed a republic were to be enlisted from a relatively narrow circle of educated, propertied, socially prominent persons who would represent others.

Classical republicanism was also notable for a deterministic attitude toward social change. The attitude has been described as a "stages" theory of cultural development: nations, like individuals, inexorably passed through a cyclical course of birth, maturity, decline, and rebirth. Societies in the earliest stages were primitive; in the middle stages pastoral; in the later stages luxurious or corrupt. Societal decay, like human decay, was inevitable. Republics were forms of social organization identified with the middle stages of the process: they were continually subjected to the pressures of corruption. The preservation of the republican stage, if possible at all, was possible only by the periodic purification of social institutions that had become corrupt.

While classical republican theorists regularly spoke of liberty as a predominant value and freedom from corruption and tyranny as one of the ends of a republican form of government, the ideology was essentially one of restraint. The concept of virtue subordinated individual self-interest to the good of society as a whole, and citizen participation was essentially a disinterested exercise. Here classical republicanism found its posture in awkward juxtaposition to the loosening of hierarchical economic relationships that marked the emergence of a capitalist economy in seventeenth-century Western Europe. Trade, commerce, and the growth of an economy with market features had made it possible for individuals to make money from their participation in economic exchange, not merely from their position in a social hierarchy. Individual participation in a market emerged as a means of gaining wealth and modifying status; it also had the effect of improving standards of living and conveying other related cultural benefits. The pursuit of market activity by individuals thus came to be perceived as a socially useful phenomenon, and individual economic initiative came to be characterized as a worthy endeavor. During the seventeenth and eighteenth centuries a reformulation of the value of commercial growth and participation in markets was undertaken by theorists of political economy, especially in Scotland, with the result that the individual pursuit of trade and commerce in capitalist markets became identified as an activity governments should encourage.

The redefinition of the value of individual economic activity in a market has been identified as the dominant factor in fostering the emergence of an ideology that was in a sense competitive with classical republicanism; an ideology to which historians have given the name "liberalism," although contemporaries tended to use the word "liberal" in a less sweeping sense. Liberalism, in its eighteenth- and early-nineteenth-century forms, was founded on the premise that individual self-fulfillment could be best encouraged by allowing individuals to pursue their economic, and to some extent their political, self-interests. Liberalism was an ideology of permissiveness rather than an ideology of restraint: it encouraged free markets, restricted governmental intervention in the affairs of individual citizens, and to a limited degree promoted a broadening of the political base of government. While liberalism shared with classical republicanism a sense that property was an important foundation of society, its advocates tended to emphasize the role of property as a source of economic freedom and productivity rather than as a source of political and social stability. Liberalism also tended to encourage the pursuit of commerce for both individual self-fulfillment and social improvement; commerce had been identified by classical republicanism as a source of luxury and decay. It is possible to characterize many of the important debates of early-nineteenth-century political economy, such as the role of corporations or the status of economic transactions based on credit, as being clashes between classical republican and liberal points of view.

Republicanism and liberalism were two trans-Atlantic ideologies with obvious relevance to early-nineteenth-century American thought, since a republican form of government existed in America and since the cultural changes described in the previous sections of this chapter had the effect of furthering the growth of a commercial economy organized around the principles of market capitalism. There were two other trans-Atlantic ideologies that also appeared relevant. One was the tradition, observable in the writings of Continental, English, and Scottish theorists from the Middle Ages onward, of "natural rights" and "natural law." That tradition, recent scholarship has suggested, was more conservative and authoritarian than radical and individualistic, but in the movement for American independence the "natural rights of man" was made the basis for a radical break not only with England but with the theory of government to which English subjects adhered. Moreover, as we shall see in the next chapter, theories of natural law, originally posited as a means of harmonizing positivist edicts with traditional religious principles, also became a device by which American judges avoided reliance on distasteful English common law precedents. Appeals to natural rights, natural law, and the American version of republican government became combined, we will see, in Marshall Court Justices' invocation of "natural justice" and "first principles" in their opinions.

Another relevant ideological source was the common law itself. The common law was not simply a source of precedents or rules to American judges; it itself had an ideological character. The ideology of the common law was an ideology of adapting general principles to changing specific circumstances, of qualifying legal rules by the contexts in which the rules were announced, of instituting change by gradual adaptation rather than by a sudden positivist edict. The common law, as administered by English judges, bequeathed to American judges distinctive methods of professional reasoning, received interpretations of the exercise of power, a bundle of justifications for judicial authority, and so on. Since any theoretical propositions announced in Marshall Court opinions were being promulgated in the context of legal disputes, the common law experience could hardly have failed to be relevant to justices charged with resolving those disputes.

In addition to these four trans-Atlantic ideologies, the variant of republicanism dominant in the Marshall Court drew upon an indigenous ideology. This last source, previously alluded to, was American exceptionalism, the idea that the United States was a unique and specially favored nation, with an opportunity to reach levels of economic prosperity and social enlightenment not available to other cultures. One can see the idea of exceptionalism in sources as diverse as pressures for the expansion of the nation's territorial boundaries, patriotic music and poetry, the proposals of people such as Joseph Story that ''great national institutions'' be created, and the belief among some republican theorists, such as Thomas Jefferson, that the ''middle stage'' of cultural development might be prolonged indefinitely in America because of the vastness of her land mass and the abundance of her natural resources. Exceptionalism made the modification of English customs, practices, or legal rules seem a more obvious and habitual part of American life.

The version of republicanism that became most influential on the Marshall Court, then, was a distinctive, and to some extent a provincial, blend of a variety of sources. It was by no means the only version of republicanism extant in early-nineteenth-century American culture; its eventual emergence as a temporarily dominant jurisprudential ideology did not mean that it was shared by the bulk of or even a majority of the population at large. Its assumptions about the fundamental principles and great purposes of republican government did not go unchallenged, and, as we shall see, it contained some internal contradictions that emerged as its adherents sought to understand and to respond to the changing conditions of early-nineteenth-century American life.

The greatest influence of this version of republicanism lay in its ability to set the boundaries of mainstream ideological discourse for the years of Marshall's tenure, and thereby tacitly suppress alternative ideologies which otherwise might have become part of that discourse. While there was sharp disagreement among theorists on the implications of republican ideology in given situations—the balance of power between the nation and the states in the American federated republic being the prime example—few quarreled with the starting premises: America was a republic; property rights were to be protected; commerce was to be encouraged; liberty and virtue were to be furthered; sovereignty was to be divided among respective spheres of influence. Neither a monarchical organization of society, with despotic power concentrated in a royal personage, nor a feudal organization, with power concentrated in ruling families that perpetuated each other through birth, nor an organization modeled on a theory of a collectivist state or on fraternal activity, nor an organization modeled on mass democracy was an alternative seriously contemplated in early-nineteenth-century political discourse. This is not to say that some institutional structures in early-nineteenth-century American culture do not fairly deserve the characterization of "monarchical," "feudal," "collectivist," or "democratic"; but republicanism, in the modified version described above, was nonetheless the accepted framework within which political debate occurred.

The succeeding section of this chapter considers the manner in which cultural change in nineteenth-century America posed certain acute dilemmas for the variant of republicanism previously described. Students of American republicanism have identified certain code words that encapsulate some of its central premises, words such as "virtue," "property," "commerce," and "decay." Each of these words can be associated with the starting propositions of republican theory previously identified. "Virtue" symbolized the commitment of citizens at the higher level of a hierarchical social structure to disinterested public service. "Property" and "commerce" symbolized the two potentially competing bedrocks of the economic order: the acquisition of security, independence, and power to use one's own resources, and the participation in market affairs. "Decay" symbolized the fragility of republican institutions over time and the inexorable decline of all civilized societies. Cultural change in early-nineteenth-century America presented republican theorists with dilemmas in political organization, economic theory, and the reconciliation of the past and the future.

Republican theory assumed that political activity was simply a reflection of the existing structure of society, not an independent, partisan enterprise. Republicanism was, as noted, a theory of representative government, that is, government in which certain persons were given the power and responsibility to make political decisions for others. The persons given political power were, by and large, the persons who already had social and economic power. While republican theory located sovereignty in the people, the people, as a practical matter, did not rule; their representatives ruled. In Templeton, we have seen, the representatives were all persons of established wealth and status or their appointees. Templeton politics was deference politics in which influence determined outcome. The political culture was dominated by hierarchical social relationships rather than partisan political relationships.

The political vocabulary of eighteenth- and early-nineteenth-century advocates of a republican form of government reflected their assumption that social and political activity were inseparable. Among the recurrent words in that vocabulary, we have seen, were "corruption," "virtue," and "interest": to them may be added the word "standing." Each of these words encapsulated certain features of the image of society on which republicanism was based. "Corruption" suggested the tendency of all societies, including republics, to decay under the inevitable pressures of human profligacy and selfishness; "virtue" represented a republic's best hope against corruption, the attitude of civic responsibility among its elite members; "interest" signified the self-regarding nature of social beings, who tended to pursue their own selfish goals, but could unite in the pursuit of matters of mutual benefit. "Standing" referred to the rank or status of a person in society: his or her station. Standing was not something that was easily acquired or lost; it was rather a product of the comparatively fixed nature of the class system.

Words such as "corruption," "virtue," "interest," and "standing" not only had distinctive connotations but also were intertwined in a complex relationship. A mixed or balanced system of government, with power diffused among institutions representing the few or the many, was assumed to be a check against corruption. Virtue was promoted by that governmental system because the cohesiveness of a republic came from the commitment of the leaders of its various branches to civic principles, such as liberty, justice, or patriotism, that they shared with the people as a whole. Such a commitment might run counter to their individual self-interest in the short run, and was thus evidence of their virtue.

To achieve virtue in the face of mankind's innate tendency toward corruption, however, it was necessary to create incentives for powerful individuals to make a commitment to the solidarity of a republic. Interest, as noted, was the concept used to signify the creation of such incentives. Republican forms of government could flourish and resist corruption only if they appealed to men's interests: they needed to enact policies which not only appealed to one's sense of civic-mindedness but to one's self-preferences. The word "interest" evolved in the eighteenth-century from a synonym for the word "passion," which was associated with profligacy and decay, to a counterpoint to that word. Destructive passions were thought to be channeled by republican forms of government into constructive interests. A republic was a conglomeration of interests, each mindful of the others, but all united in mutual self-preservation and convenience.

In order to preserve themselves against the decay fostered by corruption, republics depended on a class of virtuous and interested leaders. Standing was the concept that signified the presence of such a class,

Chapter I: *The Origins of Marshall Court Jurisprudence* I

conferred respect upon members of the class, and reminded those members of their civic obligation. The term itself assumed a distinction between the leaders of a republic, who managed political affairs on behalf of the public at large, and the people, in whom sovereignty purportedly rested. Here one can see the dual message of Judge Temple's dialogue with Richard Jones in *The Pioneers:* all citizens of the republic are equal so long as they conduct themselves with propriety, but proper conduct involves a recognition of the existing class structure. In exchange for influence and deference, members of the class that has standing are to act in a virtuous manner, thus forestalling corruption, preserving their interests, and prolonging the life of the republic.

When the political vocabulary of republicanism is examined in this fashion, one striking contrast with modern politics emerges. The vocabulary does not include the term "party" as an important agent of political culture. That term was, to be sure, part of eighteenth-century political discourse. But the conception of a party was not that of a large, diffuse coalition of interests, organized for administrative convenience and solidarity in voting, but rather that of a small, homogeneous "faction," a limited group of people with distinctive opinions and preferences. The modern conception of party anticipates that the purpose of party organization or partisan politics is to unite persons of different interests, backgrounds and circumstances in a common professional objective, the election of candidates with allegiance to the party. This conception, and its incumbent techniques of organization, began to emerge in America in the early nineteenth century, and was vigorously opposed as being contrary to republican principles.[97] The opposition to this modern conception of parties reveals much about the political assumptions of republicanism. Parties were opposed because they appeared to encourage corruption, in the form of partisan loyalties and obligations; because they disturbed the balance of government by permitting the executive branch, which emerged as the center of party organization, to arrogate power through partisan influence; because partisan appeals and slogans catered to the dependent and thereby untrustworthy sectors of society; and because they transferred voter loyalty from the republic at large to the party and thus undermined national harmony and unanimity.

When the bases of the early-nineteenth-century opposition to parties are considered in light of the demographic and political changes that took place in early-nineteenth-century American culture, an explanation for the opposition surfaces. Opponents of the modern conception of parties were protesting the potential disassociation of political life from the established social structure of their times. They were concerned that the new con-

---

[97] See R. Hofstadter, *The Idea of a Party System* (1969), 9–39; Buel, *Securing the Revolution,* 3–7.

55

ception of party signified a breakdown of representative government and, potentially, a breakdown in the hierarchical nature of republican culture. The appearance of parties came at the same time that new states were being admitted into the Union, swelling and diversifying the voting population. Moreover, parties emerged on the heels of the growth of universal manhood suffrage, which created increased numbers of voters, most of them not men of standing.[98] Parties appeared to be an ominous sign of the breakdown of cultural solidarity.

The successive presidential elections of 1820, 1824, and 1828 appeared to testify to the increasing disassociation of politics from the cultural ideals of virtue and standing. In 1820 James Monroe, the handpicked candidate of an incumbent elite of Virginia gentlemen, won re-election against token opposition even though he lacked a party organization. Monroe was himself a vigorous opponent of partisan politics and of the modern conception of parties.[99] Four years later John Quincy Adams was the successful candidate in an election in which Cooper said that "the old party distinctions . . . are broken down, and the country is no longer divided into two great political factions."[100] Adams, however, owed his election to partisan bargaining with other factions that constituted the remnants of Jefferson's Republican opposition party. During the next four years the Adams administration was paralyzed by tensions between the president's resolutely antiparty stance and efforts by his supporters and opponents to partisanize issues.[101] By 1828 a new political party had emerged, with a former member of the Republican opposition, Andrew Jackson, as its candidate, and a new style of appeal and organization. The Democrats concentrated their efforts on attracting diverse interests and "dependent" voters to the party as well as to the candidate. While Jackson's election may not have represented a total repudiation of deference politics, it was widely perceived as a harbinger of social transformations in America. Moreover, the kinds of issues around which Jacksonians united, such as opposition to the Second Bank of the United States, were widely perceived as assaults on privilege.[102]

---

[98] An important recent work on the relationship between political parties and republicanism in the early nineteenth century is R. Ketcham, *Presidents Above Party* (1984). See also M. Wallace, "Changing Concepts of Party in the United States: New York, 1815–1828," *Am. Hist. Rev.*, 74:458 (1968); R. Formisano, "Deferential-Participant Politics: The Early Republic's Political Culture, 1789–1840," *Am. Pol. Sci. Rev.*, 57:473 (1974); E.

Mayo, "Republicanism, Antipartyism, and Jacksonian Party Politics," *Am. Q.*, 31:3 (1979).

[99] See Hofstadter, *Idea of a Party System*, 22–23, 190–203.

[100] Cooper, *Notions*, II, 170.

[101] See Howe, *Political Culture*, 46–52.

[102] See Hofstadter, *Idea of a Party System*, 239–52; Meyers, *Jacksonian Persuasion*, 16–32.

It is important to emphasize, however, that the apparent disassociation of political from social activity that these developments presaged was not accompanied by the emergence of a new political vocabulary. The Jacksonians, for example, regularly made appeals to virtue, denounced corruption, and sought to identify and to recognize interests in the body politic. If there was a discernible shift in the terminology of political discourse in the early nineteenth century, it came in the diminished use of openly hierarchical appeals and the greater employment of leveling and egalitarian rhetoric. But, as we have seen, deference, influence, and standing, as political practices, remained.

Republicanism, in its eighteenth-century formulation, had posited certain values that republics were designed to promote, prominent among which were liberty, security, and freedom to acquire and dispose of property. The ultimate rationale for a republican system of government was that it promoted those values through checks on corruption, virtue, a judicious channeling of men's interests, and the political principle of representation. But the structure of republican government, we have seen, sharply distinguished between participants and beneficiaries. All men were entitled to liberty, but only some actually participated in the government that sought to secure it; all had a natural right to acquire and dispose of property as they saw fit, but only some were freeholders, and in many American states in the late eighteenth century only freeholders could vote. There was thus an apparent consensus among the people and their representatives as to the "first principles" of republican government, but there was no assurance that all members of society would be equally advantaged by that tacit agreement as to first principles. This was true even as to those principles that followed from the acknowledgment of inalienable natural rights. All men may have been created equal, but they were not necessarily entitled to an equal voice in the affairs of the republic.

As American culture became more populated, more diverse, more mobile, and more economically self-sufficient in the early nineteenth century, the distinction made in political practices between the beneficiaries of and the participants in government seemed more difficult to maintain. The disassociation of politics from a stratified culture of influence and deference was a symbol of the difficulties of excluding large numbers of citizens from a political process that was ostensibly conducted for the benefit of all. The abstract goals of republicanism—liberty, justice, natural rights, and freedom from tyranny and corruption—helped undermine some of the discriminations inherent in its practices. But the result, in the period of American history covered by this study, was not an abandonment of republican ideology. It was rather a recasting of the vocabulary of republicanism to address tensions caused by an apparent gap between ideals and practices.

Consensual surrogates played an important role in the recasting process. By consensual surrogate I mean a concept invoked to produce a surface reconciliation of tensions within a culture. Appeals to consensual surrogates were appeals to principles in which "everyone"[103] in a republican polity was assumed to believe, but at the same time were ambiguous and multifaceted. Two examples of consensual surrogates that were increasingly invoked in early-nineteenth-century political rhetoric were the concepts of "Union" and of "property." The changing meaning of those concepts, and their use in Marshall Court decisions, will subsequently be discussed in some detail. At this stage a brief introduction to the concepts will suffice.

American republicanism, as exemplified by the form of government created in the Constitution, was innovative in one major respect, as we have noted: the superimposition of a federal union on state sovereignties. Studies of the evolution of the idea of "Union" in late-eighteenth-century America have shown that Union was justified on four grounds: the mutual interest of the states in protection against foreign enemies; the commercial interdependence of the states, particularly in the area of foreign trade; the need for a governmental bulwark against provincial factions and parties; and the belief that republics could be better protected against corruption and decay if they expanded across space—thereby renewing their original principles—rather than through time. The frankly experimental nature of a federated republic was widely acknowledged by its proponents.[104]

By the 1830s the conception of Union as an experiment had been replaced by one that identified Union as an absolute: a permanent and indispensable feature of American culture. In their identification of the Union as an absolute, political rhetoricians with diverse constituencies, such as Andrew Jackson and Daniel Webster, were appealing to a consensual surrogate. The appeal appeared necessary for two reasons, both of which were related to perceived implications of early-nineteenth-century cultural change. One reason, previously alluded to, was that the emergent features of American culture appeared to be centrifugal as well as centripetal, promoting diversity, provinciality, and sectional self-interest. Another was that those features appeared to threaten the balances of republicanism by undermining distinctions of rank and status, increasing the number and diversity of the class of eligible voters, and changing

---

[103] "Everyone" is not meant literally, as the quotation marks suggest. Ideologies are articulated and recast by literate elites. But the ability of literate elites to convey their ideological presuppositions to other sectors of a culture, especially through rituals, ceremonies, and other dramaturgical devices has been impressively documented. See, e.g., Isaac, *Transformation of Virginia*. For a discussion of dramaturgy, see ibid., 323–57.

[104] See Nagel, *One Nation Indivisible*, 13–29; McCoy, *Elusive Republic*, 241–52; Wilson, *Space, Time, and Freedom*, 7–12.

the nature of the political process. Older grounds of consensus, such as mutual interdependence, were seemingly shaken by the developments. The idea of Union as an absolute served as a newly articulated symbol of consensus.[105]

But the symbol of Union was invoked because of fears of a breakdown in consensual attitudes and beliefs: it was a surrogate. The concept of a Union, when employed in a federated republic, reconciled centrifugal tensions in only a surface fashion. Union could not mean absolute deference to federal sovereignty unless the American form of republican government was to be radically altered. Nor could Union compel economic cooperation, commercial uniformity, the abandonment of political partisanship, or the amelioration of diversity and sectionalism, at least not in a culture whose form of government had been designed to secure and preserve liberty from governmental tyranny and corruption. Thus appeals to the Union were largely appeals to a spirit of harmony and cooperation in the face of pressures for fragmentation.[106]

The evolution of the concept of property offers an analogous example. Property was a concept deeply embedded in republican theory, its acquisition being regarded as a natural right and its possession being thought of as essential to independence, standing, and even virtue.[107] The source of deepest internal conflict in American republicanism, slavery, represented a conflict between two ideas about property, the idea that a republican citizen had the liberty to acquire and dispose of property as he saw fit, and the idea that a human being could become the property of another and therefore lose, in an important respect, human status. As the slavery example illustrates, property in republican theory was both a democratizing and stratifying concept. Its acquisition would enable a person to increase his wealth, status, and political participation; at the same time the conditioning of prominence on property ownership made the possession of property a symbol of power over others, extending, in the case of slavery, to the power to own others and thereby deprive them of their humanity.

This dual function of property in a republican polity became increasingly apparent in the early nineteenth century as greater opportunities to acquire property were created and as at the same time more "propertyless" persons, in the traditional sense of nonfreeholders, emerged in the population. The exclusionist features of property ownership, symbolized most vividly in the power to keep propertyless persons from partic-

---

[105] See Nagel, *One Nation Indivisible*, 109–39.

[106] Ibid., 70–82.

[107] See W. Scott, *In Pursuit of Happiness: American Conceptions of Prop-* erty from the Seventeenth to the Twentieth Century (1977), 24–61; McCoy, *Elusive Republic* 67–69, 205–207; R. Faulkner, *The Jurisprudence of John Marshall* (1968), 17–20, 117–24.

ipating in political affairs and the power to restrict the use of land, became apparent. At the same time the acquisition or use of property continued to be identified as a natural liberty of American citizenship. The free beneficial enjoyment of land came into conflict with the freedom of propertied citizens to restrict the use of that land. The respective political and economic power of Judge Temple and Bumppo indicated that republican theory weighed such conflicts heavily on the side of established property owners. But the underlying sympathy generated by Bumppo's "natural" activities suggested that such a weighting might well be an unjust violation of "true" republican principles.

The response of republican ideology to changes in the use and acquisition of property in nineteenth-century America was complicated by the alternative emphasis given property in the various ideological sources of American republicanism. As noted, in classical republicanism the archetypal propertyholding was freehold land, and the virtuous citizens who were to guide republics were freehold landowners whose propertied status had given them standing and independence. In liberal theorists, such as Locke, however, one can see a different emphasis: the natural right of property was a right "to the fruits of one's labor," that is, to the economic and social benefits of land or goods with a market value. In the Scottish eighteenth-century theorists, such as Adam Smith, one can see this idea of property pressed even further: property was markedly a vehicle of commerce, and property rights were closely identified with participation in commercial activity. Finally, the English common law had defined a whole series of nonfreehold property rights as deserving of some limited protection, and recognized instances of conflict between one type of property right and another. Appeals to protection for property, then, concealed a variety of complexities. The alternative meanings and uses of property, given the invocation of property rights as a first principle of republican government by early-nineteenth-century rhetoricians, can be seen as another appeal to a consensual surrogate. In 1836 Joseph Story, in an article on natural law, declared that "one of the great objects of political society is the protection of property," and that "whatever . . . the origin of the right to property, it is . . . now . . . a creature of civil government."[108] Story's characterization of property was consistent with a series of efforts, principally made by legal scholars and judges, to identify the protection of property as one of the bedrock principles of a republican government. The appearance of those efforts, itself the subject of a subsequent chapter, suggests that the identification of property as a first principle of republican

---

[108] J. Story, "Natural Law," in F. Lieber, ed., *Encyclopedia Americana* (13 vols., 1830), IX, 150, reprinted in J. McClellan, *Joseph Story and the American Constitution* (1971), 313, 320.

government came at the very time when the concept of property in American culture had revealed itself to be fraught with ambiguities.

In the above discussion of politics we noticed, first, the pressure placed on a central assumption of classical republicanism—that politics mirrored a hierarchical social order—by the emergence of new classes of voters, new modes of voting, and new forms of political organization; and, second, the recasting of republican political theory in the face of these changes. Two concepts central to American republican theory took on enhanced significance in the recasting process: "Union" and "property" became consensual surrogates, widely shared but ambiguous ideals that demonstrated the strains inherent in the accommodation of republican ideology to cultural change. A comparable process can be seen in the realm of economic activity.

The principal characteristic of early-nineteenth-century American economic life was the emergence of a capitalist market economy, in which relationships were principally defined by bargaining power in the exchange of goods and services rather than by pre-existing social status. The advent of market capitalism was noted by contemporaries, many of whom identified a market economy as a transforming feature of American society. Two broad sets of responses to the emerging market economy may be noted: a classical republican and a liberal response. The first response tended to see the market and its institutions, such as the corporation, as a threat to republican virtue. The marketplace was a potential source of corruption, an arena in which unchecked self-interest could flourish, a vehicle for the sudden redistribution of property and wealth, and a distraction from civic pursuits. The latter response embraced the market and made it a source not only of increased prosperity, wealth, and "improvements," but as a forum in which equality, in the form of enhanced competitive opportunities, could be promoted and economic privilege broken down. Few economic theorists articulated a wholly republican or wholly liberal response to the market; most theoretical positions were a blend of the two responses. But the responses framed discussions of economic theory in the early nineteenth century.

Two economic issues received special attention from early-nineteenth-century theorists, protectionism versus free trade, as exemplified by tariff legislation, and corporate privilege versus equality of economic opportunity, as exemplified by the growth of banks. In the discussions of both issues one can see the use of the chief consensual surrogate of the discourse of early-nineteenth-century political economy, "commerce," that functioned to produce a surface reconciliation of tensions between the republican and liberal responses.

The efficacy of protective tariffs was the most widely debated economic issue of the period covered by this work. Protective tariffs were perceived as disadvantaging those sections of the nation that engaged in extensive import-export trade and favoring those sections that had developed domestic trade and manufacturing. In the early nineteenth century the South and the Northeast tended to fall into the former category and the mid-Atlantic and western states the latter. Protective tariffs raised the prices of American products headed for foreign markets, such as cotton and tobacco, and of foreign products designed for American consumption, such as cotton and woolen cloth, shoes, and molasses. They increased the competitive position of American products made for domestic markets, thereby encouraging domestic manufacturing in areas that did not have easy access to foreign markets. Tariffs also brought more money into the federal treasury, and advocates of protectionism often suggested that the resulting treasury surplus should be used to subsidize infant industries or internal improvements.

A number of "interests" were therefore thought to be affected, favorably or adversely, by tariff legislation. Protective tariffs allegedly favored manufacturers, mechanics, and domestic farmers at the expense of commercial and mercantile interests, although support or opposition to individual tariffs tended to vary with the focus of the tariff legislation in question.[109] The actual impact of tariff legislation on the early-nineteenth-century American economy appears to have been problematic. One economic historian has concluded that "no important feature in [American] economic development during [the early nineteenth century] can be attributed unmistakably to tariff legislation."[110] But the significance of protective tariffs, for present purposes, lies in their implications for contemporaries, who sought to square them with the assumptions of republican political economy.

Two discernible positions on protective tariffs can be identified with the community of early-nineteenth-century political economists. One position, especially apparent in the writings of the Virginia squire John Taylor, deplored protective tariffs as inimical to the central values of republican society. For Taylor, protective tariffs represented subsidies to the manufacturers and "capitalists" who had an interest in the growth of the factory system. As such they tended to perpetuate that system, which Taylor regarded as antithetical to republican liberty and virtue. Factories, Taylor argued, stifled individual initiative by creating a dependent class of workers, shifted attention from the development of agriculture to the

---

[109] See generally F. Taussig, *The Tariff History of the United States* (1892); Taylor, *Transportation Revolution*, 360–65.

[110] G. Callender, *Selections from the Economic History of the United States, 1765–1860* (1909), 488.

development of industry, and rewarded parasitic "capitalists" who enjoyed the fruits of others' labor. They thus ran directly counter to Taylor's image of an enlightened republican society in which individual initiative, orderly growth, economic interdependence, and social responsibility were furthered by the possession and improvement of land.[111]

In 1823, a year before Taylor's death, his free-trade approach to tariff issues was attacked by Daniel Raymond in a treatise entitled *Elements of Political Economy*.[112] Raymond's views on protective tariffs represent an instructive contrast with Taylor's because they began with similar premises and reached diametrically opposed conclusions. Raymond believed, as did Taylor, in the natural rights of liberty and property, in the necessity for social solidarity and order, in the exceptional nature of the American republic, and in the beneficial effects of individual entrepreneurship. But he identified social solidarity with positive governmental intervention in the economy, whereas Taylor had deplored such intervention. Further, Raymond condemned the spirit of accumulating property and wealth, which he saw as a logical consequence of man's self-interest, whereas Taylor saw that phenomenon as beneficial, so long as it was a consequence of individual initiative. The result was that Raymond emerged in the 1820s as a defender of the "American system," which advocated the policies of protectionism and internal improvements in order to further the growth of a national economy and domestic commerce.

Raymond's overriding goal was the health of the national economy, not individual wealth. He identified acquisitiveness with luxury and corruption; he labeled accumulated wealth stagnant and parasitic; he condemned speculation and moneylending; he was suspicious of public corporations as specially favored oligarchs. He even advocated limiting the rights of individuals to convey accumulated property to their descendants. For him property rights represented the exercise of economic initiative, with its consequences of increased labor, productivity, and consumption, rather than exclusivity of possession. Raymond did not anticipate that policies encouraging useful labor would result in unchecked acquisitiveness, the growth of a stratified factory system, or the balkanization of the

---

[111] Taylor's views on the tariff and banks can be found in J. Taylor, *Arator* (1813) and J. Taylor, *Tyranny Unmasked* (1822). On Taylor as a political economist see R. Shalhope, *John Taylor of Caroline: Pastoral Republican* (1980), 169–73, 204–12; Conkin, *Prophets of Prosperity*, 52–72; J. Dorfman, *The Economic Mind in American Civilization* (2 vols., 1946), I, 301–304.

[112] For Raymond's economic views see D. Raymond, *The Elements of Political Economy* (2 vols., 1823). On Raymond see Conkin, *Prophets of Prosperity*, 77–107; Dorfman, *Economic Mind*, II, 566–74. See generally K. Lundberg, "Daniel Raymond: Early American Economist" (Ph.D. diss., University of Wisconsin–Madison, 1953).

American economic system into competing classes or interests. On the contrary, he found increased productivity and consumption entirely consistent with facilitation of the social goals of order, harmony, and moderation. His ideal economic state, like Taylor's, was that of the self-sufficient individual entrepreneur. In Raymond's polity, however, entrepreneurs were encouraged by interventionist governmental policies designed to promote national solidarity and economic growth.

Between the appearance of the first edition of Raymond's treatise in 1823 and the re-election of Andrew Jackson in 1832 a shift of attitudes toward protectionism occurred. Advocates of the "American system" became identified with corporate privilege, the capitalist classes, and oligarchy; their political opponents, calling themselves Democrats, championed free trade as part of a general attack upon the relationship between the federal government and economic aristocracy. But in 1832, when South Carolina, reviving free-trade arguments, threatened to treat congressional protectionist legislation as null and void, President Jackson invoked the surrogate of the Union to quash that argument.[113] The volatile status of tariff issues testified to a major difficulty in accommodating republican principles of economic activity to the new conditions of nineteenth-century American life. The difficulty was that the facilitation of individual economic initiatives did not seem to result in either liberty or virtue. A healthy, balanced economy of industrious, nonaccumulative entrepreneurs could apparently be achieved only by governmental regulation, which infringed upon liberty and fostered privilege; an economy based wholly on the principles of free trade and self-aggrandizement led to social and political divisiveness, which undermined solidarity and discouraged virtue.

In addition to the tariff issue, the strains in accommodating republican theory to a market economy were evident in the most volatile economic issue of the period under consideration, the debate over the Second Bank of the United States. Chartered in 1816, the Second Bank had become by the 1820s both a significant force in the national economy and an object of political controversy. The purpose of the Bank's chartering was to promote commerce and to supplement the expansion of federal power. To these ends, the Bank was expected not only to raise revenues that had been depleted by the War of 1812, but also to control the activities of state banks, whose notes had undergone fluctuations during the war. Once in operation, the Bank began to establish branches in several states, often lending money to its state bank competitors in the process. The presence of these branch banks, some of which were mismanaged,

---

[113] See Meyers, *Jacksonian Persuasion*, 7–15; J. W. Ward, *Andrew Jackson, Symbol for an Age* (1953), 113–15.

precipitated resentment in the states, whose banks either were indebted to the Bank of the United States or wished to avoid competition.[114]

Banks and the activity of banking occupied a precarious position in republican economic theory. Taylor and Raymond, for example, agreed that banks were necessary as places for depositing money and as mediums of commercial exchange. They disapproved however, of two additional functions of banks, circulating paper bank notes as a form of currency, and making loans, based on their own notes, at high rates of interest. These last functions, typically characterized by the pejorative word "credit," represented instances in which banks had, in both the theorists' estimations, taken advantage of their privileges to issue money. Bank notes had the effect of devaluating currency, encouraging inflation, and creating conditions of economic insecurity; the loan practices of banks only aggravated the situation. Banks were, Taylor and Raymond agreed, instruments of corporate privilege. They had been chartered by the state, but operated for profit, issued stock, paid no interest on their own notes, and made money parasitically, since they produced nothing. In both Taylor's and Raymond's views of banking one can see that the theoretical assumptions of republicanism did not fully contemplate a society with a market economy. Republican theorists acknowledged that banks facilitated commercial exchange—an important social goal—but they did not expect banks to take advantage of their strengths in the commercial economy whose growth they were facilitating. Nonetheless, as it became clear that banks were not merely making loans or receiving deposits out of a social obligation but as part of exchange relationships in which they participated, banks began to conceive those relationships in terms of bargaining power. They acted, in short, just as other participants in the early-nineteenth-century American economy had begun to act, by defining their commercial transactions as if they were the sales of goods or services.

Yet the exhibition of this market behavior by the most visible bank in early-nineteenth-century America, the Second Bank of the United States, made the Bank's effort to renew its charter in 1832 one of the major controversies of the period covered by this work. The protest against the Bank, which assumed a partisan form when Jackson vetoed the Bank's recharter in July 1832, employed the conventional vocabulary of republicanism but added a new twist. The Bank's arch critic William Leggett, editor of the New York *Post,* pictured the Bank as a symbol of "monopoly," "privilege," and "corruption," an enemy of virtue and a violator of the "simple order of nature." Leggett claimed that the chartering process by which the Bank had been founded, in which the federal

---

[114] See generally R. Catterall, *The Second Bank of the United States* (1903); B. Hammond, *Banks and Pol-* *itics in America from the Revolution to the Civil War* (1957).

government had granted corporate powers and limited liability to a "privileged class," was itself suspect. The Bank was "aristocratic," Leggett argued, identified with "the grasping monopolizing spirit of capricious capitalists," supported by "the rich, the proud, the privileged," a symbol of "the vast disparity of condition" that was emerging in America.[115]

In this rhetoric one can see the fusion of republican and liberal responses to the corporate form of organization. Corporations, from a classical republican perspective, had the potential to be enlightened institutions, since they were organized on a hierarchical basis and ostensibly led by virtuous, public-spirited citizens. But in their close relationships to the states that chartered them, corporations had the potential to become instruments of corruption and privilege. Liberalism was equally ambivalent about the corporation. Corporations had the value of being able to promote economic growth by providing public goods and services that individuals lacked the resources to provide, but at the same time their size and power made them able to interfere with the right of individuals to compete on equal terms in the market. Leggett's attack on the Second Bank of the United States articulated both republican and liberal fears.

What was the solution to the problems symbolized by the Bank? Supporters of Jackson tended to believe that with the eradication of the Bank most of those problems would cease. They perceived the Bank as the center of a network of financiers, merchants, capitalists, aristocrats, and "creatures of the paper credit system." With the Bank's demise those classes would lose their stronghold on the economy. This would allow a restoration, Leggett felt, of "the national system in all matters both of politics and political economy." Property would be protected, free trade encouraged, commerce would flourish, and "honest patient industry, and prudent enterprise" would triumph. Leggett presented a vivid contrast between the corrupt Bank-dominated economic order and the restored state of affairs once the Bank had been destroyed:

> Take a hundred ploughmen . . . from their fields and a hundred merchants from their desks, and what man, regarding the true dignity of his nature, could hesitate to give the award of superior excellence, in every main intellectual, physical, and moral respect, to the band of hearty rustics, over that of the lank and sallow accountants, worn out with the sordid anxieties of traffic and the calculations of gain?[116]

---

[115] See T. Sedgwick, ed., *A Collection of the Political Writings of William Leggett* (2 vols., 1840). The above comments are quoted at I, 97; I, 95–96; I, 77; II, 333–34; I, 66–67; II, 122–25. I have used Leggett's rhetoric as representative of the Bank's most penetrating critics, although it was particularly vivid. See R. Hofstadter, "William Leggett, Spokesman of Jacksonian Democracy," *Pol. Sci. Q.* 58:581 (1943).

[116] Leggett, *Writings,* I, 107–108; II, 333, 306; I, 101–103; II, 164.

On its surface the protest against the Bank appears to be a nostalgic effort to restore the virtuous conditions of a chaste, rural, "natural" republican society. But there was another theme in the protest. The Bank was not only corrupt and tyrannical, it was "an essentially aristocratic institution" that needed to be eradicated "or the days of democracy are numbered."[117] The argument against the Bank was a leveling argument as well as a restorative argument. Destruction of the Bank meant not only the reincarnation of virtue but the triumph of democracy and equality of economic opportunity. This last message gave a different emphasis to the attack on the Bank. While couched in republican language, it contained egalitarian premises that republican theory had not embraced. Privilege, stratification, and wealth were important ingredients in republican social organizations, part of the orderly fabric of a society in which virtue flourished. Leggett's language suggested that those identified with the Bank lacked virtue because they were privileged: the "sordid anxieties" of the merchant came from his "participation in the unequal privileges which a false system of legislation has created." Leggett asked that banking, and other economic pursuits, be "left open to the free competition of all who chose to enter into [them]."[118]

The protest against the Bank can thus be seen as a kind of crisis in the language of republicanism, in which the conventional words of that language were being used to convey liberal policies that did not seem consistent with the vision of society that the language had originally sought to convey. The Bank was being condemned both for its single-minded pursuit of its own interests, something classical republican theory would have expected from economic actors, and for its privileged status, something classical republican theory would have thought necessary to social order and virtue. The dismantling of the Bank was seen as restoring the "natural order of things," a state of affairs classical republican theory was seeking to facilitate, but also as furthering democracy and equalizing economic opportunity, goals that classical republican theory regarded as unsound.

The Bank, then, was being condemned for being too privileged and too effective an economic actor in an economy whose relationships were now dominated by exchange rather than by status. The perquisites of the Bank were attacked as aristocratic and corrupt, but the ultimate goal of its critics, after the Bank had been dismantled, was a society in which more people could participate in free competition. It is as if the Bank, in its combination of privilege and bargaining power, had suggested that the imposition of republican forms of social organization on a market economy would create "vast disparit[ies] of condition." But the solution did

---

[117] Ibid., I, 56–57.                    [118] Ibid.

not seem to be to purify the behavior of economic actors, but rather to dismantle forms of privilege, make competition freer, and thereby promote democracy. This solution would seem to present a paradox. Why would the new, "equal" competitors not eventually sort themselves out into another hierarchy, this one determined by the market? And if this were to occur, how would liberty, virtue, order, and moderation be preserved? It was as if the thrust of free competition in a market economy were incompatible with the premises of republican thought.

Although the Bank issue placed severe stress on the vocabulary of republicanism, the demise of the Bank came late in the period covered by the volume. A more accurate characterization of economic thought between 1815 and 1835 would emphasize the successful accommodation of republican political economy to the significant economic changes of the period. Of all the major economic issues that Americans debated in those twenty years—the tariff, the status of corporations, the future of slavery, governmental intervention in the economy, the factory system, and banking—only the last elicited a thorough reconsideration of republican principles of political economy. Tariff rates became gradually more protectionist; corporations, especially the private variety, were increasingly tolerated; governmental promotion and regulation of the economy persisted; the factory system was embraced; and a system of economic organization based on slave labor persisted. None of these developments was entirely compatible with a philosophy of government that emphasized liberty, economic independence, and the value of freehold property, and which was suspicious of close relationships between government and privileged sectors of the population. But between 1816 and 1832 the developments were accepted, rationalized, or ignored, until the Bank War brought the strains of accommodation to the surface.

We will subsequently see, in discussing certain of the Marshall Court's constitutional cases, the importance of the term "commerce" in facilitating this accommodation. It is worth noting here that all of the economic theorists previously quoted declared their allegiance to the goal of facilitating and expanding commerce in America. It appears that "commerce," like "Union" and "property," was a concept that seemed essential to American republicanism. And yet the dislocations produced by a market economy, the prominence of parasitic economic actors such as merchants and bankers, the volatility of tariff issues, and the debates over internal improvements could all be traced to the complexity of commercial change, which seemed to both stimulate and fragment, homogenize and stratify the American economy. Commerce was one of the concepts that signified, in its widespread use and deep ambiguity, the central tensions of early-nineteenth-century American culture.

*

Commerce evoked an image, for most early-nineteenth-century Americans, of the flow of goods across space. "Space" was itself a central word in the vocabulary of republican theory, particularly in its juxtaposition with "time." The two words signified a third presupposition of American republicanism, a deterministic, cyclical theory of cultural change. As in the realms of politics and economics, this presupposition was subjected to stress by the changing conditions of early-nineteenth-century American life.

Space and time were crucial concepts for American republican thought because of the interaction of the vast expansiveness of the American continent with the dominant eighteenth-century theory of change. Contrasted with Europe, America was an unprecedentedly large, open, and abundant environment, and early-nineteenth-century administrations had followed a policy of systematically expanding the territorial boundaries of the nation, taking in much of the trans-Mississippi West in the Louisiana Purchase, acquiring Florida in 1819, and entering into a joint occupation with the British of Oregon territory a year earlier. Of the several arguments advanced in support of territorial expansion, one is particularly salient for our purposes: the argument that the spread of republican institutions into uninhabited land would help regenerate them and thereby might preserve the Republic against decay. Jefferson had said, in ruminating upon the Louisiana Purchase, that "by enlarging the empire of liberty, we multiply its auxiliaries, and provide new sources of renovation, should its principles, at any time, degenerate."[119]

Degeneration over time was assumed by classical republican thought to be an inevitable fate of societies. "The history of the world," a supporter of Jefferson wrote in 1804, "teaches that nations, like men, must decay. Ours will not forever escape the fate of others. Wealth, luxury, vice, aristocracies will attack us in our decline: these are evils of society, never to be courted, but to be put to as distant a day as possible."[120] The inevitable degeneration of nations, we have noted, was part of a cyclical theory of change, in which societies were seen as inexorably moving from primitive beginnings to pastoral middle states to luxurious, corrupt old ages. Republican institutions were emblematic of the middle stage, in which agriculture was the chief pursuit, virtue still triumphant over vice, luxury not yet widespread, and aristocracy and corruption not yet entrenched. The decay and decline of republicanism were, however, inevitable.[121]

---

[119] Thomas Jefferson, memorandum, Dec. 28, 1805, Thomas Jefferson Papers, Library of Congress. See McCoy, *Elusive Republic*, 204–208.

[120] A. Bishop, *Oration in Honor of the Election of President Jefferson* (1804), 4.

[121] On the cyclical theory of change see S. Persons, *American Minds* (1958), 122–27.

Since the cyclical theory of change assumed that all nations were ultimately alike, it ran counter to the intuitive sense many early-nineteenth-century Americans had about the exceptional qualities of their environment. By the fiftieth anniversary of the Declaration of Independence in 1826, this perception of exceptionalism was well entrenched. In the view of those who held this perception, America was the world's most significant republic: the only one that had not dissolved into anarchy or tyranny. The American continent was incomparably abundant, and vast quantities of free, unsettled land remained. The demographic and economic growth of the nation had been staggering. The basic institutional structure of the Constitution remained intact. America had survived two wars and established herself as a military power. Perhaps the experiment of federated republicanism was to become a permanent entity in this exceptional setting.[122] Perhaps, in fact, continued expansion and economic growth, even commercialization and increased luxury, were not symbols of decline but of improvement. Perhaps the steady expansion and population of the American continent had not only preserved and regenerated republican institutions, but had broken the cycle of change itself. Perhaps change could now be identified with progress.[123]

But how was America to escape history, which had apparently taught that change inevitably brought decay and degeneration? Two strikingly different responses to that question suggested themselves to early-nineteenth-century commentators. One response emphasized the exceptionalism of American culture and claimed that the history of the rest of the world had no relevance to America. One can see this response embodied in early-nineteenth-century efforts to replace "foreign," "aristocratic," or "dead" traditions and institutions with authentic, indigenous American versions. The movement to replace the English common law with American codes, accessible to the common man, provides an example of one such effort;[124] the rise of nativist, evangelical religious sects, who declared their independence from established church orthodoxies, another.[125] The response was marked by a recoil against history and by prominent emphasis on progress and the future.

---

[122] On the surfacing in the 1820s of the idea of America as an exceptional nation, see Hofstadter, *Idea of a Party System*, 23–24, 196–198.

[123] See R. Welter, *The Mind of America 1820–1860* (1975), 17–25; Howe, *Political Culture*, 73–76; Ekirch, *The Idea of Progress*, 34–37; Persons, *American Minds*, 153–57.

[124] On codification see C. Cook, *The American Codification Movement* (1981); P. Miller, *The Life of the Mind*

*in America* (1965), 239–65; R. Gordon, Book Review, *Vand. L. Rev.*, 36:431 (1983).

[125] On the emergence of evangelical religion in the late eighteenth century see Isaac, *Transformation of Virginia*. Howe, *Political Culture*, 150–70; Persons, *American Minds*, 163–77; and Miller, *Life of the Mind*, 3–72, discuss evangelical religion in the early nineteenth century.

A second response accepted the historical lesson of inevitable societal decay, but sought to postpone the process of decline by controlling the pace and direction of change. A prominent example of this response can be found in the "American system" of internal improvements, which in its very language attempted to encapsulate the belief that the exceptional conditions of life in America could be made to produce improvement rather than decline. Notwithstanding their confidence in the exceptionalism of America, advocates of the American system did not simply trust that the natural forces at work in American culture would transform decay into progress. On the contrary, they sought to regulate the course of economic growth, to establish a hierarchical relationship between the sovereignties of the federal government and the states, and to channel governmental revenues into some sectors of the market rather than to allow the economy to function without controls. Chief proponents of the American system, such as John Quincy Adams, believed in the cyclical theory of history. They sought to use the special circumstances of American life to postpone the latter stages of the cycle.[126]

In the first response history had become irrelevant; in the second it remained an inescapable, burdensome presence. In the first response the cyclical theory of history had been discarded; in the second it had been retained. The two responses may be said to have established the boundaries of early-nineteenth-century thinking about the relationship of the past to the present and the future. Within those boundaries, a new and ambivalent synthesis emerged. In that synthesis time neither obliterated space (as in the first response) nor space time (as in the second). Change across space and change over time were treated as complementary rather than contradictory phenomena; the past was seen as both relevant and malleable. History was neither ignored nor capitulated to; it was recast. The immediate revolutionary past of America—the period of the framing of national institutions—became invested with great significance, but its significance came from the way in which it illuminated the present and helped guide the future. History thus encouraged persons living in the present to look back for guidance, but then to look forward for meaning. It was both a distant experience and an immediate one, a reminder of change and a source of continuity.

In *The Pioneers* Cooper's response to history paralleled, on its surface, the synthetic response just outlined. The world of Judge Temple, Natty, and Major Effingham is surely passing away. At the novel's close Effingham is dead, Natty a fugitive from encroaching civilization, and Judge Temple's function largely that of a patriarch who has disposed of his estate and, one suspects, his immediate power and influence with it.

---

[126] See  Howe,  *Political  Culture*, 47–52, 82–84, 137–40.

Change is perceived as inevitable: forests and estates will give way to villages, artisans, and shopkeepers. But the beneficent values of the republican village culture are sought to be preserved: virtue, moderation, respect for law, order, deference, a solicitude for natural rights. The persons charged with that preservation, however, are members of a new generation, Elizabeth Temple and Oliver Effingham. Their task is to make the values personified by Judge Temple and those who support his hierarchical village culture relevant to a new age. The novel's ending suggests on its surface that Elizabeth and Oliver can and will perpetuate the traditions embodied by Judge Temple.

As we have seen, however, the surface response of *The Pioneers* is qualified by a thematic undercurrent of far greater power. That undercurrent indicates that the values of hierarchical republican village culture are disappearing along with the heroic figures of another age, Bumppo, Chingachgook, and the Judge. The undercurrent also suggests that the democratic spirit observable among the citizens of Templeton, apparent in Kirby's independence, the housekeeper's lack of deference to Elizabeth, or a lawyer's willingness to hale Judge Temple into court on a petty civil charge, will not coexist easily with Elizabeth and Oliver's nascent squirearchy. It intimates that a natural order of society, in which rights and duties are readily understood by all and justice is a simple extension of the values of liberty and virtue, is being replaced by a more complex state of affairs, in which acquisitiveness, mobility, and self-aggrandizement, each embodied in and facilitated by the "twisty ways" of law, may become paramount.

The use of history in *The Pioneers* can thus be seen as a metaphor for describing the strains produced by an effort to accommodate republican theory to cultural change. The past is at once vanishing and a source of lessons; a burden, a warning, but also potentially an irrelevancy. One notices the same response in politics and political economy. The stratified, deferential, informal theory of politics identified with republican ideology was being altered by population growth, urbanization, and the momentum of suffrage reform, but its primary goal of channeling partisanship and corruption still seemed an important social lesson. A theory of economic activity compatible with classical republicanism, which emphasized economic relationships based on status, valued individual self-sufficiency, assumed the dominance of agriculture, and sought to establish safeguards against luxury, corporate privilege, and corruption, had not adequately explained the increasingly market character of relationships in the early-nineteenth-century American economy. But at the same time rampant market behavior by economic actors seemed to raise the spectres of capitalism and anarchy. In one sense republican political economy seemed outmoded; in another, the nation's only hope against degeneration. Finally, republican theories of time and change had a similar double-edged

A view of the Erie Canal from Lockport, Niagara County, New York, "drawn from nature" by W. Wilson in 1836. Note the ten combined locks and the horses pulling the barges.
*(Library of Congress)*

Ohio and Mississippi Steamers, 1819 and 1823.

The steamboat *Caledonia*, from a wood engraving with the caption "Ohio and Mississippi Steamers, 1819 and 1823."
*(Library of Congress)*

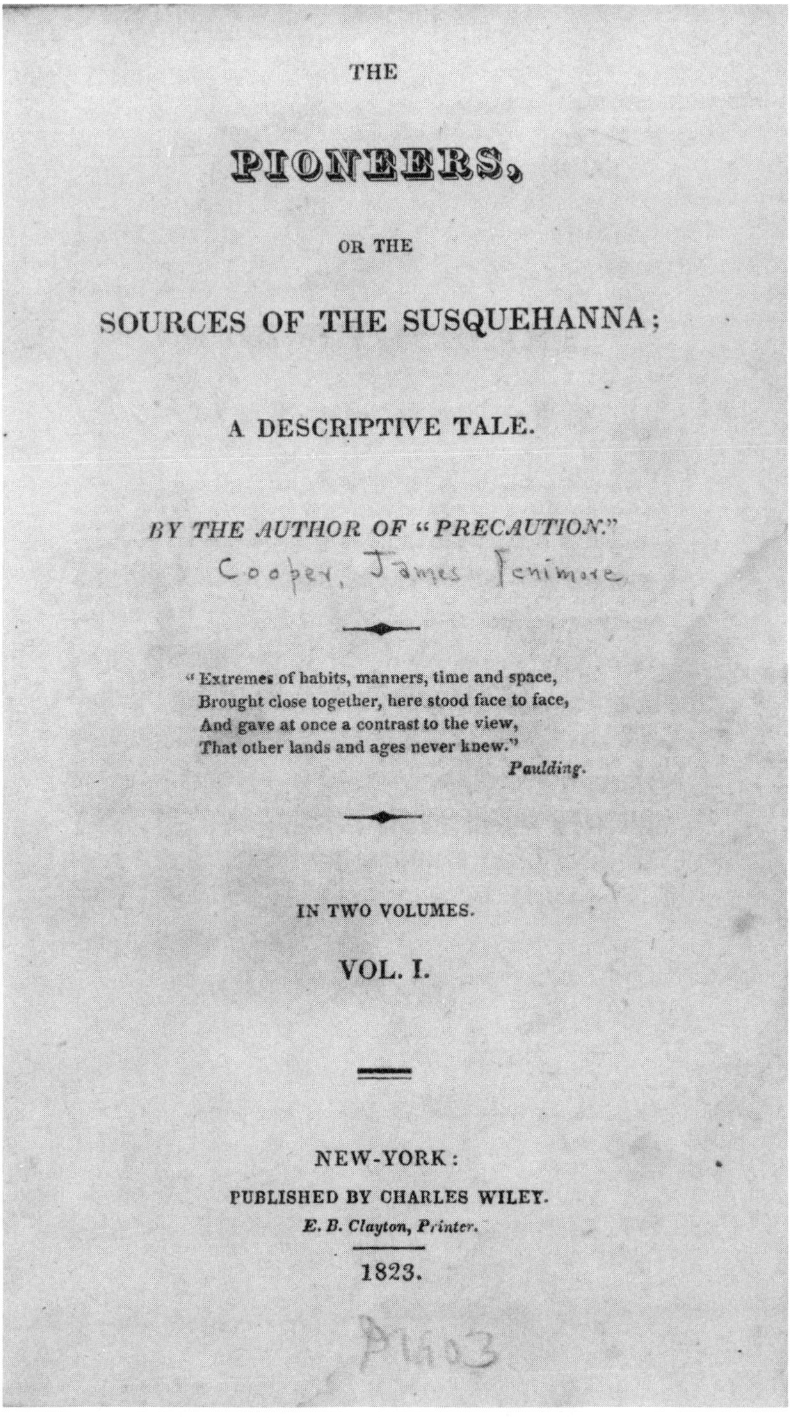

THE

# PIONEERS,

OR THE

# SOURCES OF THE SUSQUEHANNA;

## A DESCRIPTIVE TALE.

*BY THE AUTHOR OF "PRECAUTION."*

Cooper, James Fenimore

———◆———

" Extremes of habits, manners, time and space,
Brought close together, here stood face to face,
And gave at once a contrast to the view,
That other lands and ages never knew."

*Paulding.*

———◆———

IN TWO VOLUMES.

## VOL. I.

———

NEW-YORK:

PUBLISHED BY CHARLES WILEY.

*E. B. Clayton, Printer.*

1823.

PN03

The title page of the first edition of James Fenimore Cooper's *The Pioneers,*
published to great popular acclaim in 1823.
*(Library of Congress)*

An 1817 watercolor painting by Madame Hyde de Neuville, wife of a French diplomat, of the scene outside her residence at F Street and 15th Street, N.W., in Washington, D.C.

A mid-nineteenth-century photograph of the Carroll Row boardinghouses occupied by members of Congress and the Justices of the Supreme Court for most of the period between 1815 and 1835.

*(Library of Congress)*

A photograph of the restored Old Supreme Court chamber in the Capitol, looking south. The restored chamber was based in large part on the courtroom that the Justices reoccupied in 1819 and continued to use through the 1835 Term. The restoration required some modifications, such as the Justices' chairs, which were modeled on those from the Taney Court period, and lighting fixtures, also from the mid-nineteenth century. In most other respects, the restored courtroom approximates that in which the Marshall Court sat from 1819 on. Note the door south of the Justices' desks, which led to their robing room. Fireplaces behind the Justices' chairs on the east wall and one on the west wall provided heat.

*(Architect of the Capitol Collection)*

The petition for a writ of error drafted by John Marshall in *Martin* v. *Hunter's Lessee,* a case in which he had an interest in the land whose title was in dispute. He therefore declined to participate in the Supreme Court's decision. The petition was formally presented to the Supreme Court by lawyers representing a land syndicate, of which Marshall was a member, in December 1815. The petition was approved and the writ of error granted by Justice Bushrod Washington, and the *Martin* case was placed on the Supreme Court's docket for the 1816 Term.

*(National Archives Microfilm Publications)*

*The Honble Joseph Story*

*Salem*

*Massachusetts*

*...you have made in the opinion in...*
*...College case, I am highly gratified by...*
*you say respecting it. The opinion in the Bank...*
*case continues to be denounced by the old...*
*majority in Virginia. An effort is certain-...*
*ly making to induce the Legislature which...*
*the meet in December to take up the sub...*
*...to pass resolutions not very well...*

*...it but has not been acted on, Nor is there any...*
*act of the court approving the proceeding. It is in-...*
*tended to be a mere act in pais not sanctioned by...*
*the court. That it is the unauthorized act of the Marshal...*
*who might release the bond or sue upon it; and that the court...*
*cannot consider it in the place of the useful & responsi-...*
*...with great respect and esteem I am dearly your obt...*
*J Marshall*

Excerpts from a letter written by John Marshall to Joseph Story, dated May 27, 1819.
Compare the handwriting in the letter with that on the petition for the writ of error.
Note the striking upward slant of the letters in both documents, and the rendering of
the word ''Virginia.''
*(Massachusetts Historical Society)*

quality. Early-nineteeenth-century Americans wondered whether the cycle of growth and decay would be broken by American exceptionalism, or whether the rapid pace of change they observed signified a rush to oblivion. They asked themselves whether change could simply be embraced or whether it needed to be channeled.

The attempt which surfaced in the early nineteenth century to synthesize progressive and cyclical theories of change, and in the process to recast the history of the Revolutionary generation, was thus an effort with deep cultural ramifications. Succeeding chapters suggest that the opinions of the Marshall Court represented an embodiment in legal language of that attempted recasting of history. As such the Court's decisions may be seen as efforts to achieve a surface accommodation between the extant political, economic, and philosophical presuppositions of republican ideology and the new cultural features of the early-nineteenth-century American landscape. The Court, especially in its constitutional decisions, established itself as one of the primary recasters of its age, an institution that gave guidance for the future by returning to the first principles of the revolutionary past and restating them in light of the exigencies of the present.

The Court's recasting of history can be seen both as an accommodation of republicanism to the cultural changes of early-nineteenth-century America and as an effort to conceal cultural tensions and divisions. The Court's process of recasting the principles of the immediate past assumed that those principles continued to represent the bedrock values of the American nation in an age in which the framing experience had become a "memory."[127] Notwithstanding the stresses that it was encountering, federated republicanism was still the operative paradigm of political theory in America. A return to first principles meant a return to the first principles of republicanism, such as representative government, protection for property, support for the Union, promotion of commerce, distrust of partisanship, suspicion of mass democracy, homage to liberty, and the creation of opportunities for virtue. The process also assumed, however, that history evolved, so that the application of a principle could change with time even if the principle remained constant.

The role of the Marshall Court as a recaster of history can be briefly glimpsed in Chief Justice John Marshall's celebrated dictum, made in the case of *McCulloch* v. *Maryland,* that "a constitution" was "intended to endure for ages to come, and consequently to be adapted to the various

---

[127] See generally F. Somkin, *Unquiet Eagle: Memory and Desire in the* *Idea of American Freedom, 1815–1860* (1967).

crises of human affairs."[128] Just what this comment signified for Marshall is revealed in an earlier passage from *McCulloch:*

> This government is acknowledged by all to be one of enumerated powers. The principle, that it can exercise only the powers granted to it, . . . is now universally admitted. But the question respecting the extent of the powers actually granted, is perpetually arising, and will probably continue to arise, as long as our system shall exist.[129]

In this passage Marshall juxtaposed the "universality" of the principle of enumerated powers against the "perpetually arising" question of its application in changing circumstances. His approach incorporated both cyclical and progressive theories of change without acknowledging any contradiction between them. New questions of interpretation, he suggested, are constantly emerging over time, but their significance will only last "as long as our system shall exist." The "perpetual" state of republican government in America is implicitly tempered by the possibility that the system of government will degenerate.

The accommodation of republican theory to changing circumstances is revealed by the role ascribed by Marshall to the Constitution of the United States. The Constitution is simultaneously intended to "endure for ages" and "to be adapted to . . . various crises." The assumptions of republicanism, embodied in the principles of the Constitution, are to set the boundaries of constitutional interpretation, but the implications of those assumptions may vary as crises, produced by changes in the culture, arise. Marshall's approach was designed to safeguard the Republic from decay, to allow development through time as well as expansion across space, and to make the historical period in which the nation's institutions were framed both a relevant source of lessons for the future and a legacy that no longer inexorably burdens the present.

In attempting to accommodate republican theory to cultural change the Marshall Court employed the same devices used in the realms of politics and economics, consensual surrogates. The Marshall Court's approach toward history, as embodied in its theory of constitutional interpretation, provides an example. In the Court's constitutional decisions the acts of the Revolutionary generation were identified as forces that defined the identity of America as a nation; the Constitution became the vehicle through which the meaning of the Framers' experience was recorded. The Constitution was ideally suited for that function, since it was both a source of the original republican principles for which the American nation stood and a document whose language was seen as being both "permanent" and adaptive. We will see, in succeeding chapters, that

---

[128] 4 Wheat. 316, 415 (1819). | [129] Ibid., 405.

constitutional interpretation by the Marshall Court became one of the major theatres of American intellectual life in which consensual surrogates—"Union," "commerce," and "property rights" are examples—were invoked as an effort to reconcile tensions resulting from the interaction of republican ideology and dramatic cultural change.

Thus far the origins of Marshall Court jurisprudence have been associated with pervasive cultural changes in early-nineteenth-century America, with the ambivalent reactions that those changes elicited from contemporaries, and with the accommodation of the presuppositions of modified republicanism, the predominant belief structure of the period, to those changes. The preceding discussion has not considered the precise relationship between the above themes and the jurisprudential issues that emerged in the period of the later Marshall Court. That relationship is the focus of the next chapter, which explores the nature and sources of law in early-nineteenth-century American jurisprudence.

As our focus shifts to distinctively legal issues a set of questions surfaces. What was the role of the American legal profession in the process of accommodating republican theory to cultural change? I have identified that process with two rhetorical strategies, the recasting of history and the invocation of consensual surrogates. If the process is identified in such a fashion, what role did lawyers play as rhetorical strategists? In the early nineteenth century a class of elite lawyers assumed the function of juristic commentators, framing and analyzing jurisprudential issues. Why did this group of lawyers come into prominence in the early nineteenth century, what jurisprudential issues did they find most pressing, and how did they seek to reconcile those issues? Such questions are the subject of the next chapter.

# CHAPTER II

## *The Origins of Marshall Court Jurisprudence* II: *The Nature and Sources of Law*

THIS CHAPTER explores the relationship of the interaction of republican ideology with cultural change to the emergence of distinctive attitudes about the nature and sources of law in early-nineteenth-century America. Three topics are emphasized in the tracing of that relationship: the status of law and the image of lawyers in a republican society; the emergence of a class of elite lawyer-commentators in response to perceived problems with the role of the legal profession; and the characterization of the nature and sources of American law advanced by those commentators. The common assumptions implicit in that characterization may be seen as establishing the juristic boundaries of Marshall Court jurisprudence.

In *The Pioneers*, we will recall, law occupied an ambiguous position in the village culture of Templeton. On the one hand, legal offices, responsibilities, obligations, and powers were reflections of the status gradations of republican society. The principal landowner was designated "Judge," despite his lack of legal training; his friends and associates held minor legal offices; his wealth and power were enforced and perpetuated by legal documents; others of lower social and economic status were dependent upon his "laws"; he in turn felt an obligation to enforce his proprietary rights in a moderate and humane fashion. This close affinity between law and republican social practices suggests that law was perceived as, in the words of Judge Temple, a force for "wholesome restraint," cementing the interdependence and underscoring the stratification of republican society.

But law had another image as well, that of a contrast to "justice," a mysterious, unintelligible force that was capable of being "twisted" to the advantage of those with "cunning," power, and ambition. None of the lawyers in *The Pioneers* is an admirable character; none of the admirable characters, including Judge Temple, is a lawyer. Law seems both necessary to republican culture and alien to its ideals: it reinforces the social assumptions of republicanism but at the same time serves as a barrier to the achievement of "natural justice."

The characterizations of law and lawyers made in *The Pioneers* were familiar ones to early-nineteenth-century Americans. On the one hand, law was perceived as an especially vital force in the establishment and perpetuation of a republican form of government. That form of government was uniquely committed to the inalienable rights of individuals and the sovereign powers of the people, and it was imperative that a republic's citizens know what those rights and powers were. "In a representative government," two Georgia jurists declared in 1800, "it is of the utmost consequence to the body of the nation to be rightly informed of those laws and regulations by which their duties are defined and their rights secured."[1]

How were the people to learn the laws? One eighteenth-century intellectual tradition, "common sense" theory, suggested that the average citizen had an inherent capacity to grasp principles of social organization, morality, and economic behavior, and that no class of savants was necessary to render such principles intelligible. For the most part, however, lawyers were regarded as a vital link between the citizenry and the body of laws by which it was governed, a medium for making the law intelligible.

But alongside the perceived importance of law and lawyers in a republic needs to be placed the widespread criticism of the late-eighteenth- and early-nineteenth-century American legal profession as obscurantist, cunning, avaricious, and self-interested: a class of persons who reinforced the unintelligibility of the law for their own purposes. Numerous scholars have shown the persistence of antilegalism in America from the Revoluation through the Civil War. The legal profession in those years received criticism from a variety of sources on a variety of grounds. Among the complaints were the inaccessibility of legal procedures, the alien content of legal doctrines, many of them English in origin, the unnecessarily complex and time-consuming nature of legal proceedings, the high costs of legal representation, the uncertainty and unpredictability of legal rules, and the "chicanery and finesse" of practitioners. Merchants, landowners,

---

[1] R. Watkins and G. Watkins, *A Digest of the Laws of the State of Georgia* (1800), iv.

farmers, evangelicals, novelists, and politicians contributed to the criticism.[2]

Classical republican ideology was more sanguine about the presence of law in a republic than about the characteristics of representatives of the legal profession. One of the ideals of classical republicanism was "simplicity," a word that was intended to signify a lack of pretension, a disdain for artificial ceremonies and distinctions, and a repudiation of decadent or corrupt symbols of privilege. Lawyers, with their invocations of mysterious words, their fetish for ritual, even their costumes, were reminiscent of the luxurious and sinister world of monarchs and courtiers that republican government was designed to forestall.

Distrust of the courtier-like functions of lawyers may have contributed to the comparatively slow emergence in America of the practice of law as a full-time profession as distinguished from a part-time hobby or avocation. Many persons who studied law in the late eighteenth century never entered practice: a common pattern, notable among owners of large freeholds, was to read law in a law office, become admitted to a state bar, and then make use of the resultant familiarity with law in the management of an estate. Moreover, many lawyers who actually entered practice tended to retire from their profession if they inherited land or wealth,[3] using their legal training only to assist them in their private business affairs. A South Carolina magazine described one such example in 1806. The lawyer portrayed was "the proprietor of a small plantation, not far from town," who "was bred to the law . . . [and] continued in the practice of the profession for several years," but then "by the death of a near relation . . . became the owner of a plantation." The lawyer was "aware . . . that property never thrives so well as when the proprietor is on the spot, and for this reason he settled on his estate immediately after the bargain was concluded and now scarcely ever comes to town but on club nights."[4]

The pattern of lawyers becoming squires was sufficiently entrenched in late-eighteenth-century America, especially in the South, as to become an aspirational ideal. In a subsequent chapter we shall note the pursuit of this ideal by two prominent early-nineteenth-century Virginia lawyers,

---

[2] For discussions of antilegalism in late-eighteenth- and early-nineteenth-century America, see A. Roeber, *Faithful Magistrates and Republican Lawyers* (1981), 231–56; C. Cook, *The American Codification Movement* (1981), 1–18; M. Bloomfield, *American Lawyers in a Changing Society, 1776–1876* (1976), 32–58; G. Gawalt, *The Promise of Power: The Emergence*

*of the Legal Profession in Massachusetts 1760–1840* (1979), 81–118; R. Gordon, Book Review, *Vand. L. Rev.*, 36:431 (1983), 441–58.

[3] See Bloomfield, *American Lawyers*, 50–52.

[4] "The Archer, No. II," *Monthly Register, Magazine, and Review of the United States*, 1:308 (1806).

## Chapter II: *The Origins of Marshall Court Jurisprudence* II

Littleton Tazewell and William Wirt. Tazewell retired from law practice at forty-five "to draw his living from the moderate profits of agriculture . . . in the mould of our early statesmen";[5] Wirt was obsessed by a recurrent fantasy in which his law practice would yield enough income to enable him to retire to a James River plantation.[6]

The image of a squire employing his legal training in the management of his estate rather than in the practice of law testified to the strains in reconciling classical republican social ideals with the proliferation of the legal profession that took place in early-nineteenth-century America. Antilegalist sentiment and the elevation of the gentleman amateur as an aspirational ideal persisted in a culture in which practitioners were becoming more numerous and professionalized.[7] As the United States expanded geographically, its population increased, and the nation became more diverse and at the same time more economically interdependent, the demand for specialized legal services increased. The early nineteenth century was a period of growth for every segment of the legal profession—law schools, firms, the judiciary, professional journals, scholars, and publicists.

The confluence of these trends was to foster the emergence of a new class of lawyers—elite commentators—who defined their role as educating the profession and the public in the "science" of law. The most interesting characteristic of the members of this class was their ideological strategy. They self-consciously set out not only to respond to the increased demand for legal sources, specifically in the systematization and publication of legal rules and doctrines, but also to establish themselves as professional guardians of republican principles, persons whose special knowledge of "legal science" enabled them to recast law in conformity with the assumptions of republican government.

The emergence of this class of jurists did not come until after the War of 1812, but their strategy of increasing the professional power and prominence of lawyers by simultaneously rendering more efficient legal services and restating the principles of republican government was not novel. In the late eighteenth century, a version of the strategy had been adopted by lawyers in Virginia. Between 1774 and 1790, as A. L. Roeber has shown,[8] a group of republican theorists, including St. George Tucker, Thomas Jefferson, and James Madison, launched a successful campaign to reduce the influence of local county courts, which had been presided over by lay judges, and to create a system of district courts, administered

---

[5] H. Grigsby, *Discourse on the Life and Character of Hon. Littleton Waller Tazewell* (1860), 87–88.

[6] See infra, Chapter IV, pp. 261–62.

[7] See Bloomfield, *American Lawyers*, 142–51; Gawalt, *Promise of Power*, 168–91.

[8] Roeber, *Faithful Magistrates*, 160–202.

by judges and clerks with legal training. The county courts had incurred criticism for the arbitrariness of their decisions, the inefficiency and slowness of their procedures, and their purported toleration of "immoral" conduct, such as gambling, excess drinking, and swearing. Critics of the courts associated those charges with tyranny and corruption and identified the professionalization of the court system with republican virtue.

The success of late-eighteenth-century law reform in Virginia furnishes an example of the use of the generalized vocabulary of republicanism by a specialized, self-interested profession. Reform of the court system in Virginia, while justified as a campaign against vestiges of a corrupt monarchical past, was principally a response to the failure of the county court system to provide efficient, speedy, and predictable resolutions of legal disputes.[9] It also, however, illustrates the increased importance of law and legal services in a society whose population was growing and diffusing rapidly and whose economy was becoming more complex.

To summarize, the place of law in late-eighteenth-century republican culture had been an ambiguous one, and lawyers, as a professional class, had neither been fully accepted nor universally welcomed. As the nineteenth century began, considerable opposition to lawyers and their practices persisted, but at the same time a knowledge of law came to be seen as vital to the citizenry of a republican government, and legal services came to be perceived as increasingly necessary in a growing and commercializing society. Familiarity with law continued to be regarded as indispensable for the class of virtuous gentlemen who were to provide leadership for the new nation and helpful to the bulk of the populace. Moreover, an awareness of the content of legal rules and doctrines came to be regarded as important to the growing number of people engaged in commercial transactions as the nation's economy expanded and diversified. And while an image of lawyers as avaricious, cunning pettifoggers persisted, law retained its significance as a mechanism for communicating republican principles to the population at large.

Some members of the legal profession were to respond to the growing importance of law in early-nineteenth-century American life by carving out a new professional role for themselves, that of commentators who systematized and restated the content of American law. Among the purposes of the commentators were the reformulation of legal doctrines to make them more predictable and accessible, the harmonizing of existing rules with the assumptions of republican theory, and the upgrading of the prestige and power of the legal profession in an expanding market economy. While seeking to bring about those aims, the commentators precipitated new definitions of the nature and sources of American law.

---

[9] Ibid., 203–30.

✳

In 1803 St. George Tucker, who had succeeded George Wythe as professor of law at the College of William and Mary thirteen years earlier,[10] published an edition of William Blackstone's *Commentaries on the Law of England*. Tucker had contemplated an edition of Blackstone for several years. In 1797 he completed a proposal "for publishing an American edition of Blackstone's Commentaries" that would include "notes of reference to the Constitution and laws of the federal government of the United States" and "tracts upon such subjects as appeared necessary to form a systematic view of the laws of Virginia as a member of the Federal Union."[11] His edition, when it appeared, consisted of five volumes, with more than 1,400 notes on various subjects, including a "very numerous" selection on "the constitution and laws of the United States."[12] In appendices Tucker also provided the tracts he had promised, including discussions of sovereignty under the Constitution,[13] slavery,[14] freedom of speech and the press,[15] and the status of the English common law in the American federal courts.[16]

Tucker was not the only commentator of his generation, and his perspective differed in important respects from the nineteenth-century commentators who followed him, but still he can be seen as prototypical. In the preface to his 1803 edition of Blackstone, Tucker advanced a series of justifications for issuing the work. Each of the justifications can be read as a clue not only to Tucker's motivation in undertaking the edition but also to the motivations of the commentators who followed Tucker. The justifications advanced by Tucker were repeated, in less extensive form, by his successor commentators; they amounted to a rationale for the presence of juristic commentary in early-nineteenth-century America.

Tucker began his preface by asserting that until the appearance of Blackstone's *Commentaries* "the students of law in England, and its dependencies, were almost destitute of any scientific guide to conduct their studies."[17] The assumption behind this assertion was that legal study should be "scientific," an assumption that was consistently made by other early-nineteenth-century commentators. By "science" Tucker seems only to have meant systematization and organization of relevant data. He stated that "on the appearance of the *Commentaries* the laws of England, from

---

[10] See E. Bauer, *Commentaries on the Constitution* (1952), 173.

[11] S. Tucker, *Proposals for Publishing an American Edition of Blackstone's Commentaries* (1797), ix.

[12] Ibid., 3.

[13] S. Tucker, ed., *Blackstone's Commentaries: With Notes of Reference to the Constitution and Laws of the Federal Government of the United States*

and of the Commonwealth of Virginia (5 vols., 1803), II, Appendix D, 140–377.

[14] Tucker, *Blackstone*, III, Appendix H, 31–85.

[15] Tucker, *Blackstone*, III, Appendix G, 3–30.

[16] Tucker, *Blackstone*, II, Appendix E, 378–439.

[17] Ibid., iii.

a rude chaos, instantly assumed the semblance of a regular system," and referred to Blackstone as having provided "a regular and systematic guide," and a "model of methodical elegance."[18]

A "scientific" approach to the study of law, Tucker felt, was particularly necessary in America. He advanced two reasons for the importance of science. First, the American governmental system was complex, and likely to become more so as the nation grew and expanded. "Government in [America]," Tucker felt,

> may be compared to a seedling oak, that has just burst the acorn and appears above the surface of the earth with its first leaves; it advances with civilization, rears its head in proportion as the other increases; and puts forth innumerable branches till it covers the earth with an extensive shade, and is finally regarded as the king of the forest: all behold it with reverence, few have any conception of its magnitude, or of the dimensions, or number of its parts; few are acquainted with the extent of its produce, or can compare the benefits derived from its shade, with the loss of soil which it appropriates to its own support.[19]

The potential vastness and complexity of American government, then, required "painful, laborious, and incessant" efforts to "trace its figure." Science was equal to the task. Science "unfolds to its votaries those principles which ought to direct the operations" of government, "discloses the application of other powers, and demonstrates the sources from which they spring, and the effect they are calculated to produce."[20]

But why was an understanding of the principles of government so essential, especially given the effort required? Tucker's answer linked science to republican ideology. As nations passed from "savage life" to "civilization," he maintained, "society and civilization create a thousand relations [hitherto] unknown," which come to be "extended and diversified in such a manner that the machine of government becomes necessarily more complex in its parts, in proportion as its functions are multiplied." And at that point "those who administer it acquire a mechanical acquaintance with its powers, and often, by a slight alteration in the frame, produce an entire revolution in the principles of its action." Complex government, in short, was a potential seedbed of tyranny and corruption; the remedy was to return to first principles. Science was the mechanism to "unfold" those principles. "Hence," Tucker concluded, "those nations which have been most eminent in science have been most distinguished by freedom."[21]

An understanding of the principles of government and an under-

---

[18] Ibid., iii, iv, vi.
[19] Ibid., xv.

[20] Ibid., xv, xvi.
[21] Ibid., xvi.

standing of law were especially important in America, Tucker argued, because of the presence of a republican form of government. In the American republic "the force and obligation of every positive law, and of every act of government," were "immediately blended with the authority of the government itself." The "study of law, as a science" was necessary "to a full and perfect understanding" of republican principles, "for the rules of law must not infrequently be consulted to explain the principles." And "in a government founded on the basis of equal liberty among all its citizens, to be ignorant of the law . . . is to be ignorant of the rights of the citizen."[22]

At this point Tucker crowned his argument by invoking the code words of republican theory. He had sought to establish a connection between the complexity of government in a civilized society, the need for scientific study to make that complexity intelligible, the importance of penetrating complexity to reveal governing principles, and the necessity for republican citizens to comprehend those principles. He now invoked the special language of republicanism to render a shorthand summary of that argument. "Ignorance" in the citizenry, he claimed, "is invariably the parent of error; where it is blended with a turbulent and unquiet temper, it infallibly produces licentiousness, the most terrible enemy to liberty, except despotism." And "when ignorance is united with supineness, liberty becomes lethargic, and despotism erects her standard without opposition." Corruption and tyranny thus inevitably followed from an ignorance of law and government. "An enlightened people," however, "who have once attained the blessing of free government [such as in America] can never be enslaved until they abandon virtue and relinquish science." [23] Science was thus a link between "virtue" and "liberty": by penetrating the complexity of government to reveal its first principles, the citizen, if he made that difficult effort, ensured that he would be both civic-minded and free.

Tucker's conception of law as a science, and his association of scientific legal inquiry with the great ideals of republican government, virtue and freedom, was a powerful justification for juristic commentary, one that was repeatedly advanced by the commentators who succeeded Tucker.[24] The importance of scientific legal study in a republic, however, was not the only justification Tucker offered for publishing his edition of Blackstone. His remaining reasons pointed up the other major purpose of legal community in the early nineteenth century, to respond to the increased demand for legal services in a culture whose rapidly changing

---

[22] Ibid., xvii.
[23] Ibid.
[24] In addition to the discussion of legal science in this chapter, See P.

Miller, *The Life of the Mind in America* (1966), 156–85; Gordon, Book Review, 452–57.

economic and political character was perceived as affecting the scope and content of its law.

The revolution that had separated America from Great Britain had precipitated, Tucker believed, "a corresponding revolution not only in the principles of our government", but also in "the laws which relate to property, and a variety of other cases." A "revolution" in the content of American laws had produced statutes and decisions that were "contradictory . . . and irreconcilable to the principles contained in the *Commentaries*." Moreover, the new American laws were not always accessible: in Virginia they had been "stitched together . . . in a loose and slovenly manner," and "thrown [into] obscurity . . . by partial editions." There was thus a practical need to know the current state of legal rules and doctrines. Students who pursued "a systematical course of study," Tucker believed, would be "delivered from a labyrinth of uncertainty." He hoped that his notes and annotations to Blackstone would result in readers "casting [their] eye[s] to the bottom of the page, and there finding whether the statute [they were] considering still forms a part of, or has been expunged from, that code which [they wish] to understand."[25]

Tucker, then, proposed to "offer remarks upon such [sections of Blackstone] as . . . required illustration, either because the law had been confirmed, or changed, or repealed, by some constitutional or legislative act of the Federal Government or of the Commonwealth of Virginia."[26] In his preface he gave a list of examples. Contrary to Blackstone, the "principles of our government" embodied the idea that sovereignty rested in the people.[27] "Local circumstances" in America had "necessarily introduced a variety of new regulations" in court procedure.[28] A "great number of alterations in the system of our jurisprudence" had resulted because of "a desire to conform to the newly adopted principles of republican government." Among those were the abolition of primogeniture and entail, "the preference heretofore given to the male line in respect to real estates of inheritance," and the "right of survivorship between joint-tenants."[29] There had, in fact, been an "almost total change in the system of laws relative to property, both real and personal, in Virginia." Many such laws had been deemed "obsolete" or "inapplicable to our local circumstances and policy."[30] Finally, the legal ramifications of slavery could not be "pass[ed] over without attention."[31]

In his justifications for the 1803 edition of Blackstone, Tucker had articulated the dual role that elite commentators on law were to perform in early-nineteenth-century America. The commentators were both syn-

---

[25] Tucker, *Blackstone*, I, v, ix.
[26] Ibid., vi.
[27] Ibid., viii.
[28] Ibid., x.

[29] Ibid.
[30] Ibid., xi.
[31] Ibid.

thesizers of the law as it currently was and recasters of the "original principles" of government, "those principles which ought to direct the operations of the machine."[32] Their view of law was both systematic and adaptive. As new rules and doctrines came into being the commentators not only took note of them, they also "scientifically" reconciled them with "original principles."

Tucker's preface also indicated that he had a firm idea of the audience for which this edition of Blackstone was intended. He repeated that "an acquaintance with the . . . laws of our country" was "requisite to preserve the blessings of freedom to the people." Thus while Tucker prepared his commentaries for law students, they could be seen as being designed for every republican citizen. In particular, Tucker singled out one class of persons that he felt would especially profit from perusal of his edition. "Those who are to frame laws and administer the government," he suggested, "should possess a thorough knowledge of these subjects." It would be "absurd" if "one who neither understands the constitution nor the law should boldly adventure to administer the government." Tucker hoped that "men of talents and virtue" would enter public service in America, and become acquainted with law as a preparation for doing so. "The road to office" was "equally open to all" in the United States, Tucker recognized, but "men of talents and virtue" did not always travel it, being "generally more [modest] than those of inferior pretensions." Tucker hoped that this class of persons would have "their minds properly enlightened by study and application of the law"[33] as part of their preparation for public service.

The fact that Tucker intended his edition of Blackstone to be read primarily by "men of talents and virtue" who were preparing to "frame laws or administer the government" reminds us that legal knowledge was not expected to be primarily consumed by a class of specialized professionals at the time Tucker's edition appeared. Tucker's decision to include extended theoretical "inquiries and discussions of subjects," in addition to "short explanatory notes and references to [the Virginia] state code"[34] reflected his sense of his audience. Tucker proposed "to investigate the nature of the compact which the people have entered into, one with another; to consider the connection between the federal government and the state governments"; and to "survey . . . the whole complicated structure of our government, and consider how far the parts of a machine so immense, intricate, and complex, are likely to correspond, or interfere with the operations of each other." Such inquiries, he felt, "would necessarily lead to an examination of the principles of our government."[35] He hoped

---

[32] Ibid., xvi.
[33] Ibid., xvi–xviii.

[34] Ibid., vi–vii.
[35] Ibid., vii.

to reach an audience of persons for whom law and republican theory were inextricably linked.

Tucker's justifications for issuing his 1803 edition of Blackstone have been probed in some detail because of Tucker's pivotal position in the history of early-nineteenth-century legal commentary. Two of Tucker's assumptions about juristic commentary were held by all of his successors: his conception of the study of law as a "scientific" inquiry, by which he meant a systematic extrapolation and application of the principles of republican government; and his characterization of American law as constantly changing in scope and content, and thus needing to be made predictable and accessible to those whose activities were governed by it. Another of Tucker's assumptions, that he wrote as much for prospective public servants and statesmen as for practitioners, law being indistinguishable from political theory, also warrants attention. That assumption was to be reformulated by later commentators as American lawyers became more professionalized. Finally, Tucker's commentary was closely associated with legal education. He was one of the few law professors in early-nineteenth-century America, and William and Mary one of the few law schools. The link between commentaries and legal education was immediately apparent to Tucker. He had first adopted Blackstone as a text in his classes, he said, "to be useful to his pupils."[36] As the idea of university-related legal education flourished in nineteenth-century America, so did volumes of commentaries, and the two enterprises assumed a mutually supportive relationship.

Tucker's edition of Blackstone was the first of a series of commentaries on American law that appeared during the years of the Marshall Court. While Tucker can be seen as a prototype for later commentators, especially in his affiliation with legal education and his interest in approaching legal subjects "scientifically," in another sense he was unrepresentative of the writers that followed him. Tucker had approached Blackstone's commentaries from the perspective of a Virginia lawyer. His first concern, as he put it, was "being particularly useful to the students of law in his own state."[37] His explorations into "the principles of the constitution of the federal government, and the general laws of the union," were made with the idea of producing "a valuable system of federal and state jurisprudence, so far at least as relates to the Commonwealth of Virginia."[38] Tucker's substantive views on jurisprudential issues were consistent with his state-centered perspective. He was particularly concerned with the preservation of state sovereignty in a federal

---

[36] Ibid., vi.
[37] Ibid., xiv.

[38] Ibid.

republic and with the maintenance of state lawmaking prerogatives in a system of competing sources of law.

In short, Tucker's edition of Blackstone combined a provincial perspective with a methodology that was designed to emphasize both the fundamental principles of a republican legal system and the anomalies created by applying English law to the American environment. In Tucker's approach provincialism, scientific analysis, and modification of received legal doctrine were fused. In the approach of most of the commentators who succeeded Tucker that fusion was not even sought, let alone achieved. For example, the writings of Tucker's fellow Virginian John Taylor, who wrote commentary between 1810 and 1823, also made an effort to restate the fundamental principles of republican government and to emphasize the importance of state autonomy in a federal republic. But Taylor, unlike Tucker, spent no time on common law doctrine, confining his inquiries to political and constitutional theory. Moreover, Taylor's works bore no connection with legal education or law practice: they were intended as tracts to be read by "statesmen."[39]

In contrast to Taylor, most of the other commentators who followed Tucker explicitly abandoned his state-centered stance, while retaining his emphasis on scientific methodology and the reshaping of British law. A visible characteristic of most of the volumes of early-nineteenth-century American legal commentary was their resolutely nationalistic perspective. The authors of the commentaries sought to link the growth of the American legal profession with the emergence of a unique and interdependent American nation.

After the War of 1812 a distinct pattern of commentary emerged. Law schools were founded or revitalized and scholars were recruited to provide instruction. The scholars were expected to prepare lectures as part of their course of instruction, and several such lectures were published as commentaries. The published commentaries were disseminated to a wide professional audience, which extended beyond the boundaries of the state in which the commentator's law school was based and beyond the student constituency to which the lectures had been originally addressed. The commentaries were reviewed in professional journals and magazines, which were then growing rapidly. The reviewers were themselves persons who sought to promote scientific legal study, to systematize the content of American law, to increase interchange among all sections of the American legal profession, and to advance a particular political orientation. The 1817 appearance of David Hoffman's lectures, *A Course of Legal Study*, furnishes an example of this pattern.

---

[39] For discussions of Taylor's writings on legal issues, see Bauer, *Commentaries*, 182–96, 264–71; R. Shalhope, *John Taylor of Caroline: Pastoral Republican* (1980), 152–80, 188–95, 204–10.

In 1812 the University of Maryland attempted to organize a law school and shortly thereafter[40] appointed Hoffman, a Baltimore practitioner, to plan the curriculum and to give a course of lectures. Hoffman published the plan of the lectures in 1817 as *A Course of Legal Study.* That volume, while not advertised as a commentary, was in fact one. Hoffman gave a list of prescribed reading for prospective law students; he subsequently called his volume "the first manual ever arranged for law students."[41] The manual was much more than a bibliography, however. It was, as Tucker's edition of Blackstone had been, an annotated guide to authoritative legal sources. Hoffman divided the study of law into thirteen "titles" or topics, including among them "moral and political philosophy," the law of "real rights and real remedies," "the law of equity," "the civil and roman law," "the law of crimes and punishments," "the constitution and laws of the United States of America," and "political economy."[42] Each topic was accompanied by a syllabus of relevant works, with Hoffman supplying notes for many of the titles he listed. In the second edition of *A Course of Legal Study,* which appeared in 1836, Hoffman suggested the following approach to his syllabus:

> [B]efore [the student] has taken a book in hand, . . . he should read in *A Course of Legal Study* first, the Table of Contents, and the Proem [Introduction]; and then, with great care, the whole of the First Title, with its Notes. After this, and at his leisure, whilst studying the works recommended in the first title, he should read cursorily in anticipation, the whole of the Second Title. The studies of the first title being completed, the student should then, for the second time, read carefully the second title, with its notes; and whilst engaged in studying the books, etc. therein recommended, he may proceed to a cursory reading of the Third Title; which, like the preceding, is to be again carefully read, just before the student engages in the studies prescribed in it. The foregoing remarks apply equally to the other titles of the course.[43]

Hoffman felt that his *Course* was "extensive," but could be accomplished in six or seven years. That period of time was "very long," he

---

[40] There is some difference of opinion as to precisely when Hoffman's appointment took place. Charles Warren, in his *A History of the American Bar* (1911), 356, gives 1816 as the date; Francis Aumann, in *The Changing American Legal System* (1940), 109, gives 1815; and Bauer, *Commentaries,* 106, gives 1814. Only Bauer cites contemporary supporting evidence, and I am inclined to follow her designation.

[41] D. Hoffman, *An Address to Students of Law in the United States* (1824), 1.
[42] D. Hoffman, *A Course of Legal Study* (1817), 32–33. I have used both this edition and Hoffman's expanded second edition as sources of Hoffman's views, which did not change substantially in the period between the editions.
[43] D. Hoffman, *A Course of Legal Study* (2d ed., 1836), xiv–xv.

acknowledged, but appeared necessary given "the extent, difficulty, and importance of the science."[44] Being mindful of "circumstances, such as too advanced age, pecuniary necessity, etc. which may render the prosecution of our entire Course impracticable,"[45] Hoffman offered shortened versions, omitting certain of the books in the syllabus. By his second edition Hoffman had added two additional shortened courses. One reduced the time to "a three years' course" by omitting additional works; another was "adapted to the wants of those who study with a fixed view of practicing their profession in the interior; that is, out of our commercial and maritime cities." Such persons, Hoffman felt, "did not need to embrace several departments of the science," such as "the Admiralty and Maritime Law," the "laws of Nature and Nations," and even "the Constitution and Law of the United States."[46]

Most of Hoffman's *Course* consisted of commentaries on the sources he recommended, presented as notes. On Blackstone's *Commentaries,* for example, Hoffman made the following observation:

[W]e strongly urge an earnest perusal of this admirable work, the student always bearing in mind, that its principal object is to present an orderly and systematic view of a science, the outlines of which are not to be found as briefly yet completely delineated, in any other work.[47]

Hoffman felt that Blackstone's *Commentaries* were like "the general institutes of a science": they "exhibited a general map of the English law" but did not apply "particular and definite knowledge on any of its various doctrines."[48] He was subsequently to "lament that young men of fine talents, fascinated by the perspicuity of [Blackstone's] arrangement, and the charms of the style, persist in reading little else than these commentaries."[49]

Hoffman's notes were not confined to observations on other treatises or commentaries; he also discussed substantive areas of law. In Hoffman's syllabus on "personal rights and remedies," for example, he referred the student to several chapters in Matthew Bacon's 1736 *Abridgement of the Law,* which covered marriage and divorce, aliens, corporations, wills and testaments, assignment, obligations, and fraud. No work was "better known to law generally," Hoffman said in 1836, than Bacon's *Abridgement.* But Bacon's discussion of the topics of agreement, obligations, assignment, authority and bailments, while constituting "a tolerable out-

---

44 Hoffman, *Course of Legal Study* (1817), xxviii.
45 Ibid., xxix.
46 Hoffman, *Course of Legal Study* (1836), 46.

47 Hoffman, *Course of Legal Study* (1817), 91.
48 Ibid., 88.
49 Hoffman, *Course of Legal Study* (1836), 154.

line," revealed that "the English law of contracts . . . has never been cultivated with correspondent assiduity."[50] Hoffman suggested that the "flourishing maturity" of "foreign or domestic trade and commerce" in America made an inquiry into "the general doctrine of contracts" particularly fitting. He felt that "a scientific, and learned, yet elementary view of the doctrine of contracts . . . argued in the spirit of a matured philosophy, could not fail to be a work of great utility." Contract law, Hoffman felt, "must be commensurate . . . with our habits and institutions, as it is a scheme educed from the principles of common reason, and is the natural growth of the simple and hourly occurring negotiations of life."[51]

Observations of this kind ranged through Hoffman's *Course*. He commented on the "luminous . . . clear, and almost simple,"[52] if "essentially erroneous,"[53] classifications of remainders by Charles Fearne. He discussed the different species of "pure and corrupt" governments treated in Aristotle.[54] He pointed out the difficulty of defining with accuracy the law respecting confessions.[55] He noted Lord Coke's tendency to "frequently blend points of law, neither raised by the pleadings nor agitated before the court, but suggested solely by his lordship."[56] And he characterized the United States Constitution as "that happy exemplar of the practicableness and utility of philosophical codification."[57] Hoffman's view of the Constitution, as interpreted by the Marshall Court, was as follows:

> The constitutional law of the United States illustrates, we think, in the clearest manner, the coexistence of two facts, which, though perfectly in unison with each other, are at first, seemingly at variance— viz: first, a constitutional code, consisting of but a few pages, which regulates many of the most important interests of twenty-four sovereign states, and of a great nation educed out of them all; and, secondly, the exercise of interpretive powers, swelling into volumes, and yet in no instance departing from the clear letter, or manifest spirit of the instrument, and never falling into the vice of judicial legislation.[58]

The observations, selections, and organization of Hoffman's *Course* revealed his commitment to a distinctive jurisprudential perspective. Hoff-

---

[50] Ibid., 336.
[51] Ibid., 337.
[52] Ibid., 142.
[53] Ibid., 245.
[54] Hoffman, *Course of Legal Study* (1817), 65.
[55] Hoffman, *Course of Legal Study* (1836), 367.
[56] Hoffman, *Course of Legal Study* (1817), 105.
[57] Hoffman, *Course of Legal Study* (1836), 566. Hoffman also offered

some helpful hints to law students. Among the "resolutions" he suggested for a prospective student were "to guard my mind from idle thoughts, and sensual images," "to dress fairly in the fashion, but never beyond my means, and studiously to shun foppery," and "to avoid intimate association with young men of doubtful principles." Ibid., 51–52.
[58] Ibid., 565–66.

man's perspective placed special emphasis on three tasks of legal study: the "scientific" systematization of doctrines, through which their first principles would be revealed; the modification of received rules, especially the rules of English common law, to meet the altered conditions of life in America; and the promulgation of American law on a "national" scale, as manifested in efforts to state the general principles that governed a body of law and could be applied across jurisdictional and state boundaries. These tasks were complemented by Hoffman's view of constitutional interpretation, in which the "letter" and "manifest spirit" of the instrument was constantly restated in "interpretations" that never departed from it. Law, for Hoffman, was both a collection of general principles, whose integrity was revealed by scientific inquiry, and a flexible set of doctrines that could be modified as conditions changed.

Hoffman's perspective can be seen in any of his discussions of legal topics in *A Course of Legal Study*. His notes on "The Constitution and Laws of the Several States in the Union" provide one of numerous possible illustrations. In pursuing this topic, Hoffman pointed out, the student should emphasize the extent to which "the Common and Statute Laws of the mother country have been either confirmed, repealed, altered, or modified."[59] He should further "abridge analytically all the state laws then in force of an important and general nature."[60] And he should master not only "the jurisprudence of his own state, and of that of the General Government," but "the laws of each state," which in "numerous . . . respects may readily affect the rights of the citizens of any other state."[61] In those exhortations one can see Hoffman's three principles of legal study: awareness of doctrinal change, systematization of data, and attention to the "national" implications of local rules in a culture characterized by economic expansion and increased social and political interchange.

The first major review of *A Course of Legal Study* was by Joseph Story in the *North American Review* in November 1817.[62] Story revealed an awareness of Hoffman's jurisprudential point of view and warmly endorsed it. Story was, as we shall see, a singularly energetic and visible promoter of the "scientific" approach to legal study, simultaneously serving as judge, commentator, educator, and publicist; his review of Hoffman was written in the last capacity. On November 13, 1817, Story wrote the Supreme Court's Reporter, Henry Wheaton, a close friend, that "I have been applied to by the editors of the North American Review . . . to furnish them a review of Mr. Hoffman on the Study of the Law." He

---

[59] Hoffman, *Course of Legal Study* (1817), 281.

[60] Ibid., 282.

[61] Hoffman, *Course of Legal Study* (1836), 572.

[62] J. Story, "Course of Legal Study," *No. Am. Rev.*, 6:7 (1817), reprinted in W. Story, ed., *The Miscellaneous Writings of Joseph Story* (1852), 66.

added, "I have prepared one which is to be published in the next number. When it comes out, I beg you to peruse it . . . as for the coincidence with some of your favorite views. . . . Show it to Mr. Hoffman, but without intimating that I had aught to do with it."[63] The episode was typical of Story at the time. In the decade after the War of 1812 he was constantly corresponding with promising younger scholars, of whom Wheaton was one, encouraging them to engage in the writing of treatises and digests, and lobbying with them on behalf of extensive jurisdiction for the federal courts, the systematization of American law, and the "establishment of a great national policy on all subjects."[64] The unsigned review was one of several Story wrote in the *North American Review* between 1817 and 1826, each praising an effort to make American law more adaptive, generalized, and "scientific."[65]

Story's review of Hoffman spent comparatively little time on *A Course of Legal Study* itself, devoting most of its attention to a reaffirmation of the precepts of Hoffman's jurisprudence. Story announced that "the progress of moral, political, and judicial science" in the "last two centuries" had been "wonderful,"[66] and cited the "regular system," exhibiting "such a scientific arrangement and harmony of principles," that had been constructed in several areas of American law. "A spirit of scientific research," Story claimed, "has diffused itself over the . . . departments of the common law" and "giv[en] it a systematic character, so that we may . . . arrive at its principles by regular analysis [and] teach its elements and distinctions by a nice synthesis."[67]

But at the same time, Story pointed out, "the rules of the statute or common law . . . must necessarily be general in their language," so that they can take into account "the boundless circumstances of life, which may modify, limit, or affect them."[68] The common law, in Story's view, was peculiarly fitted for being "moulded and fashioned, from age to age." It "had the advantage of expanding with the improvements of the age, and of continually enlarging itself":[69] it could adapt to the changing state of the American economy. There was thus a current of new opinions and doctrines to which lawyers had to keep pace; in this task "regular systems, built up with general symmetry of parts" made "the

---

[63] J. Story to H. Wheaton, Nov. 13, 1817, in W. Story, *The Life and Letters of Joseph Story* (2 vols., 1851), I, 309.
[64] J. Story to H. Wheaton, Dec. 13, 1815, quoted in W. Story, *Life and Letters*, I, 270–71.
[65] See, e.g., "Literature of the Maritime Law" (1818), reprinted in W. Story, *Miscellaneous Writings*, 93; "Chancery Jurisdiction" (1820), re-

printed in ibid., 148; "Growth of the Commercial Law" (1825), reprinted in ibid., 262; "Digests of the Common Law" (1826), reprinted in ibid., 379.
[66] J. Story, "Course of Legal Study," in W. Story, *Miscellaneous Writings*, 66.
[67] Ibid., 69–70.
[68] Ibid., 70.
[69] Ibid., 67.

necessary investigations in new and difficult cases'' able to be conducted with more safety.[70] A scientific derivation of general principles thus complemented the adaptive capacity of the law.

The combination of this "progress" in legal science and the inherent flexibility of law, Story felt, had "greatly enlarged . . . the sphere of professional activity," and made "the mysteries of the science" more "accessible to all."[71] The study of law had "become fashionable" in America in part because of the nature of American political institutions, which made a legal education "if not a prerequisite, at least a very important qualification for political distinction and public office," and in part because of the increased demand for legal sources fostered by commercial expansion. Consequently there had been a great increase in the bar, and an "ascendancy in society" that distinguished the American legal profession.[72]

Hoffman's *Course* reinforced all those trends. It contained, in Story's opinion, "by far the most perfect system for the study of law which has ever been offered to the public." Its "precepts" were "calculated to elevate the moral as well as intellectual character of the profession." If those precepts were "steadily pursued," the American legal profession "will attain a higher elevation, an elevation which shall command the reverence of Europe."[73] The appearance of Hoffman's *Course* was "proof of the opinion that the law, as a science, never was so well understood, nor so well taught, as at the present period."[74]

But the rapidly changing character of American society, the expansion of the legal profession, and the adaptive capacity of the common law suggested to Story that "a profound or comprehensive knowledge" of the law "never was of more difficult attainment." Given the complexity and multifariousness of American law, Story felt, additional measures were necessary to ensure that the legal profession would continue to remain in "ascendancy." Foremost among those measures, for Story, was the development of university legal education. Hoffman's treatise, he felt, "will demonstrate to the understanding of every discerning man the importance, nay, the necessity, of the law school, which the government of Harvard College have, so honorably to themselves, established at Cambridge." A year at a university law school "in attendance upon the lectures" would, in Story's view, "lay a foundation of solid learning . . . in elementary principles." The aspiring attorney would "then be prepared to reap the full benefits of the practice of an attorney's office," since instead of becoming mired "in the forms of conveyancing and pleading," he could "ascend to the principles which guide and govern

---

[70] Ibid., 79.
[71] Ibid., 80.
[72] Ibid., 76.

[73] Ibid., 91.
[74] Ibid., 86.

them." Apprenticeships without previous exposure to "the guidance of a learned and discreet lecturer," Story felt, were "immethodical, interrupted, and desultory."[75]

Story's essay on Hoffman provides a convenient occasion to assess the characteristics of American juristic commentary from Tucker through the early 1820s. One was the commentators' basic agreement as to the principal purposes of their enterprise. Tucker, Hoffman, and Story all believed that juristic commentary should be scientific, by which they meant that it should emphasize the systematic derivation and application of general principles in order to make law more intelligible, predictable, and in harmony with both the axioms of republicanism and the demands of a market economy. They also all recognized the adaptive character of American law and the close connection between cultural change in America and the modification of received doctrine. They each felt that because of the nature of American political institutions, the study of law was particularly necessary and important for Americans. They each sensed the importance, in a federalized republic and an increasingly interstate economy, of understanding the extent to which laws had a greater than local impact, and the extent to which federal and state laws competed with and complemented one another. And they each saw law as a "liberal" pursuit, inseparable from moral philosophy or political economy, subjects which Hoffman included in his curriculum.

There nonetheless had been a discernible shift of emphasis from Tucker to Hoffman and Story. First, Tucker had conceived of his project as an exercise in correcting some practical deficiencies in Blackstone and as an opportunity to expound on certain jurisprudential issues that he regarded as unsettled and important. Hoffman and Story no longer regarded Blackstone as authoritative; their interest in his commentaries was as an example of scientific analysis. Second, Hoffman's orientation was distinctly more professional and nationalistic than that of Tucker, and this emphasis was reinforced in Story's review. Tucker had identified as his audiences law students and practitioners in Virginia and potential statesmen there and elsewhere, and his political perspective was decidedly solicitous of state sovereignty. Hoffman and Story, while embracing Tucker's belief in science, had linked the growth of the scientific method of legal study to broader goals: widening the impact of law throughout America, perpetuating the power and prestige of the legal profession, and increasing political and economic interchange throughout the nation. One can observe this emphasis in Story's statement that one of his "motives" for "commending" Hoffman's treatise "earnestly to the perusal of our readers" was to demonstrate the importance of university legal education, and in Hoffman's expectation that his course would appeal not only to

---

[75] Ibid., 92.

## Chapter II: *The Origins of Marshall Court Jurisprudence* II

lawyers in "commercial and maritime cities" but also to those "in country practice."[76]

In the years between 1817 and the last Term of the Marshall Court the growth of commentary continued apace. Between 1819 and 1835 appeared John Milton Goodenow's *Historical Sketches of the Principles and Maxims of American Jurisprudence*,[77] Thomas Sergeant's *Constitutional Law*,[78] James Angell's *Watercourses*,[79] Nathan Dane's nine-volume *General Abridgement and Digest of American Law*,[80] Peter Du Ponceau's *Dissertation on the Nature and Extent of the Jurisdiction of the Courts of the United States*,[81] Gulian Verplanck's *Essay on the Doctrine of Contracts*,[82] William Rawle's *A View of the Constitution of the United States of America*,[83] Joseph Chitty's *A Practical Treatise on the Law of Contracts*,[84] the first volume of Hoffman's *Legal Outlines*,[85] Henry St. George Tucker's *Commentaries on the Laws of Virginia*,[86] and James Gould's *Pleading*.[87] This wave of treatise writing was to culminate in James Kent's four-volume *Commentaries on American Law*,[88] which appeared between 1826 and 1830, and Joseph Story's *Commentaries on the Law of Bailments*,[89] his three-volume *Commentaries on the Constitution*,[90] and his *Commentaries on the Conflict of Laws*,[91] all of which were published between 1832 and 1834. Since Kent's and Story's commentaries were clearly the most visible and influential of all the works that appeared between 1817 and 1835, it seems worthwhile to consider how far they retained or modified the conception of the enterprise articulated by Tucker and Hoffman.

---

[76] Hoffman, *Course in Legal Study* (1836), 46.

[77] J. Goodenow, *Historical Sketches of the Principles and Maxims of American Jurisprudence* (1819).

[78] T. Sergeant, *Constitutional Law* (1822).

[79] J. Angell, *Watercourses* (1824).

[80] N. Dane, *A General Abridgement and Digest of American Law* (9 vols., 1823).

[81] P. Du Ponceau, *Dissertation on the Nature and Extent of the Jurisdiction of the Courts of the United States* (1824).

[82] G. Verplanck, *Essay on the Doctrine of Contracts* (1825).

[83] W. Rawle, *A View of the Constitution of the United States of America* (1825).

[84] J. Chitty, *A Practical Treatise on the Law of Contracts* (1826).

[85] D. Hoffman, *Legal Outlines* (1829).

[86] H. Tucker, *Commentaries on the Laws of Virginia* (1831).

[87] J. Gould, *A Treatise on the Principles of Pleading in Civil Actions* (1832).

[88] J. Kent, *Commentaries on American Law* (4 vols., 1826–1830).

[89] J. Story, *Commentaries on the Law of Bailments* (1832).

[90] J. Story, *Commentaries on the Constitution* (3 vols., 1833).

[91] J. Story, *Commentaries on the Conflict of Laws* (1834).

Kent's *Commentaries on American Law* originated in a course of lectures he prepared after being appointed professor of law at Columbia in 1823.[92] Kent had held the same professorship thirty years earlier, before becoming a judge on the Supreme Court of New York, and the 1823 lectures, in their coverage, followed the design of his earlier course.[93] By the 1820s, however, Kent had considerably more American materials with which to work, and he conceived his lectures as providing "an elementary and sweeping view of the subject," and "endeavour[ing] to ascertain . . . great elementary maxims of universal justice and . . . broad principles of national policy."[94] The "knowledge that is intended to be communicated in these volumes," Kent wrote in his preface to the third volume, "is believed to be, in most cases, of general application, and is of that elementary kind, which is . . . essential to every person who pursues the science of law as a practical profession."[95]

On reflecting on the changes that had taken place in the interval between his two tenures as professor at Columbia, Kent was to say that "the progress of jurisprudence was nothing in New York prior to 1793," and that when he was appointed a judge "we had no law of our own."[96] By the publication of his commentaries that situation had changed: Kent was able to cite American sources extensively. In a discussion of fraudulent sales of personal property, for example, Kent announced, after reviewing English statutes and cases, that "the law on this subject is . . . more unsettled in this country than in England."[97] He then surveyed decisions of the Marshall Court, the federal circuit courts, and the states of Virginia, South Carolina, Tennessee, Kentucky, Pennsylvania, New Jersey, Connecticut, North Carolina, New York, Massachusetts, and New Hampshire, concluding that while some American decisions "harmonize with those of England," others "have, under equal sanction, established a more lax and popular doctrine."[98]

The sweep and detail of Kent's approach in his *Commentaries* presents an obvious contrast with Tucker. The latter's edition of Blackstone had dealt primarily with one source of law, modified by the editor's extrapolation of Virginia statutes or decisions that had qualified or undermined Blackstone's conclusions. Tucker's tracts on jurisprudential issues had been offered as personal attempts to explore large unsettled questions. Kent's compilations, in contrast, were offered as authoritative

---

[92] J. Horton, *James Kent: A Study in Conservatism* (1939), 269.

[93] For a reprint of the original lectures, delivered on November 17, 1794, see *Colum. L. Rev.*, 3:330 (1903).

[94] Kent, *Commentaries*, IV, 1–2.

[95] Kent, *Commentaries*, III, iv.

[96] J. Kent to William Kent, Feb. 17, 1847, James Kent Papers, Library of Congress; J. Kent to Thomas Washington, Oct. 6, 1828, ibid.

[97] Kent, *Commentaries*, III, 410.

[98] Ibid., 410–13, 414.

compendia of rules and doctrines, based on a far wider and more detailed survey of American sources than Tucker had been able to undertake.

The clear implication of Kent's *Commentaries,* then, was that they were to be regarded as embodying legal "knowledge . . . of general application."[99] Kent underscored the "national" sweep of his effort in a passage near the end of his final volume. He had omitted a discussion of the subject of special pleading from his *Commentaries,* he said, because he had not been able "to extend such a discussion beyond the courts of New York," and was consequently unable "to give anything approaching a full and correct view of the practice of the courts in the several states." He had also foregone a discussion of "the law of crimes and punishments," which he regarded as "a very important part of our legal system," because it rested "upon an exact knowledge of local law . . . in each state," and the "object" of his *Commentaries* was "professedly national, and not local."[100]

A national orientation, an emphasis on "elementary" principles of "general application," and a commitment to "the science of the law"[101] were thus present in Kent, as they had been in Hoffman. Moreover, Kent's intended audience was not dissimilar from those of Hoffman and Tucker. He hoped that his volumes would contain "knowledge . . . which is not only essential to every person who pursues the science of law as a practical profession," but could also be "useful and ornamental to gentlemen in every pursuit, and especially to those who are to assume places of public trust, and to take a share in the business and in the councils of our country." In this last sentence one can see that while the concept of law as a science was closely linked to the growth of a professional class of practitioners who needed to have the elementary principles of law made accessible and intelligible, it continued to be associated with the education of statesmen and public servants. A scientific approach to law not only resulted in the formulation of elementary principles, it revealed the basic assumptions of republican government. As Kent put it, "the elementary principles of the common law are the same in every state, and equally enlighten and invigorate every part of the country."[102]

The appearance of Kent's *Commentaries,* however, underscored a change in the stance of commentators toward substantive issues, a change that testified to the altered status of legal commentary in America. In Tucker's edition of Blackstone the argumentative presentations of the commentator had been explicitly separated from the synthetic, "digestive" presentations. Tucker's notes on Blackstone's text typically sought to show where Blackstone's generalizations were obsolete or misleading

---

[99] Ibid., iv.
[100] Kent, *Commentaries,* IV, 1527.

[101] Kent, *Commentaries,* III, liv.
[102] Kent, *Commentaries,* II, 418.

when applied to the current state of Virginia law, and rested with that showing. The generalizations Tucker "corrected" were not often probed to reveal their philosophic assumptions. In Tucker's tracts, by contrast, an argumentative posture was openly adopted, and the questions Tucker addressed were regarded as unsettled and susceptible of abstract reasoning from principles. Both modes of commentary were offered to Tucker's audience.

In Hoffman's *Course of Legal Study* one can note a subtle shift in the commentator's argumentative stance. The thrust of Hoffman's energies was seemingly directed toward digesting and synthesizing legal source materials: Hoffman appeared as the compiler, the bibliographer, and the dispenser of practical advice. In Hoffman's notes, however, one can perceive that he was not simply regurgitating the contents of his sources, he was weighing their contributions. Little by little a general argument emerged from Hoffman's notes, an argument that American law should be adaptive to local conditions, grounded on fundamental principles, universal in scope, and systematically organized. Moreover, law should be regarded as inseparable from political economy and moral philosophy, so that the fundamental principles that lay at the root of its doctrines were indistinguishable from the organizing principles of republican government and the necessities of commercial exchange.

The principal difference between Hoffman and Tucker was that Hoffman's argumentative structure was presented inferentially. Hoffman did not make a sharp separation between digests and tracts; instead he offered his notes as the ruminations of a scientific "jurisconsult" rather than the arguments of one advocating a particular point of view. Hoffman's jurisprudential perspective, while discernible, was rendered less overtly; his ideological positions were infused with his compilations of legal doctrines rather than held apart from them.

In Kent's *Commentaries* a tendency to fuse the argumentative and synthetic modes of commentary can be seen as even more pronounced. In the third volume of his *Commentaries* Kent, in an aside, described his stance as a commentator:

> My mind has been too long disciplined by the actual business of life, to indulge in general theory on law subjects, or to think it of much value. The first duty of a law book is to state the law *as it is,* truly and accurately, and then the reason or principle of it as far as it is known; and if the author be a lecturer or commentator, he may be more free in his observations on its history and character, and he ought to illustrate it by comparison with the institutions of other countries and ages, and, in strong cases, to point out its defects, to show its false doctrines, and modestly and temperately to suggest alterations and improvements. All this I have endeavoured to do. . . ; but still the existing and leading

rules ought to be laid open to the inspection of the lawyer and the scholar, with mathematical precision, and absolute certainty.[103]

A surface impression gleaned from the text of Kent's *Commentaries* appears to support the claim that Kent's purpose was to state "the law as it is." On a typical group of pages Kent made declarative pronouncements of rules and doctrines, supported by citations, conveying the sense that he was simply "laying . . . existing and leading rules" open to "inspection." But a closer reading of the text reveals that the commentator had engaged in some shaping of his materials. In Kent's discussion of marine insurance, to take a random example, he took up the "very unsettled question" of whether underwriters who had stipulated in their policies that they would not be liable for "partial loss" of designated articles would nonetheless be responsible if such articles, though not "lost," had been sufficiently damaged as to render them valueless. After citing cases resolving this question in contradictory ways, Kent noted that

> in France . . . the insurer is not holden, though part of the subject insured be totally destroyed. The principle is that the parties have a right to make their own contracts, and if the contract be lawful, it becomes a law to the court, and it would introduce uncertainty and confusion to undertake to modify the contract . . . upon amended principles of equity.[104]

He then added that "[t]he French law positively requires that goods, subject by their nature to particular detriment or diminution, be specified in the policy, otherwise the insurer is not liable for the losses. . . ." This was "a valuable rule," Kent said, "calculated to guard against dispute and imposition." In the midst of these references to French law he noted that two Marshall Court cases had followed the position of the French law, and that "the rule" in those cases (no liability for the "partial loss" of designated articles, however deteriorated in value) "may now be considered as the settled law of this country on the subject."[105]

In the above discussion Kent was, of course, not merely stating the law "as it was." He was analyzing an "unsettled question" that had been adjudicated both in favor of and against liability, introducing a civil law response to that question which favored no liability, offering reasons (the sanctity of contracts and the value of avoiding uncertainty and confusion) on behalf of the no-liability rule, calling the civilian response "valuable," and claiming that the question had been "settled" by a Marshall Court decision in favor of no liability. He had done more than

---

[103] Kent, *Commentaries*, III, 88–89.
[104] Ibid., 246.

[105] Ibid., 247.

"illustrate" the rule "by comparison with the institutions of other countries": he had used a civil law country's rule, together with a Marshall Court decision, as a basis for justifying one rather than another approach to the question. Moreover, the rule recognized the primacy of market relationships by substituting the "intent of the parties" in a bargained-for exchange for any considerations of "equity" a court might introduce. Having engaged in his gloss, Kent then pronounced the law as settled. Story, in the first of his commentaries, recognized Kent's artful use of civilian sources to "restate" American doctrine. "I have long entertained the belief," Story wrote in his preface to *Commentaries on the Law of Bailments,* "that an enlarged acquaintance with the continental jurisprudence, and especially with that of France, would furnish the most solid means of improvement of commercial law, as it now is, or hereafter may be, administered in America. Mr. Chancellor Kent has already led the way in this noble career; and has, by an incorporation of some of the best principles of the foreign law into ours, infused into it . . . a more persuasive cogency and spirit."[106]

Story's treatises revealed a more obviously self-conscious attitude toward the role of the commentator as advocate for a substantive point of view. Tucker had explicitly made "inquiries, and discussions of subjects which neither form a part of, nor even bear any relation to, the laws of England."[107] Kent had referred to the "freedom" of "a lecturer or commentator to make "observations" and to "modestly and temperately . . . suggest alterations and improvements," but he had principally defined his task as stating the law. Story was more cautious still. In his volume on bailments he spoke of "avail[ing] myself occasionally of the freedom belonging to a commentator to express a doubt or deny a doctrine." But he had "rarely done so," Story informed his audience, "except when the point has been purely speculative or the Common Law authorities justified one in the suggestion."[108]

When Story was preparing his *Commentaries on the Constitution* in 1831 and 1832, he and his close friends in the legal community were well aware that the treatise was likely to be controversial. By that time Story's positions on matters such as state sovereignty and the permanence of the Union were well known, and he was expected strongly to oppose nullification and other states' rights doctrines in his *Commentaries.* As early as September 1832, before the treatise appeared, John Marshall had written Story, "I anticipate much pleasure as well as information from perusing the work, and can assure you in anticipation that I shall not be among those who bring on the charge of '*apostasy*' and 'ultraism.' "[109]

[106] J. Story, *Bailments,* vii.
[107] Tucker, *Blackstone,* I, vii.
[108] J. Story, *Bailments,* ix.
[109] J. Marshall to J. Story, Sept. 22,

Three months later Story sent Marshall "a proof sheet of the title page," and Marshall responded, "I . . . am certain in advance that I shall read every sentence with entire approbation." Marshall believed that his and Story's theories of constitutional interpretation were "identical," but "[n]ot so with Virginia or the South generally."[110]

This assessment of the *Commentaries* continued after their publication in early 1833. Marshall wrote in April of that year, "I greatly fear that south of the Potomac, where it is most wanted, it will be least used." The "heresies of your *Commentaries*," Marshall felt, could "give our orthodox nullifyer a fever." A "whole school might be infected by the atmosphere if a single copy should be placed on one of the shelves of a bookcase."[111] On June 3 Marshall, on learning that Story had prepared an abridgment of *The Commentaries* for use "in all our colleges and universities," hoped that "your book, if read, will . . . remove . . . prejudices." "Our young men," Marshall maintained, "grow up in the firm belief that liberty depends on construing our constitution into a league instead of a government; that it has nothing to fear from breaking these United States into numerous petty republics. Nothing in their view is to be feared but that bugbear, consolidation; and every exercise of legitimate power is construed into a breach of the constitution."[112] These observations of Marshall were made before he had read any of the contents of *Commentaries on the Constitution*.

Marshall's sense of the point of view Story would take in *Commentaries on the Constitution* was based, of course, on a long and intimate friendship, and his suppositions proved accurate. About two weeks after Story received the last quoted letters from Marshall one arrived from Kent. "I not only applaud, but admire," Kent wrote, "your bold and free defense of sound doctrine, against the insidious, mischievous, and malignant attacks of Jefferson . . . I am very much pleased to observe the skill and address with which you handle the most delicate and debatable points in our constitutional contests, and . . . I consider your work to be an incomparable monument of sound and healthy constitutional principles."[113] Kent's reference to Story's handling of Jefferson, whom Marshall, Kent, and Story identified as the fountainhead of states' rights doctrines, paralleled an allusion Marshall had made in his September 1832 letter. "I shall like to see," Marshall had written Story, "how in your quotations from the sage . . . you imitate the bee in extracting honey

---

1832, quoted in *Proc. Mass. Hist. Soc.*, 14:351 (1901).
[110] J. Marshall to J. Story, Dec. 25, 1832, quoted in ibid., 352.
[111] J. Marshall to J. Story, Apr. 24, 1833, quoted in ibid., 354, 356.

[112] J. Marshall to J. Story, June 3, 1833, quoted in ibid., 357, 358.
[113] J. Kent to J. Story, June 19, 1833, quoted in W. Story, *Life and Letters*, III, 135.

from poison. I have no doubt, however dexterous the operation, that you will be well stung in requittal for your skill and industry."[114]

Given the expectations that Story's *Commentaries* would be extremely controversial,[115] the stance Story took in his preface was remarkably modest. He spoke of the *Commentaries* as having been composed "with a degree of uninviting labour, and dry research, of which it is scarcely possible for the general reader to form any adequate estimate." He referred to his compilations of "loose and scattered" materials, "obscure private and public documents," and "irregular fragments." He identified as his "two great sources" the *Federalist* papers ("an incomparable commentary of three of the greatest statesmen of their age") and the "extraordinary Judgments of Mr. Chief Justice Marshall upon constitutional law." He had merely "transferred into my own pages all which seemed to be of permanent importance" in *The Federalist;* and he had not advanced "any novel views and novel constructions of the Constitution." He disavowed "the ambition to be the author of any new plan of interpreting the theory of the Constitution, or of enlarging or narrowing its powers by ingenuous subtleties and learned doubts." He had simply tried to "bring before the reader the true view of [constitutional] powers maintained by its founders." The "expositions" in his *Commentaries* were to be regarded "less . . . as my own opinions than as those of the

---

[114] J. Marshall to J. Story, Dec. 12, 1832, quoted in *Proc. Mass. Hist. Soc.,* 14:351(1901).

[115] On the flyleaf of a copy of the 1833 edition of Story's *Commentaries on the Constitution* in the library of the University of Virginia School of Law, a student made the following notation: "The Devil himself [could] not have written a worse book—1845." See also the discussion of Story's *Commentaries on the Constitution* in A. Upshur, *A Brief Enquiry Into the True Nature and Character of Our Federal Government* (1840), and H. Tucker, *Lectures on Constitution Law* (1843). Another distinction between Kent's and Story's commentaries was their implicit attitude toward the relationship of one legal subject to another. Tucker had followed Blackstone in treating law as a field composed of several subjects but presented as an integrated whole. Subsequent commentators who sought to treat American law in its entirety, such as Nathan Dane, Hoffman, or Kent, followed this pattern. Kent, for example, divided his volumes of commentaries into various subjects, but presented the volumes as a unified treatment of the law. Story's attitude was different: he sought to produce individual volumes on legal subjects, the aggregate of which would represent a survey of American law. With Story a new pattern became established: the commentators who followed Story confined their treatments to subject areas, such as contracts, property, criminal law, or evidence.

It is suggestive that the time period between the appearance of Kent's *Commentaries* (1826) and Story's first volume (1832) has been associated with the emergence in America of a "public-private distinction," that is, a separation of society into "public" and "private" realms, the latter realm ostensibly free from state interference. By separating "public" and "private" legal subjects Story may have tacitly reinforced this distinction. See M. Horwitz, "The History of the Public/Private Distinction," *U. Pa. L. Rev.,* 130:1423 (1982).

great minds which framed the constitution." He had exhibited "a solicitude, not to go incidentally beyond the line pointed out by the authorities."[116]

In short, if one took Story's stance as a constitutional commentator at face value, he had merely found and digested the authoritative views of others. His task, he implied, had been that of a compiler of obscure data and recorder of the opinions of the framers. While he admitted that he drew heavily from interpretations of the Constitution made by a Court on which he sat, he stressed that the "extraordinary Judgments" that he had relied upon had been those of Marshall. He, the commentator, had expressed no "novel views." These claims were startling, given the context in which Story's *Commentaries on the Constitution* appeared, the correspondence surrounding its appearance, the reaction of allies such as Marshall and Kent to the work, and the position of Story himself as a Justice in the Supreme Court and a visible champion of the Union and "consolidation." In a similarly charged context, thirty years earlier, Tucker had been explicit about the argumentative and speculative modes of his commentary. Story took pains to de-emphasize those modes.

When one examines commentaries on American legal subjects in the period between Tucker's and Story's volumes, a discernible pattern emerges. The more authoritative the volume of commentary purports to be, the less openly free the commentator regards himself to take substantive jurisprudential positions. The changes from Tucker through Hoffman and Kent to Story are not so much changes in what the commentator does—each of the successive commentaries identifies itself as a scientific synthesis and arrangement of legal subjects—but in what the commentator admits to doing. In Kent, and especially in Story, one can see the presence of "policy" arguments made inferentially, as in Kent's discussion of the French rule governing partial loss in marine insurance, or attributed to sources other than the commentator. And as the sources of American law, including commentary itself, increased in the early nineteenth century, those inferences and attributions were easier to make.

Several of these inferential "policy" arguments can be found in Story's *Commentaries on the Constitution*. An example is Story's discussion of the question whether "independent of the constitution of the United States, the nature of republican and free governments does not necessarily impose some restraints upon the legislative power."[117] Story answered that question as follows:

> It seems to be the general opinion, fortified by a strong current of judicial opinion, that since the American revolution no state government can be presumed to possess the transcendental sovereignty to

---

[116] J. Story, *Constitution*, I, v–vii.   [117] J. Story, *Constitution*, III, 268.

take away vested rights of property; to take away the property of A and transfer it to B by a mere legislative act."[118]

He then gave a justification for that "general opinion":

> The fundamental maxims of a free government seem to require that the rights of personal liberty, and private property, should be held sacred. At least no court of justice, in this country, would be warranted in assuming, that any state legislature possessed a power to violate and disregard them. . . . The people ought not to be presumed to part with rights, so vital to their security and well-being, without very strong and positive declarations to that effect.[119]

This language was accompanied by a footnote, which included references to five Marshall Court decisions and one volume of commentary. Three of the five decisions had been written by Story.[120] The commentary cited, Thomas Sergeant's 1830 treatise on constitutional law, had based its support for the so-called "vested rights" principle on three of those decisions.[121] The language in which Story advanced his justification for protecting vested rights of property because of their intimate connection with the nature of republican and free governments was virtually identical to language he had employed in his opinion for the Court in *Wilkinson* v. *Leland*,[122] the first case he cited. Story the commentator had established the primacy of a "general opinion" largely through citations to the decisions of Story the judge. Nowhere did he explicitly declare this "general opinion" to be largely his own. "General opinion" was treated as an apolitical, neutral concept.

The appearance of Story's *Commentaries* revealed, then, not only the changed stance of commentators but the increasing opportunities for writers of legal commentary to frame and to influence jurisprudential issues. As noted, the emergence of legal commentary in the early nineteenth century can be seen as a conscious response by one segment of the legal profession to the increased demand for legal services in America. That response took the form of syntheses and digests of American law that claimed the status of authoritativeness and thereby increased the stat-

---

[118] Ibid.

[119] Ibid., 268–69.

[120] Terrett v. Taylor, 9 Cranch 43 (1815); Town of Pawlet v. Clark, 9 Cranch 292 (1815); Wilkinson v. Leland, 2 Pet. 627 (1829).

[121] T. Sergeant, *Constitutional Law* (2d ed., 1830), 359–60. Sergeant cited Terrett v. Taylor, supra, note 120, Town of Pawlet, supra, note 120, and

Fletcher v. Peck, 6 Cranch 87 (1810), which Story had also cited.

[122] See 2 Pet. at 657. The only difference between Story's language in *Wilkinson* and that quoted above from his *Constitution* was the substitution in the latter of "strong and positive declarations to that effect" for "strong and direct expressions of such an intention."

ure and visibility of the lawyers whose commentaries identified them as authorities. The increased domain of American law, the growing complexity of legal doctrine, the growth of a market economy whose transactions had legal ramifications, a tradition of modification of and adaptation of established rules, and the perceived importance of law in a republican form of government combined to make "authoritative" statements of legal rules and doctrines a service of considerable utility. In exchange for performing this service commentators were tacitly granted the power not merely to collect and synthesize legal doctrines but also to participate in their formulation. They were a group of political theorists whose professional ideals, such as legal science, tended to mask the political dimensions of their work.

By the appearance of Story's first volumes of commentaries an informal network of people having an interest in the production and dissemination of judicial opinions and legal commentary was well established. The network included federal judges, such as Story, Marshall, Bushrod Washington, and Joseph Hopkinson, who in 1829 had become a federal district judge in Pennsylvania;[123] treatise writers such as Nathan Dane, Kent, Hoffman, Timothy Walker, and Peter Du Ponceau; reporters of judicial decisions, such as Henry Wheaton, William Johnson, Richard Peters, John Gallison, William Mason, and Henry Gilpin; and legal educators, such as Hoffman, Kent, Story, and Simon Greenleaf. Story's correspondence between 1815 and 1835 testifies to the efforts made by these men to facilitate the publication and dissemination of judicial opinions; encourage the production of digests, collections of documents, and treatises; secure judgeships, reporterships, and professorships for persons committed to the scientific study of law; and write unsigned reviews of each other's published works.

Story appears to have been the center of this informal network. He was an intimate of both Washington and Marshall and exchanged correspondence with them about legal issues that surfaced in federal circuit court decisions.[124] He had pressed hard for Hopkinson's appointment to the federal bench.[125] Dane had made a bequest of a chaired professorship to Harvard Law School on the condition that Story occupy it.[126] Kent and Story began in 1819 a correspondence that was to continue until

---

[123] See B. Konkle, *Joseph Hopkinson* (1931), 267.

[124] See discussion in Chapter III, at 173–74.

[125] Story had been interested in securing a federal judgeship for Hopkinson as early as 1826. See J. Story to J. Hopkinson, Mar. 8, 1826, in Joseph Hopkinson Papers, Historical Society of Pennsylvania, Philadelphia, Pa. See also the discussion in Konkle, *Hopkinson*, 253–60.

[126] See W. Story, *Life and Letters*, II, 1–7.

Story's death: one of its central concerns, as Story put it in his initial letter, was "to preserve in the profession a steady spirit of original investigation, and to unite a deep respect for authorities with an habitual inquiry into their consonance with principles."[127] Story had reviewed Hoffman's *Course of Legal Study* favorably, and encouraged Walker, one of his first students at Harvard, to write an *Introduction to American law*, which was to appear in 1837, dedicated to Story.[128]

Of all of Story's efforts to "preserve . . . a steady spirit of original investigation . . . in the profession," the most important to him were reporting and legal education. Reporting was the mechanism by which judicial opinions reached the profession and the public, and Story took pains to observe, encourage, and publicize the efforts of reporters. His involvement with Henry Wheaton and Richard Peters forms the subject of a subsequent chapter, and he assiduously cultivated the friendship of John Gallison and William Mason, reporters of his federal circuit court decisions. In 1821 he told William Johnson, Kent's reporter, that "you have conferred the highest honor on [New York] State; and . . . its judicial character abroad has been greatly elevated by your excellent Reports."[129] Three years later, on Johnson's retirement, Story wrote him that "your thirty volumes of Reports will form an era, not merely in the jurisprudence of New York, but of America."[130]

Perhaps the most important to Story of all the reporters he cultivated was Simon Greenleaf, with whom he had become acquainted in 1819, when Greenleaf was practicing law in Portland, Maine, and Story was holding federal circuit court in the same city. Greenleaf wrote Story of his interest in publishing an annotated edition of Henry Hobart's *Reports*[131] and of his general interest in legal scholarship and commentary. Story responded by expressing pleasure "that there are gentlemen of the Bar who are willing to devote their leisure to the correction and ministration of the noble science of the law," and encouraged Greenleaf "to give public notice" of his proposed edition.[132] A year later Story wrote Greenleaf that he was "perfectly satisfied" with Greenleaf's "plan of editing Hobart"[133] and by 1821 noted that Greenleaf had planned a list of "Overruled Cases," a digest of the "Rules of the Federal and

---

[127] J. Story to J. Kent, Aug. 21, 1819, quoted in ibid., I, 330.
[128] T. Walker, *Introduction to American Law* (1837), v.
[129] J. Story to W. Johnson, Nov. 11, 1821, quoted in W. Story, *Life and Letters*, I, 407.
[130] J. Story to W. Johnson, May 16, 1824, quoted in ibid., 429.
[131] H. Hobart, *Reports* (1671).
[132] J. Story to S. Greenleaf, Nov. 11, 1819, quoted in W. Story, *Life and Letters*, I, 329.
[133] J. Story to S. Greenleaf, June 9, 1820, Simon Greenleaf Papers, Harvard Law School Library. I am indebted to Professor Alfred S. Konefsky of the Faculty of Law of the State University of New York at Buffalo for making transcripts of the Story–Greenleaf correspondence available to me.

State Courts,'' and volumes of the reports of cases decided in the new state of Maine, which had entered the Union in 1820.[134] By 1822 Greenleaf had sent Story a copy of his Maine Reports, which Story pronounced ''highly creditable to the Bar and Court'' and urged Greenleaf to call ''Greenleaf's Reports.''[135]

Four years later three volumes of Greenleaf's Maine Reports had appeared, and Story hailed the last ''as a new proof of your talents, which adds one more to the monuments of your fame and professional learning.''[136] Greenleaf was sufficiently encouraged by these comments to approach Story in October 1826 about the possibility of succeeding Henry Wheaton as the Reporter of the Marshall Court, Wheaton having intimated that he would resign. Story responded that he had already committed himself to support Richard Peters for the Reportership, but that had he known of Greenleaf's interest he would have supported him instead.[137] In the last sentence of the letter Story promised Greenleaf, ''I will remember you hereafter in better season.'' Peters succeeded Wheaton in 1827, and Greenleaf continued his law practice in Portland and his editions of the Maine Reports. Story acknowledged another volume in 1829, noting that ''the Court and the Reporter have fully maintained their reputation.''[138]

In 1829 Greenleaf wrote Story that he was giving up the practice of reporting Maine decisions, and asked Story again about the Supreme Court Reportership. Story responded, ''[I]t is by no means improbable that Mr. Peters may not incline . . . much longer to remain Reporter; in which event I shall sustain your claims with all my might.'' Story also indicated ''that I have other thoughts also respecting you in events, which may occur hereafter, which may bring you back to Massachusetts.''[139] Those events occurred four months later, when Professor John Ashmun, who had been Story's colleague on the faculty of Harvard Law School, died in April 1833 at the age of thirty-two. Ashmun, who had practiced law in addition to his teaching responsibilities, had been ill for several years, and Story may well have anticipated his death. On April 6, however, five days after Ashmun's death, Story dispatched a letter to Greenleaf in which he referred to ''the unexpected death of Professor Ashmun,'' which had placed Harvard ''in a sad predicament.'' He then asked Green-

---

[134] J. Story to S. Greenleaf, June 2, 1821, Greenleaf Papers; J. Story to S. Greenleaf, Dec. 11, 1821, quoted in W. Story, *Life and Letters*, I, 404; J. Story to S. Greenleaf, July 7, 1821, Greenleaf Papers.

[135] J. Story to S. Greenleaf, May 25, 1822, Greenleaf Papers.

[136] J. Story to S. Greenleaf, Aug. 26, 1826, ibid.

[137] J. Story to S. Greenleaf, Oct. 10, 1826, ibid.

[138] J. Story to S. Greenleaf, Oct. 10, 1829, ibid.

[139] J. Story to S. Greenleaf, Dec. 19, 1832, ibid.

leaf "whether if you were elected you would accept the appointment."[140] Greenleaf responded that "the opportunity to return to Massachusetts under circumstances so flattering is one I feel every disposition to embrace," but felt that he could not leave Maine before "the middle of July."[141] Further letters followed, discussing details, and on April 24 Story wrote that "you were unanimously elected Royall Professor of Law to fill the vacancy occasioned by the death of Professor Ashmun."[142] Greenleaf accepted three days later.[143]

The Story–Greenleaf relationship provides a detailed example of the simultaneous functions commentators saw themselves as serving. As noted, Story was a judge, a professor, a contributor to legal and popular journals, a reviewer, and a publicist as well as a commentator; Greenleaf at various times in his career had been a reporter, a practitioner, and a scholar in addition to joining Story on the Harvard Law School faculty and subsequently publishing an important treatise on the law of evidence.[144] For Story and Greenleaf, compiling digests of English cases, reporting state judicial decisions, writing treatises, giving lectures, and deciding cases were all pursuits of one devoted to legal science. By "tracing every principle to its original foundations, through all the shifting authorities,"[145] Story, Greenleaf, and their juristic associates were claiming the authority to articulate the prevailing rules and doctrines and to formulate the principal legal issues of their times. They were creating and publicizing their interpretations of American law, and in the process enhancing their own authority and the image of their profession.

In sum, the scholarship of Kent, Story, and other commentators in the Story network amounted to a claim on the part of one sector of the legal profession to establish the terms not only of legal discourse but of political discourse as well. In Kent's and Story's commentaries issues of moral philosophy and political economy, issues that Tucker had regarded as unsettled and Hoffman as auxiliary to law, were cast in legal terms. Story ended his *Commentaries on the Constitution* with the following admonition:

> The future . . . may well awaken the most earnest solicitude, both for the virtue and the permanence of our republic. The fate of other republics, their rise, their progress, their decline, and their fall, are written but too legibly on the pages of history . . . They have

---

[140] J. Story to S. Greenleaf, Apr. 6, 1833, ibid.
[141] S. Greenleaf to J. Story, Apr. 11, 1833, ibid.
[142] J. Story to S. Greenleaf, Apr. 24, 1833, quoted in W. Story, *Life and Letters*, II, 149.

[143] S. Greenleaf to J. Story, Apr. 27, 1833, Greenleaf Papers.
[144] S. Greenleaf, *Treatise on the Law of Evidence* (1846).
[145] Story to Kent, Aug. 21, 1819, supra, note 127.

perished; and perished by their own hands. Prosperity has enervated them, corruption has deposed them, and a venal populace has consummated their destruction . . . Patronage and party, the triumph of a leader, and the discontents of a day, have outweighed all solid principles and institutions of government. Such are the melancholy lessons of the past history of republics down to our own. . . .

[T]he slightest attention to the history of the national constitution must satisfy every reflecting mind, how many difficulties attended its formation and adoption, from real or imaginary differences of interests, sectional feelings, and local institutions. It is an attempt to create a national sovereignty, and yet to preserve the state sovereignties; though it is impossible to assign definite boundaries in every case to the powers of each. The influence of the disturbing causes, which, more than once in the convention, were on the point of breaking up the Union, have since immeasurably increased in concentration and vigor. . . . If, under these circumstances, the Union should once be broken up, it is impossible that a new constitution should ever be formed, embracing the whole Territory. We shall be divided into several nations or confederacies, rivals in power and interest. . . . Let the history of the Grecian and Italian republics warn us of our dangers.[146]

In this passage Story conveyed an explicit and an implicit message. The explicit message was communicated in the conventional language of republican theory and advanced the standard republican version of cultural change. Republics declined and fell; their decline was caused by luxury, corruption, and venality; demagoguery, patronage, and partisanship were manifestations of the decline. The problem of decline was accentuated in America by the federated character of American government, the inevitable presence of legal and sectional interests, and the "concentration and vigor" of centrifugal forces in the culture. Dissolution would inevitably bring about decay; the lessons of history were too plain. Only through the continued presence of the "national constitution" could decay be warded off. The "structure" of the Constitution, Story said, "has been created by architects of consummate skill and fidelity; its foundations are solid . . . its arrangements are full of wisdom and order. . . . It has been reared for immortality. . . . It may, nevertheless, perish in an hour by the falling or corruption, or negligence of . . . the people."[147] The integrity of a republican constitution, then, was a bulwark against the disintegrating forces of cultural change and an antidote against corruption, decay, and decline. The "national constitution" being that bulwark, those who advocated "disturbing causes" that might break up the Union, and with it the Constitution, were fostering cultural disintegration.

---

[146] J. Story, *Constitution*, III, 756–59.

[147] Ibid., 759–60.

The implicit message of Story's remarks can be discerned when one notes the place in his *Commentaries* where this passage appeared. His invocation of a "national constitution" as the savior of republican government in America came only after he had spent three volumes detailing the Constitution's history and origins, discussing its "nature," setting forth rules for its interpretation, and painstakingly analyzing each of its textual provisions. What Story meant by a "national constitution" was the Constitution that had been set forth in the pages of his *Commentaries*. His claim that fidelity to that Constitution was necessary to save the Republic was in effect an argument for the vindication of his interpretation of the document. He had made a claim for the primacy of legal commentary as an authoritative technique for articulating the relationship of republican ideology to cultural change.

Story's warning at the close of his *Commentaries* thus gives us a clear picture of the central purposes of early-nineteenth-century legal commentary. The scientific articulation of legal rules and doctrines was, among other things, an exercise in elevating legal discourse to a position of centrality in early American thought. It represented a claim that the interaction of republicanism with cultural change in America most significantly represented itself in legal issues, and therefore that persons with legal training could most authoritatively respond to the social pressures engendered by that interaction. The emergence of legal commentary in early-nineteenth-century America was thus one of the principal ways in which an articulate segment of the legal profession responded to the complex interaction of republican ideology and cultural change.

The response of the commentators, however, was not offered as political theory but as "scientific" digests of the law "as it was." The claim of commentary to be authoritative rested on the purported neutrality and disinterestedness of the commentator. Even Tucker had made a version of this claim, separating his avowedly theoretical "tracts" from his "digest" of Blackstone in light of Virginia law, as if the latter exercise were apolitical in nature. Hoffman, Kent, and Story had progressively subsumed their role as speculative theorists to their role as digesters and compilers, even though contemporaries recognized the political orientation of their work.

The lesson for future jurisprudential commentators offered by the early-nineteenth-century practitioners of that art appeared to be clear: political interpretations of legal issues gain more legitimacy if they are offered as professional, neutral, "scientific" efforts. While Tucker and Story, for example, held radically different views on the proper distribution of sovereignty in a federalized republic, they both could offer their views as part of an enterprise designed to make American law more scientific. Thus the most significant contribution of the elite commentators to early-nineteenth-century jurisprudence was not their assiduous digests and compilations. It was rather their implicit judgment that while law and political ideology in America were closely linked, they should be treated as capable of being separated. Professional commentary was claimed to be distinct from political theory even though it was a version of it. The image of law fostered by the commentators was that of an entity above or apart from politics.

The appearance of legal commentary thus not only suggested that American law was capable of being synthesized and thereby made more accessible and intelligible to a wider audience, but also that legal discourse was an important medium through which social change could be interpreted and ideology recast. In the implicit claims of Story and his "scientific" colleagues one gets a fuller sense of the meaning of Tocqueville's observations in *Democracy in America,* made at the same time that Story's commentaries began to appear,[148] that "scarcely any political question arises in the United States that is not resolved, sooner or later, into a judicial question."[149] One also begins to get a fuller sense of the role of the Marshall Court Justices as actors in their culture. The Court was seeking to perform a function analagous to that of the commentators: to establish itself as a guardian of the principles of republican government and an authoritative, apolitical expounder of the relevance of those principles to a rapidly changing cultural environment. In the process it was also seeking to perpetuate the same image of law fashioned by the commentators. The irony in that effort was that the very persons most dedicated to perpetuating the image of law as distinct from politics were those in the best position to appreciate how tenuous that distinction was.

If legal discourse in the early nineteenth century is regarded not merely as a medium for discussing specialized professional issues but also as a vehicle for the airing of larger ideological disputes, the central issues of American jurisprudence in the period take on an expanded historical significance. Jurisprudential inquiry and debate become not simply features of a dialogue among professional savants but one of the several efforts of articulate persons in positions of power and prominence to explore the application of republican ideology to cultural change. Juris-

---

[148] Story believed that Tocqueville's analysis of American legal institutions in *Democracy in America* had borrowed extensively from *Commentaries on the Constitution.* In a letter to Francis Lieber, written on May 9, 1840, Story said that Tocqueville had "borrowed the greater part of his reflections from American works, and little from his own observations." "The main body of [Tocqueville's] materials," Story claimed, "will be found in the Federalist and in Story's Commentaries on the Constitution." Quoted in W. Story, *Life and Letters,* II, 330.

[149] A. de Tocqueville, *Democracy in America* (2 vols., 1835), II, 180.

prudence, in the early nineteenth century, can be seen as a form of ideological communication, possessing the special language of a professional medium but not restricted in its scope to lawyers and judges. Central jurisprudential issues of the period can likewise be seen as having wider implications than their specialized vocabulary might suggest.

The most fundamental, and at the same time the most unsettled, issue of early-nineteenth-century American jurisprudence involved the nature and sources of law in the American republic. Since "frequent recurrence to first principles" was taken to be a vital exercise in the preservation and development of republican forms of government, and republican governments were acknowledged to be quintessentially governments of laws, it seemed necessary to identify what was meant by "law" in America and where legal principles originated. But the changing character of early American culture made that effort a formidable one. Acknowledging that America was a government of laws did not make the meaning of law any more intelligible.

American law, in early-nineteenth-century jurisprudence, was implicitly considered to be an amalgam of seven discrete sources. While each of the sources was considered proper material on which to base a judicial decision—and the term "law" as used in this section refers to the rules and principles declared in the opinions of courts—the sources were not given identical weight as authorities. A precise description of the nature and sources of American law at the time of the Marshall Court requires the designation not only of source categories but of subcategories within those categories and of hierarchies among the categories. In rough outline, and in descending order of authority, the sources were the Constitution; the common law, which contained numerous subcategories within it; the law of nature, or of nations, a source of unwritten principles of natural justice; the civil law, which included not only principles established in civilian codes but the writings of civilian commentators; and specialized sources whose pertinence was restricted to discrete areas, such as equity, the law merchant as laid down in specialized mercantile courts in England and on the Continent, the lex loci, which referred to the local law of a jurisdiction on a matter peculiarly confined to that jurisdiction, the "law admiralty and maritime," as manifested in the decisions of British and Continental admiralty courts, and American federal and state statutes. Statutes and other specialized sources were regarded as not so much within the hierarchy of authority as to one side of it: while being confined to discrete situations, in those situations (an "admiralty" case, a case arguably governed by a federal or state statute, a "local law" case, an "equity" case) they had a significant claim to authoritativeness.

The system of jurisprudence that these sources and their interaction represented had certain interpretive conventions, which themselves represented tacitly shared ideological assumptions. No jurist in the early nineteenth century, for example, seriously questioned a proposition that to moderns might seem worth debating, that in declaring the law judges could look to a variety of sources, some written and some unwritten, some foreign and some indigenous, some specific and some general in their nature. A significant corollary to that proposition was that judges could themselves fashion the rules for deciding which sources to give more prominence than others. Thus not only was the theory of American law as an amalgam of various sources entrenched, the more radical theory that judges could themselves decide which sources to rely upon in specific cases was also entrenched.

An important distinction of early-nineteenth-century jurisprudence requires attention at this point. While jurists conceded the amalgamated character of American law, and conceded that the choice among potential sources in a given case was a judicial choice, they implicitly reserved the right to suggest that the choice was inapposite. If in an admiralty case, for example, a judge chose to use a common law rule as a source of authority, that choice might be attacked as an unwarranted exercise of judicial discretion. Admiralty cases, critics might suggest, were to be governed by admiralty and maritime rules, not by common law rules. Such criticism was regarded as appropriate even though American law was conceived of as a blend of diverse sources and even though the process of investigating, weighing, and applying sources was tacitly delegated to judges.

This distinction may help to explain the presence of an issue that numerous early-nineteenth-century commentators invested with great significance. The issue was the relationship between the jurisdiction of a court and the substantive rules that court declared. As we will see, jurists at the time of the Marshall Court were vitally concerned about the jurisdictional limits of the federal courts created by the Constitution. Some jurists advanced the argument that if the common law were adopted in the federal courts federal court jurisdiction would be unlimited; others countered that those courts were of limited jurisdiction, fixed by Congress, and that they could declare rules—common law rules or otherwise—only within the limits of their jurisdiction.

The debate over this issue, which will be subsequently reviewed, can be seen as a debate that revealed an internal inconsistency in early-nineteenth-century jurisprudence. The inconsistency stemmed from the simultaneous presence of an amalgamated conception of law and a partitioning of the various sources of law. While American law was taken as a blend of multiple sources, at the same time certain types of cases were taken to be governed by certain types of authorities. If judges could pick and choose among sources, could they not also, by the technique of analogy, derive rules for one area from another? And who was to determine whether analogies were appropriate in given cases?

These questions—questions, I will suggest, about the limits of judicial discretion in an age in which judges were not considered lawmakers in the modern sense—were particularly acute in two areas of early-nineteenth-century jurisprudence, constitutional interpretation and common law interpretation by the federal courts. They were also present in natural rights cases and admiralty cases, which are considered in subsequent chapters; and they were present in equity cases as well. But they engendered the greatest amount of attention and debate in the first two areas.

In subsequent chapters discussing the Marshall Court's constitutional law opinions we will note that the Justices drew upon a range of sources to justify their decisions: the text of the Constitution, the plain or ordinary meaning of words, common law definitions or principles, natural law, local practices and rules, principles of equity, and what they termed "general principles of republican government." One of the habitual tasks of the Court in these cases, we will see, was to fashion a relationship between the positive words of the Constitution and these extraconstitutional sources, and the chapters on constitutional adjudication will suggest that the Court's principal response to this task was to pack the Constitution's text with meaning derived from a variety of other places.

Many of the Court's efforts to pack constitutional language were controversial, such as its finding that the Contract Clause embodied the unwritten principle that a legislature cannot take property from A and give it to B without compensation, or its finding that enumerated powers given to Congress gave rise to additional unenumerated "implied" powers. The controversiality of the Court's decisions emanated not only from the results the Court reached but also from the jurisprudential attitude with which it approached constitutional interpretation. Critics suggested that even if one granted the Court a general authority to interpret the Constitution, as claimed by Marshall in *Marbury* v. *Madison*,[150] what gave the Justices the power, in its interpretation, to apply one set of legal sources—"general principles," common law rules, etc.—to an area of law ostensibly governed by another source, the Constitution's own language? One might acknowledge the interpretive power, they argued, but insist that "interpretation" was to be strictly limited to the words of the document, with no room for extraconstitutional sources.

In his *Commentaries on the Constitution* Story responded to this criticism by proposing "rules of interpretation" in constitutional adjudication.[151] If such rules were "correctly laid down," he suggested, "it will save us from many embarrassments in examining and defining" the Constitution's language. He then promulgated nineteen rules of constitutional interpretation, in order, he said, to establish "some fixed

---

[150] 1 Cranch 137 (1803).    |    [151] J. Story, *Constitution*, I, 382.

standard."[152] He listed various authorities for the rules, ranging from decisions by the Marshall Court to treatise writers to the *Federalist* papers. Of the nineteen rules Story advanced, eight were supported by reference to Marshall Court decisions, four by reference to treatise writers, and three by reference to *The Federalist*. For the remaining four rules Story cited no authorities at all.

The question raised by Story's exercise is how he could claim that his nineteen propositions amounted to "rules." He had supported his rules by outside authorities in only seven of nineteen instances: the other twelve were rules that Story had either asserted to be correct or had supported by reference to decisions of the Marshall Court, on which he himself sat. A disinterested party might wonder how "uniform rules of interpretation" of the Constitution could be "expressly or tacitly agreed on by . . . disputants."[153] when most of the rules were being declared either by the judges who were themselves engaging in the interpretation or by one of those judges in a subsequent commentary.

That Story was aware of the capacity of interpretive rules to be convenient rubrics for reaching particular results can be seen in his discussion of a competing set of rules for constitutional interpretation that he ascribed to Jefferson. "Mr. Jefferson," Story said in his *Commentaries on the Constitution,*

> has laid down two rules, which he deems perfect canons for the interpretation of the constitution. The first is, "the capital and leading object of the constitution was, to leave with the states all authorities, which respected their own citizens only, and to transfer to the United States those, which respected citizens of foreign or other states; to make us several as to ourselves, but one as to all others. In the latter case, then, constitutions should lean to the general jurisdiction, if the words will bear it; and in favour of the states in the former, if possible, to be so construed." . . .
>
> The second canon is, "on every question of construction [we should] carry ourselves back to the time, when the constitution was adopted; recollect the spirit manifested in the debates; and instead of trying, what meaning may be squeezed out of the text, or invented against, conform to the probable one in which it was passed."[154]

Story then attacked both of those rules. The first, he argued, was "contradicted" by provisions of the Constitution that gave powers to the states that affected their relations with other states or with foreign countries. Moreover, the first rule ignored "the intent or objects of . . . particular clause[s]"; it insisted that state power be preferred "if possible" in all

---

[152] Ibid., 383.
[153] Ibid.

[154] Ibid., 390.

clauses respecting state citizens.[155] The second rule was "utter[ly] loose and incoheren[t]." The "spirit of the debates" at the time of the framing was difficult to decipher, diverse, potentially manifest in a variety of sources, and on many issues out of date.[156] The rules smacked of convenience: they harmonized well with Jefferson's own conviction that the constitutional interpretations of the Marshall Court had been insufficiently respectful of state sovereignty and overly inclined to advance novel readings of the constitutional text that were more in keeping with a consolidationist ideology than with the spirit of the Framers.

But if Jefferson's rules for constitutional interpretation were purposive, what about Story's own? Consider his discussion of the question whether the language and powers of the Constitution were to be construed strictly, as Tucker had argued in his edition of Blackstone. After summarizing Tucker's argument, Story took fourteen pages to refute it. He suggested that Tucker had wrenched the proposition out of context from the writings of Vattel.[157] He challenged Tucker's reading of the reserved powers in the Tenth Amendment.[158] He then denied that the Constitution was a social compact, as Tucker had claimed,[159] argued that it had been established by the people, not the states,[160] noted that nowhere in the Constitution was there any language calling for strict construction of federal powers,[161] and concluded that a "strict interpretation" would be "subversive of the great interests of society" and would "derogate" the Constitution "from the inherent sovereignty of the people."[162] The appropriate construction for the Constitution was "a reasonable construction."[163]

Virtually all the sources cited by Story to support his critique of Tucker were Marshall Court decisions, including one written by himself. He gave almost no reasons for his conclusion that the Constitution should be construed "reasonably" rather than "strictly." In fact, as we will see in the Court's sovereignty cases, the question of construction of the Constitution was difficult to separate from the theory of sovereignty held by the interpreter. If a clause in the Constitution delegated power to the federal government, or restricted the powers of the states (as most of the clauses construed by the Marshall Court in its constitutional cases did), whether one interpreted the clause "reasonably" or "strictly" produced an outcome that either expanded or contracted the sovereignty of the federal government, or restricted or entrenched the sovereignty of the states. Since there was no language in the Constitution declaring how its

---

[155] Ibid.
[156] Ibid., 391.
[157] Ibid.
[158] Ibid., 395.
[159] Ibid., 397.
[160] Ibid., 400.
[161] Ibid., 402.
[162] Ibid., 407.
[163] Ibid.

Chapter II: *The Origins of Marshall Court Jurisprudence* II

text should be construed, nothing except one's theory of sovereignty compelled one interpretive rule or another. That Story and other Marshall Court Justices had favored a "reasonable" rather than a "strict" construction of constitutional provisions did not establish reasonable construction as a uniform rule of interpretation.

Many of Story's "rules" could be subjected to a similar analysis. They were rules that had aided the Marshall Court in reaching particular results that were consistent with an ideological perspective, one that for the most part was sympathetic to restrictions on state power in the name of private rights or in the name of national sovereignty. One might suggest that rather than the rules of interpretation having produced the outcomes in these Marshall Court decisions, the outcomes had dictated the particular canon of interpretation chosen. But Story's rules were offered as "uniform" guides, to "save us from many embarrassments" in constitutional interpretation.

What, then, was the purpose of Story's rules? Taken together, the rules appear designed neither to promote uniformity in constitutional adjudication nor to avoid "embarrassments" in construction, but to maintain an image of judges as being bound by professional conventions while at the same time affording judicial interpreters of the Constitution as much freedom as possible to draw on a range of extraconstitutional sources in the interpretation of the constitutional text. Such rules as the "fundamental rule," Rule I, that "the interpretation of all instruments is to construe them according to [their] intention," and that "the intention of the law is gathered from . . . the context . . . the effects and consequence, or the reason and spirit of the law";[164] or Rule XII, that questions of concurrent power "must be decided by [themselves] upon [their] own circumstances or reasons";[165] or Rule XV, that "every word in the constitution is to be expounded in its plain obvious and common sense,"[166] explicitly support this view of the purpose of Story's rules, and the other rules can also be said to be consistent with that purpose.

Here we notice the same distinction identified earlier. In formulating his rules Story did not seem overly concerned with the fact that judges were laying down their own interpretive rules or buttressing those rules by citing their own decisions: he treated those acts as the mere expounding of already existing legal principles. His concern was more with the fact that constitutional interpretation might be confined to the words of the text itself, a positivistic document with the potential to be "strictly" read, rather than to the variety of other sources—history, common law analogies, context, common sense, changing circumstances—that a judge could

[164] Ibid., 383.
[165] Ibid., 431.

[166] Ibid., 436.

117

draw upon in declaring constitutional law. Story's rules were thus designed to give judges as much freedom as possible to blend constitutional and common law. The rules were announced, however, as if they were themselves time-honored legal conventions that constrained judicial interpretation within proper analytical boundaries.

Story's rules of interpretation thus had major ramifications for two of the great jurisprudential questions of early-nineteenth-century America, the proper sources and methodology of constitutional interpretation and the proper sources and methodology of common law interpretation. It is one of the purposes of the remainder of this section to show that while the two questions can be viewed as conceptually distinct, early-nineteenth-century jurists perceived them as necessarily bound together.

Reconstructing the jurisprudential universe of the Marshall Court thus requires abandoning several of the premises governing modern analyses of the Court's actions. Modern Supreme Court Justices are perceived as "making law" in their interpretations of the Constitution, statutes, or common law doctrines; early-nineteenth-century judges were not similarly perceived. The task of finding and declaring a source of law, and applying it to a particular case, was not regarded as lawmaking. However, serious questions of judicial discretion remained, one being whether a judge was entitled to apply the particular source he had deemed appropriate to a given case, another being whether the court in which the judge sat was entitled to decide that sort of case at all. The objection to federal court judges' declaring common law rules, for example, was not that in so doing those judges would be making rather than finding law, but that they either had no authority to use the common law or other source in the particular case they were deciding, or that they had no authority to declare common law rules at all in a given substantive area.

The paradox of early-nineteenth-century jurisprudence was thus the absence of a theory of judicial decisionmaking that treated interpretation or rule declaration by judges as the equivalent of lawmaking, and at the same time the presence of an assumption that the federal judges and the federal courts would reflect the political interests and goals of the federal government. This paradox helps to explain why so many of the major jurisprudential controversies of the Marshall Court were controversies about the scope of federal court jurisdiction. Whether the admiralty jurisdiction of the federal courts was broad or narrow in scope, whether the federal courts had jurisdiction over common law crimes, and whether the Supreme Court of the United States could review the final decisions of state courts on constitutional questions were among the major legal issues of the time. In each case the issue was not joined on the legitimacy of given Supreme Court interpretations of the Constitution or given declarations of common law rules by the lower federal courts. The Court's critics tacitly assumed that if the federal courts, including the Supreme Court, could decide admiralty or criminal law cases at all, or could substitute their interpretations of the Constitution for those of state courts, they would fashion rules that furthered the interest of the federal government and those who wished to augment its powers. The issue was joined on the power of the federal courts to claim legal authority over an area of American life.

Over time, the term "common law" underwent a change in meaning that reflected early-nineteenth-century jurists' effort to make this paradox intelligible. At first the term, as used in early nineteenth-century commentary, signified a specific area of law, the body of doctrines associated with the nonconstitutional and nonstatutory decisions of English and early American courts. Over time the term came to have an extended meaning, signifying the use of a discretionary methodology in which judges found, declared, and applied legal principles, employing a variety of sources. In this second sense the "common law" came to be seen as part of a broader jurisprudential effort to make American law more scientific, that is, predictable, uniform, systematic, and less susceptible to judicial discretion. But common law judging in this second, methodological sense actually had the effect of enhancing both judicial discretion and judicial power.

A parallel evolution can be seen in the area of constitutional interpretation. Those who criticized the Marshall Court's constitutional decisions regularly did so on the ground that the Court had no jurisdiction to entertain the cases it was hearing—no power, in other words, to decide the cases at all. Once the Court's jurisdiction was established, attention shifted to the Court's interpretations of the constitutional text. In the course of its decisions, however, the Court itself established interpretive canons for constitutional exegesis, canons that were, of course, supportive of the results it reached. While the Court's results were criticized, and its interpretive canons opposed by others, critics did not focus on the Court's discretion, once its jurisdiction was established, to fashion the canons themselves, and the Court treated its process of establishing interpretive canons as indistinguishable from finding or declaring the law itself.

The result was a fusion in early-nineteenth-century American jurisprudence of a methodology by which common law rules were promulgated by courts and a methodology by which the text of the Constitution was interpreted. While commentators regularly perceived the partisan consequences of this fusion from the point of view of results, they did not for the most part emphasize that the methodology actually strengthened the discretionary lawmaking powers of judges. Where intimations of this sort surfaced, apologists for the methodology quickly de-emphasized the subjective or partisan features of judging.

The generalizations made in the last paragraphs can be illustrated by revisiting[167] one of the major political and jurisprudential controversies of the late eighteenth and early nineteenth centuries. In 1798, in the federal circuit court case of *United States* v. *Worrall*,[168] an indictment for bribery, Supreme Court Justice Samuel Chase and district court judge Richard Peters had taken different positions on the question of whether, as Chase put it, "the United States, as a federal government, have [a] common law."[169] Chase concluded that, at least with respect to crimes and punishments, "the common law authority . . . has not been conferred upon the government of the United States, which is a government in other respects also of a limited jurisdiction." Congress could confer such a power of statute, Chase suggested, but until Congress did it would be "improper [for federal judges] to exercise a discretion" to make bribery punishable by resort to common law precedents.[170] Peters, on the other hand, concluded that "the power to punish misdemeanors, [which was] originally and strictly a common law power" was one "of which . . . the United States are constitutionally possessed." Peters's reasoning was as follows:

> Whenever a government has been established . . . a power to preserve itself, was a necessary, and an inseparable concomitant. But the existence of the federal government would be precarious, it could no longer be called an independent government, if, for the punishment of offences of this nature, tending to obstruct and prevent the administration of its affairs, an appeal must be made to the state tribunals. . . .
> The power to punish misdemeanors, is originally and strictly a common law power. . . . It might have been exercised by congress in form of a legislative act; but it may, also . . . be enforced in a course of judicial proceeding. Whenever an offence aims at the subversion of any federal institution . . . it is an offence against the well-being of the United States; from its very nature, it is cognizable under their authority; and consequently it is within the jurisdiction of [the federal] court[s].[171]

Peters's position was supported a year later by Chief Justice Oliver Ellsworth in *United States* v. *Williams*,[172] a case involving an indictment

---

[167] Additional discussions of the issues treated in the next several pages may be found in C. Warren, *The Supreme Court in United States History* (3 vols., 1922), II, 160–64; C. Haines, *The Role of the Supreme Court in American Government and Politics* (1944), 174–75; W. Crosskey, *Politics and the Constitution in the History of the United States* (2 vols., 1953), I,

626–40; M. Horwitz, *The Transformation of American Law, 1780–1860* (1977), 9–15. See also Dwight Henderson's *Congress, Courts and Criminals* (1985) for a discussion of federal criminal law between 1801 and 1829.
[168] 2 Dall. 384 (1798).
[169] Ibid., 394.
[170] Ibid., 395.  [171] Ibid.
[172] The *Williams* decision was re-

of an American seaman who had voluntarily renounced his citizenship to accept a foreign commission, and in a charge to a South Carolina grand jury in another criminal case. In the latter case Ellsworth's reasoning approximated that of Peters:

> An offence consists in transgressing the sovereign will, whether that will be expressed, or obviously implied. Conduct, therefore, clearly destructive of a government or its powers, which the people have ordained to exist, must be criminal.[173]

The issue of whether there was a "common law of the United States," as distinguished from the received and modified English common law doctrines that existed in the courts of the states, contained within it three questions that modern jurisprudence has tended to separate. The first question, which formed the basis of most of Peters's and Ellsworth's reasoning, was whether the newly created federal government, merely by virtue of its sovereignty, could criminalize and punish conduct "destructive" to its "well being" even though it had not specified in advance the conduct sought to be punished. Peters and Ellsworth answered that question affirmatively, and Chase negatively, and the question has been rendered, in shorthand, as the "federal common law of crimes" question.[174] We shall subsequently have occasion to consider that question in more detail.

The second question lurking in the phrase "common law of the United States" was whether Congress, in exercising its constitutional power to create federal courts, could give those courts discretionary power to fashion substantive common law rules and subjects. Answering this question affirmatively required a fusion of two arguably discrete concepts, the concept of jurisdiction and the concept of substantive rulemaking. Article III of the Constitution had given Congress the power to "ordain and establish" federal courts, and had defined the "judicial Power" of those courts as extending to "all Cases, in Law and Equity, arising under [the] Constitution [and] the Laws of the United States."[175] Did this mean that the Constitution had given the federal courts power to declare their own common law rules? In debating the constitutionality of the Alien and Sedition Acts in 1798, Harrison Gray Otis assumed that the answer to that question was obvious. The distinction in Article III between cases "arising under the Constitution" and cases arising under federal statutes, Otis claimed, could mean only that the former set of cases were common

---

ported in the *Connecticut Courant* (Hartford, Conn.), Sept. 30, 1799.
[173] Ellsworth's charge to the grand jury was reported in the *Virginia Argus* (Richmond, Va.), Aug. 9, 1799.

[174] See, e.g., Horwitz, *Transformation*, 9–11.
[175] U.S. Const., Art. I, Sect. 1; Art. I, Sect. 2.

law cases. The effect of the clause was to give to the federal courts "that legal discretion which has been exercised in England since time immemorial."[176] In making this argument, Otis, as one of his opponents in the debate pointed out, had assumed that discretionary rule-declaration power in "all" cases meant that the jurisdiction of the federal courts was unlimited.[177] This question has come to be rendered as the "jurisdiction/ substantive law" question, and that question shall also receive further attention in this section.[178]

There was a third separable question embedded in the issue of whether a "common law of the United States" existed. This question has attracted comparatively little attention from modern scholars, but it was of great significance to contemporaries of the Marshall Court. The question was whether, if the Constitution vested Congress with authority to give the federal courts power to declare the common law in "all Cases," that act not only conceivably made the jurisdiction of the federal courts unlimited, it made the jurisdiction of Congress itself, or any branch of the federal government, also unlimited. Answering this question affirmatively may seem quixotic to moderns, since an affirmative answer appears to ignore separation of powers principles and to assume an identity of interest among the federal judiciary and the federal executive and legislature.[179] But at the time the "common law of the United States" issue first arose the concept of judicial review was not firmly established, Congress was not clearly perceived as the source of opposition to as well as support for the executive, and the departments of the federal government were conceived in some quarters as just that—departmental associates engaged in partisan struggles with the states. An example of contemporary

---

[176] Otis's argument is reported in *Debates and Proceedings in the Congress of the United States*, 5th Cong., 2d sess. (1797–98), 2145–57. Hereafter cited as *Annals*.

[177] Albert Gallatin in *Annals*, 2141, 2157.

[178] The distinction between the jurisdiction of the federal courts and the substantive rulemaking powers of those courts was addressed by several early-eighteenth-century commentators. See the discussion infra, pp. 137–44.

[179] Morton Horwitz, in his *Transformation of American Law*, suggests that "it is difficult to understand precisely what . . . the assertion that if the federal judiciary possessed jurisdiction to impose criminal sanctions without a statute it would be able to obliterate al constitutional limitations on the federa

government . . . was all about." Horwitz cites James Sullivan, who published a treatise on the constitutionality of freedom of the press in 1801, as "under[standing] that the question of common law jurisdiction involved no special constitutional difficulties, for all that it required was that federal common law jurisdiction be limited to those substantive crimes over which Congress had legislative power." Horwitz, *Transformation*, 10. The subsequent discussion in the text is intended to suggest that the assertions described by Horwitz emanated from widely, although not universally, held assumptions by contemporaries of the Marshall Court about the relationship between the powers of the respective branches of the federal government.

perceptions can be seen in a comment from the *Virginia Argus,* responding to that portion of Ellsworth's charge to the South Carolina grand jury in which he stated that the "common law of the United States" extended to "acts manifestly subversive of the National government, or of some of the powers specified in the Constitution." The *Argus* commented:

> It has long been feared that the Government of the United States tended to a consolidation, and consolidation would generate monarchy. Nothing can so soon produce the first as the establishment of the doctrine that the common law of England is the law of the United States; it renders the State governments useless burthens; it gives the Federal Government and its Courts jurisdiction over every subject that has hitherto been supposed to belong to the states; instead of the General Government being instituted for particular purposes, it embraces every subject to which government can apply.[180]

In this passage one can see all of the questions separated in the preceding paragraphs linked in one argument. "Common law of the United States" means common law doctrines on all subjects, including political crimes such as sedition and treason. Common law rulemaking power in the federal courts gives these courts "jurisdiction over every subject." And the "General Government," with the jurisdiction of its courts thereby expanded, now "embraces every subject to which government can apply." The assumptions made in the *Argus*'s comment render more intelligible an often quoted remark of Thomas Jefferson's, made a year later, that "the principle of a common law being in force in the United States" would "possess . . . the general government at once of all the powers of the State Governments and reduce . . . us to a single consolidated government."[181] The *Argus*'s comment also fleshes out a passage in Tucker's commentaries which at first glance might seem obscure:

> Judge Ellsworth is reported, on a late occasion, to have laid it down as a general rule, that the common law of England is the unwritten law of the United States, in their national, or federal capacity. . . .
>
> This question is of very great importance, not only as it regards the limits of the jurisdiction of the *federal* courts; but also, as it relates to the extent of the powers vested in the *federal government.* For, if it be true that the common law of England, has been adopted by the United States in their national, or federal capacity, the jurisdiction of the *federal courts* must be coextensive with it; or, in other words, *unlimited:* so also, must be the jurisdiction and authority of the *other*

---

[180] *Virginia Argus* (Richmond, Va.) Aug. 9, 1799.
[181] T. Jefferson to Gideon Granger, Aug. 18, 1800, quoted in P. Ford, ed., *The Writings of Thomas Jefferson* (10 vols., 1892–99), VII, 451.

*branches* of the federal government; that is to say, their powers respectively must be, likewise, *unlimited*.[182]

The "musts" in Tucker's passage designate his assumptions that common law rulemaking power in the federal courts was not only synonymous with unlimited jurisdiction for those courts under the Constitution but also synonymous with unlimited constitutional power for Congress. Those assumptions led him to answer the third "common law of the United States" question affirmatively: if the federal courts could declare their own common law, there would be no constitutional limits on the jurisdiction of those courts and of other branches of the federal government. We shall designate the question Tucker answered affirmatively as the "coterminous power" question.

The proposition that the judicial power of the federal government was coextensive with its legislative power, while maintained by both supporters and critics of the doctrine of a federal common law, and, as we shall see, by both the Justices of the Marshall Court and those who deplored the Court's extension of the powers of Congress and the judicial courts, was rarely subjected to searching analysis by late-eighteenth- and early-nineteenth-century commentators. A representative example of the treatment of the coterminous power question can be found in Hamilton's *Federalist* essay No. 80. The subject of that essay was the "extent of the authority of the [federal] judiciary." Hamilton argued that the authority of the federal courts ought to extend to several categories of cases, including "all those which concern the execution of the provisions expressly contained in the Articles of Union,"[183] by which he meant the express text of the Constitution. He then justified the inclusion of that category of cases as follows:

> [I]t is impossible, by any argument or comment, to make it clearer than it is in itself. If there are such things as political axioms, the propriety of the judicial power of a government being coextensive with its legislature may be ranked among the number. The mere necessity of uniformity in the interpretation of the national laws decides the question. Thirteen independent courts of final jurisdiction over the same cases, arising from the same laws, is a hydra in government, from which nothing but contradiction and confusion can proceed.[184]

Why was coterminous power a "political axiom"? One reason seemed to lie in the nature of government itself; as Peters said in *Worrall*, an "independent" government needed "the power to preserve itself,"

---

[182] Tucker, *Blackstone*, I, Appendix E, 380. Emphasis in original.
[183] Publius [Alexander Hamilton],

*The Federalist* No. 80 (C. Rossiter, ed., 1961), 438.
[184] Ibid., 439.

which was associated with the process by which its laws were implemented. Another was "uniformity": the implementation of "national" laws needed to be made by national courts lest "confusion and contradiction" result from different constructions by different state courts. But neither of these reasons seem dispositive, at least to moderns. Judicial implementation of laws is not indistinguishable from legislative promulgation: laws have to be applied to discrete situations and thereby interpreted, and in the process their meaning may change. Nor does it follow that if only federal courts interpret a federal law "uniformity" will result, as the presence of conflicts among the modern federal circuit courts of appeal repeatedly demonstrates. In describing the coterminous power principle as a "political axiom," Peters, Hamilton, Tucker, and their contemporaries seem to have made two assumptions that we no longer hold: the assumption that the interests of the federal legislature in making laws and the federal judiciary in implementing them were identical, and the assumption that the federal law embodied in the Constitution, congressional statutes, and perhaps common law doctrines would always be declared by the federal courts in a "uniform" fashion.

Thus while coterminous power theory assumed an identity of interest among the departments of the federal government (and, parenthetically, among the departments of an individual state), it also assumed that federal judges would simply be declaring the will of federal legislatures, that is, the will of the law. But this assumption does not seem to have been carried over into the common law decisionmaking of federal judges; there the declarations appeared more discretionary to contemporaries, and thus more potentially partisan.

The assumption made by Tucker and other contemporaries of the Marshall Court that federal legislative or executive power was coterminous with federal judicial power thus reveals another dimension of the jurisprudential climate in which the Court functioned. Once that assumption was seriously held, every potential expansion of federal judicial power, if warranted by the Constitution, was a potential expansion of legislative power, and every potential extension of Congress's power at the expense of the states a potential increase in the jurisdiction of the federal courts. The phenomenon triggering this dramatic expansion of the powers of the federal government, for Tucker, Jefferson, and other critics of the position advanced by Peters and Ellsworth, was the claim that the Constitution implicitly and explicitly delegated power to the federal courts to declare their own common law doctrines. Thus one can see that from the time the "common law of the United States" issue first surfaced constitutional law and common law, in early-nineteenth-century jurisprudence, were inextricably linked.

Two themes that were to be continuously repeated throughout Marshall's tenure emerged from the perceived linkage of constitutional law and common law in early-nineteenth-century jurisprudence. The first theme provided the ideological backdrop for the great constitutional sovereignty cases of the Marshall Court. It was the theme of "consolidation," a catchword for the aggrandizement of the sovereignty of the federal government at the expense of the sovereignty of the states. While the Marshall Court's contribution to theories of sovereignty in early American jurisprudence and its response to the theme of consolidation will primarily be covered in Chapter VIII, a brief note on the relationship between that theme and the "common law of the United States" issue seems in order here.

Consolidation, in the eyes of those who opposed it, beginning with Tucker and Jefferson at the turn of the century and extending through Spencer Roane, Thomas Ritchie, William Brockenbrough, John Taylor, and John Calhoun, the "states' rightists" of the 1820s and 1830s, was predicated on two unfounded premises and two unfortunate consequences of those premises. One of the premises was that in the formation of the Constitution the ultimate sovereign powers being delegated to the federal government were not those of the states but those of the people as individuals. There had, on the contrary, been a compact of the states and the federal government at the Constitution's creation, anticonsolidationists argued; the result was that many sovereign powers had been reserved by the states as distinguished from the people at large. The other unfounded premise was that the federal judiciary, in the guise of interpreting the Constitution, could review the activities of state courts and legislatures. Judicial review of the acts of other *federal* departments might have been anticipated in the constitutional design, but not judicial review of the sovereign acts of the states. The Constitution had not been designed to bring about so radical a transfer of power.

The above two premises could be seen to be unfounded, anticonsolidationists believed, because of their consequences. The first consequence of diminished state sovereignty was the aggrandizement of every branch of the federal government. If one assumed an identity of interest among the federal departments, the expansion of one branch's jurisdiction would result in the expansion of the powers of another. Eventually the only check on the government would be the people as individuals; state sovereignty would disappear. The importance of preserving state sovereignty and the idea of the Constitution as a compact, then, were augmented by the anticonsolidationists' assumption that federal power was coterminous.

Similarly the premise that federal judicial review could extend to sovereign acts of states was revealed to be unfounded by the assumption that no distinction existed between the jurisdiction of the federal courts and their substantive rulemaking powers. If the federal courts could review and constitutionally invalidate acts of state courts and legislatures, their powers would become unlimited once they were given the discretion to declare their own common law rules. Common law rulemaking power was assumed by anticonsolidationists to be synonymous with the power to review cases in the first place, and the jurisdiction of the federal courts, the rulemaking powers of those courts, and the legislative or executive powers of the federal government were all lumped together.

By this reasoning Tucker, Jefferson, and other anticonsolidationists were able to erect a powerful chimera. By rejecting compact theory, installing judicial review, and adopting the common law in the federal courts, they claimed, those intent on radically transforming sovereign relationships in the new American nation had prepared the way for total consolidation. Each expansion of federal power in one area, or in one department, meant an expansion of the federal government as a whole.[185] It was in this context, with the "consolidation theme" sounding all around them, that Marshall and the other Justices of the Supreme Court made their decisions and sought to articulate their theories of constitutional interpretation. While the Justices may have had a clean constitutional slate to write upon in the sense that the Constitution they were interpreting had rarely been interpreted before, they were not operating in an ideological vacuum. Their jurisprudential universe was bound in by the ideological assumptions of their peers, among those the assumptions of the anticonsolidationists.

Thus one major consequence of the early articulation of the "common law of the United States" issue was the emergence of the consolidation chimera as an ideological backdrop to constitutional adjudication on the Marshall Court. While that consequence has received the greatest attention from previous commentators, and will receive considerable attention in this work, it was arguably not the most fundamental jurisprudential controversy that surfaced during Marshall's tenure. An even more significant controversy concerned the nature of judging itself, and was likewise embedded in the all-encompassing phrase "common law." Buttressing the assumption that if the common law were received in the federal courts the jurisdiction of those courts and that of the other federal departments would be unlimited was an implicit theory about the judicial declaration of legal rules. While that theory should not be confused with modern theories, which tend to conceive of judges as making rather than finding or declaring law, it anticipated the possibility that judging might be a partisan political exercise. The debate about the common law in the federal courts during Marshall's tenure was to an important extent a debate about judicial discretion and, ultimately, about whether judges could be expected to make decisions in a nonpartisan, disinterested fashion, merely following the will of the law, not their own wills, in their interpretations.

---

[185] See the correspondence cited in Warren, *Supreme Court*, I, 163–64.

To reach that level of the debate, however, we need to pass temporarily from constitutional jurisprudence and return first to the "common law of crimes" question as it was considered in early-nineteenth-century commentary, and then to the evolving meaning of "common law" itself.

"Common law," to early-nineteenth-century American jurists, was a term that was capable of several different meanings. It referred, first, to English law generally; second, to a specific kind of English law, the adjudications of the common law courts, King's Bench, Common Pleas, and Exchequer, as distinguished from other types of adjudications, such as those of equity, admiralty, or mercantile courts; third, any law declared by courts, as opposed to that declared by legislatures; fourth, a body of principles, derived over time by courts in specific case settings, and often unwritten in the sense of unreported and available only through memory; and fifth, a methodology by which judges, drawing on a variety of sources, gradually adapted principles to new contexts and conditions. In early-nineteenth-century juristic commentary, then, the term could mean several things, and could evoke quite different responses. One of the purposes of the subsequent discussion will be to trace the shifting meanings of the term and to explore their implications.

In addition, the place of the common law in American law came over time to be perceived as subsuming a bundle of related but distinguishable questions. Were Americans, being previously subjects of England, to be governed by English common law rules? Were judicial decisions handed down before the American Revolution to be given effect? Were the substantive rules of decision in the new federal courts that had been created by the Constitution to be common law rules? And were the rules of decision employed by the federal courts to be identical to, or different from, those employed by state courts? Those questions, while logically related, came to be invested with different degrees of significance, the last two questions being perceived as much more significant.

The first two questions were commonly given a uniform answer by eighteenth-century American judges and jurists: that Americans, having been English subjects before the revolution, took "as much of . . . the common law of England . . . with [them] as the nature of things will bear."[186] In practice, this meant that the rules of decision in the newly formed American states would be English common law rules, subject to modification if conditions warranted. Twelve of the thirteen original states passed "reception" provisions between 1776 and 1798. The practice of receiving the English common law in American courts was made in the face of language in two of its most respected commentaries, those of

---

[186] Richard West (1720), quoted in S. Sioussat, *The English Statutes in* *Maryland* (1903), 21.

Chapter II: *The Origins of Marshall Court Jurisprudence* II

Coke and Blackstone, both of whom had argued that the common law had no force in America.[187]

After independence, reception of the common law did not require strict adherence to English precedents, although that practice seems to have existed earlier in the eighteenth century.[188] English doctrines were increasingly treated as open to modification if inapplicable to New World conditions. But at the same time the common law was treated as a source of timeless principles, consistent with natural justice, founded in reason, conforming to custom, and influenced by divine revelation. As a consequence common law doctrines, as articulated by judges, were seen as principles that had been discovered rather than new laws that were being made. A sharp distinction can be seen in eighteenth-century jurisprudence between common law, which, although articulated by judges and capable of being modified to suit changing conditions, was invested with qualities of universality, permanence, and even mystery, and statute law, which was recognized as the willful and positivistic acts of legislators. One late-eighteenth-century judge expressed concern lest "the distinct boundaries of law and legislation be confounded," and identified judges as "expositors of existing [law]," rather than "makers of new law."[189]

Americans were thus bound by those common law rules that seemed consistent with principles of natural justice in America. American judges were conceded to be the expositors of common law rules, but since the rules themselves needed to retain their consonance with fundamental principles, exposition was not the same as lawmaking. The conception of law implicit in the term "common law" was thus a complex one. Law was not easily separable from justice, custom, or even religion, and as such was conceived as a repository of timeless or universal principles, but at the same time it was a body of doctrines whose applicability to the conditions of American life needed to be regularly evaluated.

The complexities inherent in the term "common law" became readily apparent when the Constitution was framed. While the text of the Constitution was conceded to be a paramount source of law in those areas included within its coverage, many areas were not included.[190] Congress,

[187] Coke took that position in Calvin's Case, 7 Coke Rep. 1, 17 (1608); Blackstone agreed in W. Blackstone, *Commentaries on the Law of England* (4 vols., 1765–69), IV, 107. For a discussion of "reception" statutes, see E. Brown, *British Statutes in American Law, 1776–1834* (1964).
[188] See the discussion in Horwitz, *Transformation*, 6–7.
[189] James Iredell in Chisholm v. Georgia, 2 Dall. 419, 448 (1793).

[190] Robert Cover, in his imaginative and provocative study, *Justice Accused* (1973), argued that "[t]hroughout the sixty year period following the Revolution . . . the courts uniformly recognized a hierarchy of sources of law for application in which 'natural law' was subordinate to constitutions, statutes, and well-settled precedents" (p. 34). It is difficult to know what to make of that statement in light of the numerous contemporary references, documented

for example, was given enumerated powers, and an assumption of the constitutional design was that if Congress exercised those powers through legislation, its laws would supersede any competing ones. But Congress's enumerated powers were limited, and it did not choose to exercise all the enumerated powers it possessed. Where Congress had not acted or the text of the Constitution did not seem applicable, other law—state statutes or the common law—arguably governed. But what did common law mean in the constitutional design?

The most immediate application of this question involved the law to be applied in the new federal courts that Congress, via Article I of the Constitution, had the power to create. The Constitution said only that Congress could create the courts, nothing about what kind of law they should administer. In the Judiciary Act of 1789 Congress exercised its powers to some extent, creating federal district and circuit courts in eleven districts, which in most cases conformed to the boundaries of existing states. Congress then added the following language:

> And be it further enacted, that the laws of the several states, except where the constitution, treaties or statutes of the United States shall otherwise require or provide, shall be regarded as rules of decision in trials at common law in the courts of the United States in cases where they apply.[191]

The origins of this language are shrouded in mystery, and its interpretation has been a matter of considerable debate. Section 34 of the Judiciary Act of 1789, in which the language appeared, was added to the judiciary bill sometime between June 12 of that year, when "a bill to establish the Judicial Courts of the United States" was first read in Congress,[192] and September 22, when the bill was passed by both houses of Congress and sent to President Washington for his signature.[193] The sec-

---

throughout the bulk of this chapter, to law in America as a conglomerate of multiple sources, including "natural law" and "natural justice." Cover may have intended to limit his remarks to constitutional adjudication, and it does seem fair to say that where the language of a statute or a constitution explicitly governed a situation, the courts acknowledged the primacy of that source. But in the numerous areas where no such coverage existed, early-nineteenth-century judges and commentators clearly felt free to draw on a variety of sources, including natural law.

Moreover, the question whether natural law was superseded by positive laws or took primacy over them was unsettled. The relationship between natural law and constitutional law on the Marshall Court is the subject of Chapter X.

[191] 1 Stat. 73 (1789).

[192] *Journal of the Senate of the United States of America* [from the First Session of the First Congress through the Second Session of the Sixth Congress], 1:50 (1789–81). Hereafter cited as *Senate Journal*.

[193] *Senate Journal*, 1:144.

tion was not in the original bill that was first presented to the Congress[194] but appeared in the eventual enacted version. There is no surviving record of when or how it was added, although a draft copy of its text, allegedly authored by Oliver Ellsworth, has survived.[195]

The genesis of Section 34 provides an illustration of the significance contemporaries attached to the role of the common law in the newly framed American government. It also reveals the ambiguities that emanated from that concept in the late eighteenth century. In June 1789 the attorney general of Delaware wrote to one of the senators from his state, detailing his concerns about the pending judiciary bill. Among them he listed the fact that

> indefinite expressions unavoidably made use of will create difficulties. Common law and statute law are referred to in the act. Have the states the same accurate and fixed idea of both or either as applied to themselves individually or to the States generally? Do we refer to the common law and statute law of England? This is derogatory. What then, is the common and statute law of the United States? It is difficult to answer. Yet the dignity of America requires that it be ascertained, and that where we refer to laws they should be laws of our own country. If the principles of the laws of any country are good and worthy of adoption, incorporate them into our own.[196]

A month later a Pennsylvania lower court judge, Edward Shippen, wrote to one of the Pennsylvania senators expressing similar views. "It is of the utmost consequence," Shippen argued, "that the Judiciary law should establish in express terms by what law we are to be governed. There are some loose Expressions in the Bill concerning the Common Law, but it is no where said the Judges should decide according to it." Shippen believed that "[t]he American states have generally adopted the common law," and felt that "[t]he United States should likewise adopt it." He also noted that "the common law alone [might] not be sufficient," and that American states had already "improve[d]" it and "amend[ed]" it through statutes.[197]

These letters reveal that contemporaries of the framers of the Judiciary Act were aware, first, that the term "common law" was capable

---

[194] See C. Warren, "New Light on the History of the Federal Judiciary Act of 1789," *Harv. L. Rev.,* 37:49, 51 (1923).

[195] Ibid., 85 ("[T]he original slip of paper on which the amendment containing Section 34 was written. . . , with little doubt, in Ellsworth's handwriting").

[196] Gunnery Bedford, Jr., to George Read, June 24, 1789, in W. Read, ed., *Life and Correspondence of George Read* (1870), 482–83.

[197] E. Shippen to Robert Morris, July 13, 1789, Edward Shippen Papers, Historical Society of Pennsylvania, Philadelphia, Pa.

of multiple meanings; second, that the common law of England had already been received by American states; and, third, that the reception of the common law did not preclude its modification or supplementation by other laws. They were also interested, for practical as well as patriotic reasons, that such modifications take place ("where we refer to laws they should be laws of our own country"). And they were well aware that one of the most important jurisprudential questions being addressed in the Judiciary Act was whether the federal courts of the United States would receive the common law.

An answer to that question was provided by the language of Section 34 of the Judiciary Act, but the answer was marvelously ambiguous. The only extant draft of Section 34 that has survived was a chit in the handwriting of Oliver Ellsworth, which contained an original and an edited text.[198] The language of the edited text was that which appeared in the final printed bill that Congress adopted. The original text read:

> And be it further enacted, that the statute law of the several States in force for the time being and their unwritten or common law now in use, whether by adoption from the common law of England, the ancient statutes of the same or otherwise, except where the constitution, treaties or statutes of the United States shall otherwise require or provide, shall be regarded as rules of decision in the trials at common law in the courts of the United States in cases where they apply.[199]

This language was apparently not edited by Ellsworth himself, as has been surmised,[200] but by someone else, perhaps a clerk or another member of the Senate Judiciary Committee charged with drafting the Judiciary Act. Ellsworth's original text contained two alternative versions, the version quoted above and a shorter one in the margin that substituted the phrase "the Laws of the several states" for all the language between "statute law" and "the same or otherwise" in the longer version. Bracket marks were placed before "statute" and after "otherwise." When the editor made a decision to use Ellsworth's shorter version, he crossed out the language in the margin, crossed out the words "statute law" and all of the language from "in force" through "otherwise" in the longer version, and inserted the word "Laws" in place of "statute law." The insertion was made in handwriting plainly different from the hand that had written the original text.

Ellsworth's original text conveys a clearer sense of the assumptions

---

[198] Charles Warren discovered the chit in 1923 "in the attic of the capitol." Warren, "New Light," 50.

[199] A copy of the text of the chit is reproduced in Warren, "New Light," 87.
[200] Ibid., 86.

late-eighteenth-century American lawyers made about the content of American law. Ellsworth's original version distinguished between "statute law," "unwritten or common law," and "the constitution, treaties or statutes of the United States." He assumed that in the federal courts constitutional provisions, federal treaties, and federal statutes would supersede other forms of law. He also assumed that common law was not statutory law; that its content would not be constant ("their unwritten or common law now in use"); and that American common law could be derived from "adoption from the common law of England," adoption of "the ancient statutes of the same," or from some other source. Finally, he assumed that "the statute law of the several states" was "in force for the time being." Those assumptions are consistent with a theory of American law, both in its statutory and common varieties, as flexible and changing in its content; as not, in its latter form, the equivalent of the common law of England; and as capable of being derived from sources other than English cases and statutes. Law, as conceived by Ellsworth in his original text of Section 34 of the Judiciary Act, was an entity with multifarious sources, with a changing content, and of an uncertain duration.

The editing of Ellsworth's text converted his illustrative language to a single, highly ambiguous phrase, "the Laws of the several states." That editing has resulted in a continuing controversy over the content of substantive law in the federal courts, an explanation of which will not detain us here. It should be pointed out, however, that Ellsworth's original text, by particularizing what he meant by "the Laws of the several states," lends support to the view that that phrase probably did not mean "the law of the particular state in which a given federal court sits," but rather something like "the collective laws of all of the states, whether statutory or common, taken as sources of rules and doctrines."[201] This meaning may also be said to be consistent with the general theory of American law implicit in Ellsworth's language.

---

[201] Contemporaries of Ellsworth used the word "several" to describe a collective mass and the word "respective" to describe individual components in that mass. In St. George Tucker's 1803 edition of Blackstone, for example, Tucker spoke of "several sovereign and independent states" as "unite[d] . . . together," and the Constitution as having been "solemnly entered into by the several states of North America." Tucker, *Blackstone*, I, Appendix D, 140. In the same discussion he noted that "a convention was . . . summoned in every state by the authority of their respective legislatures" (p. 151) . Note the use of the adjective "several" to refer to states as a body and the adjective "respective" to refer to states as individual units. My understanding of the evolution of the Judiciary Act of 1789 has been enhanced by the research and commentary of Professor Wilfred Ritz of Washington and Lee Law School.

Since many early-nineteenth-century jurists conceived of American law as an entity whose sources and content were not fixed, they regarded the use of a federal common law in the new federal courts as a significant and controversial development. We have noted that the potential dangers in a concession that a "common law of the United States" existed were identified by Tucker in his 1803 edition of Blackstone. We have previously considered Tucker's constitutional argument, emphasizing its assumption that the adoption of the common law by the federal courts would result in an unwarranted extension of federal judicial and, because of the coterminous power doctrine, federal legislative powers. But the bulk of Tucker's critique was based on the nature of the common law itself.

Fifty-five of Tucker's pages in his tract on "the common law of the United States" issue were devoted to describing the nature of the common law in America. He examined the transmutation of English common law to the American colonies,[202] the adoption and modification of the common law of the colonies,[203] the abrogation or retention of the common law after the Revolution,[204] and the "engraft[ing]" of English common law "upon . . . the constitution of the United States."[205] His conclusions were summarized in two paragraphs:

> We may fairly infer from all that has been said that the common law of England stands precisely upon the same footing in the federal . . . courts of the United States . . . as the civil and ecclesiastical laws stand upon in England: that is to say, its maxims and rules of proceeding are to be adhered to, whenever the written law is silent, in cases of a similar or analogous nature, the cognizance whereof is by the constitution vested in the federal courts; it may govern and dissect the course of proceeding in such cases, but cannot give jurisdiction in *any case,* where jurisdiction is not expressly given by the constitution. . . .
>
> In short, as the matters cognizable in the federal courts belong . . . partly to the law of nations, partly to the common law of England; partly to the civil law; partly to the maritime law; . . . partly to the general laws and action of merchants; and partly to the municipal laws of any foreign nation, or of any state in the union, where the cause of action may happen to arise, or where the suit may be instituted; so, the law of nations, the common law of England, the civil law, the law maritime, the lex loci, or law of the foreign nation, or state in which the cause of action may arise, or shall be decided, must in their turn be resorted to as the rule of decision, according to the nature and circumstances of each case, respectively. So that each of these laws may be regarded, so far as they apply to such cases, respectively, as the law of the land.[206]

---

[202] Tucker, *Blackstone,* I, Appendix E, 381.
[203] Ibid., 384.
[204] Ibid., 403.
[205] Ibid., 412.
[206] Ibid., 429–30.

Few clearer statements of the prevailing early-nineteenth-century conception of the nature and sources of law in America can be found. For Tucker the common law of England was one of a variety of sources that American courts, state or federal, could draw upon in their decisions. Its "maxims and rules" could furnish "analogies" or guidance in cases where "the written law" (here Tucker meant statute law, as distinguished from "unwritten" or common law) was "silent" and where the "matter" was "cognizable" by the court in question. American law was, he assumed, a composite of English common law, civil law, natural law, maritime law, the law merchant, and local law (the lex loci); and the choice of any of those sources depended upon "the nature and circumstances of each case." Where the circumstances of a case made application of a particular source of law appropriate, that law was "the law of the land."

The conception of American law employed by Tucker provides a clue to his concern that the adoption of the common law by the federal courts might give them, and the federal government, potentially unlimited jurisdiction under the Constitution. Tucker had taken pains throughout the tract to show how English doctrines, in their unmodified form, were inconsistent with republican principles or inapplicable to the conditions of American life. He cited example after example of the modification of common law doctrines by American legislatures. He emphasized the "opposite, discordant, and conflicting . . . codes" of the American colonies.[207] He indicated that most of the modification of English common law in the colonies had been undertaken by legislatures, and pointed out that in his state of Virginia, "it would be a violation of the [state] constitution for the *courts* to undertake to supply all defects of the common law not already supplied by statute."[208] In short, he sought to paint a picture of obsolete English common law rules being modified by American state statutes. This suggests that part of his concern about the consequences of an adoption of the common law by the federal courts was based on a belief that if the federal courts were permitted to use the English common law as their predominant source of rules, they might undo some of the work of American state legislatures.

This belief of Tucker becomes more intelligible if one remembers that in his preface to his 1803 edition of Blackstone he had alluded to the paucity of published sources of law in America, and that throughout his tract on the introduction of the English common law into the federal courts he had distinguished between "written" (statute) and "unwritten" (common) law. If the decisions of American courts were to remain unwritten, and if the English common law were to be installed as the *predominant*

---

[207] Ibid., 403.  [208] Ibid., 405.

source of law in the federal courts, what was to prevent the federal courts from slavishly following English rules, or fashioning their own rules, inspired by English examples? And would not those rules be treated in the federal courts as superseding the statutory laws of American states? And might not those rules, being unwritten, form a potentially vast, amorphous sphere of jurisprudence whose content was known only by federal judges?

The installation of English common law in the federal courts, then, placed the states in what Tucker felt was a double bind. With an unwritten, "foreign" common law established as the predominant source of law in American courts, the judges who declared that law would either be following English rules, which might well be inappropriate to American life, or modifying "defects of the common law" in what Tucker felt was an unauthorized fashion, since the task of supplying defects in the common law was the exclusive province of state legislatures. At this point one encounters another reason why Tucker and his Virginia contemporaries equated a pre-eminent status for the common law in the federal courts with unlimited federal jurisdiction. They believed that a group of federal judges, using an unwritten, foreign body of law as the predominant basis for their substantive rules of decision, was in effect claiming the power to substitute that law for the written rules of state legislatures. In Tucker's view this claim amounted to a potentially unlimited expansion of the jurisdiction of the federal courts and, given his theory of coterminous power, of the federal government itself. Every time a case was cognizable in a federal court, it ran the risk of being decided in a way that ignored state modifications of the common law.

Tucker's argument thus assumed that the cognizability of a case in the federal courts—whether a federal court could take jurisdiction over it—could itself become a question of unwritten federal law. He did not seem to expect that federal judges would be scrupulous about constitutional limits on their jurisdiction, or he believed—as it turned out, quite presciently—that questions of federal jurisdiction would be regarded as questions of substantive law that federal judges could resolve. Despite having concluded in his analysis that the common law "may direct the course of proceeding" in cases in the federal courts, "but cannot give jurisdiction *in any case,* where jurisdiction is not expressly given by the constitution," he nonetheless asserted that federal court jurisdiction would become "co-extensive with [the common law]," or "unlimited." He was thus using the term "common law" in two ways: first, to signify a substantive body of English cases; second, to signify a methodology by which courts exercised discretionary power to reshape substantive rules of law. If the federal courts adopted the substantive English rules, he believed, they would also tacitly adopt the methodology. And the methodology might be employed not only to determine substantive rules but also to determine the jurisdiction of courts themselves. In this second belief Tucker was arguably correct, for although the Constitution of the United States defined the limits of federal court jurisdiction, the question of what branch of the federal government would interpret the Constitution and thereby declare the substance of those limits was unsettled. *Marbury* v. *Madison,* handed down in the same year that Tucker's tract on the reception of the common law by the federal courts appeared, gave an answer to that question which may have confirmed Tucker's worst fears. The Marshall Court held in *Marbury* that the Constitution had mandated that the institution charged with determining the substantive constitutional limits of the jurisdiction of the federal courts was to be the Supreme Court of the United States, a federal court.

The prescience of Tucker's belief that the scope of the jurisdiction of the new federal courts in America was to be affected not only by theories of sovereignty under the Constitution but also by the nature of the common law can be seen by revisiting the "federal common law of crimes" question in juristic commentary between 1812, when the question was first decided by the Marshall Court, and the 1830s, when Story's volumes of commentaries, including his *Commentaries on the Constitution,* were first published. Two issues immediately surfaced in federal common law of crimes cases, the issue whether such cases were cognizable in the federal courts at all, and the issue as to what criminal law those courts could apply if the cases were cognizable. Between 1812 and the 1820s juristic commentary developed sharply different responses to those two issues.

There was little dispute among early-nineteenth-century jurists that the federal courts could entertain certain criminal cases. Crimes committed on the high seas ("admiralty and maritime" crimes), crimes involving federal officials, and crimes in which citizens of different states participated were all considered to be potentially within federal court jurisdiction. At the same time, however, jurists demonstrated concern about, and in some instances overt hostility toward, the idea of federal judges declaring unwritten substantive criminal law rules. An 1800 resolution by the Virginia legislature, charging that the presence of "a new tribunal for the trial of crimes" would "open a new code of sanguinary criminal law, both obsolete and unknown"[209] reflected that hostility, and in 1812 the Marshall Court, in the case of *United States* v. *Hudson and Goodwin,*[210] announced, in an opinion by Justice William Johnson, that the question whether "the Circuit Courts of the United States can exercise a common

---

[209] Quoted in ibid., 405.  |  [210] 7 Cranch 32 (1812).

law jurisdiction in criminal cases" had "been long since settled in public opinion."[211] Johnson argued that the lower federal courts did not derive their jurisdiction from the Constitution, but from Congress; that Congress had not expressly given them jurisdiction over nonstatutory crimes; and that to imply such jurisdiction would be to give the lower federal courts "a . . . much more extended" and "in its nature very indefinite" power to make unwritten substantive criminal law rules.[212]

Johnson's opinion seems to have followed Tucker in equating extensive jurisdiction with "extended" and "very indefinite" substantive common law rulemaking. But another opinion he wrote a year later demonstrated that he recognized a distinction between jurisdiction and substantive rule declaration. In *Hudson and Goodwin* he had said that it was "not necessary to inquire whether [Congress] possesses the power of conferring on [the lower federal courts] any common law jurisdiction in criminal cases."[213] In a circuit court opinion in 1813, however, he admitted that "if Congress had by law vested in [the Supreme Court] jurisdiction over all cases in which the punishing power of the United States might . . . be extended," the Court would then have the power "to decide . . . to what cases that jurisdiction extended."[214] This came close to saying that while the federal courts had been established by Congress as courts of limited jurisdiction, once Congress granted them jurisdiction over a given area they might well have the power to establish substantive rules within the ambit of that jurisdiction, and perhaps even to define its limits themselves.

The distinction hinted at by Johnson between limited federal court jurisdiction and broad substantive rulemaking power within that jurisdiction was also employed, from a different perspective, by Story in his circuit court opinion in *United States* v. *Coolidge*, another 1813 decision.[215] Unlike Johnson, Story was sympathetic to the use of the common law by the federal courts in criminal cases; he had silently dissented from Johnson's opinion in *Hudson and Goodwin*.[216] In his opinion in the *Coolidge* case, which was eventually appealed to the Marshall Court, Story said:

> I admit in the most explicit terms that the courts of the United States are courts of limited jurisdiction, and cannot exercise any authorities, which are not confided in them by the constitution and laws made in pursuance thereof. But I do contend that when once an au-

---

[211] 7 Cranch at 32.
[212] Ibid., 33.
[213] Ibid.
[214] *The Trial of William Butler for Piracy* (1813), 34–35, quoted in Horwitz, *Transformation*, 271. A copy of

the *Butler* opinion, which was unreported, is in the Harvard Law School Library.
[215] United States v. Coolidge, 25 F. Cas. 619 (1813).
[216] See ibid., 621.

thority is lawfully given, the nature and extent of that authority, and the mode, in which it shall be exercised, must be regulated by all rules of the common law. In my judgment, the whole difficulty and obscurity of the subject has arisen from losing sight of this distinction.[217]

Story was, as we shall subsequently see, an advocate not only of extensive jurisdiction for the federal courts but of discretionary authority for those courts to employ a variety of substantive rules, including those of the English common law. But the point of his distinction in *Coolidge* was not merely to argue that there should be a federal common law of crimes; it was to separate jurisdictional powers from substantive rulemaking powers. When one recognizes that this separation was being urged by a jurist who believed in extensive and aggressive activity by federal judges, the distinction Story urged appears to be strategic. By separating jurisdiction from substantive law Story was attempting to remind his audience that the federal courts, after all, were purely creations of Congress: whatever rulemaking power they had was what Congress had given them. His purpose was to minimize the fears Tucker and others had expressed about unlimited federal court jurisdiction. But once jurisdiction had been granted by a federal legislature, Story argued, the power to determine ''the nature and extent'' of that jurisdiction was part of the substantive rulemaking powers of a federal court. Was Story's distinction a distinction without a difference? Here again one confronts the difficulty of reconciling a limited theory of federal jurisdiction with an open-ended conception of the nature and sources of law, which assumed that courts had considerable latitude to search for authorities, analogies, and principles.

The debate over the existence of the common law of crimes also stimulated the next major early-nineteenth-century jurisprudential treatment of the relationship between federal jurisdiction and substantive law. In 1819 John Milton Goodenow, an Ohio lawyer, published ''an *unfinished* composition'' entitled *Historical Sketches of the Principles and Maxims of American Jurisprudence, in contrast with The Doctrines of the English Common Law on the Subject of Crimes and Punishments.*[218] Goodenow's book consisted of ''a series of juridical inquiries,'' including ''whether the common law was adopted by the Constitution and government of the U[nited] States.'' Goodenow had ''withdr[awn] myself from my office . . . in the vacation after our December term, 1818, and prepared [the book] in the course of Eight Weeks.'' He had been ''moved to contemplate such a task from the occasional agitation in [Ohio] courts, of the question of common law jurisdiction.'' He apologized for the book,

---

[217] Ibid., 619.

[218] Goodenow, *Historical Sketches,* iii.

feeling "no pride" in its "matter and execution," but at the same time he announced that "the opinions which I have advanced are as near and dear to me as the liberties I enjoy."[219]

Goodenow's *Historical Sketches* represents an important example of the evolution of American jurisprudential attitudes since Tucker. Goodenow's purpose was to deny the applicability of the English common law of crimes not only to the federal courts but to state courts as well. He invoked some familiar arguments on behalf of this purpose, including the argument that the English common law was "suited to an ignorant and blood-thirsty people," the creation of "haughty, sacrilegious tyrants and dictators," "without beauty, symmetry or even shape," and "entirely diverse and repugnant to the philosophy . . . of this country."[220] All of these arguments had been made by Tucker, and were common to the language of early-nineteenth-century opponents of the common law of crimes.

Goodenow's strong interest in curtailing the power of federal and state courts to fashion substantive rules in criminal cases led him to advance some eccentric jurisprudential theories. He first defined "human laws" as "necessarily of a positive, local existence," "arbitrary" and "not universal."[221] But this characterization turned out not to apply to all laws, but only "those of criminal law." Civil actions were "founded in the private rights and private wrongs of individuals," and thus should be decided by appeal to "natural justice and right reason." Goodenow divided law into "public" and "private" spheres, permitting judicial appeals to reason, justice, and even the common law in the latter sphere, but confining the former sphere exclusively to legislation. In criminal cases, then, the federal courts had no authority at all.

Goodenow's interest in denying the federal courts power to declare any rules in the "public sphere" led him to scrutinize Story's claim that while the federal courts had a limited jurisdiction, they had full discretionary power to declare common law rules within their jurisdictional limits. In *Coolidge* Story had maintained, as noted, that "once an authority is lawfully given [to the federal courts], the nature and extent of that authority, and the mode in which it shall be exercised, must be regulated by the rules of the common law." Goodenow set out to show that Story's distinction rested "almost entirely on verbal disputation instead of principle."[222] Story had used the term "authority," Goodenow argued, in a way that made it synonymous with "jurisdiction."[223] If the

[219] Ibid., iii, iv.
[220] Ibid., vi.
[221] Ibid., 3.
[222] Ibid., 288.

[223] After saying in his *Coolidge* opinion that "the courts of the United States are courts of limited jurisdiction," Story added that they could not "exercise any authorities." 25 F. Cas. at 619.

terms "authority" and "jurisdiction" were regarded as synonymous, Goodenow pointed out, to say that "the nature and extent of the authority and the mode in which it shall be exercised, must be regulated by the rules of the common law" made no sense. Since the jurisdiction of the federal courts was established by Congress, it could not be "regulated" by the common law.

If, however, the terms "authority" and "jurisdiction" were not synonymous, Story, in Goodenow's view, was making a bold claim. The claim was that "authority" meant "a discretion" in the "court . . . in construing their own authority, possessing the qualities of elongation and contraction."[224] In other words, Story was claiming that the nature and extent of the "limited" jurisdiction of the federal courts could be determined by those courts themselves. He was claiming that implicit in Congress's granting of jurisdiction to the federal courts had been a delegation of discretionary power to establish the limits of that jurisdiction in a given case. The power delegated was power to "elongate" or "contract" a jurisdiction that was defined as "limited."

In this critique of Story Goodenow had raised two very significant issues for early-nineteenth-century jurisprudence. The first was whether juristic distinctions between jurisdiction and substantive law could truly be made. It was all very well to say, as Justices on the Marshall Court and commentators regularly said, that a grant of limited powers necessarily involved the authority to implement those powers to their fullest extent within the granted limits, but what did such language mean if the limits were themselves open to interpretation in concrete cases? Congress may have granted limited jurisdiction to the federal courts, or the Constitution enumerated powers to Congress. But if the limits on that jurisdiction or those powers were to be determined by the federal courts, it would seem that those courts had a discretion to ascertain not only the scope of enumerated congressional powers but the scope of their own jurisdiction. Such discretionary determinations, Goodenow intimated, were the equivalent of declaring substantive rules of law.

As Goodenow's critique of Story unfolded, then, its emphasis shifted to the second significant issue. Goodenow had taken pains to show that in civil cases a judicial declaration of common law rules was not only appropriate, but desirable, because judges would necessarily conform law to the immutable principles of reason, justice, and republican ideology. Nowhere in Goodenow's discussion was there a hint that judges, in civil cases, were making law rather than declaring it; that the content of rules was anything but the received wisdom of others. Why, then, this suggestion that discretion in the federal courts in criminal law cases was inappropriate? We shall have occasion to return to the issue of

---

[224] Goodenow, *Historical Sketches*, 288.

judicial discretion subsequently: suffice it to say here that Goodenow had touched a deeper juristic nerve than he perhaps knew.

Five years after Goodenow's *Historical Sketches* the common law of crimes issue stimulated another treatment of the relationship between jurisdiction and substantive rulemaking in the federal courts. Peter Du Ponceau, the provost of the Law Academy of Philadelphia, published his 1824 "valedictory address" to his students under the title *A Dissertation on the Nature and Extent of the Jurisdiction of the Courts of the United States*. The stated purpose of Du Ponceau's "discourse," as he styled it, was to inquire "whether it is competent for the [federal] judicial department, whose sphere of action the Constitution has been peculiarly careful to limit and define, to assume rights in themselves by their decisions *a priori,* and to carry them *provisionally* into effect, before the legislature has made any law upon the subject." While his inquiry had been stimulated by the common law of crimes debate, Du Ponceau felt that the center of his focus should be on "the ambiguous words *common law jurisdiction.*"[225] That focus provides a clue to the primary normative purpose of Du Ponceau's essay: he had set out to recast, and to revitalize, the meaning of common law in America.

Du Ponceau began his analysis by attempting to determine what the phrase "common law" meant, and turned to history for guidelines. "In England," he argued, there was "a metaphysical being called common law," which had originally been a composite of custom, the law of nations, the law merchant, the maritime law, the unwritten British constitution, and religion. The extent and boundaries of the common law, he suggested, were "unlimited" and "unknown." The common law was thus the "source of power or jurisdiction" for those who declared its principles and maxims; it defined and limited not only substantive legal rights and responsibilities but also the "conflicting jurisdictions of the different tribunals in which justice is admonishable." When particular English tribunals engaged in "gradual and successive assumptions of power," their authoritative status was established and consolidated by the common law.[226]

In America, by contrast, political institutions depended on "express written compacts" rather than "uncertain traditions," and thus the common law was "only occasionally referred to for the interpretation of passages in our textual constitutions and statutes." It was "no longer the source of power or jurisdiction, but the means or instrument through which it is exercised."[227] That distinction was designed to be the major contribution of Du Ponceau's *Dissertation,* and it served two functions. Specifically, the distinction suggested that the common law could never

---

[225] Du Ponceau, *Dissertation,* vi.
[226] Ibid., viii, vii.

[227] Ibid., xi.

serve to create federal court jurisdiction where it had not been given by the Constitution or Congress, but that once jurisdiction had been given, the common law could serve as "the national law of the Union, as well as that of the individual states."[228] This was essentially the same distinction Story had advanced in his *Coolidge* opinion. But Du Ponceau's characterization of the common law as a "means or instrument" rather than a "source" had a more general purpose: to suggest that the common law's principal impact was methodological. Because American law was an amalgam of a variety of sources, Du Ponceau suggested, the challenge for American judges was to use those sources in a way that fostered the generation of intelligible and useful "principles." The methodology of the common law, with its emphasis on the derivation of general rules through time and the gradual adaptation of those rules to changed circumstances, was especially suited to judicial decisionmaking in America.

Du Ponceau concluded his essay with an exhortation that might at first appear curious to moderns. After spending several pages detailing the flexibility, adaptability, and susceptibility to change of the common law, he ended with a plea for "the study of general jurisprudence." When "the principles of that science are sufficiently disseminated," he claimed,

[t]hey will fructify, and statutes and judicial decisions will gradually take their colour from them. System will be introduced where it is wanted. Sound theories will take the place of false ones, and the rules of genuine logic will direct their application to particular cases.[229]

This passage reveals the growing investment of early-nineteenth-century jurists in legal science. The great need of American law, Du Ponceau assumed, was for substantive rules that "made sense" in the American environment: rules that identified obligations, protected rights, made economic interchange more certain and predictable, and reflected the unique features of American culture. The common law was an excellent source of those rules because of its adaptive capacity. But that very adaptability and flexibility could engender chaos, illogic, and unsound theorizing. The law in America could become synonymous with a welter of parochial, discordant, anomalous decisions. Science, with its emphasis on system, logic, and the articulation of first principles, was the antidote to the common law run amok.

But were the goals of legal science compatible with a conception of American law as composed of multifarious sources and in a constant state of change? How could a methodology oriented toward the systematization of legal doctrine, whose ultimate end was the derivation and dissemination, through logic, reason, natural justice, and republican the-

---

[228] Ibid., xv.

[229] Ibid., 128–29.

ory, of a series of guiding principles, be reconciled with a theory of American law as inherently adaptive? At a point in his analysis—the very point at which, to modern observers, paradox enters—Du Ponceau took a leap of faith. Science was to yield first principles whose unchallenged logic, justice, wisdom, and truth made them "immutable." The very permanence of those principles produced the "system" Du Ponceau yearned for. Legal science can thus be seen as the second stage in a two-stage juristic effort to transform early-nineteenth-century American law. Law was first to be made "American," next "scientific." The first stage was a loosening process, with an emphasis on the multiplicity of sources available to those charged with declaring substantive legal rules. The second stage was a tightening process, with the rules being reorganized and recast in the form of immutable, scientific principles.

This exercise in examining Du Ponceau's jurisprudential assumptions has brought us far from the debate over the common law of crimes but close to the center of Marshall Court jurisprudence. Du Ponceau, in his essay, defined the central tasks of the Marshall Court as "improving" American law and making it more "scientific." The first required a rejection of obsolete, wrongheaded, or despotic doctrines; the second a recasting of "improved" doctrine so as to harmonize it with fundamental principles, and a systematic application of those principles to new controversies as they arose. "[T]he common law," Du Ponceau noted in his preface, "appears more and more dignified with *American features*. It is observed with pleasure that the opinions of Mr. Chief Justice Marshall are more generally founded upon principle than upon authority."[230] Du Ponceau then continued:

> [W]ith the same satisfaction we see that Judge Washington, while he pays proper respect to modern English decisions, does not hesitate to reject those doctrines which to his discriminating mind do not appear consonant to our American system of jurisprudence. . . .
> Thus the law in this country, as every other science, tends to improvement. This laudable spirit requires only to receive a proper direction. . . . I have ventured to give a few hints to shew the importance of sound principles. The peculiar situation in which we are placed appeared to me to require [that] we rally under the standard of principle, [or] we shall be reduced to choose between a perpetual dependence in foreign opinions, and plunging into an inextricable labyrinth of confusion and uncertainty.[231]

By bringing in two Marshall Court judges as examples of enlightened common law jurists Du Ponceau had added another dimension to

---

[230] Ibid., xxiv.  [231] Ibid., xxiv–xxv.

his argument. Not only was the common law in America primarily a methodology, a metaphor for judicial reasoning that emphasized principle and thereby furthered legal science, visible exponents of that methodology could be found in the federal judiciary, specifically on the Marshall Court. The systematization of American law was, Du Ponceau estimated, a process requiring a national orientation, familiarity with general jurisprudence, and, perhaps, service on a federal court or in an educational or professional community with a national orientation.

In light of the original concerns expressed by the *Virginia Argus,* Jefferson, and Tucker about the consequence of adoption of the common law in the federal courts, Du Ponceau's intimation is worth lingering over. In his insistence that federal court jurisdiction could be kept separate from federal common law rulemaking, Du Ponceau appeared to be assuaging the anticonsolidationists' earlier fears. But by converting the common law from a body of rules to a methodology of judicial decisionmaking, and by suggesting that federal court judges had been particularly skillful in that methodology, Du Ponceau had made an association between judging resting on general principles, a scientific approach to the law, and the federal courts that represented a significant departure from Tucker. The common law in the federal courts had been a problem for Tucker precisely because its rules were suspect, and the judges declaring those rules equally suspect. Nowhere in Tucker's vision of law as a science had he made room for even discriminating federal judges promulgating common law doctrines. Du Ponceau had sought to complicate the perceived connection between the adoption of the common law and unlimited federal power by insisting that jurisdiction was not the same as substantive law, but when he came to make his own definition of the common law, it had a strikingly nationalized tone.

The culmination of a conception of the common law as a methodology designed to yield a body of scientific principles can be seen in the writings of Story in the 1820s and 1830s. Tucker, Goodenow, Du Ponceau and others[232] had formulated a conception of American law as indigenous, multifarious, and adaptable, and had then made some suggestions as to how American law could become more principled, systematized and thus scientific. In his tracts Tucker had explored a variety of substantive topics, from sovereignty to criminal law, real property, and freedom of religion, speech, and the press. Goodenow had surveyed the reception of English criminal law in America and analyzed

---

[232] Space does not permit a discussion here of all the commentators whose writings are cited at notes 78–87. In many instances their jurisprudential contributions informed the Court's discussions of substantive legal issues, as will be seen in subsequent chapters.

the place of nonstatutory criminal law in the federal and state courts. Du Ponceau had offered a general analysis of the relationship of federal jurisdiction to the promulgation of substantive rules, and had analyzed specific issues in federal jurisdiction, discussing pertinent state and federal cases in the process. Kent, in his *Commentaries,* had pursued a "scientific" analysis of substantive issues with far greater detail and comprehensiveness than any of his predecessors: he had begun to implement the juristic blueprint Tucker and Du Ponceau had sketched. It remained for Story, in his writings and commentaries, to undertake a full-blown "scientific" survey of American law, cataloguing the "improvements" made since the Revolution and presenting them in a consciously systematic format.

My concern here, however, is not to explore Story's treatment of substantive issues, but to inquire how far his conception of the common law retained or modified prevailing early-nineteenth-century theories of the nature and sources of American law. In tracing conceptions of the common law from Tucker through Goodenow to Du Ponceau we have noted explicit agreement on certain propositions and implicit agreement on others. While the commentators differed sharply in the role of the common law in America, they each expressly stated that the source of American law included, in addition to the constitutional text and statutes currently in force, a variety of unwritten sources, such as civil law maxims, natural law precepts, "reason," "justice," and "first principles of republican government." One commentator, Goodenow, found that the use of such unwritten sources by judges constituted undue discretion, but his reservations about discretion, for the most part, seemed directed at the employment of "wrong" (despotic, barbarous, or outmoded) criminal law rules. Only occasionally did Goodenow hint that judges had discretion to set the limits of their own jurisdictional powers, notwithstanding the demarcation of those powers by a legislature. The logic of Goodenow's hint threatened to expose the entire process of substantive law declaration by judges as discretionary in the modern, subjective sense of that word. But no other commentator saw fit to follow up Goodenow's lead.

The tacit agreement among the commentators that American law was multifarious, open-ended, and flexible was itself to reinforce the hope that it could be reduced to a system of fundamental principles that would be seen to have a universal and timeless meaning. Du Ponceau pointedly made the connection between an amalgamated body of law and scientific methodology in his essay. "The common law, the civil law, the law commercial and maritime, the law of nature and nations, the constitutional and federal law of our country, and the jurisprudence of the different states," he announced, "form together the aggregate of the great body of American law. It is impossible that such a diversified field of knowledge can be well or successfully cultivated without the aid of academical instruction." And the "object" of legal education, he maintained, should be "the promotion of legal science."[233]

Science would eventually lead, the commentators hoped, to the promulgation of universal governing principles. The improvement of American law would, it was hoped, reach a stage in which substantive legal doctrines stood in harmony with the first principles of society, ethics, and government. Goodenow seems to have doubted that this stage would ever come to pass in the "public sphere" of life. His division of the legal realm into public and private spheres was not, however, part of the jurisprudence of Tucker or Du Ponceau. Nor was Goodenow's public-private division followed by Kent, whose *Commentaries* implicitly classified legal doctrines into public or private categories but applied the same methodology to each, a methodology designed to identify first principles that could be articulated, disseminated, and applied. All of the commentators, even Goodenow, can be said to have conceived of law as ultimately resting on a set of principles whose origins were diverse—sometimes not even strictly "legal"—but whose nature was timeless. "Pure ethics and sound logic," Du Ponceau said, were "parts of the common law."[234] With the exception of Goodenow's "public" sphere, law for the commentators was a holistic and universal entity, indistinguishable from moral philosphy, political economy, "right reason" and natural justice.

Were these views retained by Story in his mature jurisprudential writing? In addition to his commentaries on legal subjects, which he began in 1830 after having been appointed Dane Professor of Law at Harvard Law School, Story also produced numerous miscellaneous writings on jurisprudential topics during his years on the Marshall Court. In two of those writings he spoke particularly to the nature and sources of American law and to the role of the common law in America. The first such essay was an 1821 address to the Suffolk bar entitled "Progress of Jurisprudence";[235] the other was Story's 1831 essay on "Law, Legislation, and Codes," written for the *Encyclopedia Americana,* edited by Francis Lieber.[236]

A characteristic of Story as a writer, whether essayist, correspondent, or judge, was his penchant for articulating, in a vivid and repetitious manner, the intellectual assumptions of his age. Consider, for example, the following excerpt from "Progress of Jurisprudence":

---

[233] Du Ponceau, *Dissertation,* 181–82, 190.

[234] Ibid., 132.

[235] J. Story, "Progress of Jurisprudence," reprinted in W. Story, *Miscellaneous Writings,* 198.

[236] J. Story, "Law, Legislation, and Codes," reprinted in J. McClellan, *Joseph Story and the American Constitution* (1971), 350.

In government purely despotic, the laws rarely undergo any considerable changes through a long series of ages. The fundamental institutions, . . . whether modeled at first by accident or design . . . assume a settled course, which is broken in upon only by the positive edicts of the sovereign, suited to some temporary exigency. . . . In such countries the law can scarcely be said to have existence as a science. . . . It assumes no general rules, by which rights or actions are to be governed. Causes are decided summarily, and more with reference to the condition and character of the parties than with reference to principles; and judges are ministers of state to execute the policy of the cabinet, rather than jurists to interpret rational doctrines.[237]

In this paragraph are embedded a bundle of interconnected assumptions about republican government, legal science, the articulation of general principles, and the role of judges as "interpreters" of "rational doctrines," assumptions that have previously been discussed in detail. Story's language describes the antithesis of the American legal system (despotic, fortuitous, static, positivistic, subjectivist, cabinet-dominated, irrational) and by implication defines republican law in America. A subsequent paragraph spelling out the contrast ("in free governments . . . when the popular interests have obtained some representation or power . . . we can trace a regular progress from age to age in their laws, a gradual adaptation, . . . a substantial improvement [and the rise of] a system . . . to administer justice [dominated by] the judicial powers")[238] seems hardly necessary.

In both the essays Story acquiesced in the prevailing view of his generation of jurists that American law was, and should be, a composite of multiple sources. Among the sources Story included in American jurisprudence were "the common law, [with its] local usages and peculiarities,"[239] state "canons of descent" for the transfers of property,[240] "commercial law,"[241] "maritime law,"[242] and "principles of equity,"[243] which consisted of "the general doctrines of the English chancery . . . modified by local statutes, usages, and decisions."[244] These multiple sources, Story felt, "justify the suggestion . . . that American jurisprudence can never acquire a homogeneous character."[245]

But the multifarious character of American law was not perceived by Story, as it had been by earlier jurists, as a welcome symbol of America's independence and enlightenment. The "increasing discrepancies" Story felt might appear in the future content of American legal doctrines

---

[237] J. Story, "Progress of Jurisprudence," 198–99.
[238] Ibid., 199.
[239] Ibid., 213.
[240] Ibid., 214.
[241] Ibid.
[242] Ibid.
[243] Ibid., 223.
[244] Ibid., 222.
[245] Ibid., 224.

were "of no small moment." He expressed concern "lest . . . the profession . . . become devoted to mere state jurisprudence." He was anxious that "those more enlightened and extensive researches, which form the accomplished scholar, and elevate the refined jurist" not be "abandon[ed]."[246] And he proposed a solution:

> The establishment of the National Government, and of courts to exercise its constitutional jurisdiction, will, it is to be hoped, in this respect, operate with a salutary influence. Dealing, as such courts must, in questions of a public nature, such as . . . the domestic relations of the states with each other, and with the General Government; such as that of the great doctrines of prize and maritime law; such as involve the discussion of grave constitutional powers and authorities—it is natural to expect that these courts will attract the ambition of some of the ablest lawyers in the different states. . . . And thus . . . if I do not indulge in an idle dream, the foundations may be laid for a character of excellence and professional ability . . . in which minute knowledge of local law will be combined with the most profound attainments in general jurisprudence, and with that instinctive eloquence which . . . grasps principles which fix the destiny of nations, or strike down to the very roots of civil policy.[247]

With this passage the close connection between elite commentary and the reformulation of "general jurisprudence" in America along more national lines once more surfaces. Story conceded the "Americanness" of American jurisprudence, but associated the adaptability of doctrines, at the state level, with provinciality, and proposed an antidote. In the federal courts, he argued, where "questions of a public nature" were presented, opportunities for "general jurisprudence" existed. That jurisprudence could be "national" in scope, "uniform" in content, and "eloquent" in its articulation of "principles" that constitute "the very roots of civil policy." It could be propounded by "the ablest lawyers in the different states."

It was, of course, no coincidence that Story followed this passage with a series of paragraphs illustrating his conviction that "the principal improvements [in] the future prospects of the jurisprudence of our country . . . must arise from a more thorough and deep-laid juridical education, a more exact preparatory discipline, and a more methodical and extensive range of studies."[248] He then called for, respectively, attention to "those general principles which constitute the foundation of actions"; the employment of "that close and systematical logic, by which success in the profession is almost always secured"; study of the essentially rational

---

[246] Ibid.
[247] Ibid.

[248] Ibid., 232.

and "enlarged and elevated . . . principles" of equity; investigation of "the stores of juridical wisdom and policy" in "foreign jurisprudence"; speculations on "the origin and extent of moral obligations," the "great truths and dictates of natural law," and the "immutable principles that regulate right and wrong in social and private life"; and, above all, systematization of "those portions of our jurisprudence which, under the forming hand of the judiciary, shall from time to time acquire scientific accuracy."[249] In short, provinciality in American jurisprudence should be countered by a "scientific" search for the sources of general principles, followed by the digesting and dissemination of those principles which had achieved "accuracy" and therefore a kind of permanence.

The contribution of Story, then, was in forging a series of connected entities, each part of a grand jurisprudential design. The reception of English law in America had engendered modifications, adaptations, and improvements. That pattern of modification had given American jurisprudence its uniquely multifarious character, but it had also threatened to lead to provincialism as local usages proliferated. The pattern, however, had also engendered a methodology: in selecting from a multiplicity of sources American judges, most particularly, were implicitly resting their decisions on "principles." That methodology, founded on common law techniques, could now be understood as "scientific" in character, resting on the logical derivation of great principles, their accommodation to republican government, and their dissemination. The most fertile fields for legal science were three: education, juristic commentary, and the decisions of federal judges. Those three fields could be made to reinforce the "progress" of one another through the recognition of the contributions made in each field and through the continued "scientific" promulgation of the principles of general jurisprudence.

Ten years after "Progress of Jurisprudence" appeared Story returned to the subject of the common law in America.[250] The intervening time had altered the context of his topic, and Story's emphasis on "law, legislation and codes" was consequently different. He was no longer concerned with the potential balkanization and provincialism of American law but with a development on the other side of the jurisprudential continuum: the possibility of general codification. Arguments that American law, particularly common law, was unwieldy, inaccessible, overly technical, unnecessarily diverse, and mysterious to nonprofessionals had surfaced in the late 1820s, and the promulgation of a general code of American law had been proposed by "reformers."[251] Story was both

---

[249] Ibid., 232, 233–34, 235.
[250] J. Story, "Law, Legislation, and Codes," 351.
[251] By "reformers" Story meant such advocates of codification as William Sampson, Thomas Smith Grimke, and Robert Rantoul. See C. Cook, *The American Codification Movement*, 96–

sympathetic and hostile to codification. He had been on record as an opponent of diversification and a proponent of general jurisdiction, and he was especially attracted to the idea that commercial law could be made uniform and predictable, possibly through codification.[252] A general code, however, came to be anathema to Story because it threatened to strip judges of their power to declare substantive rules. By the 1830s Story had come to identify the common law, and even American law generally, with judicial declarations. "Where . . . in America . . . it is asked what the law is," he announced in 1831, "we are accustomed to consider what it has been declared to be by the judicial department, as the true and final exposition."[253] General codification ran the risk, in Story's view, of transferring law declaration from the judiciary to those—probably legislators or their agents—who would draft the code.

Story's 1831 inquiry into the sources of American law was thus a pointed defense of the common law, as declared by the judiciary, as the center of American jurisprudence. The most interesting facet of Story's argument was his attempt to link a "historico-philosophical view of the sources of laws" with a claim for the primacy of the method of judicial declaration of common law rules. The first part of Story's 1831 essay surveyed and evaluated "the schools of modern jurisconsults,"[254] concluding that the historical school was correct in maintaining that "laws can be properly comprehended only by an historical examination of their development" and that the "philosophical school" was also correct in recognizing "a universal right, which exists prior to all positive legislation."[255] "Law," Story concluded, "is founded, not upon any will, but on the discovery of a right already existing; which is to be drawn either from the internal legislation of human reason, or the historical development of the nation." While law was "not irrevocable," as long "as it existe[d]" it was "of irresistible and universal force."[256]

The ultimate justification for substantive legal rules, then, was that they were declarations of "already existing rights." The rights themselves were based on reason, history, justice, or principles of republican government; whatever their basis, they were, while they were in existence, "universal." Judges were permitted to declare rules because anyone with proper historical and philosophical training could identify and articulate

---

168. Gordon, Book Review, 452–58, and Miller, *Life of the Mind*, 241–53, argue that only in its most radical, de-professionalizing implications was the codification movement threatening to the established legal profession, and that codification had the virtue, from an established practitioner's point of view, of reducing uncertainty, arbitrariness, and confusion as to the source of law.

[252] In "Progress of Jurisprudence," 237, Story professed an interest in "reducing to a text the exact principles of the law . . . and thus . . . pav[ing] the way to a general code."

[253] J. Story, "Law, Legislation, and Codes," 358.

[254] Ibid., 351.

[255] Ibid., 354.

[256] Ibid., 355.

the proper rule in a given case. The "rule," Story claimed, "controls the arbitrary discretion of judges, and puts the case beyond the reach of temporary feelings and prejudices, as well as beyond the peculiar opinions and complexional reasoning of a particular judge."[257] Once declared, rules were "conclusive and obligatory." The "sense of a law once fixed by judicial interpretation," Story argued, "is forever deemed its true and only sense."[258]

The image of American law that Story sought to create in his 1831 essay was that of a body of fixed rules, themselves declarations of pre-existing rights or manifestations of universal principles, which was from time to time interpreted by judges. The creation of such an image was, even for so bold a rhetorician as Story, an extraordinary performance. He equated law in America with common law, and common law with the declaration of substantive rules by American judges. He divorced law from legislation: "Our legislatures," Story said, "can only declare what the law shall be, not what it has been, or is."[259] He claimed that common law rules were inevitably declaratory of pre-existing rights and needed always to be regarded as "irresistible" and "universal." He suggested that the power to declare common law rules constrained rather than enhanced judicial discretion. He associated common law rules with values such as "certainty," "exactness," and "uniformity," and claimed that "a general and settled course of interpreting the laws" had emerged "in countries governed by the common law."[260] He even went so far as to suggest that "the changes which have been wrought in the fabric of the laws, have not so much arisen from misapplication of principles by the courts, as from the new state of society having rendered the old . . . laws inexpedient or inconvenient."[261]

It appears that a primary concern of Story's in writing the essay was to protect the process by which judges declared substantive rules from being attacked as inherently arbitrary, dominated by "peculiar opinions," "complexional reasoning," and "temporary feelings and prejudices"; in a word, as discretionary. Story's attribution of impersonality, "irrefutability," and universality to common law rules appears as a strategy to deflect too probing an inquiry into their flexibility, diversity, close affinity with local usage, provinciality, and occasional injustice and irrationality—features Story had hinted at in his 1821 article. We have noted a version of the same strategy in Story the treatise writer: the more he perceived that jurists shaped their materials, the less he was willing to declare that shaping function openly. Story wanted his treatises to be "authoritative" and thus took pains to downplay his opinionated and

---

[257] Ibid., 359.
[258] Ibid., 360.
[259] Ibid.

[260] Ibid., 359–60.
[261] Ibid., 359

interventionist posture. He also wanted judges to continue to have the power to declare substantive rules, whether based on the common law or not; therefore he claimed that the rules themselves controlled discretion, just as he claimed did the rules for constitutional interpretation he proposed in his *Commentaries on the Constitution.*

Story's essays had thus modified earlier conceptions of the common law in America in two respects. For him the common law was not only best described as a scientific methodology, it was a methodology that imposed constraints on the discretion of its judicial practitioners. Moreover, the body of principles that constituted the common law were principles derived from the other substantive areas that had been identified as sources of American law. Those areas were thus *subordinate* to the common law in the hierarchy of authoritative sources: the common law was composed of those areas rather than being separate from them. Moreover, the methodology of the common law was of universal application: it could provide techniques for the derivation of scientific principles of equity, commercial law, natural law, and so on. Indeed Story's own treatises represented efforts to derive such principles and present them in a scientific manner.

By 1831 one can observe two changes in the conception of the common law that has been traced from Tucker onward. Tucker had begun his consideration of the nature and sources of American law by rejecting the common law as having any applicability to American jurisprudence. Further analysis revealed that Tucker had not quite meant what he said. By "common law" he meant unmodified English common law doctrines, most particularly those in the area of criminal law; and by "American jurisprudence" he principally meant the federal courts. Tucker's definition of American law was gradually replaced, partly because of Tucker's own work, by a much broader and looser conceptualization in which the common law was perceived as only one of a variety of laws American judges and jurists might draw upon in deciding rules and formulating principles. That conceptualization persisted in the writings of Goodenow, Du Ponceau, and Kent, and in Story's 1821 essay. But Du Ponceau had realized that the term "common law" carried a broader meaning than merely one source of law: the term, he said, was "interwoven with the very idiom that we speak, and we cannot learn another system of laws without learning at the same time another language."[262] By 1831 the common law, as embodied in judicial declarations of substantive rules, had been made synonymous with American law itself.

The last sentence hints at the second change: American law had increasingly become identified with its judicial as distinguished from its legislative formulations. None of the jurists considered in this chapter, in

---

[262] Du Ponceau, *Dissertation,* 91.

his exploration of the nature of American law, directed his attention to statutes. While Tucker, Goodenow, Du Ponceau, and Story all included statutory law as a source of law, their focus was on cases, treatises, and other sources of principles—such as foreign jurisprudence, natural justice, history, custom, and reason—not on statutes. Story claimed that the decisions of courts, not statutes, represented what the law was, and Goodenow identified statutory law as a positivistic, arbitrary, time-bound medium, contrasting it with the universal, timeless, principle-laden medium of the law of civil rights and wrongs. A growing tendency to equate law, especially of the "general," "scientific," or "universal" kind, with the common law decisions of judges is apparent in the treatise writers.

Thus a precise formulation of the prevailing conception of law in early-nineteenth-century American jurisprudential writings should speak in terms of layers. In its surface construction, American law was conceived of as an entity with multiple sources, diverse manifestations, and a constantly changing content. But underneath the surface lay another vision, one in which the law, in a not-too-distant future state, would become synonymous with a body of fundamental and universal principles, consonant with reason and justice, scientifically formulated and disseminated, and declared by judges. The sources of law most commonly associated with that vision were the Constitution and the common law; other sources were implicitly delegated to a position of less authority.

The decisions of the Marshall Court were made within a jurisprudential universe bounded by these surface and underlying conceptions. The Marshall Court has traditionally been identified with its constitutional law decisions, and those decisions are of sufficient importance and interest to merit prominent attention in this study. But the constitutional jurisprudence of the Marshall Court cannot be separated from its jurisprudence as a whole, and the juristic world in which the Court functioned was one in which the Constitution, while assumed to be a predominant source of law within the limits of its coverage, was not sharply differentiated from other sources of "general jurisprudence." Both of the central prevailing assumptions of early-nineteenth century jurisprudence—the inherent open-endedness of American law and the special importance of a recast common law—affected constitutional as well as nonconstitutional decisionmaking on the Marshall Court. In the Court's constitutional opinions we will have occasion to observe uses of multiple sources, appeals to nonlegal principles, "scientific" derivations of substantive rules, and other common law methodologies. We will also have occasion to observe regular efforts on the part of the Court to minimize, control, or even deny the presence of judicial discretion. We will, in addition, note an underlying pressure on Marshall Court Justices to forge their declarations of substantive rules, or their interpretations of the text of the Constitution, in as authoritative a fashion as possible, as if the Court were seeking to elevate its interpretations to the status of permanent and universal principles. We will note the confidence with which the Court supplied meaning not only to nonconstitutional areas but also to the Constitution itself, as if the same interpretive methodology were appropriate to both areas. And finally, we will note, despite the efforts of some commentators and the Marshall Court Justices themselves to downplay the political and ideological significance of the Court's role as a federal court, the persistence of the associations made by early critics of the common law in the federal courts.

With the elevation to juristic prominence of a scientific methodology, relevant to both constitutional and common law adjudication, and with the identification of that methodology with curbs on judicial discretion and the conception of law as a body of timeless, yet adaptive principles, the elite commentators of the early nineteenth century had crystallized their response to the cultural problem with which this chapter began: the simultaneous importance of law to all the citizens of a republic and the obscurantist, self-interested image of the legal profession. Science provided the metaphors through which the nature of American law and the role of the legal and judicial professions could be recast; its goals were clarity, intelligibility, the derivation of universal rules, and the eradication of judicial discretion. A scientific approach to legal issues made law more comprehensible to the average citizen and less susceptible to being "twisted" by cunning lawyers.

The commentators who achieved this recasting of the nature and sources of American law had not emphasized how significantly their work had enhanced the power and status of two segments of the legal profession, judges, especially federal judges, and commentators themselves. While one can note a progressive emphasis in early-nineteenth-century legal commentary on the constraining effects of common law methodolgy and scientific jurisprudence, it is also possible to read the enhanced authority of the common law and the triumph of early-nineteenth-century legal science as having liberating effects, most particularly upon those who engineered those developments. Since the common law—increasingly characterized as "general principles" of jurisprudence—came to be the principal source of authority employed by the federal courts outside criminal cases, recasting the common law as an incorporation of the numerous other sources of American law increased the flexibility and discretion of federal judges in their efforts to declare rules. Since a scientific approach to legal subjects was regarded as conducive to the development of sound "principles," sources that employed such an approach—most conspicuously the treatises published by commentators—

enhanced their authoritativeness in the process. And since common law methodology, when scientifically conducted, made law more accessible and curbed judicial discretion in the process, the decisions of judges could be seen as both more important and less partisan or idiosyncratic. In the person of Story one finds the most vivid example of a beneficiary of the recast conception of American law: the judge/commentator whose judicial decisions support his commentary, whose commentary explains his judicial decisions, and whose theories of judging and of commentary increase his own importance in both fields. In Story one also finds the commentator most self-conscious about the two great jurisprudential issues of his age: consolidation and judicial discretion. Finally, in Story one finds the strongest exponent on the Marshall Court of the very design Jefferson, Tucker, and the *Argus* had seen being fashioned in the federal courts: a design to use the common law to expand the powers of the national government in a republic with a constitutional structure.

For all his protean energy, Story would have been a far less significant figure in early-nineteenth-century American jurisprudence had he not also been a Justice on the Marshall Court. It is to the Court that the narrative now turns, in a series of chapters designed to detail the institutional setting of its decisions and to provide sketches of the personalities closely involved with those decisions. The first of these focuses on the process by which cases came to the Marshall Court, its internal deliberative process, and its institutional goals: what I have called its "working life." While the emphasis of the next chapter may at first seem to constitute a radical shift from abstract jurisprudential issues to concrete and technical matters, themes identified in earlier chapters, particularly the themes of the relationship of law to politics and the nature of judicial discretion, will resurface.

# CHAPTER III

*The Working Life of the Court*

To re-create the working life of the Supreme Court of the United States between 1815 and 1835 is to confront the remarkable capacities of change. Imagine a Court in session for as little as six weeks instead of the current nine months, composed of seven Justices rather than nine, conducting its business not in a massive marble building but in a basement room of an unfinished Capitol, and rendering less than a third the number of opinions per year as the modern Court. Imagine Supreme Court Justices living and working together in a boardinghouse; sitting during arguments not behind a long single bench but at individual desks; announcing the decisions of cases sometimes within days, and nearly always within two to three weeks, after they were argued; often not knowing when the official reports of their decisions would appear. Imagine a Court with no library, no secretaries or law clerks, no typewriters, no duplicating machines, no office space, no published docket, and no time limit for oral arguments. Imagine a Supreme Court Justice not only deciding cases in Washington, but also traveling on horseback, in a stagecoach, or by steamboat from one United States Circuit Court to another to hear an additional set of cases. To summon up these images is to enter another world, but such a suspension of time and of belief is necessary to understand the Marshall Court. It was a Court of a different century, with a character fundamentally different from its modern counterpart.

This chapter details some of the features of the Marshall Court's working life that give it an aura of differentness to a modern observer. It also considers, at its conclusion, the most fundamental way in which the Marshall Court was different—the set of implicit starting assumptions about law and judging held by the Justices and their contemporaries. My focus, for the most part, is on more tangible items: the routine of the Court's work; the Justices' lodgings and working conditions; the manner by which cases came to the Court; and the process by which they were heard, decided, published, and disseminated. Such items may seem trivial or devoid of intellectual significance, but they assist the modern observer in recreating what it was like to hold the office of Supreme Court Justice between 1815 and 1835. They also help remind us that the mundane and prosaic features of an age reveal that age's sensitivity as fully as its grander achievements.

When the 1815 Term began, the Supreme Court had no courtroom in which to conduct its business. L'Enfant's original plan for Washington had included a site, approximately equidistant between the proposed White House and the proposed Capitol, on which a building for the Court would be erected.[1] That plan had been approved in 1791, and by 1815 the skeletons of an executive mansion and a legislative building were evident on the Washington landscape. At the Supreme Court site, however, there was nothing except the swamps of Goose Creek, the estuary that flowed between Capitol Hill and the White House, creating "wet, marshy ground covered with weeds and wancopins where sportsmen shot ortolan, where cattle formed paths in zigzag courses, . . . and where fishermen often took their spoil, especially at full tide."[2]

The Supreme Court was therefore forced to hold court in a room in the Capitol, originally on the first floor and after 1810 in the basement. In 1814 the Court lost even those quarters when British troops burned the Capitol, seriously damaging the basement courtroom. An 1816 report to Congress by Benjamin Latrobe, the architect of the Capitol, noted that "[g]reat efforts were made to destroy the Court-room, which was built with uncommon solidity, by collecting into it and setting fire to the furniture of the adjacent rooms." The result was that "the columns [of the courtroom] were cracked exceedingly" and its "condition [rendered] dangerous."[3]

The uninhabitable condition of the courtroom forced the Justices to hold court in a nearby private home for the next two years. In 1817 they returned to the Capitol in "a room temporarily filled up for this occupation,"[4] and by the 1819 Term they were back in their basement courtroom. Even the refurbished courtroom was apparently unimpressive. A newspaper correspondent noted in 1824 that visiting the courtroom was "like going down cellar." To find the room, "[a] stranger might traverse the dark avenues of the Capitol for a week [seeking] a room which is hardly capacious enough for a ward justice." Another observer suggested

---

[1] J. Young, *The Washington Community 1800–1828,* (1966), 6.

[2] B. Sunderland, *A Sketch of the Life of William Gunton* (1878), 15, quoted in Young, *Washington Community,* 75. The United States Court of Appeals building now stands approximately on the site. See generally Young at 1–10.

[3] Report from Benjamin Latrobe to Congress, Nov. 28, 1816, quoted in C. Warren, *The Supreme Court in United States History* (3 vols., 1922, I, 459.

[4] Notebook entry of Henry Wheaton (February 1817), in Henry Wheaton Papers, Pierpont Morgan Library, New York, N.Y.

that the courtroom had "a certain cellarlike aspect," giving "the impression of justice being done in a corner."[5]

Inside the courtroom a rail separated the Justices from lawyers arguing cases; another rail separated the lawyers from the public. The Justices' seats, chairs behind individual mahogany desks, were slightly elevated. From that elevation steps led down to the chairs and tables for lawyers, then led up, to a point higher than the Justices' area, to enable spectators in chairs, settees, and sofas to observe the proceedings. Adjacent to the courtroom was a tiny robing room for the Justices; they often put on their robes in full view of the spectators. They wore no wigs. Visitors to the Court passed in and out with no apparent restrictions. A florid speech by a famous lawyer such as William Pinkney or Daniel Webster might pack the galleries, but at the close of the oration the courtroom would be nearly empty. An argument before the Court was regarded as something of a social occasion; numerous eyewitnesses testified to the desirability of the courtroom as a place to meet members of the opposite sex.[6]

Between 1815 and 1835 the Supreme Court sat from the first Monday in February or the second Monday in January[7] through the second or third week in March. The Justices heard arguments from 11 A.M. to 4 P.M. with no break for lunch. No time limits were imposed on lawyers arguing before the Court, and arguments sometimes lasted as long as six days. The work load of the Marshall Court was fairly substantial. During their brief sessions in Washington, the Justices rendered an average of forty majority opinions per year.[8] Although this is less than a third of the 139 opinions the Court averaged between 1970 and 1980,[9] the Marshall Court had less than a fourth of the time the current Court has to consider a case.

---

[5] Warren, *Supreme Court,* I, 461, quoting New York *Statesman,* Feb. 7, 1824; T. Hamilton, *Men and Manners in America* (2d Am. ed., 1833), 66, quoted in Young, *Washington Community,* 76.

[6] For contemporary descriptions of the courtroom, see Warren, *Supreme Court,* I, 460–62; "The Supreme Court of the U.S. in 1853–4," *Am. L. Reg.,* 2:705, 706 (1854). On the courtroom as a social rendezvous, see C. Ingersoll, *Inchiquin, The Jesuit Letter,* (1810), 51–55; M. Smith, *The First Forty Years of Washington Society* (1906), 96–97, 146. An informative secondary source on the courtroom is "When the Supreme Court Was in the Capitol," *A.B.A. J.,* 61:949 (1975).

[7] After 1827, and through the 1835 Term, the Court began its sessions on the second Monday in January. Prior to that time, the Court started its Term on the first Monday in February. Minutes of the Supreme Court of the United States (Feb. 1, 1790–Aug. 4, 1828), National Archives, reprinted in National Archives Microfilm Publications, Microcopy No. 215, Roll No. 1.

[8] These figures are taken from Volumes 13–34 (9 Cranch through 9 Pet.) of the United States Reports (1815–35).

[9] These figures are taken from Volumes 400–53 of the United States Reports (1970–80).

When the Justices were not hearing oral arguments, they spent little time working at the Capitol. Although there is some evidence that they met irregularly in a conference room there,[10] the Justices had no offices or chambers in the building. Nor did they have a support staff to manage, nor a library in which to do research. The Justices had little reason to remain at the Capitol other than to hear oral arguments.

On the conclusion of formal argument, the Justices tended to retire to their boardinghouse. From 1815 to 1830 all the Justices lived together, without their families, in one of these houses. The particular boarding-house varied from year to year, and during the summer months the Justices would correspond with one another about arrangements.[11]

Boardinghouses were a principal focus of political and social relationships in early-nineteenth-century Washington. The unfinished character of the city—roads ranged from dusty or muddy to nonexistent, a swamp separated Capitol Hill from the White House, and Georgetown, the most established population center, was five virtually impassable miles from the Capitol—combined with the temporary residency of members of Congress to produce a clustering of boardinghouses around the Capitol. Although the executive branch of government had more permanence among its staff and tended to draw all but its highest-level employees from the pool of local residents, Congress was staffed by a transient population who saw the boardinghouses in which they resided as symbols of their regional and political identities.[12] In choosing to live in a Capitol Hill boardinghouse and to remain in Washington for only a temporary period, the Justices, although ostensibly permanent members of the Wash-

---

[10] Most descriptions of the Marshall Court's years in the Capitol do not mention the presence of a conference room, and Charles Warren did not refer to any such room in his history of the Supreme Court. See supra, note 5. Joseph Story, however, in his 1835 eulogy of Marshall, referred to a "conference room" immediately after describing Marshall's delivery of opinions in the Capitol courtroom. J. Story, "Life, Character, and Services of Chief Justice Marshall" in W. Story, ed., *The Miscellaneous Writings of Joseph Story* (1852), 639, 692. Moreover, Albert Beveridge, in his biography of Marshall, stated that "each case was . . . fully examined in the consultation room at the Capitol" where "the court had a regular 'consultation day.' " A. Beveridge, *The Life of John Marshall* (4 vols.,

1916–19), IV, 87. Finally, an eyewitness account of Supreme Court arguments in 1827 spoke of the Justices "coming in from their side-room" to the Capitol courtroom. O. Smith, *Early Indiana Trials and Sketches* (1858), 137. It is possible that Story and Smith referred to the robing room, but the size of that room would seem to have precluded conferencing. Story may have meant a designated room in a boarding-house.

[11] See infra, text accompanying note 163.

[12] On the significance of boarding-houses as social and political centers in early Washington, see C. Green, *Washington: A History of the Capitol, 1800–1950* (1962), 107–108; Young, *Washington Community,* 98–109.

ington community by virtue of their life tenure, adopted the congressional rather than the executive pattern of residence. The boardinghouse became the nerve center of their existence in Washington.

Not all of the Justices' time, however, was spent either in the courtroom or in the boardinghouse. Although one study of Washington life concluded that the Marshall Court Justices "lived . . . a reclusive existence,"[13] the Justices' correspondence suggests a more active social life. John Marshall's letters to his wife, who remained in Richmond, testify to regular attendance at dinners, balls, and other social functions. Marshall would complain of the demands on his time,[14] but he did not seem to turn down many invitations.[15] In 1818 a New York newspaper noted that Washington's "season of greatest festivity" began "after the Supreme Court commenced its session" and that "[t]here are now tea and dining parties daily."[16] Five years later Charles Ingersoll remarked that the Justices "begin a day's session . . . after robing & taking their places, by receiving from the Marshal their cards of invitation and taking up their pens to answer them before the list of cases is called for hearing." Ingersoll criticized the Justices "for dining out so continually," although he asked, "[H]ow can they help it under this raging star."[17] In the face of this evidence, Joseph Story's remark that "I scarcely go to any places of pleasure or fashion"[18] needs to be taken in context.

One should remember, however, that the Justices spent only between six weeks and two months in Washington. A much larger portion of their time was spent serving as judges on the United States Circuit Courts. There were six of these courts before 1807 and seven thereafter to the end of Marshall's tenure.[19] The circuit courts embraced various regions and varied widely in size and accessibility: the Third Circuit, consisting of Pennsylvania and New Jersey, was the most compact and manageable, and the Seventh Circuit, consisting of Kentucky, Ohio, and

---

[13] Young, *Washington Community,* 77.

[14] Letter from J. Marshall to Mary Ambler Marshall, Feb. 14, 1817, reprinted in F. Mason, *My Dearest Polly* (1961), 235.

[15] See letters from J. Marshall to M. A. Marshall, Feb. 14, 1817; Mar. 12, 1826; Feb. 1, 1829; Feb. 14, 1830; reprinted in Mason, *My Dearest Polly,* 235, 293–94, 304, 319. For a letter in which Marshall did turn down an invitation, see letter from J. Marshall to M. A. Marshall, Feb. 12, 1826, reprinted in Mason, *My Dearest Polly,* 292–93.

[16] Warren, *Supreme Court,* I, 471, quoting New York *Commercial Advertiser,* Feb. 7, 1818.

[17] Diary entries of Charles Ingersoll, Feb. 14 and 20, 1823, quoted in W. Meigs, *The Life of Charles Jared Ingersoll* (1900), 123, 137.

[18] Letter from J. Story to Ezekiel Bacon, Mar. 12, 1818, reprinted in W. Story, *The Life and Letters of Joseph Story* (2 vols., 1851), I, 310.

[19] Judiciary Act of 1802, 2 Stat. 156, 157; Act of Feb. 24, 1807, 2 Stat. 420.

Tennessee, was by far the most expansive and time consuming.[20] The circuits were conceived primarily as courts of original jurisdiction for certain kinds of cases, such as serious crimes, copyrights and patents, piracy, slave and Indian cases, designated civil suits involving amounts over $500, and diversity of citizenship cases.[21] Their jurisdiction, in all but the first three sets of cases, was concurrent with the state courts, and cases in which diversity of citizenship existed and the amount in dispute exceeded $500 could be removed from state to federal courts. In addition, the circuit courts had appellate jurisdiction from the limited class of cases that originated in the federal district courts. The district courts were located within the boundaries of states, most states containing one court.[22]

The staffing of the circuit courts was peculiar in that no circuit court judges were appointed. Instead the circuit courts were composed of the Supreme Court Justice assigned to that circuit and a district judge from the locality in which the circuit court had been established. In theory, the Supreme Court Justices would serve as itinerant "experts," bringing "the sense of the Supreme Court" to the localities, and the district judges would be conversant in local law.[23]

Joseph Story's travels on the First Circuit, embracing the states of New Hampshire, Massachusetts, and Rhode Island, provide a representative picture of circuit-riding.[24] Story's yearly circuit duties commenced

---

[20] See F. Frankfurter and J. Landis, *The Business of the Supreme Court* (1928), 49–50. In 1838, in repsonse to Senate consideration of a proposal to abolish circuit riding, the Justices listed their yearly mileage on their respective circuits. The purpose of the inquiry makes the Justices' estimates as to mileage somewhat suspect, especially Justice Henry Baldwin's estimate of 2,000 miles for the Third Circuit, which included only Pennsylvania and New Jersey, and Justice John McKinley's estimate of 10,000 miles for the new Ninth Circuit, which included Alabama, Louisiana, Mississippi, and Arkansas. McKinley added, "I have never yet been at Little Rock, the place of holding the court in Arkansas; but, from the best information I can obtain, it could not be conveniently approached in the spring of the year, except by water, and by that route the distance would be greatly increased." Frankfurter and Landis, *Business of the Supreme Court,* 49, quoting S. Doc. No. 50, 25th Cong., 3d Sess. 39 (1838). The 1838 estimation of distances by Justices ranged from 458 (The Fourth Circuit) to McKinley's 10,000 miles. Frankfurter and Landis, *Business of the Supreme Court,* 49, quoting S. Doc. No. 50, 25th Cong., 3d Sess. 32 (1838). In contrast, an 1826 speech in Congress listed the distances on the then seven circuits as ranging from 116 (Third Circuit) to 2,600 miles (Seventh Circuit). Ibid., citing 2 Cong. Deb. 1047 (1826).

[21] See T. Sergeant, *Constitutional Law* (2d ed., 1830), 34–141.

[22] See generally Frankfurter and Landis, *Business of the Supreme Court,* 11–33; J. Goebel, *Antecedents and Beginnings to 1801* (1971), 472–508; S. Law, *The Jurisdiction and Powers of the United States Courts* (1852), 133–214; Sergeant, *Constitutional Law,* 34–141.

[23] R. Newmyer, "Justice Joseph Story on Circuit and a Neglected Phase of American Legal History," *Am. J. Legal Hist.,* 14:112, 133 (1970), quoting 11 *Annals of Congress* 103 (1802).

[24] See generally Newmyer, "Justice Joseph Story on Circuit"; R. Newmyer, *Supreme Court Justice Joseph Story: Statesman of the Old Republic* (1985).

with the opening of court in Boston on or about May 1. From Boston he went to Portland or Wiscasset, Maine; then to Portsmouth or Exeter, New Hampshire; then to Providence or Newport, Rhode Island, ending his spring circuit about June 27. Another circuit term began on or about October 1 and lasted until about November 27. The geography of Story's circuit, which consisted of almost two thousand miles of traveling, made it possible for him to return sporadically to Salem, Massachusetts, where he lived until September 1829, when he moved to Cambridge to assume the Dane Professorship at Harvard Law School.[25] Story's letters reveal that his time in court was not particularly extensive, nor did he spend considerable time in transit.[26] The very fact that Story accepted the Dane Professorship suggests that he anticipated being able to be in Cambridge for a good portion of the academic year notwithstanding his circuit duties. Other Justices, however, with less compact circuits, needed to allow much more time for travel. Before being appointed to the Court and assigned to the new Ninth Circuit, Justice John McKinley allegedly called his prospective position "certainly the most onerous and laborious of any in the United States."[27]

The Justices therefore had to allocate approximately six months of each year to holding court either in Washington or on their respective circuits. Even during their stays at home, the Justices apparently could not completely relinquish their judicial burdens, for, as Story mentioned in an 1823 letter, there were "many important cases . . . upon which I am obliged to spend a great deal of time in vacation."[28]

The life of a Marshall Court Justice was clearly a strenuous one. In exchange for a comparatively paltry salary,[29] a Justice was forced to leave his family and home for extended periods of time each year and travel through a largely undeveloped country. The job was not without its rewards, however. As illustrated below, a clever and ambitious Supreme

---

[25] W. Story, *Life and Letters*, II, 22–23.

[26] Of the letters collected in W. Story, *Life and Letters*, many written by Story between April and June or between September and December were dispatched from Salem or Cambridge.

[27] F. Gatell, "John McKinley," in L. Friedman and F. Israel, eds., *The Justices of the United States Supreme Court 1789–1969*, (4 vols., 1969), I, 773.

[28] Letter from J. Story to John Bailey, Dec. 8, 1823, Joseph Story Papers, Massachusetts Historical Society, Boston, Mass.

[29] From 1789 until 1819, the salary of the Chief Justice was $4,000 and the other Justices received $3,500. Act of Sept. 23, 1789, ch. 18, 1 Stat. 72. After 1819, Chief Justice Marshall received $5,000, in salary, and the other Justices received $4,500. Act of Feb. 20, 1819, ch. 27, 3 Stat. 484. Prominent lawyers such as William Pinkney and Daniel Webster earned as much as $17,000–$20,000 a year in the same time period. See J. McIntyre, ed., *The Writings and Speeches of Daniel Webster* (18 vols., 1903), XVII, 545; R. Ireland, "William Pinkney: A Revision and Re-emphasis," *Am. J. Legal Hist.*, 14:235, 238 (1970).

Court Justice could use the powers of his office to channel some of the most important political questions of the day to his Court.

Although a description of the Justices' working environment and way of life gives some idea of the context in which the Marshall Court made its decisions, it reveals little about the processes through which the Justices heard and decided cases. One of the most important of those processes was the selection of cases for the Court to hear. The suggestion that the Marshall Court chose the issues that came before it may seem implausible, because, unlike the modern Court, it had no statutory power to select the cases that appeared on its docket. Nonetheless, individual Marshall Court Justices, taking shrewd advantage of their jurisdictional powers, devoted a portion of their energies to channeling lower court cases up to the Supreme Court.

Between 1801 and 1835, the years of Marshall's tenure, the Supreme Court's appellate jurisdiction generated most of its business.[30] The Court did have original jurisdiction over a constitutionally prescribed class of cases, such as boundary disputes between states, and its docket sometimes included such cases. These cases, however, came to the Court as a matter of course once they met the constitutional requirements.[31] The appellate cases were not only more numerous, but they also allowed the Marshall Court a certain amount of discretion over its docket. Discretion as practiced by the Marshall Court must be contrasted with the Supreme Court's current discretionary powers, which since 1916 have been fixed by statute.[32] The current statutory framework gives the Justices, through the device of granting or denying certiorari, considerable freedom to control their docket[33] and thus formalizes the discretion of the Court. The jurisdictional system during the Marshall era in theory gave the Justices relatively little discretion to control their docket but in practice permitted such discretionary control.

The Marshall Court exercised appellate jurisdiction through one of four procedural devices: a writ of error from a federal circuit court or from a highest level state court; an appeal from a circuit court; a certification of division of opinion between the Supreme Court Justice and the district judge sitting on a given circuit; and a miscellaneous category of other writs, including mandamus, prohibition, habeas corpus, certiorari,

[30] See G. Haskins and H. Johnson, *Foundations of Power: John Marshall, 1801–15* (1981) 377–78.
[31] "In all cases affecting Ambassadors, other public Ministers and Consuls, and those in which a State shall be a Party, the Supreme Court shall have original Jurisdiction." U.S. Const., Art. III, sect. 2.
[32] Act of Sept. 6, 1916, 39 Stat. 726; Act of Feb. 13, 1925, 43 Stat. 936.
[33] For a discussion of the history and policy of the 1916 Act, see Frankfurter and Landis, *Business of the Supreme Court*, 203–16.

and procedendo.[34] Of these devices, the writ of error and the certificate of division were the most conducive to informal control by Marshall Court Justices. The appeals procedure was available only in statutorily designated cases, with stipulated requirements for the amounts at issue, and it therefore did not allow the Justices any leeway to decide what types of cases they wanted to hear. The Justices also could not make discretionary use of the miscellaneous writ cases because each writ could be employed only in a designated class of cases. The writ of error and the certificate of division, however, required affirmative participation by Justices and thereby provided opportunities to shape the content of the Court's docket, as two examples will illustrate.

A writ of error was the appropriate form of Supreme Court review whenever a case involved the validity or construction of the Constitution, or of federal treaties, statutes, "commissions or authorities."[35] Although the writ could be used to review cases from both the highest state courts and the lower federal courts, most of the significant cases that reached the Marshall Court through the writ came from state courts. In the typical state writ of error cases, an act of a state legislature was claimed to violate the Constitution, and a state supreme court had upheld that act's constitutionality. Such major Marshall Court cases as *Fletcher* v. *Peck*,[36] *Martin* v. *Hunter's Lessee*,[37] *Cohens* v. *Virginia*,[38] and *Gibbons* v. *Ogden*[39] came to the Court in this manner.

To initiate the writ of error process from a state case, counsel for the petitioning party would draft a writ of error petition and sign it. Either a judge of the state's highest court or a Supreme Court Justice then had to approve this petition before the Court could consider the case. Given the fact that the state supreme court had just upheld the validity of its own state legislature's act against a federal constitutional challenge, it was unlikely, in many writ of error cases, that a judge of the state court would sign the petition. A Supreme Court Justice's signature was thus often required, and that Justice purportedly had to be convinced, by the substance of the petition for the writ of error itself, that Supreme Court review was appropriate. Once the petition was approved, the Supreme Court would order the state court to transmit a certified record of the case.

In *Martin* v. *Hunter's Lessee*,[40] a case ultimately decided in 1816, Marshall Court Justices intervened in this process to secure appellate

---

[34] Judiciary Act of 1789, ch. 20, 1 Stat. 73; Act of Mar. 2, 1793, ch. 22, 1 Stat. 333; Act of Apr. 29, 1802, ch. 31, 2 Stat. 156. See A. Conkling, *A Treatise on the Organization and Jurisdiction of the Supreme, Circuit, and District Courts of the United States* (2d ed., 1842), 435–67; Sergeant, *Constitutional Law*, 49–71.

[35] Judiciary Act of 1789, 1 Stat. 73, 85–87.
[36] 6 Cranch 87 (1810).
[37] 1 Wheat. 304 (1816).
[38] 6 Wheat. 264 (1821).
[39] 9 Wheat. 1 (1824).
[40] 1 Wheat. 304 (1816).

review on a writ of error. The complicated facts of the *Martin* case do not warrant extensive discussion here. The principal question in the case originally concerned the validity of titles to a large tract of land in Virginia. One group of litigants, a syndicate of which John Marshall and his brother James Marshall were members, claimed title through a British subject, Denny Martin, whose interest was ostensibly protected by the 1783 Treaty of Paris between the United States and Great Britain.[41] A second group claimed that an escheat act passed by the Virginia legislature in 1779[42] had forfeited to the state lands held by hostile British subjects.

In 1810 the Virginia Supreme Court of Appeals held that the claim to title originating under the Virginia escheat acts should prevail.[43] Because the Virginia court's decision drew into question the validity of a treaty made by the United States government, a writ of error was the appropriate form of appeal to the Marshall Court. The writ was routinely secured, with the cooperation of one of the Virginia Supreme Court of Appeals judges who had disagreed with part of the Virginia court's decision.[44] Justice Story, for an apparent majority[45] of the Supreme Court,

---

[41] The Jay Treaty of 1797 also affected land owned in the United States by British subjects and their heirs. Beveridge, *John Marshall*, II, 206.

[42] Act of May 3, 1779, 1779 Va. Acts 98.

[43] Hunter v. Fairfax's Devisee, 1 Munf. 218 (1810), rev'd, 7 Cranch 603 (1813).

[44] The judge in question was William Fleming, the President Judge of the Virginia Supreme Court of Appeals. The Supreme Court of Appeals sat in three-judge panels, and one of the panel, Judge St. George Tucker; did not sit in the case as a result of "being nearly related to a person interested." 1 Munf. at 223. That person was his son, Henry St. George Tucker, who was one of the attorneys for David Hunter, the claimant whose title derived from the Virginia escheat acts. The third judge on the panel was Spencer Roane, a long-time opponent of the Marshall Court.

[45] Fairfax's Devisee v. Hunter's Lessee, 7 Cranch 603 (1813). Charles Warren, in his history of the Supreme Court of the United States, claimed that the *Fairfax* decision was "that of less than a majority of the full Court." Warren, *Supreme Court*, I, 446. Warren based

his claim on the supposition that "Chief Justice Marshall and Judge [Bushrod] Washington absented themselves from the argument; Judge [Thomas] Todd was absent at the decision; and Judge [William] Johnson dissented." Ibid. This would leave only Story, Brockholst Livingston, and Gabriel Duvall as the "Court." A check of Cranch's Reports reveals, however, that although Marshall and Washington were absent from the arguments of the *Fairfax* case, which began on February 27, 1812, Todd was not, and although Marshall and Todd were absent when Story delivered the opinion in that case on March 15, 1813, Washington was not. Marshall's consistent refusal to participate in the *Fairfax* litigation because of his involvement with the litigation from its origins accounts for his absence. Washington, although a resident of Virginia, had no reason to disqualify himself, and it cannot be presumed that he did not take part in deliberations even though he did not hear argument. Moreover, one cannot presume that Todd's absence when the opinion was delivered meant that he had not voted on it, because the Justices had two Terms (1812 and 1813) in which to discuss the case, and Todd missed only the 1813 Term.

reversed, in the process lecturing the Virginia judges on Virginia land law. The Virginia Supreme Court of Appeals responded two years later by claiming that their judgments on matters of Virginia law were definitive, by arguing that the Supreme Court's assertion of appellate power was unconstitutional, by declaring that the writ of error in the original case had been "improvidently allowed," and by refusing to cooperate with the decision.[46]

Given the stance of the Virginia Supreme Court of Appeals, it was inconceivable that any judge on that court would sign the petition for a writ of error that was necessary to take the case to the Marshall Court a second time. The claimants therefore had to get a Supreme Court Justice to sign the petition on short notice. The Virginia Supreme Court of Appeals had handed down its decision in December 1815, and the Supreme Court's Term was to begin within six weeks.

A logical choice to sign the petition would have been John Marshall. Marshall, a Virginian, was well acquainted with the controversy, and his views on a strong federal judiciary were well known. Marshall, however, had publicly recused himself from any participation in the litigation because of his financial interests in the land in dispute.[47]

Although Marshall did not openly participate in *Martin*, he did the next best thing. He not only arranged for his close friend and fellow Justice Bushrod Washington to sign the writ of error petition, he drafted

---

[46] Hunter v. Martin, 4 Munf. 1, 58–59 (1815), rev'd sub nom. Martin v. Hunter's Lessee, 1 Wheat. 304 (1816).

[47] The syndicate of which Marshall was a member had brought the original action to settle title to the land, using the name of Denny Martin, who had attempted to sell them the land. Marshall thus had a strong interest in the outcome of the litigation and felt he could not openly participate in it.

As early as 1805 Marshall had indicated that he would recuse himself from any case involving legal questions similar to the one in *Martin*. In that year a case from North Carolina involving a comparable question came before Marshall's Fourth Circuit Court in Raleigh. The case involved a dispute over North Carolina land, one claimant basing his title on North Carolina escheat acts and the other deriving his title from a British subject. Marshall declined to hear the case, stating that he had "formed an opinion" on the issue in question and that he could "not consistently with his duty and the delicacy he felt, given an opinion in the cause." Raleigh *Register*, June 24, 1805, quoted in H. Connor, "The Granville Estate and North Carolina," *U. Pa. L. Rev.* 62:671, 689 (1914). One of the supporters of the British title noted, however, that despite Marshall's recusal he had "said enough to convince our opponents he was unfavorable to their construction of the law," and, in recommending appeal of the case to the Marshall Court, speculated that "it is no doubt much in our favor what has already dropt from the Chief Justice." Letter from John London to William Gaston, July 8, 1805, quoted in ibid., 690.

the petition himself.[48] Several pieces of evidence point to this conclusion. The most compelling is that the handwriting on the petition was in the same upright slant, with the same distinctive running together of letters and the same angular strokes, as numerous letters and draft opinions written by Marshall around the same time.[49] It did not resemble the handwriting of Benjamin Leigh or William Wirt, the lawyers who were representing Denny Martin and the Marshall syndicate in the litigation.[50] It did not resemble the handwriting of James Marshall, John Marshall's brother, who was also a party to the litigation.[51] It did not resemble any of the handwriting on standard-form petitions copied by the Supreme Court's Clerk.[52] Moreover, the petition was not signed by counsel, thereby suggesting that the author wanted to remain anonymous except to those who were familiar with his handwriting.

The presence of John Marshall is also reflected in the substance of the petition. The petition quoted at length from the judgment of the Virginia Supreme Court of Appeals, which had defied the authority of the Marshall Court, thereby emphasizing the gravity of the conflict between the two courts. The purpose was to make clear what was at stake in *Martin* v. *Hunter's Lessee:* the power of the Marshall Court to review certain final state court decisions on questions of federal constitutional law.

Marshall had taken no chances that the Supreme Court would not hear *Martin* v. *Hunter's Lessee.* He made certain that Bushrod Washington would be presented with a writ of error petition, without a signature, that he had drafted and that Washington, a frequent correspondent of his, would know that he had drafted. When the petition was presented to Washington, the Justice approved it, writing "allowed by Bush. Washington one of the assoc. Just. Sup. Ct. U.S." on the margin of the formal

---

[48] Petition for writ of error, Martin v. Hunter's Lessee, 1 Wheat. 304 (1816). The petition was found in the Appellate Case Files of the Supreme Court, National Archives. A copy is available in National Archives Microfilm Publications, Microcopy No. 214, Roll No. 39, Case No. 793. The similarity between the handwriting on the petition and John Marshall's handwriting was first pointed out to me by Professor Gerald Gunther; professional archivists specializing in the period of the early Marshall Court have concurred. The petition is reproduced in the illustration section following p. 72.

[49] See, e.g., letter from J. Marshall to Richard Peters, Jr., July 21, 1815, Historical Society of Pennsylvania, Philadelphia, Pa.; manuscript opinion in Walden v. Gratz, 1 Wheat. 291

(1816), available in National Archives. See also Marshall's May 27, 1819, letter to Joseph Story, reproduced in the illustration section following p. 72.

[50] See, e.g., letter from B. Leigh to Henry Lee, Nov. 29, 1824, Virginia Historical Society, Richmond, Va.; letter from W. Wirt to William Jones, June 12, 1818, William Wirt Papers, Library of Congress.

[51] See, e.g., letter from James Marshall to Messrs. LeRoy, Bayard, et al., May 26, 1801, Historical Society of Pennsylvania, Philadelphia, Pa.

[52] See, e.g., Petition for writ of error, Patterson v. United States, 2 Wheat. 221 (1817), reprinted in National Archives Microfilm Publications, Microcopy No. 214, Roll No. 39, Case No. 787.

writ.[53] The formal writ "commanded" the Virginia judges to "distinctly and openly send the record and process in the suit" to the Marshall Court.[54]

The Virginia Supreme Court of Appeals, however, refused to respond to the formal writ of error, not even making a record of its refusal.[55] This put the attorneys for the Marshall syndicate in a quandary, because no "record and process" would be forthcoming. The attorneys eventually produced a makeshift record, consisting of a copy of the Virginia court's earlier decision, a certification by a Virginia state judge that the copy was authentic, and a certification by the governor of Virginia that the clerk who had furnished the record was actually the clerk of the Virginia Supreme Court of Appeals.[56] The form of the record was irregular, but the Marshall Court nonetheless set the case for oral argument less than six weeks after the documents had been filed in Washington. Less than a week after arguments concluded, the Court rendered an opinion, again by Story, upholding the constitutionality of the writ of error procedure. Henry St. George Tucker, one of the counsel for the respondent, objected to the unusual procedure by which the case had come to the Court,[57] but Story's opinion in *Martin* disposed of the procedural claim in a paragraph.[58]

---

[53] Formal writ of error, Martin v. Hunter's Lessee, 1 Wheat. 304 (1816), reprinted in National Archives Microfilm Publications, Microcopy No. 214, Roll No. 39, Case No. 793.

[54] Ibid.

[55] Typically the materials accompanying a writ of error contained a copy of the state court's disposition of the case. No disposition appears either in the Court's files or in the Virginia Reports.

[56] The documents are available in National Archives Microfilm Publications, Microcopy No. 214, Roll No. 39, Case No. 793.

[57] Reporter Henry Wheaton's notes had Tucker arguing as follows:

At common law the writ of error must be returned by the court itself. It is imperfect in this case . . . [T]here is no error; the [Virginia] court of appeals have done nothing; and, therefore, there is no error in their proceedings. It is a mere omission to do what they ought to have done, and no judgment can be rendered here to reverse what they have not done.

1 Wheat. at 315–16.

[58] Justice Story held:

The forms of process, and the modes of proceeding in the exercise of jurisdiction are, with few exceptions, left by the legislature to be regulated and changed as this court may, in its discretion, deem expedient. By a rule of this court, the return of a copy of a record of the proper court, under the seal of that court [which had been obtained by Leigh on December 19, 1815], annexed to the writ of error, is declared to be "a sufficient compliance with the mandate of the writ." [Story did not indicate where or when that rule had originated.] The record, in this case, is duly certified by the clerk of the court of appeals, and annexed to the writ of error. The objection, therefore, which has been urged [by Tucker] to the sufficiency of the return, cannot prevail.

Ibid., 361. Johnson, in his partial concurrence and partial dissent, simply stated that "[t]he remaining points in the case being mere questions of practice, I shall make no remarks upon them." Ibid., 382.

Marshall's goal of a favorable disposition of the cause was thus realized, but one needs to consider more fully why he felt it necessary to intervene personally in the case, having ostensibly withdrawn from it. He of course regarded the case as a very significant one, not only on the issue of appellate jurisdiction but also on the issue of the disputed title. The power of the Supreme Court to review state court decisions when those decisions conflicted with federal statutes, treaties, or the Constitution could well have been regarded by Marshall as "the keystone of the whole arch of Federal judicial power."[59] Moreover, the challenge to the Court's authority had come from judges in Marshall's home state and from persons, such as Spencer Roane, whom Marshall regarded as bitter political opponents. When one adds to these elements Marshall's own "deep interest" in the disputed land, *Martin* emerges as a case whose prompt disposition Marshall felt vitally necessary.[60]

Given the great significance of the *Martin* case to Marshall, he may have thought his intervention necessary to strengthen the case's shaky procedural standing. The Virginia court had not cooperated with the original decision and was not cooperating to facilitate review; a Marshall Court Justice's approval of the writ was therefore necessary. John Marshall was well aware of the need for a Supreme Court Justice's involvement, but he had publicly dissociated himself from the case. Marshall may have thought the procedural status of *Martin* too questionable not to take action himself.

Although one might therefore understand why Marshall chose to involve himself in *Martin,* the question remains why he chose the particular method of involvement: drafting an unsigned writ petition in his own hand. Marshall could have taken obvious steps that would have shielded his participation. He could have had someone else copy the writ petition; such was common practice at the time.[61] Through intermediaries, such as his brother James, he could have encouraged counsel for the syndicate to draft a petition in the language he suggested. Instead, he allowed a

---

[59] Warren, *Supreme Court,* I, 449.

[60] The prompt settlement of the dispute over title to the Fairfax lands had been an abiding concern of Marshall's from 1796 on. See Beveridge, *John Marshall,* II, 203–13. "It was, then," Beveridge commented, "a very grave matter to the Marshalls [and] all others deriving their titles from Fairfax, that the question be settled quickly and permanently." Ibid., 208. The amount John and James Marshall had invested in the Fairfax lands was fourteen thousand British pounds. Ibid., 211, quot-

ing Records at Large of Circuit Court of Fauquier County, Va.

[61] The appellate case files of the Marshall Court contain numerous writ petitions in which the language of the petition is written in a stylized scroll and the dates of the petition are filled in by the lawyer who signs the petition. See, e.g., Petition for writ of error, Patterson v. United States, 2 Wheat. 221 (1817), reprinted in National Archives Microfilm Publications, Microcopy No. 214, Roll No. 39, Case No. 787.

petition in his own handwriting to be filed in the Clerk's office,[62] thereby opening himself up to discovery by interested parties, such as the opposing counsel in *Martin*. Among the opposing lawyers in *Martin* were people, such as Henry St. George Tucker, who knew John Marshall well and had corresponded with him.[63] Why would Marshall risk that his handwriting would be noticed and his surreptitious involvement in the *Martin* litigation discovered?

There are at least three possible reasons for Marshall's behavior. One is that Marshall thought that the importance of the case outweighed the risk of subsequent disclosure. As previously discussed, Marshall's personal and political stakes in the case were significant. At the same time, Marshall may have considered the possibility of discovery minimal. He had not signed the petition and could perhaps, if pressed, disclaim it. The lawyers for the Marshall syndicate surely knew of his intervention and could claim authorship. Bushrod Washington, an old friend, was hardly likely to alert anyone else to Marshall's involvement. Marshall even may have believed that no one who happened to come across the petition would attach any significance to the hand in which it had been drafted. Perhaps Marshall's celebrated absentmindedness and disorderliness extended in this instance to his forgetting that the writ would remain in the Clerk's office, and he therefore underestimated the risk of discovery.

A second possibility is that Marshall regarded himself as free to participate in the *Martin* litigation because he had recused himself from the case. He may then have considered himself a private citizen, not a Supreme Court Justice, with reference to that case and felt free to take an argumentative rather than a disinterested posture toward it. He was, of course, a member of the Virginia bar. He might have reasoned that because he was not actually participating in the deliberation or disposition of *Martin,* his views, if known, would simply be the views of a person who, being identified with one of the litigants, naturally desired a particular outcome in the litigation.

A third possibility, that Marshall simply did not regard his behavior as unethical or even irregular for a Supreme Court justice, requires the greatest amount of abstraction. Although he was unwilling to make his participation in *Martin* known to the general public, he was willing to

---

[62] Records filed with the Clerk could not be taken out of his office except by consent of the Court. Records of docketed cases were kept in the Clerk's office with the intent of preserving them for posterity, and inventories were taken in 1800 and 1827. Telephone interview with James R. Perry, Editor, Documentary History of the Supreme Court of the United States, 1789–1800, Feb. 22, 1983.

[63] See, e.g., letter from J. Marshall to H. Tucker, Feb. 3, 1813, John Marshall Papers, College of William and Mary Library.

take the risk that it might be known to those familiar with the case because he did not regard his intervention as outside the approved ambit of activities in which Supreme Court Justices could engage. To assume that Marshall approached his intervention in *Martin* in this fashion is to assume a different conception of judicial behavior, and indeed a different theory of the nature of law itself, from that which governs current expectations about judicial behavior.

On balance, a combination of the first and third possibilities seems to provide the most plausible explanation for Marshall's conduct. *Martin* was unquestionably an emotional case for him, raising the kinds of issues that make even prudent persons sometimes take risks. At the same time, we have already noticed that Marshall and his contemporaries held conceptions of law and judging that would have made his actions far less incriminating than they would be today. The concluding portions of this chapter consider those conceptions in more detail. At this point it suffices to say that Marshall may not have been unduly concerned about discovery of his involvement, at least by lawyers who were familiar with Supreme Court practice, because his actions did not appear to be clearly outside the limits of judicial propriety.

The second possibility must be rejected. There is no indication that the office of Supreme Court justice, even in its earliest stages, included opportunities to practice law. By becoming a Justice of the Supreme Court a lawyer does not lose his eligibility to practice law; Justices have regularly resumed practice after resigning or retiring from the Court. Eligibility to practice and participation in practice, however, are two different states, and the correspondence of Justices suggests that they regarded holding the office of Supreme Court Justice as incompatible with continuing in active law practice.[64] Thus, although Marshall might have regarded himself as eligible to render informal legal advice while on the Court, and Marshall Court Justices such as Story did openly render such advice,[65] there is no evidence that Marshall or any of the Marshall Court Justices defined their jobs as including private law practice. It would have

---

[64] See, e.g., letter from J. Story to Nathaniel Williams, Nov. 30, 1811, reprinted in W. Story, *Life and Letters,* I, 200–201; letter from J. Story to N. Williams, May 22, 1816, reprinted in ibid., 279; letter from J. Story to Stephen White, Feb. 26, 1817, reprinted in ibid., 278. See also letter from John W. Treadwell to William W. Story, Aug. 25, 1847, reprinted in ibid., 204, 206. This letter was written by an old friend of Story's to his son when the latter was collecting materials for his father's biography. It alluded to Story's decision to leave a lucrative practice to accept his appointment to the Court in 1811. For an account describing Story's dilemma in 1816 about whether to leave the Court and take over William Pinkney's private practice, see G. Dunne, *Justice Joseph Story and the Rise of the Supreme Court* (1970), 151–52.

[65] See Dunne, *Joseph Story,* 144–48; R. Newmyer, "A Note on the Whig Politics of Joseph Story," *Miss. Valley Hist. Rev.,* 48:480 (1961).

been clearly inconsistent with even a broad definition of judicial functions for a Justice of the Supreme Court to provide legal services for one of the litigants before that Court. So even if one hypothesizes that Marshall, once having declined to sit in *Martin,* regarded himself as a private citizen, it is inconceivable that he or his contemporaries assumed that a Justice, even in a private capacity, could litigate before the Supreme Court while remaining a member of that Court.

*Martin* v. *Hunter's Lessee* is therefore much more than a landmark in constitutional history. It is a case in which Chief Justice John Marshall surreptitiously intervened in the judicial process to secure appellate jurisdiction. *Martin* therefore sheds a new light on a complex historical personage[66] and reminds moderns to consider the historical context of ethical judgments made by past Supreme Court Justices. *Martin,* however, was not an isolated instance of intervention by Marshall Court Justices in the appellate process. Another major Marshall Court decision evoked similar but less successful efforts.

Although Marshall Court Justices could intervene in the writ of error procedure to secure appellate jurisdiction in a particular case, the certificate of division procedure constituted the principal opportunity by which they could control their docket. The certificate of division procedure, which originated in the Judiciary Act of 1802, gave the Supreme Court appellate review over cases where circuit judges stipulated that they held differences of opinion over a question of law.[67] The initial rationale for the procedure was a change in the manner of staffing the circuit courts. Whereas Justices had previously rotated among the circuits, the 1802 act assigned individual Justices to designated circuits, with the result that subsequently the same district judge and Supreme Court Justice would always compose each circuit court. This situation required a method for settling differences between the two judges,[68] and thus Congress created the certificate of division procedure. In enacting the procedure, Congress apparently anticipated that differences between the district judge and Supreme Court Justice would be genuine and would be expressed in the form of opinions, but a different practice soon emerged.

Marshall Court Justices soon became aware of the opportunities provided by the certificate of division to create appellate jurisdiction in a case. The Justices, while holding court on their respective circuits or "in

---

[66] There has been speculation that Marshall practically dictated Story's opinion in *Martin.* Story's son and biographer noted that the opinion had "all the peculiar merits of the best judgments of Marshall." W. Story, *Life and Letters,* 276. Story himself wrote to George Ticknor in 1831 that Marshall "concurred in every word" of the opinion in *Martin.* Letter from J. Story to G. Ticknor, Jan. 22, 1831, reprinted in W. Story, *Life and Letters,* II, 49.

[67] Judiciary Act of 1802, 2 Stat. 156, 159–61.

[68] United States v. Daniel, 6 Wheat. 542–548 (1821).

vacation,'' would exchange letters about points of law that had emerged in the cases they encountered on circuit.[69] These letters frequently discussed the desirability for the full Court to resolve a point that a Justice had encountered on circuit and thought particularly significant. To accomplish this, the Supreme Court Justices, when sitting on circuit, would divide the circuit court by agreeing to disagree with the district judge on a point of law. Such a division was "resorted to by agreement, without the actual expression or even formation of hostile opinions between the judges of the Circuit Court.''[70]

Although the certificate of division procedure was available in a large number of cases, in certain instances a Supreme Court Justice's efforts to use the certificate of division were frustrated. For example, a Justice could divide the circuit court only when both he and the district judge were present. When the Supreme Court judge sat alone as circuit judge, sometimes because the district judge had already heard the case,[71] the case could not be appealed by the certificate of division. In an 1819 letter to Story, Marshall discussed this predicament, writing that "[a]nother admiralty question of great consequence has occurred at the last [circuit] term which I would carry before the Supreme Court, if I could . . . [but] I have not the privilege of dividing the Court when alone. . . .''[72]

In *Trustees of Dartmouth College* v. *Woodward*,[73] Story, a regular user of the pro forma division procedure, attempted to employ the practice to bring the case before the Marshall Court. Story was closely involved from the outset with the litigation in the *Dartmouth College* case, the internal history of which has been recounted on several occasions.[74] The emphasis here is on a feature of the *Dartmouth College* controversy that at one time was expected to be crucial but ended up being of only technical importance. That feature was the effort on the part of lawyers for the College, the most notable of whom was Daniel Webster, to elicit the

---

[69] See, e.g., letter from J. Marshall to J. Story, July 13, 1819, quoted in C. Warren, *The Story–Marshall Correspondence* (1942), 4; letter from J. Story to Bushrod Washington, Jan. 13, 1821, New-York Historical Society, New York, N.Y.; letter from Smith Thompson to J. Story, July 27, 1827, Joseph Story Papers, Library of Congress.

[70] Conkling, *Organization and Jurisdiction*, 465.

[71] An example of this problem is De Lovio v. Boit, 7 F. Cas. 418 (C.C.D. Mass. 1815), a significant admiralty case that came before Story's circuit

court. *De Lovio* is discussed in Chapter VII.

[72] Letter from Marshall to Story, July 13, 1819, supra, note 69.

[73] 4 Wheat. 518 (1819).

[74] See generally M. Baxter, *Daniel Webster and the Supreme Court* (1966), 65–109; J. Shirley, *The Dartmouth College Causes and the Supreme Court of the United States* (1895); F. Stites, *Private Interest and Public Gain: The Dartmouth College Case* (1972), 18–19. *Dartmouth College* v. *Woodward* is discussed in more detail in Chapter IX.

cooperation of Story in carrying the case to the Marshall Court through a pro forma certificate of division.

The *Dartmouth College* case involved an 1816 act of the New Hampshire legislature that changed the name of Dartmouth College to Dartmouth University, increased the number of overseeing trustees, and provided for state officials, including the governor, to make periodic inspections of the institution. The existing trustees of Dartmouth College challenged the constitutionality of the legislature's actions, making two principal arguments. First, they argued that the royal charter by which the College was created was a contract within the meaning of the Contract Clause of the federal Constitution and that the New Hampshire legislature's act interfered with "the Obligation of Contracts."[75] Secondly, they argued that under the New Hampshire constitution they had vested rights in the college of which they could not be deprived.[76] Both of these arguments depended upon the classification of Dartmouth College as a private corporation, which would then, at common law, take on the rights of a private individual.

The classification of Dartmouth College was a delicate and disputed matter, and that classification ended up being the heart of the case. But equally significant for the lawyers on both sides was the case's procedural posture. When the trustees of Dartmouth College sought to challenge the New Hampshire legislature's efforts to change the college's educational practices, they were originally advised to make that challenge in the New Hampshire state courts.[77] This advice rested on the belief that it would be impolitic to avoid the state courts on a matter so clearly involving the state of New Hampshire, and that patently artificial procedural steps, such as the creation of a friendly suit involving nonresident supporters of the College, were necessary to meet the jurisdictional requirements of the federal courts. Lawyers for the College believed that although they might well lose in the New Hampshire courts because a policy decision of the New Hampshire legislature was being challenged, they could still appeal to the United States Supreme Court.[78]

The existing appellate jurisdiction of the Supreme Court, however, necessitated that the appeal take the form of a writ of error and therefore be limited to those acts of the New Hampshire state legislature that had been claimed to violate the federal Constitution. This meant that the Marshall Court would hear only the Contract Clause issue and not the broader issue of whether a state legislature could infringe on vested rights.

---

[75] "No State shall . . . pass any . . . Law impairing the Obligation of Contracts . . ." U.S. Const., Art. 1, sect. 10.

[76] See Trustees of Dartmouth College v. Woodward, 1 N.H. 111, 129 (1817), rev'd, 4 Wheat. 518 (1819).

[77] See Stites, *Private Interest*, 40–41.

[78] Ibid.

The narrow ground of review concerned counsel for the College because it was by no means clear that a royal charter, imposing no limitations on its recipient, was a contract within the meaning of the Constitution. Moreover, some lawyers for the College believed that several Marshall Court Justices, including William Johnson, Washington, Story, and the Chief Justice, would be sympathetic to the vested rights argument.[79]

In November 1817 the Supreme Court of New Hampshire unanimously held against the College.[80] Shortly thereafter the lawyers for the College began to plan an alternate course of action. Daniel Webster, whom the College had retained to appeal the decision to the Supreme Court, wrote one of the College's trustees that, in addition to the appeal from the New Hampshire court's decision, cases should be instituted in the circuit court of New Hampshire "which should present *both* & all our points, to the Supreme Court."[81]

Webster had in mind a cognate action, structured to qualify for jurisdiction in Story's circuit court. Eventually three such actions were brought in the form of actions of ejectment.[82] The College leased some of its land, possession of which it continued to claim during the litigation, to citizens of Vermont, and those citizens claimed that they had been ejected by officials of the newly created Dartmouth University. The action of ejectment raised the validity of the respective titles of Dartmouth College and Dartmouth University to the land, and a stipulation that the worth of the land was over $500 guaranteed jurisdiction based on diversity of citizenship.

The cognate suits were brought before Story in Portsmouth on May 1, 1818. Earlier Webster had argued the Contract Clause issue before the Supreme Court in Washington, and the Court had announced, on March 13, that the case would be continued until its next term, which would begin on February 1, 1819.[83] Justice Story would therefore have to agree fairly quickly to issue a certificate of division for the cognate actions to be heard the following term in the Supreme Court. Webster clearly felt that Story would be willing to cooperate. In a letter to another one of the College's lawyers, Webster stated that

---

[79] Ibid., 40–41, 69.

[80] Trustees of Dartmouth College v. Woodward, 1 N.H. 111 (1817), rev'd, 4 Wheat 518 (1819).

[81] Letter from D. Webster to Charles Marsh, Dec. 8, 1817, Daniel Webster Papers, Dartmouth College Library. Emphasis in original.

[82] *Hatch* v. *Lang, Marsh* v. *Allen,* and *Pierce ex dem. Lyaman* v. *Gilbert.*

None of the cases was reported. See Stites, *Private Interest,* 90–91, 149. A fourth case was brought, *Allen* v. *College,* but it did not raise the vested rights issues as squarely as the others and was treated separately. See Shirley, *Dartmouth College Causes,* 3–4, 298–301.

[83] See Stites, *Private Interest,* 68.

I have no doubt [that Justice Story] will [be] incline[d] to send up the new cause in the most convenient manner, without giving any opinion, and probably without an argument. If the district judge will agree to divide without argument, *pro forma,* I think Judge Story will incline so to dispose of the cause.[84]

Justice Story was indeed so inclined. When counsel for the University argued that the ejectment suits were fictitious, Story dismissed their objections. One observer sympathetic to the University likened Story's action to "an assumption of power equivalent to French despotism," but found it consistent with Story's insistence on continually extending the jurisdiction of the federal courts.[85] The University then asked for a continuance to the October circuit term, which Story granted. Yet at the same time, as a trustee of the College observed, Story

made the most positive injunction on the defendants to plead in season and be prepared for trial early the next term, and it was suggested that an adjourned term [of circuit court] would be holden for their trial if necessary in order that some one or more of [the cognate cases] might be entered in the Supreme Court at next term [1819]. The Judge intimated that this was of great importance as the action now there . . . did not perhaps present all the questions that would naturally arise out of the controversy. . . . [He] assured the parties that nothing should be wanting on the part of the court to place the actions in such train as would insure their final decision.[86]

Webster, commenting on Story's actions, said that there was "a good deal of ingenious painstaking effort to defeat the suit . . . but without success. The *Judge* said it was important that a cause should go up embracing all the questions. I should not have great doubt of *his* opinion, when we get the question *fairly & broadly up.*"[87]

In October, when Story's circuit reconvened in Exeter, Story and John Sherbourne, the district judge, agreed to issue a certificate of division, rendering no opinions and hearing no arguments. Both sides stipulated that the sole question at issue in the case was the constitutionality of the 1816 New Hampshire bill, and both sides were given leave to add or delete facts in the record, providing the opposing side consented. The lawyers for the University had discovered some new facts pertaining to

---

[84] Letter from D. Webster to Jeremiah Mason, Apr. 23, 1818, reprinted in McIntyre, *Writings and Speeches,* XVII, 280, 281.

[85] Letter from Richard Ela to William Plumer, Jr., May 19, 1818, noted in Stites, *Private Interest,* 151.

[86] Letter from C. Marsh to Francis Brown, May 2, 1818, quoted in Baxter, *Daniel Webster,* 93. See Stites, *Private Interest,* 93.

[87] Letter from D. Webster to Joseph Hopkinson, July 3, 1818, emphasis in original, quoted in Stites, *Private Interest,* 151, note 27.

the original purpose of the charter, which they thought strengthened their position that Dartmouth College was a public institution, and they sought to use the records of the cognate cases to introduce these facts. By early January 1819 the records of the cognate cases were apparently complete,[88] and the cases were entered on the Court's docket on February 1, 1819.[89]

The cognate cases were never heard by the Marshall Court, however, because on February 2 Chief Justice Marshall declared that the Court had come to a decision on *Dartmouth College* and began reading from the draft of his opinion. The text of Marshall's opinion focused principally on the Contract Clause argument, although Marshall's language invested that argument with overtones of natural law and the fundamentality of vested property rights. Meanwhile Story, anticipating that the cognate cases might also be heard in the 1819 Term, had prepared and circulated a draft opinion.[90] Story's opinion went well beyond the Contract Clause argument to consider "the nature, rights and duties of . . . corporations"; it sought to make a distinction between public and private corporations which would have been useful in the disposition of the cognate cases.[91] Story's opinion was eventually published as a concurrence, with which Justice Livingston, who had read Story's draft, joined,[92] and from which Justice Johnson specifically disassociated himself.[93]

The subsequent history of the cognate cases was ironic. When Marshall began reading the opinion of the Court in *Dartmouth College,* counsel for the University were apparently not even in the courtroom.[94] Perhaps because of this, or perhaps because of the presence of the cognate cases, the Supreme Court did not enter a final judgment disposing of *Dartmouth College* v. *Woodward* at that time but asked counsel for the

---

[88] Counsel for the University, however, had not actually included the "new facts" in the papers it prepared for submission to the Supreme Court, only a statement indicating that counsel planned to introduce new facts. See Stites, *Private Interest,* at 94–95; letter from Salma Hale (a trustee of Dartmouth University), to William Allen (president of Dartmouth University), Dec. 16, 1818, Dartmouth College Library.

[89] Dockets of the Supreme Court of the United States (Aug. 4, 1791–Aug. 2, 1834), vol. C, at 1022, National Archives, reprinted in National Archives Microfilm Publications, Microcopy No. 216.

[90] See letter from Brockholst Livingston to J. Story, Jan. 24, 1819, re-

printed in W. Story, *Life and Letters,* 323; letter from William Prescott to J. Story, Jan. 9, 1819, reprinted in ibid., 324.

[91] 4 Wheat at 667, 668–69.

[92] Ibid., 666.

[93] Ibid.

[94] A February 2, 1819 letter from Cyrus Perkins, a supporter of the University, to University president William Allen stated:

The Opinion of the Court has been given this afternoon most unexpectedly on the cause as argued last term—*and against us*!! . . . and even our counsel was not there, 'til just the close of the Opinion!! They had no intimation that it was to have been delivered without a new argument.

University and the College whether they would agree to the admission of any new facts raised by the cognate cases. Webster, who had been prepared to argue the cognate cases, now refused to admit any new facts, and so shortly thereafter[95] the Supreme Court entered judgment against the University. Webster argued to the Justices that the cognate cases had come to the Marshall Court only "for a direction [to Story's circuit court on] what judgment to give on the verdict" and that the proper disposition of the cognate cases was to remand them to Story's circuit.[96] Marshall agreed, and the cases were remanded on February 25. Webster was confident that Story would quickly dispose of the cases, for on April 13 he wrote that "the judge will tell the defendants [the University] that the new facts which they talk of, were presented to the minds of the judges at Washington, and that, if all proved, they would not have the least effect on the opinion of any judge."[97]

Webster was substantially correct. When Story's circuit court opened on May 1 the University lawyers asked for a continuance, and Story granted one until May 15. At the same time, however, he read an opinion, granting judgment for the College, which was apparently substantially the same as his concurrence to the Supreme Court opinion.[98] He and counsel for both sides then agreed that the May 1 judgment would stand unless any new facts presented by the University altered his views. The University lawyers eventually presented some new facts to Story, principally information from papers of Dartmouth College's original founder, Eleazer Wheelock, and argued that this information demonstrated that the College had always been considered a public institution. On May

---

Letter from C. Perkins to W. Allen, Feb. 2, 1819, Dartmouth College Archives. Daniel Webster, in a letter to Jeremiah Mason, claimed that William Pinkney, whom the university had retained to reargue the cases, had been present when Marshall began reading the opinion. Letter from D. Webster to J. Mason, Feb. 4, 1819, reprinted in McIntyre, *Writings and Speeches*, XVI, 43. Neither source can be regarded as disinterested, but it seems clear that the Justices were well aware of efforts to reargue the case; they had, after all, set it down for reargument.

[95] Several letters by Daniel Webster indicate that the Court entered its final judgment on February 23. Letter from D. Webster to F. Brown, Feb. 23, 1819, reprinted in McIntyre, *Writings and Speeches*, XVII, 301; letter from D. Webster to J. Mason, Feb. 24, 1819, reprinted in McIntyre, *Writings and Speeches*, XVI, 44; letter from D. Webster to Jeremiah Smith, Feb. 28, 1819, reprinted in ibid., 45. The Minutes of the Supreme Court, supra, note 7, vol. C at 83, indicate February 25. Webster's date seems more reliable because he would have been eager to communicate the news, and his first two letters were written before the date designated by the Supreme Court minutes.

[96] Letter from Webster to Brown, Feb. 23, 1819, supra, note 95.

[97] Letter from D. Webster to J. Mason, Apr. 18, 1819, reprinted in McIntyre, *Writings and Speeches*, XVI, 49.

[98] See Stites, *Private Interest*, 97–98, 152.

27 counsel for the University presented the new facts, but Story "saw nothing to vary at all the case, as it had been considered and decided."[99]

The above examples of discretionary use of procedure—one might be tempted to say manipulation of procedure—by Marshall Court Justices may or may not have been unusual, as comparable documentation is lacking for most of the Marshall Court's cases. The responses of Marshall in *Martin* and Story in *Dartmouth College* were certainly products of the special significance attributed by those Justices to the cases involved, and the responses illustrate the ample opportunities Marshall Court Justices had to control the manner by which significant cases came to the Court. Although one may question the desirability of these practices, modern observers should not draw hasty conclusions about their ethical implications. Story's relationship with Webster in *Dartmouth College* and Marshall's surreptitious intervention in *Martin* may have crossed the line of ethical behavior, even by nineteenth-century standards, and there is evidence that both Story and Marshall took pains to create a public impression that they had approached the *Martin* and *Dartmouth College* cases in a disinterested fashion.[100] As previously mentioned, however, Justices

---

[99] Letter from D. Webster to F. Brown, May 30, 1819, in McIntyre, *Writings and Speeches,* XVII, 306. See Stites, *Private Interest,* 98.

[100] Marshall, of course, had recused himself in *Fairfax, Martin,* and the North Carolina circuit case. Story had no immediate financial interest at stake in *Dartmouth College,* but, like Marshall, he seems to have distinguished the impressions he wanted to create among lawyers directly involved with the case from the impressions he wanted to create among the general public. He was willing to have conversations about the case not only with Webster but with Jeremiah Mason, Webster's co-counsel; word of his action as a "feed counsellor" reached the ears of counsel for the College, who were outraged. See R. Newmyer, "Daniel Webster As Tocqueville's Lawyer: The *Dartmouth College* Case Again," *Am. J. Legal Hist.,* 11:127, 135 (1967); letter from J. Hopkinson to C. Marsh, Dec. 31, 1817, quoted in Shirley, *Dartmouth College Causes,* 274–75. But in his letter to Mason, Webster reported Story as having "said he had had a correspondence with you about 'things'; but *company being present,* did not say what things." Let-

ter from Webster to Mason, January 1818, supra (emphasis added).

Joseph Hopkinson's reaction to Story's interventionist attitude in *Dartmouth College* is particularly interesting. Hopkinson wrote in the above letter to Marsh:

The situation in which, if you are not misinformed, Judge Story has placed himself is much more alarming to us—and so disreputable to him should he sit in the case—that I confess I am inclined to believe that your information in this respect, must be mistaken. [S]hould it however be otherwise and he is about to sit as judge in a cause in which he has been a feed counsellor, I should have no hesitation in resorting to any legal and proper means to prevent such an abuse of power and office.

Letter from Hopkinson to Marsh, Dec. 31, 1817, supra. Hopkinson made this comment in the middle of a letter that exclusively discussed litigation strategy in the *Dartmouth College* case, so it is hard to know whether his use of the language "abuse of power" and "disreputable" was primarily that of an adversary or reflected deeper, and perhaps

of the Marshall Court labored under different conceptions of the proper role of the judiciary. To understand fully early-nineteenth-century ethical standards one needs to examine those conceptions. But at this point still more detail on the Court's inner life is necessary, so that the texture in which those conceptions were set can be firmly established.

If one takes a superficial look at the reported decisions of the Supreme Court during the Marshall era, two important characteristics of the Supreme Court's deliberative processes would seem to emerge. The Court's decisions were swift, and they were almost always unanimous. The Justices often handed down opinions within a few days of argument, and the opinions were rarely accompanied by dissents. The Marshall Court's reported decisions do not, however, adequately disclose the true nature of the Court's deliberative practices; one must look further to appraise the speed and unanimity of the Court's decisions.

By contemporary standards, the Marshall Court was breathtakingly quick to render decisions. Although between 1815 and 1835 the Court usually did not hear arguments before February 1, it routinely handed down decisions in cases argued in early February by the last two weeks of that month. In many years the Court disposed of, with opinion, every case on its docket for that term by the middle of March. Moreover, the time between argument and the announcement of decisions was astonishingly short. Of sixty-six constitutional cases decided with full opinion between 1815 and 1835, the Marshall Court decided seventeen no more than five days after the conclusion of the argument.[101] This would mean, if modern practices were followed, that within a space of five days or less the Justices held a conference on the case, came to a decision, assigned the opinion, produced and circulated a draft of the opinion, registered concurrences or dissents, and delivered the opinion in open court. Nor were the "five days or less" cases insignificant cases: included in their number were *Cohens* v. *Virginia,*[102] *Willson* v. *Black-bird Creek*

---

widely shared, professional sentiments. Story may, of course, have believed that nothing he said to Webster or Marsh would be repeated to anyone else. If so, this belief was ill founded and perhaps naive.

[101] Minutes of the Supreme Court of the United States (Feb. 1, 1790–Aug. 4, 1828), National Archives, reprinted in National Archives Microfilm Publications, Microcopy No. 215, Roll No. 1; ibid. (Jan. 12, 1829–Aug. 7, 1837), reprinted in National Archives Microfilm Publications, Microcopy No. 215, Roll No. 2.

[102] 6 Wheat. 264 (1821). The *Cohens* case was divided into two parts, the jurisdictional issue, which was argued on February 18, 1921, ibid. at 290, and decided on March 3, and the merits, which were argued on March 2 and decided on March 5. Ibid. at 430.

*Marsh Co.*,[103] *Cherokee Nation* v. *Georgia,* [104] and *Barron* v. *Mayor of Baltimore*.[105]

Although the Marshall Court disposed of cases more quickly than the modern Court, one must recognize that several internal practices of the Marshall Court which are not followed today led to these extraordinary results. One such practice was that opinions delivered by one Justice in court had not been subscribed to, in all their language, by the other Justices, not even the ones joining in the opinion. A Marshall Court opinion was typically rendered in the form of an "opinion of the Court," delivered by one Justice, with no disclosure of the positions of other Justices. In many instances where the decision represented the views of only a majority of the Justices, there was no indication to that effect in the United States Reports and there were no published concurrences or dissents. This made it unnecessary in many cases for all the Justices to react to the content of an opinion delivered in court. Given the relative absence of pressure on a Justice purportedly writing for the Court to clear his language with each of his peers, one of the principal factors that serve to delay current Supreme Court opinions was eliminated.

The unlimited time given to oral arguments during Marshall's tenure also may have contributed to the speedy production of opinions. Eyewitnesses suggest that oral arguments before the Marshall Court more resembled orations than colloquies; the Justices sat largely silent.[106] Marshall has been reported, perhaps apocryphally, to have said that the "acme of judicial distinction means the ability to look a lawyer straight in the eyes for two hours and not hear a damned word he says."[107] Perhaps, in fact, Marshall and the other Justices were using time during oral argument to prepare the skeleton of opinions.

Because arguments in major cases invariably lasted longer than a day, the Justices could also find time to discuss a pending case at the boardinghouse. Nothing prevented them from having an informal conference on the case while it was still being argued; conceivably nothing

---

[103] 2 Pet. 245 (1829)
[104] 5 Pet 1 (1831)
[105] 7 Pet. 243 (1833).
[106] A contemporary newspaper correspondent reported:

The Courts sits from eleven o'clock in the morning until four in the afternoon. It is not only one of the most dignified and enlightened tribunals in the world, but one of the most patient. Counsel are heard in silence for hours, without being stopped or interrupted. . . . The Judges of the Court say nothing, but when they are fatigued and worried by a long and pointless argument . . . their feelings and wishes are sufficiently manifested by their countenances.

New York *Statesman*, Feb. 7, 1824, quoted in Warren, *Supreme Court,* I, 467.
[107] Beveridge, *John Marshall,* IV, 83. The anecdote is too good not to repeat, but it has the aura of embellishment.

prevented them from taking informal votes on the case while it was still pending. As Justice Story put it, the justices "moot[ed] every case as we proceed[ed]."[108] Even if one doubts the Justices would have acted so precipitately, surely nothing prevented an individual Justice—say Marshall, Story, or Johnson, who wrote the overwhelming majority of opinions in constitutional cases—from making up his mind early and using counsel's arguments in creating an embryonic opinion. If one therefore expands the time for producing the draft opinion to include days during which the case was still being argued but was being discussed in the boardinghouse, the speedy dispatch of Marshall Court business becomes more comprehensible.

Occasionally historians have claimed that Marshall Court opinions were written beforehand. *McCulloch v. Maryland*[109] has received particular attention,[110] and in *Dartmouth College*,[111] as previously discussed, there is clear evidence that Justice Story prepared and circulated an opinion which would have been "prewritten" had the court actually heard the case a second time.[112] With the exception of *Dartmouth College*, the "pre-written" theory cannot be proved or disproved because those manuscript opinions of the Justices that have survived bear no dates, and even if some were to surface with dates, it is hardly likely that a draft opinion would be given a date that identified it as having been written before arguments on the case had been completed.

Even though the Marshall Court decided cases quickly, the opinions themselves were not published for an extended period of time. After delivering their opinions in court, the Justices gave the text of their manuscripts to the Court Reporter, whose duty was "to abridge arguments, to state facts, [and] to give the opinions of the Court substantially as they [were] delivered."[113] The process was typically completed months, occasionally years, after the opinion had been delivered in court.[114]

Thus one should not conclude that the Marshall Court Justices were able to reach swift results simply because of sheer determination and hard work. Several practices that have been rejected over time enabled the Court to act so quickly; here comparisons between the modern Court, which operates in a very different setting, and the Marshall Court are

---

[108] Letter from J. Story to Samuel P. P. Fay, Feb. 24, 1812, reprinted in W. Story, *Life and Letters*, 215.

[109] 4 Wheat. 316 (1819).

[110] See, e.g., Beveridge, *John Marshall*, IV, 290.

[111] Supra, note 73.

[112] See Stites, *Private Interest*, 83–84; letter from B. Livingston to J. Story, Jan. 24, 1819, reprinted in W.

Story, *Life and Letters*, I, 323; letter from W. Prescott to J. Story, Jan. 9, 1819, reprinted in ibid., 324.

[113] Letter from J. Story to R. Peters, Jr., May 7, 1836, reprinted in W. Story, *Life and Letters*, II, 231–32.

[114] See generally C. Swisher, *The Taney Period, 1836–64* (1974), 293–318.

fruitless. In rejecting the above procedures of the Marshall Court, the modern Court has sacrificed a certain amount of speed in exchange for greater accountability and collegial exchange in its process of producing opinions. This was a sacrifice, as illustrated below, that Chief Justice Marshall was not willing to make.

Throughout most of Marshall's tenure, the Court had a remarkable percentage of unanimous or near unanimous decisions, with a select group of Justices producing the majority of the Court's opinions. For example, between 1816 and 1823, a period in which the Court's composition was unchanged, the Justices produced a total of 302 majority opinions. In all these cases, only twenty-four dissents and eight concurrences were recorded, and eight of the dissents and four of the concurrences can be attributed to Justice William Johnson. Chief Justice Marshall wrote 124 of the majority opinions, dissenting only four times; Justice Story wrote 66 majority opinions, also dissenting on only four occasions, and Justice Johnson wrote 47 majority opinions. Together the remaining Justices produced only 65 majority opinions.[115] To observers of the modern Court, which often seems to speak in a cacophony of voices, such a record seems puzzling and in need of further investigation.

One prominent explanation for such unanimity must be the setting within which the justices worked. The use of a boardinghouse as a residence, a common dining establishment, and a shared office greatly enhanced the Justices' opportunities to discuss and dispose of cases informally. Although individual Justices were periodically absent from the boardinghouse for recreational[116] or social pursuits, until 1830 the Marshall Court Justices slept under the same roof, ate together at meals, and worked within the same small building. Story's comments when he first took his seat on the Court in 1812 suggest the effects of boardinghouse living on the Justices. He wrote to Nathaniel Williams on February 16 of that year that "[w]e live very harmoniously and familiarly," and "moot questions as they are argued, with freedom";[117] to Samuel Fay on February 24 that "[m]y brethren are very interesting men with whom I live in the most frank and unaffected intimacy";[118] and to his wife on March 5 that "the Judges here live with perfect harmony."[119] In the letter to Fay he was most explicit:

---

[115] These figures are taken from volumes 14–21 (1–8 Wheat.) of the United States Reports (1816–23).

[116] John Marshall, for exmaple, regularly walked three miles before breakfast. See letters from J. Marshall to M. A. Marshall, Feb. 12, 1826, Jan. 31, 1830, reprinted in Mason, *My Dearest Polly*, 292–93; 317–18.

[117] Letter from J. Story to N. Williams, Feb. 16, 1812, reprinted in W. Story, *Life and Letters*, I, 214.

[118] Letter from Story to Fay, Feb. 24, 1812, supra, note 108.

[119] Letter from J. Story to Sarah Waldo Story, Mar. 5, 1812, reprinted in W. Story, *Life and Letters*, I, 217.

# Chapter III: *The Working Life of the Court*

[W]e are all united as one, with a mutual esteem which makes even the labors of Jurisprudence light. The mode of arguing causes in the Supreme Court is excessively prolix and tedious; but generally the subject is exhausted, and it is not very difficult to perceive at the close of the cause, in many cases, where the press of the argument and of the law lies. We moot every question as we proceed, and [our] familiar conferences at our lodgings often come to a very quick, and, I trust, a very accurate opinion, in a few hours. . . .

. . . One great cause of the Holland Land Company, of which I had a printed brief of two hundred and thirty pages, lasted five days in argument, and has now been happily decided. It was my first cause, and though excessively complex, I had the pleasure to find that my own views were those which ultimately obtained the sanction of the whole Court.[120]

The "Holland Land Company" case to which Story referred was *United States* v. *Crosby*,[121] handed down the same day he wrote the letter. Story's opinion in the *Crosby* case did not reveal its "excessively complex" nature. The case, which involved a dispute over land originally claimed by the Dutch West India Company, presented the question whether the validity of a contract passing title to land was controlled by the law of the jurisdiction where the contract was signed or that where the land was located. In *Crosby* a contract transferring land in Maine had been executed, without a seal, on the West Indian island of Grenada. The United States government, claiming title under the Grenadian contract, sought to eject Jonah Crosby, the possessor of the land. Grenadian law provided that contracts executed without a seal were valid; Maine law required that land be conveyed by contracts under seal. Story's entire opinion for the Court read: "The court entertain no doubt on the subject; and are clearly of opinion, that the title to land can be acquired and lost only in the manner prescribed by the law of the place where such land is situate."[122] Notwithstanding the five days it had taken counsel to argue the *Crosby* case, and notwithstanding the presence of a 230-page brief, the Court disposed of it in less than two weeks. Story had previously written on the very question in dispute, and the other justices apparently deferred to his expertise.[123] "[M]y first strong views [on the Holland Company Cause]," he had written Williams eight days before the formal delivery of his opinion, "have been those which the Court have ultimately supported."[124]

---

[120] Letter from Story to Fay, Feb. 24, 1812, supra, note 108, at 215–16.
[121] 7 Cranch 115 (1812).
[122] Ibid., at 116.
[123] See Dunne, *Joseph Story,* 92; K. Nadelmann, "Joseph Story's Contri-

bution to American Conflicts Law: A Comment," *Am. J. Legal Hist.,* 5:230, 238 (1961).
[124] Letter from Story to Williams, Feb. 16, 1812, supra, note 117.

Although the boardinghouse setting could lead to a unanimous result in certain cases, it does not totally explain the phenomenal record of unanimity of the Marshall Court. A look at the United States Reports of the period would compel one to believe that all seven Justices were able to agree on practically every case. Although they well may have been able to agree on many decisions, two practices of the Court gave the appearance of unanimity even when the Justices did not agree.

The first of the practices, common in the earlier years of the Marshall Court, was the delivery of opinions on seniority grounds, the Chief Justice being regarded as most senior and the other Justices ranked by years in service.[125] Under this system, one could not tell whether the judge who delivered the opinion in Court had actually written the opinion[126] or even joined in the result. Although there is some evidence that by 1815 seniority had ceased to become an overwhelming consideration in the delivery of opinions, as late as 1810 only four opinions were delivered by Justices when more senior Justices were present.[127] The seniority practice, if followed, ensured that the Chief Justice, who did not miss a full term of Court during his entire tenure, would deliver the opinion in the great bulk of cases.

A second feature, the "opinion of the Court" practice, also could give a false impression of unanimity. Under this practice, as Johnson put it, a Justice was appointed "to deliver the opinion of the majority," and other Justices were given "discretion to record their opinions."[128] As a consequence there is no way of ascertaining whether unrecorded opinions

---

[125] See Haskins and Johnson, *Foundations of Power*, 385–88.

[126] An 1822 letter from William Johnson to Thomas Jefferson testifies to the importance of seniority in delivering the Court's opinions. Johnson stated that on coming in the Court in 1805 he found Marshall "delivering all the opinions in cases in which he sat, even in some instances when contrary to his own judgment & vote." Letter from W. Johnson to T. Jefferson, Dec. 10, 1822, Thomas Jefferson Papers, Library of Congress. When Johnson protested against this practice, he recalled, "the answer was [Marshall] is willing to take the trouble, & [the practice] is a mark of respect to him." Ibid. Johnson claimed that later in his tenure "I got them to adopt the course they now pursue, which is to appoint someone to deliver the opinion of the majority, but leave it to the discretion of the rest of the judges to record their opinions or not. . . ." Ibid. The Johnson letter sup-

ports the existence of opinions being delivered by the most senior Justice present; it also suggests that it was not even necessary for the Justice delivering the opinion to have voted with the majority.

Other evidence has surfaced that indicates that in the early years of the Marshall Court the deliverer of the opinion had not always written it. In several cases there is language that suggests that the justice delivering the opinion was not necessarily the author. See M'Ilvaine v. Coxe's Lessee, 4 Cranch 209 (1808); M'Ferran v. Taylor, 3 Cranch 270, 281 (1806); Stuart v. Laird, 1 Cranch 299, 308 (1803). This issue is discussed in Haskins and Johnson, *Foundations of Power*, 383–85.

[127] See Haskins and Johnson, *Foundations of Power*, 386–87.

[128] Letter from Johnson to Jefferson, Dec. 10, 1822, supra, note 126.

would have been concurrences or dissents. Occasionally Marshall Court opinions from this period intimated that an opinion of the Court, from which there had been no recorded dissents, was only an opinion of a majority,[129] and sometimes a division in the Court would reveal itself in a later case;[130] but the practice of openly revealing unrecorded dissents seems to have been followed sporadically and frowned upon generally.[131] Story, in an 1818 letter to Henry Wheaton, stated that "the habit of delivering dissenting opinions on ordinary occasions weakens the authority of the Court, and is of no public benefit."[132]

A significant consequence of the "opinion of the Court" practice was to free those Justices who declined to publicize their concurrences or dissents from being formally accountable for their votes. If in the "familiar conferences" a Justice concluded that his position would be

---

[129] Compare, e.g., Green v. Biddle, 8 Wheat. 1, 94 (1823) ("the opinion of a majority of the Court") with The Frances & Eliza v. Coates, 8 Wheat. 398, 406 (1823) ("the unanimous opinion of the Court"). In both cases the Reporter introduced the opinion by stating that a particular Justice had delivered the opinion of the Court. *Green*, 8 Wheat. at 69; *The Frances & Eliza*, 8 Wheat. at 404.

[130] In Ogden v. Saunders, 12 Wheat. 213, 272–73 (1827), Justice William Johnson stated that in Sturges v. Crowninshield, 4 Wheat. 122 (1819), "the Court was . . . greatly divided in their views of the doctrine, and the judgment partakes as much of a compromise as of a legal adjudication." In the *Sturges* opinion the Reporter stated only that "Mr. Chief Justice Marshall delivered the opinion of the Court." 4 Wheat. at 191.

[131] One can see evidence of the practice in instances in which Justices decided to depart from it. In 1814 Story wrote in dissent that "I have the misfortune to differ from a majority of the Court. . . . Had this been an ordinary case I should have contented myself with silence. . . ." The Nereide, 9 Cranch 388, 455 (1815) (Story, J., dissenting). In 1827 Marshall, in one of his rare dissents, said that he "should now, as is my custom, when I have the misfortune to differ from this Court, acquiesce silently in its opinion," had he not believed that his circuit court opinion, which the Court was reversing,

was right in the first place. Bank of the United States v. Dandridge, 12 Wheat. 64, 90 (1827) (Marshall, C.J., dissenting). That same term Washington, in a dissent, indicated that "[i]t has never been my habit to deliver dissenting opinions in cases where it has been my misfortune to differ from those which have been pronounced by a majority of this Court." Mason v. Haile, 12 Wheat. 370, 379 (1827) (Washington, J., dissenting). Only Johnson, who announced in 1824 that "in questions of great importance and great delicacy, I feel my duty to the public best discharged by an effort to maintain my opinions in my own way," openly opposed the practice. Gibbons v. Ogden, 9 Wheat 1, 223 (1824) (Johnson, J., dissenting).

[132] Letter from J. Story to H. Wheaton, Apr. 8, 1818), reprinted in W. Story, *Life and Letters*, I, 303–304. In another letter to Wheaton, written two days later, Story indicated that "a majority of the Court," including himself, had "suppressed from motives of delicacy" the disposition of one issue that ran counter to the treatment of that issue in an opinion of the Court written by Marshall. The issue in question—"exemptions of a public shop of war from State jurisdiction"—was not necessary to decide, given Marshall's opinion. The case was United States v. Bevans, 3 Wheat. 336 (1818). See letter from J. Story to H. Wheaton, Apr. 10, 1818, reprinted in W. Story, *Life and Letters*, I, 305.

outvoted, he could then choose not to record an opinion, and not only his views but his vote would remain unknown. As Thomas Jefferson had suggested to Johnson, the practice ensured that "nobody knows what opinion any individual member gave in any case, nor even that he who delivers the opinion, concurred in it himself."[133] Jefferson may not have been fair in insinuating that the silent Justices on the Court were "lazy," "modest," and "incompetent,"[134] but he was correct in noting that the practice insulated silent Justices from accountability.

The practice of allowing Justices the discretion whether or not to record their opinions also had a marked effect on the circulation of draft opinions among the members of the Marshall Court. Because Justices were unlikely to register a dissent or concurrence, the author of the opinion had no reason to circulate his opinion so that separate opinions could be prepared. In fact, there was an incentive not to circulate a draft opinion because circulation only gave other Justices who concurred in the result an opportunity to object to the opinion's language or reasoning. At the same time, because Justices were not going to be on record as having subscribed individually to the language of the opinion of the Court, they had no incentive to quarrel about its wording. In short, neither the author of an opinion of the Court nor any other Justice had an interest in seeing drafts of opinions, except in the comparatively rare circumstances[135] when an individual had decided to register a concurrence or a dissent.[136]

---

[133] Letter from T. Jefferson to W. Johnson, Oct. 27, 1822, reprinted in P. Ford, ed., *The Writings of Thomas Jefferson* (10 vols., 1892–99), X, 222, 225.

[134] Ibid.

[135] Only 32 dissents were filed in 305 cases between 1816 and 1823. These figures are taken from volumes 14–21 (1–8 Wheat.) of the United States Reports (1816–23).

[136] Contemporary evidence demonstrates that there was little circulation and editing of Supreme Court manuscript opinions. The internal correspondence of Justices and those Marshall Court draft opinions that have survived from the period suggest that although there was regular discussion among the Justices about circuit court cases, there was comparatively little editing of Supreme Court manuscript opinions by other Justices, and that alterations, if any, were usually made by the Court Reporter or the author of the opinion. Research for this study has unearthed 70 draft opinions, some only partially preserved. Of these the great bulk (51) are from the 1832 Term. Only 12 draft manuscripts exist for the 1816 and 1817 Terms, and none thereafter until the 1828 Term. Five opinions— Bank of the United States v. Green, 6 Pet. 26 (1832); Dufau v. Couprey's Heirs, 6 Pet. 170 (1832); Leland v. Wilkinson, 6 Pet. 317 (1832); New Jersey v. New York, 6 Pet. 323 (1832); United States v. M'Daniel, 6 Pet. 634 (1832)—are signed by Marshall but appear to be in Story's handwriting rather than Marshall's. Two other opinions, *Ex parte* Bradstreet, 6 Pet. 774 (1832), and Gassies v. Balloon, 6 Pet. 761 (1832), again signed by Marshall, appear to be in the handwriting of Reporter Richard Peters. No other manuscript opinions bear signs of editing by persons other than the author. Copies of the manuscript opinions are available in the National Archives. Marshall had had a serious prostrate operation in October 1831 and was still convalescing at the opening of the 1832 Term. See Beveridge, *John Marshall*, IV, 518–24.

# Chapter III: *The Working Life of the Court*

The result of noncirculation was to make an opinion of the Court a highly individualized product that certainly cannot be considered a concerted effort of a unified court. An opinion of the Court merely reflected one Justice's effort to advance a formal justification for a majority decision made orally and informally. Thus the perception of a united Court speaking in one voice that represented all its members is illusory. The Marshall Court sacrificed individual expression in favor of an impression of unanimity.

Although these practices help explain how the Marshall Court was able to convey an aura of unanimity, they do not explain why dissenting or concurring Justices were willing to acquiesce in such practices. Again, the boardinghouse setting serves as a partial explanation. The boardinghouse provided not only an informal forum in which the Justices could discuss issues until they were resolved but also a fraternal setting in which one Justice might not want to disagree openly with another Justice. Even Justices who would have liked to disagree or to explain their reasoning were likely not to dissent to avoid discord among the Court's members. The changing attitude of William Johnson illustrates this point.

Johnson was appointed to the Court in 1805 by Jefferson, who regarded the appointment as an opportunity to put a Justice of unquestionable Republican sympathies on a Court that Jefferson suspected of being highly unsympathetic to his views.[137] Johnson, for his part, not only supported Jefferson's political views but also was a loyal confidant and frequent correspondent of Jefferson. After an initial period in which he wrote a handful of concurrences and dissents, however, Johnson apparently lapsed into acquiescence; he opposed almost no opinions of the Court from 1819 to 1822.[138] In that last year, infuriated by the Court's "consolidationist" tendencies, Jefferson wrote to Johnson deploring the practice of silent Court opinions.[139]

Responding to Jefferson's letter, Johnson described the internal atmosphere of the Marshall Court:

> Some case soon occurred [after Johnson's appointment] in which I disagreed from my brethren & I thought it a thing of course to deliver my opinion. But, during the rest of the session I heard nothing but lectures on the indecency of judges cutting at each other, & the loss of reputation which the Virginia appellate court had sustained by pursuing such a course etc. At length I found that I must either submit to circumstances or become such a cypher in our consultations as to effect no good at all. I therefore bent to the current. . . .[140]

---

[137] See D. Morgan, *Justice William Johnson: The First Dissenter* (1954), 41–54.

[138] Ibid., 176–89.

[139] Letter from Jefferson to Johnson, Oct. 27, 1822, supra, note 133, at 223–25.

[140] Letter from Johnson to Jefferson, Dec. 10, 1822, supra, note 126.

The practices described in this exchange were in some sense the inevitable product of a Court whose members lived and worked together and who saw themselves as transients in the Washington community, linked by a common boardinghouse residence. One may view internal harmony, a mutual concern to minimize each other's labors, and an indisposition to have "judges cut at each other" as goals of a community of persons who live and work in close contact with one another and collectively perform a visible public function. In advocating seriatim opinions Johnson was opposing the group psychology of the boardinghouse.

The boardinghouse setting can be considered only a partial explanation, however, for the Justices' willingness to conform to practices that gave a false impression of unanimity and resulted in certain Justices' delivering a large majority of opinions. Another key factor was the dominating personality of John Marshall. The question of Marshall's dominance has been a common theme of the literature on the Marshall Court, earlier studies tending to emphasize Marshall's leadership and later works seeking to qualify Marshall's importance.[141] In arguing that his position on the Court was less dominant than previously suggested, the later studies have pointed to one or another of the distinctive features of the Marshall Court's deliberative process. A 1956 article by Donald Morgan is illustrative. Morgan, after suggesting that "even the reasonably well-informed student [of the Marshall Court] assumes that Marshall completely dominated his brothers," then set forth to show that "Marshall's influence was not the same as commonly supposed."[142] In questioning the assumption of Marshall's dominance Morgan pointed to the fact that "[w]hen the Court divided, the size of the majority and the identity of the dissenters often remained a mystery."[143]

All of the features previously discussed, however, were innovations made or refined by Marshall himself. The Court had met so infrequently prior to Marshall's becoming Chief Justice in 1801 that the practice of quartering the Justices, without their families, in a boardinghouse cannot be said to have been institutionalized. Under Marshall the boardinghouse setting became an integral part of the Court's working pattern. Marshall

---

[141] Compare Beveridge, *John Marshall,* and Warren, *Supreme Court* (Marshall dominant figure on the Court) with D. Morgan, "Marshall, The Marshall Court and the Constitution," in M. Jones, ed., *Chief Justice Marshall: A Reappraisal* (1956), 168, and D. Roper, "Judicial Unanimity and the Marshall Court—A Road to Reappraisal," *Am. J. Legal Hist.*, 9:118 (1965) (emphasizing role of other Justices). For a fuller discussion, see G. White, "The Art of Revising History: Revisiting the Marshall Court," *Suffolk U.L. Rev.,* 16:659 (1982). See also R. Seddig, "John Marshall and the Origins of Supreme Court Leadership," *U. Pitt. L. Rev.*, 16:785 (1975).

[142] Morgan, "Marshall Court," 168–69.

[143] Ibid., 173.

regularly informed himself about prospective boardinghouse arrangements for the next term, corresponded with other Justices about those arrangements, and worried that should the Justices "scatter ad libitum," not only would the Court be unable to "carry on our business as fast as usual," but an increasing number of cases would "probably be carried off by seriatim opinions."[144] Marshall clearly associated collective residence in a boardinghouse with the production of collective opinions of the Court and was therefore willing to work to ensure the boardinghouse setting.

Marshall was also responsible for the "opinion of the Court" practice[145] and for institutionalizing the practice of delivering opinions by seniority, which had sporadically occurred on the Ellsworth Court. Although the seniority principle had been modified by 1815, the "opinion of the Court" practice remained established for the duration of Marshall's tenure, and between 1815 and 1823 not even Johnson regularly took the opportunity to concur with or dissent from collective opinions.[146] In the later years of the Marshall Court, more dissents and an occasional seriatim opinion appeared,[147] but for the great bulk of Marshall's tenure the collective, anonymous opinion of the Court was the norm.

The "opinion of the Court" practice, as noted, resulted in one Justice being appointed to deliver an opinion and the remaining Justices unaccountable for their votes. In a large number of cases, the appointed Justice was John Marshall. In Marshall's thirty-four year tenure on the Court, he wrote 547 opinions of the Court. By contrast, in twenty-three years Justice Duvall wrote only fifteen such opinions, and in eighteen years Justice Todd wrote only fourteen. In fact, during Marshall's tenure, all the other Marshall Court Justices combined wrote 574 such opinions.[148] By instituting the "opinion of the Court" practice, Marshall was not only able to project a unanimous front for the Court, he was also able to take on the burden of writing and delivering a large number of opinions. By appointing himself the deliverer of opinions, Marshall was certainly exerting a type of dominance.

Finally, the absence of circulated draft opinions meant that in a very high number of cases the language of Supreme Court opinions would be the language of John Marshall. Although there is evidence that Marshall drew on his fellow Justices, especially Story and Washington, for ad-

---

[144] Letter from J. Marshall to J. Story, Nov. 10, 1831, quoted in Warren, *Correspondence*, 28.

[145] Prior to Marshall's tenure the Justices wrote seriatim opinions. See Goebel, *Antecedents and Beginnings*, 777; Haskins and Johnson, *Foundations of Power*, 382–83.

[146] See Morgan, *Justice William Johnson*, 179–81.

[147] For an example of a case in which seriatim opinions were rendered in this period, see Ogden v. Saunders, 12 Wheat. 213 (1827).

[148] These figures are taken from volumes 5–34 (1 Cranch–9 Pet.) of the United States Reports (1801–35). A similar count is in Seddig, "John Marshall," 800.

vice,[149] and some of Marshall's opinions contain language that seems designed to placate silently dissenting Justices,[150] the fact remains that most of the Marshall Court's pronouncements on major legal issues, especially constitutional issues, were written in the unedited language of John Marshall. To imagine a comparable situation in a modern Supreme Court—the Chief Justice writing lengthy per curiam opinions on major cases that, although subscribed to by the Associate Justices, had not even been read by the subscribers—boggles the mind. Those who have claimed that Marshall's dominance of his Court was not as overwhelming as it might first appear may well be correct, but for reasons other than those that have been commonly advanced.

Consideration of Marshall's impact on the Marshall Court in terms of internal norms of procedure and deliberation, as distinguished from substantive legal issues, aids in refining a now common theory that the Marshall Court was not a static entity but an institution that went through discernible "phases."[151] The "phases," which include a so-called "golden age" (1812–25)[152] and a so-called "transition" period (1826–35),[153] have traditionally been characterized in terms of the major constitutional themes of the Court's tenure: nationalism, state sovereignty, property rights, and regulation of the economy.[154] The Marshall Court has been said to have been "united" on such issues in the "golden age" and to have been "fragmented" on such issues in the period of "transition."

Historians have repeatedly found that such doctrinal characterizations are of limited value,[155] but a tendency to identify phases in the Marshall Court with changing attitudes toward issues of constitutional law

---

[149] In addition to the letters cited supra, note 75, see J. McClellan, *Joseph Story and the American Constitution* (1971), 294–96 for evidence of Marshall's solicitation of Story's views "on [a] variety of legal questions." Ibid., 294, quoting Beveridge, *John Marshall*, 120.

[150] See, e.g., Sturges v. Crowninshield, 4 Wheat. 122, 206–208 (1819), discussed in Chapter IX.

[151] On the "phases" of the Marshall Court, see R. Newmyer, *The Supreme Court under Marshall and Taney* (1968), 83–88; Seddig, "John Marshall," 794–833.

[152] See H. Carson, *The History of the Supreme Court of the United States* (2 vols., 1904), I, 242; Seddig, "John Marshall," 810–22.

[153] The term "transition," as used by Seddig, "John Marshall," 822, and implied by C. Haines, *The Role of the Supreme Court in American Govern-*

*ment and Politics 1789–1835* (1944), 590, assumes a movement on the Court from one political point of view to another, in this instance from a "Federalist" perspective to "a point of view which veered in the direction of . . . democratic ideas and principles." Haines, supra. See also Newmyer, *Supreme Court*, 92 ("To the immense discomfiture of conservatives, President Jackson was able to bring the Supreme Court into harmony with Jacksonian Democracy by virtue of seven appointments").

[154] See the emphasis in Carson, *History of the Supreme Court*, I, 195–287. See also Haines, *Role of the Supreme Court*, 641–44; Newmyer, *The Supreme Court*, 91–94, 113–18; Seddig, "John Marshall," 794–833.

[155] See, e.g., Roper, "Judicial Unanimity and the Marshall Court," supra, note 141.

has persisted. A more satisfying explanation for the Marshall Court's phases may rest in a comparison of the character of the Court's deliberative process in various periods. Between 1801 and 1810, for example, the Court's personnel changed regularly, the Justices commonly followed the practice of delivering opinions through the seniority principle, concurrences and dissents were infrequent, and Marshall's name appeared above the great majority of the opinions. Between 1812 and 1823[156] the Court's personnel remained constant and the "opinion of the Court" practice became the norm, with the seniority principle waning in importance. The Justices issued even fewer dissents (compared to the increased number of majority opinions), and Marshall wrote comparatively fewer opinions of the Court, although he continued to write more than any other Justice. After 1823, and especially after 1827, the Court's personnel fluctuated, more concurring and dissenting opinions appeared,[157] and Marshall wrote still fewer opinions for the Court, as compared with the other Justices, than he had in the 1812–23 period. Moreover, after 1829 the Justices modified their custom of living in the same boardinghouse: Justices McLean and Johnson did not take meals nor sleep in the Court's quarters.

Thus, three different stages of the Court's deliberative practices emerge. When one applies these three stages to the small-group decisionmaking processes of the Court,[158] three different types of groups can be identified. In its first phase, the Marshall Court seemed to be a group in which the leader's (in this instance the Chief Justice's)[159] views, both

---

[156] There was no session in 1811 because only three of the seven Justices were able to be present in Washington.

[157] Several examples can illustrate this point. In 1827, in Ogden v. Saunders, 12 Wheat. 213 (1827), the Justices temporarily resurrected seriatim opinions, thereby openly communicating divisions within the Court. Three years earlier Johnson had announced that in constitutional cases he would invariably write an opinion, and he repeated this in 1829 in Weston v. City Council, 2 Pet. 449, 470 (1829), and in 1831 in Cherokee Nation v. Georgia, 5 Pet. 1, 20 (1831). Washington openly dissented in an 1827 case and noted that such action ran counter to his usual practice. Mason v. Haile, 12 Wheat. 370, 379 (1827). Story, in an 1830 case, also openly dissented, stated that "[i]t is not without reluctance, that I deviate from my usual practice of submitting in silence to the decisions of my brethren, when I dissent from them." Inglis v. Trustees of the Sailor's Snug Harbour, 3 Pet. 99, 145 (1830). Even Marshall himself dissented openly on occasion. See, e.g., Bank of the United States v. Dandridge, 12 Wheat. 64, 90 (1827).

[158] See W. Murphy, *Elements of Judicial Strategy* (1964); W. Murphy, "Courts as Small Groups," *Harv. L. Rev.*, 79:1565 (1966).

[159] The designation of the Chief Justice as "leader" assumes that "leader" is defined as "the individual in the group who directs and coordinates . . . group activities." F. Fiedler, "A Contingency Model of Leadership Effectiveness," *Advances in Experimental Soc. Psychology*, 1:149, 153 (1964). See also D. Danelski, "The Influence of the Chief Justice in the Decisional Process," in W. Murphy and C. Pritchett, eds., *Courts, Judges and Politics: An Introduction to the Judicial Process* (1961), 497. Citation of this literature should not be taken as an endorsement of its applicability to every facet of internal Supreme Court decisionmaking.

on substantive issues and on internal practices, overwhelmed those of the other members. In its second stage, the Court became a group in which the other members of the group adopted the leader's views on internal practices, and those practices fostered an *appearance* of harmony on substantive issues. In its final stage, the Court was a group in which the presence of new members,[160] coupled with the group's continued involvement with visible and difficult social issues, made it more difficult for the leader to maintain his views on internal practices. Because those practices had placed a high value on the appearance of internal harmony on doctrinal issues, a lessening of agreement on practices resulted in more open divisions on matters of doctrine.

It is possible, then, that the Marshall Court was never as "harmonious" doctrinally as it appeared in its "Golden Age." The harmony came in matters of internal procedure. Fragmentation on the late Marshall Court, from this perspective, can be seen as the public disclosure of features of the Court's decisionmaking that had existed throughout the Marshall Court's tenure but had been suppressed. The "transition" that historians have associated with the late Marshall Court was not so much a transition toward novel doctrines as it was a transition toward a more open revelation of the roles of individual Justices in the Court's decisionmaking process. The model of decisionmaking in the Marshall Court was overwhelmingly collective because the "opinion of the Court" practice served to conceal the views of most individual Justices. The model

---

[160] The new Justices on the Marshall Court refused to become socialized in existing practices. When John McLean was appointed to the Court for the 1830 Term, he declined to live in the designated boardinghouse. See letter from Marshall to Story, Nov. 10, 1831, supra, note 144. Justice McLean had already been a resident of Washington before being appointed to the Court, having served as postmaster general of the United States. See F. Weisenburger, *The Life of John McLean* (1937), 34–35. That same term, after becoming aware of McLean's break with custom, Justice Johnson resolved to "quarter to himself," letter from Marshall to Story, Nov. 10, 1831, supra, note 144, the result being that for the last six Terms of the Marshall Court all the Justices did not live together.

Meanwhile, Henry Baldwin joined the Court, beginning with the 1830 Term, and almost immediately established himself as disinclined to follow existing practices. Baldwin published seven dissents in the 1831 Term and allegedly threatened to resign after that Term. See F. Gatell, "Henry Baldwin," in Friedman and Israel, *Justices,* I, 576. Baldwin became emotionally unstable shortly after his appointment and was confined to a mental hospital for the first 1833 Term. He took extensive notes of conferences and regularly drafted concurring or dissenting opinions which he threatened to file but never released; he argued against the views of other Justices in an erratic and vociferous fashion. In 1837 he published a pamphlet in which he attacked Story's writings and revealed the internal deliberations of certain late Marshall Court cases. H. Baldwin, *A General View of the Origin and Nature of the Constitution and Government of the United States* (1837). Baldwin's presence changed the tone of the Marshall Court's "familiar conferences." For a fuller discussion of Baldwin, see Chapter V.

of decisionmaking on the Taney Court was strikingly less collective, although it could not be called individualistic.[161] The late Marshall Court may be said to represent a "transition" from one model to another.

In 1834 Marshall acknowledged the Court's new divisiveness on internal procedures by making public the Justices' posture toward opinions of the Court in constitutional cases. "The practice of this court," he said, "is, not (except in cases of absolute necessity) to deliver any judgment in cases where constitutional questions are involved, unless four judges concur in opinion, thus making the decision that of a majority of the whole court."[162] Such a posture seemed to assume the likelihood of fragmentation among the Justices on major issues. It was one more effort by Marshall to convey to his colleagues the importance he placed on unanimity. It was also a concession to the "revolutionary spirit" which, in an 1831 letter to Story, he had found "displayed . . . in our circle," working "inconvenience and mischief."[163]

But there is an additional question that lurks behind this analysis of the Marshall Court's deliberative practices: why did the Justices care so much about preserving an appearance of unanimity? Dissent and discord are common features of the modern Court, and the practice of multiple opinions and open disagreement has been institutionalized since at least the mid-nineteenth century. Even if the boardinghouse, Marshall's presence, and the absence of several contentious Justices may have been important factors fostering Court harmony, why was the "appearance of harmony" argument itself so compelling? At this point one confronts the conceptions of law and judging that characterized the age of the Marshall Court.

The preceding sections of this chapter have demonstrated that the Marshall Court Justices not only worked in an environment that only tangentially resembles that of current Justices, they also engaged in procedures clearly unacceptable by current ethical standards and in internal practices notable for their informality and lack of accountability. Their procedures and practices invite speculation as to why contemporaries did not deplore the Justices' actions and why the Justices felt it necessary to engage in them.

Explanation of these questions requires attention to two of the most significant jurisprudential propositions of the Marshall Court's intellectual universe, both of which we have previously encountered. The first prop-

---

[161] See Swisher, *The Taney Period,* 93–98.
[162] Briscoe v. Commonwealth's Bank, 8 Pet. 118, 121 (1834).

[163] Letter from J. Marshall to J. Story, May 3, 1831, Story Papers, Massachusetts Historical Society, Boston, Mass.

osition was that judges did not make law but rather only discovered certain universal or fundamental principles. Once a judge identified the applicable principles, he applied them to the facts of a case and thus reached the correct result. These principles were regarded as distinct from the personal biases of judges: they represented the will of the law, not the wills of the judges. The identification and declaration of principles was itself a check on judicial "discretion."[164]

The second proposition was that law, especially constitutional law, embraced politics and political theory, so that a stark separation of legal and political questions was unnecessary. That proposition was reinforced by a distinction in early American political culture between politics and partisanship. On the one hand, consensual political theory, which in the period of the Marshall Court was derived from republican ideology, was perceived as incorporating law; on the other hand, partisan politics were regarded, despite the activities of Jefferson and his supporters in the 1790s, as suspect and potentially subversive activity. Moderns have run together the term "politics" and "partisan politics"; early-nineteenth-century political culture sought to hold them firmly apart.[165]

From a modern perspective, the Marshall Court appears to be a

---

[164] See the discussion in Chapters I and II. See also E. Bauer, *Commentaries on the Constitution 1790–1860* (1952), 25–31; R. Faulkner, *The Jurisprudence of John Marshall* (1968), 58–64, 195–206, 255–60; B. Wright, *American Interpretations of National Law* (1931), 149–241; J. Nedelsky, "Confining Democratic Politics: Anti-Federalists, Federalists, and the Constitution," *Harv. L. Rev.,* 96:340, 352–60 (1982).

[165] See the discussion in Chapters I and II. Several commentators have noted that the Marshall Court Justices attempted to depoliticize the Court by downplaying their partisan political affiliations and avoiding overt political activity. From this evidence, the commentators have concluded that a central theme of the Marshall Court was an effort to invest law with a neutral non-political character and thereby achieve a separation of law from politics. See Haskins and Johnson, *Foundations of Power,* 7, 648–49; G. Haskins, "Law Versus Politics in the Early Years of the Marshall Court," *U. Pa. L. Rev.,* 130: 1 (1981); W. Nelson, "The Eighteenth-Century Background of John Marshall's Constitutional Jurisprudence," *Mich.*

*L. Rev.,* 76:893 (1978); W. Nelson, Book Review, *U. Pa. L. Rev.,* 131:489, 1982. But the withdrawal of the Marshall Court Justices from partisan political activities was, in concrete terms, an attempt to extricate the judicial branch from its traditionally close ties with the executive branch, and, in abstract terms, an effort to distinguish consensual political theory from partisanship. The Justices did not stop deciding political issues; indeed, they increased their involvement with them, and contemporaries commented on that increased involvement. The Justices did take pains, however, to avoid any identification of their decisions with the credos of a political party. But in the period between 1812 and 1823, when the Court achieved its greatest unanimity on constitutional issues, American political culture was dominated by an "antiparty" ideology. See generally R. Formisano, *The Transformation of Political Culture: Massachusetts Politics, 1790s–1840s* (1983); R. Hofstadter, *The Idea of a Party System: The Rise of Legitimate Opposition in the United States, 1780–1840* (1970). See also the discussion of political parties in Chapter VIII.

partisan political body, but it took pains to avoid being perceived as one. It did not, however, take pains to avoid being perceived as "political" in the early-nineteenth-century sense of that term. By appealing to immutable principles of early-nineteenth-century political culture, such as the inviolability of private property or the superiority of republican forms of government, the Court was clearly making political decisions, but it presented these decisions in the official, purportedly neutral, language of the law. The most striking example of the Court's political influence was its establishment of the federal government as the locus of sovereignty in the new Republic. The Court's decisions in this area, remarkably activist efforts at the expense of the state governments, were legitimated by appeals to the fusion of law and politics. Because law was conceived of as embracing such political choices, the Justices were able to elevate their decisions above the plane of partisan politics, to transform political issues into legal ones, and thereby to increase the political power of the Court.

The first proposition was consistent with a view of the proper role of judges that has since been abandoned. Modern conceptions of judicial behavior, including not only standards of judicial ethics but also theories of judicial performance, presuppose that the decisions of judges are not merely reflections or discoveries of the law, a universalistic, finite entity, but are rather the law itself.[166] Modern jurisprudence regards the distinction Marshall Court Justices sought to make between the will of the judge and the will of the law as a distinction without a difference. The legal decisions of judges are, in the modern consciousness, necessarily personal and creative. Given that assumption, various canons for judicial performance follow. Judges should avoid conflicts of interest; judges should not establish private relationships with lawyers that affect cases before them; judges should reveal the reasons for their votes in a case, or, at a minimum, their votes; judges, in short, should recognize and seek to minimize their subjectivity.

Modern judges readily accept these canons. The present Supreme Court practice in most cases is to register the vote of every Justice who participated in the decision. Justices routinely disqualify themselves if they perceive conflict-of-interest issues in a case before them, and an apparent unconcern for this canon has proved fatal to the careers of some recent holders of and aspirants to seats on the Supreme Court.[167] Moreover, judges as well as commentators have propounded a variety of theories in this century about the appropriate posture a Supreme Court Justice

---

[166] I have discussed the triumph of these presuppositions about the nature of law and the function of judges in G. White, *The American Judicial Tradition* (1976), 54–56, 196–66, 230–31, 292–94; and G. White, *Patterns of American Legal Thought* (1978), 99–143.

[167] See, e.g., R. Shogan, *A Question of Judgment: The Fortas Case and the Struggle for the Supreme Court* (1972).

ought to take toward the decision of cases.[168] Modern canons for judicial behavior and modern theories of judicial performance presuppose that judges make law and that judicial will and legal will are thus inseparable.

In contrast, the Marshall Court Justices and their contemporaries based their theories of judicial action on the belief that the essential function of judges was to discover legal principles and apply them to particular situations. Nineteenth-century judges, commentators, and treatise writers, we have seen, regularly grounded results in particular cases or justified particular legal rules and doctrines through appeals to "universal," "fundamental," or "general" principles of law. A passage from one of Marshall's 1824 opinions expresses this attitude. Marshall stated that "[c]ourts are the mere instruments of the law, and can will nothing. When they are said to exercise a discretion, it is a mere legal discretion, a discretion to be exercised in discerning the course prescribed by law. . . ."[169]

The perceived absence of judicial will, in the sense of modern discretionary lawmaking power, meant that the Marshall Court Justices were freer to involve themselves in extrajudicial activities. Because judges were seen as deciding cases by resort to immutable principles and not by reference to their own subjective values, their contemporaries were less concerned that outside interests or bias would affect the judicial decisionmaking process. Thus, in the early nineteenth century one could find Supreme Court Justices openly drafting congressional legislation, advising presidents, sitting on cases in which, according to modern standards, they had apparent conflicts of interest, and regularly holding ex parte conversations and communications with lawyers.[170] Although modern observers might feel that these activities would affect a Justice's perspective, to Marshall Court contemporaries a Justice's "discretion" was circumscribed by the law itself.

This is not to say that there were no limits on the Marshall Court Justices' extrajudicial activities, or no awareness that the Court's decisions represented political choices of a sort. The obvious financial interest of a Justice in a case, for example, was regarded as sufficient to encourage him to deviate from fixed principles of justice. The Justices were well aware of these perceived limits, and, as has been repeatedly catalogued

---

[168] Recent works by judges resting on the above presuppositions include F. Coffin, *The Ways of a Judge: Reflections from the Federal Appellate Bench* (1980). B. Cardozo, *The Nature of the Judicial Process* (1921), is a classic early-twentieth-century concession that judges make law, coupled with an exhortation that judges therefore constrain their own subjectivity.

[169] Osborn v. Bank of the United States, 9 Wheat. 738, 866 (1824).

[170] For a survey of such activities, see B. Murphy, *The Brandeis/Frankfurter Connection* (1982), 345–56.

by historians,[171] they avoided political activity that would have been considered "interested" or partisan, and at times they recused themselves from cases. The fact nevertheless remains that these limits were far less restrictive than the strict standards placed on Justices today, and consequently the opportunities for the exercise of unfettered judicial "discretion," in the modern sense of the term, were far greater.

In this light, one can understand why there was relatively little contemporary criticism of the "irregular" procedures of the Marshall Court. The Justices were not seen by their contemporaries as acting in ways that were inconsistent with the then current perception of how judges should act. Because the Justices were ultimately bound to declare the law, they could be interventionist and politically conscious in selecting and shaping the litigation that resulted in the law being declared. Intervention of the kind engaged in by Marshall in *Martin* and by Story in *Dartmouth College* involved "mere questions of practice," and such practices were not thought of as affecting the legal result. Although both Marshall and Story reached the outer boundaries of judicial propriety in their actions, their intervention was arguably still within the tacit limits of proper extrajudicial activity.

The proposition that judges did not make law in the modern sense also helped to legitimize the Court's deliberative practices, which presented a false impression of unanimity and minimized the individual Justice's accountability. Because the role of the Court was not to make law but merely to discover and apply it, it was unnecessary for each Justice to explain the reasoning behind his decision. Once the Court collectively discovered the law and applied the right principle, it had done its job. More than one opinion by the Court only brought into question whether the Court had discovered the right result.

Just as the first proposition helps to clarify the Justices' interventionist posture and some of the Court's deliberative practices, so does the second proposition. Once one realizes that law was perceived of as inseparable from political theory, but politics as separable from partisanship, the Justices' great concern with promoting an appearance of unanimity becomes explicable. Indeed, the inquiry leads to one of those deep paradoxes that help define the jurisprudence of an age. The limits on judging imposed by early-nineteenth-century jurisprudence were not so much limits focusing on subjectivity, nor limits focusing on politics as separate from law, as they were limits focusing on partisanship. Human beings were seen as self-interested and potentially corrupt; political parties were by no means fully legitimated. Law, conceived of in its constitu-

---

[171] See, e.g., Haskins and Johnson, *Foundations of Power,* 363–65; War- ren, *Supreme Court,* I, 20–23; Haskins, "Law Versus Politics."

tional form as inseparable from republican political theory, was a check on partisanship. One might quarrel over the application of republican theory to an individual case: that was a quarrel over politics in the grand, consensual sense. Critics of the Court instituted such quarrels. But the jurisprudential assumptions of the time did not typically conceive such disputes as disputes about judicial partisanship and subjectivity. Moderns think of this attitude as paradoxical because of contemporary assumptions about politics and partisanship. But Marshall Court Justices sought to claim political power by demonstrating their apparent avoidance of partisanship. The most severe criticism directed at the Court's opinions, we will see, came in connection with its decisions in sovereignty issues, where the theories of sovereignty and constitutional interpretation advanced were attacked as not merely unsound and unfaithful to the intent of the Constitution's Framers but as "consolidationist" and thereby partisan.

The distinctive features of the working life of the Marshall Court thus can be seen not only as a mirror of the uniqueness of early-nineteenth-century American intellectual culture but also as a testament to the ability of tacitly shared ideas and values to define the roles played by persons who have held power in American society. Moderns may examine the procedures and practices of the Marshall Court, or its general interventionist stance in political affairs, and conclude that bias, cover-ups, conflicts of interest, and judicial arrogations of power were rampant in the early history of the United States Supreme Court. Such observations are in the main anachronistic. They are not based on more penetrating or more enlightened theories of human nature; they stem instead from radically altered conceptions of law and judging.

# CHAPTER IV

## Prominent Lawyers
## Before the Marshall Court

INSTITUTIONAL HISTORIES sometimes convey the impression that the institution under study transcends in importance the individuals comprising it. In the case of the Supreme Court of the United States one can see how such an impression might be generated: not only has the institution survived individual occupants, it dwarfs them. But any close student of the Court, or of the judiciary at large, comes to realize that it is people who principally give a judicial institution its character. The Marshall Court's identity can be seen as forged, to an important extent, by the personalities who shaped its decisions. Because the Marshall Court was not blessed or burdened with a significant legacy of prior Supreme Court decisions, practices, or customs, it was largely free to create its own doctrines and to develop its own working patterns. Given that freedom, the attitudes and characteristics of individuals were themselves creative forces, albeit confined by the boundaries of time, circumstance, and culture.

The next three chapters provide sketches of a variety of persons who participated in the life of the Marshall Court. This chapter deals with lawyers; the succeeding two with Justices and Reporters. The sketches of lawyers who argued cases before the Supreme Court between 1815 and 1835 are selective; my purpose is to produce encapsulated rather than detailed portraits and to treat individuals as representatives of the diverse early-nineteenth-century Supreme Court bar.

A specialized Supreme Court bar came into existence in the last twenty years of the Marshall Court. The growth of specialists resulted from increased Court business, especially business generated in the lower federal courts, and from difficulties in transportation. Between 1801 and 1815 the overwhelming percentage of cases litigated before the Marshall Court had been of two types, those involving the jurisdiction and procedure of the federal courts and those involving admiralty and marine insurance.[1] While the two sets of cases were conceptually distinct, they bore a practical relationship to one another, since most Marshall Court cases in this period concerned maritime matters. It is not too much to say that the federal courts in the early years of the Marshall Court were essentially maritime courts. They sat principally in seacoast jurisdictions; their cases repeatedly involved incidents affecting ships, such as crimes committed by seamen, piracy or prize disputes, losses to ships or cargo, and maritime insurance contracts. All but the last group of cases were assumed to be federal matters; all took on increased significance with the War of 1812. The result was that the Supreme Court, as supervisor of the federal courts, became a visible forum by settling maritime disputes, which had significant economic consequences, for seacoast trade was still a major component of the American economy.[2]

The Supreme Court, however, met in the District of Columbia, where relatively few maritime disputes originated and where comparatively little law business was generated. The District's minor role as a legal center was a result of its small population, which was only 24,023 people in 1810 and 39,834 by 1830.[3] This situation induced certain attorneys to specialize in a Supreme Court practice. Attorneys from the more populous seacoast cities, such as Baltimore, Philadelphia, New York, Boston, and Charleston, would be retained to argue cases before the Supreme Court and, once having done so, would tend to repeat the journey. Because Washington was relatively inaccessible to any major city save Philadelphia and Baltimore, the majority of lawyers that practiced before the Marshall Court in its early years came from those two cities. As transportation conditions improved after the War of 1812,[4] New York, Boston, and Charleston became better represented, and the number of lawyers from other jurisdictions increased. But throughout Marshall's tenure the Supreme Court bar was a small, selective group, with the same attorneys appearing in Washington with regularity.

Arguing a case before the Marshall Court was not only a professional challenge, it was often a physical adventure. As late as 1812 Joseph Story anticipated that the trip from Washington to Boston would take twelve days;[5] from Washington to Charleston took even longer.[6] The extended time in transit resulted partially from primitive transportation.

---

[1] See G. Haskins and H. Johnson, *Foundations of Power: John Marshall, 1801–15* (1981), 377–89.

[2] See G. Taylor, *The Transportation Revolution* (1951), 3–14.

[3] C. Green, *Washington: Village and Capital, 1800–1878* (1962), 20–21, 182–83.

[4] Taylor, *Transportation Revolution,* 15–29.

[5] J. Story to Sarah Waldo Story, Mar. 12, 1812, in W. Story, *The Life and Letters of Joseph Story* (2 vols., 1851), I, 219.

[6] C. Warren, *A History of the American Bar* (1911), 255–56.

# Chapter IV: *Prominent Lawyers Before the Marshall Court*

Story's descriptions of his adventures, noted in Chapter I, are paralleled by one in a letter from Congressman Elijah Mills of Massachusetts to his wife, recounting Mills's efforts to get from Washington to Northampton in 1815:

> From Washington to Baltimore we went in the first day. There we took passage in a packet for French-Town [Maryland], in the Chesapeake Bay, and were delayed by a dead calm, so that we were twenty-four hours performing a passage usually completed in six. On Wednesday, we left our packet and went overland to Newcastle [Delaware]. There we again took a packet, and arrived in Philadelphia late in the evening. On Thursday we remained in that city, the stage being too full to receive us that day. . . . This morning we left it at two o'clock, and ought to have arrived in New York this evening. But the excessive badness of the roads has arrested our progress at a distance of about forty miles from it. I shall make no stay in New York, but shall press my journey with all the rapidity in my power, and shall be with you, my dear Harriette, I hope by the Friday stage.[7]

In addition to proximate residency, seacoast affiliations, and a capacity for adventure, the prospective advocate before the Marshall Court required oratorical skills. As we have seen, there were no time limits on arguments before the Court, the Justices put relatively few questions to counsel, and the courtroom, despite its stuffy and cramped basement location, was regarded as something of a social and entertainment hall. All of these factors tended to invest oral advocacy before the Court with some of the emotional features of modern trial practice, such as impassioned language, dramatic forms of delivery, and "extralegal" appeals. Despite superficial similarities, however, the conception of oral argument prevalent at the time of the Marshall Court was fundamentally different from current conceptions.

Advocacy before the Marshall Court was an essentially oral medium. Written briefs were rare and, as noted, were not required; collected volumes of precedents were sparse; written treatises were neither numerous nor widely available. And while the Supreme Court bar was a highly literate stratum of American society and writing a frequent form of activity for both lawyers and Justices, the oral presentation—a lecture, a speech, even the open declaration of one's voting preferences—was still a major form of communication in early-nineteenth-century American culture. Oratory was a high art; listening to lengthy speeches was an established social and intellectual activity.[8]

---

[7] E. Mills to Harriette Mills, Mar. 8, 1815, in *Proc. Mass. Hist. Soc.*, 19:19–20 (1881).

[8] On the place of oratory in early-nineteenth-century American culture,

see B. Baskerville, *The People's Voice* (1979), 7–87; R. Osterweis, *Romanticism and Nationalism in the Old South* (1967), 94–96.

The oratorical advocacy at the time of the Marshall Court differed in its emphasis from modern forensic modes of argument. Early-nine-teenth-century orators did not expect to be interrupted frequently; they sought to persuade by the content or the emotion of their discourse rather than by riposte, clarification, and counterpoint. While advocates before the Marshall Court anticipated argument, as we employ that term, at some point, their modes of argumentation presupposed that an advocate would have ample undisturbed time to put forward his claims before being chal-lenged by his opponent. Consequently, lawyers appearing before the Court made regular use of two techniques of advocacy: the rhetorical flourish and the dogmatic generalization. Both techniques were based on deeply held jurisprudential assumptions. A commentator, analyzing the performance of one Marshall Court advocate, made those assumptions explicit:

> There are many advocates . . . who make a parade of their learning; who quote decisions without an accurate discrimination of what they tend to prove. Legal distinctions are not less nice and delicate than those of a moral order. Law and ethics are in fact intimately blended. A system of jurisprudence embraces rules of action for all the concerns of human life. . . . No rule of law can be sound and salutary unless it be consistent with justice, when carried through in all its bearings and in its full application to all cases to which it can even pertain. . . . The law deals in general rules. All its axioms are general. All its maxims are intended to be universal.[9]

In this passage "law" appears as both "intimately blended" with ethics ("consistent with justice") and as a "system" of "general rules" and "universal" maxims. The effective advocate was one who could infuse his arguments with ethical appeals and who could present particular cases or applications of general principles. The oratorical mode facilitated both tasks. Rhetorical flourishes, in which the advocate made emotional ap-peals, were tacit reminders that law and ethics could not be separated; dogmatic generalizations demonstrated the principle that rules of law were not "sound and salutary" unless they could be applied "to all cases to which [they] could even pertain." The use of the oratorical mode in legal advocacy was thus founded on a widely shared presupposition: law would be seen to be more ethical and more just if the universality of its maxims was demonstrated and its inner emotion revealed.

The commentator previously quoted made his remarks in the course of a celebration of the advocacy of Thomas A. Emmet, who argued cases before the Supreme Court between 1815 and 1824. Few of the lawyers

---

[9] C. Haines, *Memoir of Thomas Addis Emmet* (1812), 100.

who appeared before the Marshall Court had as vivid a personal history as Emmet. He had come to America from Ireland, via France, in 1804, having been previously imprisoned for treason against the British government. His father had been appointed to the government post of State Physician by the Viceroy of Ireland and settled in Dublin; his elder brother, Temple, was a promising lawyer who died of overwork at the age of twenty-seven; his younger brother, Robert, was an Irish nationalist who was hanged in 1803, at the age of twenty-five, for treason.[10]

Thomas Emmet had originally studied medicine and had been admitted to practice in 1784, at the age of twenty. After his brother Temple's death four years later, Emmet was encouraged by his father to study law and, after receiving an LL.B. from Trinity College, was admitted to the bar in 1790. Five years later he joined the Society of United Irishmen, an organization dedicated to the preservation of Ireland's national parliament against unionist pressures from England, and his law practice took on a decidedly political cast. In 1798 he was arrested for participating in a rebellion, and spent the next four years in prison. He was released in 1802 on the condition that he leave Ireland, and he temporarily settled in France, hoping to get French support for Irish resistance against England. By 1804 insurgency in Ireland had been suppressed by the British, Emmet's brother had been hanged, and the possibility of French support had evaporated. Emmet decided to immigrate to America, fixing on New York state, whose governor, George Clinton, was a native of Ireland and a strong supporter of Irish nationalism.[11]

On arriving in New York Emmet almost immediately became involved in controversy. He applied to be admitted to the New York bar shortly after his arrival, seeking to have residency requirements waived on his behalf. He was opposed on the ground that he was an alien but, with Clinton's support, he prevailed. The incident precipitated a change in the New York bar's rules that made American citizenship a condition of admission to practice in the state.[12] By 1806 Emmet had become a naturalized citizen and had argued a case before New York's highest state court. He had also visited Washington and been admitted to practice before the Supreme Court.[13]

---

[10] For information on Temple, Robert, and Thomas Emmet, and the Emmet family in Ireland, see T. Emmet, *Memoir of Thomas Addis Emmet and Robert Emmet* (2 vols., 1915). The statement about Temple's death is from ibid., I, 191. Historical details on Thomas Emmet's life, unless otherwise cited, are from ibid., I, 149–406.

[11] Emmet, *Memoir*, I, 202–406; Haines, *Memoir of Emmet*, 36–87. For an account of New York politics in the early nineteenth century, see A. Kass, *Politics in New York State 1800–1830* (1965).

[12] Compare 2 Carnes 386 (1805) with 1 Johns. 528 (1815). For an account of the controversy, see O. Hall, "Thomas Addis Emmet," *Green Bag* 8:273 (1896).

[13] Compare Hall, "Thomas Addis Emmet," 275, with Emmet, *Memoir*, I, 406.

Between 1806 and 1815 Emmet established himself as one of the leading lawyers in New York state, whose legal community, while thought by Story in 1807 "not to be equal to what it has been,"[14] still included several distinguished lawyers and judges.[15] Emmet's rise had been accompanied by conspicuous forays into politics: the climate of early-nineteenth-century New York was intensely political, and Emmet was a zealous and experienced political advocate. Despite the fact that "a combination [of] the great men of the New York bar turned their forces against Mr. Emmet," the newcomer, taking advantage of what one memorialist called his "dauntless . . . spirit" and "ready talent of successful and over-awing reply," prevailed "in the wars against the combination," and "business flowed in."[16]

The candidacy of Rufus King, a prominent Federalist, for governor of New York in 1807 provides an example of Emmet's involvement in controversial political issues. Emmet was a warm supporter of the opposing Clinton faction, which he correctly thought more sympathetic to Irish autonomy and "republican principles" than its opponents.[17] Emmet also had been embittered by King's actions during the latter's tenure as minister to England in 1798 and 1799, when King had exhibited an antipathy to Irish nationalism and a conviction that "a large proportion of the emigrants from Ireland" had "arranged themselves on the side of the malcontents."[18] Emmet was well aware that King was among those who had sought to prevent his immigration to New York. When King announced his candidacy, Emmet wrote him two open letters, published in New York City newspapers, one of which contained the following paragraphs:

[O]n being pressed to know what reason Mr. King could have for preventing us, who were avowed republicans, from emigrating to America, [the British authorities] significantly answered, "perhaps Mr. King does not desire to have republicans in America." Your interference was then, sir, made the pretext of detaining us for four years in custody, by which very extensive and useful plans of settlement in these states were broken up. The misfortunes which you brought upon the objects of your persecution were incalculable. Almost all of us wasted four of the best years of our lives in prison. As to me, I should have brought along with me my father and his family, including a

[14] J. Story to Samuel P. P. Fay, May 21, 1807, in W. Story, *Life and Letters*, I, 146. Alexander Hamilton had been assassinated by Aaron Burr in 1804, and Story felt that the New York bar's "splendor has been obscured since Burr . . . and Hamilton have departed." Ibid.

[15] See J. Horton, *James Kent* (1939), 96–122.

[16] Haines, *Memoir of Emmet*, 89–90.

[17] On the Clinton faction see Kass, *Politics in New York State*, 70–92.

[18] R. King to Henry Jackson, Aug. 23, 1799, quoted in Emmet, *Memoir*, I, 412.

brother, whose name even you will not read without emotions of sympathy and respect. Others nearly connected with me would have come as partners in my emigration. But all of them have been torn from me. . . .

But I mean to confine myself to an examination of your conduct, as far as it is of public importance.

The step you took was unauthorized by your own Government. . . . [Y]ou had . . . forty-two days, in the calms of summer, for [receiving authorization that King's views on Irish emigration were official views of the American government]. As you had no [such] order, what was the motive of your unauthorised act?[19]

The letter to King was characteristic of Emmet's capacity, remarked upon by contemporaries, to infuse his arguments with emotion. While not prepossessing in personal exchanges (one contemporary called him "modest, unassuming, unobtrusive, and perfectly polite, . . . not . . . an eloquent or a powerful man in ordinary conversation"),[20] Emmet could become galvanized in a public setting such as the courtroom, "indul[ging] in bursts of lofty and noble sentiments" and "display[ing] wonderful powers of eloquence."[21] Story, in a commemorative reminiscence of Emmet written in 1829, said that Emmet "kindled as he spoke"; that he was "quick, vigorous, searching, and buoyant."[22] But the paragraphs from the King letter were not completely emotional in their impact. Emmet did not forget the point that King had overstepped his legal authority as minister to England. Emotion suffused Emmet's legal arguments rather than supplanting them. "His object seemed to be," Story suggested, "not to excite wonder or surprise, to captivate by bright pictures and varied images and graceful groups and startling apparitions; but by earnest and due reasoning to convince the judgment, or to overwhelm the heart by awakening its most profound emotions." In Story's view Emmet's eloquence "was most striking for its persuasiveness. . . . The tones of his voice . . . were utterances of the soul as well as of the lips."[23]

A contemporary of Emmet's has been quoted as saying that his response to controversy was "to carry the war into the enemy's coun-

---

[19] T. Emmet to R. King, Apr. 4, 1807, quoted in ibid., I, 413–16. The letter appeared in the New York *American Citizen,* Apr. 5, 1807.

[20] Haines, *Memoir of Emmet,* 116. Another commentator said that "Emmet's appearance in court was rather that of a rollicking middle-aged Irish squire, fond of the hunt and the bottle." Hall, "Thomas Addis Emmet," at 275. Story said that "[Emmet's] appearance is not that of an orator, and his voice is rather thick and guttural," W. Story, *Life and Letters,* I, 145, but Hall claimed that Emmet "used a musical, expressive and variable voice, pleasantly tinctured with a winning Corkonian brogue." Hall, "Thomas Addis Emmet," 275.

[21] Haines, *Memoir of Emmet,* 102.

[22] J. Story to William Sampson, Feb. 27, 1829, in W. Story, *Life and Letters,* I, 569.

[23] Ibid., 570.

try."[24] By 1815 that terrain had widened beyond New York. Emmet, who had been named Attorney General of New York in 1812 and had come to command an income of about $10,000 a year,[25] appeared for the first time before the Marshall Court in 1815 and immediately became embroiled in a memorable dispute. Emmet was counsel in four prize cases,[26] and in the first of them, *The Mary*, he encountered William Pinkney, then at the very height of his career as an advocate.[27] Pinkney, who argued over half the cases before the Marshall Court in the 1814 Term, was intimately familiar with Supreme Court advocacy and with prize cases, and in *The Mary* he had the better of the substantive argument. George Ticknor, who was in the audience, reported that Pinkney, who was charged with rebutting Emmet,

> sprang into the arena like a lion who had been loosed by his keepers on the gladiator that awaited him. . . . The display was brilliant . . . by the force of eloquence, logic, and legal learning, by this display of naked talent, he made his way over my prejudices. . . . He left his rival far behind him."[28]

In the course of his remarks Pinkney "treated Mr. Emmet . . . with somewhat coarse contempt,"[29] apparently alluding "to the fact of Mr. Emmet's migration to the United States,"[30] and Emmet's combative nature was prodded. He rose after Pinkney's argument, although he was technically not permitted to do so, and according to one account,

> after correcting a trifling error in one of Mr. Pinkney's statements . . . took up the mode and manner in which his opponent had treated him. He said he was Mr. Pinkney's equal in birth, in rank, in his connexions, and he was not his enemy. It was true that he was an Irishman. It was true . . . that he had come to America for refuge, and sought protection beneath her constitution and her laws; and it was also true that his learned antagonist would never . . . add lustre to his well earned fame, by alluding to these facts in a tone of malicious triumph.[31]

According to another eyewitness, Emmet then continued,

> The gentleman yesterday announced to the court his purpose to show that I was mistaken in every statement of facts and every conclusion

---

[24] Haines, *Memoir of Emmet*, 90.
[25] Ibid., 95, 90.
[26] The cases were The Mary, 9 Cranch 126 (1824) The Frances, 9 Cranch 183 (1824), The Adeline, 9 Cranch 244 (1824), and The Nereide, 9 Cranch 388 (1824).
[27] Pinkney's career is treated below, pp. 241–54.

[28] G. Ticknor to Elisha Ticknor, Feb. 21, 1815, in F. Greenslet, ed., *Life, Letters, and Journals of George Ticknor* (2 vols., 1909), I, 40.
[29] Ibid.
[30] Haines, *Memoir of Emmet*, 111.
[31] Ibid.

of law which I had laid before it. Of his success to-day the court alone have a right to judge, but in my estimation, the manner of announcing his threat of yesterday, and of attempting to fulfill it to-day was not very courteous to a stranger, an equal, and one who is so truly inclined to honor his talents and learning. It is a manner which I am persuaded he did not learn in the polite circles in Europe, to which he referred, and which I sincerely wish he had forgotten there, wherever he may have learnt it.[32]

Pinkney reportedly responded to Emmet's remarks "in a few words of cold and inefficient explanation."[33] But about two weeks later[34] that same Term, in another prize case, Pinkney publicly apologized to Emmet. In his argument in *The Nereide,* according to Henry Wheaton, who took notes at the argument, Pinkney digressed at a point to

beg my learned opponents to . . . believe that I respect them both too much to be willing to give umbrage to either. To one of them, indeed, I have heretofore given unintentional pain, by observations to which the influence of accidental excitement imparted the appearance of un-kind criticism. The manner in which he replied to those observations reproached me by its forbearance and urbanity, and could not fail to hasten the repentance which reflection alone would have produced, and which I am glad to have so public an occasion of avowing. I offer him a gratuitous and cheerful atonement—cheerful because it puts me to rights with myself, and because it is tendered not to ignorance and presumption, but to the highest worth in intellect and morals, enhanced by such eloquence as few may hope to equal—to an interesting stranger whom adversity has tried and affliction struck severely to the heart—to an exile whom any county might be proud to receive, and every man of a generous temper would be ashamed to offend.[35]

---

[32] G. Ticknor to E. Ticknor, Feb. 21, 1815, supra, note 28, 41.

[33] Ibid.

[34] The precise dates are uncertain. The minutes of the Supreme Court for the 1815 Term show *The Mary* being argued on February 18 and *The Nereide* being argued on March 10, an interval of twenty days. Minutes of the Supreme Court of the United States (Feb. 1, 1790–Aug. 4, 1828) National Archives, reprinted in National Archives Microfilm Publications, Microcopy No. 215, Roll No. 1. The Supreme Court's Docket for the 1815 Term, however, has *The Nereide* being argued on March 6. Reporter William Cranch did not list the dates of arguments in his Reports,

only the dates opinions were delivered in Court. In general, the dates listed in the Court's Minutes for this time period are more reliable than the dates listed in its Docket.

[35] Wheaton had not yet succeeded Cranch as the Court's Reporter, but he recorded and published the argument in H. Wheaton, *Some Account of the Life, Writings, and Speeches of William Pinkney* (1826), 500. Another account of the Emmet–Pinkney exchange, un-reliable because of its excessively apol-ogetic posture, appears in W. Pinkney, *The Life of William Pinkney* (1853), 100–105, a memoir written by Pink-ney's nephew.

Emmet's impromptu rejoinder to Pinkney illustrated his distinctive combination of contentiousness and grace; Pinkney's apology underscores the emotional impact that Emmet's history and presence made on contemporaries. George Ticknor remarked on the "appearance of premature age in [Emmet's] person, and of a settled melancholy in his countenance," which "may be an index to all that we know of himself and his family." Ticknor thought Emmet "more advanced in life" than Pinkney, whom he also observed in the 1815 Term; actually Emmet and Pinkney were both fifty at the time.[36] Story commented that when he "first became acquainted with Mr. Emmet . . . in the winter of 1815 . . . deep lines of care were marked upon his face . . . although . . . he could have been but little, if any, turned of fifty years of age." Story associated Emmet's appearance with "the sad remembrances . . . of past sufferings, and of those anxieties, which wear themselves into the heart, and corrode the very elements of life." There was, Story felt, "an age of subdued thoughtfulness" about Emmet; "he was cheerful, but rarely, if ever, gay; frank and courteous, but he soon relapsed into gravity, when not excited by the conversation of others."[37]

The culmination of Emmet's career as an advocate before the Marshall Court came in *Gibbons* v. *Ogden*. *Gibbons* was the famous 1824 "steamboat case" in which the Court declared that the state of New York's effort to grant Robert Fulton and his associates "the exclusive navigation of all the waters within the jurisdiction of that State, with boats moved by fire and steam" for "thirty years after 1808"[38] violated the Constitution's Commerce Clause. Fulton, the first successful American promoter of the steamboat, had been a close acquaintance of Emmet's since their initial meeting in Paris in 1803, when both were interested in obtaining the support of Napoleon's government, Emmet on behalf of an independent Ireland and Fulton on behalf of a projected submarine with torpedos.[39] An August 5, 1803, diary entry of Emmet's, written in Paris, recorded that "Fulton . . . promised if the affair [an insurrection in Ireland] should become so serious as to leave him room to work, he would go over and commence his plan of [submarine] operations."[40] When both men settled in New York, Emmet represented Fulton, his partner Robert Livingston, and their assignees in their scores of efforts, of which *Gibbons* v. *Ogden* was the last, to obtain and to protect an exclusive steamboat

[36] Greenslet, *George Ticknor*, I, 39.
[37] Story to Sampson, Feb. 27, 1829, supra, note 22, at 567. Francis Walker Gilmer, commenting on Emmet in the 1820s, said that "he possesses . . . the natural and simple pathos of his nation, with all the openness of heart, and generosity of temper, which can excite the admiration, or win the affections of men." F. Gilmer, *Sketches, Essays, and Translations* (1828), 27.
[38] Gibbons v. Ogden, 9 Wheat. 1, 2, 7 (1824).
[39] See M. Baxter, *The Steamboat Monopoly Case* (1972), 11–12.
[40] Quoted in Emmet, *Memoir*, I, 357.

franchise they had first been granted by the New York legislature in 1798.[41]

*Gibbons* v. *Ogden* was, for many contemporaries, the most stirring of all the great Marshall Court cases. Its doctrinal and cultural dimensions, and its practical implications, are discussed in a subsequent chapter. *Gibbons* has also been acknowledged as the high point of advocacy on the Marshall Court. Justice James Wayne's remark in his seriatim opinion in *The Passenger Cases*, decided in 1849, has been frequently quoted: "the case of *Gibbons* v. *Ogden*, in the extent and variety of learning, and in the acuteness with which it was argued by counsel, is not surpassed by any other case in the reports of courts."[42] William Wirt, the attorney general of the United States, who had been retained to oppose Emmet in *Gibbons*, wrote a close friend from Washington at the opening of the 1824 Term that "about tomorrow week will come on the great steamboat question from New York. Emmet and [Thomas] Oakley on one side, [Daniel] Webster and myself on the other. Come down and hear it. Emmet's whole soul is in the cause, and he will stretch all his powers."[43]

Emmet did indeed "stretch all his powers" in his *Gibbons* argument. It filled eighty pages in Wheaton's Reports, the bulk of which were devoted to an intricate interpretation of the Commerce Clause, studded with citations, that sought to establish a concurrent power in the states to regulate commerce on state waters in the absence of affirmative congressional regulatory legislation. The argument, which was not adopted by the Court in *Gibbons* but was to surface in later Commerce Clause cases,[44] also included some typical Emmet flourishes, one of which prompted a "classic" rejoinder from Wirt. At the close of his argument Emmet said that

---

[41] Baxter, *Steamboat Monopoly Case*, 8–12. Even Fulton's death can be attributed to his relationship with Emmet and to the "steamboat case." In January and February, 1824, Emmet and Fulton attended hearings before the New Jersey legislature at which the repeal of an exclusive franchise New Jersey had granted a competitor of Fulton's was at issue. Emmet and Fulton's position prevailed by a narrow vote. The two men were then returning from Trenton, the site of the hearings, to New York City and sought to take a ferryboat across the North River (now the Hudson). The river being frozen, no boat was available, and Emmet and Fulton attempted to walk across on the ice. Emmet, "the heavier of the two, broke through," and Fulton success-

fully rescued him. In the process Fulton "exposed himself by getting overheated, with the result that he caught a severe sore throat," and on February 24, died in his home in New York. The quoted passages are from Emmet, *Memoir*, I, 427–28. See also Baxter, *Steamboat Monopoly Case*, 30–32.

[42] 7 How. 283, 437 (1849).

[43] W. Wirt to Dabney Carr, Feb. 1, 1824, quoted in J. Kennedy, *Memoirs of the Life of William Wirt* (2 vols., 1850), II, 143.

[44] Emmet's position was, however, adopted, in the main, by the Taney Court in Cooley v. Board of Wardens, 12 How. 299 (1852). For a full discussion of Commerce Clause issues in the Taney Court, see C. Swisher, *The Taney Period, 1836–64* (1974), 357–422.

[t]he State of New York, by a patient and forbearing patronage of ten years to Livingston and Fulton . . . has called into existence the noblest and most useful improvement of the present day. . . . New York may raise her head . . . and case her eyes over the whole civilized world; there she may see its countless waters bearing on their surface countless offsprings of her munificence and wisdom. . . . [C]onscious of the value of her own good works, she may turn the mournful exclamation of Aeneas into an expression of triumph, and exultingly ask,
Quae regio in terris, nostri non plena laboris?[45]

Wirt, himself an accomplished classicist, then responded at the close of his rebuttal on behalf of Thomas Gibbons, the Fulton monopoly's potential competitor:

[My] learned friend [has] eloquently pictured the State of New York, casting her eyes over the ocean, witnessing everywhere this triumph of genius, and exclaiming, in the language of Aeneas,
"Quae regio in terris, nostri non plena laboris?" Sir, it was not in the moment of triumph, nor with feelings of triumph, that Aereas uttered that exclamation. It was when . . . he was surveying the works of art with which the palace of Carthage was adorned, and his attention had been caught by a representation of the battles of Troy. . . . The whole extent of his misfortunes—the loss and desolation of his friends—the fall of his beloved country, rush upon his recollection. "Constitit, et *lachrymans;* Quis jam locus, inquit, Achate [Aeneas' "faithful" friend Achates], Quae regio in terris nostri non plena laboris?"

Wirt then indulged in a rhetorical flourish of his own:

Sir, the passage may, hereafter, have a closer application to the cause than my eloquent and classical friend intended. . . . Civil wars have often arisen from far inferior causes, and have desolated some of the fairest provinces of the earth. . . . It is a momentous decision which this Court is called on to make. Here are three States [New York, New Jersey, and Connecticut] almost on the eve of war. It is the high province of the Court to interpose its benign and mediatorial influence . . . [I]f you do not interpose your friendly hand, and extirpate the seeds of anarchy which New York has sown, you *will* have civil war. . . . Your republican institutions will perish in the conflict. Your constitution will fall. The last hope of nations will be gone. . . . Then, sir, when New

---

[45] 9 Wheat. at 157–58. My rough translation would be "What country of the world is not full of ("buzzing" about) our work?" The reference is Book I, lines 459–60 of Virgil's *Aeneid.*

York shall look upon this scene of ruin, with a voice suffocated with despair, *well* may she *then* exclaim,

"Quis jam locus, quae regio un terris nostri non plena laboris!"[46]

The above example suggests what Emmet's own contemporaries noted: his eloquence occasionally led to his undoing. During the term that Emmet argued *Gibbons* v. *Ogden* he stayed at the same boardinghouse with Charles Glidden Haines, a New York lawyer who was then arguing the famous bankruptcy case of *Ogden* v. *Saunders*.[47] Emmet told Haines a good deal about his life, including his activities "connected with the contemplated revolution of Ireland," with the expectation that Haines would "reduce some things thus told to form and shape."[48] The result was an authorized "memoir," which appeared five years later. When Haines came to list, in his sketch of Emmet, "some defects . . . of a professional description," he noted that Emmet's "zeal sometimes clouds his judgment, and obscures the perceptions of his mind." In "the worst of causes," Haines felt, "I have known him to struggle with the same ardour and assurance as though he was perfectly persuaded of the justice of his suit. This has diminished his influence in our courts. They have imbibed a habit of listening to his legal doctrines with suspicion."[49] While Haines was not seeking to equate "zeal" with "eloquence," one could make that association: Emmet occasionally trapped himself in his own eloquence, just as he bred "suspicion" with his zeal. Perhaps the most affecting and least affected of the leading Marshall Court advocates, he suffered at times from "putting his whole soul" in his cases. When he died, having collapsed from a stroke while arguing a case in court, the New York *American* reported in its November 15, 1827, issue:

The circumstances of this distinguished man's death are in themselves singularly affecting. He had been constantly and more arduously employed for some weeks in causes of the greatest importance.[50] He had prepared himself in them with his usual labor and research. . . . Without allowing himself any respite . . . he forthwith . . . entered upon the important contested claim of the Sailors' Snug Harbor. In attendance upon this cause, it was yesterday that the hand of death was laid upon him. In a full court, it was suddenly perceived that Mr. Emmet had drooped upon the table. The Attorney-General [of New York] who was sitting near, addressed him, but finding him speechless, the alarm

---

[46] 9 Wheat. at 183–86. "He stood still, and weeping, said, 'Now, what country of the world is not full of our work?' " The italicization of "lachrymans" was supplied by Wirt.

[47] An anonymous biographical sketch of Haines appears in Haines, *Memoir of Emmet*, 5–32. That sketch states that Haines was born "about the year 1793." Ibid., 5. *Ogden* v. *Saunders* is treated in Chapter IX.

[48] Haines, *Memoir of Emmet*, 5.

[49] Ibid., 119.

[50] Carver v. Jackson *ex dem*. Astor, 4 Pet. 1 (1830); Inglis v. Trustees of the Sailor's Snug Harbor, 3 Pet. 99 (1830).

was immediately communicated to the court—which thereupon forthwith adjourned—medical aid was sent for. . . .

The blood flowed indeed from the arms and the temples;[51] but sense, consciousness, and intelligence had fled forever. . . . He was removed in a litter about 3 o'clock, to his own house, where he died. Yet is there in the manner of this death something glorious and consolatory.[52]

The narrative now passes from Emmet to Littleton W. Tazewell, whose professional base was in Norfolk and who served as a United States congressman and senator, and as governor of Virginia, in addition to sixty-four years in private law practice. In passing from Emmet to Tazewell the contrast in personality tempts one to indulge in regional stereotypes. Emmet sought out public controversy, Tazewell single-mindedly retreated from it; Emmet's "bold and spreading fluency, which belongs to Irish eloquence" may be juxtaposed against Tazewell's lack of "exultation" and "ambition"[53] and his self-conscious efforts to emulate the life of a self-contained Virginia squire. And yet no one accused Littleton Tazewell of lacking flair or force of personality. William Wirt's portrait of Tazewell in his mid-twenties, based on their encounter in Richmond in 1799, when Wirt was clerk of the Virginia House of Delegates and Tazewell a member of that body, testifies to the vivid impression Tazewell made on others:

[Tazewell was] a spare young man of good figure, whose face seemed formed on the finest model of antiquity, and whose large eye, of a soft deep blue, habitually expanded, as if looking upon a wide and boundless surface, might well be called an eye of ocean. [He was] cool, collected, vigorous, and self-balanced. . . . There was no broken lumber nor useless trash in his mind. . . . [H]is memory appeared to have possessed a facility of discriminating among the subjects offered to its retention, and rejecting the incumbrance of what was worthless, to have seized and holden with indissoluble tenacity everything that was useful, together with all its roots and ramifications. . . . [H]is mind . . . had such a power of compression and expansion of versatility and strength, that it seemed capable of anything and everything that he pleased. . . . With what closeness and unanswerable coping he would maintain truth! And with what illusion and almost irrefutable sophistry he would dispose and metamorphise error! . . . His fault seemed to consist in the

---

[51] Under standard medical practice at the time, Emmet was "bled." See F. H. Garrison, *An Introduction to the History of Medicine* (1929), and sources cited in Chapter I.

[52] New York *American*, Nov. 15, 1827.

[53] The characterizations are from Gilmer, *Sketches*, 26, 36.

abuse of his strength; in that laxity of colloquial morals . . . which led him to triumph, with equal pleasure, in every victory, right or wrong.[54]

Wirt's sketch, while representing Tazewell early in his career, identified characteristics that contemporaries were to identify with Tazewell all his life. Among them were a striking physical appearance,[55] a remarkable capacity to cut to the heart of an argument, a remorseless logic, a continual interest in the practical consequences of ideas, an intensity and a competitiveness, and a seemingly greater interest in the mechanics of an argument than in the intrinsic rightness of the proposition he was arguing. All of these features of Tazewell's character were alluded to by Wirt, each was remarked upon by others. When Tazewell's consummate interest in public issues and his constant and determined withdrawal from public offices is added to these characteristics, the result is a complex and fascinating figure, worthy of greater attention than he has received in scholarly literature.[56]

---

[54] W. Wirt, *The Old Bachelor* (1814), 149–50.

[55] Tazewell's physical appearance was regularly marked by contemporaries. In his memoir of Tazewell, Hugh Grigsby gave portraits of his subject at several stages in his life:

In a physical view he is said by one who knew him [in his twenties] to have been the most elegant and brilliant young man of his age. His tall stature, which reached six feet, his light and graceful figure, his blue, wide, intellectual eye, his features noble and prominent. . . .

[At the Virginia state convention in 1829, when Tazewell was fifty-five] his large stature, his full stern features, lighted by a wide grave blue eye, his solemn gait . . . were in fair keeping with [an] intellectual image of him. . . .

He was without exception in middle life the most imposing, and in old age the most venerable person I ever beheld. . . . In middle life he was very thin, though lithe and strong. . . . But for the last thirty-five years [1825–60] . . . during which I have been familiar with his person, all those traces of early beauty which had marked his youthful face . . .

had disappeared, and he was altogether on a more developed scale. His stature had become large, his features were massive, his silver hair fell in ringlets about his neck, and his bearing was grave. . . .

H. Grigsby, *Discourse in the Life, and Character of Hon. Littleton W. Tazewell* (1860), 15, 65, 96. Tazewell gave a physical description of himself in 1826, in response to being called the "venerable Senator from Virginia" while serving in the United States Senate:

My bushy locks now become quite white, hang in loose profusion over my shoulders, resembling very much the representation of Judge Blackstone's wig; and the numerous furrows in my face, ploughed by various causes, stamp upon me the appearance of at least so many years as unnecessary to make up the time part of the character of "venerable."

L. Tazewell to John Wickham, May 9, 1826, in Littleton Waller Tazewell Papers, Virginia State Library, Richmond, Va.

[56] A recent biography of Tazewell, N. Peterson, *Littleton Waller Tazewell* (1984), had appeared, but its portrait of Tazewell is rarely penetrating.

Tazewell was one of the successive generations of tidewater Virginia gentry who studied law at William and Mary, were elected to the House of Delegates from safe seats in the English tradition, and came to maturity well aware of each other's strengths and failings. He was born in Williamsburg, attended Walker Maury's preparatory school (where John Randolph was a classmate), was tutored by George Wythe, graduated from William and Mary at eighteen, read for the bar in Richmond (where he met John Marshall), entered law practice at twenty-one in 1796, and was elected that same year to the Virginia House of Delegates from James City County. His father, Henry Tazewell, had been a state judge and was a United States senator when Tazewell entered law practice. In January 1799 Henry Tazewell died suddenly while in Philadelphia to attend a Senate session. A year later Littleton Tazewell was elected to Congress as a Republican to fill the vacated seat of John Marshall, who had resigned to become secretary of state.

The pattern of a promising son following in the footsteps of an accomplished father is not unusual. Given the early life of Littleton Tazewell, however, his decisions to enter law practice in Norfolk in 1796 and to run for political office were gestures fraught with significance, for his father had other plans for him. Tazewell had no recollection of his mother, Dorothea Waller, who died at twenty-three, three years after Littleton was born.[57] His first close attachments were to his father and to his maternal grandfather, Judge Benjamin Waller of Williamsburg, with whom Littleton was sent to live after his mother's death. When Judge Waller died in 1786, Littleton, who was then twelve, was reportedly "inconsolable."[58] He was taken under the care of John Wickham, a Richmond lawyer, who "heard and corrected [his] recitations," and under whom Littleton "complete[d] [his] education."[59]

After graduating from Maury's school and from William and Mary, Littleton began studying law under Wickham in Richmond in 1792. He soon became ill, however, and had to abandon his legal studies. He returned to his father's home in Kingsmill, Virginia, to recuperate under a prescribed regimen of vigorous exercise. In an autobiographical sketch of his career, Tazewell recounted what then occurred:

> I continued this course until December, 1794, when my father, being elected to the Senate of the U.S., determined to take me with him to Philadelphia. My health at this time was completely reestablished. We left Kingsmill the later end of December, & . . . arrived in Philadelphia early in January, 1795. . . .

---

[57] Grigsby, *Discourse*, 9.
[58] Ibid. at 10.
[59] Letter from L. Tazewell to William F. Wickham, quoted in Grigsby,

*Discourse*, 12. The letter, undated, was written in 1839. A copy is in the Virginia State Library, Richmond, Va.

## Chapter IV: *Prominent Lawyers Before the Marshall Court*

Soon after our arrival in Philadelphia I was directed by my father to attend Mr. Edmund Randolph, who was then the Secretary of State, and, who I was told, could advise me which course of reading and study I ought to follow. As Mr. Randolph was a lawyer of much distinction, I took it for granted that I was placed under his care for the purpose of prosecuting the study of the law. . . . [B]ut instead of telling me what books I should read . . . so soon as I appeared I was put to transcribing some public document or other. I kept at this employment until 3 o'clock, when the office was closed, and I saw nothing of the Secretary. . . .

I continued this course for some weeks, when discovering no change, I mentioned to my father how my time was wasting, and begged of him to place me in some other situation, where I might prosecute my legal studies to more advantage. . . . He then for the first time informed me of his wish to bring me up for diplomatic employment, & that this was the reason for placing me in the office of the Secretary of State. I was utterly confounded at this communication, which seemed to render useless all I had acquired for some years past, and this under my father's own advice. . . .

I had made up my mind to become a lawyer, if I could, and already began to derive pleasure from the study. I felt, moreover, much aversion to public life, and was conscious that I never could qualify myself to be a diplomatist. I expressed these opinions to my father freely, and begged of him to suffer me to return to Virginia and study the law with my friend Mr. Wickham. He could not consent to it, however, but directed me to continue my attendance at the Secretary's Office as before. . . .[60]

Shortly after this confrontation with his father, Littleton "was presented to the President General Washington," in order to be considered for "the appointment of Secretary to some of our foreign Ministers." Washington "received [Tazewell] very courteously," inquired about his education, reminisced about Judge Waller, "for whom he expressed very high respect," and "made many inquiries as to [Waller's] family and descendants."[61] But the result of the meeting was that

in a few weeks my father informed me that if I still persisted in my inclination to study the law, and wished to go to Mr. Wickham, he had no objection to my doing so. I was highly gratified at this, and as anxious was I to get away from Philadelphia lest something might occur to change my father's purpose . . . I set off for Richmond on the very next day. I arrived at Mr. Wickham's early in February, 1795.

---

[60] L. Tazewell, "Sketches of His Own Family Written for His Children" (unpublished manuscript, 1823), 146–48, Tazewell Papers.
[61] Ibid., 149.

My situation was most agreeable indeed with Mr. Wickham . . .
With Mr. Wickham I had been brought up . . . I found myself placed
in the bosom of my own family.[62]

The short month Tazewell spent with his father in Philadelphia in
1795 was to take on considerable significance in his subsequent career.
Several suggestive themes appear in the excerpt from Tazewell's autobiography: a sense of being betrayed and humiliated by his father, while
also being dominated by him; an "aversion to public life"; a conception
of legal study as a counterweight to, rather than a complement of, a public
career; and an association of John Wickham as a member of Tazewell's
"family," into whose "bosom" Tazewell was retreating after his confrontation in Philadelphia with his father. These themes were to surface
again in Tazewell's later life.

When Tazewell was elected to Congress in 1800 it appeared that
national politics was to become his career. "[H]e was [then] universally
regarded by his political friends as the first young man in the state, and
the most dazzling honors which a victorious [Republican] party could
confer upon him seemed to be within his reach."[63] But a year later
Tazewell resigned from Congress and moved his law practice to Norfolk.
With this act a pattern of voluntary withdrawals from public life, and
grudging re-entries into it, began, finally to end in 1835 when Tazewell
resigned the governorship of Virginia. Years later, when a companion
expressed regret that Tazewell had retired from public life so early,
Tazewell reportedly said, "I'm only sorry that I ever entered it at all!"[64]
And yet Tazewell never declined nominations for public office in Virginia. He wrote Hugh Grigsby in December 1824 that "there is no office,
place, or appointment within the gift of man which I wish, and none I
would accept save from my native state. To her I have never felt myself
at liberty to refuse myself under any circumstances, when she thought
proper to call me to her side."[65] That formula allowed him to re-enter
the Virginia House of Delegates in 1816; to run successfully for the United
States Senate in 1824 (his old friend Grigsby called Tazewell's election
"one of the severest trials in his life");[66] and to serve, after his retirement
from the senate in 1833, as governor of Virginia. He voluntarily resigned
all the public offices he held. Francis Gilmer, another friend, apologized
to Tazewell in the 1820s "for dragging his name from the obscurity which
he seems to court." Tazewell "has shrunk from the great national am-
phitheatre," Gilmer noted, "to an obscure seaport town."[67]

---

[62] Ibid.
[63] Grigsby, *Discourse,* 22.
[64] Ibid.
[65] L. Tazewell to H. Grigsby, Dec.

1, 1824, quoted in ibid., 120.
[66] Ibid., 57.
[67] Gilmer, *Sketches,* 35.

# Chapter IV: *Prominent Lawyers Before the Marshall Court*

In Tazewell's middle years his principal respite from public life was his law practice, where he specialized in criminal law and admiralty. Tazewell was aided as a criminal lawyer, his longtime friend Hugh Grigsby thought, by "that perfect self-possession which not only conceals his own fears and weakness, but avails itself of the fears and weakness of others."[68] In addressing juries he reportedly talked to them in an unpretentious, "natural" fashion: "he formed his theory of the case, and unfolded it to the jury in the simplest possible way." This straightforwardness was not incompatible, however, with "great adroitness": Tazewell "either knew himself or learned from others the calling of every juryman; and . . . if he saw a dangerous man among them he . . . made the man believe that his standing in his own business depended upon his bringing in a verdict in [Tazewell's client's] favor."[69]

Tazewell's admiralty litigation involved appellate cases as well as trial cases, and it was in that capacity that he first appeared before the Marshall Court. *The Santissima Trinidad*[70] was one of a series of cases decided between the 1819 and 1827 Terms in which the Court clarified the legal status of Spanish or Portuguese ships that had been captured by South American privateers and returned to American ports. The privateering was related to revolutionary activity by Spanish and Portuguese colonies in Mexico, Central America, and South America. The modus operandi of the privateers was simple enough. A merchant ship, showing no colors, would be cleared for a routine commercial voyage from an American port (typically Baltimore, Norfolk, Charleston, or New Orleans) to a Caribbean location. Once over the high seas, the ships would fly the colors of the newly formed Mexican, Argentinian, or Venezuelan republics, and attack Spanish or Portuguese commercial vessels. They would then enlist the captured vessels in their service, bringing them into American ports. On some occasions practices were even bolder: the fiction of a commercial voyage was dropped and American ports provided supplies, guns, ammunition, and mercenaries to the privateers.[71] The privateer activity was at once highly profitable to mercantile interests in certain American seaport cities and embarrassing to the Monroe and Adams administrations, which sought to improve diplomatic relations with Spain and Portugal but without encouraging any European presence in the Western Hemisphere. The federal courts became a natural forum in which the issue of America's response to privateering could be debated, and the Marshall Court moved swiftly to dissociate the American gov-

---

[68] Grigsby, *Discourse*, 76.
[69] Ibid., at 68.
[70] 7 Wheat. 283 (1822).
[71] For background in early-nineteenth-century American piracy and privateering, see C. Griffin, *The United States and the Disruption of the Spanish Empire* (1937); G. Dangerfield, *The Era of Good Feelings* (1952). For a discussion of prize law cases before the Marshall Court, see Chapter XIII.

ernment from the privateers, seeking to dispel, as Bushrod Washington put it in a grand jury charge, "the unmerited stigma of society taking part in a war which our Government is unwilling to countenance."[72]

*The Santissima Trinidad* was a typical privateering case. Two Spanish ships, the *Santissima Trinidad* and the *St. André*, were seized by "two armed vessels called the *Independencia del Sud* and the *Altravida*," and a portion of their cargo, including "eighty-nine bales of cochineal," was confiscated. The captors claimed "to be citizens of the United Provinces of the Rio de La Plata," that is, Argentina.[73] The *Independencia*, however had been "built and equipped at Baltimore as a privateer"; her captain, James ("Don Diego") Chayton, was "a native citizen of the United States" and a resident of Baltimore; and while Chayton claimed that the *Independencia* had been "sold to the government of Buenos Aires," no bill of sale of the vessel was produced.[74]

Tazewell had entered the case because the *Independencia* and the *Altravida* had taken their cargo to Norfolk. When they arrived "the captured property . . . was . . . landed for safe keeping in the custom-house store,"[75] and Don Pablo Chacon, the Spanish consul in Norfolk, filed a libel on behalf of the original owners of the *Santissima Trinidad* and the *St. André* for the return of the cochineal bales. Tazewell, who represented Chacon, argued that the bales were improperly seized and should be returned to the Spanish government. He won at both the federal court in Norfolk and Marshall's circuit court in Richmond. Several significant, if technical, points of prize law were raised in the case, one of which involved a 1795 treaty between the United States and Spain governing privateering. Tazewell suggested to Chacon that Daniel Webster be retained to argue the construction of that treaty and later, after working with Webster, commented that the latter was "excessively clever, but a lazy dog."[76]

William Pinkney, the acknowledged leader of the Supreme Court bar from the close of the War of 1812 to his death in 1822, was retained to oppose Tazewell and Webster, and contemporaries buzzed over the anticipated confrontation.[77] Pinkney's law practice was based in Baltimore, and, as noted, admiralty and prize cases were his specialty. According to John Quincy Adams, he had "bullied and browbeaten" the Baltimore federal district judge and Justice Gabriel Duvall on the Third

---

[72] Quoted in *Niles' Weekly Register*, 13:171 (Nov. 8, 1817). The name of the circuit court case was not listed.
[73] 7 Wheat. 283, 285–86 (1822).
[74] Ibid., 286.
[75] Ibid., 280.
[76] L. Tazewell to H. Grigsby, quoted in Grigsby, *Discourse*, 45.

[77] Francis Gilmer wrote, "I had long been curious to see the natural vigour, fertility, and adroitness of Mr. Tazewell, contrasted with the consummate art and accomplished prowess of Mr. Pinkney." Gilmer, *Sketches*, 37.

Circuit; he had "saved all [the] riches of [the privateers] from the richly merited halter."[78] Pinkney died suddenly, however, on February 25, 1822, just three days before arguments in *The Santissima Trinidad* began.[79] Francis Walker Gilmer, in noting the "publick disappointment . . . when the death of Mr. Pinkney rendered [his clash with Tazewell] impossible," suggested that Pinkney's "preparation for his argument with Mr. Tazewell . . . was too intense; his strength and health, and life, sunk under it."[80] Gilmer's supposition has been doubted,[81] but in any event Tazewell's principal arguments prevailed before the Marshall Court, and the cochineal bales were returned to the Spanish government.

Tazewell argued, first, that the United States courts had jurisdiction to inquire into the legality of the capture of the Spanish ships, even if the "sovereign rights of an independent state" were affected by the inquiry; second, that "an illegal outfit and augmentation of force" had been employed "by the capturing vessels"; and, third, that an alleged condemnation of the cargo by a Buenos Aires tribunal was no bar "to the present proceedings, since the property was at the time in the custody of [American courts]."[82] Story's opinion for the Court upheld, in the main, each of these arguments. Webster, whose argument followed that of Tazewell, wrote Jeremiah Mason in March of 1822, "Your friend Tazewell . . . made a good speech in one of those Baltimore Privateering cases. He is a correct, fluent, easy, & handsome speaker and a learned, ingenuous & *subtle* lawyer."[83]

Tazewell again represented the Spanish government before the Marshall Court in *The Palmyra,* another prize case, which he argued in the 1827 Term. The case, in which Tazewell's position only partially prevailed, provides a good example of his singular combination of pride, sensitivity, and competitiveness. Tazewell was serving in the Senate at the time and had been prominently involved in presidential politics. He had broken with the Adams administration after John Quincy Adams's celebrated "deal" with Henry Clay by which Adams, who had received fewer popular votes than Andrew Jackson in the divided and inconclusive election of 1824, received Clay's electoral votes in the House of Representatives, and thereby the presidency, in exchange for Clay's being named secretary of state. The maneuver fragmented the Republican party and precipitated the formation of the Democratic party. Tazewell, never

---

[78] J. Q. Adams, entries for May 26, 1819 and Aug. 21, 1819, in C. Adams, ed., *The Memoirs of John Quincy Adams, Comprising Portions of His Diary from 1795 to 1848* (12 vols., 1874–77), IV, 372, 415, 416.
[79] Pinkney's death will be treated later in this chapter, at p. 254.

[80] Gilmer, *Sketches,* 37.
[81] Grigsby, *Discourse,* 44.
[82] 7 Wheat. at 316.
[83] D. Webster to J. Mason, Mar. 3, 1822, Daniel Webster Papers, Library of Congress.

a strong partisan, temporarily threw his support to Jackson and denounced the "Coalition," as the Adams–Clay forces were termed.

Latin American relations posed difficulties for the Adams administration, which was identified with the Monroe Doctrine, Adams having been Monroe's secretary of state when the doctrine was pronounced in 1823. When Clay, with Adams's blessing, attempted to send United States delegates to a conference of new Latin American nations held in Panama in 1826, anti-Coalition forces in Congress balked, seeking to embarrass Adams and Clay and to dissociate themselves from rapprochement with revolutionary regimes.[84] Tazewell was a visible opponent of the Panama conference and, in his capacity as a member of the Senate's Committee on Foreign Affairs, delivered a critical report on the proposed Panama mission. The "Coalition jurists" responded, Tazewell wrote his old friend John Wickham, by labeling him " 'an intellectual gladiator,' 'a most ingenuous subject,' 'a subtle reasoner,' [and] 'a practiced lawyer trained to make the worse appear the better cause.' "[85]

Tazewell's rift with the Adams administration was to serve as a backdrop to his argument in *The Palmyra*.[86] The ship at issue in the case was a brig, outfitted as a privateer and commissioned by the Spanish government, which had been captured by an American warship, the *Grampus*, on August 15, 1822, and brought to Charleston for possible condemnation. The Spanish government sued in federal district court to prevent condemnation and to recover damages. The district court restored the *Palmyra* to her owners and acquitted her crew of piracy, but denied damages. The *Palmyra*'s captors appealed to Justice Johnson's circuit court and received a damage award of $10,288.58. A further appeal was then taken to the Supreme Court by both the captors and the United States government.[87] Tazewell's principal policy argument on behalf of the Spanish government was that "foreign nations must ever find quick cause for discontent, if their own ships are taken as piratical vessels, and condemned to the use of the U.S. . . . [I]n the particular case, Spain . . . might perhaps suspect that our friendship for our enemies, the new republics of South America, rather than the public law, had required the capture and caused the decision. And if so war must be the result."[88] In making that argument Tazewell linked the *Palmyra* case to the Panama Conference and to the congressional debates over Latin American affairs. Tazewell had also argued before the Court that the original claim filed by the *Palmyra*'s captors "was defective in not charging with sufficient pre-

---

[84] See Dangerfield, *Era of Good Feelings*, 356–64.
[85] L. Tazewell to J. Wickham, Jan. 21, 1827, Tazewell Papers.
[86] 12 Wheat. 1 (1827).
[87] Ibid., 2–3.
[88] L. Tazewell, "Argument Notes," Tazewell Papers.

cision the particular acts of practical aggression, and in omitting to allege a previous prosecution and conviction of the captured persons of the crime of piracy.''[89]

Tazewell had presented his arguments on January 10, 1827. On January 15 Story read a draft opinion, for a divided court,[90] reversing the decision of Johnson's circuit court with respect to the damages but affirming the return of the brig to Spain. Tazewell was not present in court when Story read the draft, and asked Story to see the text of his opinion. After reading it Tazewell wrote an outraged letter to John Marshall, dated January 18, 1827, which contained the following paragraph:

[I]n reading this opinion I found in it the following sentence, "The other point of objection is of a far more subtle and novel nature." Had these expressions been used in the heat and animation of debate, however singular the *coincidence* of the language with that which had been used elsewhere, it could not have attracted my observation. Could I consider them as only the words of Mr. Justice Story, they would not certainly have exacted any other feeling, than that of mere regret. But when they are handed out as the deliberate . . . written judicial language of the Supreme Court, I think I have a right to call the attention of the other Judges to the terms employed, to the end they may not go forth to the world, without being noticed and approved by at least a majority of them. Such, sir, is the single purpose of this letter . . .[91]

Marshall, who was perhaps unaware of Tazewell's belief that "[t]hese very words have often been applied to my political arguments by the Coalition [pamphlets] . . . to weaken the force and effect of the arguments used, by infusing into the public mind the opinion that I am very capable of using a subtle argument upon any subject,''[92] immediately replied, possibly with his tongue in his cheek:

I very much regret that any expression should have found its way into any opinion given by the Court which wounds any gentleman of the bar. There is certainly no member of the bench who would not wish very sincerely to avoid such a circumstance. I do not understand you when you speak of the "singular coincidence of the words used with

---

[89] 12 Wheat. at 7.

[90] The Justices were unanimous in finding that "the case is clearly not a case for damages." With respect to the question whether the *Palmyra*'s crew had committed piracy, "the Judges are divided in opinion; and consequently, according to the known practice of the Court, the decree of the Circuit Court, so far as it pronounced a decree of acquittal, must be affirmed." 12 Wheat. at 15.

[91] L. Tazewell to J. Marshall, Jan. 18, 1827, Tazewell Papers.

[92] Tazewell to Wickham, Jan. 21, 1827, supra, note 85.

those which have been used elsewhere." I did not know that similar words had been used elsewhere in reference to any argument of yours. Nor do I believe that anything offensive to you came into the mind of Mr. Story when he employed them.

Without inquiring however into the circumstance, or whether I should have myself felt equal sensitiveness on a similar occasion, it is enough for me that the words pain you and I shall apply to Mr. Story without showing him your letter to expunge them.[93]

Tazewell dashed off a reply,[94] attempting unsuccessfully to distinguish between "[my] interest in acquaint[ing] the judges with the fact [of the "singular coincidence" of language], and "my morbid sensibility."[95] Marshall spoke to Story, and in the official text of the opinion in *The Palmyra* in *Wheaton*'s the sentence was changed from "the other point of objection is of a far more subtle and novel nature" to "the other point of objection is of a far more important and difficult nature."[96]

Tazewell's extreme reaction to a sentence in Story's opinion is curious, given the unmistakable allusions to the Coalition in his own argument before the Court. It should first be noted that his association of Story with the Coalition was accurate. Story had been a longtime friend and supporter of John Quincy Adams,[97] and on hearing Adams's inaugural address in 1823, had written his wife, Sarah Waldo Story, "His speech was one of the best I ever heard—strong, sustained, correct, and liberal, beating down party distinctions, and leading the way to a manly exposition of the Constitution."[98] Story even reported a "strange rumor" that "if Mr. Clay declined the appointment of Secretary of State, Judge Story would be appointed." However "laugh[able]" that "tale,"[99] suggested that Story was closely associated with the Adams administration. Moreover, in an 1826 letter Story identified "the Panama Mission" as "the great point on which the opposition [to Adams] now hinges,"[100] and in another letter that "the Panama Mission . . . will be made the test of party attachments, and probably fix their course for the term of Mr. Adams' Presidency."[101] Tazewell could thus have fairly felt that Story was using pointed language in his draft opinion for political reasons.[102]

But regardless of whether Tazewell had exposed Story in an effort

[93] J. Marshall to L. Tazewell, Jan. 19, 1827, Tazewell Papers.
[94] L. Tazewell to J. Marshall, Jan. 20, 1827, ibid.
[95] Tazewell to Wickham, Jan. 21, 1827, supra, note 85.
[96] 12 Wheat. at 14.
[97] See G. Dunne, *Joseph Story and the Rise of the Supreme Court* (1971), 233–37.

[98] J. Story to S. W. Story, Mar. 4, 1825, in W. Story, *Life and Letters*, I, 485.
[99] J. Story to S. W. Story, Feb. 20, 1825, in ibid., at 482.
[100] J. Story to S. Fay, Mar. 8, 1826, in ibid., 492.
[101] J. Story to J. Evelyn Denison, Mar. 15, 1826, in ibid., 494.

to be sly, the form of his reaction was remarkable. His letter to Marshall gave the appearance of extreme sensitivity and perhaps of pettiness; moreover, it could have been taken as a presumptuous effort on the part of counsel in a Supreme Court case to insist on a privilege to edit the Court's opinion. Some clues to the explanation for Tazewell's response may be gleaned from his letter to Wickham, considered in light of other incidents in his career. Tazewell associated the phrase "subtle and novel" with efforts, as he put it to Wickham, to "put the people upon their guard against me" by the insinuation that "I am very capable of using a subtle argument upon any subject." An old charge of sophistry and artifice had recurred, and the charge had struck deep.[103] "All this I heed not," Tazewell said to Wickham.[104] One suspects otherwise. One suspects that Tazewell feared that his opponents might have uncovered something fundamental about his character, and he was determined, in his proud, bluff fashion, to set things straight. One finds in Tazewell, as evidenced by the *Palmyra* incident, a blend of pride and defensiveness, of aloofness and combativeness, of sensitivity and calculation.

The 1827 Term marked Tazewell's last appearance before the Marshall Court. He argued, and lost, *Bank of the United States* v. *Dandridge;*[105] his argument was not reported.[106] In the *Dandridge* case Marshall, who had decided the case on circuit and was reversed by the full Court, wrote a long dissent which began by saying that "I should now . . . acquiesce silently in [the Court's] opinion, did I not believe that the judgment of the Circuit Court of Virginia gave general surprize to the

---

[102] Benjamin Watkins Leigh, a close friend of Wickham and of Tazewell, attributed such motives to Story. In a letter written to Tazewell on January 24, 1827, in which Leigh discussed Tazewell's January 18 and January 20 letters to Marshall, Leigh said:

I think you were perfectly right in taking exception to that imputation of subtilty [*sic*] in Mr. Story's opinion. I believe that abuse and slander of their opponents, through the medium of the ministerial newspapers, constitute a part of the regular system of administration. . . . In regard to you, particularly, the imputation of *subtilty* is the chief method they have fallen upon to disparage you . . . I hope . . . that in the present instance the offensive imputation is imputable only to *the judge.*

B. Leigh to L. Tazewell, Jan. 24, 1827, Tazewell Papers. Emphasis in original.

[103] The characterization was not limited to Tazewell's opponents. Francis Gilmer said that Tazewell's "fault is subtlety, and a provoking minuteness of detail in his argument," and that "he sometimes shews legal and rhetorical artifice when there is not the least occasion for either." Gilmer, *Sketches,* 36.

[104] Tazewell to Wickham, Jan. 21, 1827, supra, note 85.

[105] 12 Wheat. 64 (1827).

[106] "This cause was very elaborately argued by the Attorney General (William Wirt) and Mr. Webster for the plaintiffs, and by Mr. Tazewell, for the defendants. But as the arguments are very fully stated, and the authorities cited and commented on, in the opinions of the learned judges, it has not been thought necessary to insert them." Henry Wheaton, the Court's Reporter, 12 Wheat. at 64.

profession, and was generally condemned."[107] Whether Tazewell took any consolation in this disarming piece of humor by the Chief Justice is unknown. He did not return to the Marshall Court, nor, apparently, to any courtroom practice, for the rest of his life, although he encountered Marshall again in the Virginia Convention of 1829, and according to Grigsby, who was a delegate, "fairly 'sunk the boat' under the Chief Justice" in an exchange over the constitutionality of legislative efforts to abolish judicial courts.[108]

What a commentator has called the "enigma" of Tazewell's career[109] becomes more fathomable if one regards him as a man of strong convictions and limited patience who was deeply ambivalent about public service, disliked compromises, and hated to lose. He broke with the Republican party over the Jefferson administration's Embargo Act of 1807; he opposed the candidacy of Madison in 1808; he refused to support the War of 1812, although it was sponsored by a Republican administration; he denounced what he regarded as unconstitutional efforts on the part of the John Quincy Adams administration to execute foreign policy without senatorial consent; he opposed both nullification and the Jackson administration's claim that the federal government had the right to resist nullification with force; and he vigorously opposed Jackson's removal of deposits from the Bank of United States in 1833.[110] In each case Tazewell deplored the effort of another body to assert power to affect matters in which he had a deep personal interest. As a Norfolk lawyer and member of the landed gentry who stood to benefit from seacoast commerce, he opposed Jefferson and Madison; as a member of a rival branch of government he opposed Adams's and Jackson's efforts to assert executive power; as a Virginia states' rights theorist, he opposed nullification and extreme Unionism.[111] While there may well have been some truth in the remark, attributed to Tazewell, that he entered politics only because "my father made me,"[112] he voluntarily left it when a combination of pique,

---

[107] 12 Wheat. at 90.
[108] Grigsby, *Discourse,* 67. Albert Beveridge, in his appreciative biography of Marshall, was more cautious, merely stating that Tazewell and Marshall debated the issue, and that a compromise view prevailed. A. Beveridge, *The Life of John Marshall* (4 vols., 1919), IV, 489–91.
[109] R. Walke, "Littleton Waller Tazewell," *Va. L. Reg.,* 4:409 (1898).
[110] See Grigsby, *Discourse,* 47–60.
[111] Grigsby, a great admirer of Tazewell, wrote of Tazewell's relationship with John Marshall:

The subdued manner and tone in which Mr. Tazewell spoke of Judge Marshall would convey a stronger impression of the character of the judge than any mere words of eulogy could well do. . . . Yet from the beginning of Mr. Tazewell's career to its close, [he and Marshall] differed from each other on most of the great constitutional questions of their times. Candor compels me to say . . . that the decisions of the judge in the case of McCulloch against the Bank of Maryland, and in the case of Cohens against the State of Virginia, greatly disappointed [Tazewell].

Grigsby, *Discourse,* 17.
[112] Quoted in ibid., 22.

pride, and a shrewd appraisal of the prospective success of his views convinced him to do so.

More puzzling is Tazewell's abandonment of his law practice after returning from Virginia politics. He had continued to argue cases before the Marshall Court as a senator, and at the time he left public life in 1835 "he stood," according to Grigsby, "almost without a rival in his profession in Virginia and . . . in the Supreme Court of the United States; and he might have received as large an annual income as was ever derived from the practice of law in this country." Instead, after resigning from the governorship of Virginia in 1835, Tazewell retired to Norfolk, where for twenty-five additional years he "attend[ed] mainly to his private affairs."[113]

Supervising and managing one's estate in the early-nineteenth-century subculture of which Tazewell was a part was not simply an avocation of the leisured class. The image of the virtuous republican citizen, closely connected to land, mindful of his civic duties, concerned with principles rather than partisan affiliations, proud of his ancestral roots, and scornful of those who would debase the republic with their greed, corruption, or partisanship, was a compelling one for early-nineteenth-century Americans. This was especially true for Virginians, who by the 1830s could point to four presidents, Washington, Jefferson, Madison, and Monroe, who had retired from public life to pursue "agriculture." The power of such an image can be seen in a characterization Grigsby made of Tazewell in 1860:

> [T]ake your model of a man who draws his sustenance from the plough, a private citizen, who lives privately, not because he cannot obtain office, but because, having won the highest honors, he withdraws from the scene and leaves the glittering rewards of public service to be divided among those who seek them. Look for his name in the newspapers, and you will not find it. . . ; look for deep intrigues in local politics, and you will find no finger of his in the dirty wash. Look at the ill success of those who have engaged in public affairs, their pecuniary entanglements, their deferred hopes, their sleepless nights. . . ; these and such things you may find, and find easily, but not at the door of Tazewell. He is strictly a private citizen, engaged in his private affairs . . . showing to all the highest faculties are as practical as the lowest . . . [L]iving as became a gentleman of his position in life and affairs, he yet accumulated a larger fortune than was probably ever before accumulated by a Virginia farmer or a lawyer beginning life without patrimony; and when wealth was obtained, living with that modesty and simplicity so becoming to great genius and great wealth, ever looking with just contempt on that most piteous of all spectacles, the spectacle of lofty genius debruised and debased by the accursed thirst for gold. . . .[114]

---

[113] Ibid., 91.

[114] Ibid., 78.

There is much revealing in that passage, both of its author and of its subject. Grigsby praises "sustenance from the plough," a sense of privacy, practicality, the life of a gentleman, modesty, and simplicity. He condemns political intrigue, "pecuniary entanglements," and, most severely of all, "lofty genius debruised and debased by the accursed thirst for gold." Yet Grigsby cannot forbear mentioning that Tazewell accumulated a larger fortune than any of his peers who began their careers without substantial family assets. The virtuous republican citizen was also "scrupulously exact . . . in matters of business," so much so that he "may have given offence, and subjected himself to the charge of closeness."[115]

Behind the "enigma" of Tazewell, then, lay pride, rigidity, a heightened self-awareness, and a conscious effort to live a life approximating that of an archetypal republican citizen. The combination of Tazewell's formidable physical and intellectual strengths and his self-absorption and purposiveness sometimes appeared to others as selfishness or coldness. One can see Wirt, a loyal friend, seeking to deflect that impression in his portrait of the youthful Tazewell:

> There was . . . something . . . unfortunate in this bold and commanding character . . . : I mean an apparent frigidity of manner which I feared the world would consider as the evidence of a cold and sordid heart. . . . I know that those appearances . . . are entirely fallacious; that his laxity in conversation is only sportiveness; that his attention to his own interests does not surpass the bounds of ordinary prudence; that, in a proper occasion, no man is more charitable, generous, or munificent; . . . that his apparent coldness is the effect only of mental abstraction and of judicious caution and reflection. . . . But the world at large can never have that knowledge of him that I have . . . I fear his country will never know him well enough to do him justice.[116]

Seven years later Wirt wrote again of Tazewell, this time not for public perusal:

> My friend Tazewell does not carry half the breadth of row to which he is entitled. He is admitted, indeed, to be one of the greatest men of the American nation, but they are afraid of him. . . . [N]otwithstanding his uncommon powers, [he] never did and never will command the full & secure confidence and warm support of any public body; and this is very easily explained. . . . His father, from every account, was one of the most generous mortals on earth; . . . but his mother was a Waller, [and] he was taken, in his early childhood, to his grandfather Waller's roof—where the giant shoots of his affections were trained to hug the wall—and from this hopeful school he was transferred to the office of Mr. Wickham—where he was further primed and clipped and trimmed

---

[115] Ibid., 91.

[116] Wirt, *Old Bachelor,* 155–56.

by the rules of cold-blooded prudence and caution. The Wallers are a narrow, contracted, reptile, sordid tribe—cunning, cold-hearted, and grasping—and at the same time proud, disgustingly full of themselves, and most intolerably sneering and sarcastic towards others. . . . Hence Tazewell has two sides to his character: and, unfortunately for him, the Waller side is that which predominates in his general intercourse with the world . . . in the business of life he is too cool, too calculating, too close, too deep—in conversation too subtle, too anxious to carry his point without regard to the means, too prone to run cruel rigs and expose to ridicule the opinions of others whom he can talk down at pleasure—. . . his arguments have too much of the cunning and sophistry of the lawyer . . . his manner is too composed, too sly, too much like the crouching of the panther when preparing to spring upon his prey. . . .[117]

When Wirt contrasted the "Waller tribe" with Henry Tazewell, he was unaware of Henry's assertiveness about his son's career, or of Littleton Tazewell's recoil from his father's pressure. This additional theme in Tazewell's life—the loss of his mother at an early age, the death of an assertive and "public-minded" father, the years in which he had been raised in Benjamin Waller's household—informs our understanding of the "Waller side" of Tazewell's character. The Wallers, for all their allegedly "cunning, coldhearted and grasping" ways, were young Littleton Tazewell's refuge in a life where he was deprived of a mother and given only intermittent contact with his father. When he came to maturity with his marked talents, he was confronted with another deprivation: the combination of his father's insistence on molding his son's career and his father's sudden death. That Tazewell would again seek refuge in familiar surroundings, in which the "Waller tribe" figured predominantly, was natural; that he would assume the "Waller side" in his "general intercourse with the world" was perhaps inevitable. The result was a walling up in his private affairs, a renunciation of public life, a "closeness" in his dealings with all but intimates. "Sophistry and artifice" were Tazewell's barriers against a world that he feared would impose upon him. The other side of his "coolness" was his "morbid sensibility." The combination, when superimposed on a mind of considerable range, depth, and acumen, produced one of the memorable Marshall Court advocates.

From the "extreme temperance" of Tazewell, who "ate more sparingly than any of those who sat at the table with him," and drank only "a glass of toddy or a glass of wine at dinner,"[118] we pass to the decidedly

---

[117] W. Wirt to F. Gilmer, Jan. 26, 1817, in Francis W. Gilmer Papers, Alderman Library, University of Virginia.
[118] Grigsby, *Discourse,* 85.

less temperate presence of Luther Martin, who by the time the 1815 Term of the Marshall Court opened was renowned not only for his "iron memory" and his "fullness of legal knowledge"[119] but also for "often appear[ing] in Court evidently intoxicated."[120] Martin was sixty-seven by 1815, and four years later, in August 1819, he suffered a severe stroke and never argued a case again. His career thus belongs largely to an earlier time, but his remarkable disposition and his memorable argument in *McCulloch* v. *Maryland,* made four months before his stroke, justify a brief sketch of him here.

Martin was a contemporary of John Marshall; he was born in 1748, seven years before Marshall, and died in 1826, nine years before the Chief Justice. By 1772, six years after his graduation from Princeton, Martin had established a law practice in Accomock and Northampton counties on the Eastern Shore of Virginia, and had also become licensed to practice in the adjoining state of Maryland. Martin had taught school while studying law and entered law practice in debt, but by 1774 he was earning "nearly or quite equal to a thousand pounds a year, with every prospect of increase."[121] During his early years on the Eastern Shore Martin became acquainted with Samuel Chase; the resulting friendship endured until Chase's death in 1810. Chase and Martin were both involved in Revolutionary politics, and after independence Chase used his influence to help Martin become attorney general of Maryland in 1778, a position in which he remained until 1805. On becoming attorney general, Martin moved to Baltimore, which was to become his home for the rest of his professional life,[122] and continued his private law practice. During his years as attorney general Martin had been a delegate to the 1787 Constitutional Convention, where he had been a thorn in the side of the Madisonian majority that eventually prevailed. He also developed a reputation as an "excessively voluble orator," based principally on a speech he delivered on June 27 and 28.[123] Martin's role at the Convention was that of champion of the small states, advocate of equal representation for all states in the Senate, and opponent of extensive powers in the federal government. He was subsequently to modify all of these positions, be-

---

[119] Chief Justice Roger B. Taney in S. Tyler, *Memoir of Roger Brooke Taney* (1872), 67.

[120] Ibid., 65.

[121] L. Martin, *Modern Gratitude* (1801), 150. This curious pamphlet, engendered by an acrimonious dispute Martin had with his son-in-law, Richard Reynal Keene, who eloped with Eleonora, one of Martin's daughters, in 1802, when Eleonora was fifteen, serves as a kind of autobiography, although it was not primarily written for that purpose. For more detail on Martin's domestic life, see P. Clarkson and R. S. Jett, *Luther Martin of Maryland* (1970), 195–97, 291–92.

[122] On Chase's role in Martin's career see Beveridge, *John Marshall,* III, 186; Clarkson and Jett, *Luther Martin,* 41–42.

[123] J. Beck, *The Constitution of the United States* (1924), 90; see M. Farrand, *Records of the Federal Convention* (4 vols., 1937), IV, 20–28.

coming a Federalist in the early nineteenth century and remaining so until his death.[124]

The year he resigned as attorney general Martin also participated in the most famous case of his career, the impeachment of his old friend, Samuel Chase, who his opponents claimed had engaged in excessively biased conduct in trying some sedition cases. This is not the place to review the Chase trial, which has been widely commented upon elsewhere,[125] but Martin's performance at that proceeding was among his finest. Henry Adams's characterization of Martin's performance, while regularly quoted, is still apt. Adams called Martin then "the most formidable of American advocates . . . rollicking, witty, audacious . . . drunken, generous, slovenly, grand," and felt that "nothing can be finer in its way than Martin's [argument]," with "its rugged and sustained force; its strong humor, audacity, and dexterity; its even flow and simple choice of language; free from rhetoric and affections; its close and compulsive grasp of the law; [and] its good natured contempt for the obstacles put in its way."[126] One passage from Martin's argument captures its flavor. He said, in response to charges that Chase had "prejudged" cases,

> To *prejudge* any case, I consider as meaning, that a person without competent knowledge of facts hath formed an opinion injurious to the merits of the case. If the term, prejudication, is used in this sense, there is no pretence that my honorable client gave a *prejudicated* opinion in the case of Fries; for it is not alleged that the opinion given was not strictly legal and correct . . .
>
> But if by a prejudicated opinion, is meant, that a judge, from his great legal knowledge, and familiar acquaintance with the law, as relative to the doctrine of treason . . . had formed a clear decided opinion that the facts stated in the indictment against Fries, if proved, as laid, amounted to treason, I will readily allow that I have no doubt my honorable client had *thus* prejudicated the law. . . . But if this manner of prejudicating the law, is thought improper, nay, criminal in a judge, a prejudication which is nothing more than an eminent and correct knowledge of the law, why I pray are gentlemen of great talents and high legal attainments sought in your appointments of judges?[127]

---

[124] See Clarkson and Jett, *Luther Martin*, 72–134; C. Warren, *The Making of the Constitution* (1929), 245–47.

[125] C. Evans, *Report of the Trial of the Honorable Samuel Chase* (1805), is a contemporary account of the Chase trial. Among the secondary treatments are H. Adams, *History of the United States of America during the Administration of Jefferson and Madison* (9 vols., 1891), II, 147–57; Beveridge, *John Marshall*, III, 157–222; C. Warren, *The Supreme Court in United States History* (3 vols., 1922); I, 269–99; Haskins and Johnson, *Foundations of Power*, 215–45.

[126] H. Adams, *John Randolph* (1882), 141, 147.

[127] Quoted in Evans, *Report of Chase Trial*, 193–94. Italics in original.

One can see in this passage qualities that contemporaries commonly ascribed to Martin as an advocate: a tendency to "mix up . . . his points together and [to] argue without order, with much repetition," and at the same time an ability "never [to] miss the strong points in his case."[128] Martin's qualities served Chase well: despite having committed what modern commentators agree were serious political blunders, possibly justifying impeachment as it was then understood,[129] Chase was narrowly acquitted.

Martin then defended an even more controversial figure, Aaron Burr, who was indicted for treason in 1807 in connection with his mysterious "Western expedition," which now appears to have been a combination of entrepreneurial activity in the delta South and a prospective invasion of Mexico rather than an effort to encourage Southern states to separate from the Union.[130] The trial of Aaron Burr and his confederates has been covered in detail elsewhere and lies chronologically outside the scope of this work, but since the trial cemented Martin's national reputation as an advocate and formed the basis for the extreme antagonism to Jefferson that characterized his subsequent career, some attention to Martin's participation in it seems pertinent.

The Burr trial, held before John Marshall's circuit court in Richmond, was the *cause célèbre* of the early Marshall Court years. Momentous legal issues were involved, including the scope of executive privilege and the constitutional and common law definitions of treason. The trial's political dimensions were equally significant: at stake was the reach of Thomas Jefferson's influence over the federal courts and the power of John Marshall to limit Jefferson's influence. Burr's name was a household word for villainy: he had been Jefferson's vice-president and archenemy, and the slayer of Alexander Hamilton. At the time of the trial, Burr was, according to one recent commentator, "a ruined man, hopelessly in debt, his law practice gone, and his personal reputation close to destruction."[131]

Martin entered the trial when he was retained by Dr. Justus E. Bollman, a physician with a taste for intrigue, who had been caught delivering an allegedly treasonous code message from Aaron Burr to General James Wilkinson in 1806.[132] Wilkinson, who had previously

---

[128] Taney in Tyler, *Memoir of Taney*, 66.

[129] See the discussion in R. Berger, *Impeachment* (1973), 224–51.

[130] Various accounts of the Burr trial are found in T. Abernethy, *The Burr Conspiracy* (1954); L. Levy, *Jefferson and Civil Liberties* (1960), 70–92; W. McCaleb, *A New Light on Aaron Burr* (1963); F. Philbrick, *The Rise of the West, 1754–1830* (1965), 234–52; D. Malone, *Jefferson the President: Second Term 1805–09* (1974), 215–370; Haskins and Johnson, *Foundations of Power*, 246–91.

[131] George L. Haskins in Haskins and Johnson, *Foundations of Power*, 248.

[132] On Bollman see W. McCaleb, *The Aaron Burr Conspiracy* (1936), 68–70; Philbrick, *Rise of the West*, 248–51; Beveridge, *John Marshall*, III, 307.

cooperated with Burr, now reversed himself, dissociated himself from Burr's plans, and informed Jefferson that Burr's message to him confirmed the existence of a plot to separate some southern states from the Union. In January 1807, in response to pressure from Congress, Jefferson delivered a "special message" in which he claimed that a conspiracy existed and that Burr's and Bollman's "guilt is placed beyond question."[133] Jefferson then interviewed Bollman, pledging confidentiality, but Bollman was subsequently imprisoned. Bollman sought release on a writ of habeas corpus, retaining Martin in his defense.[134]

In February 1807 the Marshall Court dismissed the case against Bollman on jurisdictional grounds (he had not committed an indictable offense in the District of Columbia)[135] and invited the Jefferson administration to "institute fresh proceedings" elsewhere.[136] Jefferson's prosecutors responded by beginning proceedings directly against Aaron Burr in Richmond in March 1807, and Martin subsequently joined Burr's defense.[137] On June 9 Burr himself first raised the executive privilege issue when he demanded that the prosecution produce a letter written by Wilkinson to Jefferson on October 21, 1806, allegedly revealing the existence of a conspiracy to dismember the Union. Burr asked that Jefferson be served with a *subpoena duces tecum,* and when counsel for the prosecution refused, on grounds of executive privilege, John Marshall asked that the point be argued. Martin, in the course of his argument, said:

> This is a peculiar case, sir. The president has undertaken to prejudge my client by declaring that "of his guilt there can be no doubt." . . . He has proclaimed him a traitor in the face of that country, which has rewarded him. He has let slip the dogs of war, the hell-hound of persecution, to hunt down my friend. And would this president of the United States, who has raised all this absurd clamour, pretend to keep back the papers which are wanted for this trial, where life itself is at stake? . . .
>
> It may be suggested that this is a private and confidential letter from General Wilkinson to the president. . . . [I]f General Wilkinson had reposed as much confidence; if he had instilled as much poison into the ear of Eve, the president would have been still responsible to a court of justice, and bound to disclose his communications. . . . It

---

[133] Quoted in J. Richardson, comp., *A Compilation of the Messages and Papers of the Presidents, 1798–1897* (10 vols., 1899), I, 405. See also *Annals of Congress,* 9th Cong., 2d Sess. 11 (1806).

[134] United States v. Bollmann, 24 F. Cas. 1189 (C.C.D.C. 1807); see Baltimore *Federal Gazette,* Feb. 12, 1807.

[135] *Ex parte* Bollman, 4 Cranch 75, 127 (1807).

[136] Ibid., 136.

[137] Among the other counsel for Burr were Littleton Tazewell's mentor John Wickham and Henry Tazewell's friend Edmund Randolph. See D. Robertson, *Trials of Aaron Burr* (2 vols., 1808), I, 1–8.

233

is a sacred principle that in all such cases the accused has a right to all the evidence which is necessary for his defense. . . .[138]

Marshall ruled that except for "matters whose disclosure would endanger the public safety," the president was constitutionally required to produce subpoenaed documents and appear in court.[139] Jefferson had already agreed "voluntarily to furnish, on all occasions, whatever the purposes of justice may require," although he reserved the right to decide for himself "what papers . . . the public interests permit to be communicated."[140] Nonetheless, Jefferson was furious at Martin for his remarks, and suggested to George Hay, the government's chief prosecutor, that Martin be indicted for treason, since Jefferson claimed that he had evidence that Martin "knew all about the criminal enterprise" by the summer of 1806. Jefferson stated to Hay that an indictment of Martin would "put down this unprincipled and imprudent federal bull-dog, and add another proof that the most glamorous defenders of Burr are all his accomplices."[141]

The Burr trial lasted until September 1807, when the jury acquitted Burr and one of his alleged accomplices, Harman Blennerhassett,[142] of treason and of conspiring against the government. While Martin had won the case, he suffered both personally and financially from his association with Burr. He had twice stood surety for Burr's bail,[143] and when Burr fled the country after his 1807 trial he forfeited his bail, since a charge of conspiracy against the government was still pending against him in Ohio.[144] Martin was accordingly made responsible for the payment of

---

[138] Quoted in ibid., I, 127–28.
[139] United States v. Burr, 25 F. Cas. 25, 33 (C.C.D. Va. 1807).
[140] T. Jefferson to G[eorge] Hay, June 17, 1807, in P. Ford, ed., The Works of Thomas Jefferson (12 vols., 1905), X, 400.
[141] Ibid.
[142] For an ornate, and highly purposive, sketch of Blennerhassett, see William Wirt's remarks at the Burr trial, quoted in Robertson, Trials of Burr, II, 96–98. Wirt, who was aiding in the prosecution, said, in part, of Blennerhassett:

Who is Blennerhassett? A native of Ireland, a man of letters, fled from the storms of his own country to find quiet in ours. His history shows that war is not the natural element of his mind. If it had been, he never would have exchanged Ireland for America. . . .

Wirt then went on to suggest that Burr had "wound himself into the open and unpractised heart of the unfortunate Blennerhassett," infusing "into it the poison of his own ambition." The Harman Blennerhassett family were close friends with the Thomas Emmets: when Emmet arrived in New York in 1806 Blennerhassett came to visit him, and in 1809, after Blennerhassett had been acquitted of treason, the two corresponded about their children's educational prospects. Blennerhassett eventually returned to Ireland in 1822, leaving his family in New York, where they came into regular contact with the Emmets. See Emmet, Memoir, I, 405, 422, 455.
[143] See Robertson, Trials of Burr, I, 106; W. Safford, ed., The Blennerhassett Papers (1864), 461.
[144] Clarkson and Jett, Luther Martin, 292.

Burr's bail, which came to about $20,000.[145] In addition, Martin, Burr, Blennerhassett, and Marshall were hanged in effigy by a mob in Baltimore in November 1807, the participants referring to Martin as "Lawyer Brandy Bottle."[146] The association with Burr also affected Martin's political ambitions: when he ran for the Maryland House of Delegates in 1811, an unfriendly newspaper contributed to Martin's defeat by reminding its readers of his defense of Burr and of the mock hanging.[147] The Burr trial also revealed, as had the Chase trial before it, Martin's tendency to personalize his advocacy. He defended Chase because Chase was an old friend; he attacked Jefferson because he felt Jefferson was using the presidency to persecute his client. In both trials he felt no compunction about presenting his arguments as his own theories or about making outspoken comments on his adversaries. He was, as Adams noted, "audacious" and candid: he did not conceal his feelings in "rhetoric and affectations."

Despite the unpopularity of some of his causes, Martin's law practice continued to thrive, and he began to appear in the Supreme Court with increasing frequency, arguing principally prize and insurance cases. He appeared twenty-five times between 1808 and 1813.[148] The most famous case he argued in that period was *Fletcher v. Peck,* the first major Contract Clause case decided by the Marshall Court.[149] Martin's professional responsibilities also increased. In 1813 he was named chief justice of the municipal criminal court for Baltimore city and county, a position he held until the court was abolished in 1816. He continued to practice law and serve as "unofficial attorney general" of the state of Maryland in this period (the office being temporarily abolished),[150] and in 1818 was officially reappointed to the office when it was re-established.[151] Martin was now seventy, and he continued to thrive despite a tendency toward chronic alcoholism. As attorney general of Maryland, he was among the distinguished group of lawyers—Webster, Wirt, Pinkney, Joseph Hopkinson, and Walter Jones—who argued the great case of *McCulloch v. Maryland*[152] in 1819.

Martin's life was intimately bound to his profession. Like many

---

[145] F. Wandell and M. Minnegrode, *Aaron Burr* (2 vols., 1925), II, 308.

[146] See Baltimore *Federal Gazette,* Nov. 4, 1807.

[147] Baltimore *Whig,* Sept. 28, 1811; Baltimore *Federal Republican,* Oct. 8, 1811.

[148] See 4 Cranch (1808)–7 Cranch (1812 and 1813). There was no 1811 Term of Court because of the absence of a quorum, Justices Chase and Cushing having died after the 1810 Term,

their replacements, Justices Duvall and Story, not having been appointed in time to begin hearing cases by February 1811, and Justice Todd having been absent for the 1811 Term.

[149] 6 Cranch 87 (1810). *Fletcher v. Peck* is briefly discussed in Chapter IX.

[150] Clarkson and Jett, *Luther Martin,* 290–91.

[151] Ibid., 292.

[152] 4 Wheat. 316 (1819). See the discussion in Chapter VIII.

famous lawyers, Martin's whole being seemed to be reflected in his performances as a lawyer, whether inside or outside the courtroom. Three accounts by contemporaries who encountered Martin in his career give some flavor of the interaction of his personal traits with his professional activities. The first account is by Story in 1808; the second by Harman Blennerhassett a year earlier; the third by Roger Taney about the same time. [153] Story wrote that Martin was

> a singular compound of strange qualities. With a professional income of $10,000 a year, he is poor and needy; generous and humane, but negligent and profuse. . . . He is about middle size, a little bald, with a common forehead, pointed nose, inexpressive eye, large mouth, and well-formed chin. His dress is slovenly. . . . But every one assures me that he is profoundly learned, and that though he shines not now in the lustre of his former days, yet he is at times very great. He never seems satisfied with a single grasp of his subject; but urges himself to successive efforts, until he models and fashions it to his purpose. You should hear of Luther Martin's fame from those who have known him long and intimately, but you should not see him. [154]

A similar impression of Martin's stamina, of his lack of discipline, of the power of his intellect, and of his tendency toward dissipation was gleaned by Blennerhassett at the time of the Burr trial. Blennerhassett recalled a meeting with Martin at a Richmond tavern:

> I was too much interested in the little I had seen, and the great things I had heard, of [Martin's] powers and passions, not to improve the present opportunity to survey him in every light the length of his visit would permit. I accordingly recommended our brandy as superior, placing a pint tumbler before him. No ceremonies retarded the libation; no inquiries solicited him upon any subject. . . . Were I now to mention only the subjects of law, politics, news, et cetera, on which he descanted, I should not be believed when I said his visit did not exceed thirty-five minutes. Imagine a man capable, in that space of time, to deliver some account of an entire week's proceedings in the trial, with extracts from memory of several speeches on both sides; . . . to caricature Jefferson; to give a history of his acquaintance with Burr, expatiate on [Burr's] virtues and sufferings, maintain his credit, embellish his fame . . .—some estimate, with these preparations, may be found of this man's powers, which are yet shackled by a preternatural secretion or excretion of saliva, which embarrasses his delivery. [155]

---

[153] Taney's account was actually written in 1854, when he first began his memoirs, but was based on his impressions of Martin from 1796 to 1822. See Tyler, *Memoir of Taney*, 56–69.

[154] J. Story to S. Fay, Feb. 16, 1808, in W. Story, *Life and Letters,* I, 163–64.

[155] Blennerhassett in Safford, *Blennerhassett Papers,* 377.

Taney, who came to know Martin well while Taney was a young lawyer in Maryland, added some complexity and detail to the portrait:

> His dress was a compound of the fine and the coarse, and appeared never to have felt the brush. He wore ruffles at the wrists, richly edged with lace—although every other person had long before abandoned them—and these ruffles, conspicuously broad, were dabbed and soiled, and showed that they had not been changed for a day or more. His voice was not musical, and when much excited it cracked. . . . [I]n his speech . . . he seemed to delight in using vulgarisms. . . . I have heard him say he *catch* him, instead of *caught* him, and he *sot* down, instead of *sat* down, and many other words and phrases not much better. He seemed to take pleasure in showing his utter disregard of good taste and refinement in his dress and language and his mode of argument. He was as coarse and unseemly at a dinner-table, in his manner of eating, as he was in everything.
>
> He introduced so much extraneous matter, or dwelt so long on unimportant points, that the attention was apt to be fatigued and withdrawn, and the logic and force of his argument lost . . . . But these very defects arise in some measure from the fulness of his legal knowledge. He had an iron memory, and forgot nothing that he read, and he read a great deal on every branch of the law; and took pleasure in showing it when his case did not require it.[156]

The impression generated by these comments is that of a man who, consciously or unconsciously, imposed his will on his surroundings rather than adapting to them. His indifference to refined speech, notwithstanding his background and education; his passion for alcohol; his soiled, old-fashioned clothes; his rambling, digressive arguments; his outspoken criticism; his fierce loyalty to his clients, however unpopular their status; even his "coarse and unseemly" table manners suggest a person who did not take pains to temper his passions to the dictates of fashion or convention. Whether Martin's personal style was a deliberate defiance of the socially conscious public world in which he functioned, or whether it was the product of drives and appetites that could not be constrained, seems unimportant: Luther Martin was what he was, take it or leave it. He made his clients, his adversaries, even his legal arguments part of himself.

The manner in which Martin's personality interacted with his role as an advocate can be seen in his argument in *McCulloch*. Martin argued that case in his capacity as attorney general of Maryland. The same day he was reappointed to that office the Maryland legislature established a tax on notes issued by banks that had not been created by "authority from the state."[157] The tax, unmistakably aimed at the Bank of the United

---

[156] Taney in Tyler, *Memoir of Taney,* 65–67.

[157] Act of Feb. 11, 1818; see 4 Wheat. at 320–22.

States, which had a branch office in Baltimore, led to *McCulloch* v. *Maryland*, a case for which the Marshall Court was waiting. Not only was the constitutionality of state taxation of a national bank at issue; the case also had clear ramifications for federal internal improvements programs, whose constitutionality was in doubt at the time. *McCulloch* was speedily dispatched to the Marshall Court. A Maryland state official sued James William McCulloch, the cashier of the Baltimore office of the Bank of the United States, to enforce the tax. The Maryland Court of Appeals, in an unreported per curiam decision, upheld the state's power to collect the tax, and attorneys for the Bank immediately filed a writ of error to the Marshall Court, accompanied by a stipulated set of facts.[158] The *National Intelligencer* identified *McCulloch* as a "great case" even before arguments began.[159]

The Court, recognizing the significance of *McCulloch*, waived its customary rule "permitting only two counsel to argue for each party,"[160] and six lawyers took part in the argument. Daniel Webster, for James McCulloch, opened the arguments on February 22, followed by Hopkinson for Maryland, William Wirt for McCulloch, and Walter Jones for Maryland. On Thursday afternoon, February 5, Martin began his argument, with William Pinkney to follow in rebuttal for McCulloch. Martin spoke through Saturday afternoon, February 27. Wheaton's Reports give a bare summary of the argument, which, contemporary accounts reveal, was characteristically long, rambling, and exhaustive,[161] and was also highly personalized. Martin devoted the bulk of his argument to "the contemporary exposition of the constitution by its authors,"[162] of which he was one, to show that the doctrine of implied powers, on which supporters of the Bank's constitutionality relied, had been "rejected by the friends of the new constitution [and], . . . if [it] had been fairly avowed at the time, would have prevented its adoption." The "only safe rule," Martin contended, "is the plain letter of the constitution." And since "the power of establishing corporations" was "not delegated [by the Framers] to the United States, nor prohibited to the individual states, [i]t is therefore reserved to the States . . . or to the people."[163] But even if one concluded "that Congress has a right to incorporate a banking company," Martin continued, the States could still tax banks "within their

---

[158] 4 Wheat. at 317.
[159] Washington *National Intelligencer*, [Saturday], Feb. 20, 1819. Arguments began on the following Monday.
[160] See 4 Wheat. at 322.
[161] William Pinkney began his rebuttal to Martin and his co-counsel by saying: "We have had the affecting retrospections of Mr. Martin upon scenes

. . . [the Convention debates] which . . . , luckily for the time of the court, had their commencement at an epoch considerably subsequent to the flood." Quoted in Wheaton, *Some Account,* 163–64.
[162] 4 Wheat. at 372.
[163] Ibid., 373–74.

territory." Again he used original constitutional language and debates to buttress a point. "[T]he [Philadelphia] Convention," he argued, "found . . . the subject of taxation . . . impossible to solve in a manner entirely satisfactory." But "the debates in the state conventions show that the power of State taxation was understood to be absolutely unlimited, except as to imports and tonnage duties." The states, Martin claimed, "would not have adopted the constitution upon any other understanding."[164]

By concentrating on the history of the Constitution Martin reminded the Court of his direct participation as a Framer and of his venerable status. He also reminded the Justices of their own close connections with the Framers' generation.[165] Near the close of his argument, in the course of reading from state ratifying convention debates on the taxing power, Martin announced to the Justices that "he had one last authority which he thought the Court would admit to be conclusive," and then read passages from the dictates of the Virginia ratifying convention of 1788. The speaker whose words Martin called to the Court's attention was John Marshall, who reportedly drew a deep breath as Martin began his recitation.[166] Marshall had said, in 1788, that "the powers not denied to the states are not vested in them by implication, because, being possessed of them antecedent to the adoption of the government, and not being divested of them, by any grant or restruction in the Constitution, the states must be as fully possessed of them as ever they had been."[167] Marshall reportedly told Story, "I was afraid I had said some foolish things in that debate; but it was not so bad as I expected";[168] and Martin's side lost the *McCulloch* case: Marshall's unanimous opinion held that Congress could create a bank and that the states could not tax its "operations."[169] But Martin's argument has been remembered as one of his best performances. Albert Beveridge characterized it as "the last worthy of re-

---

[164] Ibid., 375–76.

[165] Martin interjected in his references to the Philadelphia convention a parenthetical paraphrase of the Aeneid, "quorum pars [minima] fuit," thereby reminding his audience that he had "played a very [small] part" in the deliberations that resulted in the Constitution. Pinkney in rebuttal then responded,

"quorum pars *magna* (or minima) fuit" (for I will not object to [Martin's amendment of the original Latin], lest I should distress the modesty that suggested it. . . .

Quoted in Wheaton, *Some Account,* 163–64.

[166] The quotation from Martin's argument, and Marshall's response, are taken from an anecdote told by Story in late 1844 or early 1845 to Alexander H. Stephens, then a congressman from Georgia, quoted in R. Johnson and W. Browne, *Life of Alexander H. Stephens* (1870), 183. For the context of the anecdote, see ibid., 176–83.

[167] Quoted in D. Robertson, *Debates and Other Proceedings of the Convention of Virginia* (2d ed., 1805), 298.

[168] Quoted in Johnson and Browne, *Alexander H. Stephens,* 183.

[169] Ibid., 437. See discussion in Chapter VIII.

mark which that great lawyer ever made," and "not much inferior to those of Webster, Hopkinson, and Pinkney," whose arguments he had respectively described as "meticulous," "superb," and "great."[170] Martin's argument in *McCulloch* also had its personal drama, with Martin, by 1819 one of the few surviving participants in the Philadelphia Convention, making his own history part of his advocacy.[171]

Martin was seventy-one at the time of his appearance in *McCulloch*, but there was one sad chapter in his life yet to come. A stroke in August 1819 temporarily incapacitated him, although as late as 1821 he could write a letter giving an interpretation of a Maryland insolvency statute.[172] He began, however, to wander aimlessly into courtrooms, staring vacantly and munching gingerbread, appearing to one observer as a "trembling old dotard."[173] In 1822 the Maryland legislature, in an unprecedented gesture, passed a resolution assessing each member of the Maryland bar five dollars annually "to the use of . . . Luther Martin." The resolution referred to the "afflicting disposition of divine Providence" that had "bereaved [Martin] of his intellectual powers" and to the fact that Martin was "poor and unable to procure support."[174] That resolution was repealed less than a year later, however, because Aaron Burr, who had returned to America in 1812, re-established his law practice, and reversed his financial misfortunes, offered to take Martin in as a boarder in Burr's New York home. A strange friendship was thus renewed, and the two veterans of the Burr trial lived together until 1826, when Martin died.[175]

Of all the lawyers portrayed in this chapter, Martin was the least able to benefit from his considerable talents. His "unfortunate habits," Taney said, "made him reckless in money matters. . . . He was kind to

---

[170] Beveridge, *John Marshall*, IV, 285–87.

[171] *McCulloch* was not Martin's last Marshall Court argument. Ten days later he appeared in Sergeant's Lessee v. Biddle, 4 Wheat. 508 (1819), a routine civil procedure case in which his argument was not reported.

[172] Luther Martin to Richard Peters, Jr., August [no date given] 1821, Richard Peters Papers, Historical Society of Pennsylvania, Philadelphia, Pa.

[173] Henry P. Goodard, as recounted in Goodard, "Luther Martin: 'The Federal Bulldog,' " *Md. Hist. Soc. Pub.*, 24:10–11 (1887). The gingerbread references are from John H. B. Latrobe's recollections of seeing Martin when Latrobe was in his early twenties:

[I]t was an affecting sight. [Martin] was in his dotage. He used to come

into the Courts when they were in session, an aged man, decrepit in his movements, dressed in the style of the past generation . . . eating a star ginger head as a child would do, and smiling with a vacant lack lustre eye as the members of the bar made way for him.

Quoted in J. Semmes, *John H. B. Latrobe and His Times* (1917), 204. Latrobe, a Baltimore practitioner who argued before the Taney Court, was born in 1803 and died in 1891.

[174] Resolution No. 60, Feb. 23, 1822, quoted in Clarkson and Jett, *Luther Martin*, 303.

[175] For the last years of Martin's life, see Clarkson and Jett, *Luther Martin*, 302–303.

young members of the profession, and liberal, and indeed profuse, in his charities, and easily imposed upon by unworthy objects."[176] His private life had some unfortunate aspects, including the early death of his wife, some unsuccessful infatuations, the elopement of one daughter at the age of fifteen, and the institutionalization of another for mental illness.[177] His excessive drinking throughout his professional life occasionally led to skirmishes in court and caused him personal embarrassment.[178] But one has the sense that Martin, for all the unhappiness of his domestic life and the sad circumstances of his death, defied life rather than being buffeted by it. He was, in a self-conscious, elegant, and circumspect age, an independent, ebullient, and vivid spirit.

We have noted the contrasts in styles and temperaments in passing from Emmet to Tazewell and then to Martin; another striking contrast occurs in passing from Martin to William Pinkney. In this instance the contrast is one any spectator witnessing arguments in the Marshall Court could easily have marked. Pinkney was once reported as "writh[ing] as if in pain when listening to Martin speaking in his slovenly way in broken sentences, using the most indefensible vulgarisms and sometimes mispronouncing his words."[179] If Martin's mode of discourse offended Pinkney, so surely must his mode of dress, for whereas Martin was probably the most "slovenly" of the leading Marshall Court advocates in his appearance, Pinkney was undoubtedly the most resplendent. "The personal appearance of Mr. P.," Story recalled, "was as polished as if he had been taken right from the drawer; his coat of the finest blue, was nicely brushed; his boots shone with the highest polish; his waistcoat, of perfect whiteness, glittered with gold buttons; he played in his hand with a light cane; in short, he seemed perfectly satisfied with himself."[180] Taney's portrait went further:

> [Pinkney] was very attentive to his dress, indeed more so than was thought suitable for his age and station. It approached to dandyism, if it did not reach it. He was always dressed in the extreme of the newest

[176] Taney in Tyler, *Memoir of Taney,* 61.

[177] See Clarkson and Jett, *Luther Martin,* 192–96, 255, 291.

[178] Goddard, "Luther Martin," 31–32, and Clarkson and Jett, *Luther Martin,* 279–80, report examples, as does Tyler, *Memoir of Taney,* 122–23, recounting an anecdote told to him by Taney. Martin was quoted as defining "drunk" as "when after drinking liquor [a man] says or does that which he would not otherwise have said or done." Quoted in Goddard, "Luther Martin," 37.

[179] Taney in Tyler, *Memoir of Taney,* 70.

[180] J. Story, "Notes for a Lecture on William Pinkney," in W. Story, *Life and Letters,* II, 491.

fashion, and, for some time . . . took notes at the bar and spoke with [amber-colored doeskin] gloves on, nice enough to wear in a ball-room.[181]

Other accounts of Pinkney emphasize what Taney called his "over-dressed" manner.[182] George Ticknor, after observing Pinkney in 1815, said that he was "possessed with the ambition of being a pretty fellow," and noted that Pinkney "[wore] corsets to diminish his bulk, use[d] cosmetics . . . and dresse[d] in a style which would be thought foppish in a much younger man."[183] Theophilus Parsons, Jr., who accompanied Pinkney to Russia in 1816 and 1817 when the latter was named minister to St. Petersburg by President Monroe, gave an extended account of Pinkney's "vanity":

> While I was in Russia, I and another attache were sitting in [Pinkney's] parlor, waiting for him to come to dinner. He came in, after a long while, black and dirty as any man. Without saying a word, he walked up to the sofa, jerked off his hat, threw it and his sword down. At last Mrs. Pinkney returned, and asked, "What is the matter?" "Matter! I have been, insulted, madam!" . . . Turning to me, he said, "Sir! Is not a man of my name, my position, my country, insulted when he is to get up at 8 o'clock to pay homage to a little girl [a Russian princess]?" I ventured to suggest that we were invited at 11. "Can a gentleman dress in less than three hours?"
> He used to bathe every day, and after bathing he would throw a thin gauze over himself, and had two body servants throw fine salt at him. He had heard, he said, "Salt would preserve the skin." . . . [T]here was a rumor spread that he painted [used cosmetics]. . . . He paraded his efforts in making this show. He liked to hear such rumors of himself. . . . He was laced [corseted] in every direction. . . . His whole dress was faultless and beautiful, as well as most fashionable. . . . I should say his lacing contributed much to his death.[184]

Pinkney's foppishness and vanity were often seen by contemporaries as indications of more significant character flaws. Henry Wheaton, who wrote an appreciative biography of Pinkney, nonetheless felt that Pinkney "cared for nothing but what contributed to his individual vanity and self-gratification."[185] Lawyers who argued against Pinkney regularly were made the objects of his humor or derision, and often responded angrily.

---

[181] Taney in Tyler, *Memoir of Taney*, 64–70.

[182] Ibid., 72.

[183] G. Ticknor to E. Ticknor, February 1815 [no date given], in Greenslet, *George Ticknor*, I, 39.

[184] "Notes of a Lecture by Theophilus Parsons, Jr.," *Albany L.J.*, 2:126, 129–30 (1870).

[185] H. Wheaton, conversation with James Kent, quoted in W. Kent, *Memoirs and Letters of James Kent* (1898), 247–48.

Emmet's 1815 rejoinder has been previously noted; William Wirt nearly challenged Pinkney to a duel after being insulted by Pinkney in a case in 1818.[186] On one occasion Daniel Webster, after having been insulted by Pinkney in court, allegedly "invited [Pinkney] into a room in the Capitol, locked the door and put the key in his pocket," with the result that "the next morning Mr. Pinkney appeared in court and tendered a very courteous apology to Mr. Webster."[187] Wirt was especially competitive with and critical of Pinkney, describing him, on successive occasions, as "despotic,"[188] having "a false manner,"[189] possessed of a "childish foppery and coxcomb puerility"[190] and "a forensic tyrant as bloody in his proscriptions as Scylla."[191] In an 1816 letter Wirt fulminated against Pinkney:

> He has nothing of the rapid and unerring analysis of Marshall, but he has, in lieu of it, a dogmatizing absoluteness of manner which passes with the minions . . . for an evidence of power; and he has acquired with those around him a sort of papal infallibility. That manner is a piece of acting: it is artificial, as you may see by the wandering of his eye, and is as far removed from the composed confidence of enlightened certainty as it is from natural modesty . . . Pinkney would make you believe that he knows everything.
>
> At the bar he is despotic, and cares as little for his colleagues or adversaries as if they were men of wood. . . . Give him time . . . and he will deliver a speech which any man might be proud to claim. You will have good materials, very well put together, and clothed in a costume as magnificent as that of Louis XIV. But you will have a vast quantity of false fire, besides a vehemence of intimation for which you see nothing to account in the character of the thought.[192]

Alongside criticisms such as these went tributes of comparable magnitude, lending credence to Wheaton's observations that Pinkney "was one of the brightest and meanest of mankind."[193] From 1815 to 1822 Pinkney was, by nearly all accounts, the most eminent of the Marshall Court advocates. Marshall reportedly said that "he never knew [Pinkney's] equal as a reasoner—so clear and luminous was his method of argumentation";[194] Taney called him "a profound lawyer in every de-

---

[186] For the circumstances of the abortive duel, see note 294.

[187] L. Proctor, "William Pinkney," *Albany L.J.*, 36:464, 467 (1887).

[188] W. Wirt to F. Gilmer, Apr. 1, 1816. Gilmer Papers.

[189] W. Wirt to D. Carr, Apr. 7, 1816, in William Wirt Papers, University of North Carolina Library.

[190] W. Wirt to F. Gilmer, Mar. 18, 1819, in Gilmer Papers.

[191] W. Wirt to F. Gilmer, Oct. 15, 1819, in ibid.

[192] W. Wirt to F. Gilmer, Apr. 1, 1816, supra, note 188.

[193] Wheaton to Kent, supra, note 185.

[194] Quoted by J. Story in "Notes for a Lecture on William Pinkney," in W. Story, *Life and Letters*, II, 494.

partment of the science," who "always saw the strongest point in his case." "I have heard almost all the great advocates of the United States," Taney wrote in 1854, "but I have seen none equal to Pinkney."[195] Samuel Tyler, in the course of preparing a biography of Taney that appeared in 1872, reported a conversation in which Walter Jones of the District of Columbia bar and Marshall discussed Pinkney; Marshall called Pinkney "the greatest man he had ever seen in a Court of justice," and Jones added that "no such man has ever appeared in any country more than once in a century."[196] Francis Gilmer, in a sketch written before Pinkney's death in the 1820s, said that "the powers of his mind seemed to strengthen with his years," and that "the force of his genius was . . . most conspicuous and overwhelming, and enough, of itself, to entitle him to the first place among living orators."[197] About the same time, a correspondent in the Charleston *City Gazette* reported that Pinkney was said to "combine and concentrate" in his person "the splendid imagination and burning words of Sheridan, the terseness of Pitt, the spontaneous and overflowing resources of Fox, the magnificent originality and comprehension of Burke, and the dignity of . . . Chatham."[198] Finally, there is the testimony of Story:

> [Pinkney's] clear and forcible manner of putting his case before the Court, his powerful and commanding eloquence, occasionally illuminated with sparkling lights, but always logical and appropriate, and, above all, his accurate and discriminating law knowledge, which he pours out with wonderful precision—give him in my opinion a great superiority over every other man whom I have known. I have seen in a single man each of these qualities separate, but never before contained in so extraordinary a degree. I candidly acknowledge that Mr. Pinkney is my favorite at the Bar.[199]

These comments, taken together, catalogue some of the skills that made Pinkney so redoubtable: intense preparation and thorough recall of his sources; a sense for significant distinctions; an understanding of the strengths, and the weaknesses, of the position he was advancing; a "luminous" clarity in his presentation; and an ability to infuse his arguments with oratory without having his eloquence serve as a distraction from his central logical purposes. As William Wirt put it in 1818; "[A] debate with Pinkney is exercise and health. . . . His reputation is so high that

---

[195] Taney in Tyler, *Memoir of Taney*, 71.
[196] Tyler in ibid., 141.
[197] Gilmer, *Sketches*, 53.
[198] Charleston *City Gazette*, 1820 (no month or date given), in Henry

Wheaton notebook, Henry Wheaton Papers, Pierpont Morgan Library, New York, N.Y.
[199] J. Story to Nathaniel Williams, Mar. 6, 1814, in W. Story, *Life and Letters*, I, 252.

there is no disparagement in being foiled by him, and great glory in even dividing the palm."[200]

Pinkney was at the very prime of his career as the 1815 Term opened; during the preceding Term he had appeared in approximately half of all the cases argued before the Court.[201] But only rarely in his career did he devote his full time to private law practice; the bulk of his working life was spent in public service. Pinkney was born in Annapolis, Maryland, in 1764, "of obscure parents," and "at an early age attracted the notice of several distinguished men . . . who were patrons to genius."[202] Among these was Samuel Chase, who apparently helped Pinkney financially as well as professionally.[203] By 1786 Pinkney had entered practice in Hartford County, Maryland; in 1788 he was elected to the Maryland legislature; and in 1789 he married Ann Maria Rodgers, who was reported by Pinkney's nephew to be a person of "easy manner, affability of disposition, and strong vigorous intellect."[204] Ten children were born to the Pinkneys.

In 1796 Pinkney began the first of several assignments related to diplomatic affairs when he was sent by President Washington to London to administer prize claims arising out of the Revolutionary War. While the position gave Pinkney "opportunities of intercourse with the accomplished lawyers of [England]," and "imparted new strength and beauty to his forensic style,"[205] it was a thankless job, combining periods of delicate negotiation with periods of boredom. Three years into it Pinkney wrote a friend that "the business of the Commission does not occupy me significantly. . . . I begin to languish for my profession—I want active employment."[206] A year later he felt that the administration of prize claims had been "wretchedly bungled" and "it is time for me to think seriously of revisiting my country, and of employing myself in a profitable pursuit."[207] By 1804, however, Pinkney was still in England. In a letter written in February of that year he spoke of planning on his return to "do as well as I can with my own resources," and to "rely upon Providence and my own efforts in my profession."[208] He returned to America in August and settled in Baltimore.

By 1806 Pinkney had argued his first case in the Supreme Court[209]

---

[200] W. Wirt to William Pope, Oct. 13, 1818, quoted in Kennedy, *Memoirs of Wirt*, II, 74.

[201] See 8 Cranch (1814).

[202] Gilmer, *Sketches*, 55.

[203] Pinkney, *William Pinkney*, 16. See also A. Niles, "William Pinkney," in W. Lewis, ed., *Great American Lawyers* (6 vols., 1907), II, 180; Parsons, "Notes of a Lecture," 129.

[204] Pinkney, *William Pinkney*, 20.

[205] Wheaton, *Some Account*, 45–46.

[206] W. Pinkney to Jonathan Pinkney, Apr. 26, 1799, quoted in ibid., 30.

[207] W. Pinkney to J. Pinkney, Aug. 27, 1800, quoted in ibid., 35.

[208] W. Pinkney to [Mr.] Cooke, Feb. 15, 1804, quoted in ibid., 43.

[209] Manella v. Barry, 3 Cranch 415 (1806).

and established himself as a specialist in admiralty, marine insurance, and international law.[210] But the next year he was named minister to England, and remained abroad until 1811. He returned to Baltimore that year and resumed his law practice, "surpass[ing] every conjecture that had been formed of his improvement."[211] In 1816, however, he entered diplomatic service, this time as special minister to Italy and as minister to Russia, not returning from the latter post until the summer before the 1819 Term. He was then elected a United States senator from Maryland in 1820, a position he retained until his death. All told, Pinkney appeared in only six terms of the Marshall Court while employed solely as a private practitioner. But his diplomatic experience served him well. He "was long enough [in England]," Francis Gilmer felt, "not only to discipline his manner, but to enrich his dictum, by intermixing the more varied and splendid phrases of its literary circles."[212]

In addition, Pinkney was continually retained, when available, for the great cases of the Marshall Court—*Dartmouth College* v. *Woodward, McCulloch* v. *Maryland, Cohens* v. *Virginia, Gibbons* v. *Ogden*—and he made the most of his opportunities. Story said of Pinkney's argument in *McCulloch*, "I never, in my whole life, heard a greater speech; it was worth a journey from Salem to hear it; his elocution was excessively vehement, but his eloquence was overwhelming. . . . All the cobwebs of sophistry and metaphysics about state rights and state sovereignty he brushed away with a mighty besom."[213] And Charles Hammond, a lawyer from Ohio, wrote the following satiric comment, based on Pinkney's argument in *Cohens:*

---

[210] Henry Wheaton said in 1826 that Pinkney had "the most extensive and lucrative practice ever acquired by any American lawyer." Ibid. at 179. Robert Ireland has reported his income in 1816 as over $20,000 a year. R. Ireland, "The Legal Career of William Pinkney" (Ph.D diss., University of Nebraska, 1967), 220–23. In 1816, Pinkney, on being appointed minister to Russia, offered Story his law practice, provided Story resigned from the Court. Story wrote to a friend:

He promises to give me the whole of his business, and to introduce and support me exclusively among his friends. He states that his profits are now twenty-one thousand dollars per annum. . . . He is the retained counsel of all the [Marine] Insurance Companies at Baltimore. . . .

J. Story to Stephen White, Feb. 26, 1816, in W. Story, *Life and Letters,* I, 278.
[211] Gilmer, *Sketches,* 29.
[212] Ibid.
[213] J. Story to S. White, Mar. 3, 1819, in W. Story, *Life and Letters,* I, 325. This passage has been among the most frequently quoted in the history of literature on the Supreme Court, but until now none of the quoters has felt the need to define the meaning of the word "besom." Perhaps they all knew it, or thought it easily derivable from context. This unfortunate modern was less acute, and looked it up. A "besom" is defined as a bundle of twigs attached to a broom handle, or, more colloquially, as a broom itself.

# Chapter IV: *Prominent Lawyers Before the Marshall Court*

If Mr. Pinkney wishes to play the principal character in an oratorical exhibition, he always makes the hall of the Supreme Court his theatre. The [*National*] *Intelligencer* gravely announces that upon such and such a day, Mr. Pinkney will make a speech. It is fashionable to hear Mr. Pinkney make a set speech, so that all the beauty, if not all the intelligence, of the city crowd the Hall. Mr. Pinkney enters a la dandy, makes his bow to the audience and then to the Court, who sit as kind of managers of the farce. Five or six hours are consumed, part in traversing the bar, part in argument, part in rhodomontade. The ladies go home marvelously delighted. And in due season an opinion is delivered, reiterating and adopting all the argument of Mr. Pinkney's exhibition of himself, put forward with "it has been said" and "it has been truly said" and "would not this be its effect?" Upon which the orator and his admirers never fail to whisper that the opinion is a mere adoption and reiteration.[214]

Hammond's comments raise a fundamental question about all the lawyers pictured in this chapter: how much did Marshall Court opinions rely upon, or derive from, the arguments of counsel who appeared before the Court? As previously noted, the Marshall Court's internal practices and procedures were at once conducive and inimical to contributions by lawyers to judicial opinions. Since the Justices normally had no written briefs before them as they deliberated, to the extent they recollected lawyers' arguments it was through notes or memory. On the other hand, the Justices rendered opinions shortly after argument, discussed cases while arguments were pending, and retired to the boardinghouse directly after hearing counsel's presentations. Some lawyers who argued before the Court claimed virtual authorship of opinions,[215] and commentators have suggested that certain leading Marshall Court opinions were heavily influenced by the arguments of a particular advocate.[216] Pinkney seems an especially strong candidate on which to base such a suggestion. Two of his arguments, that in *McCulloch* and that in *Cohens,* bear striking parallels to the positions taken by Marshall in his opinion for the Court in those cases. The following excerpts underscore those parallels. The left-hand column represents Pinkney's language; the right-hand, Marshall's.

---

[214] 'Hampden' [Charles Hammond], Washington *Gazette,* Aug. 20, 1821. Hammond wrote eleven Hampden essays in the *Gazette* in the summer of 1821: the originals are in the Charles Hammond Papers, Ohio Historical Society, Columbus, Ohio.

[215] The most famous of which, doubtless, is Daniel Webster's comment that Marshall's opinion in *Gibbons* v. *Ogden* was "little else than a recital of my argument." See infra, text at notes 397–411. See also P. Harvey, *Reminiscences and Anecdotes of Webster* (1877); 142; Warren, *Supreme Court,* I, 611.

[216] See R. Ireland, "William Pinkney: A Revision and Reemphasis," *Am. J. Legal Hist.,* 14:235, 238 (1970); R. Newmyer, "Daniel Webster As Tocqueville's Lawyer," *Am. J. Legal Hist.,* 11:127 (1967).

*Pinkney* in *McCulloch*

It is said, too, that the powers of the State governments are original, and therefore more emphatically sovereign than those of the national government. But the State powers are no more original than those belonging to Union. There is no original power but in the people, who are the fountain and source of all political power. . . .

The constitution by which those authorites and the means of executing them are given, and the laws made in pursuance of it, are declared to be the supreme law of the land. The legislatures and judges of the States are to be bound by oath to support that constitution.[217]

*Marshall* for the Court in *McCulloch*

The powers of the general government, it has been said, are delegated by the States, who alone are truly sovereign. But when . . . it was deemed necessary to change [the confederation] into an effective government . . . the necessity of referring it to the people . . . was felt and acknowledged by all. The government of the Union, then . . . is emphatically and truly a government of the people. In form and in substance it emanates from them. . . .

The nation, on those subjects on which it can act, must necessarily bind its component parts. . . . [T]his question is not left to mere reason; the people have, in express terms, decided it, by saying "this constitution, and the laws of the United States, which shall be made in pursuance thereof, shall be the supreme law of the land, and by requiring that the members of the State legislatures, and the officers of the executive and judicial departments of the States, shall take the oath of fidelity to it."[218]

And in a later portion of *McCulloch:*

*Pinkney*

[W]e are told that the [Necessary and Proper Clause] . . . excludes all such [means] as are not strictly and absolutely necessary. But it is certain that this clause is

*Marshall*

[T]he argument on which most reliance is placed is drawn from the peculiar language of the clause. . . . The word "necessary" is considered as controlling the whole sen-

---

[217] Quoted in Wheaton, *Some Account,* 551–52.

[218] 4 Wheat. at 404–406.

not restrictive. . . . Compare [its language] . . . with the qualified manner [of the language of] the 10th section of the [first] article. In the latter, it is provided that "No State shall, without the consent of Congress, lay any imposts, or duties on imports or exports, except what may be *absolutely necessary* for carrying into execution the foregoing powers," etc. There is here, then, no qualification of the necessity. It need not be absolute. It may be taken in its ordinary grammatical sense. The word *necessary,* standing by itself, has no inflexible meaning; it is used in a sense more or less strict, according to the subject. . . . It may be qualified by the addition of adverbs of diminution or enlargement. . . . But that it is not always used in this strict and rigorous sense may be proved by tracing its definition and etymology in very human language.[219]

tence. Does [the word] always import an absolute physical necessity . . . ? We think it does not. . . . A thing may be necessary, . . . absolutely or indispensably necessary. . . . This comment on the word is well illustrated . . . by . . . the 10th section of the 1st article of the constitution. It is . . . impossible to compare the sentence which prohibits a State from laying "imposts, or duties on imports or exports, except which may be *absolutely necessary* for executing its inspection laws," with that which authorizes Congress "to make all laws which shall be necessary and proper for carrying into execution" the powers of the general government, without feeling a conviction that the convention understood itself to change materially the meaning of the word "necessary" by prefixing the word "absolutely." This word, then, like others, is used in various senses. . . .[220]

Finally, in *Cohens:*

*Pinkney*

*Marshall* (for the Court)

It is an axiom of political science, that the judicial power of every government must be commensurate with its legislative authority: it must be adequate to the protection, enforcement, and assertion of all the other powers of the government. . . . [In] suits between citizen and citizen on contract . . . the State courts must necessarily have original jurisdic-

The powers of the Union, on the great subjects of war, peace, and commerce, and on many others, are in themselves limitations of the sovereignty of the States. . . . The maintenance of these principles within purity is certainly among the great duties of government. One of the instruments by which this duty may be peaceably performed, is the

---

[219] Quoted in Wheaton, *Some Account,* 563–64. Emphasis in original.

[220] 4 Wheat. 414–15. Emphasis in original.

tion; but if the party defendant gets up a defence . . . and the decision of the State Court is in favour of the law thus set up, the judicial authority of the Union must be exerted over the cause. There is nothing in the constitution which prohibits the exercise of such a controlling authority. On the contrary, it is expressly declared, that where the *case* arises under the constitution and laws of the Union, the judicial power of the Union shall extend to it. It is the *case,* then, and not the *forum* in which it arises, that is to determine whether the judicial power of the Union shall extend to it.[221]

judicial department. It is authorized to decide all cases of every description, arising under the constitution or laws of the United States. From this general grant of jurisdiction, no exception is made of those cases in which a State may be a party. When we consider the situation of the Union and of a State, in relation to each other; the nature of our Constitution; the subordination of the State governments to that constitution . . . are we at liberty to insert, in this general grant, an exception of those cases in which a State may be a party? . . . We think . . . not. We think a case arising under the constitution or laws of the United States, is cognizable in the Courts of the Union, whoever may be the parties to that case. . . .[222]

To this evidence of Pinkney's impact one might add a comment made by Taney in his recollections of Pinkney. "The strong impression [Pinkney] made upon those who were accustomed to hear him," Taney said, "may, I think, be discovered in the language and style of the opinions delivered in the Courts at that period. It will be found, upon looking into them, that in many of the cases argued by [Pinkney] the language of the opinion is more ornate and embellished than usual at other sessions. . . . Mr. Pinkney's speeches must have been admired, or his ornamented style would not have been imitated."[223] Taney's comment suggests, at a minimum, that Pinkney's arguments were closely heeded.

There was another dimension to the "irresistible impetuosity"[224] of Pinkney's language. One recalls John Quincy Adams's comments that Pinkney "domineer[ed] . . . over," or "bullied and browbeat" Judges Houston and Duvall on the Third Circuit; as Gilmer put it, Pinkney's "eloquence is too constantly tempestuous." Gilmer also noted that Pinkney's "arrogant and strutting manner . . . never fails to alienate the hearts of his hearers."[225] Such comments raise once more the undertone of disaffection Pinkney engendered in nearly everyone whom he encoun-

---

[221] 4 Wheat. at 354–55.
[222] Ibid., 382–83.

[223] Taney in Tyler, *Memoir of Taney,* 74.
[224] Gilmer, *Sketches,* at 30.

tered. The gist of the disaffection seems to have been a sense that Pinkney's attitude toward others, both in court and in personal contacts, was insincere and self-serving. Taney, whose commentary was especially insightful, put it this way:

> [W]hen replying to [opposing arguments] he took particular pleasure in assailing the weaker points, and dwelling upon them in a tone and manner that sometimes made the adversary ashamed of them, and sometimes provoked his resentment. . . . His voice and manner and intonations did not appear to be natural, but artificial and studied. . . . This want of naturalness in tone and manner was unpleasant to those who heard him for the first time. . . . But a man who, at the age of fifty, spoke in amber-colored doeskin gloves, could hardly be expected to have a taste for simple or natural elocution.[226]

Others made similar observations. Story referred to Pinkney's "air of . . . *hauteur*, of superiority, . . . of abrupt and crusty precision";[227] Wirt called Pinkney's "dogmatizing absoluteness of manner" a "piece of acting," "artificial," "the half-contemptuous confidence of a charlatan," and ultimately "stiff, harsh . . . repulsive, and . . . disgusting."[228]

The discordance between Pinkney's unquestionably superior forensic talents (which even Wirt conceded) and his apparent inability to evoke admiration at a personal level among his contemporaries is worth attention. Part of the explanation for the discordance lies in the competitive, self-conscious world that Pinkney frequented, a world of talented and often caustic individuals who marked each other's abilities and used letters and anecdotes to communicate their animosities as well as their enthusiasms. In such a world Pinkney was an especially formidable and annoying presence. He did not leave incompetence unremarked; he had a tendency to ridicule and to humiliate his adversaries; his manner and his person, as Taney said, were "overdressed." The result, Gilmer felt, was that, "paradoxical as it may seem, Mr. Pinkney, with his violent manner, his vigorous thoughts, his animated metaphor, is often . . . cold, and sometimes even . . . repulsive."[229]

But the reaction to Pinkney's "too studied and artificial . . . style, matter, and manner"[230] does not explain the origins of those characteristics. Here, as with Tazewell, one finds a suggestive theme surfacing early in life. Pinkney "began life," according to Theophilus Parsons, "as a poor boy," who first became acquainted with the law because "he went into a lawyer's office to sweep his floors."[231] Pinkney's nephew,

---

[225] Ibid. at 32.
[226] Taney in Tyler, *Memoir of Taney*, 71–72.
[227] J. Story to S. Fay, Feb. 24, 1812, in W. Story, *Life and Letters*, I, 215.

[228] Wirt to Gilmer, supra, note 188.
[229] Gilmer, *Sketches*, 32.
[230] Ibid.
[231] Parsons, "Notes of a Lecture," 129.

who wrote an authorized biography, put it less starkly: "poverty" was "the portion of his early childhood."[232] Pinkney left school at the age of thirteen, and while his nephew claimed that he had "the rudiments of a first-rate education," he conceded that "it is more than probable that [Pinkney's] reading in the classics . . . was not extensive."[233] Economic and educational disadvantages, however, had not been constant features of Pinkney's youth. His father, "from one of the most respectable and ancient families of Britain,"[234] had remained loyal to the British during the Revolution, and as a consequence had seen his property confiscated by the state of Maryland.[235] Until the Revolution, Pinkney had apparently been given "the best and most skillful instruction," with "no expense spared";[236] after his eleventh or twelfth year, altered financial circumstances radically changed that course. There was, then, in Pinkney's youth a stark and sudden juxtaposition of a cultivated, "liberal," gentlemanly pattern of life with "the rough and appalling realities of life, when poverty settles down."[237] Pinkney's nephew referred to the "struggles of pride and a lofty aspiration" that the sudden change of circumstances produced in his uncle.

When Pinkney was encouraged by his patrons to take up the profession of law, he rapidly "acquired an enviable preeminence," according to his nephew, but he "did not dare . . . to enjoy it in ease."[238] The insecurity that undergirded his rise in his profession is suggested by an incident from Pinkney's first mission to London, where he encountered "the prominent men of England."[239] Pinkney told the incident to Story, who subsequently embellished it.[240] As Story recalled,

[Pinkney's] position, as American Commissioner, gave him a privilege, offered to but few of his countrymen, of frequenting the first circles, which were then filled with men of wit and learning. Mr. P. told me that at one of these parties, at which were Pitt, Fox, and other great scholars of the time, the conversation turned upon a passage in Euripides. The debate was carried on for a long time with a great deal of spirit—each side quoting many passages from Euripides and other such actions. "Of course," says Mr. P., "I took no part in all this, and after a while, one of the disputants, noticing that I took no part in the conversation, turned to me, saying, 'Why, Mr. Pinkney, you don't share in this talk—come, sir, what is your opinion of this passage?' I was obliged," said Mr. P. "to confess that I was listening to acquire

---

[232] Pinkney, *William Pinkney*, 13.
[233] Ibid., 14.
[234] Ibid., 12.
[235] Ibid., 13.
[236] Ibid., 14.

[237] Ibid., 16.
[238] Ibid., 17.
[239] Ibid., 15.
[240] See *Albany L.J.*, 13:190 (1876).

information rather than to impart any; but I resolved from that time to study the classics, and from that time I did."[241]

The anecdote is interesting in several respects. First, Pinkney was himself the source of the story, and he told it to Story, who was one of Pinkney's closest professional friends but also an inveterate gossip. Although the anecdote might seem self-deprecatory, it actually reflected Pinkney's pride in his acknowledged mastery of classical allusion in oratory. Pinkney had thus accomplished, he was suggesting, what the embarrassing dinner table conversation had motivated him to do: he had become a classicist. But the anecdote also has the ring of one of those special memories in a person's life, a tale told frequently and remembered often. In light of Pinkney's youth one can reconstruct other possible associations in the anecdote. The dinner table conversation may have brought home to Pinkney the lost opportunities of his adolescence: others had had the leisure and the wealth to enjoy a liberal, cultivated youth while he had scraped and struggled to make his mark, fearful of enjoying his success lest it vanish and poverty return. In that encounter with Pitt, Fox, and others in the "first circles," Pinkney's own marginal status as a gentleman and a scholar was confirmed. In his eventual emergence as an orator who reminded others of both Pitt and Fox, there may have been an uneasy kind of vindication, the adoption of a role that for Pinkney was more a means of survival than a pose.

One senses in Pinkney contempt toward those for whom life had not been such a struggle, and at the same time a fear of being exposed in his marginality. He may have played the dandy, down to his amber-colored gloves, in order to impress or to befuddle his contemporaries, and perhaps in order to keep them from getting to know him too well. Nothing was spontaneous about Pinkney, observers noted: his professed lapses of memory were studied efforts to demonstrate his thorough preparation; his "excessive vehemence" was an effort to intimidate his opponents or to attract the attention of the galleries; even his apologies, as in the case of the one made to Emmet, were prepared passages of eloquence. Wirt, in the course of his attacks on Pinkney, spoke of the latter's "miserable attempts at bawdy puns" and his "coarse . . . manners," and mocked his pronunciation. "I cannot love the man," Wirt wrote a close friend, "for he has no heart but for himself—and there is so much unfeeling and savage rudeness about him towards others, and so much coarse vulgarity, so much of the English porter cellar and the boasting jockey, that my affections cannot take hold of him."[242]

---

[241] J. Story, "Notes for a Lecture on William Pinkney," in W. Story, *Life and Letters,* II, 491.

[242] Wirt to Gilmer, Apr. 1, 1816, supra, note 188.

Wirt was being uncharitable—there were deeper reasons for Pinkney's acting, posing, and bullying—but Wirt's impressions were widely shared. Pinkney's great strengths as a lawyer—preparation, rigor, logic, competitiveness, presence, determination, intimidation—were also weaknesses, part of a mask he fashioned to wear in the public gaze of a world he may well have feared and even hated. When Pinkney died suddenly in 1822, at the height of his reputation, his death was attributed to overexertion in the face of a mild illness. Wirt wrote:

> Poor Pinkney! He died opportunely for his fame. It could not have risen higher. . . . He was a great man. . . . He is a real loss to the bar. No man dared to grapple with him without the most perfect preparations, and the full possession of all his strengths. . . . Poor Pinkney!—After all, how long will he be remembered? He left no monument of genius behind him, and posterity will, therefore, know nothing of such a man but by the report of others.[243]

And Story wrote:

> [T]he real truth is that [Pinkney] . . . had an influenza for some days, and having last week exerted himself in Court to a very high degree, and being of a very plethoric habit, he probably accelerated a disease to which he was constitutionally inclined. The event has filled many of us who knew his great power and eloquence, his great brilliancy, genius, learning, and wit, with profound melancholy. And yet this calamity made but a momentary impression; and the next day it was as little thought of . . . as if it were an event of a century ago. We were just sitting down to table, when the news reached us. It occasioned but a moment's pause; the dinner went on, and the laugh and joke circulated as if it were nothing worthy of notice.[244]

In the end the difficulties others found in Pinkney's "manner," characterized by Gilmer as "very brilliant to the eye but cold to the feeling," detracted not only from his contemporary stature but from his place in history. While acknowledged to be the greatest advocate of his age, he has inspired only a filiopietistic biography and a century of indifference.

William Wirt has figured prominently in these sketches as a commentator; he now becomes a subject. The numerous quotations from Wirt testify to his prominence as a literary stylist. Of the Marshall Court law-

---

[243] W. Wirt to F. Gilmer, May 9, 1822, quoted in Kennedy, *Memoirs of Wirt,* II, 122.

[244] J. Story to S. W. Story, Feb. 21, 1822, in W. Story, *Life and Letters,* 414–15.

## Chapter IV: *Prominent Lawyers Before the Marshall Court*

yers portrayed in this chapter, Wirt was clearly the most at home in the world of literature and letters. Even Daniel Webster, for all his memorable speeches, produced nothing like the volume of literature that Wirt produced, and Wirt was a well-known author before he became a well-known advocate. Wirt's inclination toward literature was more than a sidelight to his professional life: it provides insight into his character. Although Wirt is included in this chapter because of his accomplishments as an advocate before the Marshall Court, it is fair to say that had he had his choice, he would have devoted his career to writing rather than to law.

Two themes dominated Wirt's early life and strongly influenced his professional career: his social and economic marginality and his excessively imaginative temperament. In a culture in which many lawyers were also landed and monied gentlemen, regarding their profession as more of a social and political symbol than as a financial necessity, Wirt had no family connections, little money, and no well-established roots. As the nineteenth century matured, successful lawyers tended to be men who established themselves in urban centers, cultivating clients, forming associations, taking advantage of their family connections, identifying themselves as fixtures in the urban landscape. Wirt remained a transient.

Wirt's lack of a professional base was partially the result of his long tenure as attorney general of the United States at a time when Washington was still a community of transients. But Wirt's own tendency to move about accentuated the problem. Of the forty-two years (1792–1834) Wirt practiced law, twenty-one were spent as clerk of the Virginia House of Delegates (1800–1802), chancellor in the Eastern District of Virginia (1802–1804), and attorney general (1817–29). In those forty-two years Wirt practiced law and lived successively in Culpeper and Albemarle counties in Virginia and then in the cities of Richmond, Norfolk, Richmond again, Washington, and Baltimore. The other lawyers treated in this chapter had a constant professional base during their years as advocates before the Marshall Court. They may have held public office, but their private practice was in one location, to which they continually returned. Wirt had no such professional constancy in his life.

Wirt's transiency was produced by a combination of factors. He was regularly beset with financial troubles; he never quite accumulated the capital necessary to become professionally or personally independent. At the same time his tendency to indulge his passions, to invent charming fantasies, to engage the sympathies of others, and to become captured by his own dreams lent a continual sense of motion to his life. He was by all accounts a gregarious, convivial, lighthearted person, inclined to pursue the flights of his imagination and not inclined to pay careful attention to his financial affairs. He also had self-destructive tendencies, which he tried hard to control. His health was often delicate, and some of his peregrinations were attempts to relocate to ostensibly healthier climates.

He needed periodically to escape from his own delight in the pleasures of the flesh. In 1802 he wrote Dabney Carr, an intimate friend, that "I wished to leave Richmond" because "I dropped into a circle dear to me for the amiable and brilliant traits which belonged to it, but in which I had found, that during several months, I was dissipating my health, my time, my money, and my reputation."[245]

The dominant features of Wirt's character were apparent at a young age. He was born in 1772 of Swiss and German parents in Bladensburg, Maryland, now a suburb of Washington but then "a thrifty, business-doing, little seaport, profitably devoted to the tobacco trade," and "inhabited by wealthy factors . . . whose mode of living . . . communicated a certain show of opulence."[246] He was the youngest of six children, described by his biographer as "a lively, shrewd, pleasant-tempered and beautiful boy, upon whom many eyes were turned in kindly regard."[247] Wirt's father, Jacob, was a tavern-keeper: when he died two years after William's birth and left him a one-sixth share of his estate, the total amount was estimated as "not more than three or four thousand dollars."[248] In 1779 Wirt's mother died as well, and he was sent away to schools by a family friend, first attending "a classical academy . . . in Georgetown, eight miles from Bladensburg," then "a classical school in Charles County, Maryland, kept by Aaron Dent, in the vestry-house of Newport Church," and finally "the grammar school . . . of the Rev. James Hunt . . . in Montgomery County."[249] Wirt remembered that on realizing that he was an orphan "a deep sadness fell upon me . . . [w]hen I could no longer see a face that I knew, or an object that was not strange"; a "sense of total desertion and forlornness . . . seized upon my heart."[250]

But Wirt, like Emmet, possessed qualities that made others want to help him. James Hunt served as an intellectual patron, and Peter Carnes, "the owner of a considerable landed estate in Charles County," who was both a lawyer and "a cultivator of tobacco," a financial one.[251] Carnes first met Wirt when he stayed at the Wirts' tavern in Bladensburg. Wirt's biographer felt that Carnes may have "assumed the direction of the education of William . . . chiefly out of his own pocket."[252] A third patron was Benjamin Edwards, a lawyer from Montgomery County, who in 1788 hired Wirt to tutor his son, a former classmate of Wirt's at Hunt's school.

---

[245] W. Wirt to D. Carr, Feb. 12, 1802, quoted in J. Kennedy, *The Life of William Wirt* (2 vols, 1849 ed.), I, 88. John Pendleton Kennedy's biography of Wirt remains the most extensive treatment of his career and the largest printed source of Wirt's letters.
[246] Kennedy, *William Wirt*, 19.

[247] Ibid.
[248] Ibid., 17.
[249] W. Wirt, "Autobiographical Fragment," quoted in ibid., 28, 29, 30.
[250] Quoted in ibid., 28.
[251] Ibid., 49.
[252] Ibid., 50.

Wirt wrote Edwards later in his life that "[y]ou have taught me to love you like a parent. . . . [T]o you, to the influence of your conversation, your precepts, and your example in the most critical and decisive period of my life, I owe whatever of useful or good there may be in the bias of my mind and character."[253]

Wirt had become attracted to the law while attending the Reverend Hunt's school (Hunt used to take his pupils on outings to the Montgomery County courthouse, four miles away), and resolved to train for the bar. After a brief trip to Georgia in 1789, undertaken as a precaution against possible tuberculosis, Wirt began the study of law in the Montgomery County office of William P. Hunt, the son of the Reverend James Hunt. In November 1792, Wirt wrote Peter Carnes that a friend had "informed me of a very advantageous station for a lawyer in the state of Virginia." He "removed my residence immediately," took five months' apprenticeship under Thomas Swann, "manoeuvre[d]" his way past the twelvemonth Virginia residency requirement, and opened up a law practice in Culpeper County.[254]

Wirt's early life was in one sense a testament to his ability to overcome his familial and economic difficulties by the force of his personality and by his perseverance and intelligence. Edwards had noted that Wirt, in his youth, was "shy and timid in any public exhibition of himself," and that "his enunciation was thick and indistinct, marked by a nervous rapidity of utterance."[255] By maturity Wirt was well known not only for the "rich and melodious quality of his voice"[256] and the "force, purity, variety, and splendour" of "his diction"[257], but also for his "genuine eloquence,"[258] illustrated by the selection of two of his orations in a collection of works entitled *Eloquence of the United States*.[259] This transformation was doubtless aided by his physical appearance. "He had, from nature," his first biographer wrote, "a good person and carriage;"[260] another contemporary remarked on his "dignified and commanding . . . person" and his "open, manly, and playful . . . countenance."[261] After Wirt's death, John Pendleton Kennedy recalled

[t]he massive and bold outline of his countenance, the clear, kind, blue eye, the light hair falling in crisp and numerous curls upon a broad forehead, the high arching eyebrow, the large nose and ample chin . . .

---

[253] W. Wirt to B. Edwards, undated, quoted in ibid., 52.

[254] W. Wirt to P. Carnes, November 1792, quoted in ibid., 55–56.

[255] Ibid., 52.

[256] Ibid., 58, 57.

[257] Gilmer, *Sketches,* 38.

[258] Ibid.

[259] See E. Williston, *Eloquence of the United States* (1829), IV, 394, V, 454.

[260] P. Cruse, "Biographical Sketch of William Wirt," in W. Wirt, *The Letters of the British Spy* (10th ed., 1836), 35.

[261] Gilmer, *Sketches,* 38.

height rather above six feet, . . . [the] broad shoulders, capacious chest and general fullness of development. . . ."[262]

It was not long before Wirt emerged as one of the promising lawyers of his generation in Culpeper and Albemarle counties. He formed close friendships in the bar with James Barbour, Dabney Carr, and Francis Walker Gilmer, all of whom lived near Charlottesville. In 1795 he married Mildred Gilmer, Francis's sister, thereby joining an established and affluent family and increasing his professional connections. At the same time Wirt became acquainted with Jefferson, Madison, and Monroe, all at the early stages of their careers; he "whetted his appetite for elegant literature" and "gave fresh vigour to his taste and fancy."[263] He became, according to one account, "an admired object in the court-house during the day, [and] a leading spirit in the evening coterie." He was not only "eloquent on the field of justice," he was "not less elegant at the table or mess-room."[264] The result of this high living was some "misadventures" and some "occasional irregularities of conduct." Wirt was at times "too susceptible to the influences of good-fellowship," and his antics led to what his principal biographer called "the fabrication of coarse and disgusting charges of vulgar excess."[265] All these "golden days"[266] suddenly came to an end, however, in 1799, when Mildred Wirt died. Wirt "placed a tablet over [her] grave," and "determined to establish his residence in Richmond."[267] His marriage into the Gilmer family had given him security and stability; with Mildred's death marginality and transience returned, and Wirt again changed residence.

While Wirt had been affiliated with the Gilmer household, he "drank deep draughts" from Dr. Gilmer's library, which included selections from English philosophers, poets, and political theorists. At grammar school he had been conspicuous for his skillful use of language, and "letters" had become his "passion . . .—a passion foredoomed against enjoyment."[268] By the year of his wife's death he had established a local reputation as a letter-writer,[269] but as he concerned himself again with his legal prospects, his literary activities were necessarily confined. By 1803, however, before he had become fully established as a lawyer, Wirt suddenly became a popular writer. The occasion was the publication of a series of sketches entitled "The Letters of the British Spy," in the *Virginia Argus*. In letters to Dabney Carr, written in January and June, 1804, Wirt described the origins and nature of "The British Spy" and its effects on his personal and professional reputation:

---

[262] Kennedy, *William Wirt*, I, 15.
[263] Ibid., 64.
[264] Ibid., 67–68.
[265] Ibid., 68.

[266] Ibid., 73.
[267] Ibid., 75.
[268] Ibid., 65, 48.
[269] Ibid., 72.

# Chapter IV: *Prominent Lawyers Before the Marshall Court*

It was to divert my own mind, during this period of uneasiness and alarm, that I began to write. But after the project was thus started, I will acknowledge . . . that there were secondary considerations which supported and warmed me throughout the enterprise. I was gratified by the encomiums which were generally pronounced on the composition, and I was still more delicately gratified in observing the pleasure with which my wife heard those encomiums. . . .

I endeavoured to forget myself; to fancy myself the character which I assumed; to imagine how, as a Briton, I should be struck with Richmond . . . Unfortunately, however, in my zeal to support my adopted character, I forgot myself too far in some of the letters . . . Hence the portraits of living characters, which I drew with a mind . . . perfectly absorbed in the contemplation of the originals, and . . . forgettive of personal consequences. . . .

I am very sure that a great part of the public interest excited by the Spy is imputable to those portraits of prominent characters. . . . [W]hen I shall have reached their age in which I may be supposed to have touched the zenith of my mind, I should be . . . gratified in seeing my intellectual portrait set in a popular work. . . .

The letters bespeak a mind rather frolicsome and sprighty, than thoughtful and penetrating; and therefore a mind qualified to amuse, for the moment, but not to benefit either its proprietor, or the world, by the depth and utility of its researches. The style, although sometimes happy, is sometimes, also, careless and poor. . . .[270]

Upon the whole, the work is too tumid and too light; yet these, perhaps, are the very properties which gave it the degree of admiration which it excited . . .

My friend Tazewell . . . does not approve of such engagements. He says that it gives a man a light and idle appearance, in the eye of the world, and might, therefore, impede one in my profession. . . .[271]

As these examples demonstrate, Wirt's letters were his most revealing writings. Several themes in the excerpted passages are worth commenting upon. One is Wirt's association of writing with diversion from "uneasiness and alarm." He perceived his literary endeavors as an antidote to the legal profession, as well as an ornament to it; he wrote to indulge an imagination that law practice did not sufficiently exercise. Another theme is Wirt's love of "encomiums" from the public, which repeatedly motivated him to choose short-term attention and gratification to long-term financial security. The passage also furnishes testimony to Wirt's vivid and fertile imagination, which enabled him to play the role of his "stranger" narrator so completely that he dissected some of his

---

[270] W. Wirt to D. Carr, Jan. 16, 1804, ibid., 109–12.

[271] W. Wirt to D. Carr, June 8, 1804, in ibid., 115–16.

acquaintances with a merciless and impolitic objectivity. It also reveals Wirt's capacity for self-reflection and self-analysis, which coexisted with an equally strong susceptibility to fantasies and illusions, evidenced by a recurrent projection of himself at the age of forty-five as an independently wealthy squire and man of letters. Finally, the latter excerpt suggests that Wirt felt that the legal establishment, personified by Littleton Tazewell, considered literary exercises "light and idle," and that he ran a professional risk in continuing them.

Wirt nonetheless did continue his writing, authoring a series of essays, "The Rainbow," in the Richmond *Enquirer* between August and October, 1804, another series of sketches of Virginians, "The Old Bachelor," in the *Enquirer* in 1810, and *The Life of Patrick Henry,* a biography, in 1817. The first of these efforts received almost no attention, but the second has been called "the best of all [Wirt's] literary composition."[272] The third, while less favorably received by reviewers,[273] elicited a letter from John Adams, who said that the book had "given me a rich entertainment," and that he "congratulate[d] the nation on the acquisition of an Attorney General of such talents and industry as your sketches demonstrate."[274]

Adams's allusion to the attorney generalship brings the chronology of Wirt's professional life forward in a rush. By the time "The British Spy" appeared in 1803 Wirt had remarried, this time to Elizabeth Gamble, had his first child, Laura, and resigned from the chancellorship to take up law practice in Norfolk. He wrote Dabney Carr in June 1803 that he "was drawn to Norfolk by the attractions of her bank" and that he expected "that my annual income will be twelve hundred pounds," and that "by the time I am . . . forty-five, I shall be able to retire from the bar, in ease and independence, and spend the remainder of my life . . . in whatever part of the country I please."[275] Between 1804 and 1817, the year he was named attorney general by Monroe, Wirt had established a reputation as a lawyer. The most conspicuous event determining his stature was his performance at the 1807 Burr trial. On Jefferson's urging,[276] Wirt was retained to assist George Hay in the prosecution, and on Tuesday, August 25, Wirt, in the opening section of his argument, delivered a characterization of Blennerhassett and one of Burr. Those sketches, according to Albert Beveridge, "enraptured [the audience] with an eloquence that has lived for a century." Wirt's "charming and powerful" argument in the Burr trial, Beveridge felt, was notable for its "firm

---

[272] John Pendleton Kennedy in ibid., 260.
[273] For an assessment of some of the reviews, see ibid., II, 35–42.
[274] J. Adams to W. Wirt, Jan. 23,

1818, in ibid., II, 47–48.
[275] W. Wirt to D. Carr, June 6, 1803, in ibid., I, 97.
[276] See Clarkson and Jett, *Luther Martin,* 245–46.

logic and wealth of learning," and was "second only to Jefferson's [address to Congress] in fixing, perhaps irremovably, public opinion as to Aaron Burr and Harman Blennerhassett."[277] Wirt called Burr

the author and professor of the plot . . . a soldier, bold, ardent, restless, and aspiring, the great actor whose brain conceived, and whose hand brought the plot into operation . . . the contriver of the whole conspiracy. . . .

and suggested that he had seduced the "innocent" Blennerhassett "by the dignity and elegance of his demeanor, the light and beauty of his conversations, and the . . . fascinating power of his address."[278]

By the time of the Burr trial Wirt had returned to Richmond to live, having yielded to his wife's desires to leave Norfolk and to his fears of yellow fever, which was prevalent in the tidewater seacoast area. For the next ten years Wirt's reputation prospered and his opportunities expanded, but his financial situation did not stabilize to the extent he had hoped. Anxiety over his "fortune"[279] led him to decline an invitation by Jefferson to run for Congress,[280] and while he served briefly in the Virginia legislature, he concluded that "the course of politics is neither for my happiness nor fortune."[281] But he continued to enjoy public attention: when he was retained to argue a case in the Supreme Court in 1814 he noted that fact with delight,[282] and three years later he wrote of the "rejuvenescence" arguments before the Court had "given to [his] emulation."[283]

All the while Wirt was possessed by the same recurrent image:

In the course of ten years . . . I have reason to hope that I shall be worth near upon or quite one hundred thousand dollars in cash, besides having an elegant and well-furnished establishment in [Richmond]. I propose to vest twenty-five thousand dollars in the purchase, improvement and stocking of a farm somewhere on James River, in as healthy a county as I can find, having also the advantage of fertility. There I will have my books, and with my family spend three seasons of the

---

[277] Beveridge, *John Marshall*, III, 495, 497.

[278] Quoted in Robertson, *Trials of Burr*, II, 110–112.

[279] W. Wirt to Thomas Jefferson, Jan. 14, 1808, quoted in Kennedy, *William Wirt*, I, 210.

[280] T. Jefferson to W. Wirt, Jan. 10, 1808, quoted in ibid., 208.

[281] W. Wirt to D. Carr, Dec. 21, 1808, quoted in ibid., 244.

[282] W. Wirt to D. Carr, Dec. 10,

1814, quoted in ibid., 340.

[283] "Could I have supposed when you and I were threading the hog-paths through the wilds of Fluvanna, and trying to make our way at the bar of that miserable court, that a day would even come when I could care to hold up my head in the Supreme Court of the United States, and take by the beard the first champions of the nation!" W. Wirt to D. Carr, Feb. 27, 1817, quoted in ibid., II, 18–19.

year—spring, summer and fall. Three months I shall devote to the improvement of my children, the amusement of my wife, and perhaps the endeavour to raise by my pen a monument to my name. The winter we will spend in Richmond. . . . The remainder of my cash I will invest in some stable and productive fund, to raise portions for my children. . . . It is true I love distinction, but I can only enjoy it in tranquility and innocence. . . .[284]

This passage, written when Wirt was thirty-seven, is principally significant for the idealized image of life that it reflects. The attainment of an "elegant . . . establishment" in Richmond and the James River estate would symbolize that the orphaned son of a tavern-keeper had become part of the Virginia squirearchy. Other features of the passage also inform us about Wirt's attitudes: the description of the James River farm as being in "healthy" country; Wirt's sense that his "pen" could be the source of his reputation; the comment that he could only enjoy "distinction" in "tranquility and innocence." We have noted before in Wirt his strong sense that the same qualities which produced his fertile imagination made it difficult for him to live a moderate life. He "forgot himself" in high living, just as he could forget himself in his character sketches. The farm was to be his refuge from indulgence, just as it was to be a symbol of his social acceptance and the financial base for his literary efforts. One should note, finally, that nowhere in this romantic image was there room for the practice of law.

In 1817 distinction came to Wirt, but not in any of the forms anticipated by his vision in 1809. He was named attorney general of the United States, and with it given an opportunity to become one of the elite members of the American bar. By 1829, when Andrew Jackson's assumption of the presidency caused him to resign as attorney general, Wirt was as famous as any full-time practitioner in the nation. His exposure and success as attorney general generated continued business and acclaim on his resignation from that office. He was retained to argue significant Supreme Court cases, such as *Cherokee Nation* v. *Georgia;* and when he died of erysipelas[285] in February 1834, both houses of Congress adjourned for his funeral, and the president and vice-president marched in his funeral procession.

---

[284] W. Wirt to Benjamin Edwards, June 23, 1809, quoted in ibid., I, 240–41.

[285] The medical definition of erysipelas is an "acute febrile disease that is associated with intense local inflammation of the skin and subcutaneous tissues." Erysipelas is caused by a hemolytic streptococcus bacteria. It produces lesions, redness and swelling, and splotches on the face. It is now treated by sulfur drugs and penicillin. W. Thomson, ed., *Black's Medical Dictionary* (31st ed., 1978), 313–14.

But Wirt's vision of the good life never quite became a reality. In 1828, when he was reflecting on where to locate after leaving Washington, he wrote a friend that "I have long since learned that golden harvests are oftener found in the dreams of poets than in real life."[286] Familiar themes of his youth—notably financial instability and precarious physical health—continued to plague him. In 1822 Elizabeth Wirt wrote to her sister that "a good diet and a windfall of $100,000 would alleviate [Wirt's] troubles."[287] In 1830 his youngest daughter died suddenly at the age of sixteen, a misfortune that allegedly "affected [Wirth's] health and caused him to "lose [his] . . . buoyancy of spirit."[288] The next year his house in Baltimore, which he had rented because he did not have enough capital to buy it, was "taken by one of the Banks from our first landlord, for a debt," and the Wirts moved into "Newcombs Hotel."[289] The "golden harvest" of an independently wealthy country squire and man of letters, so compelling for Wirt and apparently within his grasp, had nonetheless been relegated to a poet's fancy.

Wirt's law practice, his principal means of financial support and public attention, imposed its own costs upon him. His years as attorney general particularly evidenced his tendency to become emotionally and physically drained by legal work. He had become ill after intense legal work as early as the Burr trial,[290] and as he grew older his susceptibility increased. An 1825 letter written by his daughter Elizabeth referred to Wirt's "annual supreme court sickness,"[291] and Wirt's own letters written during the period of his Attorney Generalship make regular reference to his absence from arguments because of illness or fatigue.[292] In 1834, just before his death, one of his daughters wrote a friend that the "Supreme Court" had always been considered "a terrible bugbear" by Wirt's family because his participation in arguments "suffered him to pore over his books and papers half the night . . . totally unconscious of the lateness of the hour." She doubted whether during Wirt's tenure as attorney general "he would have come off . . . well had dear mother not been present to keep him in check."[293]

---

[286] W. Wirt to Lane L. Gouverner, Dec. 4, 1828, William Wirt Papers, New York Public Library, New York, N.Y.

[287] E. Wirt to Mrs. Agnes Gamble Cabell, Jan. 31, 1822, William Wirt Papers, Library of Congress.

[288] Kennedy, *William Wirt*, I, 289.

[289] E. Wirt to Catherine Gamble, June 5, 1831, Wirt Papers, Library of Congress.

[290] W. Wirt to D. Carr, Sept. 1, 1807, in Kennedy, *William Wirt*, I, 202.

[291] E. Wirt to W. Wirt, Dec. 10, 1825, Wirt Papers, Library of Congress.

[292] See, e.g., W. Wirt to D. Carr, May 14, 1821, quoted in Kennedy, *William Wirt*, II, 107; W. Wirt to John H. Rice, Feb. 1, 1822, quoted in ibid., 119; W. Wirt to F. Gilmer, Apr. 2, 1825, quoted in ibid., 170; W. Wirt to William H. Cabell, Dec. 5, 1826, quoted in ibid., 194–95.

[293] Ellen Wirt to Peachey Gilmer, Feb. 5, 1834, Wirt Papers, Library of Congress.

Wirt's physical problems while attorney general were undoubtedly related to his temperament. His correspondence reveals a high-strung, resonant person of considerable nervous energy and a thirst for life; a person who felt things acutely, deeply, and with passion; a person who could not be counted on to restrain his impetuousness. He was immoderate both in his consumption of food and drink and in his daily routine. He rarely exercised; he loved company and conversation, and was oblivious to time when engaged intellectually or emotionally. He had considerable powers of concentration, was remarkably sensitive and perceptive, was occasionally enraged by the actions of other lawyers,[294] and in general lived life with intensity. Wirt family letters continually refer to his health being restored through vacations, travel, reduced working hours, and moderation in habits. Both he and his family were aware that for him tranquility was a necessity.

But the circumstances of Wirt's life made tranquility hard to come by, as advocacy before the Marshall Court became a frequent and consuming enterprise. In the period covered by this study Wirt appeared before the Court more frequently than any other lawyer, arguing 170 cases between 1815 and 1835. He participated in nearly all the great Marshall Court constitutional cases—*Dartmouth College, Sturges v. Crowninshield, McCulloch, Cohens, Gibbons, Ogden v. Saunders, Cherokee Nation,* and *Proprietors of the Charles River Bridge v. Proprietors of the Warren Bridge*[295]—as well as other significant private law cases. And he was, according to contemporary accounts, among the Marshall Court's finest advocates. Wirt may have lacked the comprehensiveness of Martin,

---

[294] In 1818 Wirt and William Pinkney were opponents in a trial in Baltimore and Pinkney, as was his wont, made some insulting remarks to Wirt in court. "A demand for an explanation was made" by Wirt, and "a short correspondence occurred." Kennedy, *William Wirt,* II, 76. Apparently Wirt contemplated a duel: as late as December 1818 Story alluded to "the recent disagreement" between Pinkney and Wirt, and volunteered that "I am quite persuaded, without having heard a word of the facts, that . . . Mr. Pinkney is wrong." Story suggested that Pinkney be made to "feel he has much to lose, and nothing to gain, by the course he sometimes pursues." J. Story to Henry Wheaton, Dec. 9, 1818, in W. Story, *Life and Letters,* I, 312. Kennedy, in recounting the incident, said that "the resort to the duel . . . cannot but be regarded as the tyranny of a most

wicked custom," but acknowledged that "at the time [of the incident] this tyranny of custom swayed the society of Maryland with a dominion too absolute for the resistance even of such men as those." Kennedy, *William Wirt,* II, 77.

[295] 11 Pet. 420 (1837). The "Bridge case" was first argued in the 1831 Term, Wirt representing the Warren Bridge supporters, who eventually prevailed. For Wirt's argument see Simon Greenleaf, "Arguments of Counsel in the case *Charles River Bridge v. Warren Bridge,*" unpublished notes, Harvard Law School Library. The Marshall Court was badly divided in the *Charles River Bridge* case, see J. Story to John H. Ashmun, Mar. 1, 1832, in W. Story, *Life and Letters,* II, 91–92, and never came to a decision on it. See discussion in Chapter IX.

# Chapter IV: *Prominent Lawyers Before the Marshall Court*

the intellectual sophistication of Pinkney, the "intuitive perceptions" of Tazewell, or the emotional force of Emmet. But at his best he combined some of the skills of each of them, and added what Francis Gilmer called a "prompt, pure, and brilliant . . . wit." Gilmer said of his close friend:

> I have seen no one who has such natural advantages and so many qualities requisite for genuine eloquence. . . . His diction invites force, purity, variety, and splendor. . . . The march of his mind is direct to its object, [but] the evolutions by which he attains it are so new and beautiful, and apparently necessary to the occasion, that your admiration is kept alive, your fancy delighted, and your judgment convinced, through every stage of the process. . . .[296]

Some other contemporary observers were more reserved in their assessments. John Latrobe, while acknowledging that "few persons" had the "noble features, . . . majestic carriage, . . . sweetness of . . . voice, [and] charm" of Wirt, was "never satisfied that Mr. Wirt was a profound lawyer," although he was "a most laborious one."[297] George Ticknor, while acknowledging that Wirt "is undoubtedly a powerful advocate and thorough lawyer, by general consent," found him in 1815 "perhaps affected in his manners and remarks," and indicated that "I might have set him down for one of those who were 'pretty fellows in their day,' but who were now rather second-hand in society."[298]

Wirt's manner as an advocate, unlike that of many of the other lawyers pictured in this chapter, was not a vivid extension of his distinctive human qualities, nor was it a studied and artificial pose. It was rather a careful circumscription of what his principal biographers called Wirt's "florid imagination," coupled with his instinctive gracefulness and good humor. John Pendleton Kennedy suggested that "in early life" Wirt's imagination and "power of vivid declamation" had served to identify his advocacy with "that flimsier eloquence which more captivates the crowd without the bar than the Judge upon the bench." Wirt became aware of "this disadvantage," Kennedy said, "and labored with matchless perseverance to disabuse the tribunals . . . of this disparaging impression."[299] Kennedy's comment rings true: we have seen that Wirt's professional life as a whole may be characterized as a struggle to restrain and to channel his "florid imagination." Contemporaries used adjectives such as "calm," "deliberate," "smooth," "pleasant," "agreeable," and "gentlemanly"[300] to describe him in court; in Wirt's case the calmness

---

[296] Gilmer, *Sketches,* 38.
[297] Quoted in Semmes, *John H. B. Latrobe,* 201–202.
[298] Greenslet, *George Ticknor,* 33.
[299] Kennedy, *William Wirt,* II, 383.

[300] Boston *Daily Advertiser,* July 2, 1829, quoted in D. Webster to W. Wirt, July 3, 1829, Wirt Papers, Library of Congress; Kennedy, *William Wirt,* II, 384–85.

and the deliberation were exercises in self-restraint. When Wirt was to argue a case he inevitably took "time to adjust his ideas and arrange the order of his discourse" before speaking; he "avoided . . . extemporary speaking . . . where possible." This "industry" and "aversion to [extemporaneous] speech"[301] might be thought unremarkable in a person of different temperament, but Wirt was known for his gaiety, lightheartedness, and love of repartee.

The career of Wirt presents, ultimately, an example of a man subordinating, channeling, and perhaps guarding against the passions of his nature, and profiting as well as suffering from the process. The very qualities that made Wirt a boon companion, a loving husband and father, a penetrating observer of others, a gifted stylist, a devoted friend, and a spinner of fantasies ensured that his idyll as a James River squire and man of letters would never come to pass. The practice of law was both a protective and a stifling force in Wirt's life: it gave him financial stability, respectability, and prominence, but it also reined in his imaginative temperament and caused him largely to forego literature in order to prepare and argue cases in court. His finest Supreme Court arguments— *Gibbons* v. *Ogden* and *Cherokee Nation* come to mind—were themselves a kind of literature, but not the sort Wirt had in mind when he wrote Benjamin Edwards in 1809 that he hoped, with his pen, to raise "a monument to [his] name." Another sort of monument was erected to Wirt after he succumbed to erysipelas in 1834, "sadly altered" by the "hideous" effects of the disease. He had transformed the office of attorney general of the United States by his long tenure and the consistently high quality of his advocacy; he was to be remembered as the great "government lawyer" of the Marshall Court. In a eulogy former president John Quincy Adams, then a congressman from Massachusetts, said of Wirt:

> If a mind stored with all the learning appropriate to the profession of the law, and decorated with all the elegance of classical literature; if a spirit . . . chastened by the mediations of a profound philosophy; if a brilliant imagination, a discerning intellect, a sound judgment, an indefatigable capacity, and vigorous energy of application, vivified with an ease and rapidity of elocution, copious without redundance and select without affectation; if all these, united with a sportive vein of humor, an inoffensive temper, and an angelic purity of heart—if all these in their combination are the qualities suitable for an Attorney General of the United States—in him they were all eminently combined.[302]

Adams sensed that life had "chastened" Wirt's "spirit"; he also sug-

---

[301] Kennedy, *William Wirt*, II, 385. | [302] Quoted in ibid., 371.

## Chapter IV: *Prominent Lawyers Before the Marshall Court*

gested that the early-nineteenth-century American legal profession had been benefited by that chastening. It was a perceptive and a fitting tribute.

In turning our attention from Wirt to Daniel Webster we encounter the most famous, the most controversial, and perhaps the most charismatic of all the leading Marshall Court advocates. We also encounter, for the first time in this chapter, the phenomenon of historiographic imagery. Assessing Webster's character requires stripping away layers of characterization engrafted on him by successive generations of commentators for whom he has been at times hero and at times villain. An assessment of Webster also requires one to confront the layers of myth, half-truth, and deception Webster himself erected between his person and the world. Webster has fascinated scholars to a degree that no other Marshall Court advocate has, because of his significance as a public figure and because of the strength and complexity of his personality,[303] but he has not been an altogether cooperative subject.

---

[303] The first significant volume on Webster was George Curtis's *Life of Daniel Webster* (2 vols., 1872), an authorized biography. Curtis relies heavily on reminiscences by George Ticknor, Webster's literary executor, and the volume, while detailed and well-written, stops well short of being a penetrating analysis. Peter Harvey's *Reminiscences and Anecdotes of Daniel Webster* (1877) is at once a fascinating source of memorabilia and a highly suspect account: one cannot be sure whether a given tale was varnished by Webster in the telling, Harvey in the retelling, or both. Henry Cabot Lodge, *Daniel Webster* (1883) is a remarkably full analysis of Webster's life, but dominated by Lodge's indignation over Webster's compromises on the politics of slavery in the 1850s. Claude Fuess's *Daniel Webster* (2 vols., 1930) is reliable and sprightly, but openly charitable to its subject and not attentive to manuscript sources. Five specialized studies, Richard Current, *Daniel Webster and the Rise of National Conservatism* (1955), Maurice Baxter, *Daniel Webster and the Supreme Court* (1966), Norman Brown, *Daniel Webster and the Politics of Availability* (1969), Robert Dalzell, *Daniel Webster and the Trial of American Nationalism* (1972), and Sydney Nathans, *Daniel Webster and Jacksonian Democracy* (1973), as their titles indicate, address certain of the major themes of Webster's career in depth. All are useful; none is concerned to explore Webster's character and personality in much detail. Irving Bartlett's biography, *Daniel Webster* (1978), while realizing that "in Webster's case . . . outward simplicity frequently masked our inner complexity" (p. 10), retreats to largely undocumented and not particularly convincing explanations rooted in Webster's "boyhood and adolescence" (p. 11). The breadth of Webster's interests and the multiple levels of his approach to others have made him, like many other accomplished actors, difficult to characterize, and it is perhaps no surprise that scholars have tended to analyze what Webster did rather than who he was. See, in this vein, Maurice Baxter's recent biography, *One and Inseparable: Daniel Webster and the Union* (1984), which has a heavy emphasis on the details of Webster's life but relatively little on his character. Baxter at 428. Future scholarship on Webster will be indebted to the excellent edition of his legal papers, two volumes of which have appeared, under the editorship of Alfred S. Konefsky and Andrew J. King. See Konefsky and King, *The Legal Papers of Daniel Webster* (2 vols., 1982).

Whether assessing Webster as a lawyer or as a person, contemporaries regularly began by remarking on his physical appearance. Observers seemed aware that their physical descriptions of Webster were more than superficial exercises: they sensed that Webster's looks held some clue to his character. The jet-black hair, the high, sloping forehead, the massive head, the huge, dark, piercing eyes, the bushy, prominent eyebrows, the austere expression, the slowness of movement, the sonorous voice, the startlingly white teeth, the swarthy complexion, the imposing carriage—taken together, these features seemed more than striking; they seemed suggestive of a powerful inner force. Thomas Carlyle noted the "tanned complexion," the "amorphous, raglike face," the "dull black eyes under the precipice of brows like dull anthracite furnaces needing only to be blown," and the "mastiff mouth," and concluded that "I have not traced so much of silent berserker rage . . . in any other man."[304]

Webster's imposing physical appearance was accompanied by voracious appetites. His capacity to eat and drink was constantly noted by contemporaries and spoofed by critics; his death was traced to a "mortal disease in one of the great organs of the abdomen"[305] and may have been "hastened by cirrhosis of the liver."[306] Webster suffered periodically from dysentery, gout, and indigestion, which on occasion produced violent sickness. In 1827, when Webster was forty-five, Ralph Waldo Emerson, a fellow passenger on a steamboat, wrote that Webster "was tremendously sick off Pt. Judith. . . . He spouted like a whale and roared like a leviathan, outroared the steam engine and vomited as he wd. address the House."[307] Webster's voraciousness engendered a constant flow of gossip about him.[308] His heavy drinking was so common a theme that Webster remarked on it himself: in 1832, for example, he wrote a friend that "it is not often that good wine is under any roof where I am without my knowing about it."[309] There were also persistent rumors about Webs-

---

[304] Quoted in W. Schaffer, "Daniel Webster—The Lawyer," *Temple L.Q.,* 7:3, 50 (1932).
[305] D. Webster to Millard Fillmore, Oct. 8, 1852, in J. McIntyre, ed., *The Writings and Speeches of Daniel Webster* (18 vols., 1903), XVIII, 557.
[306] Fuess, *Daniel Webster,* II, 383. Webster's stock response to inquiries about his health was that he was suffering from "catarrh" (an inflammation of the mucous membranes in the nose and throat, often the result of an allergic condition). In an earlier letter to Fillmore he had written of his health: "To all others, I gave the general answer, that it is the reason for my catarrh, but

that the disease is light." D. Webster to M. Fillmore, Sept. 28, 1852, in McIntyre, *Writings and Speeches,* XVIII, 554. He then told Fillmore that his stomach, arms, and legs were badly swollen.
[307] R. W. Emerson to William Emerson, June 24, 1827, in R. Rusk, ed., *The Letters of Ralph Waldo Emerson* (6 vols., 1939) I, 202.
[308] See Bartlett, *Daniel Webster,* 200–201; Fuess, *Daniel Webster,* II, 379–83.
[309] Webster to S. White, Sept. 14, 1832, in McIntyre, *Writings and Speeches,* XVII, 525.

ter's sexual affairs. He was reputed to have fathered "a family of eight mulattos," to have had a long-time liaison with his cook, whose portrait he had painted and hung in his house in Marshfield, Massachusetts,[310] and, in general, to have "trod the path of the gross libertine."[311] A recent biographer of Webster has questioned this last characterization, suggesting that it was politically inspired and citing Webster letters that profess outrage toward sexual infidelity.[312]

But documentation of these characteristics of Webster, or any of the numerous features of his personality, confronts the problem of separating fact from carefully fashioned fiction. Webster was anxious to create an estimable public image of himself and was assiduous in his efforts to polish and to preserve that image. At the same time he was vulnerable to his passions and to his driving ambition. The result was a life filled with self-promotional schemes, accompanied by exaggerations and misrepresentations and by promises that went unfulfilled. His financial affairs provide an example. Few nineteenth-century public figures without inherited wealth amassed as much income as Webster did in the forty years between 1812 and his death, yet few were as debt-ridden and financially overextended.[313] Webster's flamboyance, shrewdness, and affinity for power made him remarkably successful at generating income and obtaining credit, but his profligacy (one scholar has claimed that he "seem[ed] to be emotionally comfortable only when he was free to spend")[314] and his love of amenities and accoutrements made him equally successful at squandering whatever money he acquired. In 1842 Webster drew a revealing portrait of himself in a letter to Samuel Lyman:

> It will be said, or may be said hereafter, Mr. Webster was a laborious man in his profession and other pursuits; he never tasted of the bread of idleness; his profession yielded him, at some times, large amounts of income: but he seemed never to have aimed at accumulation, and perhaps was not justly sensible of the importance and duty of preservation. . . . He always said, also, that he was never destined to be

---

[310] J. Swisshelm, *Half a Century* (1880), 128. This statement was an embellishment of charges made thirty years earlier by Jane Swisshelm, an editor of the Pittsburgh *Saturday Visitor,* who wrote an account of Webster's private life in 1850, when she visited Washington. Swisshelm was an abolitionist, and her story was avowedly politically motivated. See Bartlett, *Daniel Webster,* 384–86.

[311] J. Rhodes, *History of the United States* (8 vols., 1913), I, 160.

[312] E.g., D. Webster to G. Ticknor,

Apr. 8, 1833, in McIntyre, *Writings and Speeches,* XVII, 533.

[313] Webster earned over $21,000 from private law practice in 1836, for example, McIntyre, *Writings and Speeches,* XVII, 545, and also received a salary of between $5,000 and $7,500 a year as a cabinet officer, congressman, or senator. An annual income of $25,000 in the 1830s would be worth about $250,000 today; recall that Wirt felt he could retire for life if he had accumulated an estate of $100,000.

[314] Bartlett, *Daniel Webster,* 207.

rich; that no such star presided over his birth. . . . [H]e used to say, when spoken to on such subjects, "Gentlemen, if you have any projects for money-making, I pray you keep me out of them; my singular destiny mars everything of that sort, and would be sure to overwhelm your better fortunes."[315]

Even so apparently candid a self-assessment was not exactly what it seemed. Though Webster may have admitted his profligacy to intimates, or warned them not to enter into financial dealings with him, he was neither diffident nor candid in his efforts to obtain money from others. On the contrary, he regularly approached others for money, made unfulfilled promises of remuneration, and extended himself in new ventures before satisfying outstanding obligations. He incurred a debt in 1827 to a miniaturist who painted the Webster family; that debt was still outstanding in 1851. A series of loans amounting to $10,000 that Webster undertook between 1837 and 1843 was still unpaid at his death.[316]

Webster also attempted to trade his political influence for financial perquisites. He "rarely paid for room or meals" at his favorite hotels, the Revere House in Boston and the Astor House in New York, during the years he was a cabinet official or a senator; the proprietors of those establishments "were accustomed to charge his bills off to good advertising."[317] He borrowed more than $111,000 from the Bank of the United States, one of his clients, between 1837 and 1840, and when Bank officials asked for payment he used his political clout to reduce the debt. (He was eventually relieved of the debt altogether when the Bank ceased operations in 1842.)[318] His negotiations with the Bank made it clear that he was prepared to trade patronage for favorable terms.[319] Throughout his career in politics Webster was given financial support by wealthy persons in Boston who felt he might facilitate their political or economic interests, and Webster was highly receptive to such arrangements.[320]

Webster's financial affairs provide insights into his character. His ability to acquire money, notwithstanding his "singular destiny" on financial matters, testifies to his charisma. All his adult life he attracted

---

[315] D. Webster to S. Lyman, Jan. 15, 1849, in McIntyre, *Writings and Speeches,* XVI, 511.
[316] D. Webster to Sarah Goodrich, Jan. 2, 1851, in C. Wiltse, ed., *Microfilm Edition of the Papers of Daniel Webster* (1971), No. 32013; D. Webster to Caleb Cushing, Sept. 30, 1852, in McIntyre, *Writings and Speeches,* XV, 502. See also C. Fuess, *The Life of Caleb Cushing* (2 vols., 1923), II, 88–91.
[317] Fuess, *Daniel Webster,* II, 380.

[318] See Wiltse, *Papers of Webster,* No. 39835; Bartlett, *Daniel Webster,* 204–205.
[319] See, e.g., Nicholas Biddle to D. Webster, Apr. 3, 1841, in Wiltse, *Papers of Webster,* No. 18720; T. Govan, *Nicholas Biddle, Nationalist and Public Banker* (1959), 389; Bartlett, *Daniel Webster,* 205–206.
[320] For the details, see Fuess, *Daniel Webster,* II, 388–91; Bartlett, *Daniel Webster,* 203–206.

followers and charmed multitudes. Supporters saw him as larger than life, marked for greatness, or as a political potentate: in any case a good man to invest in. Because of his passions and appetites he was vulnerable to others, but he converted that vulnerability into a source of his appeal. He sought out and thrived upon affection, loyalty, and praise; at the same time he became accustomed to relying on and even using those who offered their services. Emerson, a close observer of Webster, spoke of Webster's "three rules of living": "never to pay any debt that can by any possibility be avoided; never to do anything today that can be put off till tomorrow; [and] never to do anything himself which he can get anybody else to do for him."[321] But Webster was also extraordinarily active and hardworking, constantly interested in projects for acquiring new possessions or improving the possessions he held, and generous to excess with friends and strangers. He was at once ingenuous and deceptive, selfish and softhearted. He was kind to animals and "children instinctively sought shelter on his lap or in his arms";[322] at the same time he was perceived by adult contemporaries as "cold and didactic,"[323] "cold and forbidding,"[324] "joining the instinctive egotism of passion with the self-conscious, voluntary, deliberate, calculating egotism of ambition."[325]

Some of the paradoxes in Webster's character resolve themselves if one reminds oneself that he was an instinctive actor, able to disarm others with the force of his personality, and that his acting ability concealed a basic self-absorption and perhaps, down deep, a lack of self-esteem. To intimate personal friends, such as George Ticknor and Peter Harvey, Webster was "simple in manners, and often boyish in spirits . . . hearty, hospitable, and affectionate, steadfast in his love of his family and his attachment to his friends."[326] With them he dropped most of his poses and his need for companionship and support became manifest. To close professional colleagues, such as Jeremiah Mason and Joseph Story, Webster also avoided posturing, although the self-deprecating tone he sometimes adopted in letters to Mason and Story was not always genuine. In 1824 he wrote Mason that he had published a congressional speech "against my own judgment," as it was "clumsy, wanting in method, & tedious," Webster not having "expect[ed] to speak . . . nor [being] ready so to do."[327] When Story requested a copy of the speech Webster had

---

[321] R. W. Emerson, entry for Feb. 7, 1843, in E. Emerson and W. Forbes, eds., *Journals of Ralph Waldo Emerson*, 344 (10 vols., 1909), VI, 344.

[322] Fuess, *Daniel Webster*, II, 407.

[323] [Anonymous], *Sketches of United States' Senators of the Session of 1837–8* (1839), 19.

[324] T. Hamilton, *Men and Manners*

*in America* (2 vols., 1834), II, 152.

[325] T. Parker, *A Discourse Occurred by the Death of Daniel Webster* (1853), 81.

[326] Harvey, *Reminiscences*, 316.

[327] D. Webster to J. Mason, Apr. 19, 1824, in Webster Papers, Library of Congress.

delivered in honor of Story's receipt of the Dane Professorship of Law at Harvard, Webster replied, "I find it quite impossible to recall the recollection of my observation," reminding Story that he had "spoke[n] without preparation & without notes," and suggesting that his speech "may as well be forgotten as not."[328] These disclaimers were not quite candid. Webster carefully prepared his speeches, rewrote them significantly for print, was entirely aware of his exalted reputation as an orator, and took special care to polish his speeches when he thought they would be widely disseminated.

As Webster moved beyond the circle of his close acquaintances to the world at large, his behavior became more studied. He could be "freezingly indifferent" to strangers who sought him out in Congress;[329] he frequently suggested to correspondents that they destroy letters from him; he threatened to turn down speaking engagements if he felt he would not be given featured billing;[330] he gravely professed the absence of a financial or personal interest in issues where such an interest clearly existed.[331] In short, he consistently acted a part and sought to foster and to preserve a public image. The constant acting that characterized Webster's response to others, when coupled with his tendency to manipulate even his closest friends, and his regular resort to disingenuous or dishonest explanations for his conduct, tempts one to revive an earlier characterization of him as a calculatingly selfish egotist. But Webster's egotism was accompanied by a strong need to have close relationships with others, and he became dependent on the persons with whom he was intimate. When his first wife, Grace Fletcher Webster, died suddenly of tuberculosis in 1828, Webster wrote a friend that he felt "a vacuum, an indifference, a want of motive which I cannot well describe."[332] Webster's dependence on

---

[328] D. Webster to J. Story, Sept. 5, 1829, in *Proc. Mass. Hist. Soc.*, 14:406 (1901).

[329] O. Dyer, *Great Senators of the United States Forty Years Ago* (1889), 238.

[330] See, e.g., D. Webster to Edward Everett, Feb. 23, 1825, in Wiltse, *Papers of Webster*, No. 04864; Bartlett, *Daniel Webster*, 108–109.

[331] Compare Webster's speech in the Senate in January 1835, on the settlement of claims made by merchants whose property had been damaged by France in the Revolutionary War, with two letters he wrote to Henry Kinsman, on January 11 and January 17, 1834. In these letters Webster assured Kinsman, his law partner in Boston, that he was prepared to use his authority in the Senate to push for settlement of the claims

out of the federal treasury and that he expected to be compensated for the processing of certain Boston merchants' claims. In the Senate speech he said that he had "not the slightest interest in these claims," and that he had "never been conferred with or retained by anyone, or spoken to as counsel for any one of them." The Senate speech is in McIntyre, *Writings and Speeches*, VII, 152; the letters to Kinsman are, respectively, in ibid., XVI, 283 and in Wiltse, *Papers of Webster*, No. 11390. See also Bartlett, *Daniel Webster*, 199–200. On Webster's ethics while a congressman, see Konefsky and King, *Legal Papers*, II, 306–43.

[332] D. Webster to Eliza Buckminster Lee, May 18, 1828, in McIntyre, *Writings and Speeches*, XVII, 457.

his intimates was not always obvious to them; a year before her death Grace had written him that "I sometimes feel that if I did not obtrude myself upon you I should be a thing quite forgotten."[333]

Such was the man—with the memorable childhood nickname "Black Dan"—who first appeared in the Marshall Court in the 1814 Term, arguing two minor prize cases.[334] His career to that point had followed the same pattern we have seen in other Marshall Court advocates. Born in moderate circumstances near Salisbury, New Hampshire, in 1782, Webster was encouraged by his father, Ebenezer, a farmer, tavern-keeper, and lay judge, to attend Phillips Exeter Academy in 1796, so that he might become a schoolteacher. Webster expected that his formal education would conclude with Exeter, but in 1797 Ebenezer resolved to send him to Dartmouth College, then a momentous step for the Webster family. Webster wrote in his autobiography, "I was quite overcome, and my head grew dizzy. . . . Excellent, excellent parent! I cannot think of him, even now, without turning child again."[335] At college Webster emerged as a convivial, free-spending, sometimes overbearing student who was nonetheless well respected by his peers, although not conspicuously successful in his academic performance.[336] He conceived the idea of studying law while at Dartmouth, and when he returned to Salisbury in 1801 he began reading law in a desultory fashion. Shortly thereafter he temporarily abandoned his legal studies to teach school in Fryburg, Maine, and then returned to Salisbury, all the while complaining that legal works were as "dry, hard and stubborn as an old maid."[337] He would later suggest that "a boy of twenty, with no previous knowledge of such subjects, cannot understand Coke," and "it is folly to set him upon such an author." In two letters written at the time he claimed that "it is not he who spends most hours over his books that is the most successful student," but also complained that "if [a man] would be a great lawyer, he must first consent to be a great drudge."[338] Academic learning, in law or elsewhere, was never to become a passion of Webster's; his intelligence was essentially intuitive.

By 1805 Webster had been admitted to the New Hampshire bar, thanks in part to the patronage of Christopher Gore, who had hired Webs-

---

[333] G. F. Webster to D. Webster, Feb. 15, 1827, in C. Van Tyne, *Letters of Daniel Webster* (1902), 568.

[334] The St. Lawrence, 8 Cranch 434 (1814); The Grotus, 8 Cranch 456 (1814).

[335] D. Webster, "Autobiography," in McIntyre, *Writings and Speeches*, XVII, 12.

[336] For background on Webster's college years see Fuess, *Daniel Webs-* ter, 5–61; Bartlett, *Daniel Webster*, 22–27.

[337] D. Webster to Thomas Merrill, Jan. 4, 1803, in McIntyre, *Writings and Speeches*, XVII, 128.

[338] D. Webster, "Autobiography," ibid., 14; D. Webster to James H. Bingham, Dec. 23, 1803, ibid., 154; Webster to Merrill, Jan. 4, 1803, supra, note 337.

ter as an apprentice in his Boston office a year earlier. After his admission to practice Webster settled in Boscaven, New Hampshire, six miles from Salisbury, so that he could be near his parents. A year later his father died, and in 1807 his brother Ezekiel was also admitted to practice law. An arrangement was made between Daniel and Ezekiel in which the latter remained in the Salisbury area, taking over Daniel's office in Boscaven and the management of the family farm, while Daniel transferred his practice to Portsmouth, where he was to live "nine . . . very happy years,"[339] and where he first established his reputation as a remarkable courtroom presence. In 1810 William Plumer, Jr., a colleague of Webster, gave this assessment of Webster in Portsmouth:

> As a speaker he is perhaps the best at the bar. His language is correct, his gestures good; and his delivery slow, articulate, and distinct. He excels in the statement of facts; but he is not thought to be a deep-read lawyer. His manners are not pleasing, being haughty, cold, and over-bearing.[340]

Webster thrived in Portsmouth, rapidly making money, acquiring property, getting involved in politics, and coming to the attention of notable members of the New Hampshire bar, such as Jeremiah Mason and Jeremiah Smith. By 1812, when Webster was thirty, he had become a visible force in political and legal circles, and had been elected to Congress as a Federalist. He had also married Grace Fletcher (in 1808) and had fathered two children.[341] In December 1812, now established in Washington, Webster wrote a friend that while "wholly inexperienced in public affairs," he intended to "comprehend the objects, understand the maxims, and imbibe the spirit of [Washington's] administration, persuaded as I am that the principles which [then] prevailed . . . form the only anchorage in which our political prosperity and safety can find any hold in this dangerous and stormy time."[342] The idea that the "principles" of the early Republic could be a point of "anchorage" in the nineteenth century was to become a recurrent theme of Webster's political rhetoric.

Webster's entry into politics, far from detracting from his legal career, facilitated it. His regular attendance in Washington made him much more accessible to the Supreme Court than the average New Eng-

---

[339] D. Webster, "Autobiography," in McIntyre, Writings and Speeches, XVII.
[340] W. Plumer, Jr., diary entry, August 1810, quoted in ibid., 546–47. For more detail on Webster's early professional career, see Konefsky and King, Legal Papers, I, 9–58.

[341] Fuess, Daniel Webster, I, 103–21.
[342] D. Webster to Timothy Pickering, Dec. 11, 1812, in McIntyre, Writings and Speeches, XVI, 12.

land lawyer; indeed, until 1830 comparatively few lawyers from the New England states appeared before the Marshall Court.[343] From 1814 until his death in 1852 Webster was in Washington, in some official capacity, every year except those between 1818 and 1821, when he was practicing law full-time in Boston. During the period of the Marshall Court covered by this study, Webster appeared as counsel in every Term save those of 1816 and 1833. He continued to argue cases in the Taney Court, appearing consecutively between 1836 and 1852, with the sole exception of the 1845 Term. All told, Webster argued 168 cases before the Court, 119 in the years between 1815 and 1836.[344] Of Webster's Marshall Court cases, 14 involved issues of constitutional law, 9 of which were actually decided on constitutional grounds.[345] Webster's position prevailed in six of those nine cases.

Webster's first major case before the Marshall Court, the tenth he argued, was *Dartmouth College*. One student of Webster's legal career has said that as a result of his performance in the *Dartmouth College* case "he became one of the leaders of the bar";[346] and in 1901 the president of Dartmouth College said that "it is doubtful if the name of any educational institution in the land is so inseparably blended with the name of a graduate, or even of a founder, as is the name of Dartmouth with that of Daniel Webster."[347] Webster's triumph in *Dartmouth College* ushered in the most successful decade in his career: in the eleven years after *Dartmouth College* Webster had his greatest legal and political successes, established a new standard for lawyers' salaries, and delivered three of his most historic speeches. The halcyon years of Webster's legal career coincided with the major phase of the Marshall Court; in that period both Webster and the Court came to be identified in the public minds as guardians of the Constitution, the first principles of the Framers, and the Union itself.

The list of Webster's Marshall Court cases between the 1819 and the 1830 Terms reads like a primer in early American constitutional history. He argued and won *Dartmouth College, McCulloch v. Maryland, Cohens v. Virginia, Gibbons v. Ogden, Osborn v. Bank of the United States,* and *Mason v. Haile.* During those terms *Ogden v. Saunders* was the only major constitutional case he lost. This record would itself have made him a major figure in the history of the Marshall Court. But Webs-

---

[343] See Warren, *History of the American Bar,* 367–68, 408–409.
[344] The number of cases argued by individual attorneys from the 1815 through the 1835 Terms can be determined by the (tedious) process of counting names in the United States Reports.

[345] For a list of Webster's reported Marshall Court cases, see Baxter, *Daniel Webster and the Supreme Court,* 247–51.
[346] Ibid., 108.
[347] W. Tucker, *My Generation* (1901), 290.

ter's greatest contribution to the Court arguably lay outside his courtroom performances. In his role as the greatest orator of his age he was an apologist for, and a publicist of, the propositions of Marshall Court jurisprudence. In his orations in the 1820s Webster argued, as had a majority of the Court, on behalf of the primacy of the Union and the use of federal powers to promote the "great objects" of the Constitution; against unrestrained actions on the part of state legislatures, especially when such actions sought to restrict the jurisdictional reach of the federal judiciary; on behalf of private property when threatened by state activity; and on behalf of promotion for "commerce" and "improvements." These propositions were not simply arguments advanced by Webster in the course of representing clients; they were articles of faith, articulated as well in his less partisan and more popularly directed role as orator. Even when Webster had nothing at stake except his "patriotic duty," he continued his efforts to articulate and to justify the maxims of Marshall Court jurisprudence. Three orations from the 1820s will illustrate.

Webster was, as students of his career have regularly acknowledged, the leading orator of his time. In early-nineteenth-century America, as we have seen, oratory, legal discourse, and political discourse were closely intermingled, and in the hands of accomplished practitioners oratory became the principal medium of mass communication for the age. Webster was particularly adept at fusing the multiple appeals of oratory: his orations effectively commingled physical presence, tone of voice, imagery, and logical argument. The effect on his audience was sometimes overwhelming, as a passage from one of George Ticknor's letters reveals. After hearing Webster deliver an oration celebrating the bicentennial of the Plymouth landing on December 22, 1820, Ticknor wrote:

> His manner carried me away completely. . . . It *must* have been a great, a very great performance. . . . I never was so excited by public speaking before in my life. Three or four times I thought my temples would burst with the gush of blood. . . . When I came out I was almost afraid to come over to him. It seemed to me as if he was like the mount that might not be touched, and that burned with fire. I was beside myself, and am so still.[348]

The Plymouth speech was the first of Webster's major orations in the 1820s. Its theme was "the point of time where we now stand, both in relation to our ancestors and to posterity."[349] Such a theme was especially significant for Webster's contemporaries. The idea that the past, present, and future were logically and inevitably linked to one another, as we have seen, was an emergent feature of elite American intellectual

---

[348] Greenslet, *George Ticknor,* 330. | [349] Ibid.

276

culture in the early nineteenth century. Those who listened to Webster at Plymouth had come to take as axiomatic the proposition that the destiny of the American nation was closely tied to an understanding of the meaning of its recent history. As we shall see, the Marshall Court was to claim authority to define the meaning of the immediate past; moreover, the Court was able to use its reconstructions of history to enhance its contemporary authority. Webster performed an analogous function in his Plymouth speech; he set forth the "meaning" of the first settlement in New England. "It is a noble faculty of our nature," he began,

> which enables us to connect our thoughts, our sympathies, and our happiness with what is distant in place and time; and, looking before and after, to hold communion at once with our ancestors and our posterity. . . . We live in the past by a knowledge of its history, and in future by hope and anticipation. By ascending to our association with our ancestors . . . we seem to mingle our own existence with theirs. . . . And in like manner, by running along the line of future time, by contemplating the probable fortunes of those who are coming after us, . . . we protract our own earthly being, and seem to avoid whatever is future, as well as all that is past, into . . . our earthly existence."[350]

Webster then described vividly the history of the New World: the "bloody Indian wars,"[351] the "violent measures . . . pursued against the Colonies in the reign of Charles the Second,"[352] and the eventual rise in New England of a "commercial character,"[353] so that Boston became "a place of great wealth and trade."[354] Having completed more than half of his oration, he then turned to "the point on which we stand" in "look[ing] back."[355] A sanguine catalogue of the features of early-nineteenth-century American civilization followed. Population "has overflowed its boundaries": "nor do rivers, or mountains, or seas resist the principles of industry and enterprise. . . . The imagination hardly keeps pace with the progress of population, improvement, and civilization."[356] The "establishment and prosperous commencement of the present government" had fostered "internal improvement": "more has been done for roads, canals, and other public works, within the last thirty years than in all our former history."[357] Moreover, "literature and taste have not been stationary": "some advancement has been made in the elegant as well as in the useful arts."[358]

---

[350] D. Webster, "A Discourse Delivered at Plymouth, on the 22d of December, 1820," in McIntyre, *Writings and Speeches*, I, 181–82.
[351] Ibid., at 203.
[352] Ibid.
[353] Ibid., 205.
[354] Ibid., 206.
[355] Ibid.
[356] Ibid., 206–207.
[357] Ibid., 210.
[358] Ibid.

Webster then sought to define the meaning of the events he had just described; to show how a judicious description of America's past and present clarified "the nature and constitution of society and government in this country."[359] Here the purpose of his speech became clear. History was a link to the present, and it was also a vindication of the present: a source of first principles. Through historical exegesis one identified the fundamental values of American civilization. The persistence of such values over time demonstrated their fundamentality; once asserted as fundamental those values became guides for the future.

The culmination of Webster's Plymouth oration was thus a statement of the "entirely popular . . . privileges"[360] on which American civilization was based. The first was "the rights of property." Since "the true principle of a free and popular government" was "to construct it as to give to . . . a very great majority, an interest in its preservation," it was "political wisdom" to "found government on property; and to establish such distribution of property . . . as to interest the great majority of society in the support of the government." And that wisdom, Webster suggested, was "the true theory and the actual practice of our republican institutions."[361] He then traced the connection in republican thought between "division of property" and the "system of representation"[362] and reminded his audience that in America "salutary checks" had been made "[on] government altogether elective."[363] Webster then skimmed over the remaining first principles of republican theory—virtue and liberty— and then went on to tie the maintenance of those principles to the continued preservation of the Union as governed by a properly interpreted Constitution. He saw nineteenth-century public education as "inspiring a salutary and conservative principle of virtue . . . at an early age."[364] He declared that his generation was "bound to maintain public liberty" and "to convince the world that order and law, religion and morality, the rights of conscience, and the rights of property, may all be preserved and secured in the most perfect manner."[365] And then he turned directly to constitutional law. "It is now more than thirty years," he said, "that [the] states have been united under the Federal Constitution, and . . . it is impossible that this period of their history should not be regarded as distinguished by signal prosperity and success. . . . We can entertain no better wish for our country than that this government may be preserved; nor have a clearer duty than to maintain and support it in the full exercise of all its just constitutional powers."[366]

In the last sentences Webster claimed that property, virtue, and

---

[359] Ibid.
[360] Ibid., 211.
[361] Ibid., 214–15.
[362] Ibid., 216.

[363] Ibid., 217.
[364] Ibid., 218.
[365] Ibid., 221.
[366] Ibid., 223–24.

liberty—the bedrock values of American civilization as he defined it—could be preserved by the "full exercise" of the "constitutional powers" of the federal government. With *McCulloch* and *Dartmouth College* having been decided in the preceding year, and *Cohens* v. *Virginia* slated for argument two months later, Webster's message was unmistakable. His survey of history was intended to demonstrate not only that "the country has risen from a state of colonial subjection; it has established an independent government, and is now in the undisturbed enjoyment of peace and political security,"[367] but also that continued maintenance of that felicitous state might well depend on support for the constitutional doctrines of the Marshall Court.

Ticknor's comments, quoted above, suggest the mesmerizing effect Webster's Plymouth oration had on his audience; when the speech was published a year later its impact was no less considerable. John Adams, now in his eighty-seventh year, wrote Webster that "the observations . . . on the past, present and future of America are sagacious, profound, and affecting in a high degree. Mr. Burke is no longer entitled to the phrase—the most consummate orator of modern times."[368] James Kent added that "the reflections, the sentiments, the morals, the patriotism, the eloquence, the imagination of this admirable production are exactly what I anticipated: elevated, just, and true."[369] Webster had not only established himself as the "consummate orator" of his time, he had emerged as a guardian and interpreter of the American past for his generation.

In 1825 Webster was asked to deliver an oration on the fiftieth anniversary of the Battle of Bunker Hill. He again took the occasion to venerate and to recast the Revolutionary past.[370] He sought, as he had at Plymouth, to "show our deep sense of the value and importance of the achievements of our ancestors," and to "foster a constant regard for the privileges of the Revolution."[371] He also added some contemporary themes, more in evidence in the mid-1820s: "the general progress . . . in legislation, in commerce . . . and, above all, in liberal ideas";[372] the fact that with expanded suffrage "the people have begun, in all forms of government, to think, and to reassess, our affairs of state."[373] His point

---

[367] Ibid., 224.
[368] J. Adams to D. Webster, Dec. 23, 1821, quoted in Curtis, *Daniel Webster*, I, 194.
[369] J. Kent to D. Webster, Dec. 29, 1821, quoted in ibid.
[370] Webster also kept the crowd under control when some temporary seating collapsed. For a contemporary account, see J. Quincy, *Figures of the Past* (2 vols., 1883), I, 136–39. Quincy

recalled Webster saying after his speech, "I never desire to behold again the awful spectacle of so many human faces all turned towards me." Quoted in ibid., 139. See also Fuess, *Daniel Webster*, I, 296–99.
[371] For this address I have used Williston, *Eloquence*, V, 299–321 as my source; the quoted passage is at 302.
[372] Ibid., 304.
[373] Ibid., 316.

was that the new features of life in America—improvements, commerce, liberal ideas, extended voter participation—were vindications of the first principles: property led to improvements and commerce, liberty and virtue to liberal ideas and extended suffrage. He closed with a passage that, in its celebration of the future possibilities of a properly guided nation, was reminiscent of *McCulloch* v. *Maryland* or *Gibbons* v. *Ogden:*

> Let our age be the age of improvement. . . . Let us develop the resources of our land, call forth its powers, build up its institutions, promote all its great interests, and see whether we also, in our day and generation, may not perform something worthy to be remembered. Let us cultivate a true spirit of union and harmony. In pursuing the great objects, which our condition points out to us, let us act under a settled conviction, and an habitual feeling, that these twenty-four states are one country. Let our conceptions be enlarged to the circle of our duties. Let us extend our ideas over the whole of the last field in which we are called to act. . . .[374]

Webster's third great oration in the 1820s was his eulogy on John Adams and Thomas Jefferson, delivered on August 2, 1826, about a month after their deaths. His eulogy took the form, familiar in Webster's time, of a "discourse on the life, character and services" of his subjects; it required more attention to human personalities, and less to glittering generalities, than the Plymouth or Bunker Hill orations. Nonetheless, Webster took an occasional opportunity to link past, present, and future in the manner of his two earlier speeches. One such example came in a passage on Charles Carroll, with Adams's and Jefferson's deaths the last surviving of the signers of the Declaration:

> [W]hat thoughts, what interesting reflections must fill his elevated and devout soul! If he dwell on the past, how touching its recollections; if he survey the present, how happy, how joyous, how full of the fruition of that hope, which his ardent patriotism indulged; if he glance at the future, how does the prospect of his country's advancement almost bewilder his weakened conception![375]

Here again Webster performed his familiar role as guardian and recaster of the Revolutionary experience. The past was "touching": an experiment that had been vindicated; the present was "full of the fruition of that hope"; the future was "bewildering" in its sense of "advancement." Americans could be "joyous" because the spirit of the Revolution had been vindicated and expanded upon. Lest anyone miss the point, Webster concluded by asserting that

---

[374] Ibid., 321.

[375] Ibid., 374, 412.

with America, and in America, a new era commences in human affairs. This era is distinguished by Free Representative Governments, by . . . improved systems of national intercourse, by a newly awakened, and an unconquerable spirit of free inquiry, and by diffusion of knowledge throughout the community. . . .[376]

Property, liberty, virtue, improvement, commerce, the liberal pursuit of knowledge, and union—the identified first principles of the Founding Fathers and the code words of patriotic discourse in the 1820s—surfaced again in the most famous of all of Webster's speeches, his "Second Reply to Hayne,"[377] delivered on Tuesday, January 26, and Wednesday, January 27, 1830. The Hayne speech had a little something for everybody; its principal significance for us is as a popularization of and apology for the constitutional doctrines of the Marshall Court. The pretext for the speech was a debate over the management of the public lands, with Webster and Senator Robert Hayne of South Carolina taking predictable sectional positions.[378] Webster then expanded the debate to include slavery and nullification, two positions on which South Carolinians in the late 1820s were both aggressive and defensive. Hayne, prompted by John C. Calhoun, responded in kind, giving an articulate exposition of the compact theory of sovereignty—the idea, on which the nullification doctrine rested, that the states had not surrendered their basic sovereign powers in forming the Union. Compact theory was not novel constitutional doctrine, having appeared as early as the Virginia and Kentucky Resolutions of 1798 and having been vigorously argued by critics of *McCulloch* v. *Maryland, Cohens* v. *Virginia,* and *Green* v. *Biddle.*[379] In the Webster–Hayne exchange, however, compact theory was combined with nullification for the first time in Congress.[380] Nullification upped the political ante, since it converted compact theory from an abstract proposition to a concrete procedure by which states denied the powers of Congress or the Supreme Court to be "the exclusive judge of the extent as well as the limitations of [their] powers."[381]

---

[376] Ibid., 413.

[377] The speech has come to be known by that name: see Fuess, *Daniel Webster,* I, 361–85; Dalzell, *Webster and Nationalism,* 5; Bartlett, *Daniel Webster,* 117. It is termed "Second Speech on Foote's Resolution" in McIntyre, *Writings and Speeches,* VI, 3, referring to the public lands resolution introduced by Senator Samuel A. Foote that ostensibly prompted it. My source here is McIntyre, *Writings and Speeches,* VI, 366.

[378] At the time of the Hayne–Webster debate the New England states favored a policy limiting cheap sales of public lands in the Mississippi Valley, and southern states tended to oppose such a policy. Foote was a senator from Connecticut, whose resolution instructed the Senate Committee on Public Lands to limit sales. See W. Freehling, *Prelude to Civil War* (1966), 176–86.

[379] For a fuller discussion of compact theory, see Chapter VIII.

[380] See Fuess, *Daniel Webster,* 371; Freehling, *Prelude,* 176–86.

[381] Hayne, quoted in Fuess, *Daniel Webster* I, 371.

Webster took the opportunity to restate the articles of his political creed, which emerged as simplified and dramatized versions of the doctrinal propositions handed down by the Court in such cases as *Martin, McCulloch, Cohens, Green,* and *Osborn* v. *Bank of the United States.*[382] The timing was auspicious: eighteen days before Webster's speech Marshall, with the nullification doctrine in mind, had written Story that "the crisis of our Constitution is now upon us," and "a strong dispensation to prostrate the Judiciary has shown itself."[383] When Story arrived in Washington he reportedly expressed concern over the impact Hayne's defense of nullification had made, and "offered to aid [Webster] in looking up materials to be used in his reply." Webster told Story to "give yourself no uneasiness . . . I will grind [Hayne] as fine as a pinch of snuff."[384] And Webster did: his reaffirmation of the belief that "liberty and union" were "one and inseparable" was just what a majority of his contemporaries wanted to hear. "I never spoke in the presence of an audience so eager and so sympathetic," Webster wrote to Warren Dutton. "The public feeling here was on our side almost universally."[385] "I never knew what the constitution really was," Webster's son Fletcher wrote him, "till your last . . . speech. I thought it was a compact between the states."[386]

Webster made three central points in his reply to Hayne, two of which were taken directly from Marshall Court cases, the third a practical rather than a theoretical argument. His first point was a vivid restatement of the Marshall Court's logical sequence for justifying judicial review of the actions of state legislatures where constitutional issues were at stake. The nullification doctrine, of course, denied that such review was inevitable. The Court's logic, itself based on appeals to first principles, had been embodied in the syllogism (step one) "government of the people"; (step two) "Constitution as mandate of the people"; (step three) "federal judiciary as final interpreter of Constitution." Webster's dramatized version of that syllogism ran as follows:

[Step One]
I hold [the American government] to be a popular government, elected by the people. . . . This government . . . is the independent offering of the popular will. It is not the creature of State legislatures; nay, more, if the whole truth must be told, the people brought it into exist-

---

[382] 9 Wheat. 738 (1824).
[383] J. Marshall to J. Story, Jan. 8, 1830, quoted in Warren, *Supreme Court,* II, 187.
[384] The story is told in Harvey, *Reminiscences,* 156.

[385] D. Webster to W. Dutton, Mar. 8, 1830, in McIntyre, *Writings and Speeches,* XVII, 494.
[386] D. F. Webster to D. Webster, Mar. 23, 1830, in Wiltse, *Papers of Webster,* No. 8592.

ence, established it, and have hitherto supported it, for the very purpose
. . . of imposing certain salutary restraints on State sovereignties . . .[387]

[Step Two]
Who, then, shall construe this grant of the people? . . . With whom
do they require this ultimate right of deciding on the powers of the
government. . . . They have left it with the government itself, in its
appropriate branches. . . . The people have wisely provided, in the
Constitution itself, a proper, suitable mode and tribunal for settling
questions of constitutional law. . . . The Constitution has itself pointed
out, ordained, and established that authority. . . . [b]y declaring . . .
that "the Constitution, and the laws of the United States made in pursuance thereof, shall be the supreme law of the land, any thing in the
constitution or laws of any State to the contrary notwithstanding". . . .[388]

[Step Three]
No State law is to be valid which comes in conflict with the constitution,
or any law of the United States passed in pursuance of it. But who
shall decide this question of interference. . . . Thus . . . the Constitution decides also, by declaring, "that the judicial power shall extend
to all cases arising under the Constitution and laws of the United
States. . . ." In pursuance of these clear and express provisions, Congress established, at its very first session, in the judicial act, a mode
for carrying them into full effect, and for bringing all questions of
constitutional power to the final decision of the Supreme Court. It then
. . . became a government.[389]

In these passages one can find vivid evidence of what Story called
Webster's "clearness and downright simplicity of statement" and "his
power of disentangling a complicated proposition, and resolving it into
elements so plain as to reach the most common minds."[390] If the Court's
original syllogism justifying its power had been inaccessible, it could not
have remained so after Webster's version. Advocates of nullification denied the syllogism's conclusion, but could they deny its premise, that the
American Constitution was a mandate of the people? Having placed
Hayne in an awkward theoretical posture, Webster then turned to the
practical difficulties of nullification, exhibiting in the process what commentators termed "his fertility in illustrations drawn from practical
sources"[391]:

---

[387] McIntyre, *Writings and Speeches,*
VI, 66.
[388] Ibid., 67.
[389] Ibid., 68.
[390] J. Story, unpublished manuscript,
quoted in E. Wheeler, *Daniel Webster,
The Expounder of the Constitution*
(1905), 59–60.
[391] Ibid.

And now . . . let me run [Hayne's] doctrine a little into its practical application. . . . We will take the existing case of the tariff law. South Carolina . . . will, we must suppose, pass a law of her legislature, declaring the [federal] tariff laws null and void. . . . But the collector at Charleston is collecting the duties imposed by these tariff laws. He therefore, must be stopped. . . . The militia of the State will be called out to sustain the nullifying act. . . . But . . . the collector would probably not desist. . . . He would show [the militia] the law of Congress, the treaty instruction, and his own oath of office. . . .

Here would ensue a pause. . . . [The militia] would inquire whether it was not somewhat dangerous to resist a law of the United States. What would be the nature of their offence . . . if they, by military force and array, resisted the execution in Carolina of a law of the United States, and it should turn out, after all, that the law *was* *constitutional?* [The answer would be] Treason. . . .

Direct collision, therefore, between force and force, is the unavoidable result of that remedy for the revision of unconstitutional laws which [Hayne] contends for.[392]

Having suggested that nullification "[led] directly to disunion and civil commotion,"[393] Webster then turned to his last theme and to the basic premise of his speech, a premise again derived from the Marshall Court. He reasserted the theme of his earlier orations, that maintenance of the Constitution, "preservation of our Federal Union," and "happiness, property, and renown" for America were linked:

It is to that Union we owe our safety at home and our consideration and dignity abroad. . . . That Union we reached only by the discipline of our virtues in the severe school of adversity. It had its origin in the necessities of disordered finance, prostrate commerce, and ruined credit. Under its benign influences these great interests immediately awoke as from the dead, and sprang forth with newness of life. . . . Although our territory has stretched out wider and wider and our population spread farther and farther, they have not outrun its protection or its benefits. . . .

While the Union lasts we have high, exciting, gratifying prospects spread out before us and our children. Beyond that I seek not to penetrate the veil. God grant that in my day, at least, the curtain may not rise! . . . When my eyes shall be turned to behold for the last time the sun in heaven, may I not see him shining on the broken and dishonored fragments of a once glorious Union; on States dissevered, descendant, belligerent; on a land rent with civil feuds. . . . Let their last feeble and lingering glance [not contemplate] . . . those other words of delusion and folly, "Liberty first and Union afterwards"; but everywhere

---

[392] McIntyre, *Writings and Speeches,* VI, 71–72.

[393] Ibid., 72.

. . . that other sentiment—Liberty *and* Union, now and for ever, one and inseparable![394]

Liberty, "the great interests" of property and commerce, Union, virtue, and the Constitution had all been linked in a seemingly unbreakable chain of logic. Two weeks after Webster concluded his speech Story wrote Sarah Waldo Story that it was "the ablest [Webster] ever delivered at any time in Congress," and that it was above all "a discussion of the great Constitutional principles of the Government."[395] And in December 1832, a month after his re-election, Andrew Jackson, in response to a nullification ordinance drafted by South Carolina, declared that no state could constitutionally repeal a federal law and that he would force compliance with the law if necessary. "The Constitution of the United States forms a Government," Jackson said, "not a league."[396] Marshall Court doctrine had become executive policy.

The preceding pages have sought to provide evidence that Webster's greatest contribution to the Marshall Court was as a publicist for its doctrines rather than as a catalyst in his capacity as an advocate for the generation of those doctrines themselves. Webster was, however, of another view. Asked late in his life to name the most important single speech he had made, Webster said that it was not his reply to Hayne, but his "forensic efforts."[397] He singled out his arguments in *Dartmouth College* and *Gibbons* v. *Ogden* as those of his contributions "that have given me the most satisfaction." He claimed, in addition, that in *Gibbons* "the opinion of the court, as rendered by the chief justice, was little else than a recital of my argument." The "chief justice told me," Webster said, "that he had little to do but to repeat that argument, as that covered the whole ground."[398]

Webster made this assessment in a conversation to a young protégé whom Webster expected might at some point commit it to print, so it may well have been more authorized than authoritative. There is evidence suggesting that Webster's "forensic efforts" in *Dartmouth College* and *Gibbons* did not in fact have the kind of impact that he claimed. We have seen that his great success in *Dartmouth College* was less as an expositor of constitutional doctrine than as a behind-the-scenes operator, with a keen sense for the nuances of getting cases heard, and decided, in the most advantageous procedural form. Only if one widens the term "forensic" to include lawyering skills practiced out of court—skills that

---

[394] Ibid., 74–75.
[395] J. Story to S. W. Story, Jan. 29, 1830, in W. Story, *Life and Letters,* II, 34.
[396] The language from Jackson's proclamation is in J. Richardson, comp., *A Compilation of the Message and Papers of the Presidents, 1789–1905* (11 vols., 1907), II, 647.
[397] Quoted in Harvey, *Reminiscences,* 140.
[398] Quoted in ibid., 142.

Webster unmistakably demonstrated in the *Dartmouth College* case—does Webster's assessment of his influence on the Court in that case seem accurate.

*Gibbons* presents a more striking contrast between Webster's recollections and his actual contributions. In that case Webster not only claimed that Marshall's opinion in *Gibbons* was ''a mere recital of my argument,'' he went on to comment on William Wirt's performance in the case. In the conversation in which Marshall reportedly said that he had only to repeat Webster's argument in writing the opinion, Marshall also, as Webster recalled it,

> never referred to the fact that Mr. Wirt had made an argument. He did not speak of it once. That was very singular. It was an accident, I think. Mr. Wirt was a great lawyer, and a great man. But sometimes a man gets a hunch, and doesn't hit right. That was one of the occasions. But that was nothing against Mr. Wirt.[399]

According to Peter Harvey, who related Webster's remarks, Webster and Wirt had competing theories of the *Gibbons* case. Webster supposedly felt that an argument emphasizing exclusive federal power to regulate commerce would be most likely to prevail; Wirt preferred an argument based on congressional power under the Patents Clause to ''promote the Progress of Science and useful Arts.'' In Wheaton's Reports Webster was reported as arguing that the latter power was relevant to the *Gibbons* case, but that ''he should insist . . . the less of [this point], as . . . he had said so much upon what appeared to him the more important and interesting part of the argument.''[400]

A reading of Wheaton's Reports, however, contradicts Webster's recollections. While Webster's argument was devoted almost exclusively to the Commerce Clause argument, he did mention the Patents Clause, and claimed that ''to confer reward by exclusive grants, even if it were but a part of the use of the writing or invention, was not supposed to be a power properly to be exercised by the States.''[401] Moreover, of the twenty-seven pages of Wirt's argument reported by Wheaton, fifteen were devoted either explicitly to the Commerce Clause argument or, more generally, to the issue of exclusive versus concurrent federal regulatory power.[402] As for the quality of Wirt's argument, the Richmond *Enquirer* called it ''the finest effort of human genius ever exhibited in a Court of Justice.''[403] In a letter in which Wirt described his preparations for *Gibbons* v. *Ogden,* he noted that Webster was as ''ambitious as Caesar,'' and ''will not be outdone by any man, if it is within the compass of his

---

[399] Ibid., 142–43.
[400] 9 Wheat. at 33.
[401] Ibid., 32.

[402] Ibid., 159–65, 176–85.
[403] Richmond *Enquirer,* Mar. 2, 1824.

power to avoid it.'' Wirt had previously written ''ambitious as Lucifer,'' but thought better of it.[404]

Webster's argument was not exactly ''take[n] in'' by Marshall ''as a baby takes in its mother's milk.''[405] Webster had stressed the exclusiveness of the commerce power and the presence of a federal coastal regulation licensing steamboats that purportedly conflicted with New York's grant. Wirt had reiterated these positions, but also stressed, as an alternative, that commerce was a ''complex, multifarious and indefinite'' subject, and that ''one or more branches . . . might be given exclusively to Congress; the others may be left open to the states.'' The ''proposition,'' Wirt said, ''was not that all the commercial powers are exclusive, but that those powers being separated, there are some which are exclusive in their nature; and among them, is that power which concerns navigation.'' To Wirt it was ''immaterial, so far as this case is concerned, whether the power of Congress to regulate commerce be exclusive or concurrent.'' This was because ''it could not be denied that where Congress has legislated concerning a subject on which it is authorized to act, all State legislation which interferes with it is absolutely void.'' And congress had ''regulated . . . the coasting trade.''[406]

Marshall's majority opinion in *Gibbons* followed exactly the sequence of Wirt's alternative argument: the parallels are nearly as striking as those noted earlier between Pinkney's argument and Marshall's opinion in *McCulloch*. Marshall conceded that ''in our complex system . . . one general government['s] action extends over the whole, but . . . possesses only certain enumerated powers; and the states ''retain and exercise all powers not delegated to the Union.''[407] But since the regulation of commerce was an enumerated power, ''Congress may control the State laws, so far as may be necessary . . . for the regulation of commerce.'' And in *Gibbons* ''the laws of New York . . . have . . . come into collision with an act of Congress.''[408] The act was one ''regulating . . . the coastal trade.''[409] Since the New York statute granting exclusive rights to Fulton to operate steamboats in interstate waters was ''in direct collison with that act,'' the conflict ''decide[d] the cause.'' An examination ''of that part of the constitution which empowers Congress to promote the progress of science and the useful arts'' was therefore ''unnecessary.''[410] Marshall may have ''taken in'' Webster's argument—at one point he did say that Webster's intimation that ''the word 'to regulate' implie[d] full power over the thing to be regulated'' had ''great force''[411]—but his opinion

---

[404] Wirt to Carr, Feb. 1, 1824, supra, note 43. A handwritten copy of the letter is in Wirt Papers, Library of Congress.
[405] D. Webster to P. Harvey, quoted in Harvey, *Reminiscences,* 142.

[406] 9 Wheat. at 180–81.
[407] Ibid., 204–205.
[408] Ibid., 210.
[409] Ibid., 211.
[410] Ibid., 221.
[411] Ibid., 209.

rested at least as heavily on Wirt's. Once again Webster had sought to recast history for his own purposes.

But while one might quarrel with Webster, and others, over the precise nature of his contribution to the Marshall Court, no one can deny that Webster, in all his parts, was the most important of the Marshall Court lawyers. No advocate before the Court served simultaneously as a regular representative of clients litigating before the Court, as a celebrated publicist for the Court's doctrines, and as a close professional acquaintance and confidant of one of the Court's most influential justices. In the last role, Webster had so sufficiently impressed contemporaries by his access to Story that in 1830 a supporter of Andrew Jackson referred to Story as a "miserably frivolous book worm, destitute of solid understanding" who "is but the wretched tool of Mr. Webster."[412] The characterization of Story was excessive—Story and Webster's relationship was one of mutually advantaged equals—but it testified to Webster's prominence. Between 1819 and 1827, in the Marshall Court's most significant years, Webster was there, often on the winning side; he was there as promotor of the Court's version of history; he was there to support the Court's controversial sovereignty cases; and he was there to "overshadow all others in the importance of cases argued, and in the mastery of the great principles of constitutional law."[413]

Webster's eminence in the halcyon years of the Marshall Court underscores the close connection between law, history, and contemporary politics that the Court sought to establish in its decisions and which contemporaries recognized as one of its major goals. Important political issues invariably had constitutional ramifications in the years between 1815 and 1835, in significant part because the Marshall Court defined them as having such. The great Marshall Court advocates not only supplied arguments for the Court, they helped supply cases: they recognized the Court's intellectual tendencies and devoted their energies, in part, to the shaping and polishing of "legal" disputes which were sometimes contrived and which were often perceived, from their origins, as having distinct political ramifications. No one was more tireless nor more aggressive in this shaping than Webster, who not only served to profit from skillful shepherding of cases to the Court but also was personally committed, as a politician and public figure, to the versions of law, history, and politics that the Court expounded in its most influential years.

Ironically, Webster's great success as a popularizer of the Court's majoritarian positions on sovereignty, commerce, and property rights proved to be his undoing as a statesman. He became so identified with

---

[412] Louis McLane to Martin Van Buren, July 20, 1830, quoted in Warren, *Supreme Court,* II, 180.

[413] Charles Warren in Warren, *History of the American Bar,* 367–68.

ostensibly dispassionate and nonpartisan appeals to the Constitution and to the Union that when he sought political compromise on issues such as slavery, states' rights, and suffrage, he appeared inconsistent, hypocritical and machiavellian to critics. But although he never obtained his ultimate ambition, the presidency, Webster largely prevailed in the face of attack. It is perhaps a telling commentary on the legal and political professions that Webster's craftiness, relentless ambition, prevarication, and braggadocio rewarded rather than hampered him as a lawyer and as a politician. In the last year of his life he still held a cabinet position and argued his most lucrative case.[414] Although his credibility became tarnished in his later life, he always found a client ready to pay for the magic of his name, an administration willing to appoint him to a position, a friend willing to forego calling in debts owed. He died not in disgrace but with the honors of a carefully staged funeral; he even predicted the date of his death and, for once, made good on a promise.[415]

The lawyers portrayed here were not the only leading Marshall Court advocates. Other lawyers appeared as regularly, including Walter Jones, United States attorney for the District of Columbia, who argued 169 cases during the period covered by this study, and John Sergeant, general counsel for the Bank of the United States, who appeared 63 times. Some lawyers not portrayed here had exalted reputations, such as Robert Goodloe Harper, Joseph Hopkinson, and David Ogden. Harper was the most frequent advocate before the Court from 1800 to 1815;[416] he became a United States senator from South Carolina after the close of the War of 1812. Hopkinson, based in Philadelphia, argued *Dartmouth College* along with Webster, and was reported by the Boston *Daily Advertiser* as "close[ing] the cause for the College with great ability, and in a manner which gave perfect satisfaction and delight to all who heard him."[417] Ogden allegedly "argued more important cases before [the Marshall Court] than any other American lawyer save Webster and Wirt"; John Marshall reportedly said of Ogden "that when he had stated his case, it was already argued."[418] Other frequent advocates included Henry Wheat-

---

[414] The case was *Goodyear v. Day,* a patent dispute involving vulcanized rubber, which Webster argued in federal circuit for the District of New Jersey (in Trenton) in March 1852. Webster represented the inventor, Charles Goodyear. He was paid $10,000 for his services and another $5,000 if he won the case, which he did. See Fuess, *Daniel Webster,* 319–21; Harvey, *Reminiscences,* 104–105.

[415] See Curtis, *Daniel Webster,* II, 696.

[416] Warren, *History of the American Bar,* 261.

[417] Boston *Daily Advertiser,* Mar. 23, 1818.

[418] Warren, *History of the American Bar,* 304.

on, the Court's Reporter from 1816 through 1827, who appeared with Webster in *Ogden* v. *Saunders*;[419] Thomas Swann from the District of Columbia, who had an "immense" Supreme Court practice,[420] appearing eighty times in the period under consideration; and Charles J. Ingersoll, United States district attorney from Phildelphia, who was something of an orator himself, delivering an address in 1823 in which he argued that "the brutal, ferocious and inhuman law of the feudalists," the "arbitrary rescripts of the Civil Law, and the harsh doctrines of the Common Law have all been melted down by the general mildness of American institutions."[421]

In addition to these, a handful of notables appeared before the Marshall Court as lawyers on their way to illustrious careers in other occupations or professions. These included Francis Scott Key, the author of "The Star-Spangled Banner"; future politicians Henry Clay, James Knox Polk, Thomas Hart Benton, and William Crawford; and Roger Taney, who succeeded Wirt as attorney general of the United States in 1827 and who was to follow Marshall as Chief Justice. The federal bar in the last twenty years of the Marshall Court was a highly educated, multitalented elite, still comprised largely of men from eastern seaboard cities who often combined advocacy with elective office, who for the most part earned ample salaries, who engaged in scholarship and other literary pursuits, and who were usually trained orators. All told, the period from 1815 to 1835 was one of the highwater marks in the history of the Supreme Court bar.

What were the consequences of this proliferation of charismatic and talented advocates? One should recall here the modes of appellate advocacy and internal Court deliberation obtaining at the time. Given the character of the Marshall Court's litigation process, it seems likely that oral advocacy made a significant contribution to Marshall Court decisions, often forming the sole basis of the Justices' information about a case. While some Justices might have previously heard a case on circuit, and even decided it on that level, the Court as a whole was free to regard the circuit decisions of Justices as having no binding effect.[422] In the context of the Court's deliberative process Tazewell's succinct presentations of the facts and issues, Webster's telling appeals to the predispositions of individual Justices, Emmet's impassioned eloquence, Martin's thorough canvass of authorities, Wirt's graceful logic, or Pinkney's authoritative pronouncements might well have clarified a Justice's position on a case he and his colleagues were about to moot.

---

[419] Wheaton is portrayed in this volume in Chapter VI.
[420] Warren, *History of the American Bar*, 261.

[421] As quoted in ibid., 509.
[422] See Justice Johnson's remarks in *The Amanda*, reported in Charleston *City Gazette*, Jan. 18, 1822.

## Chapter IV: *Prominent Lawyers Before the Marshall Court*

When the breadth of oral advocacy before the Marshall Court is compared with the relative paucity of other authorities, and when one recalls that the arguments of counsel were regarded as themselves sources of law, one must conclude that Marshall Court advocacy had a significant effect on Marshall Court decisions. But the contribution of even the greatest advocates should not be overestimated. Line-by-line parallels between arguments and opinions, such as that between Pinkney and Marshall in *McCulloch* or Wirt and Marshall in *Gibbons,* were the exception rather than the rule. A more common result of advocacy was that the seeds of doctrines, and the authorities on which they rested, were planted in Justices' minds by counsel. Decisions evolved when those ideas were combined in discussions at the boardinghouse with views held by the Justices themselves. The great Marshall Court decisions could not have occurred without the contributions of counsel, but neither the nonpareil Pinkney, the "godlike" Webster, nor their gifted peers could take full credit for a Marshall Court opinion. The men portrayed in this chapter, for all their impressive contributions, are in a sense opening acts; the featured players are yet to appear.

# CHAPTER V

## *The Justices of the Marshall Court*

O NE OF THE MANY WAYS in which the Marshall Court altered the place of law in American culture was through a transformation of the office of Supreme Court Justice. When Marshall was appointed Chief Justice of the United States in 1801 the office was of dubious prominence and uncertain duration. John Jay had eagerly resigned the Chief Justiceship to serve as governor of New York; Oliver Ellsworth had held the position a mere three years. The independent review powers of the federal judiciary were not yet established; a differentiation of judges from commissioners, port collectors, and other minor agents of the executive had not yet been clearly made. By the time of Marshall's death in 1835, however, the office of Supreme Court Justice had become a major source of power in American government. The Marshall Court had demonstrated that great political issues could regularly be cast in legal terms and were susceptible of legal resolution; that the Supreme Court's interpretations of the Constitution had the status of paramount authority; that judges were beholden neither to the executives who appointed them nor to the legislative will; and that legal rhetoric could be as stirring a source of a culture's values and aspirations as any other. It was during Marshall's tenure as Chief Justice that the appointment of a Justice to the Supreme Court became a major event, having significant consequences, engendering active competition among candidates and their supporters, and requiring serious scrutiny by the appointing administration.

But if the office of Supreme Court Justice was transformed and elevated in status during the Marshall Court years, its grounding in the culture of American politics remained constant. In both the early and later Marshall Court political involvement had characterized the careers of all the Justices before their appointments, and some individual Justices used their offices as launching pads for prospective candidacies in elective politics. Political affiliations and inclinations not only contributed to the selection of persons to sit on the Court, they contributed to the outcome of decisions.

The process by which Supreme Court Justices were appointed during Marshall's tenure reflected contemporary awareness of the politically charged nature of the office. Two considerations were decisive in almost all appointments made between 1801 and 1835: geography and political affiliation. Seats on the Court were rigidly identified with particular regions of the country, and when a Justice from one region died or retired the candidates for his position invariably came from the geographic area comprising his circuit. That a Justice's circuit affiliation, and not his residency, dictated the choice of his successor is illustrated by the case of Bushrod Washington. Washington was a native Virginian who had originally been assigned to the Sixth Circuit, covering the deep South. When William Johnson was appointed to the Court in 1804 Washington switched to the Third Circuit, covering Pennsylvania and New Jersey. Upon Washington's death in 1829 all of the candidates for his spot on the Court were Pennsylvanians, despite the fact that Washington had continued to live in Virginia throughout his tenure. The theory of circuit-riding itself provided one justification for tying Supreme Court seats to particular regions. Supreme Court Justices were regarded as emissaries between a national Court and the various local jurisdictions. Having a Justice affiliated with a particular jurisdiction, and thereby purportedly acquainted with its practices, was thought to facilitate a process of interchange between the two. In addition, the geographic criterion for appointments reflected a conviction among students of American politics that sectional interests were invariably present and needed to be considered. If a New England or western Justice left the Court, another representative from that area should replace him, lest the area's provincial concerns fail to reach the Court. While the assumption that a judge would embody the provincial mores of his region sometimes proved erroneous— John Marshall's disavowal of the dominant constitutional theories of early-nineteenth-century Virginia intellectuals is a particularly conspicuous example—that assumption continued to be made. The result was that South Carolinian William Johnson was replaced by Georgian James Wayne, New Yorker Brockholst Livingston by New Yorker Smith Thompson, Kentuckian Thomas Todd by Kentuckian Robert Trimble, and so on.

But while geography was an acknowledged criterion of Court appointments, political affiliation was clearly more decisive. As the ability of the Court to affect political issues became obvious, appointing presidents sought to assure themselves that persons named to the Court were politically sympathetic to their administration's policies. Unsympathetic candidates were eliminated, as were persons who had not actively participated in politics or declared their views. All of the Justices sketched in this chapter had been involved in some form of political activity or had aspired to political office. The tradition of drawing Supreme Court appointees from a circle of politically active persons was established during the Marshall Court's tenure.

James Wayne's appointment to the Court serves as a case in point. Wayne played no significant part in the history of the Marshall Court, joining the Court only in Marshall's last Term. But Wayne was a typical Marshall Court appointee in that his selection clearly reflected geographical and political concerns. He was from the appropriate geographic region, a southerner filling the seat of William Johnson, who was from South Carolina and had sat on the Sixth Circuit. Wayne had been active in politics as well, serving in the Georgia legislature, as mayor of Savannah, as a Georgia state judge, and as a congressman. In Congress he had endeared himself to the Jackson administration by opposing nullification and supporting Jackson in his dispute with the Bank of the United States. When Johnson died in 1834 Jackson was embroiled in nullification disputes with South Carolina and thus was not inclined to select a candidate from that state. Wayne was simply there at the right time, embodying all the right criteria: not much effort was made to scrutinize his prospective ability as a judge. James Buchanan wrote a friend after Wayne's appointment that he would "[n]ever make [an] able judge,"[1] and Buchanan's prophecy proved accurate. Wayne served on the Court for thirty-two years without making any conspicuous contribution.[2]

In addition to Wayne, eleven other Justices served on the Marshall Court. They may be roughly divided into three groups, reflecting their relative significance on the Court. One group consisted of Justices John McLean, Henry Baldwin, Robert Trimble, and Smith Thompson. These Justices, principally because of the relative shortness of their tenure and in part because of the nature of their juristic contributions, exercised only a marginal influence on the Court. A second group, consisting of Justices Thomas Todd, Gabriel Duvall, Brockholst Livingston, William Johnson, and Bushrod Washington, were important figures whose presence contributed to the Court's tone and identity, especially during its years of greatest cohesiveness, 1815 to 1827, during which all, save Livingston, were in continuous service on the Court. The third group, Justice Joseph Story and Chief Justice John Marshall, was composed of the giants of the Court. Story, the most ubiquitous legal figure of his time, served simultaneously as Supreme Court Justice, author of treatises and commentaries, professor of law at Harvard Law School, and behind-the-scenes publicist and lobbyist for the judiciary. Marshall, arguably the

---

[1] J. Buchanan to Levi Woodbury, July 4, 1835, Levi Woodbury Papers, Library of Congress.
[2] On Wayne's career see A. Lawrence, *James Moore Wayne, Southern Unionist* (1943), and F. Gatell, "James M. Wayne," in L. Friedman and F. Israel, *The Justices of the United States*

*Supreme Court* (4 vols., 1969), I, 601. Lawrence said that Wayne "was not an original or a profound thinker" and "played a secondary role" on the Court (p. 215). Gatell called Wayne's judicial career "not brilliant," although "admirably consistent" (p. 610).

most influential and most renowned judge in the history of American law, was assuredly the most powerful and respected member of his Court.

John McLean's tenure, like that of Wayne, took place largely during the period of Taney's Chief Justiceship. McLean was appointed in 1829 and served until his death in 1861. His judicial career, despite its longevity, was not memorable, perhaps because he was regularly mentioned as a presidential candidate and, always mindful of that office, was anxious not to offend in his public pronouncements. McLean first came to prominence in political circles when Monroe made him postmaster general of the United States in 1823. The office was notable for its control of patronage, but McLean actually spent more of his time expanding and improving the mail service than he did dispensing jobs and favors. A reluctant supporter of Adams in 1824, McLean saw his influence reduced when Henry Clay, an old opponent of McLean's, joined the Adams administration. McLean complained that "the imprudent movements of Mr. Clay are doing more for Jackson than all the exertions of his friends,"[3] but as the election of 1828 drew closer, he tried not to offend the Jacksonians, writing a friend that "I have done nothing to injure the reputation or affect the interests of anyone."[4]

McLean had come to Washington from Ohio, and felt that he could present himself as a presidential candidate acceptable to the growing bloc of voters in the Mississippi Valley. But when he tested the waters,[5] nothing materialized, and McLean decided to court the Jacksonians. This resulted in an unsuccessful attempt by Clay to remove McLean from the office of postmaster general. Though Adams had completely lost confidence in McLean by the spring of 1828, he conceded that McLean "plays his game with so much cunning and duplicity that I can fix upon no positive act that would justify the removal of him."[6]

When Jackson won the election of 1828, then, McLean was neither fully identified with the Adams administration nor an overt Jackson supporter. He was consulted by Jackson and considered for positions in the cabinet. Eventually Jackson and his advisers conceived of the idea of appointing McLean to the Supreme Court. According to Story, who reported the decision to his brother-in-law,

---

[3] J. McLean to James Monroe, Feb. 1, 1827, James Monroe Papers, Library of Congress.

[4] J. McLean to Allen Trimble, Dec. 4, 1828, quoted in A. Trimble, *Autobiography and Correspondence* (1909), 178.

[5] See Thomas J. Brown to J. McLean, June 17, 1828, John McLean Papers, Library of Congress; F. Weisenberger, *The Life of John McLean* (1937), 52–53.

[6] J. Q. Adams, diary, in C. Adams, ed., *The Memoirs of John Quincy Adams, Comprising Portions of His Diary from 1795–1848* (12 vols., 1874–77), VIII, 51. See Weisenberger, *John McLean*, 59–61.

The truth is that [McLean] told the new President that he would not form a part of the new Cabinet, or remain in office, if he was compelled to make removals upon political grounds. The President assented to this course, but the governing ultras [Jackson's advisers] were dissatisfied, and after much debate and discussion, Mr. McLean remaining firm to his purpose, they were obliged to remove him from the Cabinet, and to make the matter fair, to appoint him (not much to his will) a Judge.[7]

Some of Story's surmises were not entirely accurate. McLean himself had apparently floated the idea of his going on the Court, although he would have preferred a cabinet post.[8] McLean felt that being on the Court would not prevent his campaigning for the presidency: in June 1829 Edward Everett reported to his brother that McLean had attacked Jackson and "intends to be a candidate himself."[9]

McLean thus went on the Court with a clear intention of continuing his active interest in politics while there,[10] which he did for the remainder of Marshall's tenure and beyond. Between 1829 and 1832 he was mentioned as a possible vice-presidential candidate on a Van Buren ticket,[11] supported for the presidency by a Massachusetts newspaper, and linked with the candidacy of Calhoun.[12] In 1831 the Anti-Mason party held a national convention and invited McLean to be considered for their presidential candidate, but he declined.[13] After Jackson's re-election McLean flirted with the new opposition Whig party, but eventually withdrew his name as a possible candidate in 1835.[14] Similar flirtations were to take place during McLean's years on the Taney Court, but nothing ever came of them.

McLean had previously served as a judge on the Ohio Supreme Court, but there is no indication that the Jackson administration gave any consideration to his jurisprudential views in appointing him. As Story said, McLean's "appointment . . . was produced by other causes than his fitness."[15] When McLean supported Marshall's view in *Worcester v.*

---

[7] J. Story to William Fettyplace, March [no date given] 1829, in W. Story, *The Life and Letters of Joseph Story* (2 vols., 1851), I, 564.

[8] See Weisenberger, *John McLean*, 67.

[9] E. Everett to A. H. Everett, June 8, 1829, Edward Everett Papers, Massachusetts Historical Society, Boston, Mass.

[10] J. H. Stull to Henry Clay, Mar. 28, 1829, Henry Clay Papers, Library of Congress.

[11] G. C. Verplanck to Martin Van Buren, Dec. 6, 1828, Martin Van Buren Papers, Library of Congress.

[12] John Sloane to J. McLean, July 6, 1826, McLean Papers.

[13] See J. McLean to Thurlow Weed, Sept. 7, 1831, in H. Weed, ed., *The Autobiography of Thurlow Weed*, vol. I of *The Life of Thurlow Weed Including His Autobiography and a Memoir* (2 vols., 1883), 389–90.

[14] J. McLean to Elisha Whittlesley, Dec. 12, 1835, Elisha Whittlesley Papers, Western Reserve Historical Society, Cleveland, Ohio.

[15] Story to Fettyplace, March 1829, supra, note 7.

*Georgia* that states had no power to regulate the affairs of Indians within their territory, Jackson was reportedly upset,[16] and Lewis Cass, Jackson's secretary of war, attacked the decision, including McLean's separate opinion, in the Washington *Globe.* McLean drafted a reply, writing as "A Member of Congress," but was unable to get it published.[17] The episode may have cost McLean any possibility of succeeding Marshall as Chief Justice.

McLean's only major Marshall Court opinion was in *Wheaton v. Peters,* a case involving a copyright dispute between the present and the past Reporters of the Court. McLean was probably chosen to write that opinion because his dislike of controversy had prevented his engaging himself on either side of the dispute.[18] McLean's principal impact on the Court was not in his opinions but in his interpretation of the office of Supreme Court Justice. He did not regard the position as incompatible with political activity, although he kept his political maneuverings covert; indeed, he thought of the office as a possible springboard for political campaigns. The fact that none of his efforts was successful did not affect his conception of the office, a radically different conception from that of Story, Marshall, Johnson, Livingston, or Duvall. Other Justices in the late Marshall Court—Thompson, most particularly—shared McLean's views, and the emergence of Supreme Court Justices as potential presidential candidates was to become commonplace on the Taney and Chase Courts.

McLean also contributed, perhaps unwittingly, to a change in the Court's internal atmosphere. Having been postmaster general in Washington before becoming a Justice, he had previously brought his family to that city, and after he went on the Court Mrs. McLean continued to live with him in Washington. While the McLeans stayed with the Justices in the boardinghouse during some Terms, they ate separately; their presence undoubtedly changed the intimacy of the Court's lodgings. After McLean joined the Court, William Johnson, never comfortable with the subtle pressures generated by boardinghouse living, resolved to live alone, and Johnson, Thompson, Baldwin, and McLean showed a tendency to express their views separately, especially in constitutional cases. McLean's contribution to the fragmentation of the Court was somewhat ironic, since he tended to side with the established majority on issues such as federalism and property rights. He was, one commentator wrote in 1833, "as sound as Chief Justice Marshall himself"[19] on such ques-

---

[16] See J. McLean to E. Whittlesley, June 26, 1832, Whittlesley Papers.

[17] Weisenberger, *John McLean,* 156–57. For Cass's attack on the *Worcester* decision, see Washington, *Globe,* Mar. 31, 1832.

[18] *Wheaton v. Peters* and the role of the Reporters in the Marshall Court are discussed in Chapter VI.

[19] Charles Hammond, in Cincinnati *Gazette,* Nov. 15, 1833.

tions. McLean's appointment, while having no particular substantive effect on Marshall Court jurisprudence, yet signaled that a new kind of appointee was populating the Court, one who identified the office with political issues generally and who regarded it as a stepping-stone to elective politics. This suggested a different constituency for the Court's opinions. McLean's efforts could be characterized less as ringing appeals to principles than as deliberately inoffensive and evasive messages to potential supporters.

If McLean's political concerns sometimes made him a distracted presence on the Court, Henry Baldwin's presence was surely a distracting one. From the moment of his appointment in 1830 Baldwin changed the atmosphere of internal Court deliberations. A week after he took office he wrote Joseph Hopkinson that "my association with the Judges is of the most pleasant kind," and the Court "a delightful [retreat] from the turbulence of politics,"[20] but by the end of the next Term he had given President Jackson "notice of his intention to resign," citing the "unwarrantable extension of its powers by the Court."[21] Baldwin was particularly vociferous in conferences, threatening to publish dissents, complaining about the practices of the Reporter, quarreling with Story, and even provoking Marshall, who wrote Story in November that he hoped "that the next term will exhibit dispositions [from Baldwin] more resembling those in the [1830 Term] than in the last."[22] In 1833 Story, who had originally found Baldwin's appointment "quite satisfactory,"[23] gave this assessment of Baldwin to Joseph Hopkinson, the federal district judge who sat with Baldwin on circuit:

> What you say respecting [Baldwin] is exactly what I expected. I have long thought you could find him uncomfortable, conceited, willful, and wrongheaded—the opinions, which you refer to, are so utterly wrong in principle and authority, that I am sure he cannot be sane. And indeed, the only charitable view which I can take of any of his conduct is that he is partially deranged at all times. His distaste for the Supreme Court and especially for [Chief Justice Marshall] is so familiarly known to us that it excites no surprise.[24]

---

[20] H. Baldwin to J. Hopkinson, Feb. 8, 1830, Joseph Hopkinson Papers, Historical Society of Pennsylvania, Philadelphia, Pa.

[21] The language is Martin Van Buren's, in J. Fitzpatrick, ed., *The Autobiography of Martin Van Buren* (1920), 578.

[22] J. Marshall to J. Story, Oct. 12, 1831, in *Proc. Mass. Hist. Soc.*, 14:347, (1901).

[23] J. Story to Sarah Waldo Story, Jan. 9, 1830, Joseph Story Papers, University of Texas Library.

[24] J. Story to J. Hopkinson, May 9, 1833, Hopkinson Papers.

# Chapter V: *The Justices of the Marshall Court*

The letter from Story to Hopkinson was written in May 1833. At the close of the preceding year Baldwin apparently suffered some kind of mental disorder. In December 1832 a lawyer in Philadelphia, where Baldwin's Third Circuit was primarily held, wrote, "I have just learned that the Honorable Judge Baldwin was seized today with a fit of derangement" while sitting in court.[25] The following January another observer testified that "Judge Baldwin is out of his wits,"[26] and on January 4 Daniel Webster wrote Warren Dutton,

> You may probably have heard of the breaking out of Judge Baldwin's insanity. When I was in Philadelphia he was under medical treatment and had become somewhat calm.[27]

Baldwin missed the 1833 Term because of mental illness, apparently brought on by concern about his financial situation. He had been "engaged . . . in several of the manufacturing enterprises which . . . were so rapidly starting up in [his home town of] Pittsburgh" and had become "involved in purchases of lands of great extent."[28] When he left Pittsburgh to serve in Congress in 1817 he relinquished the "personal control so essential to [the] successful management" of those affairs, and eventually suffered "extensive and distressing [financial] embarrassments" that eventually caused him to take bankruptcy. The result of those financial setbacks, a commentator noted, was that Baldwin's

> former free and warm-hearted commonality was, with a few rare exceptions, abandoned, and . . . he would dwell, with diseased interest, on incidents which, in his sounder mind, never could have attracted his notice, and could too often regard his truest friends with suspicion and distrust . . . [Eventually a] malady manifested itself which . . . made him temporarily incapable of public duties.[29]

Baldwin's early career had followed the typical pattern of political involvement and fortuitous affiliation with a president who was given the opportunity to make a Supreme Court nomination. Originally from New Haven, Connecticut, Baldwin settled in Pittsburgh after graduating from Yale in 1797 and reading law with Alexander Dallas in Philadelphia. After gaining the reputation of "an intellect whose power of comprehension, analysis, and argumentation has rarely been equalled,"[30] Baldwin

---

[25] Henry Etting to L. Woodbury, Dec. 22, 1832, Woodbury Papers.
[26] P. C. Brooks to E. Everett, Jan. 3, 1833, Everett Papers.
[27] D. Webster to W. Dutton, Jan. 4, 1833, Daniel Webster Papers, Dartmouth College Library.

[28] [Anonymous], "The Late Mr. Justice Baldwin," *Pa. L.J.*, 6:1, 6, (1846).
[29] Ibid., 13.
[30] Ibid., 4.

entered public service, where he became "one of General Jackson's most early and ardent supporters."[31] In 1829, when Bushrod Washington died, Baldwin became a candidate for a seat on the Court. He was pitted against Chief Justice John Bannister Gibson of the Pennsylvania Supreme Court and Horace Binney, a leading member of the Philadelphia bar. These were strong opponents, and Baldwin's selection was largely due to the Jackson administration's desire to embarrass John C. Calhoun, who had declared himself in favor of Gibson, and whose political supporters had attacked Baldwin, but who was in the process of becoming anathema to the Jacksonians.

Baldwin was never able to articulate a consistent jurisprudential posture while on the Court. After an amiable and unobtrusive first Term in 1830, he became agitated in the next Term, complaining about what he called, in a dissent in *Ex parte Crane*, "consequences of the most alarming kind" that would follow from the Court's "extension of its powers." He felt, he said in the *Crane* case, that "on the discreet exercise of the powers of this court much of the strength and public usefulness of the government depends."[32]

In 1837 Baldwin published a book that purported to summarize his views on constitutional adjudication. Entitled *A General View of the Origin and Nature of the Constitution and Government of the United States*,[33] the book sought to state Baldwin's "peculiar views of the Constitution" and to distinguish his position from "that which is usually taken."[34] Interpreters of the Constitution, Baldwin felt, could be divided into three classes, those who "adopt the most liberal rules of construction, in order to enlarge the granted powers of the federal government,"[35] those who "adopt the most narrow construction . . . in order to contract the granted powers of the [Union],"[36] and those "who were willing to take the Constitution . . . as it is, and to expound it by the accepted rules of interpretation."[37] Baldwin put himself "in the ranks of the third class," and sought "to find out the meaning of the Constitution by its expressed intention, to be collected from its parts by old settled rules, the history of the times which preceded, and the state of the times at its adoption."[38] In his search for the "expressed intention" of the Constitution he resolved not to invoke "the aid of any commentator except this Court," and not to "consult any other commentaries" save those "found in the opinions of the Court; delivered, with few exceptions, by the late venerated Chief

[31] Ibid., 6–7.
[32] *Ex parte* Crane, 5 Pet. 190, 223 (1831).
[33] H. Baldwin, *A General View of the Origin and Nature of the Constitution and Government of the United States* (1837).

[34] Ibid., 1.
[35] Ibid., 36.
[36] Ibid., 37.
[37] Ibid.
[38] Ibid.

Justice.''[39] These last sentences were pointed responses to the appearance, four years earlier, of Story's *Commentaries on the Constitution*.

Baldwin's *General View* was a bizarre performance. He ranged from ''the political condition of the colonies of Great Britain''[40] through ''the proceedings of the Congress of 1774''[41] to ''the Ordinance of 1787''[42] in an effort to show that ''the ultimate absolute sovereignty is in 'the several states' and the people thereof.''[43] This might appear to be an endorsement of a states' rights theory of constitutional interpretation, especially in light of Baldwin's claim to have found ''an early solution of all questions arising under [the Constitution]'' by taking it as ''the grant of the people of the several states.''[44] But along the way Baldwin quoted with approval, among his numerous citations to authorities, the language of Marshall in *Gibbons* v. *Ogden* deploring the efforts of ''powerful and ingenious minds'' to ''contract . . . the powers expressly granted to the government of the Union . . . into the narrowest possible compass.''[45] Like Marshall, Baldwin sought ''to recur to safe and fundamental principles,'' but those principles, if they were comprehensible at all, appeared to be the opposite of the ones Marshall's language was endorsing.

But in the end one could not be sure what position Baldwin was advancing in *A General View*. He had strung together such a rag-bag of disparate sources, citing each of them as an authoritative proposition, and he had drawn so fine a distinction between the ''people of the several states'' and ''the people in their aggregate collective capacity,''[46] that his position was virtually unintelligible. Only one thing was sure: he did not endorse Story's view of sovereignty. He cited ''an able and learned commentary on the constitution, published in 1833,'' as an example of ''the antagonist propositions to those which I have endeavored to establish.''[47] Story, for his part, once characterized Baldwin's opinions as ''bringing together materials . . . very foreign to the main subject'' and containing ''misapplication[s] of learning.''[48]

It is hard to say how much of Baldwin's incoherence as a jurist resulted from his mental problems; whatever its source, his incoherence has denied him any historical reputation. Despite his obscurity, however, Baldwin's unpredictability, coupled with his aggressive and outspoken behavior, must have resulted in his being a somewhat formidable presence on the late Marshall Court. At a time when both the informal habits and

---

[39] Ibid., 7.
[40] Ibid., 19.
[41] Ibid., 68.
[42] Ibid., 88.
[43] Ibid., 24.
[44] Ibid., 1.

[45] Ibid., 42.
[46] Ibid., 37.
[47] Ibid., 108.
[48] J. Story to J. Hopkinson, Mar. 23, 1839, Hopkinson Papers.

the established doctrines of earlier years were breaking down, the addition of a contentious, erratic, vehement maverick into the boardinghouse circle may have had profoundly disruptive effects. While Baldwin was never consistent enough in his views to establish a position of intellectual stature on the Court, he may have encouraged others, such as Johnson, Thompson, or McLean, to resist too prompt a capitulation to orthodoxy on constitutional matters. In a small group of people that relies on close contact and oral discussion to generate consensual positions, the pressures generated by one disruptive presence can result, as Story put it to Hopkinson, in "sacrifices . . . for the sake of peace and dignity."[49]

Richard Peters, the Court's Reporter during Baldwin's tenure, had a more jaundiced view of Baldwin's influence. Writing to Hopkinson in 1831, Peters first complained of Baldwin's "malignity and injustice and baseness toward me (he has told the Chief Justice *that as long as* I am reporter he will not take a single case for an opinion)," and then went on to characterize "the effect [Baldwin's] whole conduct during the Court had produced":

> I venture the assertion without fear of contradiction . . . that no one who visits the court or has an opportunity of seeing him speaks of him with respect. It is the opinion of more than the proportion I mention *that his mind is out of order.* I have heard in one day not less than five persons . . . say "he is crazy" . . . I know that some laugh at him, and one of the persons whom I have named asked Dr. Hunt "if he was not out of his senses." He sits in his room for three or four hours in the dark—jumps up and runs down into the judges' consultation room in his stocking feet, and remains in that condition while they are deliberating.[50]

When John McLean wrote Peters, after Baldwin died in 1844, that "we shall miss him on the bench," he could not forswear adding that while Baldwin "had generous impulses," his "mind was unhappily unfit for the exercise of the social virtues in a continued intercourse."[51]

In the case of Robert Trimble, who was appointed to the Court in April 1826 and died in August 1828, one is presented with a tantalizing example of a potentially distinguished judicial career cut short before it could be fully assessed. Trimble, who served only two terms on the Marshall Court, must be relegated to a minor part in its history. But there were signs that had Trimble not succumbed to a "malignant bilious

---

[49] Story to Hopkinson, May 9, 1833, supra, note 24.

[50] R. Peters, Jr. to J. Hopkinson, Mar. 18, 1838, Hopkinson Papers.

[51] J. McLean to R. Peters, Jr., May 15, 1844, Richard Peters Papers, Historical Society of Pennsylvania, Philadelphia, Pa.

fever"[52] he might have become one of the leading judges on the late Marshall Court and a strong supporter of jurisprudential orthodoxy. Marshall wrote after Trimble's death that "his superior cannot be found" for "mind sense, uprightness of intuition, and legal knowledge."[53] And Story, in a eulogy published in the *Boston Columbian Centinel,* said that "no man ever on the Bench gained so much, in so short a period of his judicial career," and that "had he lived ten years longer . . . from the expansibility of his talents, and his steady devotion to jurisprudence, he would have gained still a higher rank."[54]

Trimble's appointment to the Court had been marked by the usual political intrigues that routinely surrounded the nominations of Marshall Court Justices. He was a native of Kentucky, a state considered politically significant by the Adams administration and legally significant to the Supreme Court because of the number of contested land claims that regularly came up to the Court from there. Robert Wickliffe wrote Henry Clay in March 1826, before Trimble had been appointed, that "the adhesion of Kentucky to the administration . . . depends much upon the appointment of Trimble."[55] Earlier that year Francis Blair, a Kentucky politician, had written to Clay that Trimble had been "running from town to town with ready made recommendations in his pocket to obtain subscribers" for his prospective nomination. Blair disapproved of the activity, and doubted whether Trimble was "honest and upright," but Trimble's candidacy prevailed.[56] Story later said that Justice Thomas Todd, who "was sensible that his health was declining, and that he might soon leave the Bench" had "communicated his earnest hope that Mr. Justice Trimble might be his successor."[57]

Trimble's pre-Court career had been typical of the Marshall Court nominees. He had come to Kentucky as a small child, his father one of numerous western Virginia settlers who sought "to improve his fortune by obtaining a grant of land"[58] in the new state. In addition to "hunting game and scouting in search of the Indians,"[59] Trimble attended "com-

---

[52] [B. Mills], *American Jurist* 151 (1829). The *American Jurist* obituary of Trimble was based on a letter Mills wrote to Henry Clay on November 13, 1828. The original is in the Joseph Story Papers, Library of Congress. Mills was described in the *American Jurist* as "an eminent judicial character of Kentucky, who was [Trimble's] school-fellow and afterwards his neighbor, and has been his intimate friend for a long course of years." Ibid.

[53] J. Marshall to H. Clay, Nov. 28, 1828, Clay Papers.

[54] The eulogy may be found in the September 17, 1828, issue of the Boston *Columbian Centinel.* It is reprinted in W. Story, *Life and Letters,* I, 541–43.

[55] R. Wickliffe to H. Clay, Mar. 7, 1826, Clay Papers.

[56] F. Blair to H. Clay, Jan. 30, 1826, Clay Papers.

[57] Memorandum, reprinted in W. Story, *Life and Letters,* I, 498–99.

[58] [Mills], supra, note 52, 151.

[59] Ibid.

mon schools," and eventually taught at private academies in order to finance his continued education. He eventually graduated from Transylvania University and began to read law in the offices of George Nicholas and James Brown. In 1800 he opened a law practice in Paris, Kentucky. He pursued his practice "with unabated assiduity and undiminished success," becoming "engaged in every important cause in the courts where he appeared."[60] At the same time he became involved in politics, serving in the Kentucky legislature for two years beginning in 1802 and twice declining nominations to the United States Senate. He also served as a judge on the Kentucky Supreme Court for a year beginning in 1807, and declined a subsequent offer to be chief justice of that court. His reason for declining the Senate nominations and the judgeship was financial: Trimble "found that his compensation [for the offices] afforded him but scanty means of supporting his increasing family."[61]

But in 1817 Trimble became a federal district judge for the Eastern District of Kentucky, a position he held until he was nominated to the Supreme Court. It is unclear why Trimble found it possible to accept this office after declining the others. His financial situation may have improved, or he may have been more sympathetic to Unionist ideas than was the Kentucky state judiciary. In the course of his service as a district court judge Trimble construed a number of Kentucky land laws in ways that offended residents and earned the enmity of Senator John Rowan of Kentucky, who was himself a large landowner.[62] Rowan was able to delay Trimble's Supreme Court nomination for twenty-eight days, the longest of any nominated Justice up to that time, but was unable to defeat it. Henry Clay said that while Rowan had "made a violent opposition to Trimble's nomination," Rowan was "perfectly impotent in the Senate."[63]

Trimble's confirmation gave the Court its full complement of seven Justices for the 1827 Term, when some major cases were on the docket. In perhaps the most important of those, *Ogden* v. *Saunders*,[64] Trimble delivered a seriatim opinion. This was itself highly unusual, as we have seen. But in *Ogden* v. *Saunders*, as Marshall noted in his dissent, "it [was] well known that the Court [had] been divided in opinion,"[65] and neither Marshall nor Story, forces for unanimity and harmony on the Court, was with the majority. As a result, the four Justices in the majority,

---

[60] Ibid., 153.
[61] Ibid.
[62] See H. Clay to John Crittenden, Mar. 10, 1826, quoted in A. Coleman, *The Life of John J. Crittenden* (2 vols., 1871), I, 63. See also C. Warren, *The Supreme Court in United States History* (3 vols., 1922), II, 144.

[63] H. Clay to J. Crittenden, May 11, 1826, quoted in Coleman, *John J. Crittenden*, 65.
[64] 12 Wheat. 213 (1827).
[65] 12 Wheat. at 332.

Washington, Johnson, Thompson, and Trimble, resolved to write separately.

The case of *Ogden* v. *Saunders* will be discussed in some detail in Chapter IX. It was in many respects a jurisprudential turning point for the Marshall Court, the first major obligation of contracts case in which the Justices sustained a state bankruptcy or insolvency statute against constitutional attack. Had the case been decided otherwise, it would have scuttled insolvency legislation, for the issue in *Ogden* v. *Saunders* was whether a state debtor relief statute could operate to discharge a person from contractual obligations incurred after the passage of the statute. In *Sturges* v. *Crowninshield*[66] the Court had already held that debtor relief laws could not constitutionally affect obligations incurred before their passage. *Ogden*, had it been decided the other way, would have left no room for relief laws to have any effect.

*Ogden* v. *Saunders* was significant not only because of its practical effects on the status of bankruptcy in America—in the early nineteenth century Congress repeatedly declined to enact federal bankruptcy legislation[67]—but also because of the jurisprudential theory governing the case, which was that property rights were "natural rights," rights that Marshall characterized as "anterior of and independent of society," "not given by society but . . . brought into it."[68] According to this theory "the right to contract [was] not surrendered with the right to coerce performance"; it was "intrinsic . . . created by the contract itself, [and] not . . . dependent on the laws made to enforce it."[69] Being intrinsic, the right to contract could not be regulated by state legislatures, whether prospectively or retrospectively, without causing an "impairment of the obligation of contracts."

This argument was not easily refuted, given the jurisprudential assumptions of the time. It combined two propositions that were deeply embedded in early-nineteenth-century American philosophical discourse, the idea that property was an inalienable natural right and the idea that law was not a source of natural rights but rather an embodiment of them. Such rights, Marshall argued, were "brought with man into society" rather than being "given by human legislation." The strength of these ideas helps explain some of the distinctive features of Marshall Court jurisprudence, such as the periodic resort to extraconstitutional arguments based on "first principles" of "justice," "nature," or "republican governments." Positivistic conceptions of law, emphasizing that written legislative or judicial acts created and defined the full scope of human rights

---

[66] 4 Wheat. 122 (1819).
[67] See P. Coleman, *Debtors and Creditors in America* (1974), 18–23.

[68] 4 Wheat. at 345, 346.
[69] Ibid., 353.

and responsibilities, had not, we have noted, fully displaced natural law conceptions in jurisprudential discourse.

Trimble's opinion in *Ogden* v. *Saunders* attempted to refute Marshall's conclusion without denying the twin propositions at the heart of Marshall's argument. Consequently Trimble was forced to confront Marshall at the level of philosophical abstraction. He conceded that "men have, by the laws of nature, the right of acquiring and possessing property and the right of contracting engagement"; that "these natural rights have their correspondent natural obligations"; and that "[these] natural obligation[s] [are] founded solely in the principles of natural or universal law."[70] But he then claimed that while "no express, declaratory, municipal law [was] necessary for their creation," it was "equally true that these rights . . . are subject to be regulated, modified, and sometimes absolutely restrained by the positive enactments of municipal law." The "natural obligation of private contracts," Trimble argued, are "converted into a civil obligation," and "the right and power of enforcing performance exists . . . only in the law of the land." Thus if "the positive law of the State declares the contract shall have no obligation," it "can have no obligation, whatever may be the principles of natural law."[71]

Such an argument subverted the conception of natural rights as having independent significance, because Trimble claimed that the "obligations" correlative to those rights were dependent for their enforcement on the will of the state. It was thus hard to see what remained left of the "natural right" to contract beyond an abstract proposition, giving rise to no enforceable powers but those a government might choose to enforce. Later schools of jurisprudence were to develop this conception of rights, and conclude that natural rights in the abstract were meaningless. But Trimble sought to retain the idea of natural rights as independent of positive law. "The law of the state," he argued, "is no part of the contract itself," although "it constitutes the obligation of the contract."[72] Rights were at once independent of positive law and dependent upon it.

To modern readers Trimble's distinctions between contracts and their obligations and between the creation and the enforcement of natural rights appear to undermine the idea of legal rights as separable from the power of the state, but for his contemporaries Trimble's distinctions were significant. His opinion in *Ogden* v. *Saunders* was a skillful effort to invest his reasoning with the code words and the unchallenged assumptions of his contemporaries' discourse. At the conclusion of his argument he announced that the Framers of the Constitution were fundamentally concerned with "the protection of personal security, and of private rights, from the despotic and iniquitous operation of retrospective legislation":

---

[70] Ibid., 319.
[71] Ibid., 320.

[72] Ibid., 325.

this was "the grand principle" they "intended to . . . establish."[73] Of those words all but the word "retrospective" were code words, invocations of widely supported maxims. The word "retrospective" was the distinction that decided *Ogden* v. *Saunders*. It had been smuggled into an otherwise stock appeal to "first principles." This was reasoning in the tradition of John Marshall himself.

Thus, had Trimble served even an average length of service on the Marshall Court, he might well have become one of its distinguished Justices. Moreover, his position in *Ogden* v. *Saunders* suggests that as some of the doctrines of the early Marshall Court, such as vested rights, were pressed to the logical extremes in the 1820s and 1830s, he might have joined those Justices prepared to give a more expansive reading of state power to infringe on established property rights. But Trimble was not granted the "ten years" in which Story thought he "would have gained a still higher rank . . . among the first judges of the nation."[74] Oliver Hampton Smith, a congressman from Indiana who attended an argument in the 1827 Term, later noted that "to all appearances" Trimble possessed "a robust and strong constitution," but that while "he looked as if he would be one of the last to be called away," he was one of the first.[75]

With Smith Thompson we reach the last of the Justices whose contributions to the Marshall Court are here characterized as comparatively slight. In the case of Thompson such a characterization seems counterintuitive. Thompson served on the Marshall Court for twelve years, thus having the opportunity to decide a significant number of cases and to write a fair number of opinions. He also resolved early in his career to write separately in constitutional cases, and thus produced, by Marshall Court standards, a sizable number of concurrences. His views on the major constitutional issues of his tenure can be distinguished from those of the extant court majority: one commentator has called him a "frontrunner in the judicial reaction to John Marshall's centralist federalism."[76] Finally, his tenure covered a period in which the Court's ethos changed, both with respect to substantive doctrine and with respect to internal practices. In some respects Thompson's approach to judging typified the late Marshall Court: he was less enthusiastic about national powers, and more willing to express himself separately, than his predecessors had been. Since internal fragmentation and doctrinal debate, especially on

---

[73] Ibid., 331.

[74] Story in W. Story, *Life and Letters*, I, 542–43.

[75] O. Smith, *Early Indiana Trials and Sketches* (1858), 138.

[76] G. Dunne, "Smith Thompson," in Friedman and Israel, *Justices*, I, 475.

issues of federalism, were common themes of the late Marshall and Taney Courts, Thompson might seem a prescient "frontrunner" whose jurisprudence was more "modern" than that of his entrenched colleagues. But Thompson's service was less influential, and his substantive positions less uniform, than a surface characterization might suggest.

The most innovative feature of Thompson's tenure on the Marshall Court had little to do with his jurisprudential stance; it was his attitude toward the active participation of Supreme Court Justices in politics. Along with McLean, Thompson challenged the unwritten rules of the Marshall Court that Justices should eschew open identification with partisan political issues. Marshall, Story, and Washington, in particular, made plain their disavowal of partisanship and withdrew, at least apparently, from political life. While this stance was largely symbolic and did not prevent them from paying close attention to political developments, it became an entrenched norm of the Court, symbolized by Marshall's declining to vote in presidential elections and by the Justices' refusal to endorse political candidates.

With his succession to Brockholst Livingston's seat in 1823, Thompson revived an older custom of open judicial participation in elective politics. In 1828, in his fifth Term on the Court, he ran for governor of New York, as his predecessor John Jay had done.[77] While claiming that "the [Adams] administration have put me in nomination for Governor . . . without my consent and against my wishes," and that his nomination was "a circumstance I most sincerely regret, particularly if I should be so unfortunate as to be elected,"[78] Thompson never withdrew his candidacy nor resigned from the Court. In this decision he had the support of John Quincy Adams[79] as well as the precedent of Jay, but his actions were in striking contrast to the circumspection of other Justices who had served with Marshall.

From the outset of his service Thompson had conceived of the position of Supreme Court Justice as intimately concerned with politics. He may have derived this conception from his experiences in New York, where he had served for sixteen years as a justice of the state supreme court and had customarily participated in partisan politics, although holding office only briefly. Thompson's sympathies, in the shifting vicissi-

---

[77] Thompson married the daughter of Gilbert Livingston and Jay the daughter of his cousin William Livingston. Jay and Thompson were members of different factions within the Livingston clan and political opponents. See G. Dangerfield, *Chancellor Robert R. Livingston* (1960), 298–306; D. Roper, "Mr. Justice Thompson and the Con-

stitution" (Ph.D. diss., Indiana University, 1963), 1–6.
[78] S. Thompson to B. Washington, Sept. 16, 1828, Smith Thompson Papers, Huntington Library, San Marino, Calif.
[79] See Dunne, "Smith Thompson," 485; Roper, "Mr. Justice Thompson," 25–26.

tudes of New York political culture, were against Federalism and against DeWitt Clinton's Republican faction, making him, in New York politics, a "Bucktail" and an ally of Martin Van Buren. He was also closely associated with James Kent, with whom he had read law in Poughkeepsie after graduating from Princeton in 1788, and with Gilbert Livingston, a member of the powerful family whose influence in New York was confirmed by Jefferson's election in 1800. Thompson married Livingston's daughter Sarah in 1794, and then went into practice with his father-in-law and Kent. He ran successfully for the state legislature as a Republican in 1800, and was named to the Supreme Court of New York (now the Court of Appeals) two years later. Kent was already on that court, and Brockholst Livingston, Gilbert's cousin, was to join it in 1804. Judicial appointments were regarded by the Republicans, and their opponents, as part of political patronage.[80]

Though Thompson continued to serve as a state judge, succeeding Kent to the chief justiceship of New York in 1814, he did not relinquish his political associations. He was offered the mayoralty of New York City in 1807 and was considered as a candidate to oppose DeWitt Clinton for governor in 1816.[81] Martin Van Buren later recalled that "all admitted the Chief Justice to be honest and sincere, but it was thought he did not understand the feeling of the party sufficiently."[82] At this time Van Buren and Thompson were friends as well as political associates: Van Buren wrote Rufus King in 1820 that "I think I know [Thompson] as well as any man living." He then characterized Thompson as "unambitious for himself, wish[ing] nothing so much as retirement."[83] Van Buren's characterization was peculiar, given his perspicacity and the fact that Thompson was anything but "unambitious"; his comment was probably designed to quiet the fears of King, a longtime Federalist, about the prospects of Thompson, a Republican. Thompson did, however, like to play his cards close to his vest, as his remarkable interchange with Van Buren over his prospective appointment to the Marshall Court revealed.

In 1818 Thompson, possibly on Van Buren's recommendation, had been named secretary of the navy by President Monroe. While Thompson was not Monroe's first choice,[84] he had accepted the poisition with enthusiasm, feeling it would improve his political prospects, and he had come to enjoy Washington. The "labors" on the New York Supreme

---

[80] In tracing Thompson's career in New York politics I have followed Roper, "Mr. Justice Thompson," 8–31.

[81] Van Buren, *Autobiography,* 77; Roper, "Mr. Justice Thompson," 25.

[82] Van Buren, *Autobiography, 94.*

[83] M. Van Buren to R. King, Jan. 19, 1820, quoted in C. King, ed., *The*

*Life and Correspondence of Rufus King* (6 vols., 1900), VI, 253.

[84] J. Monroe to Benjamin Crowninshield, Oct. 18, 1818, James Monroe Papers, New York Public Library, New York, N.Y.; see Roper, "Mr. Justice Thompson," 21.

Court, he later wrote Van Buren, were "too severe and arduous for me," and "the change to the Cabinet very helpful in that regard."[85] Moreover, the Thompsons had become active participants in Washington society, notwithstanding their apparently modest financial position. The Philadelphia lawyer, Charles Ingersoll, in a diary kept for the amusement of a British friend during a trip to Washington in February 1823, made the following comment after having been invited to the Thompsons on February 20.

> We had a very elegant entertainment today, with a sherry plateau . . . some varieties of wines, and altogether a costly and handsome . . . dinner for twenty or thirty persons, most of them in full dress too, from a plain, rather puritanical, and poor family, who, I dare swear, till transplanted from Albany to the seat of government, never saw or dreamed of such things.[86]

Five years after Thompson had come to Washington to become secretary of the navy, Brockholst Livingston died, and on March 24, 1823, six days after Livingston's death, Monroe offered the Supreme Court vacancy to Thompson.[87] The vacancy was the first in twelve years on the Court. It was understood to be reserved for a New York resident, and Thompson was an obvious choice, being a member of Monroe's cabinet and an experienced judge. When rumors circulated, after Livingston fell ill in late February, that Thompson might be his successor, Thompson was not surprised by them.[88] But he had more widespread ambitions, and sought to enlist the aid of his friend Van Buren in pursuing them.

On March 17 Thompson wrote Van Buren seeking to enlist his support for a possible Thompson campaign for the presidency in 1824. Van Buren, then a congressman from New York, was well situated to play a significant role in the 1824 campaign. The National Republican party, after twenty years in office and an avowedly antiparty stance during the Monroe administrations, was crumbling, and sectional candidates were emerging. Since presidential candidates were still created by state party caucuses and elected by electors, the position of certain large states was crucial in the process, and Van Buren had considerable influence in New York's Republican caucus. William Crawford of Georgia, Henry Clay of Kentucky, John Quincy Adams of Massachusetts, and Andrew Jackson of Tennessee were regarded as candidates, but Thompson be-

---

[85] S. Thompson to M. Van Buren, Mar. 25, 1823, Van Buren Papers.
[86] Charles Ingersoll, diary entry, Mar. 5, 1823, Charles Ingersoll Papers, Historical Society of Pennsylvania, Philadelphia, Pa.

[87] Thompson to Van Buren, Mar. 25, 1823, supra, note 85.
[88] R. King, diary entry, Mar. 4, 1823, in C. King, *Life and Correspondence*, VI, 511.

lieved that a New York candidate, backed by a state caucus, would be in a strong position. He accordingly told Van Buren, in the March 17 letter, to regard him as willing to run for the presidency, to take steps to ascertain the state legislature's views, to assure him that a caucus would be forthcoming, and to indicate his own position on the 1824 race. Rumors had linked Van Buren to Crawford, and Thompson sensed some "apparent reserve" on Van Buren's part to declare himself, hence this declaration of his ambitions, made in the spirit of "candor and frankness."[89]

Thompson wrote the letter to Van Buren in Albany, but Van Buren was in New York at the time and as a result did not immediately receive it. The delay engendered a bizarre series of events that culminated in the destruction of Thompson and Van Buren's friendship. On March 21 Thompson wrote another letter to Van Buren, asking him to dispel rumors that he was about to come out for Crawford. This letter was also not received immediately. Meanwhile Van Buren wrote Thompson, also on March 21, saying only that he had heard of Livingston's death and that he hoped that Thompson would accept the Supreme Court nomination if it were offered.[90] Thompson apparently took Van Buren's silence on his presidential ambitions in this letter to mean that he was not enthusiastic about them. In his reply to Van Buren, written on March 25, he indicated that he had received an offer from Monroe to serve in the Court, but that he was not inclined to take it, and that he wanted to recommend Van Buren for the position. And in a postscript to that letter he noted that "I have written you two letters since you left [Washington] addressed to you at Albany."[91]

Van Buren, who was not aware that Thompson had explicitly asked for his support in the prospective presidential campaign, was stunned by the letter. In it Thompson had said that he was inclined to decline the nomination "solely from my state of health," but had then given other reasons, such as "the constant confinement and study day and night . . . for six or seven weeks" that the job of Supreme Court Justice required, the low salary, which was "not adequate to the expense of living here where you are unavoidably exposed to much company," and the fact that "I like the place I now hold." Thompson concluded by saying that "assuming I am out of the question, will you permit me to offer your name to the President."[92]

The seriousness with which Van Buren took Thompson's offer demonstrates the stature that the office of Supreme Court Justice had achieved

[89] S. Thompson to M. Van Buren, Mar. 17, 1823, Miscellaneous Papers, New York State Library, Albany, N.Y.
[90] M. Van Buren to S. Thompson, Mar. 21, 1823, Van Buren Papers.

[91] Thompson to Van Buren, Mar. 25, 1823, supra, note 85.
[92] Ibid.

by the 1820s, and the apparent compatibility of the office with political involvement. The fact that Martin Van Buren, one of the architects of partisan politics, was given serious consideration for, and gave serious thought to, serving on the Marshall Court demonstrates how the office of Supreme Court Justice was then viewed. While Justices were expected to be aloof from politics, they were also expected to have experienced and sound political judgment.

Rufus King articulated that conception of the office in two communications related to the Thompson–Van Buren episode. After receiving the letter from Thompson, Van Buren solicited King's advice as to whether he should go on the Court. King said that the office of Supreme Court Justice could not "tolerate the interference of the Judge's party or personal politics," and that if Van Buren were to go on the Court he "must be wholly and forever withdrawn and separated from the connexions." Entering "the Judicial Department," King felt, was "like taking the vow and veil in the Catholic Church": membership on the Supreme Court "forever divorce[d] [one] from the political world."[93] But when Van Buren agreed to pursue the nomination, and assured King that he could remove himself from politics, King then wrote a letter on his behalf to Monroe. In it he referred to Van Buren's "great public experience," "uncommon sagacity," and "prudence." These qualities were especially helpful in a Justice, King argued, because the Court "decide[d] . . . questions . . . [involving] the nice and complicated balance of our political system." It was important, given the Court's role, to appoint persons who possessed the "master spirit of the Chief Justice," who was, above all, prudent.[94]

In dangling the possibility of an appointment to the Court before Van Buren, Thompson believed he was acting most "prudently." His letter of March 25, taken together with his letters of March 17 and 21, made it clear that his withdrawal, and recommendation of Van Buren, was to be a quid pro quo for Van Buren's promotion of his presidential candidacy. But since Van Buren had not received the earlier letters by March 25, he took Thompson's offer as unconditional, and wrote Thompson back on March 30 to say that he was willing to let his interest in the position be communicated to Monroe, and enclosing a formal "affidavit" of his interest for that purpose.[95] The result was that while Van Buren thought Thompson would decline the nomination once Van Buren had agreed to allow his name to be put forth, Thompson was waiting for

---

[93] R. King, memorandum, Apr. 7, 1823, in C. King, *Life and Correspondence*, VI, 521–22.
[94] R. King to J. Monroe, Apr. 2, 1823, in ibid., 513–14.

[95] M. Van Buren to S. Thompson, Mar. 30, 1823, Van Buren Papers.

another issue to be resolved, that of Van Buren's presidential posture. And on that issue Van Buren's March 30 letter was silent. Instead he spoke warmly of Thompson for the vice-presidency, a position in which Thompson had no interest.

Meanwhile Thompson had indicated to Monroe that he had doubts about the position of Justice, "fear[ing] that the labour of the office [would] injure his health," as had the labor of judicial office in New York. But Thompson never actually declined the position, and Monroe had given him "time to deliberate."[96] When Thompson received Van Buren's formal letter of interest on April 1 he communicated it to Monroe, but he did not endorse Van Buren's candidacy, and a week later Monroe noted to Samuel Gouverner, his son-in-law, that Van Buren's name had been submitted "merely for consideration."[97] Van Buren, who had expected his nomination to follow directly from Thompson's withdrawal and endorsement, became agitated, and on April 15 wrote Thompson, "I will be glad to be informed whether your declension has been definitive and whether Mr. Monroe so understands it."[98] Thompson did not reply until the twenty-fifth, and then as follows:

> I certainly meant to be understood that I did decline taking the office. I am not certain that I told him absolutely and in terms that I could not accept it. And I recollect that on my leaving him at the time of our last conversation, he observed to me in substance that if I should change my views on the subject I must let him know it.[99]

From that point on relations between Thompson and Van Buren rapidly deteriorated. In May, with no action yet taken on the nomination, rumors circulated that Thompson had undermined Van Buren's candidacy to Monroe, and Van Buren and Thompson took pains to assure one another that nothing had transpired to change their "understanding." But Van Buren had emerged as an active supporter of Crawford, thereby making it highly unlikely that Monroe would give him any further consideration for the Court vacancy.[100] In June Van Buren wrote Thompson an angry letter stating that his candidacy was being ridiculed ("the President would sooner appoint an alligator than me,") and accusing Thompson of having "expressed your sentiments hostile to" his appointment.[101]

---

[96] J. Monroe to S. Gouverner, Mar. 31, 1823, Monroe Papers, New York Public Library.

[97] J. Monroe to S. Gouverner, Apr. 8, 1823, ibid.

[98] M. Van Buren to S. Thompson, Apr. 15, 1823, Smith Thompson Papers, New-York Historical Society, New York.

[99] S. Thompson to M. Van Buren, Apr. 25, 1823, Van Buren Papers.

[100] M. Van Buren to S. Thompson, May 23, 1823, Van Buren Papers; Thompson to M. Van Buren, May 24, 1823, ibid.

[101] M. Van Buren to S. Thompson, June 4, 1823, ibid.

Thompson eventually replied, denying that he or anyone else had made fun of Van Buren ("the story is utterly false and unfounded"), but at the same time reminding Van Buren that since "so many new points seem to be arising between us, I am afraid you are losing sight of some old ones, as they remain unanswered."[102] The last reference was unmistakably to Van Buren's silence on Thompson's presidential feeler.

Finally in July Thompson decided to accept the nomination to the Court. He wrote Van Buren on July 11 that "nothing has as yet been definitely decided upon relative to filling the vacancy," and wondered "whether, after what has passed between you and myself on the subject, you think I could with propriety as it respects yourself take the office."[103] Van Buren took some time and care to reply, forwarding alternative drafts of a letter to King,[104] but Thompson did not wait for an answer. On July 20, five days before Van Buren dispatched his response, Thompson notified Monroe of his acceptance.[105]

The judgments of contemporaries who were involved in the episode were consistent in their condemnation of Thompson's machinations and also in their explanations for this conduct. Rufus King, who had first taken Thompson's offer to withdraw seriously and become genuinely enthusiastic about Van Buren's candidacy, could barely restrain himself after hearing of Thompson's eventual acceptance. He wrote Van Buren that

> not only have the proceedings at Washington been vacillating, and I believe unprincipled, but the correspondence of Mr. S. T. has been so extraordinary, that were the case my own, I should in reply observe much caution with a decided reserve, . . . If the first letter to you was not intended in the sense in which it was understood, but aimed at quite another and different object, your answer ought to have put him right, by making straight what was intentionally crooked. . . . To have made such communication [to Van Buren], while his mind continued undecided, was a violation of the duties of friendships; and . . . could not be reconciled with the principles of honor. . . . There neither is, nor can be, on like occasions an innocent or excusable failure. Mutual reservation, or the suppression of what should be expressed, is the part of rogues and Jesuits, who, being without honor, are incapable of the offices of friendship."[106]

---

[102] S. Thompson to M. Van Buren, June 26, 1823, ibid.
[103] S. Thompson to M. Van Buren, July 11, 1823, ibid.
[104] See R. King to M. Van Buren, July 22, 1823; copy of M. Van Buren to S. Thompson, July 25, 1823, in C. King, *Life and Correspondence*, VI, 526–527.

[105] J. Monroe to S. Gouverner, July 20, 1823, James Monroe Papers, New-York Historical Society, New York, N.Y.
[106] R. King to M. Van Buren, July 22, 1823, in C. King, *Life and Correspondence*, VI, 526.

William Crawford, writing Van Buren in connection with the oncoming presidential campaign, referred to a "secret history" of Thompson's appointment, and suggested that Thompson was "induced to take [the Court seat] from an unequivocal declaration that another office, of which some supposed he wished, was not obtainable."[107] As early as April 6, Daniel Webster had speculated to Story that "Mr. Thompson will be appointed if he chooses to take the office, but he has not made up his mind . . . I cannot account for his hesitation, but on a supposition, which I have heard suggested, but cannot credit, that he thinks it possible events may throw another and a brighter office in his way."[108]

Webster's intelligence was accurate, as was often the case. Moreover, his explanation for Thompson's conduct went close to the mark. "When a man finds himself in a situation he hardly ever dreamed of," Webster said, "he is apt to take it for granted that he is a favorite of fortune and to presume that this blind patroness may have yet greater things in reserve for him."[109] And Van Buren himself suggested a similar streak of hubris in Thompson in recollecting the episode thirty-one years later, after he had retired from political life. He reread his exchange of letters with Thompson in the spring of 1823, and concluded that

> previous to the offer of his influence in obtaining the Judgeship for me [Thompson] . . . had solicited in his straightforward way my support of himself for the Presidency, and became not a little impatient of my silence. This circumstance . . . may throw some light upon the course and disposition of the judicial appointment after it was ascertained that my inclinations in regard to the Presidential Question were not in that direction. I have myself fancied on rereading [the correspondence] now that I could discover traces of views and feelings on the part of others which . . . did not occur to me at the time.[110]

Van Buren, in his old age, concluded that the episode had had a kind of justice to it: he recalled that it had culminated by his encouraging Thompson to accept the Justiceship, "for which, by the way, he was as eminently qualified as he was unfit for political life."[111]

But while "political life" may have ceased for Thompson when he took his seat late in the 1823 Term, political involvement had not. A letter from John Calhoun to a supporter written in September 1823 suggested that Calhoun regarded Thompson as his first choice for the vice-

---

[107] W. Crawford to M. Van Buren, Aug. 1, 1823, Van Buren Papers.
[108] D. Webster to J. Story, Apr. 6, 1823, in *Proc. Mass. Hist. Soc.*, 14:404 (1901).

[109] Ibid.
[110] Van Buren, *Autobiography*, 141.
[111] Ibid.

presidency on an 1824 Calhoun ticket.[112] An October 1824 letter from Thompson to Calhoun warned the Adams administration to stay out of New York politics, and especially not to become identified with DeWitt Clinton and his supporters.[113] In 1827 Thompson had a conversation with one of Henry Clay's advisers in which he recommended that Clay run for vice-president with Adams and speculated "that Calhoun will be the Jacksonian candidate for the Vice Presidency." Clay's supporter described Thompson as "ha[ving] evidently taken much pains to inform himself touching the political matters of the day," and as being a "zealous support[er]" of the Adams administration. In that same conversation Thompson expressed a hope that should the Jacksonians win the 1828 election, their dedication to "Virginia school" policies would alienate "the middle and northern states," and result in the demise, "forever," of such Jacksonian supporters as Van Buren.[114]

After his unsuccessful campaign for governor of New York in 1828, Thompson reconciled himself to staying on the Court and being removed from circles of political influence while the Jacksonians held power. Thompson's gubernatorial candidacy, while anticipated by his opponent Van Buren, had been engaged in reluctantly. Calhoun wrote a friend in September 1828 that he was surprised that "one so experienced and sensible as Judge Thompson should permit himself to be so easily entrapped." Calhoun felt that Thompson's losing the election "would be his least misfortune."[115] Thompson confessed to Bushrod Washington that he would not have run "had it not been that it would have thrown the [National Republican] party into confusion and put at hazard some of the Presidential electors."[116] Thompson felt it would be "unfortunate" if he should be elected. He received 106,444 votes to Van Buren's 136,794.[117]

Thompson's political affiliations suggest that he would have been sympathetic to the Marshall Court's resistance to "Virginia school" doctrines. Between 1824 and 1832 he had vigorously supported Adams and Clay, opposed Jackson, broken decisively with Van Buren, and condemned the supporters of William Crawford as "radicals." But Thompson did not seem as committed to the internal norms of the Marshall Court as earlier Justices had been. While he took the unusual step of selling his

[112] J. Calhoun to Ogden Edwards, Sept. 21, 1823, Ogden Edwards Papers, Huntington Library, San Marino, Calif.

[113] S. Thompson to J. Calhoun, Oct. 24, 1824, Miscellaneous Papers, New York State Library, Albany, N.Y.

[114] William B. Rochester to H. Clay, Nov. 4, 1827, Clay Papers.

[115] J. Calhoun to John A. Dix, September [no date given] 1828, John A. Dix Papers, Columbia University.

[116] S. Thompson to B. Washington, Sept. 16, 1828, Thompson Papers, Huntington Library.

[117] E. Werner, *Civil List and Constitutional History of the Colony and State of New York* (1884), 156.

house in Washington in order to move in with the Justices at their boardinghouse,[118] he resolved to express his opinions separately in constitutional cases. As other Justices, such as Johnson, Baldwin, and McLean, followed suit, the result was less outward harmony and internal compromise in later Marshall Court opinions.[119]

On the major constitutional issues of the late Marshall Court Thompson took a vocal and often a nonconformist position. He was disinclined to follow the majoritarian position on Commerce Clause cases, giving greater weight to concurrent state regulatory powers[120] and anticipating a functional test, based on the subjects to be regulated, that eventually came to prevail in the Taney Court.[121] In Contract Clause cases Thompson joined the new majority formed in *Ogden* v. *Saunders,* in reversing previous trends so as to allow prospective debtor relief legislation. He also sustained a Rhode Island law abolishing imprisonment for debt against a Contract Clause challenge.[122] He dissented from the Court's ruling in *Craig* v. *Missouri*[123] that states were prevented by the Contract Clause from issuing bank certificates as tender for the payment of state debts. He also dissented in *Wheaton* v. *Peters,*[124] concluding that Reporter Henry Wheaton's copyright in the Court's Reports had "vested" at common law. In the *Charles River Bridge* case,[125] not decided until after Marshall's death, Thompson voted with Story in dissent. This pattern demonstrated more a willingness to take positions in opposition than any consistency of views. One study of Thompson's career has suggested that he tended to favor state power to regulate commerce because he thought it would encourage promotional ventures, and did not see this promotion as necessarily inconsistent with support for vested rights in other contexts.[126]

Thompson's inclination to state his views separately may have provided a significant example for other Justices in the late Marshall Court. Between 1815 and 1823, the year Thompson joined the Court, the Justices issued only 9 concurrences and 11 dissents; in the years between 1823 and 1835, 12 concurrences and 47 dissents were issued. Thompson himself contributed 7 dissents to the total, and judges named to the Court after Thompson were responsible for another 26 of the dissents. Moreover, Justice Johnson, the leading dissenter in both periods, wrote 15 of

---

[118] Ann Polk to S. Thompson, Apr. 1, 1824, Miscellaneous Papers, New York Public Library, New York, N.Y.

[119] See Chapter III, pp. 193–94, for statistics relevant to this assertion.

[120] Brown v. Maryland, 12 Wheat. 419 (1827) (dissent); Weston v. Charleston, 2 Pet. 449 (1829) (dissent).

[121] The Taney Court case typically cited for this proposition is Cooley v.

Board of Wardens, 12 How. 299 (1852), anticipated by Thompson in Brown v. Maryland, supra, note 120.

[122] Mason v. Haile, 12 Wheat. 370 (1827).

[123] 4 Pet. 410 (1830).

[124] 8 Pet. 591 (1834).

[125] 11 Pet. 420 (1837).

[126] Roper, "Mr. Justice Thompson," 182–83.

his 22 dissents after Thompson had joined the Court. In contrast, there was no significant change in the pattern of more senior Justices: Washington, Marshall, Story, Duvall, and Todd continued to write almost no separate opinions after Thompson's appointment. The inference one might draw is that Thompson presented to his associates a departure from existing patterns of socialization—a Justice disinclined to suppress his views to achieve the outward appearance of harmony—and that some other Justices, either distressed with the established norms (Johnson), or unfamiliar with them (Baldwin and McLean) welcomed his posture.

In his reluctance to be socialized and in his continued political activity, Thompson was a new type of Marshall Court appointee. Rather than regarding the Court as a retreat from politics, he thought of it as a base from which a political career might be launched. In making this assumption he set a new tone for the aspirations of future appointees, and others, such as McLean, came to the Court with comparable ambitions. This new interpretation of the role and potential constituency of a Supreme Court Justice was inconsistent with the norms Marshall and his confederates had sought to develop, norms that discouraged partisanship, emphasized the suppression of individual views in the furtherance of an apparent harmony and solidarity, and treated an appointment to the Court as a withdrawal from political life. The increased political power of the Marshall Court had, paradoxically, been built on its eschewal of partisan politics; Thompson's open espousal of continued political involvement was a challenge to the edifice Marshall and his colleagues had carefully erected.

One of the likeliest candidates for obscurity among Marshall Court Justices is Thomas Todd, who appears to be best known for the large number of terms (five out of nineteen) that he missed because of illness, injury, or travel difficulties, the extraordinary amount of time he spent on circuit travel, and the conspicuously few opinions he wrote during his tenure (eleven majority opinions, and only fourteen all told in nineteen years).[127] Todd's anonymity has been abetted by the small number of his

---

[127] Two law review articles have claimed that Todd was either the "most insignificant justice" in the entire history of the Court, or at least a prime candidate for that honor. See D. Currie, "The Most Insignificant Justice: A Preliminary Inquiry," U. Chi. L. Rev., 50:466, 470 (1983), and F. Easter-brook, "The Most Insignificant Justice: Further Evidence," U. Chi. L. Rev., 50:481, 492–96 (1983). The fact that the articles were intended as efforts at humor should not detract from their significance. In scholarship the line between seminality and absurdity is sometimes blurred.

private papers that have survived and by his unobtrusive personality. His most conspicuous act as a Supreme Court Justice was to fall in love with and marry Dolley Madison's sister. The president's wife wrote of Todd at the time (1812) that he was "a man of the most estimable character, best principles, and high tolerance."[128] Todd himself welcomed his connection to "our estimable friends at the White House."[129]

In fact, Todd was a strategic member of the Marshall Court in several respects. First, he appears to have been fully dedicated to the Court's internal policies, writing only one dissent during his entire tenure and never differing from Marshall's position on a constitutional issue. Todd's loyalty was especially important since he came from Kentucky, a state that was often dissatisfied with the Court's decisions, especially in the areas of land claims and insolvency legislation. While the prevalent attitude in Kentucky was one of hostility toward consolidationist tendencies on the part of the Court and of sympathy for debtor relief legislation,[130] Todd stood with the Marshall Court majority in resisting state autonomy and construing the Contract Clause so as to invalidate debtor relief laws. Although he was absent when the Court decided *Green v. Biddle,* correspondence makes it clear that he supported the majority's position that a Kentucky debtor relief statute ran afoul of the Contract Clause.[131]

Second, Todd's experiences in law practice in Kentucky had made him conversant with the intricacies of western lands title claims, a subject that regularly appeared on the Marshall Court's docket. The principal locus of western lands cases was Kentucky, whose land titles had been in a chaotic state since the partitioning of Kentucky from Virginia in 1796. Particularly troublesome was the interaction between nonresident landowners and squatters. The Kentucky legislature encouraged squatters to make improvements on land and then claim ownership; *Green v. Biddle* involved such a case. Todd's expertise in the area of land law, combined with his resolute opposition to the Kentucky legislature's efforts to protect occupying claimants, made him a valuable ally for the Court majority.

---

[128] D. Madison to Richard Cutts, Mar. 10, 1812, McGregor Papers, University of Virginia Library.

[129] T. Todd to R. Cutts, June 19, 1814, ibid.

[130] For samples of the mood, see the editorials of three newspapers in the 1820s, the *Kentucky Gazette* (Lexington, Ky.), the *Argus of Western America* (Frankfort, Ky.), and the Louisville *Gazette.* See also Warren, *Supreme Court,* II, 93–111.

[131] In writing Todd, who was absent for the 1823 Term but not for the 1821 Term (when the case was first argued and Story produced a unanimous opinion of the Court), Story referred to that opinion, which was eventually withdrawn, as "our opinion," and indicated that "we wanted your firm vote on many occasions." J. Story to T. Todd, Mar. 14, 1823, in W. Story, *Life and Letters,* I, 422–23.

In addition, Marshall and Washington, both long-term residents of Virginia but owners of land in Kentucky, needed Todd's advice in threading their way through the unfamiliar complexities of Kentucky land law.[132] "We all missed you exceedingly during this term," Story wrote to Todd in 1823, "and particularly in the Kentucky Causes, many of which have been continued, solely on account of your absence."[133]

Finally, Todd was a strong supporter of the Bank of the United States and of the Court's efforts to prevent states from taxing the Bank out of existence or otherwise infringing on its operations. He joined the Court's support of the Bank in *McCulloch* v. *Maryland*[134] and *Osborn* v. *Bank*,[135] two decisions exceedingly unpopular in Kentucky, a hotbed of opposition to the Bank. Reacting to the *Osborn* decision, one Kentucky newspaper identified the Bank as "the chief cause of all the aggressions upon the sovereignty of the States . . . which have proceeded from the Federal authorities," and suggested that the Bank was "leaning on the judicial arm, which not only awards to the corporation all the claims but seeks every occasion to humble the states."[136]

Todd had been an organizer, supporter, and original stockholder of the Bank. In 1816 and 1817 he wrote letters to directors of the Bank in Philadelphia attempting to ensure that the directors of the Kentucky branch would be Republicans, and his own name was suggested for a directorship.[137] In September 1818, when the *McCulloch* case was on its way to the Supreme Court, Todd wrote William James, one of the Bank's officers, asking him to advance money to Todd's stepson should an arrangement whereby a portion of Todd's salary (paid through the Bank of the United States) was diverted to his stepson fail because of defects in mail service. Todd asked Jones to "excuse the presumption in making this application to you," and offered "a tender of my services in any way to which they can be employed to your advantage" as "remuneration."[138]

In three important respects, then, Todd supported the Marshall Court in conflicts with his own state. While Todd's opinions were infrequent,

---

[132] See T. Todd to B. Washington, Aug. 20, 1820, and Mar. 22, 1824, Bushrod Washington Papers, Free Library of Philadelphia. Marshall disqualified himself in *Green* v. *Biddle* because he had "near relatives deeply interested in that judgment." Charles F. Mercer, 19th Cong., 1st Sess., Jan. 6, 1826, at 903. *Green* v. *Biddle* is discussed in Chapter IX. The Marshall Court's western lands cases are discussed in Chapter XI.

[133] Story to Todd, Mar. 14, 1823, supra, note 131.

[134] 4 Wheat. 316 (1819).

[135] 9 Wheat. 738 (1824).

[136] *Argus of Western America* (Frankfurt, Ky.), May 12, 1824.

[137] See T. Todd to Morrison Jones, Oct. 14, 1816, Miscellaneous Papers, Historical Society of Pennsylvania, Philadelphia, Pa.; T. Todd to William Jones, Dec. 21, 1816, ibid.; Joseph Taylor to W. Jones, Jan. 14, 1817, ibid.

[138] T. Todd to W. Jones, Sept. 19, 1818, ibid.

and almost exclusively in the field of land law,[139] his presence lent harmony and cohesiveness to the Court in the years in which it emerged as a major force in American political life. As Story put it, Todd "steadfastly supported the constitutional doctrines which Mr. Chief Justice Marshall promulgated in the name of the Court." Although "bred in a different political school from that of the Chief Justice," Story noted, Todd "never failed to sustain those great principles of constitutional law on which the security of the Union depends. He never gave up to party, what he thought belonged to the country." The other Justices found Todd a person of "uncommon patience and candor in investigation, great clearness and sagacity of judgment; a cautious but steady energy; [and] a well-balanced independence." He held "the legal confidence of all who knew him."[140]

If Todd's career on the Court has remained obscure, that of Gabriel Duvall has been virtually unknown. Duvall, where noted at all, has been chiefly recognized for his deafness, for his "long, thin, and snowy locks," which were tied in a "white curl hanging down to his waist";[141] for a controversy over the spelling of his name, which, Albert Beveridge declared in 1919, was "often, incorrectly, spelled with two 'l's,"[142] but which was unmistakably spelled with two l's by Duvall in his own correspondence; and for the undistinguished impression he made on some contemporaries, one of whom called him "not . . . even up to mediocrity on the Bench."[143] Duvall himself did little during his tenure to forestall this subsequent image. He produced only fifteen opinions in twenty-three years on the Court, none in major cases. His significant votes, such as his dissent in *Dartmouth College* and his joining Marshall's dissenting opinion in *Ogden* v. *Saunders,* were unaccompanied by opinions. He might have been a pivotal vote in the *Charles River Bridge* case,[144] but since that case was not decided until after Duvall's retirement, his position remains unknown. Duvall's apparent insignificance has placed a heavy burden on commentators, who in their quest to lend some drama to his career have had to resort to claims that Duvall's dissent in *Dartmouth College* was "an act of outstanding boldness," suggesting "courage to a rare degree."[145]

---

[139] Of Todd's thirteen opinions, ten involved land cases. See L. Blandford and P. Evans, eds., *Supreme Court of the United States 1789–1980: An Index of Opinions Arranged by Justice* (1983), 55.

[140] J. Story in W. Story, *Life and Letters,* I, 498.

[141] Smith, *Early Indiana Trials,* 138.

[142] A. Beveridge, *The Life of John Marshall* (4 vols., 1819), IV, 60.

[143] Smith, *Early Indiana Trials,* 138.

[144] See C. Swisher, *The Taney Period, 1836–64* (1974), 76–78; S. Kutler, *Privilege and Creative Destruction* (1971), 174–75. The Marshall Court's deliberations on the *Charles River Bridge* case are discussed in Chapter IX.

[145] I. Dilliard, "Gabriel Duvall," in Friedman and Israel, *Justices,* I, 419,

Duvall's private letters, while not contributing to an understanding of his performance as a judge, help to flesh out his portrait. Duvall's pre-Court career was typical of many of the Justices here portrayed: he received a liberal education, read law, became involved in state politics, served briefly in Congress, and had some state judicial experience; he was chief justice of the General Court of Maryland and a recorder (the equivalent of a judge) of the Mayor's Court of Annapolis. Roger Taney's first argument in court came before Duvall in 1799, and Taney remembered that

> just as we had empannelled the jury, and felt quite brave . . . to our utter dismay in walked Recorder Duvall, with his grave face and dignified deportment, and took his seat on the bench.
>
> I do not know whether my associate or myself was the more frightened. We had both been accustomed to see him administering justice in the General Court, and listening to the first lawyers of the state, and we thought he would hardly, in his own mind, fail to contrast our efforts with theirs.[146]

Duvall at this time was forty-seven years old and an experienced Maryland lawyer and politician. He had been chief justice of the General Court and recorder of the Mayor's Court since 1796, had been a member of the electoral college that year (and was to repeat that role in 1800), and had served seven years in the Maryland legislature. He was an early supporter of Jefferson, and that support was ultimately to result in his being named to the Court.

In November 1802, Jefferson wrote Duvall offering him the position of comptroller of the United States. The office was "in its nature," Jefferson said, "partly Executive and partly judiciary, as the Comptroller decides in the first instance all questions of law arising in matters of account between the U.S. and individuals."[147] Duvall accepted, and served in the position until 1811, when Madison appointed him to the Court. A miscellaneous collection of correspondence from Duvall as comptroller reveals that Jefferson's characterization of the position was accurate. Duvall admonished collectors "to be particularly vigilant in guarding the revenue against . . . false invoices at some of the custom-houses,"[148] construed acts of Congress, interpreted Supreme Court decisions bearing on claims in bankruptcy and insolvency, asked for information about custom-house practices, issued opinions on the imple-

---

[146] Taney in S. Tyler, *Memoir of Roger Brooke Taney* (1872), 76–77.
[147] Thomas Jefferson to G. Duvall, Nov. 5, 1802, Gabriel Duvall Papers, Library of Congress.

[148] G. Duvall, memorandum, May 31, 1803, Miscellaneous Papers, New York Public Library.

mentation of treasury regulations, and responded to inquiries from collectors. Most of Duvall's cases concerned United States ports, and he had considerable opportunity to construe maritime legislation, including the Embargo Acts imposed by Jefferson in 1807.

In 1806 Duvall was tempted to return to Maryland to accept two judicial appointments, chief judge of the Maryland district court for the first district and chancellor of the Maryland equity courts. He wrote his son, "I would have preferred either appointment to my present arduous office," but "there is a consistency of conduct which I cannot abandon." He had resigned a Maryland judgeship to accept an appointment with the federal government, and "to quit the latter would have too much the appearance of levity of character."[149] Duvall's loyalty to the Jefferson and Madison administrations was eventually rewarded when Samuel Chase died in June 1811, and Duvall, being from the same state, was named Chase's successor.

Duvall's new position made it possible for him to return to his birthplace, the plantation Marietta near Buena Vista in Price George's County. The circuit to which he was assigned, the Fourth, consisted only of Baltimore, Maryland, and Dover, Delaware; in 1839 Chief Justice Taney estimated his annual mileage on that circuit to be 458 miles.[150] Duvall thus was able to spend a significant amount of time at home, where he gave attention to his horses, his farm, and his family life, which had its unfortunate aspects. In 1790 Duvall's first wife became ill and died after giving birth to their only child, a son. Duvall wrote his father that "nothing in this world can be more severe than parting with so endearing, so affectionate, virtuous and tender a wife, who possessed all that is amiable and good among women." Duvall chastised himself for "weakness in wishing the longer continuance of our dearest friends in this evil world," but confessed that "so great was my affection for her . . . that were she now living and single, if I had my choice of all the world I would prefer her."[151] Four years later Duvall was remarried, to Jane Gibbons, with whom he lived until her death in 1834. His second marriage was the subject of some wry commentary by William Wirt, who visited the Duvalls in October 1826, when Duvall was in his seventy-fifth year. Wirt arrived "between two and three o'clock," and

the old lady insisted on boiling a fowl for my dinner which kept it off till four o'clock, and asked me twice whether I slept with the bed or mattress uppermost before she would finally make any arrangements

---

149 G. Duvall to Edmund Duvall, Jan. 25, 1806, Duvall Papers, Library of Congress.
150 Quoted in Senate Report No. 50, 25th Cong., 3rd Sess. (1839), at 32.

151 G. Duvall to Benjamin Duvall, Mar. 28, 1790, Duvall Papers, Library of Congress.

for the night. Whenever the old lady left the room I had a most interesting talk with the old judge about the times and characters long since past, especially in Bladensburg, which he had known before my birth—but the good old lady was continually breaking in upon us with her tiresome gossip—at eight she threw her head back against the couch and, with open mouth, fell fast asleep—but she waked up every half hour and broke in upon us again, regardless of our subject . . .

She is, I verily believe, an excellent old lady, but she makes rather too much parade of her kindness and seems rather too anxious for everybody to know it. They are quite snugly fixed, but her clack manifestly harasses the old judge about to death—and would kill me dead if I had no retreat from it. The old judge, I suspect, makes a retreat in his newspapers and books and sleep, real or affected.[152]

Duvall's son, Edmund Bryce Duvall, was also something of a trial for the "old judge." In an 1806 letter to Edmund, filled with observations on his education (Duvall recommended mathematics, Latin, and French as subjects for concentration and agreed that dancing was a "genteel, if not a necessary, accomplishment," although it should not "interrupt your studies more that what may be unavoidable") and homilies on life ("a well deserved popularity is the highest recommendation which a man can possess"), Duvall concluded by noting that Edmund was "not attentive enough to your diction, nor to your handwriting."[153] While these admonitions did not augur any serious difficulties, and were characteristic of father–son correspondence at the time (if Supreme Court Justices are a representative sample), as an adult Edmund's problems became more troublesome. He successfully graduated from college, entered the army (eventually becoming a colonel), married and fathered five children, but his mental health began to deteriorate severely in the 1820s. By January 1829, Duvall was writing the Supreme Court Reporter, Richard Peters, that the reports on Edmund were "disturbing indeed," and that "I cannot but be apprehensive of his approaching dissolution."[154] Edmund was at that time in a mental institution in Philadelphia. In July of the same year Duvall wrote out a prayer for his son, asking that he be "restore[d] . . . to sanity and health."[155] In February 1830 Duvall was forced to leave Washington for Marietta because of "a return of [Edmund's] insanity." Story reported to his wife that Edmund's illness was "a melancholy affliction to the old gentleman, who may be said never before to have felt

---

[152] W. Wirt to Elizabeth Wirt, Oct. 22, 1826, William Wirt Papers, Maryland Historical Society, Annapolis, Md.

[153] G. Duvall to E. Duvall, Jan. 25, 1806, supra, note 149.

[154] G. Duvall to R. Peters, Jr., June 11, 1829, Peters Papers.

[155] G. Duvall, memorandum, July 1829, Duvall Papers, Library of Congress.

a serious affliction in his whole life." (Story seemed unaware of the death of Duvall's first wife.) "As proof of [Duvall's] extraordinary equanimity and quiet temperament," Story continued, "he told me a short time since that he had scarcely lost a night's sleep in his life. So easily and smoothly the world moves on with him."[156] A year later Edmund died.

Duvall's relative anonymity as a judge, or his equanimity, should not be taken as a lack of interest in his job. Observers suggested that he was dominated by Pinkney on the Fourth Circuit, and there was a marked absence of tribute to his intellectual strengths in Story's eulogy on his death. Normally effusive in his praise of the intellects of all departed Justices save those, such as Johnson, whom he disliked, Story referred only to Duvall's "urbanity, his courtesy, his gentle manners, his firm integrity and independence."[157] But while there is no evidence that Duvall contributed intellectually to the Marshall Court, there is evidence that he was well aware of the political consequences of his decisions. When the case of *McCulloch* v. *Maryland* was pending, Edward W. DuVal, a cousin of the judge and a minor office-seeker, wrote William Jones, one of the officers of the Bank of the United States, revealing the outcome of the decision three days before it was announced. DuVal said that "the opinion of the Court is not yet known, but I beg you will take it for a certainty that the opinion will be in favor of the Bank," and that it "will be unanimous." "If any advantages are derivable from a knowledge of this fact," DuVal continued, "do not hesitate as to its indubitable certainty."[158] Jones responded three days later, indicating that he would be "greatly benefitted" by the decision, but that it was "neither convenient nor perhaps prudent for me to hazard any new speculations."[159] The correspondence suggests that Duvall was not above leaking the results of Supreme Court cases to relatives who sought to use them to their advantage.

In his last years on the Court Duvall suffered a loss of hearing. In 1831 Marshall wrote Story, in connection with the Court's lodgings for the 1832 Term, that "Brother Duvall must be with us as he will be unable to attend consultations."[160] In a letter to Warren Dutton in January 1833, Webster said that Duvall's "ability to hear causes is not so good as formerly," but "his capacity for deciding them" was "unimpaired."[161]

---

[156] J. Story to S. W. Story, Feb. 17, 1830, Story Papers, University of Texas Library.
[157] J. Story, remarks on Duvall's death, quoted in W. Story, *Life and Letters*, II, 470.
[158] E. W. DuVal to W. Jones, Mar. 4, 1819, Miscellaneous Papers, Historical Society of Pennsylvania, Philadelphia, Pa.

[159] W. Jones to E. W. DuVal, Mar. 7, 1819, ibid.
[160] J. Marshall to J. Story, June 26, 1831, in *Proc. Mass. Hist. Soc.*, 14:344, (1901).
[161] D. Webster to W. Dutton, Jan. 4, 1833, Webster Papers, Dartmouth College Library.

Wirt wrote Dabney Carr in May of that year that he found Duvall, sitting on circuit in Baltimore, to be "so deaf as to be incapable [of hearing] my voice."[162] In 1835, shortly before Duvall's retirement, Congressman Benjamin Hardin of Kentucky claimed that he had not heard a legal argument for ten years.[163] And a year earlier Charles Sumner, after attending a Supreme Court argument, had noted that "Judge Duvall . . . is so deaf as to be unable to participate in conversation."[164] But "old ironsides," as Wirt called him in 1829,[165] remained on the Court until 1835, when he learned that if he resigned Jackson would appoint Roger Taney, whom Duvall admired, as his successor.[166]

There were nine years of life left for Duvall after his retirement. He remained active and in tolerable health, cultivating interests in horses and farming. He wrote a letter just before his retirement giving precise details about horses he had seen run in the 1760s: the recipient of the letter added a note that Duvall's "extraordinary memory of dates and events" meant that he was "never required to bring proof of anything he would assert as of his own knowledge."[167] In 1840, in his eighty ninth year, he inquired about "manure, & particularly . . . lime," having "read a good deal about [it]," but "never [having] met with an author who mentions the quantity necessary to an acre." In that letter Duvall said that he was "too feeble to write a word more than is necessary,"[168] though he went on to live four more years.

Both Todd's and Duvall's careers raise the issue of the intangible contributions of a relatively inarticulate judge to a court whose decisions are reached in collegial debate. If accomplishment is measured in the quantity of opinions, Duvall surely was one of the least significant judges to sit on the Supreme Court. Even the few opinions he did write are not memorable: almost none involved major cases,[169] and none was more than a few pages in length. But we have seen that the structure of Marshall

---

[162] W. Wirt to D. Carr, May 17, 1833, William Wirt Papers, University of North Carolina Library.

[163] Congressional Debates, 23d Cong., 2d Sess. (1835), at 965.

[164] C. Sumner, in E. Pierce, *Memoirs and Letters of Charles Sumner* (4 vols., 1893), I, 135.

[165] W. Wirt to E. Wirt, Jan. 5, 1829, Wirt Papers, Maryland Historical Society, Annapolis, Md.

[166] Taney's nomination as an Associate Justice was not confirmed by the Senate; the next year Jackson successfully nominated him to the Chief Justiceship. See Tyler, *Memoir of Taney*, 239–40.

[167] G. Duvall to J. S. Skinner, Feb. 15, 1835, Duvall Papers, Maryland Historical Society, Annapolis, Md.

[168] G. Duvall to J. S. Skinner, July 19, 1840, Miscellaneous Papers, New York Public Library.

[169] Arguably LeGrand v. Darnell, 2 Pet. 664 (1829), a case involving the effects on a slave's freedom on a testamentary grant of property to that slave, was an important case, although the opinion's contention (that such an act made the slave free) seems not to have been in serious dispute.

Chapter V: *The Justices of the Marshall Court*

Court decisionmaking permitted contributions by "silent" Justices, that is, Justices who participated in oral deliberations at the boardinghouse but did not choose to make public their opinions or even their votes. Given Duvall's relatively low energy level and his interest in preserving urbanity and decorum, it is hard to imagine his being a fractious force on the Court. In a letter to Duvall on his retirement, Marshall spoke of the "cordiality" and "fidelity" of Duvall's performance, and the "purity of [his] public life."[170] Marshall, in the years of his joint service with Duvall, could count on the "old judge": count on him to be present in Washington, whatever the state of his health; to be a gracious and courtly participant at the boardinghouse; and, most of all, to support Marshall's point of view, despite their original partisan differences. In a small group of people who knew each other well and relied upon each other's support, Duvall's presence was a comfort. Henry Wheaton, in a bitter letter to his wife written after the Court decided against him in *Wheaton v. Peters,* said that Duvall "never had any . . . mind," and was "in the keeping of Story."[171] But whether Duvall's regular support for the Marshall Court majority decisions rested on independent judgments or the influence of others is in a sense unimportant; for twenty-three years he was there to be counted on.

The third of the "silent" Justices of the Marshall Court's cohesive years was Brockholst Livingston, who, like Todd and Duvall, was an amiable participant in boardinghouse colloquies, a supporter of majoritarian doctrines, and a convert, after a tenure on the Supreme Court of New York in which he had written seriatim opinions, to the prevailing style of suppressed concurrences and dissents.

Livingston's altered stance on the Marshall Court gave testimony not only to his amenable temperament but to his political savvy. He came to the Court an experienced judicial politician, prepared by his membership in the Livingston family and by his service on the Supreme Court of New York, that unique institution whose members served simultaneously on the Council of Revision, a body that vetoed and redrafted legislation. The Livingston family, with its many branches and factions, was one of the dominant political forces in late-eighteenth- and early-nineteenth-century New York. Brockholst was the son of William Livingston, one of the leaders of the manor branch of the family; his cousin was Chancellor Robert Livingston and his brother-in-law John Jay, for whom

[170] J. Marshall to G. Duvall, Jan. 16, 1835, Miscellaneous Papers, Historical Society of Pennsylvania, Philadelphia, Pa.

[171] H. Wheaton to Catherine Wheaton, Mar. 21, 1834, Henry Wheaton Papers, Pierpont Morgan Library, New York, N.Y.

he was secretary when Jay became minister to Spain in 1779. Brockholst Livingston attended Princeton and read law with James Kent; he was admitted to the bar in 1783 and immediately became involved in politics, land disputes, and speculation in bank currency and securities.[172]

Brockholst was soon caught up in political squabbles, both within the family and throughout the state. He developed an animosity toward his brother-in-law Jay, and wrote unsigned polemics against Jay's candidacy for governor that prompted his sister to call his conduct "shameless" and a "disgrace."[173] Chancellor Robert Livingston regarded Brockholst as "somewhat given to duplicity,"[174] although he was to offer Brockholst the chancellorship of New York in 1801.[175] Livingston's opposition to Jay also provoked his former preceptor Kent, who said that Brockholst's "character . . . was long before publicly abandoned," and that his conduct was "execrable" and "infamous in the highest degree."[176] The biographer of Chancellor Robert Livingston asserted that because of Brockholst's involvement against Jay he was "distrusted by the whole manor family."[177] But Brockholst was "the toughest and the most persistent"[178] of the Livingstons, and he survived, largely thanks to his partnership with DeWitt Clinton and Aaron Burr, with whom he joined forces to promote the Jefferson–Burr ticket in 1800 and Clinton's candidacy for the Senate in 1802. As a result of those efforts Livingston was named to the New York Supreme Court in 1802. Kent, recalling Livingston nearly fifty years later and possibly forgetting his 1792 comments, said that he was "very polished in his address and courteous in his manners . . . tall, thin, graceful, and rapid and elegant as a speaker."[179] As a New York state judge Livingston became acquainted with maritime and prize cases and with commercial litigation, two interests he would retain on the Marshall Court. He also continued his involvement in politics, being a prominent anti-Federalist, if not always a doctrinaire Republican. In 1806, when Justice William Paterson of New Jersey died, Jefferson appointed Livingston to the Supreme Court.

Livingston entered the Court at a time when the customs of silent unanimity and deference to the Chief Justice in the writing of opinions

---

[172] Details of Livingston's early career may be found in Dangerfield, *Chancellor Robert Livingston*, and G. Dunne, "Brockholst Livingston," in Friedman and Israel, *Justices*, I, 387.

[173] Quoted in F. Monaghan, *John Jay* (1935), 336.

[174] Dangerfield, *Chancellor Robert Livingston*, 272.

[175] B. Livingston to R. Livingston, June 25, 1801, Graetz Papers, Histori-

cal Society of Pennsylvania, Philadelphia, Pa.

[176] James Kent to Moss Kent, June 15, 1792, James Kent Papers, Library of Congress.

[177] Dangerfield, *Chancellor Robert Livingston*, 281.

[178] Ibid., 299.

[179] J. Kent to William King, April 5, 1847, Kent Papers.

Thomas Emmet, from an engraving by W. G. Jastonan, based on an unknown portrait
painted late in Emmet's life, probably after 1815.
*(Library of Congress)*

Littleton Tazewell, from an unknown portrait, probably painted in the late 1820s, when Tazewell was a United States senator from Virginia.
*(Virginia Historical Society)*

Luther Martin, from an engraving by W. A. Wilmer based on an unknown portrait, probably painted around 1805.
*(Library of Congress)*

William Pinkney, in characteristically resplendent attire, from an engraving based on a portrait attributed to "Chappel," probably painted around 1811, when Pinkney was appointed Attorney General of the United States.
*(Library of Congress)*

William Wirt, from an engraving by A. B. Walter of a portrait by Charles B. King,
painted early in Wirt's tenure as Attorney General of the United States, which began in
1817.
*(Library of Congress)*

Daniel Webster, "drawn from life" by James B. Longacre, around 1833.
*(Library of Congress)*

Henry Wheaton, Reporter of the Marshall Court from 1816 to 1827. From an unknown portrait probably painted around the time Wheaton assumed the Reportership.
*(Collection of the Supreme Court of the United States)*

Richard Peters, Jr., from a portrait by Rembrandt Peale, probably painted in the 1820s. *(Library of Congress)*

had become established. Between the 1801 and 1810 Terms Marshall wrote all but one of the Court's opinions in constitutional cases, and 155 out of 182 majority opinions all told. There were only eighteen dissents filed in that entire period.[180] Beginning with the 1812 Term, however, as new Justices came on the Court and the size of the Court expanded to seven members, Marshall's dominance became less pronounced. But Livingston, Bushrod Washington, and William Johnson, the holdovers from the earlier period, were by that time inculcated in the practices, and even Johnson, who differed from the majority regularly, found it burdensome to express himself separately until the 1820s. Livingston apparently found silent acquiescence to his liking, writing only seven opinions between 1807 and 1811 and forty-nine in all, of which five were concurrences and three dissents. In 1819, notwithstanding his having taken an unequivocal position on the constitutionality of insolvency legislation in a circuit opinion two years earlier,[181] Livingston silently acquiesced in *Sturges* v. *Crowninshield*, in which Marshall, for a bare majority of the court, found that similar legislation, if retroactively applied, violated the Contract Clause.[182]

Livingston's performance on the Court suggests that he particularly welcomed its informal deliberations and its spirit of "togetherness." In 1808 Story spoke of Livingston's "accessible and easy" qualities "in private society," and his enjoyment of "the vivacities . . . of the wit and the moralist."[183] As early as 1812, after Story's first term on the Court, Livingston wrote him that he expected to have Mrs. Story stay with him "while she remains in New York," and that he would be "greatly mortified by a denial."[184] A year later Livingston wrote Story that he expected Story to stay with him before they set out for Washington for the 1814 Term. This offer was repeated in an 1821 letter: "I have only to say, that on your way [to Washington], whether your stay in this City be long or

---

[180] See R. Seddig, "John Marshall and the Origins of Supreme Court Leadership," *U. Pitt. L. Rev.*, 36:785, 800 (1975).

[181] *Adams* v. *Storey*, 1 F. Cas. 141 (C.C.D. N.Y. 1817). In a letter to Story about this opinion, William Pinkney described it as "masterful." W. Pinkney to J. Story, July 5, 1817, Story Papers, University of Texas Library.

[182] In a letter to his brother-in-law, Stephen White, written on February 17, 1819, Story intimated that Livingston did not concur in *Sturges* v. *Crowninshield*. J. Story to S. White, quoted in W. Story, *Life and Letters*, I, 326. But in the Court's official report of the case,

4 Wheat. at 191, 208 (1819), no Justices were recorded as dissenting from Marshall's opinion of the Court. Later Johnson, in *Ogden* v. *Saunders*, revealed that "the Court was greatly divided . . . and the judgment [partook] more of a compromise [than] of a legal adjudication. The minority thought it better to yield something than risk the whole." 12 Wheat. at 272–73. For a fuller discussion, see Chapter IX.

[183] J. Story to Samuel P. P. Fay, Feb. 25, 1808, in W. Story, *Life and Letters*, I. 167.

[184] B. Livingston to J. Story, June 10, 1812, Story Papers, University of Texas Library.

short, I shall expect you to make your home at No. 27 Broadway."[185] In a memorial tribute Story spoke of Livingston's "amiable manners and general kindness of disposition," and noted that he was "admired for all those qualities which constitute the finished gentleman."[186]

Livingston, like many of the other members of the Marshall Court, was well aware of the opportunities for extrajudicial influence that accompanied his position, and occasionally took advantage of them. In 1811 he apparently had an interest in a prize case that was being decided in circuit court in Baltimore; correspondence with his counsel, Robert Harper, reveals that Harper and Livingston expected that while a Baltimore jury would be prejudiced against their position, the Marshall Court would be sympathetic to it.[187] And in 1818 Charles Marsh, a trustee of Dartmouth College, had a conversation with Livingston while the *Dartmouth College* case was being reargued, and reported to the president of the College that "Justice Livingston intimated to me that the court would not hear another argument unless it might be to some new point not before urged."[188] Livingston also used the stature of his office to make recommendations to President Monroe for commissionerships,[189] to give advice on the redrafting of a fugitive slave law so as to tighten its implementation in New York state,[190] and to attempt to forestall any efforts in Congress to change the timing of his Second Circuit court sessions.[191] The last letter gave a vivid account of life on Livingston's circuit:

> The fall session is now held at Rutland [Vermont] on the 3d of October, which follows so closely on the court which is held at Hartford on the 17th day of September as to enable the Judge who holds these courts to finish the business of both without returning home or [suffering] an unnecessary detention on the road. If this term, as is contemplated, is changed to the 15th of November, the Judge must return home and set out again in a very inclement season, and when the roads in Vermont are almost impassable, and perform a Journey out and home, of between six and seven hundred miles for the sole purpose of holding a court at Montpelier. . . .
>
> At present the inhabitants on both sides of the mountains are accommodated and the courts are held in two of the pleasantest and

---

[185] B. Livingston to J. Story, Jan. 15, 1821, ibid.

[186] [Story], "Memorandum," 8 Wheat. v (1823).

[187] R. G. Harper to B. Livingston, Jan. 16, 1811, Miscellaneous Papers, Maryland Historical Society, Annapolis, Md.

[188] C. Marsh to Francis Brown, Nov. 11, 1818, Dartmouth College Library.

[189] B. Livingston to J. Monroe, Feb.

19, 1819, National Archives (recommending Henry Wheaton to be a Commissioner of Spanish Claims).

[190] B. Livingston to John Sergeant, Jan. 18, 1822, John Sergeant Papers, Historical Society of Pennsylvania, Philadelphia, Pa.

[191] B. Livingston to Timothy Pitkin, June 28, 1813, Timothy Pitkin Papers, Huntington Library, San Marino, Calif.

most convenient towns in the State, and both of them at seasons of the year when the roads are good and the traveling delightful—but what must the roads and traveling be between the middle of November and the middle of December, at which time I should be getting home? A more unfortunate day could not have been thought of and the greatest enemy of the federal courts in Vermont, and they are not without them in that State, could not have contrived to harass them more than by carrying them from the delightful villages where they now send to the dreary spot intended by this bill, and to fix on a season of the year for one of the sessions, when you must travel knee-deep in mud to get there.[192]

Livingston was present for many of the Marshall Court's great cases, voting each time, except in *Sturges* v. *Crowninshield,* with the majority. He wrote no opinions that are regarded as significant, although Story spoke of his "principal attention to the maritime and commercial law," and the "extensive experience" that "gave to his judgments in [those branches] of jurisprudence a peculiar value."[193] In *Dartmouth College,* perhaps to show his dedication to the principle of collegiality, he concurred in Marshall's opinion of the Court and in Story's and Washington's concurrences, and then declined to file a concurrence of his own that he had prepared.[194]

Livingston's geniality and good manners apparently concealed a hot temper. He fought several duels in his career, killing one of his adversaries in 1798 after the latter, angered by Livingston's political attacks on him, had "caught him by the nose [which Story described as "aquiline"] and struck him."[195] He married three times, was twice widowed, and fathered eleven children. A patron of educational institutions, he was a trustee of the American Academy of Languages and Belles Lettres, a founder of the New-York Historical Society, and a trustee of Columbia University. He was "an accomplished classical scholar, and versed in the languages and literature of the southern nations of Europe."[196]

In the winter of 1823 Livingston developed pleurisy. Rufus King reported on March 2 of that year that "Livingston continues ill, tho' not so . . . ill as had been reported to me . . . and I hope will wear through it." King commented that although Livingston was not "in immediate danger," already persons in Washington "are caballing concerning Livingston's successor. . . . This is truly the most heartless place in the

---

[192] Ibid. Note that the letter indicates that Livingston began his circuit-riding in the middle of September, earlier than Story's New England circuit. See the discussion in Chapter III.

[193] 8 Wheat. at v.

[194] Dunne, "Brockholst Livingston," 393.

[195] Story to Fay, Feb. 25, 1808, supra, note 183; Dunne, "Brockholst Livingston," 396.

[196] 8 Wheat. at v.

country.''[197] Livingston's family was notified of his illness, and his third wife, Catherine Kortright, and one of his daughters, Susan Ledyard, came to Washington to nurse him. On the fourteenth of March Story wrote Todd that Livingston was "still very ill; whether he will ever recover is doubtful."[198] Four days later William Johnson wrote John Sergeant that "poor Livingston has been dying," and that Mrs. Ledyard had "adopted the . . . project of having his Body immediately transported to New York."[199] Livingston died the same day. John Marshall later wrote to Susan Ledyard, "[Your] truly filial piety [and the] entire self-devotion with which you attended the sick bed and watched the last moments of your expiring Father, my very estimable and ever to be lamented friend, could not fail to make a deep impression on the heart of every lover of the domestic virtues."[200] Story wrote his wife, after traveling to Washington for the beginning of the 1824 Term, that he missed his "old friend Judge Livingston." During "the whole of my journey, and fifty miles of it was perfectly solitary," Story noted, "I felt exceedingly depressed by the recollections of his loss."[201] The death of Livingston marked the first change in Marshall Court personnel since 1811; it was, although not so understood at the time, the beginning of a new phase in the Court's history, a phase marked by the emergence not long after Livingston's death, of what Marshall in 1831 called a "revolutionary spirit" on the Court.

Of the senior Marshall Court Justices, the individual who had found the Court's coalescence into solidarity most trying was William Johnson. Appointed by Jefferson in 1804 with a mandate to scrutinize the Federalist sympathies of the early Marshall Court, Johnson had become by the 1820s nearly indistinguishable in his voting patterns from the Court majority. The socialization of Johnson, who was not only a great admirer of Jefferson but his confidant, has been previously discussed. As Johnson put it in the December 1822 letter, previously quoted, "I found that I must either submit to circumstances or become such a cypher in our consultations as to effect no good at all. I therefore bent to the current."[202]

Johnson was not temperamentally suited to play the role encouraged by the Marshall Court practices, that of a genial collegial majoritarian.

[197] R. King to John A. King, Mar. 2, 1823, in C. King, *Life and Correspondence*, VI, 505.

[198] Story to Todd, Mar. 14, 1823, supra, note 131.

[199] W. Johnson to J. Sergeant, Mar. 18, 1823, Sergeant Papers.

[200] J. Marshall to S. Ledyard, Nov. 6, 1825, John Marshall Papers, College of William and Mary Library.

[201] J. Story to S. W. Story, Feb. 8, 1824, Story Papers, University of Texas Library.

[202] W. Johnson to T. Jefferson, Dec. 10, 1822, Thomas Jefferson Papers, Library of Congress.

He was variously described by contemporaries as "restive, turbulent, hot-headed, [and] flaringly independent";[203] "bold, independent, eccentric, and somewhat harsh";[204] having a "mischievous obliquity of disposition," a "morbid soreness about his own character, and a perfect carelessness about the character of others";[205] "too strenuous in the maintenance of the opinions he had adopted";[206] and having a "discretion [that was] not always awake."[207] One commentator described him as inclined in discourse "to refine further than most men could follow him";[208] another, less charitable, said, "God knows how little he was fit to hold the office of judge."[209] The struggle of Johnson to accommodate himself to the practices of the Marshall Court is an interesting sidelight on that Court's history.

Johnson came to the Court at the age of thirty-two, chosen by Jefferson because of his geographic affiliation (he replaced Alfred Moore of North Carolina), his partisan Republicanism, and his comparative youth. He was Jefferson's first appointee, and clearly was intended to be something of a lieutenant in the war Jefferson hoped to wage against a Federalist-dominated Court. Thirty years later, looking back over Johnson's career on the Court, one could not say that things had worked out entirely according to plan. Johnson had retained his independence, continued his admiration for Jefferson, and engaged in some subtle partisanship (such as writing a biography of the Republican Revolutionary War general, Nathanael Greene, ostensibly to counter Marshall's life of Washington), but he had not been a persistent advocate of states' rights, as Jefferson had hoped, nor had he become a leader of the increasing number of Republican Justices. If anything, those Justices had gravitated to Marshall, Washington, and the old-boy norms and patterns of the Court; Johnson had remained a maverick.

Part of Johnson's failure to become a counterweight to Marshall on the Court can be traced to his temperament. His tendency to personalize differences of opinion, his impetuousness, and his reluctance to admit error led to periodic difficulties with other Justices. During the 1820 Term, for example, responding to Marshall's announcement that a particular admiralty case, *The Amiable Isabella*,[210] would be postponed until

---

[203] J. Q. Adams, diary entry, Mar. 27, 1820, in C. Adams, *Memoirs of Adams*, III, 43.

[204] Charles Ingersoll, *History of the Second War between the United States and Great Britain* (2d ed., 2 vols., 1852), I, 74.

[205] Thomas Cooper in Charleston *City Gazette*, Mar. 8, 1823.

[206] John Bachman in Charleston *Courier*, Aug. 18, 1834.

[207] James Madison to T. Jefferson, June 27, 1823, in J. Madison, *Letters and Other Writings* (4 vols., 1865), III, 323.

[208] Anonymous obituary in Charleston *Southern Patriot*, Aug. 18, 1834.

[209] James L. Petigru to Hugh S. Legare, Sept. 16, 1834, quoted in J. Carson, *Life, Letters, and Speeches of James Louis Petigru* (1920), 158.

[210] 6 Wheat. 1 (1821).

the next Term, Johnson declared that he had made up his mind about the case and was going to express his opinion on the spot. Henry Wheaton reported to Story, who had left Washington early because of illness in his family, that

> Mr. Justice J. announced, with great emotion, his determination to fire off—stating that as his mind was unalterably made up, and as the last argument, so far from shaking, had confirmed his first impression, he thought the party entitled to the benefit of his vote, which might be lost in case death, or *any other cause,* should prevent his being present at the next Term. He then proceeded to read the same opinion which he first drew up, and when that ended, read on: "This far was written before the last argument, which has strengthened me in my former opinion." He then proceeded, in a style which beggars all description, to ridicule Pinkney's argument, treating it with the utmost contempt as a flimsy declamation of a venal advocate for privateerism, masked under the appearance of the sanction of the Government. "If," said he, "I thought the government had authorized the use of such arguments I should blush for my Government."
>
> Pinkney was so outraged that it was with difficulty that Wirt and myself could keep him from getting up and discharging his resentment in open Court. Every person present was equally struck with the extraordinary want of dignity, or rather of decency, in the learned judge's conduct: and nothing is talked of but his tirade.
>
> The judges lament this extravagant sally, which was the more unfortunate as great numbers of persons were assembled for the purpose of hearing the decision of the court. Judge Washington assures me that everything was done that could be done to prevent it, but in vain.[211]

Behind Johnson's outburst in *The Amiable Isabella* was a controversy between him and Story over the latter's efforts to expand the admiralty jurisdiction of the federal courts, a tendency Johnson firmly opposed. In an 1821 circuit case, *The Amanda,* Johnson admitted that he had "always set my face against the extension of the jurisdiction of the Court of Admiralty" and refused to regard Story's 1815 circuit decision in *DeLovio* v. *Boit,* with its expansive reading of admiralty jurisdiction, as precedent, indicating that "I seldom, if ever, rest my opinions upon *nisi prius* decisions." [212] Johnson believed, correctly, that Story had enlisted the Court's Reporter Henry Wheaton in his efforts to expand the federal courts' admiralty jurisdiction, as the example of *The General Smith* will illustrate.

---

[211] H. Wheaton to J. Story, Mar. 17, 1820, Wheaton Papers. Emphasis in original.

[212] The decision in *The Amanda* was reported in the January 18, 1822, issue of the Charleston *City Gazette.*

Chapter V: *The Justices of the Marshall Court*

In Wheaton's notebook for Tuesday, March 9, 1819, there is an entry recording Pinkney's argument in the case of the *General Smith,* an admiralty dispute which raised the question whether mechanics who worked on a ship should be treated as having been given liens upon the ship itself in order to satisfy their claims. Wheaton's summary describes Pinkney as "not disposed to contest the jurisdiction of the Admiralty over all maritime contracts, *in personam,* and *in rem,* where the party has a right to proceed *in rem.*" Nor was Pinkney contesting, according to Wheaton, "[admiralty] jurisdiction in this case, if there is a lien," though Pinkney argued that in fact no lien had been given in *The General Smith.* After summarizing Pinkney's argument, Wheaton inserted a memorandum to himself:

> Prepare a short argument in this Case as it ought to have been argued— giving all the authorities. They will be found principally in 2 Gall. [the volume of Gallison's Reports which contained Story's *DeLovio* opinion].
> N.B. Pinkney admits the admiralty jurisdiction to its full extent.[213]

In the Reports for the 1819 Term, however, Wheaton reported only that Pinkney had argued in favor of "the admiralty possess[ing] a general jurisdiction in cases of suits by material men, *in personam,* and *in rem.*"[214] And Story's opinion for the court in *The General Smith* merely said that "the Admiralty rightfully possesses a general jurisdiction in cases of material men."[215] Eight years later, Johnson nonetheless thought he saw a conspiracy at work. In *Ramsey v. Allegre,*[216] an admiralty case decided in the 1827 Term, Johnson quoted the passage attributed to Pinkney in *The General Smith* and said that he had "too high an opinion of Mr. Pinkney's law-reading, and of his talents as an advocate, not to be well convinced that . . . he must have been misunderstood" in conceding general admiralty jurisdiction over "suits by material men *in personam* and *in rem.*"[217] After arguing that Pinkney's own citations contradicted the possibility that he made such a concession, Johnson concluded that "his reported argument [was] clearly a mistake."[218]

Wheaton, in his last year as the Court's Reporter, was unwilling to have his reputation besmirched by Johnson's accusations. He prepared a response to Johnson's allegations about the reporting of *The General Smith* and entered it as an appendix to the opinion. Pinkney's concession, Wheaton stated, was made "voluntarily . . . and it does not appear that the authorities subsequently referred to . . . were intended for that pur-

---

[213] Notebook entry, Mar. 9, 1819, in Wheaton's 1819 notebook, Wheaton Papers.
[214] 4 Wheat. at 441.

[215] Ibid., 443.
[216] 12 Wheat. 611 (1827).
[217] Ibid., 636.
[218] Ibid., 638.

pose. On this occasion, as on many other occasions,'' Wheaton surmised, "[Pinkney] probably spoke from the fulness of his learning, and with a confidence inspired by his well grounded reliance upon its accuracy.''[219] Pinkney's citations, Wheaton claimed, were intended not to justify his concession but to buttress his claim that the facts of *The General Smith* made it an exception to the usual jurisdictional rule. In responding to Johnson's implications, Wheaton said, he was "seek[ing] to vindicate . . . his own character for accuracy and integrity . . . and his own reputation to maintain the fidelity of the Reports.''[220]

The *General Smith* episode was ironic because Johnson, who was unaware of Wheaton's earlier intention to rewrite Pinkney's argument, had stumbled on a potential conspiracy of greater proportions than he had imagined, but that conspiracy, perhaps because Wheaton forgot about his own instructions or did not have time or energy to carry them out, never materialized. The most interesting feature of the episode, perhaps, is not the fact that Wheaton was tempted to put words in a Supreme Court advocate's mouth but that Johnson remembered, and commented upon, the incident eight years later. Admiralty jurisdiction was the kind of issue that engaged Johnson, one about which he felt deeply and on which he felt isolated and rebuffed by his fellow Justices. In *Ramsey* v. *Allegre* he began his opinion by stating, "I think it high time to check this silent and stealing progress of the Admiralty in acquiring jurisdiction to which it has no pretensions.''[221]

Johnson's doggedness in maintaining a position once he had adopted it, and his reluctance to modify a position in order to be congenial or politic, was well known to contemporaries. In his biography of Nathanael Greene, published in 1822, Johnson attacked various individuals involved in the Revolution, prompting indignant letters from their relatives. One correspondent, not satisfied with Johnson's response, wrote a friend that he was "fatigued by the quibbling discussions of Judge Johnson," and that he had "closed the Correspondence decisively." "It would indeed have been a folly," he continued, "to argue with a man who unblushingly states his resolution not to be convinced—and who, denying the blessing of memory to all other men, would induce his readers to believe he himself was infallible." Johnson "would make his fiat the criterion of all that is right, and having made his statement would not be persuaded that it might be erroneous.''[222]

The Greene biography brought Johnson into several skirmishes of this kind. When the *North American Review* published a review critical

---

[219] Ibid., 641.
[220] Ibid., 642–43.
[221] Ibid., 614.
[222] Alexander Garden to J. E. How-

ard, June 11, 1822, Miscellaneous Papers, Maryland Historical Society, Annapolis, Md.

of the book,[223] Johnson defended himself in the Charleston *City Gazette*.[224] When a relative of Count Casimir Pulaski sought to rescue the count's reputation as a war tactician, Johnson published a rejoinder.[225] But when Johnson stated that James Wilson had been an enemy of George Washington, Wilson's offended son enlisted a powerful ally, Bushrod Washington, Johnson's colleague and George Washington's nephew. In this case Johnson made a public apology after receiving testimony contradicting his surmises from Richard Peters, Sr., the former federal district judge from Pennsylvania who had been a contemporary of Wilson's, and from Bushrod Washington himself. Johnson thereafter attached the following "advertisement" to copies of his Life of Greene:

> Having recently ascertained, from the evidence of several highly respectable characters, that I have been led into an error in naming Mr. Wilson of Pennsylvania as one of the cabal opposed to General Washington, in justice to his memory and my own feelings I acknowledge the error, and express my extreme regret in having committed it.[226]

Even this act did not wholly assuage all of Johnson's opponents. One wrote Wilson's son that Johnson "would have done better to have candidly acknowledged his own unexcusable error than to have attempted to put it upon men of the first respectability whose name it will do no good to communicate."[227]

While Johnson was embroiled in disputes over his biography of Greene and in his usual skirmishes with his colleagues on the Marshall Court, another potential source of controversy appeared: Jefferson's letter implicitly reminding Johnson that he had failed to live up to his nominating president's expectations and suggesting that there was still time to do so. The aftermath of this letter was a correspondence between Johnson and Jefferson over the next nine months, portions of which have been quoted from. This correspondence was to furnish one of the best available sources of information about the Marshall Court's deliberative practices, and it was also to alter Johnson's posture toward public expression of his judicial opinions.

Jefferson began the letters with his previously quoted complaints

---

[223] [Edward Brooks], "Life of Nathanael Greene," *No. Am. Rev.*, 15:416 (1822).

[224] W. Johnson, "The Reviewer Reviewed," Charleston *City Gazette*, Nov. 14–16, 18–19, 1822.

[225] W. Johnson, *Remarks, Critical and Historical, on an Article in the . . . North American Review, Relating to Count Pulaski . . .* (1825).

[226] The advertisement is enclosed in a letter from C. E. Gadsden to W. Bird Wilson, June 17, 1823, W. Bird Wilson Papers, Historical Society of Pennsylvania, Philadelphia, Pa.

[227] C. H. Charnay to W. B. Wilson, Jan. 20, 1823, ibid.

about "the habitual mode of making up and delivering the opinions of the Supreme Court of the US." He then attacked the Marshall Court's practice "of making up opinions in secret and delivering them as the Oracles of the court, in mass." Such a practice, Jefferson felt, had "completely withdrawn" the Justices from their "two responsibilities: impeachment [and] individual reputation." No one could tell "what opinion any individual member gave in any case," and thus even if an opinion were "impeachable, having been done in the dark it can be proved on no one." As for an individual's reputation, it was "shielded completely" by the practice, since judges did not have to "develop their opinion[s] methodically," or even, unless assigned an opinion of the Court, "make up an opinion at all."

In the same letter Jefferson sought reassurance that Johnson's political views were as "sound" as ever. He addressed "the state of parties at this time" and concluded that while the Federalist Party had become "amalgamated" with the National Republican party, that amalgamation was "of name only, not of principle." There remained those who, "finding that monarchy is a desperate wish in this country, . . . rally to the point which they think next best, a consolidated government." Their purpose was "to break down the rights reserved by the Constitution to the states as a bulwark against that consolidation." Jefferson hoped "that the friends of the real constitution and union will prevail against consolidation." He "scarcely knew . . . which is the most to be deprecated, a consolidation, or dissolution of the states." He concluded by noting that he had "committed to [Johnson] thoughts which I would do to few others" because of his continued "confidence in the rectitude of your mind and principles."[228]

That letter was written on October 27, 1822. On December 10 Johnson responded with a twenty-one-page letter, previously alluded to. In it he ranged through a variety of subjects, including his troubles with the reaction to the Greene biography, his interest in writing a history of political parties, and the recent response in Charleston to rumors of slave uprisings, which had resulted in arrests, summary proceedings, and executions of suspected rebels. Johnson felt that the proceedings in the slave trials had been "unprecedented and illegal." He had lived to see, he wrote, "what I really never believed it possible I should see—courts held with closed doors, and men dying by scores who had never seen the faces nor heard the voices of their accusers." He intervened in the controversy, warning of the dangers of overreacting to rumors,[229] was severely criti-

---

[228] T. Jefferson to W. Johnson, Oct. 27, 1822, in P. Ford, ed., *The Works of Thomas Jefferson* (12 vols., 1905), XII, 246.

[229] W. Johnson, letter to Charleston *Courier,* June 21, 1822.

cized by supporters of the local courts, who felt "injured and defamed,"[230] and attacked them in turn.[231] Developments such as the Charleston uprising had spawned such "symptoms of anti-federal feeling, as to alarm the fears of some of those who feel most sensibly for the preservation of the union in the pure spirit of the constitution."[232]

Jefferson was undoubtedly more interested in the portions of Johnson's December 10 letter that discussed the internal practices of the Marshall Court. In that portion of his letter, we have seen, Johnson described the procedure followed at the time he joined the Marshall Court; revealed that he had opposed this practice, and resolved to deliver his opinions when "I disagreed from my brethren"; indicated he had been remonstrated with for this effort; and claimed that he had been responsible for the practice of silent acquiescence.[233]

Jefferson responded to that letter by sending a copy of it on January 6, 1823, to Madison (Johnson's "views of things . . . are so serious and sound, that they are worth your reading")[234] and, on March 4, by writing Johnson directly.[235] Again Jefferson sought to link "the consolidation of our government by the . . . supreme court" with Marshall Court internal practices. After stating that "there is no danger I apprehend so much" as "consolidation by the noiseless, and therefore unalarming, instrumentality" of the Court, Jefferson returned to his theme of "the importance and the duty of [the Justices'] giving their country the only evidence they can give of fidelity to its constitution and integrity in the administration of its laws; that is to say by everyone's giving his opinion *seriatim* and publicly on the cases he decides." The "very idea of cooking up an opinion in conclave," Jefferson felt, "begets suspicions that something passes which fears the public eye."

Johnson received that letter in Washington and waited until he had returned to Charleston, on April 11, to reply.[236] He said that "on the subject of seriatim opinions in the supreme court I have thought much, and I have come to the resolution to adopt your suggestion on all subjects of general interest, particularly constitutional questions." He then asked Jefferson to "amicably and confidentially examine" with him "the question how far the supreme court has yet trespassed upon their neighbors' territory or advanced beyond their own constitutional limits." Johnson conceded that he was interested in "bringing about a change of your opinions on the subject," or at a minimum "to have my own fairly and

---

[230] Charleston *Courier*, June 29, 1822.

[231] W. Johnson, *To the Public of Charleston* (pamphlet, 1822).

[232] Johnson to Jefferson, Dec. 10, 1822, supra, note 202.

[233] Ibid.

[234] T. Jefferson to J. Madison, Jan. 6, 1823, in Ford, *Works*, XII, 244.

[235] T. Jefferson to W. Johnson, Mar. 4, 1823, in ibid., 246.

[236] W. Johnson to T. Jefferson, Apr. 11, 1823, Jefferson Papers.

fully tried.'' He believed ''that in the main the country is satisfied with our decisions,'' although he acknowledged that ''some things have fallen from particular Judges which are exceptionable.'' He also believed that ''all [the decisions] in which I ever concurred [would] stand constitutional scrutiny.'' He cautioned Jefferson that ''it will be impossible to avoid . . . conducting the most of our business in conclave; for I do verily believe that there is no body of men . . . who could preserve the public respect for a single year, if the public eye were permitted always to look behind the curtain.'' He had ''never met but one man who could absolutely leave his vanity and weaknesses at home,'' and he had ''often [been] absolutely astonished at the predominance of little passions over men in the most elevated stations.''

Johnson's April 11 letter had been an effort to dissociate the ''conclave'' practice in the Court from the substantive merits of the Court's opinions, on which he pronounced ''the country . . . satisfied.'' Jefferson took some time, apparently, to consider whether Johnson's challenge to submit the Court's opinions to constitutional scrutiny was worth the effort, but on June 12 he responded.[237] ''You request me,'' Jefferson wrote, ''confidentially, to examine the question, whether the Supreme court has advanced beyond its constitutional limits, and trespassed on those of the State authorities?'' Jefferson's answer was that ''I do not undertake it . . . because I am unable.'' He cited ''[a]ge and the wane of mind consequent on it,'' which had ''disqualified me from investigations so severe, and researches so laborious.'' But he could not resist adding that ''others'' had done the job ''with a logic and learning to which I could add nothing.'' He referred to Judge Spencer Roane's attacks on *Cohens* v. *Virginia* in the Richmond *Enquirer,* which, he said, ''appeared to me to pulverize every word which had been delivered by Judge Marshall.'' Jefferson then went on to recall *Marbury* v. *Madison* and Marshall's ''practice . . . of travelling out of his case to prescribe what the law would be in a moot case not before the court,'' which to Jefferson was ''very irregular and very censurable.''

Warming up, Jefferson next formulated two ''canons'' by which constitutional issues could be tried: first, that ''the capital and leading object of the constitution was to leave with the states all authorities which respected their own citizens only''; second, that ''on every question of construction, [interpreters should] carry [themselves] back to the time when the constitution was adopted, recollect the spirit manifested in the debates, and instead of trying [to see] what meaning may be squeezed out of the text, or invented against it, conform to the probable one in which it was passed.'' He then proceeded to ''try Cohen's case by these canons only.'' The result was a rejection of Marshall's opinion in *Cohens,*

---

[237] T. Jefferson to W. Johnson, June 12, 1823, in Ford, *Works,* XII, 226.

which was based on' "a licentiousness of construction and inference," and "metaphysical subtleties, which may make anything mean everything or nothing, at pleasure." Jefferson "rejoiced in the example [Johnson had] set of *seriatim* opinions." Some of the other Justices, he hoped, "will be encouraged to follow it occasionally, and in time it may be felt by all as a duty, and the sound practice of the primitive court be again restored." Finally, to assure Johnson that their differences on questions of federalism did not override more fundamental areas of agreement, Jefferson reminded him that while "you and I may differ occasionally in details of minor consequence, . . . our general objects are the same, to preserve the republican form and principles of our constitution and cleave to the salutary distribution of powers which that has established."

Jefferson was sufficiently buoyed by his success in persuading Johnson to write Madison in the hope of persuading other Justices on the Marshall Court to dispense with the "conclave" practice. "In a late letter," Jefferson told Madison,

[Johnson] expresses his concurrence with me on the subject of seriatim opinions. This last being of primary importance, I enclose you a copy of my answer to the judge [the June 12 letter] because if you think of it as I do, I suppose your connection with Judge Todd and your ancient intimacy with Judge Duval might give you an opening to say something to them on the subject. If Johnson could be backed by them in the practice, the others would be obliged to follow suit and this dangerous engine of consolidation would feel a proper restraint by their being compelled to explain publicly the grounds of their opinions."[238]

But while Jefferson had repeatedly linked the "conclave" procedure to consolidationist learnings, Johnson had never made such a link: he was prepared to defend the Court's decisions restricting state powers while at the same time expressing concern about the "opinion of the court" practice. As for Jefferson's roundabout effort to enlist Todd and Duvall, it had no effect; those two Justices did not deviate from their earlier practice of writing almost no opinions at all.

The Jefferson–Johnson correspondence came to a close in the summer of 1823, Jefferson writing on July 31 that he had been incapacitated by a fever and merely alluding to Roane's articles on *Cohens;*[239] Johnson, now obsessed with the separatist tone of South Carolina politics,[240] enclosing a draft of an opinion he had written invalidating on commerce power grounds an attempt on the part of South Carolina to prohibit black seamen from entering the state.[241] Johnson's opinion read federal power

[238] T. Jefferson to J. Madison, June 13, 1823, in ibid., 259.
[239] T. Jefferson to W. Johnson, July 31, 1823, Jefferson Papers.
[240] W. Johnson to T. Jefferson, Aug. 11, 1823, ibid.
[241] Elikson v. Deliesseline, 8 F. Cas. 493 (C.C.D. S.C., 1823).

over commerce very broadly, concluding that there was "nothing for the states to act upon," given the language of the Constitution.[242] This opinion foreshadowed Johnson's concurrence in *Gibbons* v. *Ogden* six months later, in which he concluded that federal commerce power was exclusive and broad in sweep.[243] Jefferson, for his part, continued his attacks on consolidation in the Marshall Court almost until his death. He wrote a friend in February 1824 repeating the themes of his earlier letters to Johnson and claiming that the Marshall Court was comprised, "almost to a man," of Federalist sympathizers.[244]

What is one to conclude about Johnson from this correspondence? First, there is no question that at the time he felt isolated from his colleagues on the Marshall Court. While he tended to agree with the majority that the Commerce Clause and the Contract Clause served as significant restraints on state power, he resented the encroachment of federal admiralty jurisdiction, supported state bankruptcy legislation,[245] and felt that some Contract Clause opinions had unnecessarily provoked the states.[246] He disliked Story, was suspicious of Washington, appeared to be intimidated by Marshall, had no close friends on the Court, and fought with both Reporter Wheaton and his successor, Richard Peters. Given the nature of his relationships with Washington, Jefferson was a refuge for a person who felt lonely on the Court.[247]

But Johnson's reaching out to Jefferson, and his subsequent decision to write separately in "questions of great importance," which he announced in 1824,[248] should not give rise to the inference that he was Jefferson's pawn. On issues of federalism, we have seen, the two men diverged; indeed the only point of major agreement between Jefferson and Johnson seems to have been on the desirability of seriatim opinions, a procedure Johnson had welcomed from the start of his tenure. Even had Johnson been Jefferson's lieutenant on the Court, there is little evidence that between 1812 and 1823, the period of the Marshall Court's greatest internal harmony, Johnson would have had any particular influence.

With the deaths of Livingston, Todd, Trimble, and Washington, Johnson saw major personnel changes on the Court and the emergence of a new type of Justice, less wedded to established practices and more anxious to make his mark as an individual. With these developments in mind, and aware of the striking increase in separate opinions among the Justices after 1829, one commentator has argued that "Johnson, not Mar-

---

[242] Ibid., 495.
[243] 9 Wheat. 1, 223 (1824).
[244] T. Jefferson to Robert J. Garrett, Feb. 14, 1824, in Ford, *Works*, X, 294.
[245] Sturges v. Crowninshield, supra, note 182.

[246] Green v. Biddle, 8 Wheat. 1, 106 (1823).
[247] Johnson to Jefferson, supra, note 202.
[248] Gibbons v. Ogden, 9 Wheat. 1, 223 (1824).

shall, is perhaps the key figure'' of the last years of the Marshall Court.[249] But it is hard to make so independent, impetuous, and tactless a figure as William Johnson into a leader. Indeed in the last five years of the Marshall Court, beginning with the 1831 Term, Johnson lived separately from the other Justices, missed two Terms altogether, and died before the 1835 Term began. What the commentator noticed is perhaps more accurately described as a fortuitous parallel between Johnson's own interest in individual expression and debate and the tendency of several new Justices, for their own idiosyncratic reasons, to prefer to express their views separately. In his doctrinal positions, Johnson may have anticipated some of the decisions of the Taney Court, and his growing concern for individual rights may have tempted twentieth-century commentators to portray him as an early civil libertarian.[250] But he was a maverick rather than a figure of genuine influence on the Marshall Court.

In 1831 Johnson suffered the first of a series of recurrent illnesses that culminated in his death three years later. The Charleston *Courier* reported that he had been taken ill while visiting Raleigh, North Carolina.[251] Story, in discussing Johnson's illness in a letter written the following March, said that he had "been confined the whole autumn and winter" in Raleigh and that "he is in a bad way."[252] Johnson confirmed the poor state of his health in a letter to Franklin Bache in June 1832,[253] and Story continued to give gloomy reports and to make inquiries about Johnson during the course of that year.[254] In February 1833 Johnson returned to Washington, but his health problems continued. In the summer of 1833 he contracted "a bilious remittant fever" while vacationing in Pennsylvania, but was well enough to sit on circuit in Charleston in June and in Milledgeville, Georgia, in November.[255] In 1834, however, he missed the Supreme Court Term again, and wrote Bache in June that he was suffering from "serious indisposition."[256] That same month he made out his will, and the next month he set off on a journey for New York, where he scheduled an operation on his jaw. Anesthetics not being available, the operation involved "the most excruciating tortures," and a

---

[249] Seddig, "John Marshall and the Origins of Supreme Court Leadership," 825.

[250] See, e.g., D. Morgan, *Justice William Johnson* (1954), 190–229.

[251] Charleston *Courier*, Nov. 21, 1831.

[252] J. Story to John H. Ashmun, Mar. 1, 1832, in W. Story, *Life and Letters*, II, 91.

[253] W. Johnson to F. Bache, June 28,

1832, Archives, American Philosophical Society, Philadelphia, Pa.

[254] J. Story to Thomas Wetmore, Jan. 1, 1832, Story Papers, University of Texas Library; J. Story to R. Peters, Jr., Oct. 28, 1832, Peters Papers.

[255] See Morgan, *Justice William Johnson*, 277–78.

[256] W. Johnson to F. Bache, June 28, 1834, Archives, American Philosophical Society, Philadelphia, Pa.

newspaper report suggested that Johnson's sudden death, a half hour after the operation, was attributable to "exhaustion."[257]

The manner of Johnson's death was emblematic of his life. He died alone and in strange surroundings, far from Charleston, where the nullification controversy had intensified his estrangement from South Carolina politics. He left instructions that he was to be buried in "the same simple unostentatious manner"[258] in which he had tried to live; no family or friends attended his funeral. He had been advised by the surgeon who performed his last operation not to undertake it, since he would likely not survive; he elected the surgery anyway. Richard Peters described his last days:

> It is stated that without anyone of his family to attend him, he went to New York, and passed on to Brooklyn where he had an operation performed on his jaw, by the removal of a cancerous bone. It was exceedingly painful, but it was finished with entire success, and he appeared to be doing well for some minutes afterwards. But in half an hour he sank into death from exhaustion without a friend being near him to close his eyes.
>
> Why he passed through Philadelphia without consulting Dr. Physick [who had successfully removed a kidney stone from Marshall a year earlier] I have not heard, and who the surgeon was who made the extraction, I have not been informed. You will recollect Judge Johnson always considered that he had considerable medical skill—I fear his confidence in his own judgment has misled him.[259]

When Johnson first came to the Marshall Court and attempted to render his opinions separately, he was resisting a practice which had been followed since the opening of Marshall's tenure as Chief Justice. In seeking to explain why the other Justices would allow Marshall to write all the Court's opinions, even "when contrary to his own judgment and vote," Johnson discovered, as he said to Jefferson,

> the real cause. Cushing was incompetent. Chase could not be got to think or write—Paterson was a slow man and willingly declined the trouble, and the other two judges you know are commonly estimated as one judge.[260]

---

[257] New York *Evening Star*, Aug. 5, 1834.

[258] W. Johnson, will, June 17, 1834, Probate Judge's Office, Charleston, S.C., quoted in Morgan, *Justice William Johnson*, 280.

[259] R. Peters, Jr., to J. Story, Sept. 1, 1834, Story Papers, Library of Congress.

[260] Johnson to Jefferson, Dec. 10, 1822, supra, note 202.

## Chapter V: *The Justices of the Marshall Court*

The "other two judges" were John Marshall and Bushrod Washington.

Despite Johnson's words, Bushrod Washington was no cipher on the Marshall Court, though his reputation has never quite escaped that close affinity with Marshall which Johnson's remarks suggested. He was, in fact, one of its stalwarts, who helped establish practices, promote the Court's reputation, and shape the form of its judgments. A Federalist appointee from an earlier period in the Court's history, Washington welcomed the increased prominence and power of the Court under Marshall and contributed significantly to the development of internal practices by which the Court sought to enhance its reputation. Washington contributed particularly in three respects: as a firm supporter and intimate friend of Marshall, as a conscientious and informed circuit judge with an eye for significant cases, and as a spokesman for the Court's norms of collegiality and professed unanimity in the decision of cases.

When Justice James Wilson died in 1798, the appointment of a successor fell to John Adams, who conducted an informal poll of the Virginia and Pennsylvania bars; Wilson had lived in Virginia, and Pennsylvania did not then have a representative on the Court. Two names surfaced from Virginia, the state that Adams resolved to select from, John Marshall and Bushrod Washington. Both had attended George Wythe's law school at William and Mary, practiced in Richmond, and supported the Federalist party. Washington, like Marshall, had been a member of the Virginia House of Delegates and a delegate to the Virginia convention that ratified the Constitution. In late August 1798, Marshall and Washington had been summoned by George Washington to the Washington family farm in Mount Vernon and encouraged to run for Congress as Federalists.[261]

Both Marshall and Washington were thus involved in congressional campaigns when Adams resolved to make them his first and second choices for the Supreme Court vacancy. Adams preferred Marshall, citing his "experience and seniority at the bar,"[262] and offered the position to him. Marshall, however, preferred to run for Congress, and recommended Washington in his stead; on October 6, 1798, Washington was sent a commission.[263] He wrote his uncle that "I have felt much uneasiness lest my acceptance of this appointment should be disagreeable to you . . . [k]nowing the wish you had that I should be a candidate for Congress." "I flatter myself," Washington continued, "that my services will not be less useful to my Country in the office I now hold than they would have

---

[261] G. Washington to B. Washington, Aug. 27, 1798, George Washington Papers, Library of Congress.

[262] J. Adams to Timothy Pickering, Sept. 26, 1798, in C. Adams, ed., *The*

*Works of John Adams* (10 vols., 1850), VIII, 597.

[263] T. Pickering to B. Washington, Oct. 6, 1798, National Archives.

been in the legislative Councils."[264] George Washington acknowledged that Bushrod had been "perfectly right in accepting the appointment of Associate Judge."[265]

Washington was only thirty-six at the time of his appointment, but his nomination was not altogether surprising. He had read law in Philadelphia under James Wilson, who was recognized as one of the distinguished legal minds in the country. Washington was, by all accounts, an industrious and able student, and made "a favorable impression" on Federalist politicians in Virginia.[266] In 1788, having been admitted to practice law three years earlier, he moved his practice to Alexandria, where he made an unsuccessful effort to secure appointment as a United States district attorney. Unfortunately for his candidacy, his uncle, now president of the United States, was empowered to make the appointment, and George Washington felt that Bushrod had less "standing at the bar [than] some of the oldest and most esteemed court lawyers in your own State," and he wanted to avoid any charges of nepotism.[267] Bushrod was embarrassed, not having realized that his uncle was responsible for the nomination, and withdrew his candidacy.[268] Shortly thereafter he moved to Richmond, where his law practice flourished.

Two letters written by Washington in 1785 and 1786 to one of his close friends in Philadelphia gave some indications of the subjects that interested him at that time in his life. He had married Ann Blackburn sometime in 1784,[269] and wrote that "I am scarcely yet entitled to the appellation of husband as the ardor of a lover has not left me." After expressing hope that the two appellations could be combined in his marriage, Washington continued: "having said this, I suppose it will be unnecessary to add that I have not yet been surfeited. I take it, that this must be a very humiliating situation for a man, and therefore my maxim

[264] B. Washington to G. Washington, Oct. 19, 1798, Washington Papers.
[265] G. Washington to B. Washington, Oct. 24, 1798, Archives, Union Library, Mount Vernon, Va.
[266] G. Washington to David Stuart, Nov. 30, 1787, in J. Fitzpatrick, ed., *The Writings of George Washington* (39 vols., 1931), XXIX, 324.
[267] G. Washington to B. Washington, July 27, 1789, Washington Papers.
[268] B. Washington to G. Washington, Dec. 27, 1789, Archives, Union Library, Mount Vernon, Va.
[269] The principal secondary sources on Washington place the date of his marriage in 1785. See D. Annis, "Mr.

Bushrod Washington, Supreme Court Justice on the Marshall Court" (Ph.D. diss., University of Notre Dame, 1974), 47; A. Blaustein and R. Mersky, "Bushrod Washington," in Friedman and Israel, *Justices*, I, 244. But the February 1, 1785 letter to "Hodgdon" quoted in the text refers to earlier letters he had written Hodgdon (and Hodgdon had not received) before Hodgdon's last letter, written on December 10, 1784. In those letters, Washington said to Hodgdon, "I informed you that I [had been] married." So even if one assumes that Washington wrote Hodgdon immediately after his marriage, that would have placed it in the fall of 1784.

is, Moderation and Uniformity.''[270] He also ranged, in the letters, through politics ("we have all become politicians in Virginia . . . Paper Money, British Debts and the increase of Congressional Power are the principal topics''),[271] economics ("I think [Virginia] offers one of the most flattering Prospects for a Commercial Genius of any place in America"), social life ("I once promised to search for a Virginia wife for you. I have many in view . . . if you will put it in my power, I will make you acquainted with them all"), and his fondness for Philadelphia ("There is nothing pleases me more than the news of Philadelphia . . . I have a kind of natural affection for the place and its inhabitants").[272] In 1803, when a new judiciary act gave Washington an opportunity to change his circuit responsibilities, he asked for the Third Circuit, which included a court in Philadelphia.

Washington hoped that his appointment to the Supreme Court would enable him "to pursue [my profession] and to improve the knowledge which I have acquired in this science, without endangering my sight (already considerably injured).''[273] The last comment referred to his loss of vision in one eye in 1797, purportedly from his "indefatigable pursuit of knowledge and the business of his profession.''[274] Washington's hopes were fulfilled. Not only did he retain the vision in his other eye, he found the technical and sometimes laborious tasks of a federal judge suited to his temperament. He was a methodical, patient, cautious, firm-minded person who became easily acclimated to judging and who was prepared to focus his interests almost exclusively on his profession. Horace Binney, who argued many cases before Washington in circuit in Philadelphia, said that he was "as accomplished a Nisi Prius Judge as ever lived.''[275] Binney felt that Washington "contained two different persons in the same man." "In private life" Washington was "not above the common level of educated men," and "his conversation made little impression on the mind." His "reading . . . did not appear to be extensive," and his "taste . . . was rather unrefined.''[276] But "when his robes were upon him," Binney claimed, he was "the ablest Judge, and the best lawyer in Pennsylvania that I have known.''[277] Binney gave the following description of Washington sitting on circuit:

---

[270] B. Washington to [first name unavailable] Hodgdon, Feb. 1, 1785, Miscellaneous Papers, New York Public Library, New York, N.Y.

[271] B. Washington to Hodgdon, Sept. 15, 1786, ibid.

[272] Washington to Hodgdon, Feb. 1, 1785, supra, note 270.

[273] B. Washington to G. Washington, Oct. 19, 1798, supra, note 264.

[274] T. Pickering to J. Adams, Sept. 20, 1798, Timothy Pickering Papers, Massachusetts Historical Society, Boston, Mass.

[275] H. Binney, *Bushrod Washington* (1858), 12.

[276] Ibid., 7–8.

[277] Ibid., 10, 6.

Without the least apparent effort, he made everybody see at first sight that he was equal to all the duties of the place, ceremonial as well as intellectual. His mind was full, his elocution free, clear and accurate, his command of all about him indisputable. His learning and acuteness were not only equal to the profoundest argument, but carried the counsel to depths which they had not penetrated; and he was so cool, self-possessed and efficient at a moment of high excitement at the Bar . . . as if the nerves of fear had been taken out of his brain by the roots.[278]

Binney went on to single out Washington's "great quickness and accuracy of apprehension," "precise and expressive language," "power of logical arrangement," and "equanimity."[279]

In addition to these qualities, Washington was notably conscientious and hard working. He and Joseph Story, after the latter came on the Court in 1812, developed a practice of making "semiannual reports"[280] to one another of the cases they decided on their respective circuits. Two such reports, among the few that have survived, give testimony to the seriousness with which Washington approached his circuit responsibilities. He and Story were on the lookout for "new and interesting" cases, cases raising issues that might find their way up to the Marshall Court, perhaps with the aid of the Justices themselves. Washington's pattern was to return to Mount Vernon from his spring and fall circuits and immediately dispatch a summary of his cases to Story before "my domestic and agricultural concerns interfere to prevent me."[281] The summary was principally factual, with a brief digest of Washington's holdings, and an occasional query ("what say you as to this latter point") or aside ("this case is of the greatest importance"). It was probably intended principally as a reference guide in a period in which reported decisions were rare. Washington distinguished between cases of "a general nature" and ones that were dependent "on state laws," including only the former in his summaries. It is clear that both he and Story regarded decisions in another circuit, if not as binding precedent, at least as authority of a sort. Story apparently sent similar reports to Washington, although no copies seem to have survived.[282]

The Story–Washington correspondence raises the tantalizing question of how many communications of this sort took place among Marshall Court Justices. It is undisputed that the Justices sometimes exchanged

---

[278] Ibid., 11.
[279] Ibid., 16.
[280] B. Washington to J. Story, June 19, 1821, Joseph Story Papers, Massachusetts Historical Society, Boston, Mass.
[281] B. Washington to J. Story, Dec. 4, 1821, ibid.

[282] Washington closed his circuit summary of June 19, 1821, by indicating that "I shall be anxious to receive your report, in which there is always something new & instructive."

348

information about circuit cases: surviving letters so indicate. But how widespread was the practice? Was it institutionalized? Here one can only indulge in speculation. Very little correspondence between Marshall and Washington has survived;[283] Todd, Trimble, Duvall, and Livingston left virtually no extant papers; Marshall was a careless record-keeper; and Johnson regarded nisi prius decisions as having no authority. Story was, of course, a tireless correspondent, exchanging information at least with Marshall, Washington, Livingston, Todd, and Thompson. But it appears that some Justices were not engaged in such correspondence at all, which leads one to the suggestion that a group of Justices on the Marshall Court—Story, Washington, and Marshall conspicuous among them, with perhaps the less active support of Todd and Livingston—were self-consciously interested in shaping federal law, expanding federal jurisdiction, and creating opportunities to do so. The correspondence about circuit decisions would then serve as a vehicle for fulfilling such goals.

The conscientiousness with which Washington addressed his circuit summaries, when added to Binney's comments about his attentiveness and assiduousness as a circuit judge, gives credence to Story's observation, made in 1808, that "it requires intimacy to value [Washington] as he deserves."[284] Washington was, above all, a team player on the Marshall Court: dedicated, conscientious, discreet, willing to subordinate his own vanity or ambition to the larger goal of the Court's expanded power. His record of opinion-writing suggests a deliberately low profile. In thirty-one years on the Court, he wrote only three dissenting opinions, two concurrences, and seven seriatim opinions. Of these, three seriatim opinions were written before Marshall joined the Court, and three more in 1806, a year in which Marshall did not sit for a portion of the Term. Two of the three dissenting opinions came before 1806. Washington disagreed with Marshall only eight times in the twenty-eight years they served together on the Court and with Story only five times in their fourteen years of joint tenure. As Story once put it, referring to a case in which he had withdrawn a dissent, "Judge Washington thinks (and very correctly) that the habit of delivering dissenting opinions on ordinary occasions weaken[s] the authority of the Court, and is of no public benefit."[285]

That Washington played a pivotal role in the Marshall Court's conclave practice can be surmised from several sources. First, there is ample testimony to the respect he commanded among intimates. Joseph Hopkinson, who argued before Washington on the Third Circuit, referred in

---

[283] See L. Custer, "Bushrod Washington and John Marshall: A Preliminary Inquiry," *Am. J. Legal Hist.*, 4:34, 45–46 (1960).

[284] Story to Fay, Feb. 25, 1808, supra, note 183.

[285] J. Story to H. Wheaton, Apr. 18, 1818, in W. Story, *Life and Letters*, I, 303–304.

a eulogy to "the intellectual and moral qualifications which gave [him] so much dignity": "learning, . . . integrity . . . patient, searching, and penetrating investigation." "Where is the man," Hopkinson asked, "who, with manners so simple and free; with a disposition so kind and social; with a diffidence so true and unpresuming in his private intercourse, could yet maintain, in the discharge of his public duties, independence more uncompromising . . . than Judge Washington."[286] And Story, in his own eulogy, said:

> Few men have left deeper traces, in their judicial career, of everything which a conscientious judge ought to propose for his ambition, or his virtue, or his glory. His mind was solid, rather than brilliant; sagacious and searching, rather than quick or eager; slow, but not torpid; steady, but not unyielding; comprehensive, and at the same time cautious; patient in inquiry, forcible in conception, clear in reasoning. He was, by original temperament, mild, conciliatory and candid; and yet he was remarkable for an uncompromising firmness. . . . There was about him a tenderness of giving offense, and yet a fearlessness of consequences in his official character. . . . It was a rare combination. . . . It repressed arrogance, by overawing or confounding it. . . .
> There was a daily beauty in his life, which won every heart. He was benevolent, charitable, affectionate, and liberal. . . . He never lost his confidence in the political principles which he first embraced. He was always distinguished for moderation, in the days of their prosperity, and for fidelity to them, in the days of their adversity.[287]

In a Court whose members sometimes took occasion in their correspondence to vent their frustrations with one another, no adverse commentary on Washington has surfaced. Even Johnson, who unburdened himself of his frustrations in letters, and who clashed regularly with other Justices with whom he differed, voiced no criticism of Washington. Story's tribute is the most ample that has survived, but Duvall wrote Richard Peters, Jr., on Washington's death that "in his decease the United States have suffered a real loss"; that Washington was "an able, active, and upright judge, and his integrity was incorruptible"; and that "his talents and character were always held in high esteem by me."[288] Then there is the brief moving tribute by Marshall, Washington's intimate friend for fifty years: "no man knew his worth better or deplores his death more than myself."[289]

---

[286] J. Hopkinson, "Bushrod Washington," Am. L. Mag., 10:253 (1845).
[287] [J. Story], "The Late Judge Washington," Boston Daily Advertiser, Dec. 10, 1829, reprinted in W. Story, Life and Letters, II, 29.

[288] G. Duvall to R. Peters, Jr., Dec. 3, 1829, Peters Papers.
[289] 3 Pet. vii, xii (1832).

# Chapter V: *The Justices of the Marshall Court*

The second indication of Washington's pivotal role on the Court is his commitment to the practices that had come into being during Marshall's tenure, already documented. Separate opinions, Washington felt, had precipitated "a loss of reputation" in the Virginia Supreme Court; he believed dissents "weaken[ed] the authority of the Court." Thus he offered to his colleagues the example of a judge whose industry and learning were formidable, who was dedicated to mastering the intricacies of his profession, but who was willing to keep silent on major cases so that the Court could appear to speak with a united voice. That judges who had been outspoken on previous courts or who were otherwise gregarious and strong-minded personalities—Livingston, Story, Johnson, and Todd come to mind—were nonetheless willing to adhere to the Court's "conclave" practice no doubt owes something to the examples of Washington and Marshall, two members of the "conclave" who combined fairness with a conciliatory manner and a likable disposition.

The third factor facilitating Washington's role is that the conclave practices harmonized so well with Washington's persistent yet carefully muted political goals. He remained, as Story said, "a good old-fashioned federalist, of the school of the days of Washington"[290] throughout his tenure on the Court, and his mild, self-effacing manner belied the strength of his views. It was Washington, we have seen, to whom the lawyers in *Martin* v. *Hunter's Lessee* brought the writ of error petition John Marshall had drafted; it was Washington to whom Marshall turned for help in placing his pseudonymous defense of *McCulloch* in the Alexandria *Gazette*.[291] When Story's original opinion in *Green* v. *Biddle* produced an outcry in Kentucky and reargument was granted, it was Washington who eventually spoke for the Court, making a more moderate but equally uncompromising defense of the Court's power to scrutinize state legislation. In the most influential and most harmonious years of the Court, the positions Washington advanced regularly prevailed; he stood silent, on most occasions, not in a spirit of acquiescence but in one of satisfaction, having had his say in "consultation" and during the informal discussions at the boardinghouse.

Washington's marriage played a significant part in his life. Ann Blackburn Washington was in feeble health for most of their married life, and was apparently somewhat high-strung as well. Horace Binney told a story of making an argument before Washington on circuit when the courthouse clock struck three, the normal hour of adjournment. Washington interrupted Binney in the middle of a sentence and adjourned the

---

[290] [J. Story], "The Late Judge Washington," 32.

[291] See G. Gunther, *John Marshall's Defense of McCulloch v. Maryland* (1969), 12–13. Marshall's defense and Washington's role in the controversy over *McCulloch* are described in Chapter VIII.

Court. As he and Binney were walking out, Washington said, "The sound of that clock is distinctly heard by Mrs. Washington . . . and if I am not in her parlor within five minutes afterwards, she imagines some evil has happened to me, and her nerves are disordered for the rest of the day."[292] The Washingtons were childless and exceptionally close. Ann Washington often accompanied her husband on his circuit junkets, the Washingtons invariably traveling in a carriage rather than a stagecoach, since Ann was afraid of stagecoach travel. When Washington died in Philadelphia in late November 1829, Ann Washington was with him; he had sent for her two weeks earlier, fearing that he would not survive.[293] After his death his body was shipped back to Virginia on a steamboat for burial at Mount Vernon, and Ann Washington, together with her niece and nephew, began the journey home in a carriage. Shortly after leaving Philadelphia Ann Washington became ill, and two days after her husband's death she died.[294]

Living at Mount Vernon, which he inherited from his uncle after Martha Washington's death in 1802, was both a blessing and a burden to Washington. The farm was not economically profitable, losing between $500 and $1,000 a year between 1802 and 1822.[295] Pressure was put on the Washingtons to transfer George Washington's remains from Mount Vernon to the District of Columbia, but Washington, after rereading his uncle's will, declined.[296] Mount Vernon had slave labor, and while George Washington had emancipated his personal slaves at his death, others continued to live and work at Mount Vernon during the Bushrod Washingtons' residence there. In 1821, as a result of economic problems and some slave unrest at Mount Vernon, Washington resolved to sell more than fifty of his slaves. The sale was reported in local papers, and reprinted by the Baltimore *Morning Chronicle* and *Niles' Weekly Register,* which added editorials calling the sale "excessively revolting" and contrasting Bushrod Washington's attitude to that of his uncle.[297] Outraged, Washington wrote a letter to the Baltimore *Federal Republican* "enter[ing] a solemn protest against the propriety of any person questioning [my] right, legal or moral, to dispose of property."[298] Five years earlier Washington had been one of the founders, and had been elected the first

---

292 Binney, *Bushrod Washington,* 24.
293 B. Washington to David Calwell, Nov. 14, 1829, Archives, Union Library, Mount Vernon, Va.
294 [Anonymous], "Last Illness of Judge Washington," *Journal of Law,* 1:88, 91 (1830).
295 [Anonymous], "Judge Washington," *Niles' Weekly Register,* 21:70, 71 (1821).

296 B. Washington to William C. Nichols, Mar. 18, 1816, Miscellaneous Papers, New-York Historical Society, New York, N.Y.
297 The editorials are reprinted in "Judge Washington and His Slaves," *Niles' Weekly Register,* 21:1 (1821).
298 Reprinted in "Judge Washington," supra, note 295, 70.

president, of the American Colonization Society, an organization dedicated to the relocation of liberated slaves in Africa.[299] He sent some of his own slaves to Liberia[300] and encouraged others to emigrate there. All told, four members of the Marshall Court were slaveholders, Washington, Marshall, Johnson, and Duvall; and of the southern Justices on the Court only Johnson came to be an outspoken opponent of the system.

Mount Vernon was also besieged by a regular influx of visitors, who came by steamboat to picnic on the grounds, view George Washington's tomb, and generally invade the property. The Washingtons tolerated visitors for several years, but finally in 1822 Bushrod posted the following notice:

> The feelings of Mrs. Washington and myself, have been so much wounded by some late occurrences at this place, that I am compelled to give this PUBLIC NOTICE, that permission will not in future be granted to Steam-Boat Parties, to enter the gardens, or to walk over the grounds, nor will I consent that Mount Vernon, much less the lawns, shall be the place at which eating, drinking and dancing parties may assemble.[301]

By virtue of his prominent position and family connections, Washington was also the object of charitable requests, pleas for support from relatives, and crank letters. In 1824, for example, he received a letter from "Samuel George Washington" informing him that the writer was "doing very well, making thirteen dollars a month and abel to dress as fine as any young man in this state, and abel to ware boots up to my knees," and signed "your affectionate son." Washington wrote on the back, "from some fool or knave calling himself Samuel G. Washington & my son."[302] Another letter, apparently from a cousin of Mrs. Washington, complained of the writer's "deplorable situation . . . not having necessary clothing and nourishing food," and asked for "any small sum you will be good enough to remit me on an order in a store in Alexandria or Washington."[303] Finally, there is the remarkable letter Washington received on August 12, 1822 from "Urbain Batiery," a resident of Louisiana, referring to Washington's sale of his slaves a year earlier:

> Je take la libertie of writing to vous—Je have heard of votre character in Louisiana, where vous rend votre Slaves . . . Vous suppose you are

---

[299] J. Staudenraus, *The African Colonization Movement (1961)*, 30.
[300] C. Moore, *The Family Life of George Washington* (1926), 195.
[301] Notice, July 4, 1822, Archives, Union Library, Mount Vernon, Va.
[302] "Samuel George Washington" to

B. Washington, June 20, 1824, Bushrod Washington Papers, Washington State Historical Society, Tacoma, Wash.
[303] Elizabeth B. Scott to B. Washington, May 12, 1824, ibid.

great because named Washington—you imagine you may commit crimes with impunitee. Wretched being le time is coming when vous have to answer for votre base crimes. . . .

Le Spanish Pirate is better than vous. You send votre fellow mortals to a land of miserie. Vile petit villain how can vous look a manly man in le face. Votre withered hellish countenance black with le deeds of hell. . . . Your brains ought to be blown out, vous stinkin Cur. . . .

When Je return to Louisiana Je wil inform les planters what me hear of votre vile Character . . . Vous won't permit le innocent people to amuse themselves or dance on votre plantation, vous ill natured criminal. Adieu, Je remain votre implacable enemy.[304]

Washington methodically filed that letter with all the others he received, as imperturbable in the face of crank letters as he was when meeting high emotion in Court. When his health began to decline for the last time in the fall of 1829, he wrote a "confidential communication" to Charles Chauncey, a friend of his in Philadelphia:

[M]y desire is that when the Event happens, the sheet on which I am then lying may be employed as a covering sheet and at once thrown round my person and tied about my middle with a pocket hand-kerchief. The common practice of washing the body is to be avoided. My thumbs are not to be tied together nor anything put on my face or any restraint upon my person by bandages. My body is to be placed in an entirely plain coffin with a flat top and a sufficient number of holes bored through the lid and sides—particularly about the face and head to allow respiration if resuscitation should take place—and having been kept so long as to ascertain whether decay may have occurred or not, the coffin is to be closed up. My steward is to be written to immediately, on the event of despoliation, to come on, and under his care my body is to be conveyed to Virginia in the Steam Boat, by way of Baltimore, and landed directly at Mount Vernon to be buried there.[305]

On Washington's death these instructions were methodically carried out.[306] Story wrote that "the departure of such a man severs so many ties, interrupts so many beliefs, withdraws so many confidences, and leaves such an aching void . . . and such a sense of desolation, . . . that while we bow to the decree of Providence, our griefs cannot but pour themselves out."[307]

---

[304] "Urbain Batiery" to B. Washington, Aug. 12, 1822, ibid.

[305] B. Washington to C. Chauncey, Jan. 14, 1829, ibid.

[306] "Last Illness of Judge Washington," 91.

[307] [J. Story], "The Late Judge Washington," 33.

# Chapter V: *The Justices of the Marshall Court*

✳

We have seen that the nature of the office of Supreme Court Justice during Marshall's tenure could vary, depending how it was interpreted by an occupant, from something nearly resembling a sinecure to a remarkably active and powerful position. If one believes that the "silent judges" on the Court did not participate substantially in the boardinghouse conversations and were not excessively active on their respective circuits, their years on the Court were not years of significant activity or influence. While this is a large assumption, and may well slight the three Justices' contributions, no similar extrapolation from minimal evidence needs to be made in the case of the Marshall Court Justices on the other end of the activity spectrum.

Joseph Story was unquestionably the busiest and most productive judge of Marshall's tenure, and quite possibly the most active in the entire history of the Court. Moreover, Story left records of his varied activity, including some that he perhaps would have preferred history to be unaware of. The result is that anyone who studies the early history of the Supreme Court confronts the staggering achievements of Story's career. Thirty-four years a Justice; author of thirteen volumes of commentaries on legal subjects; Dane Professor at Harvard Law School for sixteen years; author of numerous prepared bills of legislation; regular contributor to the appendices in Wheaton's Supreme Court Reports; author of countless tributes, sketches, and comments; litigator, politician, and bank president; and one of the most prolific letter-writers of an epistolary age. As one of Story's biographers has put it, "the problem of selectivity . . . haunts the effort to describe Story's crowded and varied life."[308]

Like Washington, Story seemed ideally suited to be a judge, not in his case because of temperament but because of his flair for "juridical studies."[309] He grew up in Marblehead, Massachusetts, taught himself Greek and Latin in order to pass an entrance exam to Harvard College, graduated from Harvard at eighteen, and was admitted to practice in Essex County, Massachusetts, at twenty-one. While Story was to come to love the study of law, he was at first thrown into despair by the "intricate, crafted, and obsolete learning of Coke or Littleton," the "dry and technical principles . . . of the feudal system," and "the repulsive and almost unintelligible forms of processes and pleadings."[310] he encountered while reading law in the office of Samuel Sewall. Eventually, however, Story

---

[308] G. Dunne, *Justice Joseph Story and the Rise of the Supreme Court* (1970), 435.
[309] J. Story to Nathaniel Williams, Nov. 30, 1811, in W. Story, *Life and Letters*, 201.

[310] J. Story, "Autobiography," in W. Story, ed., *The Miscellaneous Writings of Joseph Story* (1852), 19.

"began to see daylight . . . and to feel that I could comprehend and reason upon the text and the comments," and soon had "acquired . . . a decided relish for . . . my profession."[311] In a year or two after being admitted to the bar "business flowed in upon me; and . . . I began . . . to reap the reward of my fidelity to my clients." When Story left private practice to become a Supreme Court Justice his practice was "probably as extensive and as lucrative as that of any gentleman in the county."[312]

At the Essex County bar Story made some longtime friends, such as Jeremiah Mason from New Hampshire and William Prescott, became involved in politics, and also made a few enemies. One constant critic of Story's was the Reverend William Bentley, who had first come into contact with Story when the latter, after his graduation from Harvard, became interested in the Republican party. Bentley found Story's ambition "boundless" and his mind "active, but not strong." "He skims," Bentley felt, "but does not rise."[313] Bentley watched Story's career from its earliest moments in Marblehead and Salem to Story's nomination to the Court, and as Story moved from one position to another, Bentley never had a flattering explanation for Story's conduct. Story was elected to the Massachusetts legislature in 1805, and two years later sponsored a bill to increase judicial salaries, a measure that his own party opposed since most existing judgeships were held by Federalists. The bill was defeated, and Bentley commented that Story's "ambition [had] outstepped his judgment."[314] In May 1808, Story was appointed to fill the unexpired term of Jacob Crowninshield, who had died that April. Bentley suggested that Story, named by the Republicans, would "answer as well for [the Federalists] as any man they could choose,"[315] and when Story made a vacillating speech on the Jefferson administration's embargo policies that same year, Bentley said, "give me a firm man who reflects, but decides."[316]

In the fall of 1808 the Republicans decided not to renominate Story and the Federalists were able to defeat their candidate. Bentley blamed Story, "whose duplicity," he said, "has been very injurious to us."[317] Story recalled in his autobiography that he had "declined being a candidate for reelection," and that he had "no reason to doubt that my reelection would have been sure."[318] Bentley put it somewhat differently. "While young [John Quincy] Adams is working into political favor," Bentley reported, "young Story of the law in this town is working out." Bentley regarded Story's unseating as the just desert of a "secret enemy

311 Ibid., 20.
312 Ibid., 21.
313 W. Bentley, *The Diary of William Bentley* (4 vols., 1914), III, 16.
314 Ibid., 273.

315 Ibid., 361.
316 Ibid., 363.
317 Ibid., 395.
318 J. Story, "Autobiography," 29.
319 Bentley, *Diary*,

and hypocrite,'' who would "sell at any price.''[319] At the same time Story had come to the attention of well-placed Federalists in the Boston area, who retained him to aid their efforts to enforce claims they made on disputed land in Georgia that was to become the basis of the 1810 Marshall Court case of *Fletcher* v. *Peck*. One of their members, Harrison Gray Otis, wrote to Robert G. Harper, who was managing the *Fletcher* case, that Story had been retained. "He is a young man of talents,'' Otis said, "who commenced Democrat a few years since and was much fondled by his party. [But] he . . . acted on several occasions with a very salutary spirit of independence and in fact did so much good that his party have denounced him, and a little attention from the right sort of people will be very useful to him and to us.''[320]

Story was happy to use the occasion of his representation of the land claimants to make two trips to Washington, in 1807 and 1808. On those trips he met Jefferson, Madison, and Rufus King, and observed the Justices of the Supreme Court for the first time. The trips were also respites from the melancholy of his private life: in the summer of 1805 he had lost both his wife, Mary Lynde Fitch Oliver, whom he had married only six months earlier, and his father. "I never look back upon this period of my life,'' he wrote in his autobiography, "without feeling a sense of desolation. It left a dark and melancholy train of thoughts behind. All my hopes were at once cut down and crushed. I remained for a long time like one in a painful dream.''[321] He wrote his Harvard classmate Samuel Fay, more than a year after his wife's death, of his "deep and continual regret over all I once possessed and have now forever lost,''[322] and in May 1807 wrote Fay from Washington that "life without a domestic friend is dreary and comfortless.''[323]

In the spring of 1808 the "irksome state'' of Story's "domestic life'' was relieved when he became engaged to Sarah Waldo Wetmore, a close friend of his first wife. He wrote his brother-in-law jubilantly that "all my doubts and apprehensions have vanished. I am now an affianced lover.''[324] Story's second marriage was, by all accounts, a successful and happy one, although the Storys had four successive children die in childhood. "I have many agonizing recollections on this subject,'' Story wrote in his autobiography, "and some truly pathetic touches of tenderness to tell, but I have neither the heart nor the power to go over them.''[325] In the meantime he had served his abortive term in Congress, where he had

[320] H. G. Otis to R. G. Harper, May 1, 1807, in S. Morrison, *Life and Letters of Harrison Gray Otis* (2 vols., 1913), I, 283.
[321] J. Story, "Autobiography,'' 26.
[322] J. Story to S. Fay, Dec. 19, 1806, in W. Story, *Life and Letters*, 141.
[323] J. Story to S. Fay, May 30, 1807, in ibid., 153.
[324] J. Story to Joseph White, May 28, 1808, in ibid., 170.
[325] J. Story, "Autobiography,'' 34–35.

been a wary opponent of Jefferson's embargo, and for this had earned the label "pseudorepublican" from Jefferson, "as," Story said, "everyone was in Mr. Jefferson's opinion who dared to venture upon a doubt of his infallibility."[326] Jefferson had claimed, in correspondence published after his death, that Story had helped the Federalists "inflict a wound upon our interests which can never be cured, and on our affections, which it will require time to cultivate."[327] Story felt that Jefferson had "sullied [his] character,"[328] which, Bentley remarked on Story's return to Marblehead in 1809, was "very doubtful."[329]

In 1810 Story was once more in Washington, arguing *Fletcher v. Peck* before the Marshall Court. After that, on his return in May, he was appointed again to the Massachusetts legislature, where he served through 1811.[330] Meanwhile his name surfaced as a candidate to fill the vacancy on the Supreme Court created by Justice William Cushing's death. Jefferson, of course, was adamantly opposed to the idea, writing Madison in October 1810, a month after Cushing's death, that Story was "unquestionably a tory," and "too young," and reminding Madison that Story had "deserted us" on the embargo.[331] For a variety of reasons, however, Jefferson was unsuccessful in his efforts to deny Story the nomination. Madison's first choice, Levi Lincoln, declined; his second choice, Alexander Wolcott of Connecticut, apparently named to fulfill a political debt,[332] was not confirmed by the Senate; and his third choice, John Quincy Adams, declined in order to preserve his political options. Meanwhile the support of Massachusetts Republicans became vital to the Madison administration as the United States moved closer to war with England. Massachusetts commercial interests resented that trend, and Story, having been elected Speaker of a Republican-dominated Massachusetts legislature in January 1811, had emerged as a power to be reckoned with. By November 1811 Madison had appointed him to the Court. Story wasted no time in accepting, citing "the high honor attached to it, the permanence of the tenure, [and] the respectability of the salary."[333] Dr. Bentley was, as usual, unkind in his comments on the appointment, saying that "this cringing man . . . has risen as he wished," and that the appointment must have come as "a reasonable relief when [Story's] political reputation has deserted him."[334]

---

[326] Ibid., 33.
[327] T. Jefferson to General Henry Dearborn, July 16, 1810, in Ford, *Works*, XI, 143.
[328] J. Story, "Autobiography," 34.
[329] Bentley, *Diary*, III, 412.
[330] W. Story, *Life and Letters*, 198–99.

[331] Letter from T. Jefferson to J. Madison, Oct. 15, 1810, Jefferson Papers.
[332] See Warren, *Supreme Court*, I, 412–13.
[333] Story to Williams, supra, note 309.
[334] Bentley, *Diary*, IV, 81, 69.

# Chapter V: *The Justices of the Marshall Court*

Two more features of Story's crowded pre-Court life deserve mention at this point. He had since college shown an interest in literature and engaged in some writing of his own: in 1801 he had published a volume of poems entitled *The Power of Solitude,* which was poorly received. "The critics," Story later wrote, "spoke unfavorably of it; and what was a little remarkable, finding from the preface [to the second edition, published in 1804] that some of the minor poems were not written by me, they praised highly those which they supposed were not mine (and which in fact were mine) and censured all the others. Such is critical praise and such critical sagacity. Henceforward I dropped poetry."[335] When in 1804 a group of Story's Harvard acquaintances formed a literary journal, the *Monthly Anthology and Boston Review,* one of their first critical efforts was a negative review of *The Power of Solitude.*[336] Story turned to legal subjects after that, publishing a collection on Chief Justice Theophilus Parsons, Sr.'s, opinions in 1802,[337] a *Selection of Pleadings in Civil Actions* in 1805, and three editions of treatises, Chitty on *Bills and Notes* (1809), Abbott on *Shipping* (1810), and Lawes on *Assumpsit* (1811).

During the same period Story had become involved in state banking. His friends the Crowninshield family had founded a "merchants bank" in Salem, of which Story was one of the original directors. A few years later Story was named president of the bank, and though Dr. Bentley regarded the appointment as another example of the machinations of "that ambitious wretch,"[338] the bank's cashier wrote Story's son many years later that "I owe [your father] much . . . of whatever is valuable in my business habits." Story drafted the bank's by-laws, "establish[ed] rules for the conduct of its business," and "inculcat[ed] . . . stern principles of probity and uprightness at the Director's Board."[339] When he was named to the Supreme Court he continued to serve as president of the bank until 1835. He was also influential in founding the first savings bank in Salem and was one of its trustees.[340]

The person who took Cushing's seat on the Marshall Court in its 1812 Term was therefore a man of varied interests, abundant talents, and ample energy and ambition. Story had not gone down easily for some of his contemporaries, from schoolmates who fought with him to Dr. Bentley and Jefferson, and was to remain a somewhat contentious and provoking presence on the Court. He disagreed regularly with Johnson on substantive issues and on the range of the Court's jurisdiction, and there is evidence

---

[335] J. Story, "Autobiography," 37.
[336] *Monthly Anthology and Boston Review,* 2:379 (1805).
[337] [J. Story], *American Precedents of Declarations* (1802).

[338] Bentley, *Diary,* IV, 347.
[339] John W. Treadwell to William W. Story, Aug. 25, 1847, in W. Story, *Life and Letters,* I, 205–207.
[340] Dunne, *Joseph Story,* 141–42.

359

that those disagreements spilled over into personal animosity.[341] He found Baldwin extremely trying and ridiculed Baldwin's *General View of the Constitution,* which had called Story's views "as unsound as dangerous."[342] His relations with Marshall, however, were uniformly excellent, and he appears to have got along well with Livingston, Todd, Duvall, Thompson, and Trimble. As their correspondence testifies, he and Washington were close friends, as were he and McLean.[343] All in all, Story was a gregarious and companionable member of the Court, strongly committed to the practices of conclave decisionmaking and silent acquiescence, anxious to expand the Court's jurisdiction and power, entirely aware of the political dimensions of the Court's jurisprudence, and vigorously partisan on issues such as sovereignty, property rights, and federal jurisdiction.

The most striking feature of Story's jurisprudence was his conception of law, which, to moderns, appears to have been erected on two irreconcilable propositions, the idea that judges could be aggressive, active developers of a novel American jurisprudence, and the idea that law was a science, being above politics, infused with incontrovertible propositions of morality and justice, and capable of being discovered, systematized, and declared by impartial judges. For Story, however, the propositions were self-reinforcing rather than inconsistent.

We have previously seen that a defining characteristic of the intellectual ethos of Story and his contemporaries was a distinctive attitude toward time and change. Story's generation was perhaps the last in American history to retain a prehistoricist sensibility, that is, to conceive of change as the progressive unfolding of first principles rather than as a continuous, dynamic process. While the past had meaning for the present and future, it was a selected meaning. Connections between past and future events were drawn by a backwards ("Whiggish") reading of history: the meaning of the past was found to reside in a series of general principles, embodied in past events, which were then applied as moral guidelines to the present and future. This technique required a characterization of the nature of change which seems alien to modern observers.

---

[341] Story regularly said of Johnson's opinions that they were "wanting in exactness," or "in his own peculiar way." E.g., Story to Todd, Mar. 14, 1823, supra, note 131. He also found "some of Judge Johnson's opinions . . . very uncourteous to some of his brethren," and suggested that "he errs most strikingly . . . in respect to a tenderness for the judgment of others." J. Story to H. Wheaton, Aug. 12, 1818, Wheaton Papers.

[342] Baldwin, *General View,* 107. Story said that he had read *A General View* "without surprise, and without any unsuitable emotion." J. Story to R. Peters, Jr., June 14, 1837, in W. Story, *Life and Letters,* II, 273.

[343] On Story's friendship with McLean, which largely developed after Marshall's death, see Weisenberger, *John McLean,* 154, 220.

Change, for Story's generation, was the equivalent of progress only because it represented a perfection and restoration of first principles. In times of stress brought about by the motion of American civilization, the remedy was to review and reassert the lessons of the past, so that American society could be seen as progressing in accordance with certain moral principles.

The technique by which the past was studied and its core principles extracted and reasserted was labeled "scientific" by Story and his contemporaries. The discussion in Chapter II suggested that science, for Story's generation, was both a methodological and a metahistorical concept. Legal science provided a methodology by which data from the past could be systematized and general principles extracted. And since the principles were invested with moral content, the end result was a philosophical statement of the values that served as guidelines for conduct. The great contribution made by science was as a system for achieving order. Story's generation did not accept the proposition that events in the history of a culture could be random or contingent; it was necessary that they be ordered and systematized, and their meaning extracted, for progress to be made. The code word by which this ordering, systematizing, and extraction was represented was the word "scientific." Law was a science, then, not because of the empirical nature of its data but because it was a subject capable of being ordered and systematized. And since the process of systematization ended up with a statement of governing moral principles, law was inseparable from moral philosophy.

The technique of scientific inquiry, as practiced by Story and other jurists of his day, involved considerable attention to legal history and to comparative law. But the use of such sources was unabashedly Whiggish: Story and his contemporaries were searching the sources for confirmation of principles they already "knew" to exist. Their use of history, and of comparative systems, was argumentative: authorities were cited in support of propositions that Story and the others had already taken to be established. Far from teaching that the diversity of human experience suggests that present values are relativistic and culturally determined, Story's methodology was designed to teach that there were universal principles capable of being extracted from diverse data. In this manner Story and his contemporaries gave meaning to the presence in early-nineteenth-century American culture of the Revolutionary experience, now perceived as separate from the world of their contemporaries, but at the same time significantly linked to that world. By seeing change as the continual vindication of first principles, Story and his peers structured and confined the flux they saw around them. They also confined judicial "discretion," for the methodology of legal science, if properly executed, confirmed the primacy of principles that judges were bound to propound and to follow.

I have previously suggested that this recasting of the experience of

361

the founding generation into a series of moral precepts—the first principles of republican government—was the central jurisprudential task of the Marshall Court; and in subsequent chapters we shall observe how the recasting was effectuated in legal doctrine. Story was, of course, a participant in the recasting as a judge. His impact was arguably even greater, however, in his extrajudicial writings, where he linked republican ideology to legal science and in the process revealed himself as the Court's most articulate exponent of a prehistoricist sensibility. One can see, in these writings, continued use of scientific techniques which culminated in the articulation of first principles; one can also see constant references to the code words of early-nineteenth-century ideological discourse. A Story article on the "Course of Legal Study," written in 1817, referred to the "wonderful . . . progress of moral, political, and juridical science" through "continual . . . adoption of those maxims of civil right."[344] One on the work of Kent spoke of "his researches [in] antiquated lore" to f[ind] the principles by which our own jurisprudence is to be illustrated."[345] One on the "Progress of Jurisprudence" called for "a gradual digest . . . of those portions of our jurisprudence which . . . shall acquire scientific accuracy."[346] And in an essay on the "History and Influence of the Puritans," Story gave a striking portrait of his contemporaries' attitude toward time and change:

> We involuntarily pause to look back upon the past, or to spell out the fortunes of the future. . . . We gather up the fragments of broken facts, as history or tradition has scattered them around us. We arrange them . . . and we realize their connection with ourselves. . . . Above all, we are thus enabled to extract from remote events that instruction which the vicissitudes of human life should press home . . . [T]he slow progress even of successful efforts . . . the fundamental causes, which question or retard their growth; these all furnish lessons. . . .[347]

In Story's conception of law as a science whose principles were both organizing guidelines for conduct and moral exhortations, one finds the explanation for his ubiquity. Story was simultaneously judge, jurist, professor, writer, draftsman, and publicist; in each role he was essentially performing the same function. He sought to explain the relationships between the past, present, and future, and in so doing looked to history as a source of instructive lessons. He garnered the lessons from principles he had extracted in his "scientific" digests and surveys of "fragments of broken facts." Whether those principles formed the chapter headings in

---

[344] J. Story, "Autobiography," 66–67.
[345] Ibid., 149.
[346] Ibid., 237.
[347] Ibid., 408–409.

his commentaries, the topics of his lectures, the basis of one of his Supreme Court opinions, or the grounding points for his political positions was immaterial; in each instance Story went through the same exegesis. Scattered through Story's writings one can find, if one probes thoroughly enough, nearly the entire vocabulary of early-nineteenth-century prehistoricist republican thought, each word bearing its special connotations and serving its unique metaphoric function in the process by which the conception of law as a science was communicated.

It should come as no surprise, then, that as a Supreme Court Justice Story continued to perform all of the tasks he had previously performed as a lawyer, politician, and commentator. Indeed, Story took on additional roles (educator) and widened the scope of others (commentator and publicist) while he was on the Marshall Court. He saw nothing unethical or even unusual in performing all those tasks simultaneously: since law was an all-embracing science, the development of law, in whatever form, was part of the process by which the "maxims of civil right" were revealed.

If the above were all one could say of Story, he would remain one of the singular legal minds of his age, a person whose tireless energy, persistent intellectual curiosity, and resonant sensibility enabled him to recast subject after subject, area after area. But Story was, besides, a compulsive conversationalist, whether the medium was letter or speech. Others perceived that Story's desire to talk went beyond ordinary limits. A contemporary from England noted that when Story was present "few others could get in a word; but it was impossible to resent this, for he talked evidently not to bear down others, but because he could not help it."[348] Story himself wrote, after his daughter Caroline died in 1819, that "with the world . . . I pass for a cheerful man . . . but my cheerfulness is the effect of labor and exertion to fly from melancholy recollections, and to catch at momentary joy."[349] These last comments suggest that Story's renowned gregariousness may have had psychological roots, but it was nonetheless a pronounced feature of his character. To this trait was added a relish for gossip, an insatiable curiosity, and a compulsion to convey his observations to others. The result was that Story's letters, some of which have been published but others of which remain in private collections, furnish vivid evidence of what it was like to be a Marshall Court Justice.

The letters, some of which have been previously quoted, reveal the time of Court sessions ("eleven to four o'clock"); the boardinghouse "conclaves" ("we moot questions as they are argued"); the nature of Supreme Court arguments ("the mode of arguing causes . . . is exces-

---

[348] G. Howard, *Travels in America* (1851), 23.

[349] J. Story, journal, in W. Story, *Life and Letters*, I, 333.

sively prolix and tedious''); the leading advocates (''Mr. Pinkney . . . is excessively vehement and impetuous''); the Court's spectators (''all the belles of the city have attended, and have been entranced for hours'').[350] They provide an ongoing picture of the interactions among the Justices (''As usual, the old maxim was verified—*juniores ad labores*. I worked very hard, and my brethren were so kind as to place confidence in my researches'')[351] (''At the earnest suggestion of Mr. Justice Washington, I have determined not to deliver a dissenting opinion *Olivera* v. *The United Insurance Company*''[352]) (''I should have delivered [the opinion] in Court, if I had not felt a delicacy in respect to the Chief Justice; especially as I acquiesced in the opinion he delivered''[353]); of boarding-house politics (''Upon the point as to exemption of a public ship of war from state jurisdiction, a majority of the Court held the same opinion as myself, although . . . that opinion was suppressed from motives of delicacy''[354]) (''All the Judges, except Judge Livingston, concurred in this opinion. It will have a most important bearing upon the fate of the bankrupt act now before Congress,''[355]) (''I see no reason to take back our opinion though for one, I felt a solicitude to come to that result . . . I could not change my opinion, and I have adhered to it''[356]); of circuit business (''I have the benefit of the semi-annual abstracts, which I sent to Judge Washington, and from which I can recover all the points, and often the leading grounds of my decisions''[357]); and of ceremonial occasions (''Yesterday was the inauguration of President Jackson. . . . At twelve, the Senate, with the other parts of the procession went through the Rotunda to the eastern portico, and there, in the presence of an immense multitude, the Chief Justice administered to him his oath of office and he pronounced his inaugural speech . . . [T]he reign of King 'Mob' seemed transparent''[358]).

Story's letters were full of his many other interests: politics; social life in Washington; literature; social issues, such as slavery, bankruptcy, and the suffrage; finances, especially judicial salaries; travel; religion; and legal education. There are also numerous references to his domestic life, particularly to the illnesses and deaths of his children. Two domestic letters are worth quoting at some length. The first is to the Reverend John Brazer on May 25, 1821, after the Story's lost their daughter Louisa to scarlet fever:

---

[350] J. Story to S. W. Story, Mar. 10, 1814, in ibid., 253.
[351] J. Story to S. Fay, Apr. 24, 1814, in ibid., 261.
[352] J. Story to H. Wheaton, Apr. 8, 1818, in ibid., 303.
[353] J. Story to H. Wheaton, Apr. 10, 1818, in ibid., 305.
[354] Ibid.

[355] J. Story to S. White, Feb. 17, 1819, in ibid., 326.
[356] Story to Todd, Mar. 14, 1823, supra, note 131.
[357] J. Story to Jeremiah Mason, Dec. 7, 1825, in ibid., 531.
[358] J. Story to S. W. Story, Mar. 7, 1829, in ibid., 563.

My dear little daughter was one of the best, purest, and most affectionate of human beings. . . . The Providence, which has removed her from us, is to be truly mysterious; but having a firm and unfaltering belief in the goodness of God, and in his parental wisdom, I cannot doubt that it is for the best, although I am incapable of perceiving how it is so. . . . I trust that after the anguish of my affliction shall have been diminished, by time and distance, I shall be able to realize the full force of . . . a belief in another and a better state of existence. . . . At present I am unable to do more than to bring the truth to my mind, without the power of giving to it the mastery over my feelings.[359]

The second is from Story to his young son, William, in February 1827, as the Court's Term opened:

I must tell you a little about myself. I live in a house which is five stories high on the back side and three stories for the front side, it being on the slope of a hill—I have a chamber to myself in the upper, that is the fifth story, and a fire there, when I am in the house, so that I may read and write. My bed is in the same chamber, so that when I am tired I go to bed.

Now you will ask what I am doing in this City—I will tell you. I believe you know that I am what they call a Judge, and that I sit in a court room to hear lawyers (and who lawyers are your mother will tell you) talk—well—six other Judges sit with me, and after we have heard all they have to say, we then tell them what we think ought to be done; and then it is done—and this is very hard work, for sometimes they puzzle us with very odd and strange questions.[360]

All told, Story lost five of the eight children of his two marriages. He buried each in Mount Auburn Cemetery, a place that never failed to evoke powerful feelings in him. James Kent remembered a day in 1836 when he and Story toured Mount Auburn, and Story "poured forth the rich profusion of his poetical and elegant genius and impassioned and pathetic feelings."[361] One such response to Mount Auburn appeared in the life of Story written by his son:

Here is the thick shrubbery, to protect and conceal the new-made grave; and there is the wild flower creeping along narrow path, and planting its seeds in the upturned earth. All around us there breathes a solemn calm, as if we were in the bosom of a wilderness . . . Ascend but a few steps, and what a change of scenery to surprise and delight us! We

[359] J. Story to J. Brazer, May 25, 1831, in ibid., II, 55.
[360] J. Story to W. Story, Feb. 2, 1827, Story Papers, Massachusetts Historical Society, Boston, Mass.

[361] J. Kent to W. Story, May 26, 1846, ibid.

seem, as it were, in an instant, to pass from the confines of death to
the bright and balmy regions of life. Below us flows the winding
Charles. . . . In the distance the city . . . rears its proud eminences,
its glittering spires, its lofty towers, its graceful mansions, its curling
smoke, its crowded haunts of business and pleasure. . . . Again we
turn, and the walls of our venerable University rise before us, with
many a recollection of happy days passed there in the interchange of
study and friendship. . . . Again we turn, and the cultivated form, the
neat cottage, the village church, the sparkling lake, the rich valley, and
the distant hills, are before us, . . . and we breathe admidst the fresh
and varied labors of man.

There is . . . within our reach, every variety of natural and artificial scenery. . . . We stand . . . upon the borders of two worlds,
and, as the mood of our minds may be, we may gather lessons of
profound wisdom by contrasting the one with the other, or indulge in
the dreams of hope and ambition, or solace our hearts by melancholy
meditations.[362]

The central images of Story's nonjudicial life recur in this passage: the
"graceful mansions" and "proud eminences" of Boston to which he had
aspired as a youth; the "happy days . . . passed . . . in the interchange
of study" he had spent at Harvard; the "neat cottage" and "village
church," symbols of his small-town New England youth; and overhang-
ing all of them the "new-made grave," with the "melancholy meditations" it provoked, a sad thread that ran through Story's busy, active,
and successful life.

Next to Marshall, Story made the most significant contribution to
Marshall Court jurisprudence. In the twenty-one years between 1815 and
1836 he wrote 188 opinions, far more than any other judge besides Marshall. He rendered opinions during those years in such significant cases
as *Martin* v. *Hunter's Lessee, Dartmouth College, Green* v. *Biddle,
Houston* v. *Moore,*[363] *The Thomas Jefferson,*[364] and *Wilkinson* v. *Leland.*[365] He dissented only six times in the period. Moreover, in addition
to his contributions to Wheaton's Reports, he wrote "official" eulogies
of several of the judges, continually lobbied for increased salaries for the
Justices and the Reporters, and, as we have seen, helped shepherd cases
up to the Court through the use of the certificate of division procedure,
compiled summaries of his circuit cases, communicated regularly with
other Justices about issues pending on circuit, and sought to ratify majoritarian Court doctrines in his role as a commentator.

---

[362] J. Story, address at dedication of
Mount Auburn Cemetery, Sept. 24,
1831, in W. Story, *Life and Letters*, II,
66–67.

[363] 5 Wheat. 1 (1828).
[364] 10 Wheat. 428 (1825).
[365] 2 Pet. 627 (1829).

# Chapter V: *The Justices of the Marshall Court*

It is harder to assess the intangible contributions Story made to the Court's solidarity, harmony, and increased prominence. His ebullient, combative personality was not universally appreciated, and one may surmise that his loquaciousness and indiscretion may have lessened his effectiveness in group discussion. He was, however, a zealous apostle of the "conclave," a reluctant dissenter, a cheerful presence, and a person whose multiple talents did not usually extend to searching criticism of others. Moreover, he was knowledgeable on a great many subjects, thoroughly at home with legal research, a productive writer, a devoted participant in the life of the boardinghouse, and a loyal friend to most of his fellow Justices. He was also, needless to say, thoroughly committed to the Court's self-appointed task of recasting fundamental legal principles in ways congenial to the demands of an expanding and commercially prominent yet increasingly fragmented and divided nation. Those interested in having the Constitution, through artful interpretations by the Supreme Court, serve as the linchpin linking the comparatively simple republican vision of the Framers to the more complicated and potentially more chaotic configurations of the early nineteenth century could have found no more dedicated nor ubiquitous interpreter than Story. Marshall, in reacting to the appearance of Story's *Commentaries on the Constitution*, gave an assessment that he would have undoubtedly regarded as applying more generally to Story's interpretive contributions. "It is," Marshall said, "a comprehensive and an accurate commentary . . . formed in the spirit of the original text, [with] solemn and interesting admonitions."[366]

When John Marshall succeeded Oliver Ellsworth as Chief Justice of the United States in January 1801, he permanently changed the stature of the office he occupied. John Jay, Adams's initial choice, had declined the position, citing as one of his reasons a conviction that the Court "would not obtain the energy, weight, and dignity which was essential to its affording due support to the national government, nor acquire . . . public confidence and respect."[367] By the time of Marshall's death in 1835 the Court's "dignity" and "respect" had been established, and its "due support to the national government" was abundantly clear. This transformation had been accomplished without any major change in the Court's powers or functions: in a formal sense, the only difference between the Court that sat in 1835 and its predecessor in 1801 was that it was made up of seven Justices instead of six.

---

[366] J. Marshall to J. Story, June 19, 1833, in W. Story, *Life and Letters*, II, 134.

[367] J. Jay to J. Adams, Dec. 18, 1800 in C. Adams, *Works of Adams*, IX, 91.

That the transformation was largely Marshall's doing has previously been suggested. As noted, in the years of his tenure he wrote 547 majority opinions, 45 of those in constitutional cases; all the other Marshall Court Justices combined produced 574 opinions, 31 in constitutional cases.[368] Moreover, in the early years of the Court, when the Court's independence was least secure and its stature most questionable, Marshall, taking advantage of the seniority principle and the tacit consent of his associates, wrote nearly all of the Court's opinions, even, if Johnson is to be believed, in cases in which he had voted the other way. The "conclave" practice, with its corollary of silent acquiescence, was instituted by Marshall; strictures against publicly voiced dissent, a tendency to compromise the language of opinions to preserve unanimity, and the practice of postponing a decision (such as *Dartmouth College* or *Charles River Bridge*) when the Justices were divided also originated during his tenure. Of the major cases establishing judicial review and cementing the Court's power to scrutinize the acts of state legislatures, defining the federal commerce power, clarifying the status of corporations, and preserving private contractual rights against state interference—cases from *Marbury* through *Gibbons*—Marshall wrote nearly every one. Only *Martin v. Hunter's Lessee* and *Green v. Biddle,* two cases in which Marshall did not participate, and *Ogden v. Saunders,* where he dissented, were major constitutional cases not bearing his imprint. Story said, in delivering a eulogy to Marshall, that "having sat by his side during twenty-four years . . . having heard many of those exquisite judgments, the fruits of his own unassisted mediations, from which the court has derived so much honor . . . I confess myself unable to find language sufficiently expressive of . . . his transcendent genius."[369]

In an autobiographical sketch he supplied to Story in connection with a review by the latter of Marshall's *A History of the Colonies* in 1827,[370] Marshall recalled that he "had grown up at a time when a love of union [and] patriotism [were] the maxim[s] of every orthodox American; and I had imbibed these sentiments so thoroughly that they constituted a part of my being."[371] Marshall's immediate contemporaries had encountered the movement for independence and the Revolutionary War as their principal formative experiences. Marshall was eighteen when the war broke out, and "engaged in it with all the zeal and enthusiasm which belonged to my age." In 1775 he was made a lieutenant, in charge of a company of minutemen, and the next year he was assigned to a regiment.

---

[368] Seddig, "John Marshall and the Origins of Supreme Court Leadership," 800.

[369] J. Story, "Autobiography," 696.

[370] J. Marshall, *An Autobiographical Sketch* (J. Adams, ed., 1937), xvi.

[371] Ibid., 9.

He fought in the Pennsylvania campaigns, rising to the rank of captain, and continued in service until 1781, when he resigned his commission.[372] Late in his life Marshall ascribed his support for a federal government to his experience in the army, "where I found myself associated with brave men from different states who were risking life and everything valuable in a common cause . . . and where I was conformed in the habit of considering America as my country, and Congress as my government."[373] Shortly after the war, when "the topics of the day were paper money, the collection of taxes, the preservation of public faith, and the administration of justice,"[374] Marshall entered state politics and in 1812 was elected to the Virginia legislature. "I partook largely of the sufferings and feelings of the army," Marshall recalled, "and brought with me into civil life an ardent devotion to its interests. My immediate entrance into the state legislature opened to my view the causes which had been chiefly instrumental in augmenting those sufferings, and the general tendency of state politics convinced me that no safe and permanent remedy could be found but in a more efficient and better organized central government." In particular, Marshall found in the state legislatures "perpetually recurring . . . questions . . . which brought into doubt principles which I thought most sound."[375]

Nothing in the twenty years Marshall spent between his resignation from the army and his succession to the Chief Justiceship changed the views he had formed during the Revolution. He distrusted state legislatures, believed in national institutions, favored sound money, the creditor classes, and the sanctity of contracts, venerated George Washington, and in general followed the principles of what Story called "a federalist of the good old school, of which Washington was the acknowledged head."[376] On a few issues, such as the efficacy of the Alien and Sedition Acts, Marshall differed from Federalist orthodoxy,[377] and a more refined analysis of late eighteenth-century Federalism would label him a moderate as distinguished from an ultra Federalist. That label could fairly be attached to him in 1801 as well as in 1781.

In his commitment to Federalism Marshall repeatedly clashed with Jefferson; indeed, there seems never to have been a time in the careers of those two talented Virginia lawyers when their attitude toward one another was not one of mutual antagonism and distrust. The enmity preceded partisan affiliations: as early as the Revolutionary War Marshall was among a group of Virginians with military experience who criticized

---

[372] Ibid., 4–6.
[373] Ibid., 9–10.
[374] Ibid., 7–8.
[375] Ibid., 10.
[376] See L. Baker, *John Marshall*

(1974), 303–305; R. Faulkner, *The Jurisprudence of John Marshall* (1968), 15–17.
[377] Beveridge, *John Marshall*, IV, 140–44.

Jefferson for not serving in the war effort and for fleeing from the British while governor of Virginia in 1781. It spilled over into issues as diverse as religion and foreign affairs: in 1784 Marshall and Jefferson clashed over a Virginia General Assembly provision assessing the general population fees for the benefit of established churches, and eight years later they differed over the proper approach to the new revolutionary regime in France.[378] Exasperated with Marshall's conduct in the latter episode, Jefferson wrote Madison that "nothing better could be done than to make him a judge."[379] He was to regret that suggestion.

During Washington's second term, as political divisions became more marked and aid to France a central issue, Marshall and Jefferson became more openly critical of one another. Marshall commented upon Jefferson's strong support for the French Revolution, which made him particularly unacceptable to mainstream Federalists.[380] Jefferson noted that at the same time Marshall had "come forth in the plentitude of his English principles."[381] By the 1800 election Jefferson had become a presidential contender, and after a deadlock election faced a runoff with Aaron Burr in the House of Representatives. Marshall, who was secretary of state at the time, received a letter from Alexander Hamilton urging him to campaign for Jefferson against Burr. Marshall responded by saying that "to Mr. Jefferson . . . I have felt almost insuperable objections. His foreign prejudices seem to me totally to unfit him for the chief magistry of a nation, [and he] appears to me to be a man who will embody himself with the House of Representatives [and thereby] sap the fundamental principles of the government." Marshall's conclusion was, "I cannot bring myself to aid Mr. Jefferson."[382]

As time passed, and the prominence of both Marshall and Jefferson increased, their mutual animosity deepened. They infuriated one another during the treason trial of Aaron Burr, where Jefferson sought to stage-manage the prosecution and where Marshall, we have seen, gave a narrow definition of treason that made possible Burr's acquittal. When Jefferson was sued for damages in 1810 by Edward Livingston, the suit arising out of a controversy over disputed land ("the batture") in New Orleans and being filed in Marshall's circuit court in Richmond, Jefferson tried to prevail upon President Madison to replace the current district judge, whom he considered a "cypher." "The state has suffered long enough," Jefferson wrote, "from the want of any counterpart to the rancorous hatred which Marshall bears to his country and from the cunning and

[378] Baker, *John Marshall,* 188–89.
[379] T. Jefferson to J. Madison, June 29, 1792, in Ford, *Works,* VII, 130.
[380] Baker, *John Marshall,* 195–96.
[381] T. Jefferson to J. Madison, Nov. 26, 1795 in Ford, *Works,* VII, 197.

[382] J. Marshall to A. Hamilton, Jan. 1, 1801, in J. Hamilton, *The Works of Alexander Hamilton* (7 vols., 1850), VI, 137.

sophistry within which he is able to surround himself.'' There was ''little doubt,'' according to Jefferson, ''that [Livingston's] knowledge of Marshall's character has induced him to bring this action. His twistifications of the law in the case of Marbury, in that of Burr, and the late Yazoo case [*Fletcher* v. *Peck*] show how dexterously he can reconcile law to his personal biases.''[383] While Marshall eventually agreed with Jefferson that his court had no jurisdiction over a land dispute in Louisiana, his comments suggested that he regarded such ''technical impediments'' as ''obstruct[ing] the course of substantial justice.''[384] Several years later Marshall identified the Livingston case as one of the sources of Jefferson's antagonism; ''the case of the mandamus [*Marbury*] may be the cloak, but the batture is recollected with still more resentment.''[385]

A final clash between Jefferson and Marshall was initiated by the *Cohens* decision, which provoked Jefferson to write Johnson about the ''conclave'' practice, to encourage Thomas Ritchie and John Taylor to write comments critical of the decision, and to release for public consumption letters critical of the Court. One such letter was read by Story, who wrote to Marshall that Jefferson's ''obvious design'' was ''to prostrate the judicial authority and annihilate all public references of its dignity.'' Story found that Jefferson's remarks, ''at his age and in these critical times, . . . fill me alternately with indignation and melancholy.''[386] Marshall responded:

> For Mr. Jefferson's opinion as respects this department it is not difficult to assign the cause. He is among the most ambitious and I suspect the most unforgiving of men. . . . He looks, of course, with ill will at an independent judiciary.[387]

But where Jefferson was concerned, Marshall was every bit as ''ambitious'' and ''unforgiving'' as his rival. He assigned political motives to all of Jefferson's acts, identified Jefferson with extremist positions, and created sinister conspiracies with Jefferson at their head. Jefferson responded in kind. It was the kind of charged relationship that occurs between people who know each other well, are in competition with one another, and fear each other. The more influential the people involved, the more charged the relationship is likely to be.

---

[383] T. Jefferson to J. Madison, May 25, 1810, in Ford, *Works*, XI, 139.

[384] Livingston v. Jefferson, 1 Brockenbrough 206 (1812).

[385] J. Marshall to J. Story, July 13, 1821, in *Proc. Mass. Hist. Soc.* 14:329 (1901).

[386] J. Story to J. Marshall, June 27, 1821, Marshall Papers, College of William and Mary Library.

[387] Marshall to Story, July 13, 1821, supra, note 385.

Marshall's relations with Jefferson were, however, unusual among his professional associations. He was overwhelmingly successful in engendering warmth and admiration among those with whom he worked or became acquainted. Charles Sumner spoke of Marshall as "a model of simplicity . . . ready to laugh; to joke and to be joked with";[388] George Bancroft referred to Marshall's "venerable coolness of manner, . . . great collectedness, great precision, . . . calm uniformity [and] unerring judgment."[389] Horace Binney said in a eulogy that Marshall "was evidenced by nature with a patience that was never surpassed" and had "the composure of a mind undisturbed by doubt, and . . . unsusceptible of fear";[390] Theophilus Parsons, in another, claimed that "no man had ever a stronger influence upon the minds of others," attributing Marshall's influence not only to "his intellectual superiority" but to this "true simplicity and kindness of heart."[391] Even the Richmond *Enquirer*, Marshall's longtime antagonist, said on his death that "he was as much beloved as he was respected," and that "there was something unresistedly winning about him."[392] A sketch by Story encapsulates the qualities that made Marshall so successful in his relationships with people:

> To be amiable, as well as great; to be kind, gentle, simple, modest, and social, and at the same time to possess the rarest endowments of mind . . . [I]n the domestic circle he is exactly what a wife, a child, a mother, and a friend would most desire."[393]

The only evidence that exists of any of the Marshall Court Justices' taking umbrage at Marshall's presence involves Baldwin in the early 1830s, as previously noted; and Story reported shortly after Marshall's death that "Judge Baldwin . . . took an interest in the Chief Justice's dying hours," and "there is no person on earth for whom [Baldwin] felt so much reverence and respect."[394] Even Johnson, who obviously found Marshall and the practices he had instituted an impediment to his desire to express himself on "important public questions," never in his correspondence with Jefferson took the occasion to criticize Marshall. Given the number of controversial and significant issues decided by the Marshall Court, the Chief Justice's ability to inspire affection and defuse criticism was truly remarkable.

---

[388] Quoted in Pierce, *Memoirs of Sumner*, I, 135.

[389] Quoted in M. Howe, *The Life and Letters of George Bancroft* (2 vols., 1908), I, 202.

[390] H. Binney, "Eulogy of Chief Justice Marshall," *Am. Jurist*, 14:462, 463 (1835).

[391] [T. Parsons], "Intelligence and Miscellancy," *Am. Jurist*, 14:240, 244 (1835).

[392] Richmond *Enquirer*, July 10, 1835.

[393] J. Story in W. Story, *Life and Letters*, I, 522.

[394] J. Story to R. Peters, Jr., July 24, 1835, in ibid., II, 201.

# Chapter V: *The Justices of the Marshall Court*

When one recalls that the internal practices that developed during Marshall's tenure were practices that placed a value on harmony, solidarity, and good fellowship in small-group decisionmaking, one can glean some indication of the impact of Marshall's style. He presided over a Court that contained some prickly and independent spirits—Story and Johnson, in particular—and some judges—Livingston, Todd, Thompson, and Trimble—who had come to the Court accustomed to expressing themselves individually in judicial roles. With the help of others, he was able to persuade each of his colleagues that silent acquiescence, the issuance of an opinion of the Court, suppression of dissents, and compromises in the internal language of opinions were preferable to independent expression. It is doubtful that he could have achieved this had he not set a standard of humility, good humor, flexibility, and patience in his dealings with others. A striking testament to Marshall's conciliating influence is the lack of customary cohesion seen on the occasions in which he did not stand with the majority or did not participate in a decision. On three such occasions—one group of cases in the 1805 Term,[395] another group in the 1806 Term,[396] and *Ogden* v. *Saunders* in the 1827 Term—the absence of Marshall resulted in seriatim opinions being delivered by the majority; in a fourth Term, in *Green* v. *Biddle,* another case in which Marshall did not participate, the Court withdrew one opinion and substituted another. These examples suggest that had Marshall, with his great ability to intersperse broad principles with narrower holdings and his willingness to insert compromising language, not written the great bulk of significant Marshall Court opinions, far less surface unanimity would have been produced.

Marshall was unquestionably one of the great legal reasoners of his time: contemporaries regularly testified to his ability to march from premise to conclusion.[397] While the power of Marshall's approach was conceded, little speculation has been advanced, either by contemporaries or scholars, as to why this particular approach should have had such great appeal. Syllogistic reasoning in legal opinions has not always been highly acclaimed: when the technique was revived by the late-nineteenth-century

---

[395] Lambert's Lessee v. Paine, 3 Cranch 97 (1805); Marine Insurance Company of Alexandria v. Wilson, 3 Cranch 187 (1805).

[396] Marine Insurance Co. of Alexandria v. Tucker, 3 Cranch 357 (1806); United States v. Heth, 3 Cranch 399 (1806); Randolph v. Ware, 3 Cranch 503 (1806).

[397] Jefferson is reported as once saying, "When conversing with Marshall, I never admit anything. So sure as you admit any position to be good, no matter how remote from the conclusion he seeks to establish, you are gone." Story told this anecdote in one of his lectures at Harvard Law School, and it was reported by Rutherford B. Hayes, one of Story's students. See C. Williams, *Diary and Letters of Rutherford Birchard Hayes* (5 vols., 1922), I, 116.

Supreme Court it came to be caricatured by twentieth-century critics.[398] But in Marshall's generation the argument from first principles had an unmistakable appeal; to probe the success of that appeal is to understand better the significance of the Marshall Court.

I have previously suggested that the generation of Americans that came to acknowledge the Marshall Court's power and prominence had developed a distinctive relationship with its immediate past. Previous chapters have suggested that the generation of the early nineteenth century had largely abandoned a cyclical theory of change, in which the history of nations inexorably passed from birth to maturity to decay, but had not yet embraced historicism, a stance which assumes that qualitative change is a given in the course of nations. Instead, Marshall's contemporaries conceived of the past as a source of lessons, embodied in the form of permanent principles: the restatement of these principles was conducive to progress. The contrast between the conceptions of the Constitution held by its Framers and that held by the generation of the 1820s is instructive here. The Framers considered the Constitution, like the Union it created, as an experiment, something that might or might not survive in the short term and was destined to decay in the long term. The generation of the 1820s, sensing the distance between their current experience and that of the Framers and at the same time resisting the idea of cultural decay, sought to find meaning in the past by investing the Constitution with the status of a permanent document, a repository of first principles that would be appealed to by successive generations. In this way the past became a source of lessons, and links between past, present, and future were forged.

Marshall's opinions were superbly effective at demonstrating the first principles on which constitutional language was grounded. His rhetorical style, as I have had suggested elsewhere,[399] was to articulate an unassailable principle of American government (such as ultimate sovereignty in the people), investigate certain constitutional language with that principle in mind, refine the language, and then show that a particular refinement of the language, which decided the case before him, was consistent with the principle. In *Gibbons* v. *Ogden,* for example, Marshall's first principle was a liberal construction of enumerated federal powers, his crucial language "commerce," his refinement the subsuming of navigation under "commerce" for constitutional purposes, and his jurisprudential message a potentially unlimited power in Congress to regulate navigation if it so chose.

The primary purpose of Marshall's rhetoric, of course, was to supply

---

[398] Roscoe Pound called it "mechanical jurisprudence": see Pound, "Mechanical Jurisprudence," *Colum. L. Rev.,* 8:605, 1908.

[399] For a fuller discussion see G. White, *The American Judicial Tradition* (1976), 25, 31–33.

justifications for the decisions he and his fellow Justices made in constitutional cases, most of which were controversial and of great immediate significance. But an important subsidiary purpose was to allow early-nineteenth-century Americans to recast their immediate past. In the *Gibbons* case two features of the Constitution had suddenly taken an added significance in the early nineteenth century: the designation of commerce as an area of federal concern, and the theory of sovereignty apparently implicit in that designation. Commerce, in the form of a state-created steamboat monopoly, had become a subject of contemporary significance, and the question of which sovereign entities could or could not regulate commerce had accordingly become a major political issue. The sudden importance of commerce, exemplified by the steamboat, gave nineteenth-century Americans a sense of distance from their less commercial past; Marshall's opinion helped give that past some meaning through a restatement of first principles as codified in the Constitution.

The peculiarly authoritative feature of Marshall's jurisprudence, then, was its invocation of the supposedly timeless principles of the founding age. The irony was that the principles had very likely not been conceived of as timeless by those who articulated them; only in Marshall's recasting did they become illustrations of the wisdom of republican theorists. The brilliance—and the legerdemain—of Marshall's interpretations was the partisan gloss he was able to put on the principles he extracted. Nothing about the word "commerce" *compelled* navigation to be included within it, and certainly nothing in the language or structure of the Constitution necessitated that the sole agent regulating commerce be the federal government. It was doubtful, in fact, that the Framers had even thought about state-sponsored steamboats when they thought about commerce, since the steamboat itself had not yet been invented. *Gibbons* was just the sort of case—new developments in American civilization giving potentially new meaning to constitutional language—that made Marshall's interpretive solution so compelling to his contemporaries. By showing that constitutional language was to be "adapted to the various crises in human affairs," Marshall was demonstrating that the past had continual meaning for the future. While his opinions were considered as unassailable because of the skill by which he invoked settled first principles, those principles had come to be perceived as settled because, for Marshall's audience, they signified a cultural linkage between the immediate past and the present.

If Marshall was a tireless rhetorician, he was a less energetic letter-writer. He regularly wrote his wife, Mary Ambler Marshall, called "Polly," who never accompanied him to Washington or on circuit; the letters were exclusively about nonlegal matters. He wrote Story and Washington periodically on topics such as arrangements for lodging, circuit cases, reaction to Supreme Court decisions, and politics. Other than that his correspondence seems to have been efforts to clarify opinions which others had found controversial or expressions of sympathy to a relative of a deceased lawyer or judge. Marshall's letters were rarely long or wide-ranging, as were Story's or William Wirt's: he did not take the pleasure in the medium that those more "literary" men did. But Marshall's letters nonetheless reveal his sense of humor, his subtlety with language, and his consummate tact.

In his letters to Polly Marshall the Chief Justice was unceasingly solicitous and affectionate, and was also apt to indulge his wit. He wrote as a man whose company was regularly in demand to an absent, ill, reclusive wife, and invariably understated the pleasures of his social life. A letter in 1826 indicated that he had "received three invitations for evening parties this week," but that he had declined, pleading ill health. ("If you were here and would go with me I am not sure that my influenza . . . would keep me so constantly within doors, but as it is I do not feast my eyes with gazing at the numerous belles who flock to this place during the winters.")[400] Five years earlier he had complained of "din[ing] out too frequently" and "eating . . . late and hearty dinners." "There are continual parties" he noted, "but I make it a point not to go to them."[401] In another 1826 letter he mentioned going to President Adams's "drawing room, but I see very few persons [there] whom I know or in whom I take any interest." He added that "a person as old as I am finds that his home is his place of most comfort, and his old wife the companion in the world in whose society he is most happy."[402] In 1830 he spent some time describing "the splendid dinner parties to which we are invited," and mentioned the fact that "three young ladies . . . proposed a great desire to be acquainted with the judges— . . . you would have been quite surprised to see how gay and sprightly the wine made me." The sentence following that description read, however: "I hope very sincerely that we shall not be invited out again, as I greatly prefer remaining at home."[403]

The letters to Polly also described some of Marshall's habits while at the boardinghouse. His "practice," when traveling to Washington, as he told Polly in an 1826 letter, was "to remain a day in Alexandria" after taking the stagecoach from Richmond. He had on that occasion departed from it, "while the weather is good," and come directly to Washington; he was ensconced in "an excellent room with a good fire" at the boardinghouse.[404] He arose well before sunrise, "[took] my walk

---

[400] J. Marshall to Mary Ambler Marshall, Feb. 12, 1826, Marshall Papers, College of William and Mary Library.
[401] J. Marshall to M. A. Marshall, Feb. 26, 1821. ibid.
[402] J. Marshall to M. A. Marshall, Mar. 12, 1826, ibid.

[403] J. Marshall to M. A. Marshall, Feb. 14, 1830, ibid.
[404] J. Marshall to M. A. Marshall, Feb. 5, 1826, ibid.

of three miles by seven, think of you, & then get down to business.''[405] This practice continued at least as late as 1830: "I take my walk in the morning, work hard all day, eat a hearty dinner and sleep sound all night.''[406] Later that same year he wrote that "I am just returned from my morning's walk of three miles and all my brethren are fast locked in sleep in their rooms.''[407] In one letter Marshall noted that he combed his hair before going to bed, and "while this operation is performing I always think with tenderness of my sweet barber in Richmond.''[408]

Marshall's affectionate asides to Polly were not mere reassurances to an absent spouse. The Marshalls' marriage was by all accounts an exceptional one. Polly Ambler's sister, Mrs. Edward Carrington, described the Marshalls' courtship and marriage in a letter written to her cousin in 1823:

> My father at this time accepted an opportunity which kept him almost constantly in Williamsburg. . . . It was at that time we became acquainted with our much loved brother then called Capt. Marshall; who being without a command post then, left the northern army to visit . . . friends. . . .
> The little circle of York were on tiptoe on his arrival. Our girls particularly were emulous who should be first introduced; it is remarkable that my sister [Polly], then only 14 and diffident beyond all others, declared that we were giving ourselves useless trouble, for that she had made up her mind to go to the ball, tho' she had not even ever been at dancing school, and was resolved to set her cap at him, and eclipse us all; this in the end proved true, and at the first introduction he became devoted to her. . . .
> The year after the war his marriage took place . . . it has been ill-naturedly said that my father made objections on the score of fortune. I have heard Mr. Marshall a hundred times declare that after paying the Parson he had but one solitary guinea left. . . .
> His exemplary tenderness to an unfortunate sister is without parallel. With a delicacy of frame and feeling that baffles all description, she became early after her marriage a prey to extreme nervous affection, which more or less embittered her comfort thro' life. But this has only served to increase his care and tenderness and he is, as you know, as entirely devoted as at the moment of their first being married, always, and under every circumstance an enthusiast in love.[409]

[405] J. Marshall to M. A. Marshall, Feb. 12, 1826, ibid.
[406] J. Marshall to M. A. Marshall, Jan. 31, 1830, John Marshall Papers, University of Virginia.
[407] J. Marshall to M. A. Marshall, Mar. 17, 1830, College of William and Mary Library.
[408] J. Marshall to M. A. Marshall, Jan. 31, 1830, Marshall Papers, University of Virginia.
[409] Mrs. Edward Carrington to Mrs Fisher, [no date given], 1823, John Marshall Papers, Library of Congress.

While Marshall was recovering from a broken arm as a result of a fall in 1824, he wrote Polly a letter indicating how he has passed his time in bed:

> I have a plenty of time on my hands in the night as well as in the day. How do you think I bequite it? I am almost tempted to leave you to guess till I write again. But as I suppose you will have rather more curiosity in my absense than you invariably show to hear my stories when I am present, I will tell you without waiting to be asked. You must know that I began with the ball at York [where they first met in 1780] and with the dinner . . . at your house the next day. I then retrace my visit to York, our splendid assembly at the Palace in Williamsburg, my visit to Richmond . . . my return [in the] fall and very welcome reception you gave me on our arrival from Dover. Our little tiffs and makings up, my feelings while Major Dick was courting you, my trip to the cottages, my visit again to Richmond the ensuing fall, and all the thousand indescribable but deeply affecting instances of your affection or coldness which constituted for a time the happiness or misery of my life, and will always be recollected with a degree of interest which can never be lost while recollection remains.[410]

Polly died on Christmas Day, 1830. Over a year later Story entered Marshall's room in the boardinghouse and

> found him in tears . . . I saw at once that he had been shedding tears over the memory of his own wife, and he has said to me several times during the term, that the moment he relaxes from business he feels exceedingly depressed, and rarely goes through a night without weeping over his departed wife.[411]

The letters from Marshall to Story provide an equally rich source of Marshall's private feelings, albeit on different issues. An 1821 exchange suggests that Marshall and Story regularly communicated their views on circuit court cases. Marshall wrote on June 15 that

> A & B, trading under the form of A + B & Co. were indebted to the U.S. on bonds for duties. They made an assignment of all their social effects to secure certain creditors of the firm. . . . A [then] conveyed [his own private property] to secure his individual creditors . . . the question [is] whether the first conveyance was an act of insolvency within the act of Congress so that the priority of the U.S. attached on

---

[410] J. Marshall to M. A. Marshall, Feb. 23, 1824, Marshall Papers, College of William and Mary Library.

[411] J. Story to S. W. Story, Mar. 4, 1823, in W. Story, *Life and Letters,* II, 87.

the social effects, or whether the act of insolvency was not committed until the execution of the second deed."[412]

Marshall wondered "if the case has ever occurred in your circuit," and "how it has been decided," or, if not, what Story's "opinion on it" was. In a June 27 letter Story responded that while such a case had "never occurred in my Circuit," he had "turned it in my mind," and his "present opinion was that the first conveyance did constitute "an insolvency within the Act of Congress so as to give the U.S. a priority of payment."[413]

Similar exchanges took place in letters written by Marshall on July 13 and Story on July 26, 1819, and in letters written by Story on June 22 and Marshall on July 2, 1823. In these instances the cases discussed involved, respectively, issues in the law of admiralty and corporations. The latter case was *Bank of the United States* v. *Dandridge,* involving the responsibility of sureties for cashiers of branches of the Bank of the United States. Marshall's opinion on circuit was eventually reversed by the Supreme Court in an opinion written by Story. When the circuit case was described Story wrote that "I should be very happy to see a copy of the opinion," and suggested that "the decision . . . would in the end have a salutary tendency by inducing greater caution" in cashiers and their sureties.[414] But Marshall, in his response, said that "the case . . . goes to the Supreme Court and will probably be reversed" because "the practice of banks has not conformed to my construction of the law."[415] Story, and a majority of the Justices, eventually came to vote for reversal, but Marshall publicly adhered to his position in a dissent. The exchange over *Dandridge* suggests that Marshall Court Justices were capable of reversing their own circuit opinions and that they did not regard as inappropriate prior discussion of a circuit case that was scheduled for Supreme Court review.

In addition to circuit cases, Marshall and Story discussed the political reactions to their constitutional decisions. In his June 15, 1821, letter Marshall noted that the Court's "opinion . . . in the lottery case [*Cohens* v. *Virginia*] has been assaulted with a degree of virulence transcending what has appeared on any former occasion," referring to Spencer Roane's commentary in the Richmond *Enquirer*. Marshall offered to send Story a copy of Roane's attack. In Story's response of June 27 he expressed an interest in seeing Roane's essays "if you think they would not make me too angry." Story then went on to complain about Jefferson's efforts "to

---

[412] J. Marshall to J. Story, June 15, 1821, Story Papers, Massachusetts Historical Society, Boston, Mass.
[413] J. Story to J. Marshall, June 27, 1821, ibid.

[414] J. Story to J. Marshall, June 22, 1823, ibid.
[415] J. Marshall to J. Story, July 2, 1823, ibid.

prostrate the judicial authority and annihilate all public reverence of its dignity,'' views that ''fill me alternately with indignation & melancholy.'' This prompted Marshall on July 13 to make his previously quoted remarks on Jefferson's ''ambition'' and incapacity to forgive. ''What you say of Mr. Jefferson's letter,'' Marshall wrote, ''rather grieves than surprises me.''

In other letters to Story Marshall ranged over a host of issues. An October 1828 letter commented on Story's speech on the ''History and Influence of the Puritans,'' indicating that Marshall was ''touched'' by Story's ''notice of the red man.'' Story had said, after recounting the efforts of the Puritans to ''christianiz[e] and civiliz[e] the Indians,'' that ''there is . . . in the fate of these unfortunate beings, much to awaken our sympathy, and much to disturb the sobriety of our judgment.''[416] Marshall agreed that ''every oppression now exercised on a helpless people depending on our magnanimity and justice for the preservation of their experience impresses a deep stain on the American character.''[417] A June 1829 letter revealed that Marshall had agreed to become a delegate to Virginia's constitutional convention that year (Story had been a delegate to Massachusetts's convention in 1820). ''I was in earnest when I told you I would not come into that body,'' Marshall wrote, ''but I have acted like a girl addressed by a gentleman she does not positively dislike, but is unwilling to marry.''[418]

In 1831 Marshall, now seventy-six, was troubled by uric acid stones and by the Court's increasing fractionalization. In a May 3 letter, previously quoted in part in Chapter III, he said to Story:

> I am apprehensive that the revolutionary spirit which displayed itself in our circle will, like most other revolutions, work inconvenience and mischief in its progress. I believe Mr. Brown does not count on boarding the Judges next winter. . . . The matter rests, I understand, with our younger brother [Baldwin], and he has probably committed it to some other person. . . . I think this is a matter of some importance, for if the Judges scatter ad libitum the docket, I fear, will remain quite compact, losing very few of its causes; and the few it may lose will probably be carried off by seriatim opinions.[419]

Story responded, on May 29, that ''for my own part I was entirely satisfied with Brown's,'' and suggested that ''I suppose that we shall be for the future separated, as (I cannot but believe) has been the design of some our Brethren.''[420]

---

[416] J. Marshall to J. Story, Oct. 29, 1828, ibid.
[417] Ibid.
[418] J. Marshall to J. Story, June 11, 1829, ibid.

[419] J. Marshall to J. Story, May 3, 1831, ibid.
[420] J. Story to J. Marshall, May 29, 1831, ibid.

Marshall continued the discussion in a letter of June 26. "I am greatly perplexed about our board for the next winter," he wrote Story. "You know what passed while you were with us, and how much discontent was expressed at all previous arrangements." (These comments and the earlier references to Brown's Hotel, where the Justices had boarded for several years, indicate that some members of the Court had voiced dissatisfaction with the arrangements there during the 1831 Term.) Marshall had been "unwilling to say anything" during the gripe session, since he was privately content with Brown's, or any place where all the Justices would board together, and since he was contemplating retirement and wanted to see if a timely resignation could influence the choice of his successor. But he had made an "erroneous calculation of the time of the [presidential] election," which would not take place for another year, so he now had to "look forward to our quarters for the next winter." Judge Baldwin had "said something of relying on his sister to select . . . lodgings," but "nothing had been done." Marshall hoped that at a minimum "you, Judge Thompson, Judge Duval, and myself may . . . continue to room together": Duvall "must be with us or [because of his deafness] he will be unable to attend consultations."[421] It is apparent from this letter that Marshall assumed that McLean, and probably Johnson, would not be boarding with the other Justices, and that Baldwin's status was uncertain.

Baldwin was also the subject of an October 12 letter from Marshall to Story written from Philadelphia, where Marshall was awaiting his prostate operation. Marshall, on encountering Baldwin, noted that "he seems to have resumed the dispositions which impressed us both so favorably at the first term." (Baldwin's first term was 1830.) Baldwin had "spoke[n] of [Story] in terms not indicating unfriendliness" (Marshall's double negative suggested he reserved judgment on Baldwin's sentiments). Baldwin had "mentioned our next winter's accommodations in such a manner as to show his decided preference for Mrs. Peyton's, but he has not engaged the apartments." Marshall felt that "we must make some positive engagement" immediately, or "or we shall separate."[422]

By the time of his next letter to Story, Marshall had come through his operation successfully, although he confessed to Story that "I am at present and have been all the summer very unfit for serious business." From the end of the 1831 Term until the operation, Marshall said, he "was not one moment free from pain," and "the pain increased daily and disqualified me for serious thought." He was now able, he said, to "leave my bed and walk across my room . . . with a tottering feeble step," and he remained "under the very disagreeable necessity of taking

[421] J. Marshall to J. Story, June 26, 1831, ibid.

[422] J. Marshall to J. Story, Oct. 12, 1831, ibid.

medicine continually to prevent new formations.'' But he had survived, and was eager to talk about ''our next winter's arrangement'': ''at length it seems fixed that we are to quarter with Ringold.''[423] All the Justices would be lodging together except McLean, who ''will of course preserve his former position,'' and Johnson, who ''will quarter by himself.'' As for Baldwin, Marshall noted that ''he is in good health and spirits,'' and hoped that Baldwin's eccentricities had abated.[424]

Marshall and Story were intimate friends who, by the time they engaged in active correspondence, had nearly identical political and jurisprudential sympathies. Thus the measured tone in which Marshall discussed persons (even Jefferson) and political events (even the Jackson administration) seems more natural than studied, and the modesty with which he characterized his performance not at all false. At one point in 1831 Marshall had determined to resign from the Court because the side effects of medicine he was taking for his uric acid stones had made him ''unequal to the effective consideration of any subject,'' and he did not want ''to hazard the disgrace of continuing in office a mere inefficient pageant.''[425] That he considered resigning because he could not perform up to the standards he had set for himself appears to be unquestioned; that he would do so, in contrast to some of his peers who clung to their offices despite mental or physical infirmities, is illustrative of his high self-esteem and his marked lack of vanity and pretentiousness. Of the documents that Marshall produced, his opinions give the best evidence of his mind and his letters the best evidence of his character. In both respects he was an extraordinary person. William Wirt said in 1828 that ''Marshall's mind . . . is on . . . a scale [of] an Atlantic Ocean'' while ''the minds around him are mere ponds in the comparison.'' ''To hear that man in full stretch,'' Wirt believed, was to ''feel annihilated by the comparison—and yet know that such a man is [one's] countryman.''[426] As for Marshall's character, Story said, on hearing that Marshall was dying:

> Great, good, and excellent man! I perceive we must soon, very soon, part with him forever. . . . [I]t would be grateful beyond expression to me to be with the Chief Justice, and to cheer his loneliness and soothe, if I could, his suffering. . . . [But] I confess that I should

---

[423] The reference was to Tench Ringold, who was then Marshal of the District of Columbia and owned a house on the corner of F and 18th Streets, about two miles from the Capitol.

[424] Marshall was also concerned with lodgings in an 1833 letter to Story. The Justices had been forced to move from Ringold's. Marshall wondered ''what is to become of us.'' J. Marshall to J. Story, Nov. 16, 1833, Story Papers, Massachusetts Historical Society, Boston, Mass.

[425] Marshall to Story, June 11, 1829, supra, note 418.

[426] W. Wirt to William Pope, Oct. 14, 1828, Wirt Papers, Maryland Historical Society, Annapolis, Md.

scarcely feel the courage . . . to stand in his presence and to feel that it was the last time. . . .

I shall never see his like again! His gentleness, his affectionateness, his glorious virtues, his unblemished life, his exalted talents, leave him without a rival or a peer."[427]

In addition to the Justices, lawyers, spectators, and chroniclers of the Marshall Court there was a skeletal staff, consisting, during the period covered by this work, of one Clerk, one Marshal, and one Reporter. The history of those offices during Marshall's tenure, and some account of the personalities who held them, is reserved for the next chapter, in which a significant Marshall Court case that clarified the nature of the most important staff position, that of Reporter, is considered.

---

[427] J. Story to R. Peters, Jr., June 19, 1835, in W. Story, *Life and Letters,* II, 199.

# CHAPTER VI

# The Reporters: Henry Wheaton, Richard Peters, and Wheaton v. Peters

A STUDY of the federal bureaucracy in the first quarter of the nineteenth century has found that the "judicial establishment" numbered the astonishingly small total of seven people in 1802, a total which had grown only to eight by 1829.[1] Of the seven members of the judicial department in 1802, and the eight in 1829, all but one were Justices. The additional member was recorded as being the Supreme Court's Clerk.[2]

[1] J. Young, *The Washington Community* (1966), 31.

[2] Young, *Washington Community*, 31; W. Davis, *A Register of Officers and Agents, Civil, Military, and Naval, in the Service of the United States on the 30th of September, 1829* (1830). Little information exists about the Court's Clerks for the period covered by this work. The Clerk from 1800 to 1825 was Elias B. Caldwell, a native of New Jersey, who was a lawyer, a Presbyterian minister, and a captain of light infantry in addition to his official duties. Caldwell was one of the organizers of the American Colonization Society in 1816, and served in the District of Columbia legislature in 1807 and 1808. In 1814, when the British burned the Capitol, the Court met for the next two terms at Caldwell's house, 204–206 Pennsylvania Avenue, S.E. Caldwell, whom a contemporary described in 1822 as "fast wearing himself out" in evangelical work, died in 1825 at the age of forty-nine.

Caldwell was succeeded as Clerk by William Griffith, also a native of New Jersey and a close friend of Caldwell's. Griffith was a lawyer, entrepreneur, and legal scholar who published *A Treatise on the Jurisdiction and Proceedings of Justices of the Peace in Civil Suits* (1796) and *The Scriveners Guide* in 1797. In 1818–19 and 1823–24 he served in the New Jersey legislature, and from 1824 to 1826 was mayor of Burlington, New Jersey. After his appointment Griffith died of heart disease, and never actually served in the office. He was fifty years old at his death.

Griffith was succeeded by William Thomas Carroll, a native of Maryland, in 1827. During Carroll's tenure the potential lucrativeness of the Clerk's office became an issue. The Clerk's compensation was regulated by a 1799 statute that provided that "the compensation to the clerk of the supreme court of the United States shall be . . . ten dollars a day . . . for his attendance in court [and] . . . double the fees of the clerk of the supreme court of the state in which the [Court sat] . . . for his

384

# Chapter VI: *The Reporters*

These figures, while they surely capture the impressively small size of the judicial branch of the federal government in the early nineteenth century, are not precisely accurate. There were two other members of the judicial establishment in the period covered by this study. One was the Court's Marshal, who kept order in the courtroom while the Court was in session. The other was the Court's Reporter, the official charged with recording the Court's arguments and oral decisions, collecting the Justices' draft opinions, preparing those opinions for publication, and arranging for the publication of the opinions in volumes of Reports.

The Reporter's office came into being with the Court itself, but, unlike the Clerk's and the Marshal's offices, it was not formally created. In the 1790s Alexander Dallas, a Pennsylvania attorney, published a series of annual volumes reporting the decisions of the Supreme Court of Pennsylvania. Beginning in 1793 Dallas began to include Supreme Court cases in his volumes, which he prepared until 1800.[3] In 1803 William Cranch,

---

other services." 1 Stat. 624–25 (1799). Court costs in the nineteenth century went directly into the pockets of clerks, and were quite expensive. In 1842, while Carroll was still Clerk, Congress authorized the Court to regulate the Clerk's costs, but the Court did not respond, and no regulation of fees was imposed until 1883. The chief sources of income for Clerks were litigants' fees and admission fees paid by attorneys who were admitted to practice before the Court. Carroll held the position of Clerk until his death in 1863.

For sources on the Clerks, see H. Wright, "Sketch of Elias Boudinot Caldwell," *Records of the Colum. Hist. Soc.* 24:204 (1922); *Dictionary of American Biography*, 7:625 (1931); C. Swisher, *The Taney Period, 1836–64* (1974), 293–95; John F. Davis, testimony before the Senate Committee on Post Office and Civil Service, Feb. 28, 1964, *Senate Reporter*, 930:2 (88th Cong., 2d Sess.).

[3] See 1 Dall. (1790)–4 Dall. (1807). The first of Dallas's volumes to include Supreme Court cases was 2 Dall., which, while it included cases such as *Chisholm* v. *Georgia*, decided in 1793, did not appear until 1798. Volume 3 of Dallas, containing cases through the February 1799 Term, appeared in 1799, but Volume 4, covering the cases decided in the 1800 Term, did not surface until 1807.

In the last three of Dallas's volumes Supreme Court cases were combined with Pennsylvania and lower federal court cases. More than half of Volume 2 was devoted to Pennsylvania cases, and Volume 4 contained only 45 pages of Supreme Court cases, as compared with 416 pages of Pennsylvania and lower federal court cases. Volume 3, which covered Supreme Court cases over a five-year period, devoted 465 out of 509 pages to Supreme Court cases.

Until the early 1800s it was apparently the practice of the Court not to reduce its opinions to writing. When William Cranch succeeded Dallas in 1803, he noted that "the court has adopted . . . the practice of reducing their opinion to writing, in all cases of difficulty or importance," which had "relieved [him] from much anxiety." 1 Cranch iv–v (1804). As late as 1834 the Court had no requirement that its opinions be filed with the Clerk. See 8 Pet. vii (1834).

Dallas stopped reporting Supreme Court cases after 1800, when the Court moved to Washington. In 1802 Dallas wrote a friend that "the manuscript for the 4th Volume is compleat" and that it "brings the decisions of the Supreme Court of the U.S. down to the [1800] Term." But "I have found such miserable encouragement for my Reports," Dallas noted, that "I have determined to . . . devote them to the rats in the

a resident of the District of Columbia and a judge of the District's circuit court, succeeded Dallas and issued a volume devoted exclusively to Supreme Court cases. Cranch included among his rationales for the volume an interest in curbing judicial discretion by making opinions accessible in print:

> In a government which is emphatically stiled a government of laws, the least possible range ought to be left for the discretion of the judge. Whatever tends to render the laws certain, equally tends to limit that discretion; and perhaps nothing conduces more to that object than the publication of reports. Every case decided is a check upon the judge. He cannot decide a similar case differently, without strong reasons, which, for his own justification, he will wish to make public. The avenues to corruption are thus obstructed, and the sources of litigation closed.[4]

Cranch continued reporting the Court's decisions through the War of 1812. By that time the pressure of his own judicial business, the increased work load of the Marshall Court, and Cranch's own tendencies to procrastinate meant that the Supreme Court's opinions were not appearing in print for a considerable length of time after they had been delivered. A group led by Joseph Story and Attorney General Richard Rush began to urge Cranch's removal and greater professionalism in reporting. In June 1814, Rush wrote Story that he had only then obtained "two more opinions of the Supreme Court of February Term 1812 and 1813,"[5] and Story responded that there had been an "extraordinary delay in the publication of our Reports."[6] A year later Rush had concluded that "Judge Cranch . . . ought to be supplanted as some penalty for his inexcusable delays."[7]

State-House." A. Dallas to Jonathan Dayton, Oct. 18, 1802, United States Supreme Court Archives.

On being informed by Justice Bushrod Washington that Dallas had recorded the cases for the 1800 Term, William Cranch, who began to report the Court's decisions in 1803, wrote Dallas to see if Dallas would "relinquish" them. W. Cranch to A. Dallas, July 25, 1803, United States Supreme Court Archives. Dallas eventually published those cases in his Volume 4.

For more detail on Dallas and Cranch, see C. Joyce, "The Rise of the Supreme Court Reporter," *Mich. L. Rev.*, 83:1291 (1985). I am indebted to Professor Joyce for making an earlier draft of his manuscript available to me. Professor Joyce's and my researches on the Reporter's office were carried out at approximately the same time, sometimes jointly.

[4] 1 Cranch iii–iv (1804).

[5] R. Rush to J. Story, May 25, 1814, Joseph Story Papers, Library of Congress.

[6] J. Story to R. Rush, June 26, 1814, Rush Family Papers, Princeton University Library.

[7] R. Rush to Henry Wheaton, Apr. 6, 1815, Henry Wheaton Papers, Pierpont Morgan Library, New York, N.Y. Further references to the Wheaton Papers, unless otherwise indicated, are to the Morgan Library collection.

# Chapter VI: *The Reporters*

Meanwhile Story had been agitating for formal congressional creation of a Reporter for the Court, as the legislatures of New York and Massachusetts had done for their highest courts. As early as 1813 Story had complained that he had "no compendious method of carrying the decisions with me on circuits,"[8] and noted that "at an early period of my professional life" he had become aware of "the New York Reports," and had read them with "zeal and care."[9] He was anxious that the opinions of the Marshall Court likewise be accessible, and suggested to Rush in 1814 that "Congress . . . might . . . be induced to authorize the president to appoint a reporter for the U.S. with a proper salary in the same manner as is done in Massachusetts and New York."[10]

Story's comments underscored the nature of Court reporting in its early stages. The Reporters were simply private individuals who ventured to collect the Court's decisions and arrange for their publication. They and the publishers shared the proceeds: the office was unsalaried. Indeed, the Reportership was not an office at all: the Reporter had no quarters, no staff, and no official status. He relied on being able to attend sessions of the Court and on cooperation from lawyers and Justices in reproducing their opinions. In William Cranch's case the Reporter was also motivated by his professional interest in having the Court's decisions available to him, but it is clear that reporting occupied a low priority on Cranch's scale of professional responsibilities. Moreover, Cranch had no responsibility to publish the Court's decisions within any limit of time: he simply collected them when he could. The venture was not very profitable: Cranch reported in 1828 that he had lost $1,000 during his tenure.[11] In jurisdictions where a reporter's salary had not been authorized, reporting was clearly regarded as a speculative financial undertaking. On Story's own circuit he had, together with district judge John Davis and their clerk William Shaw, subsidized the first volume of Gallison's Reports. Reporter John Gallison, in exchange for "contribut[ing] . . . the labor," was given "the copyright and an equal share of all profits."[12] In such instances the reporter's financial expectations were associated with his possession of

---

[8] J. Story to H. Wheaton, Oct. 16, 1813, Wheaton Papers.

[9] J. Story to James Kent, Oct. 21, 1819, in W. Story, *The Life and Letters of Joseph Story* (2 vols., 1851), I, 330.

[10] Story to Rush, June 26, 1814, supra, note 5.

[11] W. Cranch to Richard Peters, Jr., July 18, 1828, Richard Peters Papers, Historical Society of Pennsylvania, Philadelphia, Pa. Further references to the Peters Papers, unless otherwise in-

dicated, are to the Historical Society of Pennsylvania's collection. Richard Peters, Jr., and Richard Peters, Sr., are distinguished from one another in footnote references: see, for example, notes 86 and 104. The "Peters" in the text of this chapter refers to Richard Peters, Jr.

[12] J. Gallison, diary, July 4, 1815, Massachusetts Historical Society, Boston, Mass.

the copyright to the reported volumes. That was the pattern followed when Henry Wheaton succeeded Cranch in reporting the Court's decisions in 1816.

Wheaton was Story's candidate to replace Cranch. Wheaton and Story had met in Rhode Island, where Wheaton had been in law practice until moving to New York in late 1812.[13] Story encouraged Wheaton, who had traveled abroad and had some journalistic experience, to write a digest of the law of prizes,[14] which Wheaton eventually published in 1815.[15] In September of that year Story wrote Wheaton a long letter on various subjects, including the difficulties of publishing the decisions of courts.[16] In 1813 Story had indicated that no bookseller had expressed an interest in publishing "Cranch's manuscripts of the cases of 1812." "Law reports are not esteemed of so quick a sale," he noted, "as to induce a strong attachment to them."[17] With respect to his own Massachusetts circuit reports, Story told Wheaton in the letter, "I feel a solicitude that a sufficient number may sell to indemnify for the expense of publication," but that result was by no means foreordained. "Unless the first volume [of Gallison's Reports] succeeds," Story conceded, "[subsequent volumes] cannot be published."[18]

Wheaton continued to publish essays on maritime subjects, and in December 1815 Story wrote that he had been "much pleased" in reading that Wheaton had written "an essay on the necessity of a [federal] navigation act." Story was at that time eager to "vindicate the necessity of establishing other great national institutions," and regarded Wheaton as an ally in that endeavor. Wheaton had sent him a proposed national bankruptcy act in 1814, and Story, having "lately examined the whole bill with considerable attention," concluded that "some beneficial amendments and actions might be incorporated into your bill."[19] The correspondence revealed Wheaton's increased interest in national politics. He had visited Washington in 1814 and had met Attorney General Rush; in April of that year Rush and Wheaton were exchanging critical comments about Cranch's delays in publishing the Court's Reports.[20] By that time Wheaton had made known his interest in succeeding Cranch, and Rush

---

[13] William P. Van Ness to H. Wheaton, July 1, 1813, Wheaton Papers.

[14] H. Wheaton to Levi Wheaton, July 21, 1813, ibid.

[15] H. Wheaton, *A Digest of the Law of Maritime Capture and Prizes* (1815).

[16] J. Story to H. Wheaton, Sept. 5, 1815, in W. Story, *Life and Letters*, I, 268.

[17] J. Story to Nathaniel Williams, Aug. 3, 1813, in ibid., 246.

[18] J. Story to H. Wheaton, Sept. 5, 1815, in ibid., 268.

[19] J. Story to H. Wheaton, Dec. 13, 1815, in ibid., 270.

[20] R. Rush to H. Wheaton, June 26, 1814, supra, note 6.

was acting on his behalf.[21] By September Wheaton had the inside track for the appointment, and by the end of the year he had agreed to take the position.

At the same time, Story and Rush had been lobbying for the passage of a bill to create an official Reporter for the Court, with an annual salary. Such a bill had been introduced in the 1816 session, the first session after the War of 1812, and by March the bill had passed the Senate.[22] This bill, the Reporter's Act, provided that the Reporter would be paid a salary of $1,000 and would be responsible for publishing the Court's Reports six months after the close of each Term. He was also required to deliver fifty copies of the Reports to the secretary of state for distribution to public officials. The bill was delayed in the House, and in April 1816 Wheaton wrote Congressman John Sergeant that "a regular publication of those Reports" was of great "importance . . . both to the bench and bar." He added that the salary was necessary to make the position feasible: "I will only remark that the copyright alone will not indemnify me against the expense of time and money devoted to the object."[23] Eventually, in March 1817, Congress passed the bill, increasing the number of copies required to be delivered to the secretary of state to eighty.[24]

In light of the subsequent litigation between Wheaton and Richard Peters over the copyright implications of reporting Supreme Court decisions, the general understandings shared by Wheaton and his contemporaries about the Reportership at the time of the 1817 legislation are of interest. First, it is clear that all the parties regarded reports of a court's decisions as a source of potential income for its reporter. Wheaton continually argued that a salary was necessary because the projected income from sales of volumes, or of the copyright, would be relatively low. He lined up supporters, including Chief Justice Marshall, who made similar arguments. Marshall wrote Dudley Chase in February 1817, when the Reporter's bill was being debated, that because the circulation of the Court's decisions would be "limited" and perhaps confined to "those who practice in the courts of the United States, or in great commercial cities," publication of the decisions would "remain on a very precarious footing if the reporter is to depend solely on the sales of his work for a reimbursement of the expenses . . . and for his own compensation."[25] Those who opposed the bill believed that "the U.S. reports had a more extensive circulation than those of the state courts," and therefore "the sale of the copyright would amply pay [the Reporter] for the trouble."[26]

---

[21] R. Rush to H. Wheaton, Apr. 8, 1815, Rush Family Papers.

[22] *Annals of Congress* 20:184 (1810).

[23] H. Wheaton to J. Sergeant, Apr. 20, 1816, Wheaton Papers.

[24] *Annals of Congress,* supra, note 22, 132.

[25] J. Marshall to D. Chase, Feb. 7, 1817, Wheaton Papers.

[26] H. Wheaton to Charles Ingersoll, Jan. 6, 1817, ibid.

If the reports were promptly published, one opponent suggested, they would "afford emolument enough to secure the attention of adequate talents to that object."[27]

Second, both supporters and opponents of the bill regarded the act of reporting and collecting manuscripts of court opinions as creating a copyrightable interest in the reporter. As one member of Congress noted, in criticizing the 1817 bill, to create an official position of Reporter, with salary, "would be to give a monopoly of a privilege which ought to be free to all."[28] The theory of all those who participated in the debate over the Reporter's bill was that if a person who gratuitously served as a reporter had no copyrightable interest in the materials he had gathered, he surely acquired an interest once officially designated the Court's Reporter and given a "monopoly" of the dissemination of the Court's decisions. Wheaton's early contracts with book publishers indicated that his interest in the decisions was regarded as a copyright. In his initial contract with Mathew Carey, a Philadelphia book publisher, he sold the copyright to his first volume.[29] When, a year after the initial contract had been signed, Carey informed Wheaton that he would not publish the second volume "on any terms,"[30] Wheaton entered into another contract with New York publisher Robert Donaldson in which he retained the copyright, assigning only the right to publish the number of copies that constituted the first edition of the volume.[31] For the transfer of Wheaton's interest in the two agreements he received $1,200 in notes from Carey and, given the lack of success of the first volume, $500 in law books from Donaldson. Between 1818 and 1827, when Wheaton resigned, he received between $500 and $800 a year for the volumes, and his contracts provided for editions ranging from 1,000 to 1,500 copies. What Wheaton was regarded as "owning," these arrangements made clear, was the manuscript of the Court's decisions that he had assembled over a given Term.

Thus while Wheaton's interest in the Court's decisions was clearly recognized, it was not an interest that proved lucrative. Nor were Wheaton's duties as Reporter clearly defined. The office of Reporter was, however, one of considerable potential power. In an age when the Supreme Court had no stenographers recording its proceedings, no method of printing delivered opinions rapidly, no newspaper reporters assigned to it on a regular basis, and no requirements, as we have seen, that

---

[28] Ibid.
[29] Copy of contract dated June 17, 1816, Wheaton Papers.
[30] Wheaton memorandum to Daniel Webster, [January or February] 1834, ibid.
[27] See *Annals of Congress,* supra, note 21, 66–67.

[31] Copies of contracts between Henry Wheaton and C. S. Van Winkle and Charles Wiley, Apr. 28, 1817, and between Robert Donaldson and Van Winkle and Wiley, Apr. 29, 1817, ibid.

individual Justices record or even reveal their votes in a given case, the latitude given the Reporter to prepare opinions for publication was considerable. In Wheaton's tenure he sought to report not only the opinion of the Court but the arguments of counsel, and the authorities employed by both counsel and the Justices. He also sought to add notes on substantive points of law to his Reports, and in the early years of his Reportership received regular assistance from Story in the preparation of the notes, many of which were on admiralty and maritime topics. In 1819 Story deposited a memorandum in his papers indicating that he had authored at least one note in each of the first five volumes of Wheaton's Reports under the "express condition that the notes . . . should pass as his own."[32] The presence of the notes furnishes additional evidence that Wheaton was interested in enhancing the marketability of his volumes. As he put it in the preface to his first volume, Wheaton regarded his reprints as contributing to the development of "important principle[s]" and "general rule[s]," in order that "the uncertainty of law . . . will . . . be somewhat the more settled and corrected." If "law be a science," Wheaton added, "it must be founded on principle."[33]

Assembling the reports, however, was not simply a mechanical process. As we have seen, counsel at the time were not required to file written briefs, only one-page "summaries of argument." Some Justices, such as Story and Marshall, took extensive notes of arguments in court, but often Wheaton was forced to rely on after-the-fact summaries of arguments by counsel, who were sometimes disinclined to cooperate, who could alter their arguments with the Court's decision in mind, and who were in general less than dispassionate sources. Wheaton's correspondence between 1816 and 1823 contains numerous letters to prominent lawyers, including Wirt, Webster, Rush, Pinkney, and Robert Harper, in which Wheaton asked for re-creations of arguments they had made in Court.[34]

Wheaton was himself an aspiring Supreme Court advocate who hoped that the Reportership would enhance his business. He announced in October 1819 that he had formed a partnership with Elijah Paine, who was based in New York, to conduct "any business connected with the [New York] courts, and with the Supreme Court of the United States at Washington, which Mr. Wheaton regularly attends as a Counsellor and the Reporter of its decisions."[35] His specialty was prize, admiralty, and maritime law, and between 1816 and 1818 he argued four such cases

---

[32] The memorandum is in W. Story, *Life and Letters,* I, 283.
[33] 1 Wheat. at iv, v, vi.
[34] See, e.g., William Pinkney to H. Wheaton, June 1, 1816; R. Rush to H. Wheaton, July 2, 1817; D. Webster to H. Wheaton, Apr. 1, 1818; William Wirt to H. Wheaton, June 13, 1818; R. G. Harper to Wheaton, Sept. 28, 1823; all in Wheaton Papers.
[35] Printed announcement, Oct. 8, 1819, ibid.

before the Court.[36] These were followed by *The Langdon Cheves* in 1819, *The Amiable Isabella* and six other cases[37] in 1820, two cases in 1823,[38] and two cases in 1824, including the major constitutional law case of *Ogden* v. *Saunders*, argued that term and reargued in 1827.[39] Wheaton also argued one case in the 1825 Term,[40] two in the 1826 Term,[41] and six in the 1827 Term in addition to *Ogden* v. *Saunders*.[42] Only in the 1820 and 1827 terms was Wheaton markedly busy, and he never achieved the prominence of the leading Marshall Court advocates. He did, however, report his arguments fully and elaborately in the Reports, sometimes giving short shrift to those of his opponents in the same case.[43]

Wheaton's professional ambitions and the discretion the Reportership permitted him in reproducing the arguments of others combined to create ample temptation to engage in interventionist reporting, in which he did not merely render arguments but shaped them for his own purposes. Stating his own arguments fully and those of his opponents cryptically was a mild version of interventionism. There were more serious examples.

One such, already alluded to in Chapter V, was an outgrowth of Wheaton and Story's tacit partnership on behalf of an expanded jurisdiction for the federal courts over admiralty and maritime cases. A subsequent chapter will detail Story's preoccupation, beginning with his appointment to the Court in 1811, with increasing the opportunities of the federal courts to decide cases involving domestic disputes between shipowners and persons who furnished services or goods to ships while in port (shipwrights and "material men"). Wheaton was an early and en-

---

[36] The Antonia Johanna, 1 Wheat 159; The Friendschaft, 3 Wheat 14; United States v. Bevans, 3 Wheat. 336; The Aeolus, 3 Wheat. 392.

[37] The Bello Corrunes, 6 Wheat. 152; The Collector, 6 Wheat. 194; The Jonquille, 6 Wheat. 452; Spring v. South Carolina Ins. Co., 6 Wheat. 519; The United States v. Six Packages of Goods, 6 Wheat. 520; Otis v. Water, 6 Wheat. 583.

[38] Hunt v. Rousmanier's Adm'rs, 8 Wheat. 174; Dailey's Lessee v. James, 8 Wheat. 495.

[39] Ogden v. Saunders is reported in 12 Wheat. at 213. The other case argued in the 1824 Term was Baites v. Peters, 9 Wheat. 556.

[40] United States v. Morris, 10 Wheat. 246.

[41] Harding v. Handy, 11 Wheat. 103; Armstrong v. Toler, 11 Wheat. 258.

[42] Postmaster General v. Early, 12 Wheat. 136; Jackson v. Chew, 12 Wheat. 153; Armstrong v. Lear, 12 Wheat. 169; United States v. Tillotson, 12 Wheat. 180; Mason v. Haile, 12 Wheat. 370; General Insurance Co. v. Ruggles, 12 Wheat. 408.

[43] For one example, see Ogden v. Saunders, where, after reporting his argument for twelve pages, Wheaton then summarized the arguments of seven other lawyers in ten pages, inserting the following disclaimer:

> The Editor regrets that, from the great number of counsel who argued on this side of the question, and the great variety of topics insisted on by them, he has been obliged to condense the whole argument into [a] summary, which he hopes will be found to contain the substance of their reasoning.

12 Wheat. at 227.

thusiastic supporter of Story's position,[44] and part of the motivation for Story's extensive participation in the notes included in Wheaton's early volumes was the opportunity to establish his views on various issues in admiralty and maritime law. The Story-Wheaton partnership engendered one of Wheaton's most interventionist efforts at reporting a case.

Wheaton's intervention was first brought to light in the case of *Ramsay v. Allegre*,[45] an 1827 admiralty jurisdiction dispute. In *Ramsay* a material man from Maryland who had "found and provided various materials" for the use of the domestic schooner *Dorothea* in her home port of Baltimore sued the shipowner for services rendered. The shipowner countered by claiming that he had given a promissory note for the materials.[46] Marshall, for the Court, dismissed the case on the grounds that the material man had accepted the shipowner's note and thereby waived the admiralty jurisdiction.[47] The disposition enabled Marshall to avoid the larger question presented in the case, whether the admiralty jurisdiction of the federal courts extended to suits by home port material men against owners or masters of domestic ships (so-called *in personam* suits). Justice Johnson, however, was not satisfied with the majority's avoidance of the larger issue, and in a concurrence, as we have seen, delivered a stinging attack on the efforts of Story and Wheaton to expand—surreptitiously, he charged—the admiralty jurisdiction of the federal courts. While Johnson' charges were publicly rebuffed by Wheaton, his suspicions may have been well founded.

We have previously seen that the dispute aired by Johnson in *Ramsay v. Allegre* had begun in 1819, when William Pinkney argued another admiralty jurisdiction case, *The General Smith*.[48] That case, like *Ramsay*, was set in Maryland and involved a suit for services furnished by a material man in a domestic ship's home port. But in *The General Smith* the material man's suit was against the ship itself (a suit *in rem*) rather than an *in personam* suit against the shipowner. Pinkney, representing the merchant creditors of the ship's former owner, argued that no *in rem* suit could be brought in the federal admiralty courts in *The General Smith* because under "the common law (which is the law of Maryland on this subject)" material men "have no lien upon [a domestic] ship itself for their demands, but must look to the personal security of the owner."[49] As noted, Wheaton's published version of Pinkney's argument in the United States Reports also had Pinkney saying the following:

[44] See H. Wheaton to J. Story, May 21, 1816, Wheaton Papers; H. Wheaton to J. Story, Nov. 6, 1817. ibid.

[45] 12 Wheat. 611 (1827).

[46] Ibid., 611, 612.

[47] Ibid., 612–13.

[48] 4 Wheat. 438 (1819).

[49] Ibid., 442.

Mr. Pinkney . . . admitted the general jurisdiction of the District Court, as an Instance Court of Admiralty, over suits by material men *in personam* and *in rem*, and over other maritime contracts. . . . Had this been a suit *in personam* [against the shipowner] in the Admiralty, there would have been no doubt that the District Court could have had jurisdiction.[50]

When Story delivered the opinion of the Court in *The General Smith*, he began with the following passage:

No doubt is entertained by this Court, that the Admiralty rightfully possesses a general jurisdiction in cases of material men, and if this had been a suit *in personam*, there could have not been any hesitation in sustaining the jurisdiction of the District Court.[51]

In his headnote on *The General Smith* in the United States Reports, Wheaton reported this dictum as one of the principles of *The General Smith*,[52] and in *Ramsay v. Allegre* counsel for the material man had argued that "the District Courts, proceeding as Courts of admiralty and maritime jurisdiction, might take cognizance of material suits by material men, either *in personam* or *in rem*," citing *The General Smith*.[53] Thus the "admission" by Pinkney in *The General Smith* had evolved into a dictum by Story and then into a precedent.

Johnson took umbrage at this development. Even though he had joined Story's opinion in *The General Smith*, he admitted that "[he] had never read the report of that case . . . until the argument in [*Ramsay v. Allegre*]." On reading Wheaton's report he found that Pinkney was characterized as having "laid down a doctrine in very explicit terms which, I will venture to say, has no authority in law." He also found that "the Court . . . echoed [Pinkney] in terms which [were] not only not called for by the case, but actually . . . contradicted by the decision which [was] rendered."[54] Johnson concluded that while "I stand before the public as bearing my share of the responsibility incurred for certain opinions expressed in the case of *The General Smith* . . . at least I shall endeavor to administer the antidote if I have diffused the poison." He called *The General Smith* "a case of the most extravagant attempt ever made to enforce this supposed lien of material men." He had "too high an opinion of Mr. Pinkney's law-reading . . . not to be well convinced that [in his reported "admission"] he must have been misunderstood." (Pinkney, we will recall, had died in 1822, and was thus not in a position to clarify his position.) Johnson then sought to show that "the authority which [Whea-

---

[50] Ibid., 441–42.
[51] Ibid., 443.
[52] Ibid., 438.

[53] 12 Wheat. at 612.
[54] Ibid., 614.

ton reported Pinkney as citing] to sustain his doctrine, contradicts it in so many words.''[55]

In the course of discussing Pinkney's authorities Johnson made a few inside references. Wheaton had reported Pinkney's citation of the third edition of *Abbott on Shipping,* which had been edited by Story. Johnson argued that the passage from *Abbott* ''shows most distinctly that the law is otherwise in England'' than allegedly asserted by Pinkney in *The General Smith.* In no instance, Johnson claimed, did a citation from *Abbott* ''countenance the doctrine of a right of proceeding *in personam,* attributed to Mr. Pinkney.'' Johnson was not surprised at this, he said, ''when we find the rest of [Pinkney's] reported argument so clearly a mistake.''[56] Johnson then alluded to Story's circuit court decision in *DeLovio* v. *Boit,*[57] which had ''asserted . . . the right to proceed *in personam* in the Admiralty.'' He doubted whether ''the nisi prius decisions of the judges of this Court are of any authority [at the Supreme Court].'' If they were ''it is only necessary to observe'' that he himself had rendered ''a contrary decision . . . in the sixth circuit.''[58]

In sum, Johnson found ''the decision . . . in the case of *The General Smith* as conclusive against the doctrine which asserts the right of material men to proceed *in personam.*'' He concluded by stating that ''we are under a peculiar obligation to restrain the Admiralty jurisdiction within its proper limits.''[59] He had begun his opinion in *Ramsay* by deploring ''this silent and stealing progress of the admiralty in acquiring jurisdiction to which it has no pretensions.''[60]

Wheaton, who had resigned his Reportership effective at the close of the 1827 Term to accept the post of ambassador to Denmark, was stung. He decided to counter Johnson's attack on his treatment of *The General Smith.* In a note appended after the *Ramsay* case in the United States Reports, Wheaton argued that Pinkney's concession on admiralty jurisdiction had been made ''voluntarily,'' and that it was therefore ''superfluous for [him] to cite any authority.'' On this occasion, Wheaton felt, Pinkney ''spoke from the fullness of his learning, and with a confidence inspired by his well grounded reliance upon its accuracy.''[61]

Wheaton then examined each of the citations he had attributed to Pinkney. Wheaton had placed a footnote listing the citations after three Pinkney sentences, the first making the concession, the second admitting that ''the maritime law'' gave material men a lien where they had furnished materials to ''a foreign ship,'' and the third stating that ''in the case of a domestic ship'' the law of the state governed. So placed, the

---

[55] Ibid., 635, 636, 637.
[56] Ibid., 638.
[57] 2 Gallis. 400 (1815).
[58] 12 Wheat. at 638.

[59] Ibid., 640.
[60] Ibid., 614.
[61] Ibid., 641.

footnote was ambiguous: it could have referred only to the last sentence. But Wheaton took it to refer to at least the second and the third sentences. He then demonstrated that not only did Story's edition of *Abbott* show that the European maritime law allowed a lien in "foreign ship" cases, but that one of Johnson's own circuit court decisions, *Woodruff v. The Levi Dearborne*,[62] cited by Pinkney, followed that position. As Wheaton put it in summary:

> The error imputed to the report consists in the asserted liability of a foreign ship to such a lien, which (as it has been seen) is recognised and enforced by the general maritime law, and which appears also to have been maintained by several Admiralty judges in this country, and especially by Mr. Justice Johnson."[63]

Wheaton concluded his comments by suggesting that "in making these remarks the Editor has certainly not been influenced by any feelings of disrespect towards the learned judge by whom the above opinion was delivered." It was "his own character for accuracy and integrity as the Reporter of the decisions of this Court which the Editor feels to be assailed," Wheaton said, "and therefore seeks to vindicate."[64] There was much more than "accuracy and integrity" at stake for Wheaton in the episode, however. It was another of his periodic clashes with Johnson, whose "crudities" and "bad taste" Wheaton had previously complained of to Story.[65] In a letter to Daniel Webster, written after he had completed his final volume as Reporter, Wheaton said, "I left Judge Johnson my compliments at the end of the Reports."[66]

At first glance Wheaton seems to have stolen a march on Johnson in the *Ramsay* dispute. Particularly galling to Johnson must have been Wheaton's apparent demonstration that Pinkney's concession had been accompanied by a footnote reference to one of Johnson's own circuit opinions. But a closer comparison of Johnson and Wheaton's exchange reveals that Johnson was claiming only that Pinkney's *concession* had been misrepresented, pointing out in the process that the citations from *Abbott* did not support that concession, whereas Wheaton was claiming that the citations referred to other points in Pinkney's argument. Thus the whole dispute could be said to turn on how many sentences in the text of Pinkney's argument had been incorporated in Pinkney's footnote reference. Wheaton's placement of the footnote may have been arguably accurate, but it may also have been artful.

---

[62] *Am. L.J.*, 4:97 (1813).
[63] 12 Wheat. at 642.
[64] Ibid., 642–43.
[65] H. Wheaton to J. Story, July 2, 1820, Wheaton Papers.

[66] H. Wheaton to D. Webster, Nov. 20, 1827, ibid.

# Chapter VI: *The Reporters*

Johnson's supposition that Wheaton had been less than straightforward in his reporting of the *Ramsay* case gains credence when Wheaton's unpublished notebooks are consulted. In these notebooks Wheaton recorded the notes he took of oral arguments before the Court. As previously noted, until 1832 the Marshall Court had no requirement that attorneys arguing before it submit written briefs. Moreover, there were no stenographic devices; arguments were taken down in longhand by the Reporter or someone designated by him. When Wheaton or Richard Peters sought to reconstruct counsels' arguments for publication in the United States Reports, they had, for most of the period covered by this study, only their own notes, any notes taken by Justices (if these were available), and after-the-fact reconstructions of arguments by the attorneys themselves. We have also noted that attorneys who regularly argued before the Court, such as William Wirt, Webster, or Pinkney, tended to be lax in submitting their arguments.

The 1819 Term had been a particularly busy one, and *The General Smith* had been argued on March 9, late in the Term. Wheaton's notebook[67] indicates that he took comparatively few notes on *The General Smith,* and he apparently did not intend to report the substance of the argument at all. On the first page of Wheaton's notes on *The General Smith* he wrote, and subsequently crossed out, "don't give the Argt in this case. Merely say it was argued by Mr. Pinkney and Mr. Winder." The original notation is not striking, given the large number of cases in the 1819 Term and Wheaton's strong interest in having volumes of the Court's Reports appear promptly. But Wheaton's later decision to cross out the notation was accompanied by a memorandum he wrote to himself at the bottom of the first page of his notes on *Ramsay* v. *Allegre:*

> *Mem.* Prepare a *short* argument in this case as it ought to have been argued—giving all the authorities. They will be found principally in 2 *Gallis.*
>
> *N.B.* Pinkney admit the Adm. *jurisdiction* to its full extent.

Wheaton's memo to himself was, as far as can be determined, unprecedented in his tenure as Reporter. No other example of a decision to include a lawyer's argument which Wheaton had previously resolved to omit has been found, and, in particular, no other instance appears where Wheaton reminded himself to "prepare" an argument "as it ought have been argued." Wheaton, of course, "prepared" arguments all the time: that was part of his job. He reconstructed counsel's arguments from ar-

---

67 Wheaton's notebooks for the 1816 | through 1827 Terms are in the Wheaton Papers.

gument summaries, his own notes, and the notes of others. But the memorandum he wrote at the bottom of his notes on *The General Smith* is unique in its directions and striking in its use of the word "ought." And the reference to "authorities" included in the memorandum lists Volume 2 of Gallison's Reports. Story's opinion in *DeLovio,* an extensive brief for expansive admiralty jurisdiction, was to be found in "2 *Gallis.*" Moreover, there is the sentence "*N.B.* Pinkney admit the Adm. *jurisdiction* to its full extent," which suggests at a minimum that Wheaton wanted to emphasize the "concession" in Pinkney's argument.

Did Wheaton simply manufacture Pinkney's concession? A comparison of Wheaton's notes on the date *The General Smith* was argued with Pinkney's published argument can be made. But the comparison, premised on an assumption that Wheaton's original notes on *The General Smith* were disinterested and accurate, yields a less than definitive answer. Wheaton's notebook reads:

> [Pinkney was] not disposed to contest the jurisdiction of the Admiralty over maritime contracts—*in personam* and *in rem* where the party has a right to proceed *in rem.* Nor object to its jurisdiction in this case, if there is a lien. But I contend there is [no lien].

One possible way to read this passage is that Pinkney was in fact conceding the general jurisdiction of the admiralty courts over all *in personam* cases based on "maritime contracts." This reading of the passage was made by Wheaton when he rendered Pinkney's argument in print, adding some sentences to Pinkney's concession. Under this reading the phrase in Wheaton's notebook, "where the party has a right to proceed *in rem*" modified only "*in rem,*" and could be taken to mean "where the technical requirements for *in rem* cases are satisfied." Pinkney's next sentence in the notebook would then mean that in *this in rem* case, *The General Smith,* a technical requirement had not been met because no lien existed. Such a reading would be buttressed if Pinkney said "all" before "maritime contracts," and in Wheaton's notebook the word "all" was inserted, in different size handwriting, in the passage quoted above.

But there is another way to read the passage in Wheaton's notebook. The passage can be taken as meaning that Pinkney was conceding only that where a lien existed against a ship a material man could sue in the admiralty courts, either *in rem* in *in personam.* Under this reading the phrase "where the party has a right to proceed *in rem*" would be taken to mean "where the party has a lien against the ship and can therefore sue *in rem.*" Such a reading has Pinkney saying in effect, "I concede that the admiralty courts can entertain jurisdiction over certain 'maritime contracts' cases. The admiralty courts have both *in personam* and *in rem* jurisdiction over maritime contracts cases where the moving party has a lien against the ship. But no lien against the ship exists in this [*in rem*] case."

Which version of the argument would William Pinkney have been more likely to make? An obvious surmise would be the latter version, since that version would be more favorable to his client. If so, Pinkney's "concession" becomes merely an irrelevant truism about liens and *in personam* jurisdiction. Since Pinkney was representing a merchant creditor in *The General Smith*, that would have been the sort of concession his client would have appreciated. The practical message of the case would then be: "if one wants to avoid being sued by material men for their services in Maryland, make sure the work is done in the vessel's home port, make sure a domestic ship is involved, and don't, of course, voluntarily give the material men a lien in consideration for their services." The other version of Pinkney's argument would have produced a less heartening practical message: "any time a material man contracts to work on a domestic ship in its home port in Maryland, he will not be able to bring an *in rem* action in a state court, since Maryland common law prohibits that, but he will be able to bring an *in personam* action in federal court, since federal court admiralty jurisdiction applies to 'maritime contracts.' "

But that surmise does not consider the complexities of Pinkney's character and the relationship between the leading Marshall Court lawyers and their clients. Pinkney, as we have seen, was a self-preoccupied, vainglorious, and strikingly erudite advocate, convinced with good reason that he knew as much about admiralty and prize cases as anyone in America and possibly more than anyone on the Marshall Court. Wheaton said of Pinkney, in a memorial published one year before the *Ramsay* decision, that he "cooperated as an advocate . . . in laying the foundations of the system which [the Court] . . . built up [by] discuss[ing] anew all the leading doctrines of prize law, and conform[ing] them by . . . authority." Pinkney's "learning and peculiar experience in this science," Wheaton felt, "contributed essentially to enlighten the judgments of the court."[68] Reminding the Court that *in personam* maritime contract suits could be brought in the admiralty courts might simply have been one of Pinkney's habitual displays of his learning. "Pinkney," William Wirt once said, "would make you believe that he knows everything."[69]

Moreover, Pinkney's "concession," while perhaps not favorable to his clients in a general sense, did them no specific harm: *The General Smith* was an *in rem* rather than an *in personam* case. And Pinkney may have had his own reasons for wanting the admiralty jurisdiction of the

---

[68] H. Wheaton, *Some Account of the Life, Writings, and Speeches of William Pinkney* (1826), 17.

[69] W. Wirt to Francis W. Gilmer, Apr. 1, 1816, in J. Kennedy, *Life of William Wirt* (2 vols., 1849), I, 357.

federal courts to expand. The major specialty of his private practice in Baltimore was, as noted, admiralty, prize, and maritime contracts cases. An argument that the federal courts' admiralty jurisdiction over maritime contracts included only those *in personam* cases which could simultaneously have been filed as *in rem* cases (that is, cases where liens existed) was an argument whose effect was to reduce the maritime contracts business of the federal courts. One would not expect Pinkney to want that business reduced. And if one assumes, as some of the framers of the Judiciary Act of 1789 assumed, that the federal courts "would be strong courts, creditors' courts, businessmen's courts,"[70] Pinkney, who drew the bulk of his admiralty business from the Baltimore mercantile community, might have thought of an expansive federal jurisdiction as good for business in several respects.

Thus one cannot definitively conclude that Wheaton's effort to prepare Pinkney's argument ''as it ought to have been argued'' was a deliberate attempt at subterfuge. Wheaton's recasting of Pinkney's argument may merely have been a Reporter's usual "preparation." One might wonder why Pinkney did not howl in protest and obtain changes if Wheaton had misrepresented his argument, but in absence of extant evidence, even that supposition dissolves in conjecture. Pinkney may not even have read Wheaton's report of his argument; Johnson, after all, had not read Wheaton's report of the opinion in *The General Smith* until *Ramsay*, eight years later. The incident is, however, striking in the degree and nature of Wheaton's intervention. It is also suggestive because of the strong involvement of Wheaton, Pinkney, Story, and Johnson with the jurisprudential and political struggles over admiralty jurisdiction that were taking place at the time, struggles that will be discussed in the next chapter.

By the time the *Ramsay* v. *Allegre* dispute had surfaced Wheaton had resolved to resign the Reportership. His years as Reporter had principally been years of frustration. His law practice as a Supreme Court advocate had never really blossomed, and the sales of the Reports had not netted him the "honorable independence" he had anticipated when he accepted the position.[71] Congress had declined to raise his salary, and his efforts to use the Reportership as a stepping-stone to political or judicial office had not come to fruition. In 1823 he was mentioned as a candidate for the vacancy on the Supreme Court that had been caused by Brockholst Livingston's death,[72] but nothing came of that, and he appar-

---

[70] See H. Friendly, "The Historic Basis of Diversity Jurisdiction," *Harv. L. Rev.*, 41:483, 498 (1928), and sources therein cited.

[71] H. Wheaton to Jonathan Russell, May 11, 1816, Wheaton Papers.

[72] H. Wheaton to John Barly, Mar. 24, 1823, Washburn Papers, Massachusetts Historical Society, Boston, Mass.; H. Wheaton to L. Wheaton, June 7, 1823, Wheaton Papers.

## Chapter VI: *The Reporters*

ently was never regarded as a serious possibility.[73] And in 1826 Wheaton suffered his bitterest disappointment. He fully expected John Quincy Adams, whom he had warmly supported, to appoint him to a federal judgeship in the Southern District of New York. Throughout the fall he remained optimistic, writing his father-in-law that "the general impression here is that it will be offered to me" and that "I have always thought my destiny was to the judicial life."[74] In December 1826 Wheaton's political acquaintances in New York began to offer their congratulations,[75] but on December 20 Adams named someone else.[76]

As early as 1818 Wheaton had concluded that the Reportership was "hard work,"[77] and in 1825 he referred to it as "mechanical drudgery" and claimed that he was "born for better things."[78] While Theophilus Parsons, who observed Wheaton on a trip to Washington in 1818, said that "the best men . . . were on the most intimate and confidential terms with him" and that "universal respect was rendered to him,"[79] Wheaton's correspondence, with its deferential tone to judges and more celebrated lawyers, its constant angling for appointive positions, its complaints about the ill-treatment he received from dispensers of patronage, and its increasingly wounded tone, belies Parsons's view. Thus when John Quincy Adams appointed Wheaton ambassador to Denmark in 1827 it was quite clear, despite the relative insignificance of the post, that Wheaton would accept. One of his friends wrote Wheaton that he felt that "merit entitled you to a more distinguished and arduous trust,"[80] and Wheaton asked John Quincy Adams for "three or four months" to "consider" the offer,[81] but six weeks after receiving the appointment Wheaton wrote James Monroe that he had concluded to accept the post.[82] Story, for his part, had very soon after Wheaton's appointment concluded that "now is his chance or never . . . in the diplomatic line," and that "he will certainly accept it."[83]

---

[73] L. Wheaton to Catherine Wheaton, May 23, 1823, Wheaton Papers.
[74] H. Wheaton to L. Wheaton, [undated, December 1826], ibid.
[75] A. C. Flagg to H. Wheaton, Dec. 18, 1826, ibid.
[76] Martin Van Buren to J. A. Hamilton, Dec. 20, 1826, ibid. Adams named Samuel Rossiter Betts, a New York "Bucktail" Republican, in the hope of neutralizing the strength of Henry Clay and William Crawford among New York Republicans.
[77] H. Wheaton to Edward Wheaton, Mar. 1, 1818, ibid.
[78] H. Wheaton to E. Wheaton, Jan. 11, 1825, ibid.
[79] T. Parsons to Mrs. Charles C. Lit-

tle, May 23, 1853, ibid., recounting a visit Parsons made to Washington in 1818.
[80] J. Russell to H. Wheaton, Jonathan Russell Papers, John Hay Library, Brown University.
[81] J. Q. Adams, diary, in C. Adams, ed., *The Memoirs of John Quincy Adams, Comprising Portions of His Diary from 1795 to 1848* (12 vols., 1874–77), VII, 238.
[82] H. Wheaton to J. Monroe, Apr. 16, 1827, James Monroe Papers, Library of Congress.
[83] J. Story to Sarah Waldo Story, Mar. 8, 1827, Joseph Story Papers, Massachusetts Historical Society, Boston, Mass.

✳

Thus ended Henry Wheaton's Reportership. In many respects Wheaton's performance had been an improvement on that of his predecessors. His volumes had appeared on time, especially after congressional legislation had provided that the Reporter was required to publish his reports six (later, nine) months after the close of a Term, and that his salary would not be paid until after he had deposited the requisite number of copies with the Department of State. For a professional user of the Reports, Wheaton's version was also more accessible and reliable than previous sets. Dallas had omitted reporting many of the Court's decisions, and had apparently strung together other "opinions" from the notes of counsel rather than from manuscripts of the Justices.[84] Cranch had reported cases in a haphazard sequence and sometimes garbled them.[85] While Cranch had regularized the practice of reporting lawyers' arguments and had introduced summaries of the principal points decided in an opinion, one critic found inclusion of the arguments merely results in "unprofitable and expensive prolixity,"[86] and the summaries of points decided were difficult to read and sometimes obscure.

Wheaton's most obvious contribution was his scholarly notes. They were of two types, "marginal notes"[87] that elaborated on tangential points that had surfaced in the cases, and appendices consisting of extended discussions of doctrinal issues. The overwhelming number of appendices contained discussions of admiralty and maritime law;[88] some of those, as noted, were written by Story. Wheaton's appendices, taken together with his other published writings on prize law, established him as an authority on maritime matters. Wheaton also quickly won the confidence of the lawyers whose arguments he summarized in his volumes. He had indi-

---

[84] In his report of Ware v. Hylton, 3 Dall. 199 (1796), Dallas indicated that he had been absent when the case was argued and the opinion delivered, and had reconstructed the opinion from the notes "of Mr. W. Tilghman, to whose kindness . . . I have been frequently indebted for similar communications, in the course of the compilation of these reports." 3 Dall. at 207.

[85] "Judge Cranch was not unduly particular in the placement of his reports of cases in the proper year. As a consequence a number of cases argued and decided in the preceding term of the Supreme Court might appear with those argued and decided a year later. Similarly a case from a later year might be published in the volume for an earlier year if there were room for an additional opinion in that volume." G. Haskins and H. Johnson, *Foundations of Power: John Marshall, 1801–15* (1981), 497.

In 1829 Story wrote Peters that some of Cranch's volumes were "particularly painful and erroneous." J. Story to R. Peters, Jr., Dec. 10, 1829, Peters Papers.

[86] W. Pinkney to H. Wheaton, Sept. 3, 1818, Wheaton Papers.

[87] The term is Wheaton's. See 1 Wheat. at iv.

[88] Between 1816 and 1820 Wheaton contributed 444 pages of appendices to his volumes. Of these, 402 dealt with admiralty and maritime issues.

cated in his first volume that his summaries were simply "faithful outline[s]" that did not "do justice to the learning and eloquence of the
bar,"[89] but most of the lawyers were pleased with his efforts. Webster
instructed him on one occasion to "[c]ut & carve [my argument] . . . at
your pleasure,"[90] and Wirt admitted that "on points of law . . . I am
safer in your hands than in my own."[91] Some lawyers even furnished
Wheaton with summaries of arguments he had not received, and invited
him, as Pinkney put it in an 1818 letter, to "make it appear as your
work."[92]

In general, there seems to have been a professional consensus that
Wheaton's reports were timely, accurate, and impressive scholarship.
William Pinkney embodied this attitude in the 1818 letter to Wheaton,
quoted above, in which he referred approvingly to the "perfect clearness"
of Wheaton's summaries of arguments, the "well executed" and "useful" appendices, and the "promptitude with which the Reports follow
the decisions." Unfortunately, none of Wheaton's professional admirers
seemed inclined to review his volumes in print, and Wheaton had to enlist
Story to procure a review, written by Daniel Webster, of Wheaton's third
volume. Webster's review was subdued, partly because, Story surmised,
"he feels a little unpleasant from losing nearly all the cases which he
argued" in the Term covered by Wheaton's volume.[93] Eventually Wheaton's eighth volume was also reviewed, this time more enthusiastically;
he was referred to as an "accomplished reporter" with "a happy talent
for discriminating the leading points" in a decision.[94] This characteristic
of Wheaton's performance was to create a standard of comparison that
proved unfortunate to his successor.

All in all, then, Wheaton's performance as Reporter was well received. But there had been two nagging difficulties throughout his Reportership. One, as we have seen, was the failure of the position to serve
as a vehicle for the advancement of Wheaton's career as an advocate or
as a stepping-stone to a more distinguished office. The other was the high
cost of Wheaton's volumes. Cranch's last volumes had averaged slightly
over $5.00 a volume, while Wheaton's, from 1817 to 1826, ranged from
$6.50 to $7.50 each.[95] In 1826 Congress reduced the price to "not exceeding Five Dollars per volume," a response precipitated by a compet-

---

[89] I Wheat. at iii.
[90] D. Webster to H. Wheaton, April
1, 1818, Wheaton Papers.
[91] W. Wirt to H. Wheaton, June 3,
1813, ibid.
[92] Pinkney to Wheaton, Sept. 3,
1818, supra, note 86.
[93] J. Story to H. Wheaton, Sept. 4,
1817, Wheaton Papers. Wheaton had

even offered to have Story and himself
write a review. Wheaton to Story, Nov.
30, 1817, ibid.
[94] *No. Am. Rev.,* 9:321, (1824).
[95] See J. Story to R. Peters, Jr., June
26, 1828, Peters Papers; Robert Donaldson to H. Wheaton, August 11,
1828, Wheaton Papers.

itive proposal to change the reporting system.[96] By that time Wheaton had become "tire[d] of the mechanical drudgery of reporting" and had placed his "name on [Webster's] list of office seekers."[97]

Wheaton's dissatisfaction with the Reportership and the high cost of his volumes both contributed to his being succeeded as Reporter by Richard Peters, Jr., after the 1827 Term. Peters's ambitions for the Reportership were quite different from those of Wheaton. The son of a distinguished federal judge, Peters does not seem to have been either prominent or ambitious within the community of Philadelphia lawyers in which he was brought up. From the earliest phases of his career Peters had been engaged in reporting, beginning with his father's admiralty decisions, which he collected and published in the early nineteenth century.[98] Between 1826 and 1829 he published Bushrod Washington's Third Circuit decisions and in the process made a good impression on Washington. Peters apparently did not envisage combining reporting with extensive Supreme Court advocacy: between 1828 and 1835 he argued six cases, and he felt his argument worth reporting in full in only two of those.[99]

In 1826, when the Reporter's Act was scheduled for renewal, the publishing company of Carey & Lea, based in Philadelphia, made a confidential proposal to the chairman of the House Judiciary Committee, which was charged with reporting the Act to the full House. In the proposal Carey & Lea offered to publish a set of reports, "printed handsomely on paper equally good with the volumes of Mr. Wheaton's" and "bound in calf," to be "delivered to the profession at five dollars per volume." They promised to produce reports "as full as those heretofore published" which would appear in print "within as short a period after the close of the Session as they usually have been." They proposed to

---

[96] The reduction was drafted by Wheaton himself. See Joyce, "The Rise of the Supreme Court Reporter," 1354. A copy of the competitive proposal was found in the Wheaton Papers. See the discussion infra, text at notes 99–101.

[97] Wheaton wrote Webster on April 12, 1826: "If it were not *absolutely necessary* to me, you would not find my name in the list of *office seekers*. If I could live over again the years that are past, those who are in power should not know me as that character." Daniel Webster Papers, Library of Congress. Italics in original.

[98] R. Peters, *Admiralty Decisions of the District Court of the United States for the Pennsylvania District, 1780–*

*1807* (1807). Volume 14 of the *Dictionary of American Biography* (1934) at 509–10 credits Richard Peters, Sr., with the volume, but a letter from Richard Peters, Jr., to Samuel Hopkins, Nov. 15, 1805, Peters Papers, makes it very likely that Peters, Jr., was doing the reporting.

[99] The cases Peters argued were Satterlee v. Matthewson, 2 Pet. 380 (1829); Conolly v. Taylor, 2 Pet. at 556; United States v. State Bank of North Carolina, 6 Pet. 29 (1832); Brashear v. West, 7 Pet. 608 (1833); Jackson v. Ashton, 8 Pet. 148 (1834); and Beard v. Rowan, 9 Pet. 301 (1835). Peters's arguments were reported in full in *Satterlee* and *State Bank of North Carolina.*

provide their own reporter, "at their own cost, who shall be approved of by the Court." While they did not name their candidate, they had one in mind, someone who "would be in the highest degree satisfactory, as he is already by his publications advantageously known to the profession," and he had "received the unqualified approbation of a distinguished member of the Court."[100]

Word of the proposal reached Wheaton, who had already received a letter from Edward Everett, the chairman of the House Committee on the Library, expressing interest in a "less expensive publication" of the Court's Reports. As noted, Wheaton responded by drafting a new Reporter's Act, which he forwarded to his friend Daniel Webster, cutting the price of the official Reports to $5.00 or less. This action effectively killed Carey & Lea's proposal, but rumors of Wheaton's departure persisted, and Peters, who was very probably the unnamed candidate in the Carey proposal, began to mount an active campaign to succeed Wheaton.

In the fall of 1826, Wheaton's nomination to a district judgeship seemed probable, and Peters began to campaign. There was no formal procedure for appointing a Reporter; in Wheaton's case Story had very probably proposed his name to other Justices, and they had agreed. There was some impression from both candidates and Justices that unanimity was required, although no practice could be said to have been established. Peters began by confirming Washington's support for his candidacy and approaching Story. He wrote Story of his "anxious desire for the job" and his belief that there would be "many applications for the place."[101] Story responded that he knew of "no person who would be more acceptable to me," and that Peters would "cheerfully have my vote."[102] We have seen in Chapter III that Story's precipitate response was subsequently to embarrass him, for about two weeks after he had written Peters he received a letter from Simon Greenleaf indicating that Greenleaf was interested in the Reportership. While Story "entertain[ed] a sincere respect" for Peters, he wrote Greenleaf, Peters would never have received his support had he known Greenleaf to be a candidate.[103]

Having secured two votes, Peters next approached Marshall. He asked Washington to write Marshall on his behalf, and then forwarded a letter to Marshall from his father, Richard Peters, Sr., endorsing his son for the position. Marshall responded by writing Peters's father that the son "may be assured of my cordial support."[104] Peters then approached

---

[100] Carey & Lea, confidential proposal, supra, note 96.

[101] R. Peters, Jr., to J. Story, Sept. 22, 1826, Peters Papers.

[102] J. Story to R. Peters, Jr., Sept. 25, 1826, ibid.

[103] J. Story to S. Greenleaf, Oct. 10, 1826, Simon Greenleaf Papers, Harvard Law School Library.

[104] J. Marshall to R. Peters, Sr., Oct. 2, 1826, Peters Papers.

Smith Thompson, informing him that Washington, Story, and Marshall supported his candidacy, but Thompson declined to respond.[105] Meanwhile Gabriel Duvall was approached, again through Washington, and on November 3 Duvall wrote Peters that although his "general rule [is] to hold myself disengaged until the day of election," he had been "persuaded that no one better qualified will be presented as a candidate."[106]

All this activity proved fruitless in the fall of 1826, for Wheaton's judgeship never materialized; but in March 1827, when Wheaton was offered the Danish ministry, Peters renewed his efforts. He wrote Washington that Wheaton would surely accept the post and urged him to convey "my wishes to become his successor" to the other Justices.[107] He wrote Robert Trimble, in the midst of his first Term as a Justice, and solicited his vote.[108] Peters even wrote Wheaton, indicating that he could "count upon" replacing him, citing "the influence of my friend Judge Washington," and offering to come to Washington "to publish . . . the reports of this Session of the Court, either for your exclusive benefit or on such terms as you may yourself propose."[109] He then rushed down to Washington, consulted with several Justices, and learned that Duvall strongly favored unanimity in the selection and that Johnson, whom Peters had not approached, felt strongly that any Reporter should be a resident of the District of Columbia.[110]

Wheaton did not formally resign until June 6,[111] and as late as December 1827 Peters was not sure that he would be appointed, although Story wrote him that "you will find yourself located [in Washington] for the winter."[112] In January 1828, Peters was notified that he had been unanimously elected Reporter. Apparently Johnson had either been pacified by Peters's assurance that he would hire a clerk to transmit copies of the decisions to a printer and to return them to the Justices for proofing before publication,[113] or had simply decided to acknowledge the support

---

[105] R. Peters, Jr., to S. Thompson, Oct. 13, 1826, ibid.

[106] G. Duvall to R. Peters, Jr., Nov. 3, 1826, ibid.

[107] R. Peters, Jr., to B. Washington, Mar. 5, 1827, ibid.

[108] R. Peters, Jr., to R. Trimble, Mar. 5, 1827, ibid.

[109] R. Peters, Jr., to H. Wheaton, Mar. 5, 1827, ibid.

[110] This information can be found in a March 13, 1827, letter from Peters to Bushrod Washington, written after Peters had made a brief trip to Washington, D.C., between March 6 and March 8, and had returned to Philadelphia, where the letter was written. In the letter Peters responds to information he acquired in a conversation with Washington in Washington, D.C., on the seventh and eighth. The letter is in the Peters Papers.

[111] H. Wheaton to J. Marshall, June 21, 1827, Wheaton Papers.

[112] J. Story to R. Peters, Jr., Dec. 15, 1827, Peters Papers.

[113] Peters outlined this plan to Washington in his letter of March 13, 1827, supra, note 110.

Chapter VI: *The Reporters*

Peters had from other Justices.[114] At the end of his first Term as Reporter Peters could take satisfaction in the fact that his Reports had appeared in print by June 16, earlier than all of Wheaton's volumes save one.[115]

The preface to Peters's first volume indicated that some changes in the mode of reporting would take place. Peters made it clear that he was reducing his summaries of lawyers' arguments to "such arguments . . . as, in [Peters's] opinion, were required for a full and correct understanding of . . . the decision of the Court." It was "not within the scope of his purpose," he stated, "to give, at large, all the reasoning and learning addressed by [lawyers] to the Court." In addition, Peters announced that he was adopting a new system of reference for his headnotes. "The syllabus of each case," he noted, "contains an abstract of all the matters ruled and adjudged by the Court . . . with a reference to the page of the Report in which the particular point will be found."[116] Users of the volume could thus begin with the headnotes of cases, referring to the actual opinion only when they wanted more detail on a particular point decided. As conceived, Peters's headnote reference system resembled the system currently employed in the United States Reports and other official reports.

Conception and execution, however, were in Peters's case two different entities. Reviews of Peters's volumes (which appeared more promptly and in greater numbers than reviews of Wheaton's) quickly focused on his headnotes. A reviewer of the first volume charged that Peters had "heaped into his abstracts incidental observations, reflections, and reasonings of the court," producing a "mass of matter" that "serves to bewilder, rather than to assist the reader." The headnotes were so clumsily presented, the reviewer felt, that it was nearly as difficult "to ascertain the points from the note as from the whole case."[117] Volume 2 proved no better in this respect, according to a review in the same periodical. In the reviewer's judgment, Peters had simply extracted "a number of sentences or paragraphs [from an opinion], on what principle of selection it is difficult to say, and placed them at the head of the case." The headnotes left readers "in a painful state of uncertainty as to the points actually decided by the court." There was "scarcely a single abstract" in Volume 2 of Peters, the reviewer felt, "which states the points in the case definitively and tersely."[118] The pattern of Peters's headnotes,

---

[114] The only information in the Peters Papers indicating that Peters had been confirmed unanimously is a letter from C. C. Biddle to Peters dated January 25, 1828. The letter is somewhat suspect because Biddle was neither in Washington nor an intimate of those close to the Court.

[115] Volume 10 of Wheaton had appeared on June 2, 1824.
[116] 1 Pet. iii (1828).
[117] "Peters' Reports," *Am. Jurist & L. Mag.*, 1:177, 179–80 (1829).
[118] "Peters' Reports," *Am. Jurist & L. Mag.*, 3:101, 105–107 (1830).

a commentator noted in 1833, was "neither [to state] the *principle* nor the *case,* but to . . . present some excerpts, from which one or the other— or possibly both—may be conjectured."[119] Twenty years after Peters had left the Court the Philadelphia *Legal Intelligencer* referred to the "eminently discreditable" state of "the Reports of the Supreme Court of the United States," which had been "a vexatious burden . . . to those . . . obliged to read them . . . ever since the time . . . that Mr. Wheaton ceased to report them."[120]

The greatest strength of Henry Wheaton's Reportership had been his competency as a lawyer. Wheaton had sufficient grasp of the substance of the decisions he reported to know the difference between central and peripheral language in opinions: his headnotes were genuine summaries of the cases. Peters merely copied down the Court's language without refining his analysis. This forced readers to make their own judgments about the precise holdings of cases, the very task the headnote summaries were supposed to perform.

Peters was no more successful than Wheaton had been in avoiding controversy with individual Justices. While he enjoyed good relations with Story, Marshall, and Washington, whom he called "[t]he triple column on which the Court . . . rested for many years in balance,"[121] he was not comparably close to Thompson, Johnson, or McLean. And in Henry Baldwin Peters found a source of extreme discomfort. Baldwin was erratic and unpredictable in his early years on the Court, his difficulties apparently reaching a peak in the 1832 Term. One of the chief manifestations of Baldwin's unconventional behavior was his frequent dissent from decisions reached by Court majorities. Since the practice in the Marshall Court was to allow both members of the majority and dissenters the option of not publicizing their views, a Baldwin dissent in conference might never become known if Baldwin failed to write and to deliver such an opinion to the Reporter. Peters claimed, for example, that in the 1831 Term Baldwin had "dissented in at least two thirds of the cases,"[122] but his Reports list Baldwin as dissenting only nine times (out of forty-two reported cases). In many instances, apparently, Baldwin changed his mind after dissenting in conference; and in other instances he failed to file an opinion with Peters.

There were occasions, however, in which Peters did not report dissenting opinions that Baldwin had delivered to him. In the 1832 case of

[119] Thomas Day to Willard Phillips, Dec. 16, 1833, Willard Phillips Papers, Massachusetts Historical Society, Boston, Mass. Day was the reporter of the Connecticut state courts.

[120] Philadelphia *Legal Intelligencer,* Feb. 12, 1864.

[121] R. Peters, Jr., to J. Story, Nov. 26, 1829, Story Papers, Massachusetts Historical Society, Boston, Mass.

[122] R. Peters, Jr., to Joseph Hopkinson, Mar. 16, 1831, Joseph Hopkinson Papers, Historical Society of Pennsylvania, Philadelphia, Pa.

# Chapter VI: *The Reporters*

*Green* v. *Neal's Lessee*[123] Peters reported Baldwin as dissenting without opinion.[124] Baldwin had written an opinion, however, for a draft of one was found in Peters's papers at the Historical Society of Pennsylvania. And in the cases of *Crane* v. *Lessee of Morris and Astor*[125] and *Kelly* v. *Jackson*,[126] also decided in the 1832 Term, Peters reported Baldwin as having "dissented in writing," but added that "the opinion of Mr. Justice Baldwin was not delivered to the reporter."[127] But Peters's papers contain a Baldwin manuscript opinion designed to serve as a dissent in these companion cases. An earlier example of Peters's not having reported a Baldwin opinion can be found in the 1830 case of *Society for the Propagation of the Gospel* v. *The Town of Pawley*.[128] Peters merely listed Baldwin as "dissenting on the first point" of Story's opinion of the Court,[129] but Baldwin had produced a written dissent. It is possible, of course, that Baldwin delivered the written dissents to Peters after the Reports for the Term had gone to press; but Baldwin, as we shall see, was late in the delivery of his opinion in *Wheaton* v. *Peters,* yet Peters arranged to have it printed in a later edition of the United States Reports.

In an October 1831 letter, previously quoted, Marshall had written Story that Baldwin, whose behavior had apparently disturbed the Justices in the 1831 Term, "seems to have resumed the dispositions which impressed us both so favorably at the [1830] term."[130] A month later Marshall informed Story that Baldwin had "called on me frequently" while Marshall was recovering from his operation, and that Baldwin was "in good health and spirits." Marshall added that he "hope[d] that the next term will exhibit dispositions more resembling those displayed in the first than the last."[131] Unfortunately Baldwin's emotional problems persisted, and his difficulties with Peters came to a head. In two letters[132] to Joseph Hopkinson in February 1832, Baldwin accused Peters of reporting him as having dissented in two cases in the 1831 Term in which Baldwin claimed he was not in fact a dissenter. He also charged that Peters had allowed William Wirt, who had argued *Cherokee Nation* v. *Georgia,* to amend his argument after having had access to Baldwin's dissent in that case. In these letters Baldwin revealed that he had first brought the matter before the other Justices on January 12, and that Peters had responded by writing the Chief Justice a letter that was "directly contradictory as to facts." The Justices apparently checked with Smith Thompson, who "had

---

[123] 6 Pet. 291 (1832).
[124] Ibid., 301.
[125] 6 Pet. 598 (1832).
[126] 6 Pet. 622 (1832).
[127] Ibid., 621, 633.
[128] 4 Pet. 480 (1830).
[129] Ibid., 500.
[130] J. Marshall to J. Story, Oct. 12,
1831, *Proc. Mass. Hist. Soc.,* 14:347 (1901).
[131] J. Marshall to J. Story, Nov. 10, 1831, ibid., 348.
[132] H. Baldwin to J. Hopkinson, Feb. 6, 1832, and Feb. 13, 1832, Hopkinson Papers.

the papers"—the conference notes—on *Cherokee Nation,* and decided not to pursue the matter further. Baldwin indicated to Hopkinson that he was dropping the matter but that "the affair was [not] at an end . . . as it affects the personal relations between Mr. Peters and myself."[133]

Peters, who a year earlier had written Hopkinson that "the conduct of Judge Baldwin . . . has been marked by circumstances which have lost to him the regard of every one of his associates, and the respect of every member of the bar who has had an opportunity to know or observe it,"[134] responded by attacking one of Baldwin's opinions in a letter to Story. Baldwin's dissent in *Worcester* v. *Georgia,* Peters claimed, was "full of misquotations from the Laws of the U.S., from the Reports of the Decisions of this Court, and from the rules of court." The dissent also had made "a direct and positive misrepresentation in many points" of "the action of the court" in *Worcester.* Peters indicated that if he was not connected with the Court he "would direct myself to expose this and the other dissenting opinions of this Judge."[135] Story responded by saying that "of all you relate I can only say I am sorry—I do not say that I am wholly surprised." On "one subject," Story concluded, "I wish to speak resolutely to you—as you love the Court, do not be induced by any circumstances whatsoever to resign office—be firm and adhere—you owe it to yourself and to the public."[136] Story repeated these sentiments in an August 6 letter. "You know full well," he wrote Peters, "that there are persons, who will do all the mischief they can." In Story's "judgment," however, "your continuance in office is of very great importance to the dignity of the Court and the utility of the Reports."[137]

Meanwhile Peters had let Marshall know of his problems with Baldwin; the Chief Justice responded in two circumspect letters in 1832. In an August 11 letter Marshall said that he was "sorry to hear that you and our brother are still so far apart," and added that "you both seem inclined to carry on the war [interminably]."[138] On December 20, responding to a letter Peters had written him on the seventeenth, Marshall wrote that he "had hoped very seriously that the differences between our brother Baldwin and yourself, though not adjusted amicably, had been put so entirely at rest as never again to become a subject of inquiry for others." In his letter Peters had asked Marshall if he had preserved any of the letters exchanged between Baldwin, Peters, and himself about the alleg-

---

[133] These quotations are from the February 13 letter.

[134] R. Peters, Jr., to J. Hopkinson, Mar. 16, 1831, Hopkinson Papers.

[135] R. Peters, Jr., to J. Story, Mar. 29, 1832, Joseph Story Papers, Library of Congress.

[136] J. Story to R. Peters, Jr., Mar. 31, 1832, Peters Papers.

[137] J. Story to R. Peters, Jr., Aug. 6, 1832, ibid.

[138] J. Marshall to R. Peters, Jr., Aug. 11, 1832, ibid.

edly misrepresented dissents; Marshall replied that he had not. "The subject," he said, "was supposed to be entirely at an end, and the papers were believed to be no longer important."[139]

By late 1832 Peters was apparently convinced that Baldwin would seek to canvass the Justices and urge his resignation. In a December 2 letter Story referred to Peters's "controversy with Judge B" and promised to firmly resist any effort to poll the Justices. "I have never from the beginning," he told Peters, "had but one opinion on the subject. I shall not suffer Judge B again to draw me into any discussion of it. Others may do as they please, but it is time that he should learn that there are men who feel the pressure of public lives more than the private griefs of an offended party." Story added another plea that Peters not consider resigning the Reportership. "You must not think of resigning," he wrote. "Your duty is to remain where you are; and your honour now requires that you should so do."[140]

Peters and Baldwin never resolved their differences. As late as 1839 Peters was continuing to complain to Hopkinson about Baldwin's numerous unwritten or unfiled dissents, which Peters felt occurred "in six cases out of ten" and signified the "wandering" of "[Baldwin's] mind."[141] While Peters's difficulties with Baldwin can primarily be traced to the latter's temperament, they foreshadowed problems that Peters was to have with judges on the Taney Court. The underlying source of Peters's problems may have been politics—he had been identified as a critic of the Jackson administration and several of the Taney Court Justices were Jacksonians[142]—but the criticism of Peters centered on the accuracy of his reporting. Evidence for this can be found in Congressman Joseph R. Ingersoll's introduction of a resolution in the House of Representatives in 1836 calling for an investigation to ascertain whether the Court's decisions were being reported "with accuracy and fidelity."[143] In the debates on that resolution Congressman Benjamin Hardin of Kentucky was reported as saying that "the Reports furnished by [Peters] were grossly and palpably inaccurate and false," and that they were "of no more use than the Arabian Nights Entertainments." Peters "had falsified the decisions of the Court," Hardin asserted, "often omit[ting] whole pages, and frequently ma[king] the Judges say one thing, when in fact they had

---

[139] J. Marshall to R. Peters, Jr., Dec. 20, 1832, ibid.

[140] J. Story to R. Peters, Jr., Dec. 22, 1832, ibid.

[141] R. Peters, Jr., to J. Hopkinson, Mar. 8, 1839, Hopkinson Papers.

[142] Peters was a close acquaintance of Nicholas Biddle, the president of the

Bank of the United States, and wrote Biddle a supportive letter in 1836 during attacks on the Bank by the Jackson administration. See Swisher, *Taney Period*, 298.

[143] Congressional Globe 321 (24th Cong., 1st Sess., 1836).

asserted the reverse of it."[144] When Peters was dismissed as Reporter in 1843 by a truncated majority of Justices, inaccuracy in reporting was cited as the reason.[145]

The Peters–Baldwin dispute underscored the informality of the Court's reporting process and the consequent discretionary powers exercised by early Reporters. The Court kept no formal records of its conferences, although individual Justices took notes, which when compared against one another reveal wide discrepancies.[146] The practices of silent acquiescence by dissenters and the nonidentification of members of a majority meant that a dissent in conference could be altered after the fact without anyone except the Justices being aware that it had occurred. No opinions were deposited with the Clerk until 1834,[147] and no duplicating machines existed, so that the only copies of majority and dissenting opinions were those prepared by their authors. Reporters were given latitude to correct grammatical errors in opinions, and had to work with handwritten drafts; thus a printed version of an opinion might not fully resemble the original. A Justice, such as Baldwin, who regularly changed his mind about "dissents" or who failed to deliver opinions to the Reporter, could play havoc with the reporting process. On the other hand, an enterprising Reporter could publicize certain arguments and opinions of which he approved, as Peters did in both the *Cherokee* case and *Wheaton* v. *Peters*. In Peters's case the situation was not improved by his less than analytical reading of opinions and by his tendency to criticize Justices who had offended him.

If Peters was a less than successful analyst of the Court's decisions, and not fully capable of inspiring the confidence of each of the Justices, he was much more successful as a salesman and promoter of his Reports. In this capacity he embarked upon an ambitious scheme to increase the distribution and profitability of the United States Reports, a scheme that eventually led to the landmark copyright decision of *Wheaton* v. *Peters*. From the outset of his Reportership Peters's major interest was to increase his revenue from the sales of Reports. He attempted to achieve this goal through three separate strategies. One was to increase the sales of his volumes by reducing their price. He announced in the first volume that

---

[144] An account of Hardin's remarks is enclosed in a letter from Peters to Story, Apr. 18, 1836, Joseph Story Papers, Essex Historical Society, Essex, Mass.

[145] See Swisher, *Taney Period,* 304–305.

[146] Conference notes of Justices Baldwin and Story for the 1831, 1832, and 1833 Terms were found in the Peters Papers.

[147] For the Court's rule formalizing deposit of opinions with the Clerk, see 9 Pet. vii (1835). In an 1830 case in which William Wirt sought copies of an opinion decided that term, Marshall said that "the Reporter of the Court is the proper person to give copies of the opinions. . . . The opinions were delivered to him after they were read, and not to the Clerk. . . ." [Anonymous], 3 Pet. 397 (1830).

the price was hitherto to be set at $5.00 and continued to price the Reports at that figure throughout his tenure. This policy did not have the effect of improving sales. Whereas Wheaton had returned an average of between $500 and $800 in profits from book sales during his tenure, Peters, between 1827 and 1834, never exceeded $412. Even at the lower price, sales of Reports never exceeded 700 a year in that period.[148]

The second of Peters's strategies, and the one that engendered a lawsuit, was his decision to publish a series of Condensed Reports. These volumes would include all of the Court's Reports from Dallas's first volume through Wheaton's last. In his proposal for publishing the Condensed Reports, issued in 1828, Peters claimed that he could produce all the extant volumes of his predecessors "in a form [that would] complete the publication in not more than six volumes, the price of which shall not exceed thirty-six dollars." He proposed to omit all the arguments of counsel and Wheaton's appendix notes, and to present concurring and dissenting opinions in "abbreviated form."[149] The result would be a set of twenty-four volumes of Reports, which in their original form could not be acquired for less than $180, for $36. While Peters claimed that his Condensed Reports "will be a 'Digest' of the facts of the Cases and the opinions of the Court—no more,"[150] his Reports were not that. They did not contain summaries of the Court's opinions, but the opinions themselves.

The third strategy, if implemented, would have dramatically escalated Peters's income. It was a plan to require congressional distribution of copies of the decisions of the Supreme Court to all public offices in the United States.[151] In an 1834 letter to the chairman of the House Judiciary Committee, Peters urged that his six volumes of Condensed Reports, plus the seven volumes of his own Reports then in print, be distributed by Congress to the county clerks of "every county of the several states and territories of the Union," to "the executive departments of the states and territories," to "each diplomatic agent of the Country abroad," and to state and state court libraries. The distribution would amount to 1,250 sets of Reports, Peters calculated, which he would sell to Congress at a reduced price. He would also, in exchange for a standing order of 1,250 of his volumes each year, forgo his $1,000 salary.[152]

---

[148] R. Peters, Jr., to John Bell, Jan. 20, 1834, Peters Papers.

[149] Peters, "Proposals, For publishing, by subscription, The Cases, Decided in the Supreme Court of the United States, From its organization to the close of January term, 1827," in R. Peters, *Record of the Case of Wheaton v. Peters* (1834), 9–11.

[150] R. Peters, Jr., to W. Cranch, Aug. 14, 1828, Peters Papers.

[151] The plan is described in Peters to J. Bell, Jan. 20, 1834, ibid. (This is a different letter from that cited supra, note 148.)

[152] Ibid.

Taken together, the second and third portions of Peters's plan would have made the Reportership a lucrative position. Advance private sales of the Condensed Reports in 1831 numbered 900, more than the requests for Peters's own volume that year.[153] If Peters had been able to sell 1,500 copies of the Condensed Reports, the number projected in the publisher's printing, revenues from those sales, plus the congressional copies, would have amounted to nearly $30,000. While this figure was sure to diminish as the Condensed Reports were bought up, Peters's plan envisaged a standing order for his own Reports. Forgiving a $1,000 salary would have been a minor concession had the plan materialized.

As it was, Congress took no action on Peters's proposal for distribution. Meanwhile his Condensed Reports appeared, the first volume surfacing in late 1829. Members of the Court expressed pleasure at the project, Story writing Peters that he admired the "plan and execution" of the first volume, and Thompson referring to the first volume as a "highly useful book."[154] As Joseph Hopkinson made clear in a letter written at the same time, "the importance of a general circulation of the [Court's decisions]" was that it facilitated "the uniformity and correctness" of "the judgments of inferior courts."[155] Peters himself noted that the Condensed Reports would "diffuse . . . knowledge" through the country.[156]

The only people displeased with the appearance of the Condensed Reports seem to have been William Cranch, Robert Donaldson, and Henry Wheaton. Cranch wrote Peters in 1828, after learning of the latter's proposal for a series of condensed volumes, that he would vigorously object to the publication of any "new edition" of his own volumes. He had "not yet been reimbursed the actual expense of publishing my last 3 volumes," he told Peters; he was "one thousand dollars" out of pocket; and he "must insist upon all my legal rights."[157] Peters responded that he had no intention of reproducing any of Cranch's individual contributions in his condensed volumes, merely the facts and opinions of the Court's decisions, which could not be the subject of a copyright. His Condensed Reports, he assured Cranch, were "not . . . obnoxious to the law protecting literary property."[158]

Meanwhile Donaldson, who had declined to publish Peters's Re-

---

[153] F. Hicks, *Men and Books Famous in the Law* (1921), 208; Peters to Bell, Jan. 20, 1834, supra, note 148.

[154] J. Story to R. Peters, Jr., Dec. 10, 1829, Peters Papers.

[155] J. Hopkinson to John Grigg, Dec. 1, 1829, ibid. Grigg, Peters's publisher for the Condensed Reports, was a co-defendant in *Wheaton* v. *Peters*.

[156] R. Peters, Jr., to J. Grigg, Mar. 2, 1831, quoted in Peters, *Record of Wheaton* v. *Peters*, 14.

[157] W. Cranch to R. Peters, Jr., July 18, 1829, Peters Papers.

[158] R. Peters, Jr., to W. Cranch, Aug. 14, 1828, ibid.

ports in 1827, wishing Peters "better success than your predecessor,"[159] wrote Wheaton of the proposed appearance of the Condensed Reports, informing him that "there can be . . . no security for the labours of authors and publishers . . . until an example is made of these literary Pirates."[160] He also wrote Peters, a month later, that the effect of the proposal "would be to me literally ruinous in a large amount of property" and would "deprive . . . my absent friend Henry Wheaton Esq. . . . of the pecuniary reward due to his professional labours of 12 years."[161] Donaldson was eventually to file a bill for an injunction in federal circuit court in Pennsylvania, alleging that Wheaton's copyright had been violated and asking that Peters be enjoined from distributing any copies of Volume 3 of the Condensed Reports.

Wheaton's early reaction had been to "try . . . amicable remonstrances." On hearing from Donaldson in August 1828 about Peters's proposal, Wheaton merely suggested that Donaldson inform Peters that they were contemplating suit.[162] In November of that year Wheaton wrote Webster about Peters's proposals, and urged him to "remonstrate with [Peters] on the subject." Wheaton felt that Peters "ha[d] not duly considered the injury such a publication would do me," and indicated that he had been "very much surprised" by Peters's proposal.[163] Peters's response to any "remonstrances" was to continue his plans to publish the volumes of Condensed Reports. As his first volume neared publication, Cranch and Peters reached a settlement of Cranch's claims. Peters sent Cranch fifty copies of the Condensed Reports, and Cranch dropped his suit.[164]

*Wheaton v. Peters* formally began in May 1831 with Wheaton and Donaldson's bill in equity seeking to enjoin the publication of Volume 3 of the Condensed Reports. Earlier that year, in response to the news that Donaldson had threatened a New York bookseller with prosecution if he sold the volume, Peters had written his publisher, John Grigg of Philadelphia, indicating that he would "indemnify and save harmless from all costs and damages" those who published or sold the volumes. In the letter Peters asserted that "there does not exist a copyright, legally secured, to any . . . volume of Mr. Wheaton's Reports." Wheaton had

[159] R. Donaldson to R. Peters, Jr., Nov. 13, 1827, ibid.

[160] R. Donaldson to H. Wheaton, Aug. 11, 1828, Wheaton Papers.

[161] R. Donaldson to R. Peters, Jr., Sept. 25, 1828, Peters Papers.

[162] H. Wheaton to R. Donaldson, Sept. 30, 1828, Wheaton Papers.

[163] H. Wheaton to D. Webster, Nov. 25, 1828, Webster Papers, Library of Congress.

[164] Richard S. Coxe to R. Peters, Jr., Dec. 11, 1829, Peters Papers; R. Peters, Jr., to R. Coxe, Dec. 13, 1829, ibid. Coxe was representing Cranch in the negotiations.

not, Peters claimed, complied with the statutory formalities of the federal copyright statutes. He added that Congress itself had "authorized the purchase of seventy copies" of the Condensed Reports, and that "nothing . . . can stay the progress or success of the [work]."[165] His attorneys were to make the same arguments in response to Wheaton and Donaldson's bill, adding the arguments that no common law copyright existed in the United States and that the material contained in Wheaton's Reports was not copyrightable.

The case lingered in Joseph Hopkinson and Henry Baldwin's circuit court until 1833, with the injunction intact, because Hopkinson and Baldwin could not agree on its outcome. A final hearing had been scheduled for December 1832, but Baldwin, suffering at the time from a nervous disorder, was apparently unable to sit. Hopkinson resolved to proceed, and on January 9, 1833, dissolved the injunction, holding that Wheaton had failed to meet the statutory requirements for perfecting a copyright and that no common law copyright existed.[166] Wheaton and Donaldson appealed to the Supreme Court, as Hopkinson's opinion invited them to do.[167] Wheaton had previously written Webster, retaining him should the case be appealed,[168] and in December Elijah Paine, Wheaton's attorney, confirmed that fact.[169] Later Wheaton was to say that he would "never have sacrificed the last farthing of my paternal inheritance . . . knowing as I did that Hopkinson had corresponded with S[tory] about the case, and that the latter had agreed to confirm above what the former should decide below."[170]

Encouraged by Paine to attend the Supreme Court arguments if possible,[171] Wheaton wrote for a leave of absence from his post in Denmark, received permission, and arrived in Washington in time to assist Webster with his preparations for the argument. In January 1834 he supplied Webster with a memorandum addressing some of the central points at issue. As to the copyrightability of judicial opinions, Wheaton pointed out the absurdity that anyone "would have undertaken the risk and ex-

---

[165] Peters to Grigg, Mar. 2, 1831, supra, note 156.

[166] Hopkinson's opinion was reported in 8 Pet. at 725.

[167] "I am conscious of the importance of the questions which have been discussed in this cause, to the parties and to the public; and it is a real satisfaction to me to know that my opinion may be, and I presume will be, reviewed by another tribunal." 8 Pet. at 742.

[168] H. Wheaton to D. Webster, July 22, 1831, Webster Papers, Library of Congress.

[169] E. Paine to D. Webster, Dec. 6, 1831, Daniel Webster Papers, New Hampshire Historical Society, Concord, N.H.

[170] H. Wheaton to Eliza W. Lyman, May 14, 1837, Henry Wheaton Papers, John Hay Library, Brown University.

[171] "Peters is on the spot, alas, the face of a party does often turn a doubtful balance held by human judges." E. Paine to H. Wheaton, Aug. 28, 1833, Wheaton Papers.

pense of publishing an edition [of Reports] . . . which might be encountered the next day by a piratical edition."[172] He also noted that in his efforts to lobby with representatives of Congress for a Reporter's Act he and his supporters had assumed that he had an exclusive right to the "work" of his Reports. A letter Marshall had written on Wheaton's behalf to the Senate Judiciary Committee confirmed this view,[173] as did correspondence between Story and Wheaton, and Wheaton and others, in the period prior to his becoming Reporter. All in all, Wheaton's argument that he reasonably expected that the material in his Reports would be his property seemed a strong one, and Webster repeated it in his presentation to the Court.[174] The problem with the argument, however, was that while it suggested that Wheaton had a right to exclude others from the reproduction of some material in his Reports, it did not dispose of the difficulty that the bulk of the material was simply the opinions of other persons—Justices—that Wheaton had recorded. In addressing this difficulty Wheaton claimed in his memorandum to Webster that even if he "ha[d] no Copy Right in the written opinions of the Judges . . . it is enough if he has such right in any substantial portion of his 12 vols. which Mr. Peters has copied."[175]

Wheaton was also hard pressed to deal with some of Peters's other arguments. The 1790 and 1802 Copyright Acts[176] had set forth four steps to perfect a statutory copyright. The title of the work needed to be recorded in the office of the clerk of the federal judicial district in which the author resided; the statement of the recording of title had to be printed on the title page, or following page, of the work; within two weeks of the recording, a copy of the record had to be published in the public press for a period of four weeks; and within six months of the publication of the work a copy had to be delivered to and deposited with the Department of State. In his argument Peters had claimed that Wheaton had failed to perform the third and fourth steps. Wheaton could not produce any evidence that he had printed a copy of the recording of his volumes in the press,[177] although he could show that in the case of his first volume, his publisher, Mathew Carey, had done so.[178] Nor could he produce any

---

[172] H. Wheaton, memorandum to D. Webster, undated, Wheaton Papers, supra, note 30. The memorandum was obviously written in January or February, 1834.

[173] "[T]he judges think there is much reason to apprehend that the publication of the decisions of the Supreme Court will remain on a very precarious footing if the reporter is to depend solely on the sales of his work for a reimbursement of the expenses which must be incurred in preparing for it, and for his compen-

sation." Marshall to Chase, Feb. 7, 1817, supra, note 25.

[174] 8 Pet. at 652–53.

[175] Memorandum, supra, note 30.

[176] Act of May 31, 1790, 1 Stat. 124; Act of Apr. 29, 1802, 2 Stat. 171.

[177] Paine identified this difficulty in a letter to Wheaton of January 16, 1833; Wheaton Papers.

[178] Henry C. Carey gave evidence to that effect at the trial before the circuit court. See Peters, *Record of Wheaton v. Peters*, 23–24.

evidence that he had deposited with the State Department more than the eighty copies required by the Reporter's Act; he argued, in fact, that the deposit satisfied his copyright claims as well. When Elijah Paine came to argue these points before the Court, he dismissed the newspaper publication requirement as a "burthensome and needless regulation" that was not capable of "safe and easy proof" and asserted that Wheaton had in fact sent "eighty-one copies" to the State Department, but "the law giving the salary not requiring more than eighty, the papers in the department under the acts speak of but eighty."[179]

Of all the difficult points in Wheaton's argument, the copyrightability of the judges' opinions appeared most troublesome to his counsel, and they decided to deal with it head on. Wheaton had "acquired the right to the opinions," Paine argued, "by judges' gift." The opinions of the judges, when "new, original and unpublished," were clearly their own property. Judges were not bound "to write out such elaborate opinions." When the judges "invited [Wheaton] to attend at his own expense and report the cases," there was "a tacit engagement on their part to furnish him with such notes or written opinions as they might draw up."[180] This argument was not fanciful: Peters himself had anticipated it in 1830 when he wrote Justice McLean, "I am under some doubt whether by the mere circumstance of my being Reporter I obtain a property in the opinions of the Court," and asked "each member of the Court" to assign him "the right to each opinion delivered by [that Justice]."[181] McLean, Baldwin, and Story responded by assigning Peters whatever copyrights they may have had;[182] Johnson declined, stating his view that "our opinions were public property & not assignable by us."[183]

Counsel for Peters, Thomas Sergeant and J. R. Ingersoll, disputed all of the above arguments. The opinions of judges, they maintained, were public property;[184] Wheaton had no common law copyright in the Reports;[185] Wheaton had not complied with the provisions of the Copyright Acts.[186] Arguments in the case concluded by March 14. On March 18 Story sent Charles Sumner to deliver messages to both Wheaton and Peters, asking them to meet with him separately in his chambers. When Wheaton arrived Story presented him with a memorandum that he had

---

[179] 8 Pet. at 605, 612.
[180] Ibid., 615.
[181] R. Peters, Jr., to J. McLean, May 24, 1830, Peters Papers.
[182] J. McLean to R. Peters, Jr., June 3, 1830, ibid.; J. Story to R. Peters, Jr., June 1, 1830, ibid.; H. Baldwin to R. Peters, Jr., June 8, 1830, ibid.

[183] W. Johnson to R. Peters, Jr., June 5, 1830, ibid.
[184] 8 Pet. at 619, 624, 638, 648.
[185] Ibid., 629–30, 642.
[186] Ibid., 635–36, 644–47.

been "authorized by the Court to communicate to" both of the parties. The memorandum revealed that the Court had unanimously decided that no one had any property rights in the Court's opinions, and that the Justices could therefore not convey any copyrights to Reporters. As to the marginal notes, appendices, and other nonopinion portions of Wheaton's volumes, the Court had not reached a definitive conclusion; nor had it conclusively determined whether Wheaton had complied with the statutory prerequisites for perfecting his copyright. The memorandum concluded by suggesting that the suit was "a fit subject for honourable compromise between the parties."[187]

Wheaton was amazed and angered by Story's actions. He told Story that he had previously offered a compromise proposal to Peters that would have sent the action to arbitration, and Peters had rejected his offer. He added that he would not be able to reach Donaldson, who was in New York, in order to bring about any compromise before the Court concluded its 1834 Term, which was scheduled to end with the disposition of *Wheaton v. Peters*. He believed that he continued to have enforceable rights to the notes and appendices in his Reports, and he planned to see that they were vindicated. On this point Story responded, "in a menacing tone," that Wheaton might be misguided in supposing that his rights were "extensive." Wheaton concluded his conversation with Story by asking leave to confer with Webster, who subsequently advised him "unhesitatingly" not to compromise. Wheaton then wrote a letter to the Court, dated the same day as his conference with Story, in which he rejected the Court's suggestion.[188]

With the possibility of a compromise now removed, the Court met to attempt to dispose of the unsettled issues in *Wheaton v. Peters*. Only on the issue of the copyrightability of judicial opinions were the Justices able to achieve unanimity. As their subsequent opinions revealed, the six Justices who decided *Wheaton v. Peters* (Johnson missed the 1834 Term because of illness) divided on whether a common law copyright could exist and whether Wheaton had complied with the statutory formalities. None of the Justices, in the opinions originally included in Peters's report of the case, openly addressed the question whether, if Wheaton had per-

---

[187] Details of this episode came from a long memorandum, dated March 18, 1834, that Wheaton deposited in his files. He attached to the memorandum a letter from Story to Peters and himself, dated March 17, 1834; a memorandum, delivered by Story to Wheaton at the March 18 conference, with no date; and a letter from himself to the Court, dated March 18, 1834, rejecting the compromise. These are all in the Wheaton Papers.

[188] Wheaton's memorandum, Mar. 18, 1834, supra, note 187.

fected his statutory copyright, the material in the notes and appendices was copyrightable.[189]

McLean's opinion for the Court was sketchily reasoned and gave every sign of being hastily written. He began by addressing the question whether Wheaton had a copyright "under the common law," and concluded that he did not because "no [such] right had . . . been asserted" in the Pennsylvania courts, "no custom or usage established, [and] no judicial decision been given." While a common law "right of authors" had subsequently been held to exist in England, "no such right at the common law had been recognized . . . when the colony of Penn was organized."[190] Moreover, there was "no common law of the United States": whenever "a common law right is asserted, we must look to the state in which the controversy occurred."[191] Finally, the language of the Copyright Act of 1790 "created [a right] instead of sanctioning an existing right."[192] Thus any copyright that Wheaton had could only be statutory.

McLean then turned to the question of statutory compliance. He found that the requirements of the 1790 Act were not "unimportant": "all the conditions . . . were essential to a perfect title."[193] He acknowledged that some "doubts could be entertained whether the notice and deposit of the book in the state department were essential" under the 1790 Act. But, "in the opinion of three of the judges," the 1802 Act made the deposit of copies and publication in the newspapers "requisites" for perfecting title.[194] Thus Wheaton was required to show "a substantial compliance with every legal requisite."[195] It was unclear whether he had: the case was therefore remanded to the federal circuit court. As an afterthought, McLean noted that "it may be proper to remark that the court are unanimously of opinion, that no reporter has or can have any copyright in the written opinions delivered by this court; and that the judges thereby cannot confer on any reporter any such right."[196]

As stated by McLean, the Court's disposition was odd. The common law copyright issue had been decided, as Thompson's and Baldwin's dissents revealed, by a 4–2 vote, and McLean's statement that there "can be no common law of the United States," was clearly one to which Story,

---

[189] When Volume 8 of Peters, including the cases of *Wheaton* v. *Peters,* appeared in 1834, Baldwin was listed as dissenting without opinion. Baldwin had, however, delivered an opinion in court, which appeared in later editions of the United States Reports. In his opinion Baldwin concluded that "the opinions of the court" were clearly not . . . the subject of copyright," but "the marginal notes, or syllabus of the cases and points decided, the abstract of the

record and evidence, and the index to the several volumes, are as much literary property as any productions of the mind." 8 Pet. (33 U.S.) at 698g. (F. Brightly, ed., 1883).

[190] 8 Pet. at 659, 660.
[191] Ibid., 658.
[192] Ibid., 661.
[193] Ibid., 664.
[194] Ibid., 665.
[195] Ibid., 667.
[196] Ibid., 668.

and perhaps Marshall, were not committed. That issue had been decided on a forced reading of the 1790 Copyright Act (which could easily have been read as "securing" existing rights as well as creating them) and on the bootstrap argument that because no common law copyrights had sought to be enforced in the Pennsylvania courts, they did not exist. On the mandatory nature of the statutory provisions, McLean apparently did not have a clear majority. He had read the 1790 Act's provisions as mandatory, but he did not have a majority for that finding; and only "three of the judges" had read the 1802 Act as making the provisions mandatory. In terms of the disposition of the case, the lack of a majority on the point was irrelevant, because Hopkinson in the court below had held the provisions to be mandatory; an equal division in the Supreme Court had the effect of affirming his decision. But that meant that the issues to be retried in *Wheaton* v. *Peters* would be retried under standards that only three of seven Marshall Court Justices had found to be applicable.

The only clear future of *Wheaton* v. *Peters,* then, was McLean's last sentence about the noncopyrightability of Supreme Court opinions. This sentence was, despite its position in McLean's opinion, the key to the case and the practical end of the controversy. It settled the copyrightability not only of judicial opinions but of other analogous "public" documents that had been authored by private individuals, such as opinions of the attorneys general. It also meant that whatever "common law" copyrights public officials had to their ideas, once those ideas were deposited in the public domain the only copyright protections were statutory. *Wheaton* v. *Peters* thus reduced the Reporter's office from a literary position to that of a recording secretary. It meant that the only portion of Henry Wheaton's Reports that he could conceivably protect against being reproduced was a portion of largely esoteric value. The last sentence of *Wheaton* v. *Peters,* and its assertion that no common law copyright protection existed for public documents, made it a "great case." The rest of the opinion hardly stood for anything.

A day after Story's conference with Wheaton the Court delivered its opinion in *Wheaton* v. *Peters*. Only five Justices were present, Story having prudently decided to avoid any further contacts with the two Reporters by leaving Washington on the early stagecoach. An account of the Justices' exchanges during the delivery of their opinions has survived:[197] the scene was an extraordinary one. McLean began by reading his opinion. Thompson then delivered his dissent, and added that the Court had been equally divided on the effect of the 1802 Act's provisions. Baldwin then read his dissent, supporting Thompson, adding that he dis-

---

[197] The account can be found in two letters written by Charles Sumner, who was present in the courtroom, to Joseph Story, on March 19 and 20, 1834. Both letters are in the Story Papers, Library of Congress.

agreed with the majority's statement "that the U.S. *qua* U.S. had no common law," and finding that Wheaton had a copyrightable interest in the marginalia of his Reports.[198] McLean then attempted to clarify his position, claiming that his analysis of the statutory provisions had been"clearly stated," and was "based on the Statute of 1790." Thompson countered that "if the analysis had been clearly stated" he would not have queried the point. Marshall then intervened, indicating that "the [majority] opinion as read needed explanation," and "stated in full" the conclusions on statutory construction. McLean reread the statutory construction passages from his opinion and "added that this dialogue across from one to another was very unpleasant." Thompson was by now "in a perfect boil," and Baldwin exhibited a "strong passion . . . by looks and motions and whispers." Duvall, who was stone deaf by the 1834 Term, sat "in utter unconsciousness of the strife around him . . . add[ing] to the grotesqueness of the scene."[199]

Eventually Marshall ordered Peters not "to make any mention of the [Justices'] differences [on the bench] in his report of the case," but for a time the "altercation [was] magnified . . . ten times over" in Washington gossip.[200] Peters protested against the remand, arguing (correctly) that nothing in the majority opinion had intimated that Wheaton had any rights in any material in his volumes, but the Justices declined to modify their mandate,[201] and the case was returned to Hopkinson and Baldwin's court. There it rested until 1838, when a jury found that Wheaton did in fact have copyright rights to the notes and appendices.[202] Peters appealed again, but that appeal was not perfected until 1846, and both Peters and Wheaton died in 1848, before it was heard. In 1850 Peters's estate settled the case by paying Wheaton's estate $400.[203]

Wheaton reacted to the 1834 decision by directing a series of vituperative comments at Story. A day after the decision was announced he fired off letters to his wife and his father-in-law. In the former letter he labeled Story "the prime mover and instigator in Peters' piratical attack on my property in the Reports," and noted that Story had left Washington before the decision was announced, leaving McLean "to fire off the blunderbuss he had loaded, but had not courage to discharge."[204] He

---

[198] See 8 Pet., supra, note 189, at 698g–698l.

[199] C. Sumner to J. Story, Mar. 20, 1834, Story Papers, Library of Congress.

[200] Ibid.

[201] J. Marshall to R. Peters, Jr., May 15, 1834, Peters Papers.

[202] C. Chauncey to H. Wheaton, Apr. 11, 1834; John Cadwalader to H.

Wheaton, Apr. 24, 1834; Wheaton Papers. Chauncey and Cadwalader were the attorneys representing Wheaton on remand.

[203] W. B. Lawrence (Wheaton's executor) to. Robert Wheaton (Wheaton's son), Feb. 18, 1850, Wheaton Papers.

[204] H. Wheaton to C. Wheaton, Mar. 20, 1834, ibid.

# Chapter VI: *The Reporters*

subsequently referred to Story's "blunderbuss of infidelity," and said that Story had "betrayed me, Judas-like, with a kiss."[205] Wheaton made similar comments in subsequent letters. He claimed in a letter to one of his legal counsel that "a nominal majority" had supported the decision, a majority assembled by Story and including Duvall, who was "notoriously incapable of understanding anything about [the case]."[206] And in a letter to his sister in 1837 he asserted that Story and Hutchinson had conspired to "confirm" each other's position in the case and that Story had also duped Marshall:

> [The Chief Justice] never studied the cause. . . . He pinned his faith on the sleeve of his prevaricating brother, believing that, if the latter had any leaning, it was towards me on the score of the friendship the hypocrite once professed—of which doubtless he still continued to pour into that venerable man's ear.[207]

Wheaton had misunderstood Story's interest in the Reportership. For Story the reports of judicial decisions, whoever authored them, were part of the process of publicizing the opinions of courts and thereby enhancing their authority. While Story was undoubtedly interested in the quality of reporting and in the erudition of reporters, he was mainly interested in seeing that his decisions, and the decisions of his colleagues, were placed before the public. Thus he encouraged Wheaton to become the Reporter because he suspected, rightly, that Wheaton would be conscientious and assiduous; he contributed to Wheaton's appendices because he wanted digests and other doctrinal essays on admiralty and maritime law to be widely circulated; he supported Peters's candidacy for the Reportership because he had known of Peters's interest in reporting the decisions of Washington and other judges; and he encouraged Peters to publish the Condensed Reports because he wanted as full dissemination of the Court's decisions as possible. Story was also gregarious, amiable, and a compulsive correspondent, so both Wheaton and Peters regarded him as a friend. And so he was, which is why he left Washington before the decision in *Wheaton* v. *Peters* was delivered. But when it came to choosing between the property rights of Henry Wheaton and the wide dissemination of Court opinions, Story had no difficulty with the choice. His position was precisely the same as that expressed by Joseph Hopkinson, whose views he had confirmed on appeal. Hopkinson had said in 1829 that Peters's Condensed Reports were "almost [a] necessity" be-

---

[205] H. Wheaton to L. Wheaton, Mar. 20, 1834, ibid.

[206] H. Wheaton to C. Chauncey, June 11, 1834, John Cadwalader Papers, Historical Society of Pennsylvania, Philadelphia, Pa.

[207] Wheaton to Lyman, May 14, 1837, supra, note 170.

cause of "the importance of a general circulation of the decisions of [the Court] to the uniformity and correctness of the judgments of inferior courts."

Two months after the decision in *Wheaton* v. *Peters* Story wrote Kent about his tribulations in the case:

> I am sorry for the controversy between Mr. Wheaton and Mr. Peters, and did all I could to prevent a public discussion of the delicate subject of copyright, in which we all have so deep an interest. . . . Strict construction of the statute of Congress we adopted with vast reluctance. . . . I wish Congress would make some additional provisions on the subject, to protect authors of whom I think no one is more meritorious than Mr. Wheaton, You, as a judge, have frequently had occasion to know how many bitter cups we are not at liberty to pass by.[208]

Story had indeed attempted "to prevent a public discussion" of *Wheaton* v. *Peters:* he had hoped that his influence with the two Reporters would bring about a compromise, and the Court could avoid deciding the case. When that failed he had no choice but to side with Peters and the cause of wider judicial influence.

By the time of the decision in *Wheaton* v. *Peters* and the close of the Marshall Court, the office of Reporter had been transformed. It is unclear what the original conception of the office had been: Dallas seems to have simply happened upon the scene, had no formal responsibilities, and perhaps exercised considerable informal powers, most notable among them being the discretion to omit reporting those decisions he concluded were not worth reproduction. Cranch, likewise, was simply a local resident with legal training who had chosen to take the time and effort to report the Court's decisions. While Cranch clearly anticipated some profit from his venture, he never received any and never considered reporting even a part-time job. It was apparent to the Court that someone should report its decisions, but beyond that the Justices did not seem to have a clear picture of what obligations or powers lay in the Reporter's office.

Wheaton's appointment both professionalized the office and gave it the character of an entrepreneurial and professional venture. Wheaton was ambitious as a scholar, as an aspiring advocate, and as a businessman: he hoped to make the Reportership a position of considerable power and prestige. And it was clear that despite Wheaton's bad luck, indifferent

---

[208] J. Story to J. Kent, May 17, 1834, quoted in W. Story, *Life and Letters*, II, 181.

success as an advocate, and thwarted prospects, he was a person of some stature in the eyes of the Justices. He also was an interventionist Reporter who on at least one occasion probably made some law himself and who was permitted a certain amount of discretion in "cutting and carving" arguments and even opinions. Story had in mind Wheaton's practices when he wrote to Peters in 1836;

> I have always supposed the [the Reporter] was not a mere writer of a journal of what occurred, or a record of all that occurred. . . . This duty appears to me to involve the exercise of a sound discretion as to reporting a case; to abridge arguments, to state facts, to give the opinions of the Court substantially as they are delivered it. As to the order in which this is to be done, I have supposed it was a matter strictly of his own taste and discretion. . . .
>
> As to the correction of verbal and grammatical errors in an opinion, I can only say for myself that I have always been grateful for the kindness of any reporter of my opinions in doing me this favor. . . .[209]

The passage of the Reporter's Act during Wheaton's tenure, Wheaton's own undoubted ability as a digester and scholar, his strong interest in disseminating the Court's decisions, and his close contact with the Justices (he roomed with Story in the Justices' boardinghouse for at least two Terms)[210] meant that the Reportership under Wheaton had become a professional position of permanence and some power and influence.

The succession of Wheaton by Peters subtly altered the image of the Court's Reporter. Peters was, first of all, much more limited in his professional ambitions than Wheaton. The former aspired to be a judge, diplomat, politician, and Supreme Court advocate; the latter merely to be a reporter of legal decisions. Peters apparently found some pleasure in the company of successful and ambitious men, but did not emulate them and even tolerated their condescension. William Wirt once observed Peters on a visit to Philadelphia, and reported to his wife:

> [Mr. and Mrs. Peters] are rather infirm of intellect and garrulous, [but] exceedingly kind, good natured & apparently cheerful. . . . It is manifest [that Peters] is not considered as the first cut . . . [Joseph] Hopkinson and [Horace] Binney and [Nicholas] Biddle, who consider themselves at the top of the fashion, think it beneath them to make an effort at entertainment in conversation at Peters' dining table. . . . It is ridiculous to accept a man's invitation and then act in such a manner as to show that they take no pleasure in it but consider it a painful condescension. . . . Peters must want either discretion or the proper

---

[209] J. Story to R. Peters, Jr., May 7, 1836, quoted in ibid., I, 231–32.
[210] See H. Wheaton to J. Story, Dec.

19, 1816; J. Story to H. Wheaton, Dec. 23, 1816; H. Wheaton to J. Story, Dec. 25, 1817; Wheaton Papers.

spirit, to ask them a second time—or what is more probable, he is content to pay the tax for the sake of the honour, and is sensible that he cannot keep his place in their circle on any other terms.[211]

Moreover, Peters did not possess the intellect of his predecessor, as the headnotes of his volumes painfully showed. Nor did he have the confidence of the Justices that Wheaton had inspired, despite Wheaton's differences with Johnson. After Washington's death in 1829 and the new appointments made in the 1830s, Peters became increasingly isolated from the Justices, and in 1843, while Story, who had remained loyal, was absent, a majority of the Court summarily fired Peters and replaced him with Benjamin Howard.[212]

Peters began a tradition of pedestrian nineteenth-century Reporters, individuals to whom Justices were increasingly reluctant to delegate authority. In the Taney and Chase Courts Justices periodically clashed with Reporters over such issues as inaccurate reporting of opinions, undue liberties taken with the facts of cases, and failure to understand subtleties.[213] Congress continued to pay the Reporter a modest salary, and opportunities for private profit were considerably diminished after *Wheaton* v. *Peters*. The result was that the office became downgraded in status, and memorable clashes of the kind engaged in by Wheaton and Johnson disappeared. In the Marshall Court, however, the Reportership was an important office, in some respects the nerve center of the Court's efforts to ensure that its decisions became authorities for as many Americans as possible.

---

[211] W. Wirt to Elizabeth Wirt, April 27, 1828, William Wirt Papers, Maryland Historical Society, Annapolis, Md.

[212] See Swisher, *Taney Period*, 303–305, for the details.

[213] See Swisher, *Taney Period*, 302–319; C. Fairman, *Reconstruction and Reunion, 1864–88* (Part One, 1971), 70–80.

# CHAPTER VII

## *Admiralty Jurisdiction*

P REVIOUS CHAPTERS have suggested that two jurisprudential questions
had emerged as particularly pressing in the early years of the Marshall Court, and neither question had been authoritatively settled by the
Court's decisions. One was the relationship among the various sovereign
entities in a republican form of government, notable for its self-conscious
fragmentation of sovereign powers. The other was which sources of law
would be regarded as authoritative in the new federal courts that had been
created by the Constitution. In *Marbury* v. *Madison* the Marshall Court
had served notice that it intended to be the last word on the delineation
of sovereign relationships under the Constitution, and that case, together
with the 1810 case of *Fletcher* v. *Peck*[1] suggested that the Court was
prepared to draw on a variety of sources, ranging from the interpreted
constitutional text to "general principles common to republican governments," as an aid in its decisions. In *United States* v. *Hudson and Goodwin*,[2] however, the Court had backed away from the use of general common law principles in deciding criminal cases in the federal courts, and
the extreme caution with which it approached the federal common law of
crimes issue suggested that it viewed sovereignty and sources of law
questions as not only interrelated but politically explosive.

In short, as the Court began business again after the War of 1812
those who followed its deliberations could have easily predicted that
among the thorniest issues it would face in the immediate future would
be those dealing with the laws of sovereignty and the sources of law in
the federal courts. In the chapters that follow we will see that this hypothetical prophecy came to pass in such areas as federal jurisdiction,
"vested" rights, slavery, the rights of Indians, and the commerce power.

A less well known fact about the Court's involvement with issues
of sovereignty and the corporate sources of law for the federal courts was
that these issues were first presented to the Court in cases testing the
constitutional limits of the federal court's admiralty jurisdiction. Admi-

---

[1] 6 Cranch 87 (1810).    [2] 7 Cranch 32 (1813).

ralty jurisdiction cases were quintessentially sovereignty and sources of law cases, and because of the importance of maritime commerce in the American economy and the special role apparently carved out for the federal courts in admiralty cases by the Constitution, admiralty jurisdiction cases came early and often to the Court's docket. Because of the timing of their arrival, these were cases in which larger themes, such as the power of the federal courts to ground decisions on general principles and the power of the federal government to regulate interstate commerce, were rehearsed. They were also cases in which the Court's consciousness of the political ramifications of its decisions, its growing awareness of its power to expand and to shape its docket, and its abiding concern with minimizing public awareness of its internal decisions surfaced.

On September 8, 1815, Joseph Story sat down at his desk in Salem to write a letter to his close friend Nathaniel Williams. "I have now before me," Story began the last paragraph, "a vastly important question. A libel has been filed in the District Court on a policy of insurance, and the question is, whether it is a 'case of Admiralty and Maritime Jurisdiction,' within the Constitution." Story added that the case would be appealed to his circuit court, that he had "examined the subject with great diligence," and that he expected to "deliver an opinion next month [which] will be not short of seventy pages." The "materials" for that opinion were "great," Story felt, "and the learning spread over a wide surface."[3]

The opinion Story alluded to, which he eventually delivered in Boston on October 30,[4] was in the strange case of *DeLovio* v. *Boit,* the tangled history of which has been largely forgotten. Story's opinion in *DeLovio,* however, has had one of the longest and most controversial lives of any issued by a lower federal court. It was celebrated[5] and pointedly ignored[6] by Story's colleagues, followed[7] and criticized[8] in subse-

---

[3] J. Story to N. Williams, Sept. 8, 1815, quoted in W. Story, *The Life and Letters of Joseph Story* (2 vols., 1851), I, 263.

[4] Docket, United States Circuit Court for the District of Massachusetts, Federal Records Center, Waltham, Mass.

[5] See Henry Wheaton's characterization, infra, text at note 139.

[6] See William Johnson's treatment, infra, text at notes 181–82.

[7] Insurance Co. v. Dunham, 78 U.S. (11 Wall.) (1871).

[8] "The opinion is . . . remarkable, in my opinion, for its boldness in asserting novel conclusions, and the facility with which authentic historical evidence that contradicted them is disposed of." Justice John Campbell in his dissent in Jackson v. Steamboat Magnolia, 20 How. 296, 336 (1857).

## Chapter VII: *Admiralty Jurisdiction*

quent nineteenth-century Supreme Court admiralty cases, and acknowledged in the 1950s to be a "classic"[9] and "the leading early case"[10] on
the admiralty jurisdiction of the federal courts, while at the same time
apparently eradicated as a precedent.[11]

*DeLovio* v. *Boit* was a seminal episode in the history of the Marshall
Court, an anticipation of some of the great themes that were to help define
the Court's role. The *DeLovio* episode can be seen as seminal despite the
fact that the case was never appealed to the Court as a body, and its
issues never authoritatively resolved in Story's lifetime. The importance
of *DeLovio,* and of the preparation of Story's opinion in the case, comes
from the clues it furnishes to the Marshall Court's character.

One clue can be found in the facts and the procedural posture of
the case itself. *DeLovio* was not only a case, as was *Fletcher* v. *Peck,*
that was laden with overtones of collusion and fraud; *DeLovio* was a
convenient case, seized upon by Story as material for the larger juristic
and political campaigns he had begun to wage. These campaigns were
begun by the artful selection of cases through use of the appeal and
certificate of division processes. By 1818, three years after the parties in
*DeLovio* had resolved not to appeal Story's opinion to the Supreme Court,
William Johnson made a public protest against the procedural strategies
Story was using. "There are eleven questions certified from the circuit
court of Massachusetts," Johnson wrote in *United States* v. *Palmer,* a
piracy case. "[B]ut of those eleven, . . . two only appear to me to arise
out of the case. . . . No motion; no evidence; no demurrer *ore tenus,* or
case stated, appears upon the transcript, on which the remaining questions
could arise. . . . I have entered my protest against having these general
questions [certified] to this court. We are constituted to decide cases, and
not to discuss themes, or digest systems."[12]

*DeLovio* was one example of a case converted into a "theme" or
a "system." The case arose out of a chain of highly curious circumstances. On October 24, 1812, an insurance contract was signed at the
office of a Boston underwriter, William Stackpole. The signers were
William Page, an agent commissioned by a Spanish merchant, José
Manuel DeLovio, and Crowell Hatch, one of a group of five Boston
merchants and lawyers who chose to underwrite a particular voyage of
DeLovio's ship, *L'Esperanza,* which was engaged in the slave trade from
Cuba to Africa. The coverage of the policy was $2,700; the premium

---

[9] Justice Felix Frankfurter in Swift &
Co. Packers v. Compania Colombiana
del Caribe, S.A., 339 U.S. 684, 692
(1950).
[10] G. Gilmore and C. Black, *The
Law of Admiralty* (1st ed., 1957), 19.

[11] Wilburn Boat Co. v. Fireman's
Fund Ins. Co., 348 U.S. 310 (1955).
[12] 3 Wheat. 610, 640–41 (1818).

paid was $900. The contract provided for payment in the event of damage to *L'Esperanza* and her crew, "lost or not lost." But well before the signing of the contract *L'Esperanza* had already been lost. She had set sail from Havana under the command of Captain Francisco de Hita on March 25, 1812, with the protection of a Spanish warship. On June 9, 1812, *L'Esperanza* was captured by a British war vessel, H.M.S. *Daring*, in the course of hostilities between Great Britain and Spain precipitated by the Napoleonic Wars. The *Daring* took *L'Esperanza* and its cargo to Sierra Leone, a British colony, where the ship was condemned as wartime spoils by a British admiralty court and confiscated. Thus when Crowell Hatch and his fellow underwriters attached their signatures to the contract insuring *L'Esperanza* they were insuring a ship that had been confiscated over four months earlier.[13]

Three years later, on May 16, 1815, a suit was filed on behalf of DeLovio in Judge John Davis's federal district court in Boston, alleging that notice of the loss of *L'Esperanza* had been given to the underwriters on March 1, 1813, and that they had refused to pay the $2,700. Thomas Selfridge, a Suffolk County practitioner who had graduated from Harvard College a year before Story, represented DeLovio; Thomas Welch, another Suffolk County lawyer who was in Story's Harvard class of 1798, represented the underwriters.[14] John Boit, the named defendant in the case, was the executor of Crowell Hatch's estate, Hatch having died in the interim.[15] Three days after Selfridge had filed to enforce DeLovio's claim on the policy, Davis issued a routine summons and complaint form, directing the underwriters to appear in his court on June 27 to respond to Selfridge's claim. The summons was served on the underwriters on May 26.

John Boit responded to this summons on June 28 by filing a motion to excuse himself from the case, and the remaining underwriters filed a motion to dismiss the case on the grounds that the court lacked subject matter jurisdiction. Davis took the case under advisement and invited additional motions on the jurisdictional question. Such motions were filed by both parties during the September term of Davis's court. On September 14, 1815, Davis heard argument on the jurisdictional question.[16] Shortly thereafter Davis announced his decision, concluding that his own court lacked jurisdiction over maritime insurance contracts, a position that potentially reduced the business and power of his court, given the significance of marine insurance cases for lawyers in Massachusetts at the

[13] DeLovio v. Boit, Case Files, Federal Records Center, Waltham, Mass. Hereafter cited as *DeLovio* Case Files.
[14] Quinquennial Catalogue of the Officers and Students of Harvard University 1632–1920 (1920), 1169, 1201.
[15] *DeLovio* Case Files.
[16] Ibid.

time.[17] At the same time that Davis rendered his decision in *DeLovio* he announced that "from this Decree the libellant [Boit] claimed an appeal to the Circuit Court of the United States for the First Circuit, next to be holden on [October 16, 1815]," and that he had allowed the appeal.[18]

Before Davis had handed down his decision in *DeLovio*, Story had already crystallized his views on the scope of federal admiralty jurisdiction. In a circuit court opinion delivered in May 1815 Story had remarked that "in my judgment . . . the admiralty has always rightfully possessed jurisdiction over all maritime contracts."[19] And at least nine days before Davis announced that *DeLovio* would be appealed to Story's circuit court, Story had written a letter to Henry Wheaton, soon to become the Supreme Court's Reporter, in which he said that "there is now pending in the District Court a libel on a policy of insurance, and it will come to the Circuit Court on a plea to the jurisdiction." He was planning to "deliver, on this occasion," Story continued, "a very elaborate opinion upon the whole Admiralty jurisdiction. . . . I have, indeed, now by me a manuscript dissertation on this subject nearly finished."[20] Three days later he wrote the letter to Nathaniel Williams quoted earlier. After having delivered his opinion in *DeLovio* at the end of October, Story wrote Williams on December 3 that he had "devoted all my leisure time for more than a month to the subject," and that he had "never pronounced an opinion in which I was more entirely satisfied."[21] His opinion, needless to say, reversed Davis's finding as to subject matter jurisdiction. After what he called "a systematic review and examination of the history of the law on the subject,"[22] Story concluded that marine insurance contracts were within the admiralty jurisdiction of the federal courts.

The *DeLovio* case, however, failed to get to the Marshall Court. While Story obviously anticipated further review, stating at the close of his opinion that he could not "pretend to conjecture, how far a superior tribunal may deem fit to entertain the principles, which I have felt it my solemn duty to avow,"[23] no additional appeal was taken. "Unfortunately," Story informed Williams, "the cause will not go to the Supreme Court; the parties [had resolved not] to carry it thither."[24] The *DeLovio* case was never remanded to the district court, and never decided on the

---

[17] See M. Horwitz, *The Transformation of American Law, 1780–1860* (1977), 227–29.

[18] *DeLovio* Case Files. Davis's decree was not dated, but it could not have been rendered any earlier than September 14, 1815, the day the case had been set for argument.

[19] *The Jerusalem*, 13 F. Cas. 559, 565 (1815).

[20] J. Story to H. Wheaton, Sept. 5, 1815, W. Story, *Life and Letters*, I, 266.

[21] J. Story to N. Williams, Dec. 3, 1815, ibid., 269.

[22] Ibid.

[23] *DeLovio v. Boit*, 7 F. Cas. 418, 444 (1815).

[24] Story to Williams, Dec. 3, 1815, supra, note 21.

merits. Various interrogatories were filed, designed to clarify whether Page, DeLovio's agent, knew that *L'Esperanza* had been lost at the time he signed the contract. Such knowledge would have constituted fraud and have invalidated the contract. Eventually, in the September 1817 Term, the case was dismissed because, as an order issued by Story's court put it, "the said José DeLovio, altho solemnly called to come into Court and prosecute his appeal, does not appear." The underwriters were instructed to pay Welch $34.00 for his "proctor's fee" and William Smith Shaw (who was Story's and Davis's clerk) $9.75 for "commission and costs of executing."[25]

Why was *DeLovio* not taken up to the Marshall Court? This puzzle becomes clearer on a close examination of the jurisdictional and procedural features of the case and the parties involved in the litigation, bearing in mind the close relationship that existed between Story and Davis.[26] The Constitution and the Judiciary Act of 1789, taken together, entrusted "all cases of admiralty and maritime jurisdiction" to the federal courts, and provided that the federal "district courts . . . shall . . . have exclusive original cognizance of all civil cases of admiralty and maritime jurisdiction."[27] Despite this language, the admiralty jurisdiction of the federal courts was neither "exclusive" nor necessarily extensive. First, admiralty cases were divided into two classes, suits *in rem* (pertaining to the ship) and suits *in personam* (pertaining to the party making the suit), and the jurisdiction of the federal courts was exclusive only with respect to *in rem* cases. *In personam* cases were affected by Section 9 of the Judiciary Act of 1789, which included the famous "saving" clause: "saving to all suitors, in all cases, the right of a common law remedy where the common law is competent to give it."[28] This scheme allowed plaintiffs in *in personam* suits who thought their cases came within the admiralty and maritime jurisdiction, and who believed that they were entitled to a "common law remedy," to choose whether to proceed in federal or state court. In the *DeLovio* case the plaintiff chose a federal court, and the Judiciary Act, as noted above, required that the federal court be a district court, that is to say Davis's court.

---

[25] *DeLovio* Case Files. The order was not in Story's handwriting; the handwriting resembled that of Shaw himself.

[26] On September 12, 1845, two days after Story's death, Davis said in a memorial service:

It was my lot to be associated with him in judicial services, for nearly the whole pattern of his official life. It was throughout, to me, a pleasant and most instructive position of my life, and the recollection of its incidents, the genial influence of his happy temperament, and the ready expression of his varied and extensive learning, enriched and adorned by the felicitous action of his energetic mind, have been with me habitual themes of grateful recollection.

Quoted in W. Story, *Life and Letters*, II, 626.

[27] U.S. Const., Art. III, Sect. 2.

[28] 1 Stat. 76–77 (1789).

## Chapter VII: *Admiralty Jurisdiction*

One result of the above scheme was that Davis, after sitting in his capacity as district judge, could not himself hear an appeal from his own court to the circuit court, and thus Story would therefore be unable to invoke the certificate of division procedure to bring the case before the Supreme Court, because there was no one to "divide" against. An 1819 letter from Marshall to Story testifies to this constraint upon the certificate of division procedure. "Another admiralty question of great consequence," Marshall wrote, "has occurred at the last term [of his circuit court] which I would carry before the Supreme court, if I could, but as I have not the privilege of dividing the Court when alone, [and] as the sum is only about 1500$, it must abide by my decision."[29] When Supreme Court Justices sat alone as circuit judges, sometimes (as in *DeLovio*) because the district judge had heard the case before, they could not certify any division; and in the case Marshall referred to in the above letter the amount in dispute had failed to meet the $2,000 floor which would have permitted access to the Supreme Court on appeal.[30] The dispute in *DeLovio,* by contrast, was over $2,000, so appeal at the request of either of the parties was theoretically possible.

Before the question of why no appeal was taken in *DeLovio* is reached, another question surfaces: why had the plaintiff in *DeLovio* chosen to proceed in federal court in the first place? If Selfridge originally assumed, as he was subsequently to argue, that his case was an admiralty case, the saving clause allowed him to bring a contract suit in the Massachusetts state courts, which gave common law remedies for breaches of marine insurance contracts. In the early nineteenth century insureds rarely sued underwriters in federal court because state courts offered jury trials in marine insurance cases and juries were perceived as hostile to underwriters.[31] Story himself had noted in an 1822 case that in marine insurance cases "the insured would almost universally elect a domestic forum . . . from private convenience, the benefit of trial by jury, and the confidence that is so justly placed in our state tribunals."[32] *DeLovio* thus represented an unusual instance in which an insured had elected a federal forum.

One reason Selfridge may have sought a federal forum was the nationality of his client. José DeLovio was a Spanish citizen, and Selfridge may have feared that Massachusetts juries would not be sympathetic to claims of Spanish merchants engaged in the slave trade, which had been illegal in the United States since 1808.[33] Massachusetts juries might

---

[29] J. Marshall to J. Story, July 13, 1819, quoted in *Proc. Mass. Hist. Soc.,* 14:326 (1901).

[30] Act of Mar. 2, 1793, 1 Stat. 33 (1793); Act of Mar. 3, 1803, 2 Stat. 244 (1803).

[31] See Horwitz, *Transformation,* 228–30, 251.

[32] Peele v. Merchants Ins. Co., 19 F. Cas. 98 (1822).

[33] Act of Mar. 2, 1807, 2 Stat. 426 (1807).

have been thought to be even more hostile to Spanish slave traders than they were to insurers.[34] Quite possibly, however, José DeLovio's nationality had nothing to do with the choice of forum. DeLovio, of course, was absent throughout the proceedings and was represented by an agent and by Selfridge. Close scrutiny of the people most deeply involved with the *DeLovio* case suggests a lack of adverseness on the jurisdictional issue. Selfridge, Welch, Davis, and Story were all close acquaintances, and Selfridge's client was an agent acting on behalf of an absent nonresident whose first language was not English. Furthermore, Story's views on the importance of an extensive federal admiralty jurisdiction had been publicly expressed even before the *DeLovio* case was filed, and Selfridge, Welch, and Davis obviously knew of those views.

DeLovio's choice of a federal forum did not likely signify any strong view on the jurisdictional question Story ultimately addressed: Selfridge did not mention subject matter jurisdiction in his initial pleadings. Nor can one assume that opposing counsel, representing the underwriters, were strongly resistant to Story's eventual position. When Story handed down his opinion in *DeLovio*, he noted to Williams that "to my surprise, I have understood that the opinion is rather popular among merchants." "They declare," Story continued, "that in mercantile cases, they are not fond of juries; and in particular, the underwriters in Boston have expressed great satisfaction at the decision."[35] Why then had the underwriters in *DeLovio* challenged the subject matter jurisdiction of the federal courts over marine insurance contract cases? The underwriters who expressed satisfaction at the decision had been on the losing side of that very issue in Story's court.

The assumption that neither counsel for DeLovio nor counsel for Boit was genuinely averse to the extension of federal jurisdiction to include marine insurance contracts helps explain the parties' decision not to appeal *DeLovio* to the Marshall Court. Because DeLovio had won the jurisdictional dispute, his counsel could not have appealed. But since Story's decision, in providing an alternative forum in which marine insurance contracts could be litigated without juries, was popular among merchants and a source of satisfaction for the underwriters in Boston, it is hardly likely that the losing party in *DeLovio* v. *Boit* would have been inclined to appeal in any case. The closeness of interest among the judges and the lawyers in *DeLovio*, a closeness which appears to have created an opportunity for Story to apply his "manuscript dissertation" to an

---

[34] One has to consider the fact, however, that the underwriters had written a policy on a ship that they knew was engaging in the slave trade and could hardly take a position of moral superiority before a jury. Yet the underwriters opposed federal jurisdiction in *DeLovio*.

[35] Story to Williams, Dec. 3, 1815, supra, note 21.

actual case, also served to preclude further appeals. With so little genuine adverseness on the major issue in the case, there was nothing to appeal.[36]

The facts and the procedural posture of *DeLovio* thus have their own inherent interest. But the case's greatest impact arguably lay in the opportunity it provided Story to rehearse some of the most vital issues that were to come before the Marshall Court in the period covered by this volume. One such issue was the nature and scope of the jurisdiction of the federal courts; another was the nature and scope of federal power to promote commerce. The first issue was raised explicitly in *DeLovio;* the second was to evolve out of the admiralty experience. "Admiralty" for Story was a word packed with significance. He associated the word with expansive federal court jurisdiction and, implicitly, with the power of federal court judges to fashion new substantive rules of law; with uniform doctrinal treatment of a whole series of high seas cases, including prize cases, instance cases,[37] and marine insurance cases; with "navigation" more generally; and, in a favorite phrase of his, with "the enterprise of commerce."[38] But when Story sat down to write the manuscript dissertation that became his opinion in *DeLovio,* most commercial enterprise in the United States was of a maritime variety, and he was not focusing at that time upon any language in the Constitution about commerce. He was thinking of how his vision of the national authority could be infused into a discourse on the admiralty jurisdiction of the federal courts. That vision, outlined in a letter to Williams three months before *DeLovio* was first filed, had included "Judicial Courts which shall embrace the whole Constitutional powers . . . for the commercial and national concerns of the United States."[39]

The evolution of Story's opinion in *DeLovio* furnishes a vignette of the life of an energetic and purposeful early-nineteenth-century jurist. Maritime business, and the presence of the sea itself, had been dominant features of Story's early environment. One of his grandfathers had been Deputy Register of the Vice Admiralty Court of Massachusetts from 1759

---

[36] This suggests that Story's interest in expanding jurisdiction in *DeLovio* was predicated on the ideas of promoting the power of the federal courts and of fostering "uniformity" in the adjudication of marine insurance disputes, rather than on supporting the positions of merchants or underwriters.

[37] In the period covered by this volume, "instance" referred to a class of cases within the admiralty and maritime jurisdiction that were not prize cases and not marine insurance cases. These cases included salvage cases, bottomry bond cases, and charter party cases. See G. Haskins and H. Johnson, *Foundations of Power: John Marshall, 1801-15* (1981), 454, 473–92, for a discussion of Marshall Court instance decisions up to 1815.

[38] J. Story, "The Progress of Jurisprudence," address delivered in 1821, reprinted in W. Story, ed., *The Miscellaneous Writings of Joseph Story* (1852), 198, 207.

[39] J. Story to N. Williams, Feb. 22, 1815, in W. Story, *Life and Letters,* I, 254.

to 1765;[40] another had "accumulated a considerable property in the ship-building business in Boston."[41] Story was born in Marblehead, Massachusetts, "a secluded fishing town,"[42] the lives of whose inhabitants had "few incidents but those perilous adventures which everywhere belong to a seafaring life."[43] In his autobiography, Story remembered his youth in Marblehead:

> [M]y delight was to . . . gaze upon the sleepless ocean; to lay myself down on the sunny rocks and listen to the deep tones of the rising and falling tide; to look abroad, when the foaming waves were driven with terrific force and uproar against the barren cliffs or the rocky promontories. . . .
> But still more was I pleased, in a calm summer day, to lay myself down alone on one of the beautiful heights which overlook the harbor of Salem, and to listen to the broken sounds of the hammers in the distant shipyards. . . .[44]

Salem, across the bay from Marblehead, was the town in which Story first established his law practice in 1801. Although his practice started slowly, and he was periodically tempted to "migrate southward,"[45] by 1807 he was regularly litigating maritime cases in the Massachusetts courts.[46] Maritime law, and maritime issues generally, became Story's passion in the years between 1807 and his appointment to the Supreme Court in 1811. He began a manuscript, *Digest of the Law*,[47] which placed a heavy emphasis on the topics of prize law, admiralty jurisdiction, and marine insurance. He published in 1810 a third edition of Charles Abbott's treatise, *The Law Relative to Merchant Ships and Seamen*, writing in the preface that maritime law should be important to "the lawyer and the merchant; to the statesman and the private gentleman."[48] As a congressman from Massachusetts in the 1808–1809 session,

---

[40] J. Story, "Autobiography," in W. Story, *Miscellaneous Writings*. Story's "autobiography" consisted of a long letter he wrote to his son on January 23, 1831. See also K. Wroth, "The Massachusetts Vice Admiralty Court and the Federal Admiralty Jurisdiction," *Am. J. Legal Hist.*, 6:250, 251 (1962).
[41] J. Story, quoted in W. Story, *Life and Letters*, I, 2.
[42] Ibid., 7.
[43] Ibid.
[44] Ibid., 8–9.
[45] J. Story to Gabriel Duvall, Mar. 30, 1803, in W. Story, *Life and Letters*, I, 103. Cf. J. Story to Nathaniel Williams, June 6, 1805, in ibid., 104, 105

("I have long had a desire to sojourn in some southern clime, more congenial with my nature than the petty prejudices and sullen coolness of New England").
[46] See, e.g., Cleveland v. Fettyplace, 3 Mass. 344 (1802); Appleton v. Crowninshield, 3 Mass. 389 (1807). See also G. Dunne, *Justice Joseph Story and the Rise of the Supreme Court* (1970), 101–102.
[47] The manuscript was never published and is currently in the Harvard Law School Library.
[48] C. Abbott, *The Law Relative to Merchant Ships and Seamen* (3d ed., 1810), ix.

he favored "a gradual increase in our naval establishment,"[49] clashing with Jefferson in the process, and opposed the Embargo Acts of 1808, which in Story's view "prostrated the whole commerce of America," and resulted in "our navigation being withdrawn from the ocean," which gave "Great Britain . . . a triumphant monopoly of the commerce of the world."[50]

One can see in the last quoted sentence the association Story made in his early career between navigation on the high seas and commerce. For him, coming to maturity on the coast of New England and witnessing the dependence of that region, and of the entire eastern seaboard, on oceangoing trade, the association was obvious. Eventually the promotion and protection of commerce was to become enshrined by Story as a principle "conceived in political wisdom, justified by experience, and approved by the soundest maxims of national economy."[51] But at this point in Story's career larger theories of commerce were subordinated to the more immediate issues he saw raised by maritime law cases: issues of Union, national power, and federal court supremacy.

In an 1812 letter to Williams, Story talked first of "deliberate [efforts] to inflame animosities between the Northern and Southern people, and thereby promote more readily a separation of the States." He was "thoroughly convinced" that "the leading Federalists meditate a severance of the Union," and he "abhor[red] their conduct." In the next paragraph he began to talk of the "beautiful science" of the "Prize Law," and he expressed "a hope that you will be engaged deeply in the Admiralty." Then came the conclusion of these ruminations:

> I have no doubt that [the Admiralty] jurisdiction [of the federal courts] rightfully extends over every maritime contract and tort, and the more [that] jurisdiction is known, the more it will be courted. I hope the Supreme Court will have an opportunity to enter largely into its jurisdiction both as an Instance and a Prize Court.[52]

The above letter was written after Story had completed his first Term on the Court; its conclusion was not simply abstract juristic theory. *DeLovio* was the first of Story's judicial efforts to ensure that the hopes he had expressed in the letter would be fulfilled. He had begun preparation for the "opportunity" that *DeLovio* was to represent by collecting and digesting scholarly materials, such as his *Digest* and the edition of Abbott.

---

[49] J. Story in W. Story, *Miscellaneous Writings*, 30.

[50] Ibid., 32.

[51] J. Story, "Memorial against Restrictions on Commerce" (1820), ibid. 242, 261.

[52] J. Story to N. Williams, Aug. 24, 1812, in W. Story, *Life and Letters*, I, 229–30.

By September 5, 1815, when he was preparing his "very elaborate opinion" in *DeLovio,* Story told Henry Wheaton about the sources he had assembled:

> I have Godolphin, Zouch, Exton, and Spelman on the Admiralty Jurisdiction. They are principally controversial as to the question of Jurisdiction. Brown's Admiralty and Clarke's Praxis (which has been translated by Hall, but I have the original) are the best on points of practice. . . .[53]

In that same letter Story complained about his inability to find a copy of "Sir Leoline Jenkins's works," and asked Wheaton whether "they could be procured at New York." He also made it clear what use he intended to make of the authorities he had collected:

> In the United States the Constitution has given to the Courts of the United States cognizance of "all cases of admiralty and maritime jurisdiction," which I hope to show includes all cases *originally* within the admiralty jurisdiction . . . and that they are—all maritime contracts wherever made, and all torts and injuries on the high seas or in port within the ebb and flow of the tide."[54]

His sources assembled, his manuscript dissertation prepared, and the *DeLovio* case shepherded up to his circuit court, Story was ready to strike a blow for commerce, Union, and the federal courts.

*DeLovio* was, Story told Williams in December 1815, "the most elaborate opinion I [have yet] composed." It embraced "a complete digest of all the [relevant] cases [Story could find] at Common Law and in the Admiralty."[55] Much of Story's opinion in *DeLovio* was presented in the form of a historical morality play. According to Story's history, the "ancient jurisdiction of the admiralty"[56] had been very extensive, both on the Continent and in England. The villain Coke, however, had "entertained not only a jealousy of, but an enmity against that jurisdiction,"[57] and had erroneously interpreted (or perhaps deliberately distorted) cases "to disprove" the presence and scope of the admiralty.[58] Story reviewed Coke's cases and concluded that they "entirely fail of their intended purpose; and leave the current of ancient authority [on behalf of extensive admiralty jurisdiction] flowing with a uniform and irresistible force in its favor."[59] In passing Story noted that he found Coke's commentaries

---

[53] Story to Wheaton, Sept. 5, 1815, supra, note 20.

[54] Ibid.

[55] Story to Williams, Dec. 3, 1815, supra, note 21.

[56] 7 F. Cas. at 418.

[57] Ibid., 422.

[58] Ibid., at 425.

[59] Ibid.

# Chapter VII: *Admiralty Jurisdiction*

"laborious";[60] that Coke made "gratuitous assum[ptions]";[61] that at least one of Coke's citations was "probably . . . wrong," for there was "no case at all applicable to the subject" in the yearbook from which Coke had quoted;[62] that Coke "attempted to evade the force of . . . argument[s]" on behalf of the admiralty by making "perfectly gratuitous . . . construction[s]";[63] and that, in short, most of Coke's "very positive assertions"[64] about the jurisdiction of the admiralty courts were either disingenuous or wrong.

But although the sinister Coke had been exposed, the battle had not yet been won. Story had attempted to show that "the true nature and extent of the ancient jurisdiction of the admiralty" had been far more extensive than Coke claimed. But he conceded that statues passed at the time of Richard II, and ratified at the time of Henry IV, had arguably constricted the admiralty's original jurisdiction:[65]

> The courts of common law, [in construing those statutes], have held, that the jurisdiction of the admiralty is confined to contracts and things exclusively made and done upon the high seas; that it has no jurisdiction over torts, offenses or injuries, done in ports within the bodies of counties, notwithstanding the places be within the ebb and flow of the tide; nor over maritime contracts made within the bodies of counties or beyond sea, although they are, in some measure, to be executed upon the high seas; nor of contracts made upon the high seas to be executed upon land, touching things not in their own nature maritime, such as a contract for payment of money. . . . So that, upon the common law construction of these statutes, the admiralty, as to contracts, is left with the idle and vain authority to enforce contracts, which are made upon the high seas to be executed upon the high seas.[66]

At this point Story could have adopted the strategy of confession and avoidance, since, as he was to subsequently point out, "whatever may in England be the binding authority of the common law decisions upon this subject, we in the United States were at liberty to re-examine the doctrines."[67] A re-examination was possible not only because under American juristic practice the common law decisions of English courts were not followed in all instances, but also because of the references to admiralty and maritime jurisdiction in the Constitution and the Judiciary Act of 1789. Having made his observations about the original nature of admiralty jurisdiction, it would have been possible for Story simply to report that it had been restricted by statutes and common law decisions

---

[60] Ibid., 427.
[61] Ibid.
[62] Ibid., 428.
[63] Ibid., 430.

[64] Ibid.
[65] Ibid., 425.
[66] Ibid. 426.
[67] Ibid., 441.

that were peculiar products of English politics and culture. He rejected this strategy and continued the attack on Coke and the common law courts' construction of the statutes. That move, exemplifying a Storyesque combination of bravado, self-confidence, and combativeness, may have weakened the stature of the *DeLovio* opinion and precipitated comments such as that made in Justice Campbell's 1857 dissent, previously cited.

One can see, however, why Story thought an attack on Coke and the "silent and steady march" of "the courts of common law"[68] necessary. The reason, as he subsequently said in his *DeLovio* opinion, had to do with "etymology," by which he meant the historical associations of words or phrases. The ultimate question for Story in *DeLovio* was a question of the construction of the Constitution: he was searching for "the true interpretation of the clause 'all cases of admiralty and maritime jurisdiction.' "[69] While he recognized that American judges could "construe the jurisdiction of the admiralty upon enlarged and liberal principles," he understood that the "received use" of the words "admiralty" and "maritime jurisdiction" would play a significant part in their interpretation. And he further understood that one possible "exposition" of "received use" was "the jurisdiction of the admiralty as acknowledged in England at the American Revolution."[70] Were this exposition accepted, the English common law interpretation of admiralty jurisdiction might become the reference point for American constitutional language. Story wanted to make sure that

> [T]here is no solid reason for construing the terms of the constitution in a narrow and limited sense, or for engrafting upon them the restrictions of English statutes, or decisions at common law founded on those statutes, which were sometimes dictated by jealousy, and sometimes by misapprehension, which are often contradictory, and rarely supported by any consistent principle.[71]

The larger jurisprudential assumption that lay behind Story's remarks has been previously commented upon but bears repeating here. His strategy in *DeLovio* assumed that the meaning of constitutional language could be informed by common law, civil law, or natural law concepts. Law, while capable of separation into discrete jurisdictions and tribunals, was nonetheless a holistic entity. Story was fearful that if the *DeLovio* case were appealed to the Supreme Court "the narrow and perplexed doctrines of the common law [might be] engraft[ed] . . . upon the constitution." He was "not aware," he said, "of any superior sanctity in the decisions at common law . . . which should entitle them to outweigh

---

[68] Ibid., 426.
[69] Ibid., 441.
[70] Ibid., 441–42.
[71] Ibid., 443.

the very able and learned doctrines of the great civilians of the admiralty." He had consulted treatise writers in preparing his *DeLovio* opinion because, as he put it, "where could we so properly search for information on this subject, as in the works of those jurists who have adorned the maritime courts from age to age, and made its jurisdiction the pride and study of their lives?"[72]

With this sentence the methodology Story had employed in *DeLovio* came full circle, and the significance of the opinion as an interpretive exercise becomes apparent. All the authorities Story had assembled, in an opinion for whose "length" he "[made] no apology,"[73] were directed at a single proposition: in American jurisprudence constitutional law, civil law, common law, the decisions of past courts, the writings of commentators, and "fundamental principles of reason and justice" were all of a piece. This meant that historical forays of the kind that Story had made in the first part of *DeLovio* were not simply antiquarian exercises. They were inquiries into the meaning of law itself. History was a source of the meaning of language and language a representation of the meaning of law.

But the meaning of history was informed by present concerns. Story's own sense of the current importance of admiralty and maritime issues had motivated him to interpret purposively the ancient jurisdiction of admiralty and the statute seeking to restrict it; he had gone so far as to announce his conclusions on the scope of admiralty jurisdiction in advance of the *DeLovio* case itself. But since under the interpretive canons of early-nineteenth-century jurisprudence such a fusion of contemporary politics, history, and "liberal and enlarged" legal analysis was not only permissible but welcome, Story was no more apologetic about his historical scholarship than about the length of his opinion. One sentence at the outset of *DeLovio* captured his stance. "The vast importance and novelty of the questions which are involved in this suit," he wrote, "render it impossible to come to a correct decision without a thorough examination of the whole jurisdiction of the admiralty."[74] Story knew perfectly well what he meant by "correct" in that sentence and what he meant by "thorough." He was also entirely aware of the novelty of the questions he was asking, and he knew their answers in advance.

In his discussion of "etymology" Story had reached the most profound and revealing portion of *DeLovio;* from that point the opinion became less sophisticated and more assertive. To buttress his claim that the constitutional phrase "admiralty jurisdiction" could be illuminated by "an examination of the authority and powers of the vice admiralty courts in the United States under the colonial government," Story merely

---

[72] Ibid., 442.     [73] Ibid., 418.     [74] Ibid.

declared that "the commissions of the crown gave the courts . . . a most ample jurisdiction over all maritime contracts. . . ."[75] He then cited a "second hand" report of a "usual" court commission and added: "In point of fact the vice admiralty court of Massachusetts, before the Revolution, exercised a jurisdiction, far more extensive than that of the admiralty in England."[76] In reviewing the practice of the Massachusetts Vice Admiralty Court between 1718 and 1772, one modern scholar has concluded that "the court's exercise of the traditional broad powers of admiralty was coincidental and sporadic, hardly worthy of the claims which Story made for it," and that "in colonial Massachusetts 'admiralty' seems to have meant a specialized forum dealing primarily with wage and revenue actions."[77]

Story's next argument was even less supported by legal authorities. "The advantages resulting to the commerce and navigation of the United States from a uniformity of rules and decisions in all maritime questions," he claimed, "authorize us to believe that national policy, as well as juridical logic, require the clause of the constitution to be so construed, as to embrace all maritime contracts, torts, and injuries, or in other words, to embrace all those causes which originally and inherently belonged to the admiralty, before any statuable restriction." It was hard to know why the advantages Story cited "required" that particular construction. But he had fastened on a powerful policy argument for entrusting commercial cases to the federal courts: "uniformity," which came to be equated with the furthering of certainty, predictability, and confidence among persons who regularly engaged in commercial transactions.[78] The argument that the federal courts were designed to serve a specialized class of clients and to adjudicate a specialized type of law (whether admiralty or the common law of commercial tradesmen) and its principal corollary, that commerce among this specialized class, in all sections of the Union, would be facilitated by "a uniformity of rules and decisions," retained their viability well beyond Story's lifetime.[79] It was ironic that an argument originated by Story came to be regarded as a sop to large commercial interests, for, as we shall see, Story was interested in having the federal courts protect not only merchants but shipwrights and material men as well.

---

[75] Ibid., 442.
[76] Ibid., 442, note 47.
[77] Wroth, "Massachusetts Vice Admiralty Court," 364–65.
[78] J. Story, "Memorial against Restrictions on Commerce," in W. Story, *Miscellaneous Writings,* 247. See the discussion in Horwitz, *Transformation,* 250–52.

[79] One can see the explicit use of the "uniformity" argument in such admiralty cases as The Lottawanna, 21 Wall. 558, 575 (1874), Workman v. New York City, 179 U.S. 552 (1900), and the famous case of Southern Pacific Co. v. Jensen, 244 U.S. 205 (1917).

# Chapter VII: *Admiralty Jurisdiction*

The doctrinal significance of *DeLovio* remains to be considered. On the one hand the immediate results of Story's effort were anticlimactic; on the other, *DeLovio* can be seen as the unacknowledged but omnipresent backdrop to all the Marshall Court admiralty cases discussed in this volume. The failure of the parties in *DeLovio* to appeal left Story's opinion as a nisi prius decision, technically having authority only in Story's circuit; and the Marshall Court as a body never squarely considered the precise question raised by *DeLovio*.[80] In addition, while the logic of Story's opinion in *DeLovio* led toward exclusive federal court admiralty jurisdiction over marine insurance contracts, the saving clause and the legacy of English practice compelled him to admit that "there can be no possible question that the courts of common law have acquired a concurrent jurisdiction."[81] All *DeLovio* did, therefore, was to offer an alternative forum to suitors in marine insurance cases, and, as we have seen, that alternative was rarely elected. Seven years after *DeLovio* Story said that he "supposed the [doctrinal] point [of *DeLovio*] rather of theoretical than practical importance."[82]

But it is also possible to identify some of the major doctrinal issues confronted by the Court in the period covered by this volume as originating in *DeLovio*. In particular, it is possible to see in *DeLovio* the association of a series of code words that had deep significance in the literate culture of the Marshall Court: "commerce," "national policy," "uniformity," "etymology," "ancient authority," and "jurisdiction." For Story those words were associated in a vision linking the past to the future, a vision in which "great national interests . . . shall bind us in an indissoluble chain," and in which "enlarged and liberal institutions," such as "Judicial Courts which shall embrace the whole constitutional powers," would promote "commercial and national concerns" and "render . . . harmless . . . the factions of the great states."[83] Translated into judicial policy, the words signified an aggressive extension of the jurisdiction of the federal courts at the expense of the state courts, a promotion of "commercial and national concerns," and a facilitation of "great national interests." Out of a marine insurance case had emerged not only a vision but a source of potential analogies for the Marshall Court. Admiralty jurisdiction was to state common law jurisdiction as, potentially,

---

[80] *DeLovio* was not explicitly followed by the Court until Insurance Co. v. Dunham, supra, note 7. Two of Story's colleagues on the Marshall Court rejected the decision in circuit opinions, Johnson in *The Amanda*, discussed infra, text at notes 175–76, and Baldwin in Barns v. The James and Catherine, 2 F. Cas. 410 (1832).

[81] 7 F. Cas. at 444. Story went on to say that "upon the principles of the ancient common law, it is not easy to trace a legitimate origin to it."

[82] Peele v. Merchants Ins. Co., supra, note 32.

[83] Story to Williams, Feb. 22, 1815, supra, note 39.

the federal judiciary, exercising "the whole constitutional powers," was to state courts and, allowing for the separation of powers principle, as Congress was to state legislatures. Moreover, an expansive reading of the phrase "admiralty and maritime jurisidiction" was to a restrictive reading of that phrase as an expansive reading of the federal commerce power was to a restrictive reading.

Story had thus packed a whole series of jurisprudential and political referents into the language of *DeLovio,* and those referents were to emerge, sparking vivid and polemicized disputes, in the succeeding years of the Court's history. A question such as whether the admiralty jurisdiction of the federal courts was limited, as Story had suggested in *DeLovio,* to "ports within the ebb and flow of the tide"[84] had, in the ideological context of the time, major economic and political implications. In a sense the question posed by *DeLovio* was whether the vision motivating that opinion was to become the vision of the Marshall Court. Yet the very posture of the *DeLovio* case prevented the Court from squarely addressing Story's opinion itself.

*DeLovio* serves, finally, as a topical guidepost to the Marshall Court's admiralty cases between 1815 and 1835. In one way or another, Story's opinion touched upon each of the three principal areas into which those cases can be conveniently subdivided. It was, of course, a preview of the Court's admiralty jurisdiction cases, which were to serve as the principal forum in which the large juristic issues Story raised in *DeLovio* were aired. These issues will be explored in the remainder of this chapter. The opinion was also informed by the Court's activity in prize cases, which reached a peak in the 1814 Term and continued sporadically throughout the decades after *DeLovio,* and in which Story and Henry Wheaton took a special interest. Those cases are considered in Chapter XIII. Finally, *DeLovio* was a maritime contract case, a case that, had it been decided on the merits, would have involved an inquiry into the nature and practice of marine insurance. Marine insurance cases are also discussed in Chapter XIII. Taken together, jurisdiction cases, prize cases, and marine insurance cases made up the bulk of the Marshall Court's admiralty business between 1815 and 1835.

As he was about to leave Salem for the 1819 Term, Story wrote a letter to Sir William Scott thanking him for "the favorable manner in which you have been pleased to speak of the former volumes [of Gallison's Reports of Story's circuit opinions], the decisions in which . . . were made under an anxious desire to administer the law of Prize upon

---

[84] 7 F. Cas. at 419.

the principles which had been so luminously pointed out by yourself.'' Story then turned to more general matters. ''We had not,'' he said, referring to American federal courts at large, ''the benefit of a long-established and well-settled [admiralty] jurisdiction, and of an ancient customary law. . . . The Admiralty Law was in a great measure a new system to us; and we had to grope our way as well as we could.''[85]

In the letter Story was alluding not only to the ''minute discussions . . . indulged in on mere points of practice'' that filled the Court's early admiralty cases, but to the absence in American admiralty jurisprudence of not only a ''well-settled jurisdiction'' but ''an ancient customary law.'' Three questions were raised by any admiralty case that came to the Court. The first was whether the particular case was within the admiralty jurisdiction of the federal courts. That question was sometimes difficult, but even when it was not, a second question was immediately raised: what law were the federal courts, in the exercise of their admiralty jurisdiction, to follow? While that question was answered unequivocally by Marshall in an 1828 case, the directness of his answer was, we will see, belied by the Court's practice. And even if a case was clearly an admiralty case, and the law to be followed in admiralty cases clearly understood, a third question surfaced: what was the substantive and procedural content of that law? As Story put it in his letter to Scott, ''every case, whether of practice or principle, was required to be measured out.''[86]

Here our focus is on the first two questions: what types of cases were included in and excluded from the admiralty jurisdiction of the federal courts, and what law was to be followed by the federal courts in their exercise of admiralty jurisdiction. To a modern student of admiralty law the questions are not easily distinguishable, but here is another instance where modern conceptual schemes lead one astray in analyzing the Marshall Court.

Under modern admiralty practice the ''subject matter jurisdiction'' question is, as a practical matter, inseparable from the choice of law question. Under *Erie* v. *Tompkins*,[87] the federal courts, when entertaining diversity cases in equity or in common law, are bound to follow the substantive law rules of the states in which they sit, but the federal courts, when sitting in admiralty, continue to follow federal admiralty law. Moreover, the distinction between equity and law jurisdictions has been abolished in the federal courts, and amended jurisdictional pleas are routinely permitted. Under the saving clause, of course, plaintiffs have the election of being in federal or state court, but only where their cases are admiralty

---

[85] J. Story to Sir William Scott [Lord Stowell], Jan. 14, 1819, in W. Story, *Life and Letters*, I, 318.

[86] Ibid., 319.
[87] 304 U.S. 64 (1938).

cases. Resolution of the subject matter jurisdiction question, then, largely resolves the choice of law question.[88]

During the period covered by this volume, we have seen, clear conceptual divisions between state law and federal law did not exist. The Marshall Court and the lower federal courts sometimes followed the local law of the states in which they sat and sometimes regarded their decisions as governed by general common law, which was distinct from the decisions of state courts. At a more abstract level, the jurisprudence of the Marshall Court did not make definite divisions between systems of law (constitutional, common, or civil) or sources of law (treatises, precedents, or principles of political theory). Judges were regarded as relatively free to draw upon whatever legal sources, analogies, or authorities existed, and at the same time that discretion was not regarded as the equivalent of making law.

But if conceptual divisions among systems or sources of law were relatively blurred in the period of the Marshall Court, conceptual divisions among types of subject matter jurisdiction would appear at first glance to have been distinct. Two passages from opinions written by Marshall in admiralty cases are illustrative. In *The Sarah,* an 1823 case, Marshall said, for the Court,

> The [federal] District Courts are Courts both of common law and admiralty jurisdiction. In the trial of all cases of seizure, on land, the Court sits as a Court of common law. In cases of seizure made on waters navigable by vessels of ten tons burden and upwards, the Court sits as a Court of admiralty. . . .
>
> Although the two jurisdictions are vested in the same tribunal, they are as distinct from each other as if they were vested in different tribunals, and can no more be blended, than a Court of chancery with a Court of common law.[89]

And in *American Ins. Co. v. Canter,*[90] a case decided five years later, Marshall reaffirmed this position, and was more explicit about the relationship between subject matter jurisdiction and substantive law in admiralty cases. Among the questions raised in the *Canter* case was whether an act of Congress establishing territorial courts in the territory of Florida and vesting those courts with jurisdiction ''in all cases arising under the law and Constitution of the United States'' gave the Florida territorial

---

[88] This paragraph of course conceals myriad complexities. See D. Robertson, *Admiralty and Federalism* (1970), 271–83; Gilmore and Black, *Admiralty,* 344–58, 374–86; T. Stevens, ''Erie R.R. v. Tompkins and the Uniform General Maritime Law,'' *Harv. L. Rev.,* 64:246 (1950); D. Currie, ''Federalism and the Admiralty,'' *Sup. Ct. Rev.,* 158 (1960).

[89] 8 Wheat. 391, 394 (1823).

[90] 1 Pet. 511 (1828).

courts jurisdiction over salvage cases, which were conceded to be admiralty cases.

Marshall rephrased the question as "whether cases in admiralty and cases arising under the laws and Constitution of the United States are identical."[91] He then proceeded to answer the question, again for the Court:

> If we have recourse to that pure fountain from which all the jurisdiction of the Federal Courts is derived, we find language employed which cannot well be misunderstood. The Constitution declares that "the judicial power shall extend to all cases in law and equity, arising under this Constitution, the laws of the United States, and treaties made, or which shall be made, under their authority; to all cases affecting ambassadors, or other public ministers, and consuls; to all cases of admiralty and maritime jurisdiction."
>
> The Constitution certainly contemplates these as three distinct classes of cases; and if they are distinct, the grant of jurisdiction over one of them does not confer jurisdiction over either of the other two. . . . A case in admiralty does not, in fact, arise under the Constitution or laws of the United States. These cases are as old as navigation itself; and the law, admiralty and maritime, as it has existed for ages, is applied by our Courts to the cases as they arise."[92]

It would appear from these two passages that the Court regarded federal admiralty cases as clearly distinct from federal common law cases, and "the law, admiralty and maritime, as it has existed for ages" as equally distinct from common law, constitutional law, local law, or equity. But practice was much less clear-cut than the theoretical structure established by Marshall's two passages would suggest. First of all, the language in the saving clause referred to a "common law remedy" in the same sentence in which it spoke of "all civil causes of admiralty and maritime jurisdiction."[93] So the fact that a plaintiff had to have an admiralty cause of action to *qualify* for the saving clause did not mean that the same plaintiff was precluded from having his cause adjudicated under state *common law*, which was regarded as distinct from "the law, admiralty and maritime." A fair statement of the situation in the early nineteenth century was made by Supreme Court Justice Marlon Pitney in 1917:

> There is no doubt that throughout the entire life of the nation under the Constitution [until 1917], state courts not only have exercised concurrent jurisdiction with the courts of admiralty . . . but that in

---

[91] Ibid., 545.
[92] Ibid., 545–46.

[93] 1 Stat. 76–77 (1789).

exercising such jurisdiction they have . . . adopted as rules of decision their local laws and statutes, recognizing no obligation . . . to apply the law maritime.[94]

Designating a case as within the admiralty jurisdiction of the federal courts, then, did not automatically mean that it would be decided by reference to the law maritime. Moreover, jurisdictional and substantive rules in the federal courts were not as rigid as Marshall's language in *The Sarah* and *Canter* suggested.

In *The Sarah* itself Marshall moderated the severity of his own pronouncement. The case involved a seizure of 422 casks of wine that had been imported on the brig *Sarah*. While it was first thought that the seizure occurred on navigable waters, subsequent evidence revealed that the wine had been seized on land.[95] This meant that the case was not properly within the admiralty jurisdiction. But the claimant in *The Sarah* had asked for a jury trial, impermissible in civil admiralty cases, and the district court had allowed one. The jury found against the claimant, who then appealed to the Supreme Court. If these actions meant that the case was now "a case at common law," Marshall noted, "it would be necessary to dismiss this appeal," because the claimant had used the wrong appellate procedure: "the judgment could not be brought before this Court but by writ of error." However, if the case were "considered as a case of admiralty jurisdiction, the sentence ought to be reversed, because it could not be pronounced by a Court of Admiralty," the seizure of the wine casks having been made on land.[96] A rigid reading of the categories of jurisdiction, then, would have resulted in a dismissal of the case.

Marshall, however, thought it "most advisable to reverse all the proceedings . . . and to remand the case to the District Court . . . with directions to allow the libel [the suit in admiralty] to be amended, and to take such farther proceedings . . . as law and justice may require."[97] Wheaton added a historical note to Marshall's disposition of *The Sarah*. He reviewed the land-water distinction in seizure cases and noted that remanding to the district courts with leave to amend would be the practice in subsequent cases. That procedure was especially striking because in *The Sarah* the very courts allowing amendment of a claim in admiralty were courts that had no jurisdiction over that claim. Marshall had not strictly observed his own statement that "the two jurisdictions [of admiralty and common law] . . . are as distinct from each other as if they were vested in different tribunals."

Not only were the jurisdictional bright lines brighter in theory than

---

[94] Southern Pacific Co. v. Jensen, supra, note 79, at 254.
[95] 8 Wheat. at 391.
[96] Ibid., 395.
[97] Ibid., 395–96.

in practice, the stark division laid down in *Canter* between "the law, admiralty and maritime" and other substantive rules of decision was more blurred than Marshall's language implied. An example was the Court's treatment of violations of criminal statutes that occurred on the high seas. In *The Schooner Hoppet* v. *The United States*,[98] the question was raised whether prosecutions under the Non-Intercourse Act of 1809 (which prohibited the importation of foreign wines into the United States) were required, when brought in an admiralty court, to conform to the common law requirement that criminal indictments make specific charges. As Marshall put it for the Court, "It is not controverted that in all proceedings in courts of common law, either against the person or the thing for penalties or forfeitures, the allegation that the act charged was committed in violation of . . . the provisions of a particular statute will justify condemnation, unless, independent of this allegation, a case be stated which shows that the law has been violated."[99] In *The Schooner Hoppet* no specific "case" had been stated. Marshall then asked whether "this rule appl[ies] to . . . a Court of admiralty." His answer was that it did:

> It is not contended that all those technical niceties which are unimportant in themselves, and standing only on precedents of which the reason cannot be discerned, should be transplanted from the Courts of common law into the Courts of admiralty. But a rule so essential to justice and fair proceeding as that which requires a substantial statement of the offense upon which the prosecution is founded, must be the rule of every Court where justice is the object. . . . It would require a series of clear and unequivocal precedents to show that this rule is dispensed within Courts of admiralty.[100]

The quoted passage is particularly revealing for its use of a distinction between "technical niceties [whose] reason cannot be discerned" and rules "essential to justice." That distinction can be said to assume that "the law, admiralty and maritime" was as implicitly subject to the dictates of reason and justice as any body of law being interpreted by the Court. The law of admiralty could be infused with substantive common law rules when those rules exemplified principles that, as Marshall put it in another part of his *Schooner Hoppet* opinion, were "demanded by the free genius of our institutions" and "familiar . . . to every gentleman of the profession."[101] Only "a series of clear and unequivocal precedents" could preserve the autonomy of admiralty rules, and, as Story's letter to Scott indicated, clear and unequivocal precedents in admiralty were precisely what the Marshall Court lacked.

---

[98] 7 Cranch 389 (1813).
[99] Ibid., 393.

[100] Ibid., 394.
[101] Ibid., 393.

The issue raised in *Schooner Hoppet* also appeared in the Court's opinions on the existence of federal common law of crimes, delivered about the same time. While those opinions are discussed in detail elsewhere, they bore a relationship to the Court's admiralty jurisdiction decisions that is worth mentioning here. The Court's best known common law of crimes opinion, *United States* v. *Hudson and Goodwin,* decided in 1813, involved a domestic prosecution of newspaper editors in Connecticut for criminal libel and thus on its face had no admiralty component. But the admiralty implications of Justice Johnson's opinion in *Hudson and Goodwin,* which intimated that no federal common law of crimes existed, were immediately perceived. In cases where crimes that were not specifically covered by statutes occurred on the high seas, was *Hudson and Goodwin* or "the law, admiralty and maritime" to govern? Johnson, in an unreported circuit opinion in 1813, held that the common law of crimes should not be infused into admiralty because the result would be to allow federal judges, in cases where nonstatutory crimes were alleged, to "be left at large to be governed by their own views of the fitness of things."[102] On the other hand, Story, in an 1813 opinion in *United States* v. *Coolidge,* a case that he certified to the Court three years later, held that nonstatutory crimes committed on the high seas were "punishable by fine and imprisonment: . . . in the absence of positive law."[103]

Story delivered the *Coolidge* opinion in October 1813, two years before *DeLovio,* at a time when his research on admiralty jurisdiction was still in an embryonic state. As a result, he did not fully develop the admiralty implications of the case, nor clearly distinguish the issue of whether the federal courts had a general common law jurisdiction from the issue of whether common law rules of decision could be employed by the federal courts in the exercise of their admiralty jurisdiction. Peter Du Ponceau, in a scholarly commentary on the decision in 1824, understood the difficulties in Story's opinion:

> Whatever else it might be, [*United States* v. *Coolidge*] was clearly not a case of common law. It belonged to the admiralty jurisdiction. . . .
> It appears that the case of the *United States* v. *Hudson and Goodwin* . . . had been decided by the Supreme Court on an *ex parte* argument, the counsel for the defendant having declined the discussion of the [federal common law of crimes] point. This Mr. Justice Story . . . very properly considered as leaving the whole question still open, and as by no means setting the law upon it; but as the learned judge was well aware of the difference between that case and the one before

---

[102] Trial of William Butler for Piracy (unpublished pamphlet, Harvard Law School Library, 1813), 32.

[103] United States v. Coolidge, 25 F. Cas. 619 (1813).

450

him, and that the jurisdiction of the Court could be sustained on the latter on much stronger grounds than in the former, it is much to be regretted that he thought it necessary to travel out of his straight path, and to abandon an impregnable fortress to seek battle in the open field. . . .

[T]he difference between the case of the *United States v. Hudson and Goodwin* and the *[Coolidge]* case [can be] immediately perceived. The former was a case of libel of which no express cognisance is given by the Constitution to the federal courts, while [the *Coolidge* case] was one of admiralty jurisdiction. . . . The admiralty is governed by a peculiar law of its own, which may be called (*as it is the fashion to call everything*) a part of the common law; still it is not the common law in its usual and more restricted acceptation. . . .[104]

Du Ponceau's comments penetrated to a core set of issues in the Marshall Court's admiralty jurisdiction cases, and at the same time revealed the difficulties those issues raised for early-nineteenth-century jurists. Admiralty was an area in which the *jurisdiction* of the federal courts seemed clearly established, although it had been qualified by the saving clause. Much less clear, however, were the *substantive rules of decision* to be employed by the federal courts in the exercise of their admiralty jurisdiction. Here Du Ponceau's analysis clarified what Story's opinion in *Coolidge* had obfuscated. Story had said in Coolidge:

I admit in the most explicit terms that the Courts of the United States are courts of limited jurisdiction, and cannot exercise any authorities which are not confided to them by the Constitution and laws made in principle thereof. But I do contend, that once an authority is lawfully given, the nature and extent of that authority, and the mode in which it shall be exercised, must be regulated by the rules of the common law.[105]

He then went on to say that he used the term common law in "its broadest sense, including equity and admiralty."[106] But, as Du Ponceau noted, the "peculiar law" of the admiralty was "not the common law in its usual and more restricted acceptation," although it was "the fashion to call everything a part of the common law."

*United States v. Coolidge* eventually reached the Marshall Court in the 1816 Term, but on the more general question of "whether [Story's federal] circuit court had jurisdiction over common law offences against

---

[104] P. Du Ponceau, *A Dissertation in the Nature and Extent of the Jurisdiction of the Courts of the United States* (1824), 10–11. Emphasis supplied.

[105] 25 F. Cas. at 619.
[106] Ibid.

the United States.''[107] A variety of circumstances, which are detailed elsewhere, combined to result in the Court's not reviewing *Hudson and Goodwin* and therefore not articulating any distinction between federal court jurisdiction over nonstatutory crimes occurring on navigable waters and those occurring on land. But *Coolidge* had underscored a significant dimension of the Court's admiralty jurisdiction cases: if a decision was made in favor of federal court admiralty jurisdiction, what substantive rules would the federal courts, sitting in admiralty, employ? While Du Ponceau, in his comments on *Coolidge,* and Marshall, in the *Canter* case, acknowledged that "the law, admiralty and maritime," was not identical to the common law, practice and "fashion" ran the two "laws" together. The prospective use of common law analogies by federal court judges in admiralty cases, then, seems to have been a highly controversial if largely unexpressed issue in the Court's admiralty jurisdiction cases.

That issue brought the grand strategy Story had initiated in *DeLovio* into sharp focus. By refashioning the substantive law of admiralty through common law analogies Story intended to increase the power of the federal courts and at the same time promote uniformity and commerce. By this strategy Story necessarily raised the question of judicial discretion to fashion rules of law through the purposive judicial logic he had employed in *DeLovio*. Others, such as Johnson, saw his strategy, and worried about its juristic and political implications; still others, such as Marshall, were concerned that the general public could not sufficiently grasp Story's distinction between limited federal court jurisdiction and unlimited discretionary power on the part of federal judges to fashion substantive rules within their jurisdiction. The result was a bizarre and convoluted series of admiralty jurisdiction decisions by the Court, decisions that sought to conceal the pressures and controversies that they generated.

The first of the Court's jurisdiction decisions, *The General Smith,* has previously been discussed in connection with Henry Wheaton's role in refashioning William Pinkney's argument in that case. Wheaton's intervention in *The General Smith* reveals the nature of the Reporter's office at the time and the internal struggles within the Court over the extent of federal court admiralty jurisdiction. Correspondence between Story and Wheaton from 1815, when *DeLovio* was delivered, to the beginning of the 1819 Term indicates that the two regarded themselves as allies in a

---

[107] 1 Wheat. 415 (1816). At the conclusion of Story's circuit court opinion the reporter, John Gallison, noted:

Davis, District Judge, did not concur, with a view to bring [that] ques-

tion solemnly before the supreme court; so it was certified to the supreme court, as upon a division of the judges.

25 F. Cas. at 622.

campaign to expand the jurisdiction of the federal courts; that they regarded Johnson as their principal opponent; and that they could not count on Marshall's overt support.

The correspondence began with a letter from Wheaton to Story, dated September 2, 1815, in which Wheaton informed Story that he had just published a digest of prize cases[108] and reminded Story that "you suggested to me at Washington the idea of digesting the law and practice of the Instance Court." The "object" of that enterprise, Wheaton added, "should be . . . to restore the Admiralty to its original dominion as so ably maintained by Sir Leoline Jenkins and revived in your decision [in *The Jerusalem*]."[109] Story responded by encouraging Wheaton to write a treatise on "the jurisdiction, law, and practice of the Instance Court." He had encountered only "a few [Instance] cases . . . in my Circuit," Story continued, "but as they arise, I shall from time to time endeavor to fix the principle and practice by a general adherence to the Admiralty rules."[110]

By December 13 of that year Story, having finished *DeLovio*, "was much pleased on reading in a newspaper this morning that [Wheaton] had published an essay on the necessity of a navigation act." He let Wheaton know that he "truly rejoiced that there are found public spirited young men who are willing to devote their time and talents to the establishment of a great national policy on all subjects." Story hoped that "you will follow up the blow by vindicating the necessity of establishing other great national institutions," such as "the extension of the jurisdiction of the Courts of the United States over the whole extent contemplated in the Constitution."[111]

At the same time, we have seen, Story had been influential in supporting Wheaton for the Reportership, which Wheaton assumed in the 1816 Term. Wheaton's new position gave him and Story considerably more opportunities to collaborate on admiralty and maritime matters. In a May 21, 1816, letter Wheaton informed Story that his first volume of reports was "now ready for the press, except the notes," and asked whether Story "would find it convenient to extend your annotating" to "the common law and Instance cases."[112] Story responded on May 25 that he could "furnish [Wheaton] with notes on the Practice of the Prize Courts," which he thought "peculiarly important to rescue the practice

---

[108] H. Wheaton, *A Digest of the Law of Maritime Captures and Prizes* (1815).

[109] H. Wheaton to J. Story, Sept. 2, 1815, Henry Wheaton Papers, Pierpont Morgan Library, New York, N.Y. Hereafter cited as Wheaton Papers.

[110] Story to Wheaton, Sept. 15, 1815, supra, note 20.

[111] J. Story to H. Wheaton, Dec. 13, 1815, quoted in W. Story, *Life and Letters*, I, 270.

[112] H. Wheaton to J. Story, May 21, 1816, Wheaton Papers.

of the prize tribunals in the southern states from the most mischievous irregularity."[113] By July Story had sent a note,[114] which appeared in Wheaton's first volume, accompanied by the following disclaimer:

> It is time to draw this note to a close, and in so doing, it is proper to inform the reader that, although authorities are cited to support some of the positions, they will not always be found to support them in their full extent. Much of what is stated, as the general practice of prize courts, is to be gathered from lights scattered here and there in the books, and more frequently and accurately by attendance on the arguments of prize causes, where the points are discussed by counsel, or ruled incidentally by the court.[115]

The note had begun by announcing that "in some of the district courts of the United States . . . great irregularities have crept into the practice in prize causes."[116]

All told, Story provided Wheaton with thirteen notes for the first five volumes of Wheaton's Reports. These included "a more enlarged view of the principles and practice of prize courts"[117] and a long note on "the extent of the admiralty jurisdiction" over crimes,[118] which was precipitated by an unpublished dissent in the case of *United States v. Bevans.*[119] In the latter Story repeated many of the sources and arguments he had used in *DeLovio.* "It is not my desire," Story wrote in one of his memorandum books in June 1819, "ever to be known as the author of any of the notes in Mr. Wheaton's Reports." Nonetheless, he made a list of "those notes which I have written . . . lest . . . the fact should transpire."[120]

The intimate connection made by Story and Wheaton between expansive admiralty jurisdiction and "the establishment of a great national policy on all subjects"[121] can also be seen in places where admiralty issues would seem not immediately relevant. In Story's opinion in *Martin v. Hunter's Lessee,*[122] for example, he spoke of a series of cases "of vital importance . . . to the national sovereignty," including "cases of admiralty and maritime jurisdiction."[123] He then went on to say,

---

[113] J. Story to H. Wheaton, May 25, 1816, quoted in W. Story, *Life and Letters,* I, 281.

[114] "I transmit you enclosed the note which I promised on the Practice of the Prize Courts . . . I hope . . . that what I have written may be useful to you. . . ." J. Story to H. Wheaton, July 28, 1816, quoted in ibid., 282. For more detail on Story's notes in prize cases, see Chapter XIII.

[115] 1 Wheat. at 506.

[116] Ibid., 495.

[117] 2 Wheat., Appendix, Note 1, at 1 (1817).

[118] 5 Wheat. 106 (1820).

[119] 3 Wheat. 336 (1818).

[120] Memorandum, June 12, 1819, quoted in W. Story, *Life and Letters,* I, 283.

[121] Story to Wheaton, Dec. 13, 1815, supra, note 111.

[122] 1 Wheat. 304 (1816).

[123] Ibid., 334.

## Chapter VII: *Admiralty Jurisdiction*

This class of cases . . . affect[s] not only our internal policy, but our foreign relations. It would, therefore, be perilous to restrain [federal court jurisdiction over such cases] in any manner whatsoever, inasmuch as it might hazard the national safety . . .

[A]s to cases of admiralty and maritime jurisdiction, the admiralty jurisdiction embraces all questions of prize and salvage, in the correct adjudication of which foreign nations are deeply interested; it embraces also maritime torts, contracts, and offences, in which the principles of the law and comity of nations often form an essential inquiry. All these cases, then, enter into the national policy, affect the national rights, and may compromit the national sovereignty.[124]

Story and Wheaton were involved in one additional incident of significance between the appearance of *DeLovio* and the decision in *The General Smith*. On November 6, 1817, Wheaton wrote Story that he had "reread with lively satisfaction the [*DeLovio*] opinion on the admiralty jurisdiction, and it cannot fail to command the admiration and assent of the profession."[125] The occasion of Wheaton's rereading was his having been retained to assist the attorney general of the United States in arguing *United States* v. *Bevans* before the Marshall Court. The *Bevans* case, in which a sentry on the United States warship *Independence* had allegedly murdered a cook's mate while the ship lay in Boston harbor, had been certified up from Story's circuit. It provided, potentially, another opportunity to expand the admiralty jurisdiction of the federal courts, this time over capital crimes committed on ships within the harbors of ports "lying in waters of a sufficient depth at all times for ships of the largest class and burden."[126] In his letter Wheaton asked Story whether the defendant in *Bevans* "still remains in confinement awaiting his final sentence, as I . . . shall probably prepare myself for the next Term if it is likely to remain on the Calendar."[127]

Story responded on November 13. In his second paragraph he acknowledged Wheaton's comments on *DeLovio*:

If I have satisfied your mind that I am right as to the admiralty jurisdiction, I shall hope that my efforts to vindicate its just claims may on less accurate, candid & learned minds not be without some salutary effect. You have done a great deal by your work on captures & by your notes to your Reports to give a strong relish for the prize, maritime & civil law. . . .

---

[124] Ibid., 335.
[125] H. Wheaton to J. Story, Nov. 6, 1817, Wheaton Papers.

[126] 3 Wheat. at 338.
[127] Wheaton to Story, Nov. 6, 1817, supra, note 125.

455

Later, as an afterthought, Story added:

> P.S. I had quite forgotten to state to you that Bevans is still [in] custody; & that an argument is expected at the next term. Pray prepare yourself—it is an excellent cause to tread on new & interesting ground—I have prepared the sketch of an opinion.[128.]

Wheaton took the hint. The questions certified to the Court in *Bevans* boiled down to whether the federal courts had jurisdiction over "a murder committed in the waters of a state where the tide ebbs and flows."[129] Wheaton, in his argument on behalf of federal court jurisdiction (reported meticulously by the Court's Reporter in Volume 3 of Wheaton's Reports), maintained that "the jurisdiction of the colonial admiralty court" extended to "all offences committed 'on the sea shores, public streams, ports, fresh waters, rivers, and arms of the sea as of the rivers and coasts.' "[130] He reminded the Court that "the opinion of one of the learned judges of this court, in which all the learning on the civil and criminal jurisdiction of the admiralty is collected together, and concentrated in a blaze of luminous reasoning," had shown the ancient admiralty jurisdiction "had cognizance of all torts, and offences, on the high seas, and in ports and havens, as far as the ebb and flow of the tide."[131] *DeLovio* was prominently cited.

*Bevans,* however, turned out to be a frustrating case for both Story and Wheaton. The case was not so straightforward as Wheaton's argument seemed to suggest, for no statute was involved: it was a case of a "common law" crime that had been committed on a ship. The criminal jurisdiction of the English admiralty courts had always been treated differently from the civil jurisdiction, having jury trials and common law procedures. One contemporary commentator on *Bevans* said that "the criminal department of the admiralty jurisdiction . . . presents a singular mixture of the civil and common law, in which the latter . . . predominates." In particular, in cases involving serious crimes "the common law may be considered, if not the exclusive, at least as a legitimate and concurrent source of authority and rule of decision."[132] Thus a case presenting the question of whether the federal courts had jurisdiction over a murder committed in the harbor of a state port not only asked the Court to determine the scope of the admiralty jurisdiction, but also invited it to fashion the substantive rules of decision governing *Bevans*-type crimes. The last inquiry appeared to raise the federal common law of crimes issue once more. Was *Bevans* actually another version of *Coolidge?*

---

[128] J. Story to H. Wheaton, Nov. 3, 1817, Wheaton Papers.
[129] 3 Wheat. at 386.
[130] Ibid., 356.
[131] Ibid., 358–60.
[132] Du Ponceau, *Dissertation,* 57–58.

# Chapter VII: *Admiralty Jurisdiction*

To complicate matters further, *Bevans* was a capital murder case that had originally been brought in federal court and in which the federal jury had sentenced the defendant to death. An affirmative holding by the Court on the question of federal court jurisdiction meant the end of the prisoner's life. In addition, "the place" in which the *Bevans* murder had occurred was one where, as Wheaton put in his summary of the facts, "the civil and criminal processes of the courts of the state of Massachusetts have hitherto constantly been served and obeyed."[133] Finally, there was language in a federal statute, the Judiciary Act of 1790,[134] that seemed to assume that a public ship of war, on which the *Bevans* murder had taken place, was "a place . . . out of the jurisdiction of any particular state," and therefore within the "sole and exclusive jurisdiction of the United States."[135]

In an opinion for the Court, Marshall dodged his way around most of the issues. He made what was to become a familiar distinction in admiralty jurisdiction and Commerce Clause cases, between "the power of Congress to legislate" and the "exercise [of that power]."[136] Even though the Constitution had given the federal courts jurisdiction over admiralty and maritime cases, Marshall argued, Congress had not enacted legislation giving the federal courts jurisdiction over murders committed in harbors within the boundaries of states. In the absence of that legislation no evidence of "cession of territory" from the states to the federal government could be conferred. If the harbors of coastal cities were within the territory of states—a proposition no one denied—then power resided in the states unless Congress provided otherwise.[137]

Marshall then went on to make a strained, and unnecessary, reading of the Judiciary Act of 1790's language covering "place[s] . . . out of the jurisdiction of a particular state." He found that the word "place" had been "associated" in the statute with "fixed and territorial . . . objects," such as a fort, an arsenal, a dock-yard, or a magazine. Context thus showed "the mind of [Congress] to have been fixed on territorial objects": "place" did not mean "public ship of war."[138] This was a dubious interpretation, especially in light of an 1800 statute that had allowed murderers on "any public ship or vessel of the United States" to be punished by a court-martial.[139] But the discussion was irrelevant, since the "public ship" exception in the 1790 Act assumed that the "place" in question was "out of the jurisdiction of any particular state," which the first part of Marshall's opinion had denied.

---

[133] 3 Wheat. at 338.
[134] 1 Stat. 73 (1790).
[135] Wheaton made this argument. See 3 Wheat. at 375.
[136] Ibid., 387.

[137] Ibid., 388–89.
[138] Ibid., 390–91.
[139] Act of 1800 for the Better Government of the Navy, 2 Stat. 45 (1800).

Although Story resolved to acquiesce silently in the *Bevans* decision, he was furious about its outcome. He wrote Wheaton on April 8, 1818, "I hope you will take care to put in a note the very words of the authorities respecting the exemption of public ships, which point was held clear by a majority of the Court, although from delicacy, an opinion being unnecessary, it was withheld."[140] Two days later he sent Wheaton a copy of an opinion he had prepared in *Bevans* but decided not to deliver. "I have never changed my mind as to its legal accuracy," Story wrote,

> but as the case was a capital offence, I yielded to the opinion of my brethren. If it had been of another nature, I should have adhered to it. You will see that I have altered the opinion at the close accordingly. The truth is, I put the opinion by with a view at some future day to publish it, and I should have delivered it in Court, if I had not felt a delicacy in respect to the Chief Justice, especially as I acquiesced in the opinion he delivered; though I think it is not drawn up with his usual precision and accuracy. . . .[141]

The *Bevans* case foreshadowed Marshall's stance in admiralty jurisdiction cases. The case was a particularly suggestive one for Marshall because it combined an admiralty jurisdiction issue with a potential federal common law of crimes issue, and thereby recalled for Marshall the earlier difficulties he had had in formulating a position on federal common law crimes. In 1800 Marshall had taken the view that the "common law of England has . . . been adopted as the common law of America by the Constitution of the United States," and that crimes committed on the high seas against the United States were "clearly punishable in the federal courts."[142] But in the early 1800s attacks on the conception of a federal common law of crimes surfaced, accompanied by concerns about the apparently necessary relationship between extensive judicial power in the federal courts and extensive legislative power in Congress.[143] Marshall was well aware of these attacks: they had been made, most prominently, by Jefferson[144] and St. George Tucker.[145] By 1807, in *United States* v.

---

[140] J. Story to H. Wheaton, Apr. 8, 1818, quoted in W. Story, *Life and Letter*, I, 303.

[141] J. Story to H. Wheaton, Apr. 10, 1818, quoted in ibid., 305.

[142] J. Marshall to John Jay, Nov. 27, 1800, John Marshall Papers, Library of Congress.

[143] These issues were brought into focus in the congressional debates over the report of the Judiciary Act of 1801.

See *Annals of Congress,* 7th Cong., 1st Sess., 611–14. On the common law crimes debates in the early 1800s, see C. Warren, *The Supreme Court in United States History* (3 vols., 1922), I, 157–64, 433–34; Haskins and Johnson, *Foundations of Power,* 354–55, 633–39; Horwitz, *Transformation,* 10–16. See also the discussion in Chapter II.

[144] Jefferson had written to Gideon

# Chapter VII: *Admiralty Jurisdiction*

*Burr,* Marshall had retreated from his earlier position on common law crimes, intimating that the federal courts might have no authority to punish nonstatutory crimes.[146] He repeated this intimation in an unreported circuit court case in 1809.[147] And in 1811, in another circuit case, Marshall said that he was "decidedly of the opinion that the jurisdiction of the courts of the United States depends, exclusively, on the Constitution and laws of the United States."[148]

But one should place Marshall's comments in context. On the general question of federal court jurisdiction, Marshall may have been reluctant for the Supreme Court to augment the common law powers of the federal courts, but he was happy enough to encourage Congress to make that augmentation, and not unwilling to participate in the drafting of proposed congressional legislation. In 1816, apparently before the *Coolidge* case was set for argument,[149] Story drafted "a bill further to extend the judicial system of the United States," which included a section giving "general jurisdiction to the United States' Courts to punish crimes committed against the Federal Government."[150] In submitting the bill, along with commentary, to William Pinkney, Story revealed that

---

Granger in 1800 that "if the principle were to prevail of a common law being in force in the United States," that principle would "possess . . . the general government at once of all the powers of the state governments" and would "reduce . . . us to a single consolidated government [—] the most corrupt government on earth." T. Jefferson to G. Granger, Aug. 18, 1800, quoted in P. Ford, ed., *The Writings of Thomas Jefferson* (10 vols., 1892–99), VII, 451.

[145] Tucker, in his 1803 edition of Blackstone's Commentaries, discussing the question of "how far the common law of England is the law of the federal government of the United States," had said:

> This question is of very great importance, not only as it regards the limits of the jurisdiction of the *federal courts;* but also as it relates to the extent of the powers vested in the *federal government.* For if it be true that the common law of England has been adopted by the United States in their national or federal capacity, the jurisdiction of the federal courts must be coextensive with it; or, in other words, *unlimited . . .*

S. Tucker, *Blackstone's Commentaries: With Notes of Reference to the Constitution and Laws of the Federal Government of the United States and of the Commonwealth of Virginia* (5 vols., 1803), I, 280. Notice Tucker's assumption, characteristic of early nineteenth-century American jurisprudence, that judicial power was coextensive with legislative power. Cf. the discussion in Chapters II and VIII.

[146] United States v. Burr, 25 F. Cas. 160, 176 (1807).

[147] United States v. Smith, Richmond *Enquirer,* June 6, 1809.

[148] Livingston v. Jefferson, 15 F. Cas. 660 (1811).

[149] Gerald Dunne, in his biography of Story, suggests that Story drafted the bill and its accompanying commentary in January 1816. Dunne, *Joseph Story,* 147–48. The *Coolidge* case, which was never formally argued, was decided by the court on March 21, 1816. The Court's Term had opened that year in the first week in February.

[150] Excerpts from the bill are in W. Story, *Life and Letters,* I, 293–303. The quoted passages here are at 293, 297.

> The . . . bill was originally prepared by myself, and submitted to my brethren of the Supreme Court. It received a revision from several of them, particularly Judges Marshall and Washington. . . . Judge Johnson expressed some doubt as to the eleventh section; but, as I understood him, rather as to its expediency than the competency of Congress to enact it.[151]

One can infer from this incident that where a case raised the possibility that the jurisdiction of the federal courts might be expanded, Marshall seemed preoccupied with not exposing the Supreme Court as the active champion of that expansion. He was perfectly happy with the result of expanded jurisdiction, even willing to make private efforts to secure it, but he did not want the Supreme Court publicly identified with any such campaign. One might even see Marshall's surreptitious involvement with the writ of error process in *Martin v. Hunter's Lessee* as part of this general posture: he was concerned about exposing the Court on controversial matters.

In matters of federal jurisdiction, then, Marshall's experience with the federal common law of crimes controversy had resulted in his taking a cautious and publicly circumspect stance. He likewise adopted an attitude of diffidence on admiralty questions. He wrote Story in 1819 that he would appreciate the latter's help "on a case which to me who am not versed in admiralty proceedings has some difficulty,"[152] and his best-known biographer claimed that "of admiralty law in particular he knew little."[153] Story doubtless did not misconstrue Marshall's professed ignorance about admiralty issues;[154] he was only too happy to play the role of admiralty expert and leader of the campaign for increased federal court admiralty jurisdiction. Story, however, may have underestimated Marshall's strong desire that the Court not be unduly exposed on admiralty jurisdiction issues. Marshall may not have seen one of Jefferson's letters identifying "a common law in force in the United States of which . . . their Courts have cognizance" with "complete consolidation,"[155] but he knew the author well. And he had undoubtedly seen Tucker's comment, in the 1803 edition of Blackstone, making an explicit connection between

---

[151] Ibid., 300. Pinkney is identified as the recipient of the bill at 296.

[152] J. Marshall to J. Story, May 27, 1819, in *Proc. Mass. Hist. Soc.*, 14:325 (1901).

[153] A. Beveridge, *The Life of John Marshall* (4 vols., 1919), IV, 119.

[154] In a tribute to Marshall in 1835, Story said that while Marshall "was a man of the most unaffected modesty, . . . no one ever possessed a more entire sense of his own extraordinary talents and acquirements. . . ." J. Story, "Life, Character, and Services of Chief Justice Marshall" (1835), reprinted in W. Story, *Miscellaneous Writings*, 678.

[155] Thomas Jefferson to Charles Pinkney, quoted in Warren, *Supreme Court*, I, 164.

the use of substantive common law rules in the federal courts and unlimited federal court jurisdiction. Admiralty jurisdiction cases provided the Court with a tempting opportunity to expand the powers of the federal courts, given the language of Article III, but Marshall, sensing that the Court had the potential to become a decisive force in American society, wanted to proceed carefully.

Thus at the time *The General Smith* came to the Court, in the busy 1819 Term, any admiralty jurisdiction case could have been seen as having deep ramifications. But in a Term in which the justices were wrestling with *Dartmouth College* v. *Woodward, McCulloch* v. *Maryland,* and *Sturges* v. *Crowinshield, The General Smith* was clearly not seen by the Justices as a significant case, perhaps not even as an admiralty jurisdiction case. The narrow question in *The General Smith,* we have seen, was whether a ship could be attached and forced to be sold by material men who had not been paid for their services. The case was thus an instance case, one of the category of admiralty cases distinguished only by what it was not. The only issue of import in *The General Smith* appeared to be whether material men who had worked on a domestic ship had a lien on that ship which they could enforce in the admiralty courts.

As noted in the preceding chapter, however, Pinkney's concession about admiralty jurisdiction in *The General Smith* was converted into dictum in Story's opinion and then fortified by Wheaton's report of the case. The result was that *The General Smith* became a decision whose first proposition, as Wheaton reported it, was that "the admiralty possesses a general jurisdiction in cases of suits by material men, *in personam,* and *in rem.*"[156] This language was qualified only partially by the first paragraph of Story's opinion, which said that "where . . . the proceeding is *in rem* to enforce a specific lien, it is incumbent upon those who seek the aid of the Court, to establish the existence of such lien in the particular case."[157] This comment was followed by two sentences that have made *The General Smith,* according to one set of commentators, a prime candidate "for the distinction of being the most ill-advised admiralty decision ever handed down by the Supreme Court."[158] Story's paragraph ran:

> Where repairs have been made, or necessaries have been furnished to a foreign ship, or to a ship in a port of the state to which she does not belong, the general maritime law, following the civil law, gives the party a lien on the ship itself for its security; and he may well maintain a suit *in rem* in the admiralty to enforce his right. But in respect to

---

[156] 4 Wheat. at 438.
[157] Ibid., 443.

[158] Gilmore and Black, *Admiralty,* 526.

repairs and necessaries in the port or state to which the ship belongs, the case is governed altogether by the municipal law of that state; and no lien is implied, unless it is recognised by that law.[159]

Story did not give any citations for the propositions in these sentences. Commentators have encapsulated the propositions in the phrase "the home port doctrine,"[160] a doctrine which created major difficulties in the substantive law of admiralty throughout the nineteenth century.[161] The sentences were particularly odd, given Story's general views on the superiority of uniform federal law in commercial settings,[162] because they seemed to assume that state common law would govern commercial relations between shipowners and material men where domestic ships were involved. Moreover, counsel for the material men had reminded the Court that "the universal maritime law . . . recognizes the lien in the case of a domestic as well as a foreign ship," citing a case noted in *DeLovio,* and had suggested that commercial policy favored allowing the lien, and therefore admiralty jurisdiction, in both cases.[163] Yet Story seemed to reject that position.

This reading of *The General Smith* must be qualified, however, by a note appended to the opinion. The note mentioned a New York statute giving liens to material men on domestic and foreign ships and then stated that "[t]his lien, existing by the local law, may consequently be enforced, upon the principle of [*The General Smith*], by a suit *in rem* in the Admiralty."[164] The origins of that note remain obscure. Wheaton probably added it at some Justice's request, and the logical candidate would be Story himself. The note would appear to have been intended as an invitation to state legislatures to pass lien statutes, which many did.[165] Its clear message was that if the states wanted to protect material men, the

---

[159] Ibid., 443.

[160] E.g., F. Smith, "The Confusion in the Law Relating to Materialmen's Liens on Vessels," *Harv. L. Rev.,* 21:332 (1908); Gilmore and Black, *Admiralty,* 527.

[161] See the discussion in Gilmore and Black, *Admiralty,* 529–37.

[162] In discussing "commercial law" in an essay written two years after *The General Smith* was decided, Story said:

From mutual comity, from the natural tendency of maritime usages to assimilation, and from mutual convenience, if not necessity, it may reasonably be expected, that the maritime law will gradually approximate to a high degree of uniformity throughout the commercial world. This is, indeed, in every way exceedingly desirable.

J. Story, "The Progress of Jurisprudence" (1821), in W. Story, *Miscellaneous Writings,* 214–15.

[163] 4 Wheat. at 442. The case was Stevens v. The Sandwich, 1 Peter's Adm. Dec. 233, noted in DeLovio v. Boit, supra, note 23, at 443.

[164] 4 Wheat. at 444.

[165] Gilmore and Black, *Admiralty,* 530–31. It appears that the state statutes signified a more general delegation of admiralty matters to state courts, notwithstanding the language of Article III.

federal admiralty courts would be available to entertain suits for their protection, but only if the states passed lien statutes.

A similar message had been conveyed by Story and Marshall in *Coolidge,* where a judicially drafted congressional statute creating federal court jurisdiction over common law crimes was being formulated at the very time that the Court was wrestling with the issue of whether to create that jurisdiction itself. Could it be that in *The General Smith* the Court was reluctant to expose itself as the architect of expanded admiralty jurisdiction, and new substantive rules, for transactions involving work by material men on domestic ships? Could it be that Story's dictum about *in personam* admiralty jurisdiction over material men suits merely slipped by some of his colleagues, since the real issue in *The General Smith* was perceived as being whether the federal courts could use their jurisdictional powers to change the substantive rules of the states? And could it be that Story asked Wheaton to add the note to the Court's opinion in *The General Smith* in order to initiate, indirectly, the very expansion of *in rem* admiralty jurisdiction he had forsworn in the opinion itself?

One piece of evidence seems to suggest that Story had such goals in *The General Smith.* The critical distinction made by his "home port doctrine" sentences was not between foreign and domestic ships, in the sense of ships of other nations versus American ships, but between foreign and domestic ports, "foreign" meaning "a port of the state to which [the ship did] not belong."[166] This distinction was, as noted, unsupported by any citation. But in Wheaton's printed version of Pinkney's argument, Pinkney had "denied that a suit *in rem* could be maintained in the present case because the parties had no specific lien upon the ship for supplies furnished in the port to which she belonged." That argument was followed by a distinction between foreign and domestic ships, accompanied by a citation to the case of *Woodruff* v. *The Levi Dearborne.*[167]

*Woodruff* v. *The Levi Dearborne*[168] was a Johnson circuit court opinion, delivered from his Savannah, Georgia, court in December 1811. In that case Johnson had said:

> The lien on vessels for material men and shipwrights exists only in a foreign port. Where the owner is present and resident, the common law principle must govern. In such case, no lien on the vessel is created. In the case of the owner, who, though present when the work and materials are furnished, is transient and non-resident, I am disposed to think otherwise, and that in such cases the lien attaches. It is proper also to state, what shall be deemed a foreign, and what a domestic

---

[166] 4 Wheat. at 443.
[167] Ibid., 441–42.

[168] *Am. Law J.,* 4:97 (1813).

port, as to this question. The sea ports of the different states ought, in this respect, to be considered as foreign ports in relation to each other.[169]

This language of Johnson's is striking because of its focus on ports rather than ships, and because of its definition of foreign and domestic in terms of states rather than nations. Had Story been inclined to supply a citation for his phrase "port of the state to which she does not belong" in *The General Smith*, he could have cited *The Levi Dearborne*. And what were the implications of Johnson's language? Johnson's purpose in *The Levi Dearborne* had been to ensure that "where the owner is present and resident, the common law principle must govern": no lien and therefore no *in rem* suit in the admiralty courts. Story had adopted that language, possibly because Johnson had insisted on it in informal discussion, and used the language to dispose of *The General Smith*. But at the same time he had suggested that there were two possible techniques to bring suits in admiralty notwithstanding that language. One was "a suit *in personam*," in which "there could not have been any hesitation in sustaining the jurisdiction of the District Court,"[170] and another was through a statutory lien, which, if "existing by the local law, may consequently be enforced . . . by a suit *in rem* in the Admiralty."[171]

One can imagine Johnson's outrage when, in connection with the case of *Ramsay* v. *Allegre* in 1827, he read "the report of [*The General Smith*]" and discovered "unfounded doctrines" that "ought at once to be put down; and dicta . . . that cannot bear examination."[172] Johnson then proceeded, as we have seen, to attack Wheaton's reporting of *The General Smith* and to protest against the "silent and stealing progress" of the admiralty jurisdiction. He was also to use *Ramsay* v. *Allegre* as an opportunity to supply his own "brief history of the admiralty jurisdiction over contracts"[173] with a view toward refuting *DeLovio*. To understand Johnson's outburst, and why that outburst took eight years to surface, it is necessary to review the Justices' actions in admiralty jurisdiction cases ˙in the years between *The General Smith* and *Ramsay*.

In 1822 Johnson was confronted on his South Carolina circuit with a dispute over a bill of lading between the owner of a ship and a local merchant, both of whom were citizens of South Carolina. The case had been filed as a libel in federal district court. The district court, resting its opinion on *DeLovio*, had sustained the libel on the ground that the admiralty had jurisdiction over maritime contracts. Johnson reversed, delivering an unreported opinion that "a legal friend" sent to the Charleston

---

[169] Ibid., 101.
[170] 4 Wheat. at 443.
[171] Ibid., 444.

[172] Ramsay v. Allegre, 12 Wheat. 611, 614 (1827).
[173] Ibid., 616.

*City Gazette,* which published it as "highly interesting to the commercial community."[174]

The case, *The Amanda,* "furnishes a striking illustration," Johnson said, "of the consequences that may be anticipated from a leaning to the extension of Admiralty jurisdiction." He made clear what he thought was at stake:

> [I]t is obvious, that as most commercial transactions are blended with foreign and maritime transactions, if we begin to take cognizance of causes of a mercantile nature upon the ground of the maritime jurisdiction of the Admiralty, there is no telling where we shall stop. And the subject becomes the more serious when it is recollected that Admiralty and maritime causes are exclusively delegated to the government of the United States. The next step, therefore, will be a denial of the jurisdiction of the State Courts over such cases altogether.

In this passage Johnson revealed that he was well aware of Story's grand strategy in *DeLovio* and that he opposed every feature of it. He recognized the intimate connection between maritime transactions and commerce generally, and was concerned that since navigation and commerce were virtually synonymous, all contracts could be described as maritime contracts. This association was, of course, the viewpoint of a coastal planter, as Johnson had been, just as Story's perspective in *DeLovio* had been that of a resident of a fishing village on the Massachusetts coast. But the sense that all commerce and most contractual relations were maritime elicited a different response from Johnson than from Story, for Johnson added to that perception a "recollect[ion] that Admiralty and maritime causes are exclusively delegated to the government of the United States." Thus in Johnson's mind the pervasiveness of maritime transactions became ominously linked to efforts to expand the jurisdiction of the federal courts at the expense of the state courts. For Johnson, admiralty jurisdiction cases presented a sinister combination of commerce and federal supremacy issues; he was determined to resist Story's "great national policy."

The rest of Johnson's opinion in *The Amanda* was a strident and barely concealed attack on Story. He cited *DeLovio* ("a case decided by one of my learned brethren") as an example of the general problems quoted above. He intimated that Story's concession in *DeLovio* that the common law courts had concurrent jurisdiction in admiralty cases was temporary, and that "every decision . . . which adds a branch to the jurisdiction of the Admiralty Courts was putting it in the power of the

---

[174] Charleston *City Gazette and Commercial Daily Advertiser,* Jan. 18, 1822. All subsequent quotations from Johnson's opinion are taken from this source.

United States to assume to itself exclusive or appellate jurisdiction over that subject." He revealed that he regarded the decisions "of my brethren on circuit [as] not authority"; that he "seldom, if ever, rest[ed] [his] opinion on *nisi prius* decisions," and that he thought it "a public misfortune that [circuit opinions] are even published," since, among other things, they gave "a bias to legal opinions which ought to be received exclusively from tribunals of the last resort."

Johnson next turned to Story's use of history in *DeLovio*. He found it "altogether irrelevant to the question before me to launch into an investigation of the ancient jurisdiction of the Lord High Admirals of England." The subject, he felt, was one "for the patient antiquarian, rather than for one who . . . [was] employed in the search after useful knowledge." While dismissing Sir Leoline Jenkins's "celebrated argument" on behalf of the Admiralty as "strongly marked by . . . bias," he noted that Jenkins's style was "conspicuous" and "correct" in its "freedom from affectation, which marks the distinction between profound learning and vain parade." Despite his earlier comments about the irrelevance of history, Johnson gave a rough sketch of the controversy between the common law and the admiralty courts in England, which he reduced to the proposition "that it is not only a fact . . . that the Courts of Admiralty have in modern times been deprived of their ancient jurisdiction over all maritime contracts which the common-law Courts can administer complete justice in, but that they have been rightfully and constitutionally deprived of it."

Johnson then turned to Story's constitutional argument in *DeLovio*. "Some difficulty," he felt, "rests over the question, what is the extent of the Admiralty jurisdiction conceded by the third article of the Constitution?" This was the most troublesome hurdle in Johnson's attack, as he acknowledged. His strategy was to reason, in the manner of Marshall, from "self-evident" propositions. "Two positions," he claimed, "cannot be denied; that no more [than admiralty jurisdiction] was ceded, and that no state can be presumed to have ceded more than was known to its own jurisprudence." He then took those positions to mean that "the Admiralty jurisdiction as known to the judicatures of the respective states at the adoption of the Constitution is that which I hold to have been ceded to the U. States and no more." His next sentence was puzzling: "the Supreme Court have recognized these doctrines in the case of the Gen. Smith (considering that case . . . as authority only as to the point decided)."

What could Johnson have meant by this reference to *The General Smith?* There was nothing in that opinion about the constitutional origins of admiralty jurisdiction. But there was language in Story's opinion stating that state common law, not admiralty law, governed material men's suits against domestic vessels in their home ports. If Johnson had taken this language as a broad affirmation of the autonomy of state common law over maritime contracts (the material men and the shipowner in *The General Smith* had originally entered into a maritime contract), then his comment is not so remarkable. But of course *The General Smith* stood only for a much narrower proposition: that when state common law did not give a material man a maritime lien, and the material man had worked on a domestic ship in its home port, the admiralty courts could take *in rem* jurisdiction only if there was a state lien statute.

Thus Johnson's opinion in *The Amanda* not only repudiated *DeLovio*, it revealed that Johnson had seen *The General Smith* as a federal supremacy case, just as he had seen *Hudson and Goodwin, Coolidge,* and possibly *Bevans.* The opinion also intimated that Johnson might be hostile to the granting of maritime liens as a matter of policy. He alluded to "other questions of great commercial importance in this case" which he was declining to address. Johnson's intimation revealed yet another dimension of the Court's admiralty jurisdiction cases. They regularly involved contracts between shipwrights and shipowners and were therefore susceptible of being seen as conflicts between different interests. The economic policy implications of the cases cautions one to avoid monolithic generalizations about the economic ideology of Marshall Court Justices. Story, an acknowledged friend to the commercial classes on many occasions, was, in both *DeLovio* and *The Geneal Smith,* attempting to formulate jurisdictional rules that would give shipwrights and material men—members of the working classes—more opportunities to enforce their claims against shipowners and merchant creditors. Johnson, a supporter of state insolvency statutes that sought to give relief to debtors against their creditors,[175] was, in *The Amanda,* apparently advocating a position that favored the interests of commercial men. Indeed, as we shall subsequently see, the protection of the commercial world from excessive maritime lien suits was an explicit objective of Johnson's admiralty jurisdiction decisions.

Three years after *The Amanda* another theme introduced in *DeLovio* surfaced, and another cryptic Marshall Court admiralty jurisdiction decision resulted. The theme was the relationship between admiralty and commerce; the specific legal issue the extent of federal court admiralty jurisdiction over navigable inland waterways; and the relevant language Story's dictum in *DeLovio* that admiralty jurisdiction extended only "as far as the ebb and flow of the tide."[176] The decision came in a case

---

[175] See, e.g., Ogden v. Saunders, 12 Wheat. 213, 283 (1827):

[I]t is among the duties of society to enforce the rights of humanity; and both the debtor and the society have their interests in the administration of justice, and in the general good; interests which must not be swallowed up and lost sight of while yielding attention to the claim of the creditor.

[176] 7 F. Cas. at 441.

concerning the steamboat *Thomas Jefferson,* which had been built for service on the Missouri River. The steamboat's name may have evoked reactions in Story, Marshall, and Johnson, but their approach to *The Thomas Jefferson* was more clearly influenced by their participation in *Gibbons* v. *Ogden,*[177] a case that is rarely cited for its admiralty dimensions.

Between *The Amanda,* delivered in January 1822, and *Gibbons,* which was argued in early February 1824, had occurred Jefferson and Johnson's exchange of letters, which had motivated Johnson to give more frequent and public expression to his individual views on issues that came before the Court. *Gibbons* was the occasion, in fact, on which Johnson announced that heretofore "in questions of great importance and great delicacy," he would "maintain my opinions in my own way,"[178] a stance which, he had told Jefferson shortly after the 1823 Term ended, he would adopt "on all subjects of general interest, particularly constitutional questions."[179] *Gibbons* was also a case in which Webster, arguing against state restrictions on commerce, and Emmet, arguing on behalf of these restrictions, both analogized to the admiralty jurisdiction. Webster had argued "that the power of Congress over [commerce]" could be shown to be exclusive "by, [among other things], the grant of exclusive admiralty jurisdiction to the federal government."[180] Emmet had countered by citing *Bevans*[181] to remind the Justices that "this Court has decided that the grant to the United States in the constitution, of all cases of admiralty and maritime jurisdiction, does not extend to a cession of the waters in which those cases may arise." And Marshall's opinion in *Gibbons* had begun by announcing that "[a]ll America understands, and has uniformly understood, the word 'commerce' to comprehend navigation."[182]

The great significance of the Commerce Clause issues raised in *Gibbons* has led some commentators to see the Court's admiralty jurisdiction disputes as rehearsals for the disputes over the commerce power that took place through the mid-nineteenth century.[183] But it is also possible to see *Gibbons* and the subsequent Commerce Clause cases as the logical extension of disputes over federal supremacy and the meaning of commerce that originated with the admiralty cases themselves. Story had identified these issues in *DeLovio;* the Court had wrestled with them in *Coolidge, Bevans,* and *The General Smith;* Johnson had raised them again in *The Amanda.* When *Gibbons* appeared the issues were in place. The novel feature of *Gibbons* was the presence of inland waterways, which

---

[177] 9 Wheat. 1 (1824).
[178] Ibid., 223.
[179] W. Johnson to T. Jefferson, Apr. 11, 1823, reprinted in *S.C. Hist. Geneal. Mag.,* 1:207, 210 (1900).
[180] 9 Wheat. at 20.

[181] Ibid., 92.
[182] Ibid., 190.
[183] See, e.g., P. Stolz, "Pleasure Boating and Admiralty," *Calif. L. Rev.,* 51:661, 666–78 (1963).

were arguably not the high seas and therefore arguably not within the admiralty jurisdiction. From this perspective, *Gibbons* was more of an admiralty case than the earlier admiralty jurisdiction cases were Commerce Clause cases. The Court's experience with admiralty jurisdiction had furnished it with ample analogies once commerce power questions were raised.

But in light of *Gibbons,* with its extensive rehearsal of exclusive and concurrent theories of federal supremacy and the broad definition of commerce given by Marshall for the Court, it was obvious that the question whether federal admiralty jurisdiction applied to inland waterways had the broadest commercial implications. Not only had steamboat traffic been introduced on the Ohio and Mississippi rivers by 1816, and on the Missouri River by 1819,[184] the federal district courts in Kentucky[185] and Pennsylvania[186] had considered the question whether they had admiralty and maritime jurisdiction over inland waterways in 1819. In the Kentucky case Robert Trimble, then a federal district judge, had sustained the admiralty jurisdiction, and in *The Thomas Jefferson* itself the district court's first decision, handed down in December 1821, took the same position.[187]

Two weeks after the original decision in *The Thomas Jefferson,* Senator Richard Johnson of Kentucky introduced a bill in the Senate to limit the admiralty jurisdiction of the federal courts to "the high seas" and "places within the ebb and flow of the tide."[188] In a speech supporting the bill Johnson said that "Kentucky was about to learn from the exercise of admiralty jurisdiction that she was a maritime state." Johnson believed that "the people never . . . will submit to this extraordinary assumption of admiralty jurisdiction," and called expanded admiralty jurisdiction over rivers within states "the most serious encroachment upon the constitutional jurisdiction of the state tribunals and the most dangerous inroad upon state sovereignty."[189] Johnson's bill passed in the Senate but failed in the House, where it was vigorously supported by his brother, John T. Johnson, one of the co-owners of the steamboat *Thomas Jefferson.* Among the arguments made by supporters of Richard Johnson's bill was that shipowners and investors in steamboats would lose the use of their vessels while the ships were being subjected to *in rem* suits by

---

[184] L. Hunter, *Steamboats on the Western Rivers* (1949), 47; J. Hall, *The West: Its Commerce and Navigation* (1848), 162.

[185] Savage v. The Buffaloe, 21 F. Cas. 547 (1819).

[186] Sheckler v. The Geneva Boxer, 21 F. Cas. 1218 (1819). For a summary of the opinion in *Sheckler,* see T. Sergeant, *Constitutional Law* (2d ed., 1830), 195.

[187] Order Book H, Minutes of United States District Court, Eastern District of Kentucky, Frankfort, Ky., Dec. 13, 1821.

[188] 38 *Annals of Congress,* 48 (1821).

[189] 17th Cong., 1st Sess., Dec. 28, 1821, Feb. 13, 1822.

"carpenters and mechanics" in the admiralty courts.[190] Among the arguments made by opponents of the bill was that the scope of admiralty jurisdiction should be determined by the Supreme Court of the United States.[191]

The Thomas Jefferson, then, combined important questions of sovereignty with hotly debated economic issues, and was thus a delicate case when it finally came before the Court in the 1825 Term. If existing trends on the Court were to continue, one might have expected Story to press hard for admiralty jurisdiction over inland waterways, Johnson to resist that pressure, and Marshall to urge circumspection. And when the opinion of the Court was delivered by Story on March 18, those trends appeared to be evident. Story's opinion seemed to adopt a strategy similar to that which he had employed in The General Smith. He found no jurisdiction in the admiralty over "contracts for the hire of seamen, except where the service was substantially performed or to be performed upon the sea, or upon waters within the ebb and flow of the tide."[192] He therefore affirmed the decision of Thomas Todd's circuit court,[193] which had dismissed the case for want of subject matter jurisdiction.[194] He also dismissed, without extended analysis, two federal statutes that seemed to confer jurisdiction over "waters navigable from the sea by vessels of ten tons burthen" or "the government and regulation of seamen."[195]

Most significantly, Story distinguished between federal statutes recognizing existing jurisdiction and those "intend[ing] to confer any new jurisdiction." This was an argument, employed by Marshall in Bevans, that the Court was finding useful in its efforts to avoid being exposed as an aggressive proponent of expanded federal court powers. The next sentences of Story's opinion in The Thomas Jefferson perfectly complemented that argument:

> Whether, under the power to regulate commerce between the states, Congress may not extend the remedy, by the summary process of the admiralty, to the case of voyages on the western waters, it is unnecessary for us to consider. If the public inconvenience, from the want of a process of an analogous nature, shall be extensively felt, the attention of the legislature will doubtless be drawn to the subject.[196]

Here Story appeared to be employing the same strategic posture previously discussed in connection with Coolidge and The General Smith: that is, not exposing the Court on a federal supremacy issue while giving

---

[190] See 39 Annals of Congress, 1458–59 (1822); ibid., 40:1028 (1823).
[191] See ibid., 40:1024–29 (1823).
[192] The Steamboat Thomas Jefferson, 10 Wheat. 428, 429 (1825).
[193] Todd was absent during the 1825

Term and thus did not participate in the decision in The Thomas Jefferson. 10 Wheat. at iii.
[194] 10 Wheat. at 429.
[195] Ibid., 430.
[196] Ibid.

guidance to another branch of government as to how to bring about the very policy outcome the Court was eschewing. Story's hint as to the use of the commerce power was a new twist, signifying how fully admiralty jurisdiction and Commerce Clause issues had become linked after *Gibbons*.

But evidence exists which, while it does not contradict the supposition that Story's opinion in *The Thomas Jefferson* was strategic, at least complicates the matter. The holding of *The Thomas Jefferson* was, of course, entirely consistent with *DeLovio*: admiralty jurisdiction extended only as far as "the ebb and flow of the tide." Story was affirming a position that he had articulated early and repeated often in admiralty jurisdiction cases; a position he was to reaffirm in another "tidal waters" case that would come before the Taney Court in 1837.[197] It is possible that *The Thomas Jefferson* presented Story with an issue that tested his own consistency, or one which he felt too clear for dispute; the other Justices may have simply deferred to Story's views.

A series of letters Story wrote to Joseph Hopkinson in the 1830s gives credence to that possibility. Hopkinson, who had expressed outrage at Story's ethics in connection with the *Dartmouth College* case, had by the 1820s so impressed Story that the latter recommended him for a federal district judgeship in Pennsylvania.[198] Hopkinson began his tenure in 1828. Story wrote him after his appointment that he especially looked forward to Hopkinson's "pronouncing the public and maritime law."[199] Hopkinson's principal duties, a contemporary noted, involved "large commercial transactions . . . and questions of admiralty and maritime law."[200] On admiralty jurisdiction issues Hopkinson tended to be cautious, saying, in one opinion, "I confess that I do not expect to be able to draw a clear line, which will decide the place of every case that can occur, to be within or without the admiralty jurisdiction."[201]

Beginning in 1828 Hopkinson and Story began to exchange letters on doctrinal points, especially admiralty issues. In the first of those letters Hopkinson acknowledged that Story's "researches into the nature and the extent of the admiralty and maritime jurisdiction have opened to me all the laws on this subject," and told Story that he had consulted *DeLovio* and Story's edition of *Abbott on Shipping* in his research. He then asked Story a specific question about a district court case.[202] This pattern con-

---

[197] The Orleans v. Phoebus, 11 Pet. 175 (1837).
[198] See B. Konkle, *Joseph Hopkinson* (1931), 256–58.
[199] J. Story to J. Hopkinson, Dec. 16, 1827, in Joseph Hopkinson Papers, Historical Society of Pennsylvania, Philadelphia, Pa.

[200] Richard Peters, Sr., to John Quincy Adams, Jan. 27, 1829, Hopkinson Papers.
[201] The Farmer, 1 Gilpin 520 (1828).
[202] J. Hopkinson to J. Story, Dec. 13, 1828, Hopkinson Papers.

tinued over the next several years, and in a letter to Hopkinson written on December 12, 1833, Story, in responding to another Hopkinson inquiry, said,

> The admiralty jurisdiction . . . does rightfully, in my judgment, extend to all torts committed on the high seas, and everywhere in rivers, havens, ports and bays *as far as the tide ebbs and flows.*

"It may surprise you," Story continued, "to know that Chief Justice Marshall carried his doctrine much farther. He told me that he had very truly considered the subject upon principle, and if ever the question should come to the Supreme Court he should hold that the Admiralty Jurisdiction extended to all waters, rivers, etc. navigable from the sea at the head waters of such navigation." Story then told Hopkinson that Marshall

> took occasion to say to me last winter that he believed that on that point of admiralty jurisdiction he and I differed, that he went beyond me.

The remainder of the letter discussed Story's views on the limits of the admiralty jurisdiction in civil and criminal cases. He maintained that maritime contracts and torts were within the jurisdiction if they took place in the localities he had described above. The admiralty jurisdiction over crimes, he noted, was entirely "given by statutes of Congress in special terms."[203]

In another letter a year later, Story continued in the same vein, this time with specific reference to *The Thomas Jefferson.* Hopkinson had inquired about a case where a contract had been performed for services on a river. Was this a maritime contract? Story responded,

> I do not understand contracts for services on rivers, where the tide ebbs and flows, but which have no connexion with a voyage or trip on the high seas . . . to be in any just sense maritime contracts. . . . My opinion is, that the *locality* of the contract, if purely maritime, is of no consequence, and [on the other hand], that if the contact is not maritime, there is no jurisdiction in the Admiralty, even though the contract should actually be made *upon the sea.*

As an example, Story suggested that Hopkinson "look over the case of the Steam Boat Jefferson." He continued:

> I am a great friend to the Admiralty Jurisdiction, because it is so full of equity. But I have no inclination to stretch it beyond its legitimate boundaries.[204]

---

[203] Story to Hopkinson, Dec. 12, 1833, ibid. Emphasis in original.

[204] Story to Hopkinson, Nov. 17, 1834, ibid. Emphasis in original.

## Chapter VII: *Admiralty Jurisdiction*

Twelve days later, Story, who had received yet another letter from Hopkinson about the proper treatment of maritime contracts, returned to the subject:

> Since receiving your second letter I have read over the case of the Thomas Jefferson attentively. I know, that it was fully and carefully considered by the whole court, and that it was watched with jealously by one mind at least, hostile to Adm[iral]ty Jurisdiction (Mr. [Johnson]). There is nothing in that opinion which I can, or I incline to take back, if I could.[205]

This exchange of letters took place nearly ten years after *The General Smith* was decided, and thus the expansive view of admiralty jurisdiction Story attributed to Marshall may not in fact have been held by him in 1825. But the portraits of Johnson, Marshall, and Story suggested by the letters reveal Story to be much less strategic and Marshall much more deferential than might have been supposed. If Marshall held the views Story attributed to him in 1832 he certainly believed *The Thomas Jefferson* wrongly decided, and his silence was silent acquiescence. The language in *The Thomas Jefferson,* on the other hand, represented no compromise for Story at all. Johnson may have been watching Story's position "with jealousy," but he would have had no complaints.

One hesitates to accept unqualifiedly a version of events in which the narrator represents himself as a principled and consistent participant in contrast to his subtle and "jealous" peers. But it is clear that in *The Thomas Jefferson* Story's doctrinal formulation represented no departure from his previous positions. The evidence casts doubt on a characterization of *The Thomas Jefferson* as "a curious landmark of admiralty abnegation in a judicial career marked otherwise by determined support of a broadened scope for the American maritime courts."[206] But it does not require qualification of the suggestion that Story was behaving strategically in the case, and that other Justices were watching. From this point of view, the most interesting feature of the Hopkinson letters is that Story may have adopted his version of the *Coolidge–General Smith* strategy to placate Marshall. Was Marshall, notwithstanding his public circumspection, a vigorous supporter of extensive admiralty jurisdiction?

There is additional evidence that the position attributed by Story to Marshall in the Hopkinson letters was at least held by Marshall late in his career. In an unsigned article in the *New York Review* in 1838, the author recounted an apparent conversation with Marshall in which the Chief Justice had

---

[205] Story to Hopkinson, Nov. 29, 1834, ibid.

[206] Note, "From Judicial Grant to Legislative Power; The Admiralty Clause in the Nineteenth Century," *Harv. L. Rev.*, 67:1214, 1217 (1954).

said (and he spoke of it as one of the most deliberate opinions of his life), at a comparatively late period, that he had always been of opinion that we in America had misapplied the principle upon which the admiralty jurisdiction depended—that in England the common expression was, that the admiralty jurisdiction extended only on tide waters, and as far as the tide ebbed and flowed; and this was a natural and reasonable exposition of the jurisdiction in England, where the rivers were very short, and some of them navigable from the sea beyond the ebb and flow of the tide—that such a narrow interpretation was wholly inapplicable to the great rivers of America; that the true principle, upon which the admiralty jurisdiction in America depended, was to ascertain how far the river was navigable from the sea; and that consequently, in America, the admiralty jurisdiction extended upon our great rivers not only as far as the tide ebbed and flowed in them, but as far as they were navigable from the sea, as, for example, on the Mississippi and its trainers, up to the falls of the Ohio.[207]

Since the position attributed to Marshall in the excerpt so closely matches, both in substance and in time ("at a comparatively late period") the position attributed to him by Story in the 1833 Hopkinson letter, it is likely that Marshall had advanced it privately late in his career. It does not follow that he held it in *The General Smith,* although the excerpt has him saying that he had "always been of [that] opinion." The excerpt does, however, suggest that if Marshall held to this view in *The General Smith,* his posture in that case was one of remarkable circumspection. Two additional cases remain to be discussed, however, before Marshall's position on admiralty jurisdiction can be fully assessed.

Two years after *The General Smith* came the case of *Ramsay* v. *Allegre,*[208] in which, as we have seen, Johnson exploded over the use of *The General Smith* as a precedent and attacked Wheaton's reporting of that case. There was some additional significance to *Ramsay.* It was a case in which Johnson reasserted his holding in *The Amanda,* repeated his attack on *DeLovio,* and reaffirmed his hostility toward "this silent and stealing progress of the Admiralty in acquiring jurisdiction to which it has no pretensions."[209] It was also a case in which Marshall, in his opinion, again declined to expose the Court on an admiralty jurisdiction issue.

When *Ramsay* v. *Allegre* was argued before the Court, it appeared

---

[207] "Chief Justice Marshall," *N.Y. Review,* 3:328 (1838). The author of the article was very probably James Kent, who visited Marshall in Richmond in the spring of 1835. See J. Horton, *James Kent: A Study in Conservatism* (1939), 318. My thanks to Professor Donald Roper of the State University of New York at New Paltz for giving me his thoughts on the authorship of the review.

[208] Supra, note 172.

[209] Ibid., 614.

to present an opportunity to reaffirm, extend, or distinguish *The General Smith*. A material man had filed a libel *in personam* in the federal district court of Maryland, alleging that a "ship's husband" had not paid him for his services in furnishing supplies. The ship, the schooner *Dorothea,* was a domestic ship; the work was done in the *Dorothea's* "home port." Maryland had not initiated a lien statute.[210] So if admiralty jurisdiction was to exist at all, it was of the *in personam* variety, and *in personam* admiralty jurisdiction could be found only if Story's dictum in *DeLovio* that the admiralty possessed such jurisdiction over maritime contracts was adopted. The *Dorothea* was being outfitted from the "high seas,"[211] so no *Thomas Jefferson* problems existed.

But there was a complicating factor in *Ramsay v. Allegre*. The ship's husband had given the material man a negotiable promissory note for his services, and the material man had given him a receipt. The receipt said that the note was "at four months," and "when paid, [will] be in full for [the bill for services]." The ship's husband did not pay the note when it came due, and the material man brought an *in personam* suit.[212] What was the effect of the note? Did its being offered and accepted on land take the case out of the admiralty jurisdiction?

The Baltimore federal district court and Gabriel Duvall's circuit court held that "the jurisdiction of the admiralty was waived by the [material man's] acceptance of the promissory note."[213] Counsel for the ship's husband, in their arguments before the Marshall Court, "insisted that the promissory note . . . was a personal security taken on land," and while "locality might not be the test of admiralty jurisdiction" in all cases, "where the credit is personal, and the security of a kind exclusively cognizable at common law, the locality should fix the jurisdiction." They then made the more general argument that "in the case of contracts, the admiralty jurisdiction, *in personam,* ought to be merely co-extensive with the proceeding *in rem,*" and as "the domestic character of the vessel freed the thing from jurisdiction, the person of the owner ought also to be exonerated." For that general proposition they cited *The General Smith*.[214]

William Wirt and William Meredith, representing the material man, began by asserting that "the District Courts, proceeding as Courts of admiralty and maritime jurisdiction, might take cognizance of material suits by material men, either *in personam* or *in rem*." They cited *The General Smith* as support for this claim.[215] The rest of their argument, as reported by Wheaton, was devoted to showing that the jurisdiction had

---

210 Ibid., 611–13.
211 Ibid., 611.
212 Ibid., 611–12.

213 Ibid., 612.
214 Ibid., 613.
215 Ibid., 612.

475

not been waived by the material man's acceptance of the note. "No authority or principle could be found," they argued, "to warrant the assertion that although the original contract in this case was not extinguished, the suspension of the right of action took away the jurisdiction of the admiralty, so that it could not again be resorted to." Their point was that there had been no special agreement to consider the note as payment, and that "the consent of the creditor must be positively declared, as the law will not presume that he means to abandon his rights under the first contract."[216]

Marshall, for the Court, saw his opportunity, and took it. "[I]t did not appear by the record," he wrote in a one-paragraph opinion, "that the note had been tendered to be given up, or actually surrendered." Thus the note was still enforceable in a common law action, and the suit was therefore a domestic bills and notes action, not an admiralty case at all. Marshall affirmed the decision below and stated that it was "not necessary to consider the general question of jurisdiction."[217] His solution was artful, and his disposition received the apparent support of all the Justices, but it did not prevent Johnson from writing an extended concurrence in which he addressed the larger issues raised in *Ramsay*.

Most of Johnson's opinion in *Ramsay* consisted of a restatement of his argument in *The Amanda* that the admiralty had no jurisdiction over maritime contracts, and of a detailed examination of Wheaton's alleged misreporting of Pinkney's concession about *in personam* jurisdiction in *The General Smith*. Both of those features of Johnson's opinion have been previously discussed. Worthy of note at this juncture is some additional language revealing more explicitly the large issues Johnson perceived as being at stake in admiralty jurisdiction cases.

Johnson could not resist discussing *DeLovio* yet another time. "Of the case in 2 Gallison," he said, "I will only remark that it was a decision in the first circuit . . . and if the *nisi prius* decisions of the judges of this Court are of any authority here, it is only necessary to observe that a contrary decision has been rendered in the sixth circuit. Let them, therefore, fall together; and let the question be tested upon principle and authority, independent of those decisions." He then, in his conclusion, made more explicit what he meant by "principle":

> I am fortifying a weak point in the wall of the constitution. Every advance of the Admiralty is a victory over the common law; a conquest gained upon the trial by jury. The principles upon which alone this suit could have been maintained, are equally applicable to one half the commercial contracts between citizen and citizen. . . . In England there exists a controlling power, but here there is none. . . . [W]ho is to

[216] Ibid.　　　[217] Ibid., 614.

issue a prohibition to us, if we should ever be affected with a partiality for [the Admiralty] jurisdiction?[218]

The allusions to trial by jury and federal supremacy in this catalogue of principles were familiar Johnson themes, reminiscent of older battles on behalf of jury lawmaking and state sovereignty. The commercial contracts allusion, however, taken together with Johnson's remarks about the commercial community in *The Amanda,* threw an earlier comment he had made in his *Ramsay* concurrence into sharp relief. He had said, in discussing *The General Smith,*

[That case] was a case of the most extravagant attempt ever made to enforce this supposed line of material men. It serves to show to what embarrassments the commercial world might be exposed by pushing these maritime liens to excess. Since, upon the same principle on which the libel was there filed, however long the time that had elapsed, whatever number of voyages the vessel had made, and whatever changes of property she might have passed through, she could still have remained liable to material men.[219]

This is the voice of the steamboat owners in *The Thomas Jefferson;* the voice of the shipowners in Charleston; a voice advocating security and predictability for the commercial world. When one juxtaposes this passage with Story's admission to Hopkinson that he was "a great friend to the admiralty jurisdiction" because it was "so full of equity," it appears that at least one enthusiast for federal jurisdiction was not motivated, at least in maritime contracts cases, by solicitude for the commercial world. Moreover, Johnson did not regard state court autonomy in admiralty jurisdiction cases as incompatible with the values of the commercial community.

Marshall's role in *Ramsay* remains to be explored. The cryptic statements in his opinion for the Court are made more intelligible by a letter he wrote to Story in 1831. In that letter, precipitated by an admiralty jurisdiction case that he had encountered on circuit, Marshall said,

I felt some doubt whether the General Smith was not shaken by the case of Ramsay v. All[egre], in which the court supposed that the note certainly ousted the admiralty of its jurisdiction, without deciding whether independent of the note jurisdiction would have existed. I think there is a good deal of force in the argument of Wirt and Meredith that the original cause of action did not merge in the note.[220]

---

[218] Ibid., 640.
[219] Ibid., 636.
[220] J. Marshall to J. Story, June 26,

1831, in *Proc. Mass. Hist. Soc.,* 14:344 (1901).

The letter appears to confirm the supposition that Marshall's effort in *Ramsay* was to avoid confronting the question of admiralty jurisdiction over maritime contracts. But it suggests that Marshall viewed the decision in *Ramsay* as cutting back on the dictum in *The General Smith* that *in personam* jurisdiction attached whenever a maritime contract was involved. The letter also indicates that Marshall had not accepted Wirt and Meredith's invitation to distinguish the "original cause of action," an *in personam* maritime contracts suit, from the note, a common law domestic bills and notes suit, even though he felt it had "a good deal of force." On the contrary, he had written an opinion based on the premise "that the note certainly ousted the admiralty of its jurisdiction," even though he was not sure that "the original cause of action [had merged] in the note."

The letter, coupled with Marshall's opinion in *Ramsay,* tells a good deal about his interest in maintaining unanimity and the appearance of harmony within his Court. Given the violence of Johnson's concurrence, his sentiments about *The General Smith* were doubtless known to his colleagues when *Ramsay* was discussed. Marshall's opinion was an effort not only to avoid exposing the Court as a champion of federal court power but also to avoid open discussion of the larger jurisdictional issues. He was only partially successful in achieving this second goal. Story kept silent, even though *The General Smith* was "shaken," but Johnson did not.

How does one square Marshall's posture in *Ramsay* with his alleged statements about the scope of the admiralty jurisdiction over inland waters? A fruitful case for testing that query would appear to be one in which a maritime contracts and an "ebb and flow of the tide" issue were both raised, preferably late in Marshall's career. Such a case, *Peyroux* v. *Howard,*[221] did in fact come before the Court in 1833. But the result in that case, referred to at the time as *"The Planter,"* did not serve to clarify Marshall's position.

*The Planter* came during a Term when the Court was not robust. Marshall had survived a serious kidney stone operation in 1831; Baldwin was suffering from emotional problems and missed the entire Term; Duvall's deafness had become acute; Johnson was debilitated with illness; and Story was burdened with teaching responsibilities and his *Commentaries.* The Court delivered only forty-one opinions, its fewest since 1826, and Thompson and McLean, the only Justices apparently without one or another form of distraction, wrote twelve of those. One of Thompson's opinions was in *The Planter,* and while it provoked no dissents, it evaded most of the difficult issues.

*The Planter* involved an *in rem* action by shipwrights for work done

---

[221] 7 Pet. 324 (1833).

on a domestic ship in the port of New Orleans, her home port. Three admiralty jurisdiction issues were raised in the case. The first was whether the presence of a Louisiana state statute giving shipwrights a lien on vessels on which they had worked meant that, notwithstanding the home port doctrine, the lien could be enforced in the federal admiralty courts. The second was whether services performed in the port of New Orleans were "within the ebb and flow of the tide." The third was whether services performed on a steamboat which was to navigate waters beyond the ebb and flow of the tide were maritime services. So stated, *The Planter* appeared to be potentially a great case, for it provided the Court with an opportunity to clarify *The General Smith* and *The Thomas Jefferson* at the same time, and also to give more concrete meaning to the term "maritime contracts." Moreover, the vessel being libeled in *The Planter* was a steamboat employed in service on the great inland waterways of the Midwest, all of which ultimately flowed to the port of New Orleans on the Gulf of Mexico. If federal admiralty courts in New Orleans had no *in rem* jurisdiction over steamboats serviced in their waters, no federal admiralty courts located in states with inland water ports were likely to possess that jurisdiction. And if the Louisiana statutory lien invoked in *The Planter* was not enforceable in the admiralty, no state liens would be: Story's and Wheaton's dicta in *The General Smith* would be disapproved.

Thompson's opinion spent almost no time on the first and third issues, as if they had been settled. On the state statutory lien issue, he gave a nearly verbatim paraphrase of Story's language in *The General Smith,* adding at the end of his paraphrase the sentence, "But if the local law gives the lien it may be enforced in the admiralty."[222] On the "maritime services" issue, he again paraphrased Story directly, this time referring to the language of *The Thomas Jefferson.*[223] Thompson's two paraphrases resulted in a holding that the existence of a state statutory lien was sufficient to institute *in rem* proceedings in the federal courts, even in the case of a domestic ship in her home port; and that the meaning of "maritime services" was to be determined by asking whether the service was "performed substantially on the sea or on tide water."[224] With respect to the more general maritime contracts issue, Thompson asserted that away:

> The proceeding is *in rem* against a steamboat, for materials found and work performed in repairing the vessel in the port of New Orleans . . . under a contract entered into between the parties for that purpose. It is therefore a maritime contract.[225]

---

[222] Ibid., 341.
[223] Ibid., 343–44.

[224] Ibid., 341, 344.
[225] Ibid., 341.

The structure of Thompson's opinion in *The Planter*, in fact, made all these issues subordinate to the one on which he lingered: whether "the service was to be performed in a place within the jurisdiction of the admiralty."[226] This question "depend[ed]," Thompson said, "upon the fact whether the tide in the Mississippi ebbs and flows as high up the river as New Orleans."[227] He then spent two pages "notic[ing] . . . judicially" that the "tides have some effect upon the water at New Orleans."[228] That "notorious fact," for all intents and purposes, decided the case.[229]

Who among the admiralty jurisdiction buffs on the Court could be said to have won, and who to have lost, after Thompson's opinion? Story, of course, had fared rather well. Wheaton's note, likely added at Story's instance to *The General Smith*, had become established as a principle of admiralty law. The meaning of "maritime services" given in *The Thomas Jefferson* had been followed, and the meaning was a broad one, since a service performed "substantially on the sea or on tide water" was maritime wherever the ship subsequently went. And since maritime contracts were declared to be contracts for maritime services, that doctrinal category was also potentially broad. Finally, the case made it clear that the central question to ask in admiralty jurisdiction cases was the "ebb and flow" question, and Story had first formulated that question.

Johnson had not fared so well, and his silence suggests that the state of his health and his preoccupation with the nullification controversy in his home state had distracted him.[230] To be sure, he had never denied that the admiralty courts had *in rem* jurisdiction over maritime lien cases. But he had confined that jurisdiction to a certain class of cases, of which *The Planter* was not one; he had strenuously objected to any other form of maritime contracts jurisdiction; and he had said in *Ramsay* that "with regard to the contracts of shipwrights and material men in her home port, the vessel cannot be subjected, [to jurisdiction], unless by express hypothecation of the owner."[231] Even the "ebb and flow" limitation on inland waters may not have suited him: he had suggested in 1828 that a constitutional amendment would be necessary to extend admiralty jurisdiction to disputes on ships sailing in inland waters.[232] He had approved

---

[226] Ibid.
[227] Ibid., 342.
[228] Ibid., 342–43.
[229] Thompson spent three additional pages on the issue of whether the material men had waived their lien, which he treated as a "general" common law contracts issue and resolved in favor of the material men. Ibid., 344–46.

[230] See supra, Chapter VI; D. Morgan, *Justice William Johnson: The First Dissenter* (1954), 268–81.
[231] 12 Wheat. at 648.
[232] Steam Boat Edgefield v. Brooks (1828), Minutes, United States Circuit Court, District of South Carolina, Charleston, S.C.

the "ebb and flow" language in *The Thomas Jefferson,* but now that language had been used to allow the admiralty a foothold on the largest port of the inland waterways system.

If one assumes that Marshall held an expansive view about jurisdiction over inland waterways, his position was the most curious of all. He assigned the opinions of the Court, by virtue of practice, longevity, seniority, and stature, and he had the unquestioned option of writing any opinion whose result he endorsed. As we have seen, the Supreme Court's modern practice of delegating the assignment of opinions to the senior member of the majority when the Chief Justice votes with the minority was not followed on the Marshall Court, so Marshall could have assigned the opinion even had he disapproved of the result. And given Thompson's interpretation of the "ebb and flow" doctrine—"if the effect of the tide is so great as to occasion a regular rise and fall of the water,"[233] admiralty jurisdiction attached—it is difficult to imagine that Marshall disapproved of the result in *The Planter.* But why did he not take the opportunity to articulate the principle of admiralty jurisdiction over inland waters that he had formulated? *The Planter* was an ideal case in which to advance that position. The intermingling in the port of New Orleans of river and sea water, the significance of that port for inland steamboat traffic, the growing prominence of the steamboat in domestic commerce, the growth of that commerce itself, the relative efficiency of *in rem* admiralty proceedings, the increasing number of state lien statutes, the fact that federal judges, rather than state juries, would be deciding maritime lien cases— all of these factors suggested that the ebb and flow doctrine made little sense on America's inland waterways. In addition, Marshall could bear in mind the experience of his doctrinally bold but popular opinion in *Gibbons* and the practice in American jurisprudence of discarding English doctrines if they were inapplicable to the conditions of life in America.

The fact that Marshall kept silent in *The Planter,* despite all these apparent incentives to reshape the ebb and flow doctrine,[234] underscores the extremely cautious public posture he adopted in admiralty jurisdiction cases. He was well aware not only of Johnson's opposition to "the silent and stealing progress" of the admiralty but of Story's commitment to the ebb and flow doctrine. He had been in the habit of allowing others to

---

[233] 7 Pet. at 343.

[234] Nineteen years after *The Planter* the Taney Court took up the opportunity Marshall had declined and announced that *The Thomas Jefferson* "was founded in error, and that the error, if not corrected, must produce serious injustice as well as private inconvenience." Chief Justice Roger Taney's opinion for the Court overruled *The Thomas Jefferson* and intimated that federal court admiralty jurisdiction extended to all inland navigable waters. The Genessee Chief, 12 How. 443, 459 (1851). See the discussion in C. Swisher, *The Taney Period, 1836–64* (1974), 426–46.

engage in admiralty jurisdiction battles without publicly committing himself. Where he had written admiralty jurisdiction opinions, they had been narrow and circumspect, avoiding large issues if possible. He was not at all loath to keep silent when it was his "misfortune to differ" with his colleagues. He was, in the period in which *The Planter* was considered, also deeply preoccupied with the nullification controversy, writing to Story in September 1832, "I yield slowly and reluctantly to the conviction that our constitution cannot last,"[235] and in December of that year, "[W]e are now gathering the bitter fruits of the tree . . . planted by Mr. Jefferson."[236] All of these factors, together with his instinct not to offend those with whom he lived and worked, may have influenced his decision to assign *The Planter* to Thompson, a Justice who had not been active in admiralty jurisdiction cases but who was an experienced opinion writer and a consummate politician.

*The Planter* was the last of the Marshall Court's admiralty jurisdiction cases.[237] By the 1830s disputes over the commerce power had replaced disputes over the admiralty jurisdiction as the principal locus of federal-state tension in matters involving navigation.[238] The number of admiralty and maritime cases entertained by the Court had dropped dramatically since the period of *DeLovio*, *The General Smith*, *The Amanda*, and *The Thomas Jefferson*.[239] The steamboat and the Erie Canal had emerged as symbols of the expanded meaning of commerce in America: no longer was Story's association of that word with oceangoing traffic setting the terms of discourse.[240] But the subsequent importance of the commercial changes that began in the 1820s should not skew perceptions of the place of admiralty jurisdiction issues in the history of the Court.

[235] J. Marshall to J. Story, Sept. 22, 1832, quoted in *Proc. Mass. Hist. Soc.*, 14:352 (1901).

[236] J. Marshall to J. Story, Dec. 25, 1832, quoted in ibid., 354.

[237] In The Orleans v. Phoebus, 11 Pet. 175 (1837), an early Taney Court case, Story reaffirmed both the maritime lien implications of *The General Smith* and *The Planter* and continued the use of the "ebb and flow" test as determinative of admiralty jurisdiction.

[238] See discussion infra, Chapter VIII.

[239] Nineteen such cases (the term "admiralty and maritime" here taken as including prize cases, instance cases and marine insurance cases as well as jurisdiction cases) were decided in the 1816 Term, thirteen in 1817, twelve in 1818, ten in 1821, and nine in 1823. After 1827 only one Term, that of 1828, had a sizeable number of "admiralty and maritime" cases (eleven). The Court heard no such cases in 1830, three in 1831, two in 1833, and one in 1835. The figures are taken from the Court's Reports, 1 Wheaton (1818) through 9 Peters (1835).

[240] For a contemporary assessment of the significance of canals and steamboats, see J. Cooper, *Notions of the Americans* (2 vols., 1963 ed.), 321–22, 325–26, discussed in Chapter I.

## Chapter VII: *Admiralty Jurisdiction*

We have had occasion throughout this volume to confront cultural and ideological themes of sufficient centrality that they may be said to have helped establish the boundaries of the Court's juristic universe. One such theme, exemplified by the changing meanings and implications of the word "commerce," has been the coexistence, in both economic practices and theories of economic activity, of classical republican and liberal, communal and atomistic visions of the American economy. Another theme, embodied in federal supremacy issues, especially the issue of the limits on the jurisdiction of the federal courts, has been the locus of sovereignty in a federal Union with a governmental structure based on a separation of powers. A third theme has been the nature of law in America, both with respect to the substance and sources of legal rules and with respect to the issue of judicial discretion. A fourth theme has been the function of time in early-nineteenth-century American legal culture, as evidenced by the role of past history or present politics in legal discourse.

All of these themes surfaced, implicitly or explicitly, in the Marshall Court's admiralty jurisdiction opinions. Each was present in *DeLovio*, in which Story associated commerce with oceangoing navigation, thereby implicitly defining the phrase "admiralty and maritime"; in which he linked the expansion of admiralty jurisdiction to a larger campaign to expand the sovereignty and power of the federal government, and especially the federal courts; in which he assumed that purposive lawmaking, presented as detached digesting, was a legitimate activity for a federal judge, and therefore that jurisdictional power lead to judicial discretion to fashion substantive rules; and in which he alternatively appealed to history and to contemporary policy as authoritative legal sources. Thus in a *nisi prius* opinion that was not appealed Story set the stage for the Court's admiralty jurisdiction cases. The chief participants in those cases—Johnson, Marshall, and Story himself—knew precisely what was at stake.

The admiralty jurisdiction cases can be read on several levels and be seen as raising several issues simultaneously. The cryptic and cautious nature of the Court's decisions can be seen as testifying to the multiplicity and complexity of factors at stake in them. Issues of economic policy, such as whether the commercial community was better served by security for shipowners from claims by material men or by prompt and decisive satisfaction of those claims, became intermingled with issues of political theory, such as whether the federal or state courts should adjudicate such claims. Jurisprudential issues, such as the juristic authority of the Supreme Court to make decisions enhancing or limiting the power of federal judges, or the appropriate sources of substantive legal rules, came to raise larger epistemological questions, such as the question of how far the Court's decisions should be shaped by history, current politics or practices, or visions of the future. The intermingling of these momentous

483

issues produced, in those judges who participated extensively in admiralty jurisdiction cases, doctrinal and ideological cross-currents, strategies and hidden agendas, unexpressed fears, and, occasionally, violent outbursts. The Marshall Court's admiralty jurisdiction decisions, taken together with their context, can thus be seen as fraught with an underlying tension, the existence of which helps to define the Court itself.

# CHAPTER VIII

---

# *Sovereignty and Union: Federal Jurisdiction and Federal Limitations on State Power*

T HE PRECEDING CHAPTER, taken in connection with Chapters I and II, has emphasized the major importance for the Marshall Court Justices and their contemporaries of a perplexing and unsettled political and jurisprudential issue: the nature and limits of federal sovereignty in the American republic. The great importance of the issue, we have seen, came from the interplay in early-nineteenth-century America of two factors: the commitment made in the Constitution to a federated form of government, with divided repositories of sovereignty; and the dramatic expansion in territory, population, transportation, commerce, and wealth that occurred in the years after the War of 1812. Many of the great constitutional cases decided by the Marshall Court were sovereignty cases, delineating the competing spheres of influence of the federal government and the states. This chapter surveys several of those cases, which can be divided into two types: cases defining the constitutional scope of the jurisdiction of the federal courts, and cases determining the affirmative limits that the Constitution placed on the sovereignty of the states.

Included in the first category of cases are the celebrated decisions in *Martin* v. *Hunter's Lessee*[1] and *Cohens* v. *Virginia*,[2] testing the power of the states to resist Supreme Court review of the decision of their courts; the case of *Osborn* v. *Bank of the United States*,[3] considering the jurisdiction of the federal courts over so-called "federal questions"; and the case of *Houston* v. *Moore*,[4] examining the relationship between federal court jurisdiction and congressional power to regulate an activity and thereby preclude its being regulated by the states. Included in the second

---

[1] 1 Wheat. 304 (1816).
[2] 6 Wheat. 264 (1821).

[3] 9 Wheat. 738 (1824).
[4] 5 Wheat. 1 (1820).

category of cases are *McCulloch* v. *Maryland,*[5] upholding congressional power to establish a federal bank and declaring that bank immune from state taxation, and *Gibbons* v. *Ogden,*[6] the Court's first attempt to use the Constitution's Commerce Clause to restrict state economic regulation. Also included are two Commerce Clause cases, *Brown* v. *Maryland*[7] and *Willson* v. *Black-bird Creek Marsh Co.,*[8] that extended and qualified *Gibbons; Craig* v. *Missouri,*[9] the first construction of the constitutional clause limiting the power of the states to issue bills of credit; and *Barron* v. *Mayor of Baltimore,*[10] raising the question whether the provisions of the Bill of Rights, as interpreted by the federal judiciary, were themselves limits on state sovereignty.

These cases have conventionally been recognized as decisions that helped shape the tone and identity of the Marshall Court. But the definition of federal sovereignty collectively offered by the cases has often been loosely characterized and sometimes patently misunderstood. The cases have often been identified as decisions promoting ''nationalism,'' but very few of them facilitated the development of national institutions or sustained regulatory policies instituted by the national government. Many of the cases did not so much promote federal sovereignty as restrict state sovereignty. They prevented the states from treating the decisions of their courts or legislatures as authoritative and incapable of federal supervision; they limited the power of the states to exclude areas of American life from the control of the federal judiciary; they restricted the power of the states to regulate various kinds of economic activity; and they curtailed the states from taxing federal institutions located within their borders. The ''nationalism'' inherent in those decisions was not a nationalism in the modern sense of support for affirmative plenary federal regulatory power; the Court's posture can more accurately be described as a critique of reserved state sovereignty.

But there was an affirmative dimension to the Marshall Court's sovereignty cases, although the term ''nationalism'' captures that dimension imperfectly. By restricting state sovereignty in areas where it clashed with the sovereignty of the federal government, the cases implicitly revived and strengthened the ''political axiom,'' identified in *The Federalist* and in Tucker's edition of Blackstone, that federal judicial power was coterminous with federal legislative power.[11] Indeed, the theory of constitutional interpretation promulgated in some of the earlier cases appeared, to contemporary critics, to reinforce the boldest claims of consolidationists by combining a broad interpretation of the Article III

---

[5] 4 Wheat. 316 (1819).
[6] 9 Wheat. 1 (1824).
[7] 12 Wheat. 419 (1827).
[8] 2 Pet. 245 (1829).

[9] 4 Pet. 410 (1830).
[10] 7 Pet. 243 (1823).
[11] See the discussion in Chapter II, at pp. 122–27.

# Chapter VIII: *Sovereignty and Union*

jurisdictional powers of the federal courts with a broad interpretation of the Article I implied powers of Congress. Since that theory of interpretation was advanced at the same time that members of the Marshall Court, most particularly Story, were privately advocating the expansion of national powers and national institutions, modern scholars, mindful of the twentieth-century presence of the federal government as a ubiquitous regulating force, have been eager to characterize the Court as a "nationalistic" tribunal. This chapter will suggest, however, that the theory of national sovereignty offered by the cases was an archaic version, essentially concerned with the preservation of the Union against dissolution as the American republic expanded; and that to the extent that the cases took on additional implications, such as the implication that the economic and political growth of the nation would be accompanied by a growth in the regulatory powers of the federal government, the Marshall Court cannot fairly be identified with those implications.

The feature of the Court's constitutional sovereignty decisions that unites their negative and affirmative strands and provides the best index of their character is their juxtaposition of the concepts of "Union" and "compact." The overriding purpose of the decisions can be seen as the replacement of the idea that the Constitution was created by a compact among the states with the idea that the Constitution created a Union out of the states. Once this purpose was apparently achieved, and social compact theory discredited, the Court did not take the next logical step, the transformation, through the assumption of the legitimacy of coterminous federal power, of the government of the Union into an omnipresent force. By Marshall's death, compact theory had been severely undermined, but coterminous power theory had not produced an aggressively dominant federal government. The department of that government which had profited the most from the articulation of coterminous power theory was not Congress, the agent of federal regulation, but the Supreme Court of the United States, the self-styled preserver of the Union and the Constitution.

On April 13, 1830, at Brown's Hotel in Washington, Thomas Jefferson's eighty-seventh birthday was posthumously celebrated. Jefferson was at that time claimed as a patron by both major political parties; present at the dinner were President Andrew Jackson, John C. Calhoun, now the major spokesman for state autonomy, and Martin Van Buren, the apostle of modern party politics. The nullification controversy, which Calhoun and South Carolina would use as a trial balloon for state autonomy and potential secession, was brewing. The Republican party, which Jefferson had helped create and his eventual successor James Monroe had sought to transform into an antiparty devoted to the Union and to consensus

487

politics, had splintered, and Van Buren was organizing a new partisan coalition, the Democratic party. The nature and future of the Union were on the diners' minds. Toasts were proposed. Calhoun toasted "the Union: next to our liberty the most dear; may we remember that it can only be preserved by respecting the rights of the states and distributing equally the benefit and burden of the Union." Van Buren responded by emphasizing "mutual forbearance and reciprocal concessions." Through such gestures, he claimed, the Union had been established, and "the patriotic spirit from which they emanated will forever sustain it." Jackson's toast has become the most widely quoted: "Our federal Union: it must be preserved."[12]

In those three toasts can be found much of the central language in which early-nineteenth-century Americans expressed the concept of Union. Van Buren recalled the origins of the Union in necessity and compromise: a national government had been created as an experiment in mutual self-defense. Calhoun's toast emphasized that the central goal of the Union was the preservation of liberty, which he argued could best be achieved by respect for state autonomy and the equal distribution of the "burdens" of a federal system. Jackson's toast assumed that the Union was now a permanent feature of American civilization that needed to be preserved at all costs.

Each of the three toasts was premised on a different approach to sovereignty issues. Calhoun's use of the term "liberty," and his characterization of the Union as an entity whose central purpose was to preserve liberty by respecting the rights of the states, were conventional examples of social compact theory. Advocates of social compact theory assumed that men held certain inalienable rights anterior to the formation of government, and governments existed to secure those rights. The compacts made at the formation of governments required individuals to tolerate some restrictions on their rights in order to promote the public good, but they also required government to protect inalienable rights as far as possible. If a government restricted liberty, social compact theory suggested, the government could be dissolved.

The American experiment in federated republicanism required the creation of additional layers of compacts, those between the federal government and the states and those between the federal government and the people. Social compact theorists were most concerned that the balances among sovereign entities envisaged by a republic would be upset by usurpations of the compacts by the federal government. They argued that while the Constitution took pains to establish the federal government as one of limited, enumerated powers, state powers, specifically reserved in

---

[12] For a contemporary account of the dinner, including the toasts quoted, see *Niles' Weekly Register*, Apr. 24, 1830.

the Tenth Amendment, were only sporadically limited. St. George Tucker's edition of Blackstone, which described the Constitution as a "social compact," took pains to stress that "the union is in fact, as well as in theory, an association of states," and "the state governments . . . retain every power, jurisdiction, and right not delegated to the United States."[13]

Tucker's treatise also demonstrated some concern that the new compacts of federated republicanism might result in undue restrictions of individual liberties by the federal government. "[I]t might . . . be deemed somewhat extraordinary," he suggested, "that in the establishment of a federal republic, it should have been thought necessary to extend its operation to the persons of individuals, as well as to the states composing the confederacy." The "friends and supporters of the Constitution" had taken pains, Tucker maintained, to emphasize that the "assent and ratification of the people" on which the Constitution was founded had been made "not as individuals composing one entire nation" but as individuals "composing the distinct and independent states." Individual citizens had ratified the Constitution in their capacity as residents of states, and each state had ratified the Constitution "as a sovereign body, independent of all others, and only to be bound by its own voluntary act." Thus construction of the Constitution, Tucker believed, ought to be "strict" in two senses: "in all cases where the antecedent rights of a state may be drawn in question," and "wherever the right of personal liberty, of personal security, or of private property may become the subject of dispute."[14]

The effect of Tucker's remarks was to advance three propositions about the interplay between federal and state sovereignty in the American republic. First, after the passage of the Constitution the states retained a vast array of reserved powers. Second, the inalienable rights of man preserved in the social compact were associated with the sovereign rights of the states preserved in the federal compact: liberty and state autonomy were linked. Third, the Union was expressly not a consolidation of the states justified by the will of the people; it was a confederacy of the states based on the consent of states in their capacity as representatives of the people. State interests could not be bypassed in the name of a national entity directly representative of the people's will.

In the course of his discussion of social compact theory Tucker also identified the principal arguments supporters of an expansive concept of Union would seek to make throughout the next two decades. The elevation of the concept of Union as an alternative to the concept of a social compact

---

[13] S. Tucker, *Blackstone's Commentaries: With Notes of Reference to the Constitution and Laws of the Federal Government of the United States and of* the Commonwealth of Virginia (5 vols., 1803), I, Appendix, Note D, 140–41.
[14] Ibid., 146, 151.

rested on a repudiation of each of the three propositions Tucker advanced. His claim that reserved state powers were vast was opposed by a claim that these powers needed to be narrowed in the name of fidelity to the "great objects" of the Constitution. His claim that individual liberty and state autonomy were associated was opposed by a claim that liberty and Union were inseparable. And his claim that the Constitution was essentially a compact between the Union and the states was opposed by a claim that it was essentially a manifestation of the will of the people. Buttressing each of these claims were developments in early-nineteenth-century American culture that seemed to reinforce the need for a perpetual Union. In Chapter I we noted the evolution of the concept of Union as a consensual surrogate, a device to bring about a surface reconciliation of divisive cultural tensions. In this evolutionary process, the Union became no longer an "experiment" but an "absolute," a concept that defined and cemented American culture and whose preservation, as Jackson's toast suggested, was necessary. The evolution of the concept of Union can perhaps best be understood by recalling the original grounds advanced to justify a federated republic with a "general" government: protection against foreign enemies, promotion of commercial interdependence, the creation of an institutional bulwark against factionalism and partisan strife, and the preservation of a republican form of government by the continual, unified expansion of that government's territory. Each of those justifications demonstrated the presence of shared concerns Americans held at the framing of the Constitution. The new form of government was envisaged as responding to the inability of the Articles of Confederation to respond to these concerns.

By 1815 the new government appeared to have demonstrated its ability to resist foreign enemies. The War of 1812, despite its inconclusive resolution, had established the United States as the master of its own territory, and the Louisiana Purchase had significantly expanded that territory. The war experience was interpreted as an example of the benefits of Union: the war had been fought over a large geographical area, and only through cooperative efforts among the states and the development of a national navy and militia had American forces been able to repulse the British. The other three concerns had, if anything, been accentuated by early-nineteenth-century developments. First, the American experiment in republican government had been a success, justifying its continuation, and a vast area of uninhabited land had become part of the American nation, raising the possibility that republican principles could be perpetuated through the spread of republican institutions across space. But the cyclical interpretation of cultural change remained intact: republics were seen as susceptible to decay and dissolution. By facilitating the expansion of republican forms of government could the Union break the cycle? Or would sectional discord and state provincialism hasten decline?

Second, the pursuit of commerce had become more entrenched and had lost its moral ambiguity, but the vastness of the domestic commercial market appeared to make interstate cooperation all the more necessary. Third, organized opposition politics had emerged in America with Jefferson's "party" in the 1800 election, suggesting that American political culture would always have the potential of degenerating into numerous groups of factions, forestalling consensus and creating discord. Thus the role of the Union as "antiparty" surrogate seemed more necessary than ever.

Between the War of 1812 and the close of the Marshall Court's tenure the concept of Union was transformed to respond to these concerns. Union ceased to be characterized as an experiment and was identified as a permanent feature of American civilization. Its permanence was justified as a means for preserving republican forms of governments, as a vehicle for facilitating the expansion of commerce, and as a buffer against partisan factionalism and discord. Three comments made by public figures in the 1820s illustrate the respective justifications. In 1821 Story, in an address to the Suffolk County, Massachusetts, bar, expressed a "hope that . . . the union of the states . . . may be perpetual." The preservation of the Union, he felt, could be achieved only "by sustaining the powers of the National Government in their full vigor." Failure to preserve federal powers would result in "the Constitution['s] . . . sink[ing] into a premature and hopeless decline," making it "probably the last [of a] long list of experiments to establish a free government."[15] A year later, in arguing for the use of federal revenues to make repairs on the Cumberland Road, a turnpike linking Cumberland, Maryland, to Wheeling, Virginia, a congressman maintained that "[t]he Union cannot be preserved except by commercial inter-course, and a free and easy commerce will always keep us united."[16] And in 1825 President John Quincy Adams claimed in his inaugural address that "the harmony of the nation . . . and the whole Union" had replaced "the . . . political parties which have divided the opinions and feelings of our country."[17]

At the same time, political and economic developments served to revive the particularistic concerns of states and sections, giving enhanced credence to the idea, promulgated by Tucker and others, that the Union had been created out of the self-interest of the respective states, with that self-interest reflected in the idea of a compact. After Monroe's adminis-

---

[15] J. Story, "The Progress of Jurisprudence," in W. Story, ed., *The Miscellaneous Writings of Joseph Story* (1852), 231.
[16] Speech in Congress, Apr. 9, 1822, in *Annals of Congress*, 17th Cong., I Sess., 1508.

[17] J. Q. Adams, First Inaugural Address, in A. Koch and W. Peden, eds., *The Selected Writings of John and John Quincy Adams* (1946), 353.

tration national executive politics took on an increasingly sectional orientation: in the next three elections presidential candidates represented sectional blocs. The emergence of industrial commerce in the North and the proliferation of slavery in the South meant that the organization of the expanding American economy took on distinct regional differences. National legislative politics became dominated by regional and state concerns, as the Missouri Compromise demonstrated. In this atmosphere it was no surprise that anticonsolidationism, with its dual premises of inalienable individual liberties and compact theory, underwent a revival in the 1820s.

As the expanded conception of Union was paralleled by revitalization of compact theory in the years after the War of 1812, the two ideas were bound to collide. By the 1820s compact theorists, such as Taylor, John Randolph, and Calhoun had developed the doctrines of interposition and nullification, which posited that the states could interpose themselves between the federal government and individuals where liberties were being usurped, and that the states could even declare void acts of the federal government that violated individual rights and thus undermined the social compact. These doctrines clashed directly with the idea of Union as a permanent entity, and advocates of the expanded conception of Union responded by questioning the premises of compact theory. Van Buren's toast sought an accommodation between the extremist "Union" and "compact" positions, but the positions appeared increasingly irreconcilable by 1830.

The clash between the concepts of Union and compact was portrayed vividly in Daniel Webster's famous 1830 Senate speeches replying to the nullificationist Robert Hayne of South Carolina. Hayne had said, in discussing the sale of midwestern public lands by the federal government, that excessive revenue from the sales might help "consolidate the government," which would be "fatal to the sovereignty of the states." Hayne believed that "the very life of our system is the independence of the States" and that "there is no evil more to be deprecated than the consolidation of this government."[18] Webster, in his first response, said that he "rejoice[d] in whatever tends to strengthen the bond that unites us, and encourages the hope that our Union may be perpetual."[19] Hayne followed by saying that

> as to the doctrine that the federal government is the exclusive judge of the extent as well as the limitations of its powers, it seems to me utterly subversive of the sovereignty and independence of the States. It makes but little difference . . . whether Congress or the Supreme Court are covered with this power.[20]

---

[18] See *Register of Debates*, 21st Cong., 1st Sess., 43–58.

[19] Ibid., 41.

[20] Ibid., 83.

# Chapter VIII: *Sovereignty and Union*

Webster, in his second response, put the issue between Union and compact theory as sharply as he could:

> I hold [the Union] to be a popular government, erected by the people; those who administer it, responsible to the people; and itself capable of being amended and modified, first as the people may choose it should be. It is as popular, just as truly emanating from the people, as the state governments. It is created for one purpose; the state governments for another.[21]

If state sovereignty, then, was essential to individual liberties, so was the Union. As Webster put in his conclusion, "liberty *and* Union" were "now and forever, one and inseparable."[22]

In this atmosphere it was inevitable that a legal commentator would offer an interpretation of the Constitution designed to emphasize the close connections between the Union, individual liberty, and the will of the people, while at the same time attacking compact theory. Story's *Commentaries on the Constitution*,[23] which appeared three years after the Webster–Hayne debate, provided such an interpretation. Story set forth Tucker's "views of the nature of the constitution" at length, adding that those views "represent . . . in a general sense, the opinions of a large body of statesmen and jurists . . . recently revived under circumstances, which have given them increased importance, if not a perilous influence."[24] In particular, Story pointed out, the characterization of the Constitution as "a compact between the states" was consistent with the proposition that "each state has a right . . . to withdraw from the confederacy and dissolve the connexion, when such shall be its choice."[25] He then took some sixty pages to show that the Constitution was not a compact at all, that it was designed to establish the sovereignty of the people, not the states, and that since none of the arrangements that formed the Constitution could fairly be described as a compact, there was no inherent right on the part of states or individuals to withdraw from the Union. The majority of the people, Story claimed, could bind the minority: once "the people of the United States" had created a Constitution, it became "obligatory and binding upon all the states."[26] Story was to conclude his *Commentaries* by suggesting that his purpose had been to "inspire . . . a profound reverence for the Constitution and the Union."[27]

The alternative theories of sovereignty encapsulated in the code

---

[21] D. Webster, "Second Speech on Foot's Resolution," in J. McIntyre, ed., *The Writings and Speeches of Daniel Webster* (18 vols., 1903), VI, 75.

[22] Ibid. Emphasis in original.

[23] J. Story, *Commentaries on the Constitution of the United States* (3 vols., 1833).

[24] Ibid., I, 287.

[25] Ibid., I, 288.

[26] Ibid., I, 343.

[27] Ibid., III, 759.

words "Union" and "compact" framed the constitutional interpretation of sovereignty issues by the Marshall Court. The Court's role in the sovereignty debate has been regularly characterized as that of a constant advocate for national power and a constant critic of states' rights, as if it anticipated the theoretical position advanced by George Ticknor Curtis and Abraham Lincoln in the 1850s and 1860s, when they claimed that the states could not choose to dissolve the Union without the consent of the people.[28] In fact, as we shall see, the Court's role was more cautious. While attacking the premises of compact theory and restricting the sovereign powers of the states, the Marshall Court was neither an advocate of federal plenary power in the modern sense nor an unbridled promoter of consolidationism. As in the admiralty area, the Court recognized competing views and gave them serious attention, and while some of its most influential Justices may have been consolidationist in theory, they were careful not to be overly consolidationist in practice.

We have seen that for Tucker, Jefferson, and their contemporaries the prospective jurisdiction of the new federal courts envisaged by the Constitution raised serious political and jurisprudential problems. Tucker and Jefferson believed that those courts, if they adopted the common law as the basis of their decisions, could carve out an "unlimited" ambit of power for themselves and in the process nullify the decisions of state courts.

The issue of "unlimited" federal jurisdiction first came to a head, as noted, in cases raising the question whether a general law of non-statutory crimes existed. Mindful of the political ramifications of federal judges declaring the content of unwritten offenses, the Marshall Court declined to allow the federal courts to develop a common law of crimes. In the process enthusiasts for a common law of crimes, such as Story, and opponents of it, such as Johnson, agreed that a distinction existed between jurisdiction and the declaration of substantive rules. According to the distinction, the federal courts possessed only that jurisdiction which Congress, pursuant to the Constitution, had given them. But within the ambit of that jurisdiction, Story claimed, their power to develop substantive rules was unlimited. And, as we shall see in subsequent chapters, early-nineteenth-century jurists did not regard the federal courts, in fashioning their rules, as necessarily bound to follow the rules of the state courts in which they sat.

[28] See A. Lincoln, First Inaugural Address, in R. Buster, ed., *The Collected Works of Abraham Lincoln* (8 vols., 1953), IV, 289; G. Curtis, *History of the Origin, Formation, and Adoption of the Constitution of the United States* (2 vols., 1854), II, 123.

# Chapter VIII: *Sovereignty and Union*

We have also noted that the distinction posited by Story and others ignored a difficulty that had emerged with Marshall's suggestion in *Marbury* v. *Madison* that the federal judiciary was well suited to be the ultimate arbiter of constitutional questions. The limits on the jurisdiction of the federal courts, Story and others pointed out, were constitutional limits. The Constitution made federal court jurisdiction discretionary with Congress, and Congress, in statutes such as the Judiciary Act of 1789, defined the jurisdictional boundaries. But when the scope of federal jurisdiction was challenged as exceeding constitutional limits, the federal judiciary, in the person of the Supreme Court, established those limits, even when it ruled, as in common law crimes, that the federal courts had no jurisdiction over a particular subject. Thus not only was the federal judiciary, in such cases, determining the limits of its own jurisdiction, the jurisdictional issue being determined was a question of substantive constitutional law. At bottom the question was one of sovereignty, since when the federal courts were deemed not to have jurisdiction over an issue, power to resolve that issue reverted to the state courts.

When Tucker and Jefferson had originally expressed their concern that federal court power might become unlimited if the common law was adopted in the federal courts, the situation they seem to have anticipated was a common law case in which an unwritten federal substantive rule might subvert an opposing state court rule on the same subject. *Martin* v. *Hunter's Lessee*, the Court's first important sovereignty case in the period covered by this volume, was such a case on its merits: the issue determinative of the litigation in *Martin* was whether a federal treaty or a Virginia state statute controlled the disposition of an estate in Virginia. But *Martin* did come to the Marshall Court on that issue. It was appealed on a writ of error on the issue of whether the Court had jurisdiction to review a final judgment of a state court. That issue, rather than the merits issue, was to be the central focus of the Court's constitutionally based jurisdictional cases. The cases were descendants of *Marbury* v. *Madison,* cases in which the Court, having established in *Marbury* its authority to review acts of Congress under the Constitution, now claimed the power to review the substantive decisions of state courts on constitutional issues, or to preclude, by virtue of the subject matter of the case, state courts or state legislatures from passing on issues at all. These ''jurisdiction'' cases were truly sovereignty cases, and it was in these cases that the compact theory of sovereignty was most pointedly undermined by the Marshall Court.

*Martin* v. *Hunter's Lessee* arose out of a combination of three factors. One was the absence of construction of Section 25 of the Judiciary Act of 1789, giving the Supreme Court of the United States power to ''re-examine and reverse or affirm . . . a final judgment . . . in the highest court . . . of a State'' where federal statutes or federal treaties had been "drawn in question" and determined to be invalid, or where a state statute or common law decision had been challenged as "repugnant to the constitution, or laws of the United States," and found to be valid.[29] The second was the state of Virginia's outrage that its judges had been "instructed" and "commanded" by the Marshall Court to enforce the decision in *Fairfax's Devisee* v. *Hunter's Lessee*,[30] in which the Court had reversed the Virginia Court of Appeals's decision that Virginia escheat acts took precedence over federal treaties in determining the ownership of land held by British loyalists in Virginia. The third was the theoretical arguments used by the Virginia Court of Appeals to justify its refusal to comply with the *Fairfax* order. Among those arguments included claims that "[t]he constitution of the United States contemplates the independence of both [the national and the state] governments, and regards the *residuary* sovereignty of the states as not less inviolable, than the *delegated* sovereignty of the United States."[31]

As we have seen in Chapter III, the Marshall Court demonstrated a very strong interest in facilitating the process by which *Martin* v. *Hunter's Lessee* was reviewed. The Virginia Court of Appeals's unanimous decision "that the appellate [review] power of the Supreme Court of the United States does not extend to this court" was announced on December 15, 1815. On the following February 5, the Supreme Court of the United States opened its 1816 Term, and a writ of error was filed appealing the Virginia decision. By March 12 the Marshall Court heard the full argument in the case, and on March 20 the Court unanimously rejected the contention of the Virginia Court of Appeals and affirmed its constitutional power to compel that court to follow the *Fairfax* decision. Within three months the challenge had been posed and dismissed.

We have noted that one cannot begin to compare the timing of the Marshall Court's review process with that of modern Supreme Courts. Nonetheless, the speed by which *Martin* v. *Hunter's Lessee* was heard and disposed of is striking, as is the informality of the review process. *Martin* was one of a very few cases filed with the Court in the 1816 Term that had been decided by a previous court as late as December 1815. Despite its late arrival on the docket, it was the only case filed for the first time in 1816 that was decided with full opinions that Term. In his opinion for the Court, Story declared that the "record" of the *Martin* case had been "duly certified" to the Marshall Court "under the seal" of the Virginia Court of Appeals.[32] That statement was not quite accurate. Only the Court of Appeals's original refusal to comply with *Fairfax,* not its response to the writ of error taken out by the lawyers for the Marshall

---

[29] 1 Stat. 74 (1789).
[30] 7 Cranch 603 (1813).

[31] Hunter v. Martin, 4 Munf. 1, 8–10 (Va., 1815).
[32] 1 Wheat. 304, 361 (1816).

syndicate in *Martin,* had been filed with the Marshall Court. There was no "seal" of the Virginia court annexed to the writ of error in *Martin;* there was only the bundle of affidavits described in Chapter III.

Story's opinion for the Court in *Martin* reversed the Virginia Court of Appeals's holding that Section 25 of the Judiciary Act, authorizing federal review of state decisions, was unconstitutional. The first ground on which Story based his decision was that Article III of the Constitution required Congress to create federal courts and to vest in them the full range of Article III powers, including a power in the Supreme Court of the United States to review state court decisions. Story read the language of Article III[33] as "imperative," importing "an absolute grant of judicial power."[34] Congress, he claimed, was bound to create some inferior courts, and "the whole judicial power of the United States should be, at all times, vested either in an original or appellate form."[35] Moreover, Article III provided that the judicial power of the United States "shall extend to all cases" arising under the Constitution, laws, and treaties of the United States. This language, Story argued, contemplated that where cases had been originally brought in the state courts, and constitutional issues or issues involving the construction of federal laws and treaties were raised, the "judicial power" of the United States would extend to those cases. And since, if the cases were properly in the state courts, the power of the federal courts could not "extend by original jurisdiction," it "must . . . extend by appellate jurisdiction."[36]

Such was the structure of Story's Article III argument. A discerning anticonsolidationist would have heard echoes of coterminous power resounding through it. While the "government . . . of the United States" could "claim no powers which are not granted to it by the constitution," Story admitted, the Constitution was to "have a reasonable construction." A power expressly given to the federal government "in general terms" was not, unless context mandated it, "to be restrained to particular cases." And where the Constitution's granting of power had been made in general terms, Congress could be taken as permitted to "adopt its own means to effectuate legitimate objects."[37] Thus once power had been granted to the judiciary Congress could enlarge it; there was an implied power in the federal legislature to expand the power of the federal judiciary. The language of Article III, declaring that the judicial power of the United States shall be vested in one Supreme Court, was, Story claimed, "the voice of the whole American people solemnly declared, in establishing one great department of that government which was, in many

---

[33] "The judicial Power of the United States, shall be vested in one supreme Court, and in such inferior Courts as Congress may from time to time ordain and establish."

[34] I Wheat. at 331.
[35] Ibid.
[36] Ibid., 342.
[37] Ibid., 326–27.

respects, national, and in all, supreme.'' Then came a comment opponents of consolidation may well have marked:

> [Article III] is a part of the very same instrument which was to act not merely upon individuals, but upon states; and to deprive them altogether of the exercise of some powers of sovereignty, and to refrain and regulate them in the exercise of others.[38]

In this portion of the argument Story assumed a partnership between Congress and the federal courts to "effectuate [the] legitimate objects" of the Constitution. But even if Congress were disinclined to cooperate, the Constitution, Story next argued, required that cooperation. Article III's "imperative" language illustrated that "the object of the Constitution was to establish three great departments of government: the legislative, the executive, and the judicial departments." For Congress not to create a Supreme Court and some lower federal courts would make it "impossible to carry into effect some of the express provisions of the constitution," which needed to be "expound[ed] and enforce[d]" by the judicial department. This would enable Congress to "defeat the constitution" itself.[39]

Congress was thus in a partnership, either willingly or unwillingly, with the federal courts to extend the authority of the latter over what Story termed cases of "vital importance . . . to the national sovereignty."[40] Some of those cases were specified in Article III, but there might be others that Congress would elect to vest federal judicial power over. At any rate, Story concluded, Congress was required to vest all the enumerated Article III powers in the federal courts. As Story put it in summary:

> [I]t is manifest that the judicial power of the United States is unavoidably, in some cases, exclusive of all state authority, and in all others, may be made so at the election of congress. . . . Congress, throughout the judicial act [of 1789] . . . have legislated upon the supposition that in all the cases to which the judicial powers of the United States extended, they might rightfully vest exclusive jurisdiction in their own courts.
>
> But, even admitting that the language of the constitution is not mandatory, and that congress may constitutionally omit to vest the judicial power in courts of the United States, it cannot be denied that when it is vested, it may be excused to the utmost constitutional extent.[41]

---

[38] Ibid., 328.
[39] Ibid., 329.

[40] Ibid., 334.
[41] Ibid., 337.

Chapter VIII: *Sovereignty and Union*

There were some problems with Story's Article III argument. First, to read the federal courts as being given power to try "all cases" could conceivably mean, as the Virginia Court of Appeals had pointed out, that "it would give [the Supreme Court] appellate jurisdiction . . . over the courts of England and France."[42] Second, in the course of his discussion Story had claimed that the federal courts had exclusive jurisdiction over "all . . . cases" that "enter into the national policy, affect the national rights, and may compromit the national sovereignty."[43] He listed as examples of such cases criminal cases affecting "our internal policy" and "our foreign relations" and "cases of admiralty and maritime jurisdiction."[44] But in *Hudson and Goodwin* and *Coolidge* the Court had already suggested that the federal courts had no jurisdiction over nonstatutory criminal cases,[45] and the previous chapter has shown that the extent of the admiralty jurisdiction of the federal courts was a matter of considerable dispute within the Court, with no Justice, including Story, maintaining that that jurisdiction was exclusive or unlimited. Finally, the discretion to establish federal courts given Congress by Article III did not seem entirely compatible with those courts having exclusive jurisdiction over some cases. Could Congress decline to create a court, such as a prize court, that had exclusive jurisdiction over a class of cases, thereby ensuring that they would not be heard?

But the practical question in *Martin* was whether the Supreme Court could review final decisions of state courts, and on a variety of grounds Story's conclusion that it could was a sensible one. First, the Framers, in their discussions of the provision authorizing Congress to establish federal courts, had expressed concern that "national rights" and "uniformity of Judgments" be protected.[46] Story's attribution of a "presum[ption] . . . in the constitution" that "state attachments, state prejudices, state jealousies, and state interests, might sometimes obstruct . . . the regular administration of justice"[47] was appropriate. Uniformity of decisions would be hindered, Story pointed out, by the possibility that "judges of equal learning and integrity, in different states, might differently interpret [statutes, treaties, or the Constitution]" and there would be "no revising authority to control the jarring and discordant judgments."[48]

Story also pointed out that Supreme Court review of state court

---

[42] 4 Munf. at 14.
[43] 1 Wheat. at 335.
[44] Ibid.
[45] United States v. Hudson and Goodwin, 7 Cranch 32 (1812); United States v. Coolidge, 1 Wheat. 415 (1816). See discussion in Chapter II, pp. 137–38.

[46] See, e.g., M. Farrand, ed., *The Records of the Federal Convention* (4 vols., 1937), II, 124 (remarks of John Rutledge).
[47] 1 Wheat. at 348.
[48] Ibid.

decisions had been explicitly declared and admitted by the friends and by the opponents of the Constitution in the ratification debates, and previously sustained by the Supreme Court without any opposition from state courts.[49] The practice of Supreme Court appellate review of state court decisions had been conceded by even as dedicated a compact theorist as Tucker.[50] Finally, Story argued that federal appellate review of state court decisions was consistent with the practice of allowing litigants to remove cases from federal to state courts. It would be anomalous, he suggested, to allow persons to obtain federal review of cases before they had been decided by a state court but not after the decision had been made.[51]

The practical reasons for Supreme Court appellate review of state court decisions may have constituted the strongest basis for Story's decision in *Martin*. In light of the ratifying debates and the language of Article III, it seemed evident that Supreme Court appellate review of state court decisions was contemplated where federal or constitutional issues were at stake. But Story devoted only about ten pages of his forty-page opinion to practical arguments. What was he attempting to do in the rest of his opinion? One of his goals, we have seen, was an effort to read Article III as a mandate not only for extensive federal judicial power but for an obligatory judicial-legislative partnership to extend the authority of the national government. Given Story's established interest in having criminal and admiralty cases decided in the federal courts, that portion of his *Martin* opinion appears to have been designed to establish that certain subjects, being inherently "national" in character, should properly be adjudicated only by the federal courts, aided in their jurisdictional reach by Congress.

One major portion of Story's opinion in *Martin* can thus be seen as designed to entrench the proposition that the Constitution had created a federal government of potentially wide scope. That this was a major purpose of his can be seen in the remainder of his argument, whose purpose was to develop a theory of sovereignty arrangements in the Constitution that buttressed that proposition. The theory was openly presented as an alternative to compact theory. "The constitution of the United States," Story announced, "was ordained and established, not by the states in their sovereign capacities, but emphatically, as the preamble of the constitution declares, by 'the people of the United States.' " Since, "the people" were sovereign in a republic, "there can be no doubt," Story felt, that the people could "invest the general government with all the powers which they might deem proper and necessary" or prohibit to the states the exercise of any powers which were, in their judgment,

[49] Ibid., 352.
[50] See Tucker, *Blackstone*, I, 183–84.

[51] 1 Wheat. at 350.

"incompatible with the objects of the general compact." Given the ultimate sovereignty of the people, the Constitution could not be characterized as having been "carved out of existing state sovereignties," nor as "a surrender of powers already existing in state institutions," because "the people of every state had a right as to modify and restrain . . . the powers of the states." These "principles" were "plain and obvious": "no difference of opinion ought to be indulged" about them.[52]

While the principles may have been "plain and obvious," they made considerable inroads on state sovereignty. According to compact theory, as formulated by Tucker and the Virginia Court of Appeals in *Martin*, the Union was created out of a compact between the federal government and the states, with all powers not expressly delegated to the national government being reserved by the states. Story's interpretation of the Constitution's founding suggested that this version of compact theory ignored the role of "the people." Under Story's version the "people of every state" acted as a restraint on the states, and if the people wanted to restrict state power by making it "subordinate to [that] of the nation," they could.

As applied to the *Martin* case, these principles prevented the Virginia Court of Appeals from being the ultimate arbiter of questions of Virginia law that involved in their adjudication the construction of a federal treaty. This was because "the people" (including the people of Virginia) had delegated power to Congress to establish federal courts and had provided in the Constitution for the establishment of a Supreme Court, and Congress, exercising that power and supplementing the power of the Supreme Court, had provided, in Section 25 of the Judiciary Act of 1789, for appellate review of "final" state court decisions. In establishing a Supreme Court and in delegating power to Congress to establish lower federal courts the people were restraining the reserved powers of the states. Every time the government of the United States, in its legislative or judicial capacity, was given powers that restrained the power of the states, the justification for that grant of power was "the right" of the people "to make the powers of state governments, in given cases, subordinate to those of the nation."[53]

In his *Commentaries on the Constitution* Story was to make this argument even more pointedly. After referring to Tucker's view that the Constitution was "a compact . . . between the states (as contradistinguished from the people of the states), by which the several states have bound themselves to each other, and to the federal government,"[54] Story claimed that "this view . . . , having no foundation in the words of the

---

[52] Ibid., 324–25, 327.
[53] Ibid., 325.

[54] J. Story, *Constitution*, I, 328–29.

constitution, [was] altogether a gratuitous assumption." "No state," Story maintained, "had any power to establish a contract for the establishment of any new government over the people . . . or to delegate the powers of government in whole or in part to any other sovereignty." Only "the people . . . in their sovereign capacity" had a right "to enter into a compact, and to transfer any sovereignty to the national government."[55] The Constitution had not been established by the several states, Story concluded, but by "the people of the United States in the aggregate." As authority for this proposition he cited *Martin* v. *Hunter's Lessee*.[56]

One can thus see that much was on Story's mind in the *Martin* case: the exclusive and obligatory jurisdiction of the federal courts, the pragmatic necessity for federal appellate review, and the noxious implications of the compact theory of sovereignty. The variety of sovereignty issues that Story saw posed by the case accounts for his disinclination to rest on practical considerations. Johnson, in his concurrence, revealed more starkly the Justices' sense of what was at stake in *Martin,* calling the constitutional question raised in the case "one of the most momentous importance; as one which may affect, in its consequences, the permanence of the American union."[57]

Johnson's concurrence is worth pausing over, since it sheds additional light on the theoretical strategy adopted by Story in his opinion for the Court. Johnson first framed the issues in *Martin* as those of Union versus compact theory, exhibiting a minimalist conception of Union and far more solicitude than Story for the idea that the Constitution was a social compact. He associated Union with a power in "the general government . . . to protect . . . itself," either through "force" or the "judicial process." At the same time he acknowledged that "the American people can no longer enjoy the blessings of a free government, whenever the state sovereignties shall be prostrated at the feet of the general government."[58] He asserted *"in the name of the American people"* that "in this court, every state in the union is represented"; and that "we are constituted by the voice of union," so that "when decisions take place, which nothing but a spirit to give ground and harmonize can reconcile, ours is the superior claim upon the comity of the state tribunals."[59] The spirit of Union thus justified federal judicial supremacy. But he acknowledged that "the constitution appears, in every line of it, to be a contract" whose parties were "the people, the states, and the United States." It was reasoning "in a circle," he believed, "to contend that [the Consti-

---

[55] Ibid., 330.
[56] Ibid., 332.
[57] Ibid., 363.

[58] Ibid. Emphasis in original.
[59] Ibid., 364–65.

tution] professes to be the exclusive act of the people, for what have the people done but to form this compact?'' The states, he concluded, were clearly recognized, in ''various passages,'' as ''parties to it.''[60]

For Johnson, then, *Martin* stood only for the minimalist proposition that when ''[t]he angry vindictive persons of men . . . [had] made their way into [state] judicial tribunals, . . . there ought to be a power somewhere to refrain or punish, or the union must be dissolved.''[61] He saw nothing in the Judiciary Act of 1789 ''which amounts to an operation of the inferiority or dependence of the state tribunals.''[62] He felt that the jurisdiction of the Supreme Court to review the Virginia Court of Appeals in *Martin* was primarily based on the impossibility of having an ''endless . . . diversity of decisions throughout the union upon the constitution, treaties, and laws of the United States, a subject on which the tranquility of the union . . . may materially depend.''[63] *Martin* left the Supreme Court ''supreme over persons and areas as far as our judicial powers extend,'' but ''not asserting any compulsory control over the state tribunals.''[64]

The difference between Story's and Johnson's positions in *Martin* with respect to the potential reach of the national government, the legitimacy of compact theory, the coterminous nature of federal power, and the idea of Union was a significant one. Johnson's position on the relationship between national and state sovereignty closely resembled that of Samuel Dexter, co-counsel for Virginia in *Martin,* who had conceded that ''congress should have the right of arming the courts of the United States with every authority necessary to give complete effect to the judicial powers granted by the constitution.''[65] Later in his argument Dexter had said,

> I have long inclined to the belief, that the centrifugal force was greater than the centripetal. The danger is, not that we shall fall into the sun, but that we may fly off in eccentric orbits, and never return to our perihelion.[66]

Union, for Johnson as for Dexter, was a bulwark against the fragmentation and dissolution of the Republic, not much more. It was by no means the potential leviathan envisaged by Story: it functioned not to obliterate state sovereignty but, as Johnson put it, ''to prevent dissention and collision'' and thereby promote [t]he security and happiness of the whole.''[67]

The Richmond *Enquirer,* some three weeks after *Martin* v. *Hunter's*

[60] Ibid., 373.
[61] Ibid., 377.
[62] Ibid., 379.
[63] Ibid., 381.
[64] Ibid., 382.
[65] Ibid., 318.
[66] Ibid., 320.
[67] Ibid., 373.

*Lessee* was handed down, reported Johnson's concurrence in full, ignoring Story's opinion altogether.[68] The *Enquirer*'s response was a signal as to how Story's theories of federal sovereignty had been received in the state most prominently identified with compact theory and anticonsolidationism. Five years later, lawyers from Virginia were before the Court again, taking positions that appeared to assume that *Martin* had never been decided, or at least that Johnson's opinion had been that of the Court. Among the arguments those lawyers advanced was one claiming that "the appellate jurisdiction conferred by the constitution on the Supreme Court, is merely authority to revise the decisions of inferior Courts of the United States," not "[authority] to reexamine decisions in the State Courts." One of the lawyers observed in passing "that he wished to be distinctly understood as not yielding his assent to the doctrine of *Hunter* v. *Martin*."[69]

The case in which the Virginia lawyers expressed their defiance of *Martin* was *Cohens* v. *Virginia*. In 1819 the Virginia legislature passed a statute to become effective on January 1, 1820, that prohibited the purchase or sale of unauthorized lottery tickets within the state. Lotteries had become a common means of raising revenue in nineteenth-century America, and while they were periodically denounced as encouraging gambling and related "immoral" pursuits, they were prevalent. A purpose of the Virginia statute, in fact, was to protect in-state lotteries against outside competition. One commentator, discussing the 1820 statute in the Richmond *Enquirer,* asserted that it furthered a "double policy—preserving the morals of our people from the effects of a pernicious gambling, and . . . preventing the moneys of our people from going into the coffers of other states."[70]

On August 29, 1820, Philip and Mendes Cohen were accused in Norfolk Borough Court of selling tickets to the national lottery, a project designed to raise revenue for a city hall in Washington, D.C. The Cohens were professional lottery agents who maintained a branch office in Norfolk of J. I. Cohen, Jr., a Baltimore firm. In addition to selling tickets, lottery agents exchanged currency of various kinds and provided financial information. Despite the prosecution of the Cohens, J. I. Cohen's office flourished in Virginia, opening a branch in Richmond in 1823.

The case against the Cohens was heard on September 2 in Norfolk on a stipulated set of facts. The Cohens admitted selling the tickets, set forth a congressional statute of 1802 authorizing lotteries in the District of Columbia, and argued that Congress's action precluded the state of Virginia from prohibiting the national lottery. The borough court found

---

[68] Richmond *Enquirer,* Apr. 11, 1816.

[69] 1 Wheat. at 310.

[70] "The Last of the Republicans," Richmond *Enquirer,* Jan. 25, 1821.

that the Virginia statute was enforceable notwithstanding Congress's action and fined the Cohens $100 and court costs. Shortly after that decision a letter appeared in *Niles' Weekly Register* in Baltimore, signed by five prominent lawyers, which had been drafted on June 27, 1820, a day after the original indictment of the Cohens. The letter, signed by William Pinkney, Thomas Emmet, David B. Ogden, Walter Jones, and John Wells, the last a New York practitioner, advanced the opinion that state legislatures were prohibited by the Constitution from restricting Congress's attempts to "improve the seat of government." A lottery was alleged to be an appropriate means through which Congress could implement its power to improve the national capital.[71]

The Cohens appealed their fine to the United States Supreme Court in October 1820, citing Section 25 of the Judiciary Act of 1789 and claiming that the Virginia statute was unconstitutional, and that the decision of the borough court to sustain the Cohens' fine "drew into question" a state statute whose constitutionality had been sustained by a state court. The process of Section 25 appellate review required that a writ of error compelling the Norfolk court to transmit the record of its decision to the Supreme Court be signed by a Justice of the Court, and that a summons notify the respondent—the state of Virginia—that it was expected to appear before the Supreme Court at its next Term. While this procedure was routine, it had an unprecedented effect in the *Cohens* case: a state was being asked to defend the constitutionality of a decision by one of its courts on a matter of state criminal law. *Martin* had not raised such a situation, and *Cohens* arguably cut deeper into state prerogatives, since it involved a suit against a state by one of its own citizens and it was the first indication that Section 25 of the Judiciary Act could be involved to allow Supreme Court review of state criminal cases. On hearing that the Marshall Court had set the *Cohens* case on its docket, the Virginia legislature passed two resolutions. The first declared that the Court had "no rightful authority under the Constitution to examine and correct the judgment for which the Commonwealth has been cited and admonished to be and appear at the Supreme Court of the United States and that the General Assembly do hereby enter their most solemn protest against the jurisdiction of that Court over the matter." The second announced that the lawyers who were to argue the state's case before the Marshall Court would confine their argument "alone to the question of jurisdiction; and if the jurisdiction of the Court should be sustained, . . . they will consider their duties at an end."[72]

The swiftness of the review process in *Cohens,* and the very inferior

---

[71] The letter was printed in *Niles' Weekly Register* on September 2, 1820.

[72] Contemporary accounts of the resolutions can be found in *Niles' Weekly Register,* Jan. 20, 1821, and Feb. 24, 1821.

status of the state court from which review was taken, have led to speculation that the case was possibly feigned.[73] While the review process was
swift, as in many of the Marshall Court's major cases, there is little
evidence to suggest it was contrived. Stipulations of facts were not unusual in test cases: it was obvious from the outset that the issue in *Cohens*
v. *Virginia* was not whether the Cohens had sold the tickets but whether
the state of Virginia could constitutionally prohibit them from doing so.
Nor did the fact that a writ of error was taken directly from a lower level
state court to the Supreme Court of the United States, a point Virginia
anticonsolidationists were first inclined to emphasize, make the case irregular. The Cohens argued that "cases of this sort," which had been
decided by borough courts, were "not subject to revision by any other
Court of the Commonwealth,"[74] and were thus "final judgments" for
Section 25 purposes, and counsel for the state did not contest that argument. In the eventual Supreme Court opinion Henry Wheaton noted in
his summary of the facts that the Cohens' "appeal to the next Superior
Court of law of Norfolk County" had been "refused by the Court inasmuch as cases of this sort are not subject to revision by any other Court
of the Commonwealth."[75] This point was repeated by Marshall in his
opinion. The record had been "brought into this Court by writ of error,"
he noted, because the judgment rendered against the Cohens was in "the
highest Court of the State in which the case was cognizable."[76] *Cohens*
v. *Virginia* was thus not a feigned case, but merely a case whose peculiar
lower court setting and major national importance had streamlined
Supreme Court review.

News that the lawyers had issued their opinion letter about the District lottery, and subsequently that the state of Virginia had been summoned to appear before the Marshall Court to defend *Cohens,* prompted
a barrage of commentary in the Richmond *Enquirer* between September
1820 and the beginning of the 1821 Term. The *Enquirer,* whose editor,
Thomas Ritchie, was a firm anticonsolidationist, began by expressing
"regret to see such an opinion" from the lawyers who had signed the
letter printed in *Niles' Weekly Register,* and calling for "a more formal
investigation" of the lawyers' views. This touched off a series of articles
and editorials in which the major constitutional arguments that Virginia
was to make before the Marshall Court in *Cohens* were identified. The
first arguments focused on the merits of the case, suggesting that the
lawyers' opinion letter had confused congressional power over national
subjects with congressional power over the District of Columbia. If Congress, Ritchie declared in an editorial on September 19, decided that "a

---

[73] See, e.g., A. Beveridge, *The Life
of John Marshall* (4 vols., 1919), IV,
343.

[74] 6 Wheat. at 290.
[75] Ibid.
[76] Ibid., 376.

bank, a university, an East India company, or a hundred other institutions may improve the seat of government, do they become at once *national?*" The institutions established by Congress in the District of Columbia were "purely local." The lawyers, Ritchie said, "expect to settle the question by a *name,*" the "magical term *national.*"[77]

Ten days later one Publicola echoed Ritchie, calling the idea that Congress could delegate one of its enumerated powers to a municipal government and thereby preclude the states from competing with that government "preposterous." But Publicola (possibly Spencer Roane) went further. He felt that despite the fanciful character of the lawyers' argument, "the supreme court of the U.S. will confirm and enforce the doctrines which the [lawyers' letter] avows." Advocates of state sovereignty, Publicola felt, should not submit to such a "usurpation"; it would only encourage additional federal aggrandizement. "[N]othing but a consolidated government," he argued, "will satisfy the overwhelming ambitions of those seeking to destroy the independent sovereignty of the states." It was "not difficult to foresee that a consolidation of the states into one sovereignty would seal the death warrant of American liberty."[78]

The early comments of Publicola, for all their anticonsolidationist rhetoric, had not been directed at the Supreme Court's authority to review the *Cohens* case: indeed, they had assumed that the Court had such an authority. By October 1820, however, arguments against the Court's jurisdiction had surfaced. The shift had been precipitated by the Marshall Court's formal notice to the governor and attorney general of Virginia that they were expected to be in Court the next February to defend the *Cohens* case. The notice, in the form of a citation, was served on Governor Thomas Mann Randolph and Attorney General John Robertson on October 23, 1820.[79] Ritchie, in an editorial commentary on what he called the "singular summons" to Randolph and Robertson, maintained that he expected "the state [to] protest, in the first instance, against the jurisdiction of the court itself."[80] There were "at least three points," Ritchie said, "on which [the Cohens] case may fail": two were jurisdictional.

The first jurisdictional argument, noted by Ritchie in his October 27 editorial, was that Section 25 of the Judiciary Act of 1789 limited Supreme Court review to final judgments of "the highest court of law or equity of a State in which a decision in the suit could be had," and the borough court of Norfolk was "not the highest court of law in which a decision in the cause could be had." A writ of error "might be granted from a borough court to the superior court of law for the county—and

---

[77] Richmond *Enquirer*, Sept. 19, 1820. Emphasis in original.
[78] Richmond, *Enquirer*, Sept. 29, 1820.

[79] Richmond *Enquirer*, Oct. 27, 1820.
[80] Ibid.

afterwards from that superior court to the general court,'' Ritchie surmised. ''This objection alone may quash the proceeding.''[81] As noted, however, counsel for Virginia did not make this argument in the *Cohens* case, apparently because the Virginia state court system did not permit appeals from a borough court. We have seen that both counsel for the Cohens and Marshall, in his opinion, pointed out that an appeal from the borough court had been refused. Three months after the *Cohens* case had been decided, Marshall went so far as to write Henry Wheaton a letter, asking him to make sure that the fact that the Cohens' appeal had been refused appeared in the final printed version of the Court's opinion.[82]

The second jurisdictional argument, Ritchie believed, was the ''most solemn objection'' to the Court's entertaining the case. This was that the Constitution itself precluded Supreme Court review of state court decisions in the circumstances of the Cohens case. There were three potential strands to the argument. First, *Martin* v. *Hunter's Lessee* notwithstanding, Supreme Court review of the final decisions of state courts was a violation of the balance of federal and sovereignty established by the Constitution: Section 25 of the Judiciary Act of 1789 was unconstitutional. Ritchie did not mention this strand, although Alexander Smyth, one of Virginia's lawyers in *Cohens,* emphasized it in his argument, and, as noted, Philip Bartner, the other, announced that he had not assented to the *Martin* decision. Ritchie combined the other two strands in a paragraph:

> The suability of a state by her own citizens in the courts of the United States, does not exist, because it is not recognized by the federal constitution. . . . [T]here is strong reason to believe that the case before us is the very teeth of the constitution. If so, this summons to the commonwealth of Virginia is irregular, and must be dismissed.[83]

This passage was cryptic, but Ritchie had previously referred to Article III and the Eleventh Amendment as his sources for the proposition that ''the suability of a state by her own citizens in the courts of the United States does not exist.'' Indeed, Article III and the Eleventh Amendment were to be the major constitutional grounds on which the Court's jurisdiction was attacked.

The Article III argument was based on a literal reading of its language defining the cases to which the ''judicial power of the United States . . . shall extend.'' Two types of cases were listed, cases involving particular parties and cases involving particular subject matter. Cases af-

---

81 Ibid.
82 J. Marshall to H. Wheaton, June 2, 1821, Henry Wheaton Papers, Pierpont Morgan Library, New York, N.Y.
83 Richmond *Enquirer,* Oct. 27, 1820.

fecting "Ambassadors, other public Ministers and Consuls" were examples of the former type; cases of "admiralty and maritime jurisdiction" examples of the latter. Among the "parties" cases were three involving controversies "between citizens of different states." Among the "subject matter" cases were three "in which a State shall be Party." No mention of cases in which a state was being sued by one of its own citizens was made in the Article, and the clause conferring Supreme Court jurisdiction over "Cases . . . in which a State shall be party" specifically stated that in such cases the Court should have "original Jurisdiction." From this language came the argument that the *Cohens* case, in which the Supreme Court's jurisdiction was appellate, not original, and in which a state was being sued by one of its own citizens, was not cognizable by the Court.

The Eleventh Amendment, ratified in 1798, stated that the judicial power of the United States "shall not be construed to extend to any suit in law or equity, commenced or prosecuted against one of the United States by Citizens of another State, or by Citizens or Subjects of any Foreign State." Read strictly, it would not seem to refer to the Cohens. But the purpose of the Amendment, according to the *Enquirer*, was to prevent a sovereign state from being forced into the federal courts by a private litigant. That purpose applied equally to the *Cohens* case: the Cohens were prosecuting a suit against Virginia in the Supreme Court of the United States. The Eleventh Amendment's omission of a prohibition against citizens suing their own state in the federal courts was not significant, since the Amendment was designed to revise Article III's grant of power to the federal courts to hear suits "between a State and Citizens of another State," but Article III had granted no power to the federal courts to hear cases involving suits between a state and its own citizens.

Between October 1820 and February 1821, these jurisdictional arguments, and the argument on the merits, were regularly aired in the *Enquirer*. Between December 14 and January 2 a correspondent terming himself "State Rights" published six essays on "The Lottery Case," the last of which united arguments on the merits, arguments against jurisdiction, and more general arguments against consolidationist theories of federal sovereignty. One passage from State Rights's sixth essay is particularly deserving of attention.

The passage came in an effort on the part of State Rights to link his arguments on the merits with his arguments on jurisdiction. In the assertion of the lawyers that a District of Columbia lottery was immune from state control because of the supremacy of congressional legislation over competing state legislation, State Rights found evidence that the lawyers apparently believed that they could achieve federal court review of the constitutionality of state legislation regardless of whether competing congressional legislation was constitutional. This had the effect of subjecting the states to "a combined supremacy of congress and the federal courts.'' State Rights then made it clear what he meant by this "combined supremacy":

> If Congress can by law make a writ of error a writ of right, so as to give any jurisdiction to the federal over the state courts, every case whatsoever may be brought before the former, and the extent of their jurisdiction depends on their own will.[84]

In this passage the relationship between coterminous power theory and the *Martin–Cohens* sequence once again leaps to the surface. Expanding federal court jurisdiction and expanding congressional power were treated in this passage as part of the same consolidationist impulse. By merely asserting federal plenary power, Congress could precipitate constitutional conflicts and secure Supreme Court review; by engaging in that review the federal judiciary made it much more likely that the constitutionality of the asserted congressional power would be sanctioned. Eventually federal judicial and federal legislative power would become unlimited; state sovereignty would vanish.

*Cohens* v. *Virginia* was thus a formidable challenge for the Court, notwithstanding the *Martin* decision. Not only was that decision treated with disdain, it was alleged to be part of a more general consolidationist campaign on the part of the Court, a campaign that, as we will see, included the decision in *McCulloch* v. *Maryland*, which had come down two years before. Not only did the arguments against jurisdiction in *Cohens* appear to have considerable weight, the case, coming only five years after *Martin*, two after *McCulloch*, and one after the Missouri Compromise, had overtones of rebellion. Concluding the argument for Virginia, Alexander Smyth, invested his last paragraph with such overtones:

> The Court will maintain the powers of Congress as granted by the people, and for the purposes for which they were granted by the people; and will, if possible, to preserve harmony, prevent the clashing of federal and state powers. Let each operate within their respective spheres; and let each be confined to their assigned limits. We are all bound to support the constitution. How will that be best effected? Not by claiming and exercising unacknowledged federal power. The strength thus obtained will prove pernicious. The confidence of the people constitutes the real strength of this government. Nothing can so much endanger it as exciting the hostility of the state governments. With them it is to determine how long this government shall endure.[85]

Marshall met the challenge head on. Writing for a unanimous Court, he took up Virginia's arguments in a sequence convenient for the logic

---

[84] Richmond *Enquirer*, Jan. 2, 1821.  [85] 6 Wheat. at 344.

of his own presentation. That sequence characteristically began with an attention to "abstract propositions,"[86] in this instance "arguments drawn from the nature of government, and from the general spirit" of the Constitution.[87] The first such argument was the Article III argument, which Marshall represented as a claim that the Court's jurisdiction was "excluded by the character of the parties, one of them being a State, and the other a citizen of that State."[88] He immediately moved to deflect the strict reading of Article III offered by Barbour and Smyth by citing the clause of Article III, Section 2 in which federal court jurisdiction was given to "all Cases, in Law and Equity, arising under this Constitution." While agreeing with the Virginia lawyers that jurisdiction was given to the federal courts in two classes of cases, those involving enumerated subject matter and those involving enumerated parties, Marshall maintained that a case arising under the Constitution was clearly in the subject-matter class: it was what moderns would call a "federal question" case.

This response might have seemed so obvious as to raise the question why counsel for Virginia had overlooked it, but in fact both Barbour and Smyth had argued that despite the broad language of the provision, it ran counter to the doctrine of sovereign immunity, by which both the federal government, and by analogy the states, could not be sued without their consent.[89] Marshall noted this argument[90] and took considerable space to counter it. In his discussion he did not follow the argument, made by David Ogden and William Pinkney for the Cohens, that Virginia was not being sued but merely being made a defendant in error by virtue of the right of appeal given to persons prosecuted criminally by the state.[91] Instead he turned, as noted, to general principles.

The purpose of Marshall's disinclination to use an existing practical argument to defeat any sovereign immunity exception to the "all Cases . . . arising under this Constitution" clause of Article III, and to employ a more abstract and general argument, becomes clear on a consideration of the language he employed. He first cited the Supremacy Clause of Article VI and the Constitution's Preamble to establish the proposition that the "American States, as well as the American people, have believed a close and firm Union to be essential to their liberty and to their happiness."[92] The Constitution had thus been formed, in important part, to preserve the existence and protect the integrity of the Union. The express powers conferred to Congress, for example, "on the great subjects of war, peace, and commerce" were "limitations on the sovereignty of the states" that had the object of establishing "a close and firm Union."[93]

---

[86] Ibid., 377.
[87] Ibid., 384.
[88] Ibid., 378.
[89] Ibid., 303–308, 315.

[90] Ibid., 380.
[91] Ibid., 350, 366–67.
[92] Ibid., 380–81.
[93] Ibid., 380.

But there were other instances where the sovereignty of the states had been surrendered,

> instances where the surrender can only operate to the benefit of the people, and where, perhaps, no other power is conferred in Congress than a conservative power to maintain the principles established in the Constitution.[94]

The maintenance of a "close and firm Union" was thus "among the great duties" of the federal government, and "one of the instruments by which this duty may be peaceably performed" was "the judicial department." The states, then, had in the Constitution surrendered part of their sovereignty to the federal government to create, and implicitly to maintain, a Union; some of the powers surrendered to the federal government were "conservative" powers, designed to maintain "the principles established in the constitution in their purity"; and the federal judiciary, being an agent of the federal government, could help maintain those principles. In short, the "situation of the government of the Union and of a State, in relation to each other; the nature of our constitution; the subordination of the State governments to that constitution; and the great purpose for which jurisdiction over all cases arising under the constitution and laws of the United States is confided to the judicial department" dictated that any case "arising under the constitution or laws of the United States" be cognizable in the federal courts.[95]

But why did it follow that because the states had surrendered some express power, and even, arguably, a conservative power to maintain the Union, to Congress, they had also surrendered a power to maintain the Union to the federal judiciary? One could argue, as Virginia had, that while the states had surrendered some sovereign powers, they had retained others, and they had not explicitly surrendered their power not to be brought into federal court without their consent. Any surrender of implied maintenance powers to Congress would seem irrelevant to that issue. Here Marshall took steps to make clear why he had so quickly moved from a "conservative" power "conferred in Congress" to the implementation of that power by the federal courts.

"While weighing arguments drawn from the nature of government, and from the general spirit of an instrument," Marshall noted, it was proper to consider "principles" that supported the "full operation" of constitutional language as well as narrower interpretations.[96] One such principle, which Pinkney had mentioned in his argument,[97] was that

---

94 Ibid., 382.
95 Ibid., 382–83.

96 Ibid., 384.
97 Ibid., 354.

the judicial power of every well constituted government must be coextensive with the legislature, and must be capable of deciding every judicial question which grows out of the constitution and laws.[98]

This "proposition," Marshall declared, "may be considered as a political axiom." He believed that "[i]n reasoning upon it as an abstract question, there would, probably, exist no controversy of opinion respecting it."[99] Then came an extraordinary passage:

We do not mean to say, that the jurisdiction of the Courts of the Union should be construed to be coextensive with the legislature merely because it is fit that it should be so; but we mean to say, that this fitness furnishes an argument in construing the constitution which ought never to be overlooked, and which is most especially entitled to consideration, when we are inquiring, whether the words of the instrument which purport to establish this principle shall be contracted for the purpose of destroying it.[100]

With these passages Marshall revealed not only that he shared with Tucker, Jefferson, Roane, and the other anticonsolidationists the premise that coterminous power theory was "a political axiom," but also that it had been an axiom "establish[ed] [as a] principle" in the Constitution. The alternative to a coterminous power in the federal legislature and the federal judiciary was "prostrat[ing] . . . the [federal] government and its laws at the feet of every State in the Union." Federal legislative power could not be enforced without federal judicial power to "'correct' [state] judgments" in the enforcement process. The Supreme Court was, in this view, one of the architects of the policy of the federal government. While Marshall did not openly state this last assumption in his opinions, he did so privately. Writing to Story after the *Cohens* decision had been handed down and criticized in the *Enquirer* and elsewhere, Marshall declared that "the attack upon the Judiciary is an attack upon the Union," and particularized:

The judicial department is well understood to be that through which the government may be attacked most successfully, because it is without patronage, and of course without power. And it is equally well understood that every subtraction from its jurisdiction is a vital wound to the government itself. The attack on it, therefore, is a masked battery aimed at the government itself.[101]

---

[98] Ibid., 354.
[99] Ibid., 384.
[100] Ibid., 384–85.

[101] J. Marshall to J. Story, Sept. 18, 1821, in *Proc. Mass. Hist. Soc.*, 14:330–31 (1901).

Some comments are worth making at this early juncture. First, Marshall did not seem troubled by the potential scope of federal sovereignty that might follow from his view that judicial and legislative power were coextensive, yet the *Cohens* case itself provided an apt example of the possibility of coterminous power leading to unlimited federal jurisdiction. The *Cohens* case had been spawned by the constitutional collision of an act of Congress with a state statute. Congress's authorization of a lottery for the District of Columbia had been converted into a claim to be the exclusive proprietor of lotteries. That claim was itself the source of the constitutional issue in *Cohens* that made it a case "arising under the Constitution" and gave the Supreme Court jurisdiction to review it. One of the options presented to the Court in reviewing the case was to decide, on the merits, that the congressional statute did in fact put states out of the lottery business. In short, a claim of increased federal legislative power led to a claim of increased federal judicial power, which might, if upheld, result in the original legislative claim being sustained. This was the very kind of potential partnership among the departments of the federal government that Tucker had identified in his treatise. Thus far in the *Cohens* opinion, Marshall had appeared to endorse that partnership.

Second, Marshall had spent no time establishing the basis of his pronouncement that the Constitution embodied the coterminous power principle. He merely announced that it is a "political axiom" associated with "every well constituted government."[102] He seems to have assumed that his earlier line of reasoning about the relationship between state and federal sovereignty in a Constitution whose central purpose was to create and preserve the Union would suffice. Since, Marshall's argument suggested, the Constitution obviously contemplated the subordination in some respects of the states to a newly created federal government, that government could, through the extension of its legislative and judicial powers, continue the subordination apace. The only limits on the federal government were those imposed by the Constitution, but one of the great purposes of the Constitution was to create and to preserve that government. At this point Marshall's argument in *Cohens* seems quite compatible with a consolidationist perspective.

Third, Marshall's opinion in *Cohens* up to this point appeared to be informed by a theory of the relationship between law and politics in constitutional interpretation that drew only the haziest of lines between the two entities. The department interpreting the Constitution, Marshall claimed, needed to be given full power to do so in order to maintain the great principles of the Constitution. But that department, the judiciary, was admittedly an agent of the federal government. Thus while a principle of law, the supremacy of the Union, was embodied in the Constitution,

---

[102] 6 Wheat. at 384.

and its preservation by the judiciary was thus a duty, that principle was also one of politics, creating a presumption that national sovereignty would be favored over state sovereignty where the two collided. And in collisions, cases "arising under this Constitution," the institution whose duty it was to decide which sovereign prevailed was a department of the government whose sovereignty—reflected in the term "Union"—the Constitution had been created to establish. It was hard to know, given this theory, how the federal judiciary would be limited in its constitutional interpretations *except* by politics, that is except by a sense of how politic a given interpretation of the power of the federal government was at a given time. "Union" thus served a number of functions in the theory of constitutional interpretation advanced by Marshall in *Cohens,* but none of those functions was that of creating a legal restraint on the interpretive powers of the Supreme Court.

Finally, it is worth noting that the latitudinous conception of the scope of federal power which informed the early part of Marshall's *Cohens* opinion was not accompanied by a comparable conception of the national government as an extensive force. Only in one place in the argument just analyzed did Marshall speak of affirmative federal powers which were "in themselves limitations on the sovereignty of the states": those pertaining to "the great subjects of war, peace, and commerce." In the remainder of the argument federal power was identified with the maintenance of the Union against inroads upon it that might threaten its existence. The power of Congress was "conservative";[103] a narrow construction of Supreme Court review power would "prostrate . . . the government . . . at the feet" of the states;[104] the review power upheld in *Cohens* was to help "the government . . . protect itself and its laws";[105] "no government ought to be so defective in its organization, as not to contain within itself the means of securing the execution of its own laws";[106] the "judicial department . . . should . . . [have] the power . . . of preserving the constitution and laws of the Union . . . from all violation from every quarter"; the government should not have "constitutional inability to preserve itself against a section of the nation."[107] The image of the federal government conveyed by these excerpts is that of a beleaguered entity beset by centrifugal pressures, not that of an aggressive, expansionist force.

We shall subsequently have occasion to consider, in light of the different conceptions of federal sovereignty exhibited by Story and Johnson in *Martin,* whether the image of the Union created by Marshall in *Cohens,* which on its face appears much closer to Johnson's conception,

---

[103] Ibid., 382.
[104] Ibid., 385.
[105] Ibid., 386.

[106] Ibid., 387.
[107] Ibid., 390.

was strategic. At this point in his opinion, however, Marshall still had several arguments to address.

The first of these was Virginia's claim that even if Article III gave the federal courts jurisdiction over "all cases" raising constitutional issues, its language stating that in "all Cases . . . in which a State shall be a party" the Court should have original jurisdiction prevented its entertaining *Cohens,* which had come to it on appeal. Marshall himself had said, in *Marbury* v. *Madison,* that Congress could not "give this court appellate jurisdiction, where the constitution has declared their jurisdiction shall be original, and original jurisdiction where the constitution has declared it shall be appellate"; otherwise the distribution of jurisdiction made in Article III would be "form without substance."[108] In *Cohens* he took back those "general expressions." Article III had enumerated cases in which a state was a party as "original jurisdiction" cases, to be sure, but it had also singled out cases arising under the Constitution and laws of the United States as "appellate jurisdiction" cases. Marshall maintained that the joint enumeration had the effect of providing alternative ways in which cases could come before the Supreme Court.[109] If a case, such as *Cohens,* contained both enumerated features, the Court could entertain it either originally or through appellate review. This construction was supported by "the absence of negative words":[110] nowhere in Article III was there language indicating that the Court's appellate jurisdiction should not be exercised in cases where original jurisdiction was permitted, or vice versa. From these extrapolations Marshall drew the following "rule of construction": the Court's original jurisdiction "[could not] be enlarged" beyond those cases specified by the Constitution, but its appellate jurisdiction "may be exercised in every case cognizable under [Article III] . . . in which original jurisdiction cannot be exercised."[111] *Cohens* was a case where a state was a party, qualifying it for original jurisdiction, but even if it had not been, it was a case arising under the Constitution of the United States, therefore qualifying it for appellate jurisdiction.

The next jurisdictional argument identified by the *Enquirer* and raised by counsel for Virginia was the Eleventh Amendment argument. As noted, the text of the Eleventh Amendment denied the federal courts jurisdiction over suits "commenced or prosecuted against one of the United States by Citizens of another State," so a preliminary difficulty for Virginia was the fact that the Cohens were Virginia citizens, as conceded by their counsel.[112] But Virginia argued that by obtaining a writ

---

[108] I Cranch at 174.
[109] 6 Wheat. at 399.
[110] Ibid., 389.

[111] Ibid., 399.
[112] Ibid., 303.

of error commanding the state of Virginia to appear before the Supreme Court the Cohens were acting as "prosecutors," and that in any event the Constitution had never mentioned, in Article III or elsewhere, that the federal judiciary had jurisdiction over suits involving states and their citizens. "I contend," Smyth said, "that in no case can the federal courts revise the decisions of the state Courts; no such power is expressly given by the Constitution; and can it be believed that the greatest, the most *consolidating* of all the powers of this Government, should pass by an unnecessary implication?"[113] The purpose of the Eleventh Amendment, Smyth contended, was to prevent states from being humiliated or harassed by suits in the federal courts. "It would degrade the State governments, and divest them of every pretension to sovereignty," he said, "to determine that they cannot punish offences without their decisions being liable to a re-examination" in the federal courts.[114]

Marshall's response to this argument was twofold. First, he made the point he had declined to make earlier in connection with the Article III issues: the Cohens were defendants, not plaintiffs, and thus the purpose of their writ of error was not to "assert . . . any claim against the state, but for the purpose of asserting a constitutional defense against a claim made by a state."[115] The writ of error was not an independent Eleventh Amendment suit, but a continuation of the same suit initiated below. Lest he "be mistaken" in that argument, Marshall made the additional point that the Cohens were Virginia citizens, and that their case therefore did not come within the literal words of the Amendment: it was not a suit "commenced or prosecuted [against Virginia] by a citizen of another state."[116]

Next Marshall took up an argument not raised in the *Enquirer* but implicit in its disdain for Story's opinion for the Court in *Martin:* the contention that, as Smyth put it, "[t]he appellate jurisdiction conferred by the constitution on the Supreme Court, is merely authority to reverse the decisions of inferior [federal] Courts."[117] This claim had been dismissed by Story in *Martin,* although Johnson had reserved judgment on it as a general proposition. Nonetheless Smyth reiterated it, Barbour announced that he did not "yield his assent" to the *Martin* opinion of the Court, and Marshall devoted ten pages to dismissing it again. We need not belabor his discussion, which tracked Story's reasoning in *Martin,* except to note a central passage. Marshall began his reasoning by noting that the argument that the appellate jurisdiction of the Supreme Court was intended only to correct the errors of lower federal courts was premised on "the supposed total separation of the judiciary of a state from that of

---

[113] Ibid., 318. Emphasis in original.
[114] Ibid., 325.
[115] Ibid., 408–409.

[116] Ibid., 411–12.
[117] Ibid., 315.

the Union.'' He then suggested that this assumed "total incompatibility" be examined. Then:

> That the United States form, for many, and for most important purposes, a single nation, has not yet been denied. In war, we are one people. In making peace, we are one people. In all commercial regulations, we are one and the same people. In many other respects, the American people are one; and the government which is alone capable of controlling and managing their interests in all these respects is the government of the Union. . . . America has chosen to be, in many respects, and to many purposes, a nation; and for all these purposes, her government is complete; to all these objects, it is competent. The people have declared, that in the exercise of all powers given for these objects, it is supreme. It can then, in effectuating these objects, legitimately control all individuals or governments within the American territory. The constitution and laws of a state, so far as they are repugnant to the constitution and laws of the United States, are absolutely void. These states are constituent parts of the United States. They are members of one great empire—for some purposes sovereign, for some purposes subordinate.
>
> In a government so constituted is it unreasonable that the judicial power should be competent to give efficacy to the constitutional laws of the legislature? . . .
>
> We think it is not. We think that in a government acknowledgedly supreme, with respect to objects of vital interest to the nation, there is nothing inconsistent with sound reason, nothing incompatible with the nature of government, in making all its departments supreme, so far as respects those objects, and so far as is necessary to their attainment. The exercise of the appellate power over those judgments of the state tribunals which may contravene the constitution or laws of the United States is, we believe, essential to the attainment of those objects.[118]

The above passage repeats the central arguments Marshall made earlier in *Cohens* and links them to Story's arguments in *Martin*. The structure of the passage is designed to create a logical progression incorporating four elements: the sovereignty of the "people," as distinguished from that of the states, the necessity for some "national" powers in the Union, the supremacy of national power over state power as a result of that necessity, and the coextensive nature of legislative and judicial powers. The people, as "one," have created the government of the Union; in managing their interests the government of the Union requires certain indispensable powers, examples of which are the powers to declare war, make peace, and promote uniformity in commercial interchange. Where the government of the Union is promoting the interests of the people, it

---

[118] Ibid., 414–15.

is necessarily supreme over the governments of states; state sovereignty is thus "for some purposes subordinate." And where powers have been granted to the government of the Union to promote the interests of the people, the supremacy of that government should be reflected not only in the powers of its legislative department but in the powers of its judicial department. Judicial power "give[s] efficacy" to legislative power; it is in "the nature of government" that the powers should be coterminous. Once three assumptions are made—that the people are ultimately the sovereigns in a federal republic, that the national government must necessarily be delegated some "supreme" powers to preserve its existence, and that the judicial power of the national government should be coextensive with its legislative power—state sovereignty must yield to the sovereignty of the national government whenever the Union's existence requires it to yield.

Read in this fashion, the passage from Marshall's opinion in *Cohens* can be seen as an encapsulation of the theory of sovereignty maintained by the Marshall Court as a body from 1815 on. While the theory was not held in all its particulars by every Justice on the Court, it was articulated as an abstract proposition in all the leading sovereignty cases. As an abstract proposition, the theory was decidedly pro-"Union" and decidedly anti-"compact"; it was consolidationist in its assumptions. Two qualifications are in order, however. First, the extremely broad view of federal power maintained by the theory—a view which was accurately portrayed by anticonsolidationists as not envisaging many limits on the reach of the judicial legislature or the federal judiciary—was not inevitably accompanied by an expansive view of the functions of the federal government. It was, at least in Marshall's articulation, more of a preservationist theory in its emphasis than a theory designed to foster an affirmative federal regulatory presence. Story may have had grandiose ideas about the spread of national institutions, but Marshall's version appeared to focus only on preserving indispensable national powers so as to keep the Union secure against centrifugal attacks. Second, despite the unlimited potential for federal legislative and judicial supremacy assumed by the theory, that supremacy was to be qualified in practice. The theory may have been consolidationist in the abstract, but when cases testing the scope of national power to displace state power came before the Court, it produced much more cautious results.

Marshall was nearly done. He disposed of the objection that the law in *Cohens* was too local to be a "law of the United States" within the meaning of Section 25 of the Judiciary Act of 1789 and turned to the merits of the case. Virginia had refused to argue the case on the merits, but the Marshall Court resolved to hear argument anyway, and Daniel Webster, who appeared "in consequence of his being counsel for the state of New York in a similar case that had arisen in that state," presented

Virginia's arguments.[119] There was a state lottery in New York, and Marshall reportedly declared that the Court was hearing argument on the merits, despite Virginia's absence, because the decision in the *Cohens* case would "affect other cases in other states."[120] The timing of the argument on the merits was peculiar in that it was heard before the Court announced its opinion on the jurisdictional issues. This fact led to speculation that the eventual decision to sustain the constitutionality of Virginia's antilottery statute was intended as a palliative. One contemporary commentator, the Ohio lawyer Charles Hammond (who was strongly interested in *Cohens* because of another sovereignty case, *Osborn v. Bank of the United States,* that was pending in the federal courts), was especially pointed. Writing in the Washington *Gazette* in August 1821, Hammond said that although

> Mr. Pinkney on one side, and the counsel for Virginia upon the other, declared that they would not argue the merits, yet . . . the Court asked for an argument on the merits—and thus upon the ground of *expediency!* . . . It was a matter of great interest to the vendors of lottery tickets to know whether they were or were not as supreme as the Bank of the United States! Upon account of the great importance of this principle, the Court travelled out of their road to ask an argument on the merits. . . . The argument on the merits was had on Friday; on Saturday the jurisdiction was sustained, and on Monday the judgment was affirmed. To me all this looks like political maneuver. . . . To affirm the judgment of the state court, would serve, in some degree, to allay the apprehension that might be excited by sustaining the jurisdiction.[121]

Marshall's opinion on the merits was narrowly cast. He concluded that the congressional statute creating the national lottery was "directed to the City alone . . . and not to any extraterritorial operations."[122] It did not intend "to interfere with the penal laws of a State";[123] it was not essential to the lottery that "it should be exercised out of the city";[124] there were "no words [in the statute] indicating [an] intention" to "establish a lottery for these improvements in the City which are deemed national."[125] In short, the "operation" and "objects" of the lottery were "entirely local."[126] The "mind of Congress was not directed to any provision for the sale of tickets beyond the limits of the Corporation."[127] Thus Virginia, or other states, could restrict national lottery ticket sales within their borders. The Virginia statute had been upheld and the $100

---

[119] See Washington *National Intelligencer,* Mar. 3, 1820.
[120] Ibid.
[121] Hampden [Charles Hammond], Washington *Gazette,* Aug. 20, 1821. Emphasis in original.

[122] 6 Wheat. at 442.
[123] Ibid., 443.
[124] Ibid.
[125] Ibid., 445.
[126] Ibid., 446.
[127] Ibid., 447.

fine on the Cohens validated. Virginia had won the battle, although it had lost the war.

The decision in *Cohens* v. *Virginia* rapidly became one of the subjects of a pamphlet war taking place between the Marshall Court and the "Richmond Junto," the band of compact theorists—Roane, Ritchie, and William Brockenbrough, with the support of Taylor, John Randolph, and Jefferson—who used the *Enquirer* as their organ. The topic for debate in the pamphlet war was sovereignty theory, and the essays delivered by both sides represented articulations of the premises of "Union" and "compact."

Animosity between the Court and the Richmond Junto dated back to the original litigation that spawned *Martin*. It became a matter of public attention, as we shall see, after the Court's decision in *McCulloch* v. *Maryland*, when Brockenbrough and Roane published anonymous essays in the *Enquirer* (under the respective pseudonyms "Amphictyon" and "Hampden") attacking *McCulloch* as "endanger[ing] the very existence of states rights" and "work[ing] an entire change in the constitution," and John Marshall himself responded anonymously to those attacks in two sets of essays in the Philadephia *Union* and the Alexandria *Gazette*.[128] With the *Cohens* decision a second set of polemics began. Three sets of essays, by Algernon Sidney, Somers, and Fletcher of Saltoun, appeared in the *Enquirer* between May 15 and July 13, 1821. The essays, of which those by "Algernon Sidney" (another pen name for Roane) received the most attention, attacked the *Cohens* decision, deplored the Court's lack of seriatim opinions, prophesied the decline of state independence, and generally fulminated against the Court. *Cohens* was a product, Roane suggested, of "that love of power, which all history informs us infects and corrupts all who possess it, and from which even the high and ermined judges, themselves, are not exempted." It reflected the "ultra-federal" views of the "leader" of the Court: Marshall "must [have been] equally delighted and surprised to find his *republican* brothers going with him."

Marshall was piqued by the *Enquirer* essays. He wrote to Henry Wheaton on June 2, 1821, that the Court had been "attacked with a virulence superior even to that which was employed in the Bank question."[129] Thirteen days later, he wrote Story that "for coarseness and malignity of invective Algernon Sidney surpasses all party writers who have ever made pretensions to any decency of character."[130] And after

---

[128] The Amphictyon and Hampden essays, and Marshall's responses, have been collected and published in G. Gunther, *John Marshall's Defense of McCulloch v. Maryland* (1969). The two quotations are from pp. 54 and 154 of Gunther. Emphasis in original.

[129] J. Marshall to H. Wheaton, June 2, 1821, Wheaton Papers.

[130] J. Marshall to J. Story, June 15, 1821, in *Proc. Mass. Hist. Soc.*, 14:327 (1901).

the Algernon Sidney series had been completed, Marshall sent the essays to Story with a cover letter in which he called Roane's arguments "weak" but his language "violent." "In support of the sound principles of the constitution of the Union of the States," Marshall complained, "not a pen is drawn."[131]

Steps were being taken, however, to counter the *Enquirer* essays. In July and August, 1821, a series of articles appeared in the New York *American*, bearing the signature of "A Federalist of 1789" and written by Henry Wheaton. The essays defended the Court's decision in *Cohens*, criticized Roane, and asserted that "it is impossible to read the essays of Algernon Sidney . . . without feeling the deepest conviction that a plan is deliberately formed to pervert the general government in favour of the state governments."[132]

By the summer and fall of 1821, the debate over *Cohens* had spread to the Washington press. From June until August the Washington *Gazette*, whose editorial policies were resolutely anti-"aristocratical," published another series of Hampden essays on the *Cohens* decision, this time by Charles Hammond. Eventually the *Gazette*'s articles were to stimulate editorials in defense of the Court in the *National Intelligencer,* the "establishment" Washington newspaper. Meanwhile Story and Marshall had exchanged letters in June and July, Story informing Marshall, erroneously, that Thomas Jefferson had, in a letter to William Jarvis, a resident of Boston, "denie[d] the right of the Judges to decide constitutional questions."[133] Jefferson had in fact claimed only that the Court could not interfere with the ministerial functions of the executive branch. Marshall, however, assumed the worst, and wrote of Jefferson to Story,

He is among the most ambitious and I suspect among the most unforgiving of men. . . . He looks of course with ill will at an independent judiciary. That in a free country with a written constitution any intelligent man should wish a dependent judiciary; or should think that the constitution is not a law for the courts as well as the legislature would astonish me, if I had not learned from observation that with many men the judgment is completely controlled by the passions.[134]

By September Marshall was convinced that "the whole attack [on the Court], if not originating with Mr. Jefferson, is obviously approved and guided by him," and that while the "coarseness of the language" in Algernon Sidney's essays "belongs exclusively to the author," its "ac-

---

[131] J. Marshall to J. Story, July 13, 1821, ibid., 328.

[132] A Federalist of 1789 [Wheaton], New York *American*, Aug. 16, 1821.

[133] J. Story to J. Marshall, June 27, 1821, in C. Warren, *The Story–Marshall Correspondence* (1942), 13–14.

[134] Marshall to Story, July 13, 1821, supra, note 131.

tivity has been increased by his communications with the great Lama of the mountains."[135]

The *National Intelligencer* now entered the debate. On July 10 it asked whether "any principle [could] be more dangerous or irreconcilable to the principles of our government than that which makes . . . decisions [of the state courts] final on questions arising under the constitution or laws of the United States."[136] Throughout July and August, and into September, the *Intelligencer* elaborated upon this theme, criticizing the *Enquirer*'s editorials, reprinting articles in other papers supporting the Court, and calling for a congressional debate on Section 25 of the Judiciary Act.[137] Other papers joined in, most of the comments supporting the Court. By November 16 the *Enquirer* was bemoaning the failure of "the Press . . . which should stand like a watch tower on the hill, to sound the approach of danger." "Those presses from whose situation, principles and candour we had a right to expect cooperation," the *Enquirer* noted, "have contented themselves with ridicule or denunciation."[138]

By the end of 1821 the intensity of the debate had waned and the Court had emerged largely unscathed. Marshall, Story, and Washington continued to express anxiety, and Marshall and Story sought, successfully, to suppress a proposed reprinting of the Algernon Sidney essays in the Philadelphia-based *Journal of Jurisprudence*.[139] But Marshall's prediction that "an effort [would] certainly be made in Congress to repeal section 25 of the Judiciary Act"[140] did not come to pass. Senator William Johnson of Kentucky introduced, in the December 1821 session of Congress, a proposed constitutional amendment that would have made the Senate rather than the Court the forum for review of state court decisions where constitutional issues were raised, but not even Virginia supported that proposal. Story had also been apprehensive about the December congressional session, writing to Jeremiah Mason on January 10, 1822, that "the Judiciary in our country is essentially feeble," and expressing a hope that "if . . . the Judiciary is to be destroyed, I should be glad to have the decisive blow now struck, while I am young, and can return to the profession and earn an honest livelihood."[141] Daniel Webster, how-

---

135 J. Marshall to J. Story, Sept. 18, 1821, in Warren, *Correspondence,* 17.

136 Editorial, Washington *National Intelligencer,* July 10, 1821.

137 The *Enquirer* published remarks on the Court on July 17 and 27, August 3 and 17, and September 4, 11, 25, and 28; the *Intelligencer* responded on July 20, July 31, August 8, August 27, August 31, September 19, and October 3.

138 Editorial, Richmond *Enquirer,* Nov. 16, 1821.

139 Compare Marshall to Story, July 13, 1821, supra, note 131, with Marshall to Story, Sept. 18, 1821, supra, note 136.

140 Marshall to Story, Sept. 18, 1821, supra, note 136.

141 J. Story to J. Mason, Jan. 10, 1822, in W. Story, *The Life and Letters of Joseph Story* (2 vols., 1851), I, 411–12.

ever, had reassured Story on January 14 that while "Mr. Johnson has
. . . dealt . . . pretty freely with the Supreme Court [and] Governor Barbour is to annihilate *Cohens v. Virginia*," he saw "less *reality* in all this
smoke than I thought I should before I came here."[142]

Meanwhile, as early as August 1821 Jefferson had written Hammond that he had an "earnest wish to take no further part in public
affairs," claiming that "tranquility at my age is the supreme good of
life,"[143] and he repeated those sentiments in a letter to Senator Nathaniel
Macon of North Carolina on November 23.[144] The Virginia legislature,
in its December 1821 session, failed to take any public action against the
Court; in March 1822 the *Intelligencer* noted that "the string of resolutions, respecting state rights, was not forthcoming at the appointed
hour."[145] On March 12 the *Enquirer* conceded that Virginia "forbears at
present presenting her opinions."[146] Spencer Roane became ill that spring
and died in September 1822. The crisis of the spring and summer of 1821
had passed, although the theory of sovereignty Marshall had attacked in
*Cohens* apparently remained intact.

The next of the Court's significant federal jurisdiction cases was
*Osborn v. Bank of the United States,*[147] a case that had been litigated
with two purposes in mind but ended up serving a third and arguably
more fundamental purpose. The case was originally conceived, by lawyers representing the interests of the state of Ohio, as a means of securing
reconsideration of the Eleventh Amendment interpretation announced in
*Cohens* and of *McCulloch v. Maryland,* the Court's great 1819 decision.
But as *Osborn* was being argued, the Court, noting another case involving
the Bank of the United States that was pending in the 1824 Term, "ex-
pressed a wish that the [*Osborn*] case should be re-argued upon the point
of the constitutionality and effect of the provision in the charter of the
Bank, which authorizes it to sue in the Circuit Courts of the Union."[148]
The Court then proceeded to decide this question, holding that since the
Bank's ability to contract was based on federal law, Article III of the
Constitution, granting jurisdiction to the federal courts in "all cases, in
Law and Equity, arising under this Constitution [and] . . . the laws of

---

[142] D. Webster to J. Story, Jan. 14, 1822, in F. Webster, *The Private Correspondence of Daniel Webster* (2 vols., 1857), I, 319. Emphasis in original.

[143] T. Jefferson to C. Hammond, Aug. 18, 1821, Thomas Jefferson Papers, Library of Congress.

[144] T. Jefferson to N. Macon, Nov. 23, 1821, ibid.

[145] Editorial, Washington *National Intelligencer*, Mar. 8, 1822.

[146] Editorial, Richmond *Enquirer*, Mar. 12, 1822.

[147] 9 Wheat. 738 (1824).

[148] Ibid., 804.

the United States," gave the federal courts jurisdiction over every case in which the Bank participated. The *Osborn* case thus became another link in the chain of expanded federal jurisdiction that the Court was forging.

*Osborn* originated with an 1819 Ohio statute that imposed an annual tax of $50,000 on each branch of the Bank of the United States in the state. Pursuant to the statute, the Ohio state auditor, Ralph Osborn, was directed to issue a warrant requiring each of the branches of the Bank of the United States to pay its $50,000 annual tax. Should payment be refused, Osborn or his agents were empowered to seize the money deposited in the branch banks and deliver it to the state treasurer. On September 15, 1819, the federal bank's taxes became due, and "at high noon" on September 17 three agents of Osborn drove up to the bank branch in Chillicothe, gathered up over $100,000 in cash and bank notes, deposited them in a wagon, and entrusted them in a state bank in Chillicothe for the night, preparatory to transferring them to the state treasury in Columbus the following day.[149]

The branch officials had been well aware of the impending raid on their vaults. The day before the agents appeared, lawyers for the Bank had gone before federal judge Charles Byrd and sought a temporary injunction against state enforcement of the 1819 statute. Byrd granted the injunction, and the Bank's lawyers obtained papers from the federal court clerk restraining the state agents from entering the Chillicothe branch. But the papers were defective: they consisted only of a copy of the bill of injunction drafted by the Bank's lawyers and a subpoena for a later writ date; there was no formal injunction order issued by Judge Byrd's court. Accordingly, Osborn directed his agents to ignore the papers and proceed.

After withdrawing the funds on the seventeenth and depositing them in the Chillicothe state bank, the agents set off the next day for Columbus. The federal bank officials, realizing that their initial injunction papers may have been defective, now had a second set served on the agents en route. The agents ignored the papers, deposited the bank funds with the state treasurer, and returned to Chillicothe. The agents were arrested and imprisoned, then subsequently released when the warrants served on them proved defective. At that point the Bank's lawyers obtained a show cause order from Judge Byrd compelling the agents to declare why they had violated his injunction. The validity of the injunction and the constitutional issue of whether the state of Ohio could tax the Bank of the United

---

[149] The background details of *Osborn* can be found in the Chillicothe *Spectator*, Sept. 22, 1819, and the *Western Monitor* (Louisville, Ky.), Sept. 25, 1819, both reprinted in *Niles' Weekly Register*, Oct. 4, 1819.

States were litigated before Supreme Court Justice Thomas Todd, sitting on circuit, in February 1820.[150]

Todd ruled that the procedure by which the Bank had sought an injunction, while technically incorrect, was sufficient, and that the state of Ohio had no authority to tax the Bank. His decision was appealed, and the *Osborn* case was set down for argument in the 1823 Term, with two constitutional issues occupying prominence in the argument: the validity, after *McCulloch* v. *Maryland*, of Ohio's effort to tax the Bank, and the question whether, after *Cohens*, the Eleventh Amendment barred the federal courts from entertaining the suit. At that point a case from the United States Circuit Court in Georgia came to the Marshall Court's attention. The Georgia legislature had passed statutes designed to circumvent the Bank of the United States's requirement that Georgia state bank notes be redeemed in specie. The statutes provided that Georgia bank notes did not need to be redeemed in specie except under extraordinary circumstances, and had the effect of making the Bank of the United States unable to redeem any state notes it held. In 1821 the Planters' Bank of Georgia declined to cash any of its notes that were presented by the federal Bank. The Bank of the United States sued to redeem one set of notes held by citizens of Georgia and transferred to it. The Planters' Bank refused to honor the notes and, in addition, argued that since the state of Georgia had incorporated the Planters' Bank, the Eleventh Amendment prevented a citizen of Georgia from instituting suits against it, and the Bank of the United States's ability to sue was wholly derivative of the citizen of Georgia who had assigned the Bank his note. Justice Johnson, the presiding judge on the Georgia circuit, certified the case to the Supreme Court "on a *pro forma* difference of opinion . . . from the great importance of the questions it gave rise to."[151]

The Marshall Court decided that the argument made in *Planters' Bank* that the Bank of the United States could not sue in the federal courts had implications for the *Osborn* case and asked for reargument of *Osborn*. Reargument took place on March 10 and 11, 1824, and Marshall handed down his opinion in *Osborn* on March 19. Unlike many other Marshall Court opinions delivered a short time after argument, *Osborn* probably

---

[150] Henry Wheaton, on hearing of the events that precipitated *Osborn*, wrote Story on October 22, 1819:

I had occasion to write to Judge Todd lately, and took that opportunity of expressing my opinion as to the disgraceful and dangerous conduct of Ohio in the business of the national Bank. . . . The authors of this outrage must be punished with exemplary severity, or our Government is an empty name.

The letter is in the Wheaton Papers.

[151] 9 Wheat. at 910. This was one of the few instances in which the discretionary power of Supreme Court Justices in certificate of division cases was openly referred to in an opinion. See discussion in Chapter III.

was an opinion that had been largely prewritten. Most of its issues had been argued the year before; indeed, only the question of the constitutionality of denying the Bank access to the federal courts was new. Marshall's opinion in *Osborn* was fifty-four pages in the United States Reports. Of those, twelve pages were devoted to the right of the Bank to sue in the courts of the United States,[152] an issue that, as we shall see, Marshall decided by resorting to the now familiar principle of coterminous federal power. Fourteen more pages addressed five technical objections to Justice Todd's ruling, including the validity of the injunction granted against Osborn's agents. Marshall disposed of the objections summarily, as had Todd. The remaining twenty-nine pages were devoted to the state's Eleventh Amendment argument, an argument very similar to that made by Virginia in *Cohens,* and to a reconsideration of the constitutionality of state efforts to tax a national bank presented by *McCulloch* v. *Maryland.* Marshall and the rest of the Court were certainly familiar with those issues.

The Court's decision in *Osborn,* and Marshall's opinion, joined by all the Justices save Johnson, were strikingly broad and assertive on their sovereignty implications. The decision meant that states would be forced to go into federal courts whenever they were involved in disputes with the Bank of the United States. It also continued *Cohens*'s pattern of narrowing the reach of the Eleventh Amendment, in this instance fashioning a distinction between suits against states themselves and suits against officers of states. Marshall held that for the Amendment to bar a proceeding the state needed to be the party named in the record, not merely one that "had an interest" in its outcome. Moreover, the opinion reaffirmed *McCulloch*'s holding that the Bank of the United States was not to be considered a private corporation for the purposes of state taxation: it was akin to an agency of the federal government.

The two significant doctrinal features of *Osborn* were Marshall's readings of the Arising Under Clause of Article III, giving the federal courts jurisdiction over "federal questions," and of the Eleventh Amendment. He found that the Arising Under Clause justified federal jurisdiction in both *Osborn* and the companion *Planters' Bank* case. The Bank, Marshall argued, had been created by an act of Congress: "every faculty which it possesses" was the result of its charter. That charter was a law of the United States; hence any case involving the Bank "[arose] under a law of the United States." It was irrelevant, therefore, that a particular case in which the Bank participated did not involve a federal statute or treaty but instead turned on a matter of state common law. Thus not only was the *Osborn* case properly in federal court, so was the *Planters' Bank*

---

[152] Ibid., 817–28.

case, even though the dispute in _Planters' Bank_ was over a state note, the interpretation of which clearly involved state contract law. Marshall pointed to explicit language in the Bank's charter making it "able and capable in law to sue and be sued . . . in any Circuit Court of the United States."[153] He then read the Arising Under Clause to mean that there did not need to be a contested federal question for federal court jurisdiction to attach, at least in cases involving the Bank.

Marshall's interpretation of the Arising Under Clause in _Osborn_ gave little indication as to when the "federal question" in a case might be so marginal as to suggest that the federal courts had no concern with the dispute.[154] Marshall took for granted, in both _Osborn_ and _Planters' Bank_, that the federal courts had an interest in protecting the Bank, a federal institution, from being harassed in the state courts. Once again, in considering whether to expand the jurisdiction of the federal courts, he associated expansive federal jurisdiction with the need to preserve institutions identified with the Union from centrifugal forces. Even Johnson, in his dissent, acknowledged "a state of things [that] has grown up, in some of the states, which renders all protection necessary, that the general government can give to this bank."[155]

The linchpin of Marshall's _Osborn_ opinion was once again coterminous power theory. When the Court invited reargument on the "constitutionality and effect" of the Bank's charter authorizing it to sue in the federal courts, counsel for the Bank[156] invoked coterminous power theory to justify the constitutionality of Congress's creating a national bank and, having once created it, "erect[ing] a forum to which the Bank may resort to justice."[157] As Wheaton summarized the argument, it was a classic exposition of the coextensive power assumption:

> Those who framed the constitution, intended to establish a government complete for its own purposes, supreme within its sphere, and capable of acting by its own proper powers. They intended it to consist of three co-ordinate branches, legislative, executive, and judicial. In the construction of such a government, it is an obvious maxim, "that the judicial power should be competent to give efficacy to the constitutional laws of the legislature." The judicial authority, therefore, must be co-extensive with the legislative power. . . . The great object, then, of the constitutional provision, respecting the judiciary, must make it co-

---

[153] Ibid., 817.
[154] Johnson, dissenting, pointed out that the arising under jurisdiction established by the Court in _Osborn_ might extend to any land once acquired by the federal government. Ibid., 875.
[155] Ibid., 871–72.

[156] The Bank was represented by Henry Clay, Daniel Webster, and Thomas Sergeant. Wheaton combined their arguments in his reporting of the case. See ibid., 804–11.
[157] Ibid., 810.

extensive with the power of legislation, and to associate them inseparably, so that where one went, the other might go along with it. . . . It is a maxim applicable to the interpretation of a grant of political power, that the authority to create must infer a power effectually to protect, to preserve, and to sustain. . . . The Bank is created for the purpose of facilitating all the fiscal operations of the national government. . . . The Bank is, in effect, an instrument of the government . . . as much a servant of the government as the treasury department. [A] . . . facult[y] of the Bank . . . essential to its existence and utility [is] its capacity . . . of suing and being sued. [That faculty is lost] if Congress cannot erect a forum to which the Bank may resort for justice.[158]

In his discussion of the Article III issue in *Osborn,* Marshall merely restated that paragraph, and well he might have, since counsel for the Bank had cited Marshall's opinions in *Cohens* and *McCulloch* in support of their argument. The Arising Under Clause of Article III "enables," Marshall declared, "the judicial department to receive jurisdiction to the full extent of the constitution, laws, and treaties of the United States, when any question respecting them shall assume such a forum that the judicial power is capable of acting on it." Article III was an embodiment of the "great political principle" that "the legislative, executive, and judicial powers, of every well constituted government, are co-extensive with each other."[159] Since *Osborn v. Bank* was a case arising under a law of the United States, the judicial power of the federal courts would seem presumptively to extend to it under the coterminous power principle.

But counsel for Osborn had argued, Marshall pointed out, that since several legal questions had arisen in *Osborn,* and especially in *Planters' Bank,* that did not depend on laws of the United States, jurisdiction should not extend. Counsel had in fact gone further, and claimed that the *Osborn* case did not arise under the Bank's charter, but "under the general or local law of contract, and may be determined without opening the statute book of the United States."[160] Marshall emphasized the dire consequences of this argument:

[I]f the circumstance that other [legal] points are involved in it, shall disable Congress from authorizing the Courts of the Union to take jurisdiction of the original case, it equally disables Congress from authorizing those Courts to take jurisdiction of the whole cause, on an appeal, and thus . . . words obviously intended to secure to those who claim rights under the constitution, laws, or treaties of the United States, a trial in the federal courts, will be restricted to the insecure remedy of an appeal upon an isolated point, after it has received that

---

158 Ibid., 809–10.
159 Ibid., 818–19.

160 Ibid., 815.

stage which may be given to it by [a state] tribunal, into which he is forced against his will.[161]

But was *Osborn* a case where a federal question, as Marshall put it, "form[ed] an ingredient of the original cause"?[162] At this point, having proceeded, as had counsel for the Bank, from the general principle of federal coterminous power to the more specific principle that Congress could give the federal courts power to decide any case arising under a law of the United States, Marshall had still not established why the *Osborn* case had "arisen under a federal law."

His argument on that point was cryptic and assertive. A federal law, Congress's chartering of the Bank, had given the Bank power, he maintained, to "make contracts of any distinction [and] to sue in those contracts." When the Bank sued, the first question was whether it could sue, and whether it could make a particular contract. Those questions "depend[ed] entirely on a law of the United States." The note at issue in *Planters' Bank* "could never have been made, but under the authority of . . . the act of Congress" creating the Bank; and the Bank's claim in *Osborn* that the state agents had committed a trespass by seizing its funds depended on congressional authorization of the Bank to do business and acquire assets.

The difficulty with this argument was that it was hard to imagine any case in which Congress, simply by passing a law affecting an institution or individual, could be prevented from giving the subject of the legislation a right to sue in the federal courts, whatever legal questions were raised by the suit. Counsel for Osborn put one case, that of a citizen naturalized by an act of Congress, and suggested that the mere act of naturalization might enable that citizen to sue in the federal courts because his citizenship had "arisen under a law of the United States," even though the access of native citizens to the federal courts would be limited by the jurisdictional requirements of Article III. Marshall conceded the point, but held that the Bank was different because "all the faculties and capacities which that being possesses," including the right to sue and be sued, had been created by its federal character. "To use the language of the Constitution," Marshall said, "every act of the Bank arises out of this law." Naturalized citizens were not given any "capacities" by the federal statute that provided for their naturalization.[163]

One extreme case was thus excluded from the cognizability of the federal courts: "arising under" the laws of the United States, for the purposes of federal jurisdiction, did not simply mean "having any contact whatsoever with a federal law." But since there was little indication that

---

[161] Ibid., 823.
[162] Ibid.

[163] Ibid., 327.

in ordinary litigation involving the Bank of the United States the construction or interpretation of federal statutes would be at issue, Marshall's language in *Osborn* was consistent with a very broad reading of the Arising Under Clause. Johnson, dissenting on the Article III issue, felt that it was too broad.

Johnson admitted that the Bank of the United States was "identified with the administration of the national government": that it was "an immense machine, economically and beneficially applied to the fiscal transactions of the nation." The proliferation of state banks, with "a new description of bills of credit," was fiscally disastrous, Johnson believed, and "the good sense of a people" would thus "readily concede to the [national] Bank some need for protection from state courts and legislatures." But Johnson could not persuade himself that the Constitution sanctioned "the vesting of the right of [access to the federal courts] in this Bank . . . in any case, merely on the ground that a question might *possibly* be raised in it, involving the constitution, or constitutionality of a law of the United States."[164] Under that reasoning, Johnson argued, "the whole jurisdiction over contracts might [be] . . . taken from the State Courts, and conferred upon those of the United States"; cases involving bills executed on stamped paper and cases involving land originally acquired under laws of the United States might also come within federal court jurisdiction. Johnson believed that Congress, "with these palpable consequences in view," had not "intended to vest in the Bank of the United States, the right of suit here claimed."[165]

The principal merits issue in the *Osborn* case, Johnson pointed out, was whether the Bank could recover for trespass because of the forcible levying of its assets by Ohio officials. That was a question of state law.[166] So was the contracts issue in *Planters' Bank* a matter of state law.[167] Thus even if "the simple existence, or possibility of [a federal question's being raised in] a case is a sufficient ground of jurisdiction, and that ground sufficient to transfer the whole case to the federal judiciary," the *Osborn* and *Planters' Bank* cases were "not . . . case[s] within the mischief intended to be obviated by the constitution": they were simple common law cases.

Johnson now considered the fact that state common law cases might have implications for the Union, and therefore that Congress, using its necessary and proper powers under Article I, might "have assumed a latitude [to infringe on state common law] not foreseen at the adoption of the constitution." Here Johnson had in mind the *McCulloch* decision,

---

[164] Ibid., 874.
[165] Ibid., 876. Johnson seems here to have confused the capacity of the Bank to sue in the federal courts with the constitutional status of issues raised in suits involving the Bank.
[166] Ibid., 390.
[167] Ibid., 393.

which he had joined five years earlier; he had not changed his view on the scope of the Necessary and Proper Clause. To collect stamp duties, Congress had "exercised a power over the general law of contracts"; to secure debts due the United States, it had "controlled the state laws of estates of deceased persons; and all this [was] in the range of [congressional] discretion." But there was a limit to "this chain of implied powers." No "one branch of the general government" could "new model the constitutional structure of the other."[168]

This brought Johnson directly to coterminous power theory, which he found "altogether unnecessary to . . . the present case." He noted that "much stress was laid, on the argument, upon the necessity of giving coordinate extent to the several departments of a government." But "this consideration" was "needless, when applied to a constitution in which the judicial power so very far transcends both the others, in its acknowledged limits." Some of the "judicial power of the Union" was given to construe and enforce federal laws on "the principle . . . that every government should possess the means of protecting itself."[169] But "the most interesting province" of the federal judicial department was "to enforce the equal administration of laws, and systems of laws, over which the legislative power can exercise no control"; that is, to regulate the sovereign boundaries of the nation and the states, as manifested in their respective laws. While state courts had an undoubted interest in giving up their sovereignty to the federal courts in cases where foreign laws were involved, they had an equal interest in retaining their power over individuals by limiting the number of individuals who could bypass their jurisdictions for that of the federal courts. And in *Osborn* the federal government had taken jurisdiction over a person—the legal person of the Bank of the United States—by itself creating that person. As Johnson put it,

> Making a person, makes a case; and thus a government which cannot exercise jurisdiction unless an alien or citizens of another State be a party, makes a party which is neither alien nor citizen, and then claims jurisdiction because it is made a case. If this be true, why not make every citizen a corporation sole, and thus bring them all into the Courts of the United States.[170]

Johnson's point, however obscurely made, was that while coterminous power theory might provide a rationale for the implementation of federal legislative power by the federal judiciary (as in a broad judicial construction of implied congressional powers in the Constitution), it did

---

[168] Ibid., 895–96.
[169] Ibid., 896.

[170] Ibid., 898.

not provide a rationale for the infringement of state judicial power. The Union's "protecting itself," for Johnson, meant construing and enforcing its own laws, not altering the constitutional structure.

The Article III argument in *Osborn* was thus notable not only for the broad reading of "federal questions" jurisdiction made by Marshall's opinion, and for the coterminous power premise on which his reading was erected, but for the protest by Johnson that coterminous power theory, at least as Marshall's opinion seemed to define it, was "altogether unnecessary" to the case. This was the first instance in the sequence of decisions beginning with *Martin* in which a member of the Marshall Court, in a case with sovereignty implications, had openly dissented, and the first time that the relevance of the coterminous power principle to federal jurisdiction cases had been questioned.

Marshall next turned to the Eleventh Amendment issue and, if anything, his interpretation of that issue was even more consolidationist, for its logic scuttled the Amendment. He began by emphasizing the sovereignty dimensions of the issue. "It may not be time misapplied," he suggested, "[to] reflect on the relative situation of the Union with its members," should the Eleventh Amendment be read to prohibit suits against officials of the states from being brought in the federal courts. Such a reading could allow "the agents of a State [to] arrest the execution of any law in the United States." The "carrier of the mail, the collector of the revenue, the marshal of a district . . . [might] be inhibited, under ruinous penalties, from the performance of their respective duties." Individual states and citizens would be "capable, at [their] will, of attacking the nation, of arresting its progress at every step . . . while the nation [stood] naked, stripped of its defensive armour, and incapable of . . . execution of its laws."[171] Marshall eventually resolved the Eleventh Amendment issue by invoking a series of examples designed to show that the determination that federal court jurisdiction should not attach should not rest on a finding that a state might be affected by a decision, for that inquiry might present "the curious anomaly . . . of a Court examining the whole testimony of a cause . . . without having a right to exercise any jurisdiction in the case,"[172] but on a finding that the state was a party named in the record. In *Osborn* the agents of the Ohio state treasurer were named, not the state itself, hence the Eleventh Amendment did not prevent the suit's being brought in federal court.

This argument appeared to invite those desirous of escaping the reach of the Eleventh Amendment simply to sue officials of the state rather than the state itself. It was hard to know what was left of the Amendment after *Osborn,* since in almost all cases where a state sought

---

[171] Ibid., 847–48.     [172] Ibid., 853.

to enforce a policy hostile to federal institutions agents of the state would execute the policy. And in *Planters' Bank* Marshall intimated that there were additional limitations on the Amendment as a barrier to federal court litigation. The Bank of the United States could sue a state bank in the federal courts, he said, even when the state had chartered that bank and become a shareholder of that bank, because in chartering the bank "[the state] divests itself of its sovereign character," and because the bank, not the state, was being sued.[173] But the language of the Eleventh Amendment does not distinguish between the governmental and proprietary functions of states: the immunity appears to be absolute. Moreover, a distinction between "the bank" and "the state" appears insignificant if the state charters the bank and retains power to control its operations. Indeed, Marshall had taken pains to associate the Bank of the United States with the federal government in *Osborn*. The Bank was "the great instrument by which the fiscal operations of the government are effected."[174] It was "necessary to the legitimate operations of government."[175] It "render[ed] services to the nation."[176] The "suppression of . . . its faculties . . . would . . . essentially impair, if not totally destroy, the utility of the machine to the government."[177] As "the faculty of collecting and transmitting the money of the nation," it "must be . . . exempt from state control."[178]

In concluding in his *Osborn* opinion that a "sound construction" of the act chartering the Bank was that "it exempt[ed] the trade of the Bank, as being essential to the character of a machine necessary to the fiscal operations of the government, from the control of the States,"[179] Marshall denied that he and the Justices who joined with him were doing anything more than protecting the Bank officials "while in the line of duty." In construing statutes, he said, courts were "the mere instruments of the law." Their power, "as contradistinguished from the power of the laws," had "no existence." Judicial power was "never exercised for the purpose of giving effect to the will of the Judge"; but rather "for the purposes of giving effect to the will of the legislature; or, in other words, to the will of the law."[180]

Here we see how coterminous power theory, pressed to its logical conclusions, became in Marshall's opinions a rationale for judicial discretion. Once the axiom that federal judicial power should be coextensive with federal legislative power was taken as a given, judicial implementation of a federal law was nothing more than an act that gave effect to

---

[173] Bank of the United States v. Planters' Bank, 9 Wheat. 904, 907–908 (1824).

[174] Osborn, supra, note 3, at 860.

[175] Ibid., 861.

[176] Ibid., 863.

[177] Ibid., 865.

[178] Ibid., 867.

[179] Ibid., 866.

[180] Ibid.

legislative will. But the will of the legislature had seemingly been only to charter a national bank; it had been the Marshall Court itself that had interpreted that charter to mean that the Bank was "a machine necessary to the fiscal operations of the government," and thus that no state could ever tax it and that it could invariably obtain the protection of the federal courts. Those results had been "willed" by Supreme Court Justices. In *Osborn* Marshall may have exercised power to give effect to the "will of the law," but it was law that he had written. He had done more than merely implement the will of Congress, he had expanded the jurisdiction of the federal courts. He had taken another step toward the state of affairs predicted by Tucker and his confederates: the use of coterminous power theory to develop unlimited jurisdictional power in both Congress and the federal courts.

Thus far we have encountered two constitutional bases on which the Marshall Court grounded federal court jurisdiction: Article III, Section 1's provision for a "Supreme Court" and its grant of power to Congress to "establish . . . inferior courts"; and Article 1, Section 2's declaration that "[t]he judicial power shall extend to all cases . . . arising under this constitution [and] the laws of the United States." The first of these provisions had been used to justify Supreme Court appellate review under Section 25 of the Judiciary Act of 1789; the second to justify the use of the federal courts to vindicate "federal rights," that is, claims arising under federal law. We now meet, in *Houston* v. *Moore*,[181] the third of the primary constitutional justifications for expansive federal court jurisdiction advanced by the Marshall Court: the so-called preclusion doctrine, which prevented states from acting in an area over which Congress had been delegated powers and where Congress had occupied the field.

We will have more opportunity to consider the preclusion doctrine in the Commerce Clause cases, which involved apparently competing legislative activity by the states and the federal government with respect to a subject whose regulation had been delegated to Congress. *Houston* v. *Moore,* however, was a jurisdictional case, not a legislative regulation case. The question in *Houston* was whether state courts had jurisdiction to try cases involving the construction of federal law in an area over which Congress had been delegated, and had exercised, regulatory powers. Put more precisely, the question in *Houston* was whether, if Congress, pursuant to its power to "provide for organizing, arming, and disciplining the Militia," had passed legislation providing criminal penalties for failing to serve in the militia, but had not given federal courts-

---

[181] 5 Wheat. 1 (1820).

martial exclusive jurisdiction over the trials of "failure to serve" cases, a state could create its own courts-martial to try such cases.

Two sovereignty issues were raised by *Houston* v. *Moore,* and the Court did not reach a clear consensus on either issue. The first issue was whether the federal courts, by virtue of Congress's having been delegated power over a certain area, had exclusive jurisdiction to construe the laws governing that area. The second was whether Congress could, pursuant to its delegated power, give the federal courts that exclusive jurisdiction. Washington's seriatim opinion, which was the clearest approximation to an opinion of the Court, answered no to the first question and yes to the second. But he conceded that "the other judges," who agreed with him that the judgment below "ought to be affirmed" and thus that the state of Pennsylvania could create state courts-martial to try persons for failure to report for duty in the federal militia, "do not concur in all respects in the reasons which influence my opinion."[182] Johnson, concurring, put the disposition of the case more boldly. "The course of reasoning by which the judges have reached [their] conclusion," he said, was "various." It "coincid[ed] in but one thing, viz., that there is no error in the judgment of the State Court of Pennsylvania."[183]

*Houston* v. *Moore* shows every sign of being one of those cases in which considerable turmoil existed beneath the surface of the Court's decision. The case was argued late in the 1819 Term, and the Justices, finding themselves unable to come to a decision, postponed it "for advisement."[184] In July 1819 Marshall wrote Story,

> I had never thought of preparing an opinion in the militia case. That is committed to you and cannot be in better hands. I shall just sketch my ideas for the purpose of examining them more closely, but shall not prepare a regular opinion, as at present I do not think we shall differ."[185]

The letter suggests that Marshall may have felt that he and Story had at least a majority for their position, and that he had assigned an opinion of the Court to Story. Another possibility is that the Justices were treating *Houston* as they had treated *Dartmouth College* v. *Woodward;* as a case in which several Justices might prepare opinions and circulate them in the hope that one would secure unanimous support. Marshall's response to Story's apparent intimation that Marshall might also have been writing an opinion in *Houston* over the summer ("I had never thought of preparing an opinion") is consistent with that possibility. At any rate, Story's

---

[182] Ibid., 32.
[183] Ibid., 47.
[184] Ibid., 4.

[185] J. Marshall to J. Story, July 13, 1819, in Warren, *Correspondence,* 3.

opinion clearly did not command even a majority, since when he published it as a dissent he stated that he had "the concurrrence of one of my brethren."[186]

The letter from Marshall to Story quoted above and a circuit opinion Marshall rendered in 1815[187] suggest that the judge joining Story's opinion was the Chief Justice. The presence of seriatim opinions in *Houston* is also suggestive: during Marshall's entire tenure there was no instance in which seriatim opinions were issued in a constitutional case in which Marshall voted with the majority. Marshall's silently joining Story's dissent in *Houston,* however, meant that five Justices had rejected Story's position, which was that federal courts-martial had exclusive jurisdiction to try the cases of persons who failed to report for duty in the militia. Story's opinion also suggested that exclusive federal court jurisdiction existed in all cases involving crimes "created by the laws of the United States,"[188] a position that Johnson, in particular, and other Justices may have found unacceptable.

With exclusive federal jurisdiction to try militia courts-martial having been rejected, the Justices apparently could not agree on any theory for disposing of the case. The *Houston* case was complicated by two factors: the text of the Constitution and the unsettled state of concurrent power theory in the sovereignty jurisprudence of the time. The Constitution, in Article 1, Section 8, the same place in which it gave Congress authority to organize, arm, and discipline the militia, reserved "to the States respectively, the Appointment of the Officers, and the Authority of training the Militia according to the discipline prescribed by Congress." The scheme established in these clauses looks remarkably like a cooperative effort, with Congress establishing and setting disciplinary policy for the militia and the states training individual units and making disciplinary policy. In this vein, Pennsylvania's creation of state courts-martial to try militia delinquents appeared entirely consistent with the constitutional scheme, especially since Congress, in the 1795 statute establishing a federal militia, had not provided for federal courts-martial. When Pennsylvania passed a statute in 1814 establishing state courts-martial to enforce the 1795 statute, then, it was arguable that it was only "adding such details as were indispensably necessary to execute the acts of Congress," and that "a perfect harmony" existed "between the two [statutes]"[189]

But the problem with this analysis was that it was clear that the federal militia was an institution over which the states could not exercise independent powers. Both counsel had conceded this point in argument[190]

---

[186] 5 Wheat. at 76.
[187] Meade v. Deputy Marshal, 16 F. Cas. 1291 (1815).

[188] 5 Wheat. at 68.
[189] Ibid., 12.
[190] Ibid., 5, 9.

and, as Story noted in his dissent, "to suppose each state could have an authority to govern its own militia . . . seems utterly inconsistent with that unity of command and action, on which the success of all military operations must essentially depend." Moreover, the states had never had any sovereign powers over the federal militia, so it seemed, as Story pointed out, "a strange anomaly" to give the states that power "by a sort of process in aid" because Congress had not exercised to its full extent the power given it by the Constitution to govern the militia.

The last observations bring us to the heart of concurrent sovereignty theory in *Houston* v. *Moore*. The question whether, if Congress is delegated an exclusive regulatory power over a delineated area, and does not exercise it, or only partially exercises it, the states may exercise any regulatory powers in the area was, as we shall see, the fundamental issue in the Commerce Clause cases, which are discussed in the next section of this chapter. But as significant as this question was, it had not been addressed in detail by the Marshall Court before *Houston*. In *Martin* v. *Hunter's Lessee* Story had suggested that concurrent state power could exist only "in those cases where, previous to the constitution, state tribunals possessed jurisdiction independent of national authority."[191] But that statement was not necessary to the decision in *Martin,* and in *Houston* Johnson referred to the "exploded doctrine, that within the scope in which Congress may legislate, the states shall not legislate."[192] That doctrine had, in fact, not been exploded: the first Supreme Court case subjecting concurrent sovereignty theory to a searching analysis was *Gibbons* v. *Ogden,* four years in the future. One of the *Federalist* essays had addressed the problem, and Washington paraphrased the essay as saying that "in every case in which the state tribunals should not be expressly excluded by the acts of the national legislature, they would, of course, take cognizance of the causes . . ."[193] But the original language in *The Federalist* had referred only to civil cases, a category that did not include *Houston*.[194]

No opinion in *Houston* v. *Moore* invoked coterminous power theory, and at first blush the assumption that the authority of one branch of the federal government was coextensive with the authority of the other branches would seem irrelevant to questions about the exclusivity of federal governmental power where it allegedly clashed with state power. But, as previously noted, a broad interpretation of coextensive federal powers necessarily restricted state sovereignty, because for every increase in the breadth of the authority of one department of the national government coterminous power theory posited a like increase in the other de-

---

[191] Ibid., 53.
[192] Ibid., 45.
[193] Ibid., 25-26.

[194] See *The Federalist,* No. 82 (C. Rossiter, ed., 1961), 493.

partments. And the issue in *Houston* was not whether a congressional statute pre-empted states from enacting legislation regulating the militia but whether a clause in the Constitution, not implemented through a Congressional statute, pre-empted the state *courts* from exercising jurisdictional authority over militia cases. In concluding that exclusive federal power meant exclusive judicial power as well as exclusive legislative power, even where the Constitution was silent about any form of federal exclusivity, Story must have been assuming that the "national" character of a subject—the militia in *Houston*—meant that it was to be regulated by all the departments of the national government.

Concurrent sovereignty questions, then—the questions at the heart of *Gibbons* v. *Ogden* and the other Commerce Clause cases that followed it—can be seen as a subcategory of questions about the scope of coterminous power theory. If the exercise of power by one department of the federal government bred a like potential to exercise power by another branch, then the symbiotic process of federal judicial and legislative activity necessarily expanded the sphere of federal sovereignty. Given the assumption that the delegation of power to one federal department could precipitate the aggrandizement of authority by others, it became crucial to determine what the consequences of a delegation were. If, for example, the Constitution gave Congress power to regulate commerce, and coterminous power theory suggested that the jurisdiction of the federal courts to determine whether Congress had properly executed that regulatory power in a given case should be as broad as the regulatory power itself, was any power to regulate commerce left in the states? Did, in other words, the exercise of a constitutionally mandated power by Congress not only increase the power of the federal courts but restrict the power of state courts and legislatures?

The concept of concurrent sovereignty was responsive to these questions. By positing that a delegation of sovereignty to the federal government (either by virtue of language in the Constitution or by virtue of a congressional statute) did not in itself preclude states from exercising sovereign powers over the area which was the subject of the delegation, advocates of concurrent sovereignty sought to avoid a situation where the possession of sovereign power by one department of the federal government was converted into a simultaneous expansion of the sovereign powers of other federal departments and contraction of the sovereign powers of the states.

*Houston* v. *Moore* was perceived as an odd case because Congress, while it could, pursuant to its constitutional powers, have established federal courts-martial to try militia cases, had not only not done so but had acquiesced in the practice of state courts' trying those cases. The result of Congress's inactivity was therefore that state courts were brought into the process by which the federal militia was regulated even though they could not have regulated the militia on their own. Was this a special circumstance of the constitutional scheme for establishing and regulating the federal militia, or a manifestation of a more general principle, that where Congress could have, but had not, exercised its sovereign powers fully, some sovereignty remained in the states? *Houston,* for all its ambiguities, precipitated a clear division within the Court on that point. Washington's majority suggested that concurrent sovereignty did remain in the states where the sovereignty of the federal government had not been designated as exclusive. Story's opinion, on the other hand, maintained that the "real state of the case" was that Pennsylvania, "without the assent of the United States, insist[s] on being a principal, if not a paramount sovereign," in the "execution" of a "law of the United States."[195] When Congress had been given regulatory power, Article III and coterminous power theory made the jurisdiction of the federal courts coextensive with that power. But no such process operated to extend the jurisdiction of the state courts. Pennsylvania's effort to supplement a federal regulatory scheme was, in Story's view, "a . . . direct collision with the authority of the United States . . . ; an exercise of concurrent authority where the laws of Congress have constitutionally denied it."[196]

*Houston* can thus be seen as a transition case in the history of the ongoing sovereignty debate carried out within and around the Marshall Court: a case in which the doctrine of concurrent sovereignty emerged as a potential brake on the unlimited scope of federal sovereignty anticipated by coterminous power theory. Concurrent sovereignty was to play a more decisive role in the cases establishing affirmative limits on state powers, which are subsequently considered. Before leaving the jurisdiction cases, however, it is worth asking what they had accomplished, and not accomplished, in clarifying the respective primacy of "Union" and "compact" theories of sovereignty. First, the decisions thus far considered had been particularly effective in establishing a necessary connection between extensive supervisory jurisdiction for the federal courts and the preservation of the Union. *Martin* and *Cohens,* taken together, stood for the proposition that state courts could not avoid Section 25 review by claiming that the Court's review powers were inconsistent with the compact theory of sovereignty. One could argue that, as a practical matter, the logic of compact theory was intolerable in this context and thus the results in *Martin* and *Cohens* foreordained: if the states could have made their own judgments on matters of constitutional or federal law, parochial construction of the Constitution and federal statutes or treaties would have been inevitable and the "discordant" resolution of constitutional or federal issues Story referred to in *Martin* would have resulted. In discarding this impractical vision, however, *Martin* and *Cohens* also discarded a major

---

[195] 5 Wheat. at 71.  |  [196] Ibid., 72.

doctrine of compact theory, that the Union, having been formed from states, was required to respect the autonomy of the states. This doctrine was replaced with two others, that any "well constituted" government needed to protect itself by extending its judicial powers as far as its legislative powers; and the doctrine that the government protected by the Constitution was the Union, a government that had been created by and remained responsible to the people. That exegesis was very significant, amounting to the elevation of consolidationist dogma to the status of legal principles.

*Osborn* and *Houston,* by contrast, were not cases whose focus was the supervisory powers of the federal judiciary over the states, but rather cases seeking to expand federal sovereignty by carving out areas of exclusive federal court jurisdiction. Had Story's position prevailed in both cases, the sovereignty implications would have been very significant: the state courts would have been precluded not only from all national bank cases (and arguably from such cases involving any national institutions that Congress created) but also, conceivably, from all federal criminal cases, if Congress elected to do so. This was, of course, precisely what Story had in mind, and precisely what Tucker and Jefferson had feared when they spoke of federal judicial and legislative power being potentially unlimited.

But that scenario did not come to pass. Story was repulsed in *Houston* and the idea of concurrent state power, while confusingly articulated, was decisively embraced. Concurrent state power was to represent something of a fallback position for advocates of state sovereignty: if the states could not make wholly independent judgments on issues of constitutional and federal law, they could at least invade a variety of areas of American life unless the Constitution and Congress explicitly precluded them from so doing. The articulation of concurrent sovereignty doctrine was not to come, however, until another strand of the consolidationist argument had been woven: the idea that the Constitution permitted the federal judiciary to establish the scope of the sovereign powers of the federal legislature. To that strand, embodied in *McCulloch* v. *Maryland,* we now turn.

The cases thus far considered, while informed by the political axiom of coterminous power theory, had confined the meaning of that axiom to instances in which the jurisdiction of the federal courts was being expanded so as to implement the policies of Congress and thereby help preserve the Union against centrifugal forces. Tucker had, however, identified another potential consequence of expansive federal court jurisdiction: the enlargement of the legislative powers of the federal government. As noted, Tucker seems to have been concerned that if the federal judiciary were given wide latitude to interpret the Constitution or to fashion federal common law doctrines, judges sympathetic to the expansion of federal power would construe the Constitution or develop unwritten common law doctrines in a fashion that reflected those sympathies. Despite the mixed results in *Martin, Cohens, Osborn,* and *Houston,* the cases had tended to confirm Tucker's insight. Article III of the Constitution had consistently been read to give the federal judiciary power to determine, and on some occasions to limit, the scope of state sovereignty.

Alongside the grant of power to the federal courts in Article III was another potential source of expansive federal power: the enumerated powers given to Congress by Article I, Section 8, taken together with the general grant of a power "to make all Laws which shall be necessary and proper for carrying into Execution" the enumerated powers. How far did these federal legislative powers restrict the sovereignty of the states? While the scope of one such power, that of "organizing, arming, and disciplining the Militia," had been considered in *Houston,* the issue in that case had been the consequence of federal legislative inactivity: Congress had done nothing to provide for federal courts-martial to try militia cases. What were the sovereignty consequences of congressional activity? That question was raised in *McCulloch* v. *Maryland,* and the Court's answer set off a sovereignty debate comparable in magnitude to that which had surfaced in the wake of *Martin* and *Cohens.*

The *McCulloch* case was widely perceived by contemporaries as the most significant decision the Court rendered in its 1819 Term, which had originally included *Houston,* the bankruptcy legislation case of *Sturges* v. *Crowninshield,* and the reargument of *Dartmouth College* v. *Woodward. McCulloch* was especially important to contemporaries because in a time of economic instability it tested the legitimacy of the most powerful and controversial economic institution in the country, the Second Bank of the United States; and because observers regarded it as a kind of advisory opinion for two other issues of even greater potential importance, the constitutionality of federally sponsored internal improvements projects and the constitutionality of federal slavery legislation. Between 1815 and 1819, Congress had debated the constitutionality of federally sponsored roads and canals; President Madison had vetoed one internal improvements bill on constitutional grounds, and his successor Monroe had declined to promote another for similar reasons. Meanwhile the prospect of new states in the Union had raised the possibility that Congress might enact legislation affecting the status of slavery within their borders. *McCulloch,* in this context, was a case about how much of this sort of congressional activity would be constitutionally permissible.

The Bank of the United States, first chartered in 1791, soon became a controversial institution, whose opponents claimed that it furthered the interests of the Federalist party, its foreign stockholders, "great monied monopolies''[197] and ''aristocratical principles.''[198] Its charter lapsed in 1811 and was not renewed until 1816. During the first years of an inflationary trend between 1815 and 1818 the Bank was inactive, and state banks had emerged as the principal depositories of currency, issuing their own bank notes. When the Bank of the United States began to do business again in January 1817, it immediately established branches in numerous states, issued national bank notes, loaned money on various pledges on stock and state notes, and generally tried to compete with the state banks in what was regarded as an active, thriving economy. When cotton prices fell sharply in 1818 and depositors sought to redeem their notes in specie, the speculative efforts of the branch banks—some of them corrupt, as in Maryland—came to light. The results were a panic and general hostility to the Bank. Between 1816 and 1818 several states enacted legislation designed to regulate or to prohibit the operations of the national bank offices within their borders.[199] Maryland's version, passed in February 1818, created a stamp tax on all notes issued by banks "not chartered by the legislature," ranging from ten cents to twenty dollars, depending on the value of the note. The tax could be avoided only by an annual payment of $15,000 by the affected bank. The statute, which went into effect in May, was immediately challenged by the Baltimore branch of the Bank of the United States; a case was arranged in which James McCulloch, cashier for the Baltimore branch, circulated a bank note and refused to pay the tax; and the Supreme Court, on a writ of error from a June 1818 decision by the highest court of Maryland, set the case on its docket on September 18, 1818.

The great significance of the *McCulloch* case was evident from the lawyers selected to argue it. Webster, fresh from his performance in the *Dartmouth College* case, Wirt, who according to Albert Beveridge "had arrived at the fullness of his powers,"[200] and the legendary Pinkney represented the Bank; Martin, arguing his last important case, Joseph Hopkinson, and the ubiquitous Walter Jones represented Maryland.

The arguments of counsel in *McCulloch* made it clear that both principal issues in the case were sovereignty issues. The first issue, the constitutionality of the Bank itself, tested the ability of Congress to exercise powers that the Constitution had not expressly delegated to it.

---

[197] The language of one of the judges in Bulow v. City of Charleston, 1 Nott and McCord 527 (1821).

[198] Brutus in the Philadelphia *General Advertiser*, Mar. 26, 1819, reacting to the *McCulloch* decision.

[199] On the origins of the First and Second Banks of the United States, see

B. Hammond, *Banks and Politics in America* (1957); on antibank legislation between 1816 and 1820, see C. Warren, *The Supreme Court in United States History* (3 vols., 1922), I, 505–507.

[200] Beveridge, *John Marshall*, IV, 284.

Defining the nature and scope of Congress's implied powers was another way of defining the nature and limits of federal sovereignty in the American republic. The second issue, whether, if a national bank could consitutionally be created, a state could tax it, was also at bottom a sovereignty issue. Those who argued that issue recognized that taxation was a manifestation of sovereign power and could be carried to confiscating limits. "An unlimited power to tax," Webster said in his argument, was "a power to destroy."[201] Contemporaries thus rightly perceived *McCulloch* as "a constitutional question of . . . sovereign rights,"[202] and all six counsel discussed abstract theories of sovereignty in their arguments.

From the perspective of early-nineteenth-century sovereignty theory, *McCulloch* was both a coterminous power and a concurrent power case. The Constitution had not, in express terms, granted Congress discretionary power to create a national bank. Did the absence of express delegating language mean that such a power was reserved to the states, as the Tenth Amendment suggested? Or did the express enumeration of some federal powers imply the existence of other related or incidental powers, "implied" powers? The federal judiciary, in the person of the Court, was to determine the scope of Congress's implied powers: would it find them to be unlimited? The implied powers issue in *McCulloch* was thus not confined to the case of a national bank; indeed, when the Bank of the United States had been rechartered in 1811 few doubts had been expressed about its constitutional validity. Webster, on behalf of the Bank in *McCulloch,* suggested that "the question whether Congress constitutionally possesses the power to incorporate a bank . . . was not now to be considered as an open question."[203] What was really at stake in *McCulloch,* with respect to the implied powers issue, was not whether Congress could create national banks but whether the Court would find Congress's unenumerated but implied sovereign powers to be vast.

The first sovereignty issue in *McCulloch* thus led to the second, which was more directly relevant to the case before the Court. Taxation was one of the principal weapons by which states could express their hostility to the national government, and national banks were, in the early nineteenth century, one of the few national institutions operating within state borders. If Congress had, under Article I, broad powers to create "necessary" national institutions, did its exercise of sovereignty prohibit the states from affecting those institutions? This was a question of great practical significance. If states could tax a national bank, they could drive that bank out of the state, thereby reserving banking for their own char-

---

[201] 4 Wheat. 316, 327 (1816).
[202] Ibid. at 322 (Wheaton's note for the Court).

[203] Ibid.

tered institutions. The implications of such state activity, in an economy in which financial transactions were increasingly crossing state lines, would be considerable. The fact that the House of Representatives debated whether Congress should repeal the Bank's charter at the same time *McCulloch* was being argued demonstrates how pressing and unsettled the issue of banking policy then was.[204]

Marshall began his discussion of both issues in *McCulloch* with general statements of sovereignty theory. In considering whether Congress could constitutionally establish a national bank he noted that Jones and Martin, for Maryland, had argued that "the constitution was formed and adopted, not by the people of the United States at large, but by the people of the respective states," and was therefore "a compact between the states" in which the states "reserved . . . all the powers [they had] not expressly relinquished."[205] Marshall was not two pages into his opinion for the Court in *McCulloch* before he attacked that argument. "Counsel for the State of Maryland," he said,

> have deemed it of some importance, in the construction of the constitution, to consider that instrument not as emanating from the people, but as the act of sovereign and independent states. The powers of the general government, it has been said, are delegated by the states, who alone are truly sovereign; and must be exercised in subordination to the states, who alone possess supreme dominion.[206]

Marshall devoted the next twenty pages of his opinion to refuting that proposition. The refutation involved four steps, themselves characteristic of Marshallian logic.[207] Step one was Marshall's claim that the process by which the Constitution had been ratified, and the language in its Preamble, revealed the nature of the federal government. In the process of ratification sovereignty had not been transferred from the states to the Union, but to the people, and then to the Union. "It was deemed necessary," Marshall claimed, "to change this alliance into an effective government" that both "possess[ed] great and sovereign powers, and act[ed] directly on the people," and "deriv[ed] its powers directly from [the people]."[208] Thus the "government of the Union" was "emphatically, and truly, a government of the people." It was also a government of "enumerated powers": it could "exercise only the powers granted to it" by the people. But though limited in its powers, the government of

---

[204] For the debates see *Register of Debates*, 15th Cong., 2d Sess., Feb. 18, 22, 23, 24, 1819.

[205] 4 Wheat. at 363, 372.

[206] Ibid., 402.

[207] See the discussion of Marshall's rhetoric in G. White, *The American Judicial Tradition* (1976), 25–32.

[208] 4 Wheat. at 404.

the Union was "supreme within its sphere of action." This proposition "result[ed] necessarily from its nature."[209]

The last proposition was merely asserted to be self-evident. The federal government was to be supreme within its sphere of action, Marshall claimed, because it was "the government of all; its powers are delegated by all; it represents all; and acts for all."[210] But why did the presumed sovereignty of the people necessarily result in unlimited supremacy for the government they had enacted? That government, operating within its "sphere of action," might infringe on the sovereignty of individuals. Was a transfer of sovereignty to an "effective government" the equivalent of a surrender of sovereignty?

Marshall did not address that question. He seems to have assumed that since the people had created the federal government, the "great and sovereign powers" employed by that government to render it "effective" had thereby been legitimated. It was in the "nature" of an effective government to develop means to protect and to perpetuate itself. While "the question respecting the extent of the powers actually granted would be perpetually arising, and will probably continue to arise, as long as our system shall exist," the "system" required *some* federal supremacy. The test for when that supremacy existed appeared to be whether it came within the "sphere of action" of the federal government, whether the subject over which federal supremacy was asserted was one "on which . . . [t]he nation can act."[211]

At first glance this test would seem to lack any evaluative criteria. Since the people, the ultimate sovereigns, had transferred their sovereignty to the federal government in the Constitution, any exercise of sovereign power by the federal government would be derived from the powers of the people, and the sphere of federal action would thus be unlimited. But the federal government, Marshall suggested, could exercise only the sovereign powers granted to it in the Constitution, only "laws . . . made in pursuance of the constitution form[ed] the supreme law of the land."[212] The scope of federal power was to be limited to that constitutionally mandated. And the determination of whether federal sovereignty had been mandated in a given instance had been entrusted, also by the Constitution, to the federal judicial department. Marshall had begun *McCulloch* by underscoring the last point:

> The constitution of our country, in its most interesting and vital parts, is to be considered; the conflicting powers of the government of the Union and of its members, as marked in that constitution, are to be discussed; and an opinion given, which may essentially influence the

---

[209] Ibid., 405.
[210] Ibid.

[211] Ibid.
[212] Ibid., 406.

great operations of the government. . . . On the Supreme Court of the United States has the constitution of our country developed this important duty.[213]

In five pages Marshall had structured the question of the constitutionality of Congress's creation of a national bank in such a way as to ensure that nothing in the nature of constitutional government in America, as distinguished from the specific text of the Constitution, prevented Congress from so acting. Congress had been made the agent of the sovereign people by the ratification process; the "effective" government created by that process was necessarily supreme within the ambit of its constitutional powers; the Constitution had given the federal judiciary the responsibility of determining the ambit of congressional supremacy. All that was left was for the Court to find whether among the powers entrusted to Congress by the people in the Constitution was one of establishing a bank.

Marshall proceeded to step two of his argument, in which he provided a methodology for judicial determination of that issue. The enumeration of some powers granted to Congress by Article I of the Constitution, he argued, did not necessarily exclude powers not enumerated. "Incidental or implied powers" were not specifically excluded; the Tenth Amendment's language reserving powers "not delegated to the United States" to the states or to the people did not include the word "expressly." The "idea" of constitutional interpretation "entertained by the framers" was thus to leave "the question, whether the particular power which may become the subject of contest has been delegated to the one government or prohibited to the other" to be determined by "a fair construction of the whole instrument."[214] Such a construction required only that the "great outlines" of the Constitution "be marked, its important objects designated, and the minor ingredients which comprise these objects be deduced from the nature of the objects themselves."[215] The "nature" of the Constitution was that it did not contain "accurate detail of all the subdivisions of which its great powers may admit, and of all the means by which they may be carried into execution." It was not prolix, like a "legal code": it was an outline of "important objects," to be given "a fair and just" interpretation.[216]

At this point Marshall formulated another proposition: the Constitution assumed the existence not only of enumerated federal powers but of implied federal powers. He now sought additional support for that proposition, and thus moved to step three of his argument, in which he enlisted, in addition to this "general reasoning,"[217] the Necessary and

---

[213] Ibid., 400–401.
[214] Ibid., 406.
[215] Ibid., 407.

[216] Ibid., 407.
[217] Ibid., 411.

Proper Clause of Article I, Section 8 of the Constitution. The purpose of this clause, Marshall suggested, was "to remove all doubts respecting the right to legislate on that vast mass of incidental powers which must be invoked in the Constitution."[218] Necessary powers were not merely powers limited to "those single means without which the end would be entirely unacceptable." They were not the equivalent of "absolutely necessary" powers: the Framers had, in fact, used "absolutely necessary" in another clause, that prohibiting state import duties.[219] The Necessary and Proper Clause, taken together with the "nature" and "objects" of the Constitution, established the existence of implied federal powers.

But what were the limits on these powers? Here Marshall reached step four in his argument, and he moved from concrete textual analysis to the realm of abstractions. He had begun with the proposition that the powers of the federal government were limited: he now repeated that statement. The limits of the federal government's powers were "not to be transcended." How did one know when the limits had been reached? Marshall supplied a formula:

> Let the end be legitimate, let it be within the scope of the constitution, and all means which are appropriate, which are plainly adapted to that end, which are not prohibited, but consistent with the letter and spirit of the constitution, are constitutional.[220]

In a given implied powers case, then, the formula suggested that one look to the end to which the power was directed (its "objects"), consider whether the means to that end had been "appropriate," "plainly adapted," and "not prohibited" by the Constitution, and in so doing ascertain whether the implied power being exercised was consistent with the Constitution's "letter and spirit." The exercise thus invited one to reconsider the nature of federal powers and the nature of the Union that the people had created: it brought Marshall back to the sovereignty principles from which his argument had originated.

After painstakingly developing the argument establishing criteria for implied powers cases, Marshall then spent very little time applying it to the question whether Congress could constitutionally charter a national bank. His discussion of that point, in fact, was so abrupt and assertive that one might suspect he considered the resolution obvious and was

---

[218] Ibid., 420–21.
[219] U.S. Const., Art. I, Sect. 10. See ibid., 414.
[220] Ibid. at 421. In United States v. Fisher, 2 Cranch 358 (1805), a case that also interpreted congressional implied powers, Marshall had said that Congress "must be empowered to use any means which are in fact conducive to the exercise of a power granted by the constitution." 2 Cranch at 396. No one, including Marshall, cited *Fisher* in *McCulloch*.

primarily concerned in this portion of his opinion with the implied powers principle itself. A bank, Marshall suggested, was "a convenient, a useful, and [an] essential instrument in the prosecution of [Congress's] fiscal operations." Those facts were "not now a subject of controversy." All those "who have been concerned in the administration of our finances" had "concurred in representing [the Bank's] importance and necessity."[221] Even those who had "previous opinions against [the Bank] . . . have yielded those opinions to the exigencies of the nation." In short, "the time has passed away when it can be necessary to prove the importance of this instrument as a means to effect the legitimate objects of the government."[222]

This was the kind of reasoning in which Marshall indulged when he really did not want to examine an issue in detail, and had he, he might have been hard pressed to show how a private bank in which only 20 percent of the shares were owned by the federal government was "necessary" to administer such powers as collecting taxes, conducting wars, or supporting armies and navies. Could a series of state banks have not done as well? The United States had, after all, been without a national bank throughout the War of 1812. Critics of Marshall's opinion in *McCulloch* were quick to challenge him on the "national" functions of a bank: one said that "a bank is principally intended to benefit individual merchants and traders" rather than to "enable the federal government either to collect its taxes or to borrow money."[223]

Marshall quickly passed on, however, to summarize his argument in the first part of the *McCulloch* opinion. Having developed his premises—the sovereignty of the people, their delegation of supreme powers to the federal government, the general nature of the Constitution's grant of supreme powers, the necessary relationships between ends and means in that grant, the duty of the judiciary to emphasize that relationship through "fair and just" interpretations of a document that had only expressed "great outlines" and "important objects" in its language—and having read the Necessary and Proper Clause, taken together with some enumerated congressional powers, to have granted Congress the power to create a national bank, Marshall then asked rhetorically whether any limits on congressional implied powers existed. He answered:

> Should Congress, in the execution of its powers, adopt measures which are prohibited by the Constitution; or should Congress, under the pretext of executing its powers, pass laws for the accomplishment of objects not entrusted to the government; it would be the painful duty of

---

[221] 4 Wheat. at 422–23.
[222] Ibid., 423.
[223] Amphictyon, Richmond *En-quirer*, Apr. 2, 1819, reprinted in Gunther, *Defense*, 71–72.

this tribunal . . . to say that such an act was not the law of the land. But where the law is not prohibited, and is really calculated to affect any of the objects entrusted to the government, to undertake here to inquire into the degree of its necessity, would be to pass the line which circumscribes the judicial department, and to tread on legislative ground. This court disclaims all pretensions to such a power.[224]

The relationship between the federal judiciary and the federal legislature envisaged by that passage was not one likely to cheer those who had identified the Court as an apostle of consolidation. Once Congress had been granted a power, it was stopped from executing that power through relevant means only if the means were "prohibited" or if they could be related only to "objects not entrusted to the government." Both the question of whether a particular means was "prohibited" and the question of whether a particular object was related to an enumerated power were questions for the federal judiciary. The judiciary, if it ascertained that a congressional law was "not prohibited" and was "calculated" to implement an "object entrusted to the government," could not inquire into the degree of that law's "necessity." Any connection, then, between an "object entrusted to the government"—that is, a hypothetical purpose of an enumerated judicial power—and a piece of legislation made that legislation constitutionally permissible.

Marshall suggested that by making a more searching inquiry into the necessity of congressional legislation based on implied powers the Court would be substituting its power for that of a legislature. But that position seemed to reduce itself to one of two alternatives. Either the Court, in determining that a chosen means was prohibited, was in fact conducting an inquiry into necessity, or the Court was simply saying that any articulated congressional rationale for legislation based on the Necessary and Proper Clause would suffice. Jefferson, in protesting against an effort on the part of the federal government to charter a company to mine copper in New Jersey in 1800, gave an example of the latter interpretation of the clause. "Congress are authorized to defend the nation," he wrote to Edward Livingston. "Ships are necessary for defence; copper is necessary for ships; mines, necessary for copper; a company necessary to work the mines. Under such a process of filiation of necessities the sweeping clause makes clean work."[225]

The apparently broad scope given to congressional implied powers by Marshall in *McCulloch* made the decision immediately controversial, and much of the criticism of the Court's opinion centered on the implied powers argument. Marshall's treatment of the state taxation issue may, however, have been equally foreboding to anticonsolidationists.

---

[224] 4 Wheat. at 423.
[225] T. Jefferson to E. Livingston, | Apr. 30, 1800, quoted in Warren, *Supreme Court*, I, 501.

Marshall immediately placed the taxation issue in *McCulloch* in the context of sovereignty doctrine. Taxation, Marshall declared, was

> an incident of sovereignty, and . . . coextensive with that to which it is an incident. All subjects over which the sovereign power of a state extends, are objects of taxation; but those over which it does not extend, are upon the soundest principles, exempt from taxation.[226]

The question in *McCulloch* was therefore whether "the sovereignty of a State extends . . . to those means which are employed by Congress to carry into execution powers conferred on that body by the people of the United States."[227]

To put the question in that fashion was, of course, to answer it; the first part of Marshall's *McCulloch* opinion already had done so. "If we apply the principle for which the State of Maryland contends," Marshall argued, "we shall find it capable of changing totally the character of that instrument." He then elaborated:

> We shall find [the Constitution] capable of arresting all the measures of the government, and of prostrating it at the foot of the States. The American people have declared their constitution, and the laws made in pursuance thereof, to be supreme; but this principle would transfer the supremacy, in fact, to the States.
>
> If the States may tax one instrument, employed by the government in the execution of its powers, they may tax any and every other instrument. They may tax the mail; they may tax the mint; they may tax the papers of the custom-house; they may tax judicial process. . . . This was not intended by the American people. They did not design to make their government dependent on the States.[228]

At bottom, then, *McCulloch* was "a question of supremacy."

But while Marshall invoked his parade of horribles, and repeated the argument made by Webster that "the power to tax involves the power to destroy,"[229] he did not spend much time clarifying the constitutional basis for his conclusion that Maryland could apparently not tax the Bank of the United States at all. He alluded to a principle that "so entirely pervades the constitution . . . as to be incapable of being separated from it."[230] That principle was "that the constitution and the laws made in pursuance thereof are supreme."[231] Did he mean to suggest that since the Bank's charter was a federal law, the states, by virtue of the Supremacy Clause of Article VI, could pass no laws affecting the Bank? If this was

---

[226] 4 Wheat. at 429.
[227] Ibid.
[228] Ibid., 432

[229] Ibid., 431.
[230] Ibid., 426.
[231] Ibid.

the case his examples of federal custom-houses, courts, and mints do not seem apposite: those institutions had not been chartered. Moreover, Marshall had conceded that "the power of taxation . . . is retained by the states" and was to "be concurrently exercised by the two governments."[232] Thus state taxation was not completely foreclosed on sovereignty principles: it was, apparently, simply limited to entities over which the federal government had not exercised legislative control. This last issue was to resurface with a vengeance in the Commerce Clause cases.

In addition, the Bank's charter had not given it any immunity from state taxation; it had merely brought the Bank into being and established its internal structure and organization. The Bank, as noted, was essentially a private corporation, not regulated in any fashion by the federal government. Hopkinson, for Maryland, had argued that the Bank was a "purely private . . . institution," a "trading money lender in its business," whose mercantile character overwhelmed its sovereign character.[233] Marshall was subsequently to hold that a state could tax this sort of state bank.[234]

Thus the taxation portion of *McCulloch* seems to have been based on the Supremacy Clause. Given this feature of the opinion, it is unclear whether Marshall was suggesting that any time Congress created a federal institution pursuant to its implied power, its action immunized the institution from state regulatory activity. Marshall spoke of the Court's "conviction that the states have no power, by taxation or otherwise, to retard, impede, burden, or in any manner control, the operations of the constitutional laws enacted by Congress to carry into execution the powers vested in the general government."[235] Taken literally, this would mean that the merest federal law on any subject was enough to preclude state intervention in any form. Over the years it has become clear that the Court did not mean that, or if it did, it has taken back the pronouncement.

Marshall delivered his opinion in *McCulloch*, for a unanimous Court, on March 7, 1819. Reaction from anticonsolidationists was not long in coming. On March 30 a series of essays by Amphictyon, later identified by Marshall as William Brockenbrough,[236] began in the *Enquirer*. After first expressing disappointment that seriatim opinions had not been issued by the Justices ("the people had surely a right to expect that each judge should assign his own reasons for the vote he gave"),[237]

---

[232] Ibid., 425.
[233] Ibid., 341.
[234] In Providence Bank v. Billings, 4 Pet. 514, 560 (1830); see discussion in Chapter IX.
[235] 4 Wheat. at 436.
[236] In a letter to Bushrod Washington, Aug. 3, 1819, John Marshall Papers, Library of Congress, Marshall said that "Amphyction [*sic*] is Judge Brockenbrough/Hampden is Judge Roane."
[237] Amphictyon, Richmond *Enquirer*, Mar. 30, 1819, reprinted in Gunther, *Defense*, 54. All subsequent references to Marshall's debate with Amphictyon and Hampden are from Gunther's edition.

# Chapter VIII: *Sovereignty and Union*

Amphictyon got down to business. There had been "two principles advocated and decided on by the Supreme Court" in *McCulloch,* he said, "which . . . endanger the very existence of state rights." The first principle was "the denial that the powers of the federal government were delegated to the states"; the second was "that the grant of powers to that government, and particularly the grant of powers 'necessary and proper' to carry the other powers into effect, ought to be construed in a liberal, rather than a restricted sense." Both principles, Amphictyon claimed, "tend directly to consolidation of the states, and to strip them of some of the most important attributes of their sovereignty."[238]

It is not necessary to belabor the several arguments Amphictyon summoned to attack Marshall's principles. Suffice it to say that they represented a rehearsal of themes identified by Tucker, Jefferson, and other anticonsolidationists since 1798. Amphictyon recalled that Marshall's "Union" theory of sovereignty had been argued in that year:

> [A]fter the Congress of that time had by the force of implication passed a sedition law, and vested the President with arbitrary and despotic powers over the persons of alien friends, after many political writers, and some of the federal courts had advocated the absurd and dangerous doctrine that the common law of England made a part of the law of these states, in their united and national capacity, then it was that this doctrine, which denies that the states are parties to the federal compact, was pressed with great zeal and ability. . . . The doctrine, however, was exposed and refuted, and I did not expect that it would be brought forward at this day under the supposed sanction of the highest judicial authority.[239]

Any denial that the Union had been created out of a compact among the states, Amphictyon maintained, "would be of fatal consequence to the rights and freedom of the people of the states." It was absurd to suppose, he believed, that under the Constitution "the right of the state governments to protest against . . . encroachments of their authority" had been "taken away, and transferred to the federal judiciary, whose power extends to all cases arising under the Constitution"; and that, therefore "the supreme court is the umpire to decide between the states on the one side, and the United States on the other, in all questions touching the constitutionality of laws. . . ." The states, in his view, "never could have committed an act of such egregious folly as to agree that their umpire should be altogether appointed and paid by the other party."[240]

In his discussion of compact theory, then, Amphictyon managed to revive the common law of crimes controversy, deny the validity of the

---

[238] Ibid., 55.
[239] Ibid., 57.
[240] Ibid., 58.

*Martin* decision, and suggest that the Supreme Court of the United States could never be ''a perfectly impartial tribunal . . . when the contest was between the United States and one of its members.''[241] He closed his discussion by quoting a passage from a report of a committee of the Virginia House of Delegates in 1799, one that obviously seemed apt in light of *McCulloch*:

> However true . . . it may be that the judicial department is, in all questions submitted to by the forms of the Constitution, to decide in the last resort, [t]his result must necessarily be deemed the last in relation to the authorities of other departments of the government; not in relation to the rights of the parties to the Constitutional compact, from which the judicial as well as the other departments hold their delegated trusts. On any other hypothesis, the delegation of judicial power, would annul the authority delegating it, & the concurrence of this department with the others in usurped powers, might subvert forever . . . the very Constitutions, which all were instructed to preserve.[242]

Amphictyon's critique of Marshall's necessary and proper argument was less impassioned, although in one passage he recalled the original fears of republicans about the interaction of expansive space and consolidationist institutions:

> [A] residuary power was left in possession of the states for wise purposes. It is necessary that the laws which regulate the daily transactions of men should have a regard to their interests, their feelings, even their prejudices. This can be better done when the territory is of moderate dimensions, than when it is immense; . . . It is still more important that this division of legislative power into external and internal should be rigidly adhered to, and its proper distribution religiously observed, when we reflect that the accumulation of those powers into the hands of one government would render it too strong for the liberty of the people, and would inevitably erect a throne upon the ruins of the republic.[243]

For the most part, however, Amphictyon confined himself to attacking Marshall's reading of ''necessary'' and to prophesying the consequences of ''liberal'' constructions of the Necessary and Proper and the General Welfare clauses. His prophecies were reminiscent of Story's 1815 blueprint for national institutions. The two clauses, taken together and liberally construed, would authorize, Amphictyon feared, internal improve-

---

[241] Ibid.
[242] Ibid., 64.

[243] Ibid., 71.

554

Chapter VIII: *Sovereignty and Union*

ments, national universities, "companies for the promotion of agriculture," and national churches.

Finally, Amphictyon addressed Marshall's suggestion in *McCulloch* that if Congress exceeded its powers under the Necessary and Proper Clause "it would become the painful duty of [the Court] to say that an act of Congress was not the law of the land." He first doubted that such a case would ever arise, "where the act is one which gives power to the federal government." The Court would not be inclined to be impartial in such cases, and even if it were, Marshall's latitudinous construction of the Necessary and Proper Clause would "render it unnecessary for [the Court] to discharge a duty so 'painful' to [its] feelings."[244] The Court had conceded that "Congress . . . are the sole judges of the *necessity* [of any of their laws]; and [for the Court] to attempt to control [congressional] discretion would be treading on legislative ground."[245]

Marshall had anticipated the attack on *McCulloch,* and when it came he took steps to defend himself. He had delivered the *McCulloch* opinion on March 6, 1819, and the Court had adjourned a week later. On March 24 he wrote Story that "[o]ur opinion in the Bank case has roused the sleeping spirit of Virginia," and that "[i]t will be attacked in the papers with some asperity."[246] That letter was written in Richmond, where Marshall had returned to await the opening of his circuit court term in May. Three days later he wrote to the same effect to Bushrod Washington, noting that "[w]e shall be denounced bitterly in the papers & . . . undoubtedly be condemned as a pack of consolidating aristocratics."[247] In the letter to Story Marshall said that the Court's opinion "will remain undefended, . . . as those who favor it never write for the publick." He resolved to write an anonymous defense of *McCulloch.*

Washington, assigned to the Third Circuit, had connections in Philadelphia, and Marshall and he arranged for the publication of four essays in the Philadelphia *Union,* a paper that had been identified with the Federalist party. The essays appeared in the *Union* on April 24 and April 28. When Marshall read the printed version of his essays, he realized they had been garbled. On May 6 he wrote Washington that the printer "has cut out the middle of the first number to be inserted into the middle of the second; & to show his perfect impartiality, has cut out the middle of the second number to be inserted in the first."[248] On May 27 he wrote to Story in the same vein:

[244] Ibid., 75.
[245] Ibid., 76.
[246] J. Marshall to J. Story, Mar. 24, 1819, *Proc. Mass. Hist. Soc.,* 14:324 (1901).
[247] J. Marshall to B. Washington, Mar. 27, 1819, John Marshall Papers, College of William and Mary Library.
[248] J. Marshall to B. Washington, May 6, 1819, Marshall Papers, Library of Congress.

The piece to whom you allude . . . contained, I think, a complete demonstration of the fallacies and errors contained in those attacks on the opinion of the Court . . . but was so mangled in the publication that only those who had bestowed close attention to the subject could understand it. There were two numbers & the editor of the Union in Philadelphia, the paper in which it was published, had mixed the different numbers together so as in several instances to place the reasoning intended to demonstrate one proposition under another. The points of the arguments were so separated from each other, & so strangely mixed as to constitute a labyrinth to which those only who understood the whole subject perfectly could find a clue.[249]

The *Union* essays were published under the pseudonym "A Friend of the Union." Albert Beveridge, in writing his biography of Marshall, identified the author but found "the reading of Marshall's newspaper effort . . . exhausting," and the essays filled with "tedious columns of diffuse repetition."[250] Beveridge was working with the garbled version. In the 1960s Gerald Gunther, working from information in a May 6, 1819, letter from Marshall to Washington and in the letter to Story quoted above, surmised that the *Union* essays had been erroneously printed, and he followed Marshall's instructions for correcting them. Gunther also discovered that Marshall, again using Washington as an intermediary, had actually secured publication of the corrected version, in the Alexandria *Gazette* on May 15, 17, and 18, 1819.[251] That corrected version has been reprinted; my analysis is based on the corrected text.

Marshall's first *Union* essay defended the Court's pronouncement that the Union was a government of the people rather than of the states. He cited the Preamble of the Constitution,[252] contrasted its language with that of the Articles of Confederation,[253] quoted from the very resolution of the Virginia legislature Amphictyon had cited,[254] and recited language in the *McCulloch* opinion itself in order to show that the Constitution was created and ratified by the "people of the respective states" rather than "the state governments."[255] In short,

If Amphyction [*sic*] means to assert . . . that the powers of the general government were delegated by the state legislatures, then I say his assertion is contradicted by the words of the constitution . . . and is not supported, even by that report on which he so confidently relies.[256]

---

[249] J. Marshall to J. Story, May 27, 1819, *Proc. Mass. Hist. Soc.*, 14:325 (1901).
[250] See Beveridge, *John Marshall*, IV, 319–20.
[251] See G. Gunther, "Unearthing John Marshall's Major Out-of-Court Constitutional Commentary," *Stan. L. Rev.*, 21:449, 453 (1969).

[252] Reprinted in Gunther, *Defense*, 85.
[253] Ibid., 86.
[254] Ibid., 87–88.
[255] Ibid., 90.
[256] Ibid., 85.

# Chapter VIII: *Sovereignty and Union*

Marshall expressed "regret that a gentleman whose claims to our respect appear to be by no means inconsiderable" would "manifest such excessive hostility to the powers necessary for the preservation of the Union" and had based his attack on *McCulloch* "on principles totally repugnant to the words of the constitution and to the recorded facts respecting its adoption."[257] He then turned to Amphictyon's critique of his reading of the Necessary and Proper Clause. Here his emphasis was on the fact that the reading made in *McCulloch* was not consistent with a "liberal" or "extended" or "latitudinous" reading[258] of that clause, but only with a "fair construction which gives to language the sense in which it is used, and interprets an instrument according to its true intention."[259] The "contest" between the *McCulloch* interpretation and that advanced by Amphictyon was, Marshall claimed, "between the fair sense of the words used in the constitution and a restricted sense."[260]

Put that way, there was no contest. Marshall pointed out that a "restricted" reading of "necessary" as "indispensably necessary,"[261] if it would "not absolutely arrest the progress of the government, . . . would certainly deny to those who administer it the means of executing its acknowledged powers." Tax laws could not be collected.[262] An army could not effectively be raised.[263] Congress could not implement its power to call out the militia.[264] In sum, the Necessary and Proper Clause could not be construed "to restrain the powers of Congress, or to impair the right of the legislature to exercise its best judgment in the selection of measures to carry into execution the constitutional powers of the government."[265] Marshall restated his "let the end be legitimate" language and repeated his claim that

> the principles maintained by the counsel for the state of Maryland, and by Amphyction [*sic*] would essentially damage the constitution, render the government of the union incompetent to the objects for which it was instituted, and place all powers under the control of the state legislatures. It would, in a great measure, reinstate the old confederation.[266]

The exchange between Amphictyon and Friend of the Union had pulled together a number of the respective arguments for the "compact" and "Union" positions, but had not added many new insights. Marshall was clearly right in pointing out the presence of "the people" in docu-

---

[257] Ibid., 91.
[258] Ibid., 92.
[259] Ibid.
[260] Ibid., 93.
[261] Ibid., 95.

[262] Ibid., 94.
[263] Ibid., 95.
[264] Ibid.
[265] Ibid., 97.
[266] Ibid., 99.

ments pertinent to the formation of the Constitution, but the concession that ultimate sovereignty lay in the people had been made by both sides of the debate. The issue was to what extent recognition of sovereignty in the people meant that state sovereignty was thereby restricted and the sovereignty of the Union thereby expanded. Marshall's arguments on the Necessary and Proper Clause were basically practical ones, and although he took pains to distinguish his interpretation from a "latitudinous" one, his statement that "all means which are appropriate" to the implementation of federal powers, like his insistence that construction of the Necessary and Proper Clause be "fair and just," could not have given much solace to those who understood that the construction would be undertaken by the federal judicial department.

The public debate over *McCulloch*, however, was not exhausted with the Amphictyon–Friend of the Union exchange. In his May 6 letter to Washington, in which he had given instructions for the reconstruction of the garbled *Union* essays, Marshall had noted that "some other essays, by a very great man, are now preparing & will soon appear."[267] On the twenty-seventh he informed Story that "the opinion in the Bank case continues to be denounced by the democracy in Virginia" and that "[a]n effort is certainly mounting to induce the legislature which will meet in December to take up the subject & to pass resolutions not very unlike those which were called forth by the alien & sedition law in 1799."[268] And on June 11 the first of four essays by Hampden (whom Marshall identified as Roane) was published in the *Enquirer*. Marshall wrote Washington on the seventeenth,

> I find myself more stimulated on this subject than on any other because I believe the design to be to injure the Judges & impair the constitution. I have therefore thought of answering these essays & sending my pieces to you for publication in the Alexandria paper.[269]

Marshall arranged with Washington to send his responses to Roane, which ultimately came to nine essays, to secure their printing in the *Gazette*, and to keep his identity a secret. "I hope," he said in the June 17 letter, "that the manuscript will be given to the flames. I wish two pages of each number to be directed to T. Marshall, Oakhill, Fauquier. I do not wish them to come to me lest some suspicion of the author should be created."[270] Eventually the essays appeared in the *Gazette*, between June 30 and July 15, under the pseudonym "A Friend of the Constitu-

---

[267] Marshall to Washington, May 6, 1819, supra, note 248.
[268] Marshall to Story, May 27, 1819, supra, note 249.
[269] J. Marshall to B. Washington, June 17, 1819, Miscellaneous Manuscripts, New-York Historical Society, New York, N.Y.
[270] Ibid.

tion." Marshall's goal, as he wrote to Washington, was "to put [the essays] in the hands of some members of [the] assembly should an attempt be made to [pass any anti-Court resolutions] in the legislature." With "the refutation in those hands of some respectable members of the legislature," he believed, "it may prevent some act of the assembly both silly & wicked."[271]

Ritchie introduced the first of the Hampden essays in the *Enquirer* with a brief diatribe against the Court. "We solemnly believe," he declared, "the opinion of the supreme court in the case of the bank to be fraught with alarming consequences, the federal constitution to be misinterpreted, and the rights of the states and the people to be threatened with danger." Ritchie also "believe[d] that Hampden has refuted the opinion of the supreme court and placed it in its proper light before the public." Hampden/Roane began in a similar vein: in his first paragraph he allowed that "[n]one of . . . my fellow citizens . . . can be prepared to give a Carte Blanche to our federal rulers, and to obliterate the state governments, forever, from our political system."[272]

Hampden felt that the *McCulloch* decision was a manifestation of a convergence of "that legislative power which is everywhere extending the sphere of its activity and drawing all power into its impetuous vortex" with "[t]hat judicial power which . . . has also deemed its interference necessary."[273] The judiciary had in *McCulloch* give[n] a general letter of attorney to the future legislators of the union." There was "no earthly difference" between "an *unlimited* grant of power" to Congress and "a grant limited in its terms, but accompanied with unlimited means of carrying it into execution."[274]

In Hampden's view the Court had committed two unpardonable sins in *McCulloch:* first, vesting an unlimited legislative discretion in Congress and, second, "adjudicat[ing] away the *reserved* rights of [the states] and vest[ing] them in the general government."[275] *McCulloch* was thus heretical both on coterminous power theory and on compact theory grounds. It was the "Alpha and Omega, the beginning and the *end,* the first and the last of federal usurpations."[276]

After these introductory comments in his first essay, Hampden passed on to his argument that the words "necessary and proper" meant only "such additional powers as were *fairly incidental*"[277] to the enumerated powers of Article I. Quoting *The Federalist,*[278] James Madison's 1799 report to the Virginia legislature,[279] and "clear principle[s]" of

---

[271] J. Marshall to B. Washington, June 28, 1819, Marshall Papers, Library of Congress.
[272] Hampden [Roane] in Gunther, *Defense,* 107.
[273] Ibid., 108.

[274] Ibid., 110. Emphasis in original.
[275] Ibid., 111. Emphasis in original.
[276] Ibid., 114. Emphasis in original.
[277] Ibid., 115. Emphasis in original.
[278] Ibid.
[279] Ibid., 116.

"universal law,"[280] Hampden argued that "the words 'necessary and proper' in the constitution add nothing to the powers before given to the general government."[281] They meant only "that the means were included in the grant." They were designed only to precipitate an inquiry as to "whether the [implied] power is properly an *incident* to an express power and *necessary* to its execution." If it were not, "Congress [could] not exercise it."[282] Only means *"essential"* to implement the power were constitutionally permitted.[283]

Hampden then turned to the various reasons pronounced by the Court for following its "enlarged construction" of the Necessary and Proper Clause. While there was no expression in the Constitution "excluding implied or incidental powers," the "great principle" of "reason and justice" and the theory of reserved powers in the states placed a burden on the Court to show that a broader definition of necessary and proper had been made. None of the Court's efforts to surmount that burden succeeded. The Constitution was "a compact between the people of each state, and those of all the states," and could not be altered simply because the territory of the Union was large.[284] The Constitution conveyed only limited and specific powers to the federal government, and those powers could not be enlarged without infringing on the reserved rights of the states and the people.[285] Neither Congress nor the Court was competent to change the basic principles of the Constitution: change needed to come from the people.[286] The general government was not, contrary to the Court's assertion, "supreme within the sphere of its action": all the departments of that government were "subordinate" to the people. "A body," Hampden maintained, which is subordinate to a compact, which is subordinate to another body, can scarcely be said to be supreme."[287] Finally, the "necessity" of a national bank was dubious, but the Court had apparently given Congress carte blanche to decide "the degree of necessity" that was "appropriate" in a given case. This basically left the question of what was "necessary" under the Necessary and Proper Clause to the "will and pleasure" of Congress.

Hampden/Roane now turned from the "merits" of *McCulloch* to "the jurisdiction of the Court." His "jurisdiction" argument was not so much technical as philosophical: it proceeded "on the ground, that it is not competent to the general government, to usurp rights reserved to the states, nor for its courts to adjudicate them away." The argument, Hampden suggested, was "bottomed on the clear and broad principle, that our

---

280 Ibid., 117.
281 Ibid., 124.
282 Ibid., 123. Emphasis in original.
283 Ibid., 125. Emphasis in original.

284 Ibid., 127.
285 Ibid., 128.
286 Ibid., 129.
287 Ibid., 131.

government is a federal, and not a consolidated government.''[288] He then proceeded to sketch out the theoretical alternative to consolidation.

The Constitution, Roane argued, was not adopted by the people of the United States, ''as one people,'' but by the ''several states, in their highest sovereign character.'' The assent to the Constitution was ''that of the several states, derived from the supreme authority in each state, that of the people thereof respectively.''[289] The powers of the general government thus ''result[ed] from a *compact,* to which the *states* [were] parties.''[290] Since the state governments were ''indispensably necessary to be kept up to sustain that of the Union,'' the general government could not be ''a consolidated one.'' It was ''a *federal* government, with some features of nationality.''[291] It was ''as much a federal government, or a 'league,' as the former confederation. The only difference was that the powers of this government are much extended.''

If ''everything conspires to shew that our government is a confederal, and not a consolidated one,'' Roane continued, ''how far can a state be bound by acts of the general government violating, to its injury, rights guaranteed to it, by the federal compact?''[292] Citing Madison's report to the Virginia legislature in 1799, he argued that since the authority of constitutions was paramount over governments, and the parties to a compact ''must be the rightful judges whether the compact has been violated,'' there could ''be no tribunal above their authority.'' The federal judiciary might be the ''last resort . . . in relation to the authority of the *other* departments of the [federal] government,'' but it could not be with respect ''to the rights of the parties to the compact under which the judiciary is derived.''[293] To make his meaning unmistakably clear, at that stage of his argument[294] Roane cited the Virginia Court of Appeals's decision in *Martin.* Then came the final step in Roane's logic:

> The supreme court is but a department of the general government . . . The general government cannot decide this controversy and much less can one of its departments. They cannot do it unless we treat under foot the principle which forbids a party to decide his own cause.[295]

The Court had thus behaved in an ''extrajudicial manner'' in *McCulloch* and had established an ''abstract doctrine.'' The effect of the doctrine was ''to give to congress an unbounded authority, and enable them to

---

[288] Ibid., 138.
[289] Ibid., 140.
[290] Ibid., 141. Emphasis in original.
[291] Ibid., 145. Emphasis in original.
[292] Ibid., 140.

[293] Ibid., 148–49. Emphasis in original.
[294] Ibid., 149.
[295] Ibid., 152.

shake off the limits imposed on them by the constitution.'' The Court had thus not only ''created itself the exclusive judge in the controversy,'' it had articulated an implied powers doctrine that ''may work an entire change in the constitution, and destroy entirely the state authorities.''[296]

I have quoted Roane's argument at length because it provides a classic statement of the anticonsolidationist position, reflecting in turn the assumptions that gave coherence to that position, compact and coterminous power theory. For Roane consolidation was the sum of three elements: the denial that the Constitution was created out of a compact involving the states; the claim that the federal judiciary was the ultimate arbiter of constitutional questions, even when one of the states was a litigant in the resolution of one such question; and the interpretation of the Constitution by one branch of the federal government so as to give unlimited discretionary power to the other branch to expand its powers. Once the idea of a compact was ignored, Roane argued, the idea of coterminous power was irresistible. *McCulloch* was a perfect example.

The last of Roane's Hampden essays had appeared on June 22; six days later Marshall wrote Washington that he had written three responses and planned two more.[297] By July 13, as noted, Marshall had published nine essays responding to Roane in the *Gazette*. Taken together, the essays constitute a source of the skeleton of the Union theory of sovereignty, which can be reassembled as a series of logically interconnected propositions.

Proposition one was that the ultimate sovereignty in the American federal republic rested in the people.[298] Proposition two clarified the first: the people had created the government as representatives of states.[299] The Constitution thus assumed both the reserved powers of states and the transfer of some state power to the government of the Union by the people. The Union was not a ''league,'' whose creators retained their sovereignty, but a ''government,'' which ''act[ed] directly on the people, not through the medium of the state governments.''[300] This was Marshall's third proposition.

Two further propositions followed from the first three. Since the Union was a government, it had ''all the constituent parts of a government,'' legislative, executive, and judicial ''departments.''[301] The government could, in order to be ''effective,'' take steps to preserve itself; here Marshall repeated the axiom of eighteenth-century political theory we have previously noted. Propositions four and five were dependent upon

---

[296] Ibid., 153–54.
[297] Richmond *Enquirer*, June 22, 1819; Marshall to Washington, June 28, 1819, supra, note 271.
[298] A Friend of the Constitution [Marshall], reprinted in Gunther, *Defense*, 159.
[299] Ibid., 197.
[300] Ibid., 199.
[301] Ibid.

that axiom: "effective" governments had "constituent parts," and in "effective governments" those "parts" ("departments") were given powers. One looked to the Constitution, the act in which the people of the United States, as representatives of states, had created an "effective" government, as the source of those powers.

Two types of powers were alluded to by Marshall in his *Gazette* essays, those given to Congress and those given to the federal judiciary. Here he simply summarized arguments already made in *Martin* and *McCulloch*. The enumerated powers of Congress were concessions by the people of the supremacy of the federal legislature with respect to the objects enumerated; the implied powers needed to be read in a manner consistent with that supremacy. Similarly, the judiciary's power to decide all questions "arising under the constitution and laws of the United States" had been expressly conferred by the Constitution, as had its power to decide cases involving certain designated issues or parties, such as "admiralty and maritime" or "alien" cases. Moreover, the Constitution being "the supreme law of the land," the states, the state judges, and the people were bound by it, and the supremacy of the Constitution gave rise to a "power supreme" in those who "can give the supreme law," that is to say, the Justices of the Supreme Court.[302]

All of this took Marshall to propositions six and seven, denial of the legitimacy of compact theory and acknowledgment of the coterminous power principle. The skeleton of sovereignty established by his first five propositions had led from the supremacy of the people to the supremacy of federal institutions granted legislative or interpretive power by the document the people created. But one set of sovereigns seemed left out by the progression of Marshallian logic: the states, whose sovereign existence Marshall had openly acknowledged in the essays.[303] Here he sought to make a distinction between the conferral by the people (of the states) of limited but supreme powers on the federal government and the reservation of a power in the states themselves to dispute that supremacy. The states, and the people of the states, had reserved powers: that much was clear from the Tenth Amendment. But the states did not have the reserved power that a party to a contract has to amend or nullify that contract. Once the people of the states had surrendered some state sovereignty in the process of ratifying the Constitution, the states could not reclaim that sovereign under any compact theory of the ratification. As Marshall put it:

> [The Constitution does not] resemble a compact between [the federal government] and its members.

---

[302] Ibid., 188.  [303] Ibid., 192.

> A contract is an agreement on sufficient consideration to do or not to do a particular thing.
>
> There must be parties. These parties must make an agreement, and something must proceed to and from each.
>
> The government of the United States can certainly not be a party to the instrument by which it was created. It cannot have been concerned in making that by which it was brought into existence.
>
> Neither have the state governments made this instrument. It is the act of the people themselves. . . .
>
> Our constitution is not a compact. It is the act of the people of the United States, assembling in their respective states, and adopting a government for the whole nation.[304]

Thus in surrendering some sovereign powers of the states to the federal government the people had placed them beyond the reach of recapture except through an act of the people themselves. Among the powers surrendered had been that of the federal courts to decide cases "arising under this Constitution and laws of the United States." This meant, Marshall argued, that the reach of federal judicial interpretive power should extend as far as the reach of federal legislative power. State courts could no more reserve to themselves the power to be the formal interpreters of the Constitution than could any other state departments claim reserved sovereign powers the people had surrendered to the federal government in the ratification. The reason was obvious. Marshall cited the eightieth *Federalist* essay. "[T]hey are full and explicit to the point," he said, "that the courts of the Union have, and ought to have jurisdiction, in all cases, arising under the constitution and laws of the United States." This conclusion was based on the "political axioms [that] the judicial department should be coextensive with the legislature, and with the provisions of the constitution."[305]

Thus, under the Union theory of sovereignty, the act of the people of the states in ratifying the Constitution and creating the Union had led inexorably to the sovereignty of the federal courts in interpreting the meaning of the Constitution. But Marshall still had two sticky places in his theory, and he sought to deal with them with two final propositions. The first awkward place was the claim made by Hampden that to give the federal judiciary power to interpret the scope of the federal legislature was to make the general government the sole judge of its own authority; in opposition to that claim Marshall promulgated proposition eight, the independence of the federal judiciary. The proposition rested on two principles, the separation of powers principle and the disinterestedness principle. As Marshall put it:

---

[304] Ibid., 203.

[305] Ibid., 205.

## Chapter VIII: *Sovereignty and Union*

[Principle One]
According to [the Constitution] the judicial, is a coordinate department, created at the same time, and proceeding from the same source, with the legislative and executive departments.
. . . [T]he whole government consists of departments. Neither of these is the deputy of the whole, or of the other two. . . . Each is confined to the sphere of action prescribed to it by the people of the United States, and within that sphere, performs its functions alone. . . . On a judicial question then, the judicial department is the government, and can alone exercise the judicial power of the United States.[306]

[Principle Two]
It is the plain dictate of common sense, and the whole political system is founded on the idea, that the departments of government are the agents of the nation, and will perform, within their respective spheres, the duties assigned to them. . . .
To whom more safely than to the judges are judicial questions to be referred? They are selected from the great body of the people for the purpose of deciding them. To secure impartiality, they are made perfectly independent. They have no personal interest in aggrandizing the legislative power. Their paramount interest is the public property, in which is involved their own and that of their families. . . . It is not then the party sitting in his own cause. It is the application to individuals by one department by the acts of another department of the government. The people are the authors of all; the departments are their agents; and if the judge be personally disinterested, he is as exempt from any political interest that might influence his opinion, as imperfect human institutions can make him.[307]

Here again the linchpin of Marshall's logic was the assumption of sovereignty in the people. Judges were the people's agents, chosen "from the great body of the people," confined by the people's document, the Constitution, to a "sphere of action." There were large assumptions swallowed up by that logic, such as the assumption that "judicial" and "political" questions were easily separable, and the assumption that "independence" among judges would produce impartiality. But if one granted those assumptions the judicial department could fairly be separated from the other federal departments, or at least identified with the less partisan functions of furthering "public prosperity" and providing, as Marshall said in other places in his discussion, "the peaceful and quiet mode of carrying the laws of the union into execution."[308]
One awkward point remained: the claim of anticonsolidationists, from Tucker on, that the coextensive power axiom meant that extensive

---

[306] Ibid., 210.
[307] Ibid., 211–12.

[308] Ibid., 208.

jurisdiction in the federal courts would result in the power of both those courts and Congress being unlimited, with consolidation the result. Marshall had earlier denied that the "government of the United States . . . has . . . been termed a consolidated government": it was a "national" government, coexisting with state governments.[309] But consolidation in fact if not in name could exist, Hampden and others had suggested, if one branch of the federal government had the sole power to establish the sovereign limits of another. As an example Hampden had cited the Court's interpretation of congressional implied powers in *McCulloch:* it represented "an enlargement of the enumerated powers of congress, and contend[ed] . . . for an extension of those powers beyond the import of the words."[310] Marshall responded:

> In no single instance does the court admit the unlimited power of congress to adopt any means whatever, and thus to pass the limits prescribed by the Constitution. Not only is the discretion claimed for the legislature in the selection of its means, always limited in terms to such as are appropriate, but the court expressly says, "should congress under the pretext of executing its powers, pass laws for the accomplishment of objects, not entrusted to the government, it would become the painful duty of this tribunal . . . to say that such an act was not the law of the land.[311]

Here, in his ninth proposition, the crucial premises of the Union theory of sovereignty articulated by Marshall in his *Gazette* essays were thrown into sharpest relief. The justification for judicial power to interpret the Constitution came from an "agency" relationship between the sovereign people and "disinterested" judges who would subordinate their own "personal interests" to the public welfare. To those judges devolved the duty to decide "judicial questions" so as to provide a peaceful means of resolving disputes and executing laws.[312] Among the "judicial" questions judges were given power to decide were questions arising under the Constitution, that is, the meaning of constitutional terms. In the interpretation of some of those terms the scope of the power of the federal government, whether embodied by Congress or the federal courts, would be at issue, and thus one branch of the federal government would be "interpreting" the powers or another or even its own powers. But none of this was illegitimate because the limits on unauthorized federal power had been established by the Constitution itself, the people's document.

But what about the fact that the "appropriate" constitutional limits of Congress's implied powers, the "fair" construction of its enumerated powers, and even the jurisdictional limits of the federal courts themselves

---

[309] Ibid., 193.
[310] Ibid., 185.
[311] Ibid., 187.
[312] Ibid., 186.

were being supplied by the judges of the Supreme Court? Saying that the Constitution prescribed limits to unlimited federal power, or checks on sweeping legislative autonomy, or even means by which the people could reassert their ultimate sovereignty, meant little unless one assumed that the interpretation of the constitutional system would invariably be "impartial" or "disinterested," that the "independence" of judges would obviate their personal or partisan interests. That assumption—the idea that judicial discretion to interpret was somehow different from kinds of discretionary lawmaking—was at the center of Marshall's theory. Judges could not be agents of the people, easily confined to their "judicial functions," unless their "lawgiving" was in a different order from that of other lawgivers. "There is . . . no objection made to the opinion of the supreme court in *McCulloch,*" Marshall said at the end of his last essay, "which fails more entirely than this to its jurisdiction."[313] Yet no objection had touched a deeper nerve.

The debate engendered by *McCulloch* thus produced powerful polemical efforts on both sides, representing vivid articulations of the compact and Union positions. Although the apparently irreconcilable views expressed in the debate had comparatively insignificant consequences in the short run, they marked the beginning of a recurrent dialogue over sovereignty that was to transpose the issue of slavery into an issue affecting the future of the Union. The Virginia House of Delegates passed resolutions in February 1820 entering a "most solemn protest" against the *McCulloch* decision and recommending that a new court be created to decide questions invoking the "powers of the general and state governments under the compact."[314] As these actions were taking place, the House adopted resolutions condemning Congress's effort to condition Missouri's admission into the Union on its prohibiting slavery within its borders. "Virginia . . . will cooperate with [Missouri] in resisting . . . any attempt which Congress may make to impose restraints or restrictions on the price of admission," one resolution declared.[315] Compact theory and the issue of slavery had become intertwined.

The years immediately following *McCulloch,* as may have already become evident, were ones in which the Court seemed almost continually embroiled in disputes about the reach of state sovereignty: between 1819 and 1823 came, in addition to *Cohens* and *Osborn,* the controversial Contract Clause decisions in *Dartmouth College* v. *Woodward, Sturges* v. *Crowninshield,* and *Green* v. *Biddle,* all of which found an attempted

---

[313] Ibid., 214.
[314] *Journal,* House of Delegates, Virginia, 1819–20, 56–59.

[315] Ibid., 105.

exercise of state power constitutionally impermissible. They were also the years, we have seen, in which Jefferson re-emerged as a public critic of the Court, and Johnson, under Jefferson's encouragement, eventually declared that he would "maintain my opinions in my own way" on "questions of great importance and great delicacy."[316] The case in which Johnson made that announcement continued the Court's pattern of establishing affirmative limits on state sovereignty and employed, in Marshall's opinion for the Court, interpretive techniques similar to those used in *McCulloch*. The case, however, was perhaps the Marshall Court's greatest popular triumph: the "steamboat case" of *Gibbons* v. *Ogden*.

*Gibbons* can be seen as the next logical step from *McCulloch*'s claims about federal supremacy. If Congress, in the exercise of its implied powers, could preclude state activity by enacting laws, could it preclude state activity by *not* enacting any laws where its power to do so was not simply implicit, but explicit? *Gibbons* raised that question with respect to the federal commerce power. Article I, Section 8 of the Constitution gave Congress the "Power . . . To regulate Commerce . . . among the several States." Did the mere enumeration of that power prevent a state from regulating interstate commerce? *Gibbons,* in which a steamboat owner licensed by the state of New York attempted to prevent a competitor from operating steamboats on the Hudson River between New York and New Jersey, turned on that question.

*Gibbons* v. *Ogden* was one of those cases that, given succeeding events, appear peculiarly prophetic. It was a case involving steamboats and steamboat traffic, the great symbols of mid-nineteenth-century commercial development in America. It raised the issue of monopolistic privileges at a time when the term "monopoly" was just starting to take on sinister and pejorative connotations. It seemed to pit economic privilege against free competition, the few against the many, the resisters against the defenders of progress. And it apparently committed the Marshall Court, announced defender of the first principles of republican government, to a wholesale endorsement of commerce, that potential agent of corruption and decay.

Actually, the *Gibbons* case, for all the contemporary attention it created, did not produce a definitive doctrinal judgment. Marshall evaded the principal difficulty posed by the case, that of fixing the boundaries between state and federal regulation of commerce. *Gibbons* held only that an exclusive congressional power to regulate interstate commerce existed and had been exercised with respect to steamboats; it did not specify when a dormant federal commerce power might yield to exercised state police powers. Marshall's opinion in *Gibbons* acknowledged power in the states to regulate commerce, but apparently restricted state activity

---

[316] 9 Wheat. at 223.

affecting commerce to "those internal concerns which . . . are completely within a particular State, which do not affect other States, and with which it is not necessary to interfere, for the purpose of executing some of the general powers of the government."[317] As we will see, that language did not end litigation over the scope of the commerce power.

*Gibbons* was the outgrowth of a protracted dispute between the heirs of Robert Fulton and Robert Livingston, to whom the New York legislature had granted an exclusive license to operate steamboats in New York waters, and prospective competitors of the Fulton-Livingston monopoly.[318] The steamboat had been first successfully tested in New York in 1807; an 1808 act of the New York legislature had confirmed the exclusive rights of Fulton, Livingston, and their associates. The great success of steamboats soon prompted competitors, and by 1811 the Livingston group had attempted to secure an injunction in the federal circuit court of New York against a rival line. The circuit court held that it lacked jurisdiction over the controversy. The opinion was written by Justice Brockholst Livingston, whose brother held the monopoly.

The Livingston group then turned to the New York courts, where their request for an injunction was denied in the Court of Chancery and eventually upheld in the Court of Errors.[319] James Kent's was the most significant of the seriatim opinions issued by that unusual court, whose members included state senators as well as judges. Among the issues addressed by Kent's opinion was the question whether the New York statute creating the Livingston monopoly infringed on federal power to regulate commerce. Kent concluded that states could regulate commerce in the absence of federal involvement in the field; only when state and federal powers "[came] directly in contact" should state power yield, and "the possible contingency of a collision" was not sufficient to preclude state activity.[320]

The Livingston group, sensing the enormous possibilities of steamboat travel, responded to the Court of Errors's decision by parceling out franchises rather than completely barring competitors. One erstwhile competitor who became a franchisee was Aaron Ogden, former governor of New Jersey, who in 1815 secured a license from the Livingston group to operate a steam ferryboat from Staten and Manhattan islands in New York to Elizabethtown Point, New Jersey. Ogden's ferryboats were in competition with an unauthorized boat owned by Thomas Gibbons and piloted by Cornelius Vanderbilt, later to become notorious as a railroad magnate. Vanderbilt managed to evade attempts to prevent the Gibbons ferries from

---

[317] Ibid., 195.
[318] For background on the *Gibbons* case, see M. Baxter, *The Steamboat Monopoly* (1972).

[319] Livingston v. Van Ingen, 9 Johns. 507 (1812).
[320] Ibid., 576.

running, and the Gibbons line cut into Ogden's profits. Meanwhile Ogden and Gibbons became involved in a number of personal quarrels, including Ogden's alleged interference in a dispute between Gibbons and Mrs. Gibbons, and Gibbons's being "arrested in a suit of law in [Ogden's] home . . . after [Ogden] was on board of the steamboat returning to Elizabethtown."[321] These incidents culminated when Gibbons challenged Ogden to a duel and Ogden sued Gibbons for trespass and collected $8,000.[322]

Ogden responded to the Gibbons's steamboat competition by securing an injunction in the New York Court of Chancery against Gibbons's line. Gibbons countered that he had a coastal license from the United States government to "navigate the waters of any particular state by steamboats." Kent, for the Court, considered the effect of the coastal license and found that it did not affect the laws of states because its purposes were simply to raise revenue and to designate ships as "American," thereby giving them certain privileges.[323] For such a statute to pre-empt state action, Kent maintained, it needed to contain an explicit declaration to that effect. That decision was appealed to the New York Court of Errors, which unanimously affirmed Kent's holding; Kent himself probably participated[324] but did not write the opinion.

Gibbons then appealed on a writ of error to the Supreme Court of the United States. The appeal was filed on October 17, 1820. An undocumented account of the litigation has Cornelius Vanderbilt being dispatched to Washington by Gibbons, who was ill with diabetes, to secure the services of Daniel Webster to argue before the Supreme Court.[325] Webster was retained, as was William Wirt, and *Gibbons* v. *Ogden* was docketed for the 1821 Term. But on March 21, 1821, the Marshall Court dismissed the case on the ground that the record did not show that the decision of the New York Court of Errors was a final one within the meaning of Section 25 of the Judiciary Act.[326]

That procedural difficulty caused the case to be put off until the 1824 Term, with two principal effects. First, Brockholst Livingston, who would have had yet another opportunity to involve himself in a controversy engendered by his family, died in the spring of 1823. His successor, Smith Thompson, was also from New York, was intimately familiar with the case, and had written an opinion in *Livingston* v. *Van Ingen* in his

[321] See Ogden v. Gibbons, 5 N.J.L. 598, 599 (1819).

[322] Ogden v. Gibbons, 5 N.J.L. 987 (1820).

[323] Ogden v. Gibbons, 4 Johns. Ch. R. 150, 156–57 (1819).

[324] 17 Johns. 488 (1820). See T. Campbell, "Chancellor Kent, Chief Justice Marshall, and the Steamboat Cases," *Syr. L. Rev.*, 25:497, 513 (1974).

[325] D. Kendall, "Mr. Gibbons and Colonel Ogden," *Mich. S.B.J.*, 26:22, 24 (1947).

[326] Gibbons v. Ogden, 6 Wheat. 448 (1821).

capacity as a judge on the Court of Errors, taking the same position as Kent on the Commerce Clause issue. Thompson, however, did not sit in *Gibbons*, since he had just been appointed and the death of his daughter delayed his arrival in Washington. Second, Ogden had secured William Pinkney to represent him, which seemed to ensure that Pinkney and Webster would argue against one another for the first time in their careers. But Pinkney died in February 1822, and was replaced by Thomas Emmet, whose "whole soul" was reported to be in the case, and by Thomas Oakley, "said to be one of the first logicians of the age."[327]

February 4, 1824, was the first of five days of arguments. Justice James Wayne later said that *Gibbons* v. *Ogden* was not surpassed by any other case for "the extent and variety of learning and . . . the acuteness of distinction by which it was argued by counsel."[328] After hearing the arguments, Story wrote that "whoever . . . shall sit down to the task of perusing this argument, will find that it is equally remarkable for profoundness and sagacity, for the choice and comprehensiveness of the topics, and for the delicacy and tact with which they were handled."[329] All the advocates recognized that the *Gibbons* case was essentially a concurrent sovereignty case, testing whether regulatory powers existed in the states after they had been delegated to, but not exercised by, the federal government. The ostensible sources of exclusive federal power in *Gibbons* were two: Article I, Section 8's delegation to Congress of power to regulate commerce among the several states, and the same section's grant to Congress of "Power . . . to promote the Progress of Science and useful Arts, by securing . . . to Inventors the exclusive Right to their respective . . . Discoveries." All the lawyers except Wirt devoted the bulk of their arguments to the Commerce Clause; Wirt addressed the Patents and Copyrights Clause. Since Marshall expressly decided that "it is unnecessary to enter into an examination of that part of the constitution which empowers Congress to promote the progress of science and the useful arts,"[330] Wirt's argument has become chiefly remembered for its closing passage, in which, as we have seen in Chapter IV, he turned Emmet's use of the *Aeneid* against him.

Two alternative theories of concurrent sovereignty were advanced in the argument. The first, advanced by Webster, was that since Congress's enumerated powers were exclusive, it was immaterial whether Congress had exercised those powers or not. Webster cited statements

---

[327] These characterizations of Emmet and Oakley were made by William Wirt in a letter to Dabney Carr, Feb. 1, 1824, in J. Kennedy, *Memoirs of the Life of William Wirt* (2 vols., 1849), II, 164. See Chapter IV.

[328] The Passenger Cases, 7 How. 283, 437 (1849).

[329] J. Story, quoted in E. Wheeler, *Daniel Webster, The Expounder of the Constitution* (1905), 59.

[330] 9 Wheat. at 221.

made in Congress before the framing of the Constitution,[331] and denied that "any man speaks of a general concurrent power, in the regulation of foreign and domestic trade, as still residing in the states."[332] Pressed to its conclusion, Webster's argument, as he admitted at one point, denied the validity of the concurrent power doctrine altogether. "This doctrine of a general concurrent power in the states," he maintained, "is insidious and dangerous. If it be admitted no one can say where it will stop."[333]

The second position was that the delegation of an enumerated power to Congress did not preclude the states from concurrently exercising that power until Congress had acted so as to collide with state power and thereby occupy the field. This position was advanced by Oakley and Emmet. In support of it they cited language from Marshall in *Sturges v. Crowninshield*[334] and a passage from Story's dissent in *Houston,* both of which appeared to concede the validity of concurrent state powers. "[T]he mere grant of a power to Congress," Marshall had said in *Sturges,* "did not imply a prohibition on the states to exercise the same power."[335] "[A] mere grant of . . . powers in affirmative terms to Congress," Story suggested in *Houston,* "does [not], *per se,* transfer an exclusive sovereignty on such subjects." The states had retained "concurrent authority with Congress," Story added, "not only upon the letter and spirit of the eleventh amendment of the constitution, but upon the soundest principles of general reasoning."[336] Elaborating upon this language, Oakley concluded that states could legislate "in all cases of concurrent power" even where Congress had also acted "under the same power and upon the same subject matter."[337] Only in cases of "direct and positive [and] actual and practical collision" did state law yield to Congress. For his part, Emmet argued that exclusive power in Congress to regulate commerce would "make a wreck of state legislation," and that the states had "always exercised the power of making very material regulations respecting commerce."[338] He cited several examples, including laws regulating traffic in slaves, quarantine laws, inspection laws, and laws regulating trade with Indian tribes. Only where the exercise of state power came "practically in collision with the actual exercise of some congressional power" would the state "authority . . . be controlled," and then only where it "absolutely contravene[d] the provision of the paramount law."[339]

So stated, the arguments of opposing counsel seemed very far apart, and one might have expected Marshall, who wrote the opinion of the

---

[331] Ibid. at 11–13.
[332] Ibid. at 13.
[333] Ibid. at 17.
[334] 4 Wheat. 122 (1819).
[335] Ibid., 193.

[336] 5 Wheat. at 48–49.
[337] 9 Wheat. at 42.
[338] Ibid., 102, 107.
[339] Ibid., 130.

court in *Gibbons*,[340] to take a middle-ground position: that if the power to regulate commerce was concurrent, not exclusive, it had nonetheless been exercised in the case of steamboats on navigable waters. Marshall did endorse that position, but he also intimated that Congress's power over interstate commerce was exclusive, and that intimation can be seen as the more revealing feature of his *Gibbons* opinion.

*Gibbons* was the first Marshall Court case in which the scope of the commerce power and the doctrine of concurrent sovereignty were squarely considered. That alone might seem surprising, since the case was decided twenty-three years into Marshall's tenure. But we have previously noted two features of the cultural and jurisprudential universe in which the Marshall Court made decisions that help to explain the late surfacing of the issues in *Gibbons*. First, the steamboat was a revolutionary development in the history of the American economy in that it had the potential to make internal traffic in the American continent a relatively rapid process. Before the advent of the railroad, only three means of transportation were available to Americans seeking to move goods or people through the interior of the continent: rivers, canals, or overland roads. All these modes of traffic were exceptionally slow when compared with the speed of oceangoing vessels or steamboats. With the advent of the steamboat the enterprise of American transportation was redirected and the use of inland waterways suddenly became a central part of that enterprise.

There was no obvious provision in the Constitution pertaining to inland waterway traffic. The admiralty and maritime jurisdiction granted to the federal courts by Article III had been read by the Court to be a jurisdiction over "high seas" cases. Beyond the "high seas" context, we have seen, the Court had trod narrowly, and Johnson had identified in his circuit opinion in *The Amanda* the great expansion of federal power

---

[340] An inconclusive effort has been made to identify Story with the opinion. On February 19, 1824, ten days after the arguments in *Gibbons* ended, Marshall "had the misfortune to stumble over the cellar door of the [Justices' boarding]house in the darkness, by which his shoulder was dislocated, and he received a blow in the head, which occasioned a concussion that deprived him of his senses for a quarter of an hour." J. Story to Sarah Waldo Story, Feb. 19, 1824, Joseph Story Papers, University of Texas Library. Ten days later Marshall had still not returned to active service, and on March 3 the New York *Commercial Advertiser* reported that "the opinion of the Court has not yet been given" in *Gibbons* v. *Ogden*, "nor do we know when it will be." Marshall, the paper reported, "had commenced writing the [*Gibbons*] opinion when his labors were interrupted by his unfortunate fall; and it is understood that Mr. Justice Story is now engaged in completing it." New York *Commercial Advertiser,* Mar. 3, 1824. Marshall, however, was present in court on March 2 and delivered the *Gibbons* opinion "in a low, feeble voice," wearing his arm in a sling. Ibid., Mar. 5, 1824. The language of the opinion seems unmistakably Marshall's, although Story would have strongly endorsed the Chief Justice's views.

that might follow from a broad interpretation of admiralty jurisdiction. If inland waterways cases were not admiralty cases, were they beyond the scope of federal control? Not, perhaps, if they were commerce cases: hence a critical question in *Gibbons* was whether navigation on inland waterways was "commerce" within the meaning of Article I, Section 8 of the Constitution. If "commerce" did include navigation, and Congress could thus regulate inland waterways, it could constitutionally pass a statute extending admiralty jurisdiction over those waterways. We noted in Chapter VII that Story's opinion in *The Thomas Jefferson,* decided a year after *Gibbons,* hinted at that possibility.

The first great Marshall Court Commerce Clause case, then, surfaced when inland water traffic had emerged as a vital feature of the American economy. Had the political issues raised by the Court's admiralty jurisdiction cases between 1815 and 1824 been less delicate, *Gibbons* might have been an admiralty case; instead it was argued on the potentially safer ground of the commerce power. But in that argument a feature of the sovereignty theory that had not received much emphasis in *Martin, McCulloch,* or *Cohens* emerged as an issue of critical importance. If the vision of the Constitution as a compact had been repudiated by the Court, did it not have to concede, as Marshall apparently had in *McCulloch,* that the states still had some reserved sovereign powers? And if so, was there not, among those powers, a power in the states to police their internal economic affairs? States had enacted health laws, inspection laws, and taxes. Was this not evidence of a concurrent regulating power in the state sovereign? "Concurrent sovereignty" was, of course, not a new term. One of the *Federalist* essays had used it referring to cases in which "the exercise of concurrent jurisdiction might be productive of occasional interferences in the policy of any branch of administration, but would not imply any direct contradiction or repugnancy, in point of constitutional authority."[341] Marshall himself had said in *McCulloch,* in conceding that the taxing power of the states was "not abridged by the grant of a similar power to the government of the union," that such power was "to be concurrently exercised by the two governments."[342]

Nonetheless, the concurrent power doctrine arose as a major rationale for state sovereignty for the first time in *Gibbons.* Its late surfacing can be traced to the triumph of the Court in fusing, in the cases from *Martin* through *McCulloch* and *Cohens,* a broad reading of the Article III powers of the federal courts with a broad reading of the Article I powers of Congress. The concept facilitating this fusion was the coterminous power axiom, with its premise that an "effective" government, in order to preserve itself, needed powers to make laws to ward off disintegration

---

[341] *The Federalist,* No. 32, 207.     [342] 4 Wheat. at 193.

# Chapter VIII: *Sovereignty and Union*

(such as a law chartering a national bank) and powers to implement those laws in its own courts (by reviewing hostile treatments of those laws by other courts). Once the theoretical basis for this fusion of broad Article III and Article I powers (the Union theory of sovereignty) had been established, it became clear to those engaged with sovereignty issues in the early nineteenth century that any grant in the Constitution of sovereign power to a branch of the federal government meant that the power could not be easily reclaimed.

Concurrent power theory can be seen as a doctrine designed to resurrect state sovereignty by conceding the supremacy of federal power where it had been granted, but insisting on the continued existence of state power outside the ambit of the grant. One might contrast here the language of advocates for concurrent state power in *Gibbons* with that of Amphictyon and Hampden and the critics of the *Cohens* decision. The latter set of commentators had denied absolutely that the federal government could trespass on state sovereignty without the consent of the states, parties to a "compact." Their model of the American republic was that of an entity composed of two co-equal sovereigns. Compare Emmet, arguing for concurrent power in *Gibbons:*

> The expression, concurrent powers, is objected to, as if it implied equality in the rights vested in Congress and the States. . . . It is always understood, when so applied, that the exercise by the states must be subordinate, and never can be in collision with that of Congress.[343]

In this vein, *Gibbons* represented something of a watershed in the intellectual history of sovereignty theory during the Marshall Court's tenure. Concurrent power theory, not compact theory, was to be the principal basis on which state sovereignty was to be resurrected, especially after Marshall's tenure; that trend began with *Gibbons*. *Gibbons* hence implicitly signified the cumulative impact of the Court's sovereignty decisions from *Martin* on: the Union position had reduced the compact position to one of marginality. Compact theory had not yet lost intellectual respectability, as we shall see, but it was not offered as a basis for any of the arguments on behalf of the New York legislature in *Gibbons*. In light of what subsequently transpired in the Court's sovereignty cases, the implicit judgment to substitute concurrent power theory for compact theory proved a sagacious one.

Marshall began his opinion in *Gibbons* by restating two of his familiar principles of constitutional construction: that words in the Constitution must be understood to be employed in their natural sense,[344] and that the extent of a given constitutional power should be ascertained by

---

[343] 9 Wheat. at 88.

[344] Ibid., 188.

575

reference to "the objects for which it was given."[345] The meaning and scope of Congress's power to regulate commerce, then, was to be determined "by the language of the instrument which confers [it], taken in connexion with the purposes for which [it was] conferred."[346] Applied to *Gibbons*, these principles focused Marshall's attention on two issues: the natural meaning of the word "commerce" and the purposes of the commerce power. Once this focus has been adopted, the rest of the opinion flowed swiftly to its conclusion.

For *Gibbons* to be a Commerce Clause case, the word "commerce" needed to be read as embracing the word "navigation." Marshall had no difficulty with that task. "Commerce, undoubtedly, is traffic," he said, "but it is something more: it is intercourse."[347] This definition employed the word "commerce" in its accepted senses and repeated language used by Wirt in his argument for Gibbons.[348] It also provoked some wry commentary.[349] The 1828 edition of Webster's dictionary gave as its second definition of commerce "intercourse between individuals; interchange of work, business, civilities or amusements."[350] Marshall's claim that "[a]ll America understands, and has uniformly understood, the word 'commerce' to comprehend navigation"[351] was not an undue exaggeration; the use of admiralty analogies by counsel for both sides only reinforced his point.

But what was the extent of the federal commerce power? Marshall's disposition of that issue, given the alternative positions advanced by counsel, was odd. He first sought to give a meaning to the phrase "to regulate commerce." The word "commerce," he claimed, comprehended "every species of commercial intercourse."[352] But the phrase "among the several States" meant "intermingled with" the several states, and thus did not extend to "that commerce, which is completely internal, which is carried on between man and man in a state or between different parts of the same State." "Among" in the Commerce Clause could be "very properly

---

[345] Ibid., 188–89.
[346] Ibid., 189.
[347] Ibid.
[348] Ibid., 183.
[349] Henry Seawell, who was present at the argument, wrote to Thomas Ruffin on February 12, 1824, as follows: "[F]or according to the construction now contended for, and what is more than probable will be supported by the Supreme Court, the States can do nothing, what is not in the power of Congress to *regulate;* and there is scarcely anything they can act upon at all— trade or commerce, being subject to the regulation of Congress, is supposed to draw after it almost all power of regulation, and according to a definition given to the word 'commerce' by the Attorney-General [Wirt] that it means 'intercourse.' I shall soon expect to learn that our fornication laws are unconstitutional." Quoted in Warren, *Supreme Court*, II, 66. Emphasis in original.
[350] N. Webster, *Dictionary of the English Language* (1818).
[351] 9 Wheat. at 190.
[352] Ibid., 193.

restricted to that commerce which concerns more States than one," and therefore "the completely internal commerce of a State . . . may be considered as reserved for the State itself."[353]

This language seemed to suggest that Marshall was conceding a concurrent power in the states to regulate internal commerce. It was hard to imagine from these remarks that Congress's power to regulate all commerce was exclusive. Nonetheless, Marshall took pains in the next section of his argument to show that Congress's power to regulate "commerce among the several States" *was* exclusive. "When a State proceeds to regulate commerce . . . among the several States," Marshall declared, "it is exercising the very power that is granted to Congress, and is doing the very thing which Congress is authorized to do."[354] In passing "inspection laws, quarantine laws, health laws of every description" and "laws for regulating the internal commerce of a State," the states were not "regulating commerce among the States." Such legislation derived either from the states' police power or from their power to regulate internal commerce.

The existence of this sort of legislation, Marshall thus suggested, did not prove the existence of a concurrent power in the states to regulate interstate commerce. It only proved "that the States retain powers enabling them to pass the laws to which allusion has been made," not that those laws were examples of the states' regulating interstate commerce. Marshall then added a singular paragraph:

> It has been contended by the counsel for the appellant that, as the word "to regulate" implies in its nature, full power over the thing to be regulated, it excludes, necessarily, the action of all others that would perform the same operation on the same thing. . . . It produces a uniform whole, which is as much disturbed and deranged by changing what the regulating power designs to leave untouched, as that on which it has operated. There is great force in this argument, and the Court is not satisfied that it has been refuted.[355]

The paragraph seemed designed to cover that situation where Congress had not exercised its regulatory power over interstate commerce. In that situation, Marshall seemed to say, the states could still not act. The paragraph suggests that Marshall had concluded, first, that the states could freely regulate internal commerce; second, that Congress had exclusive power to regulate interstate commerce; and, third, that when Congress did not choose to exercise its power the states were forbidden from acting.

The last conclusion was not entirely clear, because Marshall,

---

[353] Ibid., 195.
[354] Ibid., 199–200.

[355] Ibid., 209.

through a strained construction of a federal licensing statute, found that Congress *had* acted to regulate interstate steamboat traffic. The statute designated certain ships as "entitled to the privileges of ships or vessels employed in the coasting trade," and established the procedure for granting coasting trade licenses. Marshall claimed that a license was "permission, or authority," and thereby conferred a "right to trade." He found a similar statute which enrolled and licensed steamboats, and concluded that since the purpose of such licensing statutes was to confer rights to trade, they were thus federal regulations of interstate commerce and therefore in collision with the New York statute prohibiting competitive steamboats from sailing between New York and New Jersey.[356]

Marshall's reading of the coastal license statute was immediately criticized by contemporaries. Johnson, who concurred in *Gibbons,* doubted that the license could serve as "the foundation of [a] right." The purpose of the license, he felt, was to confer on ships designated American certain privileges, and thereby to facilitate the process of imposing discriminatory rates against foreign ships engaged in the coastal trade. "The abstract right of commercial intercourse" remained to all ships, but only licensed American ships were freed from "burdensome . . . duties and formalities."[357] Kent, who, we have seen, had taken the same position in his opinion below, agreed with Johnson in the 1826 edition of his *Commentaries.* "The great objects and policy of the coasting act," he wrote in discussing *Gibbons,*

> were, to exclude foreign vessels from commerce between the states, in order to cherish the growth of our marine, and to provide that the coasting trade should be conducted with security to the revenue. The register and enrolment of the vessel were to ascertain the national character; and the license was only evidence that the vessel had complied with the requisites of the law, and was qualified for the coasting trade under American privileges.[358]

Most of Marshall's opinion in *Gibbons* was thus highly inconclusive. His interpretation of commerce as embracing navigation was clear enough, but beyond that the sources of his conclusion that New York could not establish monopolies on its waters that flowed into other states were either weak or hazy. He intimated that the New York statute establishing the Livingston-Fulton monopoly might have failed, because of the exclusivity of the federal commerce power and the dormant power dictum, even had Congress not acted. But that intimation was not necessary, he claimed, because of the coastal trade licensing statute, a statute whose

---

[356] Ibid., 213–14.
[357] Ibid., 231–32.

[358] J. Kent, *Commentaries on American Law* (4 vols., 1826), I, 435.

purpose was clearly not to regulate commerce but to establish and reward American coastal traders. He had also conceded state regulatory power over a variety of subjects—internal commerce or health among them—whose regulation might affect interstate commerce. So *Gibbons,* for all the fanfare with which it was received, settled very little and that in an awkard fashion.

The awkwardness of Marshall's posture in *Gibbons* may very possibly have been a result of his discomfort with the concurrent theory of sovereignty, even in its most modest forms. The crucial feature of the concurrent theory was that it provided a rationale for states to take action where Congress had remained inactive. An example of such a situation had been the state insolvency and bankruptcy laws declared unconstitutional by Marshall in *Sturges* v. *Crowninshield.* Article I, Section 8 of the Constitution had given Congress the power "To establish . . . uniform Laws on the subject of Bankruptcies throughout the United States": there was absolutely no question that had Congress passed a bankruptcy statute it would have collided with such laws and invalidated them. But Congress had not; its power to regulate bankruptcy was dormant; and in its stead states had acted. While the Marshall Court had struck down the result of those acts, it had not been on the ground of federal pre-emption of the field. Thus, if one presupposed that Congress would be an inactive rather than an active regulatory force, concurrent power theory was a potentially significant basis on which to justify state regulation of economic affairs.

The paragraph in which Marshall had intimated that the presence of an enumerated federal power precluded states from exercising that power even when the federal government had not acted had referred to an argument made by Webster. Webster's actual language, as reported by Wheaton, had been as follows:

> The States may legislate, it is said, wherever Congress has not made a *plenary* exercise of its power. But who is to judge whether Congress has made this *plenary* exercise of power? Congress had acted on this power; it has done all that it deemed wise; and are the States now to do whatever Congress has left undone? Congress makes such rules as, in its judgment, the case requires; and those rules, whatever they are, constitute the *system.*
>
> All useful regulation does not consist in restraint; and that which Congress sees fit to leave free, is a part of its regulation, as much as the rest.[359]

Webster had introduced that argument, we have seen, by the comment that "[t]his doctrine of a *general* concurrent power in the States, is in-

---

[359] 9 Wheat. at 17–18. Emphasis in original.

sidious and dangerous. If it be admitted, no one can say where it will stop." Marshall, in his entire opinion in *Gibbons*, had never once employed the phrase "concurrent power." It is as if he felt to concede its existence in any form was to allow "insidious and dangerous" forces to be unleashed.

*Gibbons* thus ended up a highly ambiguous and perhaps an ambivalent decision. Marshall could hardly gainsay that the states had some reserved regulatory powers, however they had come by them. He conceded that a variety of state regulatory legislation would withstand constitutional scrutiny. But at the same time he had taken the most minimal federal involvement with steamboats and converted it into a regulation of commerce; it appeared that almost any exercise of federal power would be sufficient to collide. Beyond that, he had suggested that *no* exercise of power might be sufficient, and he had refused to give the label "concurrent" to any of the reserved powers he had conceded, even though he had used that label himself with respect to state taxing power in *McCulloch*.

After establishing the "direct collision" of Congress's statute licensing coastal vessels with the New York law challenged in *Gibbons*, Marshall then concluded with a passage that showed the mood in which he had written the opinion:

> Powerful and ingenious minds, taking, as postulated, that the powers expressly granted to the government of the Union, are to be contracted by construction, into the narrowest possible compass, and that the original powers of the States are retained, if any possible construction will retain them, may, by a course of well digested, but refined and metaphysical reasoning, founded on these premises, explain away the constitution of our country, and leave it, a magnificent structure, indeed, to look at, but totally unfit for use. They may so entangle and perplex the understanding, as to obscure principles, which were before thought quite plain, and induce doubts where, if the mind were to pursue its own course, none would be perceived. In such a case, it is peculiarly necessary to recur to safe and fundamental principles to sustain those principles, and when sustained, to make them the tests of the arguments to be examined.[360]

It remained unclear what "principles" had actually been enunciated in *Gibbons*, and what "tests" would be used for future Commerce Clause cases.[361]

---

[360] Ibid., 222.
[361] Quoted in P. Harvey, *Reminiscences and Anecdotes of Daniel Webster* (1878), 142.

# Chapter VIII: *Sovereignty and Union*

*Brown* v. *Maryland*,[362] decided three years after *Gibbons*, provided the Court with an opportunity to clarify Marshall's dormant power dictum, but it failed to do so. In 1821 the state of Maryland passed a statute supplementing an 1819 act that had established duties on dry goods retailers' licenses. A section of the supplementary statute provided that "all importers of foreign articles or commodities" were required to take out a license from the state, the fee for which was fifty dollars. The statute was "one of that class," *Niles' Weekly Register* commented, "which is perpetually planning to tax Baltimore City for the benefit of the State of Maryland."[363] The "impolicy of such a law in its effects upon the commercial interests of Baltimore," the Baltimore *Gazette* noted, "was . . . obvious."[364] A Baltimore merchant declined to pay the tax and brought suit in the Maryland courts, claiming that the statute violated the Imports Clause of Article 1, Section 10 of the Constitution, which prohibited states from "lay[ing] any Imposts or Duties on Imports or Exports, except what may be absolutely necessary for executing its inspection Laws," and the Commerce Clause. The case marked the first appearance before the Supreme Court of future Chief Justice Roger Taney, who represented Maryland in his capacity as that state's attorney general. Taney was described by an eyewitness as "tall, square-shouldered, . . . flat-breasted . . . with a stoop that made his shoulders even more prominent, a face without one good feature, a mouth unusually large, in which were discolored and irregular teeth, the gums of which were visible when he smiled . . . his hands spare with projecting veins, in a word, a gaunt, ungainly man." But "when he began to speak," the observer continued, "you never thought of his personal appearance, so clear, so simple, so admirably arranged were his low-voiced words."[365]

Marshall's opinion for the Court rested primarily upon the Import-Export Clause. He showed, through his habitual technique of construing "the literal meaning of [constitutional] words" with a view to "the general objects to be accomplished by them,"[366] that the clause was designed to refer not only to the act of importing foreign goods but to the "things imported."[367] Thus a tax on business that sold imported goods was the equivalent of a tax on imports. The only question was how far the prohibition extended: an imported article might eventually be resold by its original purchaser, or an article in bulk might be broken up and sold in parts by the importer. Did these resales constitute traffic in imports? If so, as Thompson pointed out in dissent, "nothing short of a total ex-

---

[362] Supra, note 7.
[363] *Niles' Weekly Register*, Mar. 17, 1827.
[364] Baltimore *Gazette,* quoted in ibid.

[365] The description appears in J. Semmes, *The Life and Times of John H. B. Latrobe* (1917), 101–103.
[366] 12 Wheat. at 437.
[367] Ibid.

emption from State charges or taxes, under all circumstances, will answer the supposed object of the constitution.''[368]

Marshall dealt with the problem of the scope of the clause by making an arbitrary distinction, one whose "universal . . . application" he admitted "might be premature."[369] He phrased the distinction as follows:

> [W]hen the importer has so acted upon the thing imported, that it has become incorporated and mixed up with the mass of property in the country, it has, perhaps, lost its distinctive character as an import and has become subject to the taxing power of the State; but while remaining the property of the importer, in his warehouse, in the original form or package in which it is imported, a tax upon it is too plainly a duty on imports to escape prohibition in the constitution.[370]

Generations of constitutional commentators have enjoyed poking fun at this so-called "original package doctrine," and absurd examples can be conjured up, such as the case of imported wine that breaks, allowing one bottle to roll free, which is subsequently seized and taxed by a state comptroller, thereby allowing the state to tax its companions in the broken case, but not any unbroken cases that remain.[371] Marshall might have better served by emphasizing the discriminatory nature of the prepaid tax in *Brown:* it applied only to local sellers of imports, not to sellers of goods made in the state.

*Brown* seemed disposed of by the Imports-Exports Clause, but Marshall went on to discuss the Commerce Clause issue, and his discussion was fraught with the same ambiguities as his discussion in *Gibbons.* Congress, Marshall noted, had passed tariff acts: these "authorize[d] importation, and offer[ed] the privilege for sale at a fixed price to every person who chooses to be a purchaser."[372] The regulation of importation was the equivalent of the regulation of commerce, thus "any charge [by a state] on the introduction and incorporation of the articles into and with the press of property in the courts, must be hostile to the power given to Congress to regulate commerce." Prescribing the "regular means for accomplishing that introduction and incorporation" was "an essential part" of regulating commerce. One is reminded here of Marshall's use of the coastal license in *Gibbons:* he read tariff legislation as giving importers a "right to sell,"[373] just as the license in *Gibbons* had purportedly given certain American ships a right to travel in navigable waters. That construction of tariff laws seems odd, since the purpose of tariff

---

[368] Ibid., 455.
[369] Ibid., 441.
[370] Ibid., 441–42.
[371] For some other examples, see T. Powell, *Vagaries and Varieties in*

*Constitutional Interpretation* (1956), 180–82.
[372] 12 Wheat. at 447.
[373] Ibid., 448.

legislation is not to allow importers to engage in commerce but to tax certain imported goods at designated rates. Tariffs, arguably, simply distinguish foreign from domestic goods, just as the coastal license statute in *Gibbons* distinguished foreign from domestic ships. Merchants had a right to import before Congress passed any tariff legislation.

There was also a statement in *Brown* that "the power claimed by the State is, in its nature, in conflict with that given to Congress, and the greater or less extent to which it may be exercised does not enter into the inquiry concerning its existence,"[374] and one that suggested that "the powers remaining with the States may be so exercised as to come in conflict with those vested in Congress."[375] Did these comments mean that the Commerce Clause prevented the states from taxing imported goods even if Congress had not regulated them at all?

The result in *Brown* produced an uncomfortable comparison of that case with *Gibbons*. In *Gibbons* Marshall had admitted that the states could, in the exercise of their reserved powers, affect commerce, such as by passing laws inspecting products entering or leaving their borders. He had also distinguished between the "questionable" power in the states to "regulate commerce" and the "acknowledged power of the states to levy taxes."[376] Thus if Congress had not exercised power to regulate imports in *Brown*, it would seem as if the reserved taxation powers of the states could come into play. This may be why Marshall chose to treat tariff legislation as regulation, but if the decision was grounded on that treatment his intimations about the exclusivity of federal commerce power were reduced in significance.

*Willson* v. *Black-bird Creek Marsh Co.*[377] continued the Court's hesitant treatment of state power to regulate commerce. An 1822 Delaware statute had incorporated the Black Bird Creek Marsh Company and authorized it to dredge marshlands and to build a dam across Black Bird Creek. The dam obstructed the creek and prevented a sloop, possessing a coastal license similar to the one held in *Gibbons,* from navigating the creek. Counsel for the sloopowner argued that the dam "unconstitutionally impeded" the sloop "in the use of her license."[378] Delaware, he suggested, had been "deprived of the power of closing a navigable river" by the Commerce Clause. Wirt argued for the company that the body of water being obstructed was insignificant: it was "one of those sluggish reptile streams, that do not run but creep, and which, wherever it possess, spreads its venom, and destroys the health of all those who inhabit its marshes."[379] Damming unhealthy waterways was a justifiable exercise

---

[374] Ibid., 447.
[375] Ibid., 448.
[376] 9 Wheat. at 201–202.

[377] Supra, note 8.
[378] Ibid., 248.
[379] Ibid., 249.

of a state's police powers, Wirt claimed, especially since Congress had passed no legislation affecting the creek.

*Willson* was both similar to and distinguishable from *Gibbons*. In both cases the shipowner had been licensed to operate on the navigable waters of the United States. In *Gibbons*, however, the body of water was large and an obvious source for commercial traffic; in *Willson* it had limited interstate use. The state prohibition in *Gibbons* had the purely commercial purpose of restraining steamboats competing with the Livingston–Fulton monopoly. The state statute in *Willson*, although arguably for "private emolument,"[380] was also directed at improving health conditions. The distinguishing features were enough for Marshall, writing for a unanimous Court. In a brief opinion he simply noted that the statute "probably improved . . . the health of the inhabitants," and such "measures" were "undoubtedly within those which are reserved to the states."[381] He then pointed out that Congress had passed no legislation regulating small navigable creeks. Under "all the circumstances of the case," he concluded, the Delaware statute was not repugnant to the commerce power.[382]

*Willson* was thus the first genuine dormant commerce power case decided by the Court; and insofar as *McCulloch* and *Gibbons* had intimated that the states could not regulate interstate commerce at all, that intimation was withdrawn. But the difficulty with treating *Willson* as a case of doctrinal importance was the patent insignificance for interstate commerce of the waterway involved. Congress had, in fact, done nothing more with steamboats in *Gibbons* than it had with sloops in *Willson:* each type of boat had been given a coastal license. To call congressional regulatory power unexercised in *Willson* and exercised in *Gibbons* seemed to call the same act by different names. Yet even though the public health features of the legislation and the significance of the waterway were probably decisive in distinguishing the cases, Marshall ostensibly grounded *Willson* on the dormancy doctrine. "If Congress had passed any act which bore upon the case; any act in execution of the power to regulate commerce," he said, "we should feel not much difficulty in saying that a state law coming in conflict with such act would be void. But Congress has passed no such act."[383]

*Willson* thus became, despite the brevity of Marshall's discussion, one of the Marshall Court precedents employed by the Taney Court in its revival of concurrent power theory.[384] More than anything else, the case was a symbol of Marshall's implicit concession that his Court had entered a new phase, one in which unanimity on sovereignty questions would be

[380] Ibid., 248.
[381] Ibid., 251.
[382] Ibid., 252.

[383] Ibid.
[384] See C. Swisher, *The Taney Period, 1836–64* (1974), 396–422.

Chief Justice John Marshall, painted by John B. Martin in 1832, three years before
Marshall's death.
*(Library of Congress)*

Associate Justice Bushrod Washington, as he appeared in the 1820s, from a painting by an unknown artist.
*(Library of Congress)*

Associate Justice William Johnson, from an unknown painting, probably in the 1820s.
*(Library of Congress)*

Associate Justice Brockholst Livingston, from an etching of an unknown portrait, probably painted between 1815 and 1820.
*(Library of Congress)*

Associate Justice Thomas Todd, from an original painting by an unknown artist, probably done shortly after Todd's appointment to the Supreme Court in 1807.
*(Library of Congress)*

The standard portrait of Associate Justice Gabriel Duvall, by an unknown artist, with a signature clearly showing the correct spelling of his last name, which has been regularly rendered with one as well as two ''l''s.
*(Library of Congress)*

Associate Justice Joseph Story, from a painting by Chester Harding, probably around 1815.
*(Library of Congress)*

Associate Justice Smith Thompson, from an etching of an unknown painting, probably around the time of Thompson's appointment to the Supreme Court in 1823.
*(Library of Congress)*

## Chapter VIII: *Sovereignty and Union*

harder to achieve, harmony among the Justices more difficult to obtain, and pressures to compromise with new political forces mounting. The same year the *Willson* decision was handed down Andrew Jackson took the oath of office.

The two remaining cases considered in this chapter were likewise from the last phase of the Marshall Court's history. *Craig* v. *Missouri*[385] considered the affirmative limitation on state "Bills of Credit" imposed by Article 1, Section 10, and *Barron* v. *Baltimore* considered whether the provisions of the Bill of Rights were themselves limits on state sovereignty.

*Craig* was a decision that reflected the altered character of the Court in the years after 1827. Trimble's death in 1828 and Washington's in 1829, and the inauguration of the Jackson administration, changed the character of Court appointments. McLean, who replaced Trimble, and Baldwin, who succeeded Washington, were expected to be less antagonistic to state sovereignty than their predecessors. Also on the Court were Johnson, who had written separately on every major constitutional case since *Gibbons,* and Thompson, who struck the balance on sovereignty questions closer toward state autonomy than nearly any of the Justices on the Court he joined in 1823. Those factors, and, after 1830, the breaking up of the boardinghouse as an exclusive residence, precipitated fewer unanimous decisions in controversial cases. *Craig* was typical: it was a 4–3 decision, with Marshall writing for himself, holdovers Story and Duvall, and the unpredictable Baldwin, who was in his first Term and not yet a thoroughgoing maverick. Johnson, Thompson, and McLean dissented, none of them taking the time to reconcile his views with the others.

*Craig* was concededly a very close case, best summarized by Johnson's observation that the fiscal arrangement created by Missouri "approach[ed] as near to a violation of the constitution as it can well go, without violating its provision."[386] Article 1, Section 10 of the Constitution prohibited states from "emit[ting] Bills of Credit" and from "mak[ing] any Thing but gold and silver Coin a Tender in Payment of Debts." Taken together, those clauses suggested that the states could borrow money but neither issue "bills of credit" nor redeem their debts in any currency save specie. Missouri issued certain certificates in exchange for promissory notes. The certificates, in various denominations, could be redeemed as payment for state taxes or state debts. Hiram Craig, having borrowed money from the state and having been issued one such certificate in the amount of $199.99 plus interest, never made good on

---

[385] Supra, note 9.

[386] 4 Pet. at 444.

his promissory note. When the state sued him, he claimed that the consideration for his note was illegal and therefore void because the state was prohibited by the Bills of Credit Clause from emitting certificates. A majority of the Court agreed.

Counsel for the state of Missouri had made two arguments in support of the certificates: first, they were not bills of credit but simply "evidences of loans made to the state"[387] pursuant to its power to borrow money; and second, they had not been made legal tender, and therefore did not violate any constitutional obligation to redeem debts in specie. They were merely pledges on the part of the state to receive them as the equivalent of money for the purposes of repaying state taxes and state loans. Citizens could refuse to receive them and thus avoid their fluctuating value, hence they were not the equivalent of legal tender.[388]

Marshall rejected both those arguments. He first indicated that the Bills of Credit Clause embraced all attempts on the part of states to issue paper money that could be subsequently redeemed.[389] This was "the sense in which [bills of credit] have always been understood": the constitutional clause was directed at "the emission of any paper medium, by a state government, for the purpose of common circulation."[390] The certificates in *Craig,* under this definition, were clearly bills of credit.[391] In the course of his discussion Marshall again repeated his conviction that one of the great purposes of the Constitution was to end the "mischief" of "ruinous speculations" that "destroy[ed] all confidence between man and man." That "mischief," he claimed, was identified by the Framers with state legislatures and paper money. The Bills of Credit Clause was "to cut up this mischief by the roots."[392]

Nor did the fact that the certificates had not been made legal tender save them. The Bills of Credit Clause was general, extending to all bills of credit. The clause making "a substantive prohibition to the enactment of tender laws" was independent of the Bills of Credit Clause; and to allow bills of credit if they were not tender was "to expunge" the Bills of Credit Clause.[393] Moreover, "the history of our country" showed that "paper money" was considered as "fraught . . . with evils . . . whether it be or be not a legal tender."[394] Thus the Missouri certificates were bills of credit, and the note of which they formed the consideration invalid, since it amounted to a promise made in consideration of an act that was forbidden by the Constitution.

The problem with all this was that Marshall himself had conceded that the states could bind themselves "to pay money at a future day for

---

[387] Ibid., 421.
[388] Ibid., 420–22.
[389] Ibid., 432.
[390] Ibid.

[391] Ibid., 433.
[392] Ibid., 432.
[393] Ibid., 434.
[394] Ibid., 435.

services actually received, or for money borrowed for present use."[395] What was the difference between a state loan agreement and the certificates in *Craig?* Johnson put an example that showed the difficulty:

> [S]uppose a state enacts a law authorizing her officers to borrow $100,000, and to give in lieu thereof certificates of $100, each expressing an acknowledgment of the debt. . . . Then suppose, that the next year she authorizes these certificates to be broken up into ten, five, and even one dollar bills. . . . And if, at the institution of the loan, the individual had given for the script his note at twelve months instead of repaying the case; it would be but doing in another form what was here done in Missouri. . . .[396]

The line between a state's issuing the equivalent of promises to repay debts and a state's "emit[ting] Bills of Credit" was thus not very bright, and, when pressed, Marshall's opinion in *Craig* seemed to say that while the states could borrow money they could not issue any paper currency of any kind. Indeed, much of his opinion was filled with allusions to "the war of our revolution, [where] we were driven" to issue "a paper medium, intended to circulate between individuals, and between government and individuals, for the ordinary purposes of our society." This was the quintessential meaning of a bill or credit: "any paper medium, by a state government, for the purpose of common circulation."[397] History "abound[ed] with proofs of the evils with which paper money is fraught, whether it be or be not a legal tender."[398]

   *Craig* was thus in one sense an opportunity for Marshall to exercise a long-standing prejudice against paper currency. It was also an opportunity for him to recharacterize the Court's role in sovereignty cases. In the *Martin–Cohens* sequence, he had alluded to Virginia's protest about being haled into court and asked to conform to the directives of the federal government, and had spoken of the judiciary's duty to enforce the people's constitutional will. He had, in *Osborn* and in the exchange with Hampden, distinguished between the "will of the law," an impersonal force, and the "will" or "interest" of the judge, and again spoken of the duties of the judicial department to follow the Constitution. Now in *Craig* he had been "reminded by one side," he said,

> of the dignity of a sovereign state, of the humiliation of her submitting herself to this tribunal, of the dangers which may result from inflicting a wound on that dignity;

---

[395] Ibid., 432.
[396] Ibid., 443.

[397] Ibid., 431.
[398] Ibid., 434.

And he had been informed "by the other," of

> the still superior dignity of the people of the United States, who have spoken their will, in terms which we cannot misunderstand.[399]

To "these admonitions," he continued, "we can only answer" that

> if the exercise of that jurisdiction which has been imposed upon us by the constitution and laws of the United States, shall be calculated to bring on those dangers which have been indicated; or if it shall be indispensable to the preservation of the Union, and consequently, of the independence and liberty of these states; these are considerations which address themselves to those departments which may with perfect propriety be influenced by them. This department can listen only to the mandates of law; and can tread only that path which is marked out by duty.[400]

The tone of this passage, while containing echoes of themes sounded earlier, has a different sound. The statements of wounded state dignity and "the still superior dignity" of the people are reminiscent of the controversies with Virginia, Ohio, and Maryland, and judicial duty again reappears, but the Court is no longer, in doing its "duty," portrayed as the champion of the Union and the people. It does not consider whether the exercise of its jurisdiction will "bring on dangers" or preserve the Union; those are considerations for other "departments." The Court merely listens to the "mandates" of the law and treads a narrow path.

One interpretation of the passage, then, and the one Marshall intended for his audience to make, was that the Court only follows the law, does its duty, and cannot consider the consequences. But the passage itself belies that interpretation: there is no balance struck between the "dignity of the states" and the "still superior dignity of the people of the United States." The people speak "their will" in the Constitution, in terms which "we"—the Court and all Americans—"cannot misunderstand." The "dangers" of state humiliation are outweighed by the "preservation of the Union, and consequently, of the independence and liberty of these states." The Court's exercise of its duty to read the people's will in the Constitution is "indispensable" to its preservation. Again, the skeleton of the Union theory of sovereignty appears: people–Constitution–Union–Court preservation of the structure of sovereign powers. Missing, however, is the aggressive, almost defiant tone of the earlier debates: the Court seems to have retreated to legalism.

---

[399] Ibid., 437.

[400] Ibid.

# Chapter VIII: *Sovereignty and Union*

The apparently cautious stance of *Craig* can be seen as also informing *Barron* v. *Mayor of Baltimore*,[401] Marshall's last significant sovereignty opinion. *Barron* is perhaps the one Marshall Court decision that
seems of immediate contemporary significance. Had it been decided differently, the Fourteenth Amendment's language might have had much
less meaning, the modern debate about the incorporation of Bill of Rights
provisions against the states by that Amendment need not have occurred,
and the relative indifference exhibited by the states to freedom of speech
and other civil liberties throughout much of the nineteenth century might
not have been possible. And had *Barron* been decided differently, the
sovereignty of the states would have been pinched from yet another angle:
the potentially broad restrictions against infringements on individual freedom articulated in the Bill of Rights.

By the time *Barron* was argued the Marshall Court had already made
significant invasions on the sovereignty of the states, first through a liberal
reading of the restrictions of the Contract Clause, then through the steady
expansion of the jurisdiction of the federal courts, then through broad
readings of enumerated plenary federal powers. *Barron* would, in a sense,
have been the capstone of this assault on state sovereignty. But the decision went swiftly and unanimously the other way, and, ironically, one
of Marshall's justifications for the result was a rehearsal of his pet sovereignty theories.

*Barron* involved an effort by a Baltimore wharfowner to recover
damages for injuries to his "extensive and highly productive wharf,"
which had become eroded as a result of changes in the grading and paving
of streets instituted by the city of Baltimore. The wharfowner sued in
state court, claiming, alternatively, that the city had committed a private
nuisance and had engaged in an uncompensated taking of property. The
Maryland Court of Appeals dismissed the suit on both counts, holding
that the act was, if anything, an unactionable public nuisance and that
the Takings Clause of the Fifth Amendment ("nor shall private property
be taken for public use, without just compensation") did not apply against
the states. Since Marshall Court jurisdiction rested on acts of the state of
Maryland (which had delegated municipal powers to the city of Baltimore)
being in violation of the Constitution, it was necessary to consider whether
the Takings Clause, or any of the provisions of the Bill of Rights, were
limitations on state activity.

Marshall advanced three arguments in support of his conclusion that
the Bill of Rights did not apply to the states, one based on the nature of
the Constitution, one on its language, and one on its history. In his first

---

[401] Supra, note 10.

589

argument he reiterated that "the constitution was ordained and established by the people of the United States for themselves, for their own government, and not for the government of the individual states."[402] This was another version of the now-familiar Union theory of sovereignty he had repeatedly advanced: the crucial relationship of sovereign entities forged by the Constitution was between the Union and the people, with state sovereignty not prominent in the balance. Since a general government was being created by the Constitution, and the people were doing the creating, "the people of the United States framed such a government . . . as they supposed . . . best calculated to promote their interests." Thus those powers and limitations conferred on the general government were "naturally" and "necessarily" applicable to the government created by the instrument unless the states were expressly singled out.[403]

The focus of sovereign relationships in the Constitution thus helped explain its language. Three kinds of limitations on power appeared in the Constitution: express limitations on the federal government, express limitations on the states, and limitations framed in general terms. This last class of limitations, Marshall argued, of which the Takings Clause was one, should be read as applying only against the federal government. As an example he contrasted Article I, Section 9's statement that "No Bill of Attainder or ex post facto law shall be passed" with the statement in Article I, Section 10 that "No state shall . . . pass any Bill of Attainder [or] ex post facto law." The second clause expressly limited the states; it would have been unnecessary if the first clause, a general limitation, was intended to apply to the states.[404]

A difficulty with this argument was that all the specific limitations made in the Bill of Rights were limitations on the federal government. Congress was singled out in the First Amendment as prohibited from making laws establishing religion or abridging speech; the federal courts were prohibited by the Seventh Amendment from re-examining "fact[s] tried by a jury . . . otherwise . . . than according to the rules of the common law." This would suggest that the general limitations of the Bill of Rights applied against both the states and the federal government, and one contemporary commentator on the Constitution came to this conclusion before *Barron* was decided. "[T]he first amendment," William Rawle wrote in 1829, "expressly refers to the powers of Congress alone, but some of those which follow are to be more generally construed, and considered as applying to the state legislatures as well as that of the Union."[405]

---

[402] 7 Pet. at 243.
[403] Ibid., 248.
[404] Ibid.

[405] W. Rawle, *A View of the Constitution of the United States of America* (2d ed., 1829), 124.

To aid in his construction of general limitations Marshall turned to his third argument, that based on history. He noted that "had the people of the several states . . . required additional safeguards to liberty from the apprehended encroachments of their particular governments,"[406] they could have simply organized state conventions rather than resorting to the "unwieldy and cumbrous machinery" of the constitutional amendments of the Bill of Rights. Moreover, Marshall claimed, the "serious fears" that resulted in "amendments to guard against the abuse of power" recommended in almost every convention in which the Constitution was adopted were fears of "the encroachments of the general government—not against those of the local governments."[407] This focus of opposition to the Constitution was "universally understood" and "part of the history of the day."[408]

What little evidence that has survived on the origins of the Bill of Rights suggests that Marshall was correct. The debates over amending the Constitution in Congress indicate that the Bill of Rights was originally to be inserted as an additional set of limitations included in Article 1, Section 9, all of whose limitations are either general or specifically directed against Congress. Limitations on the states were also proposed, and they were to be inserted in Article I, Section 10.[409] The eventual insertion of the Bill of Rights as amendments was done as a matter of convenience and intelligibility rather than because of substantive considerations. Moreover, in the ratifying conventions of two states, Massachusetts and New Hampshire, advocates for amending the Constitution specifically expressed concern about the encroachment of the federal government on individual liberties.[410]

Finally, there is some evidence that Rawle's construction of the general language in the Bill of Rights was not widely shared, at least with respect to the Takings Clause. In *Dartmouth College,* we have seen, Webster and his co-counsel were scrambling for any additional constitutional or extraconstitutional argument they could make, and they recognized early on that the New Hampshire legislature's enforced changes in Dartmouth's governing procedures amounted to an uncompensated taking. Had they thought that the Fifth Amendment applied to the states it seems likely that they would have advanced that argument. Ultimately *Barron* presented a question of "great importance, but not of much difficulty" for the Marshall Court; even Johnson, who had intimated in *Houston* that the double jeopardy provision of the Sixth Amendment ap-

---

[406] 7 Pet. at 249.
[407] Ibid., 250.
[408] Ibid.
[409] See *Annals of Congress* (J. Gales, ed., 1789), I, 451–52.

[410] See *Documentary History of the Constitution of the United States of America* (5 vols., 1894), II, 93–96, 141–44.

plied against the states,[411] joined *Barron* and subsequently described it as having "settled" the question.[412]

One might be tempted to suggest that Marshall was sacrificing a particular outcome in *Barron* for the sake of retaining the integrity of a general theory. His argument that the general limitations on governmental power found in the Constitution applied against the federal government perfectly complemented the central premise of his sovereignty theory, that the crucial relationship in the formation of the Constitution was between the people and the Union. But the *Barron* opinion bears none of the elaborate reasoning characteristic of Marshall when he conceived himself to be beset by a truly difficult question of constitutional interpretation. On the contrary, his opinion in *Barron* was short, straightforward, and apparently free from strain. He simply read sections of the Constitution, and by that reading the "plain and marked line of discrimination it imposes on the powers of the general government, and on those of the states" was revealed. He was benefited in that reading by the knowledge that state constitutions had been drafted at about the same time as the federal version, and provided a much less cumbersome method of restricting the powers of state governments; and that "it is universally understood"[413] that the "apprehended encroachments" perceived as "dangerous to liberty" by the generation of the Framers were those "of the general government."[414]

*Barron* was in this sense another of Marshall's atmospheric opinions, helping perpetuate a vivid image of the period in which the Constitution was framed. In Marshall's portrait, the time of the framing was one of chaotic economic conditions, with insecure currencies and lack of confidence; of strained relationships among the members of the league formed by the Articles of Confederation; of an ineffectual national government, lacking power to protect itself against foreign enemies or to raise revenue; and of political unrest engendered by demagogues in the state legislatures. Beset by these difficulties, the American people resolved to create a general government, representing a Union of the states, and to give it sovereign powers, once held by those states, so that it might serve as a bulwark against the evils of the times. The Constitution was the document in which that resolution was made manifest. Every effort to depart from the sovereign relationships embodied in the Constitution, or from its central purposes, or from its establishment of a Union represented cultural disintegration, a return to the chaos of the pre-framing period. An image of chaos, and the ever-present potential for decay and dissolution, were the spectres against which Marshall's theory of sover-

---

[411] See 5 Wheat. at 34.
[412] Livingston v. Moore, 7 Pet. 469, 551–52 (1833).

[413] 7 Pet. at 150.
[414] Ibid.

eigny was erected. In *Barron* those spectres reappeared, even though, for once, state sovereign powers were not adversely affected.

In light of the ongoing sovereignty debate between the Marshall Court and its critics that has been traced in this chapter, the comments from contemporaries with which the chapter began should be more intelligible. In Calhoun's toast we find the most prominent defender of compact theory nonetheless conceding that Union was next to liberty in significance; in Van Buren's toast we find a renewed sense, reflecting the political realignments of the 1820s, that sovereignty issues would increasingly represent political compromises; in Jackson's we find the symbol of those political realignments nonetheless committed to the Union's preservation. Sovereignty controversies lay ahead, most significantly those of nullification and the Jackson administration's temporary defiance of the Court in the Cherokee cases, which are reviewed in a later chapter. But the idea that the Union, whether a creation of the people or a compact among the states, needed to be preserved had become part of American political consciousness.

One would not be surprised, in light of the Court's sovereignty decisions previously reviewed, to find that Story's *Commentaries on the Constitution,* whose first volume ended with the "hope" that the Constitution "may . . . be perpetual"[415] and whose last volume concluded with the warning that "the national constitution is our last and our only security,"[416] had taken pains not only to discredit compact theory, but to link both the Union and the Constitution to a general justification for federal judicial supremacy, summoning up the coextensive power axiom in the process.[417] With Story's treatise the strategy of the Union theory of sovereignty, as developed by federal judges, was clearly revealed: the Union, the Constitution, coextensive power, the Court's role as the final arbiter of constitutional questions, and the will of the people were all integrated. Preserving the Union meant preserving all of those entities in their pure form, as evidenced by the "two great sources" of Story's *Commentaries,* the *Federalist* essays and "the extraordinary Judgments of Mr. Chief Justice Marshall upon constitutional law."[418]

One can fairly call Story's strategy "nationalist": it envisaged the Supreme Court simultaneously extending its own jurisdiction and the plenary powers of Congress, constantly displacing state sovereignty with federal sovereignty. But the promulgation of Story's theory in his *Commentaries* did not mean that his vision had been put into practice. The political realignment that swept the Jackson administration into office,

---

[415] J. Story, *Constitution,* I, 494.
[416] Ibid., III, 759.

[417] Ibid., I, 361.
[418] Ibid., I, v.

the emergence of slavery as an entrenched rather than a moribund institution, the revival, in that context, of states' rights theories, and the identification, by Jacksonians and other politicians, of federal institutions such as the Bank of the United States with economic and social privilege resulted in a severe qualification of Story's vision. Concurrent sovereignty theory became an important doctrine with *Gibbons* and was implicitly accepted by the Court in subsequent Commerce Clause cases. The federal executive sided with a state in opposition to a Marshall Court decision restricting state sovereignty. While reaffirming his support for the Union, Jackson vetoed a congressional statute establishing the Second Bank of the United States. None of the "enlarged and liberal institutions" Story had envisaged in his 1815 plan to "extend the national authority over the whole extent of power given by the Constitution" was extant by the time of Marshall's death in 1835: there was no national bank, no national system of bankruptcy, no federal navigation act extending the admiralty jurisdiction. All that remained were "judicial courts which shall embrace the whole constitutional powers."[419] One might suggest that an implicit constitutional compromise had been arrived at in the 1830s, that compromise consisting of a retention of the extensive Article III powers claimed by the Marshall Court and a circumscription of the equally extensive Article I powers claimed for Congress.

In this vein, the most nationalistic achievement of the Marshall Court's sovereignty decision was its erection of a theoretical justification for its own power to review actions of the states that potentially collided with the Constitution. The great significance of coterminous power theory in the Court's decisions was as a rationale for unlimited federal judicial power, not unlimited federal legislative power. Through their erosion of compact theory, their continual insistence that effective governments needed to have the means to implement their laws, their warnings of the eroding effects of multifarious state court systems, and their insistence that the judicial department, albeit federal, was impartial and independent, the Court's decisions had by the 1830s cemented its place as the final interpreter of the Constitution. By that achievement the meaning of the supreme source of American law would be given by a federal court. While Marshall was Chief Justice, that fact alone ensured that the Union and the Constitution would be treated as inseparable entities.

---

[419] J. Story to Nathaniel Williams, Feb. 22, 1815, in W. Story, *Life and Letters*, I, 254.

# CHAPTER IX

# Property, Vested Rights, and Legislative Regulation: The Contract Clause Cases

" Ⓘ T SEEMS TO BE the general opinion, fortified by a strong current of judicial opinion," Story wrote in his *Commentaries on the Constitution,* "that since the American revolution no state government can be presumed to possess the transcendental sovereignty, to take away vested rights of property; to take away the property of A and transfer it to B by a mere legislative act." A government could "scarcely be deemed to be free," Story continued, "where the rights of property are left solely dependent on a legislative body, without any restraint. The fundamental maxims of a free government seem to require that the rights of personal liberty and private property, should be held sacred."[1] This language tracked identical language Story had written in the 1829 case of *Wilkinson v. Leland.*[2] He had added in that case that "a different doctrine is utterly inconsistent with the great and fundamental principles of a republican government."[3]

What "great principle" was being asserted in these excerpts? Story's language is clear enough: "vested rights of . . . private property" were ostensibly immune from "legislative acts." His remarks, however, raise three questions: why should private property rights be treated as "sacred," what sorts of property rights were to be treated as "vested," and what was the constitutional basis for protecting those rights once they were identified? Story treated the principle of protection for vested property against legislative interference as settled and self-evident, but in reality it was controversial and complex, as its evolution in the constitutional jurisprudence of the Marshall Court demonstrated.

---

[1] J. Story, *Commentaries on the Constitution of the United States* (3 vols., 1833), I, 268.

[2] 2 Pet. 627 (1829).
[3] Ibid., 657.

## The Marshall Court and Cultural Change, 1815-1835

This chapter discusses the major constitutional cases in which the Court confronted the issue of legislative infringement of vested property rights. The chapter is divided into five sections. The first discusses the intellectual origins of the problem, focusing on the status of property, and of legislative regulation of private activity, in republican and liberal theory. The second surveys early Marshall Court efforts to find legal solutions, noting the Court's alternative use of constitutional and extraconstitutional arguments. The third, fourth, and fifth sections focus on the major Marshall Court cases addressing vested rights and legislative regulation. The third section, which discusses the pivotal *Dartmouth College* case, seeks to show that the Court, after 1819, conceived the problem as soluble primarily by appeal to a reconstituted Contract Clause of the Constitution, a clause that had been "packed" with extraconstitutional arguments and analogies from other constitutional provisions. The fourth and fifth sections discuss complexities and difficulties with that solution. The sections demonstrate that alongside the Court's doctrinal consensus that a reconstituted Contract Clause was the proper vehicle by which to address vested rights issues there developed a variety of views as to how those issues ought to be resolved, and a loss of internal unity among the Justices. The last three sections, taken together, suggest that the Court's conceptualization of vested rights–legislative regulation issues as Contract Clause issues had served to mask, rather than to resolve, internal divisions among the Justices on the vested rights problem itself.

While some of the chapter's emphasis is on language, rhetoric, and doctrine, there is an important additional theme of internal strategy and negotiation and external maneuvering. The Contract Clause cases were not simply doctrinal exercises. They had important practical consequences, affecting land sales, municipal taxation, the rights of nonresident landowners, bankruptcy and insolvency legislation, and the legal powers and responsibilities of corporations. They were argued by lawyers and decided by judges who were well aware of their social and economic ramifications. They were adjudicated by a Court with a highly informal mode of doing business and a persistent awareness of its enhanced power and visibility in American political life. The choice of doctrine, the framing of arguments, even the selection of facts or of controversies were to these men anything but disembodied activities. In the great Marshall Court Contract Clause cases doctrine was the product of strategy, division, and compromise as well as of ideology.

The Contract Clause cases were, next to the sovereignty cases, the Court's most prominent and controversial decisions. They represented its first efforts to assert a review power over the actions of state legislatures, preparing the way for the more explicit sovereignty claims the Court would make in *Martin* v. *Hunter's Lessee* and *Cohens* v. *Virginia*. They dealt with a principle of republican political theory—solicitude for private

596

## Chapter IX: *The Contract Clause Cases*

property—that was both central to the consciousness of early-nineteenth-century Americans and elusive in its application. They raised, more clearly than any of the Court's other constitutional cases, the question of the sources of the Court's decisions and especially the role of nontextual general principles in constitutional cases. And they furnish us with an index of the changes in American economic and political life that took place during the Court's tenure, as a society whose primary economic indicator was speculation in and control of undeveloped land (*Fletcher v. Peck*) gave way to a society in which the corporate franchise was the primary unit of economic activity (the *Charles River Bridge* case). In the Contract Clause cases, as in the sovereignty cases, the Court announced its intention to play an active role in the emergence of the American nation.

We have seen that the idea of a "natural right" to acquire property and to use acquired property as one saw fit was one of the building blocks of republican theory. For republicans, government existed in order to secure inalienable rights: citizens consented to be governed, among other reasons, so that their freedom to acquire and to hold property would be protected. While property in republican theory was generally identified with freehold land, it was not limited to that form of propertyholding. The right was a right to possess and to make use of entities that ranged from soil to other human beings, and the right antedated the formation of government itself.

While the protection of property rights by republican government could have been justified solely on the theory that government existed to secure inalienable natural rights, another justification was advanced by republican theorists. Civic virtue was a paramount goal of republicanism, and civic virtue was ostensibly promoted if the economic security of the citizenry was protected. Having a freehold and enjoying the fruits of it gave men the security and leisure to devote themselves to civic affairs. Their interests being satisfied, their virtue could emerge. When eighteenth-century American republican theorists such as Jefferson spoke of the "pursuit of happiness," they meant the disinterested attention to educational, cultural, and civic affairs that could emerge once economic security had been gained. "Property," then, contained a bundle of associations for republicans, including autonomy, economic well-being, civic-mindedness, and the cultivation of liberal pursuits.[4]

---

[4] On the place of property in republican thought see W. Scott, *In Pursuit of Happiness* (1977), 24–132; D.

McCoy, *The Elusive Republic* (1980), 68–73.

It followed from the association of propertyholding with civic virtue that the possession of property was an index of one's worth to society. Those possessed of freeholds were felt to be, because of their disinterestedness, worthy participants in civic affairs. Their economic independence made them less susceptible to demagoguery or corruption; their wealth gave them the leisure to concentrate on virtuous pursuits. The association of a propertied status with civic-mindedness can be seen in the suffrage requirements of the late eighteenth and early nineteenth centuries: the model voter in the early American republic was an owner of a freehold, and unpropertied persons had difficulty convincing others that they could be trusted to participate in civic affairs.[5]

In the idealized conception of property rights the property that was secured and protected was private in character. The right to acquire and to hold property was not a right conferred by the state but one that existed in a state of nature and therefore preceded the formation of governments. The freeholds held by the ideal republican citizenry had been acquired through industry or lineage: they were private possessions. But another sort of property existed in early America, and its acquisition revealed the presence of a competing theory about the relationship of government to propertyholding. This property had been acquired from the state itself, by state charters to individuals or corporations and state grants of land to individuals or land companies. Bridges, roads, turnpikes, ferries, and canals were built in this fashion: the state chartered a group of individuals to provide transportation facilities, typically giving them exclusive rights to maintain and to charge for the services but retaining some power to set rates. While these charters were a common method by which states affected property rights, they were not the only method: states and cities also distributed land and taxed activities in a variety of settings.

This involvement on the part of states, set in motion by state or municipal legislation, affected the idealized republican conception of property rights in two respects. First, it illustrated that government in America was not conceived exclusively as securing existing private property rights, but also as creating new ones. The land sold to companies or individuals, and the franchises distributed to groups of investors, were not examples of wholly private property acquired by industry or lineage. The property transferred in those examples had originally been public in its ownership, and the rights of the landowners or franchisees were not pre-existing, but the creations of the state itself. Second, the state was not simply dispersing the property out of its beneficence; it expected that the property would be put to a beneficial public use. Land was being sold

---

[5] On the suffrage debates see C. Williamson, *American Suffrage from Property to Democracy, 1760–1800* (1960), 139–299; M. Peterson, ed., *Democracy, Liberty, and Property* (1966).

in the hope that it would be developed, thereby providing additional areas for settlement and population centers; franchises were being doled out in the hope that improved transportation facilities would result.

The idea that the state could participate affirmatively in the distribution of economic benefits and exert some control over the distribution process was encapsulated, in late-eighteenth- and early-nineteenth-century American thought, by the term "commonwealth." The term signified an attitude toward the interaction of the state and private individuals in economic affairs which had been well established in seventeenth- and eighteenth-century England. Briefly, the attitude assumed that the state could use its powers to create economic privileges for private individuals with the expectation of enhancing the revenues of the state. The unusual feature of the commonwealth attitude was not the idea that the state could create privileges for private persons—that had been a prerogative of the British crown for centuries—but the idea that the state could create privileges in a republican society predicated on norms of individual liberty and limited government.[6] Economic privilege and close connections between governmental offices and private individuals raised the spectre of corruption, one of the evils identified by republican theory. Yet it was clear that such intervention was not only tolerated but encouraged in late-eighteenth- and early-nineteenth-century America.

An indication of the power of the idea of commonwealth can be seen in late-eighteenth-century theorists' use of the phrase "common good" in their discussions of republican government. Although theorists agreed that the common good was a fundamental goal of society, they disagreed about the ultimate meaning of the phrase. In 1764, James Otis had defined "the end of government as the good of mankind," but had equated "good" with "the security, the quest, and happy enjoyment of life, liberty and property."[7] This formulation suggested that the purpose of government was to secure individual rights. But language in the early state constitutions indicated that the common good could be inconsistent with the pursuit of individual interests, and where it was those interests should yield. Pennsylvania's constitution distinguished the "common benefit, protection and security of the people" from "the particular emolument or advantage of any single man," and Massachusetts announced that "government is instituted . . . not for the profit, honor, or private interest of any one man."[8] In the same documents, however, appeared

---

[6] For descriptions and examples of the commonwealth concept, see O. and M. Handlin, *Commonwealth* (rev. ed., 1968); L. Hartz, *Economic Policy and Democratic Thought: Pennsylvania, 1776–1860* (1948); L. Levy, *The Law of the Commonwealth and Chief Justice Shaw* (1957).

[7] J. Otis, *Rights of the British Colonies* (1764), 10.

[8] Quoted in W. Adams, *The First American Constitutions* (1980), 222–23.

restatements of Otis's equation of the common good with the protection of natural private rights. Massachusetts, for example, defined "the end . . . of government" as "furnish[ing] the individuals who compose it with the power of enjoying in safety and tranquility their natural rights."[9]

The precise question left unsettled by these attitudes about private rights and the common good was whether governmental bodies could act to curtail property rights in the name of the commonwealth and, if so, what forms that action could take. Subsequent Marshall Court decisions suggested that that question had been addressed and answered by the Framers of the Constitution when they enacted the clause preventing states from "impair[ing] the Obligation of Contracts."[10] But the scant legislative history of that clause furnishes little evidence for the Court's claim.

In the period of the Articles of Confederation several states had responded to problems in the supply of money by passing laws designed to provide for alternative means of repaying debts. The laws allowed states to issue paper currency and made that currency legal tender in the payment of debts, provided for the payment of debts in certain commodities, extended the time for debt obligations beyond the periods fixed in contracts, and allowed debts to be paid in installments despite the absence of contract installment provisions.[11] That the Framers of the Constitution were concerned about the statutes can be seen in provisions preventing the states from "coin[ing] money," "emit[ting] Bills of Credit," and "mak[ing] any thing but gold and silver coin a Tender in Payment of Debts."[12]

In the same article containing this clause appeared the clause preventing the states from impairing the obligation of contracts. But that clause was not proposed until late in the process of drafting the Constitution, and received very little attention from the delegates. The first mention of a Contract Clause was made by Rufus King on August 28, 1787, when he "moved to add . . . a prohibition on the states to interfere in private contracts." King suggested that the language of the prohibition employ "the words in the ordinance of Congress establishing new states," by which he meant the Northwest Ordinance, enacted on July 13, which had provided that "no law ought ever to be made . . . that shall, in any manner whatever, interfere with or affect private contracts . . . previously formed."[13] Between King's motion and the eventual adoption of the clause by the Committee on Style on September 12[14] there was very

---

[9] Quoted in ibid., 223.
[10] U.S. Const., Art. I, Sect. 10.
[11] Examples can be found in A. Nevins, *The American States During and After the Revolution, 1775–1789* (1924), 386–404.

[12] U.S. Const., Art. I, Sect. 10.
[13] See M. Farrand, *Records of the Federal Convention* (4 vols., 1911), II, 439.
[14] See ibid., II, 597.

limited discussion, and it was confined to the question whether the clause had a solely retrospective effect. A proposal to insert "previous" before "Obligation" was made and rejected by the Committee on Style.[15]

In the ratifying conventions discussion of the Contract Clause was also limited. Luther Martin opposed it in the Maryland legislature on the grounds that it would prevent the states from giving relief to debtors in "times of . . . great public calamities and distress, and . . . extreme scarcity of specie";[16] James Madison defended it as "a constitutional bulwark in favor of personal security and private rights," adding that "laws impairing the obligation of contracts are contrary to the first principles of the social compact and to every principle of sound legislation."[17] Only a few documents raised the issue of whether the clause applied to public as well as private contracts. In the Virginia debates Patrick Henry, arguing that the states should be allowed to redeem currency in depreciated value, said that the clause "includes public contracts as well as private contracts between individuals," but Edmund Randolph, one of the Framers, responded that the clause had been directed at "the frequent interferences of the state legislatures with private contracts."[18] In the North Carolina debates James Galloway also suggested that the clause would compel the state of North Carolina to redeem public securities in specie, and Framer W. R. Davis suggested that the Contract Clause "refers merely to contracts between individuals."[19]

The limited evidence available about the purpose of the Contract Clause thus suggests, first, that it was designed as one of several restrictions on the power of states to give relief to debtors in periods when the supply of specie was reduced; and, second, that its scope was limited to private contracts: it did not bind the states from altering the terms of their own contracts. A subsidiary point of interest was the discussion of the retrospective effect of the clause; in the context of that discussion it is difficult to tell whether the absence of the word "previous" before "Obligation" represented a decision to give the clause prospective effect or simply a tacit understanding that it could be taken only as retrospective in character, and thus the clarifying word "previous" was unnecessary.

Three propositions may be extracted from this discussion. First, to the extent that the basic problem addressed by the Court in the Contract Clause cases was the problem of legislative regulation of property rights, republican theory encompassed two apparently contradictory approaches to that problem, one elevating property rights beyond legislative interfer-

---

[15] See ibid., II, 636; IV, 59.
[16] Quoted in ibid., III, 214–15.
[17] [J. Madison], *The Federalist* No. 44 (B. Wright, ed., 1961), 329.
[18] Quoted in J. Eliot, *Debates in the* *Several State Conventions on the Adoption of the Federal Constitution* (4 vols., 1861), III, 474.
[19] Quoted in ibid., IV, 191.

ence, the other suggesting that all individual rights could yield to the goals of the commonwealth. Second, to the extent that there was unquestioned consensus about the inalienability of property rights, that consensus was confined to the private property of individuals acquired by industry or lineage, and did not include property vested in private persons by the state. Third, to the extent that the Contract Clause was intended to be a "constitutional bedrock" in favor of property rights, the rights being protected were taken to be confined to those arising out of contracts between individuals. Thus the basic issue which would recur in the Court's Contract Clause cases—the issue whether a state could interfere with "vested" rights that it had created in its own "public" contracts— had not been settled by the actions of the Framers and was susceptible of alternative resolutions within the confines of republican theory.

✻

The early Marshall Court cases interpreting the Contract Clause were notable, we will see, for being grounded not only on the text of the Constitution but on the first principles of republican theory. Two explanations may be advanced for this feature of the cases. First, their procedural posture allowed the Court to consider them as cases of general law as well as cases of constitutional interpretation. Second, the cases were not "easy" cases involving legislative restrictions on existing private property rights but more "difficult" ones involving legislative alterations of previous acts—grants, exemptions from taxes, charters—in which a legislature itself had conferred a benefit on a private party.

*Fletcher* v. *Peck*[20] was the first such case. The Georgia legislature had passed a statute in 1795 conveying large tracts of land to four land companies. A year later allegations that the companies had bribed legislators surfaced, and a newly constituted legislature passed another statute rescinding the sales. The land in question, which included large portions of what came to be Alabama and Mississippi and had originally been inhabited by Indians, was sold at less than two cents an acre. When the companies learned of the Georgia legislature's actions, they sought relief in Congress, lobbying for six years between 1803 and 1809.[21] They also attempted to test the validity of the titles given them by the 1795 legislature through an arranged suit in the federal courts. John Peck, a resident of Boston, who had invested heavily in the Georgia lands, "sold" a portion of his holdings to Robert Fletcher, a resident of Amherst, New Hampshire.[22] Both Peck and Fletcher were shareholders in the New En-

---

[20] 6 Cranch 87 (1810).
[21] On the background of *Fletcher* v. *Peck* see C. Magrath, *Yazoo* (1966), 1–49.

[22] The sale was apparently contrived for the purposes of a collusive lawsuit. See ibid., 53–56 and note 23, infra.

# Chapter IX: *The Contract Clause Cases*

gland Missisisppi Company, one of the companies that had acquired title to the land in 1795. Fletcher then brought suit against Peck to try title to the land he had "bought"; the residency of the parties and the jurisdictional amounts were clearly designed to enable the case to be brought in federal court.[23] That the purpose of the action was to determine the validity of Georgia land titles acquired under the 1795 statute, rather than to settle a private lawsuit, was also evident from the parties' continuing it "by consent" from 1803, when it was first brought, until 1807, when it appeared that Congress was not likely to provide the land companies any relief.[24]

Although *Fletcher* v. *Peck* was first heard before Justice William Cushing on his Boston circuit in October 1807, the issues in the case had been explored for many years. In 1796 Alexander Hamilton had been retained by one of the land companies to give his opinion on the 1795 sale, and Hamilton had suggested that the 1796 revocation of the 1795 statute was "a contravention of the first principles of natural justice and social policy." In addition, Hamilton maintained, the 1796 revocation violated the Contract Clause of the Constitution. That clause, Hamilton argued, was the "equivalent of saying no state shall pass a law revoking . . . a contract," and it applied to "[e]very grant from one to another, whether the grantor be a state or an individual."[25] Moreover, a 1795 circuit opinion by Justice William Paterson employed a similar argument in invalidating a Pennsylvania statute that repealed a previous statute confirming the title of certain Connecticut settlers to Pennsylvania lands. Since the state of Pennsylvania had conveyed the title in the first place, Paterson argued, it could not, in the light of "the principles of contract," convey it to another.[26] In addition, a 1799 decision by the Supreme Judicial Court of Massachusetts had considered the validity of the very 1796 statute at issue in *Fletcher* and had found it "preposterous" on "general principles," as well as a violation of the Contract Clause.[27]

The early history of *Fletcher* v. *Peck,* then, indicates that it was perceived as a case raising issues of general law as well as constitutional law. Because the case was being argued in a federal court, Supreme Court review would be on a writ of error from that court, and the Court was not limited in its consideration to constitutional issues, as it was when

---

[23] The original copies of the pleadings filed in the federal district court in Boston show alterations in the acreage of the land that had the effect of increasing the value of the suit so as to qualify for federal jurisdiction. See the discussion in G. Haskins and H. Johnson, *Foundations of Power: John Marshall, 1801–1815* (1981), 343–45.

[24] See Magrath, *Yazoo,* 56–59.
[25] A. Hamilton, "Opinion," in R. Harper, *The Case of the Georgia Sales on the Mississippi* (1799), 88–89.
[26] 2 Dall. 304, 320 (1795).
[27] Derby v. Blake, 226 Mass. 618 (1917), originally published in the Boston *Columbian Centinel,* October 9, 1799.

reviewing the decisions of state courts.[28] The argument that the 1796 repeal was void on "general principles of contract" or "first principles of natural justice" was thus an appropriate one to make, and counsel for Peck made it both before Cushing's circuit court and the Supreme Court, which reviewed Cushing's decision in the 1810 Term, finding for Peck on all counts. The Court had previously considered *Fletcher* v. *Peck* in its 1809 Term, but had postponed decision, ostensibly because only five judges were in attendance that Term[29] and also because of "the reluctance of the Court to decide the case at all, as it appeared manifestly made up for the purpose of getting the Court's judgment upon all the points."[30]

"All the points" meant the general law issues as well as the constitutional issues, and the eventual opinions issued by the Court in *Fletcher* v. *Peck* demonstrated that the Justices were prepared to ground their decision on extraconstitutional as well as constitutional authorities. Indeed, the Justices seem to have seen *Fletcher* v. *Peck* essentially as a case raising general principles of natural justice, and only secondarily as a case raising issues of constitutional construction. Marshall's opinion for the Court, for example, began with a reference to "certain great principles of justice, whose authority is universally acknowledged, that ought not to be entirely disregarded."[31] The succeeding paragraphs made it clear what those principles were. They were the "rule of property" that the "rights of third persons who are purchasers without notice for a valuable consideration, cannot be discarded"; the "principle of equity" that concealed defects in titles of which third parties "had no notice . . . cannot be set up against [them]"; and "the principle" that "when absolute rights have vested under [a] contract, a repeal of the law [creating those rights] cannot divest [them]."[32] More generally, Marshall argued, "the nature of society and of government" prescribed "some limits to the legislative power."[33] In particular, Marshall suggested that legislative power would be unlimited "if the property of an individual, fairly and honestly acquired, may be seized without compensation." The Georgia legislature was thus restrained from divesting titles by "general principles which are common to our free institutions."[34]

Johnson's concurrence in *Fletcher* had a similar emphasis on general principles. He began by asserting that "a state does not possess the power

---

[28] See the discussion of Section 25 of the Judiciary Act of 1789 in Chapter III.

[29] Marshall's remarks were reported by John Quincy Adams (who argued the case for Peck) in his diary for March 11, 1809. C. Adams, ed., *The Memoirs of John Quincy Adams* (12 vols., 1874–77), I, 547.

[30] J. Q. Adams in C. Adams, ibid., 546.

[31] 6 Cranch at 133.

[32] Ibid., 133, 135.

[33] Ibid., 135.

[34] Ibid., 139.

of revoking its own grants'' because of a "general principle . . . the reason and nature of things." Once a legislature conveyed property to an individual, Johnson believed, it "vested in the individual [and became] intimately blended with his existence, as essentially so as the blood that circulates through his system."[35] Deeming property that had been conveyed to individuals by a legislature as "vested" in those individuals was an example of "the frequent recurrence to first principles" that was necessary to protect "the security of a people against the misconduct of their rulers."[36] Thus Johnson did not need to employ the "provision in the constitution of the United States relative to laws impairing the obligation of contracts" in order to reach a decision.[37] He had characterized *Fletcher* as a general principles case, not a constitutional one.

Marshall, however, added as a ground for his decision the Contract Clause itself. In so doing he reasoned by analogy to general common law principles: if third-party bona fide purchasers without notice were protected against the annulment of private contracts, should they not be protected against the annulment of public grants? The public grant case, we have seen, was more uncertain and complicated, given the commonwealth idea and the practice of legislative regulation in the "public good." But Marshall attempted to equate it with the private law cases. He argued, citing Blackstone, that a "grant" was a "contract" because it "amount[ed] to an extinguishment of the right of the grantor, and implies a contract not to reassert that right."[38] The problem with this argument was not its accuracy as a statement of common law doctrine but its suggestion that the Obligation of Contracts Clause was designed to cover statutes repealing state grants. Marshall had already said that the statutes amounted to seizures of property without compensation,[39] but the Fifth Amendment to the Constitution appeared only to prevent such seizures when made by the federal government.[40] Marshall pointed out, however, that the language of the Contract Clause did not distinguish between "those [contracts] which are executory and those which are executed," and added that it would be odd if contracts requiring private persons to convey land were protected, but "absolute conveyances" by the state were not.[41]

Thus far Marshall had equated "grant" with "contract"; he now sought to equate "public contract" with "private contract." He argued that since the language in the Contract Clause was "general," it should be taken to embrace "contracts made with the state" unless some excep-

---

[35] Ibid., 143.
[36] Ibid., 144.
[37] Ibid.
[38] Ibid., 137.
[39] Ibid., 135.

[40] The Court decided that point in Barron v. Baltimore, 7 Pet. 243 (1833), discussed in Chapter VIII.
[41] 6 Cranch at 137.

tion could be derived from context. But context reinforced the inclusion of state contracts. There was a "sentiment" in the Framers to shield "property from the effects of . . . [legislative] passions";[42] the Ex Post Facto Clause, included in the same section as the Contract Clause, would be vitiated if a state could annul its original grants; the language giving the federal courts jurisdiction over suits brought by individual citizens against states, repealed by the Eleventh Amendment, anticipated that "a state . . . which violated its own contract was suable in the courts of the United States for that violation."[43] Thus state grants were the equivalent of private contracts for the purpose of the Contract Clause. "Grant" meant "contract" for constitutional purposes. Moreover, the takings principle, described as one of the "general principles of our political institutions"[44] that restrained a legislature from taking property from A and giving it to B (or back to itself) had been identified as an important analogy for Contract Clause cases.

*Fletcher* was the Court's first experience with the Contract Clause, and represented only the second time that it had invalidated a state statute.[45] The evidence suggests that the Justices found the case easier because of the takings analogy, which they clearly felt violative of some great principles. The difficulty in *Fletcher* was that the analogy was imperfect in two respects. First, Georgia had not taken property from A and given it to B; Georgia had given property to A and then subsequently taken it away. Was this difference a significant one? The obvious violation of natural justice that the first example represented did not mean that the second example was equally violative of first principles, given the ideas of "commonwealth" and "public good." Second, *Fletcher* v. *Peck* was a diversity case, meaning that the Court could draw upon general principles of federal law as well as the Constitution for its sources. It was not clear how significant the takings analogy would be in a "pure" Contract Clause case, one coming to the Court under Section 25 of the Judiciary Act, which delineated Court review of state court decisions, confining it to constitutional issues.

Two years after *Fletcher* v. *Peck* came *New Jersey* v. *Wilson*,[46] in which the Court considered whether the Contract Clause could override a state's power to create an exemption from taxation. In 1758 an agreement between the Delaware Indians and the colony of New Jersey was ratified by the New Jersey legislature. By the terms of the agreement the Indians relinquished their claims to any other land in New Jersey, and New Jersey gave them a tract of land on which they could reside per-

---

[42] Ibid., 138.
[43] Ibid., 139.
[44] Ibid.
[45] The first occasion was Ware v.

Hylton, 3 Dall. 199 (1796), invalidating a state law as being in conflict with a federal treaty.
[46] 7 Cranch 164 (1812).

manently and be perpetually exempt from taxation. In 1801 the Indians, "having become desirous of migrating from the state of New Jersey, and of joining their brethren at Stockbridge, in the state of New York,"[47] obtained the consent of the New Jersey legislature to sell the tract of land, and in 1803 the land was sold to George Painter and others. The New Jersey legislature, in giving its consent, had not included any "expression . . . respecting the privilege of exemption of taxation which was annexed to [the land]."[48]

In 1804 the New Jersey legislature passed a statute repealing the portion of the 1758 agreement exempting the tract of land from taxation. The owners of the land were subsequently assessed for state taxes and responded by challenging the constitutionality of the 1804 statute. The New Jersey Supreme Court held the statute constitutional, maintaining that the tax exemption was a peculiar offshoot of relations between the American colonies and Indians, who were treated as members of foreign nations or as wards of the state rather than as citizens. The exemption from taxation, the New Jersey court concluded, could not be disassociated from the possession of the land by Indians.

The case was appealed to the Marshall Court under Section 25, and Marshall held, for a unanimous Court, that the 1804 New Jersey statute violated the Contract Clause. *Fletcher* v. *Peck* had settled that state contracts were covered by that clause, and the conveyance of land to the Indians, he announced, was clearly a "contract." "Every requisite to the formation of a contract," Marshall wrote, was "found in the [1758] proceedings between the then colony of New Jersey and the Indians." In exchange for their deed of cession of extensive claims to land, the Indians received "the privilege of exemption from taxation." Moreover, the immunity from taxation, "though for the benefit of the Indians," was "annexed . . . to the land itself, not to their persons." New Jersey could have insisted on a surrender of the immunity "as the sole condition on which a sale of the property should be allowed," but it had not. The result was a "contract . . . of unusual solemnity." Thus the new owners "succeed[ed] to all the rights of the Indians," and could "claim the benefit of their contract." That contract had "certainly [been] impaired" by the 1804 statute.[49]

There was not much new interpretation of the Contract Clause in *New Jersey* v. *Wilson:* a conveyance by the state to private individuals was the very kind of act *Fletcher* had deemed a contract for constitutional purposes. The only startling feature of the case was that the immunity given to the Indians was perpetual. Could a state legislature grant away

---

[47] Ibid., 165–66.
[48] Ibid., 166.

[49] 7 Cranch at 166–67.

its powers of taxation, binding its successors in the process? In *Fletcher* Marshall and Johnson had intimated that "one legislature [could] not infringe the powers of" another or divest itself of its "rights of jurisdiction."[50] Marshall conceded that "the state of New Jersey might have insisted on a surrender of [the exemption from taxation] as a sole condition on which a sale of the property should be allowed."[51] But by not doing so it had apparently precluded other legislatures from changing the rules: contractual rights had vested. Did this mean that a state grant to a private individual to use land in one fashion—say a fish hatchery—precluded its ever being used in any other fashion? Here one sees the power of the takings analogy in the early Contract Clause cases: the state's telling a landowner that his tract of land, previously exempt from taxation, was no longer immune was like the state's taking his land and giving it to someone else. It did not matter, apparently, that the state had donated the land in the first place, or that the taxing power was considered, by most republican theorists, as indispensable to the maintenance of government.[52]

*New Jersey* v. *Wilson* had been a Section 25 case, and while the Court avoided any recourse to general law in the opinion, the takings analogy seemed as important to the decision as it had been to *Fletcher* v. *Peck*. In *Terrett* v. *Taylor*,[53] the Court's next Contract Clause decision, the case came up on a writ of error from the federal circuit court of the District of Columbia, and general principles returned with a vengeance. Indeed, it is difficult to characterize *Terrett* v. *Taylor* as a Contract Clause case at all, since it is hard, from the case's facts, to know just what contract a state had impaired.

In *Terrett* the Episcopal Church had purchased a tract of land in Alexandria from Daniel Jennings in 1770.[54] In 1776 the Virginia state legislature had "confirmed and established" the church's title to the land, and in 1786 it had made the church "a corporation . . . to hold [its] property."[55] In 1798 the state of Virginia repealed those two statutes "as inconsistent with the principles of the constitution and of religious freedom," and in 1801, after the area on which the church property was situated had become part of the District of Columbia, the Virginia legislature "asserted their right" to the church's property, and directed that church lands should be sold and the proceeds used to care for the poor of the respective parishes.[56] Taylor, a vestryman of the church, sued

---

[50] 6 Cranch at 135, 143.
[51] 7 Cranch at 167.
[52] As Marshall was to concede in Providence Bank v. Billings, 4 Pet. 514, 563 (1830).

[53] 9 Cranch 43 (1815).
[54] Ibid., 43.
[55] Ibid., 47.
[56] Ibid., 48.

# Chapter IX: *The Contract Clause Cases*

Terrett, a county overseer for the poor, to prevent him from blocking any prospective sales of church land.

As stated, the case seemed to be absurdly easy to decide. The Virginia legislature was apparently not impairing a contract: it was attempting to take the property of A (the church) and give it to B (the overseers of the poor). It was, as a result, engaging in the paradigmatic violation of general principles previously alluded to. Moreover, the state of Virginia was attempting to regulate the disposition of territory in the District of Columbia, despite Article I, Section 8 of the Constitution, which had given Congress power to "exercise exclusive legislation in all cases whatsoever over such District." So the wonder of *Terrett* v. *Taylor* is that Story, for the Court, lingered over the case, did not have unanimous support for his opinion, and intimated that the act of the Virginia legislature may have violated the Contract Clause.

The paragraph in Story's *Terrett* opinion in which he ostensibly disposed of the case read, in pertinent part:

> [T]hat the legislature can repeal statutes creating private corporations, or confirming to them property already acquired under the faith of previous laws, and by such repeal can vest the property of such corporations exclusively in the state, or dispose of the same to such purposes as they may please, without the consent or default of the corporations, we are not prepared to admit; and we think ourselves standing on the principles of natural justice, upon the fundamental laws of every free government, upon the spirit and the letter of the Constitution of the United States, and upon the decisions of most respectable judicial tribunals, in resisting such a doctrine.[57]

Story's language suggested that the Court was invalidating the 1801 statute because it presented an example of a legislature's "dispos[ing] of vested property . . . as [it] may please," that is to say the paradigmatic "taking from A giving to B" problem. Such an action was contrary to "natural justice," the "fundamental laws of every free government," and the Constitution's "spirit and letter."

As to the last claim, three possible bases for the constitutional violation suggested themselves: the Takings Clause, the Contract Clause, and Article 1, Section 8's provision delegating to Congress all power to make laws affecting the District of Columbia. Of these three the Takings Clause could be eliminated because its language referred only to the federal government. The District of Columbia Clause seemed an obvious

---

[57] Ibid., 52.

possibility, but subsequent language in Story's opinion appeared to eliminate that. "[T]here is this farther objection," he wrote of the 1801 statute, "that it passed after the District of Columbia was taken under the exclusive jurisdiction of Congress, and as to the corporations and property within that district, the right of Virginia to legislate no longer existed."[58] It seems unlikely that Story would have designated this "objection" a "farther" one if he had meant it to be the source of his language about the "letter" of the Constitution. This leaves the Contract Clause, and there is evidence that it was that claim which Story had in mind. In his *Commentaries on the Constitution* Story cited *Terrett*, along with another case, *Town of Pawlet* v. *Clark*,[59] for the proposition that "if a state grant glebe lands, or other lands to parishes, towns, or private persons gratuitously, they constitute irrevocable executed contracts," and were within the reach of the Contract Clause. Kent, in his *Commentaries*, discussed *Terrett* in his review of "judicial decisions defining and enforcing" the Contract Clause, although his discussion stopped short of saying that clause was the basis of the Court's decision.[60] While Kent claimed that *Terrett* had held that "a legislative grant, competently made, vested an undefeasible and irrevocable title,"[61] there was no grant in *Terrett* and no language to that effect in Story's opinion. It is possible that Kent might have confused *Terrett* with *Town of Pawlet* v. *Clark*, in which Story had held for the Court that a grant of glebe lands to towns by the state of Vermont "could not afterwards be repealed by the legislature so as to divest the right of the towns under the grant."[62] But the decision in *Town of Pawlet* was based on general principles of common law, not on the Constitution.

A final unusual feature of Story's opinion in *Terrett* was that it may have had the support of only two or three additional Justices. Story conceded that the decision was that of a "majority of the Court,"[63] and Johnson and Todd were absent when the opinion was delivered. If one assumes that Justices designated as "absent" by the Reporter had not participated in the decision of the case, this left Marshall, Washington, Livingston, and Duvall in addition to Story, and at least one of those Justices had disagreed with the result. Whether that disagreement was directed at Story's reasoning or the decision itself, which declared the land to be the property of the Episcopal Church,[64] cannot be determined.

The early Contract Clause cases were notable in two respects. First, the takings analogy was sufficiently prominent to infuse its way into

[58] Ibid.
[59] 9 Cranch 292 (1815).
[60] J. Kent, *Commentaries on American Law* (4 vols., 1826), I, 387.
[61] Ibid., 389.
[62] 9 Cranch at 336.
[63] 9 Cranch at 55.
[64] Ibid., 51–52.

constitutional cases, even though it was founded on extraconstitutional principles, such as common law, natural justice, or republican theory. Not only did decisions such as *Fletcher* and *Terrett* invoke the analogy in cases purportedly of constitutional interpretation, commentators, including Story himself, included takings decisions such as *Town of Pawlet* along with constitutional decisions such as *New Jersey v. Wilson* in their discussions of the Contract Clause. Kent's claim, in his discussion, that the Contract Clause barred a state from repealing a grant it had previously made was not based on a constitutional decision but on a takings decision. Thus the Court, in early cases in which the Contract Clause appeared to be relevant, appears to have been uncertain as to whether that clause required the existence of a contract at all—even so unusual a contract as a legislative grant—or simply codified the general principle that a legislature could not take property from A and then give it to B or back to itself.

That uncertainty seemed puzzling in light of the fact that the early Contract Clause cases had come to the Court in two quite distinguishable ways. One was through Section 25, and in Section 25 cases the Court was limited to constitutional issues. Only *New Jersey v. Wilson,* of the early decisions, was such a case, and only there did the Court's opinion squarely and solely rest on a constitutional provision, albeit being laden with overtones of natural justice. In diversity cases from the lower federal courts, such as *Fletcher, Terrett,* and *Town of Pawlet,* the Court could evoke general principles as well as constitutional provisions, as it openly did in *Fletcher* and *Terrett.* In *Town of Pawlet* no constitutional issue was raised, the Court grounded its decision solely on general common law principles, and commentators subsequently transformed the case into a constitutional exercise.

What, then, was the role of the takings analogy in the early cases? The only constitutional provisions pertinent to the takings analogy were the Due Process Clause and the Takings Clause of the Fifth Amendment, which prohibited the federal government from engaging in uncompensated deprivations of private property. But none of the cases from *Fletcher* through *Terrett* involved acts of Congress. Nonetheless, the takings analogy surfaced, not only as relevant to the Contract Clause, but as a more general limitation on state legislatures. But the limitation had no express constitutional basis: its origins lay in common law and in republican theory. Thus the early cases suggested that as the Court entertained more Section 25 cases it would either have to reject the takings analogy or implant it into constitutional language itself, thereby packing the Contract Clause with the general principle that once property rights had vested, a legislature could not divest them without committing a taking. This implementation is precisely what occurred in the next series of Marshall

Court Contract Clause cases. In the process the alternative grounding of Contract Clause decisions on extraconstitutional principles was discarded.

The significance of the takings analogy, and of the jurisdictional process by which vested rights cases came to the Court, came to a head in *Trustees of Dartmouth College* v. *Woodward*.[65] The *Dartmouth College* case, in which the state of New Hampshire sought a full-scale modification of the relationship between Dartmouth College and the state, presented a classic takings situation: a subsequent legislature was seeking to modify the property rights granted to a corporation by its predecessor. At the same time the case came to the Court as a Section 25 case: The Fifth Amendment was irrelevant, and the basis of constitutional objection to New Hampshire's effort rested solely on the Contract Clause. *Dartmouth College* thus presented an ideal opportunity for the Court to constitutionalize the takings principle as a weapon against the states by reading it into the Contract Clause, and that is what Marshall, for the Court, sought to do. The case can be thought of as a dual exercise in strategy, with lawyers for Dartmouth College attempting to bring the case before the Court on diversity as well as Section 25 grounds, thereby inviting consideration of general as well as constitutional principles, and the Justices seeking to forge unanimity for the proposition that the Contract Clause constitutionalized protection for vested property rights, the doctrinal embodiment of the takings principle.

*Dartmouth College* was an ideal case for both those strategies because it arose out of a series of acts by the New Hampshire legislature that amounted to a classic taking of the property of A and giving it to B. The facts of *Dartmouth College* have been noted in Chapter III and will only be briefly summarized here. By a series of statutes passed in 1816, the legislature transformed the status of Dartmouth College, an institution that had been created by royal charter in 1769 and was governed, according to the terms of its charter, by twelve trustees who had the power to choose their successors. The statutes, we have seen, created a board of overseers, principally appointed by the governor of New Hampshire, to review the decisions of the trustees, increased the number of trustees to twenty-one, and provided that the new trustees would be appointed by the governor. In effect the statutes changed the college from a private to a public institution.

Dartmouth College had originally been chartered by the royal governor of New Hampshire, George Wentworth, who affixed George III's signature to the charter in 1769. The charter was the result of successful

---

[65] 4 Wheat. 518 (1819).

Chapter IX: *The Contract Clause Cases*

fund-raising efforts by Nathaniel Whitaker, a minister, and Samson Occom, an Indian who had been converted to Christianity, on behalf of a
school run by Eleazor Wheelock for the purpose of educating and converting young Indians in New Hampshire. The charter formally established a trust fund to support the school (to be named Dartmouth College
in honor of the earl of Dartmouth, one of the principal donors) and provided for the appointment of trustees to administer the fund and to serve
"forever thereafter [as] a body corporate and politick." The trustees "and
the successors forever" were given power to appoint and remove presidents of the College, to fill vacancies on the board of trustees, and to
make laws and regulations for the College. The trustees named Eleazor
Wheelock president, and Wheelock served in that capacity until his death
in 1779, when he was succeeded by his son John.[66]

As we have seen, various religious and political controversies surfaced at the College during John Wheelock's presidency, and by 1815
open hostility between Wheelock and certain members of the board of
trustees existed, each side publishing pamphlets attacking the other.
Meanwhile political factionalism had re-emerged in New Hampshire with
the renaissance of the Federalist party after 1810, and the Dartmouth
College schism was seen as a debate between Federalists, "the maintenance of chartered rights, and the established religious order" on one
side and Republicans, "reform in college management, and equality of
religious sects," on the other. In 1816 William Plumer, a Jeffersonian
Republican, was elected governor of New Hampshire and immediately
declared that Dartmouth's charter, with its provision for perpetual government by trustees, was "hostile to the spirit and genius of a free government."[67]

In June 1816, the New Hampshire legislature, controlled by Republicans, passed the statutes described above. The name of the College
was changed to Dartmouth University, and the institution was subjected
to periodic inspections by the governor and the Council of State. The
existing trustees of the College responded to the passage of the statutes
by resolving that "every literary institution in the State will hereafter hold
its rights, privileges and property, not according to the settled established
principles of law, but according to the arbitrary will and pleasure of every
successive legislature."[68]

---

[66] For secondary accounts of the
background to *Dartmouth College*, see
J. Shirley, *The Dartmouth College
Causes* (1879); A. Beveridge, *The Life
of John Marshall* (4 vols., 1919), IV,
220–61; M. Baxter, *Daniel Webster
and the Supreme Court* (1967), 65–80;

F. Stites, *Private Power and Public
Gain* (1972). See also the discussion in
Chapter III.
[67] Quoted in G. Barstow, *A History
of New Hampshire* (1842), 396.
[68] Quoted in J. Lord, *A History of
Dartmouth College* (1913), 694.

From the outset of the *Dartmouth College* case it was clear that the pivotal issue participants saw the case raising was, as Daniel Webster put it in his argument before the Marshall Court, whether a legislature could "take away from one . . . rights, property, and franchises, and give them to another."[69] And when the *Dartmouth College* case was argued before the New Hampshire Supreme Court, counsel for the College rested their argument entirely on general principles because the New Hamsphire constitution contained no Contract Clause. Since there was general agreement on the proposition that a legislature could not arbitrarily take private property from an individual, but at the same time it was understood that legislatures could regulate the activities of certain public corporations, such as cities or towns, attention focused on the character of Dartmouth College. Chief Justice William Richardson of the New Hampshire Supreme Court eventually grounded his decision sustaining the New Hampshire statutes on the theory that Dartmouth College was "a public corporation" whose "franchises [were] exercised for publick purposes."[70] Story's opinion for the Court in *Terrett v. Taylor* had conceded that legislatures could modify the charters of public corporations for public purposes, and Richardson seized on that language. But in the process he conceded, although it was unnecessary to do so, that the Contract Clause of the federal Constitution "embrace[d] all contracts relating to private property," and "was intended to protect private rights of property."[71] In so doing Richardson invited application of the Contract Clause should Dartmouth College be found to be a private corporation.

*Dartmouth College* came to the Marshall Court on a Section 25 writ of error, and thus the Contract Clause issue was the only one ostensibly before the court. This created concern on the part not only of Webster, who, as we have seen, wrote College trustee Charles Marsh in December 1817 that he preferred a case "which should present . . . all our points to the Supreme Court,"[72] but also of Story, who was subsequently to confess to one of the lawyers for the College, "I always had a desire that the question should be put upon the [broad] basis you have stated; and it was a matter of regret that we were so stinted in jurisdiction in the Supreme Court."[73]

An apparent opportunity to widen the scope of the *Dartmouth College* decision arose when the Justices failed to reach a consensus after the

---

[69] 4 Wheat. at 558.
[70] Dartmouth College v. Woodward, 65 N.H. 473, 628–29 (1817).
[71] Ibid., 639.
[72] D. Webster to C. Marsh, Dec. 8, 1817, Daniel Webster Papers, Dartmouth College Archives.

[73] J. Story to Jeremiah Mason, Oct. 6, 1819, in W. Story, *The Life and Letters of Joseph Story* (2 vols., 1851), I, 323.

# Chapter IX: *The Contract Clause Cases*

1818 arguments. Marshall announced on March 13, 1818, that the case would be continued until the 1819 Term because some judges had not formed opinions and others were of different opinions.[74] Webster wrote his co-counsel Jeremiah Mason in April 1818 that a reconstructed case, coming to the Court from a lower federal court, should be prepared. "[T]he question we must raise [in the reconstructed case]," Webster said, "is whether, by the general principles of our governments, the state legislatures be not restrained from divesting vested rights." Webster took this question to be "independent of the constitutional provision respecting contracts," and reminded Mason that he had "endeavoured to state . . . this proposition" in his 1818 argument before the Marshall Court, even though the issue was technically not before the Court.[75] Webster had, in fact, devoted thirty pages of his forty-nine-page argument to demonstrating that the "object and effect" of the New Hampshire statutes was "to take away from one, rights, property, and franchises, and grant them to another." Webster conceded that he was "aware of the limits which bound the jurisdiction of the Court" in *Dartmouth College,* but that the "true nature and character" of the New Hampshire statutes could be revealed by "compar[ing] them with those fundamental principles, introduced into the state governments for the purpose of limiting the exercise of the legislative power."[76]

A considerable mythology has sprung up respecting the peroration of Webster's 1818 argument. Webster had begun by attempting to demonstrate that the origins of Dartmouth College as a charitable fund-raising venture by Whitaker, Occom, and Wheelock demonstrated that it was a private institution. He then made a lengthy general principles argument, followed by a brief argument based on the Contract Clause, citing *Fletcher* and *Terrett,* and began his conclusion. At this point, observers in the courtroom reported, his tone noticeably shifted, and his last remarks were suffused with emotion. What did Webster say in his conclusion, and what reactions did he produce?

The mythology of Webster's peroration has principally emanated from an account of the argument given to Rufus Choate in 1852 by Chauncey Goodrich, a professor at Yale University, who attended the March 1818 argument. On learning that Choate would be giving a commemorative discourse on Webster at Dartmouth College in July 1853, Goodrich sent him a long letter reminiscing about Webster and included a description of Webster's peroration.[77] Goodrich had been twenty-eight

---

[74] Supreme Court Docket, Mar. 13, 1818, National Archives.

[75] D. Webster to J. Mason, Apr. 28, 1818, in F. Webster, ed., *The Private Correspondence of Daniel Webster* (2 vols., 1857), I, 282–83.

[76] 4 Wheat. at 550–51.

[77] The letter, written on March 10, 1818, is referred to in J. Sterling, *Daniel Webster and a Small College* (1965), 13–14, but the original has apparently been lost.

in 1818 and was sixty-four when he wrote to Choate. In Choate's discourse he reported Webster's peroration as follows, quoting from Goodrich's letter:

> *This, Sir is my case.* It is the case, not merely of that humble institution, it is the case of every college in our Land. It is the case of every eleemosynary institution throughout our country. . . . It is more. It is, in some sense, the case of every man who has property of which he may be stripped,—for the question is simply this: shall our State Legislatures be allowed to take *that which is not their own,* to turn it from its original use, and apply it to such ends or purposes as they, in their discretion, shall see fit? Sir, you may destroy this little institution; it is weak; it is in your hands! . . . You may put it out; but if you do, you must carry through your work! You must extinguish, one after another, all those great lights of science, which, for more than a century, have thrown their radiance over our Land! It is, Sir, as I have said, a small college. And yet *there are those who love it.* . . . Sir, I know not how others may feel, but, for myself, when I see my alma mater surrounded, like Caesar in the senate house, by those who are reiterating stab upon stab, I would not, for this right hand, have her say to me, *et tu quoque, mi fili!*[78]

Goodrich added that Webster's performance had elicited tears from spectators, and that Marshall himself was moved. The content of Webster's argument and its effect on observers, notably Marshall, have become part of the folklore of the history of the Court, and one can observe versions of Goodrich's account repeated in recent scholarly literature.[79] How much of Goodrich's account is accurate? There are four surviving contemporary recollections of the incident. None has Webster saying "it is a small college, and yet there are those who love it." One said that Webster "observed that in defending the college he was doing his duty— that it should never . . . address him in the words of the Roman dictator," and that William Wirt, arguing for Dartmouth University, had "introduced [the] ghost of [Wheelock] exclaiming to Webster 'et tu Brute.' "[80] Webster did not include his peroration when he arranged to have copies of his argument printed in April 1818, informing Mason that "all the stuff and nonsense is left out,"[81] and thus none of the material quoted by Goodrich is included in Wheaton's report of the case.

---

[78] Quoted in S. Brown, *Works of Choate* (2 vols., 1862), I, 187–88. Emphasis in original.

[79] See, e.g., Stites, *Private Power,* 64.

[80] Salma Hale to William Plumer, Mar. 24, 1818, Dartmouth College Archives.

[81] D. Webster to J. Mason, Apr. 23, 1818, in J. McIntyre, ed., *Writings and Speeches of Daniel Webster* (18 vols., 1903), XVII, 281.

## Chapter IX: *The Contract Clause Cases*

There is more support for Goodrich's claim that Webster moved his audience to tears. The Boston *Columbian Centinel* reported that Webster had made "a dignified and pathetic peroration which charmed and melted his hearers."[82] Louis McLane, writing to John Milligan shortly after the argument, said, "I heard Judge Marshall say, that when Webster opined the argument, he thought nothing could exceed the solidity, or the beauty of his conclusion, which wrapped the whole Court in tears," and that "[Robert] Harper shed tears when he repeated to me a part of Webster's conclusion."[83] Salma Hale, an eyewitness to the argument, reported that "Webster . . . appeared himself to be much affected," and that "the audience was silent as death" during the peroration.[84]

And there is also a recollection of Webster's argument by Story, written twelve years later as part of an unpublished review of a volume of Webster's speeches. Story and Webster were close friends, and the review may have been an effort to enhance Webster's national visibility. In the manuscript Story said:

> [W]hen [Webster] came to his peroration, there was in his whole air and manner, in the fiery flashings of his eye, the darkness of his contracted brow, the sudden and flying flushes of his cheeks, the quivering and scarcely manageable movements of his lips in the deep guttural tones of his voice, in the struggle to suppress his emotions, in the almost convulsive clenchings of his hands without a seeming consciousness of the act, there was in these things what gave to his oratory an almost superhuman influence. . . . There was a painful anxiety towards the close. The whole audience had been wrought up to the highest excitement; many were dissolved in tears; many betrayed the most agitating mental struggles; many were sinking under exhausting efforts to conceal their own emotion. When Mr. Webster ceased to speak, it was some minutes before anyone seemed inclined to break the silence.[85]

Story, as we have seen, had a tendency toward "vivid writing," and one wonders how he could discern that many spectators were "sinking under exhausting efforts to conceal their own emotion." Notably absent from Story's account is any reference to the Chief Justice, but Story might not

---

[82] Boston *Columbian Centinel*, Mar. 11, 1818.

[83] L. McLane to J. Milligan, Mar. 15, 1818, Dartmouth College Archives. My thanks to Professors Alfred Konefsky of the State University of New York at Buffalo and Andrew King of the University of Maryland for allowing me access to the Hale and McLane letters, which will appear in their forthcoming volume of the papers of Daniel Webster.

[84] Hale to Plumer, Mar. 24, 1818, supra, note 80.

[85] J. Story, unpublished manuscript, Joseph Story Papers, Library of Congress, quoted in E. Wheeler, *Daniel Webster, The Expounder of the Constitution* (1905), 30–31.

have wanted to convey the impression that members of the Court could be moved by the rhetorical flourishes of counsel. Story's version does, however, describe members of the audience in tears.

It seems clear that Webster's peroration was an emotional moment, and there is no reason to doubt that he used language such as "the case . . . is . . . one of every man who has property of which he may be stripped": that "general principle"was the essence of his argument. But before accepting the Choate–Goodrich version as accurate one should recall that no original record of Goodrich's letter to Choate exists,[86] that Goodrich was recalling events thirty-four years after they occurred, that Choate, himself a vivid and eloquent speaker and a disciple of Webster, was using Goodrich's account in a public eulogy, and that no other contemporary observer corroborated Webster's language. Neither did any contemporary observer, including Goodrich, refer to Marshall as being in tears, although McLean reported Marshall as having so described himself. It is of course, doubtful that Webster's peroration had any effect on the outcome of the case; Webster's omission of the peroration from a printed argument that he was distributing to help influence the outcome of the case suggests, in fact, that he thought it mere "stuff and nonsense." Thus one would be justified in concluding, absent more direct evidence, that the author of the celebrated phrase "it is a small college . . . and yet there are those who love it," was not Daniel Webster but Chauncey Goodrich.

After the 1818 argument, Story, as we have previously seen, intimated to Webster in a conversation in Massachusetts in the spring of 1818 that he would welcome a reconstructed case in the federal courts. Three diversity cases were initiated in March 1818, and in May of that year all were certified by Story to the Supreme Court on a *pro forma* certificate of division. Meanwhile Webster decided to distribute copies of his argument in the case, sending Story five copies of the argument in September 1818, adding that if Story should "send one of them to each of such of the judges as you think proper," he "of course [should] do it [in a manner] least likely to lead to a feeling that any indecorum has been committed by the plaintiff."[87] Between June and December, 1818, Webster, aware that Story was working on an opinion in the case, sent him sources and citations for reference.[88]

---

[86] There is a December 4, 1852, letter from Choate to Goodrich acknowledging Goodrich's letter in the Rufus Choate Papers, Yale University Library.

[87] D. Webster to J. Story, Sept. 9,

1818, in F. Webster, *Private Correspondence*, I, 287.

[88] See D. Webster to J. Story, June 29, 1818; July 3, 1818; Aug. 16, 1818; and Dec. 27, 1818; all in Joseph Story Papers, Massachusetts Historical Society, Boston, Mass.

# Chapter IX: *The Contract Clause Cases*

By the end of the year Story had "nearly finished an opinion" in *Dartmouth College,* he told Henry Wheaton. "You know," he reminded Wheaton, "I was without one after the [March 1818] argument."[89] That January Story circulated his opinion to some friends and fellow Justices, and Justice Livingston responded by telling Story, "I hope it will be adopted without alteration."[90] Story's opinion, which was eventually published as a concurrence, devoted forty-two of its forty-seven pages to the vested rights argument, concluding that since Dartmouth College was a private corporation "the rights legally vested in a corporation cannot be controlled or destroyed by any subsequent statute, unless a power for that purpose be reserved to the legislature in the act of incorporation." That conclusion was based on "principles . . . consonant with justice, sound policy, and legal reasoning,"[91] and with "the common sense of mankind, and the maxims of eternal justice."[92] Those principles and maxims, Story claimed, derived "from the very nature of our governments."[93] But notwithstanding the "perfect correctness" of the principles, Story conceded, "the application of them . . . does not, from our limited authority, properly belong to the appellate jurisdiction of this Court in this case." Thus he devoted his last five pages to an analysis of the Contract Clause argument, concluding that "any act of a legislature which takes away any powers . . . vested by its charter in a private corporation . . . is a violation of the obligations of that charter."[94]

Two features of Story's opinion are noteworthy. The great deal of space he devoted to the vested rights dimensions of the *Dartmouth College* case suggests that he expected that a reconstituted case would eventually come to the Court, and that the takings analogy, now expanded to the idea that a legislature could not disturb vested rights, was the fundamental principle raised by New Hampshire's actions. But Story's treatment of vested rights appeared to give a selective definition of that concept. Legislatures, he maintained, could not control or destroy vested rights unless they had reserved a power to do so when they granted the rights themselves. What did this mean? It appeared to mean, first, that vested rights were not natural rights: they were rights created by government. It also appeared to mean that the feature of a right which made it "vest" was the expectation in the possessor that it would not be subsequently infringed. Legislative retention of a reserved power to modify or abrogate rights conferred in a charter meant that the charterers had no expectation

---

[89] J. Story to H. Wheaton, Dec. 30, 1818, in Henry Wheaton Papers, Pierpont Morgan Library, New York, N.Y.
[90] B. Livingston to J. Story, Jan. 24, 1819, in W. Story, *Life and Letters,* I, 323.

[91] 4 Wheat. at 708.
[92] Ibid., 707.
[93] Ibid., 695.
[94] Ibid., 708, 710, 712.

that they could exercise the rights free from future interference. The absence of a reserved legislative power, by contrast, created an expectation of unrestricted enjoyment: it was that expectation which caused the conferred right to "vest."

As Story envisaged vested rights, then, they were solely the creation of the legislature. Indeed, legislatures could violate the takings principle if they reserved a power to do so. Story's analysis of vested rights thus contained an internal ambiguity. If vested rights were solely legal creations and could be infringed at will, so long as the infringement power was reserved at their creation, what was the "fundamental principle of republican governments" that prevented a legislature from taking property from A and giving it to B? Apparently that principle could be vitiated if the legislature simply told A, when it first conferred the property, that a subsequent taking could occur. Or perhaps the takings principle only applied to private property that had not originally been conferred by a government. But *Dartmouth College* suggested that property always came from some government entity, even if it were the British crown.

Meanwhile, Justice Johnson, who had also apparently not formed an opinion after hearing the 1818 arguments, traveled to New England during the summer of 1818, looking for papers for a biography of Major General Nathanael Greene, Washington's second-in-command in the Revolutionary War. Supporters of the College's position had been engaging in a campaign to publicize their cause that spring and summer, and Charles Marsh, a judge of the New Hampshire Supreme Court and a trustee of the College, arranged to have Webster's 1818 argument sent to James Kent, then the chancellor of New York and already a jurist of considerable reputation. Kent had read Richardson's opinion and, "on a hasty perusal," concluded that "Dartmouth College was a public establishment" and that "the legislature was competent to pass the laws in question."[95] On reading Webster's argument, however, Kent wrote Marsh, he had seen "a new complexion to the case," and "it is very probable that . . . I should be led to a different conclusion from the one I had first formed."[96]

The day after Kent wrote Marsh, August 27, 1818, Johnson visited Kent in Albany, where Francis Brown, then president of Dartmouth College, was subsequently to go to seek support from New York Governor

---

[95] J. Kent to C. Marsh, Aug. 26, 1818, quoted in Shirley, *Dartmouth College*, 263. Shirley regularly quoted from letters without revealing their location. As Albert Beveridge said of Shirley's *The Dartmouth College Causes*, it is "crammed with the results of extensive research, strange conglomeration of facts, suppositions, inferences, and insinuations . . . inextricably mingled." Beveridge, *John Marshall*, IV, 258).

[96] Kent to Marsh, ibid.

# Chapter IX: *The Contract Clause Cases*

DeWitt Clinton.[97] Brown wrote Webster from Albany in September 1818, telling him of Kent's changed views on the case and of Kent's meeting with Johnson. Kent had said to Brown, according to Brown's letter, "that [Johnson] conversed on our case, and remarked that the court had a cause of 'awful' magnitude to decide. From what I learn from other sources [Johnson] has formally requested [Kent's] opinion. This opinion, if given, will also have great influence on Judge Livingston." Brown added that Kent had "read the [original] charter [of Dartmouth College], and it is evident to me that he is satisfied."[98] A week later Brown wrote Webster that "there is no doubt that, by the argument and the charter, [Kent] is brought completely over to our side," and that he believed Kent would "take every proper and prudent measure to impart correct views to others."[99] Brown also indicated that Kent would be transmitting a copy of Webster's argument to Johnson, apparently with Kent's new views. By September 19 Brown was able to write Webster that "New England [by which he meant Story] and New York [Livingston] *are gained*" on the side of the college, and "the current of opinion from this part of the country is setting so strongly towards the South [Johnson] that we may safely trust to its force alone to accomplish whatever is necessary."[100]

While this maneuvering was going on, Marshall was preparing an opinion, which was ultimately adopted as "the opinion of the Court."[101] It is difficult to say what that nomenclature meant in the *Dartmouth College* case. Of the seven members of the Court, one, Justice Thomas Todd, missed the entire 1819 Term "on account of indisposition";[102] another, Gabriel Duvall, dissented without opinion; and four of the other five judges wrote opinions. Marshall's opinion was followed by one by Washington, in which Livingston, who did not publish his opinion, concurred. Johnson issued a statement that he concurred "for the reasons stated by the Chief Justice."[103] Story issued a separate opinion, in which Livingston also concurred, and Livingston, in addition, "concurred for the reasons stated by the Chief Justice."[104] If those actions are taken to be comparable to modern procedure, this would result in only three judges, Marshall, Johnson, and Livingston, joining "the opinion of the

[97] F. Brown to D. Webster, Sept. 8, 1818, Timothy Farrar Papers, New Hampshire Historical Society, Concord, N.H. See Shirley, *Dartmouth College*, 264–66; D. Morgan, *Justice William Johnson* (1954), 215.

[98] Brown to Webster, Sept. 8, 1818, supra, note 97.

[99] F. Brown to D. Webster, Sept. 15, 1818, quoted in Shirley, *Dartmouth College*, 268–69.

[100] F. Brown to D. Webster, Sept. 19, 1818, quoted in ibid., 270–71. Emphasis in original. It is interesting that at this late date Brown believed Story to have been recently "gained": Webster had known of Story's position since April.

[101] 4 Wheat. at 624.

[102] Ibid., iii.

[103] Ibid., 666.

[104] Ibid.

Court,'' two writing separate concurrences, one dissenting, and one taking no part.

But it is clear that the procedure followed in the *Dartmouth College* case was much more informal. After Marshall's announcement on March 13 that the case would be continued, there was little additional business to dispose of. Since the Justices would now scatter, the clear implication of Marshall's comments was that those Justices who had not made up their minds should seek to do so within the interval, and that a majority, or better, a unanimous Court, should be forged. There would be little opportunity to confer, given distances and travel; the obvious means of arriving at a decision or persuading others to adopt one's views was to write and circulate a draft opinion. Given the situation, the Justices departed from the usual practice of silent acquiescence. Marshall, Story, Washington, and Livingston prepared opinions, and Story, at least, circulated his to friends.[105] The 1819 Term opened on February 1, and on February 2 Marshall, according to Webster, announced that ''the judges had formed opinions in the college case. [Marshall] then immediately began reading his opinion.''[106]

Why was Marshall's opinion chosen as the opinion of the Court? Not much evidence exists to clarify this question. We have seen that it had been the practice of the Marshall Court to have opinions delivered on seniority grounds, even if the Justice delivering the opinion had not written it, but this practice was changing by the 1819 Term.[107] There was also a clear tendency to have Marshall write for the Court in constitutional cases: between 1802 and 1818 Marshall had written fourteen of the twenty majority opinions in cases raising constitutional issues.[108] Finally, there is abundant evidence that Marshall was a conciliatory force on his Court.[109] Nowhere, perhaps, is Marshall's ability to pacify his fellow

---

[105] *See,* e.g., William Prescott to J. Story, Jan. 9, 1819, in W. Story, *Life and Letters,* I, 324, where Prescott wrote Story, ''I have read your opinion with care and great pleasure.'' At this point the Court's opinion had not been officially rendered.

[106] D. Webster to J. Mason, Feb. 4, 1819, quoted in G. Hilliard, *Memoirs and Correspondence of Jeremiah Mason* (1873), 213.

[107] See Haskins and Johnson, *Foundations of Power,* 386–87. See also discussion in Chapter III.

[108] R. Seddig, ''John Marshall and the Origins of Supreme Court Leadership,'' *U. Pitt. L. Rev.,* 36:785, 800 (1975).

[109] Of the numerous descriptions of Marshall's role as a conciliator, a particularly vivid one is furnished by Shirley, *Dartmouth College,* 377:

[H]e had an ardent social nature, a seductive personal magnetism; he was a delightful companion, fluent and facile in conversation, and, aside from Andrew Johnson, the most eloquent listener in the Union; he was full of sly, waggish humor, genial and convivial; his temper was serene and imperturbable, his patience almost inexhaustible, and his judgment cool, wary, and calculating . . . He was a born diplomatist . . . a natural politician.

judges more apparent than in Johnson's concurrence in *Dartmouth College*. In *Fletcher* v. *Peck* Marshall had identified the Contract Clause as part of the grounds for his holding, and Johnson had explicitly rejected that argument for one based on general principles. Now in *Dartmouth College* Story issued an opinion in which a general principles argument occupied the position of prominence. Johnson, however, pointedly avoided concurring with Story and associated himself with the opinion of Marshall, which not only rested on the Contract Clause but extended the reach of that clause further than had *Fletcher* v. *Peck*. A continuation of established practices and internal politics thus appears to have resulted in Marshall's opinion standing for the Court in *Dartmouth College*.

The opinion was itself a typically Marshallian exercise in the constitutional construction of pivotal words, in particular "charter" and "corporation." The structure of Marshall's argument was as follows. The Contract Clause concededly covered only contracts involving private property. The royal charter to Dartmouth College was a contract and Dartmouth College a private corporation. Private corporations could be said to acquire property rights as much as natural persons; the rights that had vested in the *Dartmouth College* case were those of the corporation, which by its charter was to be governed by its trustees and their successors forever. And the vested rights of a private eleemosynary corporation were protected from state interference by the Contract Clause. The full argument, as one of Marshall's biographers has said, was at times "brief, clear, and pointed," and at other times "prolix, diffuse, and repetitious."[110]

Marshall disposed of the question whether Dartmouth's charter was a contract by assertion. He characterized the process by which the charter was formed as originating with "an application . . . made to the crown for a charter to incorporate a religious and literary institution."[111] This statement represented a slight tinkering with facts. The royal charter to Dartmouth College, we have seen, actually originated as a consequence of fund-raising efforts for an existing school, not at that time in New Hampshire at all. There was no "application" to the crown; there was, instead, a charter to Wheelock and the trustees to manage the funds as they saw fit "forever." The trustees incorporated because they found it convenient to do so, not because of any condition in the charter application. Marshall's claim that "the charter [was] granted, and on its faith the property [was] conveyed," appears to be an overstatement, and his summary comment that "surely in this transaction every ingredient of a complete and legitimate contract is to be found"[112] seems to beg the

---

[110] Beveridge, *John Marshall*, IV, 264.

[111] 4 Wheat. at 627.

[112] Ibid.

question. What, for example, was the consideration for the crown's gift? But the point is not particularly significant, since it was clear after *Fletcher* v. *Peck* and *Terrett* v. *Taylor* that unilateral grants were contracts, and the royal charter to the trustees was unmistakably a grant.

But were all "political relations between the government and its citizens" to be considered "contracts"? Marshall did not want to be burdened with so latitudinarian a view of the Contract Clause: he conceded that it "never has been understood to embrace other contracts, than those which respect property . . . and confer rights which may be asserted in a court of justice."[113] The Contract Clause had been inserted in the Constitution, Marshall claimed, in response to "a course of legislation [that] had prevailed in many, if not in all, of the states, which weakened the confidence of man in man, and embarrassed all transactions between individuals by dispensing with a faithful performance of engagements." Its purpose was "to restrain the legislature in future from violating the right to property."[114] The clause, then, was thus a "vested rights" clause, designed to insulate established private property from being subsequently taken by a legislature. Other "impairments" of "contracts," such as legislation "on the subject of divorces," were outside the scope of the clause.[115]

For Marshall, the crucial question in the case was thus whether the charter incorporating Dartmouth College created "a civil institution . . . to be employed in the administration of the government" or "a private eleemosynary institution, endowed with a capacity to take property for objects unconnected with government."[116] If Dartmouth College was intended to be the former, its activities could be restrained by the state of New Hampshire. Eleven pages later Marshall had "ascertain[ed] the true character" of the College. Dartmouth College was a private eleemosynary institution, incorporated "for the purpose of perpetuating the application of the bounty of the donors." Its trustees were "not public officers": it had been established "for the preservation of its property, and the perpetual application of that property to the objects of its creation."[117]

At this point the only doctrinal innovation Marshall seemed to have made was his hint that corporations could be treated as "property owners" within the meaning of the Contract Clause.[118] Grants were already understood to be contracts, and a distinction between public and private corporations for the purposes of legislative regulation had been formulated

---

113 Ibid., 629.
114 Ibid., 628.
115 Ibid., 629.
116 Ibid.
117 Ibid., 640.
118 Even this point was not all that innovative in light of Marshall's deci-

sion in Bank of United States v. Deveaux, 5 Cranch 61 (1809), which allowed the Bank of the United States to be sued in federal court, and concluded that individuals do not lose legal "privileges" by becoming members of corporations. Ibid., 87.

by Story in *Terrett* v. *Taylor*. But now Marshall took steps to make his earlier suggestion explicit: corporations were to have the protection of the Contract Clause.

When one searched for the owners of the vested rights ostensibly being infringed by the New Hampshire legislature, Marshall began, one found a peculiar situation. The "founders of the college" had "parted with the property bestowed upon it, and their representatives have no interest in that property." The "donors of land" were in a similar situation. The students of the College were "fluctuating, and no individual among our youth has a vested interest in the institution which can be asserted in a Court of Justice." And the trustees, who "alone complain, . . . have no beneficial interest to be protected." Could the Dartmouth College charter thus "be such a contract as the constitution intended to withdraw from the power of State legislation?" Marshall reminded his readers that "only . . . contracts, the parties to which have a vested beneficial interest . . . are the objects about which the constitution is solicitous."[119]

"The Court's . . . most deliberate consideration" of this issue, Marshall announced, had resulted in the corporation's being deemed the owner of the affected vested interest. The corporation "represented" the descendants of the donors. It was "the assignee of their rights, stands in their place, and distributes their bounty, as they would themselves have distributed it, had they been immortal." The corporation was also "a trustee . . . for the students who are to derive learning from this source." The "aggregate . . . interest" of those students was "asserted and protected by the corporation."[120]

It was "more than possible," Marshall conceded, that the "preservation of [the] rights [of corporations] was "not particularly in the view of the framers of the constitution" when they "introduced [the Contract Clause] into that instrument." But to show "that this particular case was not in the mind of the Convention" was not enough, he claimed, to bring the case outside the scope of constitutional coverage. Since a charter incorporating a private corporation was "within the words of the rule," it must be "within its operation likewise, unless there be something in the literal construction so obviously absurd, or mischievous, or repugnant to the general spirit of the instrument, as to justify those who experienced the constitution for making it an exception."[121]

Needless to say, Marshall found nothing "repugnant to the general spirit" of the Constitution in including corporate vested rights within the scope of those rights protected by the Contract Clause. He found no

---

[119] Ibid., 641–42.
[120] Ibid., 642–43.

[121] Ibid., 644–45.

"nature and reason of the case itself that . . . sustain a construction of the constitution not warranted by its words."[122] He found that the Copyright Clause of the Constitution indicated the Framers' interest in "contracts made for the advancement of literature."[123] And he found no "public policy [that] demand[ed] that corporate charters remain exposed to legislative alteration."[124] The only difficulty with the last point was that some of the original trustees might have been loyal to the crown; but "reasoning *a priori* one should believe that learned and intelligent men . . . would select learned and intelligent men for their successors," and one could not assume that "while the light of science and of liberal principles, pervades the whole community, these originally benighted trustees remain in utter darkness, incapable of participating in the general improvement."[125]

Marshall had one more argument to make, a particularly delicate one. He had to show that while the New Hampshire legislature was bound by the original terms of the charter, to which it had not been a party, it did not have the power to terminate the charter as well, a power that Marshall had earlier conceded to Parliament. "To annul corporate rights might have given a shock to public opinion," Marshall said of Parliament, but "its power is not questioned." Had Parliament "annulled the [charter] . . . after [its] emanation," it could have done so, even though "the perfidy of the transaction would have been universally acknowledged."[126] The colonial legislature of New Hampshire had similar powers, subject to the New Hampshire constitution: "a repeal of this charter at any time prior to the adoption of the present constitution of the United States . . . could have been contested only by the restrictions upon the legislature to be found in the constitution of the State."[127] These sentences came close to suggesting that a state legislature certainly had the power to take away property that it had previously given, unless it was restrained by some specific state constitutional provision.

But Marshall was not interested in limits on the legislative power that might be imposed by state law. He grounded his *Dartmouth College* opinion on the "additional limitation" on legislative power imposed by the United States Constitution, the Contract Clause. His reluctance to make use of a general vested rights argument might seem like an opportunity lost until one considers all that Marshall packed into his Contract Clause argument. Not only did he find that a royal charter granting perpetual rights to a group of trustees in a distant colony was a contract, he expanded the "rights to property" under the Contract Clause to include corporate rights, thereby intimating that any legislative efforts to regulate

---

122 Ibid., 645.
123 Ibid., 646.
124 Ibid., 645.

125 Ibid., 650.
126 Ibid., 643.
127 Ibid., 651.

# Chapter IX: *The Contract Clause Cases*

the activities of chartered private corporations might violate the Contract Clause. And by "private" corporations he meant not only banks or mills, but charitable institutions. Further, he had reaffirmed his view that the purpose of the Contract Clause was "to restrain the legislature . . . from violating the right to property," and laid down a rule of constitutional construction that property rights of various kinds (corporate as well as individual, charitably created as well as emanating from the marketplace) were presumed to be eligible for the protection of the Contract Clause unless "there be something . . . absurd, or mischievous, or repugnant in that construction." He had, in short, significantly broadened the scope of the Contract Clause.

Nowhere in Marshall's opinion was there a suggestion that legislatures could escape the Contract Clause of the Constitution by reserving the right to modify the terms of a corporate charter. But Story's concurrence twice indicated that the power to "control or destroy . . . rights legally vested in a corporation" could be "reserved to the legislature in the incorporating charter," citing an 1806 Massachusetts decision.[128] Given this statement, which a majority of the Court never challenged, and given a subsequent tendency on the part of some legislatures to reserve the power to alter or repeal charter provisions,[129] the *Dartmouth College* decision did not become an emancipation proclamation for corporations. Marshall may have intended to free corporations from any legislative restrictions in *Dartmouth College,* but it was more likely that his strategy was simply to remind contemporaries how much theoretical baggage was contained in the words "impair the Obligation of Contracts." It was characteristic of Marshall to interfuse "general principles" with the specific language of the Constitution, thereby remaining faithful to the text but at the same time packing its words with ideological meaning. His opinion in *Dartmouth College* suggested that the word "contract" was to be used as a shorthand expression conveying the importance of solicitude for private property rights in a republic. The general principles argument developed in *Fletcher* v. *Peck* and *Terrett* v. *Taylor,* while not strictly applicable to Contract Clause analysis, had been incorporated into that analysis.[130]

*Dartmouth College* was thus a case in which the Court tacitly elected to abandon the alternative grounding of vested rights decisions on extraconstitutional principles or on the constitutional text. After *Dartmouth*

---

[128] Ibid., 708, 712.

[129] E.g., New York (1826), Massachusetts (1831), Maine (1831), Ohio (1842), New Jersey (1846). See S. Kutler, *Privilege and Creative Destruction* (1971), 62–63.

[130] In a letter written to James Kent

in 1819 Story expressed hope that the public would become aware that "the security of private rights" was "the principle . . . on which [*Dartmouth College*] rested." J. Story to J. Kent, Aug. 21, 1819, in W. Story, *Life and Letters,* I, 331.

*College* all of the Court's vested rights cases confined themselves to an analysis of the Contract Clause. The strategy had two advantages. First, it meant that the procedural posture by which a vested rights case came to the Court would no longer be significant. Section 25 cases, confined to federal constitutional issues, would be governed by an expanded Contract Clause, a clause that had been read to incorporate the general principles available to the Court in certificate of division cases. Second, the packing of a textual provision with extraconstitutional principles avoided any difficulty that might arise from an appeal to principles that were not embodied in textual language. As the stature of natural law as a body of principles independent of the positive enactments of a nation eroded in the nineteenth century, the summoning up of general principles as a basis for a judicial decision became more problematic. But if those principles had been read into a constitutional provision, the difficulty was surmounted.

*Dartmouth College* thus began a new phase in the history of the Marshall Court's Contract Clause decisions. The principle of protection for vested rights had been identified with the clause; the question then became what sorts of contracts established vested rights and thus qualified recipients of those rights for constitutional protection. This question was another way of asking how far the takings analogy extended to legislative grants: if a grant was a contract, when was a subsequent modification of that grant a taking? When, in short, did property rights vest? These questions invited a reconsideration of the implications of protection for private property rights in America.

While *Dartmouth College* was a significant doctrinal departure from the earlier Contract Clause cases, *Fletcher, New Jersey* v. *Wilson, Terrett,* and *Dartmouth College* were of a piece in that they represented a steady broadening of the restrictive effect of the Contract Clause and a resultant widening of the autonomy of property rights in the American republic. But in the same year that the opinion in *Dartmouth College* was delivered, another vested rights case was argued before the Court, *Sturges* v. *Crowninshield,* and some inherent ambiguities contained in the area of solicitude for private property rights came to the surface. When property rights were pitted against legislative efforts to restrict them, the line of cases from *Fletcher* through *Dartmouth College* suggested that where the property rights were private they came under the protection of the Contract Clause. But when one set of property rights was sought to be regulated by a legislature so as to facilitate the exercise of another set, the choice seemed puzzling and by no means obvious. Bankruptcy legislation posed that choice.

The problem of bankruptcy signified a modification of attitudes toward the place of property in a republic. The modification can be traced to perceptions about the consequences for republican theory of a dramatic growth in the American population. To republican theorists such as Jefferson and Madison the Achilles' heel of republican polity appeared to be population expansion. Population increases would not invariably result in more people being able to acquire property, there being a limit to men's talents and to natural resources. As more propertyless persons populated the nation, gaps between the few and the many might become ominously large, large enough to threaten the stability of the republic. Jefferson felt that while "an equal division of property is impracticable," an "enormous inequality" between the propertied and the propertyless would "produc[e] so much misery to the bulk of mankind."[131] Madison agreed that "no problem in political economy [was] more puzzling than that which relates to the most proper distribution of the inhabitants of a country fully peopled." Regardless of how lands were distributed, and regardless of the demand for labor, a "great surplus" of unpropertied, dependent inhabitants would emerge. "What is to be done with this surplus?" Madison asked.[132]

The presence of an unpropertied, dependent "surplus" in the population was regarded as threatening to the ideal of a republic because this surplus was susceptible to demagoguery or class warfare. Corruption, one of the arch villains of republican theory, would inevitably occur when the "poverty and dependence" of the surplus members of the population "render[ed] them the mercenary instruments of wealth." On the one hand, if the propertyless "unite[d] against the [propertied class]," they became "the dupes and instruments of ambition," and "a despotism growing out of anarchy" resulted.[133] For a time republican theorists felt that these ominous possibilities could be avoided by the abundance of free land in America, which seemed to afford the possibility of expanding and preserving a republic in which property could be distributed properly. Jefferson had written in 1816, for example, that "a government of representation is capable of extension over a greater surface of country than one of any other form." The "enlargement of the resources of life," he noted a year later, might "go hand in hand with the enlargement of territory."[134] But by the 1820s Jefferson[135] and especially Madison were

---

[131] Thomas Jefferson to James Madison, Oct. 28, 1785, in R. Rutland, ed., *The Papers of James Madison* (15 vols., 1973), VIII, 386–87.
[132] J. Madison to T. Jefferson, June 19, 1786, in ibid., IX, 76–77.
[133] J. Madison, "Remarks on Mr. Jefferson's Draught of a Constitution," October 1788, in M. Meyers, ed., *The Mind of the Founder* (1973), 59.

[134] T. Jefferson to Pierre Samuel DuPont deNemours, Dec. 31, 1815, in D. Malone, ed., *Correspondence between Thomas Jefferson and Pierre Samuel DuPont deNemours, 1798–1817* (1930), 172–73.
[135] See McCoy, *Elusive Republic*, 253–55.

voicing fears that eventually the supply of free land would be exhausted, and then a large percentage of the population would be "without landed or other equivalent property and without the means or hope of acquiring it." At that point the twin spectres of oligarchic corruption and despotic anarchy might well become real, since massive gaps would occur between the situations of "wealthy capitalists" and those of "indigent laborers."[136]

The interaction of economic development, protection for property, and population growth thus was seen as having foreboding consequences as the American nation grew rapidly in the early nineteenth century. In particular, republican theorists came to recognize that solicitude for property rights could, in a society where population was steadily growing, have the effect of retarding opportunities to acquire property. Thus while solicitude for property rights remained a central concern of early-nineteenth-century republican theorists, some commentators came to recognize that protection for one person's property rights could preclude others from "the means or hope of acquiring" property. Out of this concern came the great debates of the 1820s about eminent domain, state-supported franchises, and property restrictions on suffrage.[137]

The problem of bankruptcy was another example of an issue that brought the ambiguities in the concept of property to the surface. The view of borrowing and lending inherited from colonial times defined the debtor as having an absolute obligation to repay the creditor according to the terms of the lending agreement, regardless of subsequent changes in the value of money, the money supply, or the circumstances of the parties. Failure to pay one's debts was socially stigmatic as well as fiscally irresponsible; it could result in imprisonment. This view was consistent with regarding the lending of money as the equivalent of the renting of real property: while the borrower (or tenant) had the use of the property, absolute property rights remained in the owner. Given that view, a clear example of property rights having vested took place when a debtor borrowed money from a creditor.

But in the face of this view several states, from the Revolution on, passed laws allowing debtors to declare themselves insolvent or to take bankruptcy and thereby reduce or wholly eliminate their outstanding obligations. Several factors contributed to the passage of this legislation. First, venture capital was exceedingly important in America, given the undeveloped state of the country, and a great many people were required to take risks in order to engage in business at all. Second, business "fail-

---

[136] J. Madison, notes made in 1821 on a speech to the constitutional convention in 1787, in Meyers, *Mind of the Founder,* 504–505.

[137] A useful compendium of the debates is Peterson, *Democracy, Liberty, and Property,* supra, note 5.

ures'' and subsequent successes were common; bankruptcy legislation prevented creditors from levying on future assets and gave embarrassed borrowers a chance to rehabilitate themselves. Third, the absence of bankruptcy or insolvency legislation meant that procedures for the enforcement of debts were not regularized and that imprisonment for debt was a likely outcome. The absence of regularized procedures meant that the first creditor could prevent others from having their obligations repaid, and imprisonment for debt meant that an insolvent would be unable to work, unable to repay debts, and likely to become a public ward. Finally, the unstable condition of the American economy in the early nineteenth century meant that debtors and creditors were both faced with constant uncertainties about the value of the money with which debts would be repaid. Creditors were sometimes paid back in money worth far less than that which they had lent; debtors were sometimes disadvantaged when the money they borrowed proved because of inflation inadequate to support their ventures. Bankruptcy legislation at least enabled those who had been adversely affected by trends in the economy to cut their losses, and ensured that creditors, if they were proper participants in the bankruptcy proceeding, might get something.[138]

Above all, bankruptcy legislation reflected a reconsideration of the meaning of property rights and the moral consequences of economic activity. It represented, first, a tacit decision to extend protection to ventures as well as holdings. Strict enforcement of debt obligations meant that those with a certain kind of property—capital—had the power to prevent others from acquiring it. Bankruptcy freed the embarrassed debtor from the strict power of the creditor, allowing the debtor, once reconstituted, to venture again. Bankruptcy legislation also assumed that the loss of one's assets was not necessarily an index of moral depravity: economic failure could be traced to the market as well as to one's character. The eradication of imprisonment for debt and the emergence of bankruptcy and insolvency statutes symbolized a recognition that propertyholding was a more fluid and a more insecure activity in early-nineteenth-century America.

The *Sturges* case, which tested the constitutionality of state bankruptcy legislation in the face of the reconstituted Contract Clause, was itself a product of economic instability in the years 1818 and 1819. A variety of sudden changes in the American economy marked those years: a fall in the prices of American staples; the end to rampant inflation in the price of land, which caused it to drop dramatically; the persistence of various forms of credit, especially negotiable instruments, as a commonplace feature of business transactions; a consequent demand for the re-

---

[138] See P. Coleman, *Debtors and Creditors in America* (1974), 16–22.

demption of notes in specie when the economy showed signs of deteriorating. All of these factors made debtors less able to pay their creditors and creditors more anxious to be paid in solid currency.[139]

A particularly common case was that of the debtor who had borrowed money from a state bank or other creditor to speculate in land or to set himself up in a trade. As state banks proliferated after the War of 1812, they were anxious to accommodate borrowers in order to facilitate the circulation of their bank notes, which were used as tender. When land and staple prices dropped sharply after 1818, the value of bank notes began to fluctuate widely, and creditors sought reimbursement to protect themselves. Often debtors did not have the capital to repay their loans since the value of bank notes had depreciated. Debts thus became a pervasive feature of the economy: "debts by individuals to their neighbours, to merchants, to banks; debts among banks unregulated by a sensible credit system; debts expressing themselves in a circulating medium that might have occasioned some surprise even among the inmates of a lunatic asylum."[140] One historian of the period has concluded that "the ultimate loser in all this was . . . the man at the bottom of the chain of debt"; the individual "who believed that [his] loans could be renewed over and over again."[141]

The "man at the bottom of the chain of debt," however, was not always one of the unpropertied, dependent masses: he was often a person seeking to hold or to acquire property. Relief for him, through state laws that allowed debtors to declare bankruptcy, absolve themselves of their outstanding debts, and await more favorable economic conditions, had the effect of facilitating the exercise of property rights. But it also curtailed the rights of creditors to receive fair returns on their investments. Bankruptcy laws were thus often efforts on the part of states to intervene in a relationship between two sets of "propertied" citizens, one of whose "property" consisted of the expectations entwined in a web of credit.[142]

State bankruptcy laws thus presented the Marshall Court with an issue that was qualitatively different from the issues in *Fletcher v. Peck* and its progeny: when two classes of property rights compete, which is to prevail? The issue was not easily solved by appeal to the vested rights principle, for both debtors and creditors could be said to have rights that had vested after their initial credit transaction. The creditor had a right to have the debt repaid in full value, but the debtor could also be said to

---

[139] See generally Coleman, *Debtors and Creditors;* B. Hammond, *Banks and Politics in America* (1957); C. Warren, *Bankruptcy in United States History* (1935); G. Dangerfield, *The Awakening of American Nationalism* (1965).

[140] G. Dangerfield, *The Era of Good Feelings* (1952), 185.
[141] Ibid., 186.
[142] This view of debtor relief legislation had surfaced as early as the 1790s: see Coleman, *Debtors and Creditors,* 17–18.

have a right to the full value of the money borrowed. Thus if changing economic conditions lowered the value of the borrowed money, the debtor was being compelled to repay in currency that was worth more than the currency he had sought to make use of when assuming the debt. Did this mean, however, that he should be allowed to avoid payment altogether?

*Sturges* v. *Crowninshield* tested the constitutionality of a New York statute passed in April 1811 that allowed debtors to list their assets and creditors, assign their property, and discharge their debts. A month before the passage of the statute, Richard Crowninshield, a textile merchant who had grown up with Story in Salem, Massachusetts, but was then a resident of New York, borrowed $1,543.74 from Josiah Sturgis,[143] a resident of Massachusetts. In November 1811, Crowninshield declared bankruptcy under the New York statute, claiming that he was "an insolvent debtor." Crowninshield then returned to Massachusetts, founded a new textile business, and began to prosper. In October 1816, Sturgis, who had unsuccessfully opposed the discharge of Crowninshield's debts in 1811, sued to recover the value of his loan, arguing that the New York statute impaired the obligation of contracts.

Sturgis's suit was filed in United States Circuit Court for the District of Massachusetts, for which Story was the designated Supreme Court Justice. Story was himself highly interested in the case, not only because one of the litigants was an old associate, but also because of his strong interest in securing the passage of a uniform federal bankruptcy law. As early as 1812 Story had taken the position that Congress's power "to establish . . . uniform laws on the subject of bankruptcies throughout the United States"[144] either pre-empted or very substantially narrowed the powers of the states to pass bankruptcy or insolvency legislation.[145] In *Sturges* he and district judge John Davis stipulated a division in order to get full Supreme Court review.[146] The result was that the constitutionality of state bankruptcy laws was argued before the Marshall Court a little more than a year after the original suit had been filed in Story's circuit court. The questions on which Story and district judge Davis stipulated

---

[143] The plaintiff's last name in *Sturges* v. *Crowninshield* was Sturgis, but was misspelled when the case was originally filed at the Supreme Court, and has remained so. The manuscript records of the case are in the National Archives. See G. Dunne, *Justice Joseph Story* (1970), 158.

[144] U.S. Const., Art. I, Sect. 8.

[145] Babcock v. Weston, 2 F. Cas. 306 (1812); Van Reimsdyck v. Kane, 28 F. Cas. 1062 (1812). Story had also

pressed for national bankruptcy legislation from at least 1815 on (see J. Story to H. Wheaton, Dec. 13, 1815, in W. Story, *Life and Letters*, I, 271) and was eventually to be the draftsman of bankruptcy legislation passed by Congress in 1841. Ibid., 407.

[146] W. Prescott to Leverett Saltonstall, May 17, 1817, Saltonstall Papers, Massachusetts Historical Society, Boston, Mass. See Dunne, *Joseph Story*, 164.

their division were calculated to test not only the reach of federal plenary power over bankruptcy legislation but the reach of the Contract Clause.

The eventual compromise that Marshall's opinion struck for the Court furnishes a good example of the manner in which the Marshall Court strove to conceal its internal divisions through the process of delivering formal opinions. Marshall's opinion was designated "the opinion of the Court,"[147] and there were no dissents. But it was clear before the case was argued that the Justices differed deeply on the plenary power issue, and subsequent comments by participants revealed that considerable bargaining took place within the Court. Prior to the certification four Justices of the six who rendered the decision in *Sturges* v. *Crowninshield* had made known their views on federal plenary power with respect to bankruptcy legislation. As indicated, Story had intimated in 1812 that the states were probably pre-empted from enacting such legislation. Justice Bushrod Washington had held in an 1814 circuit decision that congressional power over bankruptcy was exclusive and that state bankruptcy legislation impaired the Obligation of Contracts Clause.[148] Justice Brockholst Livingston, in an 1817 decision from his New York circuit court, had upheld the constitutionality of the very law being challenged in *Sturges* v. *Crowninshield,* dismissing both the plenary power and the Contract Clause arguments.[149] And Justice William Johnson had held on circuit that state power to enact insolvency legislation was concurrent to federal power.[150] Thus before the case was argued two Justices were known to oppose the legislation whose constitutionality was at stake in *Sturges,* two were known to support it, and two others, Marshall and Duvall, had not committed themselves. Daniel Webster, writing to one of his co-counsel in the *Dartmouth College* case on February 15, 1819, a week after *Sturges* had been argued, said that "the general opinion is that the six judges now here will be equally divided on the point. I confess, however, I have a strong suspicion there will be an opinion, and that that opinion will be against the state laws."[151]

Not only was there an opinion in *Sturges,* it was delivered by Marshall only two days after Webster's letter. Marshall held, for the Court, that the New York legislation violated the Contract Clause. The opinion, while purportedly unanimous, contained signs of internal division. One sign was Marshall's discussion of federal plenary power over bankruptcy. He began by asserting that "when the terms in which a power is granted

---

[147] 4 Wheat. at 191.
[148] Golden v. Prince, 10 F. Cas. 542 (1814).
[149] Adams v. Storey, 1 F. Cas. 141 (1817).
[150] Hannay v. Jacobs, an unreported case, cited by counsel for Crowninshield, 4 Wheat. at 135.
[151] D. Webster to J. Mason, Feb. 15, 1819, in McIntyre, *Writings and Speeches,* XVI, 49–50.

to Congress, or the nature of the power, require that it should be exercised exclusively by Congress, the subject is as completely taken from the State Legislatures as if they had been expressly forbidden to act in it."[152] But the grant to Congress of power to establish uniform bankruptcy laws, he added, was one of "peculiar terms": it did not extend to insolvency laws, which were different from, although hard to distinguish from, bankruptcy laws. Bankruptcy laws were "said to grow out of the exigencies of Commerce, and to be applicable solely to traders; but it is not easy to say who must be excluded from, or may be included within, this description."[153] Consequently "much inconvenience would result from that construction of the constitution which should deny to the State Legislatures the power of acting on this subject, in consequence of the grant to Congress."

The theme of "convenience" ran through Marshall's holding on the plenary power issue. "Much inconvenience" would result from denying to the states the power to pass insolvency legislation; it "may be thought more convenient" that debtor-creditor relations "be regulated by State legislation"; it did "not appear to be a violent construction of the Constitution, and it is certainly a convenient one, to consider the power of the States as existing over such cases as the laws of the Union may not reach."[154] Marshall then converted convenience into a principle of constitutional construction: "it is not the mere existence of the power, but its exercise, which is incompatible with the exercise of the same power by the States. It is not the right to establish these uniform laws, but their actual establishment, which is inconsistent with the partial acts of the States."[155]

Given the tenor of other Marshall Court opinions dealing with the issue of federal-state sovereignty, this concession seemed remarkable. The explicit grant of a power to Congress, Marshall appeared to be saying, did not preclude state legislation on the same subject if Congress had not exercised its power. What if Congress should fail to exercise its taxing or interstate commerce powers; would the states be allowed to tax national enterprises or to regulate interstate commerce? Debtor-creditor relationships often spanned state boundaries, as the *Sturges* case showed. Marshall's principle of construction appeared to permit a spate of state regulatory activity in cases, such as bankruptcy, in which political considerations dictated that federal regulatory power might remain dormant. We have seen that his remarks in *Sturges* were cited in the arguments in *Gibbons* v. *Ogden*.

Marshall's concession is all the more interesting because he was no friend of state legislative activity in the area of debtor-creditor relations.

---

[152] 4 Wheat. at 193.
[153] Ibid., 195.

[154] Ibid., 196.
[155] Ibid.

In his life of Washington he had referred to "efforts . . . increasingly directed to [the] relief . . . of the debtor" that took place "in many of the states" prior to the Constitution. Such activity created "instability in principles which ought to be rendered immutable" and fostered a "loss of confidence in the government and in individuals."[156] Eight years after *Sturges* Marshall was to voice his attitude even more pointedly. State exercise of "a power of changing the relative situation of debtor and creditor," he declared, "[broke] in upon the ordinary intercourse of society, and destroy[ed] all confidence between man and man."[157] Given these sentiments, it appears remarkable that Marshall would have tolerated the exercise of any power by the states in the area of debtor-creditor relations. His language appears to have been inserted to placate other Justices.

The *Sturges* decision, Justice Johnson was to assert eight years later, partook "as much of a compromise as of a legal adjudication." The Marshall Court judges, Johnson said, were "greatly divided in their views of the doctrine . . . The minority thought it better to yield something than risk the whole." By "the minority" Johnson meant Livingston, Duvall, and himself; by "risking the whole" he meant surrendering "the general maintenance of state power over the subject." The compromise struck, then, was Marshall's concession of a concurrent state power in the bankruptcy area in exchange for unanimous support for the proposition that the Contract Clause invalidated at least those insolvency laws that affected contracts made prior to them. "[D]enying the power to act on anterior contracts," Johnson indicated, "could do no harm, but, in fact, imposed a restriction conceived in the true spirit of the construction."[158]

In his opinion on behalf of an unrevealed "majority" (himself, Washington, Story, and possibly Todd, who has been identified with support for federal plenary power),[159] Marshall was thus trading the opportunity to make a ringing affirmation of federal plenary power over bankruptcy for an opportunity to once again protect vested property rights through the Contract Clause. If Johnson is to be believed, this was not an opportunity that other Marshall Court Justices were loath to grant: they thought that restrictions on state power to "act upon anterior contracts" were "in the true spirit of the constitution."

In short, there *was* a kind of unanimity on the Court in *Sturges* v. *Crowninshield*: unanimity for the proposition that solicitude for vested property rights precluded the passage of even that legislation whose purpose was to facilitate the acquisition of property. *Sturges* had raised an

---

[156] J. Marshall, *The Life of George Washington* (5 vols., 1804), V, 86–87.
[157] Ogden v. Saunders, 12 Wheat. 213 (1827).

[158] Ibid., 272–73.
[159] See D. Annis, *Mr. Bushrod Washington* (1977), 183.

inherent difficulty in applying the axiom of republican theory that protection for property rights was a necessary feature of enlightened social organization. Debtor relief laws were designed to facilitate some people's rights to acquire property at the expense of others. They were, as Justice Livingston had said in his circuit opinion, sustaining the New York insolvency law, "for the benefit of trade" and consistent with "the sentiments and practice of commercial men."[160]

Against the idea that insolvency and bankruptcy legislation facilitated commerce and thereby enhanced opportunity to acquire property was pitted the inexorable logic of the Court's opinion in *Sturges*. For once Marshall had accompanied his statement that "until the power to pass uniform laws on the subject of bankruptcies be exercised by Congress, the States are not forbidden to pass a bankrupt law" with the qualifying phrase "provided [that law] contain no principle which violates the 10th section of the first article of the constitution of the United States,"[161] he had framed "the great question on which the cause must depend." And to ask that question, given Marshall's construction of the Contract Clause, was to answer it.

The portion of Marshall's *Sturges* opinion dealing with the Contract Clause furnishes a good example of his ability to link linguistic construction with appeals to tacitly shared presuppositions and values. His "first inquiry," he said, was "into the meaning of words in common use." Among the words in question were "contract," "obligation," and "impair." He was hard put "to substitute words which are more intelligible, or less liable to misconstruction, than those." "Contracts" were agreements to perform "undertaking[s]," "to do or not to do a particular thing." "Obligations" were legal requirements to perform the undertaking. Any law that "releases a part of this obligation must, in the literal sense of the word, impair it." Thus a law which made an obligation "totally invalid, and entirely discharge[d] it," clearly "impaired" the obligation of a contract. The "words of the constitution, then, are express, and incapable of being misunderstood. They admit of no variety of construction."[162]

But while one might agree with Marshall's dictionary definitions in the abstract, his exegesis standing alone was insufficient, for there were examples of constitutionally sanctioned laws—statutes of limitations and statutory prohibitions against usury, for example—that interfered with contractual undertakings. If a person was precluded from suing to enforce a promise after a certain date, or prohibited from enforcing a given rate of interest in a contract, it was difficult to see, under Marshall's defini-

---

[160] Adams v. Storey, supra, note 149, at 149.

[161] 4 Wheat. at 187.
[162] Ibid., 198.

tions, how the "obligation" of his contract had not been "impaired." Thus Marshall initiated a further inquiry into the purpose of the Contract Clause in order to clarify the scope of its coverage. That inquiry was to be abetted, however, by his earlier definitions of the "meaning of words in common use." He reminded his readers, for example, that the obligation of a contract was not confined to the property mentioned in it: "industry, talents and integrity constitute a fund which is as confidently trusted as property itself." Thus to "surrender the whole" of one's existing property was not necessarily to discharge one's contractual obligations: "future acquisitions" were subsumed in the meaning of "contracts."[163] Already the dictionary definitions were being infused with tacit assumptions about the propriety of certain types of conduct.

Marshall then moved squarely to consider the intent of the Framers in drafting the Contract Clause. He was on familiar ground here, having taken up the same theme in *Fletcher* v. *Peck* and *New Jersey* v. *Wilson*. The clause embodied a "principle": the "inviolability of contracts." The principle "was to be protected in whatsoever form it might be assailed."[164] The "spirit . . . of a constitution" was "to be collected chiefly from its words." If the "plain meaning of a provision . . . is to be disregarded, because we believe the framers of that instrument could not intend what they say, it must be one in which the absurdity and injustice of applying the provision to the case would be so monstrous, that all mankind would, without hesitation, unite in rejecting the application."[165] Since the Framers had used the generic term "contracts," they meant contracts of every type; only "monstrous applications" of the prohibition against the impairment of "contracts" would be inconsistent with their intent.

By this rule of construction Marshall was able to ignore some apparent difficulties in applying the Contract Clause to state insolvency laws. States had passed insolvency laws prior to the passage of the Constitution. The "mind of the Convention" was "directed to . . . laws which were fraudulent in their character, which allowed the debtor to escape from his obligation," and not "to all bankruptcy and insolvency laws"; the "attention of the Convention . . . was particularly directed to paper money; and to acts which enabled the debtor to discharge his debt."[166] Marshall concluded that "violence would be done to [the] plain meaning [of the words in the Contract Clause] by understanding them in a more limited sense." His justification was "those rules of construction which have been consecrated by the wisdom of the ages."[167]

---

[163] Ibid.
[164] Ibid., 200.
[165] Ibid., 202–203.
[166] Ibid., 205–206.
[167] Ibid., 206.

# Chapter IX: *The Contract Clause Cases*

Thus an inquiry into "the meaning of words in common use" had led to the extraction of a "great principle," the inviolability of contracts, and that principle had been made extensive in scope through the "monstrous application" rule of construction. Marshall's opinion in *Sturges* is a striking illustration of his ability to invest the "common meaning" of language with tacitly shared values and thereby to argue that certain "great principles" are obvious. That they were not "obvious" in application Marshall was consistently aware; his purpose in connecting the common meaning of words to great principles was to convince his reader that the principles were sufficiently obvious in theory that controversial applications of them were justifiable extrapolations of their spirit.

But the inexorability of Marshall's logic in *Sturges* had not fully relieved him from pressures to compromise. Not only was he eager to forge an ostensibly unanimous opinion, he was disinclined to provoke public reaction unnecessarily. Thus he distinguished insolvency from laws prohibiting imprisonment for debt on the grounds that imprisonment was "a remedy" and "no part of the contract," and that to make "a constitutional principle" of imprisonment for debt would be to "impute to the illustrous patriots who framed our constitution" an "excess of inhumanity."[168] He also distinguished statutes of limitations and anti-usury laws on similar grounds: they "related to . . . remedies" or were not directed at contractual "obligations."[169] Those distinctions were thin; the exceptions seemed to be in actuality illustrations of his "monstrous application" rule of construction.

Finally, Marshall's *Sturges* opinion contained an additional inscrutable caveat, one that was to loom large in the next series of Marshall Court Contract Clause cases. In his discussion of statutes of limitations and usury laws Marshall referred to laws affecting "contracts already in existence" at the time of the laws' passage, and indicated that such legislation would be "clearly unconstitutional." Was he suggesting by these examples that the Contract Clause prohibited only retroactive application of debtor relief laws? Nowhere else in the opinion was there any such suggestion, and the discussion of statutes of limitation and usury laws was, as noted, apparently to distinguish them entirely from debtor relief laws. There was considerable concern in the press about the scope of the *Sturges* opinion after it was announced, and the general impression was that states had no power to pass any bankruptcy or insolvency legislation, whether prospective or retroactive in nature, that impaired the obligation of contracts. A March 31, 1819, editorial in the Augusta *Chronicle and Georgia Gazette* asked, "Under the decision of the Supreme Tribunal of the country, what were wretched debtors to do? The States can exempt

---

[168] Ibid., 200–201.      [169] Ibid., 207.

nothing but their bodies from the harrowing pursuit of the law."[170] Moreover, in the case of *McMillan* v. *McNeill*,[171] decided only one day after *Sturges*, Marshall, for a unanimous Court, had said that the case "was not distinguishable in principle from the preceding case of *Sturges* v. *Crowninshield*" and "that the circumstance of the State law, under which the debt was attempted to be discharged, having been passed before the debt was contracted, made no difference in the application of the principle."[172]

Given *McMillan* v. *McNeill* and the absence of any language in the *Sturges* decision confining its principle to retroactive application of debtor relief laws, why did the issue remain open? Part of the reason, at least, was that Marshall had ended his *Sturges* opinion with the statement that "this opinion is confined to the case actually under consideration."[173] In *Sturges* the law had been passed after the debt was contracted. But one needs to consider Marshall's statement in context. His statement that the *Sturges* decision was confined to "the case actually under consideration" was part of a paragraph that continued:

> It is confined to a case in which a creditor sues in a Court, the proceedings of which the legislature, whose act is pleaded, had not a right to control, and to a case where the creditor had not proceeded to execution against the body of his debtor, within the State whose law attempts to absolve a confined insolvent debtor from his obligation. When such a case arises, it will be considered.[174]

What is the meaning of this paragraph? It seems that the sentences following "this opinion is confined to the case actually under consideration" should be taken as a further statement about what the "case" was. In *Sturges* a creditor had sued in a federal court, located in Massachusetts, the "proceedings" of which could not be "controlled" by a state legislature. Moreover, Josiah Sturgis had not attempted to imprison Richard Crowninshield for debt; Crowninshield had in fact left the jurisdiction of New York State, and Sturgis was not "proceed[ing] . . . to execution . . . within the state." In short, the case was not one where a creditor in a state sought to "confine" an insolvent debtor in order to enforce his obligation, and that state's bankruptcy law sought to "absolve" the debtor. Such a case seems to be what Marshall meant by the "case" that "will be considered . . . when [it] arises."

There was another feature of *McMillan* v. *McNeill*, however, which rendered it less than dispositive on the retroactivity issue. The law struck

---

[170] Augusta *Chronicle and Georgia Gazette*, Mar. 31, 1819.
[171] 4 Wheat. 209 (1819).
[172] Ibid., 211–12.
[173] 4 Wheat. at 207.
[174] Ibid., 207–208.

down in the case had discharged a debtor from a debt incurred in another state; it might have been unconstitutional as an unwarranted attempt on the part of one state to regulate the commerce of another. Kent, discussing *Sturges* and *McMillan* in his commentaries, concluded that while "the general language" in *McMillan* "would seem to reach" the case of a debt incurred after the passage of an insolvency law within the state that had passed the law, the issue "remains yet to be settled."[175] That issue was argued five years after *Sturges* in *Ogden* v. *Saunders*, but before that decision the Court was to decide two additional Contract Clause cases.

Farmers and Merchants Bank v. Smith[176] was, after *Sturges*, a straightforward case, although it did appear to clarify some of the meaning of Marshall's last passage in *Sturges*. The *Sturges* case had involved citizens of different states and had been brought in a federal court; in *Farmers and Merchants Bank* both participants were citizens of Pennsylvania, and the case was originally brought in a Pennsylvania state court. The contract in question was a promissory note held by the Farmers and Merchants Bank against Smith, signed in June 1811. A Pennsylvania debtor relief statute of 1812 had provided a procedure for discharging insolvent debtors from their obligations. The constitutionality of that statute was challenged on a Section 25 writ of error from the Pennsylvania Supreme Court, which had allowed Smith to be discharged.

Marshall, in a one-paragraph opinion, said that the case "was not distinguishable from [the Court's] former decisions on the same subject," citing *Sturges* and *McMillan* v. *McNeill*. The only factual difference was that "the defendant . . . was a citizen of the same state with the plaintiffs, at the time the contract was made in that state, and remained such at the time the suit was announced in its Courts." These facts, Marshall maintained, "made no difference in the cases." The Constitution was "equally binding upon all the Courts and all the citizens."[177] The "case" Marshall had left open in *Sturges* was apparently settled in *Farmers and Merchants Bank*.

Green v. Biddle,[178] ultimately decided in 1823, was far more delicate, at least as the Court chose to approach it. The case involved a "compact" between Virginia and Kentucky made in 1789, when Kentucky separated from Virginia to form the new state that gained admission to the Union two years later. The compact provided that "all private rights and interests of lands derived from the laws of Virginia" in the former western portion of Virginia (now Kentucky) should "remain valid" and be "determined by the laws now existing" in Virginia.[179] The result of this agreement was that Kentucky land transactions were

---

175 Kent, *Commentaries*, I, 395–96.
176 6 Wheat. 131 (1821).
177 Ibid., 134.

178 8 Wheat. 1 (1823).
179 Ibid., 3.

made insecure, since Kentucky residents acquiring land could not always be sure that the title was free from an outstanding Virginia claim; purchasers might face eviction and a suit for rents and profits.

Two Kentucky statutes, popularly referred to as occupying claimant laws, sought to remedy the problem. A 1797 statute prohibited persons who could establish a "clear and connected" title to their land from being held liable for rents and profits if they were evicted on proof of a superior title. The statute also provided that before a nonoccupying claimant could secure possession of land he had to pay the occupant the value of any "permanent improvements" the occupant had made. If the claimant refused to pay, the occupant could purchase the land for its value less the improvements. An 1812 statute was even more favorable to occupants: it established commissioners to determine the value of disputed land in each case and required nonoccupying claimants to pay occupants for their possession of the land as well as for the improvements on it.[180] The heirs of a claimant, John Green, brought suit against an occupant, Richard Biddle, in federal circuit court for the District of Kentucky, and the case was certified to the Supreme Court on the familiar stipulation that the circuit judges were divided. The case was argued in the 1821 Term, with Story rendering an opinion on March 5.[181]

From the outset *Green* v. *Biddle* presented the Marshall Court with some ticklish problems. *Cohens* v. *Virginia*[182] had been handed down only two days earlier, and the Court correctly anticipated a storm of protest over its purported usurpation of state sovereignty. Story's opinion in *Green* v. *Biddle* was expected to have the same effect: it erected a constitutional barrier to a state's efforts to regularize its system of land titles. Moreover, Biddle, the occupant of the Kentucky land in dispute, had not been represented by counsel before the Court. "We should have been glad in the consideration of this subject," Story said in his opinion, "to have had the benefit of an argument on behalf of the tenant." But "no counsel has appeared for him, and the cause has been some time before the Court."[183] Three weeks, in fact, had elapsed between the argument and the delivery of Story's opinion. Henry Clay, senator from Kentucky, appeared before the Court on March 12 and moved for a rehearing, claiming that "the rights and claims of numerous occupants of land in Kentucky . . . would be irrevocably determined by this decision," and that Biddle had not been represented.[184] The Court, aware of the practical and political difficulties of upsetting established land title settlement procedures in Kentucky without hearing any defense of those

---

[180] Ibid., 4–7.
[181] Ibid., 10. See generally P. Gates, "Tenants of the Log Cabin," *J. Am. Hist.*, 49:1 (1962).

[182] 6 Wheat. 264 (1821).
[183] 8 Wheat. at 11.
[184] Ibid., 17–18.

procedures, granted the motion, and the case was reargued in March 1822.[185]

In the interval attacks on the Court had become more open and virulent. In December 1821, we have seen, Senator Richard Johnson of Kentucky proposed a constitutional amendment to give the United States Senate appellate jurisdiction over cases where the constitutionality of a state's laws was challenged and the state chose to defend them,[186] and the following January Johnson denounced the Court for "assum[ing] a guardianship over the States, even to the controlling of their peculiar municipal regulations." In particular, Johnson charged, the Court had "in one moment, subvert[ed] the deliberate policy of . . . Kentucky, affecting its whole landed property." The effect of Story's opinion in *Green* v. *Biddle*, according to Johnson, was "to legislate for the people; to regulate the interior policy of that community, and to establish their municipal code as to real estate."[187]

In the face of this controversy the Marshall Court retreated. Story's opinion, announced as "unanimous" and supported by all the Justices except Washington (who missed the entire 1821 Term because of a viral infection), was withdrawn. An alternative opinion was prepared by Washington but not delivered until February 27, 1823, and announced as a "majority" opinion.[188] Three Justices were not present when the opinion was delivered: Livingston had become seriously ill with pneumonia (he was to die on March 18); Todd, the Justice who was a resident of Kentucky, was unable to attend the 1823 Term "because of indisposition";[189] and Marshall declined to sit.[190] The "majority" therefore purportedly consisted of only Washington, Story, and Duvall; Johnson concurred separately.[191] These circumstances led to the erroneous supposition by Henry Clay, made in a letter written in early March 1823, that "the decision is that of three Judges to one, a minority therefore of the whole Court."[192] Story was probably the only Justice in the majority who did not actually approve of the opinion: he noted in a March 14 letter to Todd

---

185 Ibid., 18.
186 *Annals of Congress*, 17th Cong., 1st Sess., 68.
187 Ibid., 74, 103.
188 8 Wheat. at 94.
189 Ibid., vi.
190 Members of the Marshall family, including the Chief Justice, claimed title to over 400,000 acres of land in Kentucky. See Gates, "Tenants of the Log Cabin," 4–6.
191 Beveridge, *John Marshall*, IV, 381, has Johnson dissenting, a view that is belied by Johnson's opinion. See

8 Wheat. at 103–107. Morgan, *William Johnson*, 185, has Johnson concurring. Thus there were at least four votes for Washington's opinion, since Livingston was reported in 1826, "on unquestionable authority," to have "concurred in the sentence of the Court." See remarks of Charles Mercer in Congressional Record, 19th Cong., 1st Sess., Jan. 6, 1826.
192 H. Clay to Francis Brooke, Mar. 9, 1823, in C. Colton, ed., *The Private Correspondence of Henry Clay* (1856), 75.

that his opinion had been withdrawn, although he saw "no reason to take [it] back," and referred to "many struggles" within the Court before *Green* v. *Biddle* was "definitely settled."[193]

A comparison of Story's and Washington's opinions furnishes clues as to what may have taken place in the Court's internal deliberations. Story's opinion was unusual for him in its relative brevity and lack of documentation. Indeed, the opinion gave the impression that the unconstitutionality of the Kentucky statutes was so patent as to hardly be worth discussion. Story began by asserting that the article of the "compact" stating that "all private rights and interests of lands" in Kentucky "shall remain valid and secure under the laws of the proposed State" could not be taken as a statement that Kentucky was powerless to "regulate the content, distribution and grants of the domain within its bounds," for "the general principles of law" and "the first principles of justice" required that states could make their own rules for the transfer of land situated within their boundaries. The article was therefore intended not to constrain Kentucky's procedure for the disposition of land titles, but to assure that the "private rights and interests" of those holding title to lands previously in the State of Virginia would "remain valid and secure under the laws of Kentucky."[194]

Since the Kentucky statutes "materially impair[ed] the rights and interests of the rightful owner[s] of land," they were unconstitutional violations of the compact. To require owners of land to pay "improvements made upon them, without [their] consent of default" was to create "a direct and permanent lien upon the lands." No "such burthen" was imposed on owners under Virginia law. Owners of land were "no more bound . . . to pay for improvements which [they] had not authorized . . . than [they were] to pay a sum to a stranger for the liberty of possessing and using [their] own property."[195] The Kentucky statutes were the equivalent of laws forcing owners to "recover lands . . . upon payment . . . of the whole of their value" or to sell them "at a price to be fixed by others." The principle was the same: an owner of land had an unlimited "right and interest" to the possession and use of his duly acquired property. Thus the legislation clearly impaired the contract between Virginia and Kentucky protecting that "right and interest."

Story did not furnish a single citation in his opinion, and he made no effort to discuss the issue of whether a compact between states was the kind of transaction that was intended to be covered by the Contract Clause. This omission was peculiar given the clause in Article 1, Section

---

[193] J. Story to T. Todd, Mar. 14, 1823, in W. Story, *Life and Letters*, I, 422.

[194] 8 Wheat. at 12–13.
[195] Ibid., 16–17.

Chapter IX: *The Contract Clause Cases*

10 of the Constitution providing that "no State shall, without the Consent
of Congress . . . enter into any Agreement or Compact with another
State." The juxtaposition of that clause with the Contract Clause in the
same Article suggests that the Framers did not regard interstate compacts
as coming within the jurisdiction of the Contract Clause; they were to be
either authorized or forbidden by Congress. By avoiding the Compact
Clause and focusing on the Contract Clause Story transformed *Green* v.
*Biddle* from a federalism case to a property rights case, but at the risk of
appearing to have made an erroneous interpretation of the Constitution.
The omission of the Compact Clause was all the more puzzling because
Congress, when it admitted Kentucky to the Union in 1791, had ratified
the Virginia-Kentucky agreements.[196]

The opinion delivered by Washington in 1823 appeared to be a self-
conscious correction of some of the deficiencies in Story's earlier effort.
First, Washington took pains to buttress, by citation to common law
decisions, Story's assertion that "the law of nature" and "principles of
law and reason"[197] allowed an owner of land "the fruits or profits of the
land, [including] those that were produced by the industry of the occupant."[198] Washington then alluded to the Compact Clause, demonstrating
that Congress had "expressed by a solemn act, [its] consent . . . to the
separation" of Kentucky from Virginia, and that if Congress had not,
Kentucky would be "at this moment a part of the State of Virginia, and
all her laws . . . acts of usurpation."[199]

It remained for Washington to show that a compact between two
states was a "contract" within the meaning of the Contract Clause. He
merely cited a definition of a contract, earlier used by Marshall, as an
"agreement of two or more parties to do, or not to do, certain acts," and
asserted that "it must be obvious that the propositions" offered by Virginia and agreed to by Kentucky added up to "a contract." He then cited
Marshall's language in *Fletcher* v. *Peck* that defined a contract as "a
*compact* between two or more parties." Kentucky was thus party to a
"contract" which had "guaranteed . . . claimants to [Kentucky] land
. . . their rights," and as such "was incompetent to violate that contract
by passing any law which rendered these rights as valid and secure."[200]

Washington also took pains to communicate his sensitivity to the
political consequences of the Court's interference with Kentucky land
claims. The effect of *Green* v. *Biddle* was potentially to bring the disposition and improvement of land in Kentucky to a grinding halt. All
occupants and their prospective purchasers were accountable to absentee
claimants for any efforts they made to upgrade the value of land to which

[196] 1 Statutes at Large 189 (1791).
[197] 8 Wheat. at 75, 82.
[198] Ibid., 74–85.
[199] Ibid., 87.
[200] Ibid., 92–93.

645

Virginians or their heirs retained title. As Johnson said in his concurrence, the decision "chained [Kentucky] down to a state of hopeless imbecility— embarrassed with a thousand minute discriminations drawn from the common law . . . appropriate to a state of society, and a state of property, having no analogy whatever to the actual things in Kentucky."[201] Washington seemed to recognize this, for he reminded his readers that Kentucky could continue to pass laws in which lands were taken "for public use," provided that the owners were given just compensation. The "universal law of all free governments" embodied the takings principle, and its "admission never has been imagined by any person as rendering his right to property less valid and secure."[202] Kentucky could thus encourage improvement in land held by out-of-state claimants by seizing it, compensating the owners, and selling it to Kentucky residents.

On the surface, *Green* v. *Biddle* seems a curious, almost reckless decision. Why did Story's opinion ignore the interstate compacts clause altogether, and spend so little time buttressing its assertions about the autonomy of private rights to land? Why did Washington, who was aware of the Compact Clause, not ground his decision on that, thereby making the compact supreme over state laws by virtue of the Federal Supremacy Clause of Article VI of the Constitution and shifting the political burdens of disrupting Kentucky's land laws onto Congress, which had approved the agreement? And why did the Court withdraw one "unanimous" opinion, joined in by all of its members save an absent Justice, for another that appeared to be endorsed by only three Justices and was explicitly not unanimous?

The behavior of the Court can be clarified by reminding ourselves of its ideological presuppositions. It was taken for granted by all the Justices who approved Story's opinion, and by Washington as well, that "first principles of natural justice" conferred upon an owner of land a "right" and an "interest" in the "security" that all improvements made on the land would revert to him and that he could keep the land in an unimproved condition if he so chose. Security for property was regarded as so fundamental a value in "free governments" that it hardly needed any legal documentation. Moreover, similar declarations of the sanctity of vested property rights had been made in previous Contract Cases not involving land. Here was a case that combined vested contract rights and vested common law rights to land, both of which were being usurped by a state legislature. It seemed to be a case that required only the reassertion of settled jurisprudential principles.

---

[201] Ibid., 104.     [202] Ibid., 89.

# Chapter IX: *The Contract Clause Cases*

But three factors served to make *Green* v. *Biddle* a more treacherous case than the Marshall Court may have anticipated. First, *Green* v. *Biddle* was not properly a contract case at all: the compact between Virginia and Kentucky was more like a treaty between a sovereign nation and a former colony in which the colony acknowledged that in certain respects the dominion of the sovereign remained after independence. *Green* v. *Biddle* was in effect a takings case, a case in which the rights of land claimants and improvers were being balanced by a statute, and the question was whether the balancing so favored improvers as to amount to a taking. But since *Green* v. *Biddle* was a Section 25 case, the Court could not consider the takings issue, but was limited to the (reconstituted) Contract Clause; its attention focused on the fact that the statutes had created some impairment of the compact. That focus distorted what was really at stake in the case: whether the balance struck by the statutes between claimants and improvers, admittedly an impairment, was fair and sensible. Second, there was the sovereignty issue. Kentucky, in exchange for the privilege of being allowed to separate from Virginia and enter the Union, was being forced into a kind of vassalage with respect to the disposition of its land; it was beholden to the whims of Virginia claimants. This was not only galling, it struck at what many early-nineteenth-century Americans regarded as the heart of economic relationships, transactions in land. Kentucky residents, in many instances, could not participate in the development of their state's natural resources without the consent of nonresident landowners, many of whom had no interest in Kentucky land being improved. By invalidating the occupying claimant laws the Court was pitting itself against the desires of local citizens to use land in their locality. That was a powerful interest for a remote federal institution to be opposing.

Third, *Green* v. *Biddle* suggested, as had *Sturges*, that when state legislatures were infringing upon vested property rights they were not necessarily doing so in support of a dependent, propertyless rabble. The Kentucky laws were designed to benefit another class of propertyholders: those who sought to convert their possession of land into a claim of title that would eventually result in their obtaining the fruits of their own labor. *Green* v. *Biddle* was therefore not a case where a state had sided with those whose lack of industry, talent, or education assured they would never acquire property, independence, and leisure. On the contrary, it was a case where a state had sided with those who purportedly had the intelligence or the industry to recognize that the ownership and improvement of land was a potential source of wealth and status in nineteenth-century America. The fact that many of the occupying claimants in Kentucky were squatters, carving out a bare existence on vacant land, may have lent an abstract or even ironic character to conceptions of them as entrepreneurs. But it did not resolve the contradiction suggested by both

*Sturges* and *Green* v. *Biddle:* solicitude for vested property rights could retard the use and enjoyment of other property rights.

The confrontation between two sorts of property rights that had surfaced in *Sturges* and *Green* v. *Biddle* became acutely evident in the 1827 case of *Ogden* v. *Saunders.* Between the delivery of Washington's opinion in *Green* v. *Biddle* and the arguments in *Ogden* v. *Saunders* signs of change in the Court had occurred. Livingston's death had resulted, after some delay, in the appointment of Smith Thompson to the Court, and Thompson's record as a judge on the New York Court of Appeals suggested that he would be solicitous of state powers.[203] In addition, Justice Todd, who never failed to side with Marshall in a constitutional case during his entire tenure, had missed the 1823 and 1825 Terms because of continuing ill health. Finally, we have noted that Justice Johnson, prodded by Jefferson,[204] announced in *Gibbons* v. *Ogden,* handed down in 1824, that "in questions of great importance and great delicacy," he would issue separate opinions.[205] The carefully orchestrated "unanimity" of earlier Marshall Court cases seemed in danger of breaking down.

*Ogden* v. *Saunders* showed every sign of being the case in which divisions on the Marshall Court would come to light. The very fact that it was argued as early as the 1824 Term was remarkable, in light of *Sturges, McMillan* v. *McNeill,* and *Farmers and Mechanics Bank* v. *Smith.* There had not been a single dissenting vote in those opinions; all had invalidated debtor relief laws; and the Court had continued to widen the scope of the Contract Clause between 1819 and 1822. Yet after the original arguments in March 1824, the Court pronounced itself divided on the outcome and unable to render an opinion. In the intervening two years Todd's illness and eventual death prevented a clear majority from surfacing. The fact of a division within the Court may have been puzzling to those who had simply read its preceding debtor relief opinions, but could have come as no surprise to persons familiar with the politics of bankruptcy legislation. Between 1819 and 1824 Congress had repeatedly failed to pass a uniform bankruptcy law, despite model statutes supplied

[203] The best source on Thompson is D. Roper, "Mr. Justice Thompson and the Constitution," (Ph.D. diss., Indiana University, 1963). See also D. Roper, "Justice Smith Thompson," *N.-Y. Hist. Soc.,* 51:119 (1967); G. Dunne, "Smith Thompson," in L. Friedman and F. Israel, *The Justices of the United States Supreme Court* (4 vols., 1969), I, 475. See also discussion in Chapter V.

[204] See T. Jefferson to W. Johnson, Oct. 27, 1822, in P. L. Ford, ed., *The Works of Thomas Jefferson* (12 vols., 1905), XII, 246–52; W. Johnson to T. Jefferson, Dec. 10, 1822, Thomas Jefferson Papers, Library of Congress. See Morgan, *William Johnson,* 168–85.

[205] Gibbons v. Ogden, 9 Wheat. 1, 223 (1824).

# Chapter IX: *The Contract Clause Cases*

by Justices Story and Johnson,[206] and two weeks before the Court's decision finally came down in *Ogden* v. *Saunders* Story wrote to John Brazier Davis that "the Bankruptcy Bill has been lost and under circumstances which will forbid any attempt to revive it for many years." "I now begin to believe," Story concluded, "that the power will, in the National Government, forever remain a dead letter."[207]

The inability of Congress to pass federal bankruptcy legislation was the political issue that dominated consideration of *Ogden* v. *Saunders*. If unexercised congressional power to establish bankruptcy legislation did not preclude states from acting, as *Sturges* had intimated, it precluded state legislation once Congress had acted. Moreover, the Contract Clause did not apply to Congress. Thus a uniform federal statute not only avoided thorny constitutional questions, it provided relief to debtors, a class of persons that had remarkably widespread public support. The failure of Congress to act meant that if the *Sturges* line of cases truly meant what it seemed to say, debtors would have no recourse against the claims of their creditors, regardless of whether the agreements on which creditor claims were based had occurred prior to or subsequent to the passage of state debtor relief legislation. Counsel for the debtor in *Ogden* v. *Saunders* put the issue sharply: "if the Court should pronounce the state bankrupt codes invalid, and Congress should refuse to supply their place . . . the country would present the extraordinary spectacle of a great commercial nation, without laws on the subject of bankruptcy."[208]

As Congress continued to debate but refused to pass a national bankruptcy act in the years after *Sturges,* the problem of debtor relief plagued the Marshall Court, affecting the manner in which the Court treated *Ogden* v. *Saunders*. In *McMillan* v. *McNeill*, it will be recalled, Marshall's opinion had said that "the circumstance of the State law . . . having been passed before the debt was contracted made no difference in the application of the principle." By the word "principle" he meant, as his preceding sentence made clear, the "principle . . . of *Sturges* v. *Crowninshield*." In arguing for the creditor in *Ogden* v. *Saunders*, Henry Wheaton, the Court's Reporter, reminded the Justices that "it was supposed to be decided that . . . it was immaterial whether the contract was made before or after the passage of the [debtor relief] law." But then Wheaton conceded that "the whole question might now be considered as open for discussion."[209]

Why was the constitutionality of prospective debtor relief legislation

---

[206] For Story's effort see Dunne, *Joseph Story,* 261; for Johnson's, see Morgan, *William Johnson,* 118. Johnson's model statute was written in 1820 and Story's in 1824.

[207] J. Story to J. Davis, Feb. 4, 1827, in W. Story, *Life and Letters,* I, 514.

[208] 12 Wheat. at 237.

[209] Ibid., 215.

"open for discussion" after *McMillan* v. *McNeill?* And why, even more remarkably, did no Justice who wrote an opinion in *Ogden* v. *Saunders* regard *McMillan* v. *McNeill* as settling the issue? The opinions in *Ogden* v. *Saunders* reveal that none did, including Marshall himself. Thompson, one of the four-member majority, said that "although several cases have been before this Court which may have a bearing upon the question" during the argument before the Court, "the particular point now raised [the constitutionality of prospective debtor relief legislation] has been treated by the counsel as still open for discussion, and so considered by the Court by permitting its discussion."[210] Washington, another member of the majority, said in his seriatim opinion that in *McMillan* v. *McNeill* the fact that "the contract preceded in order of time the act of assembly under which the debtor was discharged . . . was not thought necessary to notice . . . in the opinion which was announced."[211] That statement was clearly incorrect: Marshall's opinion had made specific reference to the fact that the legislation preceded the contract in question.

Marshall, Trimble, and Johnson expressed similar views of *Mc-Millan* v. *McNeill*. Marshall said that "it is a general rule . . . that the positive authority of a decision is co-extensive only with the facts on which it is made," and that in *McMillan* v. *McNeill* "the contract, though subsequent to the passage of the act, was made in a different State . . . and consequently without any view to the law, the benefit of which was claimed by the debtor." He summarized *McMillan* v. *McNeill* as holding only "that an act which operates on future contracts is inapplicable to a contract made in a different state, at whatever time it may have been entered into."[212] After alluding specifically to *McMillan* v. *McNeill*, Trimble read that decision as covering only a case where "a discharge in one State under its laws was pleaded to a contract made in another State."[213] Johnson surmised that the "principle" referred to in *McMillan* v. *McNeill* was only that "insolvent laws have no extra-territorial operation upon the contracts of other States," a principle "of universal law," "obvious and uncontestable."[214] He said that "if the marginal note to the report, or summary of the effect of the case of *McMillan* v. *McNeal* [*sic*] presented a correct view of the report of that decision, it is obvious that there would remain very little, if anything, for this Court to decide." But "by comparing the note of the Reporter with the facts of the case," Johnson claimed, "it will be found that there is a generality of expression admitted into the former which the case itself does not justify." But Johnson's comments do not square with Marshall's opinion in *McMillan*

---

210 Ibid., 293.
211 Ibid., 254.
212 Ibid., 333.

213 Ibid., 315.
214 Ibid., 272.

v. *McNeill*. The headnote summary prepared by Henry Wheaton is virtually identical to Marshall's own language. Moreover, the retrospective-prospective distinction was specifically argued by counsel for the debtor and, as noted, specifically addressed in Marshall's opinion. If Johnson's reading had truly been the holding of *McMillan* v. *McNeill*—that a Louisiana debtor relief law had no bearing on contracts made outside Louisiana by two citizens of South Carolina—it is strange that no mention was made of the point in Marshall's opinion.

It is clear that the Marshall Court Justices wanted an opportunity to consider afresh an issue they had perhaps inadvertently settled in *McMillan* v. *McNeill* but had subsequently concluded was too delicate to merit so summary a resolution. Marshall was technically correct that a holding of a case is only coextensive with its facts, but when the holding takes no notice of facts that are later said to be central, and specifically resolves issues that are later said to be left unresolved, invocation of the "general rule" becomes contrived. Nonetheless everyone—counsel for both sides and all the sitting Justices, since Duvall and Story joined Marshall's opinion—tacitly agreed not to give *McMillan* v. *McNeill* any weight. Marshall's opinion in that case had been too summary and the issue of the constitutionality of prospective debtor relief legislation was too significant.

Another example of the pressures swirling around the Court in *Ogden* v. *Saunders* was the majority's decision to release seriatim opinions. For the first and only time in his career Marshall had been unable to forge a majority in a constitutional case. A student of Marshall's Contract Clause opinions could have comfortably predicted his vote in *Ogden* v. *Saunders:* he had previously said, after all, that the Contract Clause established "a great principle, that contracts should be inviolable."[215] Moreover, none of his opinions in the *Sturges–McMillan–Farmers and Merchants Bank* sequence had admitted any distinction between contracts made before or after debtor relief legislation. But the presence of Trimble and Todd, plus Johnson's increasingly visible discomfort with the Court's efforts to restrict state regulatory powers, resulted in three Justices' being disinclined to adopt Marshall's position, and Marshall already knew, from earlier discussions, that he was not going to have Washington's vote.

Washington's divergence from Marshall in a constitutional case was virtually unique in the twenty-nine years of their joint service, matched only by Washington's concurrence in *Dartmouth College* and by his dissent in *Mason* v. *Haile*,[216] a case decided the same term as *Ogden* v. *Saunders*. Washington had long been on record as believing that federal

---

[215] In Sturges v. Crowninshield, 4 Wheat. at 206.

[216] 12 Wheat. 370 (1827).

power over debtor relief legislation was exclusive. He had, however, joined the majority in *Sturges,* and he felt "compelled" by that decision to "admit the right of a state to discharge insolvent debtors from their debts."[217] He combined his theory of exclusive power with his adherence to *Sturges* in the observation that since the Framers of the Constitution "expected the power vested in [Congress to] be exercised so effectively to prevent its exercise by the states, it is more probable that . . . retrospective laws were alone in the contemplation of the convention."[218] In addition, Washington doubted that if a law of the state where a contract had been made "forms a part of that contract, and of its obligation," it could also be said to "at the same time impair that obligation."[219] Finally, Washington referred to the "decent respect" held by the Marshall Court for "the wisdom, the integrity, and patriotism" of "the legislative body by which any law is passed," and accordingly thought that the "validity" of legislation should be "presumed . . . until its violation of the Constitution is proved beyond all reasonable doubt."[220] The result of this blend of stubbornness and deference to precedent was a fourth vote against Marshall's position.

But the Justices upholding prospective debtor relief legislation were far from unified on their reasons. This fact and the significance of the case moved not only Johnson and Washington but the newcomers Thompson and Trimble to write separately. Marshall, for his part, prepared an opinion that he may have originally designed to serve as a majority opinion for the Court, but it ended up being subscribed to only by Story and Duvall, and was published as a dissent.

The outcome of *Ogden v. Saunders* had its own ironies, for the two Justices who endorsed Marshall's dissent ended up "assenting to the judgment," while three of the four "majority" Justices dissented. That curiosity was the result of Johnson's conclusion that while states could apply debtor relief legislation to subsequent contracts made by their own citizens (and, Johnson thought, to prior contracts as well), they had no power to affect contracts made by citizens of other states. In *Ogden v. Saunders* the legislation being challenged had been passed in New York, but at the time the contract was signed the debtor was a citizen of Kentucky. Thus the New York insolvency statute, while constitutional as applied prospectively, did not relieve the debtor from his obligation, since it could be enforced only against contracts made by New York citizens. Johnson based this conclusion on "an harmonious distribution of justice throughout the Union," which would be achieved by "confin[ing] the states, in the exercise of their judicial sovereignty, to cases between their

---

[217] Ibid., 381.
[218] Ogden v. Saunders, supra, note 157, at 256.

[219] Ibid., 260.
[220] Ibid., 270.

own citizens,'' and thus avoiding the problem of conflicting laws governing the same transaction.[221] He also seemed to feel that notice requirements and limits on the reach of the states' jurisdiction beyond their
borders might be violated if bankruptcy laws could apply to out-of-state
creditors.[222]

That the opinions in *Ogden* v. *Saunders* were massive, idiosyncratic, and repetitive testified to the political significance of the case and
to the absence of a Marshall opinion that could be endorsed by a majority.
The several opinions expressed a spectrum of views on the relationship
between property rights and legislative regulation. On one end of the
spectrum was Marshall's conviction that the ''right to acquire property''
was ''intrinsic,'' and ''not given by society but . . . brought into it'';[223]
on the other end was Johnson's claim that ''all the contracts of men
receive a relative . . . interpretation, for the rights of all must be held
and enjoyed in subserviency to the good of the whole.''[224] The division
between the Justices thus appeared, at one level, to be very deep, and
some commentators have seen the decision as a clash between ''vested
rights'' and ''social interests.''[225] But *Ogden* v. *Saunders* was noticeable
for the agreement of both the majority and dissenting Justices on two
fundamental propositions: the importance of protecting property rights
*and* the importance of facilitating commercial ventures. The striking feature of the case, for present purposes, is the fact that the significance of
both these propositions was stressed but that their potential incompatibility
was not expressly recognized.

After his string of Contract Clause opinions from *Fletcher* v. *Peck*
through *Sturges*, Marshall's dissent in *Ogden* v. *Saunders* might have
been expected to stress the inviolability of vested property rights and to
make a close connection between the Contract Clause and the Framers'
solicitude for that principle. The Chief Justice did not disappoint. Not
only had the ''authority of . . . writers on natural and national law''[226]
established the principle that property rights were anterior to social legislation, the ''state of the times'' at the framing of the Constitution ''most
urgently required'' attentiveness toward ''securing the prosperity and harmony of our citizens''[227] by protecting the security of property rights
through the Contract Clause. Marshall reminded his readers (for the third
time in twenty years)[228] that ''the State legislatures'' in the 1790s had
used ''the power of changing the relative situation of debtor and creditor,

---

[221] Ibid., 359.
[222] Ibid., 365–67.
[223] Ibid., 346.
[224] Ibid., 282.
[225] E.g., Morgan, *William Johnson*, 207–30.

[226] 12 Wheat. at 347.
[227] Ibid., 339.
[228] See Marshall, *George Washington*, V, 86–87; Marshall in *Dartmouth College*, supra, note 122.

of interfering with contracts . . . [so] as to break in upon the ordinary intercourse of society, and destroy all confidence between man and man.'' To "guard against the continuance of [this] evil," he announced, "was an object of deep interest with all the truly wise, as well as the virtuous, of this great community.''[229]

Such positions might have been expected from Marshall. But Justices Thompson and Trimble advanced them as well. Thompson spoke of the Contract Clause as "intended . . . to protect the rights of property," thereby achieving "greater security and safety [by] incorporat[ing] into [the Constitution] provisions admitted by all to be among the first principles of our government.''[230] Laws "taking away vested rights," Thompson stated, were "repugnant to . . . fundamental principles.''[231] Trimble, for his part, announced that "the protection of personal security, and of private rights . . . was . . . the grand principle intended to be established" by the Framers. "It was," he felt, "a principle of the utmost importance to a free people." The principle could also be derived from "the laws of nature," since among men's "natural rights" was "the right of acquiring and possessing property.''[232]

At the same time, Marshall, Thompson, and Johnson emphasized that a major purpose and justification of debtor relief laws was, as Marshall put it, to encourage "commercial intercourse." Thompson noted that a flexible interpretation of the effect of the Contract Clause was "indispensable to facilitate commercial intercourse''[233] and suggested that insolvency laws were "generally admitted" to be "useful, if not absolutely necessary, in a commercial community.''[234] A "bankrupt system," he noted, "deals with commercial men''; a state should be allowed to "exercise its sovereign power in relieving the necessities of men who through their commercial ventures have become incapable of performing their contracts.''[235] Johnson agreed with these observations, and associated them with the context of the Constitution's origins. Recalling the existence of insolvency legislation before the Constitution's passage, he assumed that the legislation was "vitally important to a people overwhelmed in debt, and urged to enterprise by the activity of mind that is generated by revolutions and free governments.''[236]

But not a single Justice openly acknowledged that the assertion of the fundamental importance of solicitude for property did not help judges decide cases where solicitude for one person's property rights infringed upon solicitude for another's. If Marshall's opinion in *Ogden* v. *Saunders* had prevailed, "security" for creditors whose debtors fell into financial

---

[229] 12 Wheat. at 355.
[230] Ibid., 303.
[231] Ibid., 304.
[232] Ibid., 331, 319.

[233] Ibid., 300.
[234] Ibid., 276.
[235] Ibid., 313.
[236] Ibid., 276.

Chapter IX: *The Contract Clause Cases*

difficulties would have been at least hypothetically assured, especially if Congress continued not to enter the bankruptcy field. But "insecurity" for those who sought to invest in commercial ventures would also have occurred. If a person who borrowed money from another in order to engage in "commercial activity" knew that if his enterprise failed, or if the market value of his debt changed, he could not escape the precise terms of his obligation, his commercial activity was made less secure. This was especially the case when a debtor borrowed money relying upon the fact that his state had a debtor relief law, only to find subsequently that the law could not constitutionally be applied to exempt him from the letter of his obligations.

The jurisprudential principle of solicitude for property rights thus came to be perceived, as the commercial character of American society became more evident, as requiring a further inquiry: whose property was to be protected? This inquiry was qualitatively different from that posed by the earlier Marshall Court Contract Clause cases, where the Justices had asked themselves what sorts of transactions were "contracts" and therefore entitled to the protection of the clause. Focus now shifted to cases where a transaction would clearly be considered, given earlier cases, to be a "contract," but where solicitude for one set of property rights created by that contract infringed upon other property rights. It was not so easy, in the latter set of cases, for the Court to resolve issues by invoking the close linkage between natural justice, republican theory, and solicitude for property.

*Ogden* v. *Saunders* signified, in fact, that the Court had tacitly concluded that "contracts" constitutionally protected by the Contract Clause involved only a limited set of vested rights. First, despite the importance of the takings analogy, legislative takings made incumbent to reserved legislative police powers were not impairments of contracts. Second, contractual rights not in existence at the time of restrictive legislation were not impaired by that legislation. Contractual rights, the majority opinion in *Ogden* suggested, were not anterior to society but the creations of government, and whether they had sufficiently vested to receive the protection of the Contract Clause turned on whether the owners of these rights had an expectation that they would not be infringed. Owners of contractual rights that were conferred after an insolvency statute had been passed had no legitimate expectation that the other party to the contract would not declare insolvency. The rights had thus not sufficiently vested in their owners to enable them to claim that the contract had been impaired by the statute.

After *Ogden*, the scope of the Contract Clause was thus far narrower than previous cases had intimated, and the narrowing had two facets. Not only was the definition of an impairment for constitutional purposes narrower, the definition of vested rights was narrower and, by implication, the pressure of the takings analogy of Section 25 Contract Clause cases reduced. In decisions after *Ogden,* in fact, the Court made it clear that whatever the scope of the vested rights principle, or the force of the takings analogy in nonconstitutional law, the meaning of "vested rights" in the Contract Clause was limited.

The new stance of the Court after *Ogden* was readily observable. Between *Fletcher* and *Ogden* the Court had considered nine cases in which the Contract Clause was advanced as a barrier to state activity, and in only one, *Gozler* v. *Georgetown,*[237] was the state activity upheld. Even the *Gozler* case can be seen as the exception that proved the rule, for had the Contract Clause argument prevailed there the District of Columbia would have been permanently prevented, by an earlier grant from the Maryland legislature to the town of Georgetown, from changing "the graduation and levelling of the streets, lanes, and alleys within the jurisdiction of the same town."[238] The town of Georgetown, after having been given by Maryland "full power and authority" to pass ordinances respecting the graduation of its streets, then passed an ordinance establishing graduations for certain streets and stating that "the said level and graduation . . . shall be forever thereafter considered as the true graduation of the streets so graduated."[239] On its face the ordinance appeared to contain "a promise [by the town] to all who should build in the graduated streets that the graduation should be unalterable."[240] Marshall conceded as much in his opinion for the Court, but concluded that the town of Georgetown had no power to make such a promise, especially since the power to graduate and level streets was a "continuing" power, and this promise would "bind [the town's] capacities forever thereafter."[241] In short, the consequences of calling the ordinance a contract within the meaning of the Constitution would be "monstrous." *Gozler* thus stood for nothing more than the proposition that even a Contract Clause argument could be pressed to absurd limits. Towns had to be able to continue to make adjustments in their street plans even if they had been reckless enough to promise never to do so.

The eight cases after *Ogden* v. *Saunders,* by contrast, were more delicate, and in none of them was the Contract Clause found to be a barrier against state activity. The cases can be roughly grouped into two classes. The first consisted of cases where the Court took advantage of Marshall's distinction in *Sturges* between the "obligation" of a contract and "the remedy given by the legislature to enforce the obligation," a distinction Marshall had said to "exist in the nature of things." While these cases were notable in that they seized on an opportunity to limit the

---

237 6 Wheat. 593 (1821).
238 Ibid.
239 Ibid., 594.

240 Ibid., 597.
241 Ibid., 598.

656

# Chapter IX: *The Contract Clause Cases*

reach of the Contract Clause, that opportunity had been provided by Marshall, and was based on the common sense proposition that the Contract Clause did not keep legislatures from using their remedial powers to correct obvious injustices, such as usury, fraud, or the adjudication of stale claims.

Thus the legislature of Pennsylvania could create a contractual relationship between out-of-state settlers on land and in-state claimants, even though none had previously existed; creating a contract was not the same thing as impairing it.[242] The states of Kentucky[243] and Pennsylvania[244] could also change the proceedings by which forfeited land was sold, and Pennsylvania could "cure" defective land grants by married women when the curative procedures merely effectuated the intent of the grantors.[245] The *Sturges* decision did not prevent Rhode Island from retroactively abolishing imprisonment for debt[246] or Ohio from discharging insolvent debtors from prison.[247] None of these decisions was remarkable, but each demonstrated the Court's implicit sanctioning of a variety of legislative actions that had some effect on property rights. Notable was the fact that Marshall authored none of the opinions, whereas before 1827 he had written all but two of the Contract Clause decisions.

Two of the cases in this group were especially interesting in light of the distinction hinted at in *Ogden* between protection of vested rights as a general principle and protection of a limited class of vested rights under the Contract Clause. In *Satterlee* v. *Matthewson* two men acquired land in Pennsylvania under a title derived from a Connecticut corporation. After holding the land in common, they entered into a contract in which each became the landlord of the other for portions of the land, one tenanting the east side of the Susquehanna River and the other the west side. Both parties subsequently died, and their heirs became embroiled in a dispute over the land which resulted in an ejectment suit. In 1825 that suit reached the Supreme Court of Pennsylvania, which held that under Pennsylvania common law persons holding land under a Connecticut title could not enter into the relationship of landlord and tenant. The Pennsylvania legislature responded, a year later, by passing a statute which provided that "the relationship of landlord and tenant shall exist, and be held as fully and effectually between Connecticut settlers and Pennsylvania claimants as between other citizens of this commonwealth." This

---

[242] Satterlee v. Mattewson, 2 Pet. 380 (1829).
[243] Lessee of Livingston v. Moore, 7 Pet. 469 (1833).
[244] Hawkins v. Barney's Lessee, 5 Pet. 457 (1831). *Hawkins* sustained a procedure instituted by the same statutes allegedly invalidated in *Green* v.

*Biddle*, and did so in the face of a Contract Clause argument.
[245] Watson v. Mercer, 8 Pet. 88 (1834).
[246] Mason v. Haile, supra, note 216.
[247] Beers v. Houghton, 9 Pet. 329 (1835).

statute was challenged as a violation of the Contract Clause. Thomas Sergeant, arguing against its constitutionality, claimed that "retrospective laws are always unjust, and are contrary to the fundamental principles of our social compact"; that "[p]rivate property cannot be taken, even for public use, without full compensation and process of law"; and therefore that "retrospective laws, violating the rights of property, are contrary to the contract of any society established upon a republican basis." Such laws "not only impair [the obligation of contracts]," Sergeant concluded, "they break it."[248]

Washington, for the Court, noted that the statute had been challenged under the Contract Clause and also "because it operates to divest and destroy . . . vested rights."[249] He found that a law creating a contract did not "mean the same thing" as one "destroy[ing] or impair[ing] one."[250] He then asked whether there was "any other part of the constitution of the United States to which [the statute] was repugnant."[251] In particular, he noted the vested rights argument:

> The objection . . . which was most pressed upon the court, and relied upon by the counsel of the plaintiff in error, was that the effect of this act was to divest rights which were vested by law in Satterlee. There is certainly no part of the constitution of the United States which applies to a state law of this description; nor are we aware of any decision of this . . . court, which has condemned such a law upon this ground, provided its effect be not to impair the obligation of a contract.[252]

Washington then turned to *Fletcher,* where Marshall had said that "the nature of society and of government" prescribed some limits to legislative power, one limit being the inability of a legislature to take the property of an individual without compensation. Without "impugn[ing] the correctness of the sentiments expressed" in *Fletcher,* Washington pointed out that it was "no where intimated in that opinion that a state statute, which divests a vested right, is repugnant to the *constitution of the United States.*" He noted that *Fletcher* had come to the Court "not from the supreme court of a state, but from a circuit court,"[253] and the Court was thus not limited to constitutional sources for its holding. In contrast, *Satterlee* was a Section 25 case, and "unless . . . the statute objected to [was] repugnant to the *constitution of the United States, . . .* this Court has no authority . . . to reverse the judgment" of the Pennsylvania Supreme Court.[254]

---

248 2 Pet. at 406–407.
249 Ibid., 411.
250 Ibid., 413.
251 Ibid.

252 Ibid.
253 Ibid., 419.
254 Ibid. Emphasis in original.

# Chapter IX: *The Contract Clause Cases*

The distinction offered by Washington in *Satterlee* had both procedural and substantive features. On the one hand it suggested that the Court's limiting of protection to contract rights, rather than the larger category of vested property rights, was simply a matter of the jurisdictional posture of the case: had *Satterlee* come up from a circuit court, general principles of federal law might have invalidated the statute. On the other hand, the distinction suggested that the Contract Clause did not protect all divestments of vested rights or takings: only those which had impaired contracts. This dimension of *Satterlee* represented an implicit revival of the alternative basis for property rights holdings that had been characteristic of earlier Marshall Court decisions and seemed to have been abandoned in *Dartmouth College*. Property rights cases, in this view, were both vested rights and contracts cases. If they came to the Court as federal law cases under its diversity jurisdiction, they could be decided, as *Fletcher* had been, by recourse to the Constitution or to general principles. If, however, they came to the Court under Section 25, they could be decided only by recourse to the federal Constitution, the only relevant provision of which was the Contract Clause. And the Contract Clause, after *Ogden* and *Satterlee*, protected only a certain class of property rights: vested contractual rights that had been "impaired" by a state.

*Satterlee* was followed in the 1834 case of *Watson* v. *Mercer*, in which another 1826 Pennsylvania statute, this one designed to validate titles created by conveyances by married women that had been defective because of technical errors in the acknowledgment of the deeds. One such title, "cured" by the statute, was at issue in an ejectment proceeding, and the title was challenged, among other grounds, as not being rendered valid by the statute because the statute impaired the obligation of contracts and "destroyed and impaired vested rights."[255] Story, for a unanimous Court, made short shrift of the claim, noting that *Satterlee* had "fully settled" the distinction between curative statutes that "confirm[ed]" contracts and statutes that impaired them. He also took occasion to repeat that

> [t]his court has no right to pronounce an act of the state legislature void, contrary to the Constitution of the United States, from the mere fact that it devests antecedent vested rights of property.[256]

The Court's "authority" under Section 25, Story noted, was "to examine into the constitutionality of the act of 1826," in order "to ascertain, whether it violates the constitution of the United States." The questions of whether "it violates the Constitution of Pennsylvania," or "general principles" of federal law were, "upon the present writ of error, not

---

[255] 8 Pet. at 108.      [256] Ibid., 110.

before us."[257] Again, the message of *Watson* was that the Contract Clause protected only a limited class of property rights that had not only vested but were "contractual" and had been "impaired."

The second class of cases represented a more obvious departure from the thrust of earlier contracts cases and signified the Court's awareness of the potential for the Contract Clause to cripple state regulatory power. In *Jackson* v. *Lamphire*[258] the state of New York had originally granted land to one John Cornelius in consideration for his service in the Revolutionary War. Before Cornelius's title had been perfected, which occurred in 1790, he conveyed the land to two separate persons, each of whom eventually recorded the conveyances. In 1797 a New York statute appointed land commissioners to settle disputed titles, and two years later the commissioners awarded the land to one of the claimants. James Jackson, whose title to the disputed land derived from that of the losing claimant, sued to recover the land, claiming that the 1797 statute impaired the obligation of the original grant to Cornelius.

While *Jackson* v. *Lamphire* could have been decided on the same obligation/remedy distinction made in other similar cases involving disposition of land titles, Justice Henry Baldwin added a statement that was to prove portentous. In concluding that the case did not "come fairly within the [contract] clause," Baldwin said that "the only contract made by the state [was] a grant to John Cornelius, his heirs and assigns, of the land in question," and that it contained "no covenant to do, or not to do, any further act in relation to the land." Given that fact, the Court did not "feel at liberty to create [an obligation] by implication."[259] In this passage were the seeds of the doctrine that the obligations of state grants were to be strictly construed, a doctrine that the Taney Court was ultimately to use to allow legislative destruction of vested property rights in the great case of *Charles River Bridge* v. *Warren Bridge*.[260]

Another portentous but minor case was *Mumma* v. *Potomac Co.*,[261] decided in 1834. There Maryland and Virginia statutes had dissolved a corporation, the Potomac Company, which had done business in those states and the District of Columbia. Pursuant to the dissolution, the "property, rights and privileges" of the Potomac Company were "surrendered" to the Chesapeake and Ohio Canal Company, which had been incorporated in 1828. Shortly after its dissolution, a creditor of the Potomac company attempted to revive an unenforced judgment granted against that company in 1812. Among the creditor's arguments was the argument that Virginia and Maryland had violated the Contract Clause by confirming

---

[257] Ibid., 109.
[258] 3 Pet. 280 (1830).
[259] Ibid., 289.
[260] Proprietors of the Charles River Bridge v. Proprietors of the Warren Bridge, 11 Pet. 420 (1837).
[261] 8 Pet. 281 (1834).

the deed of surrender and incorporating the new corporation. Story dismissed the argument peremptorily. "A corporation," he wrote for a unanimous Court, "by the very terms and nature of its political existence, is subject to dissolution, by a surrender of its corporate franchises." "It would be a doctrine new in the law," Story observed, "that the existence of a private contract of the corporation should force upon it a perpetuity of existence contrary to public policy." The doctrine was offensive to "general principles."[262] In short, legislatures could dissolve corporations notwithstanding the "obligations" of corporate contracts. "Every creditor," Story noted, "must be presumed to understand the nature and incidents of [a corporation]."[263]

*Mumma* v. *Potomac Co.* was also helpful to Taney's decision in *Charles River Bridge,* where Massachusetts sought to "destroy" a toll bridge franchise it had chartered by allowing a free bridge to be constructed down river from the existing bridge. Story, who stood for the vested rights of the toll bridge stockholders in *Charles River Bridge,* saw that case as different from *Mumma,* but his language stating that corporate creditors presumed the vulnerability of corporations to legislative dissolution seemed capable of being applied to corporate stockholders as well.

To *Jackson* v. *Lamphire* and *Mumma* should be added *Providence Bank* v. *Billings,*[264] an 1830 decision written by Marshall for a unanimous Court. *Providence Bank* was the only Contract Case after 1827 in which Marshall wrote an opinion; it tested the scope of three of his previous decisions, *New Jersey* v. *Wilson, Dartmouth College,* and *McCulloch* v. *Maryland.* The Rhode Island legislature had granted a charter to the Providence Bank in 1791. In 1822 the legislature passed a statute taxing the capital stock of the bank at the rate of fifty cents per thousand dollars of stock. Subsequent statutes raised the tax to $1.25 per $1,000.00. The bank challenged the constitutionality of the legislation, arguing that the charter, which had no provision for taxation, was a contract between the state and the bank that perpetually exempted the bank from taxation. As framed, the *Providence Bank* case raised three doctrinal issues: whether *New Jersey* v. *Wilson* governed a case where a state's exemption from taxation had not been made explicit; whether an unlimited legislative grant of power to a corporation, as in *Dartmouth College,* precluded the legislature from subsequently changing the terms of its grant; and whether the limitation imposed on state taxation of national banks in *McCulloch* v. *Maryland,* an opinion in which Marshall had said that "the power to tax involves the power to destroy,"[265] applied to state taxation of state banks.

---

262 Ibid., 287.
263 Ibid.

264 4 Pet. 514 (1830).
265 4 Wheat. at 431.

Marshall found all of his previous holdings inapposite. He distinguished *New Jersey* v. *Wilson* on the ground that "the stipulation exempting the land from taxation was made in express words."[266] He distinguished *McCulloch* on the ground that the "opinion in that case . . . was founded expressly on the supremacy of the laws of Congress:" states could not tax national banks because to do so would interfere with "those means which are employed by Cognress to carry into execution powers conferred on that body by the people of the United States."[267] And he distinguished *Dartmouth College* on the ground that while the trustees of Dartmouth College had expressly been given the privilege of running the College "forever," and thus the New Hampshire legislature could not withdraw that privilege, the Providence Bank had been given no such privilege against taxation. And taxation, Marshall noted, was one of the "burdens" shared by individuals in society.[268]

"The power of . . . taxation," Marshall declared, "operates on all the persons and property belonging to the body politic." This statement was "an original principle, which has its foundation in society itself." However "absolute" individual rights were, it was "still in the nature of that right, that it must bear a portion of the public burdens."[269] Thus corporations could no more claim immunity from the burdens of taxation than individuals. Moreover, the "portion of the public burdens" that "individuals or corporate bodies" were to bear "must be determined by the legislature." In a concession to state legislative power reminiscent of his disinclination to probe legislative corruption in *Fletcher*, Marshall acknowledged that "the interest, wisdom and justice of the representative body, and its relations with its constituents, furnish the only security against unjust and excessive taxation."[270] Unless a legislative charter expressly exempted a corporation from taxation, no exemption could be taken to have been made. "It would be going very far" for a court "to insert [an exemption] by construction." The Contract Clause, or indeed the Constitution itself, "was not intended to furnish the corrective for every abuse of power which may be committed by the state governments."[271]

*Providence Bank* thus construed the obligations in Rhode Island's contract with the bank strictly, acknowledged that state tax powers were indispensable to government, and conceded that the Constitution could not correct every abuse of power by state governments. Marshall's suggestion in *Providence Bank* that the obligations of states in their grants were to be strictly construed, already announced in *Jackson* v. *Lamphire*,

---

[266] 4 Pet. at 563.
[267] Ibid., 563–64.
[268] Ibid., 562.

[269] Ibid., 563.
[270] Ibid., 562–63.
[271] Ibid., 563.

was followed in two other late Marshall Court cases, *Beaty* v. *Lessee of Knowler*[272] and *United States* v. *Corredondo*,[273] both of which were unanimous opinions. This apparent shift in the Court's stance seems most easily attributable to the Justices' eventual recognition that excessive solicitude for established property rights could retard private or state opportunities to engage in or benefit from commercial activity.

*Charles River Bridge* would be the case in which that recognition was made explicit, and in which the Court's members finally confronted in an open fashion the contradictions inherent in the principle of solicitude for private property. On one side in *Charles River Bridge* stood, as Taney's majority opinion was to put it, opportunities for the "States to . . . partake of the benefit of those improvements which are now adding to the wealth and prosperity, and the convenience and comfort of the civilized world";[274] on the other side stood Story "upon the old law, [which] resist[ed] . . . encroachments upon the rights and liberties of the citizens, secured by public grants."[275] For Taney the issue was whether Massachusetts was bound from chartering future bridges by its having chartered one, and therefore whether "we shall be thrown back to the improvements of the last century, and obliged to stand still until the claims of the old turnpike corporations shall be satisfied."[276] For Story the issue was whether the "title deeds" of propertied citizens could be "shake[n] . . . by . . . speculative niceties or novelties."[277] The issue could not have been more clearly joined: should established property rights yield to prospective property rights?

The Marshall Court had never explicitly faced that issue, and it found itself unable to decide *Charles River Bridge*. The bridge case had come up from the Massachusetts Supreme Court, where in March 1830 two judges had voted to sustain and two to overturn an 1828 Massachusetts statute enfranchising a second bridge from Boston to Charlestown.[278] The judges wrote their opinions seriatim, splitting decisively on the question whether the Charles River Bridge's charter, which contained no express provisions granting the proprietors an exclusive privilege to operate a bridge across the Charles River, should be "strictly" or "liberally" construed. The opinions also demonstrated an explicit awareness that cases such as *Charles River Bridge* brought one set of property rights into confrontation with another.[279] In order to comply with the requirements

---

[272] 4 Pet. 152 (1830).
[273] 6 Pet. 691 (1832).
[274] 11 Pet. at 553.
[275] Ibid., 598.
[276] Ibid., 553.
[277] Ibid., 598.

[278] Proprietors of Charles River Bridge v. Proprietors of Warren Bridge, 7 Pick. 344 (Mass., 1830).
[279] See ibid., 420–37, 446–52, 475–83, 510–20.

of Section 25 of the Judiciary Act of 1789, the Massachusetts Supreme Court sustained the statute, permitting appeal to the Supreme Court of the United States.[280]

The Marshall Court set arguments in *Charles River Bridge* in March 1831. Between *Ogden* v. *Saunders* and the 1831 Term two more personnel changes had taken place: Trimble had died in 1828, to be replaced a year later by John McLean; Washington had died in late 1829, succeeded by Henry Baldwin. Both McLean and Baldwin were Jackson appointees and presumably resistant to the aggrandizement of the powers of the federal judiciary at the expense of the states. We have seen that Baldwin went so far as to offer to resign in 1831, claiming, as later reported by Martin Van Buren, that he opposed "an unwarrantable extension of its powers by the Court."[281] Of the Court that had decided the cases from *Fletcher* v. *Peck* through *Green* v. *Biddle,* then, only Marshall, Story, Johnson, and Duvall remained.

Story was from the first strongly interested in the *Charles River Bridge* case, and decisively partisan. He was a professor at Harvard Law School and an overseer of Harvard College, who received a portion of the Charles River Bridge's tolls as a result of originally holding ferry rights across the Charles River.[282] In addition, Story felt that the Massachusetts legislature simply could not "destroy" the economic power of a state-created franchise by chartering a competitive franchise and declining to compensate the established franchise holder: such action violated the taking principle and natural justice. By November 1831 Story had prepared an opinion and had sent it to his friend Jeremiah Mason to "see . . . whether there is any weak point which can be fortified or ought to be abandoned."[283]

By March 1832, however, Story reported that the "Charlestown Bridge case is not yet decided," that "some of the Judges had not prepared their opinions," and the Court was "greatly divided in opinion," and possibly would not decide the case in the 1832 Term.[284] On March 14, 1832, the *National Intelligencer* reported that the case would be continued for another Term.[285] Marshall was reported as justifying the continuance on the ground that "one Judge . . . [was] absent [Johnson] and

---

[280] For a thorough summary of the Massachusetts opinions, see Kutler, *Privilege*, 36–53.

[281] M. Van Buren to L. McLane, quoted in M. Van Buren, *The Autobiography of Martin Van Buren* (J. Fitzpatrick, ed., 1920), 578.

[282] See Dunne, *Joseph Story*, 357–58.

[283] J. Story to J. Mason, Nov. 19, 1831, quoted in C. Warren, *The Supreme Court in United States History* (3 vols., 1922) II, 233.

[284] J. Story to J. Mason, Mar. 1, 1832, in W. Story, *Life and Letters,* II, 91–92.

[285] Washington *National Intelligencer,* Mar. 14, 1832.

the judges differ[ed]."[286] In the 1833 Term the Court still did not have a full membership in attendance, and a motion for reargument was granted.[287]

Absences among the Justices plagued the Marshall Court in its last years. Duvall had missed the 1831 arguments in *Charles River Bridge* because of the illness of his wife, Johnson had missed the entire 1832 and 1834 Terms, Baldwin missed the 1833 Term, and Duvall missed most of the 1834 Term. Eventually Johnson died in August 1834, and Duvall resigned before the 1835 Term. When Marshall died in July 1835, the *Charles River Bridge* case had still not been resolved. Absences on the part of Justices were, however, a commonplace feature of the Marshall Court. In the years between 1815 and 1835, for example, the Court had a full membership in Washington for only seven Terms. The absence of Justices did not preclude the Court from deciding pivotal cases, as we have seen in *Dartmouth College, Sturges,* and *Green v. Biddle.* Absences were critical in *Charles River Bridge,* however, because the Justices were so closely divided. Marshall made the significance of the 1833 grant of a reargument clear a year later when he said that "the practice of this court is not (except in cases of absolute necessity) to deliver any judgment in cases where constitutional questions are involved, unless four judges concur in opinion, thus making the decision that of a majority of the whole court."[288]

Of the prospective votes of the Marshall Court Justices who considered *Charles River Bridge,* some have been relatively easy to establish and others have remained obscure.[289] No evidence has surfaced suggesting that Story's and Thompson's 1837 positions, in which they voted to invalidate the Massachusetts statute, were departures from previously held views. McLean's position in 1837 was that the Court did not have jurisdiction to decide the case, and there is no evidence indicating that this position represented a change from earlier views. An 1832 letter from Story to Jeremiah Mason hinted at McLean's position. "The doubts of some of the brethren," Story wrote, were "various" and "apply to different aspects of the case."[290]

Baldwin said in 1837 that "it now appears that I stood alone after the argument in 1831,"[291] and since Baldwin voted with the Taney Court

---

[286] Ibid.
[287] Kutler, *Privilege,* 174.
[288] 8 Pet. at 122.
[289] See Warren, *Supreme Court,* II, 233; Kutler, *Privilege,* 172–79; C. Haines, *The Role of the Supreme Court in American Government and Politics 1789–1835* (1944), 611.

[290] Story to Mason, Mar. 1, 1832, supra, note 284.
[291] H. Baldwin, *A General View of the Origin and Nature of the Constitution and Government of the United States* (1837), 2.

majority, his earlier inclination to sustain the statute seems clear. Less confidence can be placed in Baldwin's judgment that he apparently "stood alone." If he had, there would have been a clear majority to invalidate the statute, since even if Duvall had recused himself for failure to hear argument, five Justices would have opposed Baldwin, and Story's concerns about divisions among the Justices would have been unnecessary. Baldwin, we have noted, had periods of mental illness throughout his career on the Court, and his absence for the 1833 Term was on account of a nervous breakdown.[292] Thus while it is likely that Baldwin had come to a decision to sustain the statute by 1831, other Justices may well have been leaning in that direction.

Between 1832 and 1835 no four-vote majority surfaced on either side of the case. Story's behavior indicates that the chances of those opposed to the Massachusetts legislation seemed more promising than the chances of those supporting it, at least in the early stages. Daniel Webster, who represented the proprietors of the Charles River Bridge before the Court and who was a remarkably successful predictor of eventual decisions, wrote his co-counsel in the case that Justice Duvall was likely to support their side, since Duvall was "generally sound on [vested rights] subjects,"[293] and Webster was correct in that characterization: Duvall had, after all, joined Marshall in his dissent in *Ogden* v. *Saunders*. But if Duvall was prepared to vote with Story and Thompson, we know no other Justice was, because only one additional vote was needed.

Johnson's position in the case has never been clarified. His principal biographer did not discuss the case at all, and there is little extant evidence of his views. Johnson attended the 1831 Term, which produced no decision, but missed the 1832 and 1834 Terms, and died in the summer of 1834. If Johnson had voted with Story's group, it is probable that the case would have been decided, so it is unlikely that he gave any signs of supporting the Charles River Bridge proprietors. Johnson was not particularly interested in compromising his views at this stage of his career, was estranged from Story and disinclined to join Story opinions, especially in constitutional cases,[294] and was, by and large, an advocate of state powers. In 1833 Webster reported Johnson as opposing a second argument of the case,[295] so it is probable that Johnson was inclined to

---

[292] F. Gatell, "Henry Baldwin," in Friedman and Israel, *Justices,* I, 576; R. Vree, "Henry Baldwin and the Marshall Monolith" (unpublished manuscript, Stanford Law School, 1969), 18–20. See discussion in Chapter V.
[293] D. Webster to Warren Dutton,

Jan. 29, 1833, Webster Papers. See Kutler, *Privilege,* 174–75.
[294] See Dunne, *Joseph Story,* 168–170, 263–64.
[295] Webster to Dutton, Jan. 29, 1833, supra, note 293.

support the Warren Bridge proprietors but had not produced an opinion, possibly because of ill health.

The critical vote in the case was thus Marshall's. Had Marshall strongly endorsed Story and Thompson's position, a majority opinion would likely have resulted, and there would have been no need for a reargument after 1833. Baldwin's absence for the 1833 Term would then have made no difference. But if Marshall was leaning in the other direction, the case stood 3–3 on the merits, with McLean disinclined to hear it at all: a genuine deadlock. The idea of Marshall's voting to sustain the Massachusetts statute might at first glance seem improbable. But while Marshall was the author of *Dartmouth College* and *Ogden v. Saunders,* he was also the author of *Providence Bank,* and he was by all accounts an inveterate compromiser and supporter of consensual positions, especially in major constitutional cases. Had Marshall declared himself early on as an opponent of the Massachusetts statute, it is unlikely that Story would have felt obligated to write a draft opinion, for that would have probably meant four votes to strike down the statute, and Marshall, having written so many significant Contract Clause opinions, would likely have been inclined to try to write another opinion for the Court.

Professor Stanley Kutler has shown that not only did Marshall not produce a draft opinion at any stage of the *Charles River Bridge* deliberations, Story, in his 1837 dissent, did not associate Marshall, who had died two years earlier, with the views Story expressed. Since Story pointedly mentioned Marshall's concurrence with dissenting positions Story took in two other significant constitutional cases decided in 1837, it appears that he would have enlisted Marshall's posthumous support in *Charles River Bridge* had such support existed.[296] Moreover, Simon Greenleaf, who argued the case for the Warren Bridge proprietors, stated thirteen years after the case had been decided that he had been "credibly informed" that Marshall "held the charter of Warren Bridge constitutional, upon the first argument of the case [(1831)]; and that it was on account of division of the bench that a second argument was ordered."[297] That tale was subsequently repeated by William Kent, the son of James Kent, who was of course a close friend and correspondent of Story.[298]

Finally, a 3–3–1 division of votes in *Charles River Bridge* renders the continued postponement of the case intelligible. If the votes of four Justices were necessary to produce an opinion in a constitutional case, the absence of a full complement of Justices could easily prevent the

---

[296] Kutler, *Privilege,* 176–78.
[297] W. Cruise, *A Digest of the Law of Real Property* (S. Greenleaf, ed., 3 vols., 1850), II, 68.

[298] Kent, *Commentaries* (W. Kent, ed., 1851), III, 566–67.

formation of a majority in close cases. If one assumes, for example, that Marshall might have swayed Duvall's vote in the 1832, 1833, or 1834 Term, the absence of Baldwin or Johnson would still have prevented a four-man majority from surfacing. Even if one adopts the less likely possibility that Marshall had joined Story and Thompson and was prepared to vote against the Warren Bridge, but that Duvall was not,[299] then a four-man majority would have depended on Johnson's vote.

Perhaps the most appropriate way to describe the Marshall Court's posture in *Charles River Bridge* is to say that the Court *could* not decide the case: that is, the ideological issues posed by the case were not issues that the Marshall Court's governing jurisprudential assumptions were designed to resolve. The starting premise of Marshall Court Contract Clause opinions, from *Fletcher v. Peck* on, had been solicitude for the security of property rights in a republic. That premise had been shared by Justices who were sympathetic to the state's use of their regulatory powers, such as Johnson, Livingston, and Thompson; by Justices who were enthusiastic about the expansion of the national government, such as Todd and Story; by Justices who were unsympathetic to the propertyless masses, such as Washington and Duvall; and by Justices who were deeply suspicious of the soundness of state legislatures, such as Marshall. From *Fletcher v. Peck* through *Green v. Biddle,* security for property was regularly made the governing principle of the Contract Clause; once vested rights had been shown to have originated in a contract they prevailed over even state legislation that was considered expedient and sensible, as in the area of debtor relief. Only by *Ogden v. Saunders* had a countervailing principle emerged: the idea that state regulation actually *furthered* security for property by facilitating commercial transactions and providing relief for investments that collapsed.

The shift within the Marshall Court from an earlier liberal construction of contract obligations to a later strict construction can be attributed to the fusion of two perceptions. One of these had been an established, but controversial, feature of the Marshall Court's jurisprudence; the other had never fully surfaced to the level of an explicit policy argument, even after it became an important part of the Court's decisionmaking calculus.

The first perception was that aggressive construction of the scope of the Contract Clause resulted in the Court's being a monitor of state regulatory activities. The Marshall Court had recognized this consequence of its Contract Clause decisions very early on. Certain Justices, particularly Marshall, Story, Washington, Duvall, and Todd, welcomed this consequence as a matter of political philosophy: they saw themselves as

---

[299] As surmised by Warren in *Supreme Court,* II, 233.

preserving first principles of the Republic from state demagoguery. Other Justices, such as Johnson and Livingston, were less sympathetic to curbs on state power but were able to compromise their opposition because of their commitment to the principle of security for property and because of the circumspection of Marshall's majority opinions. But as the reach of the Contract Clause widened, and new Justices, less sympathetic to the role of the Court as a preservationist censor, came on the Court, enthusiasm for aggressive judicial scrutiny of state legislation under the Contract Clause waned. Adverse public reaction to the *Sturges* and *Green* v. *Biddle* decisions may well have strengthened the positions of those Justices who were concerned about state autonomy, and made politically sensitive promoters of an aggressive Court posture, such as Marshall, more willing to compromise.

But it is unlikely that the issue of state sovereignty alone could have resulted in the Marshall Court's altered posture toward Contract Clause cases after *Ogden v̇. Saunders*. After all, Story was still able to say in an 1829 opinion, as previously noted, that "government can scarcely be deemed to be free where the rights of property are left solely dependent upon the will of a legislative body," and every member of the Court joined his opinion. The Contract Clause, whatever its scope, was *intended* to be a restriction on state power to infringe upon property rights; the issue was not whether it was designed to erect barriers to state activity— that was taken for granted—but how far its barriers extended. Increasingly the Court sensed that it was making close judgments in Contract Clause cases. The states were to be deprived of some of their sovereign powers in the name of security for property, but surely not all of them. And how many times was the Court prepared to bar the execution of state powers where state activity was perceived as welcome and beneficent by the public? After *Ogden* the Court took pains to point out that not all property rights were protected by the Contract Clause.

In considering the political implications of close judgments in Contract Clause cases, the Marshall Court's calculus was clarified by the surfacing of a second perception, that some types of state legislation which infringed upon existing contractual relations could be seen as having the eventual purpose of promoting opportunities to acquire property. Livingston had articulated this perception as early as 1817; Johnson and Thompson had alluded to it in *Ogden* v. *Saunders*. By Taney's opinion in *Charles River Bridge,* state infringements on vested rights were being justified as providing enhanced economic opportunities that would ultimately lead to more citizens being propertied and to greater "progress."

But the step in logic that Taney's opinion had taken was never explicitly made on the Marshall Court. It was a step from a consciousness that identified property principally with the preservation of established rights to a consciousness that identified property with future commercial ventures as well. Late-eighteenth-century republican theory, we have seen, had been premised on certain assumptions about the nature of man, the tendency of governments, and the qualities of change; the place of property rights in society had been derived from those assumptions. If one assumes that the Justices on the Marshall Court shared these assumptions in the abstract, the origin of their property consciousness is readily identifiable. The Justices believed that they and other Americans had a stake in preserving the Republic, preventing the processes of corruption and decay from gaining momentum, resisting demagoguery, and promoting civic virtue and liberal statesmanship. Linked to all these pursuits was the idea of creating a sense of security for propertyholders so that worthy individuals could be free to lend their talents to the service of the state. That propertied individuals *were* worthy needed no documentation; their possession of property suggested that they had the industry and talents to channel their passions in constructive ways. Solicitude for a select class of independent, leisured, civic-minded, propertied citizens was thus indispensable for the preservation and purification of republican forms of government.

Late-eighteenth-century republican theorists also assumed, in the main, that the distribution of talent and industry among persons in society was sufficiently uneven that the propertied would remain the few. Their conception of property rights did not assume the possibility that every man could become propertied. Indeed, the propertied classes were regarded as a buffer against the more numerous, and more susceptible, nonpropertied classes; the latter's susceptibility to unbridled passion and demagoguery was perhaps even more threatening to the Republic than the former's susceptibility to luxuriousness and corruption. An eighteenth-century republican theorist could assume that with security and independence could come civic-mindedness; the Framers of the Constitution and the statesmen of the new nation were members of the propertied classes. But no similar attribution of virtue could be made to those without property. They were not likely to acquire it, and they were dangerous without it.

The words "no state shall impair the obligation of contracts," then, were fraught with meaning for those exposed to the assumptions of republican theory. They conveyed a belief in security for property, a fear of mobs and demagogues, the erection of constitutional barriers against these would seek to upset the balances or corrupt the forms of republican government. Since Marshall had earlier established, in *Marbury* v. *Madison,* the proposition that the judiciary was to give constitutional language its operative meaning, and since the Justices on Marshall's Court "knew" what the language of the Contract Clause meant in principle, it seemed natural for the Court to read the Contract Clause as providing security for property. Indeed for the Court to justify its holdings in Contract Clause cases it seemed only necessary to restate that principle, which is what Marshall Court opinions repeatedly did.

But the principle of solicitude for property made clearest sense in a regime where the security of the propertied class was being threatened by the nonpropertied classes; that is, where the state forces ''impairing'' contract rights could be pictured as destructive advocates of mob rule. Where the ''impairment'' of contract rights appeared to be designed to facilitate another set of property rights, the insights of republican theory did not produce as clear a solution. Was the status of being propertied valuable to society because it channeled one's destructive passions into constructive interests or because it freed its possessor to pursue civic virtue? Republican theorists had suggested that the value of being propertied was valuable in *both* respects, and that the twin features were not self-opposing. But the bankruptcy cases and the competitive franchise cases made it clear that security for property could thwart opportunities to acquire property; that, at a theoretical level, one sometimes had to balance civic virtue against the pursuit of one's interests; that classical republicanism could be hostile to economic liberalism.

Once the issue was framed as a choice between types of property-holders, as it was by Taney in *Charles River Bridge*, its resolution was apparent. But we should recognize why preference for an expansive meaning of property rights over a preservationist meaning was so ''easy'' once Taney and others had articulated the choice. The preference was easy because a central maxim of republican theory had been discarded: the assumption that change, especially economic change, facilitated decay rather than progress. Late-eighteenth-century republican theory had assumed that too much change in republican forms of government was to be resisted; first principles were to be periodically restated. That assumption had proved incompatible with the apparently inexhaustible opportunities to acquire propertied status offered by the nineteenth-century American economy. Taney spoke in *Charles River Bridge* of the costs of being ''thrown back'' to ''the last century,'' and of ''stand[ing] still.'' He was anxious to move on toward ''improvements,'' ''wealth and prospectivity,'' and ''convenience and comfort.'' His opinion appeared comfortable with the idea of ''progress.''

The jurisprudence of the Marshall Court did not fully embrace this redefinition of social and economic change as ''progress'' rather than as ''decay.'' Hints of the commercial value of some state statutes impairing contractual obligations had surfaced, but the idea that an expansion of potential opportunities to acquire property to all citizens would result in *beneficial* rather than *destructive* change had not been made explicit. That idea was so foreign to certain core assumptions of republican theory, such as the equation of industry and talent with propertied status and the belief that industriousness and ability were unequally and sparingly distributed among members of society, that one can understand why it did not explicitly surface on the Marshall Court. Yet intimations of the idea did surface, such as the perception that solicitude for vested property rights did not always facilitate "commercial intercourse," or the perception that there were limits on the freedom of private contracting parties from state regulation—limits on the vested rights principle. The interaction of these intimations with the still powerful opposing theory of solicitude for property as a barrier against decay paralyzed the Court in *Charles River Bridge*. The paralysis was caused by the confrontation of inherited assumptions of republican theory with economic liberalism in its pure form—the competitive enterprise demanding a share of a market.

The evolution of the Contract Clause cases, and of the Court's response to the problem of legislative regulation of vested rights, thus furnishes a striking example of the impact of tacit ideological beliefs on the Court's decisionmaking process. The Court had begun its investigations of the vested rights problem by invoking the takings analogy: a legislative taking of property from A and giving it to B was simply offensive to general principles. As vested rights cases evolved, the Justices, led by Marshall, recognized that these general principles could be most effectively made use of when fused in the text of the Constitution, and the Contract Clause was packed with the doctrine of solicitude for vested rights. At almost the very time that solicitude for vested rights became ostensibly established as a maxim of constitutional jurisprudence, however, the issue of protection for property rights took on a newly perceived complexity with the bankruptcy cases, which first revealed that legislative regulation that impaired one set of property rights could benefit another set. Meanwhile, extreme applications of the Contract Clause, such as *Green* v. *Biddle* and *McMillan* v. *McNeill*, elicited public criticism: not only were Contract Clause cases theoretically complex, they were politically delicate. The behind-the-scenes divisiveness that marked all the cases from *Sturges* to *Ogden* was a product of these factors.

As the Court began to recognize that its Contract Clause interpretations may have been too monolithic, its personnel began to change, and its apparent unanimity on behalf of vested rights was revealed to have existed only on the surface. The Court's informal deliberative practices and powerful collegial nouns prevented the unanimity from dissolving publicly until *Ogden* v. *Saunders*, but the very fact that *Ogden* v. *Saunders* was litigated so closely after the decisions in *Sturges* and its progeny was a signal that attitudes and personnel were changing. And once the great variety of views on the nature of property rights and the purpose of the Contract Clause was made public in *Ogden* v. *Saunders*, a new approach to property rights cases came to dominate the Court's decisions. The approach rested on a sense that property rights cases were no longer

## Chapter IX: *The Contract Clause Cases*

"easy"; that the Court should be cautious in its use of the Contract Clause as a weapon against state regulation; that contract rights were more limited than vested rights; and that the Court's Section 25 review power was limited to the investigation of only a special class of property rights cases. In addition, the Court's increasingly limited construction of the Contract Clause intimated that its members had perceived that some state restrictions on private property were not only constitutionally permissible but, in a world in which the concept of property was changing, socially necessary. But that intimation was never openly articulated, and its logical conclusion—that when "new" property rights clashed with "old" property rights vested holdings should give way to "progress"—was not explicitly reached. The Court, as a collective body, remained bound in by the older takings analogy: the idea that a legislature *could* take property from A and give it to B in the name of "competition," "commerce," and "progress" was never fully embraced. Thus the Contract Clause cases began with a bang—the "general principles" of *Fletcher* v. *Peck*—and ended with a whimper—the paralysis of *Charles River Bridge*. The Court's property consciousness had both helped elevate it to prominence and imprisoned it in time.

# CHAPTER X

# Natural Law and Racial Minorities: The Court's Response to Slaves and Indians

I N THE PRECEDING CHAPTER we noticed the qualification, in the Court's Contract Clause decisions, of the idea that the right to hold property or to make contracts existed in a state of nature. Echoes of that idea had appeared in *Fletcher* v. *Peck* and *Terrett* v. *Taylor,* and Marshall had developed it at length in his dissent in *Ogden* v. *Saunders.* The Court's contract cases could not be said, however, to have established the proposition that the natural right to hold property or to make contracts amounted to a substantive right against the state. On the contrary, while the Court's interpretation of the Contract Clause had been influenced by general principles such as the takings principle and the principle that a legislature could not arbitrarily divest propertyholders of their holdings, the rights held by the Court to be protected by the Contract Clause amounted to a limited subset of existing vested rights. The protection of rights by appeal to natural justice had been limited to a handful of diversity cases.

One of the implications of the Contract Clause cases, then, was that constitutional law and natural law were not the same. Indeed, in the later Contract Clause cases that implication seemed explicit: in *Satterlee* and *Watson* the Court expressly rejected the takings principle and any other general principle of protection for vested rights as apposite to Section 25 cases since the states were not restricted by the Constitution from taking property without just compensation or from divesting vested rights. The Court came to this conclusion despite acknowledging that in diversity cases those general restrictions on legislatures might remain relevant. The evolution of Contract Clause doctrine thus appeared to erect a distinction between constitutional and natural law, the former being limited to those principles that had been written down in the constitutional text.

674

# Chapter X: *Natural Law and Racial Minorities*

The Court's retention of discretion to consider general principles of natural justice in diversity cases, however, suggested that the distinction between constitutional and natural law did not amount to an equation of law with the positivistic enactments of legislative bodies. Judges could ground decisions, outside the constitutional area, on principles of "natural justice," "republican government," "our free institutions," and the like. And, as the Contract Clause cases illustrated, the distinction also did not preclude the Court from packing a textual provision with general principles in its interpretation of that provision. But the distinction suggested that where natural rights had not been expressly codified in the text of the Constitution, their intrinsic appeal did not in itself furnish an argument for their elevation to constitutional status.

Natural law was thus pertinent to constitutional cases but not dispositive of them. Indeed, the evolution of Contract Clause jurisprudence suggested that the pertinence of natural law to constitutional analysis was only in the tacit pressure it created to expand constitutional language to include natural rights principles, and that pressure could be counterbalanced by the obligation to stay within the boundaries of the text in constitutional interpretation. The Contract Clause cases, in fact, could be seen as lending support to the proposition that there was, after all, a bright line between natural law in the abstract and natural law that had been codified in the Constitution, and that the former, whatever moral weight it carried, did not form a basis for legal decisions.

Later in the nineteenth century the stark separation of moral and legal principles became an assumption of American jurisprudence, and natural law was not taken seriously as an authoritative source except to the extent it had been positivized. But in the period of the Marshall Court no such jurisprudential separation existed: the period was characterized instead by a fusion, in treatises and judicial decisions, of doctrines drawn from moral philosophy and doctrines extracted from the common law and other legal sources. The American Revolution had given a practical meaning to natural rights principles: natural law had evolved from its religious origins to a secular principle of late-eighteenth-century political theory, encompassed in the idea of the inalienable rights of man. Thus the distinction drawn in the Contract Clause cases between natural and constitutional rights emerged in a jurisprudential universe where natural rights principles had been endowed with considerable stature. The distinction also emerged in an area in which the rights in question had been deemed to be among the most necessary and fundamental in a republican society: rights of property. The example of the Contract Clause cases thus suggested that cases arising from violations of other natural rights, such as the rights to maintain personal liberty or not to be discriminated against because of ethnic or racial origin, would be susceptible to the same distinction. In fact the cases, when they came to the Court, were conceptualized in a fashion that separated constitutional from natural law even more sharply, and ultimately paved the way for the demise of natural law as an authoritative basis for legal decisions in American jurisprudence.

The natural rights cases came to the Court in an atmosphere that invested natural law arguments with considerable force. Both "natural law" and "natural rights," the terms that combined to create what this chapter calls the reconstituted natural law argument in early-nineteenth-century jurisprudence, were established philosophical concepts at the time of the American Revolution. The triumph of republican ideology in eighteenth-century America, however, enhanced the significance of those terms. The idea that human beings, by virtue of their humanity, had been tacitly granted certain freedoms and could anticipate certain opportunities had religious origins, and may have been formulated, in the sixteenth and seventeenth centuries, as part of a conservative resistance to monarchic or oligarchic despotism. But that idea was given a dramatic reformulation in the eighteenth century, when it was associated with republican forms of government, the sovereignty of the people, and the proposition that "all men are created equal." In this "liberal" reformulation of natural rights theory governments were seen as being created to protect the inalienable rights of man that existed anterior to the formation of society. The protection of natural rights was thus one of the first principles of republican government.[1]

Alongside the evolution of the concept of natural rights had evolved a related but distinguishable concept, natural law. In early-nineteenth-century jurisprudence the two concepts, while typically run together, continued to have somewhat separate meanings. Natural law, whose origins were clearly associated with religion and which was still sometimes identified with God's law in early-nineteenth-century treatise writing, referred to abstract principles of justice, humanity, tolerance, and "civilized" living that were "beyond dispute" in any culture which considered itself enlightened. Natural law could also refer to, or be used in conjunction with, the law of nations, principles to which all enlightened civilizations tacitly, or sometimes overtly, subscribed. A distinguishing characteristic of natural law was its unwritten character: it was conceived of as a collection of principles that, while universally subscribed to, had not been

---

[1] See R. Tuck, *Natural Rights Theories* (1979), 3–5, 82–173; P. Conkin, *Self-Evident Truths* (1974), 75–125.

codified, and for this reason it was regularly contrasted with "positive," "municipal," or "public" law, by which was meant written law.[2]

The persistence of natural law as an acknowledged source of law in early America, when combined with the reformulation of natural rights theory that accompanied American independence, invested the natural law argument with enhanced stature and with a degree of specificity. Natural law could be taken, in the American republic, as embracing natural rights principles. The inalienable rights of life, liberty, and property, even if not protected by positive laws, were regarded as embedded in the principles of natural law. The fusion of the two concepts is illustrated by certain stock phrases of early-nineteenth-century jurisprudence, such as "the fundamental principles of republican government," "great principles of natural justice," or the "reason and nature of things." For example, in an 1822 circuit opinion in the case *La Jeune Eugénie*, which will be subsequently discussed in more detail, Story declared that the slave trade was illegal in America because it was "repugnant to the great principles of Christian duty, the dictates of natural religion, the obligations of good faith and morality, and the eternal maxims of social justice." The trade could be "interdicted by public law," Story argued, because it offended "the general principles of justice and humanity."[3]

A sample of the writings of commentators from 1816 to 1836 reveals a consensus that natural law, in its reconstituted form, was a very important source of law in America. A recurrent theme of the treatise literature was the idea of natural law as the foundation of all other laws. In an 1828 collection of essays, Francis Walker Gilmer translated an 1816 essay by François Quesnay, who had argued that natural laws were "the foundation of . . . perfect government" and "positive laws" merely "laws of preservation." Positive legislation, according to Quesnay, was simply declaratory of natural law.[4] Nathan Dane, in his *General Abridgment and Digest of American Law*, advanced similar views. Statutes were "merely declaratory of the law of nature and reason"; the law of nations was identical to "the law of nature"; all laws contrary to natural law were invalid.[5] Peter Du Ponceau, writing in 1824, suggested that "universal justice" should be the "basis" of all law, and that "general jur-

---

[2] On the concept of natural law in early American jurisprudence, see B. Wright, *American Interpretations of Natural Law* (1931), 7–12, 63–148; E. Corwin, "The Higher Law Background of American Constitutional Law," *Harv. L. Rev.*, 42:149, 365 (1928). On the relationship between natural and positive law in republican thought, see R. Cover, *Justice Accused* (1975), 9–30; G. Wood, *The Creation of the American Republic* (1973), 259–305.

[3] *La Jeune Eugénie*, 26 F. Cas. 832, 846 (1822).

[4] F. Quesnay, "A Treatise on Natural Right," in F. Gilmer, *Sketches, Essays, and Translations* (1828), 198–99.

[5] N. Dane, *A General Abridgment and Digest of American Law* (9 vols., 1823), VI, 429.

isprudence'' should rest on ''eternal and immutable principles of right and wrong.''[6] And David Hoffman, in his *Legal Outlines,* published in 1829, argued that ''the very basis of government and laws'' lay in natural law and that if ''this foundation'' of natural law were to be removed, ''all instituted laws would become as the morning vapors.''[7]

Early-nineteenth-century commentators pointed to the close connection between the law of nature and the law of nations as an example of the fundamental quality of natural law. Nathaniel Chipman identified natural law as the ''foundation'' of the ''internal and customary law of nations'';[8] Dane characterized the law of nations as ''the law of nature applied to nations'';[9] Hoffman maintained that ''a large portion of [international law]'' was ''nothing more than the [law of nature] applied to nations.''[10] Story, in *La Jeune Eugénie,* made it clear that the ''fundamental'' character of natural law made it presumptively part of the law of nations and municipal law unless the customs and practices of a nation suggested otherwise. ''[I]t may be unequivocally affirmed,'' he wrote, ''that every doctrine, that may be fairly deduced by correct reasoning from . . . the nature of moral obligation, may theoretically be said to exist in the law of nations; and unless it be relaxed or waived by the consent of nations, which may be evidenced by their general practice and customs, it may be enforced in a court of justice.'' He himself, Story continued, would even ''go farther'' than that language:

> I may . . . say, that no practice whatsoever can obliterate the fundamental distinction between right and wrong, and that every nation is at liberty to apply to another the correct principle.[11]

Pressed to its logical conclusion, Story's position would appear to have elevated natural law to a status of jurisprudential primacy, a set of first principles that antedated and superseded positivistic law. But he was not prepared to press his logic that far in his *Eugénie* opinion, adding after the end of the excerpt quoted above the qualifying phrase, ''whenever both nations by their public acts recede from such practice.''

Some juristic contemporaries of Story were far less confident about the ''fundamental'' status of natural law, let alone its intelligibility as a set of unwritten principles. Henry Wheaton suggested in his treatise, *Elements of International Law,* which appeared in 1836, that the law of nations was not based primarily on ''the principles of natural justice,''

---

[6] P. Du Ponceau, *A Dissertation on the Nature and Extent of the Jurisdiction of the Courts of the United States* (1824), 126, 128.

[7] D. Hoffman, *Legal Outlines* (1829), 119, 349.

[8] N. Chipman, *Principles of Government,* (1833), 173, 175.

[9] Dane, *Abridgment,* VII, 429.

[10] Hoffman, *Outlines,* 83.

[11] 26 F. Cas. at 846.

although it might have a "remote foundation" in those principles. Wheaton divided international law into the "natural law of nations" and the "positive law of nations." He felt that the positive enactments of nations, such as treaties, adjudications of international tribunals, and national legislation, were not only a more accessible but a more meaningful source of law than unwritten principles of natural justice.[12] Ten years earlier James Kent had declared "positive law" to be the "most useful and practical part of the law of nations,"[13] thereby intimating that natural law, notwithstanding its importance, had a vague, ephemeral quality.

Story's concession that "fundamental distinction[s] between right and wrong" could best be observed in "public acts," taken together with Wheaton's and Kent's comments, illustrates an important complicating factor in the reconstituted natural law argument. While natural law was undoubtedly an important, even a fundamental, source of law, did it have any meaning independent of the "public acts" in which it appeared? Here one encounters a jurisprudential principle as important to late-eighteenth- and early-nineteenth-century Americans as the principle of natural rights itself: the principle that not only should the supreme law of the republic be a written constitution, but that laws, generally, should be written down. As we have seen in an earlier discussion of the applicability of the common law to the federal courts, early American jurists and political theorists made a connection between unwritten law and the partisan or arbitrary use of power. The preservation of the inalienable rights of human beings, theorists of the Framers' generation reasoned, would be enhanced if those rights were incorporated into written documents.

The reconciliation of the enhanced status of natural law with the principle of written laws was not free from difficulties. If natural law was the foundation of all laws, could it not serve as a corrective where positive enactments had gone wrong? But how could it serve as a corrective if its principles were not themselves written? And if they were written, who was to write them? By stressing the written laws principle early American jurists were intimating that unwritten laws were unintelligible and dangerous, but by stressing the importance of positive enactments of principles they were also intimating that those who wrote or declared laws in written form—legislators or judges—were perhaps the primary sources of natural law itself. And therein lay a dilemma: could the decisions of legislators or judges embody universal principles of natural justice and at the same time function as practical, immediate resolutions of legal problems?

We have previously seen that one of the significant responses to this dilemma by early-nineteenth-century American jurists, most notably the

---

[12] H. Wheaton, *Elements of International Law* (1836), 45, 47–48.

[13] J. Kent, *Commentaries on American Law* (4 vols., 1826), I, 2.

Justices of the Marshall Court, was to entrench the idea of the Constitution as the supreme source of American law and to pack the Constitution's language with principles derived from extraconstitutional sources. This technique, which was so effective in establishing the Constitution as a flexible and authoritative document, was of course vulnerable both to judicial interpretation and to the ideological presuppositions of the culture in which interpretations took place. In the case of racial minorities that vulnerability was to be especially poignant.

To summarize, three basic jurisprudential questions were raised by the emergence of the reconstituted natural law argument in late-eighteenth- and early-nineteenth-century American jurisprudence. The first question was whether the fusion of an older conception of natural law with republican natural rights theory would result in the proposition that certain inalienable rights enjoyed by all people were not only fundamental but amounted to substantive rights against the state. Language in both the Declaration of Independence and the Constitution could be taken to be consistent with that proposition, but such language had not been construed extensively by the Supreme Court of the United States in its early history. The second queston was whether natural law, in its unwritten, abstract form, was an intelligible source of law on which courts could ground decisions.[14] The third question was whether the constitutionalization of natural law principles would render them both intelligible and universal, or whether the fact that the constitutionalization process would be carried out through judicial interpretation would render those principles both contextual and contingent. All three questions were at the heart of the Marshall Court's decisions in cases involving racial minorities.

The reconstituted natural law argument, on its face, seemed particularly germane to cases affecting two racial minorities in the early American republic, black slaves and Indians. Black slaves were persons unquestionably deprived of liberty in a nation that had declared itself to be committed to liberty as a natural right; Indians were persons being dis-

---

[14] The first two questions can be seen as raised by Justice Samuel Chase's seriatim opinion in Calder v. Bull, 3 Dall. 386, 388 (1796), where Chase announced that "[a]n act of the legislature (for I cannot call it a law), contrary to the great first principles of the social compact, cannot be considered a rightful exercise of legislative authority." "[C]ertain vital principles in our free republican governments," Chase argued, ". . . will determine and over-rule an apparent and flagrant abuse of legislative power." Justice James Iredell, in his seriatim opinion in Calder, disagreed with Chase, maintaining that judges could not invalidate legislation "merely because it is, in their judgment, contrary to the principles of natural justice." The "ideas of natural justice," Iredell believed, "are regulated by no fixed standard." Ibid. at 399. The Chase–Iredell exchange in Calder foreshadowed the jurisprudential controversies discussed in this chapter.

possessed of property, because of their status, in a nation whose founders had taken the right to hold property to be inalienable. That these commitments had not been embodied in positive laws giving unqualified protection to the liberty and property rights of black slaves or Indians was not necessarily decisive, given the respectability of unwritten maxims of natural justice and common humanity as sources of early American law. Indeed, the stature of the natural law argument and the contradictions between natural law precepts and the treatment of slaves and Indians created pressure on positive law itself.

But the reconstituted natural law argument was not to prevail in cases involving discriminatory treatment of blacks and Indians. Those minorities remained outside the circle of groups whose rights were recognized and expanded in early-nineteenth-century America. And not only did the enslavement of blacks and the dispossession of Indians coexist with an expanded recognition of the liberty and property rights of white males, the natural law argument was itself tempered and eventually undermined in racial minority cases. Distinctions between written and unwritten rights began to creep into cases involving racial minorities, and eventually the cases could be read as standing for two propositions: first, that the unwritten natural rights of black slaves and Indians could not be used as sources for their legal protection; second, that to the extent that principles of natural justice had been incorporated into the written language of the Constitution, that language did not, in the main, apply to slaves or Indians. In short, each of the basic questions raised by the reconstituted natural law argument was answered to the detriment of blacks and Indians.

The Marshall Court contributed significantly to these trends. The Court cannot be fairly described as an apologist for the principle of slavery or as an advocate of the destruction of Indian culture. None of the Marshall Court Justices was comfortable with the presence of slavery in a nation ostensibly committed to natural rights: some hoped the problem would go away and others lent lukewarm support to antislavery advocates. Some Marshall Court Justices were upset over what they termed the "plight" of Indians, and in one celebrated episode, the attempted dispossession of the Cherokee Nation by the state of Georgia, certain Justices took pains to publicize the legal and moral arguments of the Indian community. But the Court nonetheless contributed to the practical erosion of the legal rights of racial minorities in nineteenth-century America and to the jurisprudential erosion of the natural law argument. It did so by tolerating the obvious contradictions between natural rights theory and the practice of racial discrimination; it did so by limiting the constitutionalization of natural law in the cases of black slaves and Indians; and it did so by suggesting that natural law arguments, at least in this context, were of limited stature in the face of contradictory positive law. In making this last suggestion the Court began to fashion a distinction between "legal" and "moral" arguments that was to become influential in nineteenth-century jurisprudence and which was eventually to eliminate extratextual natural law arguments as legitimate sources of legal authority in nineteenth-century America.

\*

The contradiction between the idea of inalienable natural human rights and the practice of slavery in America was frequently noted by late-eighteenth- and early-nineteenth-century political theorists and jurists. Influential English sources had attacked slavery on natural law grounds, Blackstone condemning the practice in his treatise[15] and Lord Mansfield, in *Somerset's Case*,[16] declaring, at least for American readers,[17] that "the state of slavery is of such a nature, that it is incapable of being introduced on any [abstract] reason[ing]," and "so odious, that nothing can be sufficed to support it, but positive law."[18] American advocates of independence not only echoed those views, they drew a logical connection between black slavery and the dependent condition of the colonies. James Otis, for example, had in his 1772 address, "The Rights of the British Colonies Asserted and Proved," condemned the slave trade as "the most shocking violation of the law of nature," a practice that in his view had "a direct tendency to diminish the idea of the inestimable value of liberty."[19] Otis was also partially responsible for the "slavery analogy" that Revolutionary pamphleteers invoked in the 1770s in their efforts to encourage separation from Great Britain. America, in these pamphlets, was pictured as the home of persons who possessed natural rights to liberty but were being "enslaved" by the practices of the crown and its corrupt agents.[20]

St. George Tucker's 1803 edition of Blackstone provides an illustration of the ideological frame of reference from which elite commentators in early-nineteenth-century America approached the perceived con-

---

[15] "[I]t is repugnant to reason, and the principles of natural law, that . . . [the] state [of slavery] should subsist anywhere." W. Blackstone, *Commentaries on the Law of England* (5 vols., 1803), I, 423. Blackstone had made the same statement in the first edition of his commentaries, published in 1769, volume I, at 423. Unless otherwise indicated, I have used St. George Tucker's 1803 edition of Blackstone.

[16] 1 Lofft's Rep. 1 (1772); 20 Howell's State Trials 82 (1772).

[17] The *Somerset* case was also reported in *Gentleman's Magazine*, 42:193 (1772) and in *The Scots Magazine*, 34:298 (1772). The version in Lofft's Reports was the one that reached America. See Cover, *Justice Accused*, 271.

[18] 20 Howell's State Trials at 82.

[19] J. Otis, "The Rights of the British Colonies Asserted and Proved," in B. Bailyn, ed., *Pamphlets of the American Revolution* (1965), 439.

[20] Bailyn, *Pamphlets*, 74–75.

## Chapter X: *Natural Law and Racial Minorities*

tradiction between the reconstituted natural law argument and the practice of slavery. As we have seen, Tucker's commentary was both prototypical and parochial, penetrating to the core ambiguities of republican ideology and at the same time having its particular axes to grind. Tucker was simultaneously a believer in the fundamental stature of natural law; an advocate for the proposition that the new American republic was an entity in which natural rights were truly inalienable; a proponent of the written laws principle and of the supremacy of a written Constitution; an apostle of compact theory, which posited moral limits on the positive acts of the state; and a Virginian who had come to believe in the emancipation of black slaves and had developed a plan for gradual emancipation in his home state. Many of these features of Tucker's thought can be seen in the following passage from his note, "On the State of Slavery in Virginia," which he had first published in 1796 and which he included as one of the appendices to his 1803 edition of Blackstone.[21] In the passage Tucker declared:

> [Inalienable] [c]ivil, or rather social rights, we may remember, are reducible to three primary heads: the right of personal security; the right of personal liberty; and the right of private property. In a state of slavery the two last are wholly abolished, the person of the slave being at the absolute disposal of his master; and property, what he is incapable, in that state, either of acquiring, or holding to his own use. Hence it will appear how perfectly irreconcilable a state of slavery is to the principles of a democracy, which, form the *basis* and *foundation* of our government. For our bill of rights, declares, "that all men are, by nature" *equally free*, and independent, and have certain rights "of which they cannot deprive or divest their posterity . . . namely, the enjoyment of life and *liberty*, with the means of *acquiring* and *possessing property*." This is, indeed, no more than a recognition of the first principles of the law of nature, which teaches us this equality, and enjoins every man, whatever advantages he may possess over another, as to the various qualities or endowments of body or mind, to practice the precepts of the law of nature to those who are in these respects his *inferiors*, no less than it enjoins his *inferiors* to practice them towards him. . . .
>
> It would be hard to reconcile reducing the negroes to a state of slavery to these principles, unless we first degrade them below the rank of human beings, not only politically, but also physically and mor-

---

[21] S. Tucker, *Blackstone's Commentaries: With Notes of Reference to the Constitution and Laws of the Federal Government of the United States and of the Commonwealth of Virginia,* (5 vols., 1803), II, Appendix H. Where I have quoted Tucker's language from his 1803 edition of Blackstone, I have designated the citation as Tucker, *Blackstone.*

ally. . . . . [S]urely it is time we should admit the evidence of moral truth, and learn to regard them as our fellow men, and equals, except in those particulars where accident, or possibly nature, may have given us some advantage. . . .[22]

The logical progression of Tucker's argument in the passage was as follows. He began by defining natural rights that were, in a republic (he used the term "democracy" in its classical sense in the passage), fundamental and inalienable. He then noted the irreconcilability of slavery with the idea of inalienable natural rights. His catalogue of rights (security, liberty, and property), originally merely posited, was then reinforced by a positive enactment, the Virginia bill of rights, which reduced the security, liberty, and property principles to written language. But this written enactment, Tucker argued, was "no more than a recognition of the first principles of the law of nature." His argument was now complete in the abstract: natural rights served as the "basis and foundation" for written enactments; those enactments were nothing more than the "recognition" of natural law principles. Having packed the Virginia bill of rights with natural law, Tucker then turned to the contradiction of slavery. Unless blacks were to be treated "below the rank of human beings," their enslavement could not be reconciled with the reconstituted natural law argument. "Moral truth" compelled that blacks be regarded as "fellow men and equals."

There was, of course, an escape clause in Tucker's argument, the sentences where he used the words "inferior," "degrade," and "advantage" to characterize white-black relations in America. As numerous scholars have shown, this escape clause was precisely the device used by proponents of slavery to avoid confronting the contradiction Tucker exposed.[23] Blacks were assumed to be inferior to whites in their "nature," to be below the rank of human beings, and to be morally degraded. But Tucker did not himself take advantage of the escape clause. He attached to his essay on slavery a plan for "the mode by which slaves . . . may be emancipated, and the legal consequences thereof, in [Virginia]."[24] The plan[25] was given only the most cursory consideration by the Virginia

---

[22] Tucker, *Blackstone*, II, Appendix H, 54–55. Emphasis in original.

[23] See, e.g., W. Jordan, *White over Black* (1968), 340–56; W. Wiecek, *The Sources of Antislavery Constitutionalism in America, 1760–1848* (1977), 126–49.

[24] Tucker, *Blackstone*, II, 64.

[25] Tucker's plan consisted of a proposal for legislation providing that females born after the date the legislation took effect would be born free but would be required to engage in servitude for twenty-eight years. All descendants of free-born females would also be free, but those born during their mothers' twenty-eight-year servitude period would themselves incur a twenty-eight-year obligation. See Tucker, *Blackstone*, II, 76–78.

legislature: Tucker wrote a contemporary that "nobody I believe had read it"; and "nobody could explain its contents."[26]

While one can observe from this passage in Tucker's *Commentaries* the strength of the reconstituted natural law argument as a potential limit on the powers of the state, Tucker stopped short of making that point explicitly. The question the passage left unanswered is whether a bill of rights or other such written recognition of natural law principles contravened practices explicitly sanctioned by or implicitly tolerated by the state. In an 1806 Virginia Court of Appeals decision on slavery, Tucker, who subsequent to the publication of his edition of Blackstone had become a judge on that court, gave an answer to that question.

The case was *Hudgins* v. *Wright*,[27] a suit for freedom by an Indian family that had been held in involuntary servitude by a white resident of Virginia who planned to leave the state and take the family with him. *Hudgins* v. *Wright* was appealed to the Court of Appeals from a decision by Judge George Wythe of the Richmond District Court of Chancery. Wythe, Marshall's teacher at William and Mary and an advocate of emancipation, declared the Indians free on two grounds, one an orthodox doctrine of the Virginia common law of slavery and the other a radical reading of the Virginia Declaration of Rights of 1776.[28] The common law basis for Wythe's decision was that none of the Indian family—Wythe personally observed three generations of the family—exhibited any "negroid characteristics," and therefore could not be presumed to be blacks (and therefore slaves), notwithstanding evidence that the family were the direct descendants of a slave mother. The practice of judicial observation of the characteristics of alleged slaves in freedom suits, and the associated assumptions that negroid characteristics could be discerned and that persons with such characteristics could be presumed to be slaves were established features of the common law of slavery in early-nineteenth-century America.[29]

Less commonplace was Wythe's conclusion that the Virginia Declaration of Rights, which announced that "all men are by nature equally free,"[30] applied, in varying degrees, to all men, including not only In-

---

[26] S. Tucker to Jeremy Belknap, undated (probably 1797), reprinted in "Letters and Documents Relating to Slavery in Massachusetts" in *Collections of the Massachusetts Historical Society*, 3:427–28 (1877).

[27] 1 Hen. & M. 133 (Va., 1806).

[28] Wythe's opinion was not reported; the basis of his opinion can be surmised from Tucker's summary of it on appeal.

[29] For examples of the presumption that persons with negroid characteristics were slaves, see Scott v. Williams, 1 Dev. 376 (N.C., 1828); White v. Tax Collector, 3 Rich. 136 (S.C., 1846). My thanks to Professor A. E. Keir Nash of the University of California at Santa Barbara for sharing his research on slave cases with me.

[30] J. Thorpe, ed., *The Federal and State Constitutions* (7 vols., 1909), VII, 3812–13.

dians but black slaves as well. The Declaration of Rights, Wythe suggested, created a presumption of freedom similar to the presumption created by the absence of negroid characteristics. In the case of black slaves this presumption could not be rebutted by direct evidence that a person suing for freedom was a direct descendant of a slave mother. This basis of Wythe's opinion suggests that the natural law principle embodied in the 1776 Declaration of Rights, that men are equally free, was to be taken literally, notwithstanding the practices in Virginia of enslavement of blacks, and for a limited period, enslavement of Indians. Wythe's reading not only identified the contradiction between the reconstituted natural law argument and slavery, it resolved that contradiction by appeal to a positive enactment of the state that allegedly implemented natural law.

Tucker, on appeal, upheld the negroid characteristics basis of Wythe's opinion but rejected Wythe's reading of the Declaration of Rights. "I do not concur with the Chancellor," Tucker wrote, "in his reasoning on the operation of the [all men are by nature equally free] clause of the Bill of Rights, which was notoriously framed with a cautious eye to [the] subject [of slavery]." The clause, in Tucker's view, "was meant to embrace the case of free citizens, or aliens only; and not by a side wind to overturn the rights of property."[31] Since blacks had "notoriously" been imported into Virginia as slaves, and remained in that state after the 1776 Declaration, they could not be presumed to be free. Indians without negroid characteristics, however, could be granted a limited presumption of freedom because the practice of Indian enslavement was neither widespread nor of long duration. Whites without negroid characteristics were, of course, presumed to be free.[32] Thus the Indian family in *Hudgins* v. *Wright* retained their freedom, but only because they were Indians who did not look like blacks.

Tucker's answer in *Hudgins* to the question he left open in his edition of Blackstone, then, was that in the case of black slavery local customs and practices contravened positive declarations of natural law principles. Since blacks continued to be enslaved in Virginia, notwithstanding the state's commitment to the abstract proposition that all men were by their nature equally free, "all men" could be taken not to include black persons. Blacks in Virginia could not be declared "free" because they were "notoriously" slaves, and they were slaves because they were black. Moreover, being slaves, they were perhaps not "men" in the full sense of that term: as Tucker put it, the "free and equal" clause in the Declaration of Rights was "not [meant] by a side wind to overturn the rights of property."

---

## Chapter X: *Natural Law and Racial Minorities*

One can reconcile Tucker's treatment of the natural law slavery contradiction in his edition of Blackstone with his decision in *Hudgins* by emphasizing that he thought emancipation should properly take place through legislation rather than through judicial construction of the Virginia bill of rights, or by suggesting that his initial belief that emancipation was an inevitable consequence of the triumph of natural rights principles in America had been tempered by events in Virginia between 1796 and 1806.[33] But the fact remains that the early-nineteenth-century jurist who had made the fullest and most serious effort to invest the reconstituted natural law argument with specific content in the slavery context had, ten years after the first publication of that argument, conceded that a clause in the Virginia bill of rights stating that all men were by their nature equally free was to yield to the force of established slaveholding practices. One might fairly ask whether, if this written version of natural law principles had no meaning where the treatment of black slaves was in contradiction to the enacted principles, natural law, even in written form, had any relevance to the state of black slaves in America.

Despite the significance of Tucker's efforts to confront the natural law-slavery contradiction, the relevance of his confrontation with the treatment of slavery on the Marshall Court was not marked. Tucker was a Virginian, functioning in a slaveholding culture that was not replicated everywhere in America; he was essentially concerned, both as a commentator and as a judge, with the local laws of his state. Moreover, the Virginia Declaration of Rights did not have the potential authority of a clause in the federal Constitution or even a federal statute. Judicial abolition of slavery in Virginia, as radical and explosive an act as that might have been, was not the equivalent of judicial abolition of slavery in all of America on the basis of some "natural law" reading of the Constitution. Issues of state sovereignty, state autonomy, and federal judicial power were not present in *Hudgins* v. *Wright*. The apparent legitimation of slavery by the Three Fifths and Slave Trade clauses of the Constitution was not relevant to the decision. And the Justices of the Marshall Court never confronted, on natural law grounds, the constitutionality of slavery itself.

But the contextual differences between Tucker's written efforts and the Marshall Court slave trade cases about to be discussed should not be taken as rendering Tucker's response irrelevant. Issues pertaining to the slave trade could not easily be separated, in early-nineteenth-century American jurisprudence, from the existence of slavery itself; or, more specifically, from the contradiction that Tucker had articulated between the reconstituted natural law argument and the practice of slavery. The

---

[33] See the cogent discussion of *Hudgins* in Cover, *Justice Accused,* 51–55.

Court's slave trade cases, were, from the outset, natural law cases, and the reconstituted natural law argument powerfully reinforced positive legislation on the slave trade. The contradiction that Tucker had identified, and the attempt that he had made to give specific content to abstract principles of natural justice, resurfaced as significant themes of the Marshall Court's slave trade cases.

No Justice who served on the Marshall Court for any length of time was an apologist for the institution of slavery, and all deplored the continued practice of the slave trade, which Congress had begun to outlaw, prospectively, in 1807.[34] Beyond this consensus the Justices differed in the degree of their opposition to the continued practice of slavery and in the extent of their support for its abolition. Story represented one end of the continuum. He was an early and vigorous opponent of slavery and the trade, declaring before Massachusetts and Rhode Island grand juries in 1819 that slavery was "repugnant to the natural rights of man and the dictates of justice," and that the slave trade was an enterprise "of human wretchedness and human depravity" that was being carried on "with . . . implacable ferocity and unsatiable rapacity."[35] That same year Story attended a town meeting in Salem, Massachusetts, in which he condemned the proposed Missouri Compromise and argued that "the spirit of the Constitution, the principles of our free government, the tenor of the Declaration of Independence, and the dictates of humanity and sound policy" prohibited the extension of slavery into the federal territories.[36]

On the other end of the continuum were the Court's southern Justices, Washington, Johnson, and Marshall, each of whom had come from an environment in which the practice of slavery was well established. We noted that Washington, who succeeded to the ownership of Mount Vernon on the death of his uncle George, owned numerous slaves, and in 1821 was attacked in the press for allegedly selling some of his slaves in a manner that broke up families.[37] *Niles' Weekly Register*, in reporting the alleged sale, commented that "there is something excessively revolting in . . . the nephew and principal heir of George Washington . . . dissolving the connection of husband and wife, mother and child."[38] Washington responded to the charges, defending his "right, *legal or moral*, to

---

[34] Act of Mar. 2, 1807, 2 Stat. 426.
[35] Charge to the grand jury of the circuit court, Boston, October term, 1819, reprinted in W. Story, *The Life and Letters of Joseph Story* (2 vols., 1851), I, 336. See also Story's charge to the grand jury at Portland, Maine, May term, 1820, reprinted in W. Story, ed., *The Miscellaneous Writings of Joseph Story* (1852), 140, where Story employed similar language.

[36] See W. Story, *Life and Letters*, I, 359; Salem *Gazette*, Dec. 11, 1819.
[37] The attack first surfaced in the Leesburg, Virginia, *Genius of Liberty* for August 21, 1821. It was reprinted in the Baltimore *Morning Chronicle* on August 24. See discussion in Chapter V.
[38] *Niles' Weekly Register*, 21:1 (1821).

dispose of property,'' claiming that efforts had been made to keep families together in the sales, and pointing up difficulties in the operation of Mount Vernon that had forced the sales.[39] Washington believed that the proper solution to the problem of slavery was colonization: in 1814 he became the first president of the American Colonization Society, an organization dedicated to financing the resettlement of freed blacks in Africa.[40]

William Johnson was also a slaveowner; he opposed abolition and was skeptical of colonization.[41] Slavery, he said in 1815, was ''an evil . . . which must be submitted to, until we find . . . that our lands can be more beneficially cultivated by free hands than by those of the slaves.''[42] But in 1822 Johnson severely protested the use of arbitrary procedures to try a group of slaves suspected of planning an insurrection in Charleston, South Carolina. As noted, he wrote Jefferson late that year that he had seen, in connection with the trials, ''courts held with closed doors, and men dying by the scores who had never seen the faces or heard the voices of their accusers.'' If such procedures constituted ''the law of this country,'' he added, ''this shall not long be my country.''[43] The result of Johnson's protest was to alienate him from the majority of his contemporaries in Charleston.[44]

John Marshall was not a slaveowner and was never a vocal supporter of the practice. He felt that slavery was a ''danger whose extent can scarcely be estimated'' and that ''nothing portends more calamity and mischief to the southern states than their slave population.'' On the other hand he deplored ''insane fanaticism'' in dealing with the problem.[45] As early as 1816 he had attended a meeting of the American Colonization Society[46] and had been selected president of the Society's Richmond branch in 1823 and one of its national vice presidents in 1825.[47] In two letters written in 1829 he expressed his hope that colonization might be a solution to the problem of black slavery in America. One letter suggested that proceeds from the sale of public lands be used to finance the resettlement of blacks in Liberia, and that United States warships be

---

[39] Washington's rejoinder came in the Baltimore *Federal Republican,* September 18, 1821. Emphasis in original. See D. Annis, ''Mr. Bushrod Washington, Supreme Court Justice on the Marshall Court'' (Ph.D. diss., University of Notre Dame, 1974), 198–201.

[40] Annis, ''Washington,'' 172, 203.

[41] See D. Morgan, *Justice William Johnson* (1954), 99, 135–137; W. Johnson to John Quincy Adams, June 2, 1821, Miscellaneous Records of the Department of State, National Archives.

[42] W. Johnson, *Nugae Georgicae: An Essay* (1815), 33–34.

[43] W. Johnson to T. Jefferson, Dec. 10, 1822, Thomas Jefferson Papers, Library of Congress.

[44] Ibid.

[45] J. Marshall to Timothy Pickering, Mar. 20, 1826, *Proc. Mass. Hist. Soc.,* 14:321 (1901).

[46] F. Mason, *My Dearest Polly* (1967), 252.

[47] American Society for Colonizing the Free People of Colour, *Eighth Annual Report* (1825), 3.

stationed off Africa to "interrupt the slave trade," which Marshall called "a horrid traffic detested by all good men."[48] The other characterized "the restoration of the descendants of Africans in these United States to the land of their ancestors" as a "great cause of humanity" that "promises great future advantages to [the] country."[49]

None of the remaining Marshall Court Justices seems to have been sympathetic to the practice of slavery. Smith Thompson and John McLean were openly critical, Thompson in 1819 calling the slave trade "inhuman and disgraceful,"[50] and McLean announcing two years earlier that in an abstract sense "a slave in any state or country, according to the unmistakable principles of natural justice, [should] be entitled to his freedom."[51] Even Gabriel Duvall, a Maryland plantation owner, stated in one case that he would permit slaves to establish their claims to freedom on the hearsay testimony of their relatives because "it will be universally admitted that the right to freedom is more important than the right to property."[52]

Revulsion against the slave trade or concern about the deleterious consequences of slavery itself was nonetheless not sufficient, in a majority of the Justices' views, to invalidate slavery on legal grounds. In the same case that McLean declared that slavery violated "the immutable principles of natural justice" he added that "as a judge I am sworn to support the Constitution of the United States."[53] In the process of coming to terms with slavery, an "unjust" practice nonetheless sanctioned by law, the justices encountered the distinction fashioned by Tucker between positively sanctioned customs or practices and abstract, inalienable rights. This distinction, of special moment in the slavery context, had not been confined to that context by early American republican theorists. While some versions of republican natural rights theory suggested that those rights declared to be intrinsic to human existence, such as life, liberty, and property, could not be infringed in any form, since society existed to preserve the rights, a more common position held by republican theorists was that even inalienable rights could be circumscribed if the circumscription was necessary to preserve society's foundations. A right to life did not mean that a murderer could not be put to death; a right to

---

[48] J. Marshall to R. R. Gurley, Dec. 14, 1831, quoted in American [Colonization] Society . . . , Fifteenth Annual Report (1832), vi.

[49] J. Marshall, unpublished letter, John Marshall Papers, College of William and Mary Library, quoted in R. Faulkner, The Jurisprudence of John Marshall (1968), 52.

[50] S. Thompson to Oliver H. Perry,

May 29, 1819, Secretary of the Navy's Private Letters, National Archives.

[51] Ohio v. Carneal (Ohio Supreme Court), reprinted in Cincinnati Gazette, June 16, 1817.

[52] Mima Queen v. Hepburn, 7 Cranch 290, 299 (1813).

[53] McLean in Ohio v. Carneal, supra, note 51.

liberty did not mean that a thief could not be incarcerated. Nor were property rights absolute: legislatures, for example, could abolish the privileges of primogeniture and entail with impunity.[54]

Those who denied the total inalienability of even fundamental natural rights could point, in their discussions of slavery, to constitutional provisions, such as the Three-Fifths Clause of Article I, Section 2, which distinguished between free persons and slaves in apportioning representation in the House of Representatives. The status of a slave may have been jarringly inconsistent with the theory that all men were created equal and with the presupposition that liberty was an inalienable right, but the Three-Fifths Clause seemed to accept that inconsistency. The presence of the clause suggested that the legal meaning of natural rights in America was apparently that some people had more rights than others; to find out which rights had been confined and which remained inalienable one looked to positively enacted law. And in the case of the slave trade the Constitution and positive legislation appeared to clarify that inquiry.

Article I, Section 9 of the Constitution prevented Congress from prohibiting the importation of slaves into America until 1808, and a 1794 statute, which was readopted in 1800,[55] limited the participation of United States citizens in the trade. In 1807, anticipating the end of constitutional restrictions, Congress passed a statute prohibiting the importation of slaves into the United States.[56] A succession of congressional statutes enacted between 1818 and 1820 then implemented that prohibition, making participation in the trade piracy and punishable by death;[57] authorizing national armed ships of the United States to intercept vessels that were suspected of containing American participants in the trade; and prohibiting American citizens from hiring themselves out to foreign ships engaging in traffic in slaves.

One might anticipate that this series of statutory restrictions would have had the effect of eliminating the participation of Americans in the trade, but it did not. America continued to be a flourishing market for African slaves, creating incentives to circumvent or to defy the statutes. Efforts to do so were facilitated by the established principle of international law that the municipal laws of one nation could be applied only to subjects over which the courts of that nation had jurisdiction, which in the case of the slave trade meant citizens or ships of the nation. Persons who were not citizens of the United States and not on board American ships could engage in the trade with impunity, provided that the nations to which they held allegiance, and on whose ships they were operating,

---

[54] See Conkin, *Self-Evident Truths,* 109–19.

[55] Act of Mar. 22, 1794, 1 Stat. 347 (1794); readopted at 2 Stat. 70 (1800).

[56] Act of Mar. 2, 1807, 2 Stat. 426 (1807).

[57] See 3 Stat. 450 (1818); 3 Stat. 532 (1819); 3 Stat. 600 (1820).

had not outlawed the trade. Even if foreigners or foreign ships could be identified with nations that had outlawed the trade, they could not be brought within the jurisdiction of American courts.

Given this situation, Americans routinely falsified their citizenship, signed on ships flying the flags of foreign nations, and imported slaves into America. As we will see in a later chapter, the idea of volitional allegiance and the presence of many nations that tolerated the trade, such as Spain, Portugal, and the Latin American republics that came into being in the early nineteenth century, greatly facilitated this process. The years after the War of 1812 thus presented a paradoxical situation with respect to the slave trade in America. Growing revulsion against the trade, reflected in congressional statutes and the oppositionist policies of the Monroe administration, led by Secretary of State John Quincy Adams, coexisted with the growth of trade routes brought about by the end of the war and the emergence of Latin American republics. And in those years slavery was flourishing and spreading in the American South.

The principal jurisprudential question presented by this situation was whether American courts could outlaw participation in the slave trade not only on the basis of federal statutes but also on the basis of principles of natural law. If the latter ground could be justified, the patent evasion of the slave trade statutes by Americans could be checked: participants could be seen, whatever their citizenship, as violating a law that was arguably more fundamental than municipal legislation. The slave trade context, in short, seemed to provide a perfect opportunity for the application of the reconstituted natural law argument.

in 1822 Story's circuit court decided a case involving an American ship, the *Alligator,* which had encountered a schooner flying a French flag off the western coast of Africa. The *Alligator* suspected the French ship, *La Jeune Eugénie,* of engaging in the slave trade and, pursuant to the statutes passed between 1807 and 1820,[58] captured her, brought her into the port of Boston, and claimed that she was in fact an American ship. *La Jeune Eugénie* was subsequently revealed to have been built in America, although her owners were French, and to have been fitted up with provisions for a year's voyage, including handcuffs and fetters. The crew of the *Eugénie* claimed that they were engaged in procuring palm oil from Africa. When the ship was brought into Boston the French government filed a claim alleging that she was a French ship and consequently was subject only to the jurisdiction of French courts.

Story thus had first to determine whether his circuit court had jurisdiction over the matter. Jurisdiction turned, Story suggested, on whether *La Jeune Eugénie* had engaged in the slave trade and, if so, whether that trade was a violation of the law of nations.[59]

---

[58] Supra, notes 54–57.  |  [59] 26 F. Cas. at 842.

# Chapter X: *Natural Law and Racial Minorities*

After finding that the ship had engaged in the slave trade,[60] Story argued that the trade violated the law of nations. He noted that the law of nations was to be deduced from three sources: "general principles of right and justice," "customary observances and recognitions of civilized nations," and "the . . . positive law that regulates the intercourse between states."[61] The slave trade was "repugnant to the great principles of Christian duty, the dictates of natural religion, the obligations of good faith and morality, and the eternal maxims of social justice." It was therefore inconsistent "with any system of law that purports to rest on the authority of reason."[62] Moreover, "at the present moment the traffic is vindicated by no nation, and is admitted by almost all commercial nations as incurably unjust and inhuman."[63] Finally, the African slave trade was prohibited by the "positive municipal regulations of France," and in enforcing the interdict of France, American courts were "an auxiliary in enforcing the great interests of universal justice."[64] Thus all of the sources of international law suggested that the slave trade violated its norms.

Crucial to Story's argument was his assumption that "general principles of right and justice" were a legitimate source of the law of nations. While individual nations had condemned or prohibited the slave trade, no international tribunal or treaty had done so. Earlier cases had distinguished between the abstract injustice of the practice and the legitimacy of its existence if sanctioned by particular nations. In the most recent of those cases, handed down two years before *La Jeune Eugénie*, a British court had flatly declared that a ship from a country that had not outlawed the slave trade was not "acting contrary to the law of nations." So long as some nations had reserved to themselves "the right of carrying . . . on" the trade, the British court announced, courts of other nations that had outlawed the trade could not interfere.[65] While the *Eugénie* case was distinguishable because France had outlawed the trade, Story had not rested his decision solely on France's actions. He had also claimed that the slave trade was contrary to the law of nations because it was contrary to natural law.

A year before Story delivered his opinion in *La Jeune Eugénie* Johnson had entertained a similar case, *The Antelope*, on his Georgia circuit. In that case, a privateer with a Venezuelan commission, the *Columbia*, secretly departed from Baltimore, ran the flag of the "Republic of Artega" (one of the newly created Latin American revolutionary

---

[60] Ibid., 840.
[61] Ibid., 846.
[62] Ibid.
[63] Ibid. 847.

[64] Ibid., 650.
[65] Madrazo v. Willes, 3 Barn. and Ald. 353 (1820).

states), and began raids on ships in the North Atlantic. After having captured the *Antelope,* a Spanish ship, and several others, and after having seized more than 250 African slaves as a result of the captures, the *Columbia*[66] was wrecked off the coast of Brazil. At that point her crew transferred themselves and their bounty to the *Antelope* and sailed for the United States, where the *Antelope* was found "hovering near the coast" by an American revenue cutter and ultimately taken into the port of Savannah. Among those making claims for the ship, her cargo, and her African passengers were the Spanish and Portuguese governments, under whose flags some of the captured ships had ostensibly sailed, the master of the revenue cutter, the captain of the privateer, and the United States government.[67]

In Johnson's circuit court the *Antelope*'s captain[68] claimed that he had been justified in capturing the vessels and taking their cargo because the slave trade was illegal under the law of nations, citing British and American statutes prohibiting the trade. Johnson dismissed the captain's claim, stating that the British and American prohibitions of the slave trade applied only to their own citizenry. "The laws of any country on the subject of the slave trade," he announced, "are nothing more in the eyes of any other nation than a class of the trade laws of the nation that enacts them."[69] Since the slave trade was not prohibited by Spanish or Portuguese law, and had not been abolished by any positive edict of an international tribunal, the Africans on Spanish and Portuguese vessels were the property of those governments. Even the Africans that had been on board American vessels were considered the rightful property of the United States government, despite the fact that Americans had been forbidden from engaging in the slave trade. Johnson ordered that the surviving slaves should eventually be divided among the Spanish, Portuguese, and American governments in proportion to the number orginally captured. He knew that this disposition would have the effect of freeing all those slaves made the property of the United States government, sixteen in number. He could not, however, "identify the individuals who

---

[66] Later called *The Arraganta.* See infra, notes 67, 68, and 69.

[67] These and subsequent facts about the *Antelope*'s voyage are taken from the report of the case on appeal in 10 Wheat. 66, 67–69 (1825) and from Minutes of the District Court for the District of Georgia, Savannah, Georgia, and Minutes of the Sixth Circuit Court, Savannah, Georgia.

[68] The original captain of the *Columbia* was Simon Metcalf, a resident of

Baltimore. He drowned in the wreck of the *Columbia* and was replaced by John Smith, the *Columbia*'s first mate. See Minutes of the District Court, supra, note 67.

[69] Johnson's decision in *The Antelope* was unreported. For the text see Minutes of the Sixth Circuit Court, supra, note 67. An informative and penetrating history of the case is J. Noonan, *The Antelope* (1977).

were taken from the American vessel,'' and thus he declared that the designation of sixteen slaves as "American" would be made by lot.[70]

The Antelope was appealed to the Marshall Court by United States District Attorney Richard W. Habersham. It was placed on the docket in February 1822,[71] but it was not to be decided until the 1825 Term. In the interval an international conference failed to enact any sanctions against the slave trade, and negotiations between England and the United States, which had begun with the goal of allowing either nation to seize slave ships flying the other's flag, broke down.[72] In addition, Story's opinion in *La Jeune Eugénie* had been delivered, and the Monroe administration had taken note of it.[73] In the time during which these developments occurred the United States attorney general's office, then headed by William Wirt, made no effort to argue *The Antelope*, which was accordingly postponed by the Court in 1823 and again in 1824.[74]

There was one additional factor contributing to the postponement of *The Antelope*. In 1819, in response to lobbying by the American Colonization Society, Congress had passed a statute, "The Act in Addition to the Acts prohibiting the slave trade,"[75] which gave the president authority to secure the "safe-keeping, support, and removal beyond the United States" of Africans found on ships illegally engaged in the slave trade. The Act in Addition, as it came to be called, assumed that the president would appoint "agents in Africa" to "receive" removed slaves. The Act thus clearly contemplated that any slaves found to be the property of the United States in a slave trade case would be transported back to Africa. Some supporters of the Act even suggested that it contemplated the establishment of American colonies in Africa as bases for the slaves. By providing for the return of "American" slaves to Africa the Act sought to ensure that they would not end up as slaves in America, but at the same time it made them wards of the federal government during the period of their relocation. The precise measures the federal government would take once slaves had been deemed "American" in slave trade adjudications remained a matter of debate within the Monroe administration; until a consensus on those measures had been reached the attorney general's office was reluctant to argue *The Antelope*.

Eventually, on the heels of Adams's disputed election as president

---

[70] See the allusion to the slave trade acts in 10 Wheat. at 71.

[71] Minutes of the Supreme Court of the United States, Feb. 1, 1790–Aug. 4, 1828, National Archives Microfilm Publications, Microcopy No. 215, Roll No. 1.

[72] See H. Soulsby, *The Right of Search and the Slave Trade in Anglo-* *American Relations 1814–1862* (1933), 13–38; L. Bethell, *The Abolition of the Brazilian Slave Trade* (1970), 24–26.

[73] See Noonan, *Antelope*, 76–77.

[74] Docket of the Supreme Court of the United States, 1791–1834, vol. C at 1250, National Archives Microfilm Publications, Microcopy No. 216.

[75] 3 Stat. 532 (1819).

in February 1825, the attorney general's office moved to argue the case.[76] Francis Scott Key, who had been strongly active in the American Colonization Society,[77] and Wirt represented the United States; John Berrien, United States senator from Georgia, and Charles Ingersoll, a practitioner and part-time federal district attorney from Philadelphia, represented Spain and Portugal respectively. Wirt described *The Antelope* as a conflict between "a claim to freedom [and] a claim to property."[78] "Everything," Wirt argued, "must depend upon the law prevailing at the time and place" of the slave ships' capture. He asserted that since the slave trade was contrary to international law, "these persons are free," and no one could consider them "merchandise."[79] Wirt's argument made it clear that the critical question in the case was whether American jurisprudence, as embodied in the decisions of American courts, would characterize the slave trade as unlawful even when conducted by foreign nations.

While Story's opinion in *La Jeune Eugénie* and Johnson's opinion in *The Antelope* appeared to be irreconcilable with respect to that question, the cases were not identical. No slaves had been on board the French ship; there were thus no prospective wards of the United States government to be removed to Africa if designated American property. Moreover, Story, acceding to a request by the Monroe administration, had agreed to return the *Eugénie* to the French government, which had been prepared to appeal his decision to the Marshall Court on the ground that United States courts had no jurisdiction over foreign ships.[80] Thus the *La Jeune Eugénie* opinion was not squarely applicable to *The Antelope*, and Story's disposition of the case seemed inconsistent with the idea that anyone who engaged in the "unlawful" slave trade forfeited any property associated with or garnered from that trade.

Discussions among the Marshall Court Justices after Story delivered his opinion in *La Jeune Eugénie* indicate that neither Story nor others took that case as dispositive of *The Antelope*. In a December 1821 letter to Washington, Story wrote about the *Eugénie* case:

> I dare say you will think me a bold Judge. . . . Be it so, but I must ask your patience to read before you condemn me. . . . You will find my opinion guarded and sober on all the ticklish points. I have not meddled at all with the question of the right of slavery in general, nor could I with any decent respect for the institutions of my country deem it proper to engage in such speculations.[81]

---

[76] Noonan, *Antelope*, 18–25, 81–89.
[77] Key was an officer of the Society. American [Colonization] Society . . . , *Second Annual Report* (1819), 1.
[78] 10 Wheat. at 81.
[79] *Ibid.*, 114

[80] Noonan, *Antelope*, 74–75.
[81] J. Story to B. Washington, Dec. 21, 1821, Bushrod Washington Papers, Washington State Historical Society, Olympia, Wash.

# Chapter X: *Natural Law and Racial Minorities*

While that letter did not suggest that Story would be open to compromise on the legality of the slave trade, it identified the question he expected slaveholding Justices to ask themselves about slave trade cases: were they the thin edge of the wedge in the abolition of "the right of slavery" itself? Since Story had already declared that he regarded slavery as violating natural rights principles, his use of the phrase "right of slavery" in his comments to Washington is suggestive. Equally suggestive is a letter Story wrote to Jeremiah Mason in February 1822, after discussing *La Jeune Eugénie* with his colleagues on the Court. The *Eugénie* opinion had "been read by several of the Judges here," he told Mason, "and in general, I think it not unsatisfactory to them in its results. The Chief Justice, with his characteristic modesty, says he thinks I am right, but the questions are new to his mind."[82]

It is hard to imagine that all the "questions" raised by *The Eugénie* and *The Antelope* were "new" to Marshall. He had not, to be sure, considered the precise issue of the legality of the slave trade when engaged in by foreign ships that were ultimately brought within the jurisdiction of American courts. But he had considered the larger issue of whether principles of natural justice would serve as a fundamental constraint on positive law in slavery cases. In *Mima Queen & Child v. Hepburn,* the aforementioned case in which Duvall would have allowed hearsay testimony in suits by slaves for their freedom, Marshall had written the opinion of the Court, which followed general common law in disallowing hearsay evidence "to establish any specific fact" which was susceptible of being proved by witnesses. After announcing that the Court would follow this "general principle," Marshall added,

> However the feelings of the individual may be interested on the part of a person claiming freedom, the Court cannot perceive any legal distinction between the assertion of this and of any other right, which will justify the application of a rule of evidence to cases of this description which would be inapplicable to general cases in which a right to property may be asserted.[83]

In other words, Marshall declined to distinguish cases where slaves claimed freedom from other property cases. That such claims "interested . . . the feelings of the individual" was no justification for a legal distinction. The irreconcilability of slavery with natural law, then, did not in itself provide a legal basis for liberalizing hearsay rules in freedom suits.

---

[82] J. Story to J. Mason, Feb. 21, 1822, quoted in G. Hilliard, *Memoir,* | *Autobiography and Correspondence of Jeremiah Mason* (1873), 256.
[83] 7 Cranch at 295.

The distinction between "feelings" and "law" that Marshall had made in *Mima Queen* was recast in his opinion for the Court in *The Antelope* as a distinction between the slave trade as a violation of natural law and the slave trade as a violation of the law of nations. Marshall argued that however "abhorrent" the slave trade, it had "been sanctioned in modern times by the laws of all nations who possess distant colonies," and had "claimed all the sanction which could be derived from long usage and general acquiescence."[84] He went further, and conceded that the trade was "contrary to the law of nature," since "every man has a natural right to the fruits of his own labour, and . . . no other person can rightfully deprive him of those fruits, and appropriate them against his will."[85] But he insisted that "the usages, the national acts, and the general assent of that portion of the world" relevant to *The Antelope* testified "in favour of the legality of the trade."[86] The traffic "remained lawful to those whose governments [had] not forbidden it"; it was therefore "consistent with the law of nations."[87] In making these distinctions, Marshall noted, he was "obey[ing] the mandate of the law" rather than "yield[ing] to feelings which might seduce [a court] from the path of duty"; he was acting as "a jurist" rather than "a moralist."[88]

It appears that Marshall's primary goal in *The Antelope* was the achievement of a politic disposition of its sensitive issues. He had before him the claims of two nations still engaging in the slave trade to property that they argued had been unlawfully stolen from them by a ship commandeered by Americans. He was also reviewing two widely different resolutions of the legality of the slave trade by fellow Justices of his Court, one of which invalidated it and the other of which concluded that the edicts of nations abolishing it were just so many "trade laws" to other nations. He sought a solution that would return part of the Africans to Spanish claimants, set the majority of them free, condemn the slave trade abstractly, but yet admit its legitimacy under the law of nations.

Marshall's solution was to grant the legality of the slave trade under the law of nations but to apply that principle to "the circumstances of the particular case"[89] in such a way as to favor the claims of the United States. Johnson, as noted, had treated the claims of Spain, Portugal, and the United States as all bona fide on their face, although he had remanded the case for further proof of the authenticity of the Portuguese claim. Although no proof was forthcoming on remand, Johnson and district judge Jeremiah Cuyler did not dismiss the Portuguese claim, but only reduced Portugal's share of the slaves. Marshall, for the Court, reversed that

---

84 Ibid., 115.
85 Ibid., 120.
86 Ibid., 121.

87 Ibid., 122.
88 Ibid.
89 Ibid., 123.

decree. No "subject of the crown of Portugal" had appeared in the five years that the case had been adjudicated, Marshall noted, "to assert his title to this property." This "inattention" gave rise to "serious suspicion that the real owner dares not avow himself." The real owner, Marshall suggested, belonged to some other nation in which the slave trade had been outlawed; carrying on the slave trade "under the flags of other countries" was "a fact of such general notoriety" that the Court could act upon it. The Portuguese claim was therefore dismissed.[90]

That left Spain and the United States as claimants. Johnson's disposition of the slaves on remand, prorated to take intervening deaths into account, had given 16 slaves to the United States (their identities having been determined by lot), 62 slaves to Portugal, and 126 to Spain. Marshall reviewed this decree *de novo*. Spain, in arguing before the Supreme Court, had produced witnesses who claimed that 166 slaves owned by Spanish subjects had originally been aboard the *Antelope*. The captain of the privateer had countered with a claim that only 93 slaves were found on the *Antelope* when she was captured. Marshall imposed the burden of proving the actual number on the claimant and held that Spain had not met the burden. This finding was to have the effect, after the case had been remanded again to Johnson's circuit court and the numbers had again been prorated, of reducing the Spanish share to a maximum of fifty.[91] While no precise formula for prorating the slaves was ever used, and deaths, discrepancies, and contradictory figures have made the actual numbers imprecise, Marshall's opinion clearly resulted in increasing dramatically the number of slaves designated "American" and thus free and eligible, under the 1819 Act in Addition, for transportation to Africa.

But why were any of the Africans designated slaves? The Spanish witnesses had neither proved that the Africans on the *Antelope* were slaves as opposed to free persons, nor identified them by name. How could anyone really tell which of the approximately 140 Africans that in 1825 were alive and in the custody of a federal marshal in Savannah, Georgia, had been on the Spanish ship? Johnson's original use of a lottery to determine which Africans were "American" and which foreign property had tacitly conceded that that question was unanswerable. But when his decree was reviewed an issue was raised before the Marshall Court: whether Spain had the burden of proving that the Africans on the *Antelope* were slaves and thus Spanish property. The Justices divided evenly on that issue.[92] The equal division was made possible by the fact that Justice Todd, who had been present when *The Antelope* was first docketed in the 1821 Term, missed the entire 1825 Term because of illness, leaving six

---

[90] Ibid., 130, 131.
[91] Ibid., 127–28, 132–33; see Noonan, *Antelope*, 122.

[92] No dissents were recorded in the case, but seventeen years later Story, referring to *La Jeune Eugénie*, wrote a

Justices to decide the case. After noting that the Spanish claimants had alleged only that the *Antelope* had purchased and loaded "a considerable number" of slaves before she was captured, Marshall announced the Court's conclusion on the burden of proving slave status:

> Whether, on this proof, Africans brought into the United States, under the various circumstances belonging to this case, ought to be restored or not, is a question on which much difficulty has been felt. It is unnecessary to state the reasons in support of the affirmative or negative answer to it, because the Court is divided on it, and, consequently, no principle is settled.[93]

The equal division of the Justices had, of course, the effect of affirming Johnson's decree directing restitution to the Spanish claimant of the Africans found on board the *Antelope,* and, as noted, that number was subsequently fixed at no more than fifty. But how were the individuals deemed Spanish property to be identified? Marshall said only that "the individuals . . . must be designated to the satisfaction of the Circuit Court."[94] He did not indicate what process of designation was to be used, and for three months, between December 1825 and March 1826, Johnson and Cuyler could not agree on whether "designation" could embrace the use of a lottery. Eventually Johnson gave in, and a crude and arbitrary method of identification was adopted, which resulted in thirty-nine Africans being labeled "Spanish."[95]

The *Antelope* decision did not rest there: Johnson's designation process was challenged in another appeal to the Marshall Court by District Attorney Habersham.[96] Key again argued on behalf of the United States, claiming that there had been "no credible and competent evidence to identify . . . any of [the Africans]."[97] Justice Robert Trimble, in his first Term on the Court, delivered an apparently unanimous opinion rejecting that argument. The process of designation had been based solely on testimony by an overseer of the United States government, William Richardson, who had supervised the work of some Africans "upon the fortifications at Savannah." Richardson testified that on one occasion he had

---

friend that "my decision was overruled in the Supreme Court in the case of *The Antelope,* but I always thought I was right, and continue to think so." J. Story to Ezekiel Bacon, Nov. 19, 1842, quoted in W. Story, *Life and Letters,* II, 43. Noonan speculates that Story and Thompson, both outspoken opponents of the slave trade, had been joined by Duvall in voting to reverse Johnson's circuit court decree in every par-

ticular. Noonan, *Antelope,* 115–116. I am inclined to agree with Noonan, given the attitudes toward slavery of the participating Justices.

[93] 10 Wheat. at 126.
[94] Ibid., 128.
[95] Noonan, *Antelope,* 119, 125, 127–28.
[96] The Antelope, 12 Wheat. 546 (1827).
[97] Ibid., 552.

witnessed the Africans "appear to recognise" one Grandona, a Spanish officer of the *Antelope,* who had visited the fortifications. The Court found this testimony dispositive "under the very peculiar circumstances of this case." Grandona was not present at the circuit court's designation hearing, having "disappeared."[98] The surviving "Spanish" Africans were eventually sold into slavery in Florida; the surviving "American" Africans were eventually transported to Africa.[99]

Over a nine-year period, from March 1820, when they were first loaded onto the *Antelope* in West Africa, to the summer of 1828, when thirty-odd of their number arrived in Florida to work on a sugar plantation,[100] the fate of approximately 130 Africans was intertwined with the legal and political machinery of the United States in an extraordinary fashion. The Africans were brought into Georgia and placed in the control of a federal marshal, maintained at the rate of sixteen cents per person per day,[101] and left there for approximately a year. At that point sixteen of them learned that they were "free," and possibly that they could expect to be taken back to Africa. Nothing occurred, however, for another five years, when all the Africans were visited in Savannah by Richardson and Grandona for designation purposes. Some of the Africans previously deemed "free" by lot may have been designated "Spanish" in that process; evidence suggests that at least one was. After the designation the Africans lingered another six to eight months in Savannah, when approximately 120 of them were transported to Liberia, the American Colonization Society's colony in Africa. The remaining thirty-odd Africans remained in Georgia, ostensibly to be sold into slavery in Cuba. They were, however, eventually sold to Henry Wilde, a Georgia lawyer, who shipped them to Florida as slaves. Those Africans that remained in slavery had had the bad luck to be considered, by their federal overseers, "the primest of the gang."[102]

As fateful as the human consequences of *The Antelope* were, its jurisprudential consequences were equally portentous. Marshall's strategy in *The Antelope* had created a jurisprudential distinction that was to have a significant subsequent history. In Story's analysis in *La Jeune Eugénie* natural law had figured prominently as a substantive source of legal rules. Given the presence of positive edicts by individual nations abolishing the slave trade, and the "inhuman" and "unjust" character of the traffic itself, a case could be made that the trade violated norms of international

---

98 Ibid., 553.

99 Noonan, *Antelope,* 133–52.

100 See *The Mercury,* Sept. 10, 1828, cited in Noonan, *Antelope,* 152.

101 Johnson had set the rate in his circuit court decision in 1821, according to his 1826 circuit court opinion on the remanded case. See Minutes of the Sixth Circuit Court (Dec. 1, 1826), supra, note 69. See also Noonan, *Antelope,* 124.

102 John Morel, testimony, Dec. 1, 1826, Minutes of the Circuit Court, supra, note 69.

law. The law of nations, nineteenth-century commentators acknowledged, could be derived in part from the law of nature. Marshall's analysis apparently foreclosed unwritten natural law as a substantive source of positive legal rules. Even though he admitted that the slave trade was contrary to the law of nature, he regarded that fact as having no substantive significance. The slave trade violated natural law, but not the law of nations. Why? Because the "law of nations" was composed of usages and practices, "national acts," and general customs.[103] Those were sources of international law; natural law was not among them.

Marshall's analysis in *The Antelope* thus truncated the stature of natural law as a source of Marshall Court jurisprudence. He characterized his posture as that of a "jurist" rather than a "moralist," and that of one obeying his "duty" and "the mandate of the law" rather than "feelings";[104] in another place he distinguished between "public feeling" and "strict law."[105] That the slave trade was contrary to the law of nature was not only irrelevant to the disposition of the case, it was a seductive "moral" issue, engaging "feelings" and tempting "jurists" to violate their "duty."

*La Jeune Eugénie* and *The Antelope*, taken together, thus form an instructive contrast to the Court's treatment of the natural law argument in the Contract Clause cases, previously discussed. In those cases, as noted, the Court began its conceptualization of the vested rights problem by first positing alternative sources of protection for contractual obligations, the Contract Clause itself or "general principles common to our free institutions." As the cases unfolded, however, a distinction between Section 25 cases and diversity cases emerged in which, in the former cases, only constitutional language, albeit packed with natural law overtones, was deemed controlling, with "general principles" being regarded as an appropriate ground of decision only in the latter cases. One jurisprudential message of the cases, then, was that constitutional provisions could be invested with natural law concepts such as the takings principle, but another message was that constitutional law decisions could not rely on unwritten sources such as "principles of natural justice."

In *La Jeune Eugénie* Story had again identified unwritten natural law as a source, perhaps even a fundamental source of law. He had declared that the slave trade was illegal not only because American citizens were forbidden to engage in it by federal statutes, but also because it violated abstract principles of natural justice. It was, in effect, *per se* illegal: a violation of fundamental principles of natural law. In *The Antelope*, however, Marshall had severely qualified this position. The slave trade was clearly immoral, Marshall argued, and slavery a violation of

---

[103] 10 Wheat. at 121.
[104] Ibid., 114.

[105] Ibid., 116.

the unwritten laws of nature and of natural rights theory, but those facts did not clarify legal analysis. The positive acts of certain nations had sanctioned the trade; acts of other nations had abolished it. Those acts, not abstract principles of natural justice, governed slave trade cases. The question in slave trade cases was not whether the status of slavery, being "irreconcilable" with the reconstituted natural law argument, was thus *per se* illegal; the question was whose "trade laws" governed the case. Some of the African passengers on the *Antelope* were slaves, even though slavery was a violation of natural law, because their owners were citizens of nations whose positive enactments sanctioned the slave trade. Some of the African passengers were, theoretically, free, because their ownership could not be firmly established. But none of the Africans was free because slavery violated unwritten natural law.

The constitutional basis of the *Antelope* decision, then, was the provision of Article I, Section 9 abolishing the slave trade after 1808 and the congressional legislation implementing that provision. No natural law principles were packed into constitutional language by the case; indeed, the use of an abstract natural justice argument as an alternative ground for invalidating the slave trade was explicitly rejected. The decision left slavery as a practice not only established but apparently invulnerable to attack from unwritten natural law arguments. Thus while the Court's Contract Clause cases can be treated as an example of the blending of natural law concepts and constitutional language, to the benefit of propertied white males, the Court's slave trade cases represented a separation of natural rights principles from the slavery context and an abandonment of unwritten natural law as a source reinforcing constitutional language and congressional legislation.

"Next to the case of the black race within our bosom," James Madison wrote in 1824, "that of the red on our borders is the problem most baffling to the policy of the country."[106] In one lamentable sense the status of the native Indian in early-nineteenth-century America was free of the ambiguities surrounding that of the black slave. Unlike slaves, Indians were not perceived by whites as linked to the future economic development of the nation. They were principally perceived as obstacles in the way of civilization, progress, and westward expansion: if incapable

---

[106] J. Madison to James Monroe, April 1824, quoted in A. Abel, "The History of Events Resulting in Indian Consolidation West of the Missis-sippi," *Annual Report of the American Historical Association for 1906* (2 vols., 1908), I, 255.

of being civilized, they needed to be removed. Indian removal was a stated policy of all the presidential administrations from Madison through Jackson: the differences were only matters of degree. A battery of stereotypic perceptions and attitudes was employed in the service of Indian removal: the "warlike," "savage," or "childlike" nature of Indians; the "destiny" of American whites to move westward; the inability of Indians to adopt "progressive" methods of agriculture rather than hunting; the inevitability of economic expansion in a maturing nation; even the glories of war and conquest. In contrast to the confusion and uncertainty that marked early-nineteenth-century attitudes toward black slaves, who were often seen as symbols of a problem that would somehow vanish, a clear consensus existed with respect to the presence of Indians: they needed to be civilized or to be dispossessed.[107] As we will see, this attitudinal consensus embraced, to a significant degree, all the Justices of the Marshall Court.

But if the cultural status of Indian tribes in early-nineteenth-century America was forebodingly clear, their legal status was much less so. Various clarifying features associated with the presence of black slaves were absent in the case of Indian tribes. The slaves were not original inhabitants, but aliens brought into the country. They had been imported as the property of others, their slave status part and parcel of their entry. Notwithstanding their natural rights, they were also the possessions of their masters, and their liberty and property were necessarily contingent. Indian tribes presented a distinguishable case. The Indians had been the initial possessors of the American continent: the land and, presumably, the property rights emanating from it were theirs. The Indians were also no one else's property: the great majority of them were free human beings, and some of them were themselves slaveowners. The Indian tribes had been recognized from the outset of white settlement as nations and had entered into legal relationships, such as treaties or contracts, with whites. Theoretically, then, Indian tribes holding land had not only rights of sovereignty but a bundle of natural rights deserving of legal recognition, rights related to the concepts of liberty, property, and self-determination that occupied so exalted a position in early-nineteenth-century jurisprudence.

---

[107] For discussions of early-nineteenth-century attitudes toward Indians, see F. Prucha, *American Indian Policy in the Formative Years* (1962); B. Sheehan, *Seeds of Extinction* (1973); M. Rogin, *Fathers and Children* (1975); and R. Horsman, *Race and Manifest Destiny* (1981). A sophisticated analysis of the relationship between white missionaries and the Cherokee nation in Georgia, with wider implications than its subject matter might suggest, is W. McLoughlin, *Cherokees and Missionaries, 1789–1839* (1984).

# Chapter X: *Natural Law and Racial Minorities*

But if the relationship of white master and black slave in early-nineteenth-century America was awkwardly interdependent, that of white settler and red occupant had been stripped of that awkwardness. It was clear by the 1820s that where white society had encountered Indian tribes in the eastern portions of North America, the Indians had eventually been conquered. Treaties and contracts negotiated between whites and Indians, whatever their language, had not been negotiations between equals. Indian tribes had ceded land, abandoned their settlements, or removed themselves from territory contiguous to whites because they did not have the force to resist the whites' presence.

This combination of cultural and jurisprudential factors was to invest the reconstituted natural law argument with ambiguity in cases considering the rights of Indian tribes. The cluster of natural rights theoretically possessed by the tribes provided an apparent obstacle to policies of removal and dispossession. But at the same time Indians had historically lacked the means to enforce their rights, and, moreover, had not appeared to "enjoy the fruits" of those rights in ways that were familiar to whites. If Indian tribes collectively held land, they often did not treat that ownership as a source of income, at least not income as defined by white civilizations. If individual tribesmen owned parcels of real estate, as in the white pattern, many of them appeared neither to attach much significance to the fact of individual ownership nor to remain on those parcels, and improve them, for any lengthy period of time. Most Indian tribes and individuals, in short, did not use land in the manner that the archetypal citizen of white republican America used it.

What, then, were the rights of Indian tribes? Were they the rights of foreign nations, tacitly recognized by the law of nations, and perhaps the law of nature, as autonomous and sovereign? If so, they were the rights of foreign nations who had been or were about to be conquered by the United States government. Were they the natural rights of republican citizens? If so, they were the rights of citizens whose behavior, for the most part, was perceived as not conforming to that of civilized white citizens. Were they the natural rights of human beings who owned freehold land? If so, they were the rights of persons who used and valued that land in ways that appeared unfathomable to whites and inconsistent with republican government. To advance the reconstituted natural laws argument in cases involving Indian tribes was to confront these complexities.

There was a final factor influencing the consideration of Indian cases by the Marshall Court, the implicit ideological boundaries that framed the issue of "Indian rights" in early-nineteenth-century white America. As noted, two idealized alternative positions shaped early-nineteenth-century discourse about Indian affairs: the "removal" position and the "civilize" position.[108] One position advocated the forceful dispossession of Indians, in part because of their "savage" or "primitive" nature; the other advocated the "civilizing" of tribes so that they could become assimilated into white culture and become useful republican citizens. The positions were, of course, two sides of the same coin: they both started with the assumption that Indians were different (primitive, childlike, savage) and that their differentness could not be tolerated. While the positions provoked sharp differences of policy and, as we shall see, precipitated conflict in the Court's Indian cases, they functioned to exclude from discourse a third ideological point of view, that of cultural relativism. The idea that Indians in America should be allowed to perpetuate a radically different cultural heritage from that of white settlers, and at the same time be treated as human beings having natural rights to autonomy and respect, was not seriously entertained at the time of the Marshall Court. Only a diluted version of that idea was entertained, manifested in the theory that Indian tribes were wards of the federal government and should, because of their cultural differentness, be forcibly separated from white society. That theory was subsequently to provide the principal justification for the establishment of federal Indian reservations, which began in earnest in the 1860s.[109]

The first Marshall Court cases in which the rights of Indian tribes were considered reflected the early patterns of Indian-white interchange in America. They involved land disputes between whites in which one of the disputing parties had acquired title to the land from an Indian tribe.[110] In *Fletcher* v. *Peck,* for example, the state of Georgia had granted a portion of its land to nonresident land companies even though Indians remained in possession of, and theoretically in ownership of, the land. Luther Martin, in arguing *Fletcher* for a member of one of the land companies, confronted the question of the Indian title. "What is the Indian title?" he asked. "It is a mere occupancy for the purpose of hunting. It is not like our tenures; they have no idea of a title to the soil itself. It is overrun by them, rather than inhabited. It is not a true and legal possession." The Indian title, Martin claimed, was "a mere privi-

---

[108] These two positions did not, of course, exhaust the responses of nineteenth-century white Americans to the "Indian question." Within the community of persons who adhered to the "civilize" position there was debate about whether "civilization" could take place without removal, or whether the two responses were linked. And within the white missionary community there were those who believed that the Indian tribes could become "civilized" and Christianized and at the same time retain their cultural identity as a nation. See McLoughlin, *Cherokees,* 335–352.

[109] See generally G. Harmon, *Sixty Years of Indian Affairs* (2d ed., 1969); F. Prucha, ed., *The Indians in American History* (1971).

[110] See, e.g., Fletcher v. Peck, 6 Cranch 87 (1810); Preston v. Browner, 1 Wheat. 115 (1816); Danforth's Lessee v. Thomas, 1 Wheat. 155 (1816).

lege which does not affect the allodial right.''[111] Marshall, for the Court, appeared to accept this argument. ''It was doubted,'' he said, ''whether a state can be seised in fee of lands, subject to the Indian title.'' But a ''majority of the court'' had concluded ''that the nature of the Indian title . . . is not such as to be absolutely repugnant to seisin in fee on the part of the state.''[112] Johnson, in his concurrence, disagreed. The Indians in Georgia, he maintained, were ''an independent people'' with ''an absolute right of soil.'' No ''other nation can be said to have an interest in [their land].''[113] He was later to abandon that position.

*New Jersey* v. *Wilson*,[114] discussed in Chapter IX, did little to clarify the status of Indian titles to land, although an Indian title was at the heart of the case. As we have seen, in *Wilson* the colony of New Jersey, in a 1758 statute ratifying an agreement between colonial commissioners and the Delaware tribe, had granted the Delawares a tract of land and perpetual immunity from taxation of that land in exchange for cession of Delaware claims to large portions of the southern half of the colony. The Delawares, as Marshall put it for the Court, ''continued in peaceable possession of the lands thus conveyed to them'' until 1801, when they decided to move to Stockbridge, New York, and ''obtained an act of the legislature of New Jersey authorizing a sale of their land.''[115] The land was sold two years later by state commissioners to a group of whites, and in 1804 the New Jersey legislature repealed the 1758 statute and assessed the land for taxation. The white buyers challenged the constitutionality of the 1804 repeal on the ground that it violated the Contract Clause, and Marshall held that the 1804 statute was invalid. The principal significance of the *Wilson* case was, as previously noted, Marshall's finding that a perpetual tax exemption granted before the United States finally came into being, and well before the framing of the Contract Clause, was nonetheless a ''contract'' for constitutional purposes.

There was, however, another issue implicitly posed by *New Jersey* v. *Wilson:* what was the status of the Indian title? The Delawares' original claims to New Jersey land would have been regarded, *Fletcher* suggested, as mere rights of possession, subject to being obliterated by the colony in which the land existed. But the New Jersey colonial legislature had, in 1758, formally granted the Delawares land. Was the title created by that grant more than a ''mere occupancy''? Marshall's language in *Wilson* suggested that it was. The land had ''been sold,'' he said, ''with the assent of the state, with all its privileges and immunities.'' The white purchasers ''succeed[ed] with the assent of the state, to all the rights of the Indians.'' And the privilege of exemption from taxation, while ''an-

---

[111] 6 Cranch at 121, 123.
[112] Ibid., 142–43.
[113] Ibid., 147.

[114] 7 Cranch 164 (1812).
[115] Ibid., 166.

nexed . . . to the land itself,'' was ''for the benefit of the Indians,'' since they had been granted land whose ''value would be enhanced'' by being perpetually exempt from taxation.[116]

The very fact that the white purchasers in *Wilson* could demonstrate that they had vested rights that could not be impaired by subsequent state legislation indicated that the Indian ''rights,'' based on ''the benefit of contract,'' were more than possessory.[117] But if pre-existing Indian titles were not ''absolutely repugnant'' to a conquering colony or state's subsequently claiming fee simple ownership of Indian land, what was the consideration for the Delawares' cession of their lands in exchange for receiving a tax-exempt tract? If the Delawares' ''title'' to those lands could be expunged by conquering whites at any time, they had apparently not given up any significant legal rights in relinquishing their claims to portions of southern New Jersey.

Marshall did not address this difficulty, preferring to treat the 1758 agreement between New Jersey and the Delawares as ''a contract clothed in forms of unusual solemnity,'' and emphasizing the ''rights of the Indians'' to which the white purchasers had succeeded.[118] One wonders how the case would have been decided had Delaware tribesmen themselves sought to challenge the 1804 repeal of the agreement on vested rights grounds. In any event, *New Jersey* v. *Wilson* did nothing to clarify the question whether the possession of American land by Indians created any significant legal rights in the occupants.

Eleven years after *New Jersey* v. *Wilson,* the question of the legal status of Indian titles to land was presented more squarely in *Johnson* v. *McIntosh,*[119] where the plaintiff's claim of title to disputed land in Virginia rested on a 1775 conveyance from the Piankeshaw Indians, and the defendant's claim rested on a subsequent grant from the United States. There was no question that the Indians held original possession of the land, and that their conveyance to a group of persons, including the father of the plaintiff, preceded (by nine years) Virginia's efforts to convey the same land to the defendant. If the defendant's title to the land was to be preferred, it could only be because the plaintiff's was defective. As Marshall put it, ''the inquiry'' in the case was ''confined to the power of Indians to give, and of private individuals to receive, a title which can be sustained in the Courts of this country.''[120]

Possession of freehold land, we have seen, was regarded by republican theory as providing one of the strongest sources of a natural right, the right to hold or to disperse of one's property as one saw fit. That

---

[116] Ibid., 167.
[117] Ibid.
[118] Ibid.

[119] 8 Wheat. 543 (1823).
[120] Ibid., 572.

Marshall felt the strength of this proposition can be seen in one of the early paragraphs of his opinion:

> As the right of society to prescribe those rules by which property can only be acquired and preserved is not, and cannot be drawn into question; as the title to lands, equally, is and must be admitted to depend entirely on the law of the nation in which they lie; it will be necessary, in pursuing this inquiry, to examine, not simply those principles of abstract justice . . . which are admitted to regulate, in a just degree, the rights of civilized nations, . . . but those principles also which our own government has adapted in the particular case and given us as the rule for our decision.[121]

Here again we encounter, as in the slave trade cases, a distinction between "abstract justice" and the positive edicts of a government that form "the rule for our decision." Abstract rights, Marshall was suggesting, were to be tempered by "the right of society to prescribe their rules by which property may be acquired." Practical considerations "adapted in the particular case" were to receive special emphasis.

Having announced his focus, Marshall then plunged into a discussion of the special features of Indian–white relations on the American continent. Those relations were dominated, he argued, by the "eager[ness] of Europeans," on discovering America, "to appropriate to themselves so much of it as they could respectively acquire," and by "the character and religion of [the Indian] inhabitants," which "afforded an apology for considering them as a people over whom the superior genius of Europe might claim an ascendancy."[122] Consequently, in establishing relations with the Indians, "the rights of the original inhabitants were [not] entirely disregarded; but were necessarily, to a considerable extent, impaired." While the Indians were "admitted to be the rightful occupants of the soil, with a legal as well as just claim to retain possession of it," their "power to dispose of the soil at their own will, to whomsoever they pleased, was denied by the . . . . fundamental principle that discovery gave exclusive title to those who made it."[123]

The recognition by European nations of the exclusive right of the discoverer to appropriate the lands occupied by the Indians was retained when the United States came into being. "It has never been doubted," Marshall announced, "that either the United States, or the several states, had a clear title to all the lands [relinquished by Great Britain after independence], subject only to the Indian right of occupancy, and that the exclusive power to extinguish that right was vested in [federal or state

---

[121] Ibid.
[122] Ibid., 572–73.

[123] Ibid., 574.

governments]."[124] The principle that discovery gave an exclusive right to extinguish Indian titles was "incompatible with an absolute and complete title in the Indians."[125] The jurisprudential limits of his inquiry, Marshall made clear, were set by the proposition that "conquest gives a title which the Courts or the conqueror cannot deny." The "private and speculative opinions of individuals" about the "original justice" of claims resting on the fact of conquest were not relevant, even though the Indians' possessory rights were "just" as well as "legal."

The principles governing Indian-white relations in America had, Marshall felt, been formulated because of "the character and habits of the people whose rights have been wrested away from them." The Indians inhabiting America "were fierce savages." To leave them in possession of their country was "to leave the country a wilderness." The European discoverers had been forced, given the character of the Indians, either to "abandon the country" or to "enforce [their] claims by the sword." They had therefore, in their legal relationship with the Indians, adopted "principles adapted to the condition of a people with whom it was impossible to mix." Laws that "ought to regulate . . . the relations between the conqueror and conquered" were "incapable of application to a people under such circumstances."[126] Thus the principle that discovery and conquest yielded an absolute right to remove Indians from the land, "however extravagant" its "pretension," became "the law of the land." The proposition that Indians were mere occupants, incapable of transferring their titles to others, might well "be opposed to natural right and . . . the usages of civilized nations." But it was "indispensable to [the] system under which [America] had been settled"; it was a response to "the actual condition of the two people."[127]

The message of *Johnson* v. *McIntosh*, then, was that the natural rights of human beings to dispose of property that they held by virtue of possession did not apply to Indians in America. While Marshall had intimated that the circumscription of the rights of conquered peoples was a prerogative of conquest, he had not suggested that such a circumscription would have occurred if the conquered persons had been other than "fierce savages," incapable of being "incorporated with the victorious nation" and thereby retaining "unimpaired" their rights to property.[128] The special principles of Indian-white property rights were a function of the "character and habits" of the Indians.

The natural law argument had been reduced, in *Johnson* v. *McIntosh*, to an advisory capacity. "Abstract principles," notions of "abstract justice," and the "natural right" to dispose of property had been

---

[124] Ibid., 584–85.
[125] Ibid., 588.
[126] Ibid., 590.

[127] Ibid., 591–92.
[128] Ibid., 589.

subordinated to the "laws of the land" and the "rules by which property may be acquired and preserved." The positive enactments of American states and the federal government, as distinguished from the unwritten principles of natural law, determined the treatment of Indian titles to land. Natural law, Marshall intimated in *Johnson* v. *McIntosh,* was not designed to apply to cases involving persons whose "character and habits" were so markedly different from "civilized" whites.

Between *Johnson* v. *McIntosh* and the next two major Marshall Court cases[129] dealing with the rights of Indian tribes the situation of native Indians in America became more complex and even more precarious. Encouraged by the Jackson administration, which favored removal of all Indians inhabiting territory east of the Mississippi, the federal government and certain states engaged in a variety of policies calculated to dispossess Indians of their land. Indian policy under Jackson was distinguished by a refusal on the part of the federal government to regard the Indian tribes as sovereign nations, by deference to states who attempted to compel Indians to conform to their laws, and by constant pressure on the Indians to emigrate. In the 1820s several states passed statutes (known colloquially as "Indian laws") bringing Indians within their borders under the jurisdiction of state courts. Indians were required to pay taxes, serve in the militia, and work on state highways. They could be sued in state courts for trespass or debt. Their tribal laws were declared to be superseded by state law, and punishments were prescribed for those attempting to enforce tribal laws.[130] Those statutes were predicated on the assumption that the legal status of Indians approximated that of persons owing legal obligations to the states in which they resided rather than that of members of independent nations.

Alongside the growth of state efforts to subject Indians to state law was the effort of the federal government to remove them from eastern lands. The process by which removal was sought demonstrated not only the significance early-nineteenth-century white Americans attached to property rights and landownership, but also their perceptions of Indians. By the "allotment" system, Indians who "had demonstrated their capacity for civilization by establishing farms"[131] were given the option of retaining cultivated land rather than emigrating. The lands retained were designated "allotments," which could ripen into fee simple titles in a few years, at which point the landowner could apply for state citizenship. The expectation was that few Indians would be sufficiently "civilized"

---

[129] Danforth v. Wear, 9 Wheat. 673 (1824) was a minor case, following Preston v. Browder and Danforth's Lessee v. Thomas, supra, note 110.

[130] See M. Young, "Indian Removal and Land Allotment: The Civilized Tribes and Jacksonian Justice," *Am. Hist. Rev.,* 64:31 (1958). The states included Alabama, Georgia, Mississippi, and Tennessee. For a listing of the relevant statutes, see Young at 35, note 9.

[131] Young, "Indian Removal," 37.

to choose allotments, but that those who did could be considered eligible material for citizenship by virtue of their ownership and cultivation of land. The system also assumed that those who held allotments could freely dispose of them in contracts with whites; that many would; and that Indians would often not secure favorable terms. These expectations largely came to pass.[132]

When tribes such as the Creeks in Alabama or the Cherokees in Georgia resisted efforts to encourage them to relocate and refused to recognize state laws, the states and white settlers joined forces to defraud them of their land or to force them to emigrate. As early as the 1820s a common pattern had emerged. Speculators bought land from Indians and then "borrowed" their money back, often in exchange for overpriced goods, including whiskey. The consequent loss of land reduced many Indians to a dependent status, whereupon the federal government and the states encouraged them to emigrate. After selling their allotments Indians sometimes "took to the swamps," sometimes scavenged off their settler neighbors, or sometimes lived in huts on land that had not been cleared for settlement. Eventually most became destitute or emigrated.[133]

The policy of removal, the frauds it helped perpetrate, and the dire consequences for the Indian population precipitated a growing concern among a segment of educated nineteenth-century Americans for what they termed the "plight" of Indians. Like the allotment system, this response revealed the implicit ideological boundaries limiting early-nineteenth-century white attitudes toward Indians. The choices posed to Indians by the allotment system were to acculturate or to leave. Either the owner of an allotment used land consistent with the way that "civilized" white republican citizens were expected to use land, in which case the owner could become a freeholder, or the owner demonstrated himself incapable of that acculturation and "voluntarily" dispossesed himself, with impoverishment or emigration following. A similar bipolarity framed the "plight" response. The "plight" of the Indians was deemed to be caused by their inability to acculturate. Given that fact, most Indians would inevitably be forced to emigrate. Most could not adapt to white customs and institutions: they lacked the inherent qualities of republican yeomen. While civilizing Indians was preferable to dispossessing them, for humanitarian and paternalistic reasons, the civilizing process did not take in most cases. The result was a "plight": dependency and poverty or emigration and dispossession.

In 1828, in an address commemorating the first settlement of Salem, Massachusetts, Story called attention to the "plight" of the Indians. He first argued that the principle that the initial discovery of North American colonies conferred upon the nation of the discoverer an exclusive right to

---

[132] Ibid., 39–41.  [133] Ibid.

the soil, while "flexible and convenient," "displaced" the Indians, who were in possession of the land and could "maintain their right to share in the common inheritance" by "stand[ing] upon the eternal laws of natural justice." But the natural law argument, Story felt, "was quite too refined to satisfy the ambition and lust of dominion" of the early European settlers. They therefore created the more convenient doctrine that "the natives . . . possessed a present right of occupancy . . . which might be surrendered to the discovering nation."[134]

The result, Story pointed out, was that "by a law of their nature," the Indians "seem destined to a slow, but sure extinction." At "the approach of the white man, they fade away." Their disappearance was not principally the result of famine or war, but of "a moral cancer, which has eaten into their hearts—a plague which the touch of the white man communicated—a poison which betrayed them into a lingering ruin." The eastern seaboard, Story noted, now contained not a single region occupied by Indians: "already the last feeble remnants of the race are preparing for their journey beyond the Mississippi."[135] For Story there were some lessons in this "melancholy history." The westward exodus of the Indians signified for him "the general background of their race." They were "incapable of . . . assimilation" with Western culture: "by their very nature and character, they neither unite themselves with civil institutions, nor can with safety be allowed to remain as distinct communities." Their "ferocious passions, their independent spirit, [and] their wandering life" represented a challenge to white society. By their presence they raised the question "whether the country itself shall be abandoned by civilized man, or maintained by his sword as the right of the strongest."[136] Story knew what the answer to that question would be.

Story sent a copy of his address to Marshall, who responded with a lengthy discussion of the "Indian question."

> I have been still more touched with your notice of the red man than of the white. The conduct of our forefathers in expelling the original occupants of the soil grew out of so many mixed motives that any censure which philanthropy may bestow upon it ought to be qualified. The Indians were a fierce and dangerous enemy whose love of war made them sometimes the aggressors, whose numbers and habits made them formidable, and whose cruel system of warfare seemed to justify every endeavour to remove them to a distance from civilized settlements. It was not until the adoption of our present government that respect for our own safety permitted us to give full indulgence to those

---

[134] J. Story, "History and Influence of the Puritans," Sept. 18, 1828, in W. Story, *Miscellaneous Writings,* 408, 460.

[135] Ibid., 464.
[136] Ibid., 464–65.

principles of humanity and justice which ought always to govern our conduct towards the aborigines when this course can be pursued without exposing ourselves to the most afflicting calamities. That time, however, is unquestionably arrived, and every oppression now exercised on a helpless people depending on our magnanimity and justice for the preservation of character. I often think with indignation on our disreputable conduct (as I think) in the affair of the Cherokees in Georgia.[137]

Story's address, and Marshall's comments on it, provide illustrations of the "plight" response. The "habits" of the Indians were prominent in both accounts: their "fierceness," their incompatibility with civilized society. While "humanity and justice" ought to govern relations between whites and Indians, considerations of "safety" quite naturally intervened. Both accounts also convey the practicality that tempered white philanthropy toward the Indians. When the Indians had been reduced to a "helpless" state, and had come to be dependent on the "magnanimity" of the whites, indulgence was appropriate and "oppression" a "disreputable" response. But while Indians remained "fierce and dangerous," self-preservation demanded a more hostile attitude. The dispossession response, Marshall felt, had resulted in a "deep stain on the American character" only when the Indians had been rendered helpless and continued to be oppressed: before that their forcible removal from "civilized settlements" had been simply a matter of necessity.

By the late 1820s and 1830s, as Story's and Marshall's comments suggest, the "plight" response and an acknowledgment of the difficulties attendant on "civilizing" Indians had become entrenched attitudes in a segment of the literate white community. Missionaries had begun to live among the Indian tribes and had begun to publish pamphlets dramatizing their "plight," the most notable of which, "Escape of William Penn," a tract written by missionary Jeremiah Evarts, appeared in the *National Intelligencer* in August 1829.[138] The immediate context of Evarts's essay was the situation of the Cherokee Indians in Georgia.

In 1802 Georgia and the federal government had signed an agreement in which Georgia ceded to the United States her claims to western lands that subsequently became the states of Alabama and Mississippi.[139] As part of the agreement the United States promised to acquire the title to lands within Georgia held by Indians. As *Fletcher v. Peck* and *Johnson*

---

[137] J. Marshall to J. Story, Oct. 29, 1828, quoted in *Proc. Mass. Hist. Soc.*, 14:337–38 (1901).
[138] The essays were reprinted in [J. Evarts], *Essays on the Present Crisis in the Condition of the American Indian*

. . . *Published Under the Signature of William Penn* (1829).
[139] Georgia Cession, Apr. 26, 1802, in *American State Papers: Public Lands* (1832), 126.

v. *McIntosh* indicated, Indians holding land within the boundaries of American jurisdictions were regarded as mere "occupants": their title could be displaced at any time. The 1802 agreement assumed that only the federal government could acquire land held by Indians, but it did not apply to Indian reserves and allotments, which in practice were "sold" by Indians to whites as rapidly as white settlers demanded them.

The actions of federal Indian agents and missionaries who came in contact with the Georgia Indians in the early nineteenth century, however, had impressed upon the Cherokees the benefits of cultivating land, and when the allotment policy was created in 1816, several Cherokees elected to remain on improved lands.[140] By the 1820s many Cherokee tribes had abandoned hunting, and they refused to emigrate or to sell their lands.[141] In 1827 the Cherokees adopted a constitution and allegedly declared themselves to be an independent nation. The response of the state of Georgia was the passage of a version of the so-called "Indian laws" previously described.[142] When the Cherokees asked the federal government for support, the Jackson administration took the position that the Cherokees could not establish an independent nation within Georgia and that the United States would not interfere with the internal laws of a state. The choice for the Indians, the Jackson administration suggested, was to emigrate or to comply with the new Georgia statutes.[143]

In keeping with that position, President Jackson, in December 1829, announced that he was recommending legislation setting aside federal territory west of the Mississippi for emigrating Indians. Those Indians that chose not to emigrate, Jackson emphasized, could retain allotted land if they qualified, but would be subject to state laws.[144] The Cherokees responded by petitioning Congress to vindicate their rights in the face of the recent Georgia statutes, which they argued were unconstitutional.[145] Meanwhile a number of political leaders declared themselves advocates of "Indian rights," and as Jackson's bill, known as the "removal bill," was debated in the spring of 1830, it took on a distinctly political cast. Southern congressmen overwhelmingly supported the bill, northern rep-

---

[140] Young, "Indian Removal," 37–38.
[141] See J. Kennedy, *Memoirs of the Life of William Wirt* (2 vols., 1850), II, 245.
[142] Act No. 545, Dec. 20, 1828, and Act No. 546, Dec. 19, 1829, in W. Dawson, *A Compilation of the Laws of the State of Georgia* (1831), 198.
[143] The Jackson administration's position was summarized in a letter from Secretary of War John Eaton to a delegation of Cherokees. The letter was written on April 18, 1829, and reprinted in *Niles' Weekly Register*, May 30, 1829. See also 2 Op. Att'y Gen. 305 (1829) for the legal position of the Jackson administration.
[144] Jackson, Annual Message, Dec. 8, 1829, in J. Richardson, comp., *A Compilation of the Messages and Papers of the Presidents 1769–1897* (10 vols., 1902), II, 442.
[145] See *Niles' Weekly Register*, Mar. 13, 1830.

resentatives generally opposed it, and adversaries of Jackson, such as Henry Clay and Daniel Webster, maneuvered to ensure that the issue of Indian rights would continue to receive public attention.

In the subsequent debate over Indian rights that formed a backdrop to the Marshall Court's decisions in _Cherokee Nation_ v. _Georgia_[146] and _Worcester v. Georgia_[147] it is important to keep in mind just what rights the proponents and opponents were debating. The members of the Cherokee tribes that had led the movement for independence and national autonomy were a "ruling elite"[148] that consisted of the wealthier, English-speaking, mixed-blood members of the Nation, and who were opposed in many of their goals by other members, although not on the goals of cultural diversity and separatism.[149] The "elite" Cherokees advocated separatism principally for two reasons: to avoid being subjected to the jurisdiction of Georgia, a state that had not only claimed power to regulate their affairs but had also passed laws discriminating against them; and to prove to the white community and to themselves that, left alone, they could use their land properly, acquire wealth, continue their education, and in general become virtuous republican citizens.[150] The rights claimed by the elite Cherokees, and defended by their proponents, were rights of cultural self-determination, but not in its modern connotation. The elite Cherokees, some of them slaveowners, wanted to be left alone so that they might become more rapidly acculturated; they were concerned that elements in Georgia would underestimate their ability to be "civilized." Those members of the Cherokees that favored maintenance of ancient tribal customs and practices were condemned by the elite Cherokees as "aboriginal."[151]

---

[146] 5 Pet. 1 (1831).

[147] 6 Pet. 515 (1832).

[148] McLoughlin, _Cherokees_, 221. For an analysis of the composition of the Cherokee elite between 1825 and 1835 see W. McLoughlin and W. Conser, "The Cherokees in Transition," _J. Am. Hist._, 64:678 (1977).

[149] McLoughlin, _Cherokees_, 184, 213–28.

[150] In 1828, after the Cherokee constitution was adopted, Utaletah, a member of the ruling elite, wrote in the newspaper of the Cherokee Nation that

[o]ur nation as a political body . . . bids fair for rapid progress in the path of civilization, the arts and sciences, while at the same time we can say with no ordinary degree of exultation, that agriculture is gradually gaining an ascendancy amongst us equalled by no other Indian tribe.

_Cherokee Phoenix and Indian Advocate_, May 6, 1828, quoted in McLoughlin, _Cherokees_, 233.

[151] John Ross, the leading chief of the Cherokee Nation from 1828 to 1866, delivered his addresses to the Cherokee Council in English because his Sequoyan, the principal language of the Cherokees, was so rudimentary. Ibid. at 184. Ross and two other elite Cherokees told John Quincy Adams in 1825 that they were anxious to "see the habits and customs of the aboriginal man extinguished." Quoted in W. Lowrie et al., eds., _American State Papers_ (2 vols., 1834), 651–52. See also McLoughlin, _Cherokees_, 180.

# Chapter X: *Natural Law and Racial Minorities*

Further, the rights being claimed by elite Cherokees in the debate were not only natural rights of ownership but also rights of sovereignty. The Cherokee Nation, as represented by its elite members, argued that its legal rights and responsibilities were based on treaties with the federal government and thus that its legal relationships were solely with that government. The relationships, the argument ran, were akin to the relationships of the United States and foreign nations; at a minimum, the tribes had the sovereign rights of a state. Thus the "Indian rights" argument was a sovereignty argument in a double sense, drawing both on vested rights principles and on an analogy to the principles of national sovereignty embedded in the law of nations. The two-pronged character of the argument made it particularly explosive, because while the Cherokees claimed that only the United States government could potentially regulate their affairs, the United States government, in the person of the Jackson administration, supported Georgia's position. When the Cherokees sought support for their plea to be left alone to become better republican citizens, then, they sought support neither from the citizens of Georgia nor the federal executive. The institution they asked to protect their rights was the Marshall Court, an institution known for its solicitude for individual vested rights.

The debate over Jackson's removal bill resulted in a victory for his administration: the bill was eventually passed and signed in May 1830. Shortly thereafter a group of prominent opponents of the Jackson administration, including Webster, advised the elite Cherokees to litigate their claims in the courts and recommended hiring William Wirt as counsel.[152] Wirt's emergence as an advocate of Indian rights was a bit sudden. He had been attorney general in the Monroe and Adams administrations, which had consistently recommended removal of the Indians from southeastern states. In 1824 he had written an advisory opinion arguing that the Cherokees were not a sovereign nation.[153] He had been inclined to stay on as attorney general under Jackson, despite the latter's reputation as an "Indian fighter." Only after Jackson, apparently because of fears about Wirt's views on Indian affairs, appeared resolved not to retain him did Wirt join the opposition forces.[154]

By 1830, however, Wirt was a strong Jackson opponent, and he had the advantage of being an experienced Supreme Court advocate who could point to two early pronouncements as attorney general in which he

---

[152] Some of these details are recounted in a letter from Wirt to Dabney Carr, June 21, 1830, in Kennedy, *William Wirt*, II, 253–55.

[153] 1 Op. Att'y Gen. 645 (1824).

[154] See W. Wirt to Elizabeth Wirt, Oct. 28, 1828; W. Wirt to D. Carr, Feb. 28, 1829; William Wirt Papers, Maryland Historical Society; Annapolis, Md.

had upheld the independent status of Indian tribes.[155] In a long letter written in June 1830 to his good friend Judge Dabney Carr of the Virginia Court of Appeals, Wirt described his situation:

> Some of the most distinguished men in Congress who had opposed [the] passage [of Jackson's removal bill], Webster, Judge [Ambrose] Spencer, [Peter] Frelinghuysen and others, advised the Cherokee delegates then in Washington to employ counsel to bring the various questions of their rights, under their treaties, to the Supreme Court of the United States: and for this purpose they were introduced to me . . . some two or three weeks ago. I was aware of the delicacy of the situation in which this application placed me. I saw that I was about to be made instrumental in thwarting or impeding . . . a project in which the President and State of Georgia were bent, and which, but for my interferences, might take immediate effect by the removal of the Indians—for they would sooner remove and die in the wilderness, than remain in subjection to the laws of Georgia. . . .
>
> There are many well-meaning men who think it the interest of the Cherokees to remove to a country where the whites will no longer annoy them and where they may pass their lives in peace and quiet. [But] . . . [t]here are wild Indians in the [new territory] who will probably contest the right of possession with [the Cherokees], and make that paradise a slaughter-house and a scene of mutual extermination. . . .[156]

Wirt was inclined to represent the Cherokees: he had "[taken] up the question of the right of Georgia to extend her laws over these people" and concluded that Georgia had acted unconstitutionally. He also believed, however, in the "manifest determination, both of the President and the State, that the [Georgia] law should be extended over [the Cherokees] *at every hazard.*"[157] He suspected that even if the Marshall Court held in favor of the Cherokees, Georgia might defy the decision, with the support of the Jackson administration. Even before the removal bill, Jackson had taken the position that the federal government would not "countenance . . . an independent [Cherokee] government," and that the Cherokees must "submit to the laws of . . . states."[158] Wirt suspected that Jackson might "render [any adverse] decision [of the Court] abortive, by forbidding the Marshal and people of the county from obeying it."[159]

---

[155] See 1 Op. Att'y Gen. 465 (1821); 2 Op. Att'y Gen. 110 (1828).
[156] Wirt to Carr, June 21, 1830, supra, note 152, at 254–55.
[157] Ibid., 253.

[158] Andrew Jackson, Message to Congress, Dec. 8, 1829, quoted in McLoughlin, *Cherokees,* 247.
[159] Wirt to Carr, June 21, 1830, supra, note 152, at 255.

# Chapter X: *Natural Law and Racial Minorities*

In addition, Wirt worried about how he would get a case before the Supreme Court in which the Cherokees could test the constitutionality of the Georgia statutes. He believed that a Section 25 writ of error strategy would fail because Georgia, following the course of Virginia in *Martin v. Hunter's Lessee*, would simply never create any record for the purposes of the writ of error.[160] This left him, he felt, two other options. One was a suit in a federal circuit court on behalf of an individual Cherokee against a Georgia official. The Cherokee would claim that the execution of the Georgia statutes either interfered with his property rights or so restricted his mobility as to amount to false imprisonment. While this option was apparently discussed by the Cherokees, it was never seriously entertained, possibly because William Johnson, in whose circuit court the suit would have been brought, was not receptive.[161] The circuit court suit required that individual Cherokees be designated "foreign . . . citizens" under Article III, Section 2 of the Constitution, since that Article's language did not contemplate suits in the federal courts by citizens of a state against the state itself or its officials.

The remaining option was the one Wirt eventually chose, but he recognized that it was not free from jurisdictional difficulties. He described it to Carr:

> [I]t became important to me to enquire whether [the Cherokees] had any right to apply at once to the original jurisdiction of the federal courts; and this I cannot perceive that they can do, unless the Cherokee Nation be *a foreign state* in the sense of the Constitution, in which case they would have a right under the Constitution to file an original bill against the State of Georgia, in the Supreme Court, and ask an injunction against the execution of her law within their territory; or, unless the individuals of the Cherokee Nation be *aliens*. . . .
>
> If the individuals of the Cherokee nation be *aliens,* so as to find the original jurisdiction of the Supreme Court, the principal chief of that nation might file a bill against those officers of the State of Georgia,

---

[160] Ibid., 256. Wirt's conjecture was reinforced by Georgia's response in the case of *Georgia v. Tassel,* handed down in December 1830. In that case George Tassel, a Cherokee, had been convicted by a Georgia court of a murder committed on Cherokee lands. Lawyers for Tassel filed an application for a writ of error in the Supreme Court, and Marshall issued the writ. The governor of Georgia, Wilson Lumpkin, publicly declared that Georgia would resist the writ, and Tassel was executed. See Richmond *Enquirer,* Dec. 9, 1830; *Niles' Weekly Register,* Jan. 8, 1831.

[161] Wirt to Carr, June 21, 1830, supra, note 152, at 256–57; W. Wirt to John Ross, Nov. 15, 1830, quoted in G. Woodward, *The Cherokees* (1963), 165–66. See also the account in J. Burke, "The Cherokee Cases: A Study in Law, Politics, and Morality," *Stan. L. Rev.,* 21:500, 511–13 (1969).

who will probably be engaged in executing her law, and ask an injunction against them, although he could not sue the State herself.[162]

Wirt added that Article 6, Section 2 of the Constitution provided that "all Treaties made . . . under the Authority of the United States, shall be the supreme Law of the Land; and the Judges in every State shall be bound thereby." This brought him to the argument he would make on the merits. He believed that federal treaties with the Cherokees had implicitly given the tribes the status of "a sovereign nation," and that the Supreme Court might declare itself bound to enforce the treaties, notwithstanding the Georgia statutes.[163]

Wirt's analysis of the case that would come to be *Cherokee Nation v. Georgia* was a brilliant performance. He was not only correct in anticipating Georgia's determination to resist a Section 25 case, and the Jackson administration's determination to support Georgia in its defiance, he had identified all of the jurisdictional obstacles the Cherokees faced. If the Cherokee Nation, as represented by its principal chief John Ross, brought a bill for injunctive relief against the state of Georgia and its executing officials in the Supreme Court of the United States, the bill might be dismissed on any of three grounds. The Cherokees might not be considered "foreign citizens" (aliens) for jurisdictional purposes; the Cherokee Nation might not be considered a "foreign state" for jurisdictional purposes; assuming these obstacles were cleared, the Eleventh Amendment might be read as preventing suits by "foreign citizens" against a state. The last ground was the least troublesome after *Osborn v. Bank* and *Planters' Bank,* which Wirt alluded to in his letter to Carr,[164] since those cases seemed to establish that the Amendment was not a bar to nonresident suits against state officials, but Marshall's language in those cases, as we have seen, had been assertive and cryptic.

Given all these difficulties, Wirt decided to seek an informal opinion from none other than John Marshall on the question of jurisdiction. "Will you . . . tell me," he asked Carr, "whether there would be any impropriety in your conversing with the Chief Justice on this subject, as a brother judge, and giving me his impressions . . . I would not have you conceal from him that the question may probably come before the Supreme Court." "If I were near the Chief Justice," Wirt added, ". . . I would speak to him with the confidence of a friend . . . and leave it to him to say, whether he would or would not be willing to come out with the expression of his opinion, so as to prevent embarrassment and mischief."[165]

[162] Wirt to Carr, June 21, 1830, supra, note 152, at 256–57.
[163] Ibid., 257.

[164] Ibid.
[165] Ibid., 258.

# Chapter X: *Natural Law and Racial Minorities*

Carr sent Wirt's letter on to Marshall, who then wrote Carr a response. "I have followed," Marshall said, "the debate in both houses of Congress, with profound attention and deep interest, and have wished, most sincerely, that both the executive and legislative departments had thought differently on the subject. Humanity must bewail the course which is pursued, whatever may be the decision of policy." Marshall added, however, that he "thought it his duty to refrain from indicating any opinion" on the jurisdictional issues.[166]

Meanwhile Wirt had sought to enlist other prominent persons on behalf of the Cherokees, including James Madison, who wrote Wirt that while he wanted "justice [to be] done to the [Cherokees'] cause," he was inclined to think removal the best policy. Madison advanced two reasons for his conclusion. First,

> [B]y not incorporating their labour and associating fixed improvements with the soil, they have not appropriated it to themselves, nor made the destined use of its capacity for increasing the number and the enjoyments of the human race.

Second,

> It is so evident that they can never be tranquil or happy within the bounds of a State, either in a separate or subject character . . . [R]emoval to another home, if a good one can be found, may well be the wish of their best friends.[167]

Wirt, notwithstanding his representation of the Cherokees, was inclined to agree. He replied to Madison:

> I . . . concur with you entirely, as to the best mode of solving the political problem with regard to the Indians within the bounds of the States. . . . While the [Cherokee] delegation was . . . in consultation [with me] on this subject, [I said that] there are many in the United States who will think it your wisest course to remove, *and I am among them,* [despite having given] my opinion . . . in favor of your right to remain.[168]

It is useful to note, on the eve of the great Cherokee litigations of 1831 and 1832, the persistence, among both supporters and opponents of

---

[166] See Kennedy, *William Wirt,* II, 258.

[167] J. Madison to W. Wirt, Oct. 1, 1830, quoted in Kennedy, *William Wirt,* II, 260–61.

[168] W. Wirt to J. Madison, Oct. 5, 1830, quoted in ibid, II, 261. Emphasis in original.

the Indians, of the attitudes that had been present throughout the early nineteenth century; and it is also useful to note the awkward status of the natural law argument in prospective Indian rights cases. Marshall, Story, Wirt, and Madison each regarded Indians as "savage" and largely incompatible with civilized society. Each admitted that if "civilizing" Indians could not solve their plight, dispossession and removal were the best policies. None felt that in the case of Indians mere possession of land yielded any natural rights of ownership. Wirt himself, in an October 1830 letter to Madison, pointed out the interaction of those views with natural rights theory:

> The argument against the title of the Indians to their land, compared with the argument in favour of our title to them, presents the strangest absurdity. . . . We say . . . that they can have not title but to so much land as they can now cultivate; . . . whilst we hold that we have a perfect title to millions upon million of acres confessedly beyond our present capacity for cultivation. In their improved condition as civilized agriculturists, you will perceive that the argument drawn from writers on natural law, applied to them in their savage state, is unanswerable, unless we admit the new and strange ground, now taken, that they had no right to alter their condition and become husbandmen.[169]

Wirt had identified in this passage the same phenomenon that had affected the natural law argument in the slave trade cases. When natural rights theory, or "universal principles of justice and humanity," cast aspersions on discrimination against racial minorities, natural law arguments were refined so as to weaken their force. Black slaves were human beings, and human beings had inalienable rights, among them the right not to be treated as property; yet slavery was entrenched and blacks were somehow different, and thus the natural law argument was reduced to a mere "moral" claim. Indians were likewise human beings, and as possessors of land had a natural right to the fruits of their labor, yet they could be dispossessed because of theories of discovery and conquest or because they had not cultivated the land. And when they could show that they had in fact become "civilized agriculturists," that showing was rejected because, being Indians, they had "no right to alter their condition." The refinements served to suggest that the "unanswerable" natural law argument could be dismissed when the results it compelled were too disquieting. The obvious corollary to that suggestion was that the stature of natural law and natural rights as sources of law was indeterminate or even dubious.

---

[169] Ibid., 262.

# Chapter X: *Natural Law and Racial Minorities*

Five months after Wirt's October 1830 letter to Madison he appeared before the Court in the case of *Cherokee Nation v. Georgia* and moved for an injunction to prevent Georgia from enforcing its Indian laws, claiming in the course of his argument that the Cherokee tribes in Georgia constituted a foreign nation. In the course of preparing for his argument Wirt had consulted several distinguished lawyers, including Webster, Horace Binney, and James Kent. Binney and Kent sent him opinion letters, which Wirt incorporated into his argument, declaring the Cherokees sufficiently "foreign" to meet the requirements for the Court's jurisdiction.[170] The opinion letters revealed that another potential obstacle to the Cherokee suit had surfaced: the possibility that the Court might conclude that it lacked power to enforce an injunction against a state legislature because that act would constitute an undue interference with that legislature's political powers. None of the lawyers Wirt consulted mentioned any constitutional basis for that suggestion, but Wirt was nonetheless aware of the possibility.[171]

Meanwhile, to complicate matters even further, the pending *Cherokee Nation* case showed signs of precipitating a political crisis. Congress, in its winter session of 1830–31, took the occasion of the Cherokee controversy to consider repealing Section 25 of the Judiciary Act. Story complained in two letters in early 1831 that the resistance to the Cherokee claims and "the recent nullification doctrine" were "parts of the same general scheme," and that "if the twenty-fifth section is repealed the Constitution is practically gone."[172] In addition, there was the aforementioned difficulty that if the Cherokees should win on the jurisdictional issue, and also on the merits, Georgia and the Jackson administration, with the tacit support of Congress, might well decline to endorse the Court's judgment, thereby isolating the Court.

Wirt alluded to this last possibility at the conclusion of his argument before the Court on March 14, 1831,[173] in which he gave a ringing defense of Indian rights:

> [I]f we have a government at all, there is no difficulty in [enforcing Supreme Court decrees]. In pronouncing your decree you will have declared the law; and it is part of the sworn duty of the President of the United States to "take care that the laws be faithfully executed."

---

[170] See R. Peters, *The Case of the Cherokee Nation Against the State of Georgia* (1831), Appendix 1, 225–230.

[171] See Wirt to Carr, June 21, 1830, supra, note 152, at 256.

[172] J. Story to John H. Ashmun, Jan. 30, 1831, quoted in W. Story, *Life and Letters*, II, 48; J. Story to George Ticknor, Jan. 22, 1831, quoted in ibid., 49.

[173] Minutes of the Supreme Court of the United States (Jan. 12, 1829–Aug. 7, 1837), vol. E at 156, National Archives Microfilm Publications, Microcopy No. 215, Roll No. 2).

It is not for him, nor for the [state of Georgia] to sit in appeal on your decision. . . . If he refuses to perform his duty, the Constitution has provided a remedy. . . .

The existence of this remnant of a once great and mighty nation is at stake [in this case]. . . . They are here in the last extremity, and with them must perish forever the honour of the American name. . . . We asked them for a portion of their land, and they ceded it. We asked again and again, and they continued to cede, until they have now reduced themselves within the narrowest compass that their own subsistence will permit. . . . I cannot believe that this honorable court . . . will stand by and see these people stripped of their property and extirpated from the earth, while they are holding up to us their treaties and claiming the fulfillment of our engagements.[174]

Thomas Sergeant had joined Wirt in arguing for the Cherokees; Georgia, in keeping with its position that the dispute was entirely a state matter, had refused to argue the case at all. The Justices took only four days after the conclusion of Wirt's and Sergeant's arguments to reach a decision.[175] The "opinion of the Court," written by Marshall, actually represented the views of only two Justices, himself and McLean. Duvall was absent because of the mental illness of his son;[176] Baldwin and Johnson concurred only in the result; Story and Thompson dissented. Moreover, while the opinion of the Court was ostensibly limited only to the jurisdictional issues, Marshall took occasion to anticipate the disposition of a hypothetical suit by Cherokees who had had their property confiscated by Georgia laws. A "majority of the judges," Marshall declared, had concluded that the Cherokee Nation was "a distinct political society, . . . capable of managing its own affairs, . . . uniformly treated as a state," with "an unquestionable . . . right to lands they occupy, until that right shall be extinguished by a voluntary cession to [the federal] government."[177] The "queston of [the] right [of the Cherokees]" to "the land [they] occupied" might "be decided by this court in a proper case with proper parties."[178] This was a clear intimation that only the federal government could succeed to Indian lands.

The language of Marshall's opinion quoted above suggests that he and McLean might have been prepared to restrain Georgia from interfering with the Cherokee lands, and as we shall see, two other Justices were also inclining in that direction. But the Court's disposition of *Cherokee*

---

[174] Wirt's argument was not reproduced in the United States Reports. Excerpts appear in Kennedy, *William Wirt*, II, 291–96.

[175] 5 Pet. at 15; Minutes, supra, note 172, at 1576.

[176] See supra, Chapter V, p. 324.

[177] 5 Pet. at 16–17.

[178] Ibid., 20.

Chapter X: *Natural Law and Racial Minorities*

*Nation* had, for a time, the opposite effect. While the Cherokee tribes were "a state," they were not "a state of the Union," as their own counsel, Marshall pointed out, had "conclusively shown."[179] Were they therefore a "foreign state"?

The answer to this "question of much . . . difficulty," Marshall concluded, was no. Indian tribes were neither domestic states nor foreign nations. They were "domestic dependent nations."[180] Their relationship to the United States was "marked by peculiar and cardinal distinctions."[181] That relationship most closely resembled "that of a ward to his guardian."[182] Marshall advanced two reasons for this conclusion, one based on the nature of Indians in America and the other based on constitutional language. While Indians had an "unquestionable . . . right" to the lands they occupied on the American continent, their occupancy of territory was contingent. The United States asserted title to their lands "independent of their will."[183] Indians and their lands were "considered . . . so completely under the sovereignty and dominion of the United States" that efforts by foreign nations to "form a political connexion" with Indians would be treated "by all [Americans] as . . . act[s] of hostility."[184]

Marshall did not intend, by this language, to refer only to the formal legal status of Indians, that is, to the fact that many tribes, including the Cherokees, had signed treaties ceding their lands to the United States. He also meant to refer to "the habits and usages of the Indians" in "their intercourse with their white neighbours." Indian tribes, Marshall suggested,

> look to our government for protection; rely upon its kindness and its power; appeal to it for relief to their wants; and address the president as their great father. . . .
> At the time the constitution was framed, the idea of appealing to an American court of justice for an assertion of right or a redress of wrong, had perhaps never entered the mind of an Indian or his tribe. Their appeal was to the tomahawk, or to the government.[185]

Indians were different: they were both savage, appealing to tomahawks, and dependent, appealing to the "great father" for "relief."

The nature of Indians, Marshall argued, "was well understood by the statesmen who framed the constitution of the United States." That understanding "might furnish some reason" why the Framers had

---

[179] Ibid., 16.
[180] Ibid., 17.
[181] Ibid., 16.
[182] Ibid., 17.

[183] Ibid.
[184] Ibid., 18.
[185] Ibid.

725

"omitt[ed] to enumerate [Indians] among the parties who might sue in the courts of the union."[186] The significance of the omission was clarified by other language in the Constitution. The Commerce Clause distinguished between "foreign nations," the "several states," and "Indian tribes": here was clear textual evidence of a "contradistin[ction]" between "foreign states" and Indian tribes. While the distinction, Marshall conceded, was made in Article I rather than Article III, one could not assume that the distinction "was lost in framing a subsequent article" absent explicit language to that effect. Context and language, then, compelled the conclusion that Indian tribes could not sue in the federal courts.[187]

Marshall's argument may strike one as faintly familiar. Twenty-six years after *Cherokee Nation* Chief Justice Taney was to consider in *Dred Scott* v. *Sanford* the question whether blacks could sue in the federal courts. Like Marshall, he concluded that "habits and usages" and context helped answer that question. Like Marshall, he concluded that the "nature" of the minority in question was "well understood" by the Framers. And, like Marshall, he concluded that the federal courts were not open to such persons.

In disposing of the original jurisdiction issue Marshall rendered all the other issues in *Cherokee Nation* moot, but he went on to address what he called the "case and controversy" issue. Wirt's tactic of applying for an injunction against the state of Georgia asked the Marshall Court to do something similar to what the Court had done in *Osborn:* grant an injunction preventing a state from enforcing one of its own statutes covering a matter within its borders. The rationale for *Osborn,* we have seen, was the unmistakably federal character of the Bank of the United States and the presumably ruinous effects of state laws imposing taxes on that bank. Here, if the Cherokees were a "foreign nation," the same rationale might seem to apply.[188]

Having found that the Cherokees were not a foreign nation, Marshall could have avoided the issue altogether, but he concluded that a bill for injunctive relief on these circumstances had not precipitated a "case and controversy." The "matter of the bill," he argued, was not a proper subject for judicial inquiry. It not only asked the Court to decide on the Cherokees' title to their land, but also "to control the legislature of Georgia, and to restrain the exertion of its physical force." The Supreme Court

186 Ibid.
187 Ibid., 19.
188 Thompson in his dissent argued that *Osborn* "fully sustain[ed] the . . . application for an injunction" in *Cherokee Nation.* "The laws of the state of Georgia in this case," he said, "go as fully to the total destruction of the complainants' rights as did the law of Ohio to the destruction of the rights of the bank." Ibid., 78–79.

could not "interpose," Marshall claimed, on state laws regulating the exercise of self-government by Indians within that state's borders. It might be able to decide whether a state could infringe upon the possession of land by Indians, but only, as noted, "in a proper case with proper parties."[189]

Marshall's last argument seems to have been strategic in character, since it was unnecessary to the decision of the case and Marshall made no effort to even discuss, let alone distinguish, the *Osborn* precedent.[190] One might also be inclined to ask, as contemporaries did, whether the enumeration of Indians in the Commerce Clause was simply intended to make crystal clear that states could not negotiate commercial treaties with tribes.[191] But the focus here is on the implicit and explicit judgments about natural rights and Indians made in the *Cherokee Nation* opinion. That focus is best served by an examination not only of Marshall's opinion of the Court but also of Johnson's concurrence, in which those judgments were more starkly and crudely expressed.

Johnson wasted no time in describing the state of mind with which he approached the *Cherokee Nation* case. "I cannot but think," he said in the second page of his eleven-page concurrence, "that there are strong reasons for doubting the applicability of the epithet *state,* to a people so low in the grade of organized society as our Indian tribes most generally

---

[189] 5 Pet. at 20.

[190] Nor did Marshall discuss the question whether Georgia's sovereign immunity prevented her from being sued by an Indian tribe. Thompson simply asserted that the case was outside the scope of the Eleventh Amendment, without considering the immunity issue. Ibid., 52.

[191] See E. Everett, "The Cherokee Case," *N. Am. Rev.,* 33:136 (1831) for a deferential but stinging critique of Marshall's Commerce Clause argument and the other justification he advanced for denying the Cherokees access to the federal courts. Everett, at that time a congressman from Massachusetts, had been active in the opposition to Jackson's 1830 removal bill and was a visible supporter of the Cherokees.

Edward Everett had a remarkable career. He became a Unitarian minister in 1803, at the age of nineteen, but resigned his pastorate two years later. He went abroad, and after returning he accepted an appointment as professor of Greek literature at Harvard College. In 1819 he helped found and became the editor of the *North American Review,* holding that post until 1824, when he was elected to Congress. He subsequently served as governor of Massachusetts (1836–40), ambassador to the Court of St. James's (1841–45), president of Harvard University (1846–49), secretary of state (1852), and United States senator from Massachusetts (1852–54). He was the featured speaker on the program when Abraham Lincoln delivered his Gettysburg Address on November 19, 1863.

Everett and Story were longtime friends; Everett wrote a biographical sketch of Story in the *New-England Magazine* in 1832 for which Story supplied a long autobiographical letter. W. Story, *Life and Letters,* I, 44. On January 15, 1820, Story wrote Everett, after reading an issue of *North American Review,* that "you have almost persuaded me you are right as to the Indians." Quoted in ibid., 381. For Everett's career see P. Frothingham, *Edward Everett, Orator and Statesman* (1925).

are.''[192] While he did not want to be understood by that statement as referring to the "present form of government" adopted by the elite Cherokees (that government "certainly must be classed among the most approved forms"), he doubted whether even the Cherokee government had "received the consistency which entitles that people to admission into the family of nations.''[193]

Next followed a singular revelation of the assumptions republican theorists made about Indian tribes in America. One can see in the following passage from Johnson's opinion an interaction of the stage theory of cultural change with the perception that Indians were "different":

> It is clear that [the treaties signed between the United States and the Cherokees were] intended to give [the Cherokees] no other rights over the territory than what were needed by a race of hunters. . . . But every advance, from the hunter state to a more fixed state of society, must have a tendency to impair [those] pre-emptive right[s]. . . . The hunter state bore within itself the premise of vacating the territory. . . . But a more fixed state of society would amount to a permanent destruction of the hope. . . .
>
> But it is said that we have extended to them the means and inducement to become agricultural and civilized. It is true: and the immediate object of that policy was so obvious as probably to have intercepted the view of ulterior consequences. Independently of the general influence of humanity, these people were restless, warlike, and signally cruel in their irruptions during the revolution. The policy, therefore, of enticing them to the arts of peace, and to those improvements which might lay desolate, was obvious; and it was wise . . . to incorporate them in time into our respective governments. . . . [But] their inveterate habits and deep seated enmity has altogether baffled . . . [that] policy.[194]

The Cherokees, being Indians, were "restless, warlike, and signally cruel" in their "hunter state." For practical reasons, and perhaps for humanitarian ones, elite white America had hoped to usher them into the "agricultural and civilized" stage of society. In the process the Cherokees had naturally lost pre-emptive rights to their land, because any permanent occupancy of land by Indians was inconsistent with the sovereignty of the American government. Hope had originally characterized the acculturation process: perhaps the Indians might become less warlike as their status "improved." But that hope, and the policy of acculturation itself, had been "baffled" by the "inveterate habits" of the Indians.

---

[192] 5 Pet. at 21. Emphasis in original.
[193] Ibid.
[194] Ibid., 23–24.

# Chapter X: *Natural Law and Racial Minorities*

Johnson's opinion, as a whole, was neither strikingly different from, nor an improvement on, Marshall's opinion of the Court. But Johnson's tendency to state his positions in as forthright a manner as possible, coupled with the strength of his assumptions about the "habits" of Indians and their tendency to resist acculturation, produced a powerful brief for the proposition that the natural rights of Indians were largely ephemeral. Since Indians could not become good republicans, Johnson implicitly argued, they could not be granted the inalienable rights of republican citizens. They could not be civilized, thus they needed to be left in a permanent "hunter" state, that is, dispossessed.

Given the implicit and explicit judgments made about Indians in both Johnson's and Marshall's opinions, the second paragraph of Marshall's opinion requires comment. Marshall said:

> If courts were permitted to indulge their sympathies, a case better calculated to excite them can scarcely be imagined. A people once numerous, powerful, and truly independent, found by our ancestors in the quiet and uncontrolled possession of an ample domain, gradually sinking beneath our superior policy, our arts and our arms, have yielded their lands by successive treaties, each of which contains a solemn guarantee of the residue, until they retain no more of their formerly extensive territory than is deemed necessary to their comfortable subsistence.[195]

That paragraph cannot simply be read as one of the standard disclaimers judges make when they ultimately conclude that their "sympathies" have nothing to do with the case. As his correspondence with Story suggests, Marshall was genuinely touched by the plight of Indian tribes in America. While he believed white republican "policy" to be "superior," he also acknowledged that force had had a good deal to do with the "sinking" of the Indians. In Johnson's concurrence there is the tone of self-fulfilling prophecy: Indians get what they deserve because they are what they are. In Marshall's paragraph the sympathies appear genuine.

This interpretation of Marshall's attitude toward the Cherokees is reinforced by the events surrounding the publication of the *Cherokee Nation* opinions. When the original decision was handed down, on March 18, 1831, no dissents were announced or delivered. Nine days later the *National Intelligencer* noted that it had learned for the first time that there were dissents in the case.[196] The origin of those dissents helps clarify the

---

[195] Ibid., 15.

[196] Washington *National Intelligencer*, Mar. 28, 1831. Justice Baldwin had delivered his opinion on March 18, when the majority opinion came down, and had identified himself as "concur[ring] in the opinion of the court." Later in the opinion, however, he referred to himself as dissenting. Compare 5 Pet. 31 with 5 Pet. 48.

Chief Justice's posture. The dissenters were Thompson, who wrote a long opinion disagreeing with the Court on both the jurisdictional and substantive issues, and Story, who joined Thompson's opinion. In a May 1831 letter to the Court's Reporter, Richard Peters, Story indicated that "neither Judge T. or myself contemplated delivering a dissenting opinion [in the *Cherokee Nation* case] until the Chief Justice suggested to us the propriety of it, and his own desire that we should do it."[197] Peters, for his part, collaborated with Story, Thompson, and Marshall in the publication of a pamphlet, *The Case of the Cherokee Nation Against the State of Georgia*,[198] which included, in addition to all of the opinions rendered in the case, Kent's opinion supporting the Cherokees on the jurisdictional issues and the relevant treaties and statutes. Marshall wrote Peters, "I should be glad to see the whole case" made public, because "a very narrow view has been taken in the opinion which is pronounced by the Court." The opinions which had been delivered in court, he added, looked "to one side of the question only."[199]

Marshall, then, wanted the "plight" of the Cherokees made public; he also wanted the substantive issues raised by Georgia's dispossession of the Cherokees aired. In short, he was anxious to keep the "Cherokee question" in the public domain so that pressure for a "proper case with the proper parties" would continue. He had, of course, intimated in his opinion that Georgia's sovereign powers over Indians within its borders were vast. But by the end of the 1831 Term he may have retreated from that intimation. He was, after all, no particular friend either to state sovereignty or to the Jackson administration. Story, for his part, felt that the publication of the pamphlet would "do a great deal of good." It will "unite the moral sense . . . of our people," and "sink to the very bottom of their sense of Justice," he wrote to Peters. "I am more satisfied," Story added, that "we are right. . . . There will be, in God's Providence, a retribution for unholy deeds."[200]

Retribution of a sort came the very next Term, in the case of *Worcester* v. *Georgia*.[201] One of the "Indian laws" passed by Georgia had been a statute forbidding white men from residing in the Cherokee territory without a license from the state. Samuel Worcester and Elizur Butler, two missionaries who had been living with the Cherokees, were arrested in March 1831 for violating that statute. Worcester and Butler were first

---

[197] J. Story to R. Peters, Jr., May 17, 1831, Richard Peters Papers, Historical Society of Pennsylvania, Philadelphia, Pa.

[198] Supra, note 170.

[199] J. Marshall to R. Peters, Jr., May 19, 1831, Peters Papers.

[200] J. Story to R. Peters, Jr., June 24, 1831, in W. Story, *Life and Letters,* II, 46.

[201] Supra, note 147.

released by the Superior Court of Gwinnett County, Georgia, a trial court, which claimed that they were federal employees, who were exempt from the law. Worcester and Butler continued to refuse to leave the Cherokee Nation, and Worcester was eventually removed as postmaster of a local village in order to sever all of his federal ties.[202] Worcester and Butler were then arrested again, convicted in the trial court of violating the statute, and sentenced to four years in prison. They were offered a pardon, but refused it and appealed their case to the Supreme Court of the United States on a writ of error, arguing that the Superior Court of Gwinnett County was "the highest court in [the state] in which a decision could be had in [such a] suit."[203] Remarkably, the clerk of the county court responded to this writ of error, although the judge never signed it. In a situation faintly reminiscent of *Martin v. Hunter's Lessee*,[204] a record was thus duly created in the case, and while the state of Georgia never appeared before the Court, and publicly announced that it would disregard any decree of the Court overturning the conviction, *Worcester v. Georgia* appeared on the Court's docket for the 1832 Term.

At least one Justice's sympathies were already engaged when Wirt and Sergeant, representing Worcester and Butler, again challenged the constitutionality of the Georgia statutes. On January 13 Story had written to his wife that on his way to Washington for the Term he had stopped in Philadelphia and had been

> introduced to two of the Chiefs of the Cherokee Nation, so sadly dealt with by the state of Georgia. They are both educated men, and conversed with singular force and propriety of language upon their own case, the law of which they perfectly understood and reasoned upon. I never in my whole life was more affected by the consideration that they and all their race are destined to destruction. And I feel, as an American, disgraced by our gross violation of the public faith toward them.[205]

Five weeks later, on February 20, arguments began. Story reported on February 26 that Wirt's argument was "uncommonly eloquent, forcible, and finished," and that Georgia had again declined to appear. On the merits Story's position remained unchanged. "I confess that I blush for my country," he wrote, "when I perceive that . . . legislation, destructive

---

202 For the details of Worcester's arrest and removal see U. Phillips, "Georgia and States Rights," *Ann. Rep. Am. Hist. Ass'n*, 2:75–81 (1902); Burke, "Cherokee Cases," 519–22; McLoughlin, *Cherokees*, 261–65.
203 6 Pet. at 532. The court treated Worcester's and Butler's claims as identical. Ibid., 534.
204 Marshall was to cite *Martin* in *Worcester*. Ibid., 537.
205 J. Story to Sarah Waldo Story, Jan. 13, 1832, quoted in W. Story, *Life and Letters*, II, 78.

of all faith and honor towards the Indians, is suffered to pass with the silent approbation of the present Government of the United States.''[206]

Close observers of the Court might well have predicted that the Cherokees would fare better in *Worcester* than they had in *Cherokee Nation*. Johnson, whose concurrence in *Cherokee Nation* had announced that Indians were "nothing more than wandering hordes, held together only by ties of blood and habit, and having neither laws or government, beyond what is required in a savage state,''[207] was absent because of ill health, and Duvall, a close friend of Marshall, Story, and Wirt, had returned. Story's and Thompson's support for the Cherokees was on record, and Marshall's posture might have been surmised from hints in his *Cherokee Nation* opinion. Thus when the decision in *Worcester* came down, on March 3, 1832, its finding that the Georgia statutes were unconstitutional as applied to the Cherokee tribes was probably not much of a surprise. Marshall wrote for Duvall, Story, and Thompson. McLean concurred in the result, but sought to distinguish himself from the apparent limits the opinion of the Court placed on a state's power to regulate the affairs of Indians within its borders. Baldwin dissented on the ground that the writ of error was defective and announced that on the merits he continued to believe that Georgia could constitutionally dispossess Indians within its borders. He never delivered his opinion to Reporter Peters.[208]

Marshall's opinion in *Worcester* was a fascinating exercise in converting the natural law argument to arguments based on the sovereign powers of the Union and of his Court. The opinion was all the more fascinating because its tone, in contrast to that of *Cherokee Nation,* was more sympathetic to the autonomy of Indian tribes and less stigmatic in its characterization of the "nature" of Indians. Yet when the opinion was said and done, the rights of Indian tribes occupied precisely the same jurisprudential state that they had occupied in *Johnson v. McIntosh.* A social role for Indian tribes in America was cemented by the opinion, and in a sense that role was new: the "plight" of the tribes was to be solved by making them wards of the federal government. But their natural rights remained the same—if existent in republican theory, nonexistent in practice—and their implicit options remained the same. They were to be acculturated only if they could be civilized, and only a handful of individuals could; where they could not be civilized, they were to be dispossessed of their original lands and made dependents of Congress and any supervisory federal agencies Congress might create in the future.

In the major portion of his opinion in *Worcester,* after disposing of two preliminary questions, whether the case's record was properly before

---

[206] J. Story to S. W. Story, Feb. 26, 1832, quoted in ibid., 84.

[207] 5 Pet. at 27–28.
[208] 6 Pet. at 596.

the Court[209] and whether the Court could properly exercise jurisdiction over the case,[210] Marshall, as was his wont in cases he regarded as "of the deepest interest,"[211] embarked upon an analytical survey of history and associated jurisprudential principles. In an opinion whose total length was twenty-six pages and one fraction of a sentence, history (by which Marshall meant the time between the earliest white settlements in America and the framing of the Constitution) and associated principles occupied seventeen. Of the remaining pages approximately six were devoted to the preliminary procedural and jurisdictional issues, leaving about three pages for explicit constitutional analysis. The structure of the opinion, then, was designed to make Marshall's familiar point that attention to history and to the principles embodied in that history not only clarified constitutional analysis, it went a long way toward disposing of the issues to be analyzed.

At first glance the structure of Marshall's opinion in *Worcester* may seem inconsistent with the previous suggestion that the jurisprudential purpose of the opinion was to convert natural law arguments into sovereignty arguments. This apparent inconsistency, moreover, might be reinforced by the emphasis Marshall placed, in some passages in his history, on the "original natural rights" of Indian tribes and the status of the tribes "as distinct, independent political communities."[212] There is a hint in *Worcester* of an attitude toward Indians that more resembles self-determination than paternalism, reflected in comments such as "the early journals of congress exhibit the most anxious desire to conciliate the Indian nations," and "[federal treaties] treat the Cherokees as a nation capable of maintaining the relations of peace and war."[213]

But as Marshall's history in *Worcester* unfolds, one comes to realize

---

[209] Marshall did not linger over this issue, citing a rule of Supreme Court practice; *Martin;* Buel v. Van Ness, 8 Wheat. 312 (1823); and *McCulloch* v. *Maryland.* "The law does not require [that the judge sign the record]," Marshall declared. "The [Court's] rule does not require it." Ibid., 537.

[210] Marshall took a little longer with this issue, about two pages of analysis in Peters's Reports. Worcester had pleaded not guilty to interfering with the Georgia laws on the ground that the state of Georgia had no jurisdiction over him, since he was a resident of the Cherokee Nation and a missionary "under the authority of the President of the United States." Ibid., 538. By overruling Worcester's plea and sentencing him to hard labor in the penitentiary,

the Georgia trial court had "drawn into question" both the validity of a "federal treaty"—the treaties between the United States government and the Cherokees—and the constitutionality of the Georgia "Indian laws," which the trial court had sustained. It was "too clear for controversy," then, that the case came within Section 25 of the Judiciary Act of 1789: the Court had appellate jurisdiction on a writ of error. "Those who fill the judicial department," Marshall took pleasure in reminding his readers, "have no discretion in selecting the subjects to be brought before them." Ibid., 541. Compare Chapter III.

[211] Ibid., 536.
[212] Ibid., 559.
[213] Ibid., 549, 555.

that its purpose is to contrast the idea of natural rights and self-determination with what Marshall called "principle[s] suggested by the actual state of things."[214] The Indian tribes may have had natural rights "from time immemorial," but those rights had yielded to "irresistible power."[215] They may have once had cultural autonomy and political self-determination, but they were now "under the protection of the United States of America."[216] The "situation" of the Indians made them "necessarily dependent."[217] Power, war, and conquest conferred "rights" in the conquerors which were "conceded by the world."[218] One of the original "objects" of the white settlers was "the civilization of the Indians." But "[b]loody conflicts" and the "[f]ierce and warlike character" of the Indians made the civilizing process difficult, if not impossible.[219]

Marshall then moved from this catalogue of the "actual state of things" to the jurisprudential principles of Indian-white relations that were developed as a response. The first was the familiar principle that the discovery of lands by whites yielded title to the land, notwithstanding the "original natural rights" of Indians. Principle two was that the relationship between the white discoverers and the Indians was one of "superiority" and dependency. Principle three was that the government of the United States, representing the discoverers, was responsible for the "protection" of the Indians, and "no other sovereign whatsoever" bore that responsibility. Principle four was that the Indian tribes, notwithstanding their dependency, were to be regarded as they had traditionally been regarded: as independent sovereign nations. Marshall noted that treaties and congressional statutes, passed both before and after the Constitution, "manifestly consider[ed] the several Indian nations as distinct political communities, having territorial boundaries within which their authority is exclusive."[220] The Constitution had ratified this judgment.[221] Even the state of Georgia had originally recognized the principle.[222]

Now Marshall moved to principle five, that "the whole intercourse between the United States and [the Indian] nation[s] is, by our constitution and laws, vested in the government of the United States."[223] This was a bold step, and he gave only cryptic reasons for it. He was now squarely into the portion of his opinion dealing with the precise constitutional issues raised by the case, and he was not inclined to linger over those issues. "The actual state of things" and "history," he repeated,[224] had

214 Ibid., 543.
215 Ibid., 559.
216 Ibid., 555.
217 Ibid.
218 Ibid., 543.
219 Ibid., 546.

220 Ibid., 557.
221 Ibid., 559.
222 Ibid., 560.
223 Ibid., 561.
224 Ibid., 560.

laid the groundwork for his fifth principle, the principle of exclusive federal power to regulate Indian affairs. "[S]ettled principles of our constitution" had committed the regulation of "relations . . . between the United States and the Cherokee nation . . . exclusively to the government of the union."[225]

But what were the "settled principles"? Marshall only referred, once more, to "treaties" and "acts of congress." Did he mean to suggest that in passing statutes such as that of 1819, which sought to "introduc[e] among . . . the Indian tribes . . . the habits and arts of civilization" by authorizing the president to employ teachers "to instruct [the tribes] in the mode of agriculture suited to their situation," Congress was regulating commerce among the tribes? If so, this was an extraordinary reading of the commerce power; if not, he had previously conceded in *Gibbons* that the unexercised existence of federal power to regulate commerce did not preclude the states from acting in areas where Congress had not intervened. Did he mean that treaties between the Indians and the federal government, which arguably recognized the sovereignty of Indian tribes, had created something like vested rights in those tribes? He said that the Georgia statutes were "in direct hostility with treaties . . . which mark out the boundary that separates the Cherokee county from Georgia" and "guaranty to [the Cherokees] all the land within their boundary."[226] But *Worcester* was not a property case. Georgia had imprisoned Samuel Worcester for residing within the borders of the Cherokee Nation and for preaching the gospel in an effort to facilitate "the civilization and improvement of the Indians."[227] Marshall admitted that the Georgia court's judgment against Worcester affected "personal liberty," not "property."[228]

Ultimately, then, Marshall based his finding that the Georgia laws were unconstitutional on "settled principles" embodied in "treaties" and "acts of congress," and he characterized those treaties and acts as products of "the actual state of things" and "history." The principle of exclusive federal control over Indian affairs—a principle elevating the sovereignty of the union over the states—had been derived principally from two extraconstitutional sources: the reality of Indian-white relations in America and the apparent recognition of that reality by federal law. The original natural rights of Indians had disappeared as a source of law: in their place had emerged another argument for the proposition that the Constitution placed severe restrictions on the sovereignty of the states.

At the very end of his *Worcester* opinion[229] Marshall summarily disposed of the question whether the Supreme Court could review the

---

[225] Ibid., 561.
[226] Ibid., 562.
[227] Ibid., 538.

[228] Ibid., 562.
[229] Ibid., 562.

acts of a state legislature by citing *Cohens* v. *Virginia*. In a sense the Cherokee cases had been a repetition of *Martin, Cohens,* and the sovereignty battles of an earlier phase in the Marshall Court's history. The fact that the Court had not been unanimous in either *Cherokee Nation* or *Worcester* testified to the internal changes a decade had produced, but from a sovereignty perspective the result was the same: a state had defied the Court and had been decisively rebuffed. There were, however, two ironic twists in the aftermath of the Cherokee cases that distinguish them from the earlier sovereignty cases. The first emanated from the fact that the Cherokee cases were racial minority cases as well as sovereignty cases; the second from the fact that the executive branch of the federal government, that is, the Jackson administration, was expected to support the defiant state in its confrontation with the Court.

With the delivery of Marshall's opinion in *Worcester* the Cherokees could claim that in their struggle with Georgia they had emerged as the winners. The autonomy of their boundaries had been recognized; they had been removed from the control of the state of Georgia; their nation, with its unique constitution, laws, and practices, had been preserved. But what followed from their victory? The Cherokees, and other Indian tribes, became in effect wards of the federal government. The officials of that government were acknowledged to have the power to do what Georgia had done: place Indians in the position of abandoning their cultural heritage—becoming "civilized"—or being dispossessed of their land and forced to emigrate. Being wards of the government did not mean that Indians in America would have more freedom or more respect. Their "plight," ostensibly solved, remained essentially the same.

"Thanks be to God," Story wrote his wife after *Worcester,* "the Court can wash their hands clean of the iniquity of oppressing the Indians, and disregarding their rights." The Cherokee cases, he felt, had been "an oasis in the desert" of the "hard and dry" 1832 Term.[230] But after Georgia's Indian laws had been rebuffed by the Court, engendering, Story reported, "anger and violence" in the Georgia delegation in Congress,[231] the federal government simply stepped in and itself continued the policy of dispossession. With Jackson's 1830 removal legislation in effect, the federal government began to enter into agreements with southeastern tribes for the cession of their lands. The Creeks, Choctaws, and Cherokees were all forced into signing such treaties, in which the federal government provided them with lands west of the Mississippi. While the treaties gave "civilized" Indians the option of remaining on allotted land, federal policy contributed to the speedy resale of allotments to white settlers and

---

[230] J. Story to S. W. Story, Mar. 4, 1832, quoted in W. Story, *Life and Letters,* II, 87.

[231] Story to G. Ticknor, Mar. 8, 1832, quoted in ibid., 83.

speculators. Even though most Indians preferred not to emigrate, the federal government assumed that they would, and failed to scrutinize "sales" in which the Indians were severely disadvantaged. Fraud, chaos, and the degradation of southeastern tribes resulted from the government's regulation of Indian affairs.[232] A bleak future beckoned for most Indian tribes: confinement to federal reservations and the consequent legitimation of their "dependent" status.

Meanwhile, the second irony of the Cherokee cases emerged. While Jackson was to hold for the entire course of his presidency the belief that the Cherokees lived "in the midst of a superior race and, without appreciating the causes of their inferiority or seeking to control them, . . . must yield to the force of circumstances and ere long disappear,"[233] events coinciding with the aftermath of the *Worcester* decision resulted in his forging an odd alliance with the Court. Eight months after *Worcester* was handed down, Jackson, having made considerable political capital out of his veto of the Second Bank's charter, decisively won re-election. Georgia, meanwhile, had taken no action to comply with the Court's directive to release Worcester and Butler, who remained in prison. Jackson had also suggested that he would take no action to enforce the Court's directive in *Worcester,* noting in correspondence that the decision had "fell stillborne."[234] In the same month of his re-election, however, the South Carolina legislature voted not to comply with a protectionist federal tariff on the basis of the nullification doctrine.

The nullification controversy, when coupled with the *Worcester* decision, placed the Jackson administration in an extremely awkward position. The federal government could hardly ignore the sovereignty implications of *Worcester* and at the same time insist that South Carolina's action was heresy. The Cherokees had one more stratagem at their disposal, and the Jackson administration knew of that stratagem. Wirt and Sergeant could inform the Court, at the opening of the 1833 Term, that Georgia had refused to comply with its mandate to release Worcester and Butler, and ask the Justices to certify the refusal and notify the president of the United States. On receipt of that notice Jackson would

---

[232] See generally Young, "Indian Removal"; M. Young, "The Creek Frauds: A Study in Conscience and Corruption," *Miss. Valley Hist. Rev.,* 42:411 (1955). A small group of Cherokees, the so-called "Eastern Band," avoided removal and remained in the North Carolina mountains. For their depressing subsequent history, see J. Finger, *The Eastern Band of Cherokees, 1819–1900* (1984).

[233] Andrew Jackson, Message to Congress, Dec. 3, 1833, 254 *House Executive Documents* 14 (1833). On the consistency of Jackson's attitudes toward Indians, see generally Rogin, supra, note 107.

[234] A. Jackson to John Coffee, Apr. 7, 1832, in J. Basset, ed., *Correspondence of Andrew Jackson* (6 vols., 1933), IV, 430.

have had a constitutional obligation to "take Care that the Laws be faithfully executed."[235]

Not only was the Jackson administration pressured by these developments, so were the elite Cherokees and Samuel Worcester and Elizur Butler. If the missionaries insisted on Wirt's and Sergeant's appearing before the Court in the second week of January 1833, influential Georgians informed them, Jackson would have to enforce the Court's decree, Georgia might declare the federal treaties and statutes pertaining to the Cherokees "null and void," and other southern states (Alabama and Mississippi were singled out) might support Georgia (and South Carolina). The result, according to these Georgians, might be secession, justified on the basis of the nullification doctrine, and civil war. They argued that Worcester and Butler should abandon their appeal and ask the governor of Georgia for a pardon, which they intimated would be granted.[236]

The elite Cherokees, on the other hand, argued that for Worcester and Butler to ask Governor Lumpkin for a pardon would be to admit that Georgia and other states did in fact have the authority to regulate Indian affairs within their borders. That admission, the Cherokees claimed, would not only undermine the autonomy of Indian tribes but also legitimate the sovereignty arguments implicitly advanced by Georgia in *Worcester*. The legitimation of those arguments would be as dangerous to the Union as the enforcement of the Court's mandate by the Jackson administration.[237]

Worcester and Butler first resolved to press their appeal, and on November 26, 1832, informed Lumpkin to that effect.[238] But eleven days later they changed their mind and informed their missionary superiors that they intended to seek a pardon from Lumpkin. After some debate, and delays precipitated by the mails, they received approval to do so, and on January 8, 1833, wrote Wirt and his co-counsel directing them to abandon the appeal.[239] Six days later they were pardoned by Lumpkin and released from prison. On January 16, two days after the missionaries' release, Jackson sent a message to Congress requesting that he be authorized to compel South Carolina to disclaim the nullification doctrine and comply with the tariff.[240]

On January 20 and 27 Story wrote two long letters to his wife. The Court's 1833 Term had opened on the fifteenth, he said, and all the judges

[235] U.S. Const., Art. II, Sect. 3.

[236] See McLoughlin, *Cherokees*, 265–66; E. Miles, "After John Marshall's Decision," *J. So. Hist.*, 39:519, 526–27 (1973).

[237] Miles, "John Marshall's Decision," 535–36; McLoughlin, *Cherokees*, 298, and sources therein cited.

[238] McLoughlin, *Cherokees*, 297.

[239] See Miles, "John Marshall's Decision," 541; McLoughlin, *Cherokees*, 298.

[240] Miles, "John Marshall's Decision," 541; McLoughlin, *Cherokees*, 299.

save Baldwin, hospitalized in Philadelphia with an emotional disorder, were present and in good health. Marshall had presented each of his colleagues with a copy of his biography of Washington, released in a new edition. The pace of the Court was slow, and he and Marshall had gone to the theatre to see the celebrated British actress, Fanny Kemble. Marshall had been "cheered in a marked manner" on entering their box, and Kemble's performance had "thr[own] . . . the whole audience," including the Chief Justice and himself, "into tears."[241] Ten days later, on the twenty-fifth, the Justices were invited to dinner at the White House. Story summarized their visit:

> [W]e dined with the President at [a] . . . fashionable hour [half past seven]. There were several ladies at the table, and of course I was called on, as one of the Court, to hand a lady to table. . . .
> We are on the eve of great political excitements. The debate on the bill reported in the President's late anti-nullification passage will be the cause. . . .
> I forgot to say, that notwithstanding I am [as Jackson has said] "the most dangerous man in America," the President specially invited me to drink a glass of wine with him. But what is more remarkable, since his last proclamation and message, the Chief Justice and myself have become his warmest supporters, and shall continue so just as long as he maintains the principles contained in them. Who would have dreamed of such an occurrence?[242]

In his concurrence in *Worcester* v. *Georgia* Justice McLean had declared that the "abstract right of every sector of the human race to a reasonable portion of the soil, by which to require the means of subsistence, cannot be controverted." The "law of nature," McLean announced, "is paramount to all other laws."[243] Expressions of this kind had been linked, in the Marshall Court's slave trade and Indian decisions, with results that suggested that such talk was empty. The natural rights of slaves to their liberty and their recognition as human beings had been qualified by their condition. Slavery was against the law of nature, but sometimes the law of nature had to yield to established practices. The natural rights of Indians to the possession and use of their land extended only as far as the federal government chose. The cases, taken together, affirmed a stark proposition: in the case of racial minorities whose "character" or "condition" made their amalgamation into white society precarious, natural rights principles simply did not apply in their full force.

---

[241] J. Story to S. W. Story, Jan. 20, 1833, quoted in W. Story, *Life and Letters*, II, 116.

[242] J. Story to S. W. Story, ibid., 118–19.
[243] 6 Pet. at 579.

Natural law was not only not "paramount to all other laws" in such cases, it had very little force.

The Court's reduction of the natural law argument to a moral exhortation, and its consequent abandonment of that argument as an independent source of law in cases involving racial minorities, played a part in the eventual undermining of unwritten natural law as a commonly held source of nineteenth-century American jurisprudence. Between the 1830s and the 1840s, for example, even "radical" antislavery constitutional theorists moved from a position that identified natural law as "antecedent and superior to the American Constitution" to a position that distinguished between "natural" and "municipal" law, and conceded that only the latter was a binding source of authority in American courts.[244] The Marshall Court's decisions provided grounds for that concession. Racial minorities received a message from the Marshall Court that they were to receive repeatedly in the subsequent course of American history: liberty and equality in America have been regularly contingent on whose freedom and whose equal treatment is at issue. Students of American jurisprudence received an equally stark message: natural law had no meaning as a set of abstract, extraconstitutional principles of justice. By the 1830s, as not only the slave trade and Indian cases but also the Contract Clause cases demonstrated, the concept of an "unwritten Constitution," and the larger concept of an unwritten body of principles embodying reason, justice, or the "nature of things," had been reduced to a marginal existence in American jurisprudence.

---

[244] See Wiecek, *Sources,* 168, 241, and sources therein cited.

Associate Justice Robert Trimble, from an unknown portrait, painted in the 1820s.
*(Library of Congress)*

Associate Justice John McLean, from Thomas Sully's 1831 portrait.
*(Library of Congress)*

Associate Justice Henry Baldwin, from an unknown portrait, probably painted shortly after Baldwin's appointment to the Supreme Court in 1829.
*(Library of Congress)*

Associate Justice James Moore Wayne, from an unknown portrait, about the time of his
appointment to the Supreme Court in 1834.
*(Library of Congress)*

Thomas Jefferson, painted by Bass Otis in 1816, when Jefferson was seventy-three and
"in retirement" at Monticello, while keeping close tabs on the Marshall Court.
*(Library of Congress)*

Thomas Ritchie, editor of the Richmond *Enquirer,* the most constant of the Marshall Court's newspaper critics. The engraving is based on a portrait by Thomas Sully, probably around 1815.
*(Library of Congress)*

Spencer Roane, judge of the Virginia Court of Appeals and the "Hampden" of the 1819 exchange of essays with John Marshall over the Supreme Court's decision in *McCulloch* v. *Maryland*. From an unknown portrait, probably painted around 1815. *(Valentine Museum, Richmond, Va.)*

Andrew Jackson, from a lithograph made by C. G. Childs in 1833, the year that his confrontation with the Marshall Court in the Cherokee Cases came to its conclusion.
*(Library of Congress)*

# CHAPTER XI

## *Of the Court, Time, and Change*

INSTITUTIONAL HISTORIES, by their very focus, appear designed to convey an impression of continuity over time: to write the history of an institution is to imply that it has proved to be more enduring than the individuals who have represented it or the culture surrounding it at any given time. And yet the thrust of this study has been to emphasize the uniqueness, the "differentness," and the time-boundedness of the later Marshall Court; to see the Court as a manifestation of its age rather than as a phase of the history of the Supreme Court of the United States. Such a thrust need not be incompatible with the historiographical premises of the series of which this volume is a part. While the Supreme Court of the United States has had a continuous history, that history seems most intelligible when the Court is firmly rooted in a cultural context. Such an emphasis reveals the institution to have been composed of a series of Courts, each with its own character and each reflective of, and responsive to, the changing culture in which it functioned.

The purpose of this chapter is twofold: to survey the way in which the Marshall Court was characterized by its contemporaries and then to characterize the Court from the perspective of history. The two efforts are related in that an understanding of those features of the Court that contemporary commentators found most significant—and, implicitly, least significant—can aid our sense of the fit between the Court and its times. The use of commentary as an index to attitudes in a culture at large necessarily raises problems of representativeness; the newspaper correspondents and journal writers surveyed in this chapter were members of an elite stratum of American opinion with a special interest in legal issues. No claim is made that the attitudes extracted from a survey of commentary on the Court document the Court's image in any definitive fashion. Nonetheless, the accounts of literate commentators are not only the principal sources that have been preserved, they emanate from a medium that has continually been an important mechanism in American culture for reflecting and shaping public attitudes, and whose influence was arguably even greater in the years before the emergence of electronic media.

Newspaper and journal commentary on the Court between 1815 and

1835 was for the most part directed to specific cases, and the survey that follows will reflect that emphasis. Three general tendencies of the commentary are nonetheless worth comment at this stage. First, commentary on the Court was comparatively sparse during the period. While certain cases stimulated a large output of commentary, most of the Court's decisions were either simply mentioned as having occurred or not mentioned at all. Only those newspapers or journals, such as the *National Intelligencer* or *Niles' Weekly Register,* which treated periodic reports on the official business of governmental institutions as part of their function, reported the Court's business on any regular basis. In 1826, for example, the *Intelligencer* recorded decisions of the Court for every day they were handed down during the Court's session (February 7 through March 24), sometimes summarizing the Court's opinions. On the basis of its tracking of the Court's business the *Intelligencer* was able to comment, on March 24, that the Court had "terminated its annual session . . . after an incessant occupation of more than six weeks"; and that during that time "out of an hundred and ninety cases on the docket, the Court was able to dispose of only forty-nine, leaving three-fourths of the docket untouched."[1] *Niles' Weekly Register* repeated the *Intelligencer*'s March 24 statement in its April 1 issue,[2] including the *Intelligencer*'s observation that "it cannot be denied . . . that the laws are not administered, under the present organization of the Courts of the United States, as promptly or as efficaciously as they ought to be."[3] Ten years before, the *Intelligencer* had noted that the Court had "finally disposed of" seventy cases, and commented that "[t]he records of no court of appeals in the Union exhibit such an instance of dispatch of business."[4]

Aside from the *Intelligencer* and *Niles' Weekly Register* (which often relied on the *Intelligencer*'s accounts) no newspaper closely followed the Court's deliberations. The sparseness of newspaper coverage leads us to a second tendency exhibited by commentary during the period: where newspapers and journals did mention the Court or its decisions, their observations were almost exclusively made in the context of constitutional law decisions. Occasionally a nonconstitutional decision of local interest would be reported, such as the *Intelligencer*'s report in its March 20, 1826, issue of *United States* v. *Tappan,*[5] a case involving a debt owed to the United States, but this was rare. The recorded impressions of the Supreme Court of the United States, for this period in its history, were overwhelmingly based on constitutional cases.

---

[1] Washington *National Intelligencer,* Mar. 24, 1826.

[2] *Niles' Weekly Register,* Mar. 1, 1826.

[3] Washington *National Intelligencer,* Mar. 24, 1826.

[4] Washington *National Intelligencer,* Mar. 23, 1816.

[5] *United States* v. *Tappan* was handed down by the Court on March 16, 1826, but never reported in Wheaton's Reports.

## Chapter XI: *Of the Court, Time, and Change*

Finally, the commentary was to a significant extent parasitic and derivative. An observation made by one newspaper or journal would be picked up and repeated in another, usually with attribution but often without comment. Most of the observations were necessarily not firsthand: few of the newspapers or magazines surveyed had correspondents in Washington. The result was that a misunderstanding or mischaracterization of an opinion by one source would often be reported by another, sometimes, as we will see in the case of *Sturges* v. *Crowninshield,* engendering considerable confusion. Another consequence of this feature of the commentary was that the remarks of correspondents were often directed more at the meaning another commentator had ascribed to a decision of the Court than at the Court's opinion itself. While some of the Court's decisions were reported in full in certain papers, this practice was overwhelmingly the exception rather than the rule.

These general features of the commentary directed at the Court's opinions between 1815 and 1835 require that commentary be treated as one type of historical source rather than another. Contemporary newspaper accounts, taken as a whole, do not provide an accurate record of the Court's activities. Not only was the reporting sparse and selective, it was often derivative and sometimes erroneous. Nor do the accounts provide a complete picture of the Court's business; they are significantly skewed in the direction of a few cases that engaged the commentators' interest. Newspaper and journal commentary on the Court between 1815 and 1835 is, in short, a source of what commentators thought was important in the Court's activities. It provides us with the impressions of contemporaries of the Court about its impact on early-nineteenth-century American culture.

The first two decisions of the Court in the period covered by this volume that one might have expected to provoke significant commentary were *United States* v. *Coolidge* and *Martin* v. *Hunter's Lessee.* Nonetheless, despite Story's concern that the Union would be "destroy[ed] and the Constitution crushed by factions" unless Congress gave "the Judicial Courts of the United States power to punish all crimes and offences against the Government, as at common law,"[6] and despite his association, in the draft of a bill "further to extend the judicial system of the United States" that he wrote in 1816, of a federal common law of crimes with "the establishment of a great national policy, and of great national institutions,"[7] newspapers did not find the *Coolidge* or the *Martin*

---

[6] J. Story to Nathaniel Williams, Oct. 8, 1812, quoted in W. Story, *The Life and Letters of Joseph Story* (2 vols., 1851), I, 243.

[7] The bill and Story's comment are reprinted in *Life and Letters,* I, 296.

case worth commenting on. Indeed, it was not until the Court's 1819 Term that its decisions provoked contemporaneous commentary. The Richmond *Enquirer* had reported the Virginia Court of Appeals's decision in *Hunter* v. *Martin* on four separate occasions in January and February, 1816,[8] and, as noted, had reprinted Johnson's concurring opinion in *Martin* v. *Hunter's Lessee* on April 13. The *National Intelligencer* had also reprinted Johnson's opinion on April 16 of that year and had printed summaries of *United States* v. *Bevans*,[9] *Evans* v. *Eaton*,[10] *Burton* v. *Williams*,[11] and *United States* v. *Palmer*[12] in 1818; *Bevans* had also been summarized in the *Enquirer*.[13] But unless one counts as commentary the *Intelligencer*'s praise of the Court's efficient dispatch of business in its 1816 Term and its characterizations of *Bevans* as containing "a very interesting question . . . as to the jurisdiction of the Federal Courts" and of *Palmer* as a case "which has excited some interest," the Court's decisions from 1815 through 1818 stimulated no response at all in the press.

The year 1819 ushered in a new attitude on the part of commentators. Not only were certain decisions of the Court extensively commented upon, particular organs, especially the *Intelligencer,* the *Enquirer,* and *Niles' Weekly Register,* began to report the Court's decisions on a regular basis. The *Intelligencer,* for example, reported Court business on February 3 (when the Court's session opened), 6, 8, 9, 13, 17, 18, 19, 20, and 26, and on March 1, 2, 3, 4, 5, 6, 8, 9, 10, 11, and 13 (when the Court adjourned). The *Enquirer* reported Court business on February 6, 9, 11, 13, 16, 19, and 25, and on March 2, 6, 9, 12, and 19. This began a pattern of regular attention to the Court by the *Intelligencer,* and sporadic but intense interest on the part of the other two journals, which was to last through Marshall's tenure.

The beginning of regular Court coverage in 1819 was accompanied by a significant amount of commentary on two of the Court's decisions, *Sturges* v. *Crowninshield* and *McCulloch* v. *Maryland. Sturges* was handed down on February 17, and three days later the New York *Evening Post* reported that the news "causes a very considerable sensation in the city," and advised "suspension of all opinions until the decision itself reaches us."[14] Early reports of the decision, including that of the *Intelligencer* on February 18, had the Court holding that states could not cancel or discharge debts at all, although they could "discharge the person of

---

[8] Richmond *Enquirer*, Jan. 27, 1816; Jan. 30, 1816; Feb. 1, 1816; Feb. 3, 1816.

[9] Washington *National Intelligencer*, Feb. 25, 1818.

[10] Ibid., Mar. 10, 1818.

[11] Ibid., Mar. 18, 1818.

[12] Ibid., Mar. 26, 1818.

[13] Richmond *Enquirer*, Mar. 28, 1818.

[14] New York *Evening Post*, Feb. 20, 1819.

the debtor . . . from arrest and imprisonment.''[15] These reports suggested that the decision embraced contracts made subsequent to the passage of state insolvency legislation as well as contracts made prior to it. The New York *Daily Advertiser,* in its issue of February 23, said that if *Sturges* applied to both sets of contracts

> it will be one of the most important decisions that has ever occurred, and will place a very numerous class of people in a very perplexing situation; and, as far as we can see, must give rise to an unheard of series of litigation. Insolvent acts have existed, in one form and another, in different parts of the country, for a long period, and proceedings have taken place under them in cases innumerable. Transfers of property which have been made, and they have been made to a vast extent, may, for aught we can discern, be at least put in hazard. Releases and discharges executed by trustees, etc.; under the sanction of these laws, may be in a predicament somewhat of a similar nature. In short, it is difficult to discover the end of such a state of things as such a decision may produce, both as it regards person and property.[16]

If ''all the former discharges under the state insolvent acts, so far as they go beyond the protection of the body of the insolvent from imprisonment are void,'' the *Evening Post* concluded, ''and the Congress shall persist in declining to pass a national bankrupt act, the condition of our countrymen, and especially of the mercantile portion of it, is truly deplorable.''[17]

Similar early reactions to *Sturges* were expressed by other papers. The Baltimore *Federal Republican* said that ''nothing but the publication of the entire opinion can possibly allay the fermentation that is executed . . . attachments are crowding themselves into the secret and confidential transactions of everybody, and must be put a stop to in some way or other, or the hearts and arms of many of our best citizens will be paralyzed.''[18] The *Columbian Centinel,* a Boston paper, reported that the *Sturges* decision had ''created much excitement and alarm in many states,'' where ''[p]ersons . . . who have been discharged many years from contracts by the laws of their states, and have since acquired property, have had it attached to pay their old debts.''[19] *Niles' Weekly Register,* reacting ten days after the decision came down, agreed that *Sturges* ''has given much alarm to many people,'' and that it would ''probably

---

[15] Washington *National Intelligencer,* Feb. 18, 1819.
[16] New York *Daily Advertiser,* Feb. 23, 1819.
[17] New York *Evening Post,* supra, note 14.

[18] Baltimore *Federal Republican,* quoted in Boston *Independent Chronicle,* Mar. 6, 1819.
[19] Boston *Columbian Centinel,* Mar. 6, 1819.

make some great revolutions improperly, and raise up many from penury, . . . and cause others to descend to the condition that becomes honest men, by compelling a payment of their debts—as every honest man ought to be compelled to do, if ever able."[20]

On March 1 the New York *Evening Post* announced that the *Sturges* decision apparently invalidated only those insolvency laws that sought to have an effect on contracts made prior to their passage.[21] As we have seen in Chapter IX, Marshall's last two paragraphs, while remarkably ambiguous, confined the scope of *Sturges* to "the case actually under consideration," and invalidated the New York insolvency statute "so far as it attempts to discharge this defendant from the debt in the declaration mentioned."[22] The basis of the debt was two promissory notes dated March 22, 1811; the New York insolvency statute had been passed on April 3, 1811.[23] Thus a fair reading of *Sturges* was that offered by the Baltimore *Federal Gazette,* as reported in the Richmond *Enquirer* on March 2:

> Since we first noticed the decision in the Supreme Court of the United States, as to the effect of the insolvent laws of the individual states, we learn from a New York paper, that the particular case before the court in which the decision was made, had reference to a law passed subsequent to the date of the contract, which it was attempted by counsel of the debtor to show it had discharged. If the decision of the Supreme Court went no further than that such a law is contrary to the constitution of the United States, the effect . . . would be much less extensive than has been supposed.[24]

But the confusion generated by *Sturges* had not died down by the end of March. The *Daily Advertiser* noted that "an extreme anxiety with regard to the effect of [Sturges] has been excited not only here but in various other parts of the country," and complained that "at the end of several weeks, the opinion of the Court has not been published."[25] The Augusta *Chronicle* wondered "what are wretched debtors to do . . . [u]nder the decision of the Supreme Tribunal of the country . . . The states can exempt nothing but their bodies from the harassing pursuit of the law."[26] And the *Enquirer,* notwithstanding its early reprinting of the *Federal Gazette,* concluded, on the basis of "the perusal of a letter received by a gentleman of the bar in this city from Washington," that the

[20] *Niles' Weekly Register,* Feb. 27, 1819.
[21] New York *Evening Post,* Mar. 1, 1819.
[22] 4 Wheat. 122, 207–208 (1819).
[23] Ibid., 122.

[24] Richmond *Enquirer,* Mar. 2, 1819.
[25] New York *Daily Advertiser,* Mar. 10, 1819.
[26] Augusta *Chronicle and Georgia Gazette,* Mar. 31, 1819.

*Sturges* case applied to all contracts, only allowing states to "except the body of the debtor from imprisonment." The *Enquirer* believed that the Court had "further decided, that until Congress acts upon the subject," states could "pass insolvent or bankrupt laws, which, however, can have no other effect than is above stated." The *Enquirer* nonetheless felt that "those laws may be beneficial in putting an end to the partial disposition of property which now operate so severely upon the great mass of the creditors of those who fail among us."[27] The letter quoted by the *Enquirer* had been dated February 23.

The *Sturges* commentary represented something of a milestone in the relationship of the Supreme Court to the popular press. Before the *Sturges* case occasional decisions of the Court, such as *Marbury* v. *Madison* and *Fletcher* v. *Peck*, had been reprinted in newspapers and provoked commentary,[28] but the discussions had been confined to partisan politics or to local issues. With *Sturges* a new dimension to the commentary surfaced, the sense that the Supreme Court of the United States could have a direct effect on the affairs of citizens of every part of the nation. *Sturges* had come at a time when, as noted, American commerce had taken on an expansionist and increasingly interstate character, and in which the principle of negotiability had emerged from a localistic, two-party setting to become a major mechanism of exchange. "The truth is," the *Daily Advertiser* said in commenting on *Sturges,* "no decision has ever been made by [the Court] which came more immediately home to the business and feelings of the community."[29]

*Sturges* was followed closely by *McCulloch,* and again the commentators emphasized the Court's sudden emergence as an institution whose decisions could vitally affect large segments of the public. But there was a new dimension to the commentary on *McCulloch.* The papers that reacted to *Sturges,* while occasionally praising the decision as a benefit to creditors or exhibiting distress at its potential to burden debtors, had principally concentrated on the uncertainty engendered by the decision in the commercial community and the potentially vast impact of a determination that state insolvency laws were constitutionally invalid. Little had been said about the Court's interpretation of the Contract Clause. In contrast, most of the commentators on *McCulloch* addressed Marshall's interpretation of Article I implied powers. We have had occasion to review the extended attack on *McCulloch* by Brockenborough and Roane, but their criticism, while more elaborately developed than most, was not unique. The Natchez, Mississippi, *Press,* for example, said that "[t]he last vestige of the sovereignty and independence of the indi-

---

[27] Richmond *Enquirer,* Mar. 9, 1819.
[28] See C. Warren, *The Supreme*

*Court in United States History,* (3 vols., 1922), I, 245–52, 398.
[29] Supra, note 25.

vidual states'' had been "obliterated at one fell sweep" by *McCulloch*;[30] the *Argus of Western America* said the decision "strikes at the roots of State-Rights and State Sovereignty";[31] and the Nashville *Clarion* claimed that the Court's "aristocratical character" had been revealed by "a decision that prostrates the state sovereignty entirely."[32]

General comments of this kind were accompanied by specific critiques of Marshall's reasoning in *McCulloch*. The *Argus of Western America* argued that under Marshall's reading of implied powers

> some excuse, some pretence of conveniency in carrying into effect specified powers may be found to justify the incorporation of companies with a monopoly of trade, of individuals for the purchase of public lands, and perhaps even of a National Church to correct and maintain morality among the people, without which none of the specified powers of the Constitution could be carried into effect.[33]

*Niles' Weekly Register* said that "the reasoning of the opinion exhibits a catching of words, and an establishment of facts by implication, with a Sibylline mystery thrown over things hitherto supposed to be very comprehensible." Marshall, the *Register* concluded, had "not added to his stock of reputation" by writing the *McCulloch* opinion.[34] And the Philadelphia *General Advertiser* claimed that "[a]ny man who is conscious of his own virtue and possessing a plain understanding, who will take up the opinion of Chief Justice Marshall on the Bench, will find a most lamentable sophistry, a most lame and impotent logic, and . . . the most flimsy and false attempt at reasoning that can be found in the annals of any nation."[35]

The *McCulloch* opinion had its defenders. The *Kentucky Gazette*, after saying that the decision "will furnish a happy lesson to local politicians against their right to infringe upon the National Constitution or upon the laws of Congress," called Marshall's opinion "the ablest document we recollect to have read of a judicial nature."[36] The Boston *Daily Advertiser* pronounced *McCulloch* "one of the most able judgments . . . ever delivered in [the Supreme] Court," and predicted that "when it is read [it] will satisfy all minds."[37] The *Western Monitor* said that the

---

[30] Quoted in *Niles' Weekly Register*, May 22, 1819.
[31] *Argus of Western America* (Frankfort, Ky.), Mar. 26, 1818.
[32] Nashville *Clarion*, quoted in Scioto *Gazette* (Scioto, Ga.), Apr. 16, 1819.
[33] *Argus of Western America* (Frankfort, Ky.), Apr. 16, 1819.

[34] *Niles' Weekly Register*, Mar. 13, 1819.
[35] Philadelphia *General Advertiser*, Mar. 17, 1819.
[36] *Kentucky Gazette* (Louisville, Ky.), Mar. 26, 1819; Mar. 19, 1819.
[37] Boston *Daily Advertiser*, Mar. 13, 1819.

issues in *McCulloch* had been "discussed . . . in a strong, lucid, masterly manner," and that "the constitutionality of a National Bank is supported with a strength and fairness of reasoning which we have seldom if ever seen surpassed."[38] The access of these papers and others to the opinion itself had been facilitated by the fact that the *Intelligencer* and *Niles' Weekly Register* had published the opinion in full on March 13, six days after it had been delivered.

The reaction to *McCulloch,* taken together with that to *Sturges,* demonstrated the emergence of a perception that the Court could be a vital force in national affairs. Indeed, some of the comments suggest that the Court's legitimacy as a final arbiter of constitutional questions had been established by the 1819 Term. The *Franklin Gazette,* a Philadelphia paper, spoke of "the acknowledged virtue and wisdom of the tribunal whence [*McCulloch*] emanates," and said that the Court's opinion "must be regarded as finally and conclusively settling a question which has distracted the country more, perhaps, than any that has yet been started under the Federal Constitution";[39] and the *Kentucky Gazette* spoke of "[t]he mighty arm of the Judiciary" as having "interposed its high and almost sacred functions for the purpose of giving effect to a provision of the Federal Constitution."[40] Even *Niles' Weekly Register,* while criticizing *McCulloch* extensively, acknowledged that "some seem to regard [the Court] with a species of that awful reverence in which the inhabitants of Asia look up to their princes."[41]

One critic of the decision, however, exhibited no such reverence or, for that matter, no belief in the legitimacy of the Court. In a letter to the Philadelphia *General Advertiser* he confessed that he had "never cherished the feeblest hope that impartiality, liberty, or reason would characterize [the Court's] discussion [in *McCulloch*] or bias its determination." The Court's "temper," he felt, was one "of high toned aristocracy," which "would necessarily preclude even a calculation as to the impartial, rigorous and comprehensive consideration" of the Constitution. The opinion in *McCulloch* was "a perfect model of that prejudiced judgment and *ex parte* consideration of a subject that springs from a predetermined resolution to accomplish a desired object."[42] This comment suggests that the Court had not convinced all sectors of the public that its decisions were free from bias or partisanship.

The tacit acknowledgment that the Court had become a force in

---

[38] *Western Monitor* (Lexington, Ky.), Apr. 3, 1819.
[39] *Franklin Gazette* (Philadelphia, Pa.), quoted in *Independent Chronicle,* Mar. 17, 1819.
[40] *Kentucky Gazette* (Louisville, Ky.), Mar. 26, 1819.

[41] *Niles' Weekly Register,* supra, note 34.
[42] Brutus, letter to Philadelphia *General Advertiser,* Mar. 26, 1819.

public affairs can be seen in a long article by Warren Dutton that appeared in the *North American Review* in 1820.[43] The article reviewed Timothy Farrar's edition of the *Dartmouth College* cases and Volume 4 of Wheaton's Reports. The article has regularly been mentioned as the first acknowledgment of the significance of the Court's decision in *Dartmouth College,* which, commentators have assumed, received comparatively little attention from the press in 1819. That perception of the reaction to *Dartmouth College* needs some qualification. The *National Intelligencer* had reported the Court's decision in *Dartmouth College* on February 6, but *Niles' Weekly Register* did not discuss the decision at all; and on this basis both Albert Beveridge and Charles Warren concluded that, as Warren put it, its "importance was not at all realized . . . at the time" it was handed down.[44] The "profound effect" of *Dartmouth College,* Beveridge felt, "was first noted in the *North American Review* a year after the Chief Justice delivered [the opinion]."[45]

But on February 10, 1819, the Boston *Columbian Centinel* published an extensive analysis of the *Dartmouth College* case. The *Centinel* first reprinted a letter from Washington, dated February 2, that stated that the "Chief Justice delivered the most able, and elaborate opinion, which, perhaps, has ever been pronounced in a Court of Judicature, on the far-famed question relative to *Dartmouth College.*" The letter erroneously reported that the decision was unanimous, and the *Centinel* referred to "other letters" that "mention . . . that Judge Duval [*sic*] dissented." The *Centinel* then printed an evaluation of the decision by one "A.," apparently its Washington correspondent. In the evaluation the *Dartmouth College* case was represented as having "excited a deep and lively interest in the public mind in different parts of the country," and as having "at different times . . . roused the religious and political feelings of the people." The correspondent nonetheless claimed that the issues in *Dartmouth College* had been "settled strictly upon pure principles of law," adding that "unanimity . . . exists among the judges of the Court." He stated that the decision "must be considered more important than any which has been made by our judicial tribunals since the adoption of the constitution." From the decision "must . . . result," he felt, "consequences of the utmost magnitude."

There were two principal consequences of the *Dartmouth College* case, the *Centinel'*s correspondent felt. One was that it established "the inviolability of [the] charters [of] . . . our literary and charitable institu-

---

[43] The article was unsigned. Charles Warren, in *The Supreme Court in United States History,* II, 2, identified Dutton as the author. Dutton was a Boston lawyer who argued the case of *Charles River Bridge* v. *Warren Bridge*

before the Marshall Court. See C. Warren, *A History of the American Bar* (1911), 423.

[44] Warren, *Supreme Court,* I, 457.

[45] A. Beveridge, *The Life of John Marshall* (4 vols., 1916–19), IV, 276.

tions." As a result of the decision such institutions were "under the protection and government of the general laws of the land," and thus "not . . . subject to the rise and fall of parties, and the fluctuation of religious and political opinions." This would result in "liberal benefactors to these institutions [being] multiplied," since they would "discover in this decision the certainty of effecting the object of their bounty."

The other "great and important constitutional principle" embodied in *Dartmouth College*, the *Centinel* pointed out, was the denial of "absolute supremacy [in] our legislatures by proving that their powers are limited not only by the rules of natural justice . . . but by the very letter and spirit of the constitution." Without "some salutary restraint" on legislative powers much "evil will result," the correspondent believed; and "this restraint under our government is to be found in our courts of justice." He elaborated:

> [The courts] may be considered the bulwark of the Constitution to guard it against legislative encroachments. They are an intermediate body between the people and the legislature, whose duty it is to preserve the privileges of the former, and counteract the assumption of power in the latter. It is their duty to declare all legislative acts which are repugnant to the Constitution null and void. They are bound to consider the Constitution a fundamental law of the land; a law . . . equally binding in the legislature and the most obscure member of the community. It is peculiarly within their province to ascertain the meaning of the Constitution.
>
> The theory of our government is now too well understood to admit the absurd doctrine, that the Legislative Body are themselves the constitutional judges of their own powers and acts. . . . To decide upon [such] power is the exclusive privilege of Courts of Justice. It is peculiarly gratifying to discover in these an inflexible and uniform adherence to the rights of individuals and those of the Constitution. It is matter of rejoicing to discover purity and independence in this branch of our government. These are qualities essential to the perpetuity of the Constitution. Whenever the Judiciary department becomes more corrupt than the Legislative, we must share the common fate of all Republics.[46]

Here, in the remarks of an obscure correspondent for a Boston paper remarking on the *Dartmouth College* decision, we find the outlines of the very argument the Marshall Court had sought to advance as a justification for its emergence to power. State legislatures, in the American republic, could not be the final judges of their own powers: they were restrained by principles of "natural justice," such as the vested rights principle at

---

[46] Boston *Columbian Centinel*, Feb. 10, 1819.

stake in *Dartmouth College,* and by the "letter and spirit" of the Constitution. The institution charged with implementing this restraint was the federal courts. That role for the courts was a product of their position as "an intermediate body between the people and the Legislature," protecting the sovereign rights of the former; of their "duty" to be "bound" to follow the dictates of the Constitution; of their peculiar talent for "ascertaining the meaning of the Constitution"; of their "inflexible and uniform" commitment to the rights of the people and the letter and spirit of the constitutional text; and of their "purity and independence." In the independent and incorruptible decisions of the courts lay the perpetuation of the Constitution. The absence of corruption in the judiciary was the key to the preservation of the Republic from decay.

The *Centinel* thus anticipated much of the interpretation of the *Dartmouth College* decision made by Dutton in the *North American Review* a year later. Dutton described his purpose in analyzing the *Dartmouth College* decision as "render[ing] . . . [an] acceptable service to the cause of learning in this country" by "exhibiting an outline of this important case," one, he felt, that "involved more important consequences" and "excited a deeper interest in the public mind" than any "judicial proceedings in this country."[47] But Dutton did not so much outline the arguments in *Dartmouth College* as present, quoting liberally from Marshall's and Story's opinions and Webster's argument on behalf of the College, a justification for the Court's position. His posture can be clearly observed in one passage, where, after announcing that "it is as much a maxim of common sense, as of law, that . . . the will of the donor [of a charitable institution], not of the legislature, is to be the rule," he noted that the Superior Court of New Hampshire had doubted that the donor's wish that the trustees manage the affairs of *Dartmouth College* could be insulated from legislative scrutiny. "We were sorry to see this published in [Farrar's] book as the reasoning of the highest judicial tribunal of a state," Dutton declared, "and we shall dismiss it."[48]

The *Review* was thus not really interested in constructing "a summary view of the course of argument" in *Dartmouth College;*[49] it was interested in the implications of the Marshall Court's position in the case. "The jurisdiction which the Supreme Court of the United States has asserted in the case of Dartmouth College and its final judgment therein," Dutton felt, were "pregnant with important results." Then followed, for the bulk of the article, a summary of the Marshall Court's major consti-

---

[47] [Dutton], "Constitutional Law," *No. Am. Rev.,* 10:83 (1820). I have equated Dutton with the *Review* for the purposes of commenting on the article.

[48] Ibid., 91.
[49] Ibid., 97.

tutional law decisions through the 1819 Term and a justification for the Court's role as "the ultimate expounder of the constitution."[50]

Dutton began with an attenuated statement of the justifications for an extensive jurisdiction in the Court. "According to the theory of our constitution," government was "a trust, emanating from the people, to be exercised for their benefit." The Constitution, being adopted by the people, embodied their will. In "providing for the organization of three co-ordinate departments," in giving enumerated powers to each department, including the judiciary, in limiting the powers of the states, and in declaring that the Constitution and laws of the United States should be supreme, "much reliance was placed upon the security, which the due exercise of the judicial power would accord, to the rights of states, as well as of individuals, when infringed or invaded by the encroaching spirit of legislative bodies, either in the states or in Congress."[51] In short,

> [T]he judicial power was regarded by the friends of a new and better order of things, as a being, separated from the prejudices, the passions, and the interests of men, watching and regulating the movements of a complex system, and wholly intent upon the impartial administration of justice.[52]

Then followed a series of more extended justifications for extensive judicial involvement in national affairs. The Court's "foreign jurisdiction" facilitated "great national interests" by giving the Court "great powers [to] take cognizance of cases in which the nation had a stake."[53] The Court's "domestic" jurisdiction was based on the assumption that it would "afford . . . the best protection against the injustice of rival parties, or the violence of popular passions." The personnel of the Court was "always to be selected from among the most eminent men in the profession of the law."[54] The "judgments" of the justices "must always be made public," as well as "the reasons and authorities upon which they are founded," so that "no gross departure from the law" could "ever be made, in any case, without exposure, and the immediate expression of public feeling and opinion."[55]

The Justices of the Court were "selected from places and states remote from each other," thus "local interests or passions . . . of which all more or less partake, are lost or neutralized in the communion with men who have never been within the infected region." Thus even though "human nature" suggested that the "judgment" of "a local tribunal

---

[50] Ibid., 104.
[51] Ibid., 104–105.
[52] Ibid., 105.

[53] Ibid.
[54] Ibid., 106.
[55] Ibid.

[would be moved] by the strong passions which surround it," when "these cases come before the Supreme Court of the United States, it may be presumed that there will always be a majority free from any such bias." The structure of the Constitution, the independence and stature of the Justices, their diverse sectional backgrounds, their obligation to make their judgments and reasoning public, and their commitment to "watching and regulating the movement" of the American federal republic thus made them "the friends of a new and better order of things."[56]

But Dutton acknowledged a "truth of fearful import" about Supreme Court Justices:

> [A]s party or faction is the offspring of our institutions, and always the heir apparent to the throne, men *may* be selected for this high office *because* they are known to be devoted to a great political party, and ready to become the willing instruments of its ambition or its vengeance; and that no species of oppression is so hopeless or so terrible, as that which may be practised under the forms of justice.[57]

The "only answer" Dutton could make to the possibility that Supreme Court Justices themselves might be partisan or corrupt was that if "wisdom and foresight, aided by experience," failed to discern such tendencies in advance, "they must be left like all extreme cases to provide for themselves."[58] Having confined the possibility of judicial partisanship or corruption to the "extreme case" (the *Centinel* had concluded that the American republic would founder should such a case arise), Dutton proceeded to elucidate upon the Marshall Court decisions that he had thus far found significant. All were constitutional cases: *Fletcher* v. *Peck, New Jersey* v. *Wilson, Terrett* v. *Taylor, Sturges, Marbury* v. *Madison, McCulloch, Martin* v. *Hunter's Lessee.* He also alluded to *Houston* v. *Moore,* about to be argued that year, and to the controversy out of which arose *Osborn* v. *Bank.*[59] With respect to *Houston,* Dutton noted that in an earlier militia episode the governor of Massachusetts and the supreme court of that state had concluded that the president of the United States could not call forth state militias, and commented that "we are aware of popular impressions in relation to this [issue], and we also know that they are dangerous expounders of constitutional law."[60] With respect to *Osborn,* Dutton acknowledged that "the state of Ohio has not chosen to submit to [the *McCulloch*] opinion of the Supreme Court"; and by attempting to tax the Ohio branch of the Bank of the United States had "put itself in array against the government of the Union."[61]

---

[56] Ibid.
[57] Ibid., 107. Emphasis in original.
[58] Ibid.

[59] Ibid., 107–13.
[60] Ibid., 112.
[61] Ibid., 111.

754

# Chapter XI: *Of the Court, Time, and Change*

In its discussions of all the other Court decisions it mentioned the *Review*'s posture was sympathetic to the Court. "Every decision of this sort," Dutton felt, "imparts something of solidity and durability to our constitution." A "judgment of the highest tribunal whose right and duty it is to expound the constitution," it believed, "connected as it usually is with interesting facts, is remembered, and exerts a salutary influence upon the public mind."[62] Dutton concluded his essay with a testament to the salutary effects of the Court's increased influence:

> This part of the law of the land is daily becoming more interesting, and exerting a wider influence upon the affairs of our country, from the respect that is generally felt for judicial decisions, from the intelligible form in which principles are exhibited, and from the gradual formation of a body of constitutional exposition, which will furnish precedents and analogies to future time. Within the last twenty years, we have seen the judicial department protecting the rights of the citizens of a state against the injustice of their own legislatures, and keeping within their constitutional bounds the legislative and executive powers of the union; and through the disastrous changes that await all free government, it may be found to be the strongest barrier against the tide of popular commotions, or the usurping spirit of popular assemblies. In the divisions which political opinions, or territorial lines and interests may make upon the great map of the empire, every good man would wish that the law should be supreme over all. While justice is allowed to do her work, uncorrupted and unobstructed, the ignorant prejudices, the local interests and passions of the day may mix, and ferment, and explode without danger to our civil state.[63]

It is worth probing this passage, for it represents an effort to link the previous justifications advanced on behalf of a visible, interventionist Court to the starting assumptions of republican theory. In the passage the Court emerges as an expositor of legal science and a buffer against cultural decay. The first portions of the passage identify the Court's decisions as forming "a body of constitutional exposition," a set of "intelligible . . . principles," a series of "precedents and analogies for future time." Constitutional law is thus elevated to the status of a science. But the purpose of this widening and deepening of the influence of law is not simply to provide guidance to savants. It is to make "the law supreme over all": to establish the Constitution, as interpreted by the Court, as a force "protecting the rights of the citizens . . . against . . . injustice"; as a vehicle for "keeping within . . . bounds the legislative and executive powers of the union"; and as a "barrier against the tide of popular commotions" which can produce "disastrous changes" in "all free governments."

---

[62] Ibid.

[63] Ibid., 113.

Law, as interpreted by the Court, becomes a means of cementing the republic against "divisions" spurred by "territorial lines and interests," "political opinions," "ignorant prejudices" and "passions." Law is, in short, a means of safeguarding the Republic against the disintegrative forces of change.

This series of justifications for prominent Court involvement in the affairs of American culture thus sought to convert arguments that could be characterized as partisan into arguments that sought to appeal to the shared assumptions of republican theory, assumptions that ostensibly went beyond partisanship. The argument that the diverse regional background of the Justices would function to retard parochialism in the Court evolved into an argument that nonparochial consitutional law was a force retarding the disintegrative effects of "territorial . . . interests." The argument that the obligation of the Justices to give reasons for their results will prevent "gross departures" from "the law" became part of an argument that the Court's purpose was to develop a body of constitutional exposition that would serve to elevate law as an antidote to prejudice or corruption. And the argument that the Court's decisions properly protected the rights of the people against legislative excesses became embedded in a more general argument that legislative excess was a manifestation of "the usurping spirit of popular assemblies" that threatened the stability of the Republic.

Lest there be any doubt among its readers as to the ultimate implications of the Court's increased influence, Dutton added in conclusion:

> It is our just pride, that we have attempted a mode of government, which divests itself of all the support, which is derived from the honest weakness and attachments of the human mind; which . . . trusts itself, with no other attractions than its own moral worth and dignity, to the custody of our virtues. By subjecting legislative bodies to rule, and holding them under the restraints of those fundamental principles and enactments, which we call the constitution, we have given a new dignity and higher duty to LAW, and realised the noble idea of a moral supremacy, clothed with power, to hold not only subjects of the government to a just performance of their various individual duties, but also the government itself, in all its departments, in its proper place and sphere.[64]

Dutton's essay in the *North American Review,* appearing less than a year after the dramatic increase in the Court's visibility with its 1819 decisions, signified an alteration in the Court's image among contemporaries that was to persist for the balance of Marshall's tenure. The commentary on *Sturges* and *McCulloch* had, for the most part, emphasized

---

[64] Ibid.

the partisan dimensions or immediate consequences of those cases: the effect of *Sturges* on creditors, debtors, and the commercial community generally; the pros and cons of a national bank, extensive federal implied powers, and restrictions on state sovereignty embodied in *McCulloch*. The exchange between Marshall, Brockenbrough, and Roane had sought a more abstract and theoretical level of discourse, but the theoretical positions being advanced were ones that had been previously identified with the Federalist and Republican parties. The *Review* essay was a more explicit effort to separate the Court's decisions from partisan considerations, characterizing them as an effort to establish the Constitution as a moral force and the Court as an expounder of a disembodied body of legal doctrine. The Court, in Dutton's treatment, had seemingly evolved from an agent of the federal government, identified with the views of those who supported Federalist party principles, to the promulgator of "fundamental principles and enactments" that served to establish law as a force in opposition to partisan politics.

This latter role for the Court was, of course, the very role Marshall and his colleagues had claimed for it in their decisions. The *Review's* acceptance of the Court as beyond "passion" and partisanship demonstrated that the Justices' claim had begun to take hold. But the Court's image had not been wholly transformed. From its first visible Term in 1819 to Marshall's death in 1835 two impressions of the Court were fostered by commentary: an older impression of a partisan force in a culture in which constitutional law and politics were deemed to be inseparable, and the *Review's* impression of an impartial tribunal expounding the fundamental principles of republican government, as embodied in the Constitution.

Previous chapters have emphasized commentary that stressed the Court's nonpartisan status, relying heavily on sources, such as the speeches of Webster and the writings of Story and other participants in the commentator network, that were closely identified with the Court itself. If one reads such commentary in the aggregate and takes it at face value, one might well conclude that the Marshall Court had been remarkably successful in establishing itself as a nonpartisan institution and in establishing its decisions as beyond partisan attack. But we have seen that the commentary was purposive in its de-emphasis of the "discretionary" features of constitutional interpretation and the idiosyncratic features of judging, and in its emphasis on the "scientific" and "fundamental" character of the Court's constitutional doctrines. We have concluded, in fact, that the commentary portraying the Court as nonpartisan can be offered as evidence that arguments ascribing nonpartisan status to law in a republican form of government touched deep chords in early-nineteenth-century political discourse, but not as evidence that the Court was widely perceived as nonpartisan. Indeed the commentary can

757

be seen as signifying the opposite: that the commentators were seeking to deflect or to defuse a widespread perception that the Court was a partisan body.

At any rate, there is abundant evidence that older characterizations of the Court as partisan persisted among commentators as the Court's public visibility increased after 1820. About the same time that Dutton's article appeared, the *National Intelligencer,* commenting on *Sturges,* referred to an "encroachment already made by Judicial legislation on our State-Rights," and characterized it as "the first movement in the mighty contest between the states and the federal government."[65] While the *Cohens* case was being argued, the Washington *Gazette* said that "we look with infinitely more apprehension to the Judiciary than to any other department of the government." The reasons for apprehension, the *Gazette* declared, were the Court's "permanency, its esprit de corps, its unbounded latitude, [and] its power."[66] The *Gazette* thus drew some sinister implications from the Court's increased influence, and others perceived that the Court's pronouncements of constitutional principles could mask more partisan goals. The *Dartmouth College, McCulloch,* and *Cohens* cases, the *Liberty Hall and Cincinnati Gazette* said in 1821,

> have each developed some new principle of Federal jurisdiction, not before supposed to exist. The principle of each of these cases, it may be said, sprung upon the States, without an opportunity afforded them to consider and combat the doctrines involved. They have not originated in public legislative provisions, publicly enacted, upon a theatre where public opinion can be felt, but have started up as from a lurking place, concealed under enactments made, it is conceived, for very different purposes . . . [E]ach [of] the principles of these cases . . . asserts a power in the government of the Union to cherish and protect a different species of corporation . . . It is . . . very evident that, by attaching to the General Government all these Establishments, its power and influence is greatly strengthened.[67]

These comments typified a strand of commentary on the Court in the 1820s that not only criticized the Court's constitutional decisions as consolidationist, but also intimated that the partisan consequences of the decisions were deliberately being suppressed. Jefferson's correspondence with Johnson, quoted earlier, had put the suppression theme particularly vividly. Opinions, Jefferson said, were huddled up in conclaves; the votes of judges not revealed; principles declared that were not necessary to the

---

[65] Washington *National Intelligencer,* Feb. 24, 1820.
[66] Washington *Gazette,* Feb. 20, 1821.

[67] *Liberty Hall and Cincinnati Gazette,* Apr. 16, 1821.

decisions; the law "sophisticated" to the "mind" of judges by "crafty" opinion writers such as Marshall.[68] The implication was that the Justices were simultaneously seizing opportunities to pronounce doctrines that went beyond the precise issues before them and concealing their partisan purposes in doing so. The *Enquirer's* criticism of *Gibbons* v. *Ogden* echoed that sentiment:

> Should it not be a rule with the bench never to "travel beyond the record"—but to confine itself strictly to the point, which is submitted for its decision? . . . Instead of confining itself to [the question presented in *Gibbons*], the court has gone into a series of other propositions, which did not require to be decided, and which ought only to have been decided, as the cases actually occurred, and upon the most serious argument and deliberation.
>
> The last paragraph of the [*Gibbons*] opinion states what would be the consequence of contracting "by construction into the narrowest possible compass" the powers expressly granted to the government of the Union." . . . And suppose we fly to the opposite extreme—suppose we stretch the powers of the government by a most liberal construction—suppose we consider "necessary" to be synonymous with "convenient," what would then be the state of the case. The state governments would moulder into ruins, upon which would rise up one powerful, gigantic, and threatening edifice. To which of these extremes the stream of decisions from the S. Court is sweeping, we refer to the case of McCulloch, and the case of the Cohens.[69]

*Gibbons*, which has been characterized as the only "popular" opinion Marshall ever delivered,[70] was thus not universally acclaimed. The significance of the commentary on *Gibbons* was not so much in its content as in the different tone adopted by supporters and critics. Supporters emphasized the stature of the Court that had delivered the opinion and the intellectual coherence of Marshall's opinion. The opinion was "luminous": "one of the most powerful efforts of the human mind that has ever been displayed from the bench of any Court."[71] It would "command the assent of every impartial mind competent to embrace such a subject."[72] It was a "masterpiece of judicial reasoning."[73] It had been pronounced by "a tribunal removed from the influence of . . . state and

---

[68] See also T. Jefferson to Thomas Ritchie, Dec. 25, 1820, quoted in P. Ford, ed., *The Works of Thomas Jefferson* (12 vols., 1905), XII, 175.

[69] Richmond *Enquirer*, Mar. 16, 1824.

[70] Beveridge, *John Marshall*, IV, 45.

[71] New York *Evening Post*, Mar. 5, 1824.

[72] New York *Commercial Advertiser*, Mar. 12, 1824.

[73] Philadelphia *National Gazette*, Mar. 9, 1824.

private interests."[74] It was "the duty of every citizen to cherish a spirit of respect and acquiescence in the decision of this Court."[75] Opponents, on the other hand, raised the themes of dissemblance and partisanship. One suggested that Marshall's opinion "contain[ed] a great deal that has no business there. . . . A judicial opinion should decide nothing and embrace nothing that is not before the Court;"[76] another, that *Gibbons* was one of a number of cases in which "the Federal branch of our government is advancing toward the usurpation of all the rights reserved to the States, and the consolidation in itself of all powers, foreign and domestic."[77] In a letter to the New York *Daily Advertiser,* reprinted in the New York *Evening Post* in March 1824, a critic writing under the pseudonym "Scaevola" combined these criticisms. Scaevola was "not satisfied," he said, "with the principles advanced in [*Gibbons*]" or with the "inadmissible and dangerous . . . rules of construction" employed by Marshall. He argued that Marshall's apparent endorsement of the doctrine that "the word to regulate implies, in its nature, full power over the thing to be regulated, [and thus] excludes, necessarily, the action of all others that would perform the same operation on the same thing," taken together with his claim that "commerce, as the word is used in the constitution, is a unit, every part of which is indicated by the term," amounted to a "principle of construction . . . pregnant with the most serious consequences." Scaevola particularized:

If [that principle of construction] be sound and if *commerce* be a unit, indicating *every part* of commerce with foreign nations, and among the several states, and with the Indian tribes, and if to *regulate* means a grant of exclusive power extending equally to what is left unregulated as to what is regulated, then the quarantine and health laws of the state[s] are clearly null and void . . .

The principle of construction of the Constitution [adopted by Marshall in *Gibbons* was that] "full power to regulate a particular subject, implies the whole power, and leaves no residuum; a grant of the whole is incompatible with the existence of a right in another to any part of it." Now, I ask, does not the principle go to cut up at once *all concurrent power in the states* in every case where full power to regulate a subject is given? . . . The 10th article of the amendments to the constitution is reversed, and instead of its being the fact that all power not delegated is reserved, it is that all power not reserved is delegated,

[74] *Connecticut Courant* (Hartford, Conn.), Mar. 9, 1824.
[75] Ibid.
[76] John Randolph to William Brockenbrough, Mar. 3, 1824, quoted in H.

Garland, *The Life of John Randolph* (2 vols., 1851), II, 212.
[77] Thomas Jefferson to William Giles, Dec. 26, 1825, quoted in Warren, *Supreme Court,* II, 80–81.

and the state powers are to be taken strictly as exceptions to a general grant.[78]

The point of the critics of *Gibbons,* then was twofold: the Court was using constitutional cases as opportunities to formulate broad doctrines and principles, not necessarily germane to the decision of the cases, whose purpose was to augment the power of the federal government. The doctrines announced were not only unsound in their implications, they were disingenuous, because their promulgation was not necessary to the result reached by the Court. As John Randolph put it about *Gibbons,* "if [Marshall] had said that 'a vessel, having the legal evidence that she has conformed to the regulations which Congress has seen fit to prescribe, has the right to go from a port of any state to a port of any other . . . non obstante such a law as that of the State of New York,' I should have been satisfied."[79]

Between 1819, when it emerged as a force in national affairs, and 1826, when Robert Trimble was appointed to replace Thomas Todd, who had died that February, the Court was subjected to recurrent criticism on the grounds of partisanship and disingenuousness. For the most part the criticism was provoked by the Court's invalidation of state efforts to assert sovereign powers: New Hampshire in *Dartmouth College,* Maryland in *McCulloch,* Virginia in *Cohens,* Ohio in *Osborn,* Georgia in *Planters' Bank,* Kentucky in *Green* v. *Biddle,* and New York in *Gibbons* were each repulsed. The criticism was in this sense self-serving, and its parochial nature was noted on occasion, as when the Virginia legislature expressly declined to support Kentucky's protest against *Green* v. *Biddle,* a decision restricting state sovereignty but advantaging Virginia residents.[80] But there was a swell of popular discontent about the Court's apparent lack of solicitude for state interests that spawned efforts in the 1820s to alter the jurisdiction or composition of the Court. *Niles' Weekly Register* declared in 1822 that "there are two parties in the United States, most decidedly opposed to each other as to the rights, powers, and province of the Judiciary." One party, *Niles'* claimed, "almost claims infallibility for the Judges, and would hedge them round about in such a manner that they cannot be reached by popular opinion at all;" the other "would subject them to the vacillations of popular prejudice" and seemingly "require . . . them to . . . interpret the Constitution according to the real or apparent expediency of things."[81] The "two parties" *Niles'* described were encapsulations of the two strands of commentary on the Court: one

---

[78] Scaevola, *Evening Post,* Mar. 18, 1824. Emphasis in original.

[79] Randolph to Brockenbrough, Mar. 3, 1824, supra, note 76.

[80] See Washington *National Intelligencer,* Feb. 18, 1822.

[81] *Niles' Weekly Register,* June 22, 1822.

ascribing to it an exalted status as promulgator of sacrosanct doctrine and defender of the Republic; the other attacking it as partisan, elitist, and consolidationist. When efforts to reform the judiciary surfaced in Congress in the 1820s, critics and defenders of the Court tracked similar positions.

Richard M. Johnson, a senator from Kentucky, was perhaps the most vocal critic of the Court in this period, advancing a bill restricting the Court's appellate jurisdiction in 1821 and another bill, that same year, requiring the concurrence of seven Justices in any case involving the constitutional validity of state or congressional statutes. Johnson charged that the Court had "a manifest disposition to enlarge, to the utmost stretch of constitutional construction, the powers of the general government"; that its constitutional decisions, from *McCulloch* through *Green* v. *Biddle*, had "prostrat[ed] the States, and in effect legislat[ed] for the people"; that "[j]udges, like other men, have their political views," and should not "be considered any more infallible, and their decisions any less subject to investigation" than other public servants; that "some interposition" by the states was necessary to prevent "this serious encroachment upon the first principles of self government"; and that "the purity of our political institutions" would be "preserved" by the adoption of "some remedy" curbing the Court's power.[82]

Webster was, as noted, the Court's most influential defender in public service, and his arguments were also employed by others. In a debate over the Court's jurisdiction in the Senate in 1826, Senator William Harper of South Carolina repeated the standard defense arguments of the time. Harper said that

> [t]he independence of the Judiciary is at the very basis of our institutions. . . . It is in times of friction, when party spirit runs high, that dissatisfaction is most likely to be occasioned by the decisions of the Supreme Court. I do not believe that the Supreme Court, or the Constitution itself, will ever be able to stand against the decided current of public opinion. . . . The Constitution has laid down the fundamental and immutable laws of justice for our Government; and the majority that constitutes the Government should not violate that. The Constitution is made to control the Government; it has no other object, and though the Supreme Court cannot resist public opinion, it may resist a temporary majority and may change that majority. However high the tempest may blow, individuals may hear the calm and steady voice of the Judiciary warning them of their danger.[83]

In Harper's version the Court was once again identified with the decla-

---

[82] *Annals of Congress,* 17th Cong., 1st Sess., Jan. 14, 1822.

[83] *Annals of Congress,* 19th Cong., 1st Sess., Apr. 12, 1826.

ration of "immutable" laws, with checks on the excesses of government, and with the preservation of individual liberties against political factions and transient majorities. It was the primary source of the social cement that held the Republic together.

After its visible decisions of the 1824 Term, the Court went into a kind of lull for the next two years. *Ogden* v. *Saunders*, the insolvency case that had precipitated considerable public interest and was internally divisive, was postponed for two Terms because of Todd's illness and the lack of unanimity; newspaper commentary on the Court slackened. With only six judges, the Court had difficulty keeping up with its work. *Niles' Weekly Register* reported in 1825 that it had disposed of only 38 out of 164 cases on its docket and "ha[d] matters sufficient ahead to occupy all the spare time of the Judges for nearly five years to come."[84] A Term later the *National Intelligencer* made its previously quoted comment that out of 190 cases on the docket, the Court was able to dispose of only 49, leaving three-fourths of the docket untouched.

The increased involvement of the Court in national affairs and the growing awareness of its power had, as noted, precipitated congressional efforts to curb or alter its appellate jurisdiction in the 1820s, but these were not the only examples of proposed legislative tinkering with the Court in the years between 1819 and 1827. The circuit-riding responsibilities of the Justices were perennially criticized as wasteful, time-consuming, and debilitating: in 1819, 1823, 1824, 1825, and 1826 bills were introduced to appoint additional Justices, relieve the Justices of circuit court duties, and increase the number of circuits. In 1826 one such bill, sponsored by Martin Van Buren, passed the House: the bill would have increased the number of Justices to ten and created three new circuits. Amendments to the bill, one of which would have required seven Justices to agree on any decision invalidating a state statute or an act of Congress, and a concern among the opponents of President John Quincy Adams that he would be able to appoint all the new Justices, eventually resulted in the bill's defeat. The failure of the bill left circuit-riding intact, and in order to deal with the Court's congested docket Congress passed a bill in 1826 extending the time the Justices were to hold Court in Washington from the first Monday in February to the second Monday in January. That practice began in the 1827 Term, and a year later Story wrote Jeremiah Mason that "[w]e have done a good deal of business, and shall not probably leave sixty cases behind us. This is a great victory over the old docket, and encourages me to hope much for the future course of the Court."[85]

---

[84] *Niles' Weekly Register*, Mar. 26, 1825.
[85] J. Story to J. Mason, Feb. 27, 1828, quoted in Warren, *Supreme Court*, II, 160.

It has previously been suggested that the 1827 Term marked something of a turning point in the Marshall Court's history, as new personnel and a partial break-up of the boardinghouse residency system contributed to a slight but discernible alteration in the Court's stance. *Ogden* v. *Saunders*, restricting the impact of *Sturges*, and *Brown* v. *Maryland*, apparently conceding the existence of a concurrent state power to regulate commerce, from the 1827 Term, *Willson* v. *Black-bird Creek Marsh Co.*, qualifying *Gibbons* even further, from the 1829 Term, and *Providence Bank* v. *Billings*, permitting a state to tax the capital stock of a corporation absent an express waiver of taxation in the corporate charter, could be offered as examples. Fewer opinions were issued without public dissents, with the 1830 case of *Craig* v. *Missouri*, in the pattern of older Court restrictions on state sovereignty, provoking dissents from three of the seven Justices. Marshall wrote Story after *Craig* had been handed down, "I have read in the last volume of Mr. Peters the three dissenting opinions delivered in [the Missouri] case, and think it requires no prophet to predict that the 25th section [of the Judiciary Act of 1789] is to be repealed, or to use a more fashionable phrase, to be nullified by the Supreme Court of the United States. I hope the case in which this is to be accomplished will not occur during my time, but accomplished it will be at no very distant period."[86]

The election of Jackson, the presence of a group of Justices— Thompson, Johnson, McLean, and Baldwin—who for diverse reasons were not as committed to the consolidationist policies of the earlier Court, the death of Washington, one of the strongest advocates of unanimity and federal power, the eccentricity of Baldwin, the absence of McLean and subsequently Johnson from the boardinghouse circle, and the political realignment symbolized by the election of Jackson and his 1832 veto of the bill rechartering the Bank of the United States, all testified to a more splintered Court, and one in retrenchment from the expansionist years of the 1820s. And as the Court subtly modified its stance, commentary on its decisions reflected that modification. Between 1825 and 1830 commentary attributing partisan positions to the Court or to individual Justices decreased, while commentary stressing the role of the Court as an impartial, incorruptible buffer against cultural disintegration continued. The result was a striking juxtaposition of Marshall's private fears that the Court had developed a "revolutionary spirit" that would "work inconvenience and mischief in its progress"[87] with commentary such as that provided in 1827 by the *American Quarterly Review*:

---

[86] J. Marshall to J. Story, Oct. 15, 1830, *Proc. Mass. Hist. Soc.*, 14:341 (1901).

[87] J. Marshall to J. Story, May 3, 1831, ibid., 343.

# Chapter XI: *Of the Court, Time, and Change*

In the city of Washington there exists a power, visible only two or three months in the years; a power without arms, without soldiers, without treasure; whose only weapon is the moral force of reason and truth, and yet to whose decisions the whole country submissively bows. This power is the venerable Bench of the Supreme Court of the United States. By their joint labours the mighty edifice of our constitution and laws is sustained; twenty-four free and independent states are made to move in their respective orbits, and every eccentric deviation is instantly checked. No country on earth presents such a spectacle. While this moral power exists, civil laws are not to be dreaded; and it can no longer exist than while it continues to be the unsullied organ of truth, reason, and justice.[88]

The tone of the *American Quarterly*'s comments was characteristic of writings on the Court in the late 1820s. The *North American Review*, for example, continued its practice of attributing nonpartisan status to the Court and associating the Court's decisions with respect for law and with the preservation of the Republic:

As the legislation and judicial administration of the United States, always border upon those of the several states, and are often blended with them by a concurrence of application to the same subjects and parties, it is a delicate and difficult office to disentangle the one from the other, and define their respective boundaries. Some questions on this subject have, for a time, disturbed the harmony of our government, and even threatened its stability. But fortunately most of these questions are brought in the first place before the judicial tribunals, and thus being far removed from all rash and violent proceedings, are made the subjects of elaborate investigation and solemn decision. Accordingly, as long as the Supreme Court of the United States shall continue to be an august tribunal of judges, holding their offices by a permanent and independent tenure . . . the jarrings between the general and state jurisdictions . . . are likely to terminate as they have hitherto terminated, . . . in providing, as well as adding to, the strength of our political institutions. . . . These tribunals are the central links which bind together our whole political system, and being once broken, the whole system must fall to ruin. . . .

    [T]hese questions are of vital importance, and if the constitution had not authorized those decisions of the Supreme Court, the government of the country must have been brought to a stand; . . . and the country can never be too grateful to those judges who have, with so much dignity, impartiality, and firmness, and so learnedly, ably, and laboriously, applied the principles and provisions of the constitution

---

[88] "Kent on American Law," *Am. Q. Rev.*, 1:179 (1827).

and laws to the many difficult . . . cases that have arisen. . . . [I]t is quite apparent that an able and independent judiciary is the palladium of our institutions.[89]

Even *Niles' Weekly Register,* a consistent critic of the Court in the early 1820s, acknowledged in 1828 that "though the constitutional construction of this lofty tribunal is not wholly conformable to our humble opinions of right, we have often thought that no person could behold this venerable body without profound respect for the virtue and talents concentrated on its bench." There needed to be "some power in every government having *final* effect," *Niles'* asserted, and "it could hardly be vested anywhere more safely than in the supreme court, as presently filled."[90]

Given the muted doctrinal profile of the Court after 1827, and its addition of two Jackson nominees, it may have come as some surprise to the Justices that the year 1830 ushered in a period in which the Court was more in the public eye, and its role in American politics more controversial, than at any time since the 1819 Term. The explanation for the Court's sudden return to visibility lay in the stress created by the simultaneous surfacing in 1830 of the nullification controversy and the Court's involvement with the dispute between the Cherokee tribes and the state of Georgia.

The Senate session of late 1829 and early 1830 was a forum for the expression of a series of political tensions that had mounted in the 1820s. In the Senate's debates in that session, which ranged over tariff, internal improvements, and western lands issues, the theme of partisanship on the Court was again aired. Prior to the debates one advisor of Jackson had signified that the power of the federal judiciary had again become a partisan issue. Writing to Jackson on Christmas Day in 1829, Worden Pope proposed that the Jackson administration consider several proposals limiting the power of the Supreme Court and the lower federal courts:

The Federal Courts should be limited to matters arising only out of the Constitution and the law merchant. . . . The lex loci of the states [should] in private rights [cases] govern the decisions of the Federal tribunals. . . . The whole seven Judges should be unanimous in deciding against the validity of a state Constitution or law. Sooner or later the jurisdiction of the Federal Courts must be curtailed, and we had better at once cut off every graft or inoculation upon the roots or trunk of the constitutional judicial tree. It is a dangerous encroaching power and ought thus to be limited.[91]

[89] "Kent's Commentaries on American Law," *No. Am. Rev.,* 24:345, 352, 361 (1827).
[90] *Niles' Weekly Register,* Jan. 19, 1828. Emphasis in original.
[91] W. Pope to A. Jackson, Dec. 25, 1829, quoted in Warren, *Supreme Court,* II, 178.

# Chapter XI: *Of the Court, Time, and Change*

When the Senate debates began in January 1830, a variety of senators attacked the Court. John Rowan of Kentucky declared that "[w]hen the Court asserts its right to impose restraints upon the sovereignty of the States, it should be treated as a usurper, and driven back by the States within its appropriate judicial space."[92] Levi Woodbury of New Hampshire suggested that the Court had engaged in "sliding onward to consolidation" and in "giving a diseased enlargement to the powers of the General Government."[93] Thomas Benton of Missouri, after claiming that "[t]he range of Federal authority is becoming unlimited under the assumption of implied powers," called the Court's decisions evidence of "a judicial tyranny and oppression" whose purpose was to "annihilate the States and reduce them to the abject condition of provinces of the Federal empire."[94] And Robert Hayne, the leading spokesman for state autonomy in the debates, stated that the nub of his concern was "the assumption of political power by the Supreme Court."[95]

Students of the 1830 debates have suggested that the sovereignty doctrines articulated by both sides—compact theory, interposition, and nullification by Hayne and his supporters; the "Union" theory of sovereignty, with its premise that the people had enacted the Constitution and created the Union, and were thus the ultimate repository of sovereign powers in the American system of government, by their opponents—were abstractions masking more tangible issues, such as slavery, tariff policy, and the role of the federal government in economic expansion, that were beginning to estrange certain southern states from the others in the Union. It is clear that in a sense the Court was an inadvertent participant in a debate over issues that were centered in Congress at the time. But it is also true that the sources of the federal government's authority to adjust tariff rates, establish policies toward slavery in federal territories, distribute western lands, and pre-empt the states from control of most commercial development were constitutional law doctrines propounded by the Marshall Court. Thus when defenders of the Court in the debates resurrected its role as a "dignified and impartial . . . umpire," free from "party and electioneering discussion," and "without power or patronage,"[96] any effort on the part of a state to claim the power to resist or to "nullify" acts of Congress would have to be based on a theory of sovereignty that was in opposition to that announced by the Marshall Court. The New York *Daily Advertiser*, observing the 1830 debates, said that "it is manifest that there is a settled determination in the minds of some of the warm and violent politicians of the country to circumscribe, if not

---

[92] *Annals of Congress*, 21st Cong., 1st Sess., Feb. 8, 1830.
[93] Ibid., Feb. 24.
[94] Ibid., Jan. 18, Feb. 2.

[95] Ibid., Jan. 25.
[96] Edward Livingston, ibid., Mar. 15.

destroy, the weight and influence of the National Judiciary.'' The *Advertiser* believed that ''if the Court should be broken down, . . . the strength and security of the Republic will be undermined, and the very first serious convulsion that occurs will endanger the very existence of the Republic.''[97]

It was in this atmosphere—renewed attention to the ''consolidationist'' tendencies of the Court in light of the newly perceived relevance of compact theory to political controversies of the late 1820s—that the Cherokee cases came to public attention in the 1830s. The Cherokee cases would very likely have precipitated public interest even had their sovereignty dimensions been less manifest: the presence of Indians, and their treatment by the states and the federal government, was an important social issue in the early nineteenth century. But the sovereignty aspects of the Cherokees' confrontation with Georgia, and the Jackson administration's determined effort to effectuate a removal policy toward Indians residing east of the Mississippi, transformed the Cherokee cases into a full-fledged political controversy, with the state of Georgia and the Jackson administration apparently aligned against the Cherokees and the Marshall Court.

In light of the criticism of the Court that the Cherokee controversy was to foster, it is interesting to note an article on the Court which appeared in the *American Quarterly Review* in March 1830, as the Senate debates over nullification and Jackson's Indian removal bill were taking place. On the eve of the Cherokee litigation, the *Quarterly* portrayed the Court in almost reverent terms:

The judicial power, like the great principle of grantation, keeps every other power of the government in its proper place and action; and maintains the whole in an uniform and beautiful order and motion. . . . Such is the power of the judiciary, whose protecting influence is in operation through every day and every hour, unseen and unfelt. The silent, but efficacious and unremitting security which the law, and its ministers, the Courts, give to every citizen, attracts but little attention and less gratitude. The judiciary makes no ostentatious display of its services. It enjoys no patronage; it neither contrives nor controls any measures of national policy and prosperity. . . . Every part of our complicated system, composed of various governments and ambitious sovereignties, is kept in place by the vigilance and integrity of the judiciary; and without it, a general confusion, distraction, and conflict, would speedily break up the social, as well as political order of things.

What an immense range of discussion any inquiry has been explored by this learned and diligent tribunal! What mighty questions

---

[97] New York *Daily Advertiser*, Mar. 19, 1830.

have been agitated and settled! What incalculable benefits have resulted from their labours! . . .

Few of our citizens know what this Court has done for them. They have enjoyed, and are daily enjoying, the invaluable benefits of their learning and diligence. . . . The poor and the humble know that they are secure from any invasion of their rights by the wealthy and powerful, but they have not reflected that they owe their safety to the independence and integrity of their judges. The whole value of a republican government would be lost, if the administration of justice between man and man were in the hands of weak, ignorant, or corrupt judges. . . .[98]

As the Cherokee controversy emerged in late 1830 and 1831, muted versions of the *Quarterly*'s characterization appeared, such as the statement in *Niles' Weekly Register* that "[t]he people are not ripe for [defiance of the Court]. . . . Without some high and common arbiter for the settlement of disputes of this character, the Union is not worth one cent,"[99] but they were joined by comments of a different nature. The *United States Telegraph*, the Washington organ of the Jackson administration, said that if Georgia chose to defy any judgment of the Court pertaining to the Cherokees, "the position in which the Supreme Court [would be] placed . . . demonstrates the absurdity of the doctrine which contends that the Court is clothed with supreme and absolute control over the States."[100] Another Washington paper, the *Globe*, was even less circumspect, calling the Court's involvement in the Cherokee litigation part of "a crusade carried on against the South by the party of whom the Chief Justice has always been the uniform representative." Marshall had achieved "infinitely more on the Court," the *Globe* felt, "than all the rest of the party has been able to effect elsewhere."[101] Such commentary, and reports that another effort would be made to reject Section 25 of the Judiciary Act in the 1831 Congress, prompted the New York *Daily Advertiser* to claim that "there is obviously a determination, on the part of politicians of a certain school, to curtail the constitutional jurisdiction and destroy the influence and independence of the Supreme Court of the United States."[102]

Efforts to curtail the power of the Court reached their peak, during the period covered by this volume, in the second session of the 21st Congress in early 1831. A bill was introduced in the Judiciary Committee of the House of Representatives to repeal Section 25 of the Judiciary Act,

---

[98] "Supreme Court of the United States," *Am. Q. Rev.*, 13:111, 112, 117, 124 (1830).
[99] *Niles' Weekly Register*, Sept. 18, 1830.

[100] *United States Telegraph* (Washington, D.C.), Jan. 3, 1831.
[101] Washington *Globe*, Jan. 5, 1831.
[102] New York *Daily Advertiser*, Jan. 13, 1831.

and a majority of the committee reported it favorably to the floor of the House. Story, writing to two friends in Massachusetts in January 1831, found the situation alarming. As previously noted, he told John Ashmun that "the recent attacks in Georgia, and the recent nullification doctrine in South Carolina," were "but parts of the same general scheme, the object of which is to elevate an exclusive State sovereignty upon the ruins of the general Government."[103] And after informing George Ticknor that the House Judiciary Committee had voted in favor of the repeal bill, Story suggested that "if the twenty-fifth section is repealed the Constitution is practically gone," and that "many of our wisest friends look with great gloom to the future."[104] While he wrote to his wife at the same time that he had "not any expectation" that the repeal bill would prevail, that "indeed . . . it will fail by a very large vote," he found it an "alarming measure," one which "shows the spirit of the times."[105] The bill was rejected, 158-51, on January 29; the Boston *Courier* communicated that "[t]he audacious attempt of a few hot-headed demagogues to break up the Supreme Court has been foiled."[106]

Having survived the 1831 session of Congress with its jurisdiction intact, the Court immediately plunged back into controversy with its holding in *Cherokee Nation v. Georgia* that it had no original jurisdiction to entertain complaints by the Cherokee Nation, which it determined was neither a "state" nor a "foreign state" within the meaning of Article III, Section 2 of the Constitution. The Richmond *Enquirer* chortled that the decision gave "sanction to the pretensions and conduct of [Georgia] with regard to the Indians,"[107] and the Boston *Courier* observed that "the nullifying politicians of Georgia must be not a little astonished to find themselves . . . receiving aid from [the Court] when they have been laboring so hard to convince their constituents that they were traduced, abused, and oppressed by the federal government."[108] These comments were premised on a misunderstanding of the Court's holding in *Cherokee Nation*, and on March 28, 1831, the *National Intelligencer* reported that "there seems to us to be a disposition to make the opinion of the Court to be what it is not, in order to sustain the [Jackson administration] on the ground which it has taken on this subject. . . . We repeat . . . that [all *Cherokee Nation* held was] that the Cherokees have no remedy in the Courts of the United States *in the capacity of a foreign nation*."[109]

---

[103] J. Story to J. Ashmun, Jan. 30, 1831, quoted in W. Story, *Life and Letters*, II, 47.

[104] J. Story to G. Ticknor, Jan. 22, 1831, quoted in ibid., 48-49.

[105] J. Story to Sarah Waldo Story, Jan. 28, 1831, quoted in ibid., 43-44.

[106] Boston *Courier*, Feb. 1, 1831.

[107] Richmond *Enquirer*, Mar. 25, 1831.

[108] Boston *Courier*, Mar. 25, 1831.

[109] Washington *National Intelligencer*, Mar. 28, 1831. Emphasis in original.

## Chapter XI: *Of the Court, Time, and Change*

By late 1831, commentators had become aware that the decision in *Cherokee Nation* had not ended the controversy, and a series of articles appeared that sought to remind the Court of the moral implications of failing to underscore ⎡⎤e Cherokees' claims. The *North American Review* and the *American Quarterly Review* took the publication of Richard Peters's pamphlet on the case to declare their hope that the Court would eventually support the Cherokees. "Some political writers who sustain the pretensions of the State of Georgia," the *North American Review* declared, "have affected to represent [the opinion in *Cherokee Nation*] as a decision in her favor and that of the Executive upon the merits of the case. It must be obvious, however, to every reader, that this representation is wholly incorrect." The judgment of the Court "went off upon a point of mere form": the "case was not decided on its merits."[110] Having set the record straight on what the Court had already decided in *Cherokee Nation,* the *Review* then proceeded to attack the Court's jurisdictional holding and to express its regret "that a case of this importance should have been decided upon by other principle than that of doing substantial justice between the parties."[111] In the *Review*'s opinion Indian tribes were "throughout the Constitution recognised and treated as foreign states,"[112] and thus it was "convinced . . . that the opinion of the Court is erroneous." Nonetheless, the *Review* was prepared "to acquiesce with perfect cheerfulness in [the Court's] decision," since "the case will no doubt be presented to [the Justices] in a form in which they will be able to take cognizance of it, and in which it will be tried upon its points."[113] The *Review* thus turned to the merits of the case, and found that "the extension by Georgia of her jurisdiction over the territory and persons of the Cherokee Indians was an open contravention of all the treaties with the Cherokees."[114] It also reminded its readers that "[w]e are bound to these children of the forest by solemn obligations," and that "a violation of them would disgrace us forever." The *Review* intimated that if the Court decided in the Cherokees' favor, and President Jackson refused to enforce the decision, he could be impeached.[115]

The *American Jurist* and the *American Quarterly Review* sought to defend the Court's ruling on its jurisdiction, but at the same time both periodicals made clear their sympathy for the Cherokees on the merits. The Court's refusal to accept jurisdiction in the case, the *American Jurist* felt, demonstrated that the Court could not "amplify . . . jurisdiction . . . even to amplify justice," and showed "how with equal solicitude and firmness, [Marshall] can exercise whatever jurisdiction the court has, and

---

[110] "The Cherokee Case," *No. Am. Rev.*, 33:136, 142, (1831).
[111] Ibid., 143.
[112] Ibid., 149.

[113] Ibid., 150.
[114] Ibid., 152.
[115] Ibid.

renounce whatever of jurisdiction it has not."[116] But while the *American Jurist* found the Court's reasoning "conclusive"[117] on the jurisdictional issue, it took pains to note that "[a] deep feeling in favor of the Cherokees had been exhibited throughout the greater part of the country"; and that "the conviction was general, that the character of our own nation was seriously implicated" in the Cherokee controversy.[118] Similarly, the *American Quarterly Review* distinguished between the jurisdictional issue and the moral implications of the Cherokees' treatment:

> Since the organization of our government, few subjects have arisen which have agitated the public mind more violently or generally, than the controversy between the state of Georgia and the Cherokee Indians. The sufferings inflicted, and to be inflicted, upon this powerless and miserable race, their helpless condition and imploring appeals, have enlisted, on their behalf, the humanity and generous sympathy of the American people. Such a state of feeling is not very propitious to a candid consideration of the *law* and *reason* of the case, or to any discriminations which prevent or interrupt the protection and redress to which they seem entitled . . .
>
> Actuated by feelings so natural and so honorable, the people of the United States . . . imagined that when the complaint of the [Cherokees] was brought before the Supreme Court, an immediate and full protection would be extended to them; and the disappointment, on the dismissal of the bill of complaint, was in proportion to the confidence and zeal with which a different result was expected.[119]

Having said all that, the *Quarterly* then proposed to "venture upon the task, probably an unwelcome one to many of our readers, of vindicating the decree of the Court"[120] in *Cherokee Nation*.

These comments on the first Cherokee case reflect the image of the Court that its defenders regularly fashioned during the last twenty years of Marshall's tenure: that of an incorruptible, impartial, virtuous force upholding the law against partisanship, passion, and even unreflective "justice." However much the Justices' sympathies may have been engaged by the plight of the Cherokees, the comments suggested, their decision was based on their duty to adhere to the law. "It was not for this Court to know anything in the case," the *Quarterly* said, "but that which came to them by and through the law of the land."[121] Questions of "right and wrong between Georgia and the Indians" needed to be "ke[pt] . . . out of view."[122] And yet none of the defenders of the Court

---

[116] "The Opinions in the Cherokee Case," *Am. Jurist*, 6:209, 322 (1831).
[117] Ibid., 319.
[118] Ibid., 209.
[119] "The Cherokee Case," *Am. Q.*

*Rev.* 21:1 (1832). Emphasis in original.
[120] Ibid., 2.
[121] Ibid.
[122] Ibid.

could resist voicing their support for the Cherokees and their conviction that outrages had been perpetrated on them.

The second Cherokee case, *Worcester* v. *Georgia*, produced another Court decision in which a state statute was found unconstitutional and state sovereignty was constrained, but the reaction in the press was comparatively mild. The Boston *Statesman*, a paper sympathetic to the Jackson administration, called *Worcester* "the boldest . . . [o]f all the attempts made at a 'Federal' consolidation," and "the least credible to the intellectual character of the Court."[123] The Baltimore *Republican* charged that "in indulging their sympathy for the Indians in Georgia . . . the people of the North . . . seem to lose sight of all other considerations, and to forget that the state has rights and feelings equal to their own."[124] Senator George Troup of Georgia was quoted in the *National Intelligencer* as saying that "[t]he paper of Georgia will receive with indignant feelings, as they ought, the [*Worcester*] decision, . . . so flagrantly violative of their sovereign state."[125] But on the whole, reaction to *Worcester* more resembled that of the *National Intelligencer*, which declared that it had "too much confidence in the love of country and the common sense of the Georgian to apprehend that the present collision between the judicial authorities of that State and of the United States would terminate in tragedy."[126]

As we have seen, the dispute between Georgia and the Cherokees did threaten to precipitate a constitutional crisis. During the interval between March 1832 and February 1833, when lawyers for Samuel Worcester and Elizur Butler were planning to seek a writ compelling federal authorities to enforce the *Worcester* decision and to order their release from prison, Georgia remained recalcitrant and President Johnson gave no indication that he would set the federal enforcement process in motion if asked. Because of technical difficulties in the Judiciary Act of 1789, it was unclear whether any process existed to free the missionaries if Georgia did not cooperate and its state courts made no written record of the refusal.[127] Thus without the cooperation of Georgia or the Jackson administration the Court's *Worcester* decree, ordering the release of Worcester and Butler, appeared unlikely to be enforced. By September 1832

---

[123] Boston *Statesman*, Mar. 19, 1832.

[124] Baltimore *Republican*, Mar. 21, 1832.

[125] Washington *National Intelligencer*, Mar. 24, 1832.

[126] Ibid., Apr. 5, 1832.

[127] The Judiciary Act of 1789 only allowed federal courts to issue a writ of habeas corpus, which was required to free the missionaries, when prisoners were in federal jails. And to execute a decree compelling state courts to act, the Act required a written refusal by the relevant state to comply with an earlier order of the Supreme Court, something Georgia had failed to provide in *Worcester*. See William Wirt to Lewis Williams, Apr. 28, 1832, William Wirt Papers, Library of Congress.

Marshall had confessed to Story, "I yield slowly and reluctantly to the conviction that our Constitution cannot last."[128]

Events then dissolved the crisis. Jackson won a decisive majority in the November 1832 election. South Carolina issued its Nullification Ordinance in late November 1832, claiming the right to nullify obnoxious federal laws and providing for no Supreme Court review of any decisions by its state courts pertaining to the ordinance or to congressional statutes. Jackson responded with his Nullification Proclamation in December, condemning South Carolina and asking for federal legislation to use force against any states that refused to enforce federal laws. Negotiations were begun to secure a pardon and release for Worcester and Butler in exchange for their not seeking any writs before the Marshall Court. The governor of Georgia signed a bill repealing the law under which Worcester and Butler had been convicted. Worcester and Butler were pardoned. Congress passed the Force Bill, which included among its provisions authority to federal judges to grant writs of habeas corpus where persons had been confined in state courts in violation of federal laws. Jackson "specially invited" Story "to drink a glass of wine with him."[129] In the Senate's January 1833 session the Court allegedly "received a stronger and more widely distributed support . . . than had been given to it in Congress for the past fifteen years."[130]

The last occasion for extensive commentary on the Court during the period covered by this volume was the death of Marshall on July 6, 1835, which provoked, as might have been expected, an outpouring of praise for the Chief Justice and a vigorous reaffirmation of the characterizations of the Court made by its defenders throughout the period. It also provoked a revival of the charges of partisanship and political aggrandizement that had been reflected in earlier critics. The labeling of Marshall as a partisan and a devotee of extensive federal power became itself an issue of controversy, demonstrating in the process the degree to which an image of the Court as incorruptible and nonpartisan had become entrenched in the consciousness of early-nineteenth-century Americans.

The day after Marshall died the news of his death was reported in the Philadelphia papers, and by the eighth of July the New York *Evening Post* issued a brief comment. "Judge Marshall," William Leggett, the Post's editor wrote,

> was a man of very considerable talents and acquirements, and great amiableness of private character. His political doctrines, unfortunately,

---

[128] Marshall to Story, Sept. 22, 1832, supra, note 86, 351–52.

[129] J. Story to S. W. Story, Jan. 27, 1833, in W. Story, *Life and Letters,* II, 117. For details on the events leading to Worcester and Butler's pardon, see E. Miles, "After John Marshall's Decision," *J. So. Hist.,* 39:519 (1973).

[130] Warren, *Supreme Court,* II, 236.

were of the ultra federal or aristocratic kind. He was one of those who
. . . distrusted the virtue and intelligence of the people, and was in
favour of a strong and vigorous general government, at the expense of
the rights of the States and of the people. His judicial decisions of all
questions involving political principles have been uniformly on the side
of implied powers and a free construction of the Constitution, and such
also has been the uniform tendency of his writings. That he was sincere
in these views we do not express a doubt, nor that he truly loved his
country; but that he has been, all his life long, a stumbling block and
impediment in the way of democratic principles no one can deny, and
his situation, therefore, at the head of an important tribunal, constituted
in utter defiance of the very first privileges of democracy, has always
been to us . . . an occasion of lively regret. That he is at length removed
from that station is a source of satisfaction, while at the same time we
trust we entertain a proper sentiment for the death of a good and exemplary man.[131]

The tone of the *Post*'s remarks was striking; a more representative comment was that of the *National Intelligencer* on July 9, that "in noticing
the decease of this illustrious citizen . . . who has lived for more than
half a century in the unvarying affections of his countrymen, the language
of eulogy from our pens would be as vain as unnecessary," and which
suggested that Marshall "has now descended to the tomb crowned with
a larger share of public esteem and public regret, than any citizen since
the departure of Washington."[132] But even Leggett, a tireless participant
in political debate, was unprepared for the vehemence of the reaction his
comments on Marshall engendered.

No sooner had the *Post*'s July 8 remarks on Marshall appeared than
the Philadelphia *National Gazette* attacked them as "[an] endeavour to
breathe the polluted breath of party upon the spotless ermine." "What
has democracy in federalism or any other party appellation to do with the
tribunal of justice?" the *Gazette* asked.[133] The *Post* responded on the
tenth that "democracy and federalism . . . have *much* to do with that
tribunal of justice *to which belongs* the expounding of Constitutional
questions," and reiterated its view that "in all . . . questions, the decision
of which rested wholly on the construction to be given certain clauses of
the Constitution, . . . Chief Justice Marshall threw the whole weight of
his official influence on the aristocratick side of free construction." Leggett went on to note that "we should have been pleased had [Marshall]
been removed long ago, and are pleased that he is removed at last,"
although "we never desired that he should be removed by death."[134]

---

[131] New York *Evening Post*, July 8,
1835.
[132] Washington *National Intelligencer*, July 9, 1835.

[133] Philadelphia *National Gazette*,
July 9, 1835.
[134] New York *Evening Post*, July 10,
1835. Emphasis in original.

Three days later the *Post* reprinted a eulogy to Marshall by his old enemy, the Richmond *Enquirer,* and added that "we heartily concur" with the *Enquirer*'s glowing account of "Judge Marshall's personal and intellectual character." Leggett could nonetheless not resist adding that "as a politician, [Marshall] belonged to a school the doctrines of which we consider adverse to popular government, and his situation, therefore, at the head of a tribunal to which belongs the decision of constitutional questions has always appeared to us a matter sincerely to be regretted."[135]

By July 29 the *Post* has been made well aware of the reaction its comments on Marshall had precipitated. In an editorial Leggett took pains to publicize the attacks and to respond further. "Few of our readers have the least idea of the bitterness and malignity with which this journal has been assailed by other prints for the sentiments it has expressed relative to the late Chief Justice of the United States," Leggett began. He then particularized. The *Post* had been termed "fiends," "hyenas," "vampyres," and "monsters." Its comments had been described as an "atrocious outpouring of partisan venom," the "ravings of a madman," and the "vomiting forth [of] the venom of a natural depravity." Leggett himself had been called a "rabid Jacobin," a "miserable maniack," a "savage," a "bandit," a "ruffian," an "unfortunate malignant," and, while "crazy," "to be pitied." The comments on Marshall had established the *Post* as "unquestionably the foulest vehicle now allowed to pollute the American soul," and in an "insulated position of infamy."

Leggett noted that "the newspapers from which we make the above extracts have not done us even the bare justice of copying the articles on which they comment." He also pointed out that "notwithstanding the abuse which has been copiously showered on us," no paper "has thought proper to deny our assertions." He then reiterated that Marshall "was of the ultra federal or aristocratick school"; that "his views of government were founded on rooted distrust of the virtue and intelligence of the people"; that he was "appointed to the chief seat in the supreme tribunal of the union on the very ground of his political opinions"; and that "he wished a strong general government established at the expense of state and popular rights." Leggett ended his editorial with a quotation from the Baltimore *Republican,* which said, after hearing of Marshall's death, that he was "a party man" whose "views of the constitution were known to be totally repugnant to those of the great majority of the people."[136]

Despite the vehemence with which the *Post* was attacked for its criticism of Marshall, it was not alone in attributing partisanship to his decisions or in protesting against their political thrust. Between July 22 and August 18 the *Post* quoted several other papers that had expressed

---

[135] Ibid., July 13, 1835.

[136] Ibid., July 29, 1835.

comparable sentiments. One such comment, that of the Columbia, South Carolina, *Sentinel,* suggested that commentary de-emphasizing Marshall's partisanship was hypocritical and itself partisan.

> Not all the clamour of the opposition will ever be able to drown the sentiment of disapprobation with which many of the decisions of the late Chief Justice were received, and with which they are still regarded. Much as is his memory revered and cherished for the learning and ability he displayed . . . a respectful difference of opinion, upon the fundamental prime plan of government, from those expressed by him, will be entertained by a great majority of the American people. The assertion . . . of his not having been a party man, is far from being correct . . . Judge Marshall was appointed by the elder Adams in January, 1801, near the close of his term. Politics ran as high then as now, and it is but reasonable to suppose that he was chosen with reference to his political principles.[137]

The controversy surrounding the *Post*'s comments on Marshall's death signified the tension between the two principal images of the Supreme Court during his tenure. One pictured the Court as above politics, expounding the doctrines of the Constitution, preserving the integrity of law, and in the process preserving the Union and the Republic from the disintegrative forces of partisanship and corruption. The other image characterized the Court as deeply partisan, furthering the goals of the original Federalist party, grafting onto the Constitution a set of political doctrines that were hostile to state sovereignty and to the democratization of American life. The tension between the images emerged from the fact that one of the chief justifications for the Court's authority as the final interpreter of the Constitution was the nonpartisan and impartial character of its decisions. In its interpretations it "could only look to the law"; its decisions were deemed to be authoritative because they amounted to the dispassionate expounding of legal principles that were already embedded in the sources from which they were extracted. Attributing partisan goals to the process of interpretation undermined the assumption that law was itself outside or above and beyond partisan politics.

The factor complicating evaluations of the Court by contemporaries, then, was that the Court's opinions provided support for both images. The opinions of Marshall and his colleagues were filled with language whose purpose was to foster an impression that the Court could only follow the "will of the law"; that it had a "duty" to pronounce this or that doctrine; that its jurisdiction had been fixed by Congress and the Constitution and could neither be expanded nor contracted; that the "dis-

---

[137] Columbia, S.C., *Sentinel,* quoted in ibid., Aug. 13, 1835.

cretion'' its members exercised in their interpretations was a mere legal discretion. At the same time the opinions, particularly those in constitutional cases, contained language demonstrating that the Court had elected one of a set of competing doctrines; that it had promoted the Union at the expense of the states; that it had read a constitutional clause ''liberally'' when it could have read it ''strictly,'' or vice versa; that it had chosen one definition of ''commerce'' or ''necessary and proper'' or ''contract'' over another. Contemporaries of the Court were not unaware of those choices, and not unaware of their political implications. Indeed, most of the more searching commentary on the Court's decisions started from the premise that the Court's interpretations were by no means foreclosed and inevitable; that, on the contrary, they were arguments for one interpretation of the Constitution or other authoritative legal source rather than another, an interpretation that had distinct political ramifications.

To conclude, therefore, that the Court succeeded in separating law from politics, or in establishing itself as a neutral nonpartisan force is to read only some of the contemporary commentary and to emphasize only some of the Court's language. It is clear that during Marshall's tenure the Court had an interest in fostering an impression of itself as removed from politics and faithful to the impersonal dictates of the law. It is also clear that the Court succeeded remarkably in establishing that impression in public consciousness. But it is not at all clear that the Court's opinions *were* nonpartisan, or even that they were so perceived by those who followed its actions closely. Perhaps the most one can say is that Marshall and his colleagues were convinced that the de-emphasis of overt partisanship and the emphasis of a judicial obligation to subordinate individual discretionary choice to the ''discretion of the law'' was an important means of gaining legitimacy for their pronouncements. To say that is not to say that the Court elevated law above politics. It is rather to say that the Court established a strategy whose purpose was to distinguish law from politics, and that the distinction between law and politics, and between legal and individual discretion, was accepted as a respectable intellectual proposition by the Court's contemporaries.

If contemporaries saw the Marshall Court both as a partisan force furthering consolidation and an expansive federal government and restricting the powers of the states, and as a nonpartisan force elevating the role of law as a force for social solidarity in a republic, can the two images be reconciled? Is it possible to see the Court not simply as a participant in the partisan conflicts of its day but also as an institution that performed a distinctive role in its unique culture? Is it, in other words, possible to see the Court not only as a transformative political force but also as an agent in the less discernible but more profound transformation

## Chapter XI:  *Of the Court, Time, and Change*

of American culture in its entirety? This volume has, of course, assumed that such a view of the Court is not only possible but desirable; that the Court was both a barometer and a precipitator of cultural change.

The early chapters of the volume introduced features that I have argued were central to the cultural experience of early-nineteenth-century Americans, and discussed the ways in which those cultural features were reflected in conceptions of the nature and sources of law. Contemporaries of the Marshall Court inherited a distinctive political ideology—American republicanism—and an established structure of belief that emphasized the uniqueness of that ideology, the exceptional setting in which it had appeared, and the promise that both the ideology and its setting might become permanent in America, thereby isolating the American nation from the degenerative effects of time and change. At the same time early-nineteenth-century Americans were exposed to abundant contemporary evidence that the present would not be a replication of the past and that the course of the future could not easily be predicted. While the ideological premises and physical environment of American civilization raised the prospect of immunity from change, the landscape of early-nineteenth-century America bore witness to the fact that the Revolutionary experience was passing into history. The meaning of cultural change thus became a pressing inquiry for contemporaries of the Marshall Court: did change, given the American setting, mean decay, or could the principles of the Revolutionary experience be preserved?

The conception of the nature and sources of law held by contemporaries of the Marshall Court can be associated with the central intellectual inquiry described above. The new and revolutionary character of American civilization meant that law in the New World could reflect its unique and exceptional cultural setting: it could be Americanized. The sources of American law could be open-ended: local custom, principles of equity, English common law doctrines, the law merchant, the "law, admiralty and maritime," the practices of British prize courts, the text of the American Constitution, the "first principles of republican government." American law could be shaped to fit the conditions of life in America: it could respond to change. But the function of law, in a republican society, was to inform the citizenry of their rights and responsibilities. Law was not merely a medium for facilitating change, but a force for continuity. One of the ways in which the Revolutionary experience was universalized and made permanent was through the promulgation of legal principles, principles that were conceived of as static in their nature but adaptive in their application. One source of such privileges was the constitutional text, packed with meaning drawn from extratextual sources such as the common law or general principles of natural justice; another was common law doctrine, "scientifically" promulgated. Thus articulated, legal principles were a mechanism for mediating between the

779

past and the future, for accommodating the Revolutionary experience to the altered conditions of the early nineteenth century.

The articulation of legal principles was thus one version of the larger mediating task—the task of reconciling republican ideology with cultural change—that early-nineteenth-century Americans proposed for themselves. But who was to perform this articulation? The answer early-nineteenth-century American jurists gave to this question was, increasingly, the judiciary. The authority of judges to serve as architects of cultural change was based on two grounds: their independence, in the constitutional framework of separation of powers, from the other branches of government whose laws they were reconciling with constitutional principles; and their ability to discover, extract, and expound "scientific" principles of law, whose meaning was accessible only to savants. These two grounds furnished the rationale for judicial discretion, that is, a discretion to articulate constitutional and common law principles that were already in existence but whose meaning needed to be made intelligible to the citizenry at large.

The idea of judicial discretion, while serving as the central justification for investing judicial interpretations of legal sources with authoritativeness, also necessitated some reconciliation with the premises of republican ideology. If judicial discretion, especially as practiced by federal judges, meant unwritten, partisan judicial lawmaking, it arguably violated some of the basic principles of republican government by establishing the federal judiciary as a potential agent of tyranny and corruption and as a potential usurper of the sovereignty of the states. Thus if discretion in federal judges was to be compatible with the premises of a republican society, it needed to be nonpartisan, reasoned, and mindful of the limited sovereignty of the federal government. Chapter III discussed the mechanisms created by the Marshall Court to legitimate its discretion. Among those were the emphasis on collegiality and unanimity in the delivery of opinions, with the attendant practices of silent acquiescence and the suppression of seriatim opinions, concurrences, and dissents; the Court's informal deliberative process, with its emphasis on the boardinghouse as a center for collegial exchange; the attempted disengagement of the Justices from partisan political life; and the cautious approach the Court took toward federal judicial rulemaking in areas—the common law of crimes, admiralty jurisdiction, Section 25 review of state court decisions—where discretionary rules might appear partisan or usurpatious.

These mechanisms, coupled with the state of transportation and communication in early-nineteenth-century America and the embryonic status of disseminative services for the Court's opinions, made the Marshall Court strikingly unlike its twentieth-century counterparts. In a whole series of ways—boardinghouse residency, limited tenure in Washington, circuit-riding, informal conferences, unlimited duration for oral arguments, the absence of written briefs, the paucity of reported decisions, the absence of a practice of recording the votes of individual Justices— the Marshall Court was a unique institution, its working life reflecting the ideas and conditions of its times.

The internal practices of the Marshall Court also meant that the roles of lawyers arguing cases before it and Justices serving on it differed from their modern counterparts. Advocacy before the Marshall Court was essentially an oral exercise, and, because of the unlimited time given to arguments and the absence of interruptions from Justices, an exercise in oratory. Oral arguments were the chief source of the Justices' information about a case: the Justices sat silent, taking notes, because their notes would often be their sole source of information in rendering a decision. Advocacy was performed by a specialized group of lawyers, who typically argued several cases in a given Term; the most celebrated of these lawyers were orators as well as technicians. Modern Supreme Court Justices, in addition to oral arguments, have at their disposal written briefs, opinions from lower courts, memoranda prepared by law clerks, and relevant works of scholarship when deciding cases; the Marshall Court Justices, in most instances, had only the first of these sources.

The nature of advocacy at the time of the Marshall Court thus served to magnify the contributions of advocates, as selected comparisons between the arguments of counsel and the Court's opinions have suggested. Similarly, the nature of the Court's deliberative process served to magnify the contributions of "silent" judges, those whose views were delivered orally during discussions in the boardinghouse but were not revealed in opinions or votes. The "opinion of the Court" practice, the custom of silent acquiescence, the informal nature of conferences, and the uneven distribution of opinion writing among the Justices make the contributions of silent Justices difficult to evaluate. We do not know if Justices such as Todd, Duvall, or Livingston, whose published contributions to the Court's work were astonishingly slight compared with those of their colleagues, were nonetheless significant internal presences. One thing, however, is clear: one cannot measure the significance or insignificance of a Marshall Court Justice simply by the output of his published opinions. We have seen in the case of Thomas Todd, for example, that the Court postponed deciding several western lands cases from Kentucky because of his absence; yet Todd did not deliver an opinion in any of the cases. The postponement was thus not to secure Todd's authorship, but to ensure his presence in the deliberations. While one has no evidence to assess the significance of Todd's presence, the postponement itself suggests that Todd's peers wanted to hear his views before coming to a final decision.

Just as one cannot accurately assess the contribution of Marshall Court Justices solely from their published opinions, one cannot assess the contribution of the Court's Reporters solely from the volumes of the

United States Reports which appeared under their names. Chapter VI suggests that during Henry Wheaton's Reportership the Reporter may have been tacitly granted some of the powers of a Justice. Wheaton undoubtedly supplied authorities for many of the Court's opinions during his tenure, and very probably corrected errors in style, and perhaps in substance, contained in draft opinions supplied him by the Justices. Indeed, Wheaton clearly regarded his reports as his own literary product, and thus his property, even though the bulk of the pages of his reports were made up of opinions authored by others. Wheaton's characterization of his volumes was rejected by the Court in *Wheaton v. Peters,* but Chapter VI suggests that there is strong evidence that Wheaton's conception was shared by the Justices when Wheaton assumed the office. Even the Court's distinction in *Wheaton v. Peters* between a Reporter's notes or emendations and the opinions of the Justices did not fully reflect practice, for many of the notes appearing in Wheaton's early volumes had been written by Story. There is evidence, in short, that the modern conception of the Reporter's office as an institution charged only with the faithful recording of the Court's decisions was not the conception which prevailed during the Marshall Court.

Most students of the Marshall Court have associated it not with any of the features thus far described, but with its great constitutional decisions, which are surveyed in Chapters VII, VIII, IX, and X. Here again the uniqueness and time-boundedness of the Court emerges. The central issue in the vested rights cases—whether the Contract Clause of the Constitution imposed an absolute prohibition of legislative efforts to restrict transfers of real or personal property—was an issue that surfaced because of the simultaneous presence in early-nineteenth-century America of two apparently incompatible conceptions of property, one identifying it with freehold land and the creation of a virtuous landholding citizenry, the other identifying property as a commodity to be bought and sold in the market. The vested rights cases were "hard" cases for the Court because they revealed that the republican principle of solicitude for property rights did not provide a basis for resolution of instances in which two kinds of property rights, prescriptive and developmental, were in conflict. Here was an issue in which an ideological premise of the Revolutionary generation—that the right to hold or to acquire property was anterior to society and could therefore not be restricted by positive legislation—simply did not square with the presence of an entrepreneurial society whose growth had been facilitated by competitive uses of property in a market economy. When, in *Charles River Bridge,* the Court fully confronted the clash between prescriptive and developmental uses of legislatively created property, it was unable to agree on a principle to decide the case, for it was clear that the invocation of the principle of protection for "property rights" did not answer the question of whose property was to be protected.

# Chapter XI: *Of the Court, Time, and Change*

Although contemporaries of the Marshall Court may not have acknowledged the contradictions contained within their solicitude for property, they undoubtedly recognized the contradictions present in the commitment of the Revolutionary generation to the idea of divided and federated sovereignty in a republic. The locus of sovereignty was the great issue around which political allegiances were cast in late-eighteenth-century America: Federalists versus Republicans, compact theorists versus consolidationists, Unionists versus states' rights theorists. The divisiveness of sovereignty issues, however, was produced by an issue that has not often been emphasized in commentary upon them: the implications of the coterminous power axiom of early-nineteenth-century political theory. In one sense the sovereignty disputes that came to the Marshall Court in the form of constitutional cases were not difficult to reconcile, given the ideological assumptions of the age; in another sense they were alarming and portentous.

The *Martin–Cohens–Osborn* line of decisions, for example, produced no startling results. While it was theoretically possible that a state court's construction of federal treaties or the Constitution could have been deemed dispositive within the jurisdiction of that state, such a result would have balkanized constitutional provisions and undermined the efficacy of federal legislation binding the states in a posture of mutual assistance. The result in *Martin* was thus foreordained, and with *Martin* decided so was the result in *Cohens*. *Osborn* was not much harder: where Congress had created a federal corporation, it presumably had in mind insulating that corporation from the parochial concerns of state law. If a federal corporation did not have the power to conduct its litigation in the federal courts, whether or not the issues in dispute were those of state law, it would seem to be vulnerable to the parochial sniping from which Congress was seeking to insulate it. The *Osborn* rationale particularly made sense in a jurisprudential universe where general and local law were conceptually distinct entities.

The sovereignty issues in *Martin, Cohens,* and *Osborn,* then, were "easy" issues because opposite results would have eviscerated the concept of a Union whose sovereign powers were intended as a buffer against state parochialism. But in each case the Court's assumption that federal judicial power was coextensive with federal legislative power seemed to mean that the more the federal judiciary occupied an area, the more the federal government could expand its influence; and *McCulloch* appeared to make that supposition explicit. After *McCulloch* it was not clear what, if anything, coterminous power theory and the implied powers of Article I left for the states to regulate; in this vein the Court's implicit adoption of concurrent power theory in *Gibbons* and its progeny was an important conciliatory step. Once the Court made its ambiguous rejection of the theory of unlimited plenary power in Congress to regulate commerce in *Gibbons,* and permitted limited state regulation where Congress had not occupied the field in subsequent Commerce Clause cases, the full implications of coterminous power theory were tempered.

Thus one of the most divisive features of the Court's sovereignty decisions disappeared after *Gibbons,* when it became clear that the federal government was not going to use coterminous power theory and its dominant regulatory powers as a means of keeping the states out of the area of commercial regulation. This tacit compromise did not, however, exhaust some other ticklish sovereignty issues that the Court confronted during Marshall's tenure, notably the issues of admiralty jurisdiction, the federal common law of crimes, slavery, and Indian rights. There were strong arguments, based on English precedent, on the language of the Constitution, and on the American version of federated republican sovereignty itself, that the admiralty jurisdiction of the federal courts was very extensive, embracing substantive questions of private law such as torts and contracts in a maritime setting and including not just oceangoing traffic but the inland waterways of the American continent. There were also strong arguments that the federal courts could look to general law in criminal cases, just as they could in other common law cases. Uniformity of criminal law doctrines was one such argument; the avoidance of local prejudice or hostility surrounding a particular crime was another. Slavery, given the assumptions of early-nineteenth-century jurisprudence, was an issue that, depending on one's perspective, could be seen as peculiarly local, since it dealt with the property rights of slaveowners, or peculiarly suited for the application of general principles, since slavery cases raised the question whether universal human rights could be curtailed by local practices. Cases involving the rights of Indians could, similarly, be conceptualized as "property" cases, since they invariably involved conflicts over land ownership, or "commerce" cases, since Congress had Article I power to regulate commerce with the Indian tribes.

In only one of these contexts was the Marshall Court activist in its interpretations of federal court jurisdiction or aggressive in its construction of the ambit of federal sovereignty. It confined the admiralty jurisdiction of the federal courts to the "high seas" and "the ebb and flow of the tide"; it never endorsed, as a body, Story's opinion in *DeLovio* that federal admiralty jurisdiction encompassed maritime contracts and torts; it declined to assume any jurisdiction over common law crimes, despite the fact that neither *Hudson and Goodwin* nor *Coolidge* had adequately dismissed such jurisdiction; it never heard a major slavery case and never came close to considering the constitutional ramifications of slavery. Only in the Cherokee cases, and then after declaring that it had no original jurisdiction to hear cases involving controversies between Indian tribes and states, could the Court be said to have taken a decisive position on the lack of state power to control Indian affairs. But the consequence of the Cherokee cases was not a shift in Indian policy; the decision merely meant that Indian removal would be performed by the federal government. The great significance of the Cherokee cases, in retrospect, was that they presented another opportunity for the repudiation of compact theory, this time by the federal executive branch. The compromise reached in the Cherokee cases was made possible, despite the Jackson administration's resolute antipathy toward Indians, by the ominous implications of allowing Georgia in effect to nullify the Court's *Worcester* decision. Once the nullification doctrine was deemed an unacceptable threat to the Union, some face-saving gesture had to be found.

The Court's cautious posture on slavery cases and its severe qualification of the natural rights of Indians underscores the fact that it was not, despite its members' use of the libertarian rhetoric of the Revolutionary generation, a Court particularly concerned with the protection of what later generations would call civil rights. The principal right for which the Court demonstrated solicitude was the right to hold and to acquire property, and that right was restricted to white males. Indians did not own, but merely occupied, land; slaves had no property rights. One looks in vain for a free speech case, a freedom of religion case, or a due process case in the Marshall Court, and, as Chapter X suggests, the Court's cases in which natural rights arguments were made were notable for the repudiation of those arguments.

In all the above respects the Court reflected the intellectual priorities of its age. The great constitutional issues of the early nineteenth century were issues of sovereignty and vested rights, not issues of civil liberties. The central role of property in a republican society, and the ambiguous status of property rights in a culture that simultaneously embraced the idea of a freehold as a repository of security and virtue and the idea of land as a speculative commodity, assured that vested rights cases would be perceived as both significant and divisive. The delicate balance of sovereign powers envisaged by American federated republicanism, the rapid growth of the nation, and the formidable barriers to intersectional exchange assured that the demarcation lines separating the powers of the federal government from those of the states would continually be under scrutiny. On the other hand, for all its natural rights rhetoric, republicanism was an ideology whose chief emphasis was on civic duty and social solidarity as distinguished from individual freedom. Order, moderation, and virtue were important words in the discourse of the Revolutionary generation; equality and autonomy were words of a later time. The constitutional emphasis of the Marshall Court mirrored the emphasis of its times.

We have also seen that the Marshall Court's cases furnish additional evidence of the impressive discretion of the Justices to function as substantive rulemakers. No Court in American history was freer to make up its own rules of law. No Court had more first impression cases of constitutional interpretation; none had greater opportunities to fashion common law rules; none enjoyed to as great an extent the singular freedom that comes from pressing business and the absence of decisive precedent. In no period in the history of the Supreme Court of the United States were the personal predilections of Justices arguably more important, since no Court that decided such important cases had so informal and unaccountable a set of deliberative procedures.

In some areas, most prominently those involving constitutional interpretation, the discretion of the Justices was emphasized by commentators and partisanship and even disingenuousness attributed to the Court. But alongside this view that the Court's doctrines reflected a particular political perspective was another view, not solely attributable to defenders of the Court, that judicial decisions were not discretionary in the strict partisan sense. Legal doctrines were not conceived, in early-nineteenth-century jurisprudence, as indistinguishable from political tracts. To an important extent they were conceived as repositories of authoritative and disembodied principles that existed independent of the wills of those who declared them. The term "discretion" contained within it both conceptions. When Marshall referred to "mere legal discretion" or distinguished between the "will of the judge" and the "will of the law," he meant to suggest that judges had only a very limited freedom to expound principles, the freedom attendant upon professional expertise in the art of rendering legal language and doctrine intelligible, nothing more. It is clear that not all of the Court's critics were convinced that this is all judges did: "discretion" was also used by them in a way that more closely resembles the modern sense of "lawmaking." But it is also clear that the more limited conception of discretion was strongly entrenched in early-nineteenth-century jurisprudence.

It is, of course, a puzzle to moderns how judges could simultaneously be granted the discretion to make substantive law and yet not fully be perceived as lawmakers. That puzzle, after all our attention to it, remains rooted in intellectual assumptions we no longer share. Here it is worth directing our attention once again to the distinctive facets of the culture in which the Marshall Court functioned. That culture was one in which an established belief structure was confronting unmistakable evidence of social change. The attitudes of the belief structure toward change were themselves distinctive, and three such attitudes have received particular emphasis in this volume. One was the unresolved tension between an assumption that change represented progress and an assumption that change should be equated with cultural decay and disintegration. A second was the effort to respond to change by the systematization and organization of areas of knowledge, reflected in the attempts of jurists to articulate scientific legal principles. A third was the rediscovery and recasting of the revolutionary history of the American republic reflected in Marshall

786

# Chapter XI: *Of the Court, Time, and Change*

Court opinions and in contemporary apologists for the Court. What links these three developments? One linkage, I would suggest, can be found in a distinctive attitude toward the past as a source of guidance for the present. The exercise of looking backward in time was not an exercise that yielded, for Marshall's contemporaries, the insight that civilization was in a constant process of change, nor the insight that the future could never fully replicate the past. The exercise of contrasting the past to the present and recasting the past was, for early-nineteenth-century Americans, a way of identifying and reasserting first principles, that is, values, beliefs, and rules that remained unchanged over time.

Versions of this exercise have been singled out in this study. One was the effort by Marshall's contemporaries to apply the assumptions and axioms of republican thought to the altered cultural ethos of early-nineteenth-century America through the device of cultural surrogates such as "Union" and "commerce." A second was the effort of judges and jurists to make the common law "scientific" by surveying its history, "Americanizing" its rules, and declaring those rules to be authoritative principles. A third was the effort of judges and commentators to recast the history of the Revolutionary generation as a series of permanent "great principles," embodied in the language of the Constitution, to which successive generations would frequently recur. If one were to give a descriptive epistemological label to the attitude in which this exercise were undertaken, that label might be prehistoricist: an attitude in which history was neither a source of progress nor a manifestation of decay but a constellation of principles that were both suspended in and vindicated by time.

But we might ask, as moderns, is not the extracting of principles from history, or the recasting of the Constitution, or the "Americanizing" of common law rules simply evidence of the need of every generation to make over its past? This question is a way of saying that for moderns the idea that the past, or any "authoritative" source of rules or values, can be immune from the contingencies of time and human idiosyncrasy seems problematic. But the conviction of Marshall and his contemporaries was that this skepticism was unfounded. This may be why they invested judges with the discretion to declare substantive rules: they truly believed that the timelessness of rules and principles would be established by their successive declaration. The declaration process, then, was not an indication of change but an antidote to change; the lawmaking of judges was not only evidence of human will, but, at a deeper level, evidence of the will of the law.

Of all the reorientations necessary to grasp the character of the Marshall Court, this last may be the most difficult of all. It may be easier to fathom judges riding in stagecoaches, or communicating to each other in handwritten letters with eighteenth-century calligraphy, or wearing knee breeches beneath their robes, or holding conferences in a boarding-

787

house, than to imagine their seeing their declarations of legal rules and principles as anything other than creative lawmaking. But if we can reconstruct the ideological boundaries of the universe in which those judges lived, perhaps we can surmount the gaps between them and ourselves. Their received ideological system was not one prepared to embrace the permanence of change and the necessary contingency of belief; it was, on the contrary, a system designed to ensure the permanence of an experimental form of social organization by forestalling change and asserting the universality of certain beliefs. The years of the Marshall Court may have been the first time in the history of American culture in which the possibility that the future might never replicate the past was truly grasped. But if that insight was grasped, it was not embraced. History was still to an important extent perceived as an affirmation of first principles. The Marshall Court's consciousness was affected—one might say imprisoned—by that perception; it was, in the deepest sense, a Court of its time.

# Table of Cases

# TABLE OF CASES

# Index

*For specific cases see also Table of Cases*

Baldwin (*continued*)
  Contract Clause cases and, 660, 664–667
  dissenting opinions of, 194n, 408–409
  Marshall (John) and, 372, 410–411
  Marshall (John) on, 298, 381, 409
  McLean (John) on, 302
  Peters (Richard, Jr.) and, 408–411
  portrait of, 298–302
Baltimore *Gazette*, 581
Baltimore *Federal Gazette*, 932
Baltimore *Federal Republican*, 689n, 931
Baltimore *Morning Chronicle*, 352
Baltimore *Republican*, 962
Baltimore *Whig*, 235n
Bancroft, George, 372
Bank of the United States, 542–549, 551–552
Bankruptcy legislation, 628–641, 648–655
Banner, J., 49n
Barbour, James, 258, 511, 517, 524
Barstow, G., 613n
Bartlett, Irving, 267n, 269n, 270n
Bartner, Philip, 508
"Batiery, Urbain," 353–354
Bauer, E., 88n
Baxter, Maurice, 211, 267n
Beck, J., 230n
Bedford, Gunnery, Jr., 131n
Bentley, William, 356–358
Benton, Thomas Hart, 290, 953
Bernhard, Duke of Saxe-Weimar-Eisenach, 31n
Berrien, John, 696
Berthoff, R., 49n
Beveridge, Albert, 160n, 182n, 231n, 239–240, 260, 261n, 321, 369n, 460n, 543, 556, 620n, 623n, 643n, 750, 759n
Biddle, C. C., 407n
Biddle, Richard, 642
Bill of Rights, 589–591
Bills of Credit Clause, 586
Binney, Horace, 300, 347–348, 351–352, 372n, 723
Bishop, A., 69n
Black, C., 429n, 462n
Black slave trade cases, 677, 678, 680–703, 739–740
Blackstone, William, 129, 682
*Blackstone's Commentaries: With Notes of Reference to the Constitution and Laws of the Federal Government of the United States and of the Commonwealth of Virginia* (Tucker), 81–87, 133n, 134, 135, 459n, 489, 682–687

Blair, Francis, 303
Blennerhassett, Harman, 234, 236, 260–261
Boardinghouse living, 160–161, 184–186, 189–191
Boardman, James, 31n
Boit, John, 430
Bollman, Justus E., 232, 233
Boston *Columbian Centinel*, 303, 617, 745, 750–752
Boston *Courier*, 956
Boston *Daily Advertiser*, 265n, 289, 748
Boston *Statesman*, 26n, 771
Brockenbrough, William, 126, 521, 552–555
Brooks, Edward, 337
Brooks, P. C., 229n
Brown, Francis, 620–621
Brown, Norman, 267n
Brown, S., 616n
Browne, W., 239n
Buchanan, James, 294
Buel, R., 49n
Burr, Aaron, 232–235, 240, 260–261, 328, 370
Byrd, Charles, 525

Caldwell, Elias B., 384n
Calhoun, John C., 126, 281, 300, 315–316, 487, 488, 492
Callender, G., 62n
Campbell, John, 428n
Canal construction, 16–17
Capitalist market economy, 61–69
Cardozo, B., 198n
Carey, Henry C., 417n
Carey, Mathew, 390, 417
Carey & Lea, 404–405
Carlyle, Thomas, 268
Carnes, Peter, 256
Carr, Dabney, 258
Carrington, Mrs. Edward, 377
Carroll, Charles, 280
Carroll, William Thomas, 384n–385n
*Case of the Cherokee Nation Against the State of Georgia, The*, 730
Cases: *see also* Opinions
  constitutional: *see* constitutional cases
  decision-making process and, 181–195
  selection of, 164–181
  speed of disposition of, 181–183
Cass, Lewis, 297
Certificates of division, 164, 165, 173–178
Chacon, Pablo, 220

# INDEX

# INDEX

# INDEX

Law *(continued)*
  natural law, 677–680
  status of law, 76–80
"Law, Legislation, and Codes" (Story), 147
Law merchant, 112
*Law Relative to Merchant Ships and Seamen, The* (Abbott), 436
Law schools, 87
Lawrence, W. B., 442*n*
Lawyer-commentators
  characterizations of nature and sources of law by, 111–156
  emergence of, 79–81
Lawyers
  before the Marshall Court: *see* Advocacy before the Marshall Court
  image of, 76–79
Ledyard, Susan, 332
Legal commentary: *see* Commentary
*Legal Outlines* (Hoffman), 95, 678
Leggett, William, 65–67, 774–776
Leigh, Benjamin, 168, 225*n*
*Letters and Journals of James Fenimore Cooper* (Beard, ed.), 40*n*
"Letters of the British Spy, The" (Wirt), 258–259
Lex Levi, 112
Liberalism, 50–51, 60–69
Liberty, concept of, 57, 83, 488, 490, 493
*Liberty Hall and Cincinnati Gazette,* 758*n*
Lieber, Frances, 31*n*
*Life of Daniel Webster,* 267*n*
*Life of George Washington, The* (Marshall), 33*n*
*Life of Patrick Henry, The* (Wirt), 260
Lincoln, Abraham, 494
Lincoln, Levi, 358
Living conditions, 13–14
Livingston, Brockholst, 166*n*, 293, 310, 349, 351, 360, 373, 569, 570, 637
  Contract Clause cases and, 619, 621–622, 643, 668, 669
  portrait of, 327–332
  Story (Joseph) on, 330
Livingston, Catherine, 332
Livingston, Edward, 370, 371, 953*n*
Livingston, Gilbert, 308*n*, 309
Livingston, Robert, 210, 327, 328, 569
Livingston, William, 327
Lodge, Henry Cabot, 267*n*
Lord, J., 613*n*
Louisiana Purchase, 69
Lyceum circuit, 25

Madison, Dolley, 319
Madison, James, 21, 79–80, 333*n*, 358, 370, 542, 559, 561, 601, 629–630, 703*n*, 721
Maine, 627*n*
*Maine Reports* (Greenleaf), 107
Majority opinions, 184
Mansfield, Lord, 682
Manufacturing, 22
Marine insurance cases, 202
Maritime commerce, 34–35
Maritime law, 112
Market economy, 61–69
Marryat, Frederick, 31*n*
Marsh, C., 177*n*, 330, 614, 620
Marshall, James, 166, 168, 170*n*
Marshall, John, 25, 33, 105, 166–173, 176, 182, 199, 239, 294–295, 304, 349, 353, 422, 950
  admiralty jurisdiction cases and, 433, 445, 446, 448–449, 457–460, 472–474, 476–478, 481–483
  American Indian cases and, 707–711, 714, 720–721, 724–727, 729–736
  Baldwin (Henry) and, 372, 410–411
  on Baldwin (Henry), 298, 381, 409
  Burr (Aaron) trial and, 232–234
  on the Constitution,, 73–74
  Contract Clause cases and, 604–606, 608, 615–618, 621–627, 634–640, 649–654, 656–657, 661, 665, 666, 668–669, 672
  newspaper commentary after death of, 774–778
  dominance of, 190–192
  Du Ponceau (Peter) on, 144
  on Duvall (Gabriel), 325, 327
  on essential function of judges, 198
  federal jurisdiction cases (constitutional) and, 508, 510–523, 526–531, 533–536
  federal limitations on state power cases and, 545–552, 555–558, 562–568, 572–573, 575–592
  Jefferson (Thomas) and, 369–372
  on Jefferson (Thomas), 522–523
  Johnson (William) and, 372
  linguistic analysis of Constitution by, 8
  on Livingston (Brockholst), 332
  offered Supreme Court vacancy, 345
  on Ogden (David), 289
  opinion authorship of, 181, 191–193, 368
  Peters (Richard, Jr.) and, 405, 408, 410–411
  Pinkney (William) and, 247–250, 291
  on Pinkney (William), 243, 244, 247–250

# INDEX